ACCOUNT CLASSIFICATION AND PRESENTATION			
Account Title	**Classification**	**Financial Statement**	**Normal Balance**
A			
Accounts Payable	Current Liability	Balance Sheet	Credit
Accounts Receivable	Current Asset	Balance Sheet	Debit
Accumulated Depreciation—Buildings	Plant Asset—Contra	Balance Sheet	Credit
Accumulated Depreciation—Equipment	Plant Asset—Contra	Balance Sheet	Credit
Advertising Expense	Operating Expense	Income Statement	Debit
Allowance for Doubtful Accounts	Current Asset—Contra	Balance Sheet	Credit
Amortization Expense	Operating Expense	Income Statement	Debit
B			
Bad Debt Expense	Operating Expense	Income Statement	Debit
Bonds Payable	Long-Term Liability	Balance Sheet	Credit
Buildings	Plant Asset	Balance Sheet	Debit
C			
Cash	Current Asset	Balance Sheet	Debit
Common Stock	Stockholders' Equity	Balance Sheet	Credit
Copyrights	Intangible Asset	Balance Sheet	Debit
Cost of Goods Sold	Cost of Goods Sold	Income Statement	Debit
D			
Debt Investments	Current Asset/Long-Term Investment	Balance Sheet	Debit
Depreciation Expense	Operating Expense	Income Statement	Debit
Discount on Bonds Payable	Long-Term Liability—Contra	Balance Sheet	Debit
Dividends	Temporary account closed to Retained Earnings	Retained Earnings Statement	Debit
Dividends Payable	Current Liability	Balance Sheet	Credit
E			
Equipment	Plant Asset	Balance Sheet	Debit
F			
Freight-Out	Operating Expense	Income Statement	Debit
G			
Gain on Disposal of Plant Assets	Other Income	Income Statement	Credit
Goodwill	Intangible Asset	Balance Sheet	Debit
I			
Income Summary	Temporary account closed to Retained Earnings	Not Applicable	(1)
Income Tax Expense	Income Tax Expense	Income Statement	Debit
Income Taxes Payable	Current Liability	Balance Sheet	Credit
Insurance Expense	Operating Expense	Income Statement	Debit
Interest Expense	Other Expense	Income Statement	Debit
Interest Payable	Current Liability	Balance Sheet	Credit
Interest Receivable	Current Asset	Balance Sheet	Debit
Interest Revenue	Other Income	Income Statement	Credit
Inventory	Current Asset	Balance Sheet (2)	Debit

Account Title	Classification	Financial Statement	Normal Balance
L			
Land	Plant Asset	Balance Sheet	Debit
Loss on Disposal of Plant Assets	Other Expense	Income Statement	Debit
M			
Maintenance and Repairs Expense	Operating Expense	Income Statement	Debit
Mortgage Payable	Long-Term Liability	Balance Sheet	Credit
N			
Notes Payable	Current Liability/ Long-Term Liability	Balance Sheet	Credit
O			
Owner's Capital	Owner's Equity	Owner's Equity and Balance Sheet	Credit
Owner's Drawings	Temporary account closed to Owner's Capital	Owner's Equity	Debit
P			
Patents	Intangible Asset	Balance Sheet	Debit
Paid-in Capital in Excess of Par—Common Stock	Stockholders' Equity	Balance Sheet	Credit
Paid-in Capital in Excess of Par—Preferred Stock	Stockholders' Equity	Balance Sheet	Credit
Preferred Stock	Stockholders' Equity	Balance Sheet	Credit
Premium on Bonds Payable	Long-Term Liability	Balance Sheet	Credit
Prepaid Insurance	Current Asset	Balance Sheet	Debit
Prepaid Rent	Current Asset	Balance Sheet	Debit
R			
Rent Expense	Operating Expense	Income Statement	Debit
Retained Earnings	Stockholders' Equity	Balance Sheet and Retained Earnings Statement	Credit
S			
Salaries and Wages Expense	Operating Expense	Income Statement	Debit
Salaries and Wages Payable	Current Liability	Balance Sheet	Credit
Sales Discounts	Revenue—Contra	Income Statement	Debit
Sales Returns and Allowances	Revenue—Contra	Income Statement	Debit
Sales Revenue	Revenue	Income Statement	Credit
Selling Expenses	Operating Expense	Income Statement	Debit
Service Revenue	Revenue	Income Statement	Credit
Stock Investments	Current Asset/Long-Term Investment	Balance Sheet	Debit
Supplies	Current Asset	Balance Sheet	Debit
Supplies Expense	Operating Expense	Income Statement	Debit
T			
Treasury Stock	Stockholders' Equity—Contra	Balance Sheet	Debit
U			
Unearned Service Revenue	Current Liability	Balance Sheet	Credit
Utilities Expense	Operating Expense	Income Statement	Debit

(1) The normal balance for Income Summary will be credit when there is a net income, debit when there is a net loss. The Income Summary account does not appear on any financial statement.

(2) If a periodic system is used, Inventory also appears on the income statement in the calculation of cost of goods sold.

The following is a sample chart of accounts. It does not represent a comprehensive chart of all the accounts used in this textbook but rather those accounts that are commonly used. This sample chart of accounts is for a company that generates both service revenue as well as sales revenue. It uses the perpetual approach to inventory. If a periodic system was used, the following temporary accounts would be needed to record inventory purchases: Purchases, Freight-In, Purchase Returns and Allowances, and Purchase Discounts.

CHART OF ACCOUNTS

Assets	Liabilities	Owner's and Stockholders' Equity	Revenues	Expenses
Cash	Notes Payable	Owner's Capital	Service Revenue	Advertising Expense
Accounts Receivable	Accounts Payable	Owner's Drawings	Sales Revenue	Amortization Expense
Allowance for Doubtful Accounts	Unearned Service Revenue	Common Stock	Sales Discounts	Bad Debt Expense
Interest Receivable	Salaries and Wages Payable	Paid-in Capital in Excess of Par—Common Stock	Sales Returns and Allowances	Cost of Goods Sold
Inventory	Unearned Rent Revenue	Preferred Stock	Interest Revenue	Depreciation Expense
Supplies	Interest Payable	Paid-in Capital in Excess of Par—Preferred Stock	Gain on Disposal of Plant Assets	Freight-Out
Prepaid Insurance	Dividends Payable	Treasury Stock		Income Tax Expense
Prepaid Rent	Income Taxes Payable	Retained Earnings		Insurance Expense
Land	Bonds Payable	Dividends		Interest Expense
Equipment	Discount on Bonds Payable	Income Summary		Loss on Disposal of Plant Assets
Accumulated Depreciation—Equipment	Premium on Bonds Payable			Maintenance and Repairs Expense
Buildings	Mortgage Payable			Rent Expense
Accumulated Depreciation—Buildings				Salaries and Wages Expense
Copyrights				Supplies Expense
Goodwill				Utilities Expense
Patents				

ACCOUNTING PRINCIPLES

TWELFTH EDITION

INTERNATIONAL STUDENT VERSION

Jerry J. Weygandt PhD, CPA
University of Wisconsin—Madison
Madison, Wisconsin

Paul D. Kimmel PhD, CPA
University of Wisconsin—Milwaukee
Milwaukee, Wisconsin

Donald E. Kieso PhD, CPA
Northern Illinois University
DeKalb, Illinois

WILEY

DEDICATED TO

the ***Wiley sales representatives*** *who sell our books and service our adopters in a professional and ethical manner, and to Enid, Merlynn, and Donna*

Founded in 1807, John Wiley & Sons, Inc. has been a valued source of knowledge and understanding for more than 200 years, helping people around the world meet their needs and fulfill their aspirations. Our company is built on a foundation of principles that include responsibility to the communities we serve and where we live and work. In 2008, we launched a Corporate Citizenship Initiative, a global effort to address the environmental, social, economic, and ethical challenges we face in our business. Among the issues we are addressing are carbon impact, paper specifications and procurement, ethical conduct within our business and among our vendors, and community and charitable support. For more information, please visit our website: www.wiley.com/go/citizenship.

ISBN: 978-1-118-95974-9

Printed in Asia

10 9 8 7 6 5

From the Authors

Dear Student,

Why This Course? *Remember your biology course in high school? Did you have one of those "invisible man" models (or maybe something more high-tech than that) that gave you the opportunity to look "inside" the human body? This accounting course offers something similar. To understand a business, you have to understand the financial insides of a business organization. An accounting course will help you understand the essential financial components of businesses. Whether you are looking at a large multinational company like Apple or Starbucks or a single-owner software consulting business or coffee shop, knowing the fundamentals of accounting will help you understand what is happening. As an employee, a manager, an investor, a business owner, or a director of your own personal finances—any of which roles you will have at some point in your life—you will make better decisions for having taken this course.*

"Whether you are looking at a large multinational company like Apple or Starbucks or a single-owner software consulting business or coffee shop, knowing the fundamentals of accounting will help you understand what is happening."

Why This Book? *Hundreds of thousands of students have used this textbook. Your instructor has chosen it for you because of its trusted reputation. The authors have worked hard to keep the book fresh, timely, and accurate.*

How to Succeed? *We've asked many students and many instructors whether there is a secret for success in this course. The nearly unanimous answer turns out to be not much of a secret: "Do the homework." This is one course where doing is learning. The more time you spend on the homework assignments—using the various tools that this textbook provides—the more likely you are to learn the essential concepts, techniques, and methods of accounting. Besides the textbook itself, WileyPLUS and the book's companion website also offers various support resources.*

Good luck in this course. We hope you enjoy the experience and that you put to good use throughout a lifetime of success the knowledge you obtain in this course. We are sure you will not be disappointed.

Jerry J. Weygandt
Paul D. Kimmel
Donald E. Kieso

Author Commitment

Jerry Weygandt

Jerry J. Weygandt, PhD, CPA, is Arthur Andersen Alumni Emeritus Professor of Accounting at the University of Wisconsin—Madison. He holds a Ph.D. in accounting from the University of Illinois. Articles by Professor Weygandt have appeared in the *Accounting Review, Journal of Accounting Research, Accounting Horizons, Journal of Accountancy*, and other academic and professional journals. These articles have examined such financial reporting issues as accounting for price-level adjustments, pensions, convertible securities, stock option contracts, and interim reports. Professor Weygandt is author of other accounting and financial reporting books and is a member of the American Accounting Association, the American Institute of Certified Public Accountants, and the Wisconsin Society of Certified Public Accountants. He has served on numerous committees of the American Accounting Association and as a member of the editorial board of the Accounting Review; he also has served as President and Secretary-Treasurer of the American Accounting Association. In addition, he has been actively involved with the American Institute of Certified Public Accountants and has been a member of the Accounting Standards Executive Committee (AcSEC) of that organization. He has served on the FASB task force that examined the reporting issues related to accounting for income taxes and served as a trustee of the Financial Accounting Foundation. Professor Weygandt has received the Chancellor's Award for Excellence in Teaching and the Beta Gamma Sigma Dean's Teaching Award. He is on the board of directors of M & I Bank of Southern Wisconsin. He is the recipient of the Wisconsin Institute of CPA's Outstanding Educator's Award and the Lifetime Achievement Award. In 2001 he received the American Accounting Association's Outstanding Educator Award.

Paul Kimmel

Paul D. Kimmel, PhD, CPA, received his bachelor's degree from the University of Minnesota and his doctorate in accounting from the University of Wisconsin. He is an Associate Professor at the University of Wisconsin—Milwaukee, and has public accounting experience with Deloitte & Touche (Minneapolis). He was the recipient of the UWM School of Business Advisory Council Teaching Award, the Reggie Taite Excellence in Teaching Award and a three-time winner of the Outstanding Teaching Assistant Award at the University of Wisconsin. He is also a recipient of the Elijah Watts Sells Award for Honorary Distinction for his results on the CPA exam. He is a member of the American Accounting Association and the Institute of Management Accountants and has published articles in *Accounting Review, Accounting Horizons, Advances in Management Accounting, Managerial Finance, Issues in Accounting Education, Journal of Accounting Education,* as well as other journals. His research interests include accounting for financial instruments and innovation in accounting education. He has published papers and given numerous talks on incorporating critical thinking into accounting education, and helped prepare a catalog of critical thinking resources for the Federated Schools of Accountancy.

Don Kieso

Donald E. Kieso, PhD, CPA, received his bachelor's degree from Aurora University and his doctorate in accounting from the University of Illinois. He has served as chairman of the Department of Accountancy and is currently the KPMG Emeritus Professor of Accountancy at Northern Illinois University. He has public accounting experience with Price Waterhouse & Co. (San Francisco and Chicago) and Arthur Andersen & Co. (Chicago) and research experience with the Research Division of the American Institute of Certified Public Accountants (New York). He has done post doctorate work as a Visiting Scholar at the University of California at Berkeley and is a recipient of NIU's Teaching Excellence Award and four Golden Apple Teaching Awards. Professor Kieso is the author of other accounting and business books and is a member of the American Accounting Association, the American Institute of Certified Public Accountants, and the Illinois CPA Society. He has served as a member of the Board of Directors of the Illinois CPA Society, then AACSB's Accounting Accreditation Committees, the State of Illinois Comptroller's Commission, as Secretary-Treasurer of the Federation of Schools of Accountancy, and as Secretary-Treasurer of the American Accounting Association. Professor Kieso is currently serving on the Board of Trustees and Executive Committee of Aurora University, as a member of the Board of Directors of Kishwaukee Community Hospital, and as Treasurer and Director of Valley West Community Hospital. From 1989 to 1993 he served as a charter member of the national Accounting Education Change Commission. He is the recipient of the Outstanding Accounting Educator Award from the Illinois CPA Society, the FSA's Joseph A. Silvoso Award of Merit, the NIU Foundation's Humanitarian Award for Service to Higher Education, a Distinguished Service Award from the Illinois CPA Society, and in 2003 an honorary doctorate from Aurora University.

Practice Made Simple

The Team for Success is focused on helping students get the most out of their accounting course by **making practice simple**. Both in the printed text and the online environment of *WileyPLUS*, new opportunities for self-guided practice allow students to check their knowledge of accounting concepts, skills, and problem-solving techniques as they receive individual feedback at the question, learning objective, and course level.

Personalized Practice

Based on cognitive science, **WileyPLUS with ORION** is a personalized, adaptive learning experience that gives students the practice they need to build proficiency on topics while using their study time most effectively. The adaptive engine is powered by hundreds of unique questions per chapter, giving students endless opportunities for practice throughout the course.

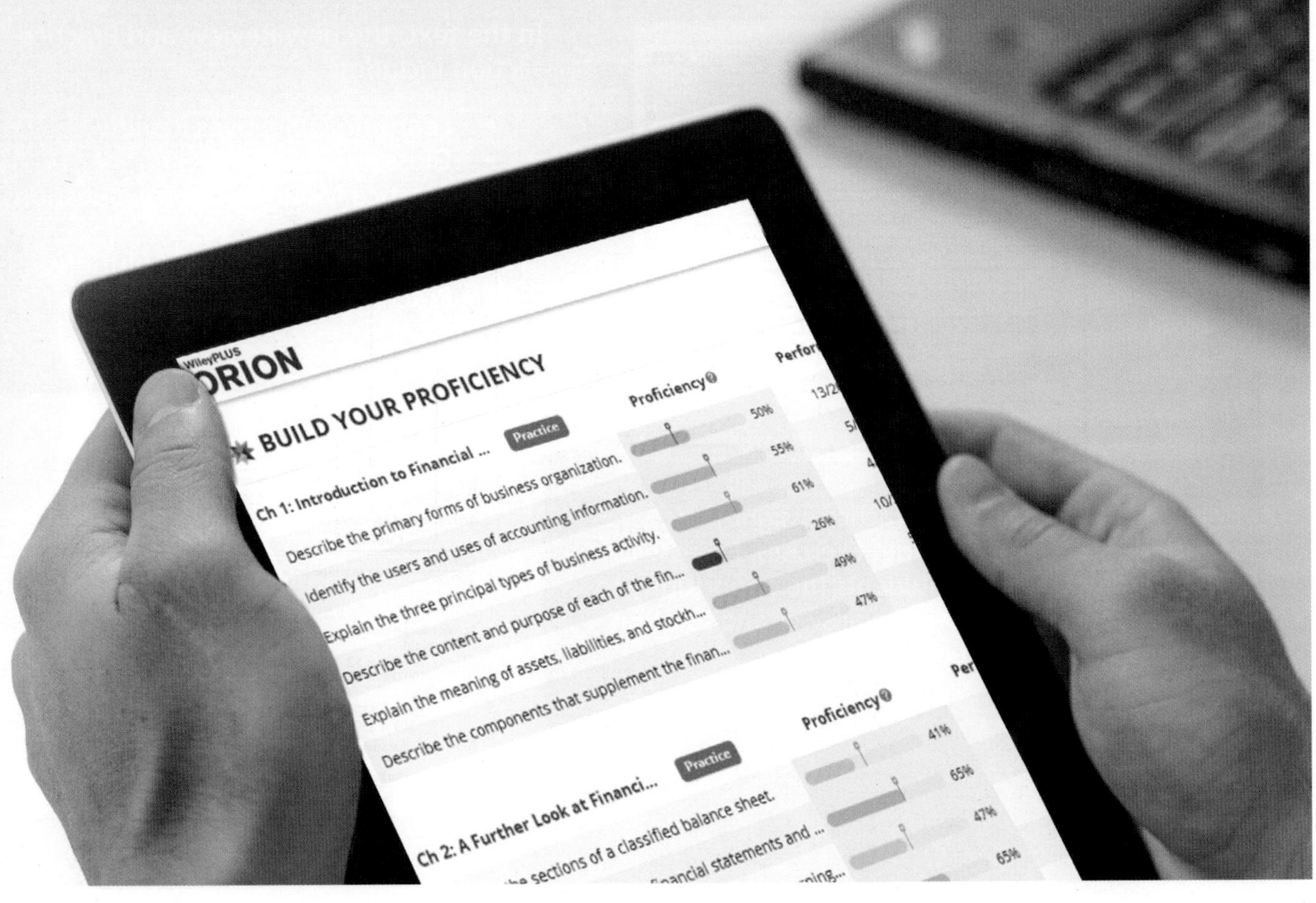

WILEY

Streamlined Learning Objectives

Newly streamlined learning objectives help students make the best use of their time outside of class. Each learning objective is addressed by reading content, answering a variety of practice and assessment questions, and watching educational videos, so that no matter where students begin their work, the relevant resources and practice are readily accessible.

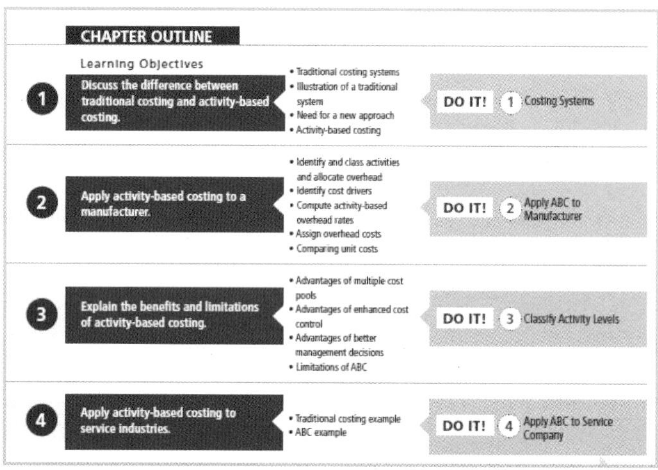

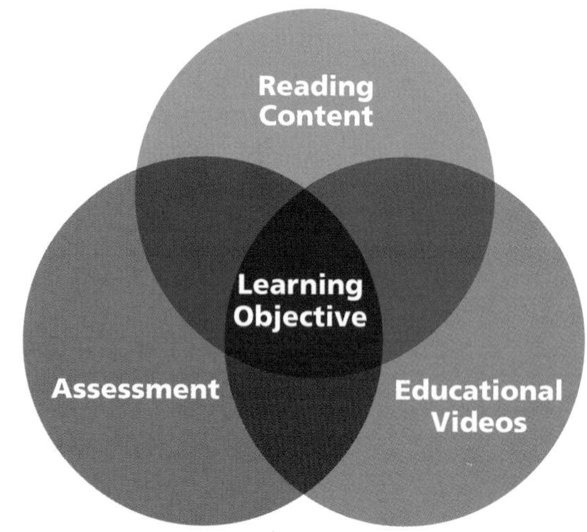

Review and Practice

A new section in the text and in **WileyPLUS** offers students more opportunities for self-guided practice.

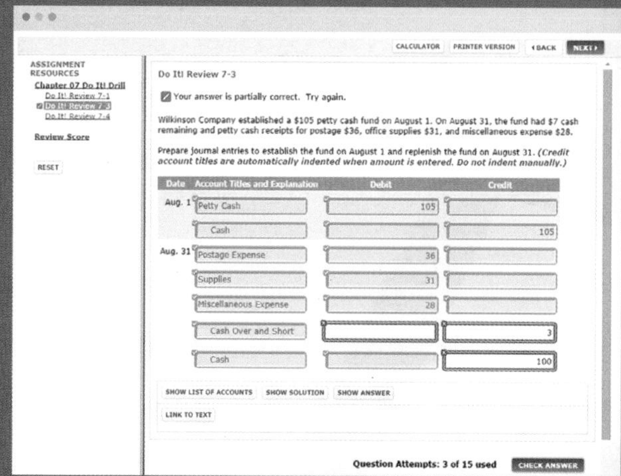

In the text, the new Review and Practice section includes:

- Learning Objectives Review
- Glossary Review
- Practice Multiple-Choice Questions and Solutions
- Practice Exercises and Solutions
- Practice Problem and Solution

In **WileyPLUS**, the new practice assignments include several Do ITs, Brief Exercises, Exercises, and Problems, giving students the opportunity to check their work or see the answer and solution after their final attempt.

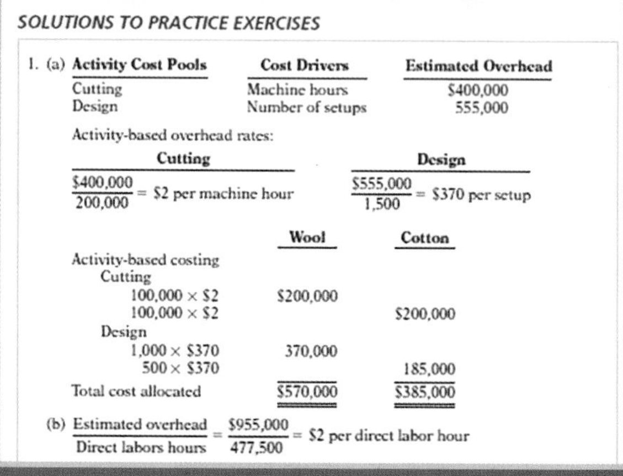

SOLUTIONS TO PRACTICE EXERCISES

1. (a)

Activity Cost Pools	Cost Drivers	Estimated Overhead
Cutting	Machine hours	$400,000
Design	Number of setups	555,000

Activity-based overhead rates:

Cutting: $\frac{\$400,000}{200,000}$ = $2 per machine hour

Design: $\frac{\$555,000}{1,500}$ = $370 per setup

	Wool	Cotton
Activity-based costing		
Cutting		
100,000 × $2	$200,000	
100,000 × $2		$200,000
Design		
1,000 × $370	370,000	
500 × $370		185,000
Total cost allocated	$570,000	$385,000

(b) $\frac{\text{Estimated overhead}}{\text{Direct labors hours}} = \frac{\$955,000}{477,500}$ = $2 per direct labor hour

What's New?

WileyPLUS with ORION

Over 5,500 new questions are available for practice and review. WileyPLUS with Orion is an adaptive study and practice tool that helps students build proficiency in course topics.

Updated Content and Design

We scrutinized all chapter material to find new ways to engage students and help them learn accounting concepts. Homework problems were updated in all chapters.

A new learning objective structure helps students practice their understanding of concepts with DO IT! exercises before they move on to different topics in other learning objectives. Coupled with a new interior design and revised infographics, the new outcomes-oriented approach motivates students and helps them make the best use of their time.

WileyPLUS Videos

Over 300 videos are available in WileyPLUS. More than 150 of the videos are new to the 12th Edition. The videos walk students through relevant homework problems and solutions, review important concepts, provide overviews of Excel skills, and explore topics in a real-world context.

Student Practice and Solutions

New practice opportunities with solutions are integrated throughout the textbook and WileyPLUS course. Each textbook chapter now provides students with a **Review and Practice** section that includes learning objective summaries, multiple-choice questions with feedback for each answer choice, and both practice exercises and problems with solutions. Also, each learning objective module in the textbook is now followed by a DO IT! exercise with an accompanying solution.

In **WileyPLUS**, two brief exercises, two DO IT! exercises, two exercises, and a new problem are available for practice with each chapter. These practice questions are algorithmic, providing students with multiple opportunities for advanced practice.

Real World Context

We expanded our practice of using numerous examples of real companies throughout the textbook. For example, new feature stories highlight operations of **Clif Bar**, **Groupon**, and **REI**. Also, in WileyPLUS, real-world Insight boxes now have questions that can be assigned as homework.

Excel

New Excel skill videos help students understand Excel features they can apply in their accounting studies. A new continuing Excel tutorial is also available at the end of each managerial accounting chapter.

More information about the 12th Edition is available on the book's website at **www.wiley.com/college/weygandt**.

Table of Contents

4 Completing the Accounting Cycle 116

5 Accounting for Merchandising Operations 165

6 Inventories 210

26 Incremental Analysis and Capital Budgeting 904

A Specimen Financial Statements: Apple Inc. A-1

B Specimen Financial Statements: PepsiCo, Inc. B-1

C Specimen Financial Statements: The Coca-Cola Company C-1

D Specimen Financial Statements: Amazon.com, Inc. D-1

E Specimen Financial Statements: Wal-Mart Stores, Inc. E-1

F Specimen Financial Statements: Louis Vuitton F-1

G Time Value of Money G-1

H Standards of Ethical Conduct for Management Accountants H-1

Cases for Managerial Decision-Making*

*Available online at **www.wiley.com/college/weygandt**.

Acknowledgments

Accounting Principles has benefited greatly from the input of focus group participants, manuscript reviewers, those who have sent comments by letter or e-mail, ancillary authors, and proofers. We greatly appreciate the constructive suggestions and innovative ideas of reviewers and the creativity and accuracy of the ancillary authors and checkers.

Twelfth Edition

Karen Andrews
Lewis-Clark State College

Sandra Bailey
Oregon Institute of Technology

Shele Bannon
Queensborough Community College

Robert Barta
Suffolk County Community College

Quent Below
Roane State Community College

Lila Bergman
Hunter College

Glen Brauchle
Dowling College

Douglas Brown
Forsyth Technical Community College

Ronald Campbell
North Carolina A&T State University

Elizabeth Capener
Dominican University of California

Beth Carraway
Horry-Georgetown Technical College

Jackie Caseu
Cape Fear Community College

Kim Charland
Kansas State University

Suzanne Cory
St. Mary's University

Paul Cox
Medgar Evers College

Joseph Cunningham
Harford Community College

Kate Demarest
Carroll Community College

Richard Dugger
Kilgore College

Bill Elliott
Oral Roberts University

Cole Engel
Fort Hays State University

Gary Ford
Tompkins Cortland Community College

Alan Foster
J.S. Reynolds Community College

Dale Fowler
Ohio Christian University

George Gardner
Bemidji State University

Willard Garman
University of California, Los Angeles

Joseph Jurkowski
D'youville College

Randy Kidd
Metropolitan Community College

Cindy Killian
Wilkes Community College

Shirly Kleiner
Johnson County Community College

David Krug
Johnson County Community College

Christy Land
Catawba Valley Community College

Anita Leslie
York Technical College

Lori Major
Luzerne County Community College

Charles Malone
North Carolina A&T State University

Ken Mark
Kansas City Kansas Community College

Barbara Michal
University of Rio Grande

Allison Moore
Los Angeles Southwest College

Brandis Phillips
North Carolina A&T State University

Mary Phillips
North Carolina Central University

La Vonda Ramey
Schoolcraft College

J. Ramos-Alexander
New Jersey City University

Michelle Randall
Schoolcraft College

Ruthie Reynolds
Tennessee State University

Kathie Rogers
Suffolk Community College

Kent Schneider
East Tennessee State University

Nadia Schwartz
Augustana College

Mehdi Sheikholeslami
Bemidji State University

Bradley Smith
Des Moines Area Community College

Emil Soriano
Contra Costa College

John Stancil
Florida Southern College

Linda Summey
Central Carolina Community College

Joan Van Hise
Fairfield University

Pat Wright
Long Island University

Judith Zander
Grossmont College

WileyPLUS Developers and Reviewers

Carole Brandt-Fink
Laura McNally
Melanie Yon

Ancillary Authors, Contributors, Proofers, and Accuracy Checkers

Bridget Anakwe
Delaware State University

Michael Barnes
Lansing Community College

Ellen Bartley
St. Joseph's College

LuAnn Bean
Florida Institute of Technology

Jack Borke
University of Wisconsin—Platteville

Sandee Cohen
Columbia College Chicago

Terry Elliott
Morehead State University

James Emig
Villanova University

Larry Falcetto
Emporia State University

Heidi Hansel
Kirkwood Community College

Coby Harmon
University of California—Santa Barbara

Karen Hern
Grossmont College

Derek Jackson
St. Mary's University of Minnesota

Laurie Larson
Valencia College

Jeanette Milius
Iowa Western Community College

Jill Misuraca
University of Tampa

Barbara Muller
Arizona State University

Yvonne Phang
Borough of Manhattan Community College

Laura Prosser
Black Hills State University

Alice Sineath
University of Maryland University College

Lakshmy Sivaratnam
Kansas City Kansas Community College

Teresa Speck
St. Mary's University of Minnesota

Lynn Stallworth
Appalachian State University

Calvin Tan
Kapiolani Community College

Mike Trebesh
Lansing Community College

Dick Wasson
Southwestern College

Lori Grady Zaher
Bucks County Community College

Advisory Board

Janice Akao
Butler Community College

Michael Barnes
Lansing Community College

Jackie Casey
Cape Fear Community College

Lisa Cole
Johnson County Community College

Susan Cordes
Johnson County Community College

Kim Gatzke
Delgado Community College

Drew Goodson
Central Carolina Community College

Thomas Kam
Hawaii Pacific University

Alfonso Maldonado
Laredo Community College

Lakshmy Sivaratnam
Kansas City Kansas Community College

Patricia Walczak
Lansing Community College

We appreciate the considerable support provided to us by the following people at Current Designs: Mike Cichanowski, Jim Brown, Diane Buswell, and Jake Greseth. We also benefited from the assistance and suggestions provided to us by Joan Van Hise in the preparation of materials related to sustainability.

We appreciate the exemplary support and commitment given to us by executive editor Michael McDonald, senior marketing manager Karolina Zarychta Honsa, customer and product development manager Christopher DeJohn, development editor Ed Brislin, assistant development editor Rebecca Costantini, market solutions assistant Elizabeth Kearns, marketing assistant Anna Wilhelm, editorial supervisor Terry Ann Tatro, editorial associate Margaret Thompson, product design manager Allie Morris, product design associate Matt Origoni, designers Maureen Eide and Kristine Carney, photo editor Mary Ann Price, indexer Steve Ingle, and Denise Showers at Aptara. All of these professionals provided innumerable services that helped the textbook take shape.

Finally, our thanks to Amy Scholz, Susan Elbe, George Hoffman, Tim Stookesberry, Douglas Reiner, Brent Gordon, Joe Heider, and Steve Smith for their support and leadership in Wiley's Global Education. We will appreciate suggestions and comments from users—instructors and students alike. You can send your thoughts and ideas about the textbook to us via email at: *AccountingAuthors@yahoo.com.*

Jerry J. Weygandt
Madison, Wisconsin

Paul D. Kimmel
Milwaukee, Wisconsin

Donald E. Kieso
DeKalb, Illinois

Chapter 1 Accounting in Action

Many students who take this course do not plan to be accountants. If you are in that group, you might be thinking, "If I'm not going to be an accountant, why do I need to know accounting?" Well, consider this quote from Harold Geneen, the former chairman of IT&T: "To be good at your business, you have to know the numbers—cold." In business, accounting and financial statements are the means for communicating the numbers. If you don't know how to read financial statements, you can't really know your business.

Many businesses agree with this view. They see the value of their employees being able to read financial statements and understand how their actions affect the company's financial results. For example, consider Clif Bar & Company. The original Clif Bar® energy bar was created in 1990 by Gary Erickson and his mother in her kitchen. Today, the company has almost 300 employees.

Clif Bar is guided by what it calls its Five Aspirations—Sustaining Our Business, Our Brands, Our People, Our Community, and the Planet. Its website documents its efforts and accomplishments in these five areas. Just a few examples include the company's use of organic products to protect soil, water, and biodiversity; the "smart" solar array (the largest in North America), which provides nearly all the electrical needs for its 115,000-square foot building; and the incentives Clif Bar provides to employees to reduce their personal environmental impact, such as $6,500 toward the purchase of an efficient car or $1,000 per year for eco-friendly improvements toward their homes.

One of the company's proudest moments was the creation of an employee stock ownership plan (ESOP) in 2010. This plan gives its employees 20% ownership of the company (Gary and his wife Kit own the other 80%). The ESOP also resulted in Clif Bar enacting an open-book management program, including the commitment to educate all employee-owners about its finances. Armed with this basic financial knowledge, employees are more aware of the financial impact of their actions, which leads to better decisions.

Many other companies have adopted this open-book management approach. Even in companies that do not practice open-book management, employers generally assume that managers in all areas of the company are "financially literate."

Taking this course will go a long way to making you financially literate. In this textbook, you will learn how to read and prepare financial statements, and how to use basic tools to evaluate financial results. Throughout this textbook, we attempt to increase your familiarity with financial reporting by providing numerous references, questions, and exercises that encourage you to explore the financial statements of well-known companies.

LEARNING OBJECTIVES

1. **Identify the activities and users associated with accounting.**
2. **Explain the building blocks of accounting: ethics, principles, and assumptions.**
3. **State the accounting equation, and define its components.**
4. **Analyze the effects of business transactions on the accounting equation.**
5. **Describe the four financial statements and how they are prepared.**

LEARNING OBJECTIVE 1

Identify the activities and users associated with accounting.

What consistently ranks as one of the top career opportunities in business? What frequently rates among the most popular majors on campus? What was the undergraduate degree chosen by Nike founder Phil Knight, Home Depot co-founder Arthur Blank, former acting director of the Federal Bureau of Investigation (FBI) Thomas Pickard, and numerous members of Congress? Accounting.[1] Why did these people choose accounting? They wanted to understand what was happening financially to their organizations. Accounting is the financial information system that provides these insights. In short, to understand your organization, you have to know the numbers.

Essential terms are printed in blue when they first appear, and are defined in the end-of-chapter ***Glossary Review****.*

Accounting consists of three basic activities—it **identifies**, **records**, and **communicates** the economic events of an organization to interested users. Let's take a closer look at these three activities.

Three Activities

As a starting point to the accounting process, a company **identifies** the **economic events relevant to its business**. Examples of economic events are the sale of snack chips by PepsiCo, the provision of cell phone services by AT&T, and the payment of wages by Facebook.

Once a company like PepsiCo identifies economic events, it **records** those events in order to provide a history of its financial activities. Recording consists of keeping a **systematic**, **chronological diary of events**, measured in dollars and cents. In recording, PepsiCo also classifies and summarizes economic events.

Finally, PepsiCo **communicates** the collected information to interested users by means of **accounting reports**. The most common of these reports are called **financial statements**. To make the reported financial information meaningful, PepsiCo reports the recorded data in a standardized way. It accumulates information resulting from similar transactions. For example, PepsiCo accumulates all sales transactions over a certain period of time and reports the data as one amount in the company's financial statements. Such data are said to be reported **in the aggregate**. By presenting the recorded data in the aggregate, the accounting process simplifies a multitude of transactions and makes a series of activities understandable and meaningful.

A vital element in communicating economic events is the accountant's ability to **analyze and interpret** the reported information. Analysis involves use of ratios, percentages, graphs, and charts to highlight significant financial trends and relationships. Interpretation involves **explaining the uses**, **meaning**, **and limitations of reported data**. Appendices A–E show the financial statements of Apple Inc., PepsiCo Inc., The Coca-Cola Company, Amazon.com, Inc., and Wal-Mart Stores, Inc., respectively. (In addition, in the *A Look at IFRS* section at the end of each chapter, the French company Louis Vuitton Moët Hennessy is analyzed.) We refer to these statements at various places throughout the textbook. At this point, these financial statements probably strike you as complex and confusing. By the end of this course, you'll be surprised at your ability to understand, analyze, and interpret them.

Illustration 1-1 summarizes the activities of the accounting process.

[1]The appendix to this chapter describes job opportunities for accounting majors and explains why accounting is such a popular major.

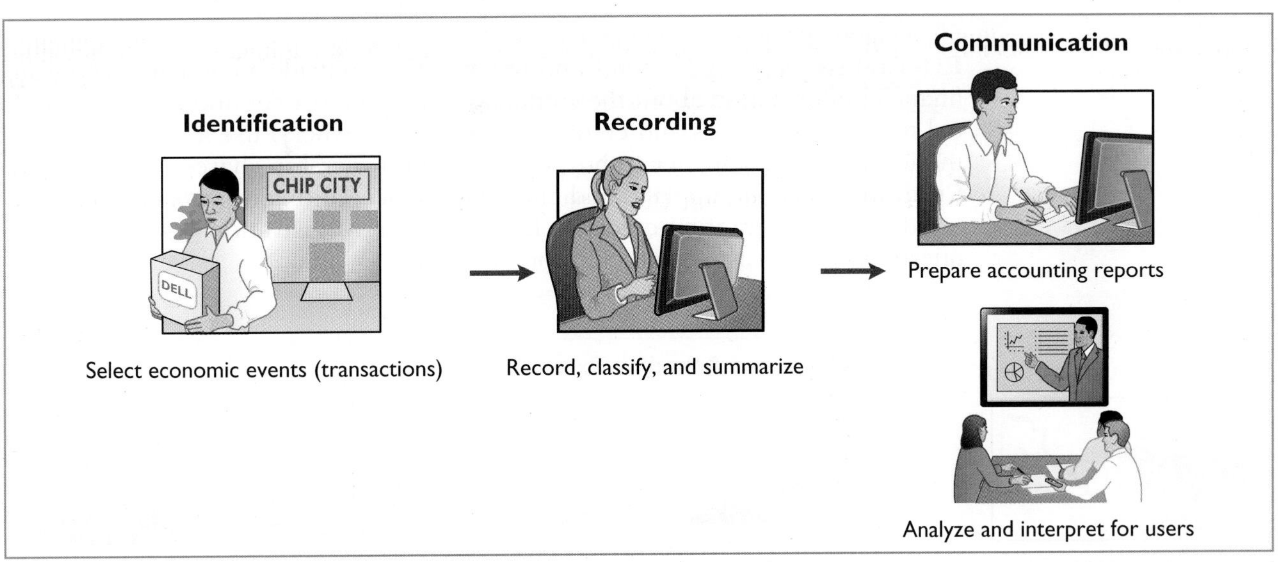

Illustration 1-1 The activities of the accounting process

You should understand that the accounting process **includes** the bookkeeping function. **Bookkeeping** usually involves **only** the recording of economic events. It is therefore just one part of the accounting process. In total, accounting involves **the entire process of identifying, recording, and communicating economic events.**[2]

Who Uses Accounting Data

The financial information that users need depends upon the kinds of decisions they make. There are two broad groups of users of financial information: internal users and external users.

INTERNAL USERS

Internal users of accounting information are managers who plan, organize, and run the business. These include marketing managers, production supervisors, finance directors, and company officers. In running a business, internal users must answer many important questions, as shown in Illustration 1-2.

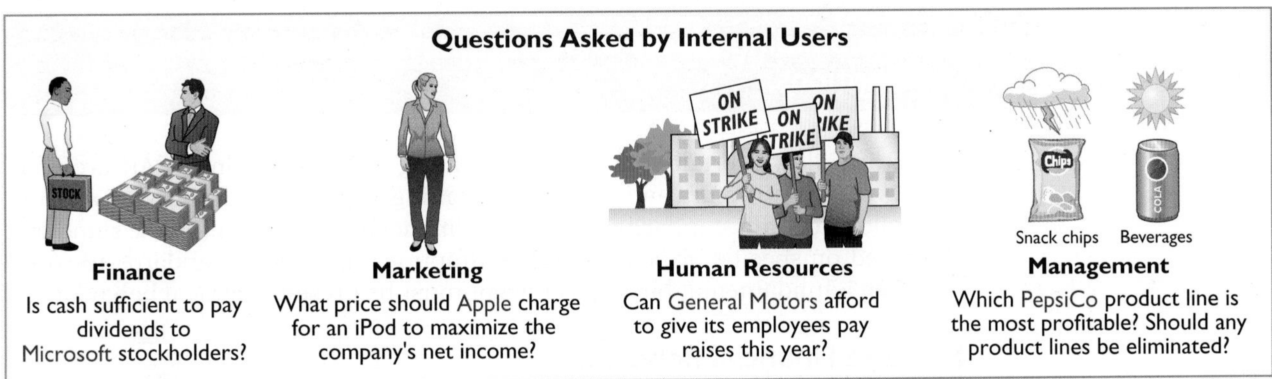

Illustration 1-2 Questions that internal users ask

To answer these and other questions, internal users need detailed information on a timely basis. **Managerial accounting** provides internal reports to help users make decisions about their companies. Examples are financial comparisons of operating alternatives, projections of income from new sales campaigns, and forecasts of cash needs for the next year.

[2]The origins of accounting are generally attributed to the work of Luca Pacioli, an Italian Renaissance mathematician. Pacioli was a close friend and tutor to Leonardo da Vinci and a contemporary of Christopher Columbus. In his 1494 text *Summa de Arithmetica, Geometria, Proportione et Proportionalite*, Pacioli described a system to ensure that financial information was recorded efficiently and accurately.

EXTERNAL USERS

External users are individuals and organizations outside a company who want financial information about the company. The two most common types of external users are investors and creditors. **Investors** (owners) use accounting information to decide whether to buy, hold, or sell ownership shares of a company. **Creditors** (such as suppliers and bankers) use accounting information to evaluate the risks of granting credit or lending money. Illustration 1-3 shows some questions that investors and creditors may ask.

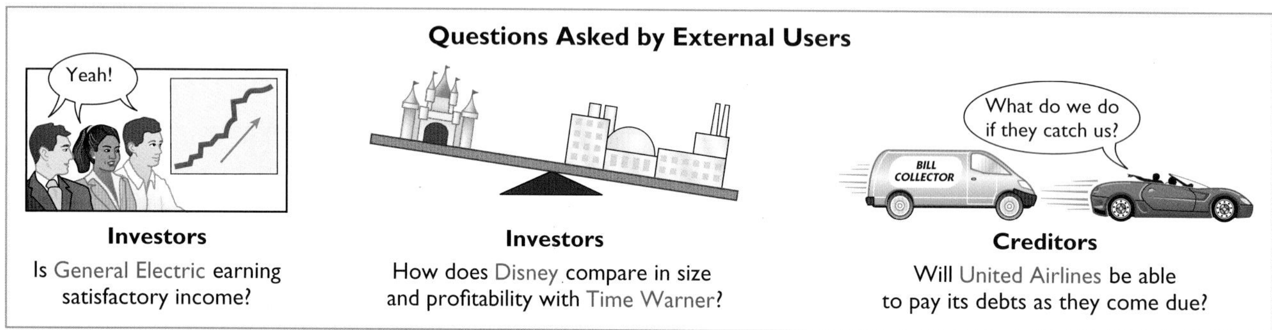

Illustration 1-3
Questions that external users ask

Financial accounting answers these questions. It provides economic and financial information for investors, creditors, and other external users. The information needs of external users vary considerably. **Taxing authorities**, such as the Internal Revenue Service, want to know whether the company complies with tax laws. **Regulatory agencies**, such as the Securities and Exchange Commission or the Federal Trade Commission, want to know whether the company is operating within prescribed rules. **Customers** are interested in whether a company like Telsa will continue to honor product warranties and support its product lines. **Labor unions** such as the Major League Baseball Players Association want to know whether the owners have the ability to pay increased wages and benefits.

LEARNING OBJECTIVE 2

Explain the building blocks of accounting: ethics, principles, and assumptions.

A doctor follows certain protocols in treating a patient's illness. An architect follows certain structural guidelines in designing a building. Similarly, an accountant follows certain standards in reporting financial information. These standards are based on specific principles and assumptions. For these standards to work, however, a fundamental business concept must be present—ethical behavior.

Ethics in Financial Reporting

People won't gamble in a casino if they think it is "rigged." Similarly, people won't play the stock market if they think stock prices are rigged. In recent years, the financial press has been full of articles about financial scandals at Enron, WorldCom, HealthSouth, AIG, and other companies. As the scandals came to light, mistrust of financial reporting in general grew. One article in the *Wall Street Journal* noted that "repeated disclosures about questionable accounting practices have bruised investors' faith in the reliability of earnings reports, which in turn has sent stock prices tumbling." Imagine trying to carry on a business or invest money if you could not depend on the financial statements to be honestly prepared. Information would have no credibility. There is no doubt that a sound, well-functioning economy depends on accurate and dependable financial reporting.

United States regulators and lawmakers were very concerned that the economy would suffer if investors lost confidence in corporate accounting because of unethical financial reporting. In response, Congress passed the **Sarbanes-Oxley Act (SOX)**. Its intent is to reduce unethical corporate behavior and decrease the likelihood of future corporate scandals. As a result of SOX, top management must now certify the accuracy of financial information. In addition, penalties for fraudulent financial activity are much more severe. Also, SOX increased the independence requirements of the outside auditors who review the accuracy of corporate financial statements and increased the oversight role of boards of directors.

The standards of conduct by which actions are judged as right or wrong, honest or dishonest, fair or not fair, are **ethics**. Effective financial reporting depends on sound ethical behavior. To sensitize you to ethical situations in business and to give you practice at solving ethical dilemmas, we address ethics in a couple of ways in this textbook:

1. Many of the *People, Planet, and Profit Insight* boxes focus on ethical issues that companies face in measuring and reporting social and environmental issues.
2. At the end of the chapter, an *Ethics Case* simulates a business situation and asks you to put yourself in the position of a decision-maker in that case.

When analyzing various ethics cases, as well as experiences in your own life, it is useful to apply the three steps outlined in Illustration 1-4.

1. Recognize an ethical situation and the ethical issues involved.
Use your personal ethics to identify ethical situations and issues. Some businesses and professional organizations provide written codes of ethics for guidance in some business situations.

2. Identify and analyze the principal elements in the situation.
Identify the **stakeholders**—persons or groups who may be harmed or benefited. Ask the question: What are the responsibilities and obligations of the parties involved?

3. Identify the alternatives, and weigh the impact of each alternative on various stakeholders.
Select the most ethical alternative, considering all the consequences. Sometimes there will be one right answer. Other situations involve more than one right solution; these situations require an evaluation of each and a selection of the best alternative.

Illustration 1-4
Steps in analyzing ethics cases and situations

Generally Accepted Accounting Principles

The accounting profession has developed standards that are generally accepted and universally practiced. This common set of standards is called **generally accepted accounting principles (GAAP)**. These standards indicate how to report economic events.

The primary accounting standard-setting body in the United States is the **Financial Accounting Standards Board (FASB)**. The **Securities and Exchange Commission (SEC)** is the agency of the U.S. government that oversees U.S. financial markets and accounting standard-setting bodies. The SEC relies on the FASB to develop accounting standards, which public companies must follow. Many countries outside of the United States have adopted the accounting standards issued by the **International Accounting Standards Board (IASB)**. These standards are called **International Financial Reporting Standards (IFRS)**.

International Note 

Over 100 countries use International Financial Reporting Standards (called IFRS). For example, all companies in the European Union follow international standards. The differences between U.S. and international standards are not generally significant.

As markets become more global, it is often desirable to compare the results of companies from different countries that report using different

International Notes highlight differences between U.S. and international accounting standards.

accounting standards. In order to increase comparability, in recent years the two standard-setting bodies have made efforts to reduce the differences between U.S. GAAP and IFRS. This process is referred to as **convergence**. As a result of these convergence efforts, it is likely that someday there will be a single set of high-quality accounting standards that are used by companies around the world. Because convergence is such an important issue, we highlight any major differences between GAAP and IFRS in *International Notes* (as shown in the margin here) and provide a more in-depth discussion in the *A Look at IRFS* section at the end of each chapter.

Measurement Principles

GAAP generally uses one of two measurement principles, the historical cost principle or the fair value principle. Selection of which principle to follow generally relates to trade-offs between relevance and faithful representation. **Relevance** means that financial information is capable of making a difference in a decision. **Faithful representation** means that the numbers and descriptions match what really existed or happened—they are factual.

HISTORICAL COST PRINCIPLE

The **historical cost principle** (or cost principle) dictates that companies record assets at their cost. This is true not only at the time the asset is purchased, but also over the time the asset is held. For example, if Best Buy purchases land for $300,000, the company initially reports it in its accounting records at $300,000. But what does Best Buy do if, by the end of the next year, the fair value of the land has increased to $400,000? Under the historical cost principle, it continues to report the land at $300,000.

FAIR VALUE PRINCIPLE

The **fair value principle** states that assets and liabilities should be reported at fair value (the price received to sell an asset or settle a liability). Fair value information may be more useful than historical cost for certain types of assets and liabilities. For example, certain investment securities are reported at fair value because market price information is usually readily available for these types of assets. In determining which measurement principle to use, companies weigh the factual nature of cost figures versus the relevance of fair value. In general, most companies choose to use cost. Only in situations where assets are actively traded, such as investment securities, do companies apply the fair value principle extensively.

Assumptions

Assumptions provide a foundation for the accounting process. Two main assumptions are the **monetary unit assumption** and the **economic entity assumption**.

MONETARY UNIT ASSUMPTION

The **monetary unit assumption** requires that companies include in the accounting records only transaction data that can be expressed in money terms. This assumption enables accounting to quantify (measure) economic events. The monetary unit assumption is vital to applying the historical cost principle.

This assumption prevents the inclusion of some relevant information in the accounting records. For example, the health of a company's owner, the quality of service, and the morale of employees are not included. The reason: Companies cannot quantify this information in money terms. Though this information is important, companies record only events that can be measured in money.

ECONOMIC ENTITY ASSUMPTION

An economic entity can be any organization or unit in society. It may be a company (such as Crocs, Inc.), a governmental unit (the state of Ohio), a municipality (Seattle), a school district (St. Louis District 48), or a church (Southern

Baptist). The **economic entity assumption** requires that the activities of the entity be kept separate and distinct from the activities of its owner and all other economic entities. To illustrate, Sally Rider, owner of Sally's Boutique, must keep her personal living costs separate from the expenses of the business. Similarly, J. Crew and Gap Inc. are segregated into separate economic entities for accounting purposes.

PROPRIETORSHIP A business owned by one person is generally a **proprietorship**. The owner is often the manager/operator of the business. Small service-type businesses (plumbing companies, beauty salons, and auto repair shops), farms, and small retail stores (antique shops, clothing stores, and used-book stores) are often proprietorships. **Usually, only a relatively small amount of money (capital) is necessary to start in business as a proprietorship. The owner (proprietor) receives any profits, suffers any losses, and is personally liable for all debts of the business.** There is no legal distinction between the business as an economic unit and the owner, but the accounting records of the business activities are kept separate from the personal records and activities of the owner.

PARTNERSHIP A business owned by two or more persons associated as partners is a **partnership**. In most respects a partnership is like a proprietorship except that more than one owner is involved. Typically, a partnership agreement (written or oral) sets forth such terms as initial investment, duties of each partner, division of net income (or net loss), and settlement to be made upon death or withdrawal of a partner. Each partner generally has unlimited personal liability for the debts of the partnership. **Like a proprietorship, for accounting purposes the partnership transactions must be kept separate from the personal activities of the partners.** Partnerships are often used to organize retail and service-type businesses, including professional practices (lawyers, doctors, architects, and certified public accountants).

CORPORATION A business organized as a separate legal entity under state corporation law and having ownership divided into transferable shares of stock is a **corporation**. The holders of the shares (stockholders) **enjoy limited liability**; that is, they are not personally liable for the debts of the corporate entity. Stockholders **may transfer all or part of their ownership shares to other investors at any time** (i.e., sell their shares). The ease with which ownership can change adds to the attractiveness of investing in a corporation. Because ownership can be transferred without dissolving the corporation, the corporation **enjoys an unlimited life**.

Although the combined number of proprietorships and partnerships in the United States is more than five times the number of corporations, the revenue produced by corporations is eight times greater. Most of the largest companies in the United States—for example, ExxonMobil, Ford, Wal-Mart Stores, Inc., Citigroup, and Apple—are corporations.

LEARNING OBJECTIVE 3

State the accounting equation, and define its components.

The two basic elements of a business are what it owns and what it owes. **Assets** are the resources a business owns. For example, Google has total assets of approximately $93.8 billion. Liabilities and owner's equity are the rights or claims against these resources. Thus, Google has $93.8 billion of claims against its $93.8 billion of assets. Claims of those to whom the company owes money (creditors) are called **liabilities**. Claims of owners are called **owner's equity**. Google has liabilities of $22.1 billion and owners' equity of $71.7 billion.

We can express the relationship of assets, liabilities, and owner's equity as an equation, as shown in Illustration 1-5.

Illustration 1-5
The basic accounting equation

Assets	=	Liabilities	+	Owner's Equity

This relationship is the **basic accounting equation**. Assets must equal the sum of liabilities and owner's equity. Liabilities appear before owner's equity in the basic accounting equation because they are paid first if a business is liquidated.

The accounting equation applies to all **economic entities** regardless of size, nature of business, or form of business organization. It applies to a small proprietorship such as a corner grocery store as well as to a giant corporation such as PepsiCo. The equation provides the **underlying framework** for recording and summarizing economic events.

Let's look in more detail at the categories in the basic accounting equation.

Assets

As noted above, **assets** are resources a business owns. The business uses its assets in carrying out such activities as production and sales. The common characteristic possessed by all assets is **the capacity to provide future services or benefits**. In a business, that service potential or future economic benefit eventually results in cash inflows (receipts). For example, consider Campus Pizza, a local restaurant. It owns a delivery truck that provides economic benefits from delivering pizzas. Other assets of Campus Pizza are tables, chairs, jukebox, cash register, oven, tableware, and, of course, cash.

Liabilities

Liabilities are claims against assets—that is, existing debts and obligations. Businesses of all sizes usually borrow money and purchase merchandise on credit. These economic activities result in payables of various sorts:

- Campus Pizza, for instance, purchases cheese, sausage, flour, and beverages on credit from suppliers. These obligations are called **accounts payable**.
- Campus Pizza also has a **note payable** to First National Bank for the money borrowed to purchase the delivery truck.
- Campus Pizza may also have **salaries and wages payable** to employees and **sales and real estate taxes payable** to the local government.

All of these persons or entities to whom Campus Pizza owes money are its **creditors**.

Creditors may legally force the liquidation of a business that does not pay its debts. In that case, the law requires that creditor claims be paid **before** ownership claims.

Owner's Equity

The ownership claim on total assets is **owner's equity**. It is equal to total assets minus total liabilities. Here is why: The assets of a business are claimed by either creditors or owners. To find out what belongs to owners, we subtract the creditors' claims (the liabilities) from assets. The remainder is the owner's claim on the assets—the owner's equity. Since the claims of creditors must be paid **before** ownership claims, owner's equity is often referred to as **residual equity**.

INCREASES IN OWNER'S EQUITY

In a proprietorship, owner's investments and revenues increase owner's equity.

INVESTMENTS BY OWNER **Investments by owner** are the assets the owner puts into the business. These investments increase owner's equity. They are recorded in a category called **owner's capital**.

REVENUES **Revenues** are the **gross increase in owner's equity resulting from business activities entered into for the purpose of earning income**. Generally, revenues result from selling merchandise, performing services, renting property, and lending money. Common sources of revenue are sales, fees, services, commissions, interest, dividends, royalties, and rent.

Revenues usually result in an increase in an asset. They may arise from different sources and are called various names depending on the nature of the business. Campus Pizza, for instance, has two categories of sales revenues—pizza sales and beverage sales.

DECREASES IN OWNER'S EQUITY

In a proprietorship, owner's drawings and expenses decrease owner's equity.

DRAWINGS An owner may withdraw cash or other assets for personal use. We use a separate classification called **drawings** to determine the total withdrawals for each accounting period. **Drawings decrease owner's equity.** They are recorded in a category called owner's drawings.

EXPENSES **Expenses** are the cost of assets consumed or services used in the process of earning revenue. They are **decreases in owner's equity that result from operating the business**. For example, Campus Pizza recognizes the following expenses: cost of ingredients (meat, flour, cheese, tomato paste, mushrooms, etc.); cost of beverages; salaries and wages expense; utilities expense (electric, gas, and water expense); delivery expense (gasoline, repairs, licenses, etc.); supplies expense (napkins, detergents, aprons, etc.); rent expense; interest expense; and property tax expense.

In summary, owner's equity is increased by an owner's investments and by revenues from business operations. Owner's equity is decreased by an owner's withdrawals of assets and by expenses. Illustration 1-6 expands the basic accounting equation by showing the items that make up owner's equity. This format is referred to as the **expanded accounting equation**.

Illustration 1-6
Expanded accounting equation

Basic Equation	Assets = Liabilities +	Owner's Equity			
Expanded Equation	Assets = Liabilities +	Owner's Capital	− Owner's Drawings	+ Revenues	− Expenses

Analyze the effects of business transactions on the accounting equation.

Transactions (**business transactions**) are a business's economic events recorded by accountants. Transactions may be external or internal. **External transactions** involve economic events between the company and some outside enterprise. For example, Campus Pizza's purchase of cooking equipment from a supplier, payment of monthly rent to the landlord, and sale of pizzas to customers are external transactions. **Internal transactions** are economic events that occur entirely within one company. The use of cooking and cleaning supplies are internal transactions for Campus Pizza.

Companies carry on many activities that do not represent business transactions. Examples are hiring employees, responding to e-mails, talking with customers, and placing merchandise orders. Some of these activities may lead to business transactions. Employees will earn wages, and suppliers will deliver ordered merchandise. The company must analyze each event to find out if it affects the components of the accounting equation. If it does, the company will record the transaction. Illustration 1-7 demonstrates the transaction identification process.

Illustration 1-7
Transaction identification process

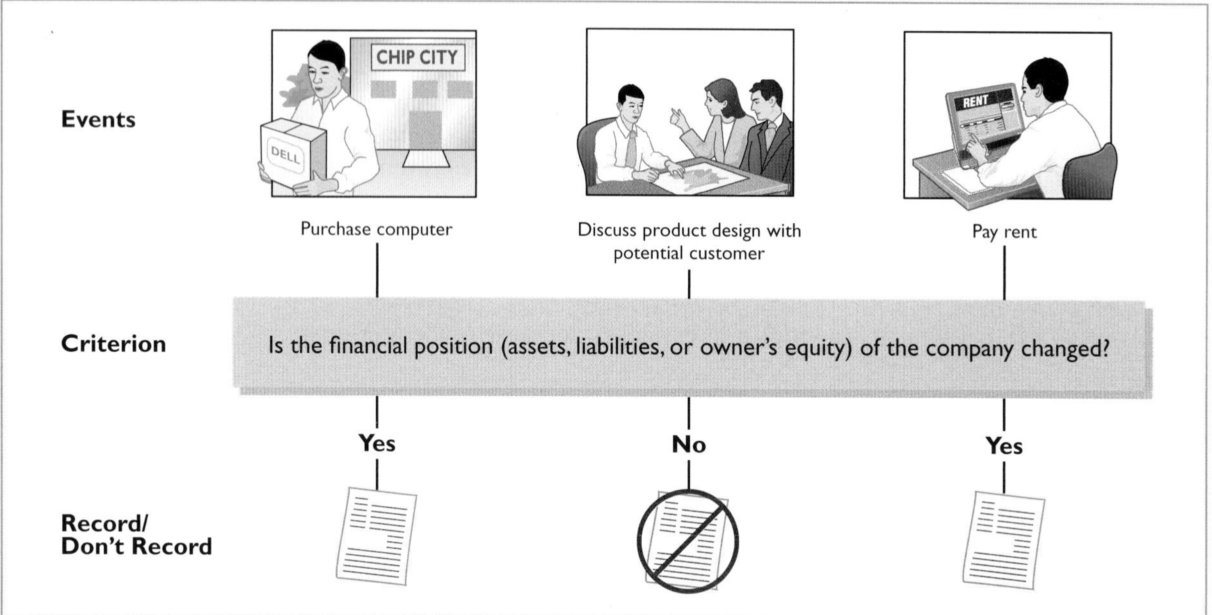

Each transaction must have a dual effect on the accounting equation. For example, if an asset is increased, there must be a corresponding (1) decrease in another asset, (2) increase in a specific liability, or (3) increase in owner's equity.

Two or more items could be affected. For example, as one asset is increased $10,000, another asset could decrease $6,000 and a liability could increase $4,000. Any change in a liability or ownership claim is subject to similar analysis.

Transaction Analysis

To demonstrate how to analyze transactions in terms of the accounting equation, we will review the business activities of Softbyte, a smartphone app development company. Softbyte is the creation of Ray Neal, an entrepreneur who wants to create focused apps that inspire and engage users of all ages. Ray was encouraged to start his own business after the success of "FoodAlert," a customizable app he developed that tracks the daily location of local food trucks. The following business transactions occur during Softbyte's first month of operations.

TRANSACTION (1). INVESTMENT BY OWNER Ray Neal starts a smartphone app development company which he names Softbyte. On September 1, 2017, he invests $15,000 cash in the business. This transaction results in an equal increase in assets and owner's equity.

Basic Analysis	The asset Cash increases $15,000, and owner's equity (identified as Owner's Capital) increases $15,000.

Equation Analysis

	Assets	=	**Liabilities**	+	**Owner's Equity**	
	Cash	=			Owner's Capital	
(1)	+$15,000	=			+$15,000	**Initial investment**

Observe that the equality of the accounting equation has been maintained. Note that the investments by the owner do not represent revenues, and they are excluded in determining net income. Therefore, it is necessary to make clear that the increase is an investment (increasing Owner's Capital) rather than revenue.

TRANSACTION (2). PURCHASE OF EQUIPMENT FOR CASH Softbyte purchases computer equipment for $7,000 cash. This transaction results in an equal increase and decrease in total assets, though the composition of assets changes.

Basic Analysis	The asset Cash decreases $7,000, and the asset Equipment increases $7,000.

Equation Analysis

	Assets			=	Liabilities	+	Owner's Equity
	Cash	+	Equipment	=			Owner's Capital
	$15,000						$15,000
(2)	**−7,000**		**+$7,000**				
	$ 8,000	+	$7,000	=			$15,000
	$15,000						

Observe that total assets are still $15,000. Owner's equity also remains at $15,000, the amount of Ray Neal's original investment.

TRANSACTION (3). PURCHASE OF SUPPLIES ON CREDIT Softbyte purchases for $1,600 from Mobile Solutions headsets and other computer accessories expected to last several months. Mobile Solutions agrees to allow Softbyte to pay this bill in October. This transaction is a purchase on account (a credit purchase). Assets increase because of the expected future benefits of using the headsets and computer accessories, and liabilities increase by the amount due to Mobile Solutions.

Basic Analysis	The asset Supplies increases $1,600, and the liability Accounts Payable increases $1,600.

Equation Analysis

	Assets					=	Liabilities	+	Owner's Equity
	Cash	+	Supplies	+	Equipment	=	Accounts Payable	+	Owner's Capital
	$8,000				$7,000				$15,000
(3)			**+$1,600**				**+$1,600**		
	$8,000	+	$1,600	+	$7,000	=	$1,600	+	$15,000
			$16,600					$16,600	

Total assets are now $16,600. This total is matched by a $1,600 creditor's claim and a $15,000 ownership claim.

TRANSACTION (4). SERVICES PERFORMED FOR CASH Softbyte receives $1,200 cash from customers for app development services it has performed. This transaction represents Softbyte's principal revenue-producing activity. Recall that **revenue increases owner's equity**.

Basic Analysis	The asset Cash increases $1,200, and owner's equity increases $1,200 due to Service Revenue.

Equation Analysis

	Assets				= Liabilities +		Owner's Equity			
	Cash	+ Supplies	+ Equipment	=	Accounts Payable	+	Owner's Capital	+	Revenues	
	$8,000	$1,600	$7,000		$1,600		$15,000			
(4)	+1,200								+$1,200	**Service Revenue**
	$9,200 +	$1,600 +	$7,000	=	$1,600	+	$15,000	+	$1,200	
		$17,800					$17,800			

The two sides of the equation balance at $17,800. Service Revenue is included in determining Softbyte's net income.

Note that we do not have room to give details for each individual revenue and expense account in this illustration. Thus, revenues (and expenses when we get to them) are summarized under one column heading for Revenues and one for Expenses. However, it is important to keep track of the category (account) titles affected (e.g., Service Revenue) as they will be needed when we prepare financial statements later in the chapter.

TRANSACTION (5). PURCHASE OF ADVERTISING ON CREDIT Softbyte receives a bill for $250 from the *Daily News* for advertising on its online website but postpones payment until a later date. This transaction results in an increase in liabilities and a decrease in owner's equity.

Basic Analysis	The liability Accounts Payable increases $250, and owner's equity decreases $250 due to Advertising Expense.

Equation Analysis

	Assets				= Liabilities +		Owner's Equity					
	Cash	+ Supplies	+ Equipment	=	Accounts Payable	+	Owner's Capital	+	Revenues	−	Expenses	
	$9,200	$1,600	$7,000		$1,600		$15,000		$1,200			
(5)					+250						−$250	**Advertising Expense**
	$9,200 +	$1,600 +	$7,000	=	$1,850	+	$15,000	+	$1,200	−	$ 250	
		$17,800						$17,800				

The two sides of the equation still balance at $17,800. Owner's equity decreases when Softbyte incurs the expense. Expenses are not always paid in cash at the time they are incurred. When Softbyte pays at a later date, the liability Accounts Payable will decrease, and the asset Cash will decrease [see Transaction (8)]. The cost of advertising is an expense (rather than an asset) because the company has **used** the benefits. Advertising Expense is included in determining net income.

TRANSACTION (6). SERVICES PERFORMED FOR CASH AND CREDIT Softbyte performs $3,500 of app development services for customers. The company receives cash of $1,500 from customers, and it bills the balance of $2,000 on account. This transaction results in an equal increase in assets and owner's equity.

Basic Analysis	Three specific items are affected: The asset Cash increases $1,500, the asset Accounts Receivable increases $2,000, and owner's equity increases $3,500 due to Service Revenue.

Equation Analysis

	Assets				= Liabilities +	Owner's Equity			
	Cash	+ Accounts Receivable	+ Supplies	+ Equipment	= Accounts Payable	+ Owner's Capital	+ Revenues	− Expenses	
	$9,200		$1,600	$7,000	$1,850	$15,000	$1,200	$250	
(6)	**+1,500**	**+$2,000**					**+3,500**		**Service Revenue**
	$10,700 +	$ 2,000 +	$1,600 +	$7,000	= $1,850	+ $15,000 +	$4,700	− $250	
	$21,300				$21,300				

Softbyte recognizes $3,500 in revenue when it performs the service. In exchange for this service, it received $1,500 in Cash and Accounts Receivable of $2,000. This Accounts Receivable represents customers' promises to pay $2,000 to Softbyte in the future. When it later receives collections on account, Softbyte will increase Cash and will decrease Accounts Receivable [see Transaction (9)].

TRANSACTION (7). PAYMENT OF EXPENSES Softbyte pays the following expenses in cash for September: office rent $600, salaries and wages of employees $900, and utilities $200. These payments result in an equal decrease in assets and owner's equity.

Basic Analysis	The asset Cash decreases $1,700, and owner's equity decreases $1,700 due to the specific expense categories (Rent Expense, Salaries and Wages Expense, and Utilities Expense).

Equation Analysis

	Assets				= Liabilities +	Owner's Equity		
	Cash	+ Accounts Receivable	+ Supplies	+ Equipment	= Accounts Payable	+ Owner's Capital	+ Revenues	− Expenses
	$10,700	$2,000	$1,600	$7,000	$1,850	$15,000	$4,700	$ 250
(7)	**−1,700**							**−600 Rent Expense** **−900 Sal. and Wages Exp.** **−200 Utilities Exp.**
	$9,000 +	$2,000 +	$1,600 +	$7,000	= $1,850	+ $15,000 +	$4,700	− $1,950
	$19,600				$19,600			

The two sides of the equation now balance at $19,600. Three lines in the analysis indicate the different types of expenses that have been incurred.

TRANSACTION (8). PAYMENT OF ACCOUNTS PAYABLE Softbyte pays its $250 *Daily News* bill in cash. The company previously [in Transaction (5)] recorded the bill as an increase in Accounts Payable and a decrease in owner's equity.

Basic Analysis	This cash payment "on account" decreases the asset Cash by $250 and also decreases the liability Accounts Payable by $250.

Equation Analysis

	Assets				= Liabilities +	Owner's Equity		
	Cash	+ Accounts Receivable	+ Supplies	+ Equipment	= Accounts Payable	+ Owner's Capital	+ Revenues	− Expenses
	$9,000	$2,000	$1,600	$7,000	$1,850	$15,000	$4,700	$1,950
(8)	**−250**				**−250**			
	$8,750 +	$2,000 +	$1,600 +	$7,000	= $1,600	+ $15,000 +	$4,700	− $1,950
	$19,350				$19,350			

Observe that the payment of a liability related to an expense that has previously been recorded does not affect owner's equity. The company recorded this expense in Transaction (5) and should not record it again.

TRANSACTION (9). RECEIPT OF CASH ON ACCOUNT Softbyte receives $600 in cash from customers who had been billed for services [in Transaction (6)]. Transaction (9) does not change total assets, but it changes the composition of those assets.

Basic Analysis

The asset Cash increases $600, and the asset Accounts Receivable decreases $600.

Equation Analysis

	Assets				=	Liabilities	+	Owner's Equity				
	Cash	+ Accounts Receivable	+ Supplies	+ Equipment	=	Accounts Payable	+	Owner's Capital	+	Revenues	−	Expenses
	$8,750	$2,000	$1,600	$7,000		$1,600		$15,000		$4,700		$1,950
(9)	**+600**	**−600**										
	$9,350 +	$1,400	+ $1,600	+ $7,000	=	$1,600	+	$15,000	+	$4,700	−	$1,950
	$19,350					$19,350						

Note that the collection of an account receivable for services previously billed and recorded does not affect owner's equity. Softbyte already recorded this revenue in Transaction (6) and should not record it again.

TRANSACTION (10). WITHDRAWAL OF CASH BY OWNER Ray Neal withdraws $1,300 in cash from the business for his personal use. This transaction results in an equal decrease in assets and owner's equity.

Basic Analysis

The asset Cash decreases $1,300, and owner's equity decreases $1,300 due to owner's withdrawal (Owner's Drawings).

Equation Analysis

	Assets				=	Liabilities	+	Owner's Equity							
	Cash	+ Accounts Receivable	+ Supplies	+ Equipment	=	Accounts Payable	+	Owner's Capital	−	Owner's Drawings	+	Revenues	−	Expenses	
	$9,350	$1,400	$1,600	$7,000		$1,600		$15,000				$4,700		$1,950	
(10)	**−1,300**									**−$1,300**					**Drawings**
	$8,050 +	$1,400	+ $1,600	+ $7,000	=	$1,600	+	$15,000	−	$1,300	+	$4,700	−	$1,950	
	$18,050					$18,050									

Observe that the effect of a cash withdrawal by the owner is the opposite of the effect of an investment by the owner. **Owner's drawings are not expenses.** Expenses are incurred for the purpose of earning revenue. Drawings do not generate revenue. They are a **disinvestment**. Like owner's investment, the company excludes owner's drawings in determining net income.

Summary of Transactions

Illustration 1-8 (page 15) summarizes the September transactions of Softbyte to show their cumulative effect on the basic accounting equation. It also indicates the transaction number and the specific effects of each transaction.

Illustration 1-8 demonstrates some significant facts:

1. Each transaction is analyzed in terms of its effect on:
   (a) The three components of the basic accounting equation.
   (b) Specific items within each component.
2. The two sides of the equation must always be equal.

	Assets				= Liabilities +	Owner's Equity				
Transaction	Cash	+ Accounts Receivable	+ Supplies	+ Equipment	= Accounts Payable	+ Owner's Capital	− Owner's Drawings	+ Rev.	− Exp.	
(1)	+$15,000					+$15,000				Initial invest.
(2)	−7,000			+$7,000						
(3)			+$1,600		+$1,600					
(4)	+1,200							+$1,200		Service Revenue
(5)					+250				−$250	Adver. Expense
(6)	+1,500	+$2,000						+3,500		Service Revenue
(7)	−600								−600	Rent Expense
	−900								−900	Sal./Wages Exp.
	−200								−200	Utilities Expense
(8)	−250				−250					
(9)	+600	−600								
(10)	−1,300						−$1,300			Drawings
	$ 8,050 +	$1,400 +	$1,600 +	$7,000	= $1,600	+ $15,000	− $1,300	+ $4,700	− $1,950	
	$18,050				$18,050					

Illustration 1-8
Tabular summary of Softbyte transactions

There! You made it through your first transaction analysis. If you feel a bit shaky on any of the transactions, it might be a good idea at this point to get up, take a short break, and come back again for a 10- to 15-minute review of the transactions, to make sure you understand them before you go on to the next section.

Describe the four financial statements and how they are prepared.

Companies prepare four financial statements from the summarized accounting data:

1. An **income statement** presents the revenues and expenses and resulting net income or net loss for a specific period of time.
2. An **owner's equity statement** summarizes the changes in owner's equity for a specific period of time.
3. A **balance sheet** reports the assets, liabilities, and owner's equity at a specific date.
4. A **statement of cash flows** summarizes information about the cash inflows (receipts) and outflows (payments) for a specific period of time.

International Note

The primary types of financial statements required by GAAP and IFRS are the same. In practice, some format differences do exist in presentations commonly employed by GAAP companies compared to IFRS companies.

These statements provide relevant financial data for internal and external users. Illustration 1-9 (page 16) shows the financial statements of Softbyte. Note that the statements shown in Illustration 1-9 are interrelated:

1. Net income of $2,750 on the **income statement** is added to the beginning balance of owner's capital in the **owner's equity statement**.
2. Owner's capital of $16,450 at the end of the reporting period shown in the **owner's equity statement** is reported on the **balance sheet**.
3. Cash of $8,050 on the **balance sheet** is reported on the **statement of cash flows**.

Illustration 1-9
Financial statements and their interrelationships

SOFTBYTE
Income Statement
For the Month Ended September 30, 2017

Revenues		
Service revenue		$ 4,700
Expenses		
Salaries and wages expense	$900	
Rent expense	600	
Advertising expense	250	
Utilities expense	200	
Total expenses		1,950
Net income		**$ 2,750** (1)

SOFTBYTE
Owner's Equity Statement
For the Month Ended September 30, 2017

Owner's capital, September 1		$ -0-
Add: Investments	$15,000	
Net income	**2,750**	17,750
		17,750
Less: Drawings		1,300
Owner's capital, September 30		**$16,450** (2)

SOFTBYTE
Balance Sheet
September 30, 2017

Assets

Cash	**$ 8,050**
Accounts receivable	1,400
Supplies	1,600
Equipment	7,000
Total assets	$ 18,050

Liabilities and Owner's Equity

Liabilities	
Accounts payable	$ 1,600
Owner's equity	
Owner's capital	**16,450**
Total liabilities and owner's equity	$ 18,050

SOFTBYTE
Statement of Cash Flows
For the Month Ended September 30, 2017

(3)

Cash flows from operating activities		
Cash receipts from revenues		$ 3,300
Cash payments for expenses		(1,950)
Net cash provided by operating activities		1,350
Cash flows from investing activities		
Purchase of equipment		(7,000)
Cash flows from financing activities		
Investments by owner	$15,000	
Drawings by owner	(1,300)	13,700
Net increase in cash		8,050
Cash at the beginning of the period		0
Cash at the end of the period		**$ 8,050**

Also, explanatory notes and supporting schedules are an integral part of every set of financial statements. We illustrate these notes and schedules in later chapters of this textbook.

Be sure to carefully examine the format and content of each statement in Illustration 1-9. We describe the essential features of each in the following sections.

Income Statement

The income statement reports the revenues and expenses for a specific period of time. (In Softbyte's case, this is "For the Month Ended September 30, 2017.") Softbyte's income statement is prepared from the data appearing in the owner's equity columns of Illustration 1-8 (page 15).

Terminology
The income statement is sometimes referred to as the *statement of operations, earnings statement,* or *profit and loss statement.*

Terminology notes introduce other terms you might hear or read.

The income statement lists revenues first, followed by expenses. Finally the statement shows net income (or net loss). **Net income** results when revenues exceed expenses. A **net loss** occurs when expenses exceed revenues.

Although practice varies, we have chosen in our illustrations and homework solutions to list expenses in order of magnitude. (We will consider alternative formats for the income statement in later chapters.)

Note that the income statement does **not** include investment and withdrawal transactions between the owner and the business in measuring net income. For example, as explained earlier, Ray Neal's withdrawal of cash from Softbyte was not regarded as a business expense.

Owner's Equity Statement

The owner's equity statement reports the changes in owner's equity for a specific period of time. The time period is the same as that covered by the income statement. Data for the preparation of the owner's equity statement come from the owner's equity columns of the tabular summary (Illustration 1-8) and from the income statement. The first line of the statement shows the beginning owner's equity amount (which was zero at the start of the business). Then come the owner's investments, net income (or loss), and the owner's drawings. This statement indicates **why** owner's equity has increased or decreased during the period.

What if Softbyte had reported a net loss in its first month? Let's assume that during the month of September 2017, Softbyte lost $10,000. Illustration 1-10 shows the presentation of a net loss in the owner's equity statement.

Illustration 1-10
Presentation of net loss

SOFTBYTE Owner's Equity Statement For the Month Ended September 30, 2017		
Owner's capital, September 1		$ -0-
Add: Investments		15,000
		15,000
Less: Drawings	$ 1,300	
Net loss	**10,000**	11,300
Owner's capital, September 30		$ 3,700

If the owner makes any additional investments, the company reports them in the owner's equity statement as investments.

Balance Sheet

Softbyte's balance sheet reports the assets, liabilities, and owner's equity at a specific date (in Softbyte's case, September 30, 2017). The company prepares the balance sheet from the column headings of the tabular summary (Illustration 1-8) and the month-end data shown in its last line.

Observe that the balance sheet lists assets at the top, followed by liabilities and owner's equity. Total assets must equal total liabilities and owner's equity. Softbyte reports only one liability—accounts payable—in its balance sheet. In most cases, there will be more than one liability. When two or more liabilities are involved, a customary way of listing is as follows.

Illustration 1-11
Presentation of liabilities

Liabilities	
Notes payable	$ 10,000
Accounts payable	63,000
Salaries and wages payable	18,000
Total liabilities	**$91,000**

The balance sheet is a snapshot of the company's financial condition at a specific moment in time (usually the month-end or year-end).

Statement of Cash Flows

The statement of cash flows provides information on the cash receipts and payments for a specific period of time. The statement of cash flows reports (1) the cash effects of a company's operations during a period, (2) its investing activities, (3) its financing activities, (4) the net increase or decrease in cash during the period, and (5) the cash amount at the end of the period.

Reporting the sources, uses, and change in cash is useful because investors, creditors, and others want to know what is happening to a company's most liquid resource. The statement of cash flows provides answers to the following simple but important questions:

1. Where did cash come from during the period?
2. What was cash used for during the period?
3. What was the change in the cash balance during the period?

As shown in Softbyte's statement of cash flows, cash increased $8,050 during the period. Net cash provided by operating activities increased cash $1,350. Cash flow from investing activities decreased cash $7,000. And cash flow from financing activities increased cash $13,700. At this time, you need not be concerned with how these amounts are determined. Chapter 17 will examine the statement of cash flows in detail.

APPENDIX 1A: Explain the career opportunities in accounting.

Why is accounting such a popular major and career choice? First, there are a lot of jobs. In many cities in recent years, the demand for accountants exceeded the supply. Not only are there a lot of jobs, but there are a wide array of opportunities. As one accounting organization observed, "accounting is one degree with 360 degrees of opportunity."

Accounting is also hot because it is obvious that accounting matters. Interest in accounting has increased, ironically, because of the attention caused by the accounting failures of companies such as **Enron** and **WorldCom**. These widely publicized scandals revealed the important role that accounting plays in society. Most people want to make a difference, and an accounting career provides many opportunities to contribute to society. Finally, the Sarbanes-Oxley Act (SOX) (see page 5) significantly increased the accounting and internal control requirements for corporations. This dramatically increased demand for professionals with accounting training.

Accountants are in such demand that it is not uncommon for accounting students to have accepted a job offer a year before graduation. As the following discussion reveals, the job options of people with accounting degrees are virtually unlimited.

Public Accounting

Individuals in **public accounting** offer expert service to the general public, in much the same way that doctors serve patients and lawyers serve clients. A major portion of public accounting involves **auditing**. In auditing, a certified public accountant (CPA) examines company financial statements and provides an opinion as to how accurately the financial statements present the company's results and financial position. Analysts, investors, and creditors rely heavily on these "audit opinions," which CPAs have the exclusive authority to issue.

Taxation is another major area of public accounting. The work that tax specialists perform includes tax advice and planning, preparing tax returns, and representing clients before governmental agencies such as the Internal Revenue Service.

A third area in public accounting is **management consulting**. It ranges from installing basic accounting software or highly complex enterprise resource planning systems, to performing support services for major marketing projects and merger and acquisition activities.

Many CPAs are entrepreneurs. They form small- or medium-sized practices that frequently specialize in tax or consulting services.

Private Accounting

Instead of working in public accounting, you might choose to be an employee of a for-profit company such as **Starbucks**, **Google**, or **PepsiCo**. In **private** (or **managerial**) **accounting**, you would be involved in activities such as cost accounting (finding the cost of producing specific products), budgeting, accounting information system design and support, and tax planning and preparation. You might also be a member of your company's internal audit team. In response to SOX, the internal auditors' job of reviewing the company's operations to ensure compliance with company policies and to increase efficiency has taken on increased importance.

Alternatively, many accountants work for not-for-profit organizations such as the **Red Cross** or the **Bill and Melinda Gates Foundation**, or for museums, libraries, or performing arts organizations.

Governmental Accounting

Another option is to pursue one of the many accounting opportunities in governmental agencies. For example, the Internal Revenue Service (IRS), Federal Bureau of Investigation (FBI), and the Securities and Exchange Commission (SEC) all employ accountants. The FBI has a stated goal that at least 15% of its new agents should be CPAs. There is also a very high demand for accounting educators at public colleges and universities and in state and local governments.

Forensic Accounting

Forensic accounting uses accounting, auditing, and investigative skills to conduct investigations into theft and fraud. It is listed among the top 20 career paths of the future. The job of forensic accountants is to catch the perpetrators of the estimated $600 billion per year of theft and fraud occurring at U.S. companies. This includes tracing money-laundering and identity-theft activities as well as tax evasion. Insurance companies hire forensic accountants to detect frauds such as arson, and law offices employ forensic accountants to identify marital assets in divorces. Forensic accountants often have FBI, IRS, or similar government experience.

"Show Me the Money"

How much can a new accountant make? Take a look at the average salaries for college graduates in public and private accounting. Keep in mind if you also have a CPA license, you'll make 10–15% more when you start out.

Illustration 1A-1
Salary estimates for jobs in public and corporate accounting

Employer	Jr. Level (0–3 yrs.)	Sr. Level (4–6 yrs.)
Public accounting (large firm)	\$51,500–\$74,250	\$71,000–\$92,250
Public accounting (small firm)	\$42,500–\$60,500	\$57,000–\$74,000
Corporate accounting (large company)	\$41,750–\$68,500	\$67,000–\$86,500
Corporate accounting (small company)	\$37,000–\$56,750	\$52,750–\$68,500

Serious earning potential over time gives CPAs great job security. Here are some examples of upper-level salaries for managers in corporate accounting. Note that geographic region, experience, education, CPA certification, and company size each play a role in determining salary.

Illustration 1A-2
Upper-level management salaries in corporate accounting

Position	Large Company	Small to Medium Company
Chief financial officer	\$189,750–\$411,000	\$96,750–\$190,500
Corporate controller	\$128,000–\$199,000	\$82,750–\$144,750
Tax manager	\$100,250–\$142,500	\$79,500–\$110,750

The Review and Practice section provides opportunities for students to review key concepts and terms as well as complete exercises and a comprehensive problem. Detailed solutions are also included.

REVIEW AND PRACTICE

LEARNING OBJECTIVES REVIEW

1 Identify the activities and users associated with accounting. Accounting is an information system that identifies, records, and communicates the economic events of an organization to interested users. The major users and uses of accounting are as follows. (a) Management uses accounting information to plan, organize, and run the business. (b) Investors (owners) decide whether to buy, hold, or sell their financial interests on the basis of accounting data. (c) Creditors (suppliers and bankers) evaluate the risks of granting credit or lending money on the basis of accounting information. Other groups that use accounting information are taxing authorities, regulatory agencies, customers, and labor unions.

2 Explain the building blocks of accounting: ethics, principles, and assumptions. Ethics are the standards of conduct by which actions are judged as right or wrong. Effective financial reporting depends on sound ethical behavior.

Generally accepted accounting principles are a common set of standards used by accountants. The primary accounting standard-setting body in the United States is the Financial Accounting Standards Board. The monetary unit assumption requires that companies include in the accounting records only transaction data that can be expressed in terms of money. The economic entity assumption requires that the activities of each economic entity be kept separate from the activities of its owner(s) and other economic entities.

3 State the accounting equation, and define its components. The basic accounting equation is:

Assets = Liabilities + Owner's Equity

Assets are resources a business owns. Liabilities are creditorship claims on total assets. Owner's equity is the ownership claim on total assets.

The expanded accounting equation is:

Assets = Liabilities + Owner's Capital − Owner's Drawings + Revenues − Expenses

Owner's capital is assets the owner puts into the business. Owner's drawings are the assets the owner withdraws for personal use. Revenues are increases in assets resulting from income-earning activities. Expenses are the costs of assets consumed or services used in the process of earning revenue.

4 Analyze the effects of business transactions on the accounting equation. Each business transaction must have a dual effect on the accounting equation. For example, if an individual asset increases, there must be a corresponding (1) decrease in another asset,

(2) increase in a specific liability, or (3) increase in owner's equity.

5 Describe the four financial statements and how they are prepared. An income statement presents the revenues and expenses, and resulting net income or net loss, for a specific period of time. An owner's equity statement summarizes the changes in owner's equity for a specific period of time. A balance sheet reports the assets, liabilities, and owner's equity at a specific date. A statement of cash flows summarizes information about the cash inflows (receipts) and outflows (payments) for a specific period of time.

***6 Explain the career opportunities in accounting.** Accounting offers many different jobs in fields such as public and private accounting, governmental, and forensic accounting. Accounting is a popular major because there are many different types of jobs, with unlimited potential for career advancement.

GLOSSARY REVIEW

Accounting The information system that identifies, records, and communicates the economic events of an organization to interested users.

Assets Resources a business owns.

***Auditing** The examination of financial statements by a certified public accountant in order to express an opinion as to the fairness of presentation.

Balance sheet A financial statement that reports the assets, liabilities, and owner's equity at a specific date.

Basic accounting equation Assets = Liabilities + Owner's equity.

Bookkeeping A part of the accounting process that involves only the recording of economic events.

Convergence The process of reducing the differences between U.S. GAAP and IFRS.

Corporation A business organized as a separate legal entity under state corporation law, having ownership divided into transferable shares of stock.

Drawings Withdrawal of cash or other assets from an unincorporated business for the personal use of the owner(s).

Economic entity assumption An assumption that requires that the activities of the entity be kept separate and distinct from the activities of its owner and all other economic entities.

Ethics The standards of conduct by which actions are judged as right or wrong, honest or dishonest, fair or not fair.

Expanded accounting equation Assets = Liabilities + Owner's capital − Owner's drawings + Revenues − Expenses.

Expenses The cost of assets consumed or services used in the process of earning revenue.

Fair value principle An accounting principle stating that assets and liabilities should be reported at fair value (the price received to sell an asset or settle a liability).

Faithful representation Numbers and descriptions match what really existed or happened—they are factual.

Financial accounting The field of accounting that provides economic and financial information for investors, creditors, and other external users.

Financial Accounting Standards Board (FASB) A private organization that establishes generally accepted accounting principles in the United States (GAAP).

***Forensic accounting** An area of accounting that uses accounting, auditing, and investigative skills to conduct investigations into theft and fraud.

Generally accepted accounting principles (GAAP) Common standards that indicate how to report economic events.

Historical cost principle An accounting principle that states that companies should record assets at their cost.

Income statement A financial statement that presents the revenues and expenses and resulting net income or net loss of a company for a specific period of time.

International Accounting Standards Board (IASB) An accounting standard-setting body that issues standards adopted by many countries outside of the United States.

International Financial Reporting Standards (IFRS) International accounting standards set by the International Accounting Standards Board (IASB).

Investments by owner The assets an owner puts into the business.

Liabilities Creditor claims against total assets.

***Management consulting** An area of public accounting ranging from development of accounting and computer systems to support services for marketing projects and merger and acquisition activities.

Managerial accounting The field of accounting that provides internal reports to help users make decisions about their companies.

Monetary unit assumption An assumption stating that companies include in the accounting records only transaction data that can be expressed in terms of money.

Net income The amount by which revenues exceed expenses.

Net loss The amount by which expenses exceed revenues.

Owner's equity The ownership claim on total assets.

Owner's equity statement A financial statement that summarizes the changes in owner's equity for a specific period of time.

Partnership A business owned by two or more persons associated as partners.

***Private (or managerial) accounting** An area of accounting within a company that involves such activities as cost accounting, budgeting, design and support of accounting information systems, and tax planning and preparation.

Proprietorship A business owned by one person.

***Public accounting** An area of accounting in which the accountant offers expert service to the general public.

Relevance Financial information that is capable of making a difference in a decision.

Revenues The gross increase in owner's equity resulting from business activities entered into for the purpose of earning income.

Sarbanes-Oxley Act (SOX) Law passed by Congress intended to reduce unethical corporate behavior.

Securities and Exchange Commission (SEC) A governmental agency that oversees U.S. financial markets and accounting standard-setting bodies.

Statement of cash flows A financial statement that summarizes information about the cash inflows (receipts) and cash outflows (payments) for a specific period of time.

***Taxation** An area of public accounting involving tax advice, tax planning, preparing tax returns, and representing clients before governmental agencies.

Transactions The economic events of a business that are recorded by accountants.

PRACTICE EXERCISES

Analyze the effect of transactions.

(LO 3, 4)

1. Selected transactions for Fabulous Flora Company are listed below.

1. Made cash investment to start business.
2. Purchased equipment on account.
3. Paid salaries.
4. Billed customers for services performed.
5. Received cash from customers billed in (4).
6. Withdrew cash for owner's personal use.
7. Incurred advertising expense on account.
8. Purchased additional equipment for cash.
9. Received cash from customers when service was performed.

Instructions

List the numbers of the above transactions and describe the effect of each transaction on assets, liabilities, and owner's equity. For example, the first answer is: (1) Increase in assets and increase in owner's equity.

Solution

1. 1. Increase in assets and increase in owner's equity.
   2. Increase in assets and increase in liabilities.
   3. Decrease in assets and decrease in owner's equity.
   4. Increase in assets and increase in owner's equity.
   5. Increase in assets and decrease in assets.
   6. Decrease in assets and decrease in owner's equity.
   7. Increase in liabilities and decrease in owner's equity.
   8. Increase in assets and decrease in assets.
   9. Increase in assets and increase in owner's equity.

Analyze the effect of transactions on assets, liabilities, and owner's equity.

(LO 3, 4)

2. Alma's Payroll Services Company entered into the following transactions during May 2017:

1. Purchased computers for $15,000 from Bytes of Data on account.
2. Paid $3,000 cash for May rent on storage space.
3. Received $12,000 cash from customers for contracts billed in April.
4. Performed payroll services for Magic Construction Company for $2,500 cash.
5. Paid Northern Ohio Power Co. $7,000 cash for energy usage in May.

6. Alma invested an additional $25,000 in the business.
7. Paid Bytes of Data for the computers purchased in (1) above.
8. Incurred advertising expense for May of $900 on account.

Instructions

Indicate with the appropriate letter whether each of the transactions above results in:

(a) an increase in assets and a decrease in assets.
(b) an increase in assets and an increase in owner's equity.
(c) an increase in assets and an increase in liabilities.
(d) a decrease in assets and a decrease in owner's equity.
(e) a decrease in assets and a decrease in liabilities.
(f) an increase in liabilities and a decrease in owner's equity.
(g) an increase in owner's equity and a decrease in liabilities.

Solution

2. 1. (c)	3. (a)	5. (d)	7. (e)
2. (d)	4. (b)	6. (b)	8. (f)

PRACTICE PROBLEM

Prepare a tabular presentation and financial statements.

(LO 4, 5)

Joan Robinson opens her own law office on July 1, 2017. During the first month of operations, the following transactions occurred:

1. Joan invested $11,000 in cash in the law practice.
2. Paid $800 for July rent on office space.
3. Purchased equipment on account $3,000.
4. Performed legal services to clients for cash $1,500.
5. Borrowed $700 cash from a bank on a note payable.
6. Performed legal services for client on account $2,000.
7. Paid monthly expenses: salaries and wages $500, utilities $300, and advertising $100.
8. Joan withdrew $1,000 cash for personal use.

Instructions

(a) Prepare a tabular summary of the transactions.
(b) Prepare the income statement, owner's equity statement, and balance sheet at July 31, 2017, for Joan Robinson, Attorney.

Solution

(a)

	Assets					=	Liabilities			+	Owner's Equity						
Transaction	Cash	+	Accounts Receivable	+	Equipment	=	Notes Payable	+	Accounts Payable	+	Owner's Capital	−	Owner's Drawings	+	Revenues	−	Expenses
(1)	+$11,000					=					+$11,000						
(2)	−800																−$800
(3)					+$3,000	=			+$3,000								
(4)	+1,500														+$1,500		
(5)	+700						+$700										
(6)			+$2,000												+2,000		
(7)	−500																−500
	−300																−300
	−100																−100
(8)	−1,000												−$1,000				
	$10,500	+	$2,000	+	$3,000	=	$700	+	$3,000	+	$11,000	−	$1,000	+	$3,500	−	$1,700
			$15,500								$15,500						

(b)

JOAN ROBINSON, ATTORNEY
Income Statement
For the Month Ended July 31, 2017

Revenues		
Service revenue		$3,500
Expenses		
Rent expense	$800	
Salaries and wages expense	500	
Utilities expense	300	
Advertising expense	100	
Total expenses		1,700
Net income		$1,800

JOAN ROBINSON, ATTORNEY
Owner's Equity Statement
For the Month Ended July 31, 2017

Owner's capital, July 1		$ 0
Add: Investments	$11,000	
Net income	1,800	12,800
		12,800
Less: Drawings		1,000
Owner's capital, July 31		$11,800

JOAN ROBINSON, ATTORNEY
Balance Sheet
July 31, 2017

Assets	
Cash	$10,500
Accounts receivable	2,000
Equipment	3,000
Total assets	$15,500
Liabilities and Owner's Equity	
Liabilities	
Notes payable	$ 700
Accounts payable	3,000
Total liabilities	3,700
Owner's equity	
Owner's capital	11,800
Total liabilities and owner's equity	$15,500

EXERCISES

Classify the three activities of accounting.

(LO 1)

E1-1 Genesis Company performs the following accounting tasks during the year:

________Analyzing and interpreting information.
________Classifying economic events.
________Explaining uses, meaning, and limitations of data.
________Keeping a systematic chronological diary of events.
________Measuring events in dollars and cents.
________Preparing accounting reports.
________Reporting information in a standard format.
________Selecting economic activities relevant to the company.
________Summarizing economic events.

Accounting is "an information system that **identifies**, **records**, and **communicates** the economic events of an organization to interested users."

Instructions
Categorize the accounting tasks performed by Genesis as relating to either the identification (I), recording (R), or communication (C) aspects of accounting.

Identify users of accounting information.

(LO 1)

E1-2 (a) The following are users of financial statements:

_______Customers	_______Securities and Exchange Commission
_______Internal Revenue Service	_______Store manager
_______Labor unions	_______Suppliers
_______Marketing manager	_______Vice president of finance
_______Production supervisor	

Instructions
Identify the users as being either **external users** or **internal users**.

(b) The following questions could be asked by an internal user or an external user.

_______Can we afford to give our employees a pay raise?
_______Did the company earn a satisfactory income?
_______Do we need to borrow in the near future?
_______How does the company's profitability compare to other companies?
_______What does it cost us to manufacture each unit produced?
_______Which product should we emphasize?
_______Will the company be able to pay its short-term debts?

Instructions
Identify each of the questions as being more likely asked by an **internal user** or an **external user**.

Discuss ethics and the historical cost principle.

(LO 2)

E1-3 Angela Duffy, president of Duffy Company, has instructed Jana Barth, the head of the accounting department for Duffy Company, to report the company's land in the company's accounting reports at its fair value of $170,000 instead of its cost of $100,000. Duffy says, "Showing the land at $170,000 will make our company look like a better investment when we try to attract new investors next month."

Instructions
Explain the ethical situation involved for Jana Barth, identifying the stakeholders and the alternatives.

Use accounting concepts.

(LO 2)

E1-4 The following situations involve accounting principles and assumptions.

1. Tisinai Company owns buildings that are worth substantially more than they originally cost. In an effort to provide more relevant information, Tisinai reports the buildings at fair value in its accounting reports.
2. Kingston Company includes in its accounting records only transaction data that can be expressed in terms of money.
3. Roger Holloway, owner of Roger's Photography, records his personal living costs as expenses of the business.

Instructions
For each of the three situations, say if the accounting method used is correct or incorrect. If correct, identify which principle or assumption supports the method used. If incorrect, identify which principle or assumption has been violated.

Classify accounts as assets, liabilities, and owner's equity.

(LO 3)

E1-5 Diehl Cleaners has the following balance sheet items:

Accounts payable	Accounts receivable
Cash	Notes payable
Equipment	Salaries and wages payable
Supplies	Owner's capital

Instructions
Classify each item as an asset, liability, or owner's equity.

Analyze the effect of transactions.

(LO 4)

E1-6 Selected transactions for Green Valley Lawn Care Company are listed below.

1. Made cash investment to start business.
2. Paid monthly rent.

3. Purchased equipment on account.
4. Billed customers for services performed.
5. Withdrew cash for owner's personal use.
6. Received cash from customers billed in (4).
7. Incurred advertising expense on account.
8. Purchased additional equipment for cash.
9. Received cash from customers when service was performed.

Instructions

List the numbers of the above transactions and describe the effect of each transaction on assets, liabilities, and owner's equity. For example, the first answer is: (1) Increase in assets and increase in owner's equity.

Analyze the effect of transactions on assets, liabilities, and owner's equity.

(LO 4)

E1-7 Falske Computer Timeshare Company entered into the following transactions during May 2017:

1. Purchased computers for $20,000 from Digital Equipment on account.
2. Paid $4,000 cash for May rent on storage space.
3. Received $17,000 cash from customers for contracts billed in April.
4. Performed computer services for Viking Construction Company for $4,000 cash.
5. Paid Tri-State Power Co. $11,000 cash for energy usage in May.
6. Falske invested an additional $29,000 in the business.
7. Paid Digital Equipment for the computers purchased in (1) above.
8. Incurred advertising expense for May of $1,200 on account.

Instructions

Indicate with the appropriate letter whether each of the transactions above results in:

(a) An increase in assets and a decrease in assets.
(b) An increase in assets and an increase in owner's equity.
(c) An increase in assets and an increase in liabilities.
(d) A decrease in assets and a decrease in owner's equity.
(e) A decrease in assets and a decrease in liabilities.
(f) An increase in liabilities and a decrease in owner's equity.
(g) An increase in owner's equity and a decrease in liabilities.

Analyze transactions and compute net income.

(LO 4)

E1-8 An analysis of the transactions made by Arthur Cooper & Co., a certified public accounting firm, for the month of August is shown below. The expenses were $650 for rent, $4,800 for salaries and wages, and $400 for utilities.

	Cash	+ Accounts Receivable	+ Supplies	+ Equipment	= Accounts Payable	+ Owner's Capital	− Owner's Drawings	+ Revenues	− Expenses
1.	+$15,000					+$15,000			
2.	−2,000			+$5,000	+$3,000				
3.	−750		+$750						
4.	+4,600	+$3,900						+$8,500	
5.	−1,500				−1,500				
6.	−2,000						−$2,000		
7.	−650								−$650
8.	+450	−450							
9.	−4,800								−4,800
10.					+400				−400

Instructions

(a) Describe each transaction that occurred for the month.
(b) Determine how much owner's equity increased for the month.
(c) Compute the amount of net income for the month.

Prepare financial statements.

(LO 5)

E1-9 An analysis of transactions for Arthur Cooper & Co. was presented in E1–8.

Instructions

Prepare an income statement and an owner's equity statement for August and a balance sheet at August 31, 2017. Assume that August is the company's first month of business.

Determine net income (or loss).

(LO 5)

E1-10 Finch Company had the following assets and liabilities on the dates indicated:

December 31	Total Assets	Total Liabilities
2016	$400,000	$250,000
2017	$460,000	$300,000
2018	$590,000	$400,000

Finch began business on January 1, 2016, with an investment of $100,000.

Instructions

From an analysis of the change in owner's equity during the year, compute the net income (or loss) for:

(a) 2016, assuming Finch's drawings were $15,000 for the year.
(b) 2017, assuming Finch made an additional investment of $45,000 and had no drawings in 2017.
(c) 2018, assuming Finch made an additional investment of $15,000 and had drawings of $25,000 in 2018.

Analyze financial statements items.

(LO 5)

E1-11 Two items are omitted from each of the following summaries of balance sheet and income statement data for two proprietorships for the year 2017, Greene's Goods and Solar Enterprises.

	Greene's Goods	Solar Enterprises
Beginning of year:		
Total assets	$110,000	$129,000
Total liabilities	85,000	(c)
Total owner's equity	(a)	80,000
End of year:		
Total assets	160,000	180,000
Total liabilities	120,000	50,000
Total owner's equity	40,000	130,000
Changes during year in owner's equity:		
Additional investment	(b)	25,000
Drawings	37,000	(d)
Total revenues	220,000	100,000
Total expenses	175,000	60,000

Instructions

Determine the missing amounts.

Prepare income statement and owner's equity statement.

(LO 5)

E1-12 The following information relates to Armanda Co. for the year 2017.

Owner's capital, January 1, 2017	$48,000	Advertising expense	$ 1,800
Owner's drawings during 2017	6,000	Rent expense	10,400
Service revenue	63,600	Utilities expense	3,100
Salaries and wages expense	29,500		

Instructions

After analyzing the data, prepare an income statement and an owner's equity statement for the year ending December 31, 2017.

Correct an incorrectly prepared balance sheet.

(LO 5)

E1-13 Abby Roland is the bookkeeper for Cheng Company. Abby has been trying to determine the correct balance sheet for Cheng Company. Cheng's balance sheet is shown below.

CHENG COMPANY
Balance Sheet
December 31, 2017

Assets		Liabilities	
Cash	$15,000	Accounts payable	$21,000
Supplies	8,000	Accounts receivable	(6,500)
Equipment	46,000	Owner's capital	67,500
Owner's drawings	13,000	Total liabilities and	
Total assets	$82,000	owner's equity	$82,000

Instructions

Prepare a correct balance sheet.

Compute net income and prepare a balance sheet.

(LO 5)

E1-14 Loren Satina is the sole owner of Clear View Park, a public camping ground near the Lake Mead National Recreation Area. Loren has compiled the following financial information as of December 31, 2017:

Revenues during 2017—camping fees	$140,000	Fair value of equipment	$140,000
Revenues during 2017—general store	65,000	Notes payable	60,000
Accounts payable	11,000	Expenses during 2017	150,000
Cash on hand	23,000	Accounts receivable	17,500
Original cost of equipment	105,500		

Instructions

(a) Determine Loren Satina's net income from Clear View Park for 2017.
(b) Prepare a balance sheet for Clear View Park as of December 31, 2017.

Prepare an income statement.

(LO 5)

E1-15 Presented below is financial information related to the 2017 operations of Sea Legs Cruise Company:

Maintenance and repairs expense	$ 95,000
Utilities expense	13,000
Salaries and wages expense	142,000
Advertising expense	24,500
Ticket revenue	410,000

Instructions

Prepare the 2017 income statement for Sea Legs Cruise Company.

Prepare an owner's equity statement.

(LO 5)

E1-16 Presented below is information related to the sole proprietorship of Alice Henning, attorney:

Legal service revenue—2017	$335,000
Total expenses—2017	211,000
Assets, January 1, 2017	96,000
Liabilities, January 1, 2017	62,000
Assets, December 31, 2017	168,000
Liabilities, December 31, 2017	100,000
Drawings—2017	?

Instructions

Prepare the 2017 owner's equity statement for Alice Henning's legal practice.

PROBLEMS

Analyze transactions and compute net income.

(LO 3, 4)

P1-1A On April 1, Julie Spengel established Spengel's Travel Agency. The following transactions were completed during the month:

1. Invested $15,000 cash to start the agency.
2. Paid $600 cash for April office rent.
3. Purchased equipment for $3,000 cash.
4. Incurred $700 of advertising costs in the *Chicago Tribune*, on account.
5. Paid $900 cash for office supplies.
6. Performed services worth $10,000: $3,000 cash is received from customers, and the balance of $7,000 is billed to customers on account.
7. Withdrew $600 cash for personal use.
8. Paid *Chicago Tribune* $500 of the amount due in transaction (4).
9. Paid employees' salaries $2,500.
10. Received $4,000 in cash from customers who have previously been billed in transaction (6).

Check figures provide a key number to let you know you are on the right track.

Instructions

(a) Prepare a tabular analysis of the transactions using the following column headings: Cash, Accounts Receivable, Supplies, Equipment, Accounts Payable, Owner's Capital, Owner's Drawings, Revenues, and Expenses.

(a) Total assets $20,800

(b) From an analysis of the owner's equity columns, compute the net income or net loss for April.

(b) Net income $6,200

P1-2A Judi Salem opened a law office on July 1, 2017. On July 31, the balance sheet showed Cash $5,000, Accounts Receivable $1,500, Supplies $500, Equipment $6,000, Accounts Payable $4,200, and Owner's Capital $8,800. During August, the following transactions occurred:

Analyze transactions and prepare income statement, owner's equity statement, and balance sheet.

(LO 3, 4, 5)

1. Collected $1,200 of accounts receivable.
2. Paid $2,800 cash on accounts payable.
3. Recognized revenue of $7,500 of which $3,000 is collected in cash and the balance is due in September.
4. Purchased additional equipment for $2,000, paying $400 in cash and the balance on account.
5. Paid salaries $2,500, rent for August $900, and advertising expenses $400.
6. Withdrew $700 in cash for personal use.
7. Received $2,000 from Standard Federal Bank—money borrowed on a note payable.
8. Incurred utility expenses for month on account $270.

Instructions

(a) Prepare a tabular analysis of the August transactions beginning with July 31 balances. The column headings should be as follows: Cash + Accounts Receivable + Supplies + Equipment = Notes Payable + Accounts Payable + Owner's Capital − Owner's Drawings + Revenues − Expenses.

(a) Total assets $16,800

(b) Prepare an income statement for August, an owner's equity statement for August, and a balance sheet at August 31.

(b) Net income $3,430
Ending capital $11,530

P1-3A On June 1, Cindy Godfrey started Divine Designs Co., a company that provides craft opportunities, by investing $12,000 cash in the business. Following are the assets and liabilities of the company at June 30 and the revenues and expenses for the month of June.

Prepare income statement, owner's equity statement, and balance sheet.

(LO 5)

Cash	$10,150	Service Revenue	$6,500
Accounts Receivable	2,800	Advertising Expense	500
Supplies	2,000	Rent Expense	1,600
Equipment	10,000	Gasoline Expense	200
Notes Payable	9,000	Utilities Expense	150
Accounts Payable	1,200		

Cindy made no additional investment in June but withdrew $1,300 in cash for personal use during the month.

Instructions

(a) Prepare an income statement and owner's equity statement for the month of June and a balance sheet at June 30, 2017.

(b) Prepare an income statement and owner's equity statement for June assuming the following data are not included above: (1) $900 of services were performed and billed but not collected at June 30, and (2) $150 of gasoline expense was incurred but not paid.

(a) Net income $4,050
Owner's equity $14,750
Total assets $24,950
(b) Owner's equity $15,500

P1-4A Trixie Maye started her own consulting firm, Matrix Consulting, on May 1, 2017. The following transactions occurred during the month of May:

Analyze transactions and prepare financial statements.

(LO 3, 4, 5)

May 1	Trixie invested $7,000 cash in the business.
2	Paid $900 for office rent for the month.
3	Purchased $600 of supplies on account.
5	Paid $125 to advertise in the *County News*.
9	Received $4,000 cash for services performed.
12	Withdrew $1,000 cash for personal use.
15	Performed $5,400 of services on account.
17	Paid $2,500 for employee salaries.
20	Paid for the supplies purchased on account on May 3.
23	Received a cash payment of $4,000 for services performed on account on May 15.
26	Borrowed $5,000 from the bank on a note payable.
29	Purchased equipment for $4,200 on account.
30	Paid $275 for utilities.

Instructions

(a) Show the effects of the previous transactions on the accounting equation using the following format.

(a) Total assets $20,800

	Assets				Liabilities		Owner's Equity			
		Accounts			Notes	Accounts	Owner's	Owner's		
Date	Cash +	Receivable +	Supplies +	Equipment =	Payable +	Payable +	Capital	− Drawings +	Revenues	− Expenses

(b) Net income $5,600
(c) Cash $14,600

(b) Prepare an income statement for the month of May.
(c) Prepare a balance sheet at May 31, 2017.

Determine financial statement amounts and prepare owner's equity statement.

(LO 4, 5)

P1-5A Financial statement information about four different companies is as follows:

	Alpha Company	Beta Company	Psi Company	Omega Company
January 1, 2017				
Assets	$ 80,000	$ 90,000	(g)	$150,000
Liabilities	41,000	(d)	80,000	(j)
Owner's equity	(a)	40,000	49,000	90,000
December 31, 2017				
Assets	(b)	112,000	170,000	(k)
Liabilities	60,000	72,000	(h)	100,000
Owner's equity	50,000	(e)	82,000	151,000
Owner's equity changes in year				
Additional investment	(c)	8,000	10,000	15,000
Drawings	15,000	(f)	12,000	10,000
Total revenues	350,000	410,000	(i)	500,000
Total expenses	333,000	385,000	350,000	(l)

Instructions

(a) Determine the missing amounts. (*Hint:* For example, to solve for (a), Assets − Liabilities = Owner's equity = $39,000.)
(b) Prepare the owner's equity statement for Alpha Company.
(c) Write a memorandum explaining the sequence for preparing financial statements and the interrelationship of the owner's equity statement to the income statement and balance sheet.

BROADENING YOUR PERSPECTIVE

FINANCIAL REPORTING AND ANALYSIS

Financial Reporting Problem: Apple Inc.

BYP1-1 The financial statements of **Apple Inc.** for 2013 are presented in Appendix A. Instructions for accessing and using the company's complete annual report, including the notes to the financial statements, are also provided in Appendix A.

Instructions

Refer to Apple's financial statements and answer the following questions.

(a) What were Apple's total assets at September 28, 2013? At September 29, 2012?
(b) How much cash (and cash equivalents) did Apple have on September 28, 2013?
(c) What amount of accounts payable did Apple report on September 28, 2013? On September 29, 2012?
(d) What were Apple's net sales in 2011? In 2012? In 2013?
(e) What is the amount of the change in Apple's net income from 2012 to 2013?

Comparative Analysis Problem: PepsiCo, Inc. vs. The Coca-Cola Company

BYP1-2 **PepsiCo, Inc.**'s financial statements are presented in Appendix B. Financial statements of **The Coca-Cola Company** are presented in Appendix C. Instructions for accessing and using the complete annual reports of PepsiCo and Coca-Cola, including the notes to the financial statements, are also provided in Appendices B and C, respectively.

Instructions

(a) Based on the information contained in these financial statements, determine the following for each company:

(1) Total assets at December 28, 2013, for PepsiCo and for Coca-Cola at December 31, 2013.

(2) Accounts (notes) receivable, net at December 28, 2013, for PepsiCo and at December 31, 2013, for Coca-Cola.

(3) Net revenues for year ended in 2013.

(4) Net income for year ended in 2013.

(b) What conclusions concerning the two companies can be drawn from these data?

Comparative Analysis Problem: Amazon.com, Inc. vs. Wal-Mart Stores, Inc.

BYP1-3 Amazon.com, Inc.'s financial statements are presented in Appendix D. Financial statements of Wal-Mart Stores, Inc. are presented in Appendix E. Instructions for accessing and using the complete annual reports of Amazon and Wal-Mart, including the notes to the financial statements, are also provided in Appendices D and E, respectively.

Instructions

(a) Based on the information contained in these financial statements, determine the following for each company:

(1) Total assets at December 31, 2013, for Amazon and for Wal-Mart at January 31, 2014.

(2) Receivables (net) at December 31, 2013, for Amazon and for Wal-Mart at January 31, 2014.

(3) Net sales (product only) for year ended in 2013 (2014 for Wal-Mart).

(4) Net income for the year ended in 2013 (2014 for Wal-Mart).

(b) What conclusions concerning these two companies can be drawn from these data?

Real-World Focus

BYP1-4 This exercise will familiarize you with skill requirements, job descriptions, and salaries for accounting careers.

Address: **www.careers-in-accounting.com**, or go to **www.wiley.com/college/weygandt**

Instructions

Go to the site shown above. Answer the following questions:

(a) What are the three broad areas of accounting (from "Skills and Talents")?

(b) List eight skills required in accounting.

(c) How do the three accounting areas differ in terms of these eight required skills?

(d) Explain one of the key job options in accounting.

(e) What is the overall salary range for a junior staff accountant?

CRITICAL THINKING

Decision-Making Across the Organization

BYP1-5 Anya and Nick Ramon, local golf stars, opened the Chip-Shot Driving Range on March 1, 2017, by investing $25,000 of their cash savings in the business. A caddy shack was constructed for cash at a cost of $8,000, and $800 was spent on golf balls and golf clubs. The Ramons leased five acres of land at a cost of $1,000 per month and paid the first month's rent. During the first month, advertising costs totaled $750, of which $100 was unpaid at March 31, and $500 was paid to members of the high-school golf team for retrieving golf balls. All revenues from customers were deposited in the company's bank account. On March 15, Anya and Nick withdrew a total of $1,000 in cash for personal living expenses. A $120 utility bill was received on March 31 but was not paid. On March 31, the balance in the company's bank account was $18,900.

Anya and Nick thought they had a pretty good first month of operations. But, their estimates of profitability ranged from a loss of $6,100 to net income of $2,480.

Instructions

With the class divided into groups, answer the following:

(a) How could the Ramons have concluded that the business operated at a loss of $6,100? Was this a valid basis on which to determine net income?

(b) How could the Ramons have concluded that the business operated at a net income of $2,480? (*Hint:* Prepare a balance sheet at March 31.) Was this a valid basis on which to determine net income?
(c) Without preparing an income statement, determine the actual net income for March.
(d) What was the revenue recognized in March?

Communication Activity

BYP1-6 Sandi Alcon, the bookkeeper for New York Company, has been trying to determine the correct balance sheet for the company. The company's balance sheet is shown below.

NEW YORK COMPANY
Balance Sheet
For the Month Ended December 31, 2017

Assets		Liabilities	
Equipment	$25,500	Owner's capital	$26,000
Cash	9,000	Accounts receivable	(6,000)
Supplies	2,000	Owner's drawings	(2,000)
Accounts payable	(8,000)	Notes payable	10,500
	$28,500		$28,500

Instructions
Explain to Sandi Alcon in a memo why the original balance sheet is incorrect, and what should be done to correct it.

Ethics Case

BYP1-7 After numerous campus interviews, Travis Chase, a senior at Great Northern College, received two office interview invitations from the Baltimore offices of two large firms. Both firms offered to cover his out-of-pocket expenses (travel, hotel, and meals). He scheduled the interviews for both firms on the same day, one in the morning and one in the afternoon. At the conclusion of each interview, he submitted to both firms his total out-of-pocket expenses for the trip to Baltimore: mileage $112 (280 miles at $0.40), hotel $130, meals $36, and parking and tolls $18, for a total of $296. He believes this approach is appropriate. If he had made two trips, his cost would have been two times $296. He is also certain that neither firm knew he had visited the other on that same trip. Within 10 days, Travis received two checks in the mail, each in the amount of $296.

Instructions
(a) Who are the stakeholders (affected parties) in this situation?
(b) What are the ethical issues in this case?
(c) What would you do in this situation?

All About You

BYP1-8 Some people are tempted to make their finances look worse to get financial aid. Companies sometimes also manage their financial numbers in order to accomplish certain goals. Earnings management is the planned timing of revenues, expenses, gains, and losses to smooth out bumps in net income. In managing earnings, companies' actions vary from being within the range of ethical activity to being both unethical and illegal attempts to mislead investors and creditors.

Instructions
Provide responses for each of the following questions.

(a) Discuss whether you think each of the following actions (adapted from **www.finaid.org/fafsa/maximize.phtml**) to increase the chances of receiving financial aid is ethical.
  (1) Spend the student's assets and income first, before spending parents' assets and income.
  (2) Accelerate necessary expenses to reduce available cash. For example, if you need a new car, buy it before applying for financial aid.
  (3) State that a truly financially dependent child is independent.

(4) Have a parent take an unpaid leave of absence for long enough to get below the "threshold" level of income.

(b) What are some reasons why a **company** might want to overstate its earnings?

(c) What are some reasons why a **company** might want to understate its earnings?

(d) Under what circumstances might an otherwise ethical person decide to illegally overstate or understate earnings?

FASB Codification Activity

BYP1-9 The FASB has developed the Financial Accounting Standards Board Accounting Standards Codification (or more simply "the Codification"). The FASB's primary goal in developing the Codification is to provide in one place all the authoritative literature related to a particular topic. To provide easy access to the Codification, the FASB also developed the Financial Accounting Standards Board Codification Research System (CRS). CRS is an online, real-time database that provides easy access to the Codification. The Codification and the related CRS provide a topically organized structure, subdivided into topic, subtopics, sections, and paragraphs, using a numerical index system.

You may find this system useful in your present and future studies, and so we have provided an opportunity to use this online system as part of the *Broadening Your Perspective* section.

Instructions

Academic access to the FASB Codification is available through university subscriptions, obtained from the American Accounting Association (at **http://aaahq.org/FASB/Access.cfm**), for an annual fee of $150. This subscription covers an unlimited number of students within a single institution. Once this access has been obtained by your school, you should log in (at **http://aaahq.org/ascLogin.cfm**) and familiarize yourself with the resources that are accessible at the FASB Codification site.

Considering People, Planet, and Profit

BYP1-10 This chapter's opening story discusses the fact that although **Clif Bar & Company** is not a public company, it does share its financial information with its employees as part of its open-book management approach. Further, although it does not publicly share its financial information, it does provide a different form of an annual report to external users. In this report, the company provides information regarding its sustainability efforts.

Address: **www.issuu.com/clifbar/docs/clif_all_aspirations_2012**

Instructions

Access the 2010 annual report of Clif Bar & Company at the site shown above and then answer the following questions:

(a) What are the Five Aspirations?

(b) What was the company 10-year compounded annual growth rate? What is the amount of 10-year organic purchases made by the company?

A Look at IFRS

LEARNING OBJECTIVE 7 **Describe the impact of international accounting standards on U.S. financial reporting.**

Most agree that there is a need for one set of international accounting standards. Here is why:

Multinational corporations. Today's companies view the entire world as their market. For example, Coca-Cola, Intel, and McDonald's generate more than 50% of their sales outside the United States. Many foreign companies, such as Toyota, Nestlé, and Sony, find their largest market to be the United States.

Mergers and acquisitions. The mergers between Fiat/Chrysler and Vodafone/Mannesmann suggest that we will see even more such business combinations of companies from different countries in the future.

Information technology. As communication barriers continue to topple through advances in technology, companies and individuals in different countries and markets are becoming more comfortable buying and selling goods and services from one another.

Financial markets. Financial markets are of international significance today. Whether it is currency, equity securities (stocks), bonds, or derivatives, there are active markets throughout the world trading these types of instruments.

Key Points

Following are the key similarities and differences between GAAP and IFRS as related to accounting fundamentals.

Similarities

- The basic techniques for recording business transactions are the same for U.S. and international companies.
- Both international and U.S. accounting standards emphasize transparency in financial reporting. Both sets of standards are primarily driven by meeting the needs of investors and creditors.
- The three most common forms of business organizations, proprietorships, partnerships, and corporations, are also found in countries that use international accounting standards.

Differences

- International standards are referred to as International Financial Reporting Standards (IFRS), developed by the International Accounting Standards Board. Accounting standards in the United States are referred to as generally accepted accounting principles (GAAP) and are developed by the Financial Accounting Standards Board.
- IFRS tends to be simpler in its accounting and disclosure requirements; some people say it is more "principles-based." GAAP is more detailed; some people say it is more "rules-based."
- The internal control standards applicable to Sarbanes-Oxley (SOX) apply only to large public companies listed on U.S. exchanges. There is continuing debate as to whether non-U.S. companies should have to comply with this extra layer of regulation.

Looking to the Future

Both the IASB and the FASB are hard at work developing standards that will lead to the elimination of major differences in the way certain transactions are accounted for and reported.

IFRS Practice

IFRS Self-Test Questions

1. Which of the following is **not** a reason why a single set of high-quality international accounting standards would be beneficial?
   (a) Mergers and acquisition activity.
   (b) Financial markets.
   (c) Multinational corporations.
   (d) GAAP is widely considered to be a superior reporting system.
2. The Sarbanes-Oxley Act determines:
   (a) international tax regulations.
   (b) internal control standards as enforced by the IASB.
   (c) internal control standards of U.S. publicly traded companies.
   (d) U.S. tax regulations.
3. IFRS is considered to be more:
   (a) principles-based and less rules-based than GAAP.
   (b) rules-based and less principles-based than GAAP.
   (c) detailed than GAAP.
   (d) None of the above.

IFRS Exercises

IFRS1-1 Who are the two key international players in the development of international accounting standards? Explain their role.

IFRS1-2 What is the benefit of a single set of high-quality accounting standards?

International Financial Reporting Problem: Louis Vuitton

IFRS1-3 The financial statements of **Louis Vuitton** are presented in Appendix F. Instructions for accessing and using the company's complete annual report, including the notes to its financial statements, are also provided in Appendix F.

Instructions
Visit Louis Vuitton's corporate website and answer the following questions from the company's 2013 annual report:

(a) What accounting firm performed the audit of Louis Vuitton's financial statements?
(b) What is the address of the company's corporate headquarters?
(c) What is the company's reporting currency?

Answers to IFRS Self-Test Questions

1. d **2.** c **3.** a

Chapter 2 The Recording Process

How organized are you financially? Take a short quiz. Answer yes or no to each question:

- Does your wallet contain so many cash machine receipts that you've been declared a walking fire hazard?
- Do you wait until your debit card is denied before checking the status of your funds?
- Was Aaron Rodgers (the quarterback for the Green Bay Packers) playing high school football the last time you verified the accuracy of your bank account?

If you think it is hard to keep track of the many transactions that make up your life, imagine how difficult it is for a big corporation to do so. Not only that, but now consider how important it is for a large company to have good accounting records, especially if it has control of your life savings. MF Global Holdings Ltd is such a company. As a big investment broker, it held billions of dollars of investments for clients. If you had your life savings invested at MF Global, you might be slightly displeased if you heard this from one of its representatives: "You know, I kind of remember an account for someone with a name like yours—now what did we do with that?"

Unfortunately, that is almost exactly what happened to MF Global's clients shortly before it filed for bankruptcy. During the days immediately following the bankruptcy filing, regulators and auditors struggled to piece things together. In the words of one regulator, "Their books are a disaster . . . we're trying to figure out what numbers are real numbers." One company that considered buying an interest in MF Global walked away from the deal because it "couldn't get a sense of what was on the balance sheet." That company said the information that should have been instantly available instead took days to produce.

It now appears that MF Global did not properly segregate customer accounts from company accounts. And, because of its sloppy recordkeeping, customers were not protected when the company had financial troubles. Total customer losses were approximately $1 billion. As you can see, accounting matters!

Source: S. Patterson and A. Lucchetti, "Inside the Hunt for MF Global Cash," *Wall Street Journal Online* (November 11, 2011).

LEARNING OBJECTIVES

1. **Describe how accounts, debits, and credits are used to record business transactions.**
2. **Indicate how a journal is used in the recording process.**
3. **Explain how a ledger and posting help in the recording process.**
4. **Prepare a trial balance.**

LEARNING OBJECTIVE 1 **Describe how accounts, debits, and credits are used to record business transactions.**

The Account

An **account** is an individual accounting record of increases and decreases in a specific asset, liability, or owner's equity item. For example, Softbyte (the company discussed in Chapter 1) would have separate accounts for Cash, Accounts Receivable, Accounts Payable, Service Revenue, Salaries and Wages Expense, and so on. (Note that whenever we are referring to a specific account, we capitalize the name.)

In its simplest form, an account consists of three parts: (1) a title, (2) a left or debit side, and (3) a right or credit side. Because the format of an account resembles the letter T, we refer to it as a **T-account**. Illustration 2-1 shows the basic form of an account.

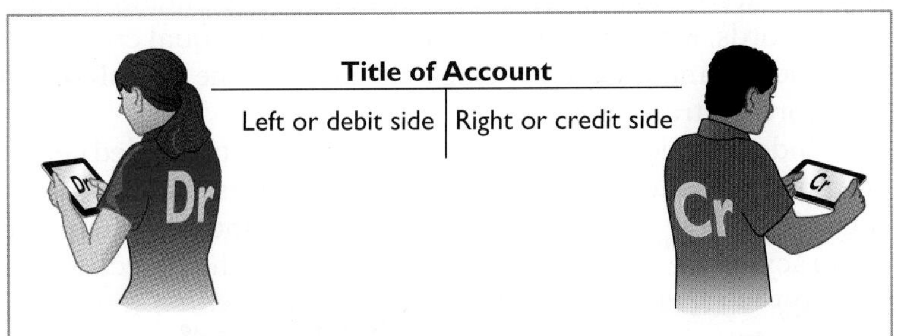

Illustration 2-1
Basic form of account

We use this form often throughout this book to explain basic accounting relationships.

Debits and Credits

The term **debit** indicates the left side of an account, and **credit** indicates the right side. They are commonly abbreviated as **Dr.** for debit and **Cr.** for credit. They **do not** mean increase or decrease, as is commonly thought. We use the terms **debit** and **credit** repeatedly in the recording process to describe **where** entries are made in accounts. For example, the act of entering an amount on the left side of an account is called **debiting** the account. Making an entry on the right side is **crediting** the account.

When comparing the totals of the two sides, an account shows a **debit balance** if the total of the debit amounts exceeds the credits. An account shows a **credit balance** if the credit amounts exceed the debits. Note the position of the debit side and credit side in Illustration 2-1.

The procedure of recording debits and credits in an account is shown in Illustration 2-2 for the transactions affecting the Cash account of Softbyte. The data are taken from the Cash column of the tabular summary in Illustration 1-8 (page 15).

Tabular Summary

Cash
$15,000
−7,000
1,200
1,500
−1,700
−250
600
−1,300
$ 8,050

Account Form

	Cash		
(Debits)	15,000	**(Credits)**	7,000
	1,200		1,700
	1,500		250
	600		1,300
Balance **(Debit)**	8,050		

Illustration 2-2
Tabular summary and account form for Softbyte's Cash account

Every positive item in the tabular summary represents a receipt of cash. Every negative amount represents a payment of cash. **Notice that in the account form, we record the increases in cash as debits and the decreases in cash as credits.** For example, the $15,000 receipt of cash (in red) is debited to Cash, and the −$7,000 payment of cash (in blue) is credited to Cash.

Having increases on one side and decreases on the other reduces recording errors and helps in determining the totals of each side of the account as well as the account balance. The balance is determined by netting the two sides (subtracting one amount from the other). The account balance, a debit of $8,050, indicates that Softbyte had $8,050 more increases than decreases in cash. In other words, Softbyte started with a balance of zero and now has $8,050 in its Cash account.

DEBIT AND CREDIT PROCEDURE

International Note

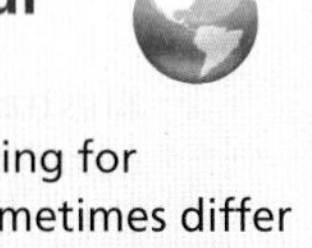

Rules for accounting for specific events sometimes differ across countries. Despite the differences, the double-entry accounting system is the basis of accounting systems worldwide.

In Chapter 1, you learned the effect of a transaction on the basic accounting equation. Remember that each transaction must affect two or more accounts to keep the basic accounting equation in balance. In other words, for each transaction, debits must equal credits. The equality of debits and credits provides the basis for the **double-entry system** of recording transactions.

Under the double-entry system, the dual (two-sided) effect of each transaction is recorded in appropriate accounts. This system provides a logical method for recording transactions and also helps ensure the accuracy of the recorded amounts as well as the detection of errors. If every transaction is recorded with equal debits and credits, the sum of all the debits to the accounts must equal the sum of all the credits.

The double-entry system for determining the equality of the accounting equation is much more efficient than the plus/minus procedure used in Chapter 1. The following discussion illustrates debit and credit procedures in the double-entry system.

DR./CR. PROCEDURES FOR ASSETS AND LIABILITIES

In Illustration 2-2 for Softbyte, increases in Cash—an asset—were entered on the left side, and decreases in Cash were entered on the right side. We know that both sides of the basic equation (Assets = Liabilities + Owner's Equity) must be equal. It therefore follows that increases and decreases in liabilities will have to be recorded **opposite from** increases and decreases in assets. Thus, increases in liabilities must be entered on the right or credit side, and decreases in liabilities must be entered on the left or debit side. The effects that debits and credits have on assets and liabilities are summarized in Illustration 2-3.

Illustration 2-3
Debit and credit effects—assets and liabilities

Debits	Credits
Increase assets	Decrease assets
Decrease liabilities	Increase liabilities

Asset accounts normally show debit balances. That is, debits to a specific asset account should exceed credits to that account. Likewise, **liability accounts normally show credit balances.** That is, credits to a liability account should exceed debits to that account. The **normal balance** of an account is on the side where an increase in the account is recorded. Illustration 2-4 shows the normal balances for assets and liabilities.

Illustration 2-4
Normal balances—assets and liabilities

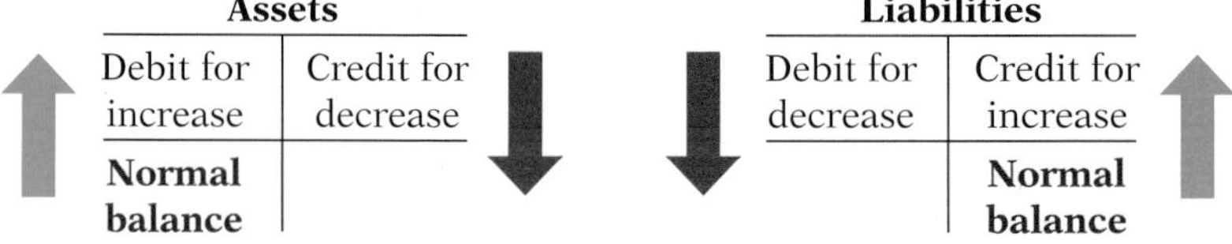

Knowing the normal balance in an account may help you trace errors. For example, a credit balance in an asset account such as Land or a debit balance in a liability account such as Salaries and Wages Payable usually indicates an error. Occasionally, though, an abnormal balance may be correct. The Cash account, for example, will have a credit balance when a company has overdrawn its bank balance (i.e., written a check that "bounced").

DR./CR. PROCEDURES FOR OWNER'S EQUITY

As Chapter 1 indicated, owner's investments and revenues increase owner's equity. Owner's drawings and expenses decrease owner's equity. Companies keep accounts for each of these types of transactions.

OWNER'S CAPITAL Investments by owners are credited to the Owner's Capital account. Credits increase this account, and debits decrease it. When an owner invests cash in the business, the company debits (increases) Cash and credits (increases) Owner's Capital. When the owner's investment in the business is reduced, Owner's Capital is debited (decreased).

Illustration 2-5 shows the rules of debit and credit for the Owner's Capital account.

Debits	Credits
Decrease Owner's Capital	Increase Owner's Capital

Illustration 2-5
Debit and credit effects—Owner's Capital

We can diagram the normal balance in Owner's Capital as follows.

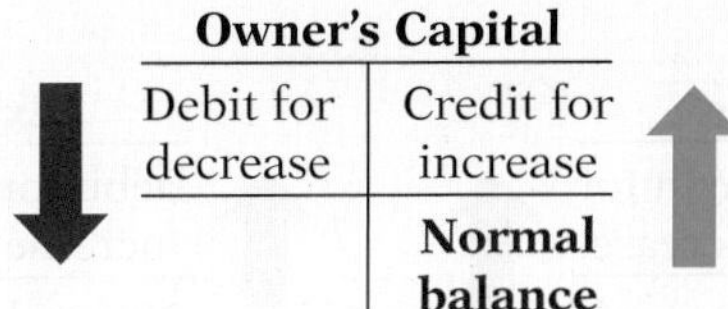

Illustration 2-6
Normal balance—Owner's Capital

OWNER'S DRAWINGS An owner may withdraw cash or other assets for personal use. Withdrawals could be debited directly to Owner's Capital to indicate a decrease in owner's equity. However, it is preferable to use a separate account, called Owner's Drawings. This separate account makes it easier to determine total withdrawals for each accounting period. Owner's Drawings is increased by debits and decreased by credits. Normally, the drawings account will have a debit balance.

Illustration 2-7 shows the rules of debit and credit for the Owner's Drawings account.

Debits	Credits
Increase Owner's Drawings	Decrease Owner's Drawings

Illustration 2-7
Debit and credit effects—Owner's Drawings

We can diagram the normal balance as follows.

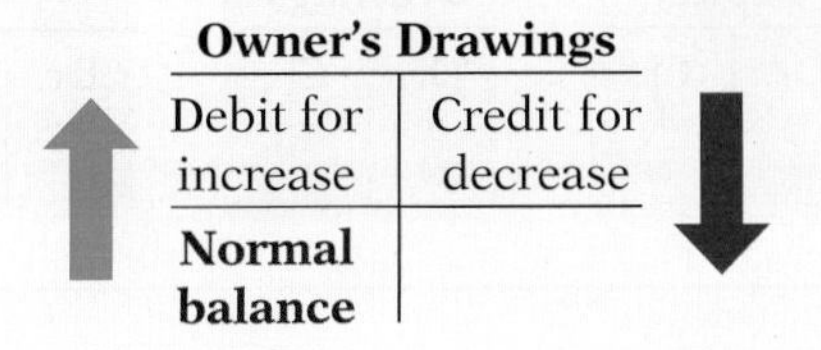

Illustration 2-8
Normal balance—Owner's Drawings

The Owner's Drawings account decreases owner's equity. It is not an income statement account like revenues and expenses.

REVENUES AND EXPENSES The purpose of earning revenues is to benefit the owner(s) of the business. When a company recognizes revenues, owner's equity increases. Therefore, **the effect of debits and credits on revenue accounts is the same as their effect on Owner's Capital**. That is, revenue accounts are increased by credits and decreased by debits.

Expenses have the opposite effect. Expenses decrease owner's equity. Since expenses decrease net income and revenues increase it, it is logical that the increase and decrease sides of expense accounts should be the opposite of revenue accounts. Thus, expense accounts are increased by debits and decreased by credits. Illustration 2-9 shows the rules of debits and credits for revenues and expenses.

Illustration 2-9
Debit and credit effects—revenues and expenses

Debits	Credits
Decrease revenues	Increase revenues
Increase expenses	Decrease expenses

Credits to revenue accounts should exceed debits. Debits to expense accounts should exceed credits. Thus, revenue accounts normally show credit balances, and expense accounts normally show debit balances. Illustration 2-10 shows the normal balances for revenues and expenses.

Illustration 2-10
Normal balances—revenues and expenses

Summary of Debit/Credit Rules

Illustration 2-11 shows a summary of the debit/credit rules and effects on each type of account. Study this diagram carefully. It will help you understand the fundamentals of the double-entry system.

Illustration 2-11
Summary of debit/credit rules

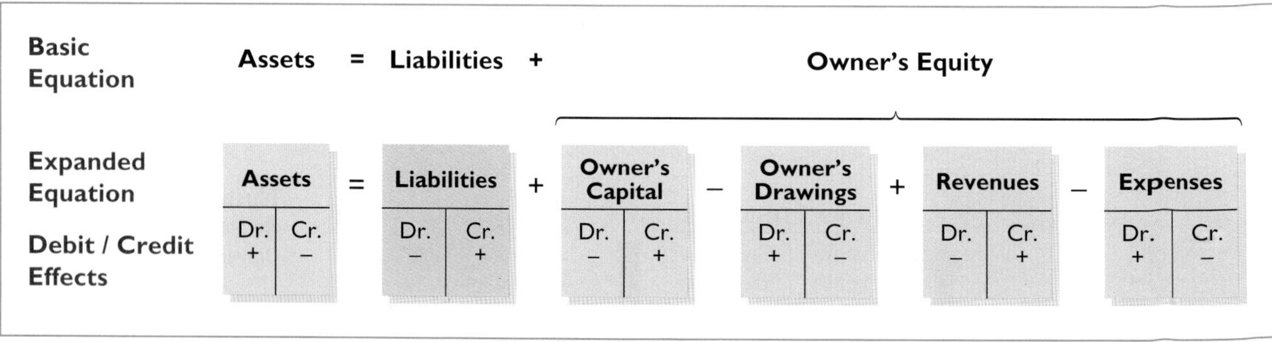

LEARNING OBJECTIVE 2

Indicate how a journal is used in the recording process.

Steps in the Recording Process

Although it is possible to enter transaction information directly into the accounts without using a journal, few businesses do so. Practically every business uses three basic steps in the recording process:

1. Analyze each transaction for its effects on the accounts.
2. Enter the transaction information in a **journal**.
3. Transfer the journal information to the appropriate accounts in the **ledger**.[1]

The recording process begins with the transaction. **Business documents**, such as a sales receipt, a check, or a bill, provide evidence of the transaction. The company analyzes this evidence to determine the transaction's effects on specific accounts. The company then enters the transaction in the journal. Finally, it transfers the journal entry to the designated accounts in the ledger. Illustration 2-12 shows the recording process.

Illustration 2-12
The recording process

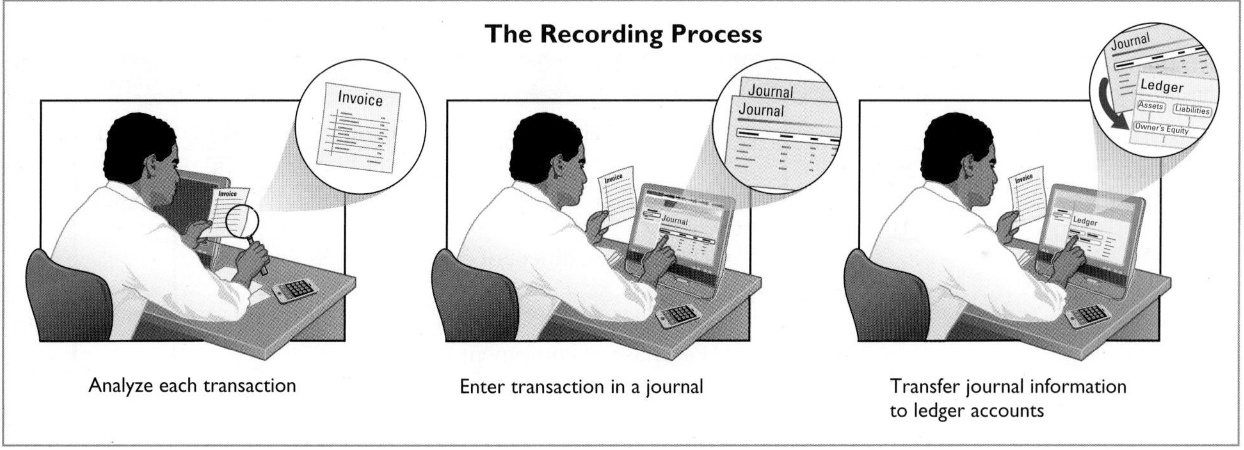

The steps in the recording process occur repeatedly. In Chapter 1, we illustrated the first step, the analysis of transactions, and will give further examples in this and later chapters. The other two steps in the recording process are explained in the next sections.

The Journal

Companies initially record transactions in chronological order (the order in which they occur). Thus, the **journal** is referred to as the book of original entry. For each transaction, the journal shows the debit and credit effects on specific accounts.

Companies may use various kinds of journals, but every company has the most basic form of journal, a **general journal**. Typically, a general journal has spaces for dates, account titles and explanations, references, and two amount columns. See the format of the journal in Illustration 2-13 (page 42). *Whenever we*

[1]We discuss here the manual recording process as we believe students should understand it first before learning and using a computerized system.

use the term "journal" in this textbook, we mean the general journal unless we specify otherwise.

The journal makes several significant contributions to the recording process:

1. It discloses in one place the **complete effects of a transaction**.
2. It provides a **chronological record** of transactions.
3. It helps to **prevent or locate errors** because the debit and credit amounts for each entry can be easily compared.

JOURNALIZING

Entering transaction data in the journal is known as **journalizing**. Companies make separate journal entries for each transaction. A complete entry consists of (1) the date of the transaction, (2) the accounts and amounts to be debited and credited, and (3) a brief explanation of the transaction.

Illustration 2-13 shows the technique of journalizing, using the first two transactions of Softbyte. Recall that on September 1, Ray Neal invested $15,000 cash in the business, and Softbyte purchased computer equipment for $7,000 cash. The number J1 indicates that these two entries are recorded on the first page of the journal. Illustration 2-13 shows the standard form of journal entries for these two transactions. (The boxed numbers correspond to explanations in the list below the illustration.)

Illustration 2-13
Technique of journalizing

GENERAL JOURNAL J1

Date	Account Titles and Explanation	Ref.	Debit	Credit
2017		[5]		
Sept. 1 [2]	Cash		15,000	
[1] [3]	Owner's Capital			15,000
[4]	(Owner's investment of cash in business)			
1	Equipment		7,000	
	Cash			7,000
	(Purchase of equipment for cash)			

[1] The date of the transaction is entered in the Date column.

[2] The debit account title (that is, the account to be debited) is entered first at the extreme left margin of the column headed "Account Titles and Explanation," and the amount of the debit is recorded in the Debit column.

[3] The credit account title (that is, the account to be credited) is indented and entered on the next line in the column headed "Account Titles and Explanation," and the amount of the credit is recorded in the Credit column.

[4] A brief explanation of the transaction appears on the line below the credit account title. A space is left between journal entries. The blank space separates individual journal entries and makes the entire journal easier to read.

[5] The column titled Ref. (which stands for Reference) is left blank when the journal entry is made. This column is used later when the journal entries are transferred to the ledger accounts.

It is important to use correct and specific account titles in journalizing. Erroneous account titles lead to incorrect financial statements. However, some flexibility exists initially in selecting account titles. The main criterion is that each title must appropriately describe the content of the account. Once a company chooses the specific title to use, it should record under that account title all later transactions involving the account.[2]

SIMPLE AND COMPOUND ENTRIES

Some entries involve only two accounts, one debit and one credit. (See, for example, the entries in Illustration 2-13.) This type of entry is called a **simple entry**. Some transactions, however, require more than two accounts in journalizing. An entry that requires three or more accounts is a **compound entry**. To illustrate, assume that on July 1, Butler Company purchases a delivery truck costing $14,000. It pays $8,000 cash now and agrees to pay the remaining $6,000 on account (to be paid later). The compound entry is as follows.

Illustration 2-14
Compound journal entry

GENERAL JOURNAL J1

Date	Account Titles and Explanation	Ref.	Debit	Credit
2017				
July 1	Equipment		14,000	
	Cash			8,000
	Accounts Payable			6,000
	(Purchased truck for cash with balance on account)			

In a compound entry, the standard format requires that all debits be listed before the credits.

LEARNING OBJECTIVE 3 **Explain how a ledger and posting help in the recording process.**

The Ledger

The entire group of accounts maintained by a company is the **ledger**. The ledger provides the balance in each of the accounts as well as keeps track of changes in these balances.

Companies may use various kinds of ledgers, but every company has a general ledger. A **general ledger** contains all the asset, liability, and owner's equity accounts, as shown in Illustration 2-15 for J. Lind Company. *Whenever we use the term "ledger" in this textbook, we are referring to the general ledger unless we specify otherwise.*

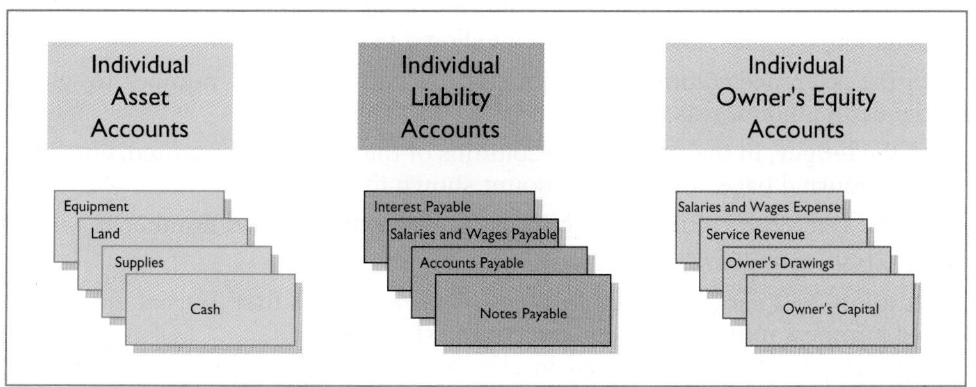

Illustration 2-15
The general ledger, which contains all of a company's accounts

[2]*In homework problems, you should use specific account titles when they are given.* When account titles are not given, you may select account titles that identify the nature and content of each account. The account titles used in journalizing should not contain explanations such as Cash Paid or Cash Received.

Companies arrange the ledger in the sequence in which they present the accounts in the financial statements, beginning with the balance sheet accounts. First in order are the asset accounts, followed by liability accounts, owner's capital, owner's drawings, revenues, and expenses. Each account is numbered for easier identification.

The ledger provides the balance in each of the accounts. For example, the Cash account shows the amount of cash available to meet current obligations. The Accounts Receivable account shows amounts due from customers. Accounts Payable shows amounts owed to creditors.

STANDARD FORM OF ACCOUNT

The simple T-account form used in accounting textbooks is often very useful for illustration purposes. However, in practice, the account forms used in ledgers are much more structured. Illustration 2-16 shows a typical form, using assumed data from a cash account.

Illustration 2-16
Three-column form of account

CASH					NO. 101
Date	**Explanation**	**Ref.**	**Debit**	**Credit**	**Balance**
2017					
June 1			25,000		25,000
2				8,000	17,000
3			4,200		21,200
9			7,500		28,700
17				11,700	17,000
20				250	16,750
30				7,300	9,450

This format is called the **three-column form of account**. It has three money columns—debit, credit, and balance. The balance in the account is determined after each transaction. Companies use the explanation space and reference columns to provide special information about the transaction.

Posting

Transferring journal entries to the ledger accounts is called **posting**. This phase of the recording process accumulates the effects of journalized transactions into the individual accounts. Posting involves the following steps:

1. In the **ledger**, in the appropriate columns of the account(s) debited, enter the date, journal page, and debit amount shown in the journal.
2. In the reference column of the **journal**, write the account number to which the debit amount was posted.
3. In the **ledger**, in the appropriate columns of the account(s) credited, enter the date, journal page, and credit amount shown in the journal.
4. In the reference column of the **journal**, write the account number to which the credit amount was posted.

Illustration 2-17 shows these four steps using Softbyte's first journal entry. The boxed numbers indicate the sequence of the steps.

Posting should be performed in chronological order. That is, the company should post all the debits and credits of one journal entry before proceeding to the next journal entry. Postings should be made on a timely basis to ensure that the ledger is up-to-date.[3]

[3] *In homework problems, you can journalize all transactions before posting any of the journal entries.*

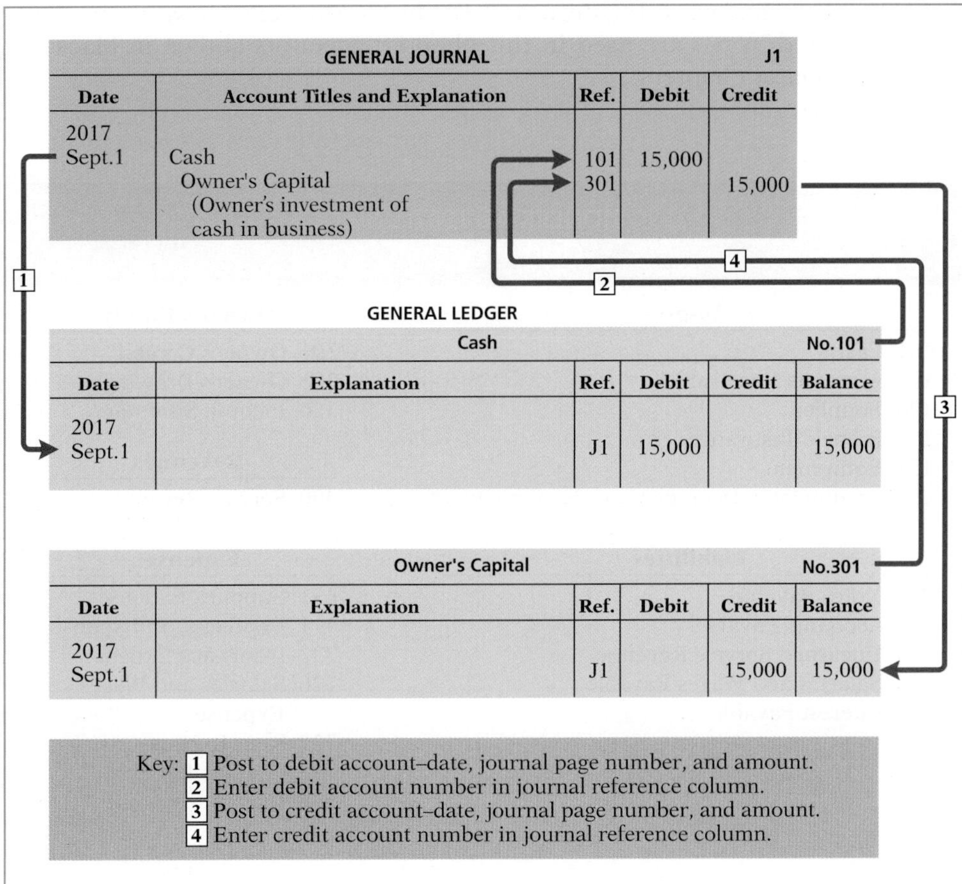

Illustration 2-17
Posting a journal entry

The reference column of a ledger account indicates the journal page from which the transaction was posted.[4] The explanation space of the ledger account is used infrequently because an explanation already appears in the journal.

CHART OF ACCOUNTS

The number and type of accounts differ for each company. The number of accounts depends on the amount of detail management desires. For example, the management of one company may want a single account for all types of utility expense. Another may keep separate expense accounts for each type of utility, such as gas, electricity, and water. Similarly, a small company like Softbyte will have fewer accounts than a corporate giant like **Dell**. Softbyte may be able to manage and report its activities in 20 to 30 accounts, while Dell may require thousands of accounts to keep track of its worldwide activities.

Most companies have a **chart of accounts**. This chart lists the accounts and the account numbers that identify their location in the ledger. The numbering system that identifies the accounts usually starts with the balance sheet accounts and follows with the income statement accounts.

In this and the next two chapters, we will be explaining the accounting for Pioneer Advertising (a service company). Accounts 101–199 indicate asset accounts; 200–299 indicate liabilities; 301–350 indicate owner's equity accounts; 400–499, revenues; 601–799, expenses; 800–899, other revenues; and

[4]After the last entry has been posted, the accountant should scan the reference column **in the journal**, to confirm that all postings have been made.

900–999, other expenses. Illustration 2-18 shows Pioneer's chart of accounts. Accounts listed in red are used in this chapter; accounts shown in black are explained in later chapters.

Illustration 2-18
Chart of accounts

PIONEER ADVERTISING
Chart of Accounts

Assets	Owner's Equity
101 Cash	301 Owner's Capital
112 Accounts Receivable	306 Owner's Drawings
126 Supplies	350 Income Summary
130 Prepaid Insurance	
157 Equipment	**Revenues**
158 Accumulated Depreciation—Equipment	400 Service Revenue
Liabilities	**Expenses**
200 Notes Payable	631 Supplies Expense
201 Accounts Payable	711 Depreciation Expense
209 Unearned Service Revenue	722 Insurance Expense
212 Salaries and Wages Payable	726 Salaries and Wages Expense
230 Interest Payable	729 Rent Expense
	732 Utilities Expense
	905 Interest Expense

You will notice that there are gaps in the numbering system of the chart of accounts for Pioneer. Companies leave gaps to permit the insertion of new accounts as needed during the life of the business.

The Recording Process Illustrated

Illustrations 2-19 through 2-28 (pages 47–51) show the basic steps in the recording process, using the October transactions of Pioneer Advertising. Pioneer's accounting period is a month. In these illustrations, a basic analysis, an equation analysis, and a debit-credit analysis precede the journal entry and posting of each transaction. For simplicity, we use the T-account form to show the posting instead of the standard account form.

Study these transaction analyses carefully. **The purpose of transaction analysis is first to identify the type of account involved, and then to determine whether to make a debit or a credit to the account.** You should always perform this type of analysis before preparing a journal entry. Doing so will help you understand the journal entries discussed in this chapter as well as more complex journal entries in later chapters.

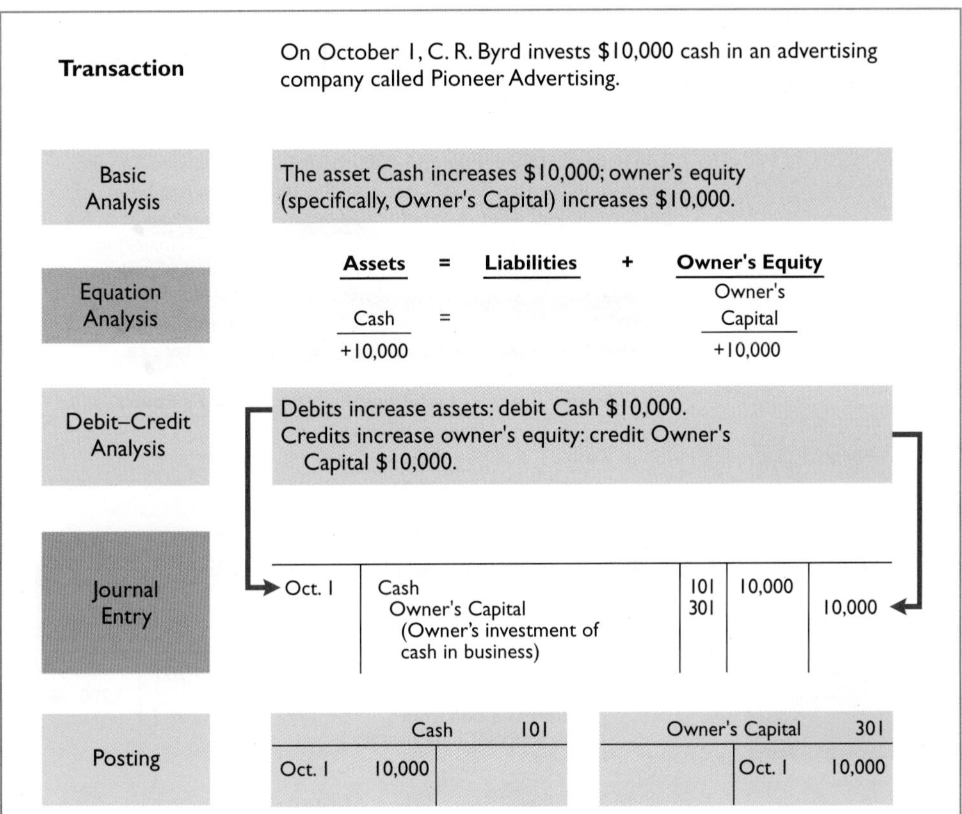

Illustration 2-19
Investment of cash by owner

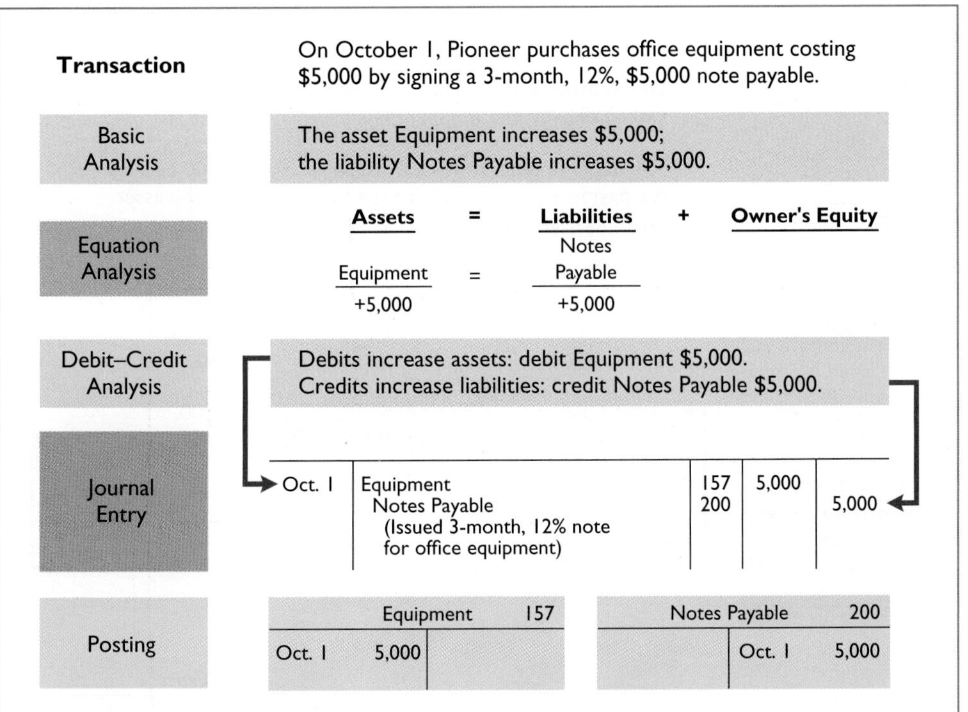

Illustration 2-20
Purchase of office equipment

Cash Flows
no effect

Illustration 2-21
Receipt of cash for future service

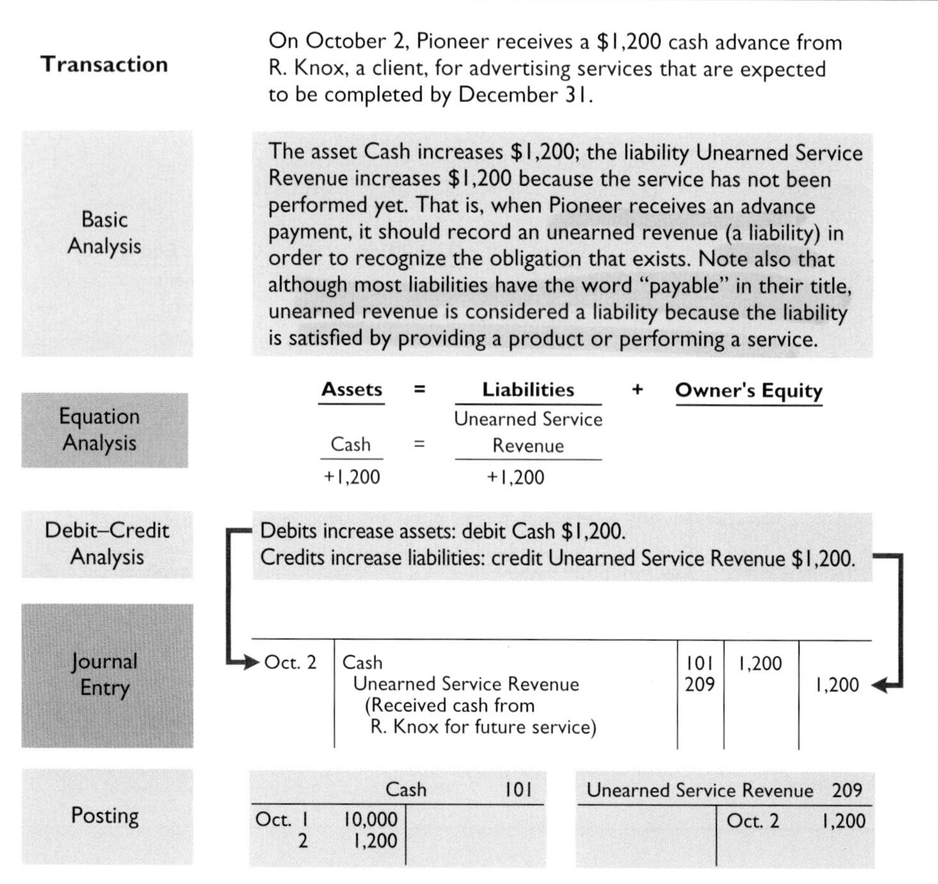

Transaction

On October 2, Pioneer receives a $1,200 cash advance from R. Knox, a client, for advertising services that are expected to be completed by December 31.

Basic Analysis

The asset Cash increases $1,200; the liability Unearned Service Revenue increases $1,200 because the service has not been performed yet. That is, when Pioneer receives an advance payment, it should record an unearned revenue (a liability) in order to recognize the obligation that exists. Note also that although most liabilities have the word "payable" in their title, unearned revenue is considered a liability because the liability is satisfied by providing a product or performing a service.

Equation Analysis

Assets	=	Liabilities	+	Owner's Equity
Cash	=	Unearned Service Revenue		
+1,200		+1,200		

Cash Flows
+1,200

Debit–Credit Analysis

Debits increase assets: debit Cash $1,200.
Credits increase liabilities: credit Unearned Service Revenue $1,200.

Journal Entry

Date	Account	Ref.	Debit	Credit
Oct. 2	Cash	101	1,200	
	Unearned Service Revenue	209		1,200
	(Received cash from R. Knox for future service)			

Posting

Cash			101
Oct. 1	10,000		
2	1,200		

Unearned Service Revenue			209
		Oct. 2	1,200

Illustration 2-22
Payment of monthly rent

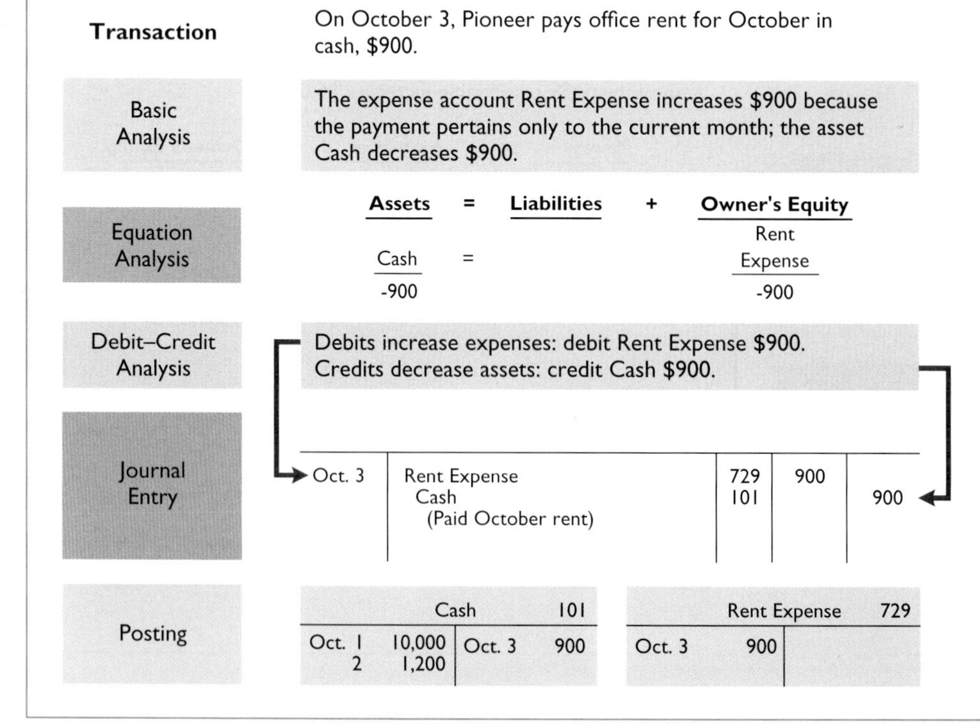

Transaction

On October 3, Pioneer pays office rent for October in cash, $900.

Basic Analysis

The expense account Rent Expense increases $900 because the payment pertains only to the current month; the asset Cash decreases $900.

Equation Analysis

Assets	=	Liabilities	+	Owner's Equity
Cash	=			Rent Expense
-900				-900

Cash Flows
−900

Debit–Credit Analysis

Debits increase expenses: debit Rent Expense $900.
Credits decrease assets: credit Cash $900.

Journal Entry

Date	Account	Ref.	Debit	Credit
Oct. 3	Rent Expense	729	900	
	Cash	101		900
	(Paid October rent)			

Posting

Cash			101
Oct. 1	10,000	Oct. 3	900
2	1,200		

Rent Expense			729
Oct. 3	900		

Illustration 2-23
Payment for insurance

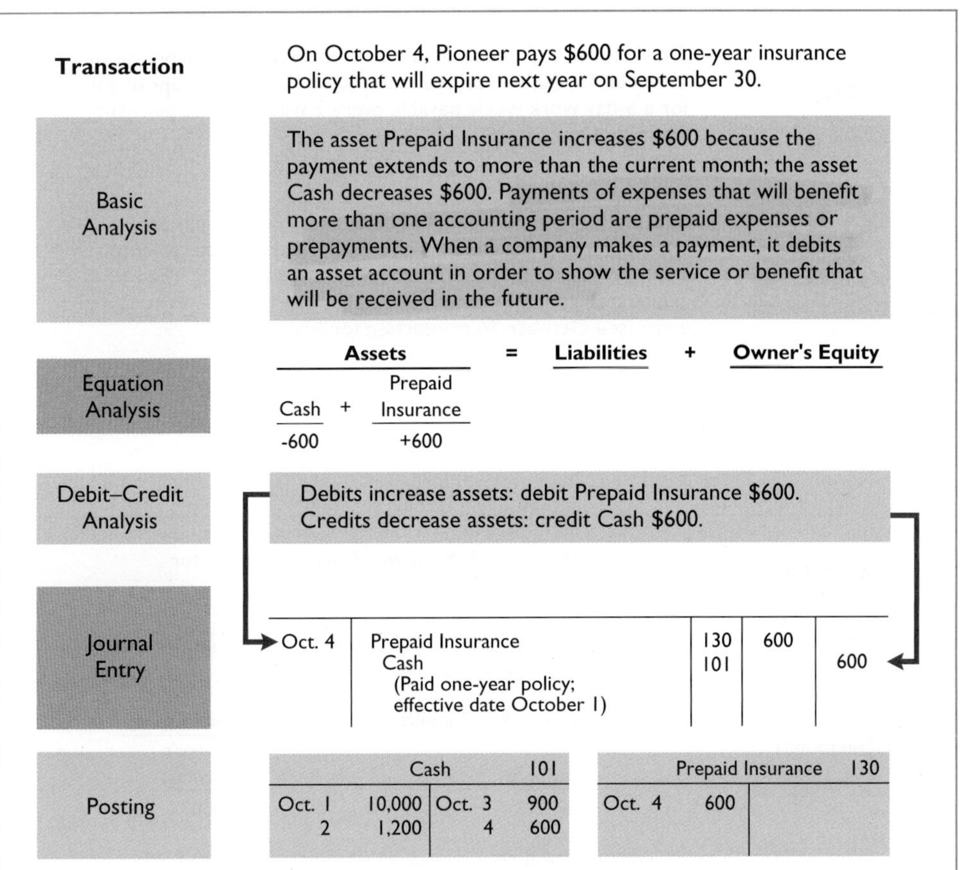

Cash Flows
−600

Illustration 2-24
Purchase of supplies on credit

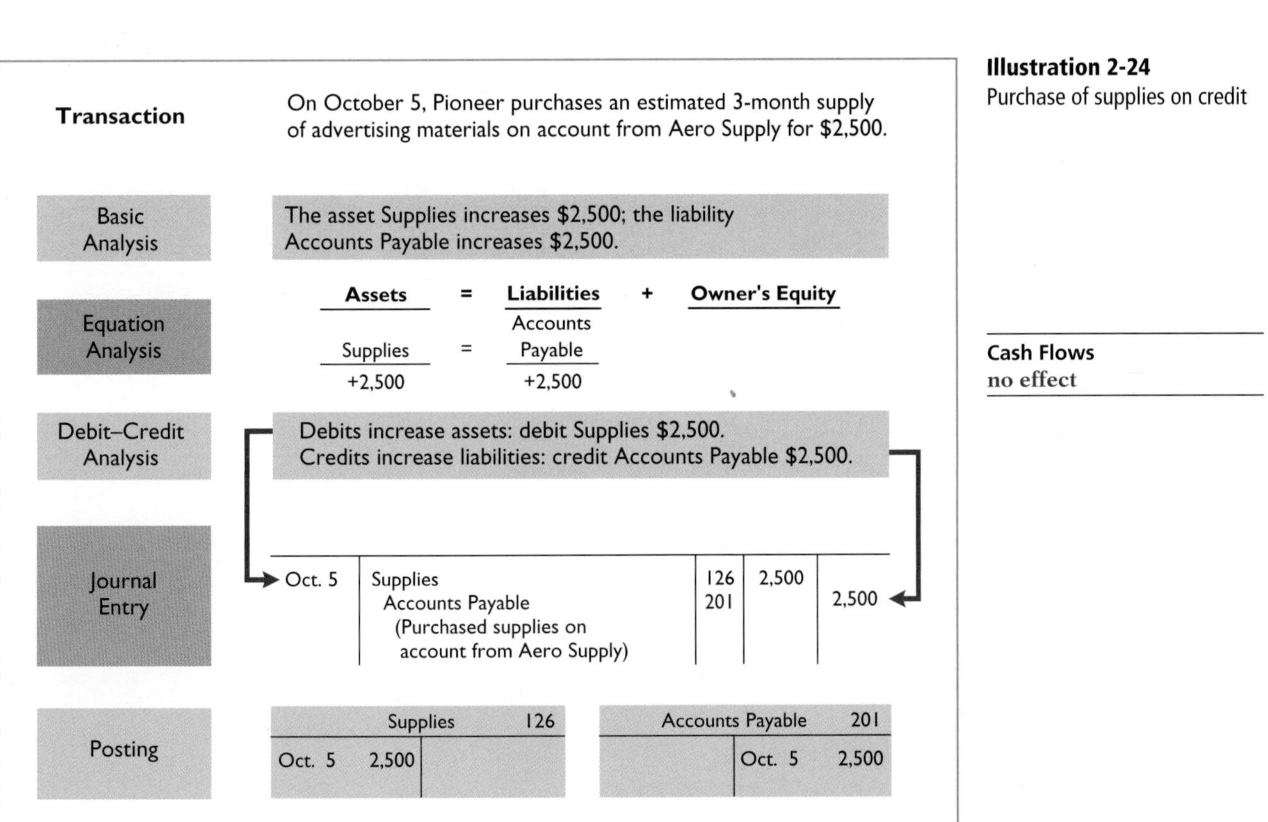

Cash Flows
no effect

Illustration 2-25
Hiring of employees

Cash Flows
no effect

Event	On October 9, Pioneer hires four employees to begin work on October 15. Each employee is to receive a weekly salary of $500 for a 5-day work week, payable every 2 weeks—first payment made on October 26.
Basic Analysis	A business transaction has not occurred. There is only an agreement between the employer and the employees to enter into a business transaction beginning on October 15. Thus, a debit–credit analysis is not needed because there is no accounting entry (see October 26 transaction for first entry).

Illustration 2-26
Withdrawal of cash by owner

Cash Flows
−500

Transaction	On October 20, C. R. Byrd withdraws $500 cash for personal use.
Basic Analysis	The owner's equity account Owner's Drawings increases $500; the asset Cash decreases $500.

Equation Analysis

Assets	=	**Liabilities**	+	**Owner's Equity**
Cash	=			Owner's Drawings
-500				-500

Debit–Credit Analysis

Debits increase drawings: debit Owner's Drawings $500.
Credits decrease assets: credit Cash $500.

Journal Entry

Oct. 20	Owner's Drawings	306	500	
	Cash	101		500
	(Withdrew cash for personal use)			

Posting

Cash			101
Oct. 1	10,000	Oct. 3	900
2	1,200	4	600
		20	500

Owner's Drawings			306
Oct. 20	500		

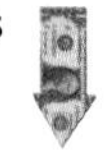

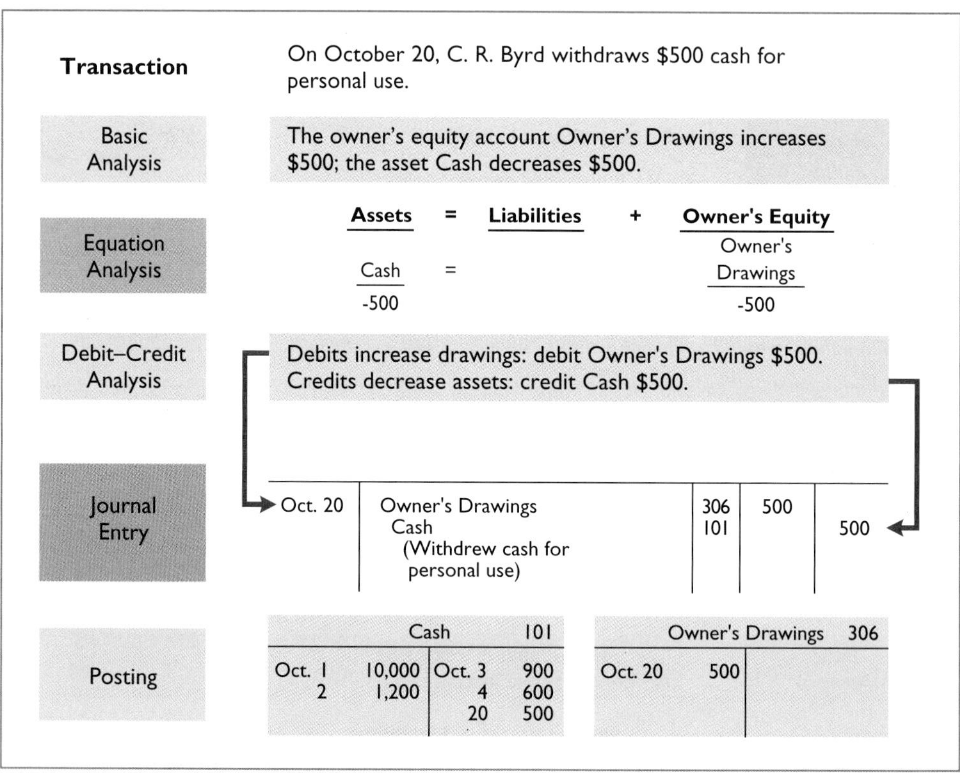

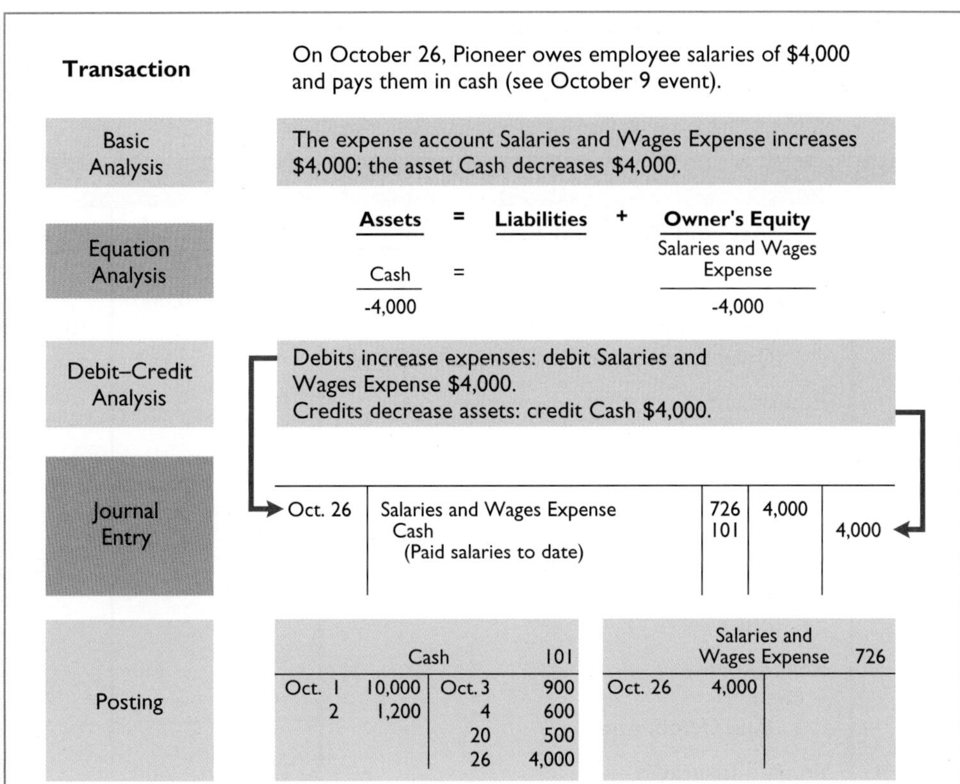

Illustration 2-27
Payment of salaries

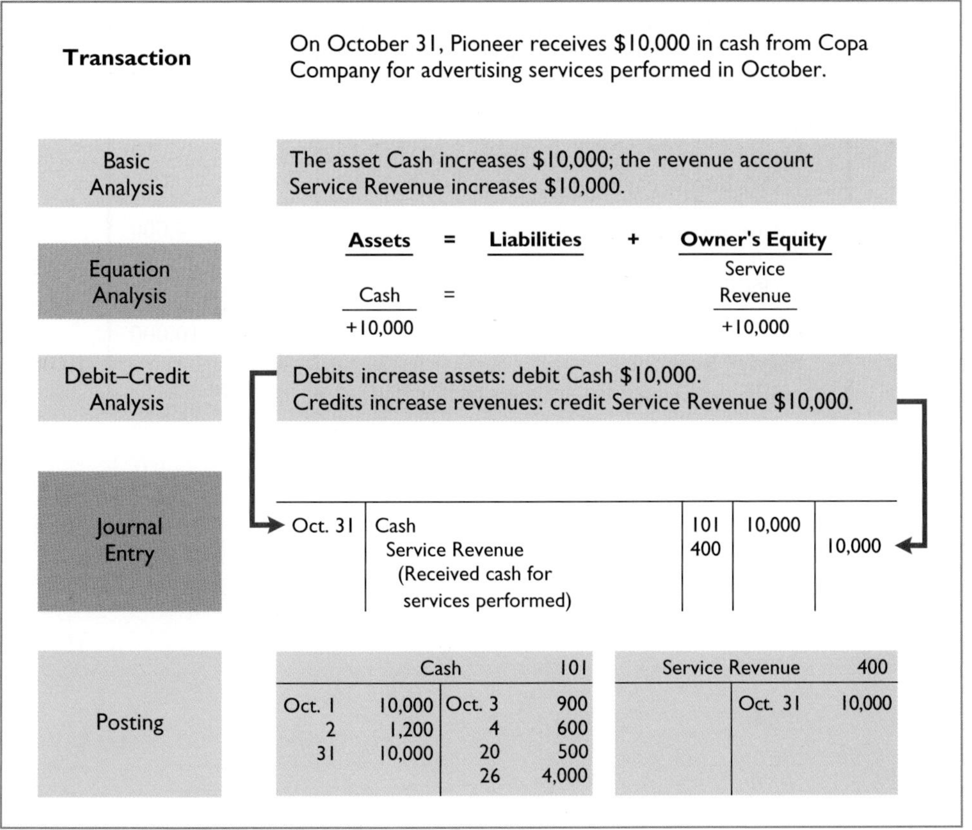

Illustration 2-28
Receipt of cash for services performed

Summary Illustration of Journalizing and Posting

Illustration 2-29 shows the journal for Pioneer Advertising for October.

Illustration 2-29
General journal entries

GENERAL JOURNAL				PAGE J1
Date	**Account Titles and Explanation**	**Ref.**	**Debit**	**Credit**
2017				
Oct. 1	Cash	101	10,000	
	Owner's Capital	301		10,000
	(Owner's investment of cash in business)			
1	Equipment	157	5,000	
	Notes Payable	200		5,000
	(Issued 3-month, 12% note for office equipment)			
2	Cash	101	1,200	
	Unearned Service Revenue	209		1,200
	(Received cash from R. Knox for future service)			
3	Rent Expense	729	900	
	Cash	101		900
	(Paid October rent)			
4	Prepaid Insurance	130	600	
	Cash	101		600
	(Paid one-year policy; effective date October 1)			
5	Supplies	126	2,500	
	Accounts Payable	201		2,500
	(Purchased supplies on account from Aero Supply)			
20	Owner's Drawings	306	500	
	Cash	101		500
	(Withdrew cash for personal use)			
26	Salaries and Wages Expense	726	4,000	
	Cash	101		4,000
	(Paid salaries to date)			
31	Cash	101	10,000	
	Service Revenue	400		10,000
	(Received cash for services performed)			

Illustration 2-30 shows the ledger, with all balances in red.

Illustration 2-30
General ledger

GENERAL LEDGER

Cash — **No. 101**

Date	Explanation	Ref.	Debit	Credit	Balance
2017					
Oct. 1		J1	10,000		10,000
2		J1	1,200		11,200
3		J1		900	10,300
4		J1		600	9,700
20		J1		500	9,200
26		J1		4,000	5,200
31		J1	10,000		**15,200**

Supplies — **No. 126**

Date	Explanation	Ref.	Debit	Credit	Balance
2017					
Oct. 5		J1	2,500		**2,500**

Prepaid Insurance — **No. 130**

Date	Explanation	Ref.	Debit	Credit	Balance
2017					
Oct. 4		J1	600		**600**

Equipment — **No. 157**

Date	Explanation	Ref.	Debit	Credit	Balance
2017					
Oct. 1		J1	5,000		**5,000**

Notes Payable — **No. 200**

Date	Explanation	Ref.	Debit	Credit	Balance
2017					
Oct. 1		J1		5,000	**5,000**

Accounts Payable — **No. 201**

Date	Explanation	Ref.	Debit	Credit	Balance
2017					
Oct. 5		J1		2,500	**2,500**

Unearned Service Revenue — **No. 209**

Date	Explanation	Ref.	Debit	Credit	Balance
2017					
Oct. 2		J1		1,200	**1,200**

Owner's Capital — **No. 301**

Date	Explanation	Ref.	Debit	Credit	Balance
2017					
Oct. 1		J1		10,000	**10,000**

Owner's Drawings — **No. 306**

Date	Explanation	Ref.	Debit	Credit	Balance
2017					
Oct. 20		J1	500		**500**

Service Revenue — **No. 400**

Date	Explanation	Ref.	Debit	Credit	Balance
2017					
Oct. 31		J1		10,000	**10,000**

Salaries and Wages Expense — **No. 726**

Date	Explanation	Ref.	Debit	Credit	Balance
2017					
Oct. 26		J1	4,000		**4,000**

Rent Expense — **No. 729**

Date	Explanation	Ref.	Debit	Credit	Balance
2017					
Oct. 3		J1	900		**900**

LEARNING OBJECTIVE 4

Prepare a trial balance.

A **trial balance** is a list of accounts and their balances at a given time. Customarily, companies prepare a trial balance at the end of an accounting period. They list accounts in the order in which they appear in the ledger. Debit balances appear in the left column and credit balances in the right column.

The trial balance proves the mathematical equality of debits and credits after posting. Under the double-entry system, this equality occurs when the sum of the debit account balances equals the sum of the credit account balances. **A trial balance may also uncover errors in journalizing and posting.** For example, a trial balance may well have detected the error at MF Global discussed in the chapter opening story. **In addition, a trial balance is useful in the preparation of financial statements**, as we will explain in the next two chapters.

The steps for preparing a trial balance are:

1. List the account titles and their balances in the appropriate debit or credit column.
2. Total the debit and credit columns.
3. Prove the equality of the two columns.

Illustration 2-31 shows the trial balance prepared from Pioneer Advertising's ledger. Note that the total debits equal the total credits.

Illustration 2-31
A trial balance

PIONEER ADVERTISING Trial Balance October 31, 2017		
	Debit	**Credit**
Cash	$ 15,200	
Supplies	2,500	
Prepaid Insurance	600	
Equipment	5,000	
Notes Payable		$ 5,000
Accounts Payable		2,500
Unearned Service Revenue		1,200
Owner's Capital		10,000
Owner's Drawings	500	
Service Revenue		10,000
Salaries and Wages Expense	4,000	
Rent Expense	900	
	$28,700	**$28,700**

A trial balance is a necessary checkpoint for uncovering certain types of errors. For example, if only the debit portion of a journal entry has been posted, the trial balance would bring this error to light.

Limitations of a Trial Balance

A trial balance does not guarantee freedom from recording errors, however. Numerous errors may exist even though the totals of the trial balance columns agree. For example, the trial balance may balance even when:

1. A transaction is not journalized.
2. A correct journal entry is not posted.
3. A journal entry is posted twice.
4. Incorrect accounts are used in journalizing or posting.
5. Offsetting errors are made in recording the amount of a transaction.

As long as equal debits and credits are posted, even to the wrong account or in the wrong amount, the total debits will equal the total credits. **The trial balance does not prove that the company has recorded all transactions or that the ledger is correct.**

Locating Errors

Errors in a trial balance generally result from mathematical mistakes, incorrect postings, or simply transcribing data incorrectly. What do you do if you are faced with a trial balance that does not balance? First, determine the amount of the difference between the two columns of the trial balance. After this amount is known, the following steps are often helpful:

1. If the error is $1, $10, $100, or $1,000, re-add the trial balance columns and recompute the account balances.
2. If the error is divisible by 2, scan the trial balance to see whether a balance equal to half the error has been entered in the wrong column.
3. If the error is divisible by 9, retrace the account balances on the trial balance to see whether they are incorrectly copied from the ledger. For example, if a

balance was $12 and it was listed as $21, a $9 error has been made. Reversing the order of numbers is called a **transposition error**.

4. If the error is not divisible by 2 or 9, scan the ledger to see whether an account balance in the amount of the error has been omitted from the trial balance, and scan the journal to see whether a posting of that amount has been omitted.

Dollar Signs and Underlining

Note that dollar signs do not appear in journals or ledgers. Dollar signs are typically used only in the trial balance and the financial statements. Generally, a dollar sign is shown only for the first item in the column and for the total of that column. A single line (a totaling rule) is placed under the column of figures to be added or subtracted. Total amounts are double-underlined to indicate they are final sums.

REVIEW AND PRACTICE

LEARNING OBJECTIVES REVIEW

1 Describe how accounts, debits, and credits are used to record business transactions. An account is a record of increases and decreases in specific asset, liability, and owner's equity items. The terms debit and credit are synonymous with left and right. Assets, drawings, and expenses are increased by debits and decreased by credits. Liabilities, owner's capital, and revenues are increased by credits and decreased by debits.

2 Indicate how a journal is used in the recording process. The basic steps in the recording process are (a) analyze each transaction for its effects on the accounts, (b) enter the transaction information in a journal, and (c) transfer the journal information to the appropriate accounts in the ledger.

The initial accounting record of a transaction is entered in a journal before the data are entered in the accounts. A journal (a) discloses in one place the complete effects of a transaction, (b) provides a chronological record of transactions, and (c) prevents or locates errors because the debit and credit amounts for each entry can be easily compared.

3 Explain how a ledger and posting help in the recording process. The ledger is the entire group of accounts maintained by a company. The ledger provides the balance in each of the accounts as well as keeps track of changes in these balances. Posting is the transfer of journal entries to the ledger accounts. This phase of the recording process accumulates the effects of journalized transactions in the individual accounts.

4 Prepare a trial balance. A trial balance is a list of accounts and their balances at a given time. Its primary purpose is to prove the equality of debits and credits after posting. A trial balance also uncovers errors in journalizing and posting and is useful in preparing financial statements.

GLOSSARY REVIEW

Account A record of increases and decreases in specific asset, liability, or owner's equity items.

Chart of accounts A list of accounts and the account numbers that identify their location in the ledger.

Compound entry A journal entry that involves three or more accounts.

Credit The right side of an account.

Debit The left side of an account.

Double-entry system A system that records in appropriate accounts the dual effect of each transaction.

General journal The most basic form of journal.

General ledger A ledger that contains all asset, liability, and owner's equity accounts.

Journal An accounting record in which transactions are initially recorded in chronological order.

Journalizing The entering of transaction data in the journal.

Ledger The entire group of accounts maintained by a company.

Normal balance An account balance on the side where an increase in the account is recorded.

Posting The procedure of transferring journal entries to the ledger accounts.

Simple entry A journal entry that involves only two accounts.

T-account The basic form of an account.

Three-column form of account A form with columns for debit, credit, and balance amounts in an account.

Trial balance A list of accounts and their balances at a given time.

PRACTICE EXERCISES

Analyze transactions and determine their effect on accounts.

(LO 1)

1. Presented below is information related to Hammond Real Estate Agency:

Oct. 1 Lia Berge begins business as a real estate agent with a cash investment of $30,000
2 Paid rent, $700, on office space.
3 Purchases office equipment for $2,800, on account.
6 Sells a house and lot for Hal Smith; bills Hal Smith $4,400 for realty services performed.
27 Pays $1,100 on the balance related to the transaction of October 3.
30 Receives bill for October utilities, $130 (not paid at this time).

Instructions

Journalize the transactions. (You may omit explanations)

Solution

1. GENERAL JOURNAL

Date	Account Titles and Explanation	Ref.	Debit	Credit
Oct. 1	Cash		30,000	
	Owner's Capital			30,000
2	Rent Expense		700	
	Cash			700
3	Equipment		2,800	
	Accounts Payable			2,800
6	Accounts Receivable		4,400	
	Service Revenue			4,400
27	Accounts Payable		1,100	
	Cash			1,100
30	Utilities Expense		130	
	Accounts Payable			130

Journalize transactions from account data and prepare a trial balance.

(LO 2, 4)

2. The T-accounts below summarize the ledger of Depot Company at the end of the first month of operations.

Cash No. 101

	Debit		Credit
4/1	16,000	4/15	700
4/12	1,200	4/25	1,600
4/29	900		
4/30	1,600		

Accounts Receivable No. 112

	Debit		Credit
4/7	2,900	4/29	900

Supplies No. 126

	Debit		Credit
4/4	1,900		

Accounts Payable No. 201

	Debit		Credit
4/25	1,600	4/4	1,900

Unearned Service Revenue No. 209

	Debit		Credit
		4/30	1,600

Owner's Capital No. 301

	Debit		Credit
		4/1	16,000

Service Revenue No. 400

	Debit		Credit
		4/7	2,900
		4/12	1,200

Salaries and Wages Expense No. 726

	Debit		Credit
4/15	700		

Instructions

(a) Prepare the complete general journal (including explanations) from which the postings to Cash were made.

(b) Prepare a trial balance at April 30, 2017.

Solution

2. (a)

GENERAL JOURNAL

Date	Account Titles and Explanation	Ref.	Debit	Credit
Apr. 1	Cash		16,000	
	Owner's Capital			16,000
	(Owner's investment of cash in business)			
12	Cash		1,200	
	Service Revenue			1,200
	(Received cash for services performed)			
15	Salaries and Wages Expense		700	
	Cash			700
	(Paid salaries to date)			
25	Accounts payable		1,600	
	Cash			1,600
	(Paid creditors on account)			
29	Cash		900	
	Accounts Receivable			900
	(Received cash in payment of account)			
30	Cash		1,600	
	Unearned Service Revenue			1,600
	(Received cash for future services)			

(b)

DEPOT COMPANY
Trial Balance
April 30, 2017

	Debit	Credit
Cash	$17,400	
Accounts Receivable	2,000	
Supplies	1,900	
Accounts Payable		$ 300
Unearned Service Revenue		1,600
Owner's Capital		16,000
Service Revenue		4,100
Salaries and Wages Expense	700	
	$22,000	$22,000

PRACTICE PROBLEM

Journalize transactions, post, and prepare a trial balance.

(LO 1, 2, 3, 4)

Bob Sample opened the Campus Laundromat on September 1, 2017. During the first month of operations, the following transactions occurred:

Sept.	1	Bob invested $20,000 cash in the business.
	2	The company paid $1,000 cash for store rent for September.
	3	Purchased washers and dryers for $25,000, paying $10,000 in cash and signing a $15,000, 6-month, 12% note payable.
	4	Paid $1,200 for a one-year accident insurance policy.
	10	Received a bill from the *Daily News* for online advertising of the opening of the laundromat $200.
	20	Bob withdrew $700 cash for personal use.
	30	The company determined that cash receipts for laundry services for the month were $6,200.

The chart of accounts for the company is the same as that for Pioneer Advertising plus No. 610 Advertising Expense.

Instructions

(a) Journalize the September transactions. (Use J1 for the journal page number.)

(b) Open ledger accounts and post the September transactions.

(c) Prepare a trial balance at September 30, 2017.

Solution

(a) **GENERAL JOURNAL** J1

Date	Account Titles and Explanation	Ref.	Debit	Credit
2017				
Sept. 1	Cash	101	20,000	
	Owner's Capital	301		20,000
	(Owner's investment of cash in business)			
2	Rent Expense	729	1,000	
	Cash	101		1,000
	(Paid September rent)			
3	Equipment	157	25,000	
	Cash	101		10,000
	Notes Payable	200		15,000
	(Purchased laundry equipment for cash and 6-month, 12% note payable)			
4	Prepaid Insurance	130	1,200	
	Cash	101		1,200
	(Paid one-year insurance policy)			
10	Advertising Expense	610	200	
	Accounts Payable	201		200
	(Received bill from *Daily News* for advertising)			
20	Owner's Drawings	306	700	
	Cash	101		700
	(Withdrew cash for personal use)			
30	Cash	101	6,200	
	Service Revenue	400		6,200
	(Received cash for services performed)			

(b) **GENERAL LEDGER**

Cash No. 101

Date	Explanation	Ref.	Debit	Credit	Balance
2017					
Sept. 1		J1	20,000		20,000
2		J1		1,000	19,000
3		J1		10,000	9,000
4		J1		1,200	7,800
20		J1		700	7,100
30		J1	6,200		13,300

Prepaid Insurance No. 130

Date	Explanation	Ref.	Debit	Credit	Balance
2017					
Sept. 4		J1	1,200		1,200

Equipment No. 157

Date	Explanation	Ref.	Debit	Credit	Balance
2017					
Sept. 3		J1	25,000		25,000

Accounts Payable No. 201

Date	Explanation	Ref.	Debit	Credit	Balance
2017					
Sept. 10		J1		200	200

Owner's Capital No. 301

Date	Explanation	Ref.	Debit	Credit	Balance
2017					
Sept. 1		J1		20,000	20,000

Owner's Drawings No. 306

Date	Explanation	Ref.	Debit	Credit	Balance
2017					
Sept. 20		J1	700		700

Service Revenue No. 400

Date	Explanation	Ref.	Debit	Credit	Balance
2017					
Sept. 30		J1		6,200	6,200

Notes Payable **No. 200**

Date	Explanation	Ref.	Debit	Credit	Balance
2017					
Sept. 3		J1		15,000	15,000

Advertising Expense **No. 610**

Date	Explanation	Ref.	Debit	Credit	Balance
2017					
Sept. 10		J1	200		200

Rent Expense **No. 729**

Date	Explanation	Ref.	Debit	Credit	Balance
2017					
Sept. 2		J1	1,000		1,000

(c)

CAMPUS LAUNDROMAT
Trial Balance
September 30, 2017

	Debit	Credit
Cash	$13,300	
Prepaid Insurance	1,200	
Equipment	25,000	
Notes Payable		$15,000
Accounts Payable		200
Owner's Capital		20,000
Owner's Drawings	700	
Service Revenue		6,200
Advertising Expense	200	
Rent Expense	1,000	
	$41,400	$41,400

EXERCISES

E2-1 Kim Yi has prepared the following list of statements about accounts:

Analyze statements about accounting and the recording process.

(LO 1)

1. An account is an accounting record of either a specific asset or a specific liability.
2. An account shows only increases, not decreases, in the item it relates to.
3. Some items, such as Cash and Accounts Receivable, are combined into one account.
4. An account has a left, or credit side, and a right, or debit side.
5. A simple form of an account consisting of just the account title, the left side, and the right side, is called a T-account.

Instructions

Identify each statement as true or false. If false, indicate how to correct the statement.

E2-2 Selected transactions for A. Mane, an interior decorator, in her first month of business, are as follows:

Identify debits, credits, and normal balances.

(LO 1)

Jan. 2 Invested $10,000 cash in business.
3 Purchased used car for $3,000 cash for use in business.
9 Purchased supplies on account for $500.
11 Billed customers $2,400 for services performed.
16 Paid $350 cash for advertising.
20 Received $700 cash from customers billed on January 11.
23 Paid creditor $300 cash on balance owed.
28 Withdrew $1,000 cash for personal use by owner.

Instructions

For each transaction, indicate the following:

(a) The basic type of account debited and credited (asset, liability, owner's equity).
(b) The specific account debited and credited (Cash, Rent Expense, Service Revenue, etc.).
(c) Whether the specific account is increased or decreased.
(d) The normal balance of the specific account.

Use the following format, in which the January 2 transaction is given as an example.

	Account Debited				Account Credited			
	(a) Basic	(b) Specific	(c)	(d) Normal	(a) Basic	(b) Specific	(c)	(d) Normal
Date	Type	Account	Effect	Balance	Type	Account	Effect	Balance
Jan. 2	Asset	Cash	Increase	Debit	Owner's Equity	Owner's Capital	Increase	Credit

Journalize transactions.
(LO 2)

E2-3 Data for A. Mane, interior decorator, are presented in E2-2.

Instructions
Journalize the transactions using journal page J1. (You may omit explanations.)

Analyze transactions and determine their effect on accounts.
(LO 1)

E2-4 The following information relates to Sanculi Real Estate Agency:

Oct. 1 Alan Sanculi begins business as a real estate agent with a cash investment of $15,000.
2 Hires an administrative assistant.
3 Purchases office furniture for $1,900, on account.
6 Sells a house and lot for R. Craig; bills R. Craig $3,800 for realty services performed.
27 Pays $1,100 on the balance related to the transaction of October 3.
30 Pays the administrative assistant $2,500 in salary for October.

Instructions
Prepare the debit-credit analysis for each transaction as illustrated on pages 47–51.

Journalize transactions.
(LO 2)

E2-5 Transaction data for Sanculi Real Estate Agency are presented in E2-4.

Instructions
Journalize the transactions. (You may omit explanations.)

Analyze transactions and journalize.
(LO 1, 2)

E2-6 Marx Industries had the following transactions:

1. Borrowed $5,000 from the bank by signing a note.
2. Paid $3,100 cash for a computer.
3. Purchased $850 of supplies on account.

Instructions
(a) Indicate what accounts are increased and decreased by each transaction.
(b) Journalize each transaction. (Omit explanations.)

Analyze transactions and journalize.
(LO 1, 2)

E2-7 Halladay Enterprises had the following selected transactions:

1. Bo Halladay invested $4,000 cash in the business.
2. Paid office rent of $840.
3. Performed consulting services and billed a client $5,200.
4. Bo Halladay withdrew $750 cash for personal use.

Instructions
(a) Indicate the effect each transaction has on the accounting equation (Assets = Liabilities + Owner's Equity), using plus and minus signs.
(b) Journalize each transaction. (Omit explanations.)

Analyze statements about the ledger.
(LO 3)

E2-8 Teresa Alvarez has prepared the following list of statements about the general ledger:

1. The general ledger contains all the asset and liability accounts but no owner's equity accounts.
2. The general ledger is sometimes referred to as simply the ledger.
3. The accounts in the general ledger are arranged in alphabetical order.
4. Each account in the general ledger is numbered for easier identification.
5. The general ledger is a book of original entry.

Instructions
Identify each statement as true or false. If false, indicate how to correct the statement.

E2-9 Selected transactions from the journal of June Feldman, investment broker, are presented below.

Post journal entries and prepare a trial balance.

(LO 3, 4)

Date	Account Titles and Explanation	Ref.	Debit	Credit
Aug. 1	Cash		5,000	
	Owner's Capital			5,000
	(Owner's investment of cash in business)			
10	Cash		2,600	
	Service Revenue			2,600
	(Received cash for services performed)			
12	Equipment		5,000	
	Cash			2,300
	Notes Payable			2,700
	(Purchased equipment for cash and notes payable)			
25	Accounts Receivable		1,700	
	Service Revenue			1,700
	(Billed clients for services performed)			
31	Cash		900	
	Accounts Receivable			900
	(Receipt of cash on account)			

Instructions

(a) Post the transactions to T-accounts.
(b) Prepare a trial balance at August 31, 2017.

E2-10 The T-accounts below summarize the ledger of Daggett Landscaping Company at the end of the first month of operations.

Journalize transactions from account data and prepare a trial balance.

(LO 2, 4)

Cash			No. 101
4/1	12,000	4/15	1,300
4/12	900	4/25	1,500
4/29	400		
4/30	1,000		

Unearned Service Revenue			No. 209
		4/30	1,000

Accounts Receivable			No. 112
4/7	3,200	4/29	400

Owner's Capital			No. 301
		4/1	12,000

Supplies			No. 126
4/4	1,800		

Service Revenue			No. 400
		4/7	3,200
		4/12	900

Accounts Payable			No. 201
4/25	1,500	4/4	1,800

Salaries and Wages Expense			No. 726
4/15	1,300		

Instructions

(a) Prepare the complete general journal (including explanations) from which the postings to Cash were made.
(b) Prepare a trial balance at April 30, 2017.

E2-11 Presented below is the ledger for Shumway Co.

Journalize transactions from account data and prepare a trial balance.

(LO 2, 4)

Cash			No. 101
10/1	3,000	10/4	400
10/10	750	10/12	1,500
10/10	4,000	10/15	350
10/20	500	10/30	300
10/25	2,000	10/31	500

Owner's Capital			No. 301
		10/1	3,000
		10/25	2,000

Owner's Drawings			No. 306
10/30	300		

Accounts Receivable			No. 112
10/6	800	10/20	500
10/20	940		

Supplies			No. 126
10/4	400		

Equipment			No. 157
10/3	2,000		

Notes Payable			No. 200
		10/10	4,000

Accounts Payable			No. 201
10/12	1,500	10/3	2,000

Service Revenue			No. 400
		10/6	800
		10/10	750
		10/20	940

Salaries and Wages Expense			No. 726
10/31	500		

Rent Expense			No. 729
10/15	350		

Instructions

(a) Reproduce the journal entries for the transactions that occurred on October 1, 10, and 20, and provide explanations for each.
(b) Determine the October 31 balance for each of the accounts above, and prepare a trial balance at October 31, 2017.

Prepare journal entries and post using standard account form.
(LO 2, 3)

E2-12 Selected transactions for Dianne Burke Company during its first month in business are presented below.

Sept.	1	Invested $10,000 cash in the business.
	5	Purchased equipment for $12,000 paying $4,000 in cash and the balance on account.
	25	Paid $3,000 cash on balance owed for equipment.
	30	Withdrew $700 cash for personal use.

Burke's chart of accounts shows: No. 101 Cash, No. 157 Equipment, No. 201 Accounts Payable, No. 301 Owner's Capital, and No. 306 Owner's Drawings.

Instructions

(a) Journalize the transactions on page J1 of the journal. (Omit explanations.)
(b) Post the transactions using the standard account form.

Analyze errors and their effects on trial balance.
(LO 4)

E2-13 The bookkeeper for J.L. Kang Equipment Repair made a number of errors in journalizing and posting, as described below.

1. A credit posting of $525 to Accounts Receivable was omitted.
2. A debit posting of $750 for Prepaid Insurance was debited to Insurance Expense.
3. A collection from a customer of $100 in payment of its account owed was journalized and posted as a debit to Cash $100 and a credit to Service Revenue $100.
4. A credit posting of $415 to Property Taxes Payable was made twice.
5. A cash purchase of supplies for $250 was journalized and posted as a debit to Supplies $25 and a credit to Cash $25.
6. A debit of $625 to Advertising Expense was posted as $652.

Instructions

For each error:

(a) Indicate whether the trial balance will balance.
(b) If the trial balance will not balance, indicate the amount of the difference.
(c) Indicate the trial balance column that will have the larger total.

Consider each error separately. Use the following form, in which error (1) is given as an example.

Error	(a) In Balance	(b) Difference	(c) Larger Column
(1)	No	$525	debit

Prepare a trial balance.

(LO 4)

E2-14 The accounts in the ledger of Overnite Delivery Service contain the following balances on July 31, 2017:

Accounts Receivable	$ 7,642	Prepaid Insurance	$ 1,968
Accounts Payable	8,396	Maintenance and Repairs Expense	961
Cash	?	Service Revenue	10,610
Equipment	49,360	Owner's Drawings	700
Gasoline Expense	758	Owner's Capital	42,000
Utilities Expense	523	Salaries and Wages Expense	4,428
Notes Payable	17,000	Salaries and Wages Payable	815

Instructions

Prepare a trial balance with the accounts arranged as illustrated in the chapter and fill in the missing amount for Cash.

PROBLEMS

Journalize a series of transactions.

(LO 1, 2)

P2-1A Holz Disc Golf Course was opened on March 1 by Ian Holz. The following selected events and transactions occurred during March:

Mar.	1	Invested $20,000 cash in the business.
	3	Purchased Rainbow Golf Land for $15,000 cash. The price consists of land $12,000, shed $2,000, and equipment $1,000. (Make one compound entry.)
	5	Paid advertising expenses of $900.
	6	Paid cash $600 for a one-year insurance policy.
	10	Purchased golf discs and other equipment for $1,050 from Stevenson Company payable in 30 days.
	18	Received $1,100 in cash for golf fees (Holz records golf fees as service revenue).
	19	Sold 150 coupon books for $10 each. Each book contains 4 coupons that enable the holder to play one round of disc golf.
	25	Withdrew $800 cash for personal use.
	30	Paid salaries of $250.
	30	Paid Stevenson Company in full.
	31	Received $2,700 cash for golf fees.

Holz Disc Golf uses the following accounts: Cash, Prepaid Insurance, Land, Buildings, Equipment, Accounts Payable, Unearned Service Revenue, Owner's Capital, Owner's Drawings, Service Revenue, Advertising Expense, and Salaries and Wages Expense.

Instructions

Journalize the March transactions.

Journalize transactions, post, and prepare a trial balance.

(LO 1, 2, 3, 4)

P2-2A Emily Valley is a licensed dentist. During the first month of the operation of her business, the following events and transactions occurred:

April	1	Invested $20,000 cash in her business.
	1	Hired a secretary-receptionist at a salary of $700 per week payable monthly.
	2	Paid office rent for the month $1,100.
	3	Purchased dental supplies on account from Dazzle Company $4,000.
	10	Performed dental services and billed insurance companies $5,100.
	11	Received $1,000 cash advance from Leah Mataruka for an implant.
	20	Received $2,100 cash for services performed from Michael Santos.
	30	Paid secretary-receptionist for the month $2,800.
	30	Paid $2,400 to Dazzle for accounts payable due.

Emily uses the following chart of accounts: No. 101 Cash, No. 112 Accounts Receivable, No. 126 Supplies, No. 201 Accounts Payable, No. 209 Unearned Service Revenue, No. 301 Owner's Capital, No. 400 Service Revenue, No. 726 Salaries and Wages Expense, and No. 729 Rent Expense.

Instructions

(a) Journalize the transactions.
(b) Post to the ledger accounts.
(c) Prepare a trial balance on April 30, 2017.

(c) Trial balance totals $29,800

Journalize transactions, post, and prepare a trial balance.

(LO 1, 2, 3, 4)

P2-3A Maquoketa Services was formed on May 1, 2017. The following transactions took place during the first month.

Transactions on May 1:

1. Jay Bradford invested $40,000 cash in the company, as its sole owner.
2. Hired two employees to work in the warehouse. They will each be paid a salary of $3,050 per month.
3. Signed a 2-year rental agreement on a warehouse; paid $24,000 cash in advance for the first year.
4. Purchased furniture and equipment costing $30,000. A cash payment of $10,000 was made immediately; the remainder will be paid in 6 months.
5. Paid $1,800 cash for a one-year insurance policy on the furniture and equipment.

Transactions during the remainder of the month:

6. Purchased basic office supplies for $420 cash.
7. Purchased more office supplies for $1,500 on account.
8. Total revenues earned were $20,000—$8,000 cash and $12,000 on account.
9. Paid $400 to suppliers for accounts payable due.
10. Received $3,000 from customers in payment of accounts receivable.
11. Received utility bills in the amount of $380, to be paid next month.
12. Paid the monthly salaries of the two employees, totaling $6,100.

Instructions

(a) Prepare journal entries to record each of the events listed. (Omit explanations.)

(b) Post the journal entries to T-accounts.

(c) Prepare a trial balance as of May 31, 2017.

(c) Trial balance totals $81,480

Prepare a correct trial balance.

(LO 4)

P2-4A The trial balance of Avtar Sandhu Co. shown below does not balance.

AVTAR SANDHU CO.
Trial Balance
June 30, 2017

	Debit	**Credit**
Cash		$ 3,340
Accounts Receivable	$ 2,812	
Supplies	1,200	
Equipment	2,600	
Accounts Payable		3,666
Unearned Service Revenue	1,100	
Owner's Capital		8,000
Owner's Drawings	800	
Service Revenue		2,480
Salaries and Wages Expense	3,200	
Utilities Expense	810	
	$12,522	$17,486

Each of the listed accounts has a normal balance per the general ledger. An examination of the ledger and journal reveals the following errors:

1. Cash received from a customer in payment of its account was debited for $580, and Accounts Receivable was credited for the same amount. The actual collection was for $850.
2. The purchase of a computer on account for $710 was recorded as a debit to Supplies for $710 and a credit to Accounts Payable for $710.
3. Services were performed on account for a client for $980. Accounts Receivable was debited for $980, and Service Revenue was credited for $98.
4. A debit posting to Salaries and Wages Expense of $700 was omitted.
5. A payment of a balance due for $306 was credited to Cash for $306 and credited to Accounts Payable for $360.
6. The withdrawal of $600 cash for Sandhu's personal use was debited to Salaries and Wages Expense for $600 and credited to Cash for $600.

Instructions

Trial balance totals $15,462

Prepare a correct trial balance. (*Hint:* It helps to prepare the correct journal entry for the transaction described and compare it to the mistake made.)

Journalize transactions, post, and prepare a trial balance.

(LO 1, 2, 3, 4)

P2-5A The Starr Theater, owned by Meg Vargo, will begin operations in March. The Starr will be unique in that it will show only triple features of sequential theme movies. As of March 1, the ledger of Starr showed: No. 101 Cash \$3,000, No. 140 Land \$24,000, No. 145 Buildings (concession stand, projection room, ticket booth, and screen) \$10,000, No. 157 Equipment \$10,000, No. 201 Accounts Payable \$7,000, and No. 301 Owner's Capital \$40,000. During the month of March, the following events and transactions occurred:

Mar.	2	Rented the three *Indiana Jones* movies to be shown for the first 3 weeks of March. The film rental was \$3,500; \$1,500 was paid in cash and \$2,000 will be paid on March 10.
	3	Ordered the *Lord of the Rings* movies to be shown the last 10 days of March. It will cost \$200 per night.
	9	Received \$4,300 cash from admissions.
	10	Paid balance due on *Indiana Jones* movies rental and \$2,100 on March 1 accounts payable.
	11	Starr Theater contracted with Adam Ladd to operate the concession stand. Ladd is to pay 15% of gross concession receipts, payable monthly, for the rental of the concession stand.
	12	Paid advertising expenses \$900.
	20	Received \$5,000 cash from customers for admissions.
	20	Received the *Lord of the Rings* movies and paid the rental fee of \$2,000.
	31	Paid salaries of \$3,100.
	31	Received statement from Adam Ladd showing gross receipts from concessions of \$6,000 and the balance due to Starr Theater of \$900 (\$6,000 × 15%) for March. Ladd paid one-half the balance due and will remit the remainder on April 5.
	31	Received \$9,000 cash from customers for admissions.

In addition to the accounts identified above, the chart of accounts includes: No. 112 Accounts Receivable, No. 400 Service Revenue, No. 429 Rent Revenue, No. 610 Advertising Expense, No. 726 Salaries and Wages Expense, and No. 729 Rent Expense.

Instructions

(a) Enter the beginning balances in the ledger. Insert a check mark (✓) in the reference column of the ledger for the beginning balance.

(b) Journalize the March transactions. Starr records admission revenue as service revenue, rental of the concession stand as rent revenue, and film rental expense as rent expense.

(c) Post the March journal entries to the ledger. Assume that all entries are posted from page 1 of the journal.

(d) Prepare a trial balance on March 31, 2017.

(d) Trial balance totals \$64,100

BROADENING YOUR PERSPECTIVE

FINANCIAL REPORTING AND ANALYSIS

Financial Reporting Problem: Apple Inc.

BYP2-1 The financial statements of Apple Inc. are presented in Appendix A. Instructions for accessing and using the company's complete annual report, including the notes to the financial statements, are also provided in Appendix A.

Apple's financial statements contain the following selected accounts, stated in millions of dollars:

Accounts Payable	Cash and Cash Equivalents
Accounts Receivable	Research and Development Expense
Property, Plant, and Equipment	Inventories

Instructions

(a) Answer the following questions:

(1) What is the increase and decrease side for each account?

(2) What is the normal balance for each account?

(b) Identify the probable other account in the transaction and the effect on that account when:
   (1) Accounts Receivable is decreased.
   (2) Accounts Payable is decreased.
   (3) Inventories are increased.
(c) Identify the other account(s) that ordinarily would be involved when:
   (1) Research and Development Expense is increased.
   (2) Property, Plant, and Equipment is increased.

Comparative Analysis Problem: PepsiCo, Inc. vs. The Coca-Cola Company

BYP2-2 PepsiCo, Inc.'s financial statements are presented in Appendix B. Financial statements of The Coca-Cola Company are presented in Appendix C. Instructions for accessing and using the complete annual reports of PepsiCo and Coca-Cola, including the notes to the financial statements, are also provided in Appendices B and C, respectively.

Instructions

(a) Based on the information contained in the financial statements, determine the normal balance of the listed accounts for each company.

PepsiCo	Coca-Cola
1. Inventory	1. Accounts Receivable
2. Property, Plant, and Equipment	2. Cash and Cash Equivalents
3. Accounts Payable	3. Cost of Goods Sold (expense)
4. Interest Expense	4. Sales (revenue)

(b) Identify the other account ordinarily involved when:
   (1) Accounts Receivable is increased.
   (2) Salaries and Wages Payable is decreased.
   (3) Property, Plant, and Equipment is increased.
   (4) Interest Expense is increased.

Comparative Analysis Problem: Amazon.com, Inc. vs. Wal-Mart Stores, Inc.

BYP2-3 Amazon.com, Inc.'s financial statements are presented in Appendix D. Financial statements of Wal-Mart Stores, Inc. are presented in Appendix E. Instructions for accessing and using the complete annual reports of Amazon and Wal-Mart, including the notes to the financial statements, are also provided in Appendices D and E, respectively.

Instructions

(a) Based on the information contained in the financial statements, determine the normal balance of the listed accounts for each company.

Amazon	Wal-Mart
1. Interest Expense	1. Net Product Revenues
2. Cash and Cash Equivalents	2. Inventories
3. Accounts Payable	3. Cost of Sales

(b) Identify the other account ordinarily involved when:
   (1) Accounts Receivable is increased.
   (2) Interest Expense is increased.
   (3) Salaries and Wages Payable is decreased.
   (4) Service Revenue is increased.

Real-World Focus

BYP2-4 Much information about specific companies is available on the Internet. Such information includes basic descriptions of the company's location, activities, industry, financial health, and financial performance.

Address: **biz.yahoo.com/i**, or go to **www.wiley.com/college/weygandt**

Steps
1. Type in a company name, or use index to find company name.
2. Choose **Profile**. Perform instructions (a)–(c) below.
3. Click on the company's specific industry to identify competitors. Perform instructions (d)–(g) below.

Instructions
Answer the following questions:
(a) What is the company's industry?
(b) What is the company's total sales?
(c) What is the company's net income?
(d) What are the names of four of the company's competitors?
(e) Choose one of these competitors.
(f) What is this competitor's name? What are its sales? What is its net income?
(g) Which of these two companies is larger by size of sales? Which one reported higher net income?

BYP2-5 The January 27, 2011, edition of the *New York Times* contains an article by Richard Sandomir entitled "N.F.L. Finances, as Seen Through Packers' Records." The article discusses the fact that the **Green Bay Packers** are the only NFL team that publicly publishes its annual report.

Instructions
Read the article and answer the following questions:
(a) Why are the Green Bay Packers the only professional football team to publish and distribute an annual report?
(b) Why is the football players' labor union particularly interested in the Packers' annual report?
(c) In addition to the players' labor union, what other outside party might be interested in the annual report?
(d) Even though the Packers' revenue increased in recent years, the company's operating profit fell significantly. How does the article explain this decline?

CRITICAL THINKING

Communication Activity

BYP2-6 Amelia's Maid Company offers home-cleaning service. Two recurring transactions for the company are billing customers for services performed and paying employee salaries. For example, on March 15, bills totaling $6,000 were sent to customers and $2,000 was paid in salaries to employees.

Instructions
Write a memo to your instructor that explains and illustrates the steps in the recording process for each of the March 15 transactions. Use the format illustrated in the text under the heading, "The Recording Process Illustrated" (p. 47).

Ethics Cases

BYP2-7 Ellynn Kole is the assistant chief accountant at Doman Company, a manufacturer of computer chips and cellular phones. The company presently has total sales of $20 million. It is the end of the first quarter. Ellynn is hurriedly trying to prepare a trial balance so that quarterly financial statements can be prepared and released to management and the regulatory agencies. The total credits on the trial balance exceed the debits by $1,000. In order to meet the 4 p.m. deadline, Ellynn decides to force the debits and credits into balance by adding the amount of the difference to the Equipment account. She chooses Equipment because it is one of the larger account balances; percentage-wise, it will be the least misstated. Ellynn "plugs" the difference! She believes that the difference will not affect anyone's decisions. She wishes that she had another few days to find the error but realizes that the financial statements are already late.

Instructions
(a) Who are the stakeholders in this situation?
(b) What are the ethical issues involved in this case?
(c) What are Ellynn's alternatives?

BYP2-8 If you haven't already done so, in the not-too-distant future you will prepare a résumé. In some ways, your résumé is like a company's annual report. Its purpose is to enable others to evaluate your past, in an effort to predict your future.

A résumé is your opportunity to create a positive first impression. It is important that it be impressive—but it should also be accurate. In order to increase their job prospects, some people are tempted to "inflate" their résumés by overstating the importance of some past accomplishments or positions. In fact, you might even think that "everybody does it" and that if you don't do it, you will be at a disadvantage.

David Edmondson, the president and CEO of well-known electronics retailer Radio Shack, overstated his accomplishments by claiming that he had earned a bachelor's of science degree, when in fact he had not. Apparently, his employer had not done a background check to ensure the accuracy of his résumé. Should Radio Shack have fired him?

YES: Radio Shack is a publicly traded company. Investors, creditors, employees, and others doing business with the company will not trust it if its leader is known to have poor integrity. The "tone at the top" is vital to creating an ethical organization.

NO: Mr. Edmondson had been a Radio Shack employee for 11 years. He had served the company in a wide variety of positions, and had earned the position of CEO through exceptional performance. While the fact that he lied 11 years earlier on his résumé was unfortunate, his service since then made this past transgression irrelevant. In addition, the company was in the midst of a massive restructuring, which included closing 700 of its 7,000 stores. It could not afford additional upheaval at this time.

Instructions

Write a response indicating your position regarding this situation. Provide support for your view.

All About You

BYP2-9 Every company needs to plan in order to move forward. Its top management must consider where it wants the company to be in three to five years. Like a company, you need to think about where you want to be three to five years from now, and you need to start taking steps now in order to get there.

Instructions

Provide responses to each of the following items:

(a) Where would you like to be working in three to five years? Describe your plan for getting there by identifying between five and 10 specific steps that you need to take.

(b) In order to get the job you want, you will need a résumé. Your résumé is the equivalent of a company's annual report. It needs to provide relevant and reliable information about your past accomplishments so that employers can decide whether to "invest" in you. Do a search on the Internet to find a good résumé format. What are the basic elements of a résumé?

(c) A company's annual report provides information about a company's accomplishments. In order for investors to use the annual report, the information must be reliable; that is, users must have faith that the information is accurate and believable. How can you provide assurance that the information on your résumé is reliable?

(d) Prepare a résumé assuming that you have accomplished the five to 10 specific steps you identified in part (a). Also, provide evidence that would give assurance that the information is reliable.

Considering People, Planet, and Profit

BYP2-10 Auditors provide a type of certification of corporate financial statements. Certification is used in many other aspects of business as well. For example, it plays a critical role in the sustainability movement. The February 7, 2012, issue of the *New York Times* contained an article by S. Amanda Caudill entitled "Better Lives in Better Coffee," which discusses the role of certification in the coffee business.

Address: **http://scientistatwork.blogs.nytimes.com/2012/02/07/better-lives-in-better-coffee**

Instructions

Read the article and answer the following questions:

(a) The article mentions three different certification types that coffee growers can obtain from three different certification bodies. Using financial reporting as an example, what potential problems might the existence of multiple certification types present to coffee purchasers?

(b) According to the author, which certification is most common among coffee growers? What are the possible reasons for this?

(c) What social and environmental benefits are coffee certifications trying to achieve? Are there also potential financial benefits to the parties involved?

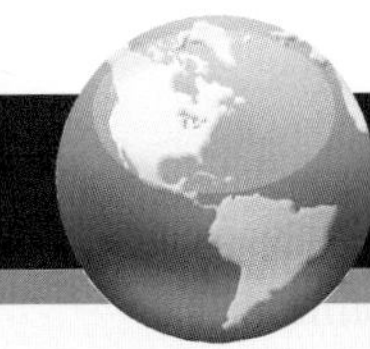

A Look at IFRS

LEARNING OBJECTIVE 5 **Compare the procedures for the accounting process under GAAP and IFRS.**

International companies use the same set of procedures and records to keep track of transaction data. Thus, the material in Chapter 2 dealing with the account, general rules of debit and credit, and steps in the recording process—the journal, ledger, and chart of accounts—is the same under both GAAP and IFRS.

Key Points

Following are the key similarities and differences between GAAP and IFRS as related to the recording process.

Similarities

- Transaction analysis is the same under IFRS and GAAP.
- Both the IASB and the FASB go beyond the basic definitions provided in the textbook for the key elements of financial statements, that is assets, liabilities, equity, revenue, and expenses. The implications of the expanded definitions are discussed in more advanced accounting courses.
- As shown in the textbook, dollar signs are typically used only in the trial balance and the financial statements. The same practice is followed under IFRS, using the currency of the country where the reporting company is headquartered.
- A trial balance under IFRS follows the same format as shown in the textbook.

Differences

- IFRS relies less on historical cost and more on fair value than do FASB standards.
- Internal controls are a system of checks and balances designed to prevent and detect fraud and errors. While most public U.S. companies have these systems in place, many non-U.S. companies have never completely documented the controls nor had an independent auditors attest to their effectiveness.

Looking to the Future

The basic recording process shown in this textbook is followed by companies across the globe. It is unlikely to change in the future. The definitional structure of assets, liabilities, equity, revenues, and expenses may change over time as the IASB and FASB evaluate their overall conceptual framework for establishing accounting standards.

IFRS Practice

IFRS Self-Test Questions

1. Which statement is **correct** regarding IFRS?
   (a) IFRS reverses the rules of debits and credits, that is, debits are on the right and credits are on the left.
   (b) IFRS uses the same process for recording transactions as GAAP.
   (c) The chart of accounts under IFRS is different because revenues follow assets.
   (d) None of the above statements are correct.
2. The expanded accounting equation under IFRS is as follows:
   (a) Assets = Liabilities + Owner's Capital + Owner's Drawings + Revenues − Expenses.
   (b) Assets + Liabilities = Owner's Capital + Owner's Drawings + Revenues − Expenses.
   (c) Assets = Liabilities + Owner's Capital − Owner's Drawings + Revenues − Expenses.
   (d) Assets = Liabilities + Owner's Capital + Owner's Drawings − Revenues − Expenses.
3. A trial balance:
   (a) is the same under IFRS and GAAP.
   (b) proves that transactions are recorded correctly.

(c) proves that all transactions have been recorded.
(d) will not balance if a correct journal entry is posted twice.

4. One difference between IFRS and GAAP is that:
   (a) GAAP uses accrual-accounting concepts and IFRS uses primarily the cash basis of accounting.
   (b) IFRS uses a different posting process than GAAP.
   (c) IFRS uses more fair value measurements than GAAP.
   (d) the limitations of a trial balance are different between IFRS and GAAP.
5. The general policy for using proper currency signs (dollar, yen, pound, etc.) is the same for both IFRS and this textbook. This policy is as follows:
   (a) Currency signs only appear in ledgers and journal entries.
   (b) Currency signs are only shown in the trial balance.
   (c) Currency signs are shown for all compound journal entries.
   (d) Currency signs are shown in trial balances and financial statements.

International Financial Reporting Problem: Louis Vuitton

IFRS2-1 The financial statements of Louis Vuitton are presented in Appendix F. Instructions for accessing and using the company's complete annual report, including the notes to its financial statements, are also provided in Appendix F.

Instructions
Describe in which statement each of the following items is reported, and the position in the statement (e.g., current asset).

(a) Other operating income and expense.
(b) Cash and cash equivalents.
(c) Trade accounts payable.
(d) Cost of net financial debt.

Answers to IFRS Self-Test Questions

1. b **2.** c **3.** a **4.** c **5.** d

Chapter 3 Adjusting the Accounts

Who doesn't like buying things at a discount? That's why it's not surprising that three years after it started as a company, Groupon was estimated to be worth $16 billion. This translates into an average increase in value of almost $15 million per day.

Now consider that Groupon had previously been estimated to be worth even more than that. What happened? Well, accounting regulators and investors began to question the way that Groupon had accounted for some of its transactions. But if Groupon sells only coupons ("groupons"), how hard can it be to accurately account for that? It turns out that accounting for coupons is not as easy as you might think.

First, consider what happens when Groupon makes a sale. Suppose it sells a groupon for $30 for Highrise Hamburgers. When it receives the $30 from the customer, it must turn over half of that amount ($15) to Highrise Hamburgers. So should Groupon record revenue for the full $30 or just $15? Until recently, Groupon recorded the full $30. But, in response to an SEC ruling on the issue, Groupon now records revenue of $15 instead.

A second issue is a matter of timing. When should Groupon record this $15 revenue? Should it record the revenue when it sells the groupon, or must it wait until the customer uses the groupon at Highrise Hamburgers? You can find the answer to this question in the notes to Groupon's financial statements. It recognizes the revenue once "the number of customers who purchase the daily deal exceeds the predetermined threshold, the Groupon has been electronically delivered to the purchaser and a listing of Groupons sold has been made available to the merchant."

The accounting becomes even more complicated when you consider the company's loyalty programs. Groupon offers free or discounted groupons to its subscribers for doing things such as referring new customers or participating in promotions. These groupons are to be used for future purchases, yet the company must record the expense at the time the customer receives the groupon. The cost of these programs is huge for Groupon, so the timing of this expense can definitely affect its reported income.

The final kicker is that Groupon, like all other companies, must rely on many estimates in its financial reporting. For example, Groupon reports that "estimates are utilized for, but not limited to, stock-based compensation, income taxes, valuation of acquired goodwill and intangible assets, customer refunds, contingent liabilities and the depreciable lives of fixed assets." It concludes by saying that "actual results could differ materially from those estimates." So, next time you use a coupon, think about what that means for the company's accountants!.

LEARNING OBJECTIVES

1. Explain the accrual basis of accounting and the reasons for adjusting entries.
2. Prepare adjusting entries for deferrals.
3. Prepare adjusting entries for accruals.
4. Describe the nature and purpose of an adjusted trial balance.

LEARNING OBJECTIVE 

Explain the accrual basis of accounting and the reasons for adjusting entries.

If we could wait to prepare financial statements until a company ended its operations, no adjustments would be needed. At that point, we could easily determine its final balance sheet and the amount of lifetime income it earned.

However, most companies need immediate feedback about how well they are doing. For example, management usually wants monthly financial statements. The Internal Revenue Service requires all businesses to file annual tax returns. Therefore, **accountants divide the economic life of a business into artificial time periods.** This convenient assumption is referred to as the **time period assumption**.

Many business transactions affect more than one of these arbitrary time periods. For example, the airplanes purchased by Southwest Airlines five years ago are still in use today. We must determine the relevance of each business transaction to specific accounting periods. (How much of the cost of an airplane contributed to operations this year?)

Time Period Assumption

Year 1 Year 10

Year 6

Terminology
The time period assumption is also called the *periodicity assumption.*

Fiscal and Calendar Years

Both small and large companies prepare financial statements periodically in order to assess their financial condition and results of operations. **Accounting time periods are generally a month, a quarter, or a year.** Monthly and quarterly time periods are called **interim periods**. Most large companies must prepare both quarterly and annual financial statements.

An accounting time period that is one year in length is a **fiscal year**. A fiscal year usually begins with the first day of a month and ends 12 months later on the last day of a month. Many businesses use the **calendar year** (January 1 to December 31) as their accounting period. Some do not. Companies whose fiscal year differs from the calendar year include Delta Air Lines, June 30, and The Walt Disney Company, September 30. Sometimes a company's year-end will vary from year to year. For example, PepsiCo's fiscal year ends on the Friday closest to December 31, which was December 29 in 2012 and December 28 in 2013.

Accrual- versus Cash-Basis Accounting

What you will learn in this chapter is **accrual-basis accounting**. Under the accrual basis, companies record transactions that change a company's financial statements **in the periods in which the events occur**. For example, using the accrual basis to determine net income means companies recognize revenues when they perform services (rather than when they receive cash). It also means recognizing expenses when incurred (rather than when paid).

An alternative to the accrual basis is the cash basis. Under **cash-basis accounting**, companies record revenue when they receive cash. They record an expense when they pay out cash. The cash basis seems appealing due to its simplicity, but it often produces misleading financial statements. It fails to record revenue for a company that has performed services but for which the company has not received the cash. As a result, the cash basis does not match expenses with revenues.

Accrual-basis accounting is therefore in accordance with generally accepted accounting principles (GAAP). Individuals and some small companies, however, do use cash-basis accounting. The cash basis is justified for small businesses because they often have few receivables and payables. Medium and large companies use accrual-basis accounting.

Recognizing Revenues and Expenses

It can be difficult to determine when to report revenues and expenses. The revenue recognition principle and the expense recognition principle help in this task.

REVENUE RECOGNITION PRINCIPLE

When a company agrees to perform a service or sell a product to a customer, it has a **performance obligation**. When the company meets this performance obligation, it recognizes revenue. The **revenue recognition principle** therefore requires that companies recognize revenue in the accounting period in which the performance obligation is satisfied. To illustrate, assume that Dave's Dry Cleaning cleans clothing on June 30 but customers do not claim and pay for their clothes until the first week of July. Dave's should record revenue in June when it performed the service (satisfied the performance obligation) rather than in July when it received the cash. At June 30, Dave's would report a receivable on its balance sheet and revenue in its income statement for the service performed.

Revenue Recognition
Satisfied performance obligation
Customer requests service
Cash received
Revenue is recognized when performance obligation is satisfied.

EXPENSE RECOGNITION PRINCIPLE

Accountants follow a simple rule in recognizing expenses: "Let the expenses follow the revenues." Thus, expense recognition is tied to revenue recognition. In the dry cleaning example, this means that Dave's should report the salary expense incurred in performing the June 30 cleaning service in the same period in which it recognizes the service revenue. The critical issue in expense recognition is when the expense makes its contribution to revenue. This may or may not be the same period in which the expense is paid. If Dave's does not pay the salary incurred on June 30 until July, it would report salaries payable on its June 30 balance sheet.

This practice of expense recognition is referred to as the **expense recognition principle** (often referred to as the **matching principle**). It dictates that efforts (expenses) be matched with results (revenues). Illustration 3-1 summarizes the revenue and expense recognition principles.

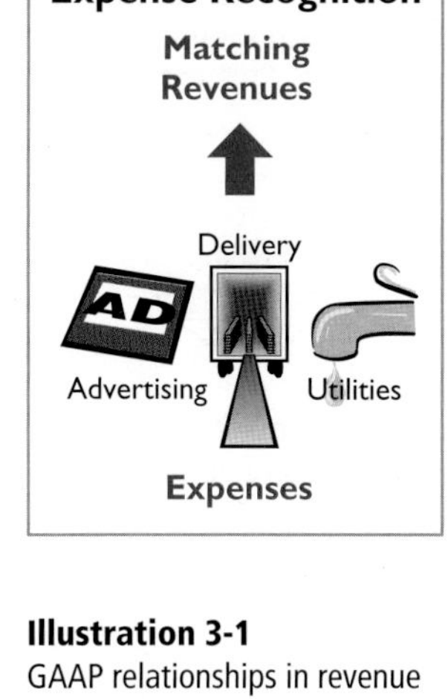

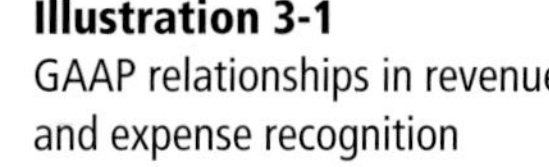

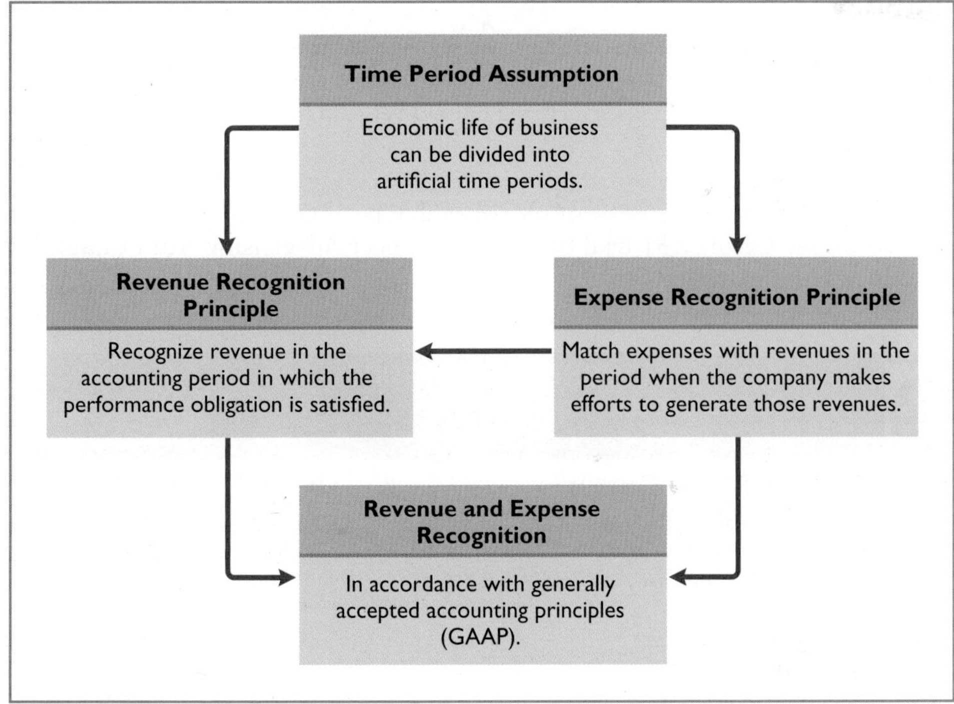

Illustration 3-1
GAAP relationships in revenue and expense recognition

The Need for Adjusting Entries

In order for revenues to be recorded in the period in which services are performed and for expenses to be recognized in the period in which they are incurred, companies make adjusting entries. **Adjusting entries ensure that the revenue recognition and expense recognition principles are followed.**

International Note

Internal controls are a system of checks and balances designed to detect and prevent fraud and errors. The Sarbanes-Oxley Act requires U.S. companies to enhance their systems of internal control. However, many foreign companies do not have to meet strict internal control requirements. Some U.S. companies believe that this gives foreign firms an unfair advantage because developing and maintaining internal controls can be very expensive.

Adjusting entries are necessary because the **trial balance**—the first pulling together of the transaction data—may not contain up-to-date and complete data. This is true for several reasons:

1. Some events are not recorded daily because it is not efficient to do so. Examples are the use of supplies and the earning of wages by employees.
2. Some costs are not recorded during the accounting period because these costs expire with the passage of time rather than as a result of recurring daily transactions. Examples are charges related to the use of buildings and equipment, rent, and insurance.
3. Some items may be unrecorded. An example is a utility service bill that will not be received until the next accounting period.

Adjusting entries are required every time a company prepares financial statements. The company analyzes each account in the trial balance to determine whether it is complete and up-to-date for financial statement purposes. **Every adjusting entry will include one income statement account and one balance sheet account.**

Types of Adjusting Entries

Adjusting entries are classified as either **deferrals** or **accruals**. As Illustration 3-2 shows, each of these classes has two subcategories.

Illustration 3-2
Categories of adjusting entries

Deferrals:

1. **Prepaid expenses**: Expenses paid in cash before they are used or consumed.
2. **Unearned revenues**: Cash received before services are performed.

Accruals:

1. **Accrued revenues**: Revenues for services performed but not yet received in cash or recorded.
2. **Accrued expenses**: Expenses incurred but not yet paid in cash or recorded.

Subsequent sections give examples of each type of adjustment. Each example is based on the October 31 trial balance of Pioneer Advertising from Chapter 2, reproduced in Illustration 3-3.

Illustration 3-3
Trial balance

PIONEER ADVERTISING
Trial Balance
October 31, 2017

	Debit	Credit
Cash	$ 15,200	
Supplies	2,500	
Prepaid Insurance	600	
Equipment	5,000	
Notes Payable		$ 5,000
Accounts Payable		2,500
Unearned Service Revenue		1,200
Owner's Capital		10,000
Owner's Drawings	500	
Service Revenue		10,000
Salaries and Wages Expense	4,000	
Rent Expense	900	
	$28,700	**$28,700**

We assume that Pioneer uses an accounting period of one month. Thus, monthly adjusting entries are made. The entries are dated October 31.

LEARNING OBJECTIVE 2 **Prepare adjusting entries for deferrals.**

To defer means to postpone or delay. **Deferrals** are expenses or revenues that are recognized at a date later than the point when cash was originally exchanged. The two types of deferrals are prepaid expenses and unearned revenues.

Prepaid Expenses

When companies record payments of expenses that will benefit more than one accounting period, they record an asset called **prepaid expenses** or **prepayments**. When expenses are prepaid, an asset account is increased (debited) to show the service or benefit that the company will receive in the future. Examples of common prepayments are insurance, supplies, advertising, and rent. In addition, companies make prepayments when they purchase buildings and equipment.

Prepaid expenses are costs that expire either with the passage of time (e.g., rent and insurance) **or through use** (e.g., supplies). The expiration of these costs does not require daily entries, which would be impractical and unnecessary. Accordingly, companies postpone the recognition of such cost expirations until they prepare financial statements. At each statement date, they make adjusting entries to record the expenses applicable to the current accounting period and to show the remaining amounts in the asset accounts.

Prior to adjustment, assets are overstated and expenses are understated. Therefore, as shown in Illustration 3-4, **an adjusting entry for prepaid expenses results in an increase (a debit) to an expense account and a decrease (a credit) to an asset account.**

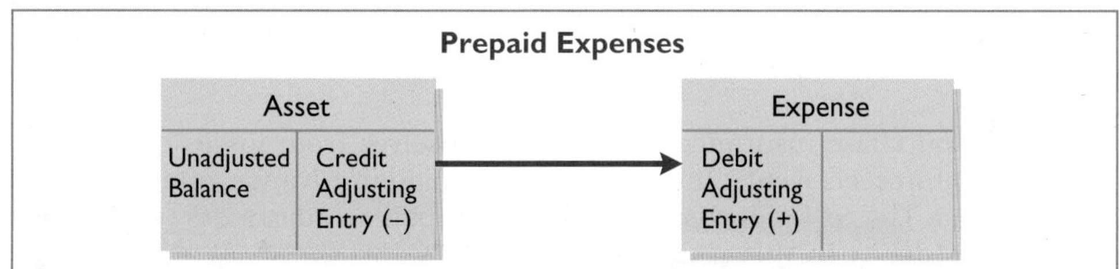

Illustration 3-4
Adjusting entries for prepaid expenses

Let's look in more detail at some specific types of prepaid expenses, beginning with supplies.

SUPPLIES

The purchase of supplies, such as paper and envelopes, results in an increase (a debit) to an asset account. During the accounting period, the company uses supplies. Rather than record supplies expense as the supplies are used, companies recognize supplies expense at the **end** of the accounting period. At the end of the accounting period, the company counts the remaining supplies. As shown in Illustration 3-5, the difference between the unadjusted balance in the Supplies (asset) account and the actual cost of supplies on hand represents the supplies used (an expense) for that period.

Recall from Chapter 2 that Pioneer Advertising purchased supplies costing $2,500 on October 5. Pioneer recorded the purchase by increasing (debiting) the asset Supplies. This account shows a balance of $2,500 in the October 31 trial balance. An inventory count at the close of business on October 31 reveals that $1,000 of supplies are still on hand. Thus, the cost of supplies used is $1,500 ($2,500 − $1,000). This use of supplies decreases an asset, Supplies. It also decreases owner's equity by increasing an expense account, Supplies Expense. This is shown in Illustration 3-5.

After adjustment, the asset account Supplies shows a balance of $1,000, which is equal to the cost of supplies on hand at the statement date. In addition, Supplies Expense shows a balance of $1,500, which equals the cost of supplies used in October. **If Pioneer does not make the adjusting entry, October expenses are understated and net income is overstated by $1,500. Moreover, both assets and owner's equity will be overstated by $1,500 on the October 31 balance sheet.**

Illustration 3-5
Adjustment for supplies

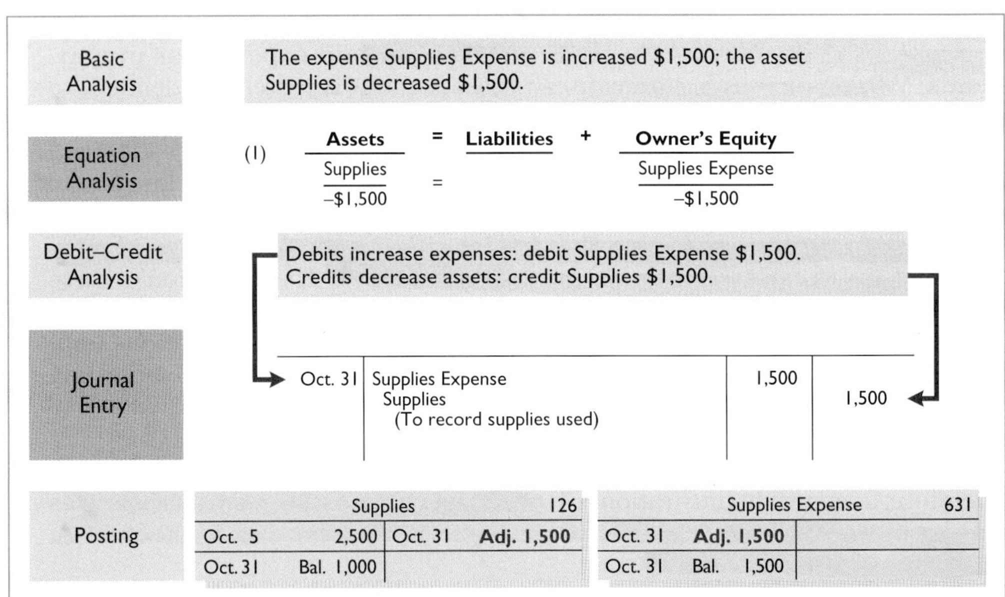

INSURANCE

Companies purchase insurance to protect themselves from losses due to fire, theft, and unforeseen events. Insurance must be paid in advance, often for more than one year. The cost of insurance (premiums) paid in advance is recorded as an increase (debit) in the asset account Prepaid Insurance. At the financial statement date, companies increase (debit) Insurance Expense and decrease (credit) Prepaid Insurance for the cost of insurance that has expired during the period.

On October 4, Pioneer Advertising paid $600 for a one-year fire insurance policy. Coverage began on October 1. Pioneer recorded the payment by increasing (debiting) Prepaid Insurance. This account shows a balance of $600 in the October 31 trial balance. Insurance of $50 ($600 ÷ 12) expires each month. The expiration of prepaid insurance decreases an asset, Prepaid Insurance. It also decreases owner's equity by increasing an expense account, Insurance Expense.

As shown in Illustration 3-6, the asset Prepaid Insurance shows a balance of $550, which represents the unexpired cost for the remaining 11 months of coverage. At the same time, the balance in Insurance Expense equals the insurance cost that expired in October. **If Pioneer does not make this adjustment, October expenses are understated by $50 and net income is overstated by $50. Moreover, both assets and owner's equity will be overstated by $50 on the October 31 balance sheet.**

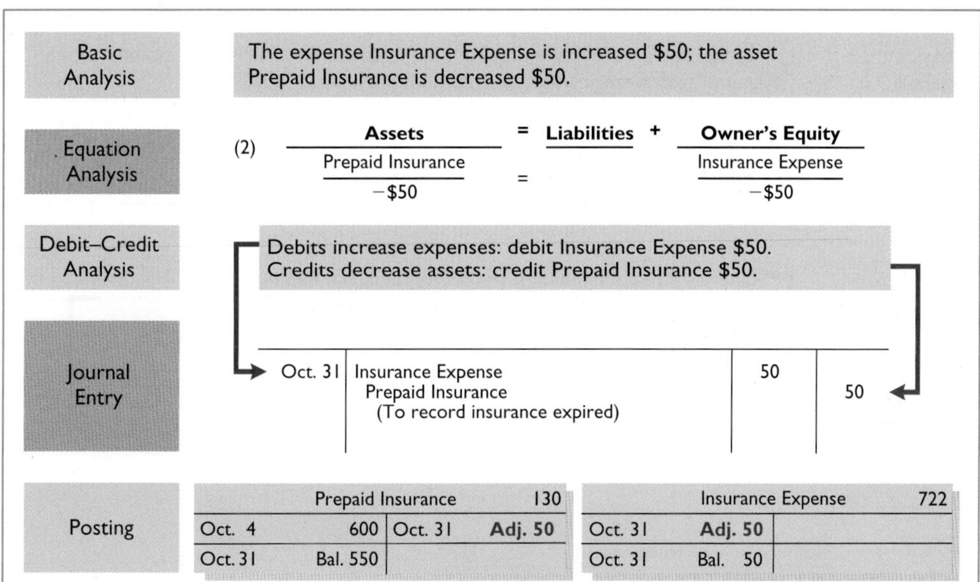

Illustration 3-6
Adjustment for insurance

DEPRECIATION

A company typically owns a variety of assets that have long lives, such as buildings, equipment, and motor vehicles. The period of service is referred to as the **useful life** of the asset. Because a building is expected to be of service for many years, it is recorded as an asset, rather than an expense, on the date it is acquired. As explained in Chapter 1, companies record such assets **at cost**, as required by the historical cost principle. To follow the expense recognition principle, companies allocate a portion of this cost as an expense during each period of the asset's useful life. **Depreciation** is the process of allocating the cost of an asset to expense over its useful life.

NEED FOR ADJUSTMENT The acquisition of long-lived assets is essentially a long-term prepayment for the use of an asset. An adjusting entry for depreciation is needed to recognize the cost that has been used (an expense) during the period and to report the unused cost (an asset) at the end of the period. One very important point to understand: **Depreciation is an allocation concept, not a valuation concept.** That is, depreciation **allocates an asset's cost to the periods in which it is used. Depreciation does not attempt to report the actual change in the value of the asset.**

For Pioneer Advertising, assume that depreciation on the equipment is $480 a year, or $40 per month. As shown in Illustration 3-7, rather than decrease (credit) the asset account directly, Pioneer instead credits Accumulated Depreciation—Equipment. Accumulated Depreciation is called a **contra asset account**. Such an account is offset against an asset account on the balance sheet. Thus, the Accumulated Depreciation—Equipment account offsets the asset Equipment. **This account keeps track of the total amount of depreciation expense taken over the life of the asset.** To keep the accounting equation in balance, Pioneer decreases owner's equity by increasing an expense account, Depreciation Expense.

The balance in the Accumulated Depreciation—Equipment account will increase $40 each month, and the balance in Equipment remains $5,000.

STATEMENT PRESENTATION As indicated, Accumulated Depreciation—Equipment is a contra asset account. It is offset against Equipment on the balance sheet. The normal balance of a contra asset account is a credit. A theoretical alternative to using a contra asset account would be to decrease (credit) the asset account by

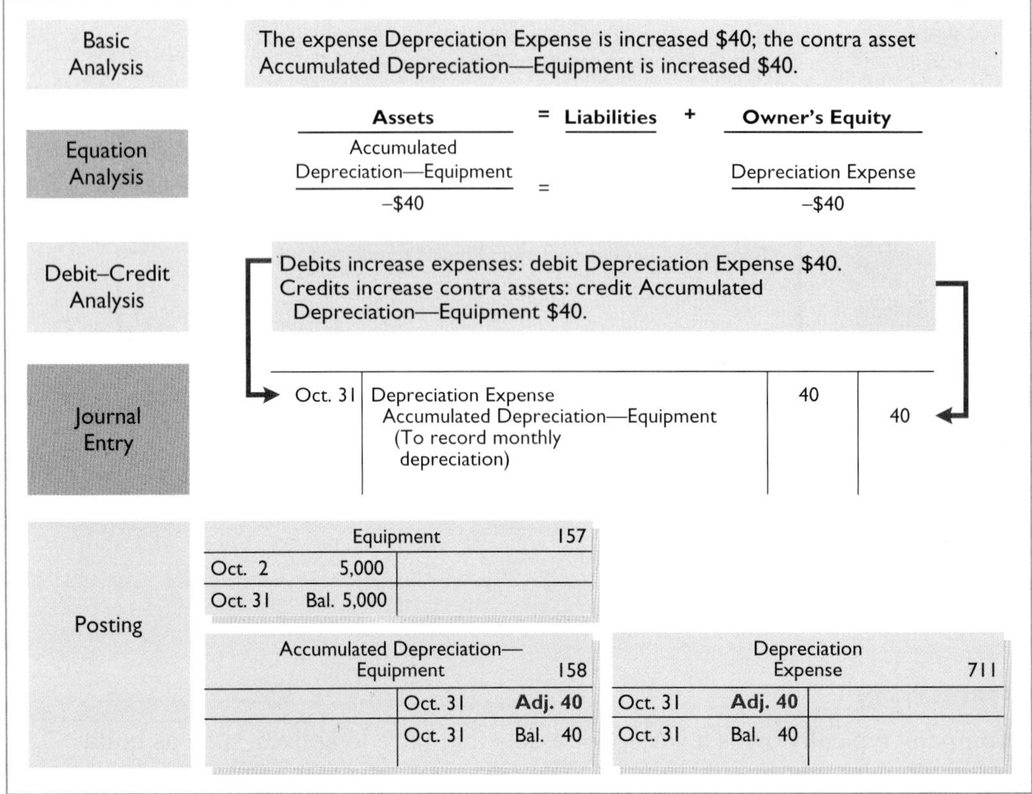

Illustration 3-7
Adjustment for depreciation

the amount of depreciation each period. But using the contra account is preferable for a simple reason: It discloses **both** the original cost of the equipment **and** the total cost that has been expensed to date. Thus, in the balance sheet, Pioneer deducts Accumulated Depreciation—Equipment from the related asset account, as shown in Illustration 3-8.

Illustration 3-8
Balance sheet presentation of accumulated depreciation

Equipment	$ 5,000
Less: Accumulated depreciation—equipment	40
	$4,960

Terminology
Book value is also referred to as *carrying value*.

Book value is the difference between the cost of any depreciable asset and its related accumulated depreciation. In Illustration 3-8, the book value of the equipment at the balance sheet date is $4,960. The book value and the fair value of the asset are generally two different values. As noted earlier, **the purpose of depreciation is not valuation but a means of cost allocation.**

Depreciation expense identifies the portion of an asset's cost that expired during the period (in this case, in October). The accounting equation shows that **without this adjusting entry, total assets, total owner's equity, and net income are overstated by $40 and depreciation expense is understated by $40**.

Illustration 3-9 summarizes the accounting for prepaid expenses.

Illustration 3-9
Accounting for prepaid expenses

ACCOUNTING FOR PREPAID EXPENSES

Examples	Reason for Adjustment	Accounts Before Adjustment	Adjusting Entry
Insurance, supplies, advertising, rent, depreciation	Prepaid expenses recorded in asset accounts have been used.	Assets overstated. Expenses understated.	Dr. Expenses Cr. Assets or Contra Assets

Unearned Revenues

When companies receive cash before services are performed, they record a liability by increasing (crediting) a liability account called **unearned revenues**. In other words, a company now has a performance obligation (liability) to transfer a service to one of its customers. Items like rent, magazine subscriptions, and customer deposits for future service may result in unearned revenues. Airlines such as **United**, **Southwest**, and **Delta**, for instance, treat receipts from the sale of tickets as unearned revenue until the flight service is provided.

Unearned revenues are the opposite of prepaid expenses. Indeed, unearned revenue on the books of one company is likely to be a prepaid expense on the books of the company that has made the advance payment. For example, if identical accounting periods are assumed, a landlord will have unearned rent revenue when a tenant has prepaid rent.

When a company receives payment for services to be performed in a future accounting period, it increases (credits) an unearned revenue (a liability) account to recognize the liability that exists. The company subsequently recognizes revenues when it performs the service. During the accounting period, it is not practical to make daily entries as the company performs services. Instead, the company delays recognition of revenue until the adjustment process. Then, the company makes an adjusting entry to record the revenue for services performed during the period and to show the liability that remains at the end of the accounting period. Typically, prior to adjustment, liabilities are overstated and revenues are understated. Therefore, as shown in Illustration 3-10, **the adjusting entry for unearned revenues results in a decrease (a debit) to a liability account and an increase (a credit) to a revenue account**.

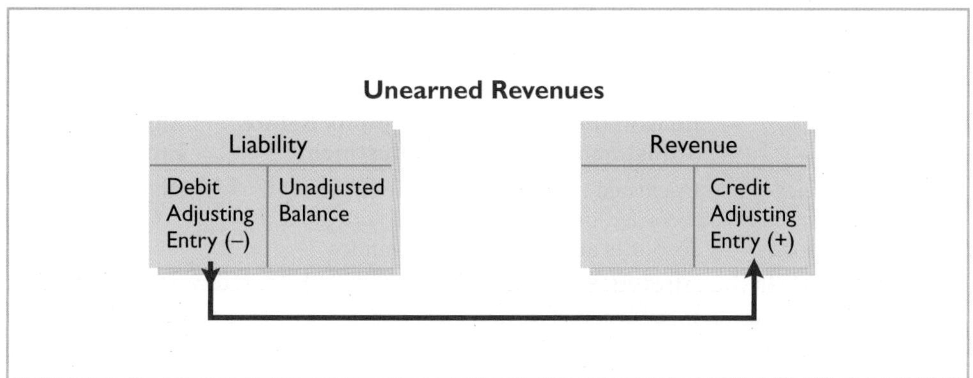

Illustration 3-10
Adjusting entries for unearned revenues

Pioneer Advertising received $1,200 on October 2 from R. Knox for advertising services expected to be completed by December 31. Pioneer credited the payment to Unearned Service Revenue. This liability account shows a balance of $1,200 in the October 31 trial balance. From an evaluation of the services Pioneer performed for Knox during October, the company determines that it should recognize $400 of revenue in October. The liability (Unearned Service Revenue) is therefore decreased, and owner's equity (Service Revenue) is increased.

As shown in Illustration 3-11, the liability Unearned Service Revenue now shows a balance of $800. That amount represents the remaining advertising services expected to be performed in the future. At the same time, Service Revenue shows total revenue recognized in October of $10,400. **Without this adjustment,**

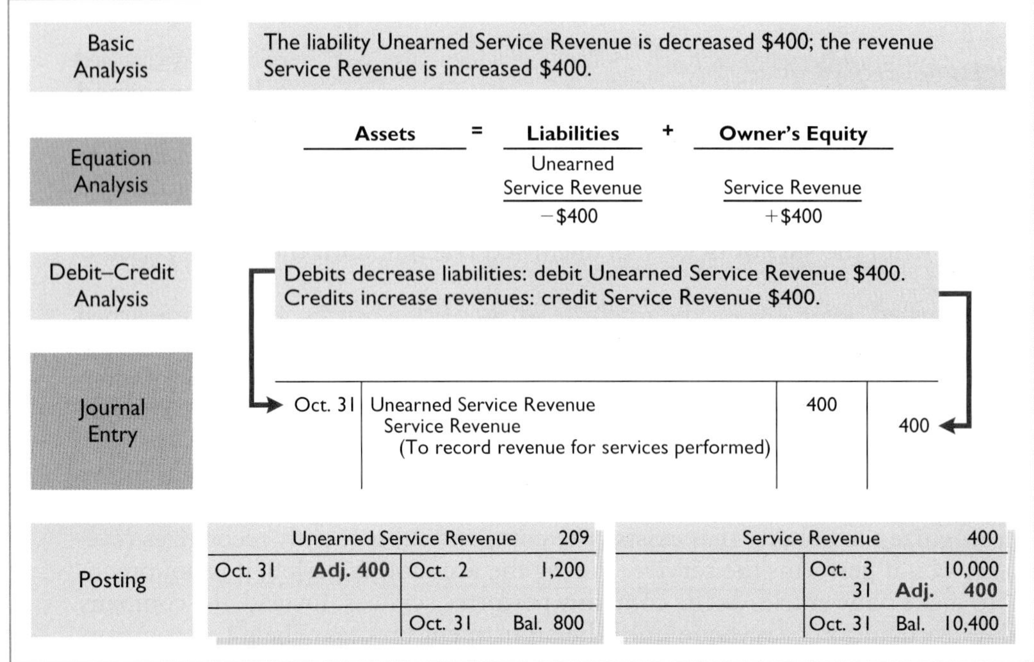

Illustration 3-11
Service revenue accounts after adjustment

revenues and net income are understated by $400 in the income statement. Moreover, liabilities will be overstated and owner's equity will be understated by $400 on the October 31 balance sheet.

Illustration 3-12 summarizes the accounting for unearned revenues.

Illustration 3-12
Accounting for unearned revenues

ACCOUNTING FOR UNEARNED REVENUES

Examples	Reason for Adjustment	Accounts Before Adjustment	Adjusting Entry
Rent, magazine subscriptions, customer deposits for future service	Unearned revenues recorded in liability accounts are now recognized as revenue for services performed.	Liabilities overstated. Revenues understated.	Dr. Liabilities Cr. Revenues

LEARNING OBJECTIVE 3

Prepare adjusting entries for accruals.

The second category of adjusting entries is **accruals**. Prior to an accrual adjustment, the revenue account (and the related asset account) or the expense account (and the related liability account) are understated. Thus, the adjusting entry for accruals will **increase both a balance sheet and an income statement account**.

Accrued Revenues

Revenues for services performed but not yet recorded at the statement date are **accrued revenues**. Accrued revenues may accumulate (accrue) with the passing of time, as in the case of interest revenue. These are unrecorded because the earning of interest does not involve daily transactions. Companies do not record interest revenue on a daily basis because it is often impractical to do so. Accrued revenues also may result from services that have been performed but not yet billed nor collected, as in the case of commissions and fees. These may be unrecorded because only a portion of the total service has been performed and the clients will not be billed until the service has been completed.

Revenue and receivable are recorded for unbilled services

An adjusting entry records the receivable that exists at the balance sheet date and the revenue for the services performed during the period. Prior to adjustment, both assets and revenues are understated. As shown in Illustration 3-13, **an adjusting entry for accrued revenues results in an increase (a debit) to an asset account and an increase (a credit) to a revenue account**.

Illustration 3-13
Adjusting entries for accrued revenues

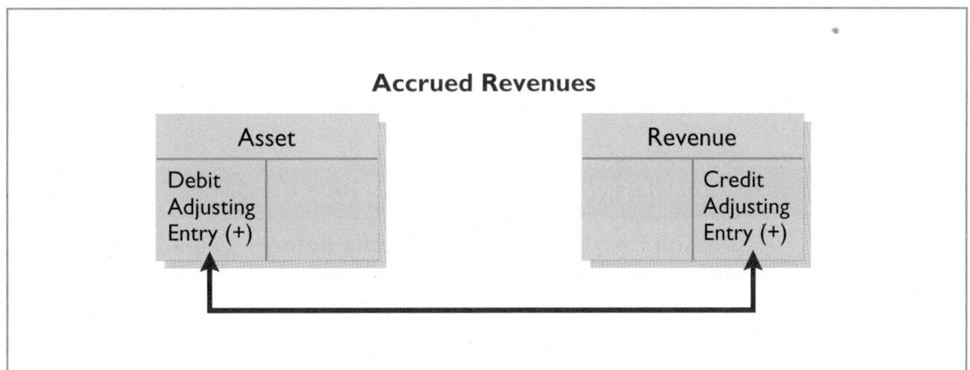

In October, Pioneer Advertising performed services worth $200 that were not billed to clients on or before October 31. Because these services are not billed, they are not recorded. The accrual of unrecorded service revenue increases an asset account, Accounts Receivable. It also increases owner's equity by increasing a revenue account, Service Revenue, as shown in Illustration 3-14.

Illustration 3-14
Adjustment for accrued revenue

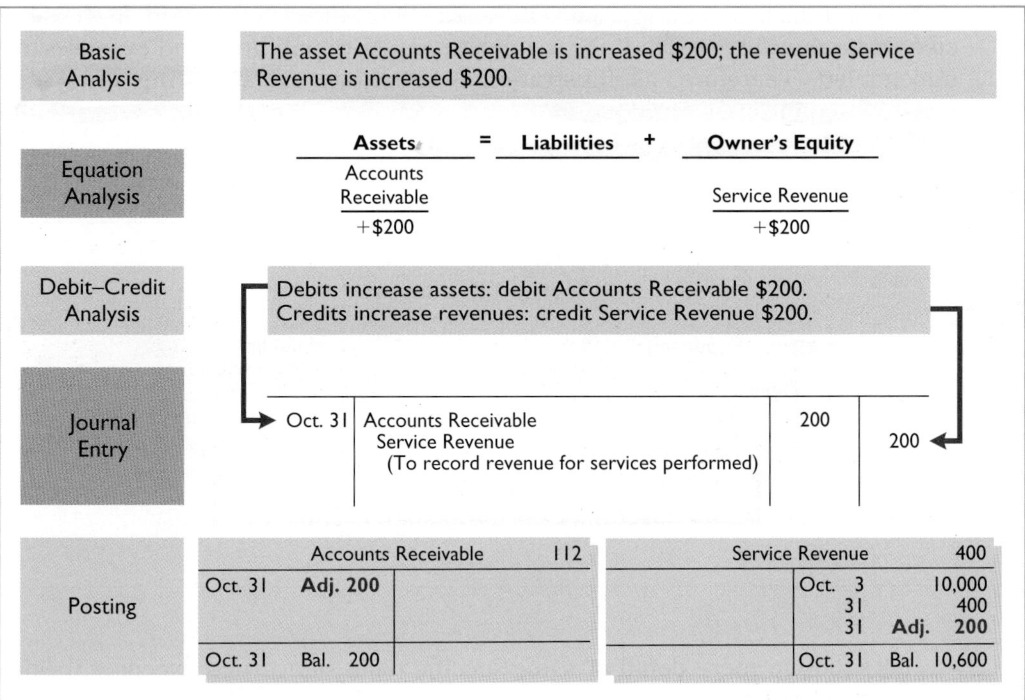

The asset Accounts Receivable shows that clients owe Pioneer $200 at the balance sheet date. The balance of $10,600 in Service Revenue represents the total revenue for services performed by Pioneer during the month ($10,000 + $400 + $200). **Without the adjusting entry, assets and owner's equity on the balance sheet and revenues and net income on the income statement are understated.**

On November 10, Pioneer receives cash of $200 for the services performed in October and makes the following entry.

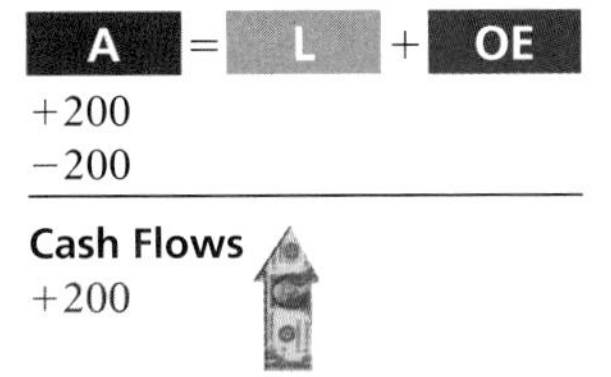

Nov. 10	Cash	200	
	Accounts Receivable		200
	(To record cash collected on account)		

Equation analyses summarize the effects of transactions on the three elements of the accounting equation, as well as the effect on cash flows.

The company records the collection of the receivables by a debit (increase) to Cash and a credit (decrease) to Accounts Receivable.

Illustration 3-15 summarizes the accounting for accrued revenues.

Illustration 3-15
Accounting for accrued revenues

ACCOUNTING FOR ACCRUED REVENUES

Examples	Reason for Adjustment	Accounts Before Adjustment	Adjusting Entry
Interest, rent, services	Services performed but not yet received in cash or recorded.	Assets understated. Revenues understated.	Dr. Assets Cr. Revenues

Accrued Expenses

Expenses incurred but not yet paid or recorded at the statement date are called **accrued expenses**. Interest, taxes, and salaries are common examples of accrued expenses.

Companies make adjustments for accrued expenses to record the obligations that exist at the balance sheet date and to recognize the expenses that apply to the current accounting period. Prior to adjustment, both liabilities and expenses are understated. Therefore, as Illustration 3-16 shows, **an adjusting entry for accrued expenses results in an increase (a debit) to an expense account and an increase (a credit) to a liability account**.

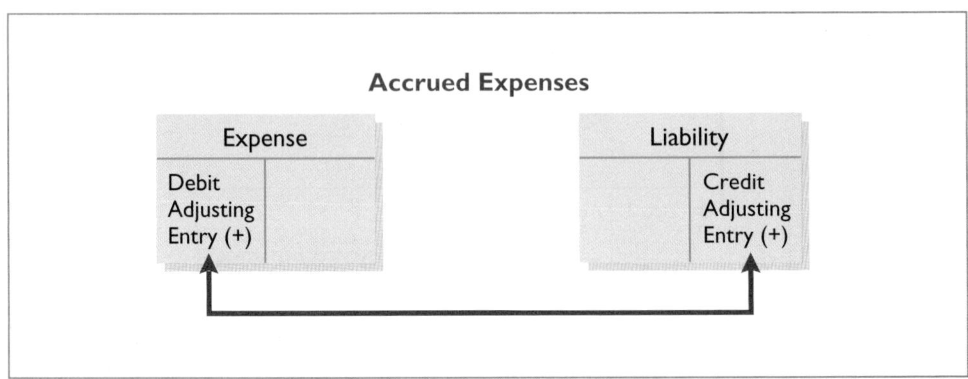

Illustration 3-16
Adjusting entries for accrued expenses

Let's look in more detail at some specific types of accrued expenses, beginning with accrued interest.

ACCRUED INTEREST

Pioneer Advertising signed a three-month note payable in the amount of $5,000 on October 1. The note requires Pioneer to pay interest at an annual rate of 12%.

The amount of the interest recorded is determined by three factors: (1) the face value of the note; (2) the interest rate, which is always expressed as an annual rate; and (3) the length of time the note is outstanding. For Pioneer, the total interest due on the $5,000 note at its maturity date three months in the future is $150 ($5,000 × 12% × $\frac{3}{12}$), or $50 for one month. Illustration 3-17 shows the formula for computing interest and its application to Pioneer for the month of October.

Illustration 3-17
Formula for computing interest

Face Value of Note	×	Annual Interest Rate	×	Time in Terms of One Year	=	Interest
$5,000	×	12%	×	$\frac{1}{12}$	=	$50

As Illustration 3-18 shows, the accrual of interest at October 31 increases a liability account, Interest Payable. It also decreases owner's equity by increasing an expense account, Interest Expense.

Interest Expense shows the interest charges for the month of October. Interest Payable shows the amount of interest the company owes at the statement date. Pioneer will not pay the interest until the note comes due at the end of three months. Companies use the Interest Payable account, instead of crediting Notes Payable, to disclose the two different types of obligations—interest and principal—in the accounts and statements. **Without this adjusting entry, liabilities and interest expense are understated, and net income and owner's equity are overstated.**

ACCRUED SALARIES AND WAGES

Companies pay for some types of expenses, such as employee salaries and wages, after the services have been performed. Pioneer Advertising paid salaries and wages on October 26 for its employees' first two weeks of work. The next payment

Illustration 3-18
Adjustment for accrued interest

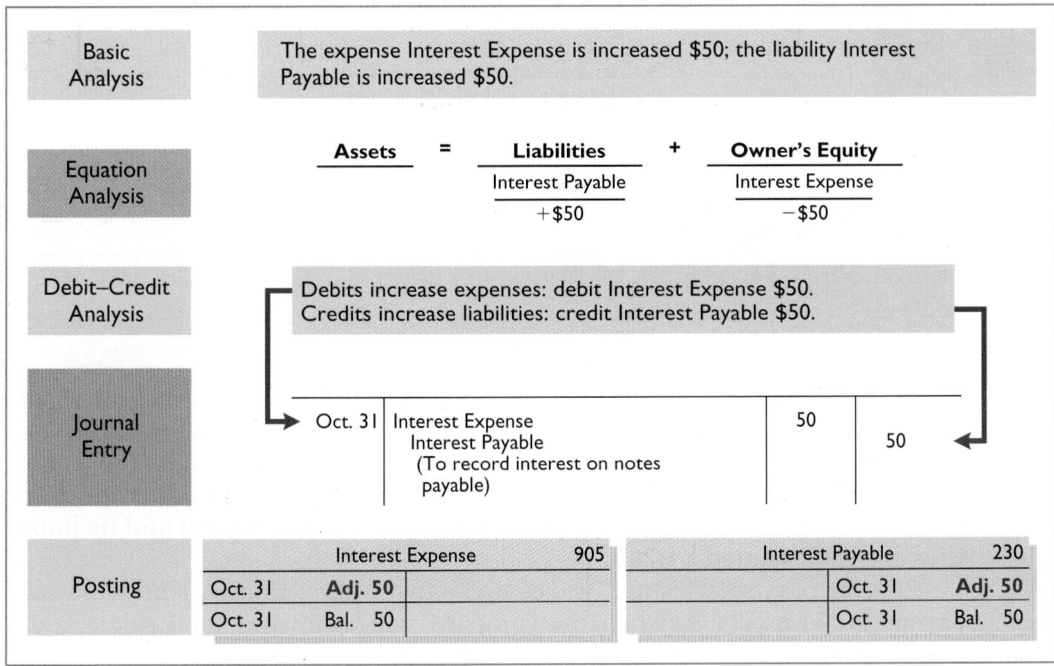

of salaries will not occur until November 9. As Illustration 3-19 shows, three working days remain in October (October 29–31).

Illustration 3-19
Calendar showing Pioneer's pay periods

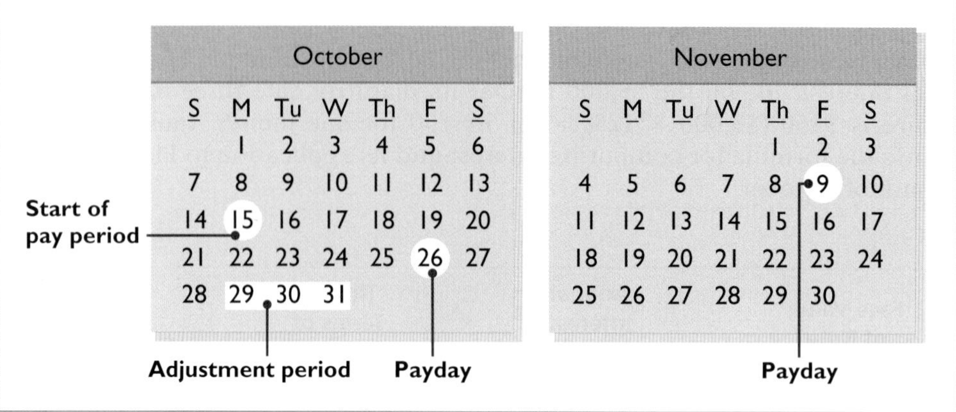

At October 31, the salaries and wages for these three days represent an accrued expense and a related liability to Pioneer. The employees receive total salaries and wages of $2,000 for a five-day work week, or $400 per day. Thus, accrued salaries and wages at October 31 are $1,200 ($400 × 3). This accrual increases a liability, Salaries and Wages Payable. It also decreases owner's equity by increasing an expense account, Salaries and Wages Expense, as shown in Illustration 3-20.

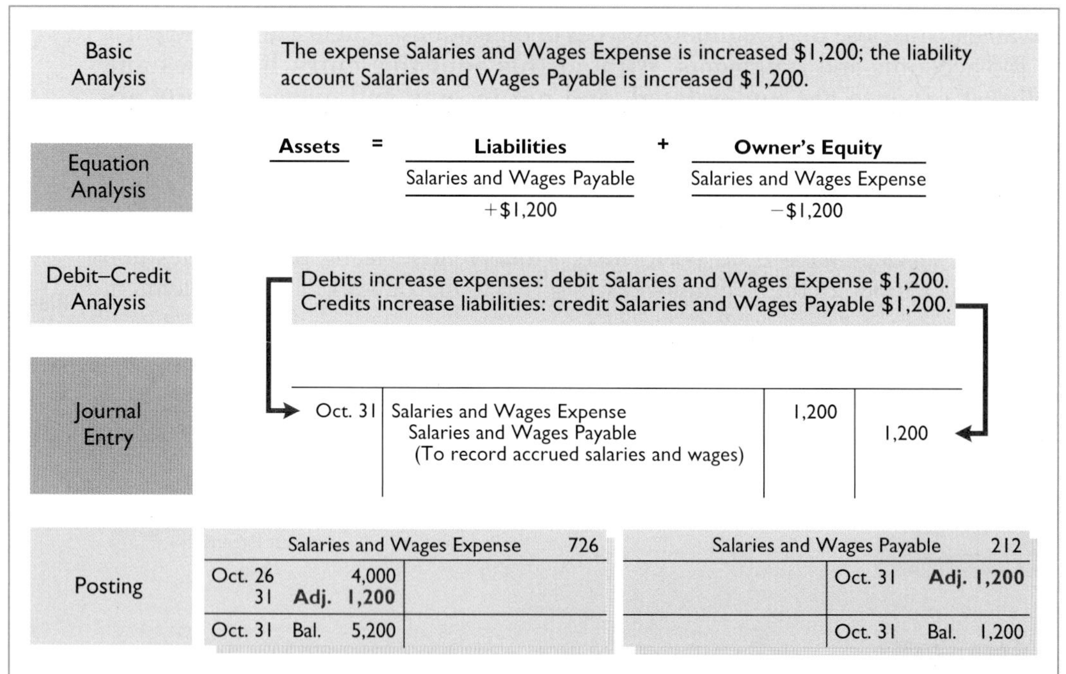

Illustration 3-20
Adjustment for accrued salaries and wages

After this adjustment, the balance in Salaries and Wages Expense of $5,200 (13 days × $400) is the actual salary and wages expense for October. The balance in Salaries and Wages Payable of $1,200 is the amount of the liability for salaries and wages Pioneer owes as of October 31. **Without the $1,200 adjustment for salaries and wages, Pioneer's expenses are understated $1,200 and its liabilities are understated $1,200.**

Pioneer pays salaries and wages every two weeks. Consequently, the next payday is November 9, when the company will again pay total salaries and wages of $4,000. The payment consists of $1,200 of salaries and wages payable at

October 31 plus $2,800 of salaries and wages expense for November (7 working days, as shown in the November calendar × $400). Therefore, Pioneer makes the following entry on November 9.

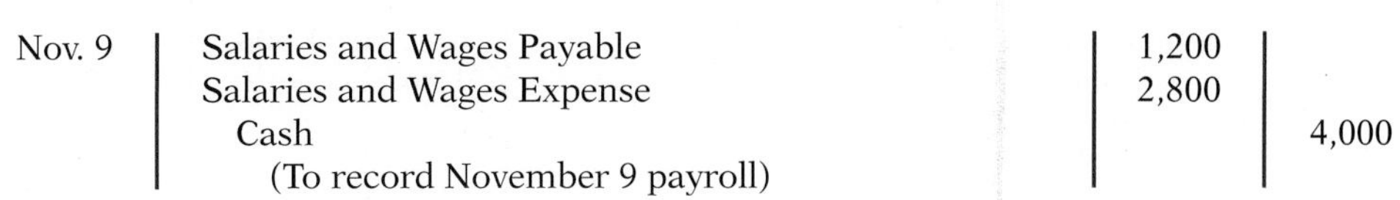

Nov. 9	Salaries and Wages Payable	1,200	
	Salaries and Wages Expense	2,800	
	Cash		4,000
	(To record November 9 payroll)		

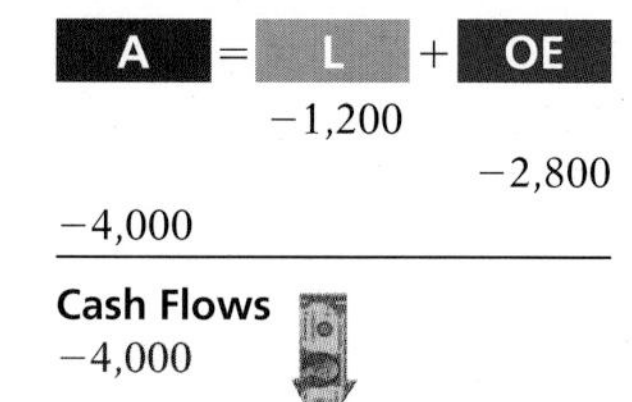

This entry eliminates the liability for Salaries and Wages Payable that Pioneer recorded in the October 31 adjusting entry, and it records the proper amount of Salaries and Wages Expense for the period between November 1 and November 9.

Illustration 3-21 summarizes the accounting for accrued expenses.

Illustration 3-21
Accounting for accrued expenses

ACCOUNTING FOR ACCRUED EXPENSES			
Examples	**Reason for Adjustment**	**Accounts Before Adjustment**	**Adjusting Entry**
Interest, rent, salaries	Expenses have been incurred but not yet paid in cash or recorded.	Expenses understated. Liabilities understated.	Dr. Expenses Cr. Liabilities

Summary of Basic Relationships

Illustration 3-22 summarizes the four basic types of adjusting entries. Take some time to study and analyze the adjusting entries. Be sure to note that **each adjusting entry affects one balance sheet account and one income statement account**.

Illustration 3-22
Summary of adjusting entries

Type of Adjustment	Accounts Before Adjustment	Adjusting Entry
Prepaid expenses	Assets overstated. Expenses understated.	Dr. Expenses Cr. Assets or Contra Assets
Unearned revenues	Liabilities overstated. Revenues understated.	Dr. Liabilities Cr. Revenues
Accrued revenues	Assets understated. Revenues understated.	Dr. Assets Cr. Revenues
Accrued expenses	Expenses understated. Liabilities understated.	Dr. Expenses Cr. Liabilities

Illustrations 3-23 (on page 86) and 3-24 (on page 87) show the journalizing and posting of adjusting entries for Pioneer Advertising on October 31. The ledger identifies all adjustments by the reference J2 because they have been recorded on page 2 of the general journal. The company may insert a center caption "Adjusting Entries" between the last transaction entry and the first adjusting entry in the journal. When you review the general ledger in Illustration 3-24, note that the entries highlighted in color are the adjustments.

Illustration 3-23
General journal showing adjusting entries

GENERAL JOURNAL				J2
Date	**Account Titles and Explanation**	**Ref.**	**Debit**	**Credit**
2017	Adjusting Entries			
Oct. 31	Supplies Expense	631	1,500	
	Supplies	126		1,500
	(To record supplies used)			
31	Insurance Expense	722	50	
	Prepaid Insurance	130		50
	(To record insurance expired)			
31	Depreciation Expense	711	40	
	Accumulated Depreciation—Equipment	158		40
	(To record monthly depreciation)			
31	Unearned Service Revenue	209	400	
	Service Revenue	400		400
	(To record revenue for services performed)			
31	Accounts Receivable	112	200	
	Service Revenue	400		200
	(To record revenue for services performed)			
31	Interest Expense	905	50	
	Interest Payable	230		50
	(To record interest on notes payable)			
31	Salaries and Wages Expense	726	1,200	
	Salaries and Wages Payable	212		1,200
	(To record accrued salaries and wages)			

Illustration 3-24
General ledger after adjustment

GENERAL LEDGER

Cash — No. 101

Date	Explanation	Ref.	Debit	Credit	Balance
2017					
Oct. 1		J1	10,000		10,000
2		J1	1,200		11,200
3		J1		900	10,300
4		J1		600	9,700
20		J1		500	9,200
26		J1		4,000	5,200
31		J1	10,000		15,200

Accounts Receivable — No. 112

Date	Explanation	Ref.	Debit	Credit	Balance
2017					
Oct. 31	**Adj. entry**	**J2**	**200**		**200**

Supplies — No. 126

Date	Explanation	Ref.	Debit	Credit	Balance
2017					
Oct. 5		J1	2,500		2,500
31	**Adj. entry**	**J2**		**1,500**	**1,000**

Prepaid Insurance — No. 130

Date	Explanation	Ref.	Debit	Credit	Balance
2017					
Oct. 4		J1	600		600
31	**Adj. entry**	**J2**		**50**	**550**

Equipment — No. 157

Date	Explanation	Ref.	Debit	Credit	Balance
2017					
Oct. 1		J1	5,000		5,000

Accumulated Depreciation—Equipment — No. 158

Date	Explanation	Ref.	Debit	Credit	Balance
2017					
Oct. 31	**Adj. entry**	**J2**		**40**	**40**

Notes Payable — No. 200

Date	Explanation	Ref.	Debit	Credit	Balance
2017					
Oct. 1		J1		5,000	5,000

Accounts Payable — No. 201

Date	Explanation	Ref.	Debit	Credit	Balance
2017					
Oct. 5		J1		2,500	2,500

Unearned Service Revenue — No. 209

Date	Explanation	Ref.	Debit	Credit	Balance
2017					
Oct. 2		J1		1,200	1,200
31	**Adj. entry**	**J2**	**400**		**800**

Salaries and Wages Payable — No. 212

Date	Explanation	Ref.	Debit	Credit	Balance
2017					
Oct. 31	**Adj. entry**	**J2**		**1,200**	**1,200**

Interest Payable — No. 230

Date	Explanation	Ref.	Debit	Credit	Balance
2017					
Oct. 31	**Adj. entry**	**J2**		**50**	**50**

Owner's Capital — No. 301

Date	Explanation	Ref.	Debit	Credit	Balance
2017					
Oct. 1		J1		10,000	10,000

Owner's Drawings — No. 306

Date	Explanation	Ref.	Debit	Credit	Balance
2017					
Oct. 20		J1	500		500

Service Revenue — No. 400

Date	Explanation	Ref.	Debit	Credit	Balance
2017					
Oct. 31		J1		10,000	10,000
31	**Adj. entry**	**J2**		**400**	**10,400**
31	**Adj. entry**	**J2**		**200**	**10,600**

Supplies Expense — No. 631

Date	Explanation	Ref.	Debit	Credit	Balance
2017					
Oct. 31	**Adj. entry**	**J2**	**1,500**		**1,500**

Depreciation Expense — No. 711

Date	Explanation	Ref.	Debit	Credit	Balance
2017					
Oct. 31	**Adj. entry**	**J2**	**40**		**40**

Insurance Expense — No. 722

Date	Explanation	Ref.	Debit	Credit	Balance
2017					
Oct. 31	**Adj. entry**	**J2**	**50**		**50**

Salaries and Wages Expense — No. 726

Date	Explanation	Ref.	Debit	Credit	Balance
2017					
Oct. 26		J1	4,000		4,000
31	**Adj. entry**	**J2**	**1,200**		**5,200**

Rent Expense — No. 729

Date	Explanation	Ref.	Debit	Credit	Balance
2017					
Oct. 3		J1	900		900

Interest Expense — No. 905

Date	Explanation	Ref.	Debit	Credit	Balance
2017					
Oct. 31	**Adj. entry**	**J2**	**50**		**50**

LEARNING OBJECTIVE 4

Describe the nature and purpose of an adjusted trial balance.

After a company has journalized and posted all adjusting entries, it prepares another trial balance from the ledger accounts. This trial balance is called an **adjusted trial balance**. It shows the balances of all accounts, including those adjusted, at the end of the accounting period. The purpose of an adjusted trial balance is to **prove the equality** of the total debit balances and the total credit balances in the ledger after all adjustments. Because the accounts contain all data needed for financial statements, the adjusted trial balance is the **primary basis for the preparation of financial statements**.

Preparing the Adjusted Trial Balance

Illustration 3-25 presents the adjusted trial balance for Pioneer Advertising prepared from the ledger accounts in Illustration 3-24. The amounts affected by the adjusting entries are highlighted in color. Compare these amounts to those in the unadjusted trial balance in Illustration 3-3 (page 74). In this comparison, you will see that there are more accounts in the adjusted trial balance as a result of the adjusting entries made at the end of the month.

Illustration 3-25
Adjusted trial balance

PIONEER ADVERTISING
Adjusted Trial Balance
October 31, 2017

	Debit	Credit
Cash	$ 15,200	
Accounts Receivable	**200**	
Supplies	**1,000**	
Prepaid Insurance	**550**	
Equipment	5,000	
Accumulated Depreciation—Equipment		**$ 40**
Notes Payable		5,000
Accounts Payable		2,500
Interest Payable		**50**
Unearned Service Revenue		**800**
Salaries and Wages Payable		**1,200**
Owner's Capital		10,000
Owner's Drawings	500	
Service Revenue		10,600
Salaries and Wages Expense	**5,200**	
Supplies Expense	**1,500**	
Rent Expense	900	
Insurance Expense	**50**	
Interest Expense	**50**	
Depreciation Expense	**40**	
	$30,190	**$30,190**

Preparing Financial Statements

Companies can prepare financial statements directly from the adjusted trial balance. Illustrations 3-26 (page 89) and 3-27 (page 90) present the interrelationships of data in the adjusted trial balance and the financial statements.

As Illustration 3-26 shows, companies prepare the income statement from the revenue and expense accounts. Next, they use the owner's capital and drawings

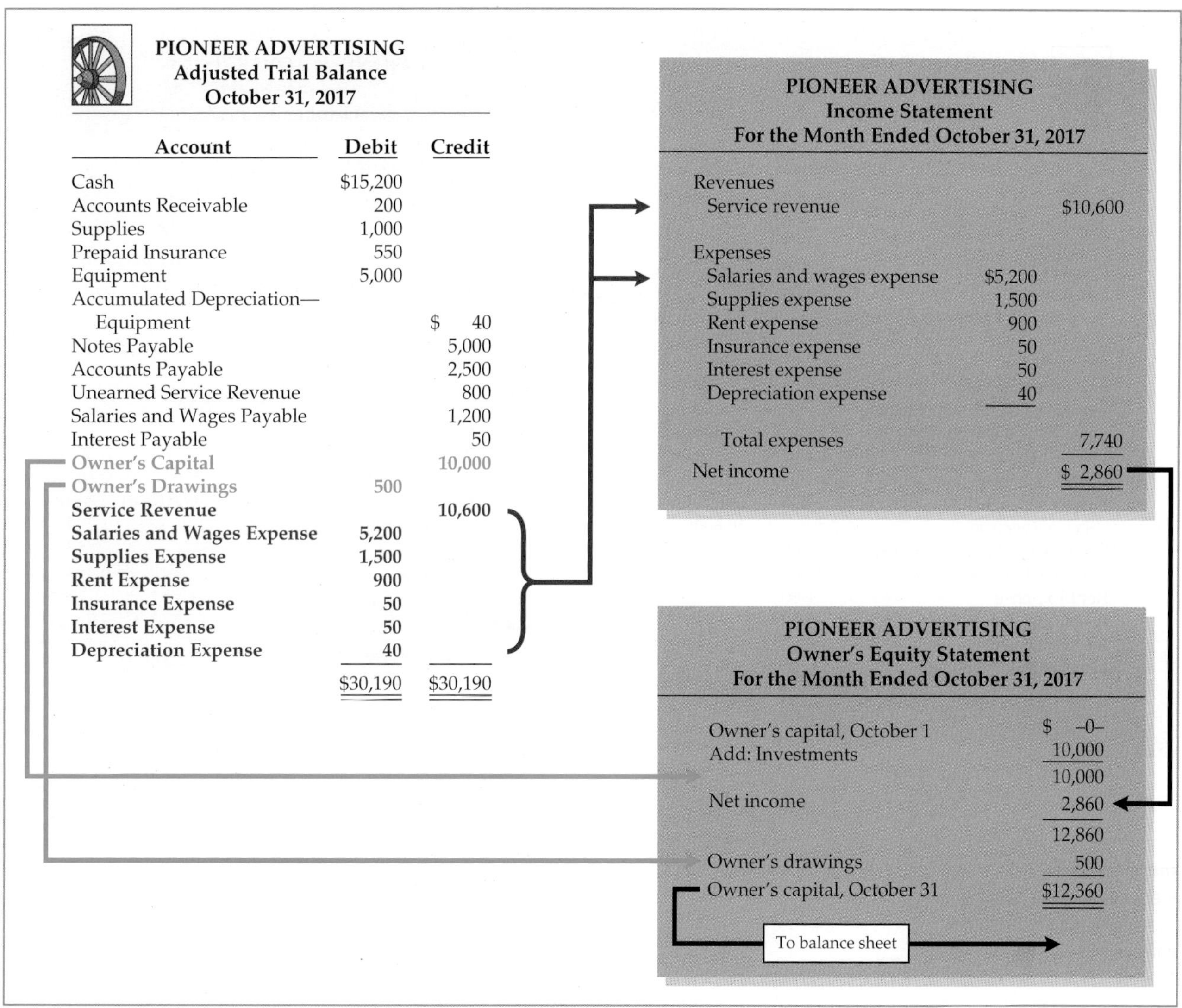

PIONEER ADVERTISING
Adjusted Trial Balance
October 31, 2017

Account	Debit	Credit
Cash	$15,200	
Accounts Receivable	200	
Supplies	1,000	
Prepaid Insurance	550	
Equipment	5,000	
Accumulated Depreciation—Equipment		$ 40
Notes Payable		5,000
Accounts Payable		2,500
Unearned Service Revenue		800
Salaries and Wages Payable		1,200
Interest Payable		50
Owner's Capital		10,000
Owner's Drawings	500	
Service Revenue		10,600
Salaries and Wages Expense	5,200	
Supplies Expense	1,500	
Rent Expense	900	
Insurance Expense	50	
Interest Expense	50	
Depreciation Expense	40	
	$30,190	$30,190

PIONEER ADVERTISING
Income Statement
For the Month Ended October 31, 2017

Revenues		
Service revenue		$10,600
Expenses		
Salaries and wages expense	$5,200	
Supplies expense	1,500	
Rent expense	900	
Insurance expense	50	
Interest expense	50	
Depreciation expense	40	
Total expenses		7,740
Net income		$ 2,860

PIONEER ADVERTISING
Owner's Equity Statement
For the Month Ended October 31, 2017

Owner's capital, October 1	$ -0-
Add: Investments	10,000
	10,000
Net income	2,860
	12,860
Owner's drawings	500
Owner's capital, October 31	$12,360

Illustration 3-26
Preparation of the income statement and owner's equity statement from the adjusted trial balance

accounts and the net income (or net loss) from the income statement to prepare the owner's equity statement.

As Illustration 3-27 (page 90) shows, companies then prepare the balance sheet from the asset and liability accounts and the ending owner's capital balance as reported in the owner's equity statement.

PIONEER ADVERTISING
Adjusted Trial Balance
October 31, 2017

Account	Debit	Credit
Cash	$15,200	
Accounts Receivable	200	
Supplies	1,000	
Prepaid Insurance	550	
Equipment	5,000	
Accumulated Depreciation—Equipment		$ 40
Notes Payable		5,000
Accounts Payable		2,500
Unearned Service Revenue		800
Salaries and Wages Payable		1,200
Interest Payable		50
Owner's Capital		10,000
Owner's Drawings	500	
Service Revenue		10,600
Salaries and Wages Expense	5,200	
Supplies Expense	1,500	
Rent Expense	900	
Insurance Expense	50	
Interest Expense	50	
Depreciation Expense	40	
	$30,190	$30,190

PIONEER ADVERTISING
Balance Sheet
October 31, 2017

Assets		
Cash		$15,200
Accounts receivable		200
Supplies		1,000
Prepaid insurance		550
Equipment	$5,000	
Less: Accumulated depreciation—equip.	40	4,960
Total assets		$21,910
Liabilities and Owner's Equity		
Liabilities		
Notes payable		$ 5,000
Accounts payable		2,500
Unearned service revenue		800
Salaries and wages payable		1,200
Interest payable		50
Total liabilities		9,550
Owner's equity		
Owner's capital		12,360
Total liabilities and owner's equity		$21,910

Capital balance at Oct. 31 from owner's equity statement in Illustration 3-26

Illustration 3-27
Preparation of the balance sheet from the adjusted trial balance

LEARNING OBJECTIVE *5

APPENDIX 3A: Prepare adjusting entries for the alternative treatment of deferrals.

In discussing adjusting entries for prepaid expenses and unearned revenues, we illustrated transactions for which companies made the initial entries to balance sheet accounts. In the case of prepaid expenses, the company debited the prepayment to an asset account. In the case of unearned revenue, the company credited a liability account to record the cash received.

Some companies use an alternative treatment. (1) When a company prepays an expense, it debits that amount to an expense account. (2) When it receives payment for future services, it credits the amount to a revenue account. In this appendix, we describe the circumstances that justify such entries and the different adjusting entries that may be required. This alternative treatment of prepaid expenses and unearned revenues has the same effect on the financial statements as the procedures described in the chapter.

Prepaid Expenses

Prepaid expenses become expired costs either through the passage of time (e.g., insurance) or through consumption (e.g., advertising supplies). If at the time of purchase the company expects to consume the supplies before the next financial statement date, **it may choose to debit (increase) an expense account**

rather than an asset account. This alternative treatment is simply more convenient.

Assume that Pioneer Advertising expects that it will use before the end of the month all of the supplies purchased on October 5. A debit of $2,500 to Supplies Expense (rather than to the asset account Supplies) on October 5 will eliminate the need for an adjusting entry on October 31. At October 31, the Supplies Expense account will show a balance of $2,500, which is the cost of supplies used between October 5 and October 31.

But what if the company does not use all the supplies? For example, what if an inventory of $1,000 of advertising supplies remains on October 31? Obviously, the company would need to make an adjusting entry. Prior to adjustment, the expense account Supplies Expense is overstated $1,000, and the asset account Supplies is understated $1,000. Thus, Pioneer makes the following adjusting entry.

Oct. 31	Supplies	1,000	
	Supplies Expense		1,000
	(To record supplies inventory)		

A	=	L	+	OE
+1,000				+1,000 Exp

Cash Flows
no effect

After the company posts the adjusting entry, the accounts show the following.

Illustration 3A-1
Prepaid expenses accounts after adjustment

Supplies

10/31 Adj. **1,000**	

Supplies Expense

10/5 2,500	10/31 Adj. **1,000**
10/31 Bal. **1,500**	

After adjustment, the asset account Supplies shows a balance of $1,000, which is equal to the cost of supplies on hand at October 31. In addition, Supplies Expense shows a balance of $1,500. This is equal to the cost of supplies used between October 5 and October 31. Without the adjusting entry, expenses are overstated and net income is understated by $1,000 in the October income statement. Also, both assets and owner's equity are understated by $1,000 on the October 31 balance sheet.

Illustration 3A-2 compares the entries and accounts for advertising supplies in the two adjustment approaches.

Illustration 3A-2
Adjustment approaches—a comparison

Prepayment Initially Debited to Asset Account (per chapter)			**Prepayment Initially Debited to Expense Account (per appendix)**		
Oct. 5 Supplies	2,500		Oct. 5 Supplies Expense	2,500	
Accounts Payable		2,500	Accounts Payable		2,500
Oct. 31 Supplies Expense	1,500		Oct. 31 Supplies	1,000	
Supplies		1,500	Supplies Expense		1,000

After Pioneer posts the entries, the accounts appear as follows.

Illustration 3A-3
Comparison of accounts

(per chapter) Supplies

10/5 2,500	10/31 Adj. **1,500**
10/31 Bal. **1,000**	

Supplies Expense

10/31 Adj. **1,500**	

(per appendix) Supplies

10/31 Adj. **1,000**	

Supplies Expense

10/5 2,500	10/31 Adj. **1,000**
10/31 Bal. **1,500**	

Note that the account balances under each alternative are the same at October 31: Supplies $1,000 and Supplies Expense $1,500.

Unearned Revenues

Unearned revenues are recognized as revenue at the time services are performed. Similar to the case for prepaid expenses, companies may credit (increase) a revenue account when they receive cash for future services.

To illustrate, assume that Pioneer Advertising received $1,200 for future services on October 2. Pioneer expects to perform the services before October 31.[1] In such a case, the company credits Service Revenue. If Pioneer in fact performs the service before October 31, no adjustment is needed.

However, if at the statement date Pioneer has not performed $800 of the services, it would make an adjusting entry. Without the entry, the revenue account Service Revenue is overstated $800, and the liability account Unearned Service Revenue is understated $800. Thus, Pioneer makes the following adjusting entry.

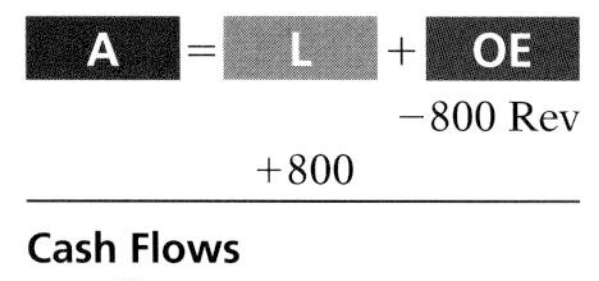

Cash Flows
no effect

Oct. 31	Service Revenue	800	
	Unearned Service Revenue		800
	(To record unearned service revenue)		

After Pioneer posts the adjusting entry, the accounts show the following.

Illustration 3A-4
Unearned service revenue accounts after adjustment

Unearned Service Revenue

Debit	Credit
	10/31 **Adj.** **800**

Service Revenue

Debit	Credit
10/31 **Adj.** **800**	10/2 1,200
	10/31 **Bal.** **400**

The liability account Unearned Service Revenue shows a balance of $800. This equals the services that will be performed in the future. In addition, the balance in Service Revenue equals the services performed in October. Without the adjusting entry, both revenues and net income are overstated by $800 in the October income statement. Also, liabilities are understated by $800 and owner's equity is overstated by $800 on the October 31 balance sheet.

Illustration 3A-5 compares the entries and accounts for initially recording unearned service revenue in (1) a liability account or (2) a revenue account.

Illustration 3A-5
Adjustment approaches—a comparison

Unearned Service Revenue Initially Credited to Liability Account (per chapter)				**Unearned Service Revenue Initially Credited to Revenue Account (per appendix)**			
Oct. 2	Cash	1,200		Oct. 2	Cash	1,200	
	Unearned Service Revenue		1,200		Service Revenue		1,200
Oct. 31	Unearned Service Revenue	400		Oct. 31	Service Revenue	800	
	Service Revenue		400		Unearned Service Revenue		800

[1]This example focuses only on the alternative treatment of unearned revenues. For simplicity, we have ignored the entries to Service Revenue pertaining to the immediate recognition of revenue ($10,000) and the adjusting entry for accrued revenue ($200).

After Pioneer posts the entries, the accounts appear as follows.

Illustration 3A-6
Comparison of accounts

(per chapter) Unearned Service Revenue		**(per appendix) Unearned Service Revenue**	
10/31 **Adj.** 400	10/2 1,200		10/31 **Adj.** **800**
	10/31 **Bal.** **800**		

Service Revenue		**Service Revenue**	
	10/31 **Adj.** **400**	10/31 **Adj.** **800**	10/2 1,200
			10/31 **Bal.** **400**

Note that the balances in the accounts are the same under the two alternatives: Unearned Service Revenue $800 and Service Revenue $400.

Summary of Additional Adjustment Relationships

Illustration 3A-7 provides a summary of basic relationships for deferrals.

Illustration 3A-7
Summary of basic relationships for deferrals

Type of Adjustment	Reason for Adjustment	Account Balances Before Adjustment	Adjusting Entry
1. Prepaid expenses	(a) Prepaid expenses initially recorded in asset accounts have been used.	Assets overstated. Expenses understated.	Dr. Expenses Cr. Assets
	(b) **Prepaid expenses initially recorded in expense accounts have not been used.**	**Assets understated.** **Expenses overstated.**	**Dr. Assets** **Cr. Expenses**
2. Unearned revenues	(a) Unearned revenues initially recorded in liability accounts are now recognized as revenue.	Liabilities overstated. Revenues understated.	Dr. Liabilities Cr. Revenues
	(b) **Unearned revenues initially recorded in revenue accounts are still unearned.**	**Liabilities understated.** **Revenues overstated.**	**Dr. Revenues** **Cr. Liabilities**

Alternative adjusting entries **do not apply** to accrued revenues and accrued expenses because **no entries occur before companies make these types of adjusting entries**.

APPENDIX 3B: Discuss financial reporting concepts.

This appendix provides a summary of the concepts in action used in this textbook. In addition, it provides other useful concepts which accountants use as a basis for recording and reporting financial information.

Qualities of Useful Information

Recently, the FASB completed the first phase of a project in which it developed a conceptual framework to serve as the basis for future accounting standards. The framework begins by stating that the primary objective of financial reporting is to provide financial information that is **useful** to investors and creditors for making decisions about providing capital. Useful information should possess two fundamental qualities, relevance and faithful representation, as shown in Illustration 3B-1.

Illustration 3B-1
Fundamental qualities of useful information

Relevance Accounting information has **relevance** if it would make a difference in a business decision. Information is considered relevant if it provides information that has **predictive value**, that is, helps provide accurate expectations about the future, and has **confirmatory value**, that is, confirms or corrects prior expectations. **Materiality** is a company-specific aspect of relevance. An item is material when its **size** makes it likely to influence the decision of an investor or creditor.

Faithful Representation **Faithful representation** means that information accurately depicts what really happened. To provide a faithful representation, information must be **complete** (nothing important has been omitted), **neutral** (is not biased toward one position or another), and **free from error**.

ENHANCING QUALITIES

In addition to the two fundamental qualities, the FASB also describes a number of enhancing qualities of useful information. These include **comparability**, **consistency**, **verifiability**, **timeliness**, and **understandability**. In accounting, **comparability** results when different companies use the same accounting principles. Another characteristic that enhances comparability is consistency. **Consistency** means that a company uses the same accounting principles and methods from year to year. Information is **verifiable** if independent observers, using the same methods, obtain similar results. For accounting information to have relevance, it must be **timely**. That is, it must be available to decision-makers before it loses its capacity to influence decisions. For example, public companies like Google or Best Buy provide their annual reports to investors within 60 days of their year-end. Information has the quality of **understandability** if it is presented in a clear and concise fashion, so that reasonably informed users of that information can interpret it and comprehend its meaning.

Assumptions in Financial Reporting

To develop accounting standards, the FASB relies on some key assumptions, as shown in Illustration 3B-2 (page 95). These include assumptions about the monetary unit, economic entity, time period, and going concern.

Principles in Financial Reporting

MEASUREMENT PRINCIPLES

GAAP generally uses one of two measurement principles, the historical cost principle or the fair value principle. Selection of which principle to follow generally relates to trade-offs between relevance and faithful representation.

HISTORICAL COST PRINCIPLE The **historical cost principle** (or cost principle, discussed in Chapter 1) dictates that companies record assets at their cost. This is true not only at the time the asset is purchased but also over the time the asset is held. For example, if land that was purchased for $30,000 increases in value to $40,000, it continues to be reported at $30,000.

FAIR VALUE PRINCIPLE The **fair value principle** (discussed in Chapter 1) indicates that assets and liabilities should be reported at fair value (the price received to sell an asset or settle a liability). Fair value information may be more useful than historical cost for certain types of assets and liabilities. For example, certain investment securities are reported at fair value because market price information is often readily available for these types of assets. In choosing between cost and

Illustration 3B-2
Key assumptions in financial reporting

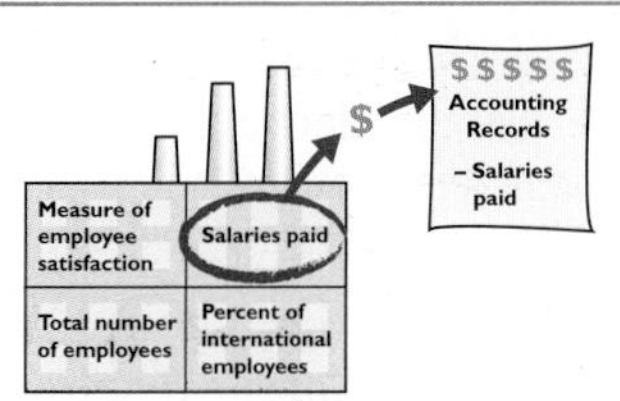

Monetary Unit Assumption The **monetary unit assumption** requires that only those things that can be expressed in money are included in the accounting records. This means that certain important information needed by investors, creditors, and managers, such as customer satisfaction, is not reported in the financial statements.

Economic Entity Assumption The **economic entity assumption** states that every economic entity can be separately identified and accounted for. In order to assess a company's performance and financial position accurately, it is important to not blur company transactions with personal transactions (especially those of its managers) or transactions of other companies.

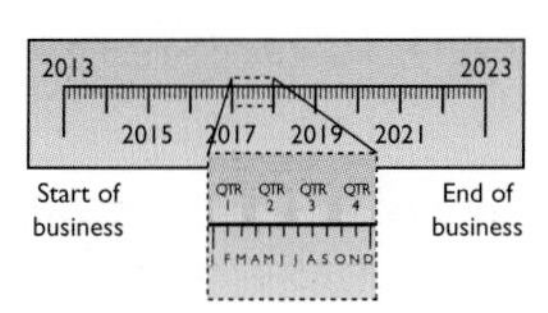

Time Period Assumption Notice that the income statement, retained earnings statement, and statement of cash flows all cover periods of one year, and the balance sheet is prepared at the end of each year. The **time period assumption** states that the life of a business can be divided into artificial time periods and that useful reports covering those periods can be prepared for the business.

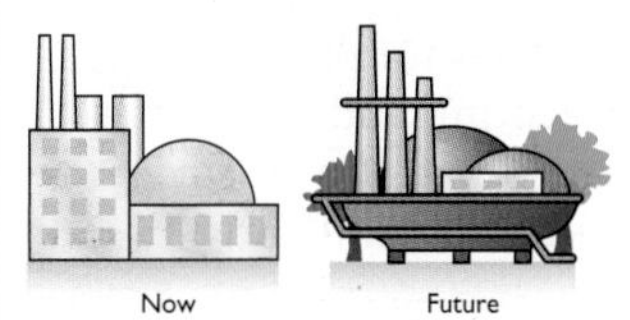

Going Concern Assumption The **going concern assumption** states that the business will remain in operation for the foreseeable future. Of course, many businesses do fail, but in general it is reasonable to assume that the business will continue operating.

fair value, two qualities that make accounting information useful for decision-making are used—relevance and faithful representation. In determining which measurement principle to use, the factual nature of cost figures are weighed versus the relevance of fair value. In general, most assets follow the historical cost principle because fair values may not be representationally faithful. Only in situations where assets are actively traded, such as investment securities, is the fair value principle applied.

REVENUE RECOGNITION PRINCIPLE

The **revenue recognition principle** requires that companies recognize revenue in the accounting period in which the performance obligation is satisfied. As discussed earlier in the chapter, in a service company, revenue is recognized at the time the service is performed. In a merchandising company, the performance obligation is generally satisfied when the goods transfer from the seller to the buyer (discussed in Chapter 5). At this point, the sales transaction is complete and the sales price established.

EXPENSE RECOGNITION PRINCIPLE

The **expense recognition principle** (often referred to as the matching principle, discussed earlier in the chapter) dictates that efforts (expenses) be matched with results (revenues). Thus, expenses follow revenues.

FULL DISCLOSURE PRINCIPLE

The **full disclosure principle** (discussed in Chapter 11) requires that companies disclose all circumstances and events that would make a difference to financial statement users. If an important item cannot reasonably be reported directly in one of the four types of financial statements, then it should be discussed in notes that accompany the statements.

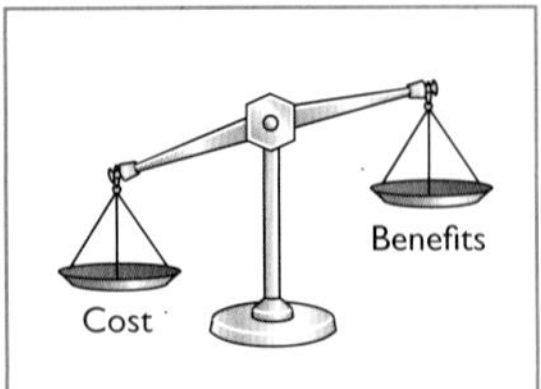

Cost Constraint

Providing information is costly. In deciding whether companies should be required to provide a certain type of information, accounting standard-setters consider the **cost constraint**. It weighs the cost that companies will incur to provide the information against the benefit that financial statement users will gain from having the information available.

REVIEW AND PRACTICE

LEARNING OBJECTIVES REVIEW

1 Explain the accrual basis of accounting and the reasons for adjusting entries. The time period assumption assumes that the economic life of a business is divided into artificial time periods. Accrual-basis accounting means that companies record events that change a company's financial statements in the periods in which those events occur, rather than in the periods in which the company receives or pays cash.

Companies make adjusting entries at the end of an accounting period. Such entries ensure that companies recognize revenues in the period in which the performance obligation is satisfied and recognize expenses in the period in which they are incurred. The major types of adjusting entries are deferrals (prepaid expenses and unearned revenues) and accruals (accrued revenues and accrued expenses).

2 Prepare adjusting entries for deferrals. Deferrals are either prepaid expenses or unearned revenues. Companies make adjusting entries for deferrals to record the portion of the prepayment that represents the expense incurred or the revenue for services performed in the current accounting period.

3 Prepare adjusting entries for accruals. Accruals are either accrued revenues or accrued expenses. Companies make adjusting entries for accruals to record revenues for services performed and expenses incurred in the current accounting period that have not been recognized through daily entries.

4 Describe the nature and purpose of an adjusted trial balance. An adjusted trial balance shows the balances of all accounts, including those that have been adjusted, at the end of an accounting period. Its purpose is to prove the equality of the total debit balances and total credit balances in the ledger after all adjustments.

***5 Prepare adjusting entries for the alternative treatment of deferrals.** Companies may initially debit prepayments to an expense account. Likewise, they may credit unearned revenues to a revenue account. At the end of the period, these accounts may be overstated. The adjusting entries for prepaid expenses are a debit to an asset account and a credit to an expense account. Adjusting entries for unearned revenues are a debit to a revenue account and a credit to a liability account.

***6 Discuss financial reporting concepts.** To be judged useful, information should have the primary characteristics of relevance and faithful representation. In addition, it should be comparable, consistent, verifiable, timely, and understandable.

The **monetary unit assumption** requires that companies include in the accounting records only transaction data that can be expressed in terms of money. The **economic entity assumption** states that economic events can be identified with a particular unit of accountability. The **time period assumption** states that the economic life of a business can be divided into artificial time periods and that meaningful accounting reports can be prepared for each period. The **going concern assumption** states that the company will continue in operation long enough to carry out its existing objectives and commitments.

The **historical cost principle** states that companies should record assets at their cost. The **fair value principle** indicates that assets and liabilities should be reported at fair value. The **revenue recognition principle** requires that companies recognize revenue in the accounting period in which the performance obligation is satisfied. The **expense recognition principle** dictates that efforts (expenses) be matched with results (revenues). The **full disclosure principle** requires that companies disclose circumstances and events that matter to financial statement users.

The **cost constraint** weighs the cost that companies incur to provide a type of information against its benefits to financial statement users.

GLOSSARY REVIEW

Accrual-basis accounting Accounting basis in which companies record transactions that change a company's financial statements in the periods in which the events occur.

Accruals Adjusting entries for either accrued revenues or accrued expenses.

Accrued expenses Expenses incurred but not yet paid in cash or recorded.

Accrued revenues Revenues for services performed but not yet received in cash or recorded.

Adjusted trial balance A list of accounts and their balances after the company has made all adjustments.

Adjusting entries Entries made at the end of an accounting period to ensure that companies follow the revenue recognition and expense recognition principles.

Book value The difference between the cost of a depreciable asset and its related accumulated depreciation.

Calendar year An accounting period that extends from January 1 to December 31.

Cash-basis accounting Accounting basis in which companies record revenue when they receive cash and an expense when they pay out cash.

***Comparability** Ability to compare the accounting information of different companies because they use the same accounting principles.

***Consistency** Use of the same accounting principles and methods from year to year within a company.

Contra asset account An account offset against an asset account on the balance sheet.

***Cost constraint** Constraint that weighs the cost that companies will incur to provide the information against the benefit that financial statement users will gain from having the information available.

Deferrals Adjusting entries for either prepaid expenses or unearned revenues.

Depreciation The process of allocating the cost of an asset to expense over its useful life.

***Economic entity assumption** An assumption that every economic entity can be separately identified and accounted for.

Expense recognition principle (matching principle) The principle that companies match efforts (expenses) with accomplishments (revenues).

***Fair value principle** Assets and liabilities should be reported at fair value (the price received to sell an asset or settle a liability).

***Faithful representation** Information that accurately depicts what really happened.

Fiscal year An accounting period that is one year in length.

***Full disclosure principle** Accounting principle that dictates that companies disclose circumstances and events that make a difference to financial statement users.

***Going concern assumption** The assumption that the company will continue in operation for the foreseeable future.

***Historical cost principle** An accounting principle that states that companies should record assets at their cost.

Interim periods Monthly or quarterly accounting time periods.

***Materiality** A company-specific aspect of relevance. An item is material when its size makes it likely to influence the decision of an investor or creditor.

***Monetary unit assumption** An assumption that requires that only those things that can be expressed in money are included in the accounting records.

Prepaid expenses (prepayments) Expenses paid in cash before they are used or consumed.

***Relevance** The quality of information that indicates the information makes a difference in a decision.

Revenue recognition principle The principle that companies recognize revenue in the accounting period in which the performance obligation is satisfied.

***Timely** Information that is available to decision-makers before it loses its capacity to influence decisions.

Time period assumption An assumption that accountants can divide the economic life of a business into artificial time periods.

***Understandability** Information presented in a clear and concise fashion so that users can interpret it and comprehend its meaning.

Unearned revenues A liability recorded for cash received before services are performed.

Useful life The length of service of a long-lived asset.

***Verifiable** The quality of information that occurs when independent observers, using the same methods, obtain similar results.

PRACTICE EXERCISES

Prepare adjusting entries. (LO 2, 3)

1. Evan Watts, D.D.S., opened a dental practice on January 1, 2017. During the first month of operations, the following transactions occurred.

1. Watts performed services for patients totaling $2,400. These services have not yet been recorded.
2. Utility expenses incurred but not paid prior to January 31 totaled $400.
3. Purchased dental equipment on January 1 for $80,000, paying $20,000 in cash and signing a $60,000, 3-year note payable. The equipment depreciates $500 per month. Interest is $600 per month.

4. Purchased a one-year malpractice insurance policy on January 1 for $12,000.
5. Purchased $2,600 of dental supplies. On January 31, determined that $900 of supplies were on hand.

Instructions

Prepare the adjusting entries on January 31. Account titles are Accumulated Depreciation—Equipment, Depreciation Expense, Service Revenue, Accounts Receivable, Insurance Expense, Interest Expense, Interest Payable, Prepaid Insurance, Supplies, Supplies Expense, Utilities Expense, and Utilities Payable.

Solution

1. JANUARY 31

Date	Account	Debit	Credit
Jan. 31	Accounts Receivable	2,400	
	Service Revenue		2,400
	Utilities Expense	400	
	Utilities Payable		400
	Depreciation Expense	500	
	Accumulated Depreciation—Equipment		500
	Interest Expense	600	
	Interest Payable		600
	Insurance Expense ($12,000 ÷ 12)	1,000	
	Prepaid Insurance		1,000
	Supplies Expense ($2,600 − $900)	1,700	
	Supplies		1,700

Prepare correct income statement.

(LO 2, 3, 4)

2. The income statement of Venden Co. for the month of July shows net income of $4,000 based on Service Revenue $8,700, Salaries and Wages Expense $2,500, Supplies Expense $1,700, and Utilities Expense $500. In reviewing the statement, you discover the following.

1. Insurance expired during July of $700 was omitted.
2. Supplies expense includes $250 of supplies that are still on hand at July 31.
3. Depreciation on equipment of $300 was omitted.
4. Accrued but unpaid wages at July 31 of $400 were not included.
5. Services performed but unrecorded totaled $650.

Instructions

Prepare a correct income statement for July 2017.

Solution

2.

VENDEN CO.
Income Statement
For the Month Ended July 31, 2017

Revenues		
Service revenue ($8,700 + $650)		$9,350
Expenses		
Salaries and wages expense ($2,500 + $400)	$2,900	
Supplies expense ($1,700 − $250)	1,450	
Utilities expense	500	
Insurance expense	700	
Depreciation expense	300	
Total expenses		5,850
Net income		$3,500

PRACTICE PROBLEM

Prepare adjusting entries from selected data.

(LO 2, 3)

The Green Thumb Lawn Care Company began operations on April 1. At April 30, the trial balance shows the following balances for selected accounts.

Prepaid Insurance	$ 3,600
Equipment	28,000
Notes Payable	20,000
Unearned Service Revenue	4,200
Service Revenue	1,800

Analysis reveals the following additional data.

1. Prepaid insurance is the cost of a 2-year insurance policy, effective April 1.
2. Depreciation on the equipment is $500 per month.
3. The note payable is dated April 1. It is a 6-month, 12% note.
4. Seven customers paid for the company's 6-month lawn service package of $600 beginning in April. The company performed services for these customers in April.
5. Lawn services performed for other customers but not recorded at April 30 totaled $1,500.

Instructions

Prepare the adjusting entries for the month of April. Show computations.

Solution

GENERAL JOURNAL J1

Date	Account Titles and Explanation	Ref.	Debit	Credit
	Adjusting Entries			
Apr. 30	Insurance Expense		150	
	Prepaid Insurance			150
	(To record insurance expired: $3,600 ÷ 24 = $150 per month)			
30	Depreciation Expense		500	
	Accumulated Depreciation—Equipment			500
	(To record monthly depreciation)			
30	Interest Expense		200	
	Interest Payable			200
	(To record interest on notes payable: $20,000 × 12% × 1/12 = $200)			
30	Unearned Service Revenue		700	
	Service Revenue			700
	(To record revenue for services performed: $600 ÷ 6 = $100; $100 per month × 7 = $700)			
30	Accounts Receivable		1,500	
	Service Revenue			1,500
	(To record revenue for services performed)			

EXERCISES

Explain the time period assumption.

(LO 1)

E3-1 Chloe Davis has prepared the following list of statements about the time period assumption.

1. Adjusting entries would not be necessary if a company's life were not divided into artificial time periods.
2. The IRS requires companies to file annual tax returns.

3. Accountants divide the economic life of a business into artificial time periods, but each transaction affects only one of these periods.
4. Accounting time periods are generally a month, a quarter, or a year.
5. A time period lasting one year is called an interim period.
6. All fiscal years are calendar years, but not all calendar years are fiscal years.

Instructions
Identify each statement as true or false. If false, indicate how to correct the statement.

Distinguish between cash and accrual basis of accounting.
(LO 1)

E3-2 On numerous occasions, proposals have surfaced to put the federal government on the accrual basis of accounting. This is no small issue. If this basis were used, it would mean that billions in unrecorded liabilities would have to be booked, and the federal deficit would increase substantially.

Instructions
(a) What is the difference between accrual-basis accounting and cash-basis accounting?
(b) Why would politicians prefer the cash basis over the accrual basis?
(c) Write a letter to your senator explaining why the federal government should adopt the accrual basis of accounting.

Compute cash and accrual accounting income.
(LO 1)

E3-3 Carillo Industries collected $108,000 from customers in 2017. Of the amount collected, $25,000 was for services performed in 2016. In addition, Carillo performed services worth $36,000 in 2017, which will not be collected until 2018.

Carillo Industries also paid $72,000 for expenses in 2017. Of the amount paid, $30,000 was for expenses incurred on account in 2016. In addition, Carillo incurred $42,000 of expenses in 2017, which will not be paid until 2018.

Instructions
(a) Compute 2017 cash-basis net income.
(b) Compute 2017 accrual-basis net income.

Identify the type of adjusting entry needed.
(LO 1, 2, 3)

E3-4 Hong Corporation encounters the following situations:

1. Hong collects $1,300 from a customer in 2017 for services to be performed in 2018.
2. Hong incurs utility expense which is not yet paid in cash or recorded.
3. Hong's employees worked 3 days in 2017 but will not be paid until 2018.
4. Hong performs services for customers but has not yet received cash or recorded the transaction.
5. Hong paid $2,400 rent on December 1 for the 4 months starting December 1.
6. Hong received cash for future services and recorded a liability until the service was performed.
7. Hong performed consulting services for a client in December 2017. On December 31, it had not billed the client for services provided of $1,200.
8. Hong paid cash for an expense and recorded an asset until the item was used up.
9. Hong purchased $900 of supplies in 2017; at year-end, $400 of supplies remain unused.
10. Hong purchased equipment on January 1, 2017; the equipment will be used for 5 years.
11. Hong borrowed $10,000 on October 1, 2017, signing an 8% one-year note payable.

Instructions
Identify what type of adjusting entry (prepaid expense, unearned revenue, accrued expense, or accrued revenue) is needed in each situation at December 31, 2017.

Prepare adjusting entries from selected data.
(LO 2, 3)

E3-5 Devin Wolf Company has the following balances in selected accounts on December 31, 2017.

Accounts Receivable	$ –0–
Accumulated Depreciation—Equipment	–0–
Equipment	7,000
Interest Payable	–0–
Notes Payable	10,000
Prepaid Insurance	2,100
Salaries and Wages Payable	–0–
Supplies	2,450
Unearned Service Revenue	30,000

All the accounts have normal balances. The information below has been gathered at December 31, 2017.

1. Devin Wolf Company borrowed $10,000 by signing a 9%, one-year note on September 1, 2017.
2. A count of supplies on December 31, 2017, indicates that supplies of $900 are on hand.
3. Depreciation on the equipment for 2017 is $1,000.
4. Devin Wolf Company paid $2,100 for 12 months of insurance coverage on June 1, 2017.
5. On December 1, 2017, Devin Wolf collected $32,000 for consulting services to be performed from December 1, 2017, through March 31, 2018.
6. Devin Wolf performed consulting services for a client in December 2017. The client will be billed $4,200.
7. Devin Wolf Company pays its employees total salaries of $9,000 every Monday for the preceding 5-day week (Monday through Friday). On Monday, December 29, employees were paid for the week ending December 26. All employees worked the last 3 days of 2017.

Instructions
Prepare adjusting entries for the seven items described above.

E3-6 Zaragoza Company accumulates the following adjustment data at December 31.

Identify types of adjustments and account relationships.

(LO 2, 3, 4)

1. Services performed but not recorded total $1,000.
2. Supplies of $300 have been used.
3. Utility expenses of $225 are unpaid.
4. Services related to unearned service revenue of $260 were performed.
5. Salaries of $800 are unpaid.
6. Prepaid insurance totaling $350 has expired.

Instructions
For each of the above items indicate the following.

(a) The type of adjustment (prepaid expense, unearned revenue, accrued revenue, or accrued expense).
(b) The status of accounts before adjustment (overstatement or understatement).

E3-7 The ledger of Passehl Rental Agency on March 31 of the current year includes the selected accounts, shown below, before adjusting entries have been prepared.

Prepare adjusting entries from selected account data.

(LO 2, 3)

	Debit	Credit
Prepaid Insurance	$ 3,600	
Supplies	2,800	
Equipment	25,000	
Accumulated Depreciation—Equipment		$ 8,400
Notes Payable		20,000
Unearned Rent Revenue		10,200
Rent Revenue		60,000
Interest Expense	–0–	
Salaries and Wages Expense	14,000	

An analysis of the accounts shows the following.

1. The equipment depreciates $400 per month.
2. One-third of the unearned rent revenue was earned during the quarter.
3. Interest of $500 is accrued on the notes payable.
4. Supplies on hand total $750.
5. Insurance expires at the rate of $300 per month.

Instructions
Prepare the adjusting entries at March 31, assuming that adjusting entries are made **quarterly**. Additional accounts are Depreciation Expense, Insurance Expense, Interest Payable, and Supplies Expense.

E3-8 Meghan Lindh, D.D.S., opened a dental practice on January 1, 2017. During the first month of operations, the following transactions occurred.

Prepare adjusting entries.

(LO 2, 3)

1. Performed services for patients who had dental plan insurance. At January 31, $875 of such services were performed but not yet recorded.

2. Utility expenses incurred but not paid prior to January 31 totaled $650.
3. Purchased dental equipment on January 1 for $80,000, paying $20,000 in cash and signing a $60,000, 3-year note payable. The equipment depreciates $400 per month. Interest is $500 per month.
4. Purchased a one-year malpractice insurance policy on January 1 for $24,000.
5. Purchased $1,600 of dental supplies. On January 31, determined that $400 of supplies were on hand.

Instructions

Prepare the adjusting entries on January 31. Account titles are Accumulated Depreciation—Equipment, Depreciation Expense, Service Revenue, Accounts Receivable, Insurance Expense, Interest Expense, Interest Payable, Prepaid Insurance, Supplies, Supplies Expense, Utilities Expense, and Utilities Payable.

Prepare adjusting entries.
(LO 2, 3)

E3-9 The trial balance for Pioneer Advertising is shown in Illustration 3-3 (page 74). Instead of the adjusting entries shown in the textbook at October 31, assume the following adjustment data.

1. Supplies on hand at October 31 total $500.
2. Expired insurance for the month is $120.
3. Depreciation for the month is $50.
4. Services related to unearned service revenue in October worth $600 were performed.
5. Services performed but not recorded at October 31 are $360.
6. Interest accrued at October 31 is $95.
7. Accrued salaries at October 31 are $1,625.

Instructions

Prepare the adjusting entries for the items above.

Prepare correct income statement.
(LO 1, 2, 3)

E3-10 The income statement of Montee Co. for the month of July shows net income of $1,400 based on Service Revenue $5,500, Salaries and Wages Expense $2,300, Supplies Expense $1,200, and Utilities Expense $600. In reviewing the statement, you discover the following.

1. Insurance expired during July of $400 was omitted.
2. Supplies expense includes $250 of supplies that are still on hand at July 31.
3. Depreciation on equipment of $150 was omitted.
4. Accrued but unpaid salaries and wages at July 31 of $300 were not included.
5. Services performed but unrecorded totaled $650.

Instructions

Prepare a correct income statement for July 2017.

Analyze adjusted data.
(LO 1, 2, 3, 4)

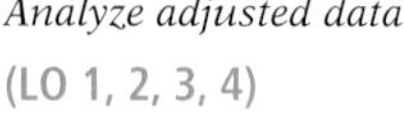

E3-11 A partial adjusted trial balance of Frangesch Company at January 31, 2017, shows the following.

FRANGESCH COMPANY
Adjusted Trial Balance
January 31, 2017

	Debit	Credit
Supplies	$ 850	
Prepaid Insurance	2,400	
Salaries and Wages Payable		$ 920
Unearned Service Revenue		750
Supplies Expense	950	
Insurance Expense	400	
Salaries and Wages Expense	2,900	
Service Revenue		2,000

Instructions

Answer the following questions, assuming the year begins January 1.

(a) If the amount in Supplies Expense is the January 31 adjusting entry, and $1,000 of supplies was purchased in January, what was the balance in Supplies on January 1?

(b) If the amount in Insurance Expense is the January 31 adjusting entry, and the original insurance premium was for one year, what was the total premium and when was the policy purchased?
(c) If $3,800 of salaries was paid in January, what was the balance in Salaries and Wages Payable at December 31, 2016?

Journalize basic transactions and adjusting entries.
(LO 2, 3)

E3-12 Selected accounts of Holly Company are shown as follows.

Supplies Expense

7/31	800		

Supplies

7/1 Bal.	1,100	7/31	800
7/10	650		

Salaries and Wages Payable

		7/31	1,200

Accounts Receivable

7/31	500		

Unearned Service Revenue

7/31	1,150	7/1 Bal.	1,500
		7/20	1,000

Salaries and Wages Expense

7/15	1,200		
7/31	1,200		

Service Revenue

		7/14	2,000
		7/31	1,150
		7/31	500

Instructions
After analyzing the accounts, journalize (a) the July transactions and (b) the adjusting entries that were made on July 31. (*Hint:* July transactions were for cash.)

Prepare adjusting entries from analysis of trial balances.
(LO 2, 3, 4)

E3-13 The trial balances before and after adjustment for Turnquist Company at the end of its fiscal year are presented below.

TURNQUIST COMPANY
Trial Balance
August 31, 2017

	Before Adjustment		After Adjustment	
	Dr.	**Cr.**	**Dr.**	**Cr.**
Cash	$10,400		$10,400	
Accounts Receivable	8,800		11,400	
Supplies	2,300		900	
Prepaid Insurance	4,000		2,500	
Equipment	14,000		14,000	
Accumulated Depreciation—Equipment		$ 3,600		$ 4,500
Accounts Payable		5,800		5,800
Salaries and Wages Payable		–0–		1,100
Unearned Rent Revenue		1,500		400
Owner's Capital		15,600		15,600
Service Revenue		34,000		36,600
Rent Revenue		11,000		12,100
Salaries and Wages Expense	17,000		18,100	
Supplies Expense	–0–		1,400	
Rent Expense	15,000		15,000	
Insurance Expense	–0–		1,500	
Depreciation Expense	–0–		900	
	$71,500	$71,500	$76,100	$76,100

Instructions
Prepare the adjusting entries that were made.

Prepare financial statements from adjusted trial balance.

(LO 4)

E3-14 The adjusted trial balance for Turnquist Company is given in E3-13.

Instructions

Prepare the income and owner's equity statements for the year and the balance sheet at August 31.

Record transactions on accrual basis; convert revenue to cash receipts.

(LO 2, 3)

E3-15 The following data are taken from the comparative balance sheets of Bundies Billiards Club, which prepares its financial statements using the accrual basis of accounting.

December 31	**2017**	**2016**
Accounts receivable from members	$16,000	$ 8,000
Unearned service revenue	17,000	25,000

Members are billed based upon their use of the club's facilities. Unearned service revenues arise from the sale of gift certificates, which members can apply to their future use of club facilities. The 2017 income statement for the club showed that service revenue of $161,000 was earned during the year.

Instructions

(*Hint:* You will probably find it helpful to use T-accounts to analyze these data.)

(a) Prepare journal entries for each of the following events that took place during 2017.
   (1) Accounts receivable from 2016 were all collected.
   (2) Gift certificates outstanding at the end of 2016 were all redeemed.
   (3) An additional $38,000 worth of gift certificates were sold during 2017. A portion of these was used by the recipients during the year; the remainder was still outstanding at the end of 2017.
   (4) Services performed for members for 2017 were billed to members.
   (5) Accounts receivable for 2017 (i.e., those billed in item [4] above) were partially collected.

(b) Determine the amount of cash received by the club, with respect to member services, during 2017.

Journalize adjusting entries.

(LO 5)

***E3-16** Zac Brown Company has the following balances in selected accounts on December 31, 2017.

Service Revenue	$40,000
Insurance Expense	2,700
Supplies Expense	2,450

All the accounts have normal balances. Zac Brown Company debits prepayments to expense accounts when paid, and credits unearned revenues to revenue accounts when received. The following information below has been gathered at December 31, 2017.

1. Zac Brown Company paid $2,700 for 12 months of insurance coverage on June 1, 2017.
2. On December 1, 2017, Zac Brown Company collected $40,000 for consulting services to be performed from December 1, 2017, through March 31, 2018.
3. A count of supplies on December 31, 2017, indicates that supplies of $900 are on hand.

Instructions

Prepare the adjusting entries needed at December 31, 2017.

Journalize transactions and adjusting entries.

(LO 5)

***E3-17** At Sekon Company, prepayments are debited to expense when paid, and unearned revenues are credited to revenue when cash is received. During January of the current year, the following transactions occurred.

Jan.	2	Paid $1,920 for fire insurance protection for the year.
	10	Paid $1,700 for supplies.
	15	Received $6,100 for services to be performed in the future.

On January 31, it is determined that $2,100 of the services were performed and that there are $650 of supplies on hand.

Instructions

(a) Journalize and post the January transactions. (Use T-accounts.)
(b) Journalize and post the adjusting entries at January 31.
(c) Determine the ending balance in each of the accounts.

***E3-18** Presented below are the assumptions and principles discussed in this chapter.

Identify accounting assumptions and principles.

(LO 6)

1. Full disclosure principle.
2. Going concern assumption.
3. Monetary unit assumption.
4. Time period assumption.
5. Historical cost principle.
6. Economic entity assumption.

Instructions

Identify by number the accounting assumption or principle that is described below. Do not use a number more than once.

_______ (a) Is the rationale for why plant assets are not reported at liquidation value. (*Note:* Do not use the historical cost principle.)
_______ (b) Indicates that personal and business recordkeeping should be separately maintained.
_______ (c) Assumes that the monetary unit is the "measuring stick" used to report on financial performance.
_______ (d) Separates financial information into time periods for reporting purposes.
_______ (e) Measurement basis used when a reliable estimate of fair value is not available.
_______ (f) Dictates that companies should disclose all circumstances and events that make a difference to financial statement users.

***E3-19** Weber Co. had three major business transactions during 2017.

Identify the assumption or principle that has been violated.

(LO 6)

(a) Reported at its fair value of $260,000 merchandise inventory with a cost of $208,000.
(b) The president of Weber Co., Austin Weber, purchased a truck for personal use and charged it to his expense account.
(c) Weber Co. wanted to make its 2017 income look better, so it added 2 more weeks to the year (a 54-week year). Previous years were 52 weeks.

Instructions

In each situation, identify the assumption or principle that has been violated, if any, and discuss what the company should have done.

***E3-20** The following characteristics, assumptions, principles, or constraint guide the FASB when it creates accounting standards.

Identity financial accounting concepts and principles.

(LO 6)

Relevance	Expense recognition principle
Faithful representation	Time period assumption
Comparability	Going concern assumption
Consistency	Historical cost principle
Monetary unit assumption	Full disclosure principle
Economic entity assumption	Materiality

Match each item above with a description below.

1. _______ Ability to easily evaluate one company's results relative to another's.
2. _______ Belief that a company will continue to operate for the foreseeable future.
3. _______ The judgment concerning whether an item's size is large enough to matter to decision-makers.
4. _______ The reporting of all information that would make a difference to financial statement users.
5. _______ The practice of preparing financial statements at regular intervals.
6. _______ The quality of information that indicates the information makes a difference in a decision.
7. _______ A belief that items should be reported on the balance sheet at the price that was paid to acquire them.
8. _______ A company's use of the same accounting principles and methods from year to year.
9. _______ Tracing accounting events to particular companies.
10. _______ The desire to minimize bias in financial statements.
11. _______ Reporting only those things that can be measured in monetary units.
12. _______ Dictates that efforts (expenses) be matched with results (revenues).

***E3-21** Speyeware International Inc., headquartered in Vancouver, Canada, specializes in Internet safety and computer security products for both the home and commercial markets. In a recent balance sheet, it reported a deficit of US$5,678,288. It has reported only net losses since its inception. In spite of these losses, Speyeware's shares of stock have traded anywhere from a high of $3.70 to a low of $0.32 on the Canadian Venture Exchange.

Comment on the objective and qualitative characteristics of accounting information.

(LO 6)

Speyeware's financial statements have historically been prepared in Canadian dollars. Recently, the company adopted the U.S. dollar as its reporting currency.

Instructions

(a) What is the objective of financial reporting? How does this objective meet or not meet Speyeware's investors' needs?

(b) Why would investors want to buy Speyeware's shares if the company has consistently reported losses over the last few years? Include in your answer an assessment of the relevance of the information reported on Speyeware's financial statements.

(c) Comment on how the change in reporting information from Canadian dollars to U.S. dollars likely affected the readers of Speyeware's financial statements. Include in your answer an assessment of the comparability of the information.

Comment on the objective and qualitative characteristics of financial reporting.

(LO 6)

***E3-22** A friend of yours, Gina Moore, recently completed an undergraduate degree in science and has just started working with a biotechnology company. Gina tells you that the owners of the business are trying to secure new sources of financing which are needed in order for the company to proceed with development of a new healthcare product. Gina said that her boss told her that the company must put together a report to present to potential investors.

Gina thought that the company should include in this package the detailed scientific findings related to the Phase I clinical trials for this product. She said, "I know that the biotech industry sometimes has only a 10% success rate with new products, but if we report all the scientific findings, everyone will see what a sure success this is going to be! The president was talking about the importance of following some set of accounting principles. Why do we need to look at some accounting rules? What they need to realize is that we have scientific results that are quite encouraging, some of the most talented employees around, and the start of some really great customer relationships. We haven't made any sales yet, but we will. We just need the funds to get through all the clinical testing and get government approval for our product. Then these investors will be quite happy that they bought in to our company early!"

Instructions

(a) What is accounting information?

(b) Comment on how Gina's suggestions for what should be reported to prospective investors conforms to the qualitative characteristics of accounting information. Do you think that the things that Gina wants to include in the information for investors will conform to financial reporting guidelines?

PROBLEMS

Prepare adjusting entries, post to ledger accounts, and prepare an adjusted trial balance.

(LO 2, 3, 4)

P3-1A Logan Krause started her own consulting firm, Krause Consulting, on May 1, 2017. The trial balance at May 31 is as follows.

KRAUSE CONSULTING
Trial Balance
May 31, 2017

Account Number		Debit	Credit
101	Cash	$ 4,500	
112	Accounts Receivable	6,000	
126	Supplies	1,900	
130	Prepaid Insurance	3,600	
149	Equipment	11,400	
201	Accounts Payable		$ 4,500
209	Unearned Service Revenue		2,000
301	Owner's Capital		18,700
400	Service Revenue		9,500
726	Salaries and Wages Expense	6,400	
729	Rent Expense	900	
		$34,700	$34,700

In addition to those accounts listed on the trial balance, the chart of accounts for Krause Consulting also contains the following accounts and account numbers: No. 150 Accumulated Depreciation—Equipment, No. 212 Salaries and Wages Payable, No. 631 Supplies Expense, No. 717 Depreciation Expense, No. 722 Insurance Expense, and No. 732 Utilities Expense.

Other data:

1. $900 of supplies have been used during the month.
2. Utilities expense incurred but not paid on May 31, 2017, $250.
3. The insurance policy is for 2 years.
4. $400 of the balance in the unearned service revenue account remains unearned at the end of the month.
5. May 31 is a Wednesday, and employees are paid on Fridays. Krause Consulting has two employees, who are paid $920 each for a 5-day work week.
6. The office furniture has a 5-year life with no salvage value. It is being depreciated at $190 per month for 60 months.
7. Invoices representing $1,700 of services performed during the month have not been recorded as of May 31.

Instructions

(a) Prepare the adjusting entries for the month of May. Use J4 as the page number for your journal.

(b) Post the adjusting entries to the ledger accounts. Enter the totals from the trial balance as beginning account balances and place a check mark in the posting reference column.

(c) Prepare an adjusted trial balance at May 31, 2017.

(c) Adj. trial balance $37,944

P3-2A Mac's Motel opened for business on May 1, 2017. Its trial balance before adjustment on May 31 is as follows.

Prepare adjusting entries, post, and prepare adjusted trial balance and financial statements.

(LO 2, 3, 4)

MAC'S MOTEL
Trial Balance
May 31, 2017

Account Number		Debit	Credit
101	Cash	$ 3,500	
126	Supplies	2,080	
130	Prepaid Insurance	2,400	
140	Land	12,000	
141	Buildings	60,000	
149	Equipment	15,000	
201	Accounts Payable		$ 4,800
208	Unearned Rent Revenue		3,300
275	Mortgage Payable		40,000
301	Owner's Capital		41,380
429	Rent Revenue		10,300
610	Advertising Expense	600	
726	Salaries and Wages Expense	3,300	
732	Utilities Expense	900	
		$99,780	$99,780

In addition to those accounts listed on the trial balance, the chart of accounts for Mac's Motel also contains the following accounts and account numbers: No. 142 Accumulated Depreciation—Buildings, No. 150 Accumulated Depreciation—Equipment, No. 212 Salaries and Wages Payable, No. 230 Interest Payable, No. 619 Depreciation Expense, No. 631 Supplies Expense, No. 718 Interest Expense, and No. 722 Insurance Expense.

Other data:

1. Prepaid insurance is a 1-year policy starting May 1, 2017.
2. A count of supplies shows $750 of unused supplies on May 31.
3. Annual depreciation is $3,000 on the buildings and $1,500 on equipment.
4. The mortgage interest rate is 12%. (The mortgage was taken out on May 1.)
5. Two-thirds of the unearned rent revenue has been earned.
6. Salaries of $750 are accrued and unpaid at May 31.

(c) Adj. trial balance $101,305
(d) Net income $4,645 Ending capital $46,025 Total assets $93,075

Instructions

(a) Journalize the adjusting entries on May 31.
(b) Prepare a ledger using the three-column form of account. Enter the trial balance amounts and post the adjusting entries. (Use J1 as the posting reference.)
(c) Prepare an adjusted trial balance on May 31.
(d) Prepare an income statement and an owner's equity statement for the month of May and a balance sheet at May 31.

Prepare adjusting entries and financial statements.
(LO 2, 3, 4)

P3-3A Alena Co. was organized on July 1, 2017. Quarterly financial statements are prepared. The unadjusted and adjusted trial balances as of September 30 are shown below.

ALENA CO.
Trial Balance
September 30, 2017

	Unadjusted		Adjusted	
	Dr.	**Cr.**	**Dr.**	**Cr.**
Cash	$ 8,700		$ 8,700	
Accounts Receivable	10,400		11,500	
Supplies	1,500		650	
Prepaid Rent	2,200		500	
Equipment	18,000		18,000	
Accumulated Depreciation—Equipment		$ –0–		$ 700
Notes Payable		10,000		10,000
Accounts Payable		2,500		2,500
Salaries and Wages Payable		–0–		725
Interest Payable		–0–		100
Unearned Rent Revenue		1,900		450
Owner's Capital		22,000		22,000
Owner's Drawings	1,600		1,600	
Service Revenue		16,000		17,100
Rent Revenue		1,410		2,860
Salaries and Wages Expense	8,000		8,725	
Rent Expense	1,900		3,600	
Depreciation Expense			700	
Supplies Expense			850	
Utilities Expense	1,510		1,510	
Interest Expense			100	
	$53,810	$53,810	$56,435	$56,435

(b) Net income $4,475 Ending capital $24,875 Total assets $38,650

Instructions

(a) Journalize the adjusting entries that were made.
(b) Prepare an income statement and an owner's equity statement for the 3 months ending September 30 and a balance sheet at September 30.
(c) If the note bears interest at 12%, how many months has it been outstanding?

Prepare adjusting entries.
(LO 2, 3)

P3-4A A review of the ledger of Remina Company at December 31, 2017, produces the following data pertaining to the preparation of annual adjusting entries.

1. Insurance expense $4,890

1. Prepaid Insurance $10,440. The company has separate insurance policies on its buildings and its motor vehicles. Policy B4564 on the building was purchased on April 1, 2016, for $7,920. The policy has a term of 3 years. Policy A2958 on the vehicles was purchased on January 1, 2017, for $4,500. This policy has a term of 2 years.

2. Rent revenue $84,000

2. Unearned Rent Revenue $429,000. The company began subleasing office space in its new building on November 1. At December 31, the company had the following rental contracts that are paid in full for the entire term of the lease.

Date	Term (in months)	Monthly Rent	Number of Leases
Nov. 1	9	$5,000	5
Dec. 1	6	$8,500	4

3. Notes Payable $120,000. This balance consists of a note for 9 months at an annual interest rate of 9%, dated November 1.
4. Salaries and Wages Payable $0. There are eight salaried employees. Salaries are paid every Friday for the current week. Five employees receive a salary of $700 each per week, and three employees earn $500 each per week. Assume December 31 is a Tuesday. Employees do not work weekends. All employees worked the last 2 days of December.

3. Interest expense $1,800

4. Salaries and wages expense $2,000

Instructions
Prepare the adjusting entries at December 31, 2017.

P3-5A On November 1, 2017, the account balances of Hamm Equipment Repair were as follows.

Journalize transactions and follow through accounting cycle to preparation of financial statements.

(LO 2, 3, 4)

No.		Debit	No.		Credit
101	Cash	$ 2,400	154	Accumulated Depreciation—Equipment	$ 2,000
112	Accounts Receivable	4,250	201	Accounts Payable	2,600
126	Supplies	1,800	209	Unearned Service Revenue	1,200
153	Equipment	12,000	212	Salaries and Wages Payable	700
			301	Owner's Capital	13,950
		$20,450			$20,450

During November, the following summary transactions were completed.

Nov.	8	Paid $1,700 for salaries due employees, of which $700 is for October salaries.
	10	Received $3,620 cash from customers on account.
	12	Received $3,100 cash for services performed in November.
	15	Purchased equipment on account $2,000.
	17	Purchased supplies on account $700.
	20	Paid creditors on account $2,700.
	22	Paid November rent $400.
	25	Paid salaries $1,700.
	27	Performed services on account and billed customers for these services $2,200.
	29	Received $600 from customers for future service.

Adjustment data consist of:

1. Supplies on hand $1,400.
2. Accrued salaries payable $350.
3. Depreciation for the month is $200.
4. Services related to unearned service revenue of $1,220 were performed.

Instructions
(a) Enter the November 1 balances in the ledger accounts.
(b) Journalize the November transactions.
(c) Post to the ledger accounts. Use J1 for the posting reference. Use the following additional accounts: No. 407 Service Revenue, No. 615 Depreciation Expense, No. 631 Supplies Expense, No. 726 Salaries and Wages Expense, and No. 729 Rent Expense.
(d) Prepare a trial balance at November 30.
(e) Journalize and post adjusting entries.
(f) Prepare an adjusted trial balance.
(g) Prepare an income statement and an owner's equity statement for November and a balance sheet at November 30.

(d) Trial balance $25,650
(f) Adj. trial balance $26,200
(g) Net income $1,770;
Ending capital $15,720
Total assets $19,250

***P3-6A** Johnson Graphics Company was organized on January 1, 2017, by Cameron Johnson. At the end of the first 6 months of operations, the trial balance contained the accounts shown on page 110.

Prepare adjusting entries, adjusted trial balance, and financial statements using appendix.

(LO 2, 3, 4, 5)

	Debit		Credit
Cash	$ 8,600	Notes Payable	$ 20,000
Accounts Receivable	14,000	Accounts Payable	9,000
Equipment	45,000	Owner's Capital	22,000
Insurance Expense	2,700	Sales Revenue	52,100
Salaries and Wages Expense	30,000	Service Revenue	6,000
Supplies Expense	3,700		
Advertising Expense	1,900		
Rent Expense	1,500		
Utilities Expense	1,700		
	$109,100		$109,100

Analysis reveals the following additional data.

1. The $3,700 balance in Supplies Expense represents supplies purchased in January. At June 30, $1,500 of supplies are on hand.
2. The note payable was issued on February 1. It is a 9%, 6-month note.
3. The balance in Insurance Expense is the premium on a one-year policy, dated March 1, 2017.
4. Service revenues are credited to revenue when received. At June 30, services revenue of $1,300 are unearned.
5. Revenue for services performed but unrecorded at June 30 totals $2,000.
6. Depreciation is $2,250 per year.

Instructions

(b) Adj. trial balance $112,975
(c) Net income $18,725 Ending capital $40,725 Total assets $71,775

(a) Journalize the adjusting entries at June 30. (Assume adjustments are recorded every 6 months.)
(b) Prepare an adjusted trial balance.
(c) Prepare an income statement and owner's equity statement for the 6 months ended June 30 and a balance sheet at June 30.

BROADENING YOUR PERSPECTIVE

FINANCIAL REPORTING AND ANALYSIS

Financial Reporting Problem: Apple Inc.

BYP3-1 The financial statements of **Apple Inc.** are presented in Appendix A at the end of this textbook. Instructions for accessing and using the company's complete annual report, including the notes to the financial statements, are also provided in Appendix A.

Instructions

(a) Using the consolidated financial statements and related information, identify items that may result in adjusting entries for prepayments.
(b) Using the consolidated financial statements and related information, identify items that may result in adjusting entries for accruals.
(c) What has been the trend since 2011 for net income?

Comparative Analysis Problem: PepsiCo, Inc. vs. The Coca-Cola Company

BYP3-2 PepsiCo, Inc.'s financial statements are presented in Appendix B. Financial statements of The Coca-Cola Company are presented in Appendix C. Instructions for accessing and using the complete annual reports of PepsiCo and Coca-Cola, including the notes to the financial statements, are also provided in Appendices B and C, respectively.

Instructions

Based on information contained in these financial statements, determine the following for each company.

(a) Net increase (decrease) in property, plant, and equipment (net) from 2012 to 2013.
(b) Increase (decrease) in selling, general, and administrative expenses from 2012 to 2013.

(c) Increase (decrease) in long-term debt (obligations) from 2012 to 2013.
(d) Increase (decrease) in net income from 2012 to 2013.
(e) Increase (decrease) in cash and cash equivalents from 2012 to 2013.

Comparative Analysis Problem: Amazon.com, Inc. vs. Wal-Mart Stores, Inc.

BYP3-3 Amazon.com, Inc.'s financial statements are presented in Appendix D. Financial statements of Wal-Mart Stores, Inc. are presented in Appendix E. Instructions for accessing and using the complete annual reports of Amazon and Wal-Mart, including the notes to the financial statements, are also provided in Appendices D and E, respectively.

Instructions

Based on information contained in these financial statements, determine the following for each company.

1. (a) Increase (decrease) in interest expense from 2012 to 2013.
   (b) Increase (decrease) in net income from 2012 to 2013.
   (c) Increase (decrease) in cash flow from operations from 2012 to 2013.
2. Cash flow from operations and net income for each company is different. What are some possible reasons for these differences?

Real-World Focus

BYP3-4 No financial decision-maker should ever rely solely on the financial information reported in the annual report to make decisions. It is important to keep abreast of financial news. This activity demonstrates how to search for financial news on the Internet.

Address: **http://biz.yahoo.com/i**, or go to **www.wiley.com/college/weygandt**

Steps:

1. Type in either Wal-Mart, Target Corp., or Kmart.
2. Choose **News**.
3. Select an article that sounds interesting to you and that would be relevant to an investor in these companies.

Instructions

(a) What was the source of the article (e.g., Reuters, Businesswire, Prnewswire)?
(b) Assume that you are a personal financial planner and that one of your clients owns stock in the company. Write a brief memo to your client summarizing the article and explaining the implications of the article for his or her investment.

CRITICAL THINKING

Decision-Making Across the Organization

BYP3-5 Happy Camper Park was organized on April 1, 2016, by Erica Hatt. Erica is a good manager but a poor accountant. From the trial balance prepared by a part-time bookkeeper, Erica prepared the following income statement for the quarter that ended March 31, 2017.

HAPPY CAMPER PARK
Income Statement
For the Quarter Ended March 31, 2017

Revenues		
Rent revenue		$90,000
Operating expenses		
Advertising	$ 5,200	
Salaries and wages	29,800	
Utilities	900	
Depreciation	800	
Maintenance and repairs	4,000	
Total operating expenses		40,700
Net income		$49,300

Erica thought that something was wrong with the statement because net income had never exceeded $20,000 in any one quarter. Knowing that you are an experienced accountant, she asks you to review the income statement and other data.

You first look at the trial balance. In addition to the account balances reported above in the income statement, the ledger contains the following additional selected balances at March 31, 2017.

Supplies	$ 6,200
Prepaid Insurance	7,200
Notes Payable	12,000

You then make inquiries and discover the following.

1. Rent revenues include advanced rentals for summer occupancy $15,000.
2. There were $1,700 of supplies on hand at March 31.
3. Prepaid insurance resulted from the payment of a one-year policy on January 1, 2017.
4. The mail on April 1, 2017, brought the following bills: advertising for week of March 24, $110; repairs made March 10, $260; and utilities, $180.
5. There are four employees who receive wages totaling $300 per day. At March 31, 2 days' salaries and wages have been incurred but not paid.
6. The note payable is a 3-month, 10% note dated January 1, 2017.

Instructions
With the class divided into groups, answer the following.

(a) Prepare a correct income statement for the quarter ended March 31, 2017.
(b) Explain to Erica the generally accepted accounting principles that she did not recognize in preparing her income statement and their effect on her results.

Communication Activity

BYP3-6 In reviewing the accounts of Kelli Taylor Co. at the end of the year, you discover that adjusting entries have not been made.

Instructions
Write a memo to Kelli Taylor, the owner of Kelli Taylor Co., that explains the following: the nature and purpose of adjusting entries, why adjusting entries are needed, and the types of adjusting entries that may be made.

Ethics Case

BYP3-7 Russell Company is a pesticide manufacturer. Its sales declined greatly this year due to the passage of legislation outlawing the sale of several of Russell's chemical pesticides. In the coming year, Russell will have environmentally safe and competitive chemicals to replace these discontinued products. Sales in the next year are expected to greatly exceed any prior year's. The decline in sales and profits appears to be a one-year aberration. But even so, the company president fears a large dip in the current year's profits. He believes that such a dip could cause a significant drop in the market price of Russell's stock and make the company a takeover target.

To avoid this possibility, the company president calls in Zoe Baas, controller, to discuss this period's year-end adjusting entries. He urges her to accrue every possible revenue and to defer as many expenses as possible. He says to Zoe, "We need the revenues this year, and next year can easily absorb expenses deferred from this year. We can't let our stock price be hammered down!" Zoe didn't get around to recording the adjusting entries until January 17, but she dated the entries December 31 as if they were recorded then. Zoe also made every effort to comply with the president's request.

Instructions
(a) Who are the stakeholders in this situation?
(b) What are the ethical considerations of (1) the president's request and (2) Zoe dating the adjusting entries December 31?
(c) Can Zoe accrue revenues and defer expenses and still be ethical?

All About You

BYP3-8 Companies must report or disclose in their financial statement information about all liabilities, including potential liabilities related to environmental cleanup. There are many situations in which you will be asked to provide personal financial information about your assets, liabilities, revenue, and expenses. Sometimes you will face difficult decisions regarding what to disclose and how to disclose it.

Instructions

Suppose that you are putting together a loan application to purchase a home. Based on your income and assets, you qualify for the mortgage loan, but just barely. How would you address each of the following situations in reporting your financial position for the loan application? Provide responses for each of the following situations.

(a) You signed a guarantee for a bank loan that a friend took out for $20,000. If your friend doesn't pay, you will have to pay. Your friend has made all of the payments so far, and it appears he will be able to pay in the future.
(b) You were involved in an auto accident in which you were at fault. There is the possibility that you may have to pay as much as $50,000 as part of a settlement. The issue will not be resolved before the bank processes your mortgage request.
(c) The company for which you work isn't doing very well, and it has recently laid off employees. You are still employed, but it is quite possible that you will lose your job in the next few months.

Considering People, Planet, and Profit

BYP3-9 Many companies have potential pollution or environmental-disposal problems—not only for electronic gadgets, but also for the lead paint or asbestos they sold. How do we fit these issues into the accounting equation? Are these costs and related liabilities that companies should report?

YES: As more states impose laws holding companies responsible, and as more courts levy pollution-related fines, it becomes increasingly likely that companies will have to pay large amounts in the future.
NO: The amounts still are too difficult to estimate. Putting inaccurate estimates on the financial statements reduces their usefulness. Instead, why not charge the costs later, when the actual environmental cleanup or disposal occurs, at which time the company knows the actual cost?

Instructions

Write a response indicating your position regarding this situation. Provide support for your view.

FASB Codification Activity

BYP3-10 If your school has a subscription to the FASB Codification, go to **http://aaahq.org/asclogin.cfm** to log in and prepare responses to the following.

Instructions

Access the glossary ("Master Glossary") to answer the following.

(a) What is the definition of revenue?
(b) What is the definition of compensation?

A Look at IFRS

LEARNING OBJECTIVE  7 **Compare the procedures for adjusting entries under GAAP and IFRS.**

It is often difficult for companies to determine in what time period they should report particular revenues and expenses. Both the IASB and FASB are working on a joint project to develop a common conceptual framework that will enable companies to better use the same principles to record transactions consistently over time.

Key Points

Following are the key similarities and differences between GAAP and IFRS as related to accrual accounting.

Similarities

- In this chapter, you learned accrual-basis accounting applied under GAAP. Companies applying IFRS also use accrual-basis accounting to ensure that they record transactions that change a company's financial statements in the period in which events occur.
- Similar to GAAP, cash-basis accounting is not in accordance with IFRS.
- IFRS also divides the economic life of companies into artificial time periods. Under both GAAP and IFRS, this is referred to as the **time period assumption**.
- The **general** revenue recognition principle required by GAAP that is used in this textbook is similar to that used under IFRS.
- Revenue recognition fraud is a major issue in U.S. financial reporting. The same situation occurs in other countries, as evidenced by revenue recognition breakdowns at Dutch software company Baan NV, Japanese electronics giant NEC, and Dutch grocer Ahold NV.

Differences

- Under IFRS, revaluation (using fair value) of items such as land and buildings is permitted. IFRS allows depreciation based on revaluation of assets, which is not permitted under GAAP.
- The terminology used for revenues and gains, and expenses and losses, differs somewhat between IFRS and GAAP. For example, income under IFRS includes both revenues, which arise during the normal course of operating activities, and gains, which arise from activities outside of the normal sales of goods and services. The term income is not used this way under GAAP. Instead, under GAAP income refers to the net difference between revenues and expenses.
- Under IFRS, expenses include both those costs incurred in the normal course of operations as well as losses that are not part of normal operations. This is in contrast to GAAP, which defines each separately.

Looking to the Future

The IASB and FASB are completing a joint project on revenue recognition. The purpose of this project is to develop comprehensive guidance on when to recognize revenue. It is hoped that this approach will lead to more consistent accounting in this area. For more on this topic, see **www.fasb.org/project/revenue_recognition.shtml**.

IFRS Practice

IFRS Self-Test Questions

1. IFRS:
   (a) uses accrual accounting.
   (b) uses cash-basis accounting.
   (c) allows revenue to be recognized when a customer makes an order.
   (d) requires that revenue not be recognized until cash is received.
2. Which of the following statements is **false**?
   (a) IFRS employs the time period assumption.
   (b) IFRS employs accrual accounting.
   (c) IFRS requires that revenues and costs must be capable of being measured reliably.
   (d) IFRS uses the cash basis of accounting.
3. As a result of the revenue recognition project by the FASB and IASB:
   (a) revenue recognition places more emphasis on when the performance obligation is satisfied.
   (b) revenue recognition places more emphasis on when revenue is realized.
   (c) revenue recognition places more emphasis on when expenses are incurred.
   (d) revenue is no longer recorded unless cash has been received.
4. Which of the following is **false**?
   (a) Under IFRS, the term income describes both revenues and gains.
   (b) Under IFRS, the term expenses includes losses.
   (c) Under IFRS, companies do not engage in the adjusting process.
   (d) Under IFRS, revenue recognition fraud is a major issue.

5. Accrual-basis accounting:
   (a) is optional under IFRS.
   (b) results in companies recording transactions that change a company's financial statements in the period in which events occur.
   (c) has been eliminated as a result of the IASB/FASB joint project on revenue recognition.
   (d) is not consistent with the IASB conceptual framework.

International Financial Reporting Problem: Louis Vuitton

IFRS3-1 The financial statements of Louis Vuitton are presented in Appendix F. Instructions for accessing and using the company's complete annual report, including the notes to its financial statements, are also provided in Appendix F.

Instructions

Visit Louis Vuitton's corporate website and answer the following questions from Louis Vuitton's 2013 annual report.

(a) From the notes to the financial statements, how does the company determine the amount of revenue to record at the time of a sale?

(b) From the notes to the financial statements, how does the company determine the provision for product returns?

(c) Using the consolidated income statement and consolidated statement of financial position, identify items that may result in adjusting entries for deferrals.

(d) Using the consolidated income statement, identify two items that may result in adjusting entries for accruals.

Answers to IFRS Self-Test Questions

1. a **2.** d **3.** a **4.** c **5.** b

Chapter 4 Completing the Accounting Cycle

When Ted Castle was a hockey coach at the University of Vermont, his players were self-motivated by their desire to win. Hockey was a game you usually either won or lost. But at Rhino Foods, Inc., a bakery-foods company he founded in Burlington, Vermont, he discovered that manufacturing-line workers were not so self-motivated. Ted thought, what if he turned the food-making business into a game, with rules, strategies, and trophies?

In a game, knowing the score is all-important. Ted felt that only if the employees know the score—know exactly how the business is doing daily, weekly, monthly—could he turn food-making into a game. But Rhino is a closely held, family-owned business, and its financial statements and profits were confidential. Ted wondered, should he open Rhino's books to the employees?

A consultant put Ted's concerns in perspective when he said, "Imagine you're playing touch football. You play for an hour or two, and the whole time I'm sitting there with a book, keeping score. All of a sudden I blow the whistle, and I say, 'OK, that's it. Everybody go home.' I close my book and walk away. How would you feel?" Ted opened his books and revealed the financial statements to his employees.

The next step was to teach employees the rules and strategies of how to "win" at making food. The first lesson: "Your opponent at Rhino is expenses. You must cut and control expenses." Ted and his staff distilled those lessons into daily scorecards—production reports and income statements—that keep Rhino's employees up-to-date on the game. At noon each day, Ted posts the previous day's results at the entrance to the production room. Everyone checks whether they made or lost money on what they produced the day before. And it's not just an academic exercise: There's a bonus check for each employee at the end of every four-week "game" that meets profitability guidelines.

Rhino has flourished since the first game. Employment has increased from 20 to 130 people, while both revenues and profits have grown dramatically.

LEARNING OBJECTIVES

1. **Prepare a worksheet.**
2. **Prepare closing entries and a post-closing trial balance.**
3. **Explain the steps in the accounting cycle and how to prepare correcting entries.**
4. **Identify the sections of a classified balance sheet.**

LEARNING OBJECTIVE 

Prepare a worksheet.

A **worksheet** is a multiple-column form used in the adjustment process and in preparing financial statements. As its name suggests, the worksheet is a working tool. **It is not a permanent accounting record.** It is neither a journal nor a part of the general ledger. The worksheet is merely a device used in preparing adjusting entries and the financial statements. Companies generally computerize worksheets using an electronic spreadsheet program such as Excel.

Illustration 4-1 shows the basic form of a worksheet and the five steps for preparing it. Each step is performed in sequence. **The use of a worksheet is optional.** When a company chooses to use one, it prepares financial statements directly from the worksheet. It enters the adjustments in the worksheet columns and then journalizes and posts the adjustments after it has prepared the financial statements. Thus, worksheets make it possible to provide the financial statements to management and other interested parties at an earlier date.

Steps in Preparing a Worksheet

We will use the October 31 trial balance and adjustment data of Pioneer Advertising from Chapter 3 to illustrate how to prepare a worksheet. In the following pages, we describe and then demonstrate each step of the process.

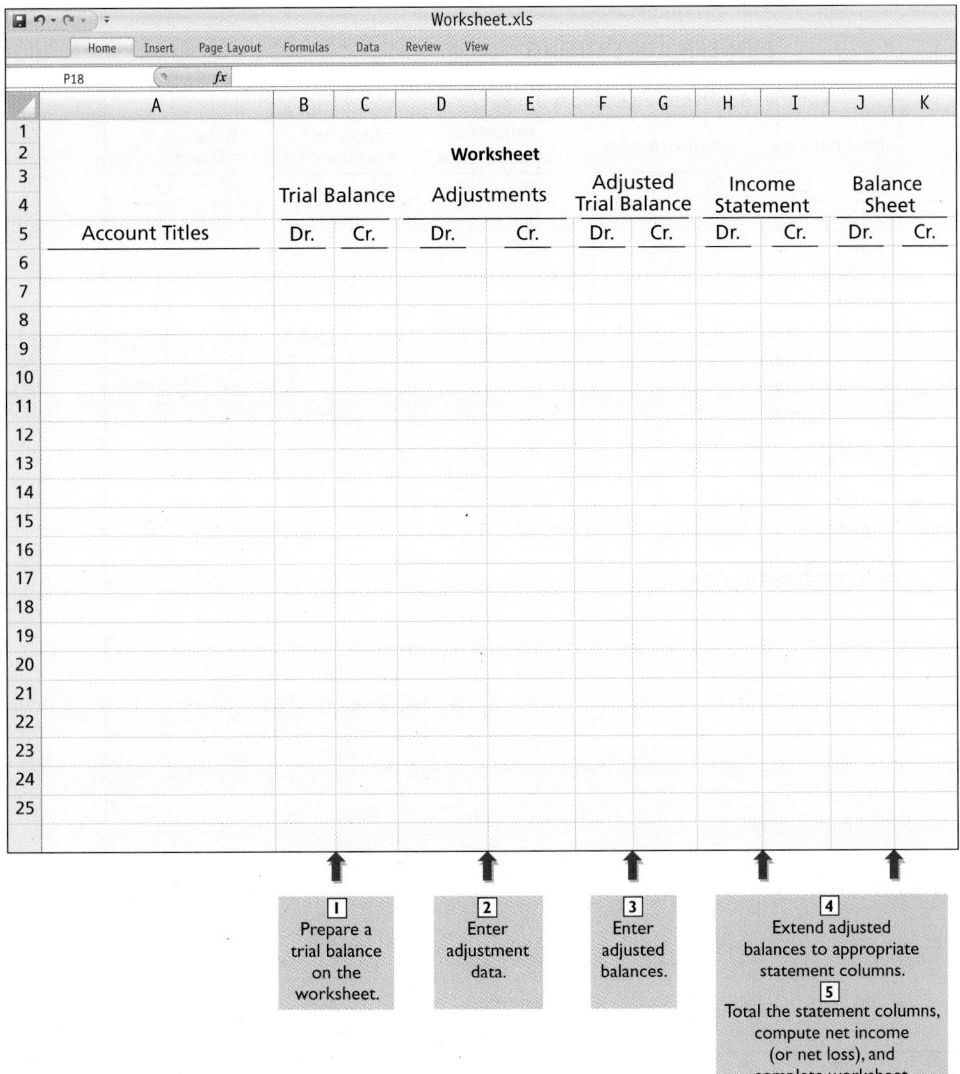

Illustration 4-1
Form and procedure for a worksheet

STEP 1: PREPARE A TRIAL BALANCE ON THE WORKSHEET

The first step in preparing a worksheet is to enter all ledger accounts with balances in the account titles column and then enter debit and credit amounts from the ledger in the trial balance columns. Illustration 4-2 shows the worksheet trial balance for Pioneer Advertising. This trial balance is the same one that appears in Illustration 2-31 (page 54) and Illustration 3-3 (page 74).

Illustration 4-2
Preparing a trial balance

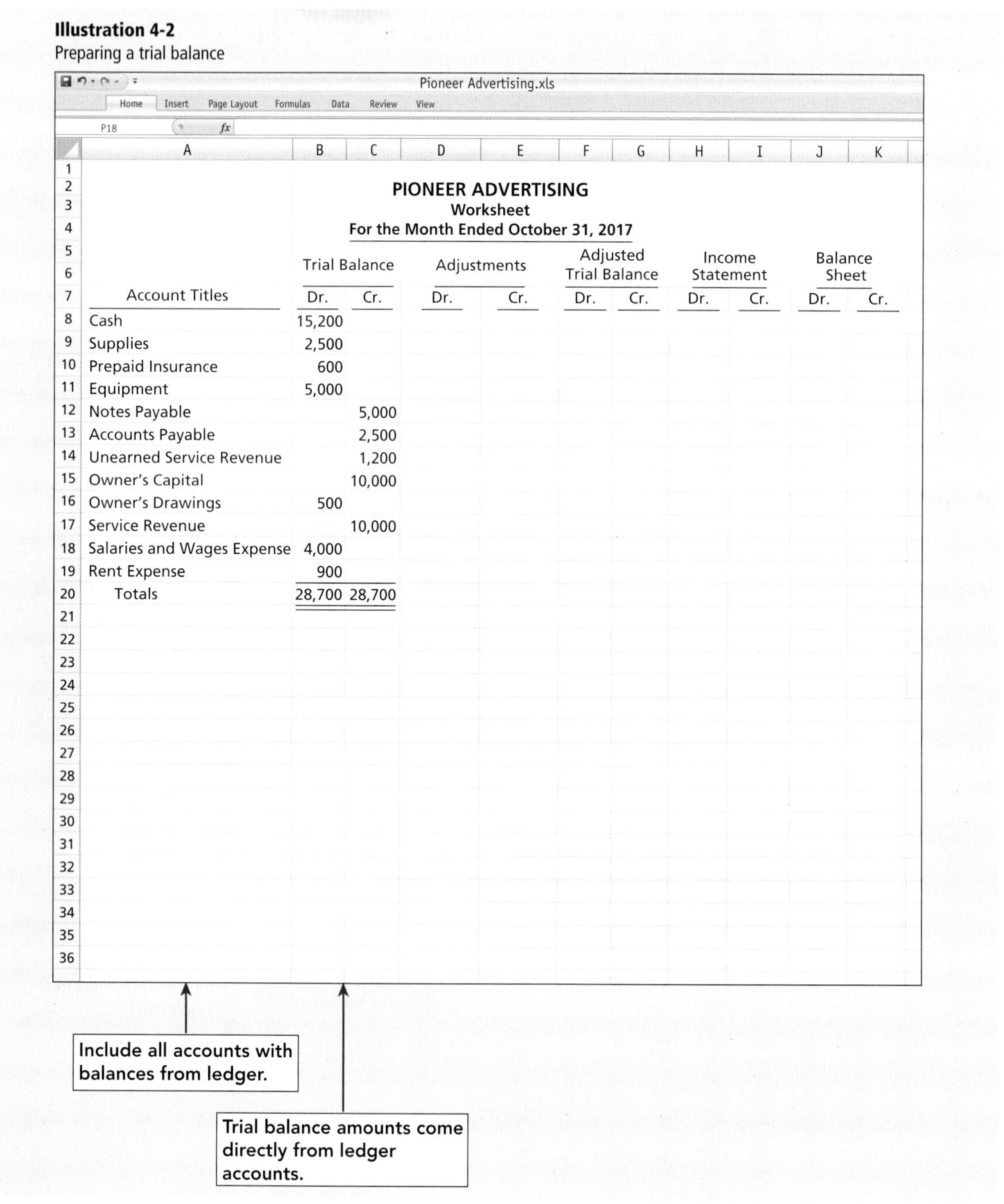

PIONEER ADVERTISING
Worksheet
For the Month Ended October 31, 2017

Account Titles	Trial Balance Dr.	Trial Balance Cr.	Adjustments Dr.	Adjustments Cr.	Adjusted Trial Balance Dr.	Adjusted Trial Balance Cr.	Income Statement Dr.	Income Statement Cr.	Balance Sheet Dr.	Balance Sheet Cr.
Cash	15,200									
Supplies	2,500									
Prepaid Insurance	600									
Equipment	5,000									
Notes Payable		5,000								
Accounts Payable		2,500								
Unearned Service Revenue		1,200								
Owner's Capital		10,000								
Owner's Drawings	500									
Service Revenue		10,000								
Salaries and Wages Expense	4,000									
Rent Expense	900									
Totals	28,700	28,700								

STEP 2: ENTER THE ADJUSTMENTS IN THE ADJUSTMENTS COLUMNS

As shown in Illustration 4-3, the second step when using a worksheet is to enter all adjustments in the adjustments columns. In entering the adjustments, use applicable trial balance accounts. If additional accounts are needed, insert them on the lines immediately below the trial balance totals. A different letter identifies the debit and credit for each adjusting entry. The term used to describe this process is **keying. Companies do not journalize the adjustments until after they complete the worksheet and prepare the financial statements.**

The adjustments for Pioneer Advertising are the same as the adjustments in Illustration 3-23 (page 86). They are keyed in the adjustments columns of the worksheet as follows.

(a) Pioneer debits an additional account, Supplies Expense, $1,500 for the cost of supplies used, and credits Supplies $1,500.

(b) Pioneer debits an additional account, Insurance Expense, $50 for the insurance that has expired, and credits Prepaid Insurance $50.

(c) The company needs two additional depreciation accounts. It debits Depreciation Expense $40 for the month's depreciation, and credits Accumulated Depreciation—Equipment $40.

(d) Pioneer debits Unearned Service Revenue $400 for services performed, and credits Service Revenue $400.

(e) Pioneer debits an additional account, Accounts Receivable, $200 for services performed but not billed, and credits Service Revenue $200.

(f) The company needs two additional accounts relating to interest. It debits Interest Expense $50 for accrued interest, and credits Interest Payable $50.

(g) Pioneer debits Salaries and Wages Expense $1,200 for accrued salaries, and credits an additional account, Salaries and Wages Payable, $1,200.

After Pioneer has entered all the adjustments, the adjustments columns are totaled to prove their equality.

Illustration 4-3A
Entering the adjustments in the adjustments columns

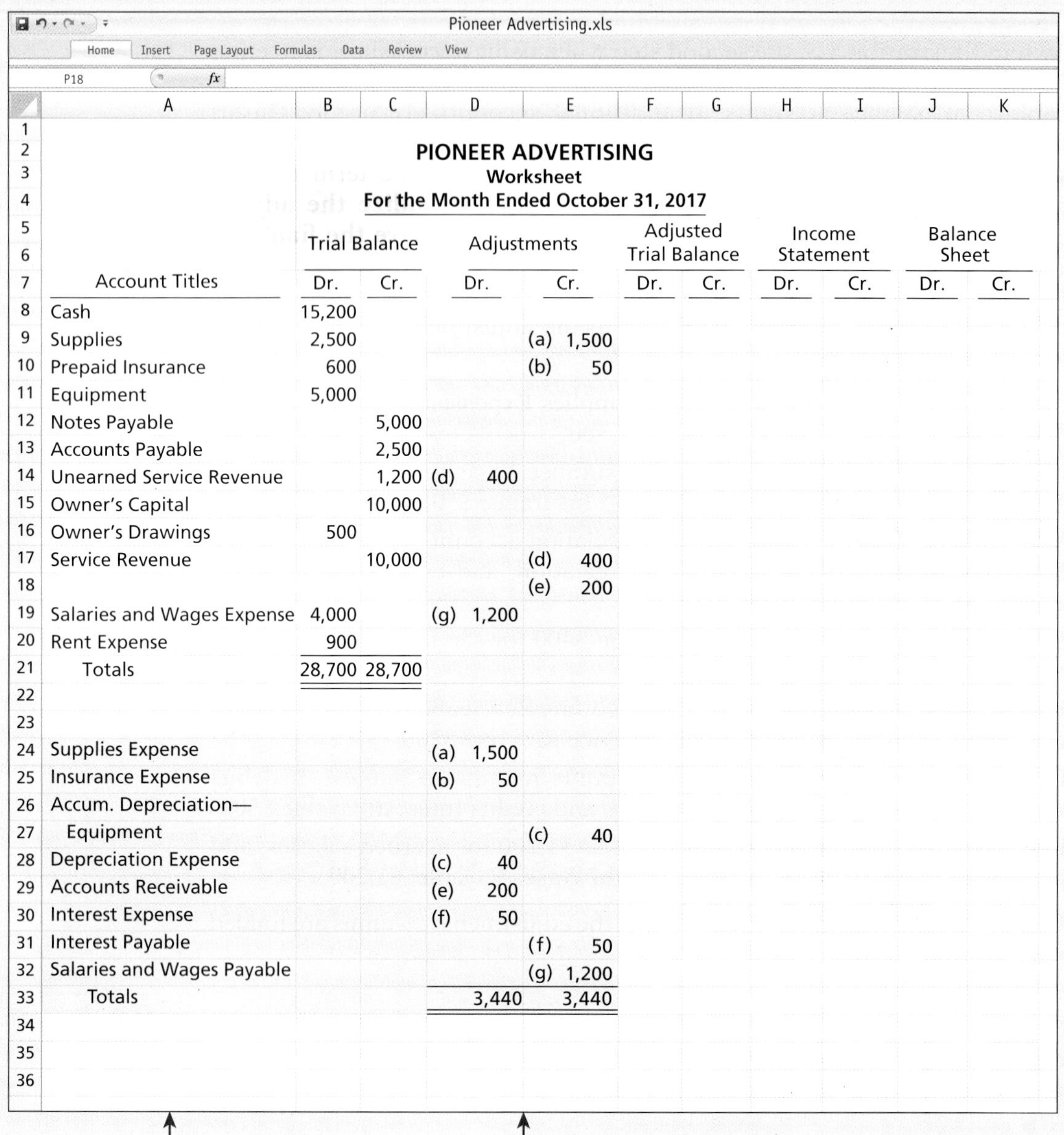
Pioneer Advertising.xls

Home Insert Page Layout Formulas Data Review View

P18 fx

PIONEER ADVERTISING
Worksheet
For the Month Ended October 31, 2017

	A	B	C	D	E	F	G	H	I	J	K
5–6		Trial Balance		Adjustments		Adjusted Trial Balance		Income Statement		Balance Sheet	
7	Account Titles	Dr.	Cr.	Dr.	Cr.	Dr.	Cr.	Dr.	Cr.	Dr.	Cr.
8	Cash	15,200									
9	Supplies	2,500			(a) 1,500						
10	Prepaid Insurance	600			(b) 50						
11	Equipment	5,000									
12	Notes Payable		5,000								
13	Accounts Payable		2,500								
14	Unearned Service Revenue		1,200	(d) 400							
15	Owner's Capital		10,000								
16	Owner's Drawings	500									
17	Service Revenue		10,000		(d) 400						
18					(e) 200						
19	Salaries and Wages Expense	4,000		(g) 1,200							
20	Rent Expense	900									
21	Totals	28,700	28,700								
22											
23											
24	Supplies Expense			(a) 1,500							
25	Insurance Expense			(b) 50							
26	Accum. Depreciation—										
27	Equipment				(c) 40						
28	Depreciation Expense			(c) 40							
29	Accounts Receivable			(e) 200							
30	Interest Expense			(f) 50							
31	Interest Payable				(f) 50						
32	Salaries and Wages Payable				(g) 1,200						
33	Totals			3,440	3,440						
34											
35											
36											

Add additional accounts as needed to complete the adjustments:
(a) Supplies Used.
(b) Insurance Expired.
(c) Depreciation Expensed.
(d) Service Revenue Recognized.
(e) Service Revenue Accrued.
(f) Interest Accrued.
(g) Salaries Accrued.

Enter adjustment amounts in appropriate columns, and use letters to cross-reference the debit and credit adjustments.

Total adjustments columns and check for equality.

STEP 3: ENTER ADJUSTED BALANCES IN THE ADJUSTED TRIAL BALANCE COLUMNS

As shown in Illustration 4-4, Pioneer Advertising next determines the adjusted balance of an account by combining the amounts entered in the first four columns of the worksheet for each account. For example, the Prepaid Insurance account in the trial balance columns has a $600 debit balance and a $50 credit in the adjustments columns. The result is a $550 debit balance recorded in the adjusted trial balance columns. **For each account, the amount in the adjusted trial balance columns is the balance that will appear in the ledger after journalizing and posting the adjusting entries.** The balances in these columns are the same as those in the adjusted trial balance in Illustration 3-25 (page 88).

After Pioneer has entered all account balances in the adjusted trial balance columns, the columns are totaled to prove their equality. If the column totals do not agree, the financial statement columns will not balance and the financial statements will be incorrect.

Illustration 4-4
Entering adjusted balances in the adjusted trial balance columns

Pioneer Advertising.xls

Home | Insert | Page Layout | Formulas | Data | Review | View

P18 | fx

PIONEER ADVERTISING
Worksheet
For the Month Ended October 31, 2017

Account Titles	Trial Balance Dr.	Trial Balance Cr.	Adjustments Dr.	Adjustments Cr.	Adjusted Trial Balance Dr.	Adjusted Trial Balance Cr.	Income Statement Dr.	Income Statement Cr.	Balance Sheet Dr.	Balance Sheet Cr.
Cash	15,200				15,200					
Supplies	2,500			(a) 1,500	1,000					
Prepaid Insurance	600			(b) 50	550					
Equipment	5,000				5,000					
Notes Payable		5,000				5,000				
Accounts Payable		2,500				2,500				
Unearned Service Revenue		1,200	(d) 400			800				
Owner's Capital		10,000				10,000				
Owner's Drawings	500				500					
Service Revenue		10,000		(d) 400		10,600				
				(e) 200						
Salaries and Wages Expense	4,000		(g) 1,200		5,200					
Rent Expense	900				900					
Totals	28,700	28,700								
Supplies Expense			(a) 1,500		1,500					
Insurance Expense			(b) 50		50					
Accum. Depreciation— Equipment				(c) 40		40				
Depreciation Expense			(c) 40		40					
Accounts Receivable			(e) 200		200					
Interest Expense			(f) 50		50					
Interest Payable				(f) 50		50				
Salaries and Wages Payable				(g) 1,200		1,200				
Totals			3,440	3,440	30,190	30,190				

Combine trial balance amounts with adjustment amounts to obtain the adjusted trial balance.

Total adjusted trial balance columns and check for equality.

STEP 4: EXTEND ADJUSTED TRIAL BALANCE AMOUNTS TO APPROPRIATE FINANCIAL STATEMENT COLUMNS

As shown in Illustration 4-5, the fourth step is to extend adjusted trial balance amounts to the income statement and balance sheet columns of the worksheet. Pioneer Advertising enters balance sheet accounts in the appropriate balance sheet debit and credit columns. For instance, it enters Cash in the balance sheet debit column, and Notes Payable in the balance sheet credit column. Pioneer extends Accumulated Depreciation—Equipment to the balance sheet credit column. The reason is that accumulated depreciation is a contra asset account with a credit balance.

Because the worksheet does not have columns for the owner's equity statement, Pioneer extends the balance in owner's capital to the balance sheet credit column. In addition, it extends the balance in owner's drawings to the balance sheet debit column because it is an owner's equity account with a debit balance.

The company enters the expense and revenue accounts such as Salaries and Wages Expense and Service Revenue in the appropriate income statement columns.

Illustration 4-5
Extending the adjusted trial balance amounts to appropriate financial statement columns

Pioneer Advertising.xls

Home Insert Page Layout Formulas Data Review View

P18 fx

PIONEER ADVERTISING
Worksheet
For the Month Ended October 31, 2017

	A	B	C	D	E	F	G	H	I	J	K
5–6		Trial Balance		Adjustments		Adjusted Trial Balance		Income Statement		Balance Sheet	
7	Account Titles	Dr.	Cr.	Dr.	Cr.	Dr.	Cr.	Dr.	Cr.	Dr.	Cr.
8	Cash	15,200				15,200				15,200	
9	Supplies	2,500			(a) 1,500	1,000				1,000	
10	Prepaid Insurance	600			(b) 50	550				550	
11	Equipment	5,000				5,000				5,000	
12	Notes Payable		5,000				5,000				5,000
13	Accounts Payable		2,500				2,500				2,500
14	Unearned Service Revenue		1,200	(d) 400			800				800
15	Owner's Capital		10,000				10,000				10,000
16	Owner's Drawings	500				500				500	
17	Service Revenue		10,000		(d) 400		10,600		10,600		
18					(e) 200						
19	Salaries and Wages Expense	4,000		(g) 1,200		5,200		5,200			
20	Rent Expense	900				900		900			
21	Totals	28,700	28,700								
22											
23											
24	Supplies Expense			(a) 1,500		1,500		1,500			
25	Insurance Expense			(b) 50		50		50			
26	Accum. Depreciation—										
27	Equipment				(c) 40		40				40
28	Depreciation Expense			(c) 40		40		40			
29	Accounts Receivable			(e) 200		200				200	
30	Interest Expense			(f) 50		50		50			
31	Interest Payable				(f) 50		50				50
32	Salaries and Wages Payable				(g) 1,200		1,200				1,200
33	Totals			3,440	3,440	30,190	30,190				
34											
35											
36											

Extend all revenue and expense account balances to the income statement columns.

Extend all asset and liability account balances, as well as owner's capital and drawings account balances, to the balance sheet columns.

STEP 5: TOTAL THE STATEMENT COLUMNS, COMPUTE THE NET INCOME (OR NET LOSS), AND COMPLETE THE WORKSHEET

As shown in Illustration 4-6, Pioneer Advertising must now total each of the financial statement columns. The net income or loss for the period is the difference between the totals of the two income statement columns. If total credits exceed total debits, the result is net income. In such a case, the company inserts the words "Net Income" in the account titles space. It then enters the amount in the income statement debit column and the balance sheet credit column. **The debit amount balances the income statement columns; the credit amount balances the balance sheet columns.** In addition, the credit in the balance sheet column indicates the increase in owner's equity resulting from net income.

What if total debits in the income statement columns exceed total credits? In that case, Pioneer has a net loss. It enters the amount of the net loss in the income statement credit column and the balance sheet debit column.

After entering the net income or net loss, Pioneer determines new column totals. The totals shown in the debit and credit income statement columns will match. So will the totals shown in the debit and credit balance sheet columns. If either the income statement columns or the balance sheet columns are not equal after the net income or net loss has been entered, there is an error in the worksheet.

Illustration 4-6 Computing net income or net loss and completing the worksheet

Home Insert Page Layout Formulas Data Review View

PIONEER ADVERTISING
Worksheet
For the Month Ended October 31, 2017

	A	B	C	D	E	F	G	H	I	J	K
5–6		Trial Balance		Adjustments		Adjusted Trial Balance		Income Statement		Balance Sheet	
7	Account Titles	Dr.	Cr.	Dr.	Cr.	Dr.	Cr.	Dr.	Cr.	Dr.	Cr.
8	Cash	15,200				15,200				15,200	
9	Supplies	2,500			(a) 1,500	1,000				1,000	
10	Prepaid Insurance	600			(b) 50	550				550	
11	Equipment	5,000				5,000				5,000	
12	Notes Payable		5,000				5,000				5,000
13	Accounts Payable		2,500				2,500				2,500
14	Unearned Service Revenue		1,200	(d) 400			800				800
15	Owner's Capital		10,000				10,000				10,000
16	Owner's Drawings	500				500				500	
17	Service Revenue		10,000		(d) 400		10,600		10,600		
18					(e) 200						
19	Salaries and Wages Expense	4,000		(g) 1,200		5,200		5,200			
20	Rent Expense	900				900		900			
21	Totals	28,700	28,700								
22											
23											
24	Supplies Expense			(a) 1,500		1,500		1,500			
25	Insurance Expense			(b) 50		50		50			
26	Accum. Depreciation—										
27	Equipment				(c) 40		40				40
28	Depreciation Expense			(c) 40		40		40			
29	Accounts Receivable			(e) 200		200				200	
30	Interest Expense			(f) 50		50		50			
31	Interest Payable				(f) 50		50				50
32	Salaries and Wages Payable				(g) 1,200		1,200				1,200
33	Totals			3,440	3,440	30,190	30,190	7,740	10,600	22,450	19,590
34											
35	Net Income							2,860			2,860
36	Totals							10,600	10,600	22,450	22,450

The difference between the totals of the two income statement columns determines net income or net loss.

Net income is extended to the credit column of the balance sheet columns. (Net loss would be extended to the debit column.)

Preparing Financial Statements From a Worksheet

After a company has completed a worksheet, it has at hand all the data required for preparation of financial statements. The income statement is prepared from the income statement columns. The balance sheet and owner's equity statement are prepared from the balance sheet columns. Illustration 4-7 shows the financial

Illustration 4-7
Financial statements from a worksheet

PIONEER ADVERTISING
Income Statement
For the Month Ended October 31, 2017

Revenues		
Service revenue		$10,600
Expenses		
Salaries and wages expense	$5,200	
Supplies expense	1,500	
Rent expense	900	
Insurance expense	50	
Interest expense	50	
Depreciation expense	40	
Total expenses		7,740
Net income		$ 2,860

PIONEER ADVERTISING
Owner's Equity Statement
For the Month Ended October 31, 2017

Owner's capital, October 1		$ -0-
Add: Investments	$10,000	
Net income	2,860	12,860
		12,860
Less: Drawings		500
Owner's capital, October 31		$12,360

PIONEER ADVERTISING
Balance Sheet
October 31, 2017

Assets		
Cash		$15,200
Accounts receivable		200
Supplies		1,000
Prepaid insurance		550
Equipment	$5,000	
Less: Accumulated depreciation—equipment	40	4,960
Total assets		$21,910
Liabilities and Owner's Equity		
Liabilities		
Notes payable	$5,000	
Accounts payable	2,500	
Interest payable	50	
Unearned service revenue	800	
Salaries and wages payable	1,200	
Total liabilities		$ 9,550
Owner's equity		
Owner's capital		12,360
Total liabilities and owner's equity		$21,910

statements prepared from Pioneer Advertising's worksheet. At this point, the company has not journalized or posted adjusting entries. Therefore, ledger balances for some accounts are not the same as the financial statement amounts.

The amount shown for owner's capital on the worksheet is the account balance **before considering drawings and net income (or loss)**. When the owner has made no additional investments of capital during the period, this worksheet amount for owner's capital is the balance at the beginning of the period.

Using a worksheet, companies can prepare financial statements before they journalize and post adjusting entries. **However, the completed worksheet is not a substitute for formal financial statements.** The format of the data in the financial statement columns of the worksheet is not the same as the format of the financial statements. **A worksheet is essentially a working tool of the accountant**; companies do not distribute it to management and other parties.

Preparing Adjusting Entries From a Worksheet

A worksheet is not a journal, and it cannot be used as a basis for posting to ledger accounts. To adjust the accounts, the company must journalize the adjustments and post them to the ledger. **The adjusting entries are prepared from the adjustments columns of the worksheet.** The reference letters in the adjustments columns and the explanations of the adjustments at the bottom of the worksheet help identify the adjusting entries. The journalizing and posting of adjusting entries **follows** the preparation of financial statements when a worksheet is used. The adjusting entries on October 31 for Pioneer Advertising are the same as those shown in Illustration 3-23 (page 86).

Prepare closing entries and a post-closing trial balance.

At the end of the accounting period, the company makes the accounts ready for the next period. This is called **closing the books**. In closing the books, the company distinguishes between temporary and permanent accounts.

Temporary accounts relate only to a given accounting period. They include all income statement accounts and the owner's drawings account. **The company closes all temporary accounts at the end of the period.**

In contrast, **permanent accounts** relate to one or more future accounting periods. They consist of all balance sheet accounts, including the owner's capital account. **Permanent accounts are not closed from period to period.** Instead, the company carries forward the balances of permanent accounts into the next accounting period. Illustration 4-8 identifies the accounts in each category.

Terminology
Temporary accounts are sometimes called *nominal accounts*, and permanent accounts are sometimes called *real accounts*.

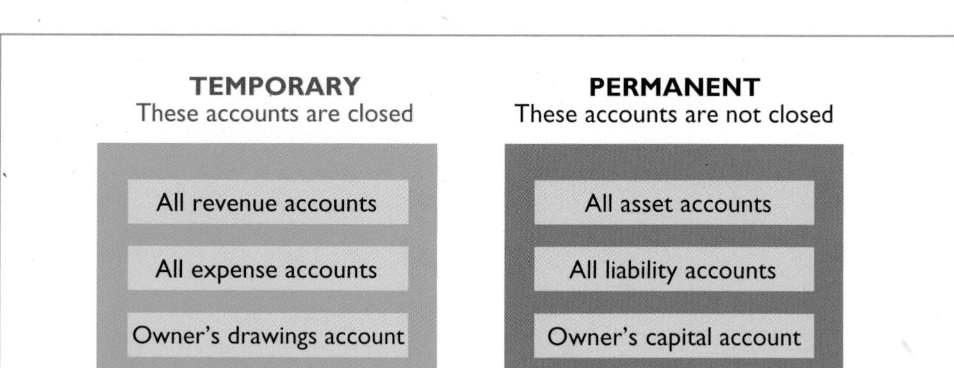

Illustration 4-8
Temporary versus permanent accounts

Preparing Closing Entries

At the end of the accounting period, the company transfers temporary account balances to the permanent owner's equity account, Owner's Capital, by means of closing entries.[1]

Closing entries formally recognize in the ledger the transfer of net income (or net loss) and owner's drawings to owner's capital. The owner's equity statement shows the results of these entries. **Closing entries also produce a zero balance in each temporary account.** The temporary accounts are then ready to accumulate data in the next accounting period separate from the data of prior periods. Permanent accounts are not closed.

Journalizing and posting closing entries is a required step in the accounting cycle. (See Illustration 4-15 on page 133.) The company performs this step after it has prepared financial statements. In contrast to the steps in the cycle that you have already studied, companies generally journalize and post closing entries **only at the end of the annual accounting period**. Thus, all temporary accounts will contain data for the entire year.

In preparing closing entries, companies could close each income statement account directly to owner's capital. However, to do so would result in excessive detail in the permanent Owner's Capital account. Instead, companies close the revenue and expense accounts to another temporary account, **Income Summary**, and they transfer the resulting net income or net loss from this account to owner's capital.

Companies **record closing entries in the general journal**. A center caption, Closing Entries, inserted in the journal between the last adjusting entry and the first closing entry, identifies these entries. Then the company posts the closing entries to the ledger accounts.

Companies generally prepare closing entries directly from the adjusted balances in the ledger. They could prepare separate closing entries for each nominal account, but the following four entries accomplish the desired result more efficiently:

1. Debit each revenue account for its balance, and credit Income Summary for total revenues.
2. Debit Income Summary for total expenses, and credit each expense account for its balance.
3. Debit Income Summary and credit Owner's Capital for the amount of net income.
4. Debit Owner's Capital for the balance in the Owner's Drawings account, and credit Owner's Drawings for the same amount.

Illustration 4-9 presents a diagram of the closing process. In it, the boxed numbers refer to the four entries required in the closing process.

[1]We explain closing entries for a partnership and for a corporation in Chapters 12 and 13, respectively.

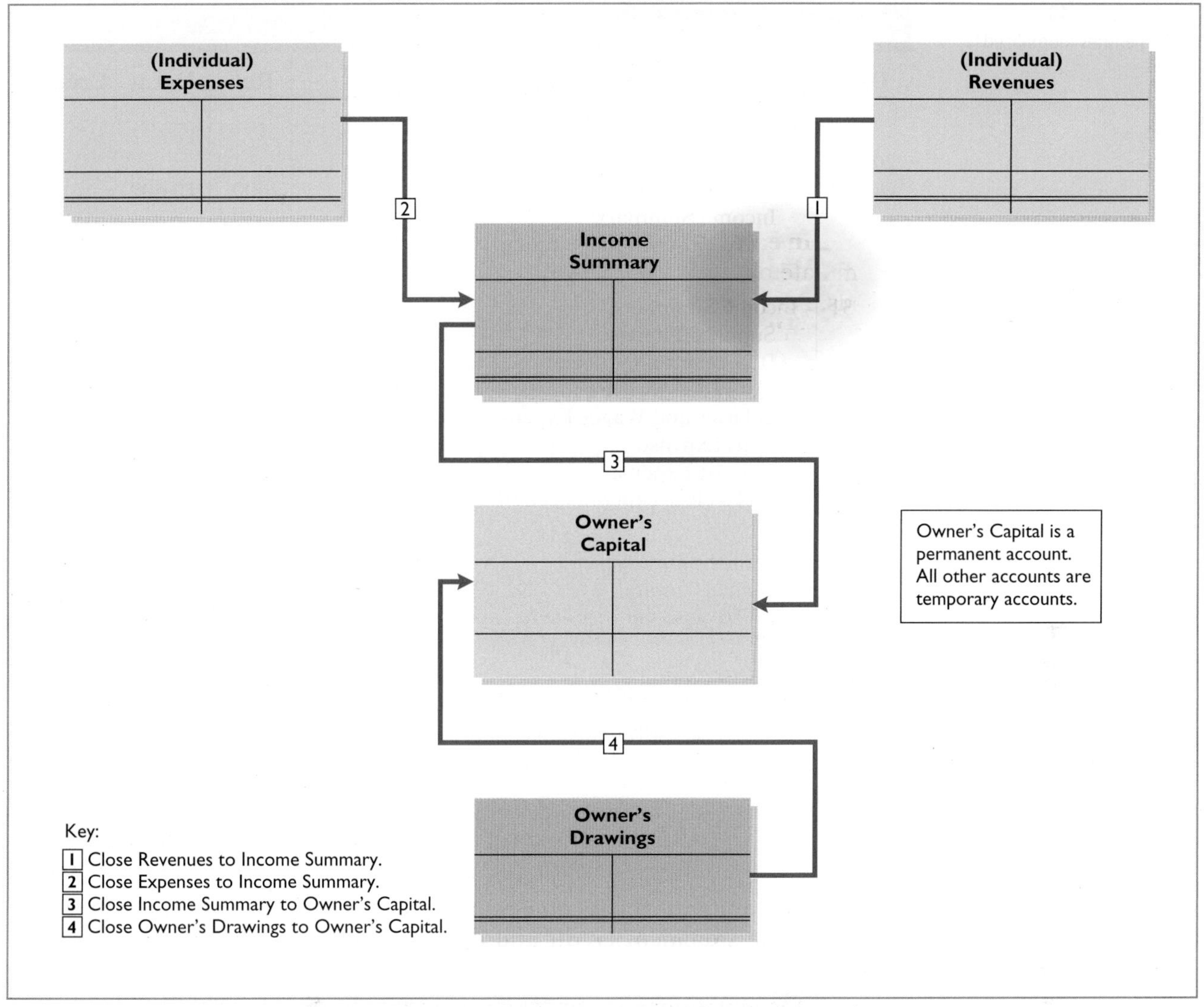

Illustration 4-9
Diagram of closing process—proprietorship

If there were a net loss (because expenses exceeded revenues), entry 3 in Illustration 4-9 would be reversed: there would be a credit to Income Summary and a debit to Owner's Capital.

CLOSING ENTRIES ILLUSTRATED

In practice, companies generally prepare closing entries only at the end of the annual accounting period. However, to illustrate the journalizing and posting of closing entries, we will assume that Pioneer Advertising closes its books monthly. Illustration 4-10 shows the closing entries at October 31. (The numbers in parentheses before each entry correspond to the four entries diagrammed in Illustration 4-9.)

Illustration 4-10
Closing entries journalized

GENERAL JOURNAL J3

Date	Account Titles and Explanation	Ref.	Debit	Credit
	Closing Entries			
2017	(1)			
Oct. 31	Service Revenue	400	10,600	
	Income Summary	350		10,600
	(To close revenue account)			
	(2)			
31	Income Summary	350	7,740	
	Supplies Expense	631		1,500
	Depreciation Expense	711		40
	Insurance Expense	722		50
	Salaries and Wages Expense	726		5,200
	Rent Expense	729		900
	Interest Expense	905		50
	(To close expense accounts)			
	(3)			
31	Income Summary	350	2,860	
	Owner's Capital	301		2,860
	(To close net income to capital)			
	(4)			
31	Owner's Capital	301	500	
	Owner's Drawings	306		500
	(To close drawings to capital)			

Note that the amounts for Income Summary in entries (1) and (2) are the totals of the income statement credit and debit columns, respectively, in the worksheet.

A couple of cautions in preparing closing entries. (1) Avoid unintentionally doubling the revenue and expense balances rather than zeroing them. (2) Do not close Owner's Drawings through the Income Summary account. **Owner's Drawings is not an expense, and it is not a factor in determining net income.**

Posting Closing Entries

Illustration 4-11 shows the posting of the closing entries and the underlining (ruling) of the accounts. Note that all temporary accounts have zero balances after posting the closing entries. In addition, notice that the balance in owner's capital (Owner's Capital) represents the total equity of the owner at the end of the accounting period. This balance is shown on the balance sheet and is the ending capital reported on the owner's equity statement, as shown in Illustration 4-7 (page 124). Pioneer Advertising uses the Income Summary account only in closing. It does not journalize and post entries to this account during the year.

As part of the closing process, Pioneer totals, balances, and double-underlines its temporary accounts—revenues, expenses, and Owner's Drawings, as shown in T-account form in Illustration 4-11 (page 129). It does not close its permanent accounts—assets, liabilities, and Owner's Capital. Instead, Pioneer draws a single underline beneath the current-period entries for the permanent accounts. The account balance is then entered below the single underline and is carried forward to the next period (for example, see Owner's Capital).

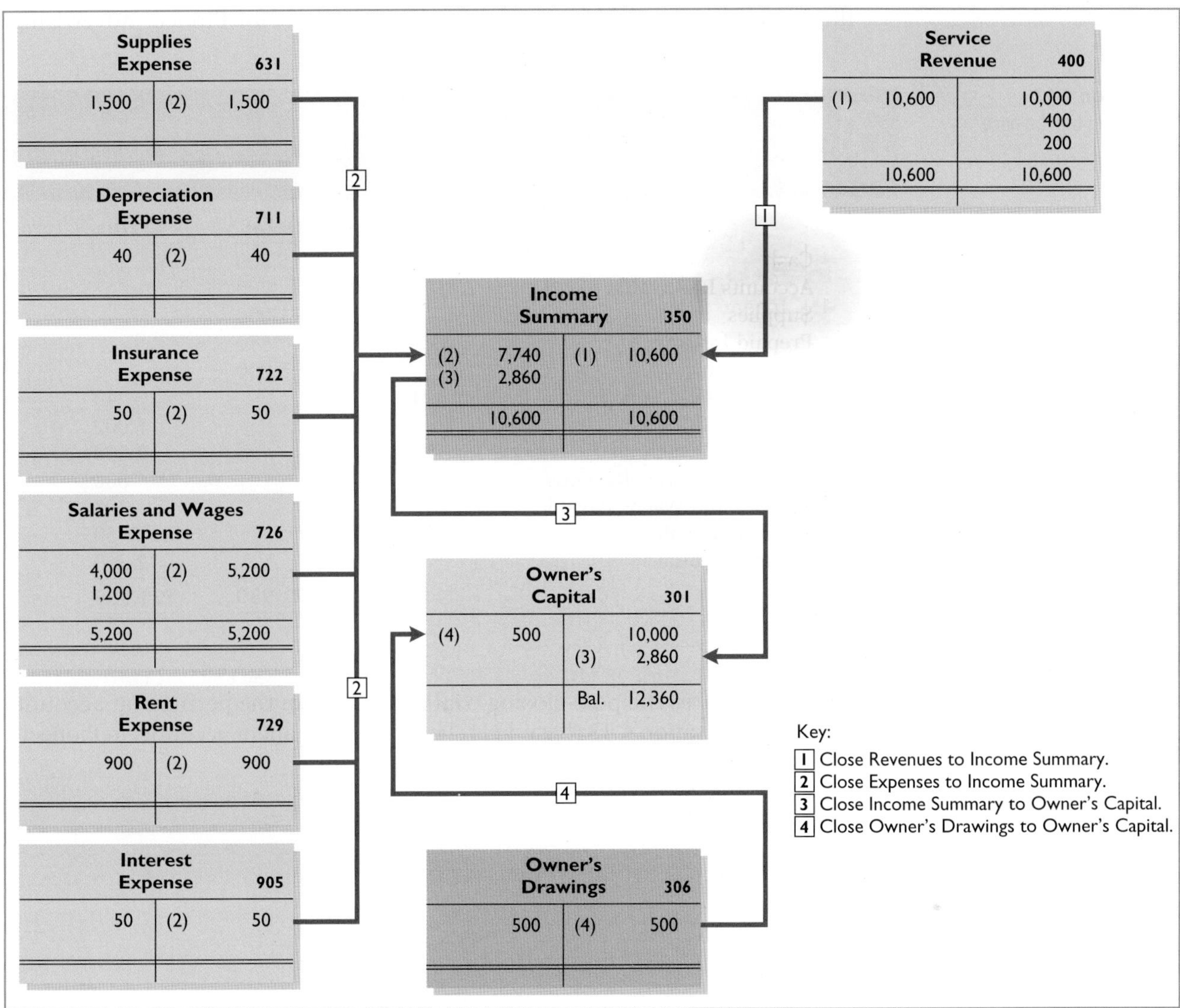

Illustration 4-11
Posting of closing entries

Preparing a Post-Closing Trial Balance

After Pioneer Advertising has journalized and posted all closing entries, it prepares another trial balance, called a **post-closing trial balance**, from the ledger. The post-closing trial balance lists permanent accounts and their balances after the journalizing and posting of closing entries. The purpose of the post-closing trial balance is **to prove the equality of the permanent account balances carried forward into the next accounting period**. Since all temporary accounts will have zero balances, **the post-closing trial balance will contain only permanent—balance sheet—accounts**.

Illustration 4-12 shows the post-closing trial balance for Pioneer Advertising.

Illustration 4-12
Post-closing trial balance

PIONEER ADVERTISING
Post-Closing Trial Balance
October 31, 2017

	Debit	Credit
Cash	$ 15,200	
Accounts Receivable	200	
Supplies	1,000	
Prepaid Insurance	550	
Equipment	5,000	
Accumulated Depreciation—Equipment		$ 40
Notes Payable		5,000
Accounts Payable		2,500
Unearned Service Revenue		800
Salaries and Wages Payable		1,200
Interest Payable		50
Owner's Capital		12,360
	$21,950	**$21,950**

Pioneer prepares the post-closing trial balance from the permanent accounts in the ledger. Illustration 4-13 (page 131) shows the permanent accounts in Pioneer's general ledger.

(Permanent Accounts Only)

GENERAL LEDGER

Cash No. 101

Date	Explanation	Ref.	Debit	Credit	Balance
2017					
Oct. 1		J1	10,000		10,000
2		J1	1,200		11,200
3		J1		900	10,300
4		J1		600	9,700
20		J1		500	9,200
26		J1		4,000	5,200
31		J1	10,000		**15,200**

Accounts Receivable No. 112

Date	Explanation	Ref.	Debit	Credit	Balance
2017					
Oct. 31	Adj. entry	J2	**200**		**200**

Supplies No. 126

Date	Explanation	Ref.	Debit	Credit	Balance
2017					
Oct. 5		J1	2,500		2,500
31	Adj. entry	J2		**1,500**	**1,000**

Prepaid Insurance No. 130

Date	Explanation	Ref.	Debit	Credit	Balance
2017					
Oct. 4		J1	600		600
31	Adj. entry	J2		**50**	**550**

Equipment No. 157

Date	Explanation	Ref.	Debit	Credit	Balance
2017					
Oct. 1		J1	5,000		**5,000**

Accumulated Depreciation—Equipment No. 158

Date	Explanation	Ref.	Debit	Credit	Balance
2017					
Oct. 31	Adj. entry	J2		**40**	**40**

Notes Payable No. 200

Date	Explanation	Ref.	Debit	Credit	Balance
2017					
Oct. 1		J1		5,000	**5,000**

Accounts Payable No. 201

Date	Explanation	Ref.	Debit	Credit	Balance
2017					
Oct. 5		J1		2,500	**2,500**

Unearned Service Revenue No. 209

Date	Explanation	Ref.	Debit	Credit	Balance
2017					
Oct. 2		J1		1,200	1,200
31	Adj. entry	J2	400		**800**

Salaries and Wages Payable No. 212

Date	Explanation	Ref.	Debit	Credit	Balance
2017					
Oct. 31	Adj. entry	J2		**1,200**	**1,200**

Interest Payable No. 230

Date	Explanation	Ref.	Debit	Credit	Balance
2017					
Oct. 31	Adj. entry	J2		**50**	**50**

Owner's Capital No. 301

Date	Explanation	Ref.	Debit	Credit	Balance
2017					
Oct. 1		J1		10,000	10,000
31	**Closing entry**	**J3**		**2,860**	**12,860**
31	**Closing entry**	**J3**	**500**		**12,360**

Note: The permanent accounts for Pioneer Advertising are shown here. Illustration 4-14 (page 132) shows the temporary accounts. Both permanent and temporary accounts are part of the general ledger. They are segregated here to aid in learning.

Illustration 4-13
General ledger, permanent accounts

A post-closing trial balance provides evidence that the company has properly journalized and posted the closing entries. It also shows that the accounting equation is in balance at the end of the accounting period. However, like the trial balance, it does not prove that Pioneer has recorded all transactions or that the ledger is correct. For example, the post-closing trial balance still will balance even if a transaction is not journalized and posted or if a transaction is journalized and posted twice.

The remaining accounts in the general ledger are temporary accounts, shown in Illustration 4-14. After Pioneer correctly posts the closing entries, each temporary account has a zero balance. These accounts are double-underlined to finalize the closing process.

(Temporary Accounts Only)

GENERAL LEDGER

Owner's Drawings — No. 306

Date	Explanation	Ref.	Debit	Credit	Balance
2017					
Oct. 20		J1	500		500
31	Closing entry	J3		500	–0–

Income Summary — No. 350

Date	Explanation	Ref.	Debit	Credit	Balance
2017					
Oct. 31	Closing entry	J3		10,600	10,600
31	Closing entry	J3	7,740		2,860
31	Closing entry	J3	2,860		–0–

Service Revenue — No. 400

Date	Explanation	Ref.	Debit	Credit	Balance
2017					
Oct. 31		J1		10,000	10,000
31	Adj. entry	J2		400	10,400
31	Adj. entry	J2		200	10,600
31	Closing entry	J3	10,600		–0–

Supplies Expense — No. 631

Date	Explanation	Ref.	Debit	Credit	Balance
2017					
Oct. 31	Adj. entry	J2	1,500		1,500
31	Closing entry	J3		1,500	–0–

Depreciation Expense — No. 711

Date	Explanation	Ref.	Debit	Credit	Balance
2017					
Oct. 31	Adj. entry	J2	40		40
31	Closing entry	J3		40	–0–

Insurance Expense — No. 722

Date	Explanation	Ref.	Debit	Credit	Balance
2017					
Oct. 31	Adj. entry	J2	50		50
31	Closing entry	J3		50	–0–

Salaries and Wages Expense — No. 726

Date	Explanation	Ref.	Debit	Credit	Balance
2017					
Oct. 26		J1	4,000		4,000
31	Adj. entry	J2	1,200		5,200
31	Closing entry	J3		5,200	–0–

Rent Expense — No. 729

Date	Explanation	Ref.	Debit	Credit	Balance
2017					
Oct. 3		J1	900		900
31	Closing entry	J3		900	–0–

Interest Expense — No. 905

Date	Explanation	Ref.	Debit	Credit	Balance
2017					
Oct. 31	Adj. entry	J2	50		50
31	Closing entry	J3		50	–0–

Note: The temporary accounts for Pioneer Advertising are shown here. Illustration 4-13 (page 131) shows the permanent accounts. Both permanent and temporary accounts are part of the general ledger. They are segregated here to aid in learning.

Illustration 4-14
General ledger, temporary accounts

Explain the steps in the accounting cycle and how to prepare correcting entries.

Summary of the Accounting Cycle

Illustration 4-15 summarizes the steps in the accounting cycle. You can see that the cycle begins with the analysis of business transactions and ends with the preparation of a post-closing trial balance.

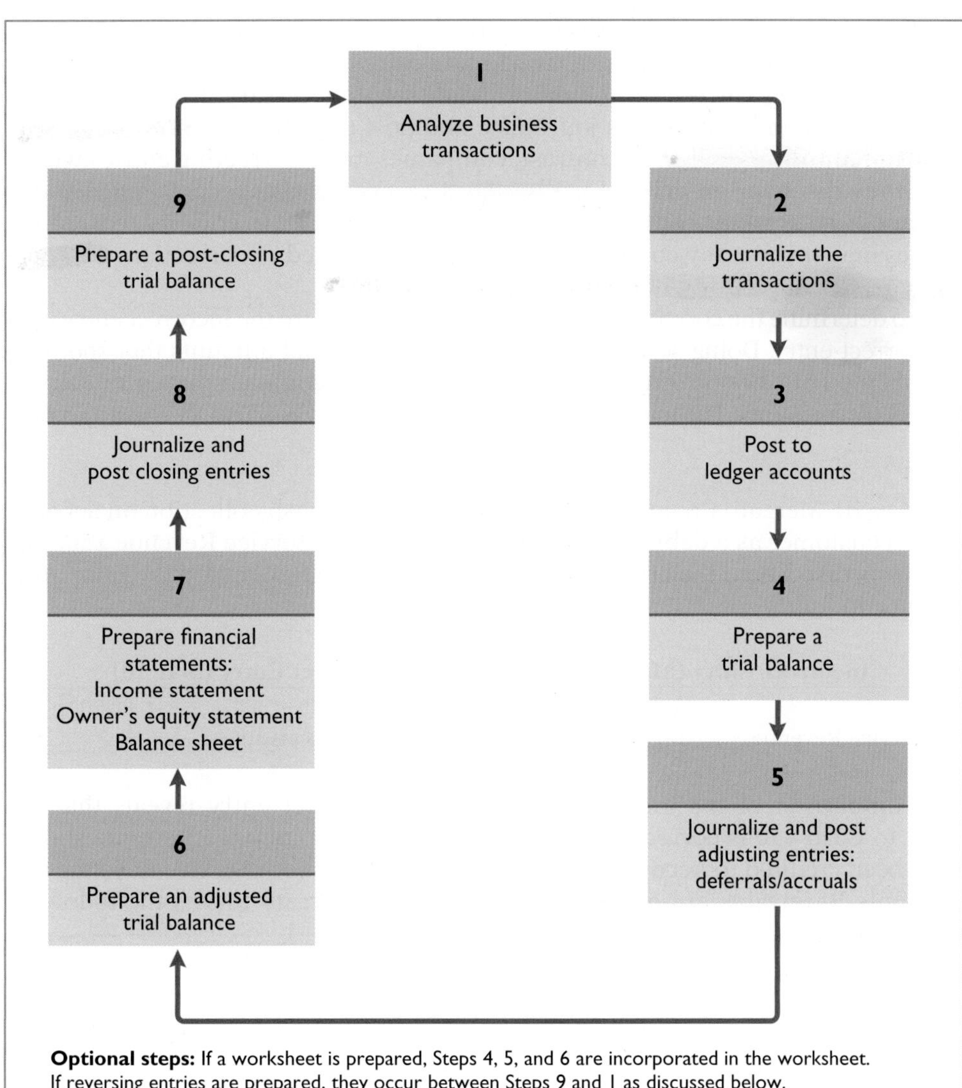

Illustration 4-15
Steps in the accounting cycle

Steps 1–3 may occur daily during the accounting period. Companies perform Steps 4–7 on a periodic basis, such as monthly, quarterly, or annually. Steps 8 and 9—closing entries and a post-closing trial balance—usually take place only at the end of a company's **annual** accounting period.

There are also two **optional steps** in the accounting cycle. As you have seen, companies may use a worksheet in preparing adjusting entries and financial statements. In addition, they may use reversing entries, as explained below.

Reversing Entries—An Optional Step

Some accountants prefer to reverse certain adjusting entries by making a **reversing entry** at the beginning of the next accounting period. A reversing entry is the exact opposite of the adjusting entry made in the previous period. **Use of reversing entries is an optional bookkeeping procedure; it is not a required step in the accounting cycle.** Accordingly, we have chosen to cover this topic in an appendix at the end of the chapter.

Correcting Entries—An Avoidable Step

Unfortunately, errors may occur in the recording process. Companies should correct errors, **as soon as they discover them**, by journalizing and posting **correcting entries**. If the accounting records are free of errors, no correcting entries are needed.

You should recognize several differences between correcting entries and adjusting entries. First, adjusting entries are an integral part of the accounting cycle. Correcting entries, on the other hand, are unnecessary if the records are error-free. Second, companies journalize and post adjustments **only at the end of an accounting period**. In contrast, companies make correcting entries **whenever they discover an error**. Finally, adjusting entries always affect at least one balance sheet account and one income statement account. In contrast, correcting entries may involve any combination of accounts in need of correction. **Correcting entries must be posted before closing entries.**

To determine the correcting entry, it is useful to compare the incorrect entry with the correct entry. Doing so helps identify the accounts and amounts that should—and should not—be corrected. After comparison, the accountant makes an entry to correct the accounts. The following two cases for Mercato Co. illustrate this approach.

CASE 1

On May 10, Mercato Co. journalized and posted a $50 cash collection on account from a customer as a debit to Cash $50 and a credit to Service Revenue $50. The company discovered the error on May 20, when the customer paid the remaining balance in full.

Illustration 4-16
Comparison of entries

Incorrect Entry (May 10)			Correct Entry (May 10)		
Cash	50		Cash	50	
Service Revenue		50	Accounts Receivable		50

Comparison of the incorrect entry with the correct entry reveals that the debit to Cash $50 is correct. However, the $50 credit to Service Revenue should have been credited to Accounts Receivable. As a result, both Service Revenue and Accounts Receivable are overstated in the ledger. Mercato makes the following correcting entry.

Illustration 4-17
Correcting entry

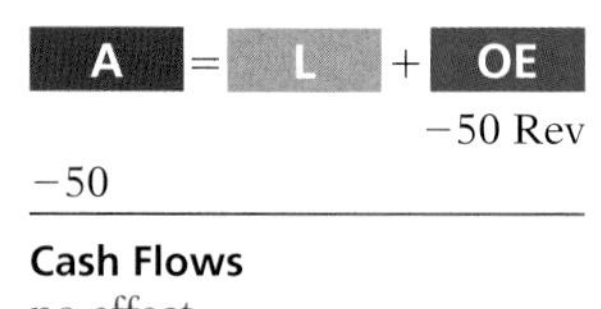

Cash Flows
no effect

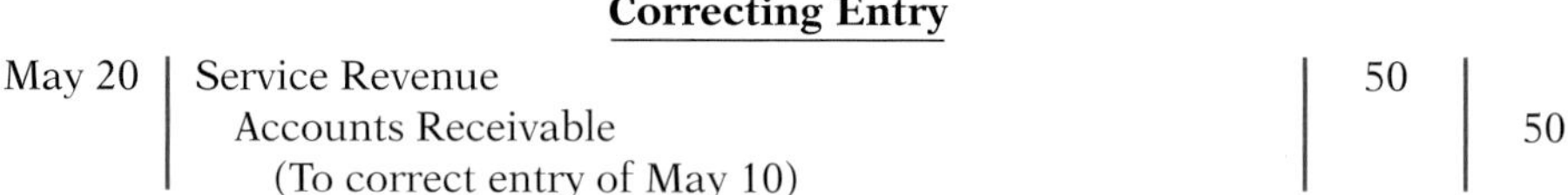

Correcting Entry

May 20	Service Revenue	50	
	Accounts Receivable		50
	(To correct entry of May 10)		

CASE 2

On May 18, Mercato purchased on account equipment costing $450. The transaction was journalized and posted as a debit to Equipment $45 and a credit to Accounts Payable $45. The error was discovered on June 3, when Mercato received the monthly statement for May from the creditor.

Illustration 4-18
Comparison of entries

Incorrect Entry (May 18)			Correct Entry (May 18)		
Equipment	45		Equipment	450	
Accounts Payable		45	Accounts Payable		450

Comparison of the two entries shows that two accounts are incorrect. Equipment is understated $405, and Accounts Payable is understated $405. Mercato makes the correcting entry shown in Illustration 4-19 (below).

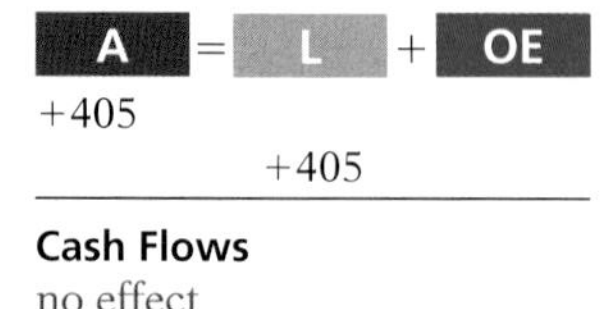

Cash Flows
no effect

Correcting Entry

June 3	Equipment	405	
	Accounts Payable		405
	(To correct entry of May 18)		

Illustration 4-19
Correcting entry

Instead of preparing a correcting entry, **it is possible to reverse the incorrect entry and then prepare the correct entry**. This approach will result in more entries and postings than a correcting entry, but it will accomplish the desired result.

LEARNING OBJECTIVE 4

Identify the sections of a classified balance sheet.

The balance sheet presents a snapshot of a company's financial position at a point in time. To improve users' understanding of a company's financial position, companies often use a classified balance sheet. A **classified balance sheet** groups together similar assets and similar liabilities, using a number of standard classifications and sections. This is useful because items within a group have similar economic characteristics. A classified balance sheet generally contains the standard classifications listed in Illustration 4-20.

Illustration 4-20 Standard balance sheet classifications

Assets	Liabilities and Owner's Equity
Current assets	Current liabilities
Long-term investments	Long-term liabilities
Property, plant, and equipment	Owner's (Stockholders') equity
Intangible assets	

These groupings help financial statement readers determine such things as (1) whether the company has enough assets to pay its debts as they come due, and (2) the claims of short- and long-term creditors on the company's total assets. Many of these groupings can be seen in the balance sheet of Franklin Company shown in Illustration 4-21 below and on the next page. In the sections that follow, we explain each of these groupings.

Illustration 4-21 Classified balance sheet

FRANKLIN COMPANY
Balance Sheet
October 31, 2017

Assets			
Current assets			
Cash		$ 6,600	
Debt investments		2,000	
Accounts receivable		7,000	
Notes receivable		1,000	
Inventory		3,000	
Supplies		2,100	
Prepaid insurance		400	
Total current assets			$22,100
Long-term investments			
Stock investments		5,200	
Investment in real estate		2,000	7,200
Property, plant, and equipment			
Land		10,000	
Equipment	$24,000		
Less: Accumulated depreciation—equipment	5,000	19,000	29,000
Intangible assets			
Patents			3,100
Total assets			$61,400

Illustration 4-21
(continued)

Liabilities and Owner's Equity		
Current liabilities		
Notes payable	$11,000	
Accounts payable	2,100	
Unearned service revenue	900	
Salaries and wages payable	1,600	
Interest payable	450	
Total current liabilities		$16,050
Long-term liabilities		
Mortgage payable	10,000	
Notes payable	1,300	
Total long-term liabilities		11,300
Total liabilities		27,350
Owner's equity		
Owner's capital		34,050
Total liabilities and owner's equity		$61,400

Current Assets

Current assets are assets that a company expects to convert to cash or use up within one year or its operating cycle, whichever is longer. In Illustration 4-21, Franklin Company had current assets of $22,100. For most businesses, the cutoff for classification as current assets is one year from the balance sheet date. For example, accounts receivable are current assets because the company will collect them and convert them to cash within one year. Supplies is a current asset because the company expects to use them up in operations within one year.

Some companies use a period longer than one year to classify assets and liabilities as current because they have an operating cycle longer than one year. The **operating cycle** of a company is the average time that it takes to purchase inventory, sell it on account, and then collect cash from customers. For most businesses, this cycle takes less than a year so they use a one-year cutoff. But for some businesses, such as vineyards or airplane manufacturers, this period may be longer than a year. **Except where noted, we will assume that companies use one year to determine whether an asset or liability is current or long-term.**

Common types of current assets are (1) cash, (2) investments (such as short-term U.S. government securities), (3) receivables (notes receivable, accounts receivable, and interest receivable), (4) inventories, and (5) prepaid expenses (supplies and insurance). **On the balance sheet, companies usually list these items in the order in which they expect to convert them into cash.**

Illustration 4-22 presents the current assets of Southwest Airlines Co.

Illustration 4-22
Current assets section

Real World

SOUTHWEST AIRLINES CO.
Balance Sheet (partial)
(in millions)

Current assets	
Cash and cash equivalents	$1,390
Short-term investments	369
Accounts receivable	241
Inventories	181
Prepaid expenses and other current assets	420
Total current assets	$2,601

As we explain later in the chapter, a company's current assets are important in assessing its short-term debt-paying ability.

Long-Term Investments

Long-term investments are generally (1) investments in stocks and bonds of other companies that are normally held for many years, (2) long-term assets such as land or buildings that a company is not currently using in its operating activities, and (3) long-term notes receivable. In Illustration 4-21, Franklin Company reported total long-term investments of $7,200 on its balance sheet.

Yahoo! Inc. reported long-term investments in its balance sheet, as shown in Illustration 4-23.

Terminology
Long-term investments are often referred to simply as *investments*.

Illustration 4-23
Long-term investments section

Real World

YAHOO! INC.
Balance Sheet (partial)
(in thousands)

Long-term investments	
Investments in securities	$90,266

Property, Plant, and Equipment

Property, plant, and equipment are assets with relatively long useful lives that a company is currently using in operating the business. This category includes land, buildings, machinery and equipment, delivery equipment, and furniture. In Illustration 4-21, Franklin Company reported property, plant, and equipment of $29,000.

Depreciation is the practice of allocating the cost of assets to a number of years. Companies do this by systematically assigning a portion of an asset's cost as an expense each year (rather than expensing the full purchase price in the year of purchase). The assets that the company depreciates are reported on the balance sheet at cost less accumulated depreciation. The **accumulated depreciation** account shows the total amount of depreciation that the company has expensed thus far in the asset's life. In Illustration 4-21, Franklin Company reported accumulated depreciation of $5,000.

Illustration 4-24 presents the property, plant, and equipment of Cooper Tire & Rubber Company.

Terminology
Property, plant, and equipment is sometimes called *fixed assets* or *plant assets*.

International Note

Recently, China adopted International Financial Reporting Standards (IFRS). This was done in an effort to reduce fraud and increase investor confidence in financial reports. Under these standards, many items, such as property, plant, and equipment, may be reported at current fair values rather than historical cost.

Illustration 4-24
Property, plant, and equipment section

Real World

COOPER TIRE & RUBBER COMPANY
Balance Sheet (partial)
(in thousands)

Property, plant, and equipment		
Land and land improvements	$ 41,553	
Buildings	298,706	
Machinery and equipment	1,636,091	
Molds, cores, and rings	268,158	$2,244,508
Less: Accumulated depreciation		1,252,692
		$ 991,816

Intangible Assets

Many companies have long-lived assets that do not have physical substance yet often are very valuable. We call these assets **intangible assets**. One significant intangible asset is goodwill. Others include patents, copyrights, and trademarks or trade names that give the company **exclusive right** of use for a specified period of time. In Illustration 4-21, Franklin Company reported intangible assets of $3,100.

Illustration 4-25 shows the intangible assets of media giant Time Warner, Inc.

Illustration 4-25
Intangible assets section

Real World

TIME WARNER, INC. Balance Sheet (partial) (in millions)	
Intangible assets	
Goodwill	$40,953
Film library	2,690
Customer lists	2,540
Cable television franchises	38,048
Sports franchises	262
Brands, trademarks, and other intangible assets	8,313
	$92,806

Current Liabilities

In the liabilities and owner's equity section of the balance sheet, the first grouping is current liabilities. **Current liabilities** are obligations that the company is to pay within the coming year or its operating cycle, whichever is longer. Common examples are accounts payable, salaries and wages payable, notes payable, interest payable, and income taxes payable. Also included as current liabilities are current maturities of long-term obligations—payments to be made within the next year on long-term obligations. In Illustration 4-21, Franklin Company reported five different types of current liabilities, for a total of $16,050.

Illustration 4-26 shows the current liabilities section adapted from the balance sheet of Marcus Corporation.

Illustration 4-26
Current liabilities section

Real World

MARCUS CORPORATION Balance Sheet (partial) (in thousands)	
Current liabilities	
Notes payable	$ 239
Accounts payable	24,242
Current maturities of long-term debt	57,250
Other current liabilities	27,477
Income taxes payable	11,215
Salaries and wages payable	6,720
Total current liabilities	$127,143

Users of financial statements look closely at the relationship between current assets and current liabilities. This relationship is important in evaluating a company's **liquidity**—its ability to pay obligations expected to be due within the next year. When current assets exceed current liabilities, the likelihood for paying the liabilities is favorable. When the reverse is true, short-term creditors may not be paid, and the company may ultimately be forced into bankruptcy.

Long-Term Liabilities

Long-term liabilities are obligations that a company expects to pay **after** one year. Liabilities in this category include bonds payable, mortgages payable, long-term notes payable, lease liabilities, and pension liabilities. Many companies report long-term debt maturing after one year as a single amount in the balance sheet and show the details of the debt in notes that accompany the financial statements. Others list the various types of long-term liabilities. In Illustration 4-21, Franklin Company reported long-term liabilities of $11,300.

Illustration 4-27 shows the long-term liabilities that **The Procter & Gamble Company** reported in its balance sheet.

Illustration 4-27
Long-term liabilities section

Real World

THE PROCTER & GAMBLE COMPANY
Balance Sheet (partial)
(in millions)

Long-term liabilities	
Long-term debt	$23,375
Deferred income taxes	12,015
Other noncurrent liabilities	5,147
Total long-term liabilities	$40,537

Owner's Equity

The content of the owner's equity section varies with the form of business organization. In a proprietorship, there is one capital account. In a partnership, there is a capital account for each partner. Corporations divide owners' equity into two accounts—Common Stock (sometimes referred to as Capital Stock) and Retained Earnings. Corporations record stockholders' investments in the company by debiting an asset account and crediting the Common Stock account. They record in the Retained Earnings account income retained for use in the business. Corporations combine the Common Stock and Retained Earnings accounts and report them on the balance sheet as **stockholders' equity**. (We discuss these corporation accounts in later chapters.) **Nordstrom, Inc.** recently reported its stockholders' equity section as follows.

Terminology
Common stock is sometimes called *capital stock*.

Illustration 4-28
Stockholders' equity section

Real World

NORDSTROM, INC.
Balance Sheet (partial)
(in thousands)

Stockholders' equity	
Common stock, 271,331 shares	$ 685,934
Retained earnings	1,406,747
Total stockholders' equity	$2,092,681

LEARNING OBJECTIVE *5

APPENDIX 4A: Prepare reversing entries.

After preparing the financial statements and closing the books, it is often helpful to reverse some of the adjusting entries before recording the regular transactions of the next period. Such entries are **reversing entries**. Companies make **a reversing entry at the beginning of the next accounting period**. Each reversing entry **is the exact opposite of the adjusting entry made in the previous period**. The recording of reversing entries is an **optional step** in the accounting cycle.

The purpose of reversing entries is to simplify the recording of a subsequent transaction related to an adjusting entry. For example, in Chapter 3 (page 83), the payment of salaries after an adjusting entry resulted in two debits: one to Salaries and Wages Payable and the other to Salaries and Wages Expense. With reversing entries, the company can debit the entire subsequent payment to Salaries and Wages Expense. **The use of reversing entries does not change the amounts**

reported in the financial statements. What it does is simplify the recording of subsequent transactions.

Reversing Entries Example

Companies most often use reversing entries to reverse two types of adjusting entries: accrued revenues and accrued expenses. To illustrate the optional use of reversing entries for accrued expenses, we will use the salaries expense transactions for Pioneer Advertising as illustrated in Chapters 2, 3, and 4. The transaction and adjustment data are as follows.

1. October 26 (initial salary entry): Pioneer pays $4,000 of salaries and wages earned between October 15 and October 26.
2. October 31 (adjusting entry): Salaries and wages earned between October 29 and October 31 are $1,200. The company will pay these in the November 9 payroll.
3. November 9 (subsequent salary entry): Salaries and wages paid are $4,000. Of this amount, $1,200 applied to accrued salaries and wages payable and $2,800 was earned between November 1 and November 9.

Illustration 4A-1 shows the entries with and without reversing entries.

Illustration 4A-1
Comparative entries—not reversing vs. reversing

Without Reversing Entries (per chapter)				**With Reversing Entries (per appendix)**			
	Initial Salary Entry				Initial Salary Entry		
Oct. 26	Salaries and Wages Expense	4,000		Oct. 26	(Same entry)		
	Cash		4,000				
	Adjusting Entry				Adjusting Entry		
Oct. 31	Salaries and Wages Expense	1,200		Oct. 31	(Same entry)		
	Salaries and Wages Payable		1,200				
	Closing Entry				Closing Entry		
Oct. 31	Income Summary	5,200		Oct. 31	(Same entry)		
	Salaries and Wages Expense		5,200				
	Reversing Entry				Reversing Entry		
Nov. 1	No reversing entry is made.			Nov. 1	**Salaries and Wages Payable**	**1,200**	
					Salaries and Wages Expense		**1,200**
	Subsequent Salary Entry				Subsequent Salary Entry		
Nov. 9	Salaries and Wages Payable	1,200		Nov. 9	**Salaries and Wages Expense**	**4,000**	
	Salaries and Wages Expense	2,800			**Cash**		**4,000**
	Cash		4,000				

The first three entries are the same whether or not Pioneer uses reversing entries. The last two entries are different. The November 1 **reversing entry** eliminates the $1,200 balance in Salaries and Wages Payable created by the October 31 adjusting entry. The reversing entry also creates a $1,200 credit balance in the Salaries and Wages Expense account. As you know, it is unusual for an expense account to have a credit balance. The balance is correct in this instance, though, because it anticipates that the entire amount of the first salaries and wages payment in the new accounting period will be debited to Salaries and Wages Expense. This debit will eliminate the credit balance. The resulting debit balance in the expense account will equal the salaries and wages expense incurred in the new accounting period ($2,800 in this example).

If Pioneer makes reversing entries, it can debit all cash payments of expenses to the expense account. This means that on November 9 (and every payday) Pioneer can debit Salaries and Wages Expense for the amount paid, without regard to any accrued salaries and wages payable. Being able to make the **same entry each time** simplifies the recording process. The company can record subsequent transactions as if the related adjusting entry had never been made.

Illustration 4A-2 shows the posting of the entries with reversing entries.

Salaries and Wages Expense

10/26 Paid	4,000	10/31 Closing	5,200
31 Adjusting	1,200		
	5,200		5,200
11/9 Paid	4,000	**11/1 Reversing**	**1,200**

Salaries and Wages Payable

11/1 Reversing	**1,200**	10/31 Adjusting	1,200

Illustration 4A-2
Postings with reversing entries

A company can also use reversing entries for accrued revenue adjusting entries. For Pioneer, the adjusting entry was Accounts Receivable (Dr.) $200 and Service Revenue (Cr.) $200. Thus, the reversing entry on November 1 is:

Nov. 1	Service Revenue	200	
	Accounts Receivable		200
	(To reverse October 31 adjusting entry)		

A	=	L	+	OE
				−200 Rev
+200				

Cash Flows
no effect

When Pioneer collects the accrued service revenue, it debits Cash and credits Service Revenue.

REVIEW AND PRACTICE

LEARNING OBJECTIVES REVIEW

1 Prepare a worksheet. The steps in preparing a worksheet are as follows. (a) Prepare a trial balance on the worksheet. (b) Enter the adjustments in the adjustments columns. (c) Enter adjusted balances in the adjusted trial balance columns. (d) Extend adjusted trial balance amounts to appropriate financial statement columns. (e) Total the statement columns, compute net income (or net loss), and complete the worksheet.

2 Prepare closing entries and a post-closing trial balance. Closing the books occurs at the end of an accounting period. The process is to journalize and post closing entries and then underline and balance all accounts. In closing the books, companies make separate entries to close revenues and expenses to Income Summary, Income Summary to Owner's Capital, and Owner's Drawings to Owner's Capital. Only temporary accounts are closed. A post-closing trial balance contains the balances in permanent accounts that are carried forward to the next accounting period. The purpose of this trial balance is to prove the equality of these balances.

3 Explain the steps in the accounting cycle and how to prepare correcting entries. The required steps in the accounting cycle are (1) analyze business transactions, (2) journalize the transactions, (3) post to ledger accounts, (4) prepare a trial balance, (5) journalize and post adjusting entries, (6) prepare an adjusted trial balance, (7) prepare financial statements, (8) journalize and post closing entries, and (9) prepare a post-closing trial balance.

One way to determine the correcting entry is to compare the incorrect entry with the correct entry. After comparison, the company makes a correcting entry to correct the accounts. An alternative to a correcting entry is to reverse the incorrect entry and then prepare the correct entry.

4 Identify the sections of a classified balance sheet. A classified balance sheet categorizes assets as current assets; long-term investments; property, plant, and equipment; and intangibles. Liabilities are classified as either current or long-term. There is also an owner's (owners') equity section, which varies with the form of business organization.

***5 Prepare reversing entries.** Reversing entries are the opposite of the adjusting entries made in the preceding period. Some companies choose to make reversing entries at the beginning of a new accounting period to simplify the recording of later transactions related to the adjusting entries. In most cases, only accrued adjusting entries are reversed.

GLOSSARY REVIEW

Classified balance sheet A balance sheet that contains standard classifications or sections.

Closing entries Entries made at the end of an accounting period to transfer the balances of temporary accounts to a permanent owner's equity account, Owner's Capital.

Correcting entries Entries to correct errors made in recording transactions.

Current assets Assets that a company expects to convert to cash or use up within one year.

Current liabilities Obligations that a company expects to pay within the coming year or its operating cycle, whichever is longer.

Income Summary A temporary account used in closing revenue and expense accounts.

Intangible assets Noncurrent assets that do not have physical substance.

Liquidity The ability of a company to pay obligations expected to be due within the next year.

Long-term investments Generally, (1) investments in stocks and bonds of other companies that companies normally hold for many years, and (2) long-term assets, such as land and buildings, not currently being used in operations.

Long-term liabilities Obligations that a company expects to pay after one year.

Operating cycle The average time that it takes to purchase inventory, sell it on account, and then collect cash from customers.

Permanent (real) accounts Accounts that relate to one or more future accounting periods. Consist of all balance sheet accounts. Balances are carried forward to the next accounting period.

Post-closing trial balance A list of permanent accounts and their balances after a company has journalized and posted closing entries.

Property, plant, and equipment Assets with relatively long useful lives and currently being used in operations.

Reversing entry An entry, made at the beginning of the next accounting period that is the exact opposite of the adjusting entry made in the previous period.

Stockholders' equity The ownership claim of shareholders on total assets. It is to a corporation what owner's equity is to a proprietorship.

Temporary (nominal) accounts Accounts that relate only to a given accounting period. Consist of all income statement accounts and owner's drawings account. All temporary accounts are closed at end of the accounting period.

Worksheet A multiple-column form that may be used in making adjusting entries and in preparing financial statements.

PRACTICE EXERCISES

Journalize and post closing entries, and prepare a post-closing trial balance.

(LO 2)

1. Hercules Company ended its fiscal year on August 31, 2017. The company's adjusted trial balance as of the end of its fiscal year is as shown below.

HERCULES COMPANY
Adjusted Trial Balance
August 31, 2017

No.	Account Titles	Debit	Credit
101	Cash	$10,900	
112	Accounts Receivable	6,200	
157	Equipment	10,600	
167	Accumulated Depr.—Equip.		$ 5,400
201	Accounts Payable		2,800
208	Unearned Rent Revenue		1,200
301	Owner's Capital		31,700
306	Owner's Drawings	12,000	
404	Service Revenue		42,400
429	Rent Revenue		6,100
711	Depreciation Expense	2,700	
720	Salaries and Wages Expense	37,100	
732	Utilities Expense	10,100	
		$89,600	$89,600

Instructions

(a) Prepare the closing entries using page J15 in a general journal.

(b) Post to Owner's Capital and No. 350 Income Summary accounts. (Use the three-column form.)

(c) Prepare a post-closing trial balance at August 31, 2017.

Solution

1. (a)

GENERAL JOURNAL — **J15**

Date	Account Titles	Ref.	Debit	Credit
Aug. 31	Service Revenue	404	42,400	
	Rent Revenue	429	6,100	
	Income Summary	350		48,500
	(To close revenue accounts)			
31	Income Summary	350	49,900	
	Salaries and Wages Expense	720		37,100
	Utilities Expense	732		10,100
	Depreciation Expense	711		2,700
	(To close expense accounts)			
31	Owner's Capital	301	1,400	
	Income Summary	350		1,400
	(To close net loss to capital)			
31	Owner's Capital	301	12,000	
	Owner's Drawings	306		12,000
	(To close drawings to capital)			

(b)

Owner's Capital — **No. 301**

Date	Explanation	Ref.	Debit	Credit	Balance
Aug. 31	Balance				31,700
31	Close net loss	J15	1,400		30,300
31	Close drawings	J15	12,000		18,300

Income Summary — **No. 350**

Date	Explanation	Ref.	Debit	Credit	Balance
Aug. 31	Close revenue	J15		48,500	48,500
31	Close expenses	J15	49,000		(1,400)
31	Close net loss	J15		1,400	0

(c)

HERCULES COMPANY
Post-Closing Trial Balance
August 31, 2017

	Debit	Credit
Cash	$10,900	
Accounts Receivable	6,200	
Equipment	10,600	
Accumulated Depreciation—Equipment		$ 5,400
Accounts Payable		2,800
Unearned Rent Revenue		1,200
Owner's Capital		18,300
	$27,700	$27,700

2. The adjusted trial balance for Hercules Company is presented in **Practice Exercise 1**.

Prepare financial statements. (LO 4)

Instructions

(a) Prepare an income statement and an owner's equity statement for the year ended August 31, 2017. Hercules did not make any capital investments during the year.

(b) Prepare a classified balance sheet at August 31, 2017.

Solution

2. (a)

HERCULES COMPANY
Income Statement
For the Year Ended August 31, 2017

Revenues		
Service revenue	$42,400	
Rent revenue	6,100	
Total revenues		$48,500
Expenses		
Salaries and wages expense	37,100	
Utilities expense	10,100	
Depreciation expense	2,700	
Total expenses		49,900
Net loss		$ (1,400)

HERCULES COMPANY
Owner's Equity Statement
For the Year Ended August 31, 2017

Owner's capital, September 1, 2016		$31,700
Less: Net loss	$ 1,400	
Owner's drawings	12,000	13,400
Owner's capital, August 31, 2017		$18,300

(b)

HERCULES COMPANY
Balance Sheet
August 31, 2017

Assets		
Current assets		
Cash	$10,900	
Accounts receivable	6,200	
Total current assets		$17,100
Property, plant, and equipment		
Equipment	10,600	
Less: Accumulated depreciation—equip.	5,400	5,200
Total assets		$22,300
Liabilities and Owner's Equity		
Current liabilities		
Accounts payable	$2,800	
Unearned rent revenue	1,200	
Total current liabilities		$ 4,000
Owner's equity		
Owner's capital		18,300
Total liabilities and owner's equity		$22,300

PRACTICE PROBLEM

Prepare worksheet and classified balance sheet, and journalize closing entries.

(LO 1, 2, 4)

At the end of its first month of operations, Pampered Pet Service has the following unadjusted trial balance.

PAMPERED PET SERVICE
August 31, 2017
Trial Balance

	Debit	Credit
Cash	$ 5,400	
Accounts Receivable	2,800	
Supplies	1,300	
Prepaid Insurance	2,400	
Equipment	60,000	
Notes Payable		$40,000
Accounts Payable		2,400
Owner's Capital		30,000
Owner's Drawings	1,000	
Service Revenue		4,900
Salaries and Wages Expense	3,200	
Utilities Expense	800	
Advertising Expense	400	
	$77,300	$77,300

Other data:

1. Insurance expires at the rate of $200 per month.
2. $1,000 of supplies are on hand at August 31.
3. Monthly depreciation on the equipment is $900.
4. Interest of $500 on the notes payable has accrued during August.

Instructions

(a) Prepare a worksheet.

(b) Prepare a classified balance sheet assuming $35,000 of the notes payable are long-term.

(c) Journalize the closing entries.

Solution

(a)

PAMPERED PET SERVICE
Worksheet for the Month Ended August 31, 2017

Account Titles	Trial Balance Dr.	Trial Balance Cr.	Adjustments Dr.	Adjustments Cr.	Adjusted Trial Balance Dr.	Adjusted Trial Balance Cr.	Income Statement Dr.	Income Statement Cr.	Balance Sheet Dr.	Balance Sheet Cr.
Cash	5,400				5,400				5,400	
Accounts Receivable	2,800				2,800				2,800	
Supplies	1,300			(b) 300	1,000				1,000	
Prepaid Insurance	2,400			(a) 200	2,200				2,200	
Equipment	60,000				60,000				60,000	
Notes Payable		40,000				40,000				40,000
Accounts Payable		2,400				2,400				2,400
Owner's Capital		30,000				30,000				30,000
Owner's Drawings	1,000				1,000				1,000	
Service Revenue		4,900				4,900		4,900		
Salaries and Wages Expense	3,200				3,200		3,200			
Utilities Expense	800				800		800			
Advertising Expense	400				400		400			
Totals	77,300	77,300								
Insurance Expense			(a) 200		200		200			
Supplies Expense			(b) 300		300		300			
Depreciation Expense			(c) 900		900		900			
Accumulated Depreciation—Equipment				(c) 900		900				900
Interest Expense			(d) 500		500		500			
Interest Payable				(d) 500		500				500
Totals			1,900	1,900	78,700	78,700	6,300	4,900	72,400	73,800
Net Loss								1,400	1,400	
Totals							6,300	6,300	73,800	73,800

Explanation: (a) insurance expired, (b) supplies used, (c) depreciation expensed, and (d) interest accrued.

(b)

PAMPERED PET SERVICE Balance Sheet August 31, 2017		
Assets		
Current assets		
Cash	$ 5,400	
Accounts receivable	2,800	
Supplies	1,000	
Prepaid insurance	2,200	
Total current assets		$11,400
Property, plant, and equipment		
Equipment	60,000	
Less: Accumulated depreciation—equipment	900	59,100
Total assets		$70,500
Liabilities and Owner's Equity		
Current liabilities		
Notes payable	$ 5,000	
Accounts payable	2,400	
Interest payable	500	
Total current liabilities		$ 7,900
Long-term liabilities		
Notes payable		35,000
Total liabilities		42,900
Owner's equity		
Owner's capital		27,600*
Total liabilities and owner's equity		$70,500

*Owner's capital $30,000 less drawings $1,000 and net loss $1,400.

(c)

Date	Account Titles and Explanation	Debit	Credit
Aug. 31	Service Revenue	4,900	
	Income Summary		4,900
	(To close revenue account)		
31	Income Summary	6,300	
	Salaries and Wages Expense		3,200
	Depreciation Expense		900
	Utilities Expense		800
	Interest Expense		500
	Advertising Expense		400
	Supplies Expense		300
	Insurance Expense		200
	(To close expense accounts)		
31	Owner's Capital	1,400	
	Income Summary		1,400
	(To close net loss to capital)		
31	Owner's Capital	1,000	
	Owner's Drawings		1,000
	(To close drawings to capital)		

EXERCISES

Complete the worksheet.
(LO 1)

E4-1 The trial balance columns of the worksheet for Dixon Company at June 30, 2017, are as follows.

DIXON COMPANY
Worksheet
For the Month Ended June 30, 2017

Account Titles	Trial Balance Dr.	Trial Balance Cr.
Cash	2,320	
Accounts Receivable	2,440	
Supplies	1,880	
Accounts Payable		1,120
Unearned Service Revenue		240
Owner's Capital		3,600
Service Revenue		2,400
Salaries and Wages Expense	560	
Miscellaneous Expense	160	
	7,360	7,360

Other data:

1. A physical count reveals $500 of supplies on hand.
2. $100 of the unearned revenue is still unearned at month-end.
3. Accrued salaries are $210.

Instructions
Enter the trial balance on a worksheet and complete the worksheet.

Complete the worksheet.
(LO 1)

E4-2 The adjusted trial balance columns of the worksheet for Savaglia Company are as follows.

SAVAGLIA COMPANY
Worksheet (partial)
For the Month Ended April 30, 2017

Account Titles	Adjusted Trial Balance Dr.	Adjusted Trial Balance Cr.	Income Statement Dr.	Income Statement Cr.	Balance Sheet Dr.	Balance Sheet Cr.
Cash	10,000					
Accounts Receivable	7,840					
Prepaid Rent	2,280					
Equipment	23,050					
Accumulated Depreciation—Equip.		4,900				
Notes Payable		5,700				
Accounts Payable		4,920				
Owner's Capital		27,960				
Owner's Drawings	3,650					
Service Revenue		15,590				
Salaries and Wages Expense	10,840					
Rent Expense	760					
Depreciation Expense	650					
Interest Expense	57					
Interest Payable		57				
Totals	59,127	59,127				

Instructions
Complete the worksheet.

Prepare financial statements from worksheet.
(LO 1, 4)

E4-3 Worksheet data for Savaglia Company are presented in E4-2. The owner did not make any additional investments in the business in April.

Instructions
Prepare an income statement, an owner's equity statement, and a classified balance sheet.

Journalize and post closing entries and prepare a post-closing trial balance.
(LO 2)

E4-4 Worksheet data for Savaglia Company are presented in E4-2.

Instructions
(a) Journalize the closing entries at April 30.
(b) Post the closing entries to Income Summary and Owner's Capital. Use T-accounts.
(c) Prepare a post-closing trial balance at April 30.

Prepare adjusting entries from a worksheet, and extend balances to worksheet columns.
(LO 1)

E4-5 The adjustments columns of the worksheet for Becker Company are shown below.

Account Titles	Adjustments	
	Debit	Credit
Accounts Receivable	1,100	
Prepaid Insurance		300
Accumulated Depreciation—Equipment		900
Salaries and Wages Payable		500
Service Revenue		1,100
Salaries and Wages Expense	500	
Insurance Expense	300	
Depreciation Expense	900	
	2,800	2,800

Instructions
(a) Prepare the adjusting entries.
(b) Assuming the adjusted trial balance amount for each account is normal, indicate the financial statement column to which each balance should be extended.

Derive adjusting entries from worksheet data.
(LO 1)

E4-6 Selected worksheet data for Rosa Company are presented below.

Account Titles	Trial Balance		Adjusted Trial Balance	
	Dr.	Cr.	Dr.	Cr.
Accounts Receivable	?		34,000	
Prepaid Insurance	26,000		20,000	
Supplies	7,000		?	
Accumulated Depreciation—Equipment		12,000		?
Salaries and Wages Payable		?		5,600
Service Revenue		88,000		97,000
Insurance Expense			?	
Depreciation Expense			10,000	
Supplies Expense			4,500	
Salaries and Wages Expense	?		49,000	

Instructions
(a) Fill in the missing amounts.
(b) Prepare the adjusting entries that were made.

Prepare closing entries, and prepare a post-closing trial balance.
(LO 2)

E4-7 Victoria Lee Company had the following adjusted trial balance.

VICTORIA LEE COMPANY
Adjusted Trial Balance
For the Month Ended June 30, 2017

Account Titles	Adjusted Trial Balance Debit	Credit
Cash	$ 3,712	
Accounts Receivable	3,904	
Supplies	480	
Accounts Payable		$ 1,382
Unearned Service Revenue		160
Owner's Capital		5,760
Owner's Drawings	550	
Service Revenue		4,300
Salaries and Wages Expense	1,260	
Miscellaneous Expense	256	
Supplies Expense	1,900	
Salaries and Wages Payable		460
	$12,062	$12,062

Instructions

(a) Prepare closing entries at June 30, 2017.
(b) Prepare a post-closing trial balance.

Journalize and post closing entries, and prepare a post-closing trial balance.

(LO 2)

E4-8 Okabe Company ended its fiscal year on July 31, 2017. The company's adjusted trial balance as of the end of its fiscal year is shown below.

OKABE COMPANY
Adjusted Trial Balance
July 31, 2017

No.	Account Titles	Debit	Credit
101	Cash	$ 9,840	
112	Accounts Receivable	8,780	
157	Equipment	15,900	
158	Accumulated Depreciation—Equip.		$ 7,400
201	Accounts Payable		4,220
208	Unearned Rent Revenue		1,800
301	Owner's Capital		45,200
306	Owner's Drawings	16,000	
400	Service Revenue		64,000
429	Rent Revenue		6,500
711	Depreciation Expense	8,000	
726	Salaries and Wages Expense	55,700	
732	Utilities Expense	14,900	
		$129,120	$129,120

Instructions

(a) Prepare the closing entries using page J15.
(b) Post to Owner's Capital and No. 350 Income Summary accounts. (Use the three-column form.)
(c) Prepare a post-closing trial balance at July 31.

Prepare financial statements.

(LO 4)

E4-9 The adjusted trial balance for Okabe Company is presented in E4-8.

Instructions

(a) Prepare an income statement and an owner's equity statement for the year. Okabe did not make any capital investments during the year.
(b) Prepare a classified balance sheet at July 31.

E4-10 Renee Davis has prepared the following list of statements about the accounting cycle.

Answer questions related to the accounting cycle.
(LO 3)

1. "Journalize the transactions" is the first step in the accounting cycle.
2. Reversing entries are a required step in the accounting cycle.
3. Correcting entries do not have to be part of the accounting cycle.
4. If a worksheet is prepared, some steps of the accounting cycle are incorporated into the worksheet.
5. The accounting cycle begins with the analysis of business transactions and ends with the preparation of a post-closing trial balance.
6. All steps of the accounting cycle occur daily during the accounting period.
7. The step of "post to the ledger accounts" occurs before the step of "journalize the transactions."
8. Closing entries must be prepared before financial statements can be prepared.

Instructions
Identify each statement as true or false. If false, indicate how to correct the statement.

E4-11 Selected accounts for Tamora's Salon are presented below. All June 30 postings are from closing entries.

Prepare closing entries.
(LO 2)

Salaries and Wages Expense			
6/10	3,200	6/30	8,800
6/28	5,600		

Service Revenue			
6/30	18,100	6/15	9,700
		6/24	8,400

Owner's Capital			
6/30	2,100	6/1	12,000
		6/30	5,000
		Bal.	14,900

Supplies Expense			
6/12	600	6/30	1,300
6/24	700		

Rent Expense			
6/1	3,000	6/30	3,000

Owner's Drawings			
6/13	1,000	6/30	2,100
6/25	1,100		

Instructions
(a) Prepare the closing entries that were made.
(b) Post the closing entries to Income Summary.

E4-12 Noah Bahr Company discovered the following errors made in January 2017.

Prepare correcting entries.
(LO 3)

1. A payment of Salaries and Wages Expense of $700 was debited to Equipment and credited to Cash, both for $700.
2. A collection of $1,000 from a client on account was debited to Cash $100 and credited to Service Revenue $100.
3. The purchase of equipment on account for $760 was debited to Equipment $670 and credited to Accounts Payable $670.

Instructions
(a) Correct the errors by reversing the incorrect entry and preparing the correct entry.
(b) Correct the errors without reversing the incorrect entry.

E4-13 Patel Company has an inexperienced accountant. During the first 2 weeks on the job, the accountant made the following errors in journalizing transactions. All entries were posted as made.

Prepare correcting entries.
(LO 3)

1. A payment on account of $750 to a creditor was debited to Accounts Payable $570 and credited to Cash $570.
2. The purchase of supplies on account for $560 was debited to Equipment $56 and credited to Accounts Payable $56.
3. A $500 withdrawal of cash for N. Patel's personal use was debited to Salaries and Wages Expense $500 and credited to Cash $500.

Instructions
Prepare the correcting entries.

E4-14 The adjusted trial balance for McCoy Bowling Alley at December 31, 2017, contains the following accounts.

Prepare a classified balance sheet.
(LO 4)

	Debit		Credit
Buildings	$128,800	Owner's Capital	$115,000
Accounts Receivable	14,520	Accumulated Depreciation—Buildings	42,600
Prepaid Insurance	4,680	Accounts Payable	12,300
Cash	18,040	Notes Payable	97,780
Equipment	62,400	Accumulated Depreciation—Equipment	18,720
Land	67,000	Interest Payable	3,800
Insurance Expense	780	Service Revenue	17,180
Depreciation Expense	7,360		$307,380
Interest Expense	3,800		
	$307,380		

Instructions

(a) Prepare a classified balance sheet; assume that $20,000 of the note payable will be paid in 2018.

(b) Comment on the liquidity of the company.

Classify accounts on balance sheet.

(LO 4)

E4-15 The following are the major balance sheet classifications.

Current assets (CA)	Current liabilities (CL)
Long-term investments (LTI)	Long-term liabilities (LTL)
Property, plant, and equipment (PPE)	Owner's equity (OE)
Intangible assets (IA)	

Instructions

Classify each of the following accounts taken from Faust Company's balance sheet.

________	Accounts payable	________	Accumulated depreciation—equipment
________	Accounts receivable	________	Buildings
________	Cash	________	Land (in use)
________	Owner's capital	________	Notes payable (due in 2 years)
________	Patents	________	Supplies
________	Salaries and wages payable	________	Equipment
________	Inventory	________	Prepaid expenses
________	Stock investments (to be sold in 7 months)		

Prepare a classified balance sheet.

(LO 4)

E4-16 The following items were taken from the financial statements of J. Pineda Company. (All amounts are in thousands.)

Long-term debt	$ 1,000	Accumulated depreciation—equipment	$ 5,655
Prepaid insurance	880	Accounts payable	1,444
Equipment	11,500	Notes payable (due after 2018)	400
Stock investments (long-term)	264	Owner's capital	12,955
Debt investments (short-term)	3,690	Accounts receivable	1,696
Notes payable (due in 2018)	500	Inventory	1,256
Cash	2,668		

Instructions

Prepare a classified balance sheet in good form as of December 31, 2017.

Prepare financial statements.

(LO 4)

E4-17 These financial statement items are for Basten Company at year-end, July 31, 2017.

Salaries and wages payable	$ 2,080	Notes payable (long-term)	$ 1,800
Salaries and wages expense	48,700	Cash	14,200
Utilities expense	22,600	Accounts receivable	9,780
Equipment	34,400	Accumulated depreciation—equipment	6,000
Accounts payable	4,100	Owner's drawings	3,000
Service revenue	63,000	Depreciation expense	4,000
Rent revenue	8,500	Owner's capital (beginning of the year)	51,200

Instructions

(a) Prepare an income statement and an owner's equity statement for the year. The owner did not make any new investments during the year.

(b) Prepare a classified balance sheet at July 31.

***E4-18** Lovrek Company pays salaries of $12,000 every Monday for the preceding 5-day week (Monday through Friday). Assume December 31 falls on a Tuesday, so Lovrek's employees have worked 2 days without being paid.

Use reversing entries.

(LO 5)

Instructions

(a) Assume the company does not use reversing entries. Prepare the December 31 adjusting entry and the entry on Monday, January 6, when Lovrek pays the payroll.
(b) Assume the company does use reversing entries. Prepare the December 31 adjusting entry, the January 1 reversing entry, and the entry on Monday, January 6, when Lovrek pays the payroll.

***E4-19** On December 31, the adjusted trial balance of Shihata Employment Agency shows the following selected data.

Prepare closing and reversing entries.

(LO 2, 5)

Accounts Receivable	$24,500	Service Revenue	$92,500
Interest Expense	7,700	Interest Payable	2,200

Analysis shows that adjusting entries were made to (1) accrue $5,000 of service revenue and (2) accrue $2,200 interest expense.

Instructions

(a) Prepare the closing entries for the temporary accounts shown above at December 31.
(b) Prepare the reversing entries on January 1.
(c) Post the entries in (a) and (b). Underline and balance the accounts. (Use T-accounts.)
(d) Prepare the entries to record (1) the collection of the accrued revenue on January 10 and (2) the payment of all interest due ($3,000) on January 15.
(e) Post the entries in (d) to the temporary accounts.

PROBLEMS

P4-1A The trial balance columns of the worksheet for Warren Roofing at March 31, 2017, are as follows.

Prepare a worksheet, financial statements, and adjusting and closing entries.

(LO 1, 2, 4)

WARREN ROOFING
Worksheet
For the Month Ended March 31, 2017

Account Titles	Trial Balance Dr.	Trial Balance Cr.
Cash	4,500	
Accounts Receivable	3,200	
Supplies	2,000	
Equipment	11,000	
Accumulated Depreciation—Equipment		1,250
Accounts Payable		2,500
Unearned Service Revenue		550
Owner's Capital		12,900
Owner's Drawings	1,100	
Service Revenue		6,300
Salaries and Wages Expense	1,300	
Miscellaneous Expense	400	
	23,500	23,500

Other data:

1. A physical count reveals only $480 of roofing supplies on hand.
2. Depreciation for March is $250.
3. Unearned revenue amounted to $260 at March 31.
4. Accrued salaries are $700.

(a) Adjusted trial balance $24,450
(b) Net income $2,420
Total assets $17,680

Instructions

(a) Enter the trial balance on a worksheet and complete the worksheet.
(b) Prepare an income statement and owner's equity statement for the month of March and a classified balance sheet at March 31. T. Warren made an additional investment in the business of $10,000 in March.
(c) Journalize the adjusting entries from the adjustments columns of the worksheet.
(d) Journalize the closing entries from the financial statement columns of the worksheet.

Complete worksheet; prepare financial statements, closing entries, and post-closing trial balance.

(LO 1, 2, 4)

P4-2A The adjusted trial balance columns of the worksheet for Thao Company, owned by D. Thao, are as follows.

THAO COMPANY
Worksheet
For the Year Ended December 31, 2017

Account No.	Account Titles	Adjusted Trial Balance Dr.	Cr.
101	Cash	5,300	
112	Accounts Receivable	10,800	
126	Supplies	1,500	
130	Prepaid Insurance	2,000	
157	Equipment	27,000	
158	Accumulated Depreciation—Equipment		5,600
200	Notes Payable		15,000
201	Accounts Payable		6,100
212	Salaries and Wages Payable		2,400
230	Interest Payable		600
301	Owner's Capital		13,000
306	Owner's Drawings	7,000	
400	Service Revenue		61,000
610	Advertising Expense	8,400	
631	Supplies Expense	4,000	
711	Depreciation Expense	5,600	
722	Insurance Expense	3,500	
726	Salaries and Wages Expense	28,000	
905	Interest Expense	600	
	Totals	103,700	103,700

(a) Net income $10,900
(b) Current assets $19,600
Current liabilities $14,100
(e) Post-closing trial balance $46,600

Instructions

(a) Complete the worksheet by extending the balances to the financial statement columns.
(b) Prepare an income statement, owner's equity statement, and a classified balance sheet. (*Note:* $5,000 of the notes payable become due in 2018.) D. Thao did not make any additional investments in the business during the year.
(c) Prepare the closing entries. Use J14 for the journal page.
(d) Post the closing entries. Use the three-column form of account. Income Summary is No. 350.
(e) Prepare a post-closing trial balance.

Prepare financial statements, closing entries, and post-closing trial balance.

(LO 1, 2, 4)

P4-3A The completed financial statement columns of the worksheet for Bray Company are shown as follows.

BRAY COMPANY
Worksheet
For the Year Ended December 31, 2017

Account No.	Account Titles	Income Statement Dr.	Income Statement Cr.	Balance Sheet Dr.	Balance Sheet Cr.
101	Cash			8,800	
112	Accounts Receivable			10,800	
130	Prepaid Insurance			2,800	
157	Equipment			24,000	
158	Accumulated Depreciation—Equip.				4,200
201	Accounts Payable				9,000
212	Salaries and Wages Payable				2,400
301	Owner's Capital				19,500
306	Owner's Drawings			11,000	
400	Service Revenue		60,000		
622	Maintenance and Repairs Expense	1,700			
711	Depreciation Expense	2,800			
722	Insurance Expense	1,800			
726	Salaries and Wages Expense	30,000			
732	Utilities Expense	1,400			
	Totals	37,700	60,000	57,400	35,100
	Net Income	22,300			22,300
		60,000	60,000	57,400	57,400

Instructions

(a) Prepare an income statement, an owner's equity statement, and a classified balance sheet.

(b) Prepare the closing entries. L. Bray did not make any additional investments during the year.

(c) Post the closing entries and underline and balance the accounts. (Use T-accounts.) Income Summary is account No. 350.

(d) Prepare a post-closing trial balance.

(a) Ending capital $30,800
Total current assets $22,400

(d) Post-closing trial balance $46,400

P4-4A Vang Management Services began business on January 1, 2017, with a capital investment of $120,000. The company manages condominiums for owners (Service Revenue) and rents space in its own office building (Rent Revenue). The trial balance and adjusted trial balance columns of the worksheet at the end of the first year are as follows.

Complete worksheet; prepare classified balance sheet, entries, and post-closing trial balance.

(LO 1, 2, 4)

VANG MANAGEMENT SERVICES
Worksheet
For the Year Ended December 31, 2017

Account Titles	Trial Balance Dr.	Trial Balance Cr.	Adjusted Trial Balance Dr.	Adjusted Trial Balance Cr.
Cash	13,800		13,800	
Accounts Receivable	28,300		28,300	
Prepaid Insurance	3,600		2,400	
Land	67,000		67,000	
Buildings	127,000		127,000	
Equipment	59,000		59,000	
Accounts Payable		12,500		12,500
Unearned Rent Revenue		6,000		1,500
Mortgage Payable		120,000		120,000
Owner's Capital		144,000		144,000
Owner's Drawings	22,000		22,000	
Service Revenue		90,700		90,700
Rent Revenue		29,000		33,500
Salaries and Wages Expense	42,000		42,000	
Advertising Expense	20,500		20,500	
Utilities Expense	19,000		19,000	
Totals	402,200	402,200		

Account Titles	Trial Balance Dr.	Trial Balance Cr.	Adjusted Trial Balance Dr.	Adjusted Trial Balance Cr.
Insurance Expense			1,200	
Depreciation Expense			6,600	
Accumulated Depreciation—Buildings				3,000
Accumulated Depreciation—Equipment				3,600
Interest Expense			10,000	
Interest Payable				10,000
Totals			418,800	418,800

(a) Net income $24,900
(b) Total current assets $44,500

(e) Post-closing trial balance $297,500

Instructions

(a) Prepare a complete worksheet.
(b) Prepare a classified balance sheet. (*Note:* $30,000 of the mortgage note payable is due for payment next year.)
(c) Journalize the adjusting entries.
(d) Journalize the closing entries.
(e) Prepare a post-closing trial balance.

Complete all steps in accounting cycle.

(LO 1, 2, 4)

P4-5A Anya Clark opened Anya's Cleaning Service on July 1, 2017. During July, the following transactions were completed.

July	1	Anya invested $20,000 cash in the business.
	1	Purchased used truck for $12,000, paying $4,000 cash and the balance on account.
	3	Purchased cleaning supplies for $2,100 on account.
	5	Paid $1,800 cash on a 1-year insurance policy effective July 1.
	12	Billed customers $4,500 for cleaning services.
	18	Paid $1,500 cash on amount owed on truck and $1,400 on amount owed on cleaning supplies.
	20	Paid $2,800 cash for employee salaries.
	21	Collected $3,400 cash from customers billed on July 12.
	25	Billed customers $6,000 for cleaning services.
	31	Paid $350 for the monthly gasoline bill for the truck.
	31	Withdraw $5,600 cash for personal use.

The chart of accounts for Anya's Cleaning Service contains the following accounts: No. 101 Cash, No. 112 Accounts Receivable, No. 126 Supplies, No. 130 Prepaid Insurance, No. 157 Equipment, No. 158 Accumulated Depreciation—Equipment, No. 201 Accounts Payable, No. 212 Salaries and Wages Payable, No. 301 Owner's Capital, No. 306 Owner's Drawings, No. 350 Income Summary, No. 400 Service Revenue, No. 631 Supplies Expense, No. 633 Gasoline Expense, No. 711 Depreciation Expense, No. 722 Insurance Expense, and No. 726 Salaries and Wages Expense.

Instructions

(a) Journalize and post the July transactions. Use page J1 for the journal and the three-column form of account.

(b) Trial balance $37,700
(c) Adjusted trial balance $41,900

(b) Prepare a trial balance at July 31 on a worksheet.
(c) Enter the following adjustments on the worksheet and complete the worksheet.
   (1) Unbilled and uncollected revenue for services performed at July 31 were $2,700.
   (2) Depreciation on equipment for the month was $500.
   (3) One-twelfth of the insurance expired.
   (4) An inventory count shows $600 of cleaning supplies on hand at July 31.
   (5) Accrued but unpaid employee salaries were $1,000.

(d) Net income $6,900 Total assets $29,500

(d) Prepare the income statement and owner's equity statement for July and a classified balance sheet at July 31.
(e) Journalize and post adjusting entries. Use page J2 for the journal.

(g) Post-closing trial balance $30,000

(f) Journalize and post closing entries and complete the closing process. Use page J3 for the journal.
(g) Prepare a post-closing trial balance at July 31.

P4-6A Casey Hartwig, CPA, was retained by Global Cable to prepare financial statements for April 2017. Hartwig accumulated all the ledger balances per Global's records and found the following.

Analyze errors and prepare correcting entries and trial balance.

(LO 3)

GLOBAL CABLE
Trial Balance
April 30, 2017

	Debit	**Credit**
Cash	$ 4,100	
Accounts Receivable	3,200	
Supplies	800	
Equipment	10,600	
Accumulated Depreciation—Equip.		$ 1,350
Accounts Payable		2,100
Salaries and Wages Payable		700
Unearned Service Revenue		890
Owner's Capital		12,900
Service Revenue		5,450
Salaries and Wages Expense	3,300	
Advertising Expense	600	
Miscellaneous Expense	290	
Depreciation Expense	500	
	$23,390	$23,390

Casey Hartwig reviewed the records and found the following errors.

1. Cash received from a customer on account was recorded as $950 instead of $590.
2. A payment of $75 for advertising expense was entered as a debit to Miscellaneous Expense $75 and a credit to Cash $75.
3. The first salary payment this month was for $1,900, which included $700 of salaries payable on March 31. The payment was recorded as a debit to Salaries and Wages Expense $1,900 and a credit to Cash $1,900. (No reversing entries were made on April 1.)
4. The purchase on account of a printer costing $310 was recorded as a debit to Supplies and a credit to Accounts Payable for $310.
5. A cash payment of repair expense on equipment for $96 was recorded as a debit to Equipment $69 and a credit to Cash $69.

Instructions

(a) Prepare an analysis of each error showing (1) the incorrect entry, (2) the correct entry, and (3) the correcting entry. Items 4 and 5 occurred on April 30, 2017.

(b) Prepare a correct trial balance.

(b) Trial balance $22,690

COMPREHENSIVE PROBLEM: CHAPTERS 2 TO 4

CP4 Ashley Williams opened Ashley's Maids Cleaning Service on July 1, 2017. During July, the company completed the following transactions.

July	1	Invested $14,000 cash in the business.
	1	Purchased a used truck for $10,000, paying $3,000 cash and the balance on account.
	3	Purchased cleaning supplies for $800 on account.
	5	Paid $2,160 on a 1-year insurance policy, effective July 1.
	12	Billed customers $3,800 for cleaning services.
	18	Paid $1,000 of amount owed on truck, and $400 of amount owed on cleaning supplies.
	20	Paid $1,600 for employee salaries.
	21	Collected $1,400 from customers billed on July 12.
	25	Billed customers $1,900 for cleaning services.
	31	Paid gasoline for the month on the truck, $400.
	31	Withdrew $700 cash for personal use.

The chart of accounts for Ashley's Maids Cleaning Service contains the following accounts: No. 101 Cash, No. 112 Accounts Receivable, No. 126 Supplies, No. 130 Prepaid Insurance, No. 157 Equipment, No. 158 Accumulated Depreciation—Equipment, No. 201 Accounts Payable, No. 212 Salaries and Wages Payable, No. 301 Owner's Capital, No. 306 Owner's Drawings, No. 350 Income Summary, No. 400 Service Revenue, No. 631 Supplies Expense, No. 633 Gasoline Expense, No. 711 Depreciation Expense, No. 722 Insurance Expense, and No. 726 Salaries and Wages Expense.

Instructions

(a) Journalize and post the July transactions. Use page J1 for the journal.

(b) Trial balance totals $26,100

(b) Prepare a trial balance at July 31 on a worksheet.

(c) Enter the following adjustments on the worksheet, and complete the worksheet.

(1) Unbilled fees for services performed at July 31 were $1,300.

(2) Depreciation on equipment for the month was $200.

(3) One-twelfth of the insurance expired.

(4) An inventory count shows $100 of cleaning supplies on hand at July 31.

(5) Accrued but unpaid employee salaries were $500.

(d) Net income $3,420 Total assets $23,620

(d) Prepare the income statement and owner's equity statement for July, and a classified balance sheet at July 31, 2017.

(e) Journalize and post the adjusting entries. Use page J2 for the journal.

(f) Journalize and post the closing entries, and complete the closing process. Use page J3 for the journal.

(g) Trial balance totals $23,820

(g) Prepare a post-closing trial balance at July 31.

BROADENING YOUR PERSPECTIVE

FINANCIAL REPORTING AND ANALYSIS

Financial Reporting Problem: Apple Inc.

BYP4-1 The financial statements of Apple Inc. are presented in Appendix A at the end of this textbook. Instructions for accessing and using the company's complete annual report, including the notes to the financial statements, are also provided in Appendix A.

Instructions

Answer the questions below using Apple's Consolidated Balance Sheets.

(a) What were Apple's total current assets at September 28, 2013, and September 29, 2012?

(b) Are assets that Apple included under current assets listed in proper order? Explain.

(c) How are Apple's assets classified?

(d) What was Apple's "Cash and cash equivalents" at September 28, 2013?

(e) What were Apple's total current liabilities at September 28, 2013, and September 29, 2012?

Comparative Analysis Problem: PepsiCo, Inc. vs. The Coca-Cola Company

BYP4-2 PepsiCo, Inc.'s financial statements are presented in Appendix B. Financial statements of The Coca-Cola Company are presented in Appendix C. Instructions for accessing and using the complete annual reports of PepsiCo and Coca-Cola, including the notes to the financial statements, are also provided in Appendices B and C, respectively.

Instructions

(a) Based on the information contained in these financial statements, determine each of the following for PepsiCo at December 31, 2013, and for Coca-Cola at December 31, 2013.

(1) Total current assets.

(2) Net amount of property, plant, and equipment (land, buildings, and equipment).

(3) Total current liabilities.

(4) Total equity.

(b) What conclusions concerning the companies' respective financial positions can be drawn?

Comparative Analysis Problem: Amazon.com, Inc. vs. Wal-Mart Stores, Inc.

BYP4-3 Amazon.com, Inc.'s financial statements are presented in Appendix D. Financial statements of Wal-Mart Stores, Inc. are presented in Appendix E. Instructions for accessing and using the complete annual reports of Amazon and Wal-Mart, including the notes to the financial statements, are also provided in Appendices D and E, respectively.

Instructions

(a) Based on the information contained in these financial statements, determine the following for Amazon at December 31, 2013, and Wal-Mart at January 31, 2014.
  (1) Total current assets.
  (2) Net amount of property and equipment (fixed assets), net.
  (3) Total current liabilities.
  (4) Total equity.

(b) What conclusions concerning these two companies can be drawn from these data?

Real-World Focus

BYP4-4 Numerous companies have established home pages on the Internet, e.g., the soda companies Capt'n Eli Root Beer Company **(www.captneli.com/rootbeer.php)** and Cheerwine **(www.cheerwine.com)**.

Instructions

Examine the home pages of any two companies and answer the following questions.

(a) What type of information is available?
(b) Is any accounting-related information presented?
(c) Would you describe the home page as informative, promotional, or both? Why?

CRITICAL THINKING

Decision-Making Across the Organization

BYP4-5 Whitegloves Janitorial Service was started 2 years ago by Jenna Olson. Because business has been exceptionally good, Jenna decided on July 1, 2017, to expand operations by acquiring an additional truck and hiring two more assistants. To finance the expansion, Jenna obtained on July 1, 2017, a $25,000, 10% bank loan, payable $10,000 on July 1, 2018, and the balance on July 1, 2019. The terms of the loan require the borrower to have $10,000 more current assets than current liabilities at December 31, 2017. If these terms are not met, the bank loan will be refinanced at 15% interest. At December 31, 2017, the accountant for Whitegloves Janitorial Service Inc. prepared the balance sheet shown below.

WHITEGLOVES JANITORIAL SERVICE
Balance Sheet
December 31, 2017

Assets		**Liabilities and Owner's Equity**	
Current assets		Current liabilities	
Cash	$ 6,500	Notes payable	$10,000
Accounts receivable	9,000	Accounts payable	2,500
Supplies	5,200	Total current liabilities	12,500
Prepaid insurance	4,800	Long-term liability	
Total current assets	25,500	Notes payable	15,000
Property, plant, and equipment		Total liabilities	27,500
Equipment (net)	22,000	Owner's equity	
Delivery trucks (net)	34,000	Owner's capital	54,000
Total property, plant, and equipment	56,000		
Total assets	$81,500	Total liabilities and owner's equity	$81,500

Jenna presented the balance sheet to the bank's loan officer on January 2, 2018, confident that the company had met the terms of the loan. The loan officer was not impressed. She said, "We need financial statements audited by a CPA." A CPA was hired and immediately realized that the balance sheet had been prepared from a trial balance and not from an adjusted trial balance. The adjustment data at the balance sheet date consisted of the following.

1. Unbilled janitorial services performed were $3,700.
2. Janitorial supplies on hand were $2,500.
3. Prepaid insurance was a 3-year policy dated January 1, 2017.
4. December expenses incurred but unpaid at December 31, $500.
5. Interest on the bank loan was not recorded.
6. The amounts for property, plant, and equipment presented in the balance sheet were reported net of accumulated depreciation (cost less accumulated depreciation). These amounts were $4,000 for cleaning equipment and $5,000 for delivery trucks as of January 1, 2017. Depreciation for 2017 was $2,000 for cleaning equipment and $5,000 for delivery trucks.

Instructions
With the class divided into groups, answer the following.

(a) Prepare a correct balance sheet.
(b) Were the terms of the bank loan met? Explain.

Communication Activity

BYP4-6 The accounting cycle is important in understanding the accounting process.

Instructions
Write a memo to your instructor that lists the steps of the accounting cycle in the order they should be completed. End with a paragraph that explains the optional steps in the cycle.

Ethics Case

BYP4-7 As the controller of Take No Prisoners Perfume Company, you discover a misstatement that overstated net income in the prior year's financial statements. The misleading financial statements appear in the company's annual report which was issued to banks and other creditors less than a month ago. After much thought about the consequences of telling the president, Mike Flanary, about this misstatement, you gather your courage to inform him. Mike says, "Hey! What they don't know won't hurt them. But, just so we set the record straight, we'll adjust this year's financial statements for last year's misstatement. We can absorb that misstatement better in this year than in last year anyway! Just don't make such a mistake again."

Instructions
(a) Who are the stakeholders in this situation?
(b) What are the ethical issues in this situation?
(c) What would you do as a controller in this situation?

All About You

BYP4-8 Companies prepare balance sheets in order to know their financial position at a specific point in time. This enables them to make a comparison to their position at previous points in time, and gives them a basis for planning for the future. In order to evaluate your financial position, you need to prepare a personal balance sheet. Assume that you have compiled the following information regarding your finances. (*Note:* Some of the items might not be used in your personal balance sheet.)

Amount owed on student loan balance (long-term)	$ 5,000
Balance in checking account	1,200
Certificate of deposit (6-month)	3,000
Annual earnings from part-time job	11,300
Automobile	7,000
Balance on automobile loan (current portion)	1,500
Balance on automobile loan (long-term portion)	4,000
Home computer	800
Amount owed to you by younger brother	300
Balance in money market account	1,800
Annual tuition	6,400
Video and stereo equipment	1,250
Balance owed on credit card (current portion)	150
Balance owed on credit card (long-term portion)	1,650

Instructions
Prepare a personal balance sheet using the format you have learned for a classified balance sheet for a company. For the capital account, use Owner's Capital.

FASB Codification Activity

BYP4-9 If your school has a subscription to the FASB Codification, go to **http://aaahq.org/ascLogin.cfm** to log in and prepare responses to the following.

Instructions
(a) Access the glossary ("Master Glossary") at the FASB Codification website to answer the following.
  (1) What is the definition of current assets?
  (2) What is the definition of current liabilities?
(b) A company wants to offset its accounts payable against its cash account and show a cash amount net of accounts payable on its balance sheet. Identify the criteria (found in the FASB Codification) under which a company has the right of set off. Does the company have the right to offset accounts payable against the cash account?

A Look at IFRS

LEARNING OBJECTIVE 6 **Compare the procedures for the closing process under GAAP and IFRS.**

The classified balance sheet, although generally required internationally, contains certain variations in format when reporting under IFRS.

Key Points

Following are the key similarities and differences between GAAP and IFRS related to the closing process and the financial statements.

Similarities

- The procedures of the closing process are applicable to all companies, whether they are using IFRS or GAAP.
- IFRS generally requires a classified statement of financial position similar to the classified balance sheet under GAAP.
- IFRS follows the same guidelines as this textbook for distinguishing between current and noncurrent assets and liabilities.

Differences

- IFRS recommends but does not require the use of the title "statement of financial position" rather than balance sheet.
- The format of statement of financial position information is often presented differently under IFRS. Although no specific format is required, many companies that follow IFRS present statement of financial position information in this order:
  - Non-current assets
  - Current assets
  - Equity
  - Non-current liabilities
  - Current liabilities
- Under IFRS, current assets are usually listed in the reverse order of liquidity. For example, under GAAP cash is listed first, but under IFRS it is listed last.
- IFRS has many differences in terminology from what are shown in your textbook. For example, in the following sample statement of financial position, notice in the investment category that stock is called shares.

FRANKLIN COMPANY
Statement of Financial Position
October 31, 2017

Assets			
Intangible assets			
Patents			$ 3,100
Property, plant, and equipment			
Land		$10,000	
Equipment	$24,000		
Less: Accumulated depreciation	5,000	19,000	29,000
Long-term investments			
Share investments		5,200	
Investment in real estate		2,000	7,200
Current assets			
Prepaid insurance		400	
Supplies		2,100	
Inventory		3,000	
Notes receivable		1,000	
Accounts receivable		7,000	
Debt investments		2,000	
Cash		6,600	22,100
Total assets			$61,400
Equity and Liabilities			
Equity			
Owner's capital			$34,050
Non-current liabilities			
Mortgage payable		$10,000	
Notes payable		1,300	11,300
Current liabilities			
Notes payable		11,000	
Accounts payable		2,100	
Salaries and wages payable		1,600	
Unearned service revenue		900	
Interest payable		450	16,050
Total equity and liabilities			$61,400

- Both GAAP and IFRS are increasing the use of fair value to report assets. However, at this point IFRS has adopted it more broadly. As examples, under IFRS, companies can apply fair value to property, plant, and equipment, and in some cases intangible assets.

Looking to the Future

The IASB and the FASB are working on a project to converge their standards related to financial statement presentation. A key feature of the proposed framework is that each of the statements will be organized in the same format, to separate an entity's financing activities from its operating and investing activities and, further, to separate financing activities into transactions with owners and creditors. Thus, the same classifications used in the statement of financial position would also be used in the income statement and the statement of cash flows. The project has three phases. You can follow the joint financial presentation project at the following link: **http://www.fasb.org/project/financial_statement_presentation.shtml**.

IFRS Practice

IFRS Self-Test Questions

1. A company has purchased a tract of land and expects to build a production plant on the land in approximately 5 years. During the 5 years before construction, the land will be idle. Under IFRS, the land should be reported as:
   (a) land expense.
   (b) property, plant, and equipment.
   (c) an intangible asset.
   (d) a long-term investment.
2. Current assets under IFRS are listed generally:
   (a) by importance.
   (b) in the reverse order of their expected conversion to cash.
   (c) by longevity.
   (d) alphabetically.
3. Companies that use IFRS:
   (a) may report all their assets on the statement of financial position at fair value.
   (b) may offset assets against liabilities and show net assets and net liabilities on their statements of financial position, rather than the underlying detailed line items.
   (c) may report noncurrent assets before current assets on the statement of financial position.
   (d) do not have any guidelines as to what should be reported on the statement of financial position.
4. Companies that follow IFRS to prepare a statement of financial position generally use the following order of classification:
   (a) current assets, current liabilities, noncurrent assets, noncurrent liabilities, equity.
   (b) noncurrent assets, noncurrent liabilities, current assets, current liabilities, equity.
   (c) noncurrent assets, current assets, equity, noncurrent liabilities, current liabilities.
   (d) equity, noncurrent assets, current assets, noncurrent liabilities, current liabilities.

IFRS Exercises

IFRS4-1 In what ways does the format of a statement of financial of position under IFRS often differ from a balance sheet presented under GAAP?

IFRS4-2 What term is commonly used under IFRS in reference to the balance sheet?

IFRS4-3 The statement of financial position for Wallby Company includes the following accounts (in British pounds): Accounts Receivable £12,500, Prepaid Insurance £3,600, Cash £15,400, Supplies £5,200, and Debt Investments (short-term) £6,700. Prepare the current assets section of the statement of financial position, listing the accounts in proper sequence.

IFRS4-4 The following information is available for Sutter Bowling Alley at December 31, 2017.

Buildings	$128,800	Owner's Capital	$115,000
Accounts Receivable	14,520	Accumulated Depreciation—Buildings	42,600
Prepaid Insurance	4,680	Accounts Payable	12,300
Cash	18,040	Notes Payable	97,780
Equipment	62,400	Accumulated Depreciation—Equipment	18,720
Land	64,000	Interest Payable	2,600
Insurance Expense	780	Bowling Revenues	14,180
Depreciation Expense	7,360		
Interest Expense	2,600		

Prepare a classified statement of financial position. Assume that $13,900 of the notes payable will be paid in 2018.

International Comparative Analysis Problem: Apple vs. Louis Vuitton

IFRS4-5 The financial statements of Louis Vuitton are presented in Appendix F. Instructions for accessing and using the company's complete annual report, including the notes to its financial statements, are also provided in Appendix F.

Instructions

Identify five differences in the format of the statement of financial position used by Louis Vuitton compared to a company, such as Apple, that follows GAAP. (Apple's financial statements are available in Appendix A.)

Answers to IFRS Self-Test Questions

1. d **2.** b **3.** c **4.** c

Chapter 5 Accounting for Merchandising Operations

Have you ever shopped for outdoor gear at an REI (Recreational Equipment Incorporated) store? If so, you might have been surprised if a salesclerk asked if you were a member. A member? What do you mean a member? You soon realize that REI might not be your typical store. In fact, there's a lot about REI that makes it different.

REI is a consumer cooperative, or "co-op" for short. To figure out what that means, consider this quote from the company's annual stewardship report:

> As a cooperative, the Company is owned by its members. Each member is entitled to one vote in the election of the Company's Board of Directors. Since January 1, 2008, the nonrefundable, nontransferable, one-time membership fee has been 20 dollars. As of December 31, 2010, there were approximately 10.8 million members.

Voting rights? Now that's something you don't get from shopping at Wal-Mart. REI members get other benefits as well, including sharing in the company's profits through a dividend at the end of the year, which can be used for purchases at REI stores during the next two years. The more you spend, the bigger your dividend.

Since REI is a co-op, you might also wonder whether management's incentives might be a little different than at other stores. For example, is management still concerned about making a profit? The answer is yes, as it ensures the long-term viability of the company. At the same time, REI's members want the company to be run efficiently, so that prices remain low. In order for its members to evaluate just how well management is doing, REI publishes an audited annual report, just like publicly traded companies do. So, while profit maximization might not be the ultimate goal for REI, the accounting and reporting issues are similar to those of a typical corporation.

How well is this business model working for REI? Well, it has consistently been rated as one of the best places to work in the United States by *Fortune* magazine. It is one of only five companies named each year since the list was created in 1998. Also, REI had sustainable business practices long before social responsibility became popular at other companies. The CEO's stewardship report states "we reduced the absolute amount of energy we use despite opening four new stores and growing our business; we grew the amount of FSC-certified paper we use to 58.4% of our total paper footprint—including our cash register receipt paper; we facilitated 2.2 million volunteer hours and we provided $3.7 million to more than 330 conservation and recreation nonprofits."

So, while REI, like other retailers, closely monitors its financial results, it also strives to succeed in other areas. And, with over 10 million votes at stake, REI's management knows that it has to deliver.

LEARNING OBJECTIVES

1. **Describe merchandising operations and inventory systems.**
2. **Record purchases under a perpetual inventory system.**
3. **Record sales under a perpetual inventory system.**
4. **Apply the steps in the accounting cycle to a merchandising company.**
5. **Compare a multiple-step with a single-step income statement.**

LEARNING OBJECTIVE 1

Describe merchandising operations and inventory systems.

REI, Wal-Mart, and Amazon.com are called merchandising companies because they buy and sell merchandise rather than perform services as their primary source of revenue. Merchandising companies that purchase and sell directly to consumers are called **retailers**. Merchandising companies that sell to retailers are known as **wholesalers**. For example, retailer Walgreens might buy goods from wholesaler McKesson. Retailer Office Depot might buy office supplies from wholesaler United Stationers. The primary source of revenues for merchandising companies is the sale of merchandise, often referred to simply as **sales revenue** or **sales**. A merchandising company has two categories of expenses: cost of goods sold and operating expenses.

Cost of goods sold is the total cost of merchandise sold during the period. This expense is directly related to the revenue recognized from the sale of goods. Illustration 5-1 shows the income measurement process for a merchandising company. The items in the two blue boxes are unique to a merchandising company; they are not used by a service company.

Illustration 5-1
Income measurement process for a merchandising company

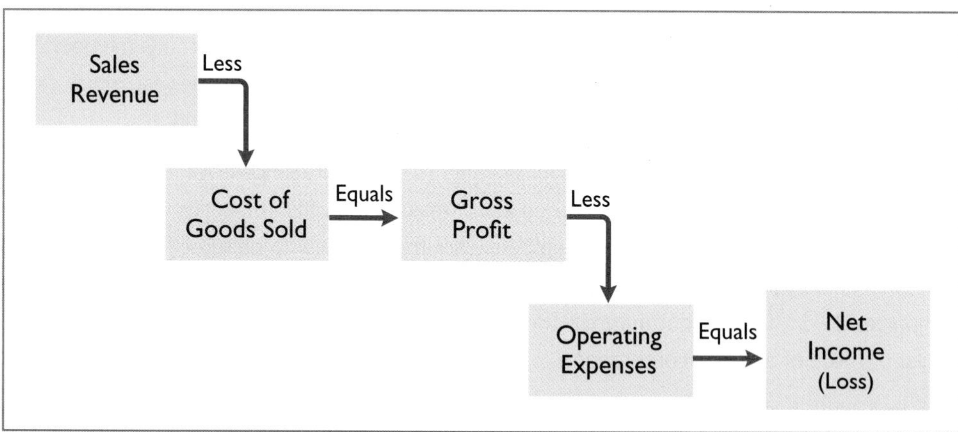

Operating Cycles

The operating cycle of a merchandising company ordinarily is longer than that of a service company. The purchase of merchandise inventory and its eventual sale lengthen the cycle. Illustration 5-2 shows the operating cycle of a service company.

Illustration 5-2
Operating cycle for a service company

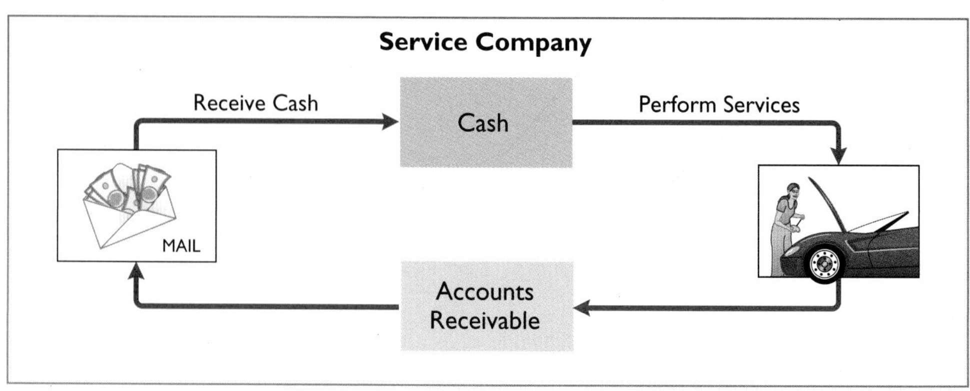

Illustration 5-3 shows the operating cycle of a merchandising company.

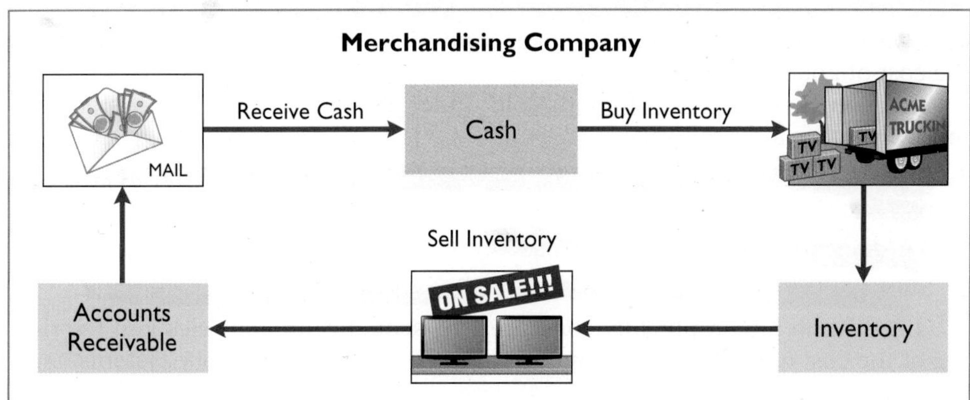

Illustration 5-3
Operating cycle for a merchandising company

Note that the added asset account for a merchandising company is the Inventory account. Companies report inventory as a current asset on the balance sheet.

Flow of Costs

The flow of costs for a merchandising company is as follows. Beginning inventory plus the cost of goods purchased is the cost of goods available for sale. As goods are sold, they are assigned to cost of goods sold. Those goods that are not sold by the end of the accounting period represent ending inventory. Illustration 5-4 describes these relationships. Companies use one of two systems to account for inventory: a **perpetual inventory system** or a **periodic inventory system**.

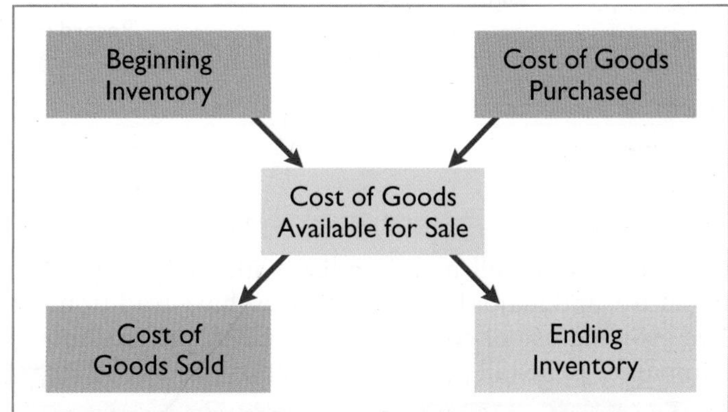

Illustration 5-4
Flow of costs

PERPETUAL SYSTEM

In a **perpetual inventory system**, companies keep detailed records of the cost of each inventory purchase and sale. These records continuously—perpetually—show the inventory that should be on hand for every item. For example, a **Ford** dealership has separate inventory records for each automobile, truck, and van on its lot and showroom floor. Similarly, a **Kroger** grocery store uses bar codes and optical scanners to keep a daily running record of every box of cereal and every jar of jelly that it buys and sells. Under a perpetual inventory system, a company determines the cost of goods sold **each time a sale occurs**.

PERIODIC SYSTEM

In a **periodic inventory system**, companies do not keep detailed inventory records of the goods on hand throughout the period. Instead, they determine the cost of goods sold **only at the end of the accounting period**—that is, periodically. At that point, the company takes a physical inventory count to determine the cost of goods on hand.

To determine the cost of goods sold under a periodic inventory system, the following steps are necessary:

1. Determine the cost of goods on hand at the beginning of the accounting period.
2. Add to it the cost of goods purchased.
3. Subtract the cost of goods on hand at the end of the accounting period.

Illustration 5-5 graphically compares the sequence of activities and the timing of the cost of goods sold computation under the two inventory systems.

Illustration 5-5
Comparing perpetual and periodic inventory systems

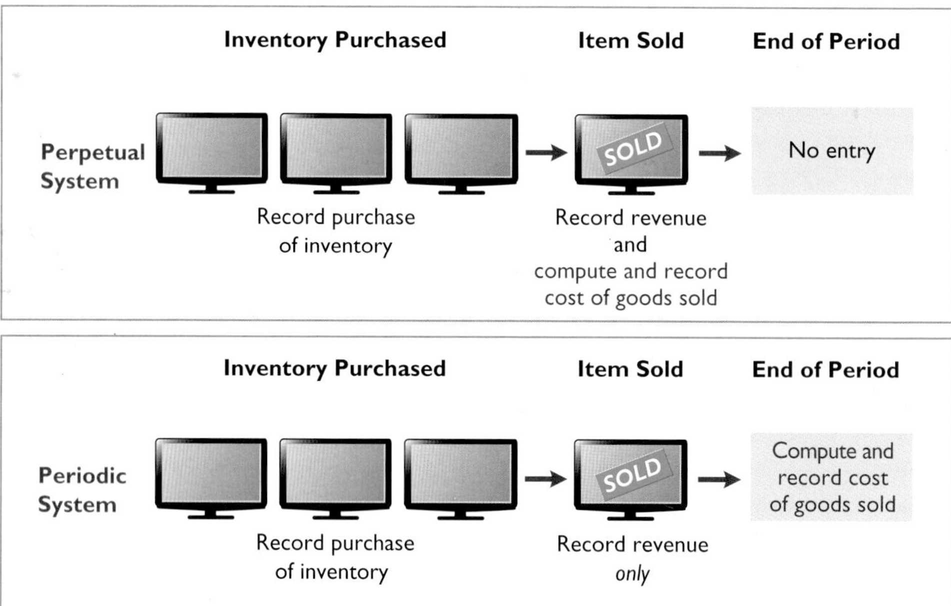

ADVANTAGES OF THE PERPETUAL SYSTEM

Companies that sell merchandise with high unit values, such as automobiles, furniture, and major home appliances, have traditionally used perpetual systems. The growing use of computers and electronic scanners has enabled many more companies to install perpetual inventory systems. The perpetual inventory system is so named because the accounting records continuously—perpetually—show the quantity and cost of the inventory that should be on hand at any time.

A perpetual inventory system provides better control over inventories than a periodic system. Since the inventory records show the quantities that should be on hand, the company can count the goods at any time to see whether the amount of goods actually on hand agrees with the inventory records. If shortages are uncovered, the company can investigate immediately. Although a perpetual inventory system requires both additional clerical work and expense to maintain the subsidiary records, a computerized system can minimize this cost. Much of Amazon.com's success is attributed to its sophisticated inventory system.

Some businesses find it either unnecessary or uneconomical to invest in a sophisticated, computerized perpetual inventory system such as Amazon's. Many small merchandising businesses find that basic accounting software provides some of the essential benefits of a perpetual inventory system. Also, managers of some small businesses still find that they can control their merchandise and manage day-to-day operations using a periodic inventory system.

Because of the widespread use of the perpetual inventory system, we illustrate it in this chapter. We discuss and illustrate the periodic system in Appendix 5B.

LEARNING OBJECTIVE  **Record purchases under a perpetual inventory system.**

Companies purchase inventory using cash or credit (on account). They normally record purchases when they receive the goods from the seller. Every purchase should be supported by business documents that provide written evidence of the transaction. Each cash purchase should be supported by a canceled check or a cash register receipt indicating the items purchased and amounts paid. Companies record cash purchases by an increase in Inventory and a decrease in Cash.

A **purchase invoice** should support each credit purchase. This invoice indicates the total purchase price and other relevant information. However, the purchaser does not prepare a separate purchase invoice. Instead, the purchaser uses as a purchase invoice a copy of the sales invoice sent by the seller. In Illustration 5-6, for example, Sauk Stereo (the buyer) uses as a purchase invoice the sales invoice prepared by PW Audio Supply (the seller).

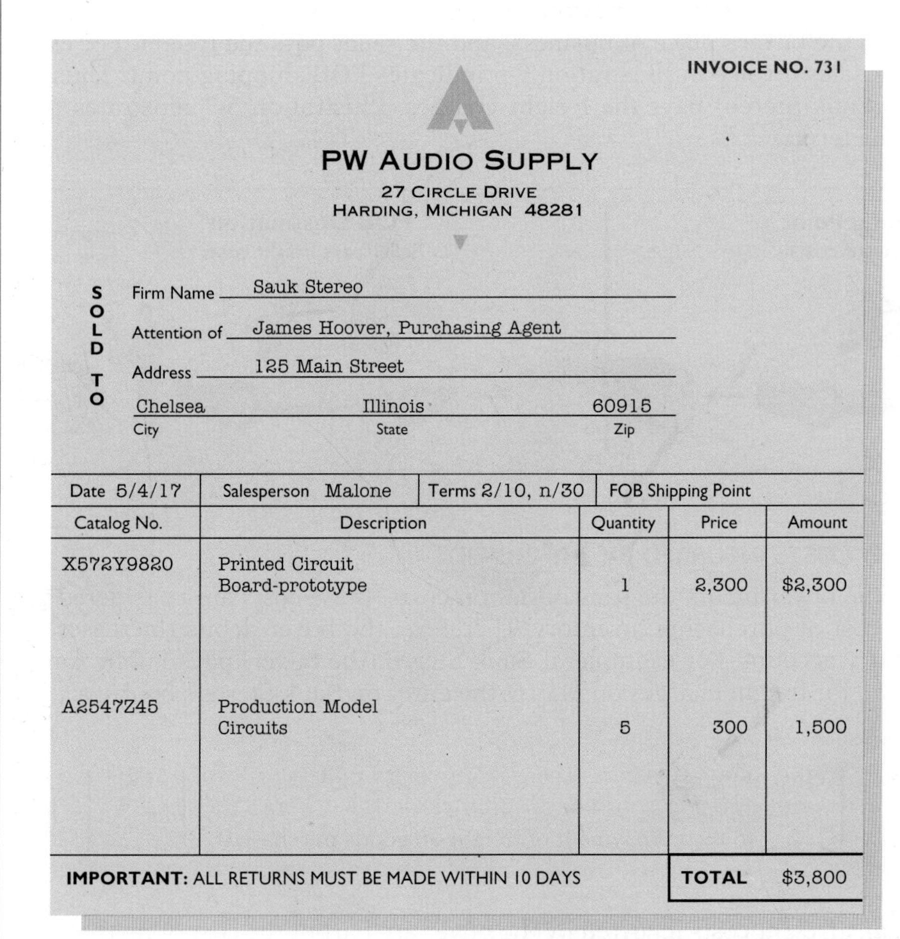

INVOICE NO. 731

PW AUDIO SUPPLY
27 CIRCLE DRIVE
HARDING, MICHIGAN 48281

SOLD TO
Firm Name: Sauk Stereo
Attention of: James Hoover, Purchasing Agent
Address: 125 Main Street
City: Chelsea State: Illinois Zip: 60915

Date 5/4/17 | Salesperson Malone | Terms 2/10, n/30 | FOB Shipping Point

Catalog No.	Description	Quantity	Price	Amount
X572Y9820	Printed Circuit Board-prototype	1	2,300	$2,300
A2547Z45	Production Model Circuits	5	300	1,500

IMPORTANT: ALL RETURNS MUST BE MADE WITHIN 10 DAYS **TOTAL** $3,800

Illustration 5-6
Sales invoice used as purchase invoice by Sauk Stereo

Sauk Stereo makes the following journal entry to record its purchase from PW Audio Supply. The entry increases (debits) Inventory and increases (credits) Accounts Payable.

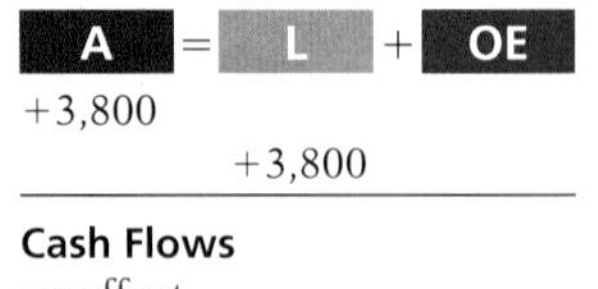

May 4	Inventory	3,800	
	Accounts Payable		3,800
	(To record goods purchased on account from PW Audio Supply)		

Under the perpetual inventory system, companies record purchases of merchandise for sale in the Inventory account. Thus, REI would increase (debit) Inventory for clothing, sporting goods, and anything else purchased for resale to customers.

Not all purchases are debited to Inventory, however. Companies record purchases of assets acquired for use and not for resale, such as supplies, equipment, and similar items, as increases to specific asset accounts rather than to Inventory. For example, to record the purchase of materials used to make shelf signs or for cash register receipt paper, REI would increase (debit) Supplies.

Freight Costs

The sales agreement should indicate who—the seller or the buyer—is to pay for transporting the goods to the buyer's place of business. When a common carrier such as a railroad, trucking company, or airline transports the goods, the carrier prepares a freight bill in accord with the sales agreement.

Freight terms are expressed as either FOB shipping point or FOB destination. The letters FOB mean **free on board**. Thus, **FOB shipping point** means that the seller places the goods free on board the carrier, and the buyer pays the freight costs. Conversely, **FOB destination** means that the seller places the goods free on board to the buyer's place of business, and the seller pays the freight. For example, the sales invoice in Illustration 5-6 indicates FOB shipping point. Thus, the buyer (Sauk Stereo) pays the freight charges. Illustration 5-7 illustrates these shipping terms.

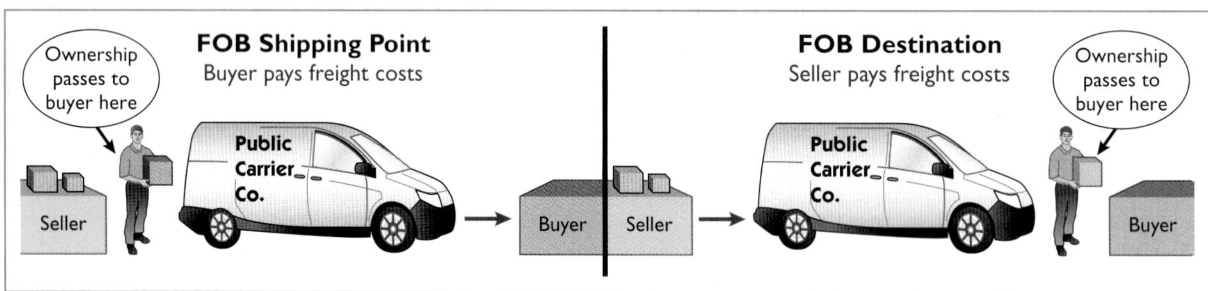

Illustration 5-7
Shipping terms

FREIGHT COSTS INCURRED BY THE BUYER

When the buyer incurs the transportation costs, these costs are considered part of the cost of purchasing inventory. Therefore, the buyer debits (increases) the Inventory account. For example, if Sauk Stereo (the buyer) pays Public Carrier Co. $150 for freight charges on May 6, the entry on Sauk Stereo's books is:

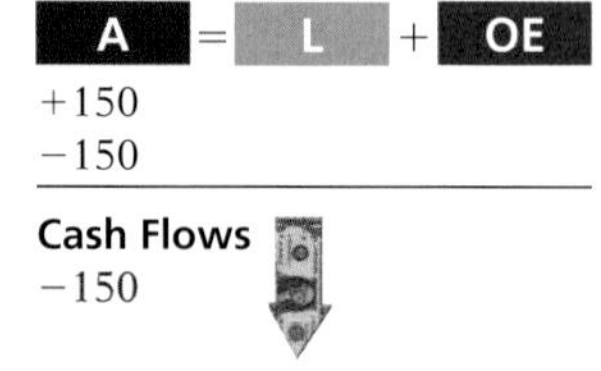

May 6	Inventory	150	
	Cash		150
	(To record payment of freight on goods purchased)		

Thus, any freight costs incurred by the buyer are part of the cost of merchandise purchased. The reason: Inventory cost should include all costs to acquire the inventory, including freight necessary to deliver the goods to the buyer. Companies recognize these costs as cost of goods sold when inventory is sold.

FREIGHT COSTS INCURRED BY THE SELLER

In contrast, **freight costs incurred by the seller on outgoing merchandise are an operating expense to the seller**. These costs increase an expense account titled Freight-Out (sometimes called Delivery Expense). For example, if the freight terms on the invoice in Illustration 5-6 had required PW Audio Supply (the seller) to pay the freight charges, the entry by PW Audio Supply would be:

Date	Account	Debit	Credit
May 4	Freight-Out (or Delivery Expense)	150	
	Cash		150
	(To record payment of freight on goods sold)		

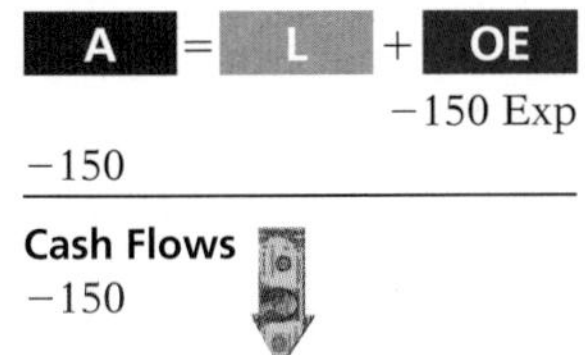

When the seller pays the freight charges, the seller will usually establish a higher invoice price for the goods to cover the shipping expense.

Purchase Returns and Allowances

A purchaser may be dissatisfied with the merchandise received because the goods are damaged or defective, of inferior quality, or do not meet the purchaser's specifications. In such cases, the purchaser may return the goods to the seller for credit if the sale was made on credit, or for a cash refund if the purchase was for cash. This transaction is known as a **purchase return**. Alternatively, the purchaser may choose to keep the merchandise if the seller is willing to grant an allowance (deduction) from the purchase price. This transaction is known as a **purchase allowance**.

Assume that Sauk Stereo returned goods costing $300 to PW Audio Supply on May 8. The following entry by Sauk Stereo for the returned merchandise decreases (debits) Accounts Payable and decreases (credits) Inventory.

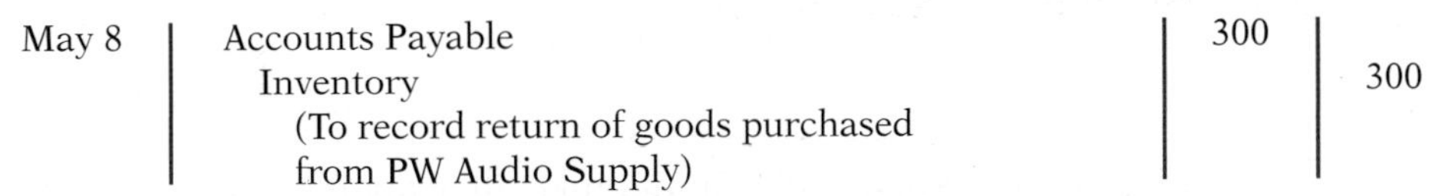

Date	Account	Debit	Credit
May 8	Accounts Payable	300	
	Inventory		300
	(To record return of goods purchased from PW Audio Supply)		

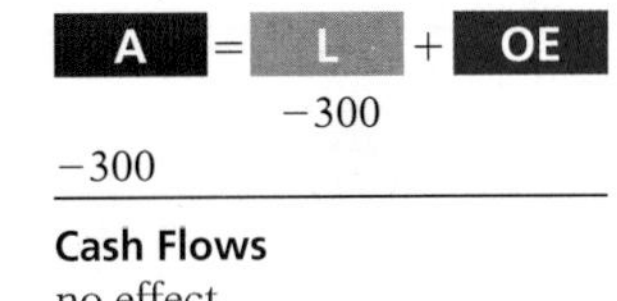

Because Sauk Stereo increased Inventory when the goods were received, Inventory is decreased when Sauk Stereo returns the goods.

Suppose instead that Sauk Stereo chose to keep the goods after being granted a $50 allowance (reduction in price). It would reduce (debit) Accounts Payable and reduce (credit) Inventory for $50.

Purchase Discounts

The credit terms of a purchase on account may permit the buyer to claim a cash discount for prompt payment. The buyer calls this cash discount a **purchase discount**. This incentive offers advantages to both parties. The purchaser saves money, and the seller is able to shorten the operating cycle by converting the accounts receivable into cash.

Credit terms specify the amount of the cash discount and time period in which it is offered. They also indicate the time period in which the purchaser is expected to pay the full invoice price. In the sales invoice in Illustration 5-6 (page 169), credit terms are 2/10, n/30, which is read "two-ten, net thirty." This means that the buyer may take a 2% cash discount on the invoice price, less ("net of") any returns or allowances, if payment is made within 10 days of the invoice date (the **discount period**). Otherwise, the invoice price, less any returns or allowances, is due 30 days from the invoice date.

Alternatively, the discount period may extend to a specified number of days following the month in which the sale occurs. For example, 1/10 EOM (end of month) means that a 1% discount is available if the invoice is paid within the first 10 days of the next month.

When the seller elects not to offer a cash discount for prompt payment, credit terms will specify only the maximum time period for paying the balance due. For example, the invoice may state the time period as n/30, n/60, or n/10 EOM. This means, respectively, that the buyer must pay the net amount in 30 days, 60 days, or within the first 10 days of the next month.

When the buyer pays an invoice within the discount period, the amount of the discount decreases Inventory. Why? Because companies record inventory at cost and, by paying within the discount period, the buyer has reduced its cost. To illustrate, assume Sauk Stereo pays the balance due of $3,500 (gross invoice price of $3,800 less purchase returns and allowances of $300) on May 14, the last day of the discount period. The cash discount is $70 ($3,500 × 2%), and Sauk Stereo pays $3,430 ($3,500 − $70). The entry Sauk Stereo makes to record its May 14 payment decreases (debits) Accounts Payable by the amount of the gross invoice price, reduces (credits) Inventory by the $70 discount, and reduces (credits) Cash by the net amount owed.

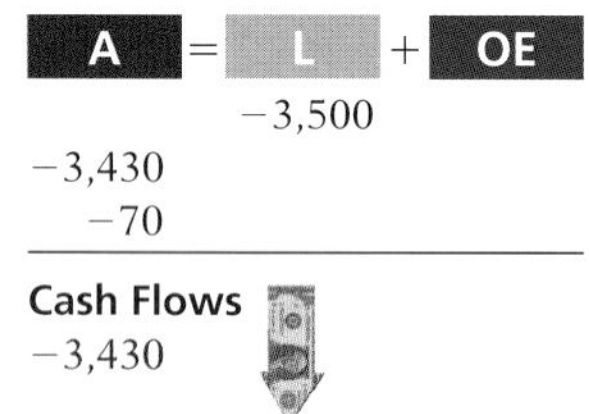

May 14	Accounts Payable	3,500	
	Cash		3,430
	Inventory		70
	(To record payment within discount period)		

If Sauk Stereo failed to take the discount and instead made full payment of $3,500 on June 3, it would debit Accounts Payable and credit Cash for $3,500 each.

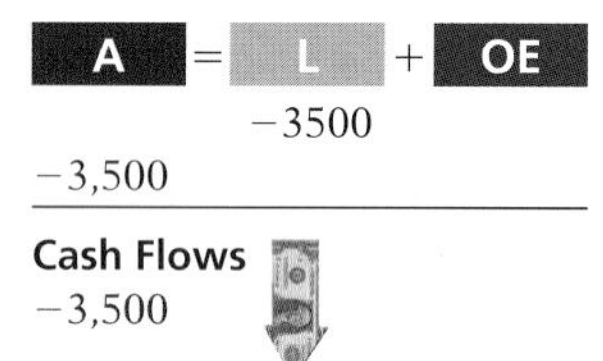

June 3	Accounts Payable	3,500	
	Cash		3,500
	(To record payment with no discount taken)		

A merchandising company usually should take all available discounts. Passing up the discount may be viewed as **paying interest** for use of the money. For example, passing up the discount offered by PW Audio Supply would be comparable to Sauk Stereo paying an interest rate of 2% for the use of $3,500 for 20 days. This is the equivalent of an annual interest rate of approximately 36.5% (2% × 365/20). Obviously, it would be better for Sauk Stereo to borrow at prevailing bank interest rates of 6% to 10% than to lose the discount.

Summary of Purchasing Transactions

The following T-account (with transaction descriptions in red) provides a summary of the effect of the previous transactions on Inventory. Sauk Stereo originally purchased $3,800 worth of inventory for resale. It then returned $300 of goods. It paid $150 in freight charges, and finally, it received a $70 discount off the balance owed because it paid within the discount period. This results in a balance in Inventory of $3,580.

	Inventory				
Purchase	May 4	3,800	May 8	300	**Purchase return**
Freight-in	6	150	14	70	**Purchase discount**
Balance		3,580			

LEARNING OBJECTIVE 3

Record sales under a perpetual inventory system.

In accordance with the revenue recognition principle, companies record sales revenue when the performance obligation is satisfied. Typically, the performance obligation is satisfied when the goods transfer from the seller to the buyer. At this point, the sales transaction is complete and the sales price established.

Sales may be made on credit or for cash. A **business document** should support every sales transaction, to provide written evidence of the sale. **Cash register documents** provide evidence of cash sales. A **sales invoice**, like the one shown in Illustration 5-6 (page 169), provides support for a credit sale. The original copy of the invoice goes to the customer, and the seller keeps a copy for use in recording the sale. The invoice shows the date of sale, customer name, total sales price, and other relevant information.

The seller makes two entries for each sale. **The first entry records the sale**: The seller increases (debits) Cash (or Accounts Receivable if a credit sale) and also increases (credits) Sales Revenue. **The second entry records the cost of the merchandise sold**: The seller increases (debits) Cost of Goods Sold and also decreases (credits) Inventory for the cost of those goods. As a result, the Inventory account will show at all times the amount of inventory that should be on hand.

To illustrate a credit sales transaction, PW Audio Supply records its May 4 sale of $3,800 to Sauk Stereo (see Illustration 5-6) as follows (assume the merchandise cost PW Audio Supply $2,400).

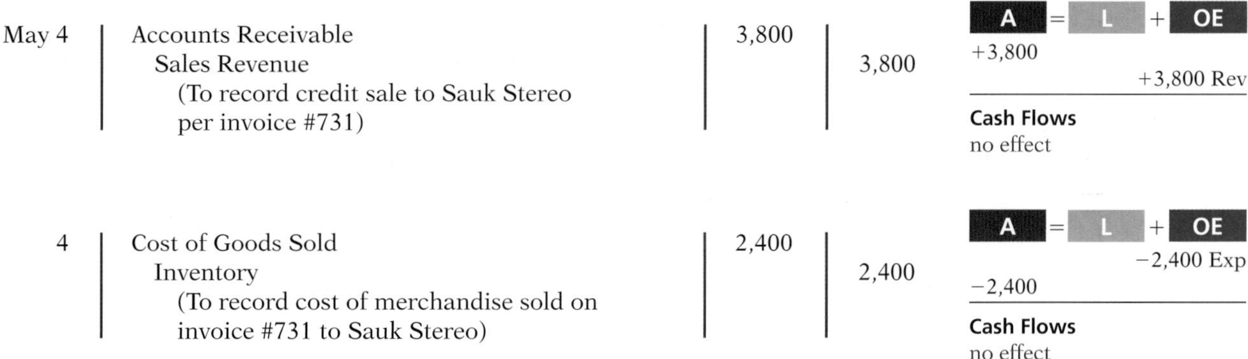

Date	Account	Debit	Credit
May 4	Accounts Receivable	3,800	
	Sales Revenue		3,800
	(To record credit sale to Sauk Stereo per invoice #731)		
4	Cost of Goods Sold	2,400	
	Inventory		2,400
	(To record cost of merchandise sold on invoice #731 to Sauk Stereo)		

For internal decision-making purposes, merchandising companies may use more than one sales account. For example, PW Audio Supply may decide to keep separate sales accounts for its sales of TVs, Blu-ray players, and headsets. REI might use separate accounts for camping gear, children's clothing, and ski equipment—or it might have even more narrowly defined accounts. By using separate sales accounts for major product lines, rather than a single combined sales account, company management can more closely monitor sales trends and respond more strategically to changes in sales patterns. For example, if TV sales are increasing while Blu-ray player sales are decreasing, PW Audio Supply might reevaluate both its advertising and pricing policies on these items to ensure they are optimal.

On its income statement presented to outside investors, a merchandising company normally would provide only a single sales figure—the sum of all of its individual sales accounts. This is done for two reasons. First, providing detail on all of its individual sales accounts would add considerable length to its income statement. Second, companies do not want their competitors to know the details of their operating results. However, Microsoft recently expanded its disclosure of revenue from three to five types. The reason: The additional categories enabled financial statement users to better evaluate the growth of the company's consumer and Internet businesses.

At the end of "Anatomy of a Fraud" stories, which describe some recent real-world frauds, we discuss the missing control activities that would likely have prevented or uncovered the fraud.

ANATOMY OF A FRAUD[1]

Holly Harmon was a cashier at a national superstore for only a short while when she began stealing merchandise using three methods. Under the first method, her husband or friends took UPC labels from cheaper items and put them on more expensive items. Holly then scanned the goods at the register. Using the second method, Holly scanned an item at the register but then voided the sale and left the merchandise in the shopping cart. A third approach was to put goods into large plastic containers. She scanned the plastic containers but not the goods within them. One day, Holly did not call in sick or show up for work. In such instances, the company reviews past surveillance tapes to look for suspicious activity by employees. This enabled the store to observe the thefts and to identify the participants.

Total take: $12,000

THE MISSING CONTROLS

Human resource controls. A background check would have revealed Holly's previous criminal record. She would not have been hired as a cashier.

Physical controls. Software can flag high numbers of voided transactions or a high number of sales of low-priced goods. Random comparisons of video records with cash register records can ensure that the goods reported as sold on the register are the same goods that are shown being purchased on the video recording. Finally, employees should be aware that they are being monitored.

Source: Adapted from Wells, *Fraud Casebook* (2007), pp. 251–259.

Sales Returns and Allowances

We now look at the "flip side" of purchase returns and allowances, which the seller records as **sales returns and allowances**. These are transactions where the seller either accepts goods back from the buyer (a return) or grants a reduction in the purchase price (an allowance) so the buyer will keep the goods. PW Audio Supply's entries to record credit for returned goods involve (1) an increase (debit) in Sales Returns and Allowances (a contra account to Sales Revenue) and a decrease (credit) in Accounts Receivable at the $300 selling price, and (2) an increase (debit) in Inventory (assume a $140 cost) and a decrease (credit) in Cost of Goods Sold, as shown below (assuming that the goods were not defective).

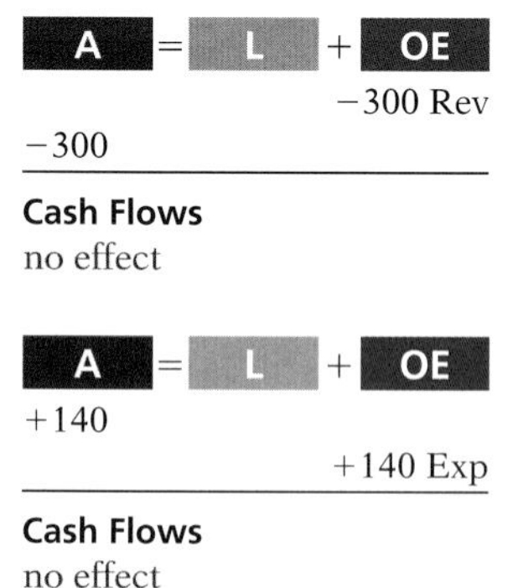

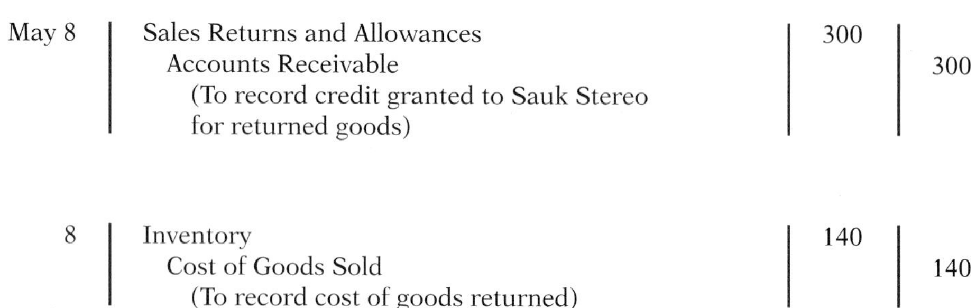

May 8	Sales Returns and Allowances	300	
	Accounts Receivable		300
	(To record credit granted to Sauk Stereo for returned goods)		
8	Inventory	140	
	Cost of Goods Sold		140
	(To record cost of goods returned)		

If Sauk Stereo returns goods because they are damaged or defective, then PW Audio Supply's entry to Inventory and Cost of Goods Sold should be for the fair

[1]The "Anatomy of a Fraud" stories in this textbook are adapted from *Fraud Casebook: Lessons from the Bad Side of Business,* edited by Joseph T. Wells (Hoboken, NJ: John Wiley & Sons, Inc., 2007). Used by permission. The names of some of the people and organizations in the stories are fictitious, but the facts in the stories are true.

value of the returned goods, rather than their cost. For example, if the returned goods were defective and had a fair value of $50, PW Audio Supply would debit Inventory for $50 and credit Cost of Goods Sold for $50.

What happens if the goods are not returned but the seller grants the buyer an allowance by reducing the purchase price? In this case, the seller debits Sales Returns and Allowances and credits Accounts Receivable for the amount of the allowance. An allowance has no impact on Inventory or Cost of Goods Sold.

Sales Returns and Allowances is a **contra revenue account** to Sales Revenue. This means that it is offset against a revenue account on the income statement. The normal balance of Sales Returns and Allowances is a debit. Companies use a contra account, instead of debiting Sales Revenue, to disclose in the accounts and in the income statement the amount of sales returns and allowances. Disclosure of this information is important to management. Excessive returns and allowances may suggest problems—inferior merchandise, inefficiencies in filling orders, errors in billing customers, or delivery or shipment mistakes. Moreover, a decrease (debit) recorded directly to Sales Revenue would obscure the relative importance of sales returns and allowances as a percentage of sales. It also could distort comparisons between total sales in different accounting periods.

Sales Discounts

As mentioned in our discussion of purchase transactions, the seller may offer the customer a cash discount—called by the seller a **sales discount**—for the prompt payment of the balance due. Like a purchase discount, a sales discount is based on the invoice price less returns and allowances, if any. The seller increases (debits) the Sales Discounts account for discounts that are taken. For example, PW Audio Supply makes the following entry to record the cash receipt on May 14 from Sauk Stereo within the discount period.

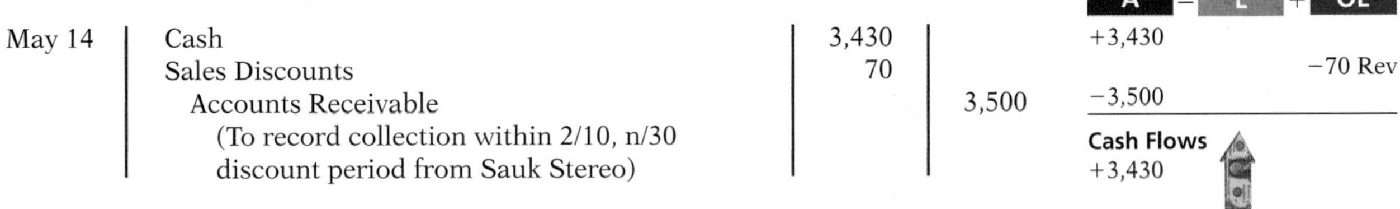

		Debit	Credit
May 14	Cash	3,430	
	Sales Discounts	70	
	Accounts Receivable		3,500
	(To record collection within 2/10, n/30 discount period from Sauk Stereo)		

Like Sales Returns and Allowances, Sales Discounts is a **contra revenue account** to Sales Revenue. Its normal balance is a debit. PW Audio Supply uses this account, instead of debiting Sales Revenue, to disclose the amount of cash discounts taken by customers. If Sauk Stereo does not take the discount, PW Audio Supply increases (debits) Cash for $3,500 and decreases (credits) Accounts Receivable for the same amount at the date of collection.

The following T-accounts summarize the three sales-related transactions and show their combined effect on net sales.

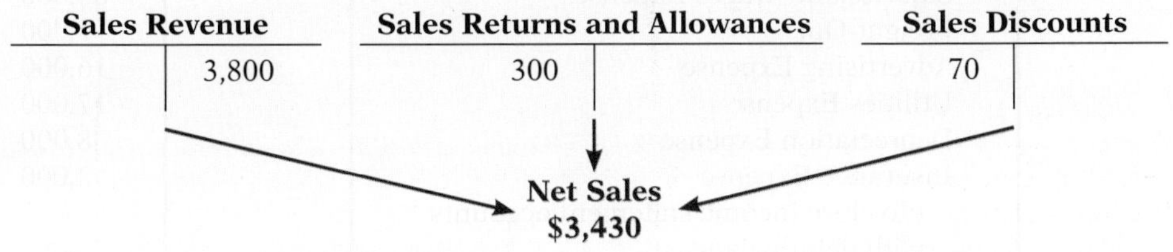

LEARNING OBJECTIVE 

Apply the steps in the accounting cycle to a merchandising company.

Up to this point, we have illustrated the basic entries for transactions relating to purchases and sales in a perpetual inventory system. Now we consider the remaining steps in the accounting cycle for a merchandising company. Each of the required steps described in Chapter 4 for service companies apply to merchandising companies. Appendix 5A to this chapter shows use of a worksheet by a merchandiser (an optional step).

Adjusting Entries

A merchandising company generally has the same types of adjusting entries as a service company. However, a merchandiser using a perpetual system will require one additional adjustment to make the records agree with the actual inventory on hand. Here's why. At the end of each period, for control purposes, a merchandising company that uses a perpetual system will take a physical count of its goods on hand. The company's unadjusted balance in Inventory usually does not agree with the actual amount of inventory on hand. The perpetual inventory records may be incorrect due to recording errors, theft, or waste. Thus, the company needs to adjust the perpetual records to make the recorded inventory amount agree with the inventory on hand. **This involves adjusting Inventory and Cost of Goods Sold.**

For example, suppose that PW Audio Supply has an unadjusted balance of $40,500 in Inventory. Through a physical count, PW Audio Supply determines that its actual merchandise inventory at December 31 is $40,000. The company would make an adjusting entry as follows.

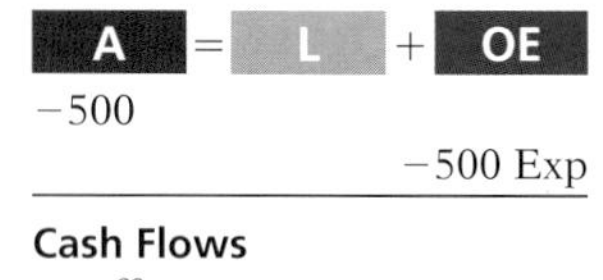

Cash Flows
no effect

Dec. 31	Cost of Goods Sold	500	
	Inventory		500
	(To adjust inventory to physical count)		

Closing Entries

A merchandising company, like a service company, closes to Income Summary all accounts that affect net income. In journalizing, the company credits all temporary accounts with debit balances, and debits all temporary accounts with credit balances, as shown below for PW Audio Supply. Note that PW Audio Supply closes Cost of Goods Sold to Income Summary.

Dec. 31	Sales Revenue	480,000	
	Income Summary		480,000
	(To close income statement accounts with credit balances)		
31	Income Summary	450,000	
	Sales Returns and Allowances		12,000
	Sales Discounts		8,000
	Cost of Goods Sold		316,000
	Salaries and Wages Expense		64,000
	Freight-Out		7,000
	Advertising Expense		16,000
	Utilities Expense		17,000
	Depreciation Expense		8,000
	Insurance Expense		2,000
	(To close income statement accounts with debit balances)		

31	Income Summary	30,000	
	Owner's Capital		30,000
	(To close net income to capital)		
31	Owner's Capital	15,000	
	Owner's Drawings		15,000
	(To close drawings to capital)		

After PW Audio Supply has posted the closing entries, all temporary accounts have zero balances. Also, Owner's Capital has a balance that is carried over to the next period.

Summary of Merchandising Entries

Illustration 5-8 summarizes the entries for the merchandising accounts using a perpetual inventory system.

Illustration 5-8
Daily recurring and adjusting and closing entries

	Transactions	Daily Recurring Entries	Dr.	Cr.
Sales Transactions	Selling merchandise to customers.	Cash or Accounts Receivable	XX	
		Sales Revenue		XX
		Cost of Goods Sold	XX	
		Inventory		XX
	Granting sales returns or allowances to customers.	Sales Returns and Allowances	XX	
		Cash or Accounts Receivable		XX
		Inventory	XX	
		Cost of Goods Sold		XX
	Paying freight costs on sales; FOB destination.	Freight-Out	XX	
		Cash		XX
	Receiving payment from customers within discount period.	Cash	XX	
		Sales Discounts	XX	
		Accounts Receivable		XX
Purchase Transactions	Purchasing merchandise for resale.	Inventory	XX	
		Cash or Accounts Payable		XX
	Paying freight costs on merchandise purchased; FOB shipping point.	Inventory	XX	
		Cash		XX
	Receiving purchase returns or allowances from suppliers.	Cash or Accounts Payable	XX	
		Inventory		XX
	Paying suppliers within discount period.	Accounts Payable	XX	
		Inventory		XX
		Cash		XX
	Events	**Adjusting and Closing Entries**		
	Adjust because book amount is higher than the inventory amount determined to be on hand.	Cost of Goods Sold	XX	
		Inventory		XX
	Closing temporary accounts with credit balances.	Sales Revenue	XX	
		Income Summary		XX
	Closing temporary accounts with debit balances.	Income Summary	XX	
		Sales Returns and Allowances		XX
		Sales Discounts		XX
		Cost of Goods Sold		XX
		Freight-Out		XX
		Expenses		XX

LEARNING OBJECTIVE 5

Compare a multiple-step with a single-step income statement.

Merchandising companies widely use the classified balance sheet introduced in Chapter 4 and one of two forms for the income statement. This section explains the use of these financial statements by merchandisers.

Multiple-Step Income Statement

The **multiple-step income statement** is so named because it shows several steps in determining net income. Two of these steps relate to the company's principal operating activities. A multiple-step statement also distinguishes between **operating** and **nonoperating activities**. Finally, the statement highlights intermediate components of income and shows subgroupings of expenses.

INCOME STATEMENT PRESENTATION OF SALES

The multiple-step income statement begins by presenting **sales revenue**. It then deducts contra revenue accounts—sales returns and allowances, and sales discounts—from sales revenue to arrive at **net sales**. Illustration 5-9 presents the sales section for PW Audio Supply, using assumed data.

Illustration 5-9
Computation of net sales

PW AUDIO SUPPLY Income Statement (partial)		
Sales		
Sales revenue		$ 480,000
Less: Sales returns and allowances	$12,000	
Sales discounts	8,000	20,000
Net sales		**$460,000**

GROSS PROFIT

Terminology
Gross profit is sometimes referred to as *gross margin*.

From Illustration 5-1, you learned that companies deduct cost of goods sold from sales revenue to determine **gross profit**. For this computation, companies use **net sales** (which takes into consideration Sales Returns and Allowances and Sales Discounts) as the amount of sales revenue. On the basis of the sales data in Illustration 5-9 (net sales of $460,000) and cost of goods sold under the perpetual inventory system (assume $316,000), PW Audio Supply's gross profit is $144,000, computed as follows.

Illustration 5-10
Computation of gross profit

Net sales	$ 460,000
Cost of goods sold	316,000
Gross profit	**$144,000**

We also can express a company's gross profit as a percentage, called the **gross profit rate**. To do so, we divide the amount of gross profit by net sales. For PW Audio Supply, the **gross profit rate** is 31.3%, computed as follows.

Illustration 5-11
Gross profit rate formula and computation

Gross Profit	÷	Net Sales	=	Gross Profit Rate
$144,000	÷	$460,000	=	31.3%

Analysts generally consider the gross profit **rate** to be more useful than the gross profit **amount**. The rate expresses a more meaningful (qualitative) relationship between net sales and gross profit. For example, a gross profit of $1,000,000 may sound impressive. But if it is the result of a gross profit rate of only 7%, it is not so impressive. The gross profit rate tells how many cents of each sales dollar go to gross profit.

Gross profit represents the **merchandising profit** of a company. It is not a measure of the overall profitability because operating expenses are not yet deducted. But managers and other interested parties closely watch the amount and trend of gross profit. They compare current gross profit with amounts reported in past periods. They also compare the company's gross profit rate with rates of competitors and with industry averages. Such comparisons provide information about the effectiveness of a company's purchasing function and the soundness of its pricing policies.

OPERATING EXPENSES AND NET INCOME

Operating expenses are the next component in measuring net income for a merchandising company. They are the expenses incurred in the process of earning sales revenue. These expenses are similar in merchandising and service companies. At PW Audio Supply, operating expenses were $114,000. The company determines its net income by subtracting operating expenses from gross profit. Thus, net income is $30,000, as shown below.

Illustration 5-12
Operating expenses in computing net income

Gross profit	$144,000
Operating expenses	**114,000**
Net income	$ 30,000

The net income amount is the so-called "bottom line" of a company's income statement.

NONOPERATING ACTIVITIES

Nonoperating activities consist of various revenues and expenses and gains and losses that are unrelated to the company's main line of operations. When nonoperating items are included, the label "**Income from operations**" (or "Operating income") precedes them. This label clearly identifies the results of the company's normal operations, an amount determined by subtracting cost of goods sold and operating expenses from net sales. The results of nonoperating activities are shown in the categories "**Other revenues and gains**" and "**Other expenses and losses**." Illustration 5-13 lists examples of each.

Illustration 5-13
Other items of nonoperating activities

Other Revenues and Gains
Interest revenue from notes receivable and marketable securities.
Dividend revenue from investments in common stock.
Rent revenue from subleasing a portion of the store.
Gain from the sale of property, plant, and equipment.
Other Expenses and Losses
Interest expense on notes and loans payable.
Casualty losses from recurring causes, such as vandalism and accidents.
Loss from the sale or abandonment of property, plant, and equipment.
Loss from strikes by employees and suppliers.

Merchandising companies report the nonoperating activities in the income statement immediately after the company's operating activities. Illustration 5-14 shows these sections for PW Audio Supply, using assumed data.

The distinction between operating and nonoperating activities is crucial to many external users of financial data. These users view operating income as sustainable and many nonoperating activities as non-recurring. Therefore, when forecasting next year's income, analysts put the most weight on this year's operating income and less weight on this year's nonoperating activities.

Illustration 5-14
Multiple-step income statement

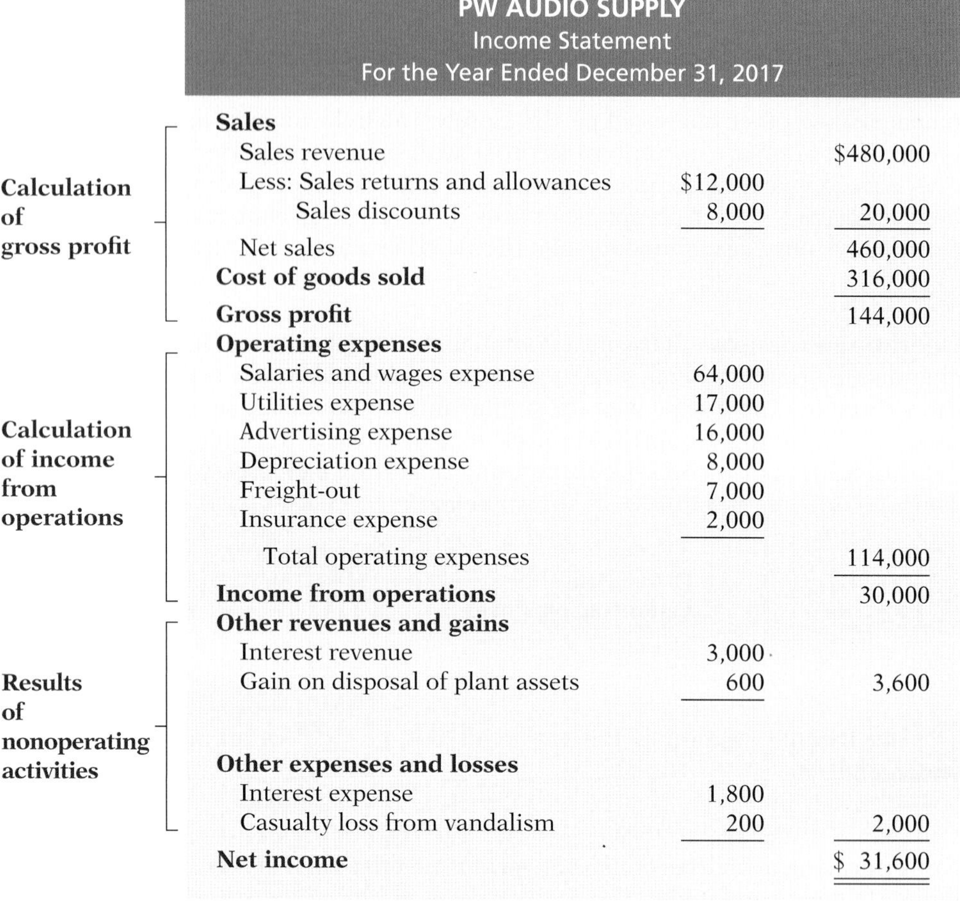

	PW AUDIO SUPPLY Income Statement For the Year Ended December 31, 2017		
Calculation of gross profit	**Sales**		
	Sales revenue		$480,000
	Less: Sales returns and allowances	$12,000	
	Sales discounts	8,000	20,000
	Net sales		460,000
	Cost of goods sold		316,000
	Gross profit		144,000
Calculation of income from operations	**Operating expenses**		
	Salaries and wages expense	64,000	
	Utilities expense	17,000	
	Advertising expense	16,000	
	Depreciation expense	8,000	
	Freight-out	7,000	
	Insurance expense	2,000	
	Total operating expenses		114,000
	Income from operations		30,000
Results of nonoperating activities	**Other revenues and gains**		
	Interest revenue	3,000	
	Gain on disposal of plant assets	600	3,600
	Other expenses and losses		
	Interest expense	1,800	
	Casualty loss from vandalism	200	2,000
	Net income		$ 31,600

Single-Step Income Statement

Another income statement format is the **single-step income statement**. The statement is so named because only one step—subtracting total expenses from total revenues—is required in determining net income.

In a single-step statement, all data are classified into two categories: (1) **revenues**, which include both operating revenues and other revenues and gains; and (2) **expenses**, which include cost of goods sold, operating expenses, and other expenses and losses. Illustration 5-15 shows a single-step statement for PW Audio Supply.

Illustration 5-15
Single-step income statement

PW AUDIO SUPPLY Income Statement For the Year Ended December 31, 2017		
Revenues		
Net sales		$460,000
Interest revenue		3,000
Gain on disposal of plant assets		600
Total revenues		463,600
Expenses		
Cost of goods sold	$316,000	
Operating expenses	114,000	
Interest expense	1,800	
Casualty loss from vandalism	200	
Total expenses		432,000
Net income		$ 31,600

There are two primary reasons for using the single-step format. (1) A company does not realize any type of profit or income until total revenues exceed total expenses, so it makes sense to divide the statement into these two categories. (2) The format is simpler and easier to read. *For homework problems, however, you should use the single-step format only when specifically instructed to do so.*

Classified Balance Sheet

In the balance sheet, merchandising companies report inventory as a current asset immediately below accounts receivable. Recall from Chapter 4 that companies generally list current asset items in the order of their closeness to cash (liquidity). Inventory is less close to cash than accounts receivable because the goods must first be sold and then collection made from the customer. Illustration 5-16 presents the assets section of a classified balance sheet for PW Audio Supply.

Illustration 5-16
Assets section of a classified balance sheet

PW AUDIO SUPPLY Balance Sheet (Partial) December 31, 2017		
Assets		
Current assets		
Cash		$ 9,500
Accounts receivable		16,100
Inventory		40,000
Prepaid insurance		1,800
Total current assets		67,400
Property, plant, and equipment		
Equipment	$80,000	
Less: Accumulated depreciation—equipment	24,000	56,000
Total assets		$123,400

LEARNING OBJECTIVE *6

APPENDIX 5A: Prepare a worksheet for a merchandising company.

Using a Worksheet

As indicated in Chapter 4, a worksheet enables companies to prepare financial statements before they journalize and post adjusting entries. The steps in preparing a worksheet for a merchandising company are the same as for a service company (see pages 117–123). Illustration 5A-1 on page 182 shows the worksheet for PW Audio Supply (excluding nonoperating items). The unique accounts for a merchandiser using a **perpetual inventory system** are in red.

TRIAL BALANCE COLUMNS

Data for the trial balance come from the ledger balances of PW Audio Supply at December 31. The amount shown for Inventory, $40,500, is the year-end inventory amount from the perpetual inventory system.

ADJUSTMENTS COLUMNS

A merchandising company generally has the same types of adjustments as a service company. As you see in the worksheet, adjustments (b), (c), and (d) are for insurance, depreciation, and salaries. Pioneer Advertising, as illustrated in Chapters 3 and 4, also had these adjustments. Adjustment (a) was required to adjust the perpetual inventory carrying amount to the actual count.

PW Audio Supply.xls

Home | Insert | Page Layout | Formulas | Data | Review | View

P18 fx

	A	B	C	D	E	F	G	H	I	J	K
1											
2		**PW AUDIO SUPPLY**									
3		**Worksheet**									
4		**For the Year Ended December 31, 2017**									
5–6		Trial Balance		Adjustments		Adjusted Trial Balance		Income Statement		Balance Sheet	
7	Accounts	Dr.	Cr.	Dr.	Cr.	Dr.	Cr.	Dr.	Cr.	Dr.	Cr.
8	Cash	9,500				9,500				9,500	
9	Accounts Receivable	16,100				16,100				16,100	
10	Inventory	40,500			(a) 500	40,000				40,000	
11	Prepaid Insurance	3,800			(b) 2,000	1,800				1,800	
12	Equipment	80,000				80,000				80,000	
13	Accumulated Depreciation—Equipment		16,000		(c) 8,000		24,000				24,000
14	Accounts Payable		20,400				20,400				20,400
15	Owner's Capital		83,000				83,000				83,000
16	Owner's Drawings	15,000				15,000				15,000	
17	Sales Revenue		480,000				480,000		480,000		
18	Sales Returns and Allowances	12,000				12,000		12,000			
19	Sales Discounts	8,000				8,000		8,000			
20	Cost of Goods Sold	315,500		(a) 500		316,000		316,000			
21	Freight-Out	7,000				7,000		7,000			
22	Advertising Expense	16,000				16,000		16,000			
23	Salaries and Wages Expense	59,000		(d) 5,000		64,000		64,000			
24	Utilities Expense	17,000				17,000		17,000			
25	Totals	599,400	599,400								
26	Insurance Expense			(b) 2,000		2,000		2,000			
27	Depreciation Expense			(c) 8,000		8,000		8,000			
28	Salaries and Wages Payable				(d) 5,000		5,000				5,000
29	Totals			15,500	15,500	612,400	612,400	450,000	480,000	162,400	132,400
30	Net Income							30,000			30,000
31	Totals							480,000	480,000	162,400	162,400
32											
33	Key: (a) Adjustment to inventory on hand. (b) Insurance expired. (c) Depreciation expense. (d) Salaries and wages accrued.										

Illustration 5A-1
Worksheet for merchandising company—perpetual inventory system

After PW Audio Supply enters all adjustments data on the worksheet, it establishes the equality of the adjustments column totals. It then extends the balances in all accounts to the adjusted trial balance columns.

ADJUSTED TRIAL BALANCE

The adjusted trial balance shows the balance of all accounts after adjustment at the end of the accounting period.

INCOME STATEMENT COLUMNS

Next, the merchandising company transfers the accounts and balances that affect the income statement from the adjusted trial balance columns to the income statement columns. PW Audio Supply shows Sales Revenue of $480,000 in the credit column. It shows the contra revenue accounts Sales Returns and Allowances $12,000 and Sales Discounts $8,000 in the debit column. The difference of $460,000 is the net sales shown on the income statement (Illustration 5-14, page 180).

Finally, the company totals all the credits in the income statement column and compares those totals to the total of the debits in the income statement column. If the credits exceed the debits, the company has net income. PW Audio Supply has net income of $30,000. If the debits exceed the credits, the company would report a net loss.

BALANCE SHEET COLUMNS

The major difference between the balance sheets of a service company and a merchandiser is inventory. PW Audio Supply shows the ending inventory amount of $40,000 in the balance sheet debit column. The information to prepare the owner's equity statement is also found in these columns. That is, the Owner's Capital account is $83,000. Owner's Drawings are $15,000. Net income results when the total of the debit column exceeds the total of the credit column in the balance sheet columns. A net loss results when the total of the credits exceeds the total of the debit balances.

LEARNING OBJECTIVE *

APPENDIX 5B: Record purchases and sales under a periodic inventory system.

As described in this chapter, companies may use one of two basic systems of accounting for inventories: (1) the perpetual inventory system or (2) the periodic inventory system. In the chapter, we focused on the characteristics of the perpetual inventory system. In this appendix, we discuss and illustrate the **periodic inventory system**. One key difference between the two systems is the point at which the company computes cost of goods sold. For a visual reminder of this difference, refer back to Illustration 5-5 (on page 168).

Determining Cost of Goods Sold Under a Periodic System

Determining cost of goods sold is different when a periodic inventory system is used rather than a perpetual system. As you have seen, a company using a **perpetual system** makes an entry to record cost of goods sold and to reduce inventory each time a sale is made. A company using a **periodic system** does not determine cost of goods sold until the end of the period. At the end of the period, the company performs a count to determine the ending balance of inventory. It then **calculates cost of goods sold by subtracting ending inventory from the cost of goods available for sale**. Goods available for sale is the sum of beginning inventory plus purchases, as shown in Illustration 5B-1.

Illustration 5B-1
Basic formula for cost of goods sold using the periodic system

	Beginning Inventory
+	Cost of Goods Purchased
	Cost of Goods Available for Sale
−	Ending Inventory
	Cost of Goods Sold

Another difference between the two approaches is that the perpetual system directly adjusts the Inventory account for any transaction that affects inventory (such as freight costs, returns, and discounts). The periodic system does not do this. Instead, it creates different accounts for purchases, freight costs, returns, and discounts. These various accounts are shown in Illustration 5B-2, which presents the calculation of cost of goods sold for PW Audio Supply using the periodic approach.

Illustration 5B-2
Cost of goods sold for a merchandiser using a periodic inventory system

PW AUDIO SUPPLY Cost of Goods Sold For the Year Ended December 31, 2017			
Cost of goods sold			
Inventory, January 1			**$ 36,000**
Purchases		$325,000	
Less: Purchase returns and allowances	$10,400		
Purchase discounts	6,800	17,200	
Net purchases		307,800	
Add: Freight-in		12,200	
Cost of goods purchased			**320,000**
Cost of goods available for sale			356,000
Less: Inventory, December 31			**40,000**
Cost of goods sold			**$316,000**

Note that the basic elements from Illustration 5B-1 are highlighted in Illustration 5B-2. You will learn more in Chapter 6 about how to determine cost of goods sold using the periodic system.

The use of the periodic inventory system does not affect the form of presentation in the balance sheet. As under the perpetual system, a company reports inventory in the current assets section.

Recording Merchandise Transactions

In a **periodic inventory system**, companies record revenues from the sale of merchandise when sales are made, just as in a perpetual system. Unlike the perpetual system, however, companies **do not attempt on the date of sale to record the cost of the merchandise sold**. Instead, they take a physical inventory count at the **end of the period** to determine (1) the cost of the merchandise then on hand and (2) the cost of the goods sold during the period. And, **under a periodic system, companies record purchases of merchandise in the Purchases account rather than in the Inventory account**. Also, in a periodic system, purchase returns and allowances, purchase discounts, and freight costs on purchases are recorded in separate accounts.

To illustrate the recording of merchandise transactions under a periodic inventory system, we will use purchase/sales transactions between PW Audio Supply and Sauk Stereo, as illustrated for the perpetual inventory system in this chapter.

Recording Purchases of Merchandise

On the basis of the sales invoice (Illustration 5-6, shown on page 169) and receipt of the merchandise ordered from PW Audio Supply, Sauk Stereo records the $3,800 purchase as follows.

May 4	Purchases	3,800	
	Accounts Payable		3,800
	(To record goods purchased on account from PW Audio Supply)		

Purchases is a temporary account whose normal balance is a debit.

FREIGHT COSTS

Terminology
Freight-In is also called *Transportation-In*.

When the purchaser directly incurs the freight costs, it debits the account Freight-In (or Transportation-In). For example, if Sauk Stereo pays Public Carrier Co. $150 for freight charges on its purchase from PW Audio Supply on May 6, the entry on Sauk Stereo's books is:

Date	Account Titles and Explanation	Debit	Credit
May 6	Freight-In (Transportation-In)	150	
	Cash		150
	(To record payment of freight on goods purchased)		

Like Purchases, Freight-In is a temporary account whose normal balance is a debit. **Freight-In is part of cost of goods purchased.** The reason is that cost of goods purchased should include any freight charges necessary to bring the goods to the purchaser. Freight costs are not subject to a purchase discount. Purchase discounts apply only to the invoice cost of the merchandise.

PURCHASE RETURNS AND ALLOWANCES

Sauk Stereo returns $300 of goods to PW Audio Supply and prepares the following entry to recognize the return.

Date	Account Titles and Explanation	Debit	Credit
May 8	Accounts Payable	300	
	Purchase Returns and Allowances		300
	(To record return of goods purchased from PW Audio Supply)		

Purchase Returns and Allowances is a temporary account whose normal balance is a credit.

PURCHASE DISCOUNTS

On May 14, Sauk Stereo pays the balance due on account to PW Audio Supply, taking the 2% cash discount allowed by PW Audio Supply for payment within 10 days. Sauk Stereo records the payment and discount as follows.

Date	Account Titles and Explanation	Debit	Credit
May 14	Accounts Payable ($3,800 − $300)	3,500	
	Purchase Discounts ($3,500 × 0.02)		70
	Cash		3,430
	(To record payment within the discount period)		

Purchase Discounts is a temporary account whose normal balance is a credit.

Recording Sales of Merchandise

The seller, PW Audio Supply, records the sale of $3,800 of merchandise to Sauk Stereo on May 4 (sales invoice No. 731, Illustration 5-6, page 169) as follows.

Date	Account Titles and Explanation	Debit	Credit
May 4	Accounts Receivable	3,800	
	Sales Revenue		3,800
	(To record credit sales per invoice #731 to Sauk Stereo)		

SALES RETURNS AND ALLOWANCES

To record the returned goods received from Sauk Stereo on May 8, PW Audio Supply records the $300 sales return as follows.

Date	Account Titles and Explanation	Debit	Credit
May 8	Sales Returns and Allowances	300	
	Accounts Receivable		300
	(To record credit granted to Sauk Stereo for returned goods)		

SALES DISCOUNTS

On May 14, PW Audio Supply receives payment of $3,430 on account from Sauk Stereo. PW Audio Supply honors the 2% cash discount and records the payment of Sauk Stereo's account receivable in full as follows.

May 14	Cash	3,430	
	Sales Discounts ($3,500 × 0.02)	70	
	Accounts Receivable ($3,800 − $300)		3,500
	(To record collection within 2/10, n/30 discount period from Sauk Stereo)		

COMPARISON OF ENTRIES—PERPETUAL VS. PERIODIC

Illustration 5B-3 summarizes the periodic inventory entries shown in this appendix and compares them to the perpetual system entries from the chapter. Entries that differ in the two systems are shown in color.

ENTRIES ON SAUK STEREO'S BOOKS

	Transaction	Perpetual Inventory System			Periodic Inventory System		
May 4	Purchase of merchandise on credit.	**Inventory**	**3,800**		**Purchases**	**3,800**	
		Accounts Payable		3,800	Accounts Payable		3,800
6	Freight costs on purchases.	**Inventory**	**150**		**Freight-In**	**150**	
		Cash		150	Cash		150
8	Purchase returns and allowances.	Accounts Payable	300		Accounts Payable	300	
		Inventory		**300**	**Purchase Returns and Allowances**		**300**
14	Payment on account with a discount.	Accounts Payable	3,500		Accounts Payable	3,500	
		Cash		3,430	Cash		3,430
		Inventory		**70**	**Purchase Discounts**		**70**

ENTRIES ON PW AUDIO SUPPLY'S BOOKS

	Transaction	Perpetual Inventory System			Periodic Inventory System		
May 4	Sale of merchandise on credit.	Accounts Receivable	3,800		Accounts Receivable	3,800	
		Sales Revenue		3,800	Sales Revenue		3,800
		Cost of Goods Sold	**2,400**		**No entry for cost of goods sold**		
		Inventory		**2,400**			
8	Return of merchandise sold.	Sales Returns and Allowances	300		Sales Returns and Allowances	300	
		Accounts Receivable		300	Accounts Receivable		300
		Inventory	**140**		**No entry**		
		Cost of Goods Sold		**140**			
14	Cash received on account with a discount.	Cash	3,430		Cash	3,430	
		Sales Discounts	70		Sales Discounts	70	
		Accounts Receivable		3,500	Accounts Receivable		3,500

Illustration 5B-3
Comparison of entries for perpetual and periodic inventory systems

Journalizing and Posting Closing Entries

For a merchandising company, like a service company, all accounts that affect the determination of net income are closed to Income Summary. Data for the preparation of closing entries may be obtained from the income statement columns of the worksheet. In journalizing, all debit column amounts are credited, and all credit columns amounts are debited. To close the merchandise inventory in a periodic inventory system:

1. The beginning inventory balance is debited to Income Summary and credited to Inventory.
2. The ending inventory balance is debited to Inventory and credited to Income Summary.

The two entries for PW Audio Supply are as follows.

	(1)		
Dec. 31	Income Summary	36,000	
	Inventory		36,000
	(To close beginning inventory)		
	(2)		
31	Inventory	40,000	
	Income Summary		40,000
	(To record ending inventory)		

After posting, the Inventory and Income Summary accounts will show the following.

Illustration 5B-4
Posting closing entries for merchandise inventory

Inventory		Income Summary	
1/1 Bal. 36,000	12/31 Close **36,000**	12/31 Close **36,000**	12/31 Close **40,000**
12/31 Close **40,000**			
12/31 Bal. 40,000			

Often, the closing of inventory is included with other closing entries, as shown below for PW Audio Supply. (*Close inventory with other accounts in homework problems unless stated otherwise.*)

Dec. 31	**Inventory (Dec. 31)**	**40,000**	
	Sales Revenue	480,000	
	Purchase Returns and Allowances	10,400	
	Purchase Discounts	6,800	
	Income Summary		537,200
	(To record ending inventory and close accounts with credit balances)		
31	Income Summary	507,200	
	Inventory (Jan. 1)		**36,000**
	Sales Returns and Allowances		12,000
	Sales Discounts		8,000
	Purchases		325,000
	Freight-In		12,200
	Salaries and Wages Expense		64,000
	Freight-Out		7,000
	Advertising Expense		16,000
	Utilities Expense		17,000
	Depreciation Expense		8,000
	Insurance Expense		2,000
	(To close beginning inventory and other income statement accounts with debit balances)		
31	Income Summary	30,000	
	Owner's Capital		30,000
	(To transfer net income to capital)		
31	Owner's Capital	15,000	
	Owner's Drawings		15,000
	(To close drawings to capital)		

After the closing entries are posted, all temporary accounts have zero balances. In addition, Owner's Capital has a credit balance of $98,000: beginning balance + net income − drawings ($83,000 + $30,000 − $15,000).

Using a Worksheet

As indicated in Chapter 4, a worksheet enables companies to prepare financial statements before journalizing and posting adjusting entries. The steps in preparing a worksheet for a merchandising company are the same as they are for a service company (see pages 117–123).

TRIAL BALANCE COLUMNS

Data for the trial balance come from the ledger balances of PW Audio Supply at December 31. The amount shown for Inventory, $36,000, is the beginning inventory amount from the periodic inventory system.

ADJUSTMENTS COLUMNS

A merchandising company generally has the same types of adjustments as a service company. As you see in the worksheet in Illustration 5B-5, adjustments (a), (b), and (c) are for insurance, depreciation, and salaries and wages. These adjustments were also required for Pioneer Advertising, as illustrated in Chapters 3 and 4. The unique accounts for a merchandiser using a **periodic inventory system** are shown in capital red letters. Note, however, that the worksheet excludes nonoperating items.

After all adjustment data are entered on the worksheet, the equality of the adjustment column totals is established. The balances in all accounts are then extended to the adjusted trial balance columns.

INCOME STATEMENT COLUMNS

Next, PW Audio Supply transfers the accounts and balances that affect the income statement from the adjusted trial balance columns to the income statement columns. The company shows Sales Revenue of $480,000 in the credit column. It shows the contra revenue accounts, Sales Returns and Allowances of $12,000 and Sales Discounts of $8,000 in the debit column. The difference of $460,000 is the net sales shown on the income statement (Illustration 5-9, page 178). Similarly, Purchases of $325,000 and Freight-In of $12,200 are extended to the debit column. The contra purchase accounts, Purchase Returns and Allowances of $10,400 and Purchase Discounts of $6,800, are extended to the credit columns.

The worksheet procedures for the Inventory account merit specific comment. The procedures are:

1. The beginning balance, $36,000, is extended from the adjusted trial balance column to the **income statement debit column**. From there, it can be added in reporting cost of goods available for sale in the income statement.
2. The ending inventory, $40,000, is added to the worksheet by an **income statement credit and a balance sheet debit**. The credit makes it possible to deduct ending inventory from the cost of goods available for sale in the income statement to determine cost of goods sold. The debit means the ending inventory can be reported as an asset on the balance sheet.

PW Audio Supply.xls

Home | Insert | Page Layout | Formulas | Data | Review | View

P18 *fx*

	A	B	C	D	E	F	G	H	I	J	K
1											
2		**PW AUDIO SUPPLY**									
3		**Worksheet**									
4		**For the Year Ended December 31, 2017**									
5–6		Trial Balance		Adjustments		Adjusted Trial Balance		Income Statement		Balance Sheet	
7	Accounts	Dr.	Cr.	Dr.	Cr.	Dr.	Cr.	Dr.	Cr.	Dr.	Cr.
8	Cash	9,500				9,500				9,500	
9	Accounts Receivable	16,100				16,100				16,100	
10	INVENTORY	36,000				36,000		36,000	40,000	40,000	
11	Prepaid Insurance	3,800			(a) 2,000	1,800				1,800	
12	Equipment	80,000				80,000				80,000	
13	Accumulated Depreciation—Equipment		16,000		(b) 8,000		24,000				24,000
14	Accounts Payable		20,400				20,400				20,400
15	Owner's Capital		83,000				83,000				83,000
16	Owner's Drawings	15,000				15,000				15,000	
17	SALES REVENUE		480,000				480,000		480,000		
18	SALES RETURNS AND ALLOWANCES	12,000				12,000		12,000			
19	SALES DISCOUNTS	8,000				8,000		8,000			
20	PURCHASES	325,000				325,000		325,000			
21	PURCHASE RETURNS AND ALLOWANCES		10,400				10,400		10,400		
22	PURCHASE DISCOUNTS		6,800				6,800		6,800		
23	FREIGHT-IN	12,200				12,200		12,200			
24	Freight-Out	7,000				7,000		7,000			
25	Advertising Expense	16,000				16,000		16,000			
26	Salaries and Wages Expense	59,000		(c) 5,000		64,000		64,000			
27	Utilities Expense	17,000				17,000		17,000			
28	Totals	616,600	616,600								
29	Insurance Expense			(a) 2,000		2,000		2,000			
30	Depreciation Expense			(b) 8,000		8,000		8,000			
31	Salaries and Wages Payable				(c) 5,000		5,000				5,000
32	Totals			15,000	15,000	629,600	629,600	507,200	537,200	162,400	132,400
33	Net Income							30,000			30,000
34	Totals							537,200	537,200	162,400	162,400
35											
36											

Key: (a) Insurance expired. (b) Depreciation expense. (c) Salaries and wages accrued.

Illustration 5B-5
Worksheet for merchandising company—periodic inventory system

These two procedures are specifically illustrated below:

Illustration 5B-6
Worksheet procedures for inventories

		Income Statement Dr.	Income Statement Cr.		Balance Sheet Dr.	Balance Sheet Cr.
Inventory	**(1)**	**36,000**	**40,000** ←	**(2)**	→ **40,000**	

The computation for cost of goods sold, taken from the income statement column in Illustration 5B-5, is as follows.

Illustration 5B-7
Computation of cost of goods sold from worksheet columns

Debit Column		Credit Column	
Beginning inventory	$ 36,000	Ending inventory	$40,000
Purchases	325,000	Purchase returns and allowances	10,400
Freight-in	12,200	Purchase discounts	6,800
Total debits	373,200	Total credits	$57,200
Less: Total credits	57,200		
Cost of goods sold	**$316,000**		

Finally, PW Audio Supply totals all the credits in the income statement column and compares these totals to the total of the debits in the income statement column. If the credits exceed the debits, the company has net income. PW Audio Supply has net income of $30,000. If the debits exceed the credits, the company would report a net loss.

BALANCE SHEET COLUMNS

The major difference between the balance sheets of a service company and a merchandising company is inventory. PW Audio Supply shows ending inventory of $40,000 in the balance sheet debit column. The information to prepare the owner's equity statement is also found in these columns. That is, the Owner's Capital account is $83,000. Owner's Drawings are $15,000. Net income results when the total of the debit column exceeds the total of the credit column in the balance sheet columns. A net loss results when the total of the credits exceeds the total of the debit balances.

REVIEW AND PRACTICE

LEARNING OBJECTIVES REVIEW

1 Describe merchandising operations and inventory systems. Because of inventory, a merchandising company has sales revenue, cost of goods sold, and gross profit. To account for inventory, a merchandising company must choose between a perpetual and a periodic inventory system.

2 Record purchases under a perpetual inventory system. The company debits the Inventory account for all purchases of merchandise and freight-in, and credits it for purchase discounts and purchase returns and allowances.

3 Record sales under a perpetual inventory system. When a merchandising company sells inventory, it debits Accounts Receivable (or Cash) and credits Sales Revenue for the **selling price** of the merchandise. At the same time, it debits Cost of Goods Sold and credits Inventory for the **cost** of the inventory items sold. Sales Returns and Allowances and Sales Discounts are debited and are contra revenue accounts.

4 Apply the steps in the accounting cycle to a merchandising company. Each of the required steps in the accounting cycle for a service company applies to a merchandising company. A worksheet is again an optional step. Under a perpetual inventory system, the company must adjust the Inventory account to agree with the physical count.

5 Compare a multiple-step with a single-step income statement. A multiple-step income statement shows numerous steps in determining net income, including nonoperating activities sections. A single-step income statement classifies all data under two categories, revenues or expenses, and determines net income in one step.

***6 Prepare a worksheet for a merchandising company.** The steps in preparing a worksheet for a merchandising company are the same as for a service company. The unique accounts for a merchandiser are Inventory, Sales Revenue, Sales Returns and Allowances, Sales Discounts, and Cost of Goods Sold.

*7 **Record purchases and sales under a periodic inventory system.** In recording purchases under a periodic system, companies must make entries for (a) cash and credit purchases, (b) purchase returns and allowances, (c) purchase discounts, and (d) freight costs. In recording sales, companies must make entries for (a) cash and credit sales, (b) sales returns and allowances, and (c) sales discounts.

GLOSSARY REVIEW

Contra revenue account An account that is offset against a revenue account on the income statement.

Cost of goods sold The total cost of merchandise sold during the period.

FOB destination Freight terms indicating that the seller places the goods free on board to the buyer's place of business, and the seller pays the freight.

FOB shipping point Freight terms indicating that the seller places goods free on board the carrier, and the buyer pays the freight costs.

Gross profit The excess of net sales over the cost of goods sold.

Gross profit rate Gross profit expressed as a percentage, by dividing the amount of gross profit by net sales.

Income from operations Income from a company's principal operating activity; determined by subtracting cost of goods sold and operating expenses from net sales.

Multiple-step income statement An income statement that shows several steps in determining net income.

Net sales Sales revenue less sales returns and allowances and less sales discounts.

Nonoperating activities Various revenues, expenses, gains, and losses that are unrelated to a company's main line of operations.

Operating expenses Expenses incurred in the process of earning sales revenue.

Other expenses and losses A nonoperating-activities section of the income statement that shows expenses and losses unrelated to the company's main line of operations.

Other revenues and gains A nonoperating-activities section of the income statement that shows revenues and gains unrelated to the company's main line of operations.

Periodic inventory system An inventory system under which the company does not keep detailed inventory records throughout the accounting period but determines the cost of goods sold only at the end of an accounting period.

Perpetual inventory system An inventory system under which the company keeps detailed records of the cost of each inventory purchase and sale, and the records continuously show the inventory that should be on hand.

Purchase allowance A deduction made to the selling price of merchandise, granted by the seller so that the buyer will keep the merchandise.

Purchase discount A cash discount claimed by a buyer for prompt payment of a balance due.

Purchase invoice A document that supports each credit purchase.

Purchase return A return of goods from the buyer to the seller for a cash or credit refund.

Sales discount A reduction given by a seller for prompt payment of a credit sale.

Sales invoice A document that supports each credit sale.

Sales returns and allowances Purchase returns and allowances from the seller's perspective. See *Purchase return* and *Purchase allowance,* above.

Sales revenue (Sales) The primary source of revenue in a merchandising company.

Single-step income statement An income statement that shows only one step in determining net income.

PRACTICE EXERCISES

Prepare purchase and sales entries.

(LO 2, 3)

1. On June 10, Spinner Company purchased $10,000 of merchandise from Lawrence Company, FOB shipping point, terms 2/10, n/30. Spinner pays the freight costs of $600 on June 11. Damaged goods totaling $700 are returned to Lawrence for credit on June 12. The fair value of these goods is $300. On June 19, Spinner pays Lawrence in full, less the purchase discount. Both companies use a perpetual inventory system.

Instructions

(a) Prepare separate entries for each transaction on the books of Spinner Company.

(b) Prepare separate entries for each transaction for Lawrence Company. The merchandise purchased by Spinner on June 10 had cost Lawrence $6,400.

Solution

1. (a)

Date	Account	Debit	Credit
June 10	Inventory	10,000	
	Accounts Payable		10,000
11	Inventory	600	
	Cash		600
12	Accounts Payable	700	
	Inventory		700
19	Accounts Payable ($10,000 – $700)	9,300	
	Inventory ($9,300 × 2%)		186
	Cash ($9,300 – $186)		9,114

(b)

Date	Account	Debit	Credit
June 10	Accounts Receivable	10,000	
	Sales Revenue		10,000
	Cost of Goods Sold	6,400	
	Inventory		6,400
12	Sales Returns and Allowances	700	
	Accounts Receivable		700
	Inventory	300	
	Cost of Goods Sold		300
19	Cash ($9,300 – $186)	9,114	
	Sales Discounts ($9,300 × 2%)	186	
	Accounts Receivable ($10,000 – $700)		9,300

Prepare multiple-step and single-step income statements.

(LO 5)

2. In its income statement for the year ended December 31, 2017, Sale Company reported the following condensed data.

Interest expense	$ 50,000	Net sales	$1,650,000
Operating expenses	590,000	Interest revenue	20,000
Cost of goods sold	902,000	Loss on disposal of equipment	7,000

Instructions

(a) Prepare a multiple-step income statement.

(b) Prepare a single-step income statement.

Solution

2. (a)

SALE COMPANY
Income Statement
For the Year Ended December 31, 2017

Net sales			$1,650,000
Cost of goods sold			902,000
Gross profit			748,000
Operating expenses			590,000
Income from operations			158,000
Other revenues and gains			
Interest revenue		$20,000	
Other expenses and losses			
Interest expense	$50,000		
Loss on disposal of equipment	7,000	57,000	(37,000)
Net income			$ 121,000

(b)

SALE COMPANY
Income Statement
For the Year Ended December 31, 2017

Revenues		
Net sales	$1,650,000	
Interest revenue	20,000	
Total revenues		$1,670,000
Expenses		
Cost of goods sold	902,000	
Operating expenses	590,000	
Interest expenses	50,000	
Loss on sale of equipment	7,000	
Total expenses		1,549,000
Net income		$ 121,000

PRACTICE PROBLEM

Prepare a multiple-step income statement.

(LO 5)

The adjusted trial balance columns of Falcetto Company's worksheet for the year ended December 31, 2017, are as follows.

	Debit		Credit
Cash	14,500	Accumulated Depreciation— Equipment	18,000
Accounts Receivable	11,100	Notes Payable	25,000
Inventory	29,000	Accounts Payable	10,600
Prepaid Insurance	2,500	Owner's Capital	81,000
Equipment	95,000	Sales Revenue	536,800
Owner's Drawings	12,000	Interest Revenue	2,500
Sales Returns and Allowances	6,700		673,900
Sales Discounts	5,000		
Cost of Goods Sold	363,400		
Freight-Out	7,600		
Advertising Expense	12,000		
Salaries and Wages Expense	56,000		
Utilities Expense	18,000		
Rent Expense	24,000		
Depreciation Expense	9,000		
Insurance Expense	4,500		
Interest Expense	3,600		
	673,900		

Instructions

Prepare a multiple-step income statement for Falcetto Company.

Solution

FALCETTO COMPANY Income Statement For the Year Ended December 31, 2017		
Sales		
Sales revenue		$536,800
Less: Sales returns and allowances	$ 6,700	
Sales discounts	5,000	11,700
Net sales		525,100
Cost of goods sold		363,400
Gross profit		161,700
Operating expenses		
Salaries and wages expense	56,000	
Rent expense	24,000	
Utilities expense	18,000	
Advertising expense	12,000	
Depreciation expense	9,000	
Freight-out	7,600	
Insurance expense	4,500	
Total operating expenses		131,100
Income from operations		30,600
Other revenues and gains		
Interest revenue	2,500	
Other expenses and losses		
Interest expense	3,600	1,100
Net income		$ 29,500

EXERCISES

Answer general questions about merchandisers.

(LO 1)

E5-1 Mr. McKenzie has prepared the following list of statements about service companies and merchandisers.

1. Measuring net income for a merchandiser is conceptually the same as for a service company.
2. For a merchandiser, sales less operating expenses is called gross profit.
3. For a merchandiser, the primary source of revenues is the sale of inventory.
4. Sales salaries and wages is an example of an operating expense.
5. The operating cycle of a merchandiser is the same as that of a service company.
6. In a perpetual inventory system, no detailed inventory records of goods on hand are maintained.
7. In a periodic inventory system, the cost of goods sold is determined only at the end of the accounting period.
8. A periodic inventory system provides better control over inventories than a perpetual system.

Instructions

Identify each statement as true or false. If false, indicate how to correct the statement.

Journalize purchase transactions.

(LO 2)

E5-2 Information related to Kerber Co. is presented below.

1. On April 5, purchased merchandise from Wilkes Company for $23,000, terms 2/10, net/30, FOB shipping point.
2. On April 6, paid freight costs of $900 on merchandise purchased from Wilkes.
3. On April 7, purchased equipment on account for $26,000.
4. On April 8, returned damaged merchandise to Wilkes Company and was granted a $3,000 credit for returned merchandise.
5. On April 15, paid the amount due to Wilkes Company in full.

Instructions

(a) Prepare the journal entries to record these transactions on the books of Kerber Co. under a perpetual inventory system.

(b) Assume that Kerber Co. paid the balance due to Wilkes Company on May 4 instead of April 15. Prepare the journal entry to record this payment.

E5-3 On September 1, Nixa Office Supply had an inventory of 30 calculators at a cost of $18 each. The company uses a perpetual inventory system. During September, the following transactions occurred.

Journalize perpetual inventory entries.

(LO 2, 3)

Sept. 6 Purchased 90 calculators at $22 each from York, terms net/30.
9 Paid freight of $90 on calculators purchased from York Co.
10 Returned 3 calculators to York Co. for $69 credit (including freight) because they did not meet specifications.
12 Sold 26 calculators costing $23 (including freight) for $31 each to Sura Book Store, terms n/30.
14 Granted credit of $31 to Sura Book Store for the return of one calculator that was not ordered.
20 Sold 30 calculators costing $23 for $32 each to Davis Card Shop, terms n/30.

Instructions

Journalize the September transactions.

E5-4 On June 10, Diaz Company purchased $8,000 of merchandise from Taylor Company, FOB shipping point, terms 2/10, n/30. Diaz pays the freight costs of $400 on June 11. Damaged goods totaling $300 are returned to Taylor for credit on June 12. The fair value of these goods is $70. On June 19, Diaz pays Taylor Company in full, less the purchase discount. Both companies use a perpetual inventory system.

Prepare purchase and sales entries.

(LO 2, 3)

Instructions

(a) Prepare separate entries for each transaction on the books of Diaz Company.

(b) Prepare separate entries for each transaction for Taylor Company. The merchandise purchased by Diaz on June 10 had cost Taylor $4,800.

E5-5 Presented below are transactions related to R. Humphrey Company.

Journalize sales transactions.

(LO 3)

1. On December 3, R. Humphrey Company sold $570,000 of merchandise to Frazier Co., terms 1/10, n/30, FOB destination. R. Humphrey paid $400 for freight charges. The cost of the merchandise sold was $350,000.
2. On December 8, Frazier Co. was granted an allowance of $20,000 for merchandise purchased on December 3.
3. On December 13, R. Humphrey Company received the balance due from Frazier Co.

Instructions

(a) Prepare the journal entries to record these transactions on the books of R. Humphrey Company using a perpetual inventory system.

(b) Assume that R. Humphrey Company received the balance due from Frazier Co. on January 2 of the following year instead of December 13. Prepare the journal entry to record the receipt of payment on January 2.

E5-6 The adjusted trial balance of Sang Company shows the following data pertaining to sales at the end of its fiscal year October 31, 2017: Sales Revenue $820,000, Freight-Out $16,000, Sales Returns and Allowances $25,000, and Sales Discounts $13,000.

Prepare sales section and closing entries.

(LO 4, 5)

Instructions

(a) Prepare the sales section of the income statement.

(b) Prepare separate closing entries for (1) sales revenue, and (2) the contra accounts to sales revenue.

E5-7 Tim Jarosz Company had the following account balances at year-end: Cost of Goods Sold $60,000, Inventory $15,000, Operating Expenses $29,000, Sales Revenue $115,000, Sales Discounts $1,200, and Sales Returns and Allowances $1,700. A physical count of inventory determines that merchandise inventory on hand is $13,600.

Prepare adjusting and closing entries.

(LO 4)

Instructions

(a) Prepare the adjusting entry necessary as a result of the physical count.
(b) Prepare closing entries.

Prepare adjusting and closing entries.

(LO 4)

E5-8 Presented below is information related to Hoerl Co. for the month of January 2017.

Ending inventory per perpetual records	$ 21,600	Insurance expense	$ 12,000
Ending inventory actually on hand	21,000	Rent expense	20,000
Cost of goods sold	218,000	Salaries and wages expense	55,000
Freight-out	7,000	Sales discounts	10,000
		Sales returns and allowances	13,000
		Sales revenue	380,000

Instructions

(a) Prepare the necessary adjusting entry for inventory.
(b) Prepare the necessary closing entries.

Prepare multiple-step income statement.

(LO 5)

E5-9 Presented below is information for Kaila Company for the month of March 2017.

Cost of goods sold	$215,000	Rent expense	$ 30,000
Freight-out	7,000	Sales discounts	8,000
Insurance expense	6,000	Sales returns and allowances	13,000
Salaries and wages expense	58,000	Sales revenue	380,000

Instructions

(a) Prepare a multiple-step income statement.
(b) Compute the gross profit rate.

Prepare multiple-step and single-step income statements.

(LO 5)

E5-10 In its income statement for the year ended December 31, 2017, Anhad Company reported the following condensed data.

Operating expenses	$ 725,000	Interest revenue	$ 28,000
Cost of goods sold	1,289,000	Loss on disposal of plant assets	17,000
Interest expense	70,000	Net sales	2,200,000

Instructions

(a) Prepare a multiple-step income statement.
(b) Prepare a single-step income statement.

Prepare correcting entries for sales and purchases.

(LO 2, 3)

E5-11 An inexperienced accountant for Stahr Company made the following errors in recording merchandising transactions.

1. A $210 refund to a customer for faulty merchandise was debited to Sales Revenue $210 and credited to Cash $210.
2. A $180 credit purchase of supplies was debited to Inventory $180 and credited to Cash $180.
3. A $215 sales discount was debited to Sales Revenue.
4. A cash payment of $20 for freight on merchandise purchases was debited to Freight-Out $200 and credited to Cash $200.

Instructions

Prepare separate correcting entries for each error, assuming that the incorrect entry is not reversed. (Omit explanations.)

Compute various income measures.

(LO 5)

E5-12 In 2017, Laquen Company had net sales of $900,000 and cost of goods sold of $522,000. Operating expenses were $225,000, and interest expense was $11,000. Laquen prepares a multiple-step income statement.

Instructions

(a) Compute Laquen's gross profit.
(b) Compute the gross profit rate. Why is this rate computed by financial statement users?

(c) What is Laquen's income from operations and net income?
(d) If Laquen prepared a single-step income statement, what amount would it report for net income?
(e) In what section of its classified balance sheet should Laquen report inventory?

E5-13 Presented below is financial information for two different companies.

Compute missing amounts and compute gross profit rate.

(LO 5)

	Summer Company	Winter Company
Sales revenue	$92,000	(d)
Sales returns	(a)	$ 5,000
Net sales	87,000	102,000
Cost of goods sold	56,000	(e)
Gross profit	(b)	41,500
Operating expenses	15,000	(f)
Net income	(c)	18,000

Instructions

(a) Determine the missing amounts.
(b) Determine the gross profit rates. (Round to one decimal place.)

E5-14 Financial information is presented below for three different companies.

Compute missing amounts.

(LO 5)

	Hardy Cosmetics	Yee Grocery	Wang Wholesalers
Sales revenue	$90,000	$ (e)	$122,000
Sales returns and allowances	(a)	5,000	12,000
Net sales	86,000	95,000	(i)
Cost of goods sold	56,000	(f)	(j)
Gross profit	(b)	38,000	24,000
Operating expenses	15,000	(g)	18,000
Income from operations	(c)	(h)	(k)
Other expenses and losses	4,000	7,000	(l)
Net income	(d)	11,000	5,000

Instructions

Determine the missing amounts.

***E5-15** Presented below are selected accounts for McPhan Company as reported in the worksheet using a perpetual inventory system at the end of May 2017.

Complete worksheet using a perpetual inventory system.

(LO 6)

Accounts	Adjusted Trial Balance		Income Statement		Balance Sheet	
	Dr.	Cr.	Dr.	Cr.	Dr.	Cr.
Cash	11,000					
Inventory	76,000					
Sales Revenue		480,000				
Sales Returns and Allowances	10,000					
Sales Discounts	9,000					
Cost of Goods Sold	300,000					

Instructions

Complete the worksheet by extending amounts reported in the adjusted trial balance to the appropriate columns in the worksheet. Do not total individual columns.

Prepare a worksheet using a perpetual inventory system.

(LO 6)

***E5-16** The trial balance columns of the worksheet using a perpetual inventory system for Balistreri Company at June 30, 2017, are as follows.

BALISTRERI COMPANY
Worksheet
For the Month Ended June 30, 2017

Account Titles	Trial Balance Debit	Trial Balance Credit
Cash	1,920	
Accounts Receivable	2,440	
Inventory	11,640	
Accounts Payable		1,120
Owner's Capital		3,500
Sales Revenue		42,500
Cost of Goods Sold	20,560	
Operating Expenses	10,560	
	47,120	47,120

Other data:
Operating expenses incurred on account, but not yet recorded, total $1,500.

Instructions
Enter the trial balance on a worksheet and complete the worksheet.

Prepare cost of goods sold section.
(LO 7)

***E5-17** The trial balance of A. Wiencek Company at the end of its fiscal year, August 31, 2017, includes these accounts: Inventory $19,500; Purchases $149,000; Sales Revenue $190,000; Freight-In $5,000; Sales Returns and Allowances $3,000; Freight-Out $1,000; and Purchase Returns and Allowances $2,000. The ending inventory is $23,000.

Instructions
Prepare a cost of goods sold section for the year ending August 31 (periodic inventory).

Compute various income statement items.
(LO 7)

***E5-18** On January 1, 2017, Brooke Hanson Corporation had inventory of $50,000. At December 31, 2017, Brooke Hanson had the following account balances.

Freight-in	$ 4,000
Purchases	509,000
Purchase discounts	6,000
Purchase returns and allowances	2,000
Sales revenue	840,000
Sales discounts	5,000
Sales returns and allowances	10,000

At December 31, 2017, Brooke Hanson determines that its ending inventory is $60,000.

Instructions
(a) Compute Brooke Hanson's 2017 gross profit.
(b) Compute Brooke Hanson's 2017 operating expenses if net income is $130,000 and there are no nonoperating activities.

***E5-19** Below is a series of cost of goods sold sections for companies B, F, L, and R.

	B	F	L	R
Beginning inventory	$ 180	$ 70	$1,000	$ (j)
Purchases	1,620	1,060	(g)	43,590
Purchase returns and allowances	40	(d)	290	(k)
Net purchases	(a)	1,030	6,210	41,090
Freight-in	110	(e)	(h)	2,240
Cost of goods purchased	(b)	1,280	7,940	(l)
Cost of goods available for sale	1,870	1,350	(i)	49,530
Ending inventory	250	(f)	1,450	6,230
Cost of goods sold	(c)	1,230	7,490	43,300

Instruction
Fill in the lettered blanks to complete the cost of goods sold sections.

***E5-20** This information relates to Nandi Co.

Journalize purchase transactions.

(LO 7)

1. On April 5, purchased merchandise from Dion Company for $25,000, terms 2/10, net/30, FOB shipping point.
2. On April 6, paid freight costs of $900 on merchandise purchased from Dion Company.
3. On April 7, purchased equipment on account for $30,000.
4. On April 8, returned some of April 5 merchandise, which cost $2,800, to Dion Company.
5. On April 15, paid the amount due to Dion Company in full.

Instructions

(a) Prepare the journal entries to record these transactions on the books of Nandi Co. using a periodic inventory system.

(b) Assume that Nandi Co. paid the balance due to Dion Company on May 4 instead of April 15. Prepare the journal entry to record this payment.

***E5-21** Presented below is information related to Chung Co.

Journalize purchase transactions.

(LO 7)

1. On April 5, purchased merchandise from Jose Company for $21,000, terms 2/10, net/30, FOB shipping point.
2. On April 6, paid freight costs of $800 on merchandise purchased from Jose.
3. On April 7, purchased equipment on account from Winker Mfg. Co. for $26,000.
4. On April 8, returned merchandise, which cost $4,000, to Jose Company.
5. On April 15, paid the amount due to Jose Company in full.

Instructions

(a) Prepare the journal entries to record these transactions on the books of Chung Co. using a periodic inventory system.

(b) Assume that Chung Co. paid the balance due to Jose Company on May 4 instead of April 15. Prepare the journal entry to record this payment.

***E5-22** Presented below are selected accounts for T. Swift Company as reported in the worksheet at the end of May 2017. Ending inventory is $75,000.

Complete worksheet.

(LO 7)

Accounts	Adjusted Trial Balance		Income Statement		Balance Sheet	
	Dr.	Cr.	Dr.	Cr.	Dr.	Cr.
Cash	9,000					
Inventory	80,000					
Purchases	240,000					
Purchase Returns and Allowances		30,000				
Sales Revenue		450,000				
Sales Returns and Allowances	10,000					
Sales Discounts	5,000					
Rent Expense	42,000					

Instructions

Complete the worksheet by extending amounts reported in the adjustment trial balance to the appropriate columns in the worksheet. The company uses the periodic inventory system.

PROBLEMS

P5-1A Kern's Book Warehouse distributes hardcover books to retail stores and extends credit terms of 2/10, n/30 to all of its customers. At the end of May, Kern's inventory consisted of books purchased for $1,800. During June, the following merchandising transactions occurred.

Journalize purchase and sales transactions under a perpetual inventory system.

(LO 2, 3)

June 1 Purchased books on account for $1,600 from Binsfeld Publishers, FOB destination, terms 2/10, n/30. The appropriate party also made a cash payment of $50 for the freight on this date.

3 Sold books on account to Reading Rainbow for $2,500. The cost of the books sold was $1,440.

6	Received $100 credit for books returned to Binsfeld Publishers.
9	Paid Binsfeld Publishers in full, less discount.
15	Received payment in full from Reading Rainbow.
17	Sold books on account to Rapp Books for $1,800. The cost of the books sold was $1,080.
20	Purchased books on account for $1,800 from McGinn Publishers, FOB destination, terms 2/15, n/30. The appropriate party also made a cash payment of $60 for the freight on this date.
24	Received payment in full from Rapp Books.
26	Paid McGinn Publishers in full, less discount.
28	Sold books on account to Baeten Bookstore for $1,600. The cost of the books sold was $970.
30	Granted Baeten Bookstore $120 credit for books returned costing $72.

Kern's Book Warehouse's chart of accounts includes the following: No. 101 Cash, No. 112 Accounts Receivable, No. 120 Inventory, No. 201 Accounts Payable, No. 401 Sales Revenue, No. 412 Sales Returns and Allowances, No. 414 Sales Discounts, and No. 505 Cost of Goods Sold.

Instructions

Journalize the transactions for the month of June for Kern's Book Warehouse using a perpetual inventory system.

Journalize, post, and prepare a partial income statement.

(LO 2, 3, 5)

GLS

P5-2A Renner Hardware Store completed the following merchandising transactions in the month of May. At the beginning of May, the ledger of Renner showed Cash of $5,000 and Owner's Capital of $5,000.

May	1	Purchased merchandise on account from Braun's Wholesale Supply $4,200, terms 2/10, n/30.
	2	Sold merchandise on account $2,100, terms 1/10, n/30. The cost of the merchandise sold was $1,300.
	5	Received credit from Braun's Wholesale Supply for merchandise returned $300.
	9	Received collections in full, less discounts, from customers billed on sales of $2,100 on May 2.
	10	Paid Braun's Wholesale Supply in full, less discount.
	11	Purchased supplies for cash $400.
	12	Purchased merchandise for cash $1,400.
	15	Received refund for poor quality merchandise from supplier on cash purchase $150.
	17	Purchased merchandise from Valley Distributors $1,300, FOB shipping point, terms 2/10, n/30.
	19	Paid freight on May 17 purchase $130.
	24	Sold merchandise for cash $3,200. The merchandise sold had a cost of $2,000.
	25	Purchased merchandise from Lumley, Inc. $620, FOB destination, terms 2/10, n/30.
	27	Paid Valley Distributors in full, less discount.
	29	Made refunds to cash customers for defective merchandise $70. The returned merchandise had a fair value of $30.
	31	Sold merchandise on account $1,000 terms n/30. The cost of the merchandise sold was $560.

Renner Hardware's chart of accounts includes the following: No. 101 Cash, No. 112 Accounts Receivable, No. 120 Inventory, No. 126 Supplies, No. 201 Accounts Payable, No. 301 Owner's Capital, No. 401 Sales Revenue, No. 412 Sales Returns and Allowances, No. 414 Sales Discounts, and No. 505 Cost of Goods Sold.

Instructions

(a) Journalize the transactions using a perpetual inventory system.

(b) Enter the beginning cash and capital balances and post the transactions. (Use J1 for the journal reference.)

(c) Prepare an income statement through gross profit for the month of May 2017.

(c) Gross profit $2,379

P5-3A Big Box Store is located in midtown Madison. During the past several years, net income has been declining because of suburban shopping centers. At the end of the company's fiscal year on November 30, 2017, the following accounts appeared in two of its trial balances.

Prepare financial statements and adjusting and closing entries.

(LO 4, 5)

	Unadjusted	Adjusted		Unadjusted	Adjusted
Accounts Payable	$ 25,200	$ 25,200	Notes Payable	$ 37,000	$ 37,000
Accounts Receivable	30,500	30,500	Owner's Capital	101,700	101,700
Accumulated Depr.—Equip.	34,000	45,000	Owner's Drawings	10,000	10,000
Cash	26,000	26,000	Prepaid Insurance	10,500	3,500
Cost of Goods Sold	518,000	518,000	Property Tax Expense		2,500
Freight-Out	6,500	6,500	Property Taxes Payable		2,500
Equipment	146,000	146,000	Rent Expense	15,000	15,000
Depreciation Expense		11,000	Salaries and Wages Expense	96,000	96,000
Insurance Expense		7,000	Sales Revenue	720,000	720,000
Interest Expense	6,400	6,400	Sales Commissions Expense	6,500	11,000
Interest Revenue	2,000	2,000	Sales Commissions Payable		4,500
Inventory	32,000	32,000	Sales Returns and Allowances	8,000	8,000
			Utilities Expense	8,500	8,500

Instructions

(a) Prepare a multiple-step income statement, an owner's equity statement, and a classified balance sheet. Notes payable are due in 2020.

(b) Journalize the adjusting entries that were made.

(c) Journalize the closing entries that are necessary.

(a) Net income $32,100
Owner's capital $123,800
Total assets $193,000

P5-4A Yolanda Hagen, a former disc golf star, operates Yolanda's Discorama. At the beginning of the current season on April 1, the ledger of Yolanda's Discorama showed Cash $1,800, Inventory $2,500, and Owner's Capital $4,300. The following transactions were completed during April.

Journalize, post, and prepare a trial balance.

(LO 2, 3, 4)

Apr.	5	Purchased golf discs, bags, and other inventory on account from Mumford Co. $1,200, FOB shipping point, terms 2/10, n/60.
	7	Paid freight on the Mumford purchase $50.
	9	Received credit from Mumford Co. for merchandise returned $100.
	10	Sold merchandise on account for $900, terms n/30. The merchandise sold had a cost of $540.
	12	Purchased disc golf shirts and other accessories on account from Saucer Sportswear $670, terms 1/10, n/30.
	14	Paid Mumford Co. in full, less discount.
	17	Received credit from Saucer Sportswear for merchandise returned $70.
	20	Made sales on account for $610, terms n/30. The cost of the merchandise sold was $370.
	21	Paid Saucer Sportswear in full, less discount.
	27	Granted an allowance to customers for clothing that was flawed $20.
	30	Received payments on account from customers $900.

The chart of accounts for the store includes the following: No. 101 Cash, No. 112 Accounts Receivable, No. 120 Inventory, No. 201 Accounts Payable, No. 301 Owner's Capital, No. 401 Sales Revenue, No. 412 Sales Returns and Allowances, and No. 505 Cost of Goods Sold.

Instructions

(a) Journalize the April transactions using a perpetual inventory system.

(b) Enter the beginning balances in the ledger accounts and post the April transactions. (Use J1 for the journal reference.)

(c) Prepare a trial balance on April 30, 2017.

(c) Total debits $5,810

***P5-5A** The trial balance of Gaolee Fashion Center contained the following accounts at November 30, the end of the company's fiscal year.

Complete accounting cycle beginning with a worksheet.

(LO 4, 5, 6)

GAOLEE FASHION CENTER
Trial Balance
November 30, 2017

	Debit	Credit
Cash	$ 20,700	
Accounts Receivable	30,700	
Inventory	44,700	
Supplies	6,200	
Equipment	133,000	
Accumulated Depreciation—Equipment		$ 28,000
Notes Payable		60,000
Accounts Payable		48,500
Owner's Capital		93,000
Owner's Drawings	12,000	
Sales Revenue		755,200
Sales Returns and Allowances	8,800	
Cost of Goods Sold	497,400	
Salaries and Wages Expense	140,000	
Advertising Expense	24,400	
Utilities Expense	14,000	
Maintenance and Repairs Expense	12,100	
Freight-Out	16,700	
Rent Expense	24,000	
Totals	$984,700	$984,700

Adjustment data:

1. Supplies on hand totaled $2,600.
2. Depreciation is $11,500 on the equipment.
3. Interest of $3,800 is accrued on notes payable at November 30.
4. Inventory actually on hand is $44,400.

(a) Adj. trial balance $1,000,000
Net loss $1,400
(b) Gross profit $248,700
Total assets $191,900

Instructions

(a) Enter the trial balance on a worksheet, and complete the worksheet.
(b) Prepare a multiple-step income statement and an owner's equity statement for the year, and a classified balance sheet as of November 30, 2017. Notes payable of $20,000 are due in January 2018.
(c) Journalize the adjusting entries.
(d) Journalize the closing entries.
(e) Prepare a post-closing trial balance.

Determine cost of goods sold and gross profit under periodic approach.

(LO 5, 7)

***P5-6A** At the end of Donaldson Department Store's fiscal year on November 30, 2017, these accounts appeared in its adjusted trial balance.

Freight-In	$ 7,500
Inventory	40,000
Purchases	585,000
Purchase Discounts	6,300
Purchase Returns and Allowances	2,700
Sales Revenue	1,000,000
Sales Returns and Allowances	20,000

Additional facts:

1. Merchandise inventory on November 30, 2017, is $52,600.
2. Donaldson Department Store uses a periodic system.

Gross profit $409,100

Instructions

Prepare an income statement through gross profit for the year ended November 30, 2017.

Calculate missing amounts and assess profitability.

(LO 5, 7)

***P5-7A** Kayla Inc. operates a retail operation that purchases and sells home entertainment products. The company purchases all merchandise inventory on credit and uses a periodic inventory system. The Accounts Payable account is used for recording inventory purchases only; all other current liabilities are accrued in separate accounts. You are provided with the following selected information for the fiscal years 2014 through 2017, inclusive.

	2014	2015	2016	2017
Income Statement Data				
Sales revenue		$55,000	$ (e)	$47,000
Cost of goods sold		(a)	14,800	14,300
Gross profit		38,300	35,200	(i)
Operating expenses		34,900	(f)	28,800
Net income		$ (b)	$ 2,500	$ (j)
Balance Sheet Data				
Inventory	$7,200	$ (c)	$ 8,100	$ (k)
Accounts payable	3,200	3,600	2,500	(l)
Additional Information				
Purchases of merchandise inventory on account		$14,200	$ (g)	$13,200
Cash payments to suppliers		(d)	(h)	13,600

(c) $4,700
(g) $18,200
(i) $32,700

Instructions

(a) Calculate the missing amounts.
(b) Sales declined over the 3-year fiscal period, 2015–2017. Does that mean that profitability necessarily also declined? Explain, computing the gross profit rate and the profit margin (Net income ÷ Sales revenue) for each fiscal year to help support your answer. (Round to one decimal place.)

***P5-8A** At the beginning of the current season on April 1, the ledger of Gage Pro Shop showed Cash $3,000, Inventory $4,000, and Owner's Capital $7,000. These transactions occurred during April 2017.

Journalize, post, and prepare trial balance and partial income statement using periodic approach.

(LO 7)

Apr. 5 Purchased golf bags, clubs, and balls on account from Tiger Co. $1,200, FOB shipping point, terms 2/10, n/60.
7 Paid freight on Tiger Co. purchases $50.
9 Received credit from Tiger Co. for merchandise returned $100.
10 Sold merchandise on account to customers $600, terms n/30.
12 Purchased golf shoes, sweaters, and other accessories on account from Classic Sportswear $450, terms 1/10, n/30.
14 Paid Tiger Co. in full.
17 Received credit from Classic Sportswear for merchandise returned $50.
20 Made sales on account to customers $600, terms n/30.
21 Paid Classic Sportswear in full.
27 Granted credit to customers for clothing that had flaws $35.
30 Received payments on account from customers $600.

The chart of accounts for the pro shop includes Cash, Accounts Receivable, Inventory, Accounts Payable, Owner's Capital, Sales Revenue, Sales Returns and Allowances, Purchases, Purchase Returns and Allowances, Purchase Discounts, and Freight-In.

Instructions

(a) Journalize the April transactions using a periodic inventory system.
(b) Using T-accounts, enter the beginning balances in the ledger accounts and post the April transactions.
(c) Prepare a trial balance on April 30, 2017.
(d) Prepare an income statement through gross profit, assuming merchandise inventory on hand at April 30 is $4,824.

(c) Tot. trial balance $8,376
Gross profit $465

COMPREHENSIVE PROBLEM

CP5 On December 1, 2017, Rodriguez Distributing Company had the following account balances.

	Debit		Credit
Cash	$ 7,200	Accumulated Depreciation—Equipment	$ 2,200
Accounts Receivable	4,600	Accounts Payable	4,500
Inventory	12,000	Salaries and Wages Payable	1,000
Supplies	1,200	Owner's Capital	39,300
Equipment	22,000		
	$47,000		$47,000

During December, the company completed the following summary transactions.

Dec. 6 Paid $1,600 for salaries and wages due employees, of which $600 is for December and $1,000 is for November salaries and wages payable.
8 Received $2,200 cash from customers in payment of account (no discount allowed).
10 Sold merchandise for cash $6,300. The cost of the merchandise sold was $4,100.
13 Purchased merchandise on account from Boehm Co. $9,000, terms 2/10, n/30.
15 Purchased supplies for cash $2,000.
18 Sold merchandise on account $15,000, terms 3/10, n/30. The cost of the merchandise sold was $10,000.
20 Paid salaries and wages $1,800.
23 Paid Boehm Co. in full, less discount.
27 Received collections in full, less discounts, from customers billed on December 18.

Adjustment data:

1. Accrued salaries and wages payable $840.
2. Depreciation $200 per month.
3. Supplies on hand $1,500.

Instructions

(a) Journalize the December transactions using a perpetual inventory system.
(b) Enter the December 1 balances in the ledger T-accounts and post the December transactions. Use Cost of Goods Sold, Depreciation Expense, Salaries and Wages Expense, Sales Revenue, Sales Discounts, and Supplies Expense.
(c) Journalize and post adjusting entries.
(d) Totals $68,340 (d) Prepare an adjusted trial balance.
(e) Net income $1,610 (e) Prepare an income statement and an owner's equity statement for December and a classified balance sheet at December 31.

BROADENING YOUR PERSPECTIVE

FINANCIAL REPORTING AND ANALYSIS

Financial Reporting Problem: Apple Inc.

BYP5-1 The financial statements of **Apple Inc.** are presented in Appendix A at the end of this textbook. Instructions for accessing and using the company's complete annual report, including the notes to the financial statements, are also provided in Appendix A.

Instructions

Answer the following questions using Apple's Consolidated Statement of Income.

(a) What was the percentage change in (1) sales and in (2) net income from 2011 to 2012 and from 2012 to 2013?
(b) What was the company's gross profit rate in 2011, 2012, and 2013?
(c) What was the company's percentage of net income to net sales in 2011, 2012, and 2013? Comment on any trend in this percentage.

Comparative Analysis Problem: PepsiCo, Inc. vs. The Coca-Cola Company

BYP5-2 PepsiCo's financial statements are presented in Appendix B. Financial statements of The Coca-Cola Company are presented in Appendix C. Instructions for accessing and using the complete annual reports of PepsiCo and Coca-Cola, including the notes to the financial statements, are also provided in Appendices B and C, respectively.

Instructions

(a) Based on the information contained in these financial statements, determine each of the following for each company.
   (1) Gross profit for 2013.
   (2) Gross profit rate for 2013.
   (3) Operating income for 2013.
   (4) Percentage change in operating income from 2012 to 2013.

(b) What conclusions concerning the relative profitability of the two companies can you draw from these data?

Comparative Analysis Problem: Amazon.com, Inc. vs. Wal-Mart Stores, Inc.

BYP5-3 Amazon.com, Inc.'s financial statements are presented in Appendix D. Financial statements of Wal-Mart Stores, Inc. are presented in Appendix E. (Use Wal-Mart's January 31, 2014, financial statements for comparative purposes.) Instructions for accessing and using the complete annual reports of Amazon and Wal-Mart, including the notes to the financial statements, are also provided in Appendices D and E, respectively.

Instructions

(a) Based on the information contained in these financial statements, determine each of the following for each company. Use Amazon's net product sales to compute gross profit information.
   (1) Gross profit for 2013.
   (2) Gross profit rate for 2013.
   (3) Operating income for 2013.
   (4) Percentage change in operating income from 2012 to 2013.

(b) What conclusions concerning the relative profitability of the two companies can you draw from these data?

Real-World Focus

BYP5-4 No financial decision-maker should ever rely solely on the financial information reported in the annual report to make decisions. It is important to keep abreast of financial news. This activity demonstrates how to search for financial news on the Web.

Address: **biz.yahoo.com/i**, or go to **www.wiley.com/college/weygandt**

Steps:

1. Type in either PepsiCo or Coca-Cola.
2. Choose **News**.
3. Select an article that sounds interesting to you.

Instructions

(a) What was the source of the article (e.g., Reuters, Businesswire, PR Newswire)?

(b) Assume that you are a personal financial planner and that one of your clients owns stock in the company. Write a brief memo to your client, summarizing the article and explaining the implications of the article for his or her investment.

CRITICAL THINKING

Decision-Making Across the Organization

BYP5-5 Three years ago, Amy Hessler and her brother-in-law Jacob Seelig opened Family Department Store. For the first two years, business was good, but the following condensed income results for 2016 were disappointing.

FAMILY DEPARTMENT STORE
Income Statement
For the Year Ended December 31, 2016

Net sales		$700,000
Cost of goods sold		553,000
Gross profit		147,000
Operating expenses		
Selling expenses	$100,000	
Administrative expenses	20,000	120,000
Net income		$ 27,000

Amy believes the problem lies in the relatively low gross profit rate (gross profit divided by net sales) of 21%. Jacob believes the problem is that operating expenses are too high.

Amy thinks the gross profit rate can be improved by making both of the following changes. She does not anticipate that these changes will have any effect on operating expenses.

1. Increase average selling prices by 17%. This increase is expected to lower sales volume so that total sales will increase only 6%.
2. Buy merchandise in larger quantities and take all purchase discounts. These changes are expected to increase the gross profit rate by 3 percentage points.

Jacob thinks expenses can be cut by making both of the following changes. He feels that these changes will not have any effect on net sales.

1. Cut sales salaries of $60,000 in half and give sales personnel a commission of 2% of net sales.
2. Reduce store deliveries to one day per week rather than twice a week. This change will reduce delivery expenses of $30,000 by 40%.

Amy and Jacob come to you for help in deciding the best way to improve net income.

Instructions

With the class divided into groups, answer the following.

(a) Prepare a condensed income statement for 2017, assuming (1) Amy's changes are implemented and (2) Jacob's ideas are adopted.
(b) What is your recommendation to Amy and Jacob?
(c) Prepare a condensed income statement for 2017, assuming both sets of proposed changes are made.

Communication Activity

BYP5-6 The following situation is in chronological order.

1. Parker decides to buy a surfboard.
2. He calls Surfing USA Co. to inquire about its surfboards.
3. Two days later, he requests Surfing USA Co. to make a surfboard.
4. Three days later, Surfing USA Co. sends him a purchase order to fill out.
5. He sends back the purchase order.
6. Surfing USA Co. receives the completed purchase order.
7. Surfing USA Co. completes the surfboard.
8. Parker picks up the surfboard.
9. Surfing USA Co. bills Parker.
10. Surfing USA Co. receives payment from Parker.

Instructions

In a memo to the president of Surfing USA Co., answer the following.

(a) When should Surfing USA Co. record the sale?
(b) Suppose that with his purchase order, Parker is required to make a down payment. Would that change your answer?

Ethics Case

BYP5-7 Tiffany Lyons was just hired as the assistant treasurer of Key West Stores. The company is a specialty chain store with nine retail stores concentrated in one metropolitan area. Among other things, the payment of all invoices is centralized in one of the departments Tiffany will manage. Her primary responsibility is to maintain the company's high credit rating by paying all bills when due and to take advantage of all cash discounts.

Jay Barnes, the former assistant treasurer who has been promoted to treasurer, is training Tiffany in her new duties. He instructs Tiffany that she is to continue the practice of preparing all checks "net of discount" and dating the checks the last day of the discount period. "But," Jay continues, "we always hold the checks at least 4 days beyond the discount period before mailing them. That way, we get another 4 days of interest on our money. Most of our creditors need our business and don't complain. And, if they scream about our missing the discount period, we blame it on the mail room or the post office. We've only lost one discount out of every hundred we take that way. I think everybody does it. By the way, welcome to our team!"

Instructions

(a) What are the ethical considerations in this case?
(b) Who are the stakeholders that are harmed or benefitted in this situation?
(c) Should Tiffany continue the practice started by Jay? Does she have any choice?

All About You

BYP5-8 There are many situations in business where it is difficult to determine the proper period in which to record revenue. Suppose that after graduation with a degree in finance, you take a job as a manager at a consumer electronics store called Impact Electronics. The company has expanded rapidly in order to compete with **Best Buy**. Impact has also begun selling gift cards for its electronic products. The cards are available in any dollar amount and allow the holder of the card to purchase an item for up to 2 years from the time the card is purchased. If the card is not used during that 2 years, it expires.

Instructions

Answer the following questions.

At what point should the revenue from the gift cards be recognized? Should the revenue be recognized at the time the card is sold, or should it be recorded when the card is redeemed? Explain the reasoning to support your answers.

FASB Codification Activity

BYP5-9 If your school has a subscription to the FASB Codification, go to **http://aaahq.org/ascLogin.cfm** to log in and prepare responses to the following.

Instructions

(a) Access the glossary ("Master Glossary") to answer the following:
  (1) What is the definition provided for inventory?
  (2) What is a customer?
(b) What guidance does the Codification provide concerning reporting inventories above cost?

A Look at IFRS

LEARNING OBJECTIVE 7 **Compare the accounting for merchandising under GAAP and IFRS.**

The basic accounting entries for merchandising are the same under both GAAP and IFRS. The income statement is a required statement under both sets of standards. The basic format is similar although some differences do exist.

Key Points

Following are the key similarities and differences between GAAP and IFRS related to inventories.

Similarities

- Under both GAAP and IFRS, a company can choose to use either a perpetual or periodic inventory system.
- The definition of inventories is basically the same under GAAP and IFRS.
- As indicated above, the basic accounting entries for merchandising are the same under both GAAP and IFRS.
- Both GAAP and IFRS require that income statement information be presented for multiple years. For example, IFRS requires that 2 years of income statement information be presented, whereas GAAP requires 3 years.

Differences

- Under GAAP companies generally classify income statement items by function. Classification by function leads to descriptions like administration, distribution, and manufacturing. Under IFRS, companies must classify expenses either by nature or by function. Classification by nature leads to descriptions such as the following: salaries, depreciation expense, and utilities expense. If a company uses the functional-expense method on the income statement, disclosure by nature is required in the notes to the financial statements.
- Presentation of the income statement under GAAP follows either a single-step or multiple-step format. IFRS does not mention a single-step or multiple-step approach.
- Under IFRS revaluation of land, buildings, and intangible assets is permitted. The initial gains and losses resulting from this revaluation are reported as adjustments to equity, often referred to as **other comprehensive income**. The effect of this difference is that the use of IFRS results in more transactions affecting equity (other comprehensive income) but not net income.

Looking to the Future

The IASB and FASB are working on a project that would rework the structure of financial statements. Specifically, this project will address the issue of how to classify various items in the income statement. A main goal of this new approach is to provide information that better represents how businesses are run. In addition, this approach draws attention away from just one number—net income. It will adopt major groupings similar to those currently used by the statement of cash flows (operating, investing, and financing), so that numbers can be more readily traced across statements. For example, the amount of income that is generated by operations would be traceable to the assets and liabilities used to generate the income. Finally, this approach would also provide detail, beyond that currently seen in most statements (either GAAP or IFRS), by requiring that line items be presented both by function and by nature. The new financial statement format was heavily influenced by suggestions from financial statement analysts.

IFRS Practice

IFRS Self-Test Questions

1. Which of the following would **not** be included in the definition of inventory under IFRS?
   (a) Photocopy paper held for sale by an office-supply store.
   (b) Stereo equipment held for sale by an electronics store.
   (c) Used office equipment held for sale by the human relations department of a plastics company.
   (d) All of the above would meet the definition.
2. Which of the following would **not** be a line item of a company reporting costs by nature?
   (a) Depreciation expense.
   (b) Salaries expense.
   (c) Interest expense.
   (d) Manufacturing expense.
3. Which of the following would **not** be a line item of a company reporting costs by function?
   (a) Administration.
   (b) Manufacturing.
   (c) Utilities expense.
   (d) Distribution.
4. Which of the following statements is **false**?
   (a) IFRS specifically requires use of a multiple-step income statement.
   (b) Under IFRS, companies can use either a perpetual or periodic system.
   (c) The proposed new format for financial statements was heavily influenced by the suggestions of financial statement analysts.
   (d) The new income statement format will try to de-emphasize the focus on the "net income" line item.

IFRS Exercises

IFRS5-1 Explain the difference between the "nature-of-expense" and "function-of-expense" classifications.

IFRS5-2 For each of the following income statement line items, state whether the item is a "by nature" expense item or a "by function" expense item.

_______	Cost of goods sold	_______	Utilities expense
_______	Depreciation expense	_______	Delivery expense
_______	Salaries and wages expense	_______	General and administrative expenses
_______	Selling expenses		

IFRS5-3 Matilda Company reported the following amounts (in euros) in 2017: Net income, €150,000; Unrealized gain related to revaluation of buildings, €10,000; and Unrealized loss on non-trading securities, €(35,000). Determine Matilda's total comprehensive income for 2017.

International Financial Reporting Problem: Louis Vuitton

IFRS5-4 The financial statements of **Louis Vuitton** are presented in Appendix F. Instructions for accessing and using the company's complete annual report, including the notes to its financial statements, are also provided in Appendix F.

Instructions

Use Louis Vuitton's annual report to answer the following questions.

(a) Does Louis Vuitton use a multiple-step or a single-step income statement format? Explain how you made your determination.

(b) Instead of "interest expense," what label does Louis Vuitton use for interest costs that it incurs?

(c) Using the notes to the company's financial statements, determine the following:

(1) Composition of the inventory.

(2) Amount of inventory (gross) before impairment.

Answers to IFRS Self-Test Questions

1. c **2.** d **3.** c **4.** a

Chapter 6 Inventories

Let's talk inventory—big, bulldozer-size inventory. Caterpillar Inc. is the world's largest manufacturer of construction and mining equipment, diesel and natural gas engines, and industrial gas turbines. It sells its products in over 200 countries, making it one of the most successful U.S. exporters. More than 70% of its productive assets are located domestically, and nearly 50% of its sales are foreign.

In the past, Caterpillar's profitability suffered, but today it is very successful. A big part of this turnaround can be attributed to effective management of its inventory. Imagine what it costs Caterpillar to have too many bulldozers sitting around in inventory—a situation the company definitely wants to avoid. Yet Caterpillar must also make sure it has enough inventory to meet demand.

At one time during a 7-year period, Caterpillar's sales increased by 100% while its inventory increased by only 50%. To achieve this dramatic reduction in the amount of resources tied up in inventory while continuing to meet customers' needs, Caterpillar used a two-pronged approach. First, it completed a factory modernization program, which greatly increased its production efficiency. The program reduced by 60% the amount of inventory the company processes at any one time. It also reduced by an incredible 75% the time it takes to manufacture a part.

Second, Caterpillar dramatically improved its parts distribution system. It ships more than 100,000 items daily from its 23 distribution centers strategically located around the world (10 million square feet of warehouse space—remember, we're talking bulldozers). The company can virtually guarantee that it can get any part to anywhere in the world within 24 hours.

These changes led to record exports, profits, and revenues for Caterpillar. It would seem that things couldn't be better. But industry analysts, as well as the company's managers, thought otherwise. In order to maintain Caterpillar's position as the industry leader, management began another major overhaul of inventory production and inventory management processes. The goal: to cut the number of repairs in half, increase productivity by 20%, and increase inventory turnover by 40%.

In short, Caterpillar's ability to manage its inventory has been a key reason for its past success and will very likely play a huge part in its future profitability as well.

LEARNING OBJECTIVES

1. **Discuss how to classify and determine inventory.**
2. **Apply inventory cost flow methods and discuss their financial effects.**
3. **Indicate the effects of inventory errors on the financial statements.**
4. **Explain the statement presentation and analysis of inventory.**

LEARNING OBJECTIVE 1

Discuss how to classify and determine inventory.

Two important steps in the reporting of inventory at the end of the accounting period are the classification of inventory based on its degree of completeness and the determination of inventory amounts.

Classifying Inventory

How a company classifies its inventory depends on whether the firm is a merchandiser or a manufacturer. In a **merchandising** company, such as those described in Chapter 5, inventory consists of many different items. For example, in a grocery store, canned goods, dairy products, meats, and produce are just a few of the inventory items on hand. These items have two common characteristics: (1) they are owned by the company, and (2) they are in a form ready for sale to customers in the ordinary course of business. Thus, merchandisers need only one inventory classification, **merchandise inventory**, to describe the many different items that make up the total inventory.

In a **manufacturing** company, some inventory may not yet be ready for sale. As a result, manufacturers usually classify inventory into three categories: finished goods, work in process, and raw materials. **Finished goods inventory** is manufactured items that are completed and ready for sale. **Work in process** is that portion of manufactured inventory that has been placed into the production process but is not yet complete. **Raw materials** are the basic goods that will be used in production but have not yet been placed into production.

For example, Caterpillar classifies earth-moving tractors completed and ready for sale as **finished goods**. It classifies the tractors on the assembly line in various stages of production as **work in process**. The steel, glass, tires, and other components that are on hand waiting to be used in the production of tractors are identified as **raw materials**. Illustration 6-1 shows an adapted excerpt from Note 7 of Caterpillar's annual report.

Illustration 6-1
Composition of Caterpillar's inventory

	December 31		
(millions of dollars)	**2013**	**2012**	**2011**
Raw materials	$ 2,966	$ 3,573	$ 3,766
Work-in-process	2,589	2,920	2,959
Finished goods	6,785	8,767	7,562
Other	285	287	257
Total inventories	**$12,625**	**$15,547**	**$14,544**

By observing the levels and changes in the levels of these three inventory types, financial statement users can gain insight into management's production plans. For example, low levels of raw materials and high levels of finished goods suggest that management believes it has enough inventory on hand and production will be slowing down—perhaps in anticipation of a recession. Conversely, high levels of raw materials and low levels of finished goods probably signal that management is planning to step up production.

Many companies have significantly lowered inventory levels and costs using **just-in-time (JIT) inventory** methods. Under a just-in-time method, companies manufacture or purchase goods only when needed for use. Dell is famous for having developed a system for making computers in response to individual customer requests. Even though it makes each computer to meet each customer's particular specifications, Dell is able to assemble the computer and put it on a truck in less than 48 hours. The success of the JIT system depends on reliable suppliers. By integrating its information systems with those of its suppliers, Dell reduced its inventories to nearly zero. This is a huge advantage in an industry where products become obsolete nearly overnight.

The accounting concepts discussed in this chapter apply to the inventory classifications of both merchandising and manufacturing companies. Our focus here is on merchandise inventory. Additional issues specific to manufacturing companies are discussed later in the managerial section of this textbook (Chapters 19–26).

Determining Inventory Quantities

No matter whether they are using a periodic or perpetual inventory system, all companies need to determine inventory quantities at the end of the accounting period. If using a perpetual system, companies take a physical inventory for the following reasons:

1. To check the accuracy of their perpetual inventory records.
2. To determine the amount of inventory lost due to wasted raw materials, shoplifting, or employee theft.

Companies using a periodic inventory system take a physical inventory for **two different purposes**: to determine the inventory on hand at the balance sheet date, and to determine the cost of goods sold for the period.

Determining inventory quantities involves two steps: (1) taking a physical inventory of goods on hand and (2) determining the ownership of goods.

TAKING A PHYSICAL INVENTORY

Companies take a physical inventory at the end of the accounting period. Taking a physical inventory involves actually counting, weighing, or measuring each kind of inventory on hand. In many companies, taking an inventory is a formidable task. Retailers such as Target, True Value Hardware, or Home Depot have thousands of different inventory items. An inventory count is generally more accurate when goods are not being sold or received during the counting. Consequently, companies often "take inventory" when the business is closed or when business is slow. Many retailers close early on a chosen day in January—after the holiday sales and returns, when inventories are at their lowest level—to count inventory. Wal-Mart Stores, Inc., for example, has a year-end of January 31.

DETERMINING OWNERSHIP OF GOODS

One challenge in computing inventory quantities is determining what inventory a company owns. To determine ownership of goods, two questions must be answered: Do all of the goods included in the count belong to the company? Does the company own any goods that were not included in the count?

GOODS IN TRANSIT A complication in determining ownership is **goods in transit** (on board a truck, train, ship, or plane) at the end of the period. The company may have purchased goods that have not yet been received, or it may have sold goods that have not yet been delivered. To arrive at an accurate count, the company must determine ownership of these goods.

Goods in transit should be included in the inventory of the company that has legal title to the goods. Legal title is determined by the terms of the sale, as shown in Illustration 6-2 and described on the next page.

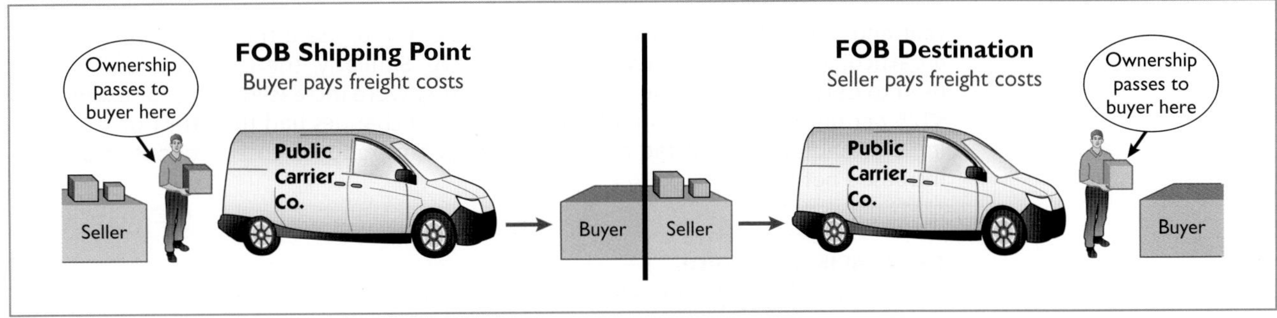

Illustration 6-2
Terms of sale

1. When the terms are **FOB (free on board) shipping point**, ownership of the goods passes to the buyer when the public carrier accepts the goods from the seller.
2. When the terms are **FOB destination**, ownership of the goods remains with the seller until the goods reach the buyer.

If goods in transit at the statement date are ignored, inventory quantities may be seriously miscounted. Assume, for example, that Hargrove Company has 20,000 units of inventory on hand on December 31. It also has the following goods in transit:

1. Sales of 1,500 units shipped December 31 FOB destination.
2. Purchases of 2,500 units shipped FOB shipping point by the seller on December 31.

Hargrove has legal title to both the 1,500 units sold and the 2,500 units purchased. If the company ignores the units in transit, it would understate inventory quantities by 4,000 units (1,500 + 2,500).

As we will see later in the chapter, inaccurate inventory counts affect not only the inventory amount shown on the balance sheet but also the cost of goods sold calculation on the income statement.

CONSIGNED GOODS In some lines of business, it is common to hold the goods of other parties and try to sell the goods for them for a fee, but without taking ownership of the goods. These are called **consigned goods**.

For example, you might have a used car that you would like to sell. If you take the item to a dealer, the dealer might be willing to put the car on its lot and charge you a commission if it is sold. Under this agreement, the dealer **would not take ownership** of the car, which would still belong to you. Therefore, if an inventory count were taken, the car would not be included in the dealer's inventory because the dealer does not own it.

Many car, boat, and antique dealers sell goods on consignment to keep their inventory costs down and to avoid the risk of purchasing an item that they will not be able to sell. Today, even some manufacturers are making consignment agreements with their suppliers in order to keep their inventory levels low.

ANATOMY OF A FRAUD

Ted Nickerson, CEO of clock manufacturer Dally Industries, was feared by all of his employees. Ted also had expensive tastes. To support this habit, Ted took out large loans, which he collateralized with his shares of Dally Industries stock. If the price of Dally's stock fell, he was required to provide the bank with more shares of stock. To achieve target net income figures and thus maintain the stock price, Ted coerced employees in the company to alter inventory figures. Inventory quantities were manipulated by changing the amounts on inventory control tags after the year-end physical inventory count. For example, if a tag said there were 20 units of a particular item, the tag was changed to 220. Similarly, the unit costs that were used to determine the value of ending inventory were increased from, for example, $125 per unit to $1,250. Both of these fraudulent changes had the effect of increasing the amount of reported ending inventory. This reduced cost of goods sold and increased net income.

Total take: $245,000

THE MISSING CONTROL

Independent internal verification. The company should have spot-checked its inventory records periodically, verifying that the number of units in the records agreed with the amount on hand and that the unit costs agreed with vendor price sheets.

Source: Adapted from Wells, *Fraud Casebook* (2007), pp. 502–509.

LEARNING OBJECTIVE 2

Apply inventory cost flow methods and discuss their financial effects.

Inventory is accounted for at cost. Cost includes all expenditures necessary to acquire goods and place them in a condition ready for sale. For example, freight costs incurred to acquire inventory are added to the cost of inventory, but the cost of shipping goods to a customer are a selling expense.

After a company has determined the quantity of units of inventory, it applies unit costs to the quantities to compute the total cost of the inventory and the cost of goods sold. This process can be complicated if a company has purchased inventory items at different times and at different prices.

For example, assume that Crivitz TV Company purchases three identical 50-inch TVs on different dates at costs of $720, $750, and $800. During the year, Crivitz sold two sets at $1,200 each. These facts are summarized in Illustration 6-3.

Illustration 6-3
Data for inventory costing example

Purchases			
February 3	1 TV	at	$720
March 5	1 TV	at	$750
May 22	1 TV	at	$800
Sales			
June 1	2 TVs	for	$2,400 ($1,200 × 2)

Cost of goods sold will differ depending on which two TVs the company sold. For example, it might be $1,470 ($720 + $750), or $1,520 ($720 + $800), or $1,550 ($750 + $800). In this section, we discuss alternative costing methods available to Crivitz.

Specific Identification

If Crivitz can positively identify which particular units it sold and which are still in ending inventory, it can use the **specific identification method** of inventory costing. For example, if Crivitz sold the TVs it purchased on February 3 and May 22, then its cost of goods sold is $1,520 ($720 + $800), and its ending inventory is $750 (see Illustration 6-4). Using this method, companies can accurately determine ending inventory and cost of goods sold.

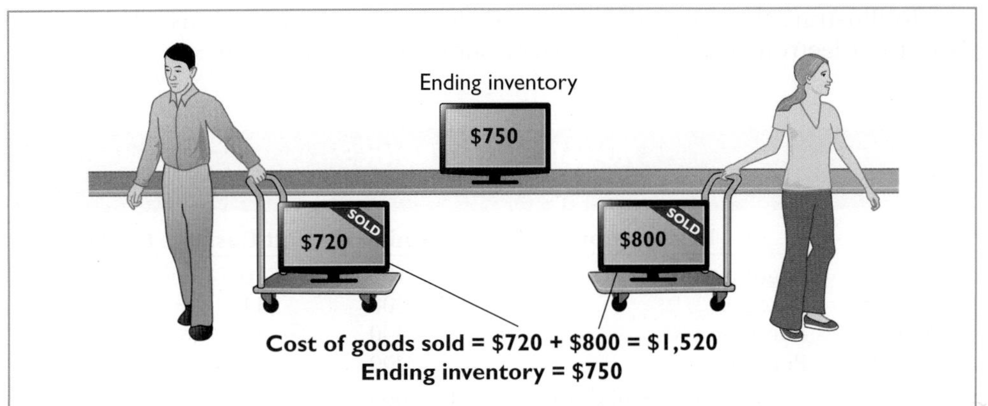

Illustration 6-4
Specific identification method

Specific identification requires that companies keep records of the original cost of each individual inventory item. Historically, specific identification was possible only when a company sold a limited variety of high-unit-cost items that could be identified clearly from the time of purchase through the time of sale. Examples of such products are cars, pianos, or expensive antiques.

Today, bar coding, electronic product codes, and radio frequency identification make it theoretically possible to do specific identification with nearly any type of product. The reality is, however, that this practice is still relatively rare. Instead, rather than keep track of the cost of each particular item sold, most companies make assumptions, called **cost flow assumptions**, about which units were sold.

Cost Flow Assumptions

Because specific identification is often impractical, other cost flow methods are permitted. These differ from specific identification in that they **assume** flows of costs that may be unrelated to the physical flow of goods. There are three assumed cost flow methods:

1. First-in, first-out (FIFO)
2. Last-in, first-out (LIFO)
3. Average-cost

There is no accounting requirement that the cost flow assumption be consistent with the physical movement of the goods. Company management selects the appropriate cost flow method.

To demonstrate the three cost flow methods, we will use a **periodic** inventory system. We assume a periodic system because **very few companies use perpetual LIFO, FIFO, or average-cost** to cost their inventory and related cost of goods sold. Instead, companies that use perpetual systems often use an assumed cost (called a standard cost) to record cost of goods sold at the time of sale. Then, at the end of the period when they count their inventory, they **recalculate cost of goods sold using periodic FIFO, LIFO, or average-cost** as shown in this chapter and adjust cost of goods sold to this recalculated number.[1]

[1]Also, some companies use a perpetual system to keep track of units, but they do not make an entry for perpetual cost of goods sold. In addition, firms that employ LIFO tend to use **dollar-value LIFO**, a method discussed in upper-level courses. FIFO periodic and FIFO perpetual give the same result. Therefore, companies should not incur the additional cost to use FIFO perpetual. Few companies use perpetual average-cost because of the added cost of recordkeeping. Finally, for instructional purposes, we believe it is easier to demonstrate the cost flow assumptions under the periodic system, which makes it more pedagogically appropriate.

To illustrate the three inventory cost flow methods, we will use the data for Houston Electronics' Astro condensers, shown in Illustration 6-5.

Illustration 6-5
Data for Houston Electronics

HOUSTON ELECTRONICS
Astro Condensers

Date	Explanation	Units	Unit Cost	Total Cost
Jan. 1	Beginning inventory	100	$10	$ 1,000
Apr. 15	Purchase	200	11	2,200
Aug. 24	Purchase	300	12	3,600
Nov. 27	Purchase	400	13	5,200
	Total units available for sale	1,000		$12,000
	Units in ending inventory	450		
	Units sold	550		

The cost of goods sold formula in a periodic system is:

(Beginning Inventory + Purchases) − Ending Inventory = Cost of Goods Sold

Houston Electronics had a total of 1,000 units available to sell during the period (beginning inventory plus purchases). The total cost of these 1,000 units is $12,000, referred to as **cost of goods available for sale**. A physical inventory taken at December 31 determined that there were 450 units in ending inventory. Therefore, Houston sold 550 units (1,000 − 450) during the period. To determine the cost of the 550 units that were sold (the cost of goods sold), we assign a cost to the ending inventory and subtract that value from the cost of goods available for sale. The value assigned to the ending inventory **will depend on which cost flow method we use**. No matter which cost flow assumption we use, though, the sum of cost of goods sold plus the cost of the ending inventory must equal the cost of goods available for sale—in this case, $12,000.

FIRST-IN, FIRST-OUT (FIFO)

The **first-in, first-out (FIFO) method** assumes that the **earliest goods** purchased are the first to be sold. FIFO often parallels the actual physical flow of merchandise. That is, it generally is good business practice to sell the oldest units first. Under the FIFO method, therefore, the **costs** of the earliest goods purchased are the first to be recognized in determining cost of goods sold. (This does not necessarily mean that the oldest units **are** sold first, but that the costs of the oldest units are **recognized** first. In a bin of picture hangers at the hardware store, for example, no one really knows, nor would it matter, which hangers are sold first.) Illustration 6-6 shows the allocation of the cost of goods available for sale at Houston Electronics under FIFO.

Illustration 6-6
Allocation of costs—FIFO method

COST OF GOODS AVAILABLE FOR SALE				
Date	**Explanation**	**Units**	**Unit Cost**	**Total Cost**
Jan. 1	Beginning inventory	100	$10	$ 1,000
Apr. 15	Purchase	200	11	2,200
Aug. 24	Purchase	300	12	3,600
Nov. 27	Purchase	400	13	5,200
	Total	1,000		**$12,000**

STEP 1: ENDING INVENTORY				STEP 2: COST OF GOODS SOLD	
Date	**Units**	**Unit Cost**	**Total Cost**		
Nov. 27	400	$13	$ 5,200	Cost of goods available for sale	$12,000
Aug. 24	50	12	600	Less: Ending inventory	5,800
Total	450		**$5,800**	Cost of goods sold	**$ 6,200**

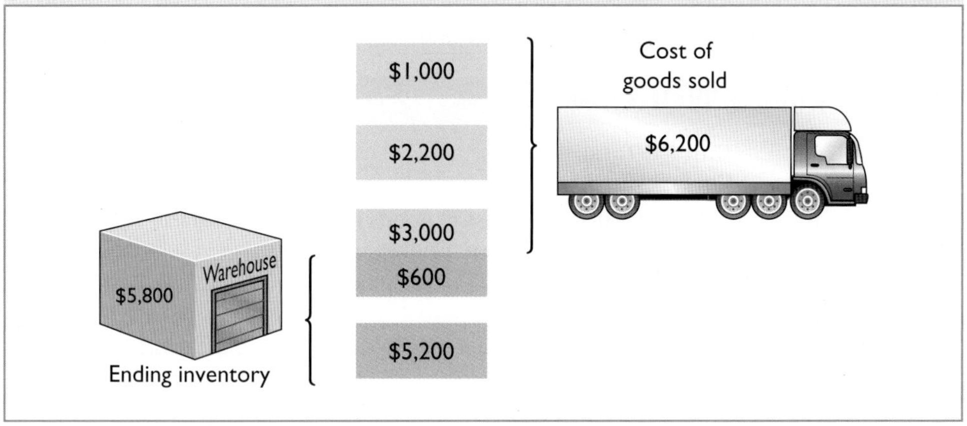

Under FIFO, since it is assumed that the first goods purchased were the first goods sold, ending inventory is based on the prices of the most recent units purchased. That is, **under FIFO, companies obtain the cost of the ending inventory by taking the unit cost of the most recent purchase and working backward until all units of inventory have been costed**. In this example, Houston Electronics prices the 450 units of ending inventory using the **most recent** prices. The last purchase was 400 units at $13 on November 27. The remaining 50 units are priced using the unit cost of the second most recent purchase, $12, on August 24. Next, Houston Electronics calculates cost of goods sold by subtracting the cost of the units **not sold** (ending inventory) from the cost of all goods available for sale.

Illustration 6-7 demonstrates that companies also can calculate cost of goods sold by pricing the 550 units sold using the prices of the first 550 units acquired. Note that of the 300 units purchased on August 24, only 250 units are assumed sold. This agrees with our calculation of the cost of ending inventory, where 50 of these units were assumed unsold and thus included in ending inventory.

Illustration 6-7
Proof of cost of goods sold

Date	Units	Unit Cost	Total Cost
Jan. 1	100	$10	$ 1,000
Apr. 15	200	11	2,200
Aug. 24	250	12	3,000
Total	550		**$6,200**

LAST-IN, FIRST-OUT (LIFO)

The **last-in, first-out (LIFO) method** assumes that the **latest goods** purchased are the first to be sold. LIFO seldom coincides with the actual physical flow of inventory. (Exceptions include goods stored in piles, such as coal or hay, where goods are removed from the top of the pile as they are sold.) Under the LIFO method, the **costs** of the latest goods purchased are the first to be recognized in determining cost of goods sold. Illustration 6-8 shows the allocation of the cost of goods available for sale at Houston Electronics under LIFO.

Illustration 6-8
Allocation of costs—LIFO method

COST OF GOODS AVAILABLE FOR SALE

Date	Explanation	Units	Unit Cost	Total Cost
Jan. 1	Beginning inventory	100	$10	$ 1,000
Apr. 15	Purchase	200	11	2,200
Aug. 24	Purchase	300	12	3,600
Nov. 27	Purchase	400	13	5,200
	Total	1,000		**$12,000**

STEP 1: ENDING INVENTORY

Date	Units	Unit Cost	Total Cost
Jan. 1	100	$10	$ 1,000
Apr. 15	200	11	2,200
Aug. 24	150	12	1,800
Total	450		**$5,000**

STEP 2: COST OF GOODS SOLD

Cost of goods available for sale	$12,000
Less: Ending inventory	5,000
Cost of goods sold	**$ 7,000**

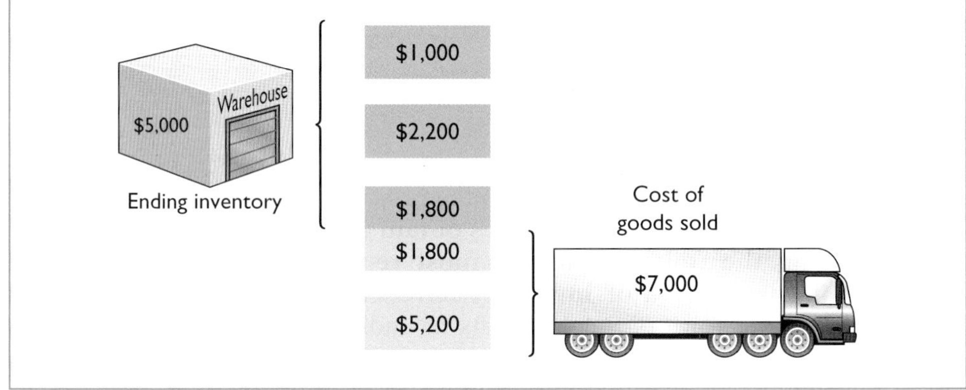

Under LIFO, since it is assumed that the first goods sold were those that were most recently purchased, ending inventory is based on the prices of the oldest units purchased. That is, **under LIFO, companies obtain the cost of the ending inventory by taking the unit cost of the earliest goods available for sale and working forward until all units of inventory have been costed**. In this example, Houston Electronics prices the 450 units of ending inventory using the **earliest** prices. The first purchase was 100 units at $10 in the January 1 beginning inventory. Then, 200 units were purchased at $11. The remaining 150 units needed are priced at $12 per unit (August 24 purchase). Next, Houston Electronics calculates cost of goods sold by subtracting the cost of the units **not sold** (ending inventory) from the cost of all goods available for sale.

Illustration 6-9 demonstrates that companies also can calculate cost of goods sold by pricing the 550 units sold using the prices of the last 550 units acquired. Note that of the 300 units purchased on August 24, only 150 units are assumed sold. This agrees with our calculation of the cost of ending inventory, where 150 of these units were assumed unsold and thus included in ending inventory.

Date	Units	Unit Cost	Total Cost
Nov. 27	400	$13	$5,200
Aug. 24	150	12	1,800
Total	550		$7,000

Illustration 6-9
Proof of cost of goods sold

Under a periodic inventory system, which we are using here, **all goods purchased during the period are assumed to be available for the first sale, regardless of the date of purchase.**

AVERAGE-COST

The **average-cost method** allocates the cost of goods available for sale on the basis of the **weighted-average unit cost** incurred. The average-cost method assumes that goods are similar in nature. Illustration 6-10 presents the formula and a sample computation of the weighted-average unit cost.

Cost of Goods Available for Sale	÷	Total Units Available for Sale	=	Weighted-Average Unit Cost
$12,000	÷	1,000	=	**$12**

Illustration 6-10
Formula for weighted-average unit cost

The company then applies the weighted-average unit cost to the units on hand to determine the cost of the ending inventory. Illustration 6-11 shows the allocation of the cost of goods available for sale at Houston Electronics using average-cost.

COST OF GOODS AVAILABLE FOR SALE

Date	Explanation	Units	Unit Cost	Total Cost
Jan. 1	Beginning inventory	100	$10	$ 1,000
Apr. 15	Purchase	200	11	2,200
Aug. 24	Purchase	300	12	3,600
Nov. 27	Purchase	400	13	5,200
	Total	1,000		**$12,000**

STEP 1: ENDING INVENTORY

$12,000 ÷ 1,000 = $12

Units	Unit Cost	Total Cost
450	$12	**$5,400**

STEP 2: COST OF GOODS SOLD

Cost of goods available for sale	$12,000
Less: Ending inventory	5,400
Cost of goods sold	**$ 6,600**

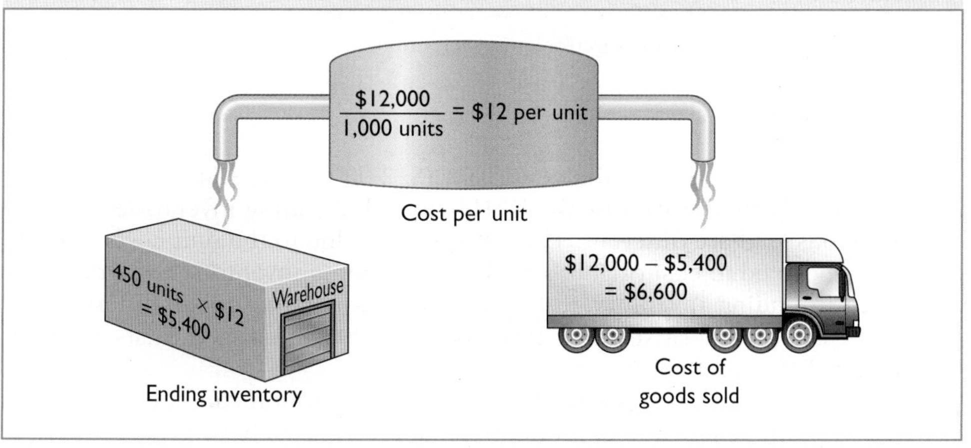

Illustration 6-11
Allocation of costs—average-cost method

We can verify the cost of goods sold under this method by multiplying the units sold times the weighted-average unit cost (550 × $12 = $6,600). Note that this method does **not** use the average of the unit costs. That average is $11.50 ($10 + $11 + $12 + $13 = $46; $46 ÷ 4). The average-cost method instead uses the average **weighted by** the quantities purchased at each unit cost.

Financial Statement and Tax Effects of Cost Flow Methods

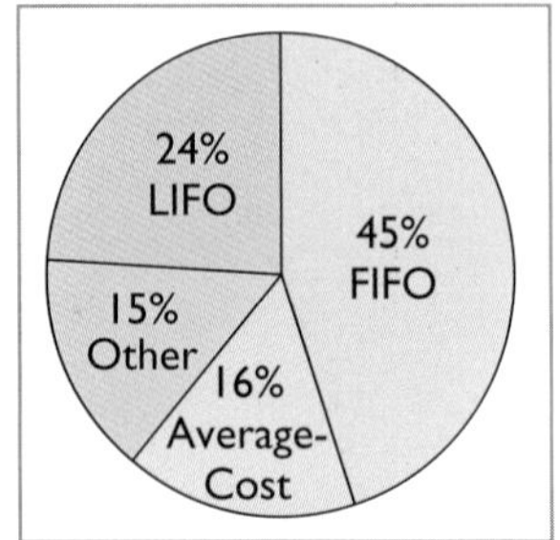

Illustration 6-12
Use of cost flow methods in major U.S. companies

Each of the three assumed cost flow methods is acceptable for use. For example, **Reebok International Ltd.** and **Wendy's International** currently use the FIFO method of inventory costing. **Campbell Soup Company**, **Kroger**, and **Walgreen Drugs** use LIFO for part or all of their inventory. **Bristol-Myers Squibb**, **Starbucks**, and **Motorola** use the average-cost method. In fact, a company may also use more than one cost flow method at the same time. **Stanley Black & Decker Manufacturing Company**, for example, uses LIFO for domestic inventories and FIFO for foreign inventories. Illustration 6-12 (in the margin) shows the use of the three cost flow methods in 500 large U.S. companies.

The reasons companies adopt different inventory cost flow methods are varied, but they usually involve one of three factors: (1) income statement effects, (2) balance sheet effects, or (3) tax effects.

INCOME STATEMENT EFFECTS

To understand why companies might choose a particular cost flow method, let's examine the effects of the different cost flow assumptions on the financial statements of Houston Electronics. The condensed income statements in Illustration 6-13 assume that Houston sold its 550 units for $18,500, had operating expenses of $9,000, and is subject to an income tax rate of 30%.

Illustration 6-13
Comparative effects of cost flow methods

HOUSTON ELECTRONICS
Condensed Income Statements

	FIFO	LIFO	Average-Cost
Sales revenue	$18,500	$18,500	$18,500
Beginning inventory	1,000	1,000	1,000
Purchases	11,000	11,000	11,000
Cost of goods available for sale	12,000	12,000	12,000
Ending inventory	**5,800**	**5,000**	**5,400**
Cost of goods sold	6,200	7,000	6,600
Gross profit	12,300	11,500	11,900
Operating expenses	9,000	9,000	9,000
Income before income taxes*	3,300	2,500	2,900
Income tax expense (30%)	990	750	870
Net income	**$ 2,310**	**$ 1,750**	**$ 2,030**

*We are assuming that Houston Electronics is a corporation, and corporations are required to pay income taxes.

Note the cost of goods available for sale ($12,000) is the same under each of the three inventory cost flow methods. However, the ending inventories and the costs of goods sold are different. This difference is due to the unit costs that the company allocated to cost of goods sold and to ending inventory. Each dollar of difference in ending inventory results in a corresponding dollar difference in income before income taxes. For Houston, an $800 difference exists between FIFO and LIFO cost of goods sold.

In periods of changing prices, the cost flow assumption can have significant impacts both on income and on evaluations of income, such as the following.

1. In a period of inflation, FIFO produces a higher net income because lower unit costs of the first units purchased are matched against revenue.
2. In a period of inflation, LIFO produces a lower net income because higher unit costs of the last goods purchased are matched against revenue.
3. If prices are falling, the results from the use of FIFO and LIFO are reversed. FIFO will report the lowest net income and LIFO the highest.
4. Regardless of whether prices are rising or falling, average-cost produces net income between FIFO and LIFO.

As shown in the Houston example (Illustration 6-13), in a period of rising prices FIFO reports the highest net income ($2,310) and LIFO the lowest ($1,750); average-cost falls between these two amounts ($2,030).

To management, higher net income is an advantage. It causes external users to view the company more favorably. In addition, management bonuses, if based on net income, will be higher. Therefore, when prices are rising (which is usually the case), companies tend to prefer FIFO because it results in higher net income.

Others believe that LIFO presents a more realistic net income number. That is, LIFO matches the more recent costs against current revenues to provide a better measure of net income. During periods of inflation, many challenge the quality of non-LIFO earnings, noting that failing to match current costs against current revenues leads to an understatement of cost of goods sold and an overstatement of net income. As some indicate, net income computed using FIFO creates **"paper or phantom profits"**—that is, earnings that do not really exist.

BALANCE SHEET EFFECTS

A major advantage of the FIFO method is that in a period of inflation, the costs allocated to ending inventory will approximate their current cost. For example, for Houston Electronics, 400 of the 450 units in the ending inventory are costed under FIFO at the higher November 27 unit cost of $13.

Conversely, a major shortcoming of the LIFO method is that in a period of inflation, the costs allocated to ending inventory may be significantly understated in terms of current cost. The understatement becomes greater over prolonged periods of inflation if the inventory includes goods purchased in one or more prior accounting periods. For example, **Caterpillar** has used LIFO for more than 50 years. Its balance sheet shows ending inventory of $12,625 million. But the inventory's actual current cost if FIFO had been used is $15,129 million.

TAX EFFECTS

We have seen that both inventory on the balance sheet and net income on the income statement are higher when companies use FIFO in a period of inflation. Yet, many companies have selected LIFO. Why? The reason is that LIFO results in the lowest income taxes (because of lower net income) during times of rising prices. For example, at Houston Electronics, income taxes are $750 under LIFO, compared to $990 under FIFO. The tax savings of $240 makes more cash available for use in the business.

Using Inventory Cost Flow Methods Consistently

Whatever cost flow method a company chooses, it should use that method consistently from one accounting period to another. This approach is often referred to as the **consistency concept**, which means that a company uses the same accounting principles and methods from year to year. Consistent application enhances the comparability of financial statements over successive time periods. In contrast, using the FIFO method one year and the LIFO method the next year would make it difficult to compare the net incomes of the two years.

Although consistent application is preferred, it does not mean that a company may never change its inventory costing method. When a company adopts a different method, it should disclose in the financial statements the change and its effects on net income. Illustration 6-14 shows a typical disclosure, using information from recent financial statements of **Quaker Oats** (now a unit of **PepsiCo**).

Illustration 6-14
Disclosure of change in cost flow method

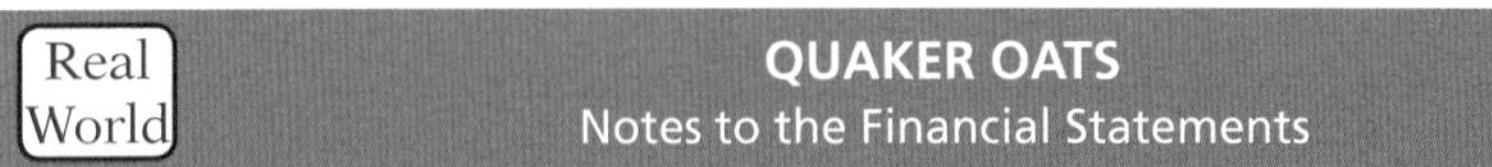

Note 1: Effective July 1, the Company adopted the LIFO cost flow assumption for valuing the majority of U.S. Grocery Products inventories. The Company believes that the use of the LIFO method better matches current costs with current revenues. The effect of this change on the current year was to decrease net income by $16.0 million.

LEARNING OBJECTIVE 3

Indicate the effects of inventory errors on the financial statements.

Unfortunately, errors occasionally occur in accounting for inventory. In some cases, errors are caused by failure to count or price the inventory correctly. In other cases, errors occur because companies do not properly recognize the transfer of legal title to goods that are in transit. When errors occur, they affect both the income statement and the balance sheet.

Income Statement Effects

Under a periodic inventory system, both the beginning and ending inventories appear in the income statement. The ending inventory of one period automatically becomes the beginning inventory of the next period. Thus, inventory errors affect the computation of cost of goods sold and net income in two periods.

The effects on cost of goods sold can be computed by first entering incorrect data in the formula in Illustration 6-15 and then substituting the correct data.

Illustration 6-15
Formula for cost of goods sold

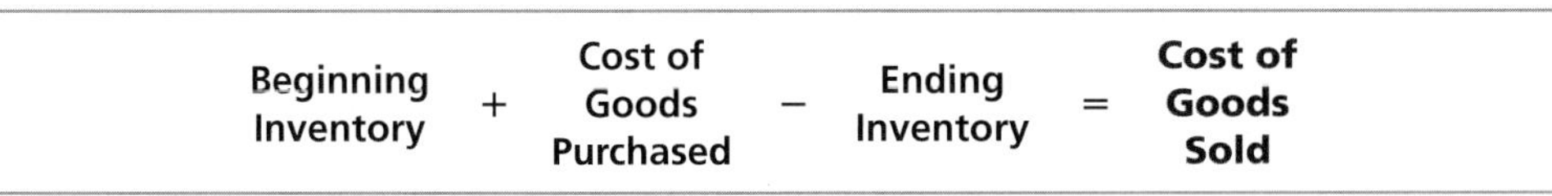

If the error understates **beginning** inventory, cost of goods sold will be understated. If the error understates **ending** inventory, cost of goods sold will be overstated. Illustration 6-16 shows the effects of inventory errors on the current year's income statement.

Illustration 6-16
Effects of inventory errors on current year's income statement

When Inventory Error:	Cost of Goods Sold Is:	Net Income Is:
Understates beginning inventory	Understated	Overstated
Overstates beginning inventory	Overstated	Understated
Understates ending inventory	Overstated	Understated
Overstates ending inventory	Understated	Overstated

So far, the effects of inventory errors are fairly straightforward. Now, though, comes the (at first) surprising part: An error in the ending inventory of the current period will have a **reverse effect on net income of the next accounting**

period. Illustration 6-17 shows this effect. As you study the illustration, you will see that the reverse effect comes from the fact that understating ending inventory in 2016 results in understating beginning inventory in 2017 and overstating net income in 2017.

Over the two years, though, total net income is correct because the errors **offset each other**. Notice that total income using incorrect data is $35,000 ($22,000 + $13,000), which is the same as the total income of $35,000 ($25,000 + $10,000) using correct data. Also note in this example that an error in the beginning inventory does not result in a corresponding error in the ending inventory for that period. The correctness of the ending inventory depends entirely on the accuracy of taking and costing the inventory at the balance sheet date under the periodic inventory system.

SAMPLE COMPANY
Condensed Income Statements

	2016				2017			
	Incorrect		Correct		Incorrect		Correct	
Sales revenue		$80,000		$80,000		$90,000		$90,000
Beginning inventory	$20,000		$20,000		**$12,000**		**$15,000**	
Cost of goods purchased	40,000		40,000		68,000		68,000	
Cost of goods available for sale	60,000		60,000		80,000		83,000	
Ending inventory	**12,000**		**15,000**		23,000		23,000	
Cost of goods sold		48,000		45,000		57,000		60,000
Gross profit		32,000		35,000		33,000		30,000
Operating expenses		10,000		10,000		20,000		20,000
Net income		$22,000		$25,000		$13,000		$10,000

$(3,000) Net income understated

$3,000 Net income overstated

The errors cancel. Thus, the combined total income for the 2-year period is correct.

Illustration 6-17
Effects of inventory errors on two years' income statements

Balance Sheet Effects

Companies can determine the effect of ending inventory errors on the balance sheet by using the basic accounting equation: Assets = Liabilities + Owner's Equity. Errors in the ending inventory have the effects shown in Illustration 6-18.

Ending Inventory Error	Assets	Liabilities	Owner's Equity
Overstated	Overstated	No effect	Overstated
Understated	Understated	No effect	Understated

Illustration 6-18
Effects of ending inventory errors on balance sheet

The effect of an error in ending inventory on the subsequent period was shown in Illustration 6-17. Recall that if the error is not corrected, the combined total net income for the two periods would be correct. Thus, total owner's equity reported on the balance sheet at the end of 2017 will also be correct.

LEARNING OBJECTIVE 4

Explain the statement presentation and analysis of inventory.

Presentation

As indicated in Chapter 5, inventory is classified in the balance sheet as a current asset immediately below receivables. In a multiple-step income statement, cost of goods sold is subtracted from net sales. There also should be disclosure of (1) the major inventory classifications, (2) the basis of accounting (cost, or lower-of-cost-or-market), and (3) the cost method (FIFO, LIFO, or average-cost).

Wal-Mart Stores, Inc., for example, in its January 31, 2014, balance sheet reported inventories of $44,858 million under current assets. The accompanying notes to the financial statements, as shown in Illustration 6-19, disclosed the following information.

Illustration 6-19
Inventory disclosures by Wal-Mart

WAL-MART STORES, INC.
Notes to the Financial Statements

Note 1. Summary of Significant Accounting Policies

Inventories

The Company values inventories at the lower-of-cost-or-market as determined primarily by the retail method of accounting, using the last-in, first-out ("LIFO") method for substantially all of the WalMart U.S. segment's inventories. The WalMart International segment's inventories are primarily valued by the retail method of accounting, using the first-in, first-out ("FIFO") method. The retail method of accounting results in inventory being valued at the lower of cost or market since permanent markdowns are currently taken as a reduction of the retail value of inventory. The Sam's Club segment's inventories are valued based on the weighted-average cost using the LIFO method. At January 31, 2014 and 2013, the Company's inventories valued at LIFO approximate those inventories as if they were valued at FIFO.

As indicated in this note, Wal-Mart values its inventories at the lower-of-cost-or-market using LIFO and FIFO.

Lower-of-Cost-or-Market

The value of inventory for companies selling high-technology or fashion goods can drop very quickly due to continual changes in technology or fashions. These circumstances sometimes call for inventory valuation methods other than those presented so far. For example, at one time purchasing managers at Ford decided to make a large purchase of palladium, a precious metal used in vehicle emission devices. They made this purchase because they feared a future shortage. The shortage did not materialize, and by the end of the year the price of palladium had plummeted. Ford's inventory was then worth $1 billion less than its original cost. Do you think Ford's inventory should have been stated at cost, in accordance with the historical cost principle, or at its lower replacement cost?

As you probably reasoned, this situation requires a departure from the cost basis of accounting. This is done by valuing the inventory at the **lower-of-cost-or-market (LCM)** in the period in which the price decline occurs. LCM is a basis whereby inventory is stated at the lower of either its cost or market value as determined by current replacement cost. LCM is an example of the accounting convention of **conservatism**. Conservatism means that the approach adopted among accounting alternatives is the method that is least likely to overstate assets and net income.

International Note

Under U.S. GAAP, companies cannot reverse inventory write-downs if inventory increases in value in subsequent periods. IFRS permits companies to reverse write-downs in some circumstances.

Companies apply LCM to the items in inventory after they have used one of the cost flow methods (specific identification, FIFO, LIFO, or average-cost) to determine cost. Under the LCM basis, market is defined as **current replacement cost**, not selling price. For a merchandising company, current replacement cost is the cost of purchasing the same goods at the present time from the usual suppliers in the usual quantities. Current replacement cost is used because a decline in the replacement cost of an item usually leads to a decline in the selling price of the item.

To illustrate the application of LCM, assume that Ken Tuckie TV has the following lines of merchandise with costs and market values as indicated. LCM produces the results shown in Illustration 6-20. Note that the amounts shown in the final column are the lower-of-cost-or-market amounts for each item.

Illustration 6-20
Computation of lower-of-cost-or-market

	Units	Cost per Unit	Market per Unit	Lower-of-Cost-or-Market	
Flat-screen TVs	100	$600	$550	$ 55,000	($550 × 100)
Satellite radios	500	90	104	45,000	($90 × 500)
Blu-ray players	850	50	48	40,800	($48 × 850)
CDs	3,000	5	6	15,000	($5 × 3,000)
Total inventory				$155,800	

Analysis

The amount of inventory carried by a company has significant economic consequences. And inventory management is a double-edged sword that requires constant attention. On the one hand, management wants to have a great variety and quantity available so that customers have a wide selection and items are always in stock. But, such a policy may incur high carrying costs (e.g., investment, storage, insurance, obsolescence, and damage). On the other hand, low inventory levels lead to stock-outs and lost sales. Common ratios used to manage and evaluate inventory levels are inventory turnover and a related measure, days in inventory.

Inventory turnover measures the number of times on average the inventory is sold during the period. Its purpose is to measure the liquidity of the inventory. The inventory turnover is computed by dividing cost of goods sold by the average inventory during the period. Unless seasonal factors are significant, average inventory can be computed from the beginning and ending inventory balances. For example, Wal-Mart reported in its 2014 annual report a beginning inventory of $43,803 million, an ending inventory of $44,858 million, and cost of goods sold for the year ended January 31, 2014, of $358,069 million. The inventory turnover formula and computation for Wal-Mart are shown below.

Illustration 6-21
Inventory turnover formula and computation for Wal-Mart

Cost of Goods Sold	÷	Average Inventory	=	Inventory Turnover
$358,069	÷	$\frac{\$44,858 + \$43,803}{2}$	=	**8.1 times**

A variant of the inventory turnover is **days in inventory**. This measures the average number of days inventory is held. It is calculated as 365 divided by the inventory turnover. For example, Wal-Mart's inventory turnover of 8.1 times divided into 365 is approximately 45.1 days. This is the approximate time that it takes a company to sell the inventory once it arrives at the store.

There are typical levels of inventory in every industry. Companies that are able to keep their inventory at lower levels and higher turnovers and still satisfy customer needs are the most successful.

LEARNING OBJECTIVE *5

APPENDIX 6A: Apply the inventory cost flow methods to perpetual inventory records.

What inventory cost flow methods can companies employ if they use a perpetual inventory system? Simple—they can use any of the inventory cost flow methods described in the chapter. To illustrate the application of the three assumed cost flow methods (FIFO, LIFO, and average-cost), we will use the data shown in Illustration 6A-1 and in this chapter for Houston Electronics' Astro condensers.

Illustration 6A-1
Inventoriable units and costs

HOUSTON ELECTRONICS
Astro Condensers

Date	Explanation	Units	Unit Cost	Total Cost	Balance in Units
1/1	Beginning inventory	100	$10	$ 1,000	100
4/15	Purchases	200	11	2,200	300
8/24	Purchases	300	12	3,600	600
9/10	Sale	550			50
11/27	Purchases	400	13	5,200	450
				$12,000	

First-In, First-Out (FIFO)

Under perpetual FIFO, the company charges to cost of goods sold the cost of the earliest goods on hand **prior to each sale**. Therefore, the cost of goods sold on September 10 consists of the units on hand January 1 and the units purchased April 15 and August 24. Illustration 6A-2 shows the inventory under a FIFO method perpetual system.

Illustration 6A-2
Perpetual system—FIFO

Date	Purchases		Cost of Goods Sold	Balance (in units and cost)	
January 1				(100 @ $10)	$ 1,000
April 15	(200 @ $11)	$2,200		(100 @ $10) (200 @ $11)	$ 3,200
August 24	(300 @ $12)	$3,600		(100 @ $10) (200 @ $11) (300 @ $12)	$ 6,800
September 10			(100 @ $10) (200 @ $11) (250 @ $12) **$6,200**	(50 @ $12)	$ 600
November 27	(400 @ $13)	$5,200		(50 @ $12) (400 @ $13)	**$5,800**

Cost of goods sold ($6,200)

Ending inventory ($5,800)

The ending inventory in this situation is $5,800, and the cost of goods sold is $6,200 [(100 @ $10) + (200 @ $11) + (250 @ $12)].

Compare Illustrations 6-6 (page 217) and 6A-2. You can see that the results under FIFO in a perpetual system are the **same as in a periodic system**. In both cases, the ending inventory is $5,800 and cost of goods sold is $6,200. Regardless of the system, the first costs in are the costs assigned to cost of goods sold.

Last-In, First-Out (LIFO)

Under the LIFO method using a perpetual system, the company charges to cost of goods sold the cost of the most recent purchase prior to sale. Therefore, the cost of the goods sold on September 10 consists of all the units from the August 24 and April 15 purchases plus 50 of the units in beginning inventory. Illustration 6A-3 shows the computation of the ending inventory under the LIFO method.

Illustration 6A-3
Perpetual system—LIFO

Date	Purchases		Cost of Goods Sold	Balance (in units and cost)	
January 1				(100 @ $10)	$ 1,000
April 15	(200 @ $11)	$2,200		(100 @ $10) (200 @ $11)	$ 3,200
August 24	(300 @ $12)	$3,600		(100 @ $10) (200 @ $11) (300 @ $12)	$ 6,800
September 10			(300 @ $12) (200 @ $11) (50 @ $10)	(50 @ $10)	$ 500
			$6,300 Cost of goods sold		
November 27	(400 @ $13)	$5,200		(50 @ $10) (400 @ $13)	**$5,700** Ending inventory

The use of LIFO in a perpetual system will usually produce cost allocations that differ from those using LIFO in a periodic system. In a perpetual system, the company allocates the latest units purchased **prior to each sale** to cost of goods sold. In contrast, in a periodic system, the latest units purchased **during the period** are allocated to cost of goods sold. Thus, when a purchase is made after the last sale, the LIFO periodic system will apply this purchase to the previous sale. Compare Illustrations 6-8 (page 218) and 6A-3. Illustration 6-8 shows that the 400 units at $13 purchased on November 27 applied to the sale of 550 units on September 10. Under the LIFO perpetual system in Illustration 6A-3, the 400 units at $13 purchased on November 27 are all applied to the ending inventory.

The ending inventory in this LIFO perpetual illustration is $5,700, and cost of goods sold is $6,300, as compared to the LIFO periodic Illustration 6-8 (page 218) where the ending inventory is $5,000 and cost of goods sold is $7,000.

Average-Cost

The average-cost method in a perpetual inventory system is called the **moving-average method**. Under this method, the company computes a new average **after each purchase**, by dividing the cost of goods available for sale by the units on hand. The average cost is then applied to (1) the units sold, to determine the cost of goods sold, and (2) the remaining units on hand, to determine the ending inventory amount. Illustration 6A-4 shows the application of the moving-average cost method by Houston Electronics (computations of the moving-average unit cost are shown after Illustration 6A-4).

Illustration 6A-4
Perpetual system—moving-average method

Date	Purchases		Cost of Goods Sold	Balance (in units and cost)	
January 1				(100 @ $10)	$ 1,000
April 15	(200 @ $11)	$2,200		(300 @ $10.667)	$ 3,200
August 24	(300 @ $12)	$3,600		(600 @ $11.333)	$ 6,800
September 10			(550 @ $11.333)	(50 @ $11.333)	$ 567
			$6,233 Cost of goods sold		
November 27	(400 @ $13)	$5,200		(450 @ $12.816)	**$5,767** Ending inventory

As indicated, Houston Electronics computes **a new average each time it makes a purchase**.

1. On April 15, after Houston buys 200 units for \$2,200, a total of 300 units costing \$3,200 (\$1,000 + \$2,200) are on hand. The average unit cost is \$10.667 (\$3,200 ÷ 300).
2. On August 24, after Houston buys 300 units for \$3,600, a total of 600 units costing \$6,800 (\$1,000 + \$2,200 + \$3,600) are on hand. The average cost per unit is \$11.333 (\$6,800 ÷ 600).
3. On September 10, to compute cost of goods sold, Houston uses this unit cost of \$11.333 until it makes another purchase, when the company computes a new unit cost. Accordingly, the unit cost of the 550 units sold on September 10 is \$11.333, and the total cost of goods sold is \$6,233.
4. On November 27, following the purchase of 400 units for \$5,200, there are 450 units on hand costing \$5,767 (\$567 + \$5,200) with a new average cost of \$12.816 (\$5,767 ÷ 450).

Compare this moving-average cost under the perpetual inventory system to Illustration 6-11 (page 219) showing the average-cost method under a periodic inventory system.

LEARNING OBJECTIVE *6

APPENDIX 6B: Describe the two methods of estimating inventories.

In the chapter, we assumed that a company would be able to physically count its inventory. What if it cannot? What if the inventory were destroyed by fire or flood, for example? In that case, the company would use an estimate.

Two circumstances explain why companies sometimes estimate inventories. First, a casualty such as fire, flood, or earthquake may make it impossible to take a physical inventory. Second, managers may want monthly or quarterly financial statements, but a physical inventory is taken only annually. The need for estimating inventories occurs primarily with a periodic inventory system because of the absence of perpetual inventory records.

There are two widely used methods of estimating inventories: (1) the gross profit method, and (2) the retail inventory method.

Gross Profit Method

The **gross profit method** estimates the cost of ending inventory by applying a gross profit rate to net sales. This method is relatively simple but effective. Accountants, auditors, and managers frequently use the gross profit method to test the reasonableness of the ending inventory amount. It will detect large errors.

To use this method, a company needs to know its net sales, cost of goods available for sale, and gross profit rate. The company then can estimate its gross profit for the period. Illustration 6B-1 shows the formulas for using the gross profit method.

Illustration 6B-1
Gross profit method formulas

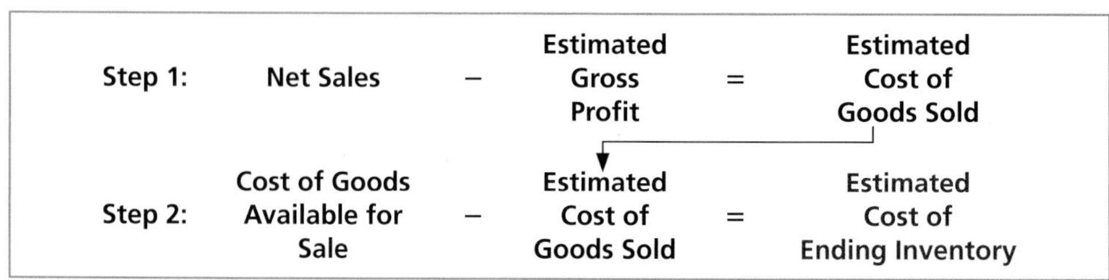

To illustrate, assume that Kishwaukee Company wishes to prepare an income statement for the month of January. Its records show net sales of $200,000, beginning inventory $40,000, and cost of goods purchased $120,000. In the preceding year, the company realized a 30% gross profit rate. It expects to earn the same rate this year. Given these facts and assumptions, Kishwaukee can compute the estimated cost of the ending inventory at January 31 under the gross profit method as follows.

Illustration 6B-2
Example of gross profit method

Step 1:	
Net sales	$ 200,000
Less: Estimated gross profit (30% × $200,000)	60,000
Estimated cost of goods sold	**$140,000**
Step 2:	
Beginning inventory	$ 40,000
Cost of goods purchased	120,000
Cost of goods available for sale	160,000
Less: Estimated cost of goods sold	140,000
Estimated cost of ending inventory	**$ 20,000**

The gross profit method is based on the assumption that the gross profit rate will remain constant. But, it may not remain constant, due to a change in merchandising policies or in market conditions. In such cases, the company should adjust the rate to reflect current operating conditions. In some cases, companies can obtain a more accurate estimate by applying this method on a department or product-line basis.

Note that companies should not use the gross profit method to prepare financial statements at the end of the year. These statements should be based on a physical inventory count.

Retail Inventory Method

A retail store such as **Home Depot**, **Ace Hardware**, or **Walmart** has thousands of different types of merchandise at low unit costs. In such cases, it is difficult and time-consuming to apply unit costs to inventory quantities. An alternative is to use the **retail inventory method** to estimate the cost of inventory. Most retail companies can establish a relationship between cost and sales price. The company then applies the cost-to-retail percentage to the ending inventory at retail prices to determine inventory at cost.

Under the retail inventory method, a company's records must show both the cost and retail value of the goods available for sale. Illustration 6B-3 presents the formulas for using the retail inventory method.

We can demonstrate the logic of the retail method by using unit-cost data. Assume that Ortiz Inc. has marked 10 units purchased at $7 to sell for $10 per unit. Thus, the cost-to-retail ratio is 70% ($70 ÷ $100). If four units remain unsold, their retail value is $40 (4 × $10), and their cost is $28 ($40 × 70%). This amount agrees with the total cost of goods on hand on a per unit basis (4 × $7).

Illustration 6B-3
Retail inventory method formulas

Step 1:	**Goods Available for Sale at Retail**	**−**	**Net Sales**	**=**	**Ending Inventory at Retail**
Step 2:	**Goods Available for Sale at Cost**	**÷**	**Goods Available for Sale at Retail**	**=**	**Cost-to-Retail Ratio**
Step 3:	**Ending Inventory at Retail**	**×**	**Cost-to-Retail Ratio**	**=**	**Estimated Cost of Ending Inventory**

Illustration 6B-4 shows application of the retail method for Valley West. Note that it is not necessary to take a physical inventory to determine the estimated cost of goods on hand at any given time.

Illustration 6B-4
Application of retail inventory method

	At Cost	At Retail
Beginning inventory	$14,000	$ 21,500
Goods purchased	61,000	78,500
Goods available for sale	$75,000	100,000
Less: Net sales		70,000
Step (1) Ending inventory at retail =		**$ 30,000**

Step (2) Cost-to-retail ratio = $75,000 ÷ $100,000 = 75%
Step (3) Estimated cost of ending inventory = $30,000 × 75% = $22,500

The retail inventory method also facilitates taking a physical inventory at the end of the year. Valley West can value the goods on hand at the prices marked on the merchandise, and then apply the cost-to-retail ratio to the goods on hand at retail to determine the ending inventory at cost.

The major disadvantage of the retail method is that it is an averaging technique. Thus, it may produce an incorrect inventory valuation if the mix of the ending inventory is not representative of the mix in the goods available for sale. Assume, for example, that the cost-to-retail ratio of 75% for Valley West consists of equal proportions of inventory items that have cost-to-retail ratios of 70%, 75%, and 80%. If the ending inventory contains only items with a 70% ratio, an incorrect inventory cost will result. Companies can minimize this problem by applying the retail method on a department or product-line basis.

REVIEW AND PRACTICE

LEARNING OBJECTIVES REVIEW

1 Discuss how to classify and determine inventory. Merchandisers need only one inventory classification, merchandise inventory, to describe the different items that make up total inventory. Manufacturers, on the other hand, usually classify inventory into three categories: finished goods, work in process, and raw materials. To determine inventory quantities, manufacturers (1) take a physical inventory of goods on hand and (2) determine the ownership of goods in transit or on consignment.

2 Apply inventory cost flow methods and discuss their financial effects. The primary basis of accounting for inventories is cost. Cost of goods available for sale includes (a) cost of beginning inventory and (b) cost of goods purchased. The inventory cost flow methods are specific identification and three assumed cost flow methods—FIFO, LIFO, and average-cost.

When prices are rising, the first-in, first-out (FIFO) method results in lower cost of goods sold and higher net income than the other methods. The last-in, first-out (LIFO) method results in the lowest income taxes. The reverse is true when prices are falling. In the balance sheet, FIFO results in an ending inventory that is closest to current value. Inventory under LIFO is the farthest from current value.

3 Indicate the effects of inventory errors on the financial statements. In the income statement of the current year: (a) If beginning inventory is understated, net income is overstated. The reverse occurs if beginning inventory is overstated. (b) If ending inventory is overstated, net income is overstated. If ending inventory is understated, net income is understated. In the following period, its effect on net income for that period is reversed, and total net income for the two years will be correct.

In the balance sheet: Ending inventory errors will have the same effect on total assets and total owner's equity and no effect on liabilities.

4 Explain the statement presentation and analysis of inventory. Inventory is classified in the balance sheet as a current asset immediately below receivables. There also should be disclosure of (1) the major inventory classifications, (2) the basis of accounting, and (3) the cost method.

Companies use the lower-of-cost-or-market (LCM) basis when the current replacement cost (market) is less than cost. Under LCM, companies recognize the loss in the period in which the price decline occurs.

The inventory turnover is cost of goods sold divided by average inventory. To convert it to average days in inventory, divide 365 days by the inventory turnover.

*5 **Apply the inventory cost flow methods to perpetual inventory records.** Under FIFO and a perpetual inventory system, companies charge to cost of goods sold the cost of the earliest goods on hand prior to each sale. Under LIFO and a perpetual system, companies charge to cost of goods sold the cost of the most recent purchase prior to sale. Under the moving-average (average-cost) method and a perpetual system, companies compute a new average cost after each purchase.

*6 **Describe the two methods of estimating inventories.** The two methods of estimating inventories are the gross profit method and the retail inventory method. Under the gross profit method, companies apply a gross profit rate to net sales to determine estimated gross profit and cost of goods sold. They then subtract estimated cost of goods sold from cost of goods available for sale to determine the estimated cost of the ending inventory.

Under the retail inventory method, companies compute a cost-to-retail ratio by dividing the cost of goods available for sale by the retail value of the goods available for sale. They then apply this ratio to the ending inventory at retail to determine the estimated cost of the ending inventory.

GLOSSARY REVIEW

Average-cost method Inventory costing method that uses the weighted-average unit cost to allocate to ending inventory and cost of goods sold the cost of goods available for sale.

Consigned goods Goods held for sale by one party although ownership of the goods is retained by another party.

Consistency concept Dictates that a company use the same accounting principles and methods from year to year.

Current replacement cost The current cost to replace an inventory item.

Days in inventory Measure of the average number of days inventory is held; calculated as 365 divided by inventory turnover.

Finished goods inventory Manufactured items that are completed and ready for sale.

First-in, first-out (FIFO) method Inventory costing method that assumes that the costs of the earliest goods purchased are the first to be recognized as cost of goods sold.

FOB (free on board) destination Freight terms indicating that ownership of the goods remains with the seller until the goods reach the buyer.

FOB (free on board) shipping point Freight terms indicating that ownership of the goods passes to the buyer when the public carrier accepts the goods from the seller.

***Gross profit method** A method for estimating the cost of the ending inventory by applying a gross profit rate to net sales and subtracting estimated cost of goods sold from cost of goods available for sale.

Inventory turnover A ratio that measures the number of times on average the inventory sold during the period; computed by dividing cost of goods sold by the average inventory during the period.

Just-in-time (JIT) inventory Inventory system in which companies manufacture or purchase goods only when needed for use.

Last-in, first-out (LIFO) method Inventory costing method that assumes the costs of the latest units purchased are the first to be allocated to cost of goods sold.

Lower-of-cost-or-market (LCM) A basis whereby inventory is stated at the lower of either its cost or its market value as determined by current replacement cost.

***Moving-average method** A new average is computed after each purchase, by dividing the cost of goods available for sale by the units on hand.

Raw materials Basic goods that will be used in production but have not yet been placed into production.

***Retail inventory method** A method for estimating the cost of the ending inventory by applying a cost-to-retail ratio to the ending inventory at retail.

Specific identification method An actual physical flow costing method in which items still in inventory are specifically costed to arrive at the total cost of the ending inventory.

Weighted-average unit cost Average cost that is weighted by the number of units purchased at each unit cost.

Work in process That portion of manufactured inventory that has been placed into the production process but is not yet complete.

PRACTICE EXERCISES

Determine the correct inventory amount.

(LO 1)

1. Matt Clark, an auditor with Grant CPAs, is performing a review of Parson Company's inventory account. Parson did not have a good year and top management is under pressure to boost reported income. According to its records. the inventory balance at year-end was $600,000. However, the following information was not considered when determining that amount.

1. The physical count did not include goods purchased by Parson with a cost of $30,000 that were shipped FOB destination on December 28 and did not arrive at Parson's warehouse until January 3.
2. Included in the company's count were goods with a cost of $150,000 that the company is holding on consignment. The goods belong to Alvarez Corporation.
3. Included in the inventory account was $21,000 of office supplies that were stored in the warehouse and were to be used by the company's supervisors and managers during the coming year.
4. The company received an order on December 28 that was boxed and was sitting on the loading dock awaiting pick-up on December 31. The shipper picked up the goods on January 1 and delivered them on January 6. The shipping terms were FOB shipping point. The goods had a selling price of $29,000 and a cost of $19,000. The goods were not included in the count because they were sitting on the dock.
5. On December 29, Parson shipped goods with a selling price of $56,000 and a cost of $40,000 to Decco Corporation FOB shipping point. The goods arrived on January 3. Decco had only ordered goods with a selling price of $10,000 and a cost of $6,000. However, a Parson's sales manager had authorized the shipment and said that if Decco wanted to ship the goods back next week, it could.
6. Included in the count was $27,000 of goods that were parts for a machine that the company no longer made. Given the high-tech nature of Parson's products, it was unlikely that these obsolete parts had any other use. However, management would prefer to keep them on the books at cost, "since that is what we paid for them, after all."

Instructions

Prepare a schedule to determine the correct inventory amount. Provide explanations for each item above, saying why you did or did not make an adjustment for each item.

Solution

1. Ending inventory—as reported	$600,000
1. No effect—title does not pass to Parson until goods are received (Jan. 3).	0
2. Subtract from inventory: The goods belong to Alvarez Corporation. Parson is merely holding them as a consignee.	(150,000)
3. Subtract from inventory: Office supplies should be carried in a separate account. They are not considered inventory held for resale.	(21,000)
4. Add to inventory: The goods belong to Parson until they are shipped (Jan. 1).	19,000
5. Add to inventory: Decco ordered goods with a cost of $6,000. Parson should record the corresponding sales revenue of $10,000. Parson's decision to ship extra "unordered" goods does not constitute a sale. The manager's statement that Decco could ship the goods back indicates that Parson knows this over-shipment is not a legitimate sale. The manager acted unethically in an attempt to improve Parson's reported income by overshipping.	34,000
6. Subtract from inventory: GAAP require that inventory be valued at the lower-of-cost-or-market. Obsolete parts should be adjusted from cost to zero if they have no other use.	(27,000)
Correct inventory	$455,000

2. Rhode Software reported cost of goods sold as follows.

Determine effects of inventory errors.

(LO 3)

	2016	2017
Beginning inventory	$ 27,000	$ 40,000
Cost of goods purchased	200,000	235,000
Cost of goods available for sale	227,000	275,000
Ending inventory	40,000	45,000
Cost of goods sold	$187,000	$230,000

Rhode made two errors: (1) 2016 ending inventory was overstated $4,000, and (2) 2017 ending inventory was understated $9,000.

Instructions

Compute the correct cost of goods sold for each year.

Solution

2.

	2016	2017
Beginning inventory	$ 27,000	$ 36,000
Cost of goods purchased	200,000	235,000
Cost of goods available for sale	227,000	271,000
Corrected ending inventory	(36,000)[a]	(54,000)[b]
Cost of goods sold	$191,000	$217,000

[a]$40,000 − $4,000 = $36,000; [b]$45,000 + $9,000 = $54,000

PRACTICE PROBLEMS

1. Gerald D. Englehart Company has the following inventory, purchases, and sales data for the month of March.

Compute inventory and cost of goods sold using three cost flow methods in a periodic inventory system.

(LO 2)

Inventory:	March 1	200 units @ $4.00	$ 800
Purchases:	March 10	500 units @ $4.50	2,250
	March 20	400 units @ $4.75	1,900
	March 30	300 units @ $5.00	1,500
Sales:	March 15	500 units	
	March 25	400 units	

The physical inventory count on March 31 shows 500 units on hand.

Instructions

Under a **periodic inventory system**, determine the cost of inventory on hand at March 31 and the cost of goods sold for March under (a) FIFO, (b) LIFO, and (c) average-cost.

Solution

1. The cost of goods available for sale is $6,450, as follows.

Inventory:		200 units @ $4.00	$ 800
Purchases:	March 10	500 units @ $4.50	2,250
	March 20	400 units @ $4.75	1,900
	March 30	300 units @ $5.00	1,500
Total:		1,400	$6,450

Under a **periodic inventory system**, the cost of goods sold under each cost flow method is as follows.

(a) **FIFO Method**

Ending inventory:

Date	Units	Unit Cost	Total Cost	
March 30	300	$5.00	$1,500	
March 20	200	4.75	950	$2,450

Cost of goods sold: $6,450 − $2,450 = $4,000

(b) **LIFO Method**

Ending inventory:

Date	Units	Unit Cost	Total Cost	
March 1	200	$4.00	$ 800	
March 10	300	4.50	1,350	$2,150

Cost of goods sold: $6,450 − $2,150 = $4,300

(c) **Average-Cost Method**

Average unit cost: $6,450 ÷ 1,400 = $4.607
Ending inventory: 500 × $4.607 = $2,303.50

Cost of goods sold: $6,450 − $2,303.50 = $4,146.50

Compute inventory and cost of goods sold using three cost flow methods in a perpetual inventory system.
(LO 5)

*2. **Practice Problem 1** on page 233 showed cost of goods sold computations under a periodic inventory system. Now let's assume that Gerald D. Englehart Company uses a perpetual inventory system. The company has the same inventory, purchases, and sales data for the month of March as shown earlier:

Inventory:	March 1	200 units @ $4.00	$ 800
Purchases:	March 10	500 units @ $4.50	2,250
	March 20	400 units @ $4.75	1,900
	March 30	300 units @ $5.00	1,500
Sales:	March 15	500 units	
	March 25	400 units	

The physical inventory count on March 31 shows 500 units on hand.

Instructions

Under a **perpetual inventory system**, determine the cost of inventory on hand at March 31 and the cost of goods sold for March under (a) FIFO, (b) LIFO, and (c) moving-average cost.

Solution

2. The cost of goods available for sale is $6,450, as follows.

Inventory:		200 units @ $4.00	$ 800
Purchases:	March 10	500 units @ $4.50	2,250
	March 20	400 units @ $4.75	1,900
	March 30	300 units @ $5.00	1,500
Total:		1,400	$6,450

Under a **perpetual inventory system**, the cost of goods sold under each cost flow method is as follows.

(a) **FIFO Method**

Date	Purchases		Cost of Goods Sold	Balance	
March 1				(200 @ $4.00)	$ 800
March 10	(500 @ $4.50)	$2,250		(200 @ $4.00) (500 @ $4.50)	$3,050
March 15			(200 @ $4.00) (300 @ $4.50) $2,150	(200 @ $4.50)	$ 900
March 20	(400 @ $4.75)	$1,900		(200 @ $4.50) (400 @ $4.75)	$2,800
March 25			(200 @ $4.50) (200 @ $4.75) $1,850	(200 @ $4.75)	$ 950
March 30	(300 @ $5.00)	$1,500		(200 @ $4.75) (300 @ $5.00)	$2,450

Ending inventory $2,450 Cost of goods sold: $2,150 + $1,850 = $4,000

(b)

LIFO Method

Date	Purchases		Cost of Goods Sold		Balance	
March 1					(200 @ $4.00)	$ 800
March 10	(500 @ $4.50)	$2,250			(200 @ $4.00) (500 @ $4.50)	$3,050
March 15			(500 @ $4.50)	$2,250	(200 @ $4.00)	$ 800
March 20	(400 @ $4.75)	$1,900			(200 @ $4.00) (400 @ $4.75)	$2,700
March 25			(400 @ $4.75)	$1,900	(200 @ $4.00)	$ 800
March 30	(300 @ $5.00)	$1,500			(200 @ $4.00) (300 @ $5.00)	$2,300

Ending inventory $2,300 Cost of goods sold: $2,250 + $1,900 = $4,150

(c)

Moving-Average Cost Method

Date	Purchases		Cost of Goods Sold		Balance	
March 1					(200 @ $ 4.00)	$ 800
March 10	(500 @ $4.50)	$2,250			(700 @ $4.357)	$3,050
March 15			(500 @ $4.357)	$2,179	(200 @ $4.357)	$ 871
March 20	(400 @ $4.75)	$1,900			(600 @ $4.618)	$2,771
March 25			(400 @ $4.618)	$1,847	(200 @ $4.618)	$ 924
March 30	(300 @ $5.00)	$1,500			(500 @ $4.848)	$2,424

Ending inventory $2,424 Cost of goods sold: $2,179 + $1,847 = $4,026

EXERCISES

Determine the correct inventory amount.

(LO 1)

E6-1 Tri-State Bank and Trust is considering giving Wilfred Company a loan. Before doing so, management decides that further discussions with Wilfred's accountant may be desirable. One area of particular concern is the inventory account, which has a year-end balance of $297,000. Discussions with the accountant reveal the following.

1. Wilfred sold goods costing $38,000 to Lilja Company, FOB shipping point, on December 28. The goods are not expected to arrive at Lilja until January 12. The goods were not included in the physical inventory because they were not in the warehouse.
2. The physical count of the inventory did not include goods costing $95,000 that were shipped to Wilfred FOB destination on December 27 and were still in transit at year-end.
3. Wilfred received goods costing $22,000 on January 2. The goods were shipped FOB shipping point on December 26 by Brent Co. The goods were not included in the physical count.
4. Wilfred sold goods costing $35,000 to Jesse Co., FOB destination, on December 30. The goods were received at Jesse on January 8. They were not included in Wilfred's physical inventory.
5. Wilfred received goods costing $44,000 on January 2 that were shipped FOB destination on December 29. The shipment was a rush order that was supposed to arrive December 31. This purchase was included in the ending inventory of $297,000.

Instructions

Determine the correct inventory amount on December 31.

Determine the correct inventory amount.

(LO 1)

E6-2 Kari Downs, an auditor with Wheeler CPAs, is performing a review of Depue Company's inventory account. Depue did not have a good year, and top management is under pressure to boost reported income. According to its records, the inventory balance at year-end was $740,000. However, the following information was not considered when determining that amount.

1. Included in the company's count were goods with a cost of $250,000 that the company is holding on consignment. The goods belong to Kroeger Corporation.
2. The physical count did not include goods purchased by Depue with a cost of $40,000 that were shipped FOB destination on December 28 and did not arrive at Depue warehouse until January 3.

3. Included in the inventory account was $14,000 of office supplies that were stored in the warehouse and were to be used by the company's supervisors and managers during the coming year.
4. The company received an order on December 29 that was boxed and sitting on the loading dock awaiting pick-up on December 31. The shipper picked up the goods on January 1 and delivered them on January 6. The shipping terms were FOB shipping point. The goods had a selling price of $40,000 and a cost of $28,000. The goods were not included in the count because they were sitting on the dock.
5. On December 29, Depue shipped goods with a selling price of $80,000 and a cost of $60,000 to Macchia Sales Corporation FOB shipping point. The goods arrived on January 3. Macchia had only ordered goods with a selling price of $10,000 and a cost of $8,000. However, a sales manager at Depue had authorized the shipment and said that if Machia wanted to ship the goods back next week, it could.
6. Included in the count was $40,000 of goods that were parts for a machine that the company no longer made. Given the high-tech nature of Depue's products, it was unlikely that these obsolete parts had any other use. However, management would prefer to keep them on the books at cost, "since that is what we paid for them, after all."

Instructions

Prepare a schedule to determine the correct inventory amount. Provide explanations for each item above, saying why you did or did not make an adjustment for each item.

Calculate cost of goods sold using specific identification and FIFO.

(LO 2)

E6-3 On December 1, Kiyak Electronics Ltd. has three DVD players left in stock. All are identical, all are priced to sell at $150. One of the three DVD players left in stock, with serial #1012, was purchased on June 1 at a cost of $100. Another, with serial #1045, was purchased on November 1 for $88. The last player, serial #1056, was purchased on November 30 for $80.

Instructions

(a) Calculate the cost of goods sold using the FIFO periodic inventory method assuming that two of the three players were sold by the end of December, Kiyak Electronics' year-end.

(b) If Kiyak Electronics used the specific identification method instead of the FIFO method, how might it alter its earnings by "selectively choosing" which particular players to sell to the two customers? What would Kiyak's cost of goods sold be if the company wished to minimize earnings? Maximize earnings?

(c) Which of the two inventory methods do you recommend that Kiyak use? Explain why.

Compute inventory and cost of goods sold using FIFO and LIFO.

(LO 2)

E6-4 Elsa's Boards sells a snowboard, Xpert, that is popular with snowboard enthusiasts. Information relating to Elsa's purchases of Xpert snowboards during September is shown below. During the same month, 121 Xpert snowboards were sold. Elsa's uses a periodic inventory system.

Date	Explanation	Units	Unit Cost	Total Cost
Sept. 1	Inventory	26	$ 97	$ 2,522
Sept. 12	Purchases	45	102	4,590
Sept. 19	Purchases	20	104	2,080
Sept. 26	Purchases	50	105	5,250
	Totals	141		$14,442

Instructions

(a) Compute the ending inventory at September 30 and cost of goods sold using the FIFO and LIFO methods. Prove the amount allocated to cost of goods sold under each method.

(b) For both FIFO and LIFO, calculate the sum of ending inventory and cost of goods sold. What do you notice about the answers you found for each method?

Compute inventory and cost of goods sold using FIFO and LIFO.

(LO 2)

E6-5 Ballas Co. uses a periodic inventory system. Its records show the following for the month of May, in which 68 units were sold.

		Units	Unit Cost	Total Cost
May 1	Inventory	30	$ 8	$240
15	Purchases	25	11	275
24	Purchases	35	12	420
	Totals	90		$935

Instructions
Compute the ending inventory at May 31 and cost of goods sold using the FIFO and LIFO methods. Prove the amount allocated to cost of goods sold under each method.

E6-6 Moath Company reports the following for the month of June.

Compute inventory and cost of goods sold using FIFO and LIFO.

(LO 2)

		Units	Unit Cost	Total Cost
June 1	Inventory	200	$5	$1,000
12	Purchase	400	6	2,400
23	Purchase	300	7	2,100
30	Inventory	100		

Instructions
(a) Compute the cost of the ending inventory and the cost of goods sold under (1) FIFO and (2) LIFO.
(b) Which costing method gives the higher ending inventory? Why?
(c) Which method results in the higher cost of goods sold? Why?

E6-7 Shawn Company had 100 units in beginning inventory at a total cost of $10,000. The company purchased 200 units at a total cost of $26,000. At the end of the year, Shawn had 75 units in ending inventory.

Compute inventory under FIFO, LIFO, and average-cost.

(LO 2)

Instructions
(a) Compute the cost of the ending inventory and the cost of goods sold under (1) FIFO, (2) LIFO, and (3) average-cost.
(b) Which cost flow method would result in the highest net income?
(c) Which cost flow method would result in inventories approximating current cost in the balance sheet?
(d) Which cost flow method would result in Shawn paying the least taxes in the first year?

E6-8 Inventory data for Moath Company are presented in E6-6.

Compute inventory and cost of goods sold using average-cost.

(LO 2)

Instructions
(a) Compute the cost of the ending inventory and the cost of goods sold using the average-cost method.
(b) Will the results in (a) be higher or lower than the results under (1) FIFO and (2) LIFO?
(c) Why is the average unit cost not $6?

E6-9 Elliott's Hardware reported cost of goods sold as follows.

Determine effects of inventory errors.

(LO 3)

	2016	2017
Beginning inventory	$ 20,000	$ 30,000
Cost of goods purchased	150,000	175,000
Cost of goods available for sale	170,000	205,000
Ending inventory	30,000	35,000
Cost of goods sold	$140,000	$170,000

Elliott's made two errors: (1) 2016 ending inventory was overstated $3,000, and (2) 2017 ending inventory was understated $5,000.

Instructions
Compute the correct cost of goods sold for each year.

E6-10 Smart Watch Company reported the following income statement data for a 2-year period.

Prepare correct income statements.

(LO 3)

	2016	2017
Sales revenue	$220,000	$250,000
Cost of goods sold		
Beginning inventory	32,000	44,000
Cost of goods purchased	173,000	202,000
Cost of goods available for sale	205,000	246,000
Ending inventory	44,000	52,000
Cost of goods sold	161,000	194,000
Gross profit	$ 59,000	$ 56,000

Smart uses a periodic inventory system. The inventories at January 1, 2016, and December 31, 2017, are correct. However, the ending inventory at December 31, 2016, was overstated $6,000.

Instructions

(a) Prepare correct income statement data for the 2 years.
(b) What is the cumulative effect of the inventory error on total gross profit for the 2 years?
(c) Explain in a letter to the president of Smart Watch Company what has happened, i.e., the nature of the error and its effect on the financial statements.

Determine ending inventory under LCM.
(LO 4)

E6-11 Freeze Frame Camera Shop uses the lower-of-cost-or-market basis for its inventory. The following data are available at December 31.

Item	Units	Unit Cost	Market
Cameras:			
Minolta	5	$170	$156
Canon	6	150	152
Light meters:			
Vivitar	10	125	115
Kodak	14	120	135

Instructions

Determine the amount of the ending inventory by applying the lower-of-cost-or-market basis.

Compute lower-of-cost-or-market
(LO 4)

E6-12 Charapata Company applied FIFO to its inventory and got the following results for its ending inventory.

Cameras	100 units at a cost per unit of $65
Blu-ray players	150 units at a cost per unit of $75
iPods	125 units at a cost per unit of $80

The cost of purchasing units at year-end was cameras $71, Blu-ray players $67, and iPods $78.

Instructions

Determine the amount of ending inventory at lower-of-cost-or-market.

Compute inventory turnover, days in inventory, and gross profit rate.
(LO 4)

E6-13 This information is available for Abdullah's Photo Corporation for 2015, 2016, and 2017.

	2015	2016	2017
Beginning inventory	$ 100,000	$ 300,000	$ 400,000
Ending inventory	300,000	400,000	480,000
Cost of goods sold	900,000	1,152,000	1,300,000
Sales revenue	1,200,000	1,600,000	1,900,000

Instructions

Calculate inventory turnover, days in inventory, and gross profit rate (from Chapter 5) for Abdullah's Photo Corporation for 2015, 2016, and 2017. Comment on any trends.

Compute inventory turnover and days in inventory.
(LO 4)

E6-14 The cost of goods sold computations for Sooner Company and Later Company are shown below.

	Sooner Company	Later Company
Beginning inventory	$ 45,000	$ 71,000
Cost of goods purchased	200,000	290,000
Cost of goods available for sale	245,000	361,000
Ending inventory	55,000	69,000
Cost of goods sold	$190,000	$292,000

Instructions

(a) Compute inventory turnover and days in inventory for each company.
(b) Which company moves its inventory more quickly?

***E6-15** Ehrhart Appliance uses a perpetual inventory system. For its flat-screen television sets, the January 1 inventory was 3 sets at $600 each. On January 10, Ehrhart purchased 6 units at $660 each. The company sold 2 units on January 8 and 5 units on January 15.

Apply cost flow methods to perpetual records.

(LO 5)

Instructions

Compute the ending inventory under (a) FIFO, (b) LIFO, and (c) moving-average cost.

***E6-16** Moath Company reports the following for the month of June.

Calculate inventory and cost of goods sold using three cost flow methods in a perpetual inventory system.

(LO 5)

Date	Explanation	Units	Unit Cost	Total Cost
June 1	Inventory	200	$5	$1,000
12	Purchase	400	6	2,400
23	Purchase	300	7	2,100
30	Inventory	100		

Instructions

(a) Calculate the cost of the ending inventory and the cost of goods sold for each cost flow assumption, using a perpetual inventory system. Assume a sale of 440 units occurred on June 15 for a selling price of $8 and a sale of 360 units on June 27 for $9.

(b) How do the results differ from E6-6 and E6-8?

(c) Why is the average unit cost not $6 [($5 + $6 + $7) ÷ 3 = $6]?

***E6-17** Information about Elsa's Boards is presented in E6-4. Additional data regarding Elsa's sales of Xpert snowboards are provided below. Assume that Elsa's uses a perpetual inventory system.

Apply cost flow methods to perpetual records.

(LO 5)

Date		Units	Unit Price	Total Revenue
Sept. 5	Sale	12	$199	$ 2,388
Sept. 16	Sale	50	199	9,950
Sept. 29	Sale	59	209	12,331
	Totals	121		$24,669

Instructions

(a) Compute ending inventory at September 30 using FIFO, LIFO, and moving-average cost.

(b) Compare ending inventory using a perpetual inventory system to ending inventory using a periodic inventory system (from E6-4).

(c) Which inventory cost flow method (FIFO, LIFO) gives the same ending inventory value under both periodic and perpetual? Which method gives different ending inventory values?

***E6-18** Shereen Company reported the following information for November and December 2017.

Use the gross profit method to estimate inventory.

(LO 6)

	November	December
Cost of goods purchased	$536,000	$ 610,000
Inventory, beginning-of-month	130,000	120,000
Inventory, end-of-month	120,000	?
Sales revenue	840,000	1,000,000

Shereen's ending inventory at December 31 was destroyed in a fire.

Instructions

(a) Compute the gross profit rate for November.

(b) Using the gross profit rate for November, determine the estimated cost of inventory lost in the fire.

***E6-19** The inventory of Hang Company was destroyed by fire on March 1. From an examination of the accounting records, the following data for the first 2 months of the year are obtained: Sales Revenue $51,000, Sales Returns and Allowances $1,000, Purchases $31,200, Freight-In $1,200, and Purchase Returns and Allowances $1,400.

Determine merchandise lost using the gross profit method of estimating inventory.

(LO 6)

Instructions

Determine the merchandise lost by fire, assuming:

(a) A beginning inventory of $20,000 and a gross profit rate of 30% on net sales.

(b) A beginning inventory of $30,000 and a gross profit rate of 40% on net sales.

Determine ending inventory at cost using retail method.
(LO 6)

***E6-20** Kicks Shoe Store uses the retail inventory method for its two departments, Women's Shoes and Men's Shoes. The following information for each department is obtained.

Item	Women's Shoes	Men's Shoes
Beginning inventory at cost	$ 25,000	$ 45,000
Cost of goods purchased at cost	110,000	136,300
Net sales	178,000	185,000
Beginning inventory at retail	46,000	60,000
Cost of goods purchased at retail	179,000	185,000

Instructions
Compute the estimated cost of the ending inventory for each department under the retail inventory method.

PROBLEMS

Determine items and amounts to be recorded in inventory.
(LO 1)

P6-1A Houghton Limited is trying to determine the value of its ending inventory as of February 28, 2017, the company's year-end. The following transactions occurred, and the accountant asked your help in determining whether they should be recorded or not.

(a) On February 26, Houghton shipped goods costing $800 to a customer and charged the customer $1,000. The goods were shipped with terms FOB shipping point and the receiving report indicates that the customer received the goods on March 2.
(b) On February 26, Crain Inc. shipped goods to Houghton under terms FOB shipping point. The invoice price was $450 plus $30 for freight. The receiving report indicates that the goods were received by Houghton on March 2.
(c) Houghton had $720 of inventory isolated in the warehouse. The inventory is designated for a customer who has requested that the goods be shipped on March 10.
(d) Also included in Houghton's warehouse is $700 of inventory that Korenic Producers shipped to Houghton on consignment.
(e) On February 26, Houghton issued a purchase order to acquire goods costing $900. The goods were shipped with terms FOB destination on February 27. Houghton received the goods on March 2.
(f) On February 26, Houghton shipped goods to a customer under terms FOB destination. The invoice price was $390; the cost of the items was $240. The receiving report indicates that the goods were received by the customer on March 2.

Instructions
For each of the above transactions, specify whether the item in question should be included in ending inventory, and if so, at what amount.

Determine cost of goods sold and ending inventory using FIFO, LIFO, and average-cost with analysis.
(LO 2)

P6-2A Glee Distribution markets CDs of the performing artist Unique. At the beginning of October, Glee had in beginning inventory 2,000 of Unique's CDs with a unit cost of $7. During October, Glee made the following purchases of Unique's CDs.

Oct. 3	2,500 @ $8	Oct. 19	3,000 @ $10
Oct. 9	3,500 @ $9	Oct. 25	4,000 @ $11

During October, 10,900 units were sold. Glee uses a periodic inventory system.

Instructions
(a) Determine the cost of goods available for sale.
(b) Determine (1) the ending inventory and (2) the cost of goods sold under each of the assumed cost flow methods (FIFO, LIFO, and average-cost). Prove the accuracy of the cost of goods sold under the FIFO and LIFO methods.
(c) Which cost flow method results in (1) the highest inventory amount for the balance sheet and (2) the highest cost of goods sold for the income statement?

(b)(2) Cost of goods sold:
FIFO $ 94,500
LIFO $108,700
Average $101,370

P6-3A Sekhon Company had a beginning inventory on January 1 of 160 units of Product 4-18-15 at a cost of $20 per unit. During the year, the following purchases were made.

Determine cost of goods sold and ending inventory, using FIFO, LIFO, and average-cost with analysis.

(LO 2)

Mar. 15	400 units at $23	Sept. 4	330 units at $26
July 20	250 units at $24	Dec. 2	100 units at $29

1,000 units were sold. Sekhon Company uses a periodic inventory system.

Instructions

(a) Determine the cost of goods available for sale.

(b) Determine (1) the ending inventory, and (2) the cost of goods sold under each of the assumed cost flow methods (FIFO, LIFO, and average-cost). Prove the accuracy of the cost of goods sold under the FIFO and LIFO methods.

(c) Which cost flow method results in (1) the highest inventory amount for the balance sheet, and (2) the highest cost of goods sold for the income statement?

(b)(2) Cost of goods sold:
FIFO $23,340
LIFO $24,840
Average $24,097

P6-4A The management of Gresa Inc. is reevaluating the appropriateness of using its present inventory cost flow method, which is average-cost. The company requests your help in determining the results of operations for 2017 if either the FIFO or the LIFO method had been used. For 2017, the accounting records show these data:

Compute ending inventory, prepare income statements, and answer questions using FIFO and LIFO.

(LO 2)

Inventories		Purchases and Sales	
Beginning (7,000 units)	$14,000	Total net sales (180,000 units)	$747,000
Ending (17,000 units)		Total cost of goods purchased (190,000 units)	466,000

Purchases were made quarterly as follows.

Quarter	Units	Unit Cost	Total Cost
1	50,000	$2.20	$110,000
2	40,000	2.35	94,000
3	40,000	2.50	100,000
4	60,000	2.70	162,000
	190,000		$466,000

Operating expenses were $130,000, and the company's income tax rate is 40%.

Instructions

(a) Prepare comparative condensed income statements for 2017 under FIFO and LIFO. (Show computations of ending inventory.)

(b) Answer the following questions for management.

(1) Which cost flow method (FIFO or LIFO) produces the more meaningful inventory amount for the balance sheet? Why?

(2) Which cost flow method (FIFO or LIFO) produces the more meaningful net income? Why?

(3) Which cost flow method (FIFO or LIFO) is more likely to approximate the actual physical flow of goods? Why?

(4) How much more cash will be available for management under LIFO than under FIFO? Why?

(5) Will gross profit under the average-cost method be higher or lower than FIFO? Than LIFO? (*Note:* It is not necessary to quantify your answer.)

(a) Gross profit:
FIFO $312,900
LIFO $303,000

P6-5A You are provided with the following information for Koetteritz Inc. for the month ended June 30, 2017. Koetteritz uses the periodic method for inventory.

Calculate ending inventory, cost of goods sold, gross profit, and gross profit rate under periodic method; compare results.

(LO 2)

Date	Description	Quantity	Unit Cost or Selling Price
June 1	Beginning inventory	40	$40
June 4	Purchase	135	43
June 10	Sale	110	70
June 11	Sale return	15	70
June 18	Purchase	55	46
June 18	Purchase return	10	46
June 25	Sale	65	76
June 28	Purchase	35	50

(a)(iii) Gross profit:
LIFO $4,330
FIFO $4,830
Average $4,546.90

Instructions

(a) Calculate (i) ending inventory, (ii) cost of goods sold, (iii) gross profit, and (iv) gross profit rate under each of the following methods.
(1) LIFO. (2) FIFO. (3) Average-cost.

(b) Compare results for the three cost flow assumptions.

Compare specific identification, FIFO, and LIFO under periodic method; use cost flow assumption to justify price increase.
(LO 2)

P6-6A You are provided with the following information for Gobler Inc. Gobler Inc. uses the periodic method of accounting for its inventory transactions.

March 1	Beginning inventory 2,000 liters at a cost of 60¢ per liter.
March 3	Purchased 2,500 liters at a cost of 65¢ per liter.
March 5	Sold 2,300 liters for $1.05 per liter.
March 10	Purchased 4,000 liters at a cost of 72¢ per liter.
March 20	Purchased 2,500 liters at a cost of 80¢ per liter.
March 30	Sold 5,200 liters for $1.25 per liter.

Instructions

(a) Prepare partial income statements through gross profit, and calculate the value of ending inventory that would be reported on the balance sheet, under each of the following cost flow assumptions. (Round ending inventory and cost of goods sold to the nearest dollar.)

(a) Gross profit:
(1) Specific identification $3,715
(2) FIFO $3,930
(3) LIFO $3,385

(1) Specific identification method assuming:
(i) The March 5 sale consisted of 1,000 liters from the March 1 beginning inventory and 1,300 liters from the March 3 purchase; and
(ii) The March 30 sale consisted of the following number of units sold from beginning inventory and each purchase: 450 liters from March 1; 550 liters from March 3; 2,900 liters from March 10; 1,300 liters from March 20.
(2) FIFO.
(3) LIFO.

(b) How can companies use a cost flow method to justify price increases? Which cost flow method would best support an argument to increase prices?

Compute ending inventory, prepare income statements, and answer questions using FIFO and LIFO.
(LO 2)

P6-7A The management of Danica Co. asks your help in determining the comparative effects of the FIFO and LIFO inventory cost flow methods. For 2017, the accounting records provide the following data.

Inventory, January 1 (10,000 units)	$ 47,000
Cost of 100,000 units purchased	532,000
Selling price of 84,000 units sold	735,000
Operating expenses	140,000

Units purchased consisted of 35,000 units at $5.10 on May 10; 35,000 units at $5.30 on August 15; and 30,000 units at $5.60 on November 20. Income taxes are 30%.

Instructions

(a) Net income
FIFO $113,120
LIFO $101,220

(a) Prepare comparative condensed income statements for 2017 under FIFO and LIFO. (Show computations of ending inventory.)

(b) Answer the following questions for management.
(1) Which inventory cost flow method produces the most meaningful inventory amount for the balance sheet? Why?
(2) Which inventory cost flow method produces the most meaningful net income? Why?
(3) Which inventory cost flow method is most likely to approximate actual physical flow of the goods? Why?
(4) How much additional cash will be available for management under LIFO than under FIFO? Why?
(5) How much of the gross profit under FIFO is illusory in comparison with the gross profit under LIFO?

Calculate cost of goods sold and ending inventory under LIFO, FIFO, and moving-average cost under the perpetual system; compare gross profit under each assumption.
(LO 5)

***P6-8A** Dempsey Inc. is a retailer operating in British Columbia. Dempsey uses the perpetual inventory method. All sales returns from customers result in the goods being returned to inventory; the inventory is not damaged. Assume that there are no credit transactions;

all amounts are settled in cash. You are provided with the following information for Dempsey Inc. for the month of January 2017.

Date	Description	Quantity	Unit Cost or Selling Price
January 1	Beginning inventory	100	$15
January 5	Purchase	140	18
January 8	Sale	110	28
January 10	Sale return	10	28
January 15	Purchase	55	20
January 16	Purchase return	5	20
January 20	Sale	90	32
January 25	Purchase	20	22

Instructions

(a) For each of the following cost flow assumptions, calculate (i) cost of goods sold, (ii) ending inventory, and (iii) gross profit.
(1) LIFO.
(2) FIFO.
(3) Moving-average cost. (Round cost per unit to three decimal places.)

(b) Compare results for the three cost flow assumptions.

(a)(iii) Gross profit:
LIFO $2,160
FIFO $2,560
Average $2,421

***P6-9A** Wittmann Co. began operations on July 1. It uses a perpetual inventory system. During July, the company had the following purchases and sales.

Determine ending inventory under a perpetual inventory system.

(LO 5)

	Purchases		
Date	Units	Unit Cost	Sales Units
July 1	5	$122	
July 6			3
July 11	7	$136	
July 14			5
July 21	8	$147	
July 27			5

Instructions

(a) Determine the ending inventory under a perpetual inventory system using (1) FIFO, (2) moving-average cost, and (3) LIFO.

(b) Which costing method produces the highest ending inventory valuation?

(a) Ending inventory
FIFO $1,029
Avg. $996
LIFO $957

***P6-10A** Bao Company lost all of its inventory in a fire on December 26, 2017. The accounting records showed the following gross profit data for November and December.

Compute gross profit rate and inventory loss using gross profit method.

(LO 6)

	November	December (to 12/26)
Net sales	$600,000	$700,000
Beginning inventory	32,000	36,000
Purchases	389,000	420,000
Purchase returns and allowances	13,300	14,900
Purchase discounts	8,500	9,500
Freight-in	8,800	9,900
Ending inventory	36,000	?

Bao is fully insured for fire losses but must prepare a report for the insurance company.

Instructions

(a) Compute the gross profit rate for November.

(b) Using the gross profit rate for November, determine the estimated cost of the inventory lost in the fire.

(a) Gross profit rate 38%

***P6-11A** Rayre Books uses the retail inventory method to estimate its monthly ending inventories. The following information is available for two of its departments at October 31, 2017.

Compute ending inventory using retail method.

(LO 6)

	Hardcovers		Paperbacks	
	Cost	Retail	Cost	Retail
Beginning inventory	$ 420,000	$ 640,000	$ 280,000	$ 360,000
Purchases	2,135,000	3,200,000	1,155,000	1,540,000
Freight-in	24,000		12,000	
Purchase discounts	44,000		22,000	
Net sales		3,100,000		1,570,000

At December 31, Rayre Books takes a physical inventory at retail. The actual retail values of the inventories in each department are Hardcovers $744,000 and Paperbacks $335,000.

Instructions

(a) Hardcovers: End. Inv. $488,400

(a) Determine the estimated cost of the ending inventory for each department at **October 31**, 2017, using the retail inventory method.

(b) Compute the ending inventory at cost for each department at **December 31**, assuming the cost-to-retail ratios for the year are 65% for Hardcovers and 75% for Paperbacks.

COMPREHENSIVE PROBLEM

CP6 On December 1, 2017, Annalise Company had the account balances shown below.

	Debit		Credit
Cash	$ 4,800	Accumulated Depreciation—Equipment	$ 1,500
Accounts Receivable	3,900	Accounts Payable	3,000
Inventory	1,800*	Owner's Capital	27,000
Equipment	21,000		$31,500
	$31,500		

*(3,000 × $0.60)

The following transactions occurred during December.

Dec. 3 Purchased 4,000 units of inventory on account at a cost of $0.74 per unit.

5 Sold 4,400 units of inventory on account for $0.90 per unit. (It sold 3,000 of the $0.60 units and 1,400 of the $0.74.)

7 Granted the December 5 customer $180 credit for 200 units of inventory returned costing $120. These units were returned to inventory.

17 Purchased 2,200 units of inventory for cash at $0.80 each.

22 Sold 2,100 units of inventory on account for $0.95 per unit. (It sold 2,100 of the $0.74 units.)

Adjustment data:

1. Accrued salaries payable $400.
2. Depreciation $200 per month.

Instructions

(a) Journalize the December transactions and adjusting entries, assuming Annalise uses the perpetual inventory method.

(b) Enter the December 1 balances in the ledger T-accounts and post the December transactions. In addition to the accounts mentioned above, use the following additional accounts: Cost of Goods Sold, Depreciation Expense, Salaries and Wages Expense, Salaries and Wages Payable, Sales Revenue, and Sales Returns and Allowances.

(c) Prepare an adjusted trial balance as of December 31, 2017.

(d) Prepare an income statement for December 2017 and a classified balance sheet at December 31, 2017.

(e) Compute ending inventory and cost of goods sold under FIFO, assuming Annalise Company uses the periodic inventory system.

(f) Compute ending inventory and cost of goods sold under LIFO, assuming Annalise Company uses the periodic inventory system.

BROADENING YOUR PERSPECTIVE

FINANCIAL REPORTING AND ANALYSIS

Financial Reporting Problem: Apple Inc.

BYP6-1 The notes that accompany a company's financial statements provide informative details that would clutter the amounts and descriptions presented in the statements. Refer to the financial statements of **Apple Inc.** in Appendix A as well as its annual report. Instructions for accessing and using the company's complete annual report, including the notes to the financial statements, are also provided in Appendix A.

Instructions

Answer the following questions. Complete the requirements in millions of dollars, as shown in Apple's annual report.

(a) What did Apple report for the amount of inventories in its consolidated balance sheet at September 29, 2012? At September 28, 2013?

(b) Compute the dollar amount of change and the percentage change in inventories between 2012 and 2013. Compute inventory as a percentage of current assets at September 28, 2013.

(c) How does Apple value its inventories? Which inventory cost flow method does Apple use? (See Notes to the Financial Statements.)

(d) What is the cost of sales (cost of goods sold) reported by Apple for 2013, 2012, and 2011? Compute the percentage of cost of sales to net sales in 2013.

Comparative Analysis Problem: PepsiCo, Inc. vs. The Coca-Cola Company

BYP6-2 PepsiCo's financial statements are presented in Appendix B. Financial statements of The Coca-Cola Company are presented in Appendix C. Instructions for accessing and using the complete annual reports of PepsiCo and Coca-Cola, including the notes to the financial statements, are also provided in Appendices B and C, respectively.

Instructions

(a) Based on the information contained in these financial statements, compute the following 2013 ratios for each company.

(1) Inventory turnover.

(2) Days in inventory.

(b) What conclusions concerning the management of the inventory can you draw from these data?

Comparative Analysis Problem: Amazon.com, Inc. vs. Wal-Mart Stores, Inc.

BYP6-3 Amazon.com, Inc.'s financial statements are presented in Appendix D. Financial statements of Wal-Mart Stores, Inc. are presented in Appendix E. Instructions for accessing and using the complete annual reports of Amazon and Wal-Mart, including the notes to the financial statements, are also provided in Appendices D and E, respectively.

Instructions

(a) Based on the information contained in these financial statements, compute the following 2013 ratios for each company.

(1) Inventory turnover.

(2) Days in inventory.

(b) What conclusions concerning the management of the inventory can you draw from these data?

Real-World Focus

BYP6-4 A company's annual report usually will identify the inventory method used. Knowing that, you can analyze the effects of the inventory method on the income statement and balance sheet.

Address: **www.cisco.com**, or go to **www.wiley.com/college/weygandt**

Instructions

Answer the following questions based on the current year's annual report on Cisco's website.

(a) At Cisco's fiscal year-end, what was the inventory on the balance sheet?

(b) How has this changed from the previous fiscal year-end?

(c) How much of the inventory was finished goods?
(d) What inventory method does Cisco use?

CRITICAL THINKING

Decision-Making Across the Organization

BYP6-5 On April 10, 2017, fire damaged the office and warehouse of Corvet Company. Most of the accounting records were destroyed, but the following account balances were determined as of March 31, 2017: Inventory (January 1, 2017), $80,000; Sales Revenue (January 1–March 31, 2017), $180,000; Purchases (January 1–March 31, 2017), $94,000.

The company's fiscal year ends on December 31. It uses a periodic inventory system.

From an analysis of the April bank statement, you discover cancelled checks of $4,200 for cash purchases during the period April 1–10. Deposits during the same period totaled $18,500. Of that amount, 60% were collections on accounts receivable, and the balance was cash sales.

Correspondence with the company's principal suppliers revealed $12,400 of purchases on account from April 1 to April 10. Of that amount, $1,600 was for merchandise in transit on April 10 that was shipped FOB destination.

Correspondence with the company's principal customers produced acknowledgments of credit sales totaling $37,000 from April 1 to April 10. It was estimated that $5,600 of credit sales will never be acknowledged or recovered from customers.

Corvet Company reached an agreement with the insurance company that its fire-loss claim should be based on the average of the gross profit rates for the preceding 2 years. The financial statements for 2015 and 2016 showed the following data.

	2016	2015
Net sales	$600,000	$480,000
Cost of goods purchased	404,000	356,000
Beginning inventory	60,000	40,000
Ending inventory	80,000	60,000

Inventory with a cost of $17,000 was salvaged from the fire.

Instructions

With the class divided into groups, answer the following.

(a) Determine the balances in (1) Sales Revenue and (2) Purchases at April 10.

***(b)** Determine the average gross profit rate for the years 2015 and 2016. (*Hint:* Find the gross profit rate for each year and divide the sum by 2.)

***(c)** Determine the inventory loss as a result of the fire, using the gross profit method.

Communication Activity

BYP6-6 You are the controller of Small Toys Inc. Pamela Bames, the president, recently mentioned to you that she found an error in the 2016 financial statements which she believes has corrected itself. She determined, in discussions with the Purchasing Department, that 2016 ending inventory was overstated by $1 million. Pamela says that the 2017 ending inventory is correct. Thus, she assumes that 2017 income is correct. Pamela says to you, "What happened has happened—there's no point in worrying about it anymore."

Instructions

You conclude that Pamela is incorrect. Write a brief, tactful memo to Pamela, clarifying the situation.

Ethics Case

BYP6-7 R. J. Graziano Wholesale Corp. uses the LIFO method of inventory costing. In the current year, profit at R. J. Graziano is running unusually high. The corporate tax rate is also high this year, but it is scheduled to decline significantly next year. In an effort to lower the current year's net income and to take advantage of the changing income tax rate, the president of R. J. Graziano Wholesale instructs the plant accountant to recommend to the purchasing department a large purchase of inventory for delivery 3 days before the end of the year. The price of the inventory to be purchased has doubled during the year, and the purchase will represent a major portion of the ending inventory value.

Instructions

(a) What is the effect of this transaction on this year's and next year's income statement and income tax expense? Why?

(b) If R. J. Graziano Wholesale had been using the FIFO method of inventory costing, would the president give the same directive?

(c) Should the plant accountant order the inventory purchase to lower income? What are the ethical implications of this order?

All About You

BYP6-8 Some of the largest business frauds ever perpetrated have involved the misstatement of inventory. Two classics were at **Leslie Fay** and **McKesson Corporation**.

Instructions

There is considerable information regarding inventory frauds available on the Internet. Search for information about one of the two cases mentioned above, or inventory fraud at any other company, and prepare a short explanation of the nature of the inventory fraud.

FASB Codification Activity

BYP6-9 If your school has a subscription to the FASB Codification, go to **http://aaahq.org/ascLogin.cfm** to log in and prepare responses to the following.

Instructions

(a) The primary basis for accounting for inventories is cost. How is cost defined in the Codification?

(b) What does the Codification state regarding the use of consistency in the selection or employment of a basis for inventory?

A Look at IFRS

LEARNING OBJECTIVE  7

Compare the accounting for inventories under GAAP and IFRS.

The major IFRS requirements related to accounting and reporting for inventories are the same as GAAP. The major differences are that IFRS prohibits the use of the LIFO cost flow assumption and determines market in the lower-of-cost-or-market inventory valuation differently.

Relevant Facts

Following are the key similarities and differences between GAAP and IFRS related to inventories.

Similarities

- IFRS and GAAP account for inventory acquisitions at historical cost and value inventory at the lower-of-cost-or-market subsequent to acquisition.
- Who owns the goods—goods in transit or consigned goods—as well as the costs to include in inventory are essentially accounted for in the same way under both IFRS and GAAP.

Differences

- The requirements for accounting for and reporting inventories are more principles-based under IFRS. That is, GAAP provides more detailed guidelines in inventory accounting.
- A major difference between IFRS and GAAP relates to the LIFO cost flow assumption. GAAP permits the use of LIFO for inventory valuation. IFRS prohibits its use. FIFO and average-cost are the only two acceptable cost flow assumptions permitted under IFRS. Both sets of standards permit specific identification where appropriate.
- In the lower-of-cost-or-market test for inventory valuation, IFRS defines market as net realizable value. GAAP, on the other hand, defines market as replacement cost.

Looking to the Future

One convergence issue that will be difficult to resolve relates to the use of the LIFO cost flow assumption. As indicated, IFRS specifically prohibits its use. Conversely, the LIFO cost flow assumption is widely used in the United States because of its favorable tax advantages. In addition, many argue that LIFO from a financial reporting point of view provides a better matching of current costs against revenue and, therefore, enables companies to compute a more realistic income.

IFRS Practice

IFRS Self-Test Questions

1. Which of the following should **not** be included in the inventory of a company using IFRS?
   (a) Goods held on consignment from another company.
   (b) Goods shipped on consignment to another company.
   (c) Goods in transit from another company shipped FOB shipping point.
   (d) None of the above.
2. Which method of inventory costing is prohibited under IFRS?
   (a) Specific identification.
   (b) LIFO.
   (c) FIFO.
   (d) Average-cost.

IFRS Exercises

IFRS6-1 Briefly describe some of the similarities and differences between GAAP and IFRS with respect to the accounting for inventories.

IFRS6-2 LaTour Inc. is based in France and prepares its financial statements (in euros) in accordance with IFRS. In 2017, it reported cost of goods sold of €578 million and average inventory of €154 million. Briefly discuss how analysis of LaTour's inventory turnover (and comparisons to a company using GAAP) might be affected by differences in inventory accounting between IFRS and GAAP.

International Financial Reporting Problem: Louis Vuitton

IFRS6-3 The financial statements of Louis Vuitton are presented in Appendix F. Instructions for accessing and using the company's complete annual report, including the notes to its financial statements, are also provided in Appendix F.

Instructions
Using the notes to the company's financial statements, answer the following questions.

(a) What cost flow assumption does the company use to value inventory?
(b) What amount of goods purchased for retail and finished products did the company report at December 31, 2013?

Answers to IFRS Self-Test Questions

1. a **2.** b

Chapter 7 Accounting Information Systems

Starting a small business requires many decisions. For example, you have to decide where to locate, how much space you need, how much inventory to have, how many employees to hire, and where to advertise. Small business owners are typically so concerned about the product and sales side of their business that they often do not give enough thought to something that is also critical to their success—how to keep track of financial results.

Small business owners today can choose either manual or computerized accounting systems. For example, Paul and Laura West were the owners of the first independent dealership of Carvin guitars and professional audio equipment. When they founded their company in Sacramento, California, they decided to purchase a computerized accounting system that would integrate many aspects of their retail operations. They wanted to use their accounting software to manage their inventory of guitars and amplifiers, enter sales, record and report financial data, and process credit card and debit card transactions. They evaluated a number of options and chose QuickBooks® by Intuit Inc.

QuickBooks®, like most other popular software packages, has programs designed for the needs of a specific type of business, which in this case is retailing. This QuickBooks® retailing package automatically collects sales information from its point-of-sale scanning devices. It also keeps track of inventory levels and automatically generates purchase orders for popular items when re-order points are reached. It even supports specialized advertising campaigns.

For example, QuickBooks® compiled a customer database from which the Wests sent out targeted direct mailings to potential customers. The computerized system also enabled data files to be emailed to the company's accountant. This kept down costs and made it easier and more efficient for the Wests to generate financial reports as needed. The Wests believed that the investment in the computerized system saved them time and money, and allowed them to spend more time on other aspects of their business.

Source: Intuit Inc., "QuickBooks® and ProAdvisor® Help Make Guitar Store a Hit," *Journal of Accountancy* (May 2006), p. 101.

LEARNING OBJECTIVES

1. **Explain the basic concepts of an accounting information system.**
2. **Describe the nature and purpose of a subsidiary ledger.**
3. **Record transactions in special journals.**

LEARNING OBJECTIVE 1 Explain the basic concepts of an accounting information system.

The **accounting information system** collects and processes transaction data and communicates financial information to decision-makers. It includes each of the steps in the accounting cycle that you studied in earlier chapters. It also includes the documents that provide evidence of the transactions, and the records, trial balances, worksheets, and financial statements that result. An

accounting system may be either manual or computerized. Most businesses use some sort of computerized accounting system, whether it is an off-the-shelf system for small businesses, like QuickBooks® or Sage 50, or a more complex custom-made system.

Efficient and effective accounting information systems are based on certain basic principles. These principles, as described in Illustration 7-1, are (1) cost-effectiveness, (2) usefulness, and (3) flexibility. If the accounting system is cost-effective, provides useful output, and has the flexibility to meet future needs, it can contribute to both individual and organizational goals.

Illustration 7-1
Principles of an efficient and effective accounting information system

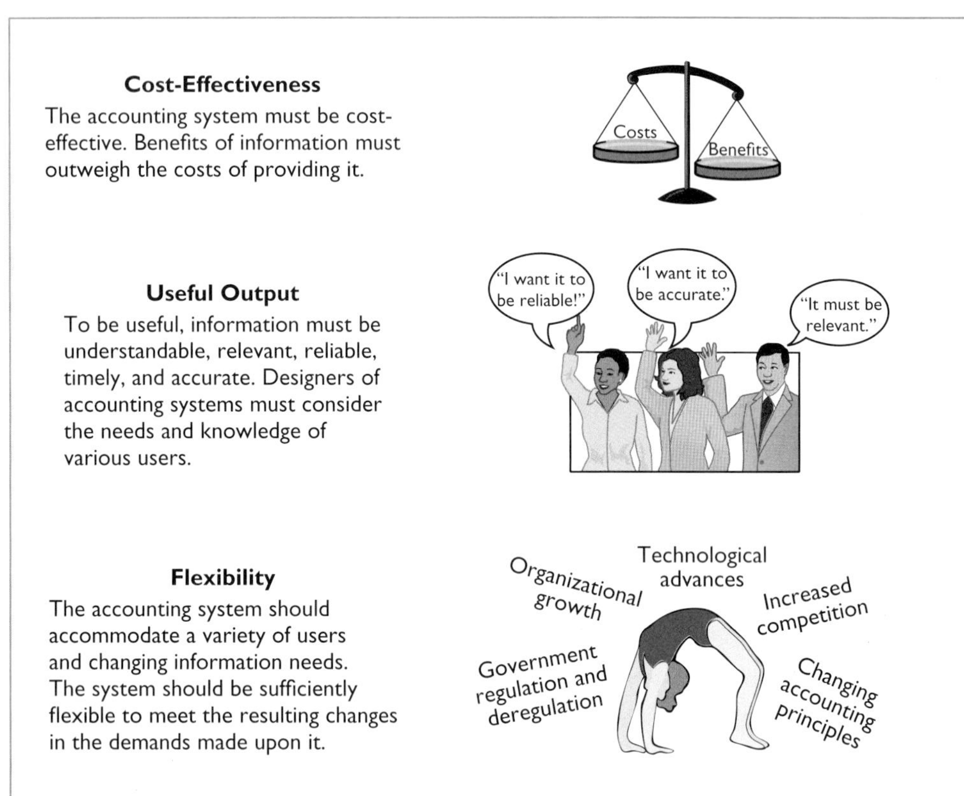

Computerized Accounting Systems

Many small businesses use a computerized general ledger accounting system. **General ledger accounting systems** are software programs that integrate the various accounting functions related to sales, purchases, receivables, payables, cash receipts and disbursements, and payroll. They also generate financial statements. Computerized systems have a number of advantages over manual systems. First, the company typically enters data only once in a computerized system. Second, because the computer does most steps automatically, it eliminates many errors resulting from human intervention in a manual system, such as errors in posting or preparation of financial statements. Computerized systems also provide up-to-the-minute information. More timely information often results in better business decisions. Many different general ledger software packages are available.

CHOOSING A SOFTWARE PACKAGE

To identify the right software for your business, you must understand your company's operations. For example, consider its needs with regard to inventory, billing, payroll, and cash management. In addition, the company might have specific needs that are not supported by all software systems. For example, you might want to track employees' hours on individual jobs or to extract information for determining sales commissions. Choosing the right system is critical because installation of even a basic system is time-consuming, and learning a new system will require many hours of employee time.

ENTRY-LEVEL SOFTWARE

Software publishers tend to classify businesses into groups based on revenue and the number of employees. Companies with revenues of less than $5 million and up to 20 employees generally use **entry-level programs**. The two leading entry-level programs are Intuit's QuickBooks® and The Sage Group's Sage 50. These programs control more than 90% of the market. Each of these entry-level programs comes in many different industry-specific versions. For example, some are designed for very specific industry applications such as restaurants, retailing, construction, manufacturing, or nonprofit.

Quality entry-level packages typically involve more than recording transactions and preparing financial statements. Here are some common features and benefits:

- **Easy data access and report preparation.** Users can easily access information related to specific customers or suppliers. For example, you can view all transactions, invoices, payments, as well as contact information for a specific client.
- **Audit trail.** As a result of the Sarbanes-Oxley Act, companies are now far more concerned that their accounting system minimizes opportunities for fraud. Many programs provide an "audit trail" that enables the tracking of all transactions.
- **Internal controls.** Some systems have an internal accounting review that identifies suspicious transactions or likely mistakes such as wrong account numbers or duplicate transactions.
- **Customization.** This feature enables the company to create data fields specific to the needs of its business.
- **Network-compatibility.** Multiple users in the company can access the system at the same time.

ENTERPRISE RESOURCE PLANNING SYSTEMS

Enterprise resource planning (ERP) systems are typically used by manufacturing companies with more than 500 employees and $500 million in sales. The best-known of these systems are SAP AG's SAP ERP (the most widely used) and Oracle's ERP. ERP systems go far beyond the functions of an entry-level general ledger package. They integrate all aspects of the organization, including accounting, sales, human resource management, and manufacturing. Because of the complexity of an ERP system, implementation can take three years and cost five times as much as the purchase price of the system. Purchase and implementation of ERP systems can cost from $250,000 to as much as $50 million for the largest multinational corporations.

Manual Accounting Systems

In **manual accounting systems**, someone performs each of the steps in the accounting cycle by hand. For example, someone manually enters each accounting transaction in the journal and manually posts each to the ledger. Other manual computations must be made to obtain ledger account balances and to prepare a trial balance and financial statements. In the remainder of this chapter, we illustrate the use of a manual system.

You might be wondering, "Why cover manual accounting systems if the real world uses computerized systems?" First, small businesses still abound. Most of them begin operations with manual accounting systems and convert to computerized systems as the business grows. You may work in a small business or start your own someday, so it is useful to know how a manual system works. Second, to understand what computerized accounting systems do, you also need to understand manual accounting systems.

The manual accounting system represented in the first six chapters of this textbook is satisfactory in a company with a low volume of transactions. However, in most companies, it is necessary to add additional ledgers and journals to the accounting system to record transaction data efficiently.

LEARNING OBJECTIVE 2

Describe the nature and purpose of a subsidiary ledger.

Imagine a business that has several thousand charge (credit) customers and shows the transactions with these customers in only one general ledger account—Accounts Receivable. It would be nearly impossible to determine the balance owed by an individual customer at any specific time. Similarly, the amount payable to one creditor would be difficult to locate quickly from a single Accounts Payable account in the general ledger.

Instead, companies use subsidiary ledgers to keep track of individual balances. A **subsidiary ledger** is a group of accounts with a common characteristic (for example, all accounts receivable). It is an addition to and an expansion of the general ledger. The subsidiary ledger frees the general ledger from the details of individual balances.

Two common subsidiary ledgers are as follows.

1. The **accounts receivable** (or **customers'**) **subsidiary ledger**, which collects transaction data of individual customers.
2. The **accounts payable** (or **creditors'**) **subsidiary ledger**, which collects transaction data of individual creditors.

In each of these subsidiary ledgers, companies usually arrange individual accounts in alphabetical order.

A general ledger account summarizes the detailed data from a subsidiary ledger. For example, the detailed data from the accounts receivable subsidiary ledger are summarized in Accounts Receivable in the general ledger. The general ledger account that summarizes subsidiary ledger data is called a **control account**. Illustration 7-2 presents an overview of the relationship of subsidiary ledgers to the general ledger. There, the general ledger control accounts and subsidiary ledger accounts are in green. Note that Cash and Owner's Capital in this illustration are not control accounts because there are no subsidiary ledger accounts related to these accounts.

Illustration 7-2
Relationship of general ledger and subsidiary ledgers

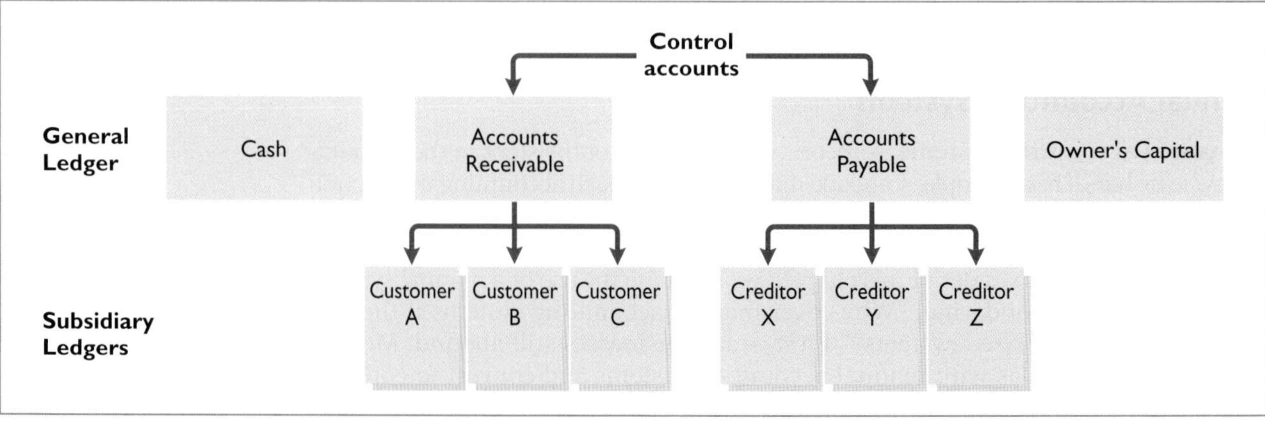

At the end of an accounting period, each general ledger control account balance must equal the composite balance of the individual accounts in the related subsidiary ledger. For example, the balance in Accounts Payable in Illustration 7-2 must equal the total of the subsidiary balances of Creditors X + Y + Z.

Subsidiary Ledger Example

Illustration 7-3 lists credit sales and collections on account for Pujols Company.

Illustration 7-3
Sales and collection transactions

Credit Sales			Collections on Account		
Jan. 10	Aaron Co.	$ 6,000	Jan. 19	Aaron Co.	$4,000
12	Branden Inc.	3,000	21	Branden Inc.	3,000
20	Caron Co.	3,000	29	Caron Co.	1,000
		$12,000			$8,000

Illustration 7-4 provides an example of a control account and subsidiary ledger for Pujols Company. (Due to space considerations, the explanation column in these accounts is not shown in this and subsequent illustrations.) Illustration 7-4 is based on the transactions listed in Illustration 7-3.

Illustration 7-4
Relationship between general and subsidiary ledgers

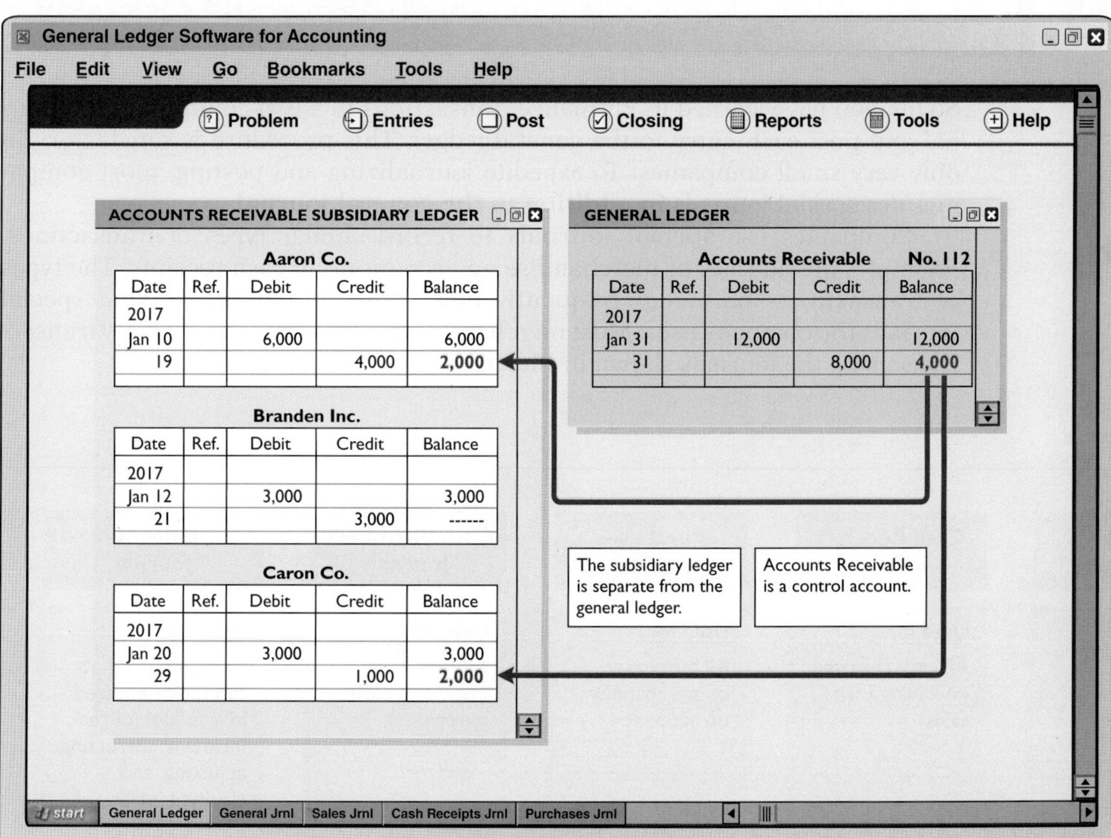

Aaron Co.

Date	Ref.	Debit	Credit	Balance
2017				
Jan 10		6,000		6,000
19			4,000	2,000

Branden Inc.

Date	Ref.	Debit	Credit	Balance
2017				
Jan 12		3,000		3,000
21			3,000	------

Caron Co.

Date	Ref.	Debit	Credit	Balance
2017				
Jan 20		3,000		3,000
29			1,000	2,000

Accounts Receivable No. 112

Date	Ref.	Debit	Credit	Balance
2017				
Jan 31		12,000		12,000
31			8,000	4,000

Pujols can reconcile the total debits ($12,000) and credits ($8,000) in Accounts Receivable in the general ledger to the detailed debits and credits in the subsidiary accounts. Also, the balance of $4,000 in the control account agrees with the total of the balances in the individual accounts (Aaron Co. $2,000 + Branden Inc. $0 + Caron Co. $2,000) in the subsidiary ledger.

As Illustration 7-4 shows, companies make monthly postings to the control accounts in the general ledger. This practice allows them to prepare monthly financial statements. Companies post to the individual accounts in the subsidiary ledger daily. Daily posting ensures that account information is current. This enables the company to monitor credit limits, bill customers, and answer inquiries from customers about their account balances.

Advantages of Subsidiary Ledgers

Subsidiary ledgers have several advantages:

1. **They show in a single account transactions affecting one customer or one creditor,** thus providing up-to-date information on specific account balances.
2. **They free the general ledger of excessive details.** As a result, a trial balance of the general ledger does not contain vast numbers of individual account balances.
3. **They help locate errors in individual accounts** by reducing the number of accounts in one ledger and by using control accounts.
4. **They make possible a division of labor** in posting. One employee can post to the general ledger while someone else posts to the subsidiary ledgers.

LEARNING OBJECTIVE 

Record transactions in special journals.

So far, you have learned to journalize transactions in a two-column general journal and post each entry to the general ledger. This procedure is satisfactory in only very small companies. To expedite journalizing and posting, most companies use special journals **in addition to the general journal**.

Companies use **special journals** to record similar types of transactions. Examples are all sales of merchandise on account or all cash receipts. The types of transactions that occur frequently in a company determine what special journals the company uses. Most merchandising companies record daily transactions using the journals shown in Illustration 7-5.

Illustration 7-5
Use of special journals and the general journal

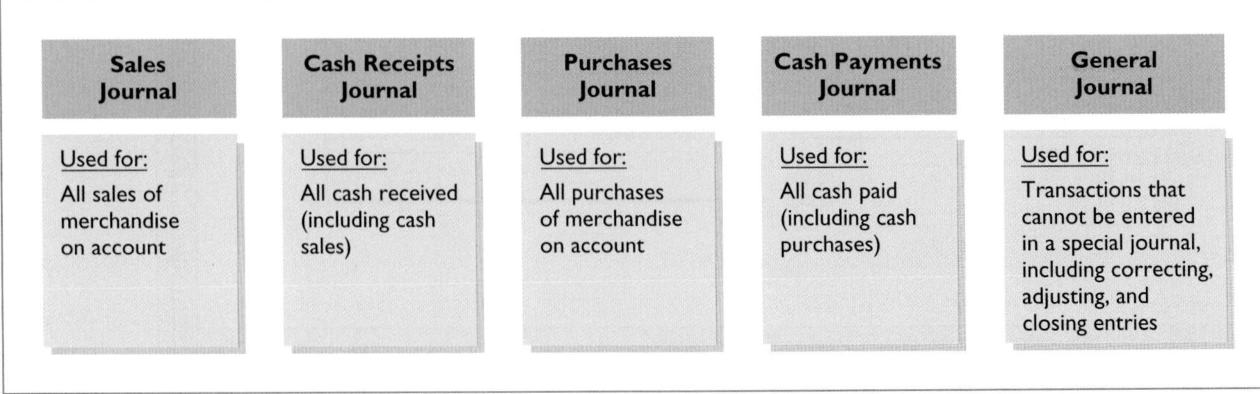

If a transaction cannot be recorded in a special journal, the company records it in the general journal. For example, if a company had special journals for only the four types of transactions listed above, it would record purchase returns and allowances that do not affect cash in the general journal. Similarly, **correcting,**

adjusting, and closing entries are recorded in the general journal. In some situations, companies might use special journals other than those listed above. For example, when sales returns and allowances that do not affect cash are frequent, a company might use a special journal to record these transactions.

Special journals **permit greater division of labor** because several people can record entries in different journals at the same time. For example, one employee may journalize all cash receipts, and another may journalize all credit sales. Also, the use of special journals **reduces the time needed to complete the posting process**. With special journals, companies may post some accounts monthly instead of daily, as we will illustrate later in the chapter. On the following pages, we discuss the four special journals shown in Illustration 7-5.

Sales Journal

In the **sales journal**, companies record **sales of merchandise on account**. Cash sales of merchandise go in the cash receipts journal. Credit sales of assets other than merchandise go in the general journal.

JOURNALIZING CREDIT SALES

To demonstrate use of a sales journal, we will use data for Karns Wholesale Supply, which uses a **perpetual inventory system**. Under this system, each entry in the sales journal results in one entry **at selling price** and another entry **at cost**. The entry at selling price is a debit to Accounts Receivable (a control account) and a credit of equal amount to Sales Revenue. The entry at cost is a debit to Cost of Goods Sold and a credit of equal amount to Inventory (a control account). Using a sales journal with two amount columns, the company can show on only one line a sales transaction at both selling price and cost. Illustration 7-6 shows this two-column sales journal of Karns Wholesale Supply, using assumed credit sales transactions (for sales invoices 101–107).

Note that, unlike the general journal, an explanation is not required for each entry in a special journal. Also, the use of prenumbered invoices ensures that all invoices are journalized and no invoices are duplicated. Finally, the reference

Illustration 7-6
Journalizing the sales journal—perpetual inventory system

General Ledger Software for Accounting

File Edit View Go Bookmarks Tools Help

Problem Entries Post Closing Reports Tools Help

SALES JOURNAL SI

Date	Account Debited	Invoice No.	Ref.	Accts. Receivable Dr. Sales Revenue Cr.	Cost of Goods Sold Dr. Inventory Cr.
2017					
May 3	Abbot Sisters	101		10,600	6,360
7	Babson Co.	102		11,350	7,370
14	Carson Bros.	103		7,800	5,070
19	Deli Co.	104		9,300	6,510
21	Abbot Sisters	105		15,400	10,780
24	Deli Co.	106		21,210	15,900
27	Babson Co.	107		14,570	10,200
				90,230	62,190

start General Ledger General Jrnl Sales Jrnl Cash Receipts Jrnl Purchases Jrnl

(Ref.) column is not used in journalizing. It is used in posting the sales journal, as explained in the next section.

POSTING THE SALES JOURNAL

Companies make daily postings from the sales journal **to the individual accounts receivable** in the subsidiary ledger. Posting **to the general ledger** is done **monthly**. Illustration 7-7 shows both the daily and monthly postings.

A check mark (✓) is inserted in the reference column to indicate that the daily posting to the customer's account has been made. If the subsidiary ledger accounts were numbered, the account number would be entered in place of the check

Illustration 7-7
Posting the sales journal

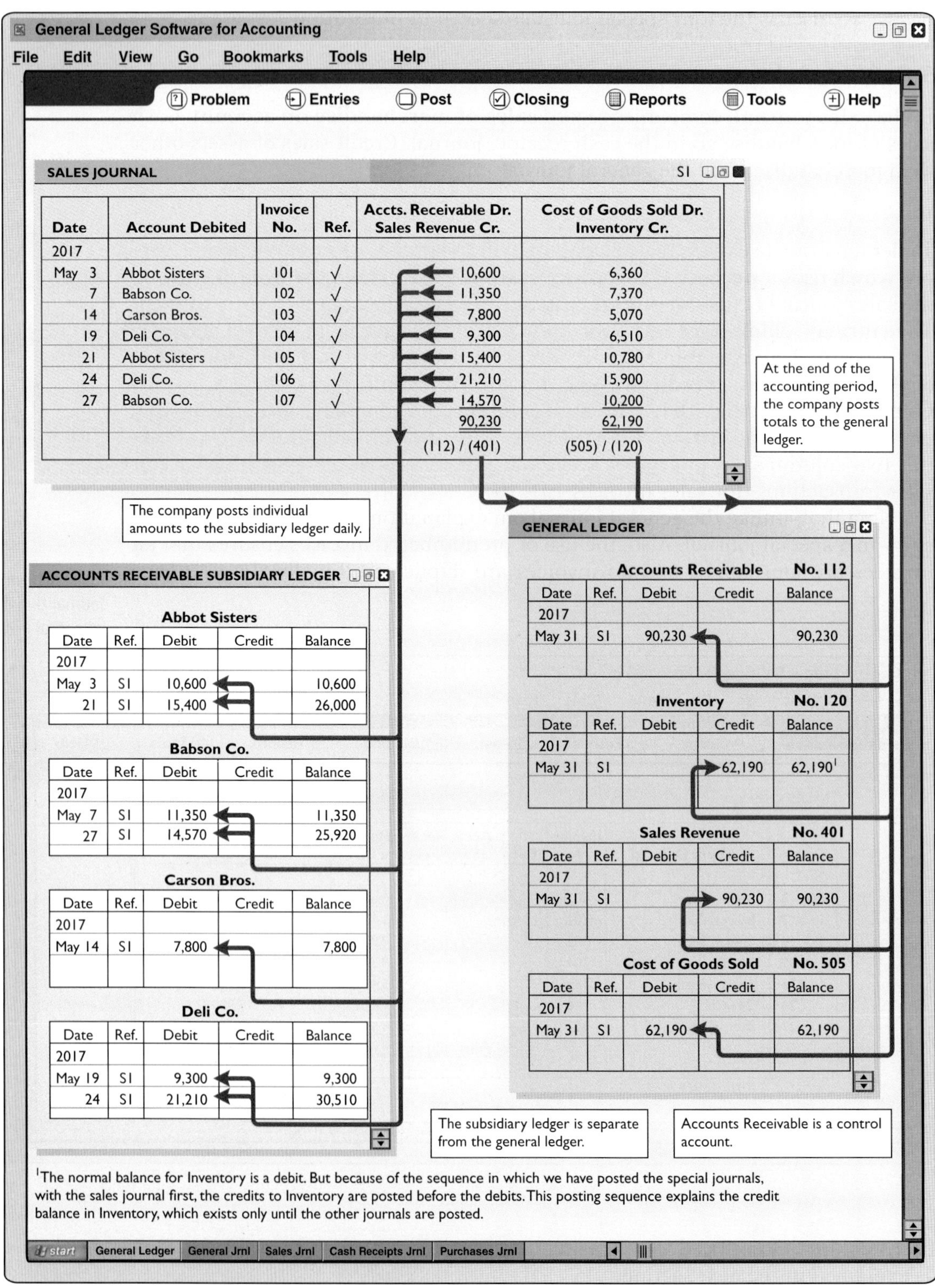

SALES JOURNAL S1

Date	Account Debited	Invoice No.	Ref.	Accts. Receivable Dr. Sales Revenue Cr.	Cost of Goods Sold Dr. Inventory Cr.
2017					
May 3	Abbot Sisters	101	✓	10,600	6,360
7	Babson Co.	102	✓	11,350	7,370
14	Carson Bros.	103	✓	7,800	5,070
19	Deli Co.	104	✓	9,300	6,510
21	Abbot Sisters	105	✓	15,400	10,780
24	Deli Co.	106	✓	21,210	15,900
27	Babson Co.	107	✓	14,570	10,200
				90,230	62,190
				(112) / (401)	(505) / (120)

ACCOUNTS RECEIVABLE SUBSIDIARY LEDGER

Abbot Sisters

Date	Ref.	Debit	Credit	Balance
2017				
May 3	S1	10,600		10,600
21	S1	15,400		26,000

Babson Co.

Date	Ref.	Debit	Credit	Balance
2017				
May 7	S1	11,350		11,350
27	S1	14,570		25,920

Carson Bros.

Date	Ref.	Debit	Credit	Balance
2017				
May 14	S1	7,800		7,800

Deli Co.

Date	Ref.	Debit	Credit	Balance
2017				
May 19	S1	9,300		9,300
24	S1	21,210		30,510

GENERAL LEDGER

Accounts Receivable No. 112

Date	Ref.	Debit	Credit	Balance
2017				
May 31	S1	90,230		90,230

Inventory No. 120

Date	Ref.	Debit	Credit	Balance
2017				
May 31	S1		62,190	62,190[1]

Sales Revenue No. 401

Date	Ref.	Debit	Credit	Balance
2017				
May 31	S1		90,230	90,230

Cost of Goods Sold No. 505

Date	Ref.	Debit	Credit	Balance
2017				
May 31	S1	62,190		62,190

[1]The normal balance for Inventory is a debit. But because of the sequence in which we have posted the special journals, with the sales journal first, the credits to Inventory are posted before the debits. This posting sequence explains the credit balance in Inventory, which exists only until the other journals are posted.

mark. At the end of the month, Karns posts the column totals of the sales journal to the general ledger. Here, the column totals are as follows. From the selling-price column, a debit of $90,230 to Accounts Receivable (account No. 112), and a credit of $90,230 to Sales Revenue (account No. 401). From the cost column, a debit of $62,190 to Cost of Goods Sold (account No. 505), and a credit of $62,190 to Inventory (account No. 120). Karns inserts the account numbers below the column totals to indicate that the postings have been made. In both the general ledger and subsidiary ledger accounts, the reference **S1** indicates that the posting came from page 1 of the sales journal.

PROVING THE LEDGERS

The next step is to "prove" the ledgers. To do so, Karns must determine two things: (1) The total of the general ledger debit balances must equal the total of the general ledger credit balances. (2) The sum of the subsidiary ledger balances must equal the balance in the control account. Illustration 7-8 shows the proof of the postings from the sales journal to the general and subsidiary ledgers.

Illustration 7-8
Proving the equality of the postings from the sales journal

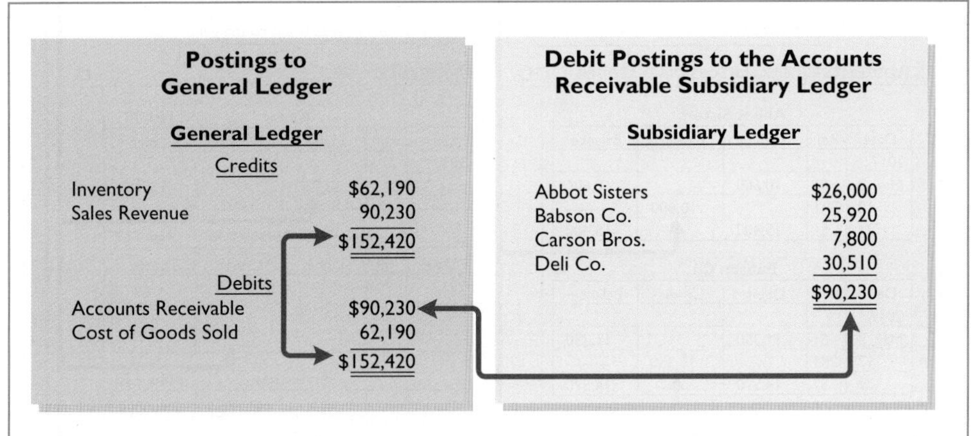

ADVANTAGES OF THE SALES JOURNAL

The use of a special journal to record sales on account has a number of advantages. First, the one-line entry for each sales transaction saves time. In the sales journal, it is not necessary to write out the four account titles for each transaction. Second, only totals, rather than individual entries, are posted to the general ledger. This saves posting time and reduces the possibilities of errors in posting. Finally, a division of labor results because one individual can take responsibility for the sales journal.

Cash Receipts Journal

In the **cash receipts journal**, companies record all receipts of cash. The most common types of cash receipts are cash sales of merchandise and collections of accounts receivable. Many other possibilities exist, such as receipt of money from bank loans and cash proceeds from disposal of equipment. A one- or two-column cash receipts journal would not have space enough for all possible cash receipt transactions. Therefore, companies use a multiple-column cash receipts journal.

Generally, a cash receipts journal includes the following columns: debit columns for Cash and Sales Discounts, and credit columns for Accounts Receivable, Sales Revenue, and "Other Accounts." Companies use the Other Accounts category when the cash receipt does not involve a cash sale or a collection of accounts receivable. Under a perpetual inventory system, each sales entry also is accompanied by an entry that debits Cost of Goods Sold and credits Inventory for the cost of the merchandise sold. Illustration 7-9 shows a six-column cash receipts journal.

Illustration 7-9
Journalizing and posting the cash receipts journal

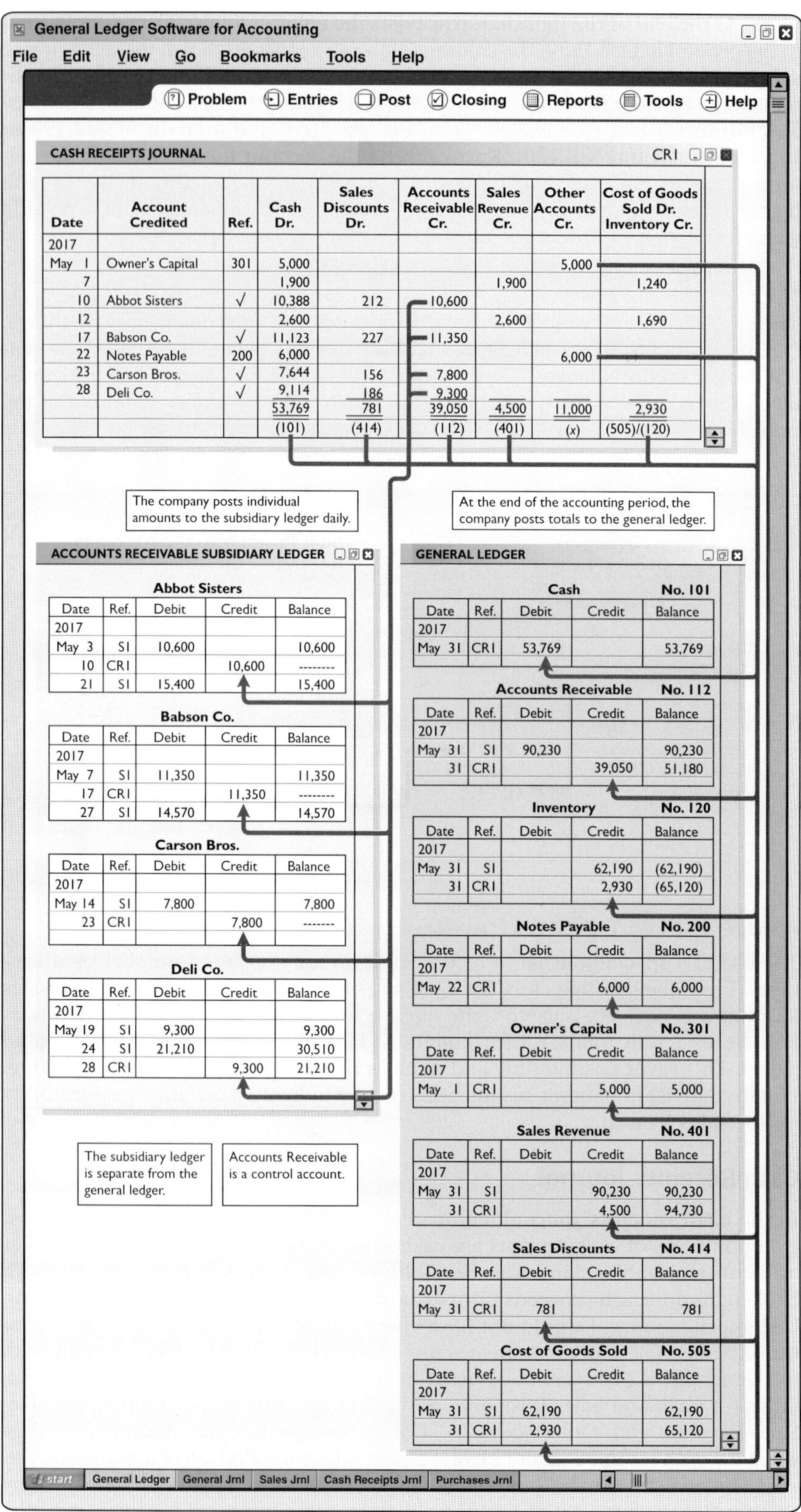

CASH RECEIPTS JOURNAL CR1

Date	Account Credited	Ref.	Cash Dr.	Sales Discounts Dr.	Accounts Receivable Cr.	Sales Revenue Cr.	Other Accounts Cr.	Cost of Goods Sold Dr. Inventory Cr.
2017								
May 1	Owner's Capital	301	5,000				5,000	
7			1,900			1,900		1,240
10	Abbot Sisters	√	10,388	212	10,600			
12			2,600			2,600		1,690
17	Babson Co.	√	11,123	227	11,350			
22	Notes Payable	200	6,000				6,000	
23	Carson Bros.	√	7,644	156	7,800			
28	Deli Co.	√	9,114	186	9,300			
			53,769	781	39,050	4,500	11,000	2,930
			(101)	(414)	(112)	(401)	(x)	(505)/(120)

ACCOUNTS RECEIVABLE SUBSIDIARY LEDGER

Abbot Sisters

Date	Ref.	Debit	Credit	Balance
2017				
May 3	S1	10,600		10,600
10	CR1		10,600	--------
21	S1	15,400		15,400

Babson Co.

Date	Ref.	Debit	Credit	Balance
2017				
May 7	S1	11,350		11,350
17	CR1		11,350	--------
27	S1	14,570		14,570

Carson Bros.

Date	Ref.	Debit	Credit	Balance
2017				
May 14	S1	7,800		7,800
23	CR1		7,800	-------

Deli Co.

Date	Ref.	Debit	Credit	Balance
2017				
May 19	S1	9,300		9,300
24	S1	21,210		30,510
28	CR1		9,300	21,210

GENERAL LEDGER

Cash No. 101

Date	Ref.	Debit	Credit	Balance
2017				
May 31	CR1	53,769		53,769

Accounts Receivable No. 112

Date	Ref.	Debit	Credit	Balance
2017				
May 31	S1	90,230		90,230
31	CR1		39,050	51,180

Inventory No. 120

Date	Ref.	Debit	Credit	Balance
2017				
May 31	S1		62,190	(62,190)
31	CR1		2,930	(65,120)

Notes Payable No. 200

Date	Ref.	Debit	Credit	Balance
2017				
May 22	CR1		6,000	6,000

Owner's Capital No. 301

Date	Ref.	Debit	Credit	Balance
2017				
May 1	CR1		5,000	5,000

Sales Revenue No. 401

Date	Ref.	Debit	Credit	Balance
2017				
May 31	S1		90,230	90,230
31	CR1		4,500	94,730

Sales Discounts No. 414

Date	Ref.	Debit	Credit	Balance
2017				
May 31	CR1	781		781

Cost of Goods Sold No. 505

Date	Ref.	Debit	Credit	Balance
2017				
May 31	S1	62,190		62,190
31	CR1	2,930		65,120

Companies may use additional credit columns if these columns significantly reduce postings to a specific account. For example, a loan company such as **Household International** receives thousands of cash collections from customers. Using separate credit columns for Loans Receivable and Interest Revenue, rather than the Other Accounts credit column, would reduce postings.

JOURNALIZING CASH RECEIPTS TRANSACTIONS

To illustrate the journalizing of cash receipts transactions, we will continue with the May transactions of Karns Wholesale Supply. Collections from customers relate to the entries recorded in the sales journal in Illustration 7-6. The entries in the cash receipts journal are based on the following cash receipts.

May	1	D. A. Karns makes an investment of $5,000 in the business.
	7	Cash sales of merchandise total $1,900 (cost, $1,240).
	10	Received a check for $10,388 from Abbot Sisters in payment of invoice No. 101 for $10,600 less a 2% discount.
	12	Cash sales of merchandise total $2,600 (cost, $1,690).
	17	Received a check for $11,123 from Babson Co. in payment of invoice No. 102 for $11,350 less a 2% discount.
	22	Received cash by signing a note for $6,000.
	23	Received a check for $7,644 from Carson Bros. in full for invoice No. 103 for $7,800 less a 2% discount.
	28	Received a check for $9,114 from Deli Co. in full for invoice No. 104 for $9,300 less a 2% discount.

Further information about the columns in the cash receipts journal is listed below.

Debit Columns:

1. **Cash.** Karns enters in this column the amount of cash actually received in each transaction. The column total indicates the total cash receipts for the month.
2. **Sales Discounts.** Karns includes a Sales Discounts column in its cash receipts journal. By doing so, it does not need to enter sales discount items in the general journal. As a result, the cash receipts journal shows on one line the collection of an account receivable within the discount period.

Credit Columns:

3. **Accounts Receivable.** Karns uses the Accounts Receivable column to record cash collections on account. The amount entered here is the amount to be credited to the individual customer's account.
4. **Sales Revenue.** The Sales Revenue column records all cash sales of merchandise. Cash sales of other assets (plant assets, for example) are not reported in this column.
5. **Other Accounts.** Karns uses the Other Accounts column whenever the credit is other than to Accounts Receivable or Sales Revenue. For example, in the first entry, Karns enters $5,000 as a credit to Owner's Capital. This column is often referred to as the sundry accounts column.

Debit and Credit Column:

6. **Cost of Goods Sold and Inventory.** This column records debits to Cost of Goods Sold and credits to Inventory.

In a multi-column journal, generally only one line is needed for each entry. Debit and credit amounts for each line must be equal. When Karns journalizes the collection from Abbot Sisters on May 10, for example, three amounts are indicated. Note also that the Account Credited column identifies both general ledger and subsidiary ledger account titles. General ledger accounts are illustrated in the May 1 and May 22 entries. A subsidiary account is illustrated in the May 10 entry for the collection from Abbot Sisters.

When Karns has finished journalizing a multi-column journal, it totals the amount columns and compares the totals to prove the equality of debits and credits. Illustration 7-10 shows the proof of the equality of Karns's cash receipts journal.

Illustration 7-10
Proving the equality of the cash receipts journal

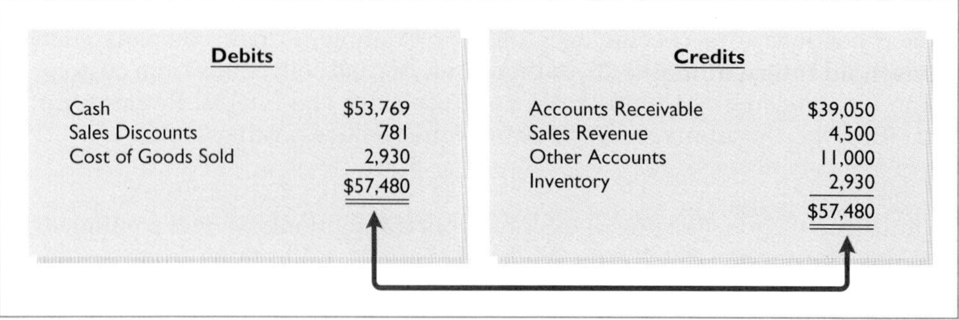

Debits		Credits	
Cash	$53,769	Accounts Receivable	$39,050
Sales Discounts	781	Sales Revenue	4,500
Cost of Goods Sold	2,930	Other Accounts	11,000
	$57,480	Inventory	2,930
			$57,480

Totaling the columns of a journal and proving the equality of the totals is called **footing** and **cross-footing** a journal.

POSTING THE CASH RECEIPTS JOURNAL

Posting a multi-column journal (Illustration 7-9, page 258) involves the following steps.

1. **At the end of the month**, the company posts all column totals, except for the Other Accounts total, to the account title(s) specified in the column heading (such as Cash or Accounts Receivable). The company then enters account numbers below the column totals to show that they have been posted. For example, Karns has posted Cash to account No. 101, Accounts Receivable to account No. 112, Inventory to account No. 120, Sales Revenue to account No. 401, Sales Discounts to account No. 414, and Cost of Goods Sold to account No. 505.
2. The company **separately posts the individual amounts making up the Other Accounts total** to the general ledger accounts specified in the Account Credited column. See, for example, the credit posting to Owner's Capital. The total amount of this column has not been posted. The symbol (X) is inserted below the total to this column to indicate that the amount has not been posted.
3. The individual amounts in a column, posted in total to a control account (Accounts Receivable, in this case), are posted **daily to the subsidiary ledger** account specified in the Account Credited column. See, for example, the credit posting of $10,600 to Abbot Sisters.

The symbol **CR**, used in both the subsidiary and general ledgers, identifies postings from the cash receipts journal.

PROVING THE LEDGERS

After posting of the cash receipts journal is completed, Karns proves the ledgers. As shown in Illustration 7-11, the general ledger totals agree. Also, the sum of the subsidiary ledger balances equals the control account balance.

Illustration 7-11
Proving the ledgers after posting the sales and the cash receipts journals

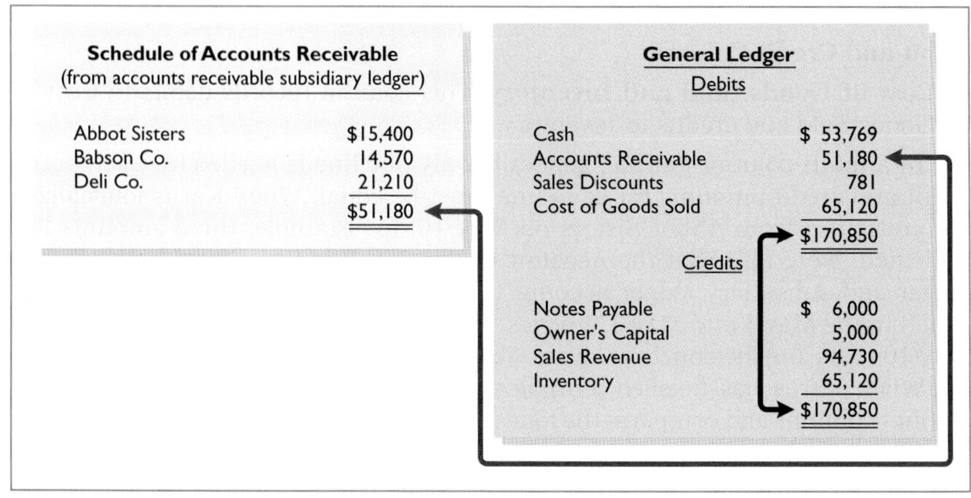

Schedule of Accounts Receivable (from accounts receivable subsidiary ledger)	
Abbot Sisters	$15,400
Babson Co.	14,570
Deli Co.	21,210
	$51,180

General Ledger	
Debits	
Cash	$ 53,769
Accounts Receivable	51,180
Sales Discounts	781
Cost of Goods Sold	65,120
	$170,850
Credits	
Notes Payable	$ 6,000
Owner's Capital	5,000
Sales Revenue	94,730
Inventory	65,120
	$170,850

Purchases Journal

In the **purchases journal**, companies record all purchases of merchandise on account. Each entry in this journal results in a debit to Inventory and a credit to Accounts Payable. For example, consider the following credit purchase transactions for Karns Wholesale Supply in Illustration 7-12.

Illustration 7-12
Credit purchase transactions

Date	Supplier	Amount
5/6	Jasper Manufacturing Inc.	$11,000
5/10	Eaton and Howe Inc.	7,200
5/14	Fabor and Son	6,900
5/19	Jasper Manufacturing Inc.	17,500
5/26	Fabor and Son	8,700
5/29	Eaton and Howe Inc.	12,600

Illustration 7-13 shows the purchases journal for Karns Wholesale Supply. When using a one-column purchases journal (as in Illustration 7-13), a company

Illustration 7-13
Journalizing and posting the purchases journal

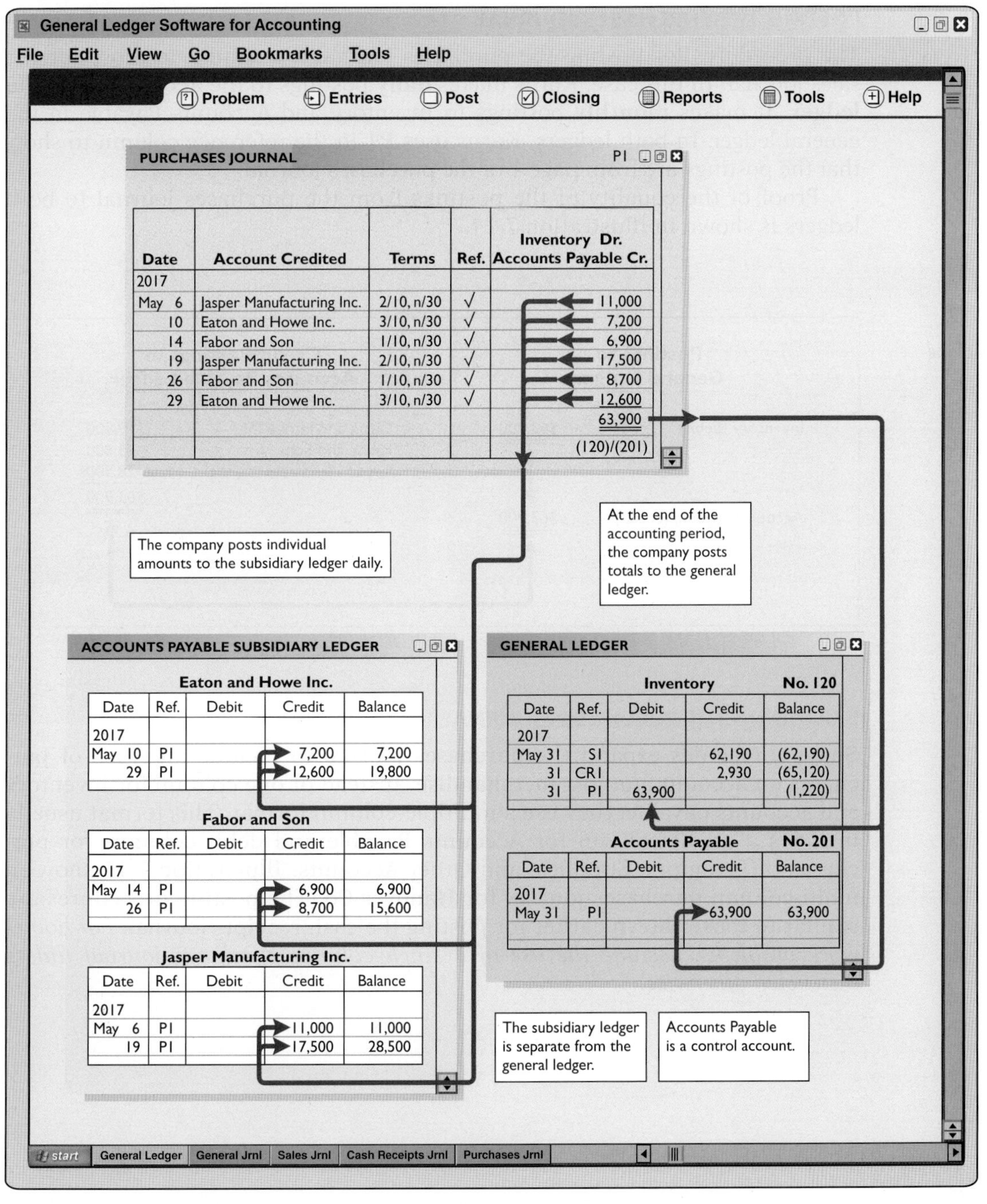

PURCHASES JOURNAL PI

Date	Account Credited	Terms	Ref.	Inventory Dr. Accounts Payable Cr.
2017				
May 6	Jasper Manufacturing Inc.	2/10, n/30	√	11,000
10	Eaton and Howe Inc.	3/10, n/30	√	7,200
14	Fabor and Son	1/10, n/30	√	6,900
19	Jasper Manufacturing Inc.	2/10, n/30	√	17,500
26	Fabor and Son	1/10, n/30	√	8,700
29	Eaton and Howe Inc.	3/10, n/30	√	12,600
				63,900
				(120)/(201)

ACCOUNTS PAYABLE SUBSIDIARY LEDGER

Eaton and Howe Inc.

Date	Ref.	Debit	Credit	Balance
2017				
May 10	PI		7,200	7,200
29	PI		12,600	19,800

Fabor and Son

Date	Ref.	Debit	Credit	Balance
2017				
May 14	PI		6,900	6,900
26	PI		8,700	15,600

Jasper Manufacturing Inc.

Date	Ref.	Debit	Credit	Balance
2017				
May 6	PI		11,000	11,000
19	PI		17,500	28,500

GENERAL LEDGER

Inventory No. 120

Date	Ref.	Debit	Credit	Balance
2017				
May 31	SI		62,190	(62,190)
31	CR1		2,930	(65,120)
31	PI	63,900		(1,220)

Accounts Payable No. 201

Date	Ref.	Debit	Credit	Balance
2017				
May 31	PI		63,900	63,900

cannot journalize other types of purchases on account or cash purchases in it. For example, if the company used the purchases journal in Illustration 7-13, Karns would have to record credit purchases of equipment or supplies in the general journal. Likewise, all cash purchases would be entered in the cash payments journal.

JOURNALIZING CREDIT PURCHASES OF MERCHANDISE

The journalizing procedure is similar to that for a sales journal. Companies make entries in the purchases journal from purchase invoices. In contrast to the sales journal, the purchases journal may not have an invoice number column because invoices received from different suppliers will not be in numerical sequence. To ensure that they record all purchase invoices, some companies consecutively number each invoice upon receipt and then use an internal document number column in the purchases journal. The entries for Karns Wholesale Supply are based on the assumed credit purchases listed in Illustration 7-12.

POSTING THE PURCHASES JOURNAL

The procedures for posting the purchases journal are similar to those for the sales journal. In this case, Karns makes **daily** postings to the **accounts payable ledger**. It makes **monthly** postings to Inventory and Accounts Payable in the general ledger. In both ledgers, Karns uses **P1** in the reference column to show that the postings are from page 1 of the purchases journal.

Proof of the equality of the postings from the purchases journal to both ledgers is shown in Illustration 7-14.

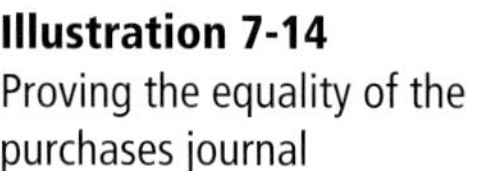
Illustration 7-14
Proving the equality of the purchases journal

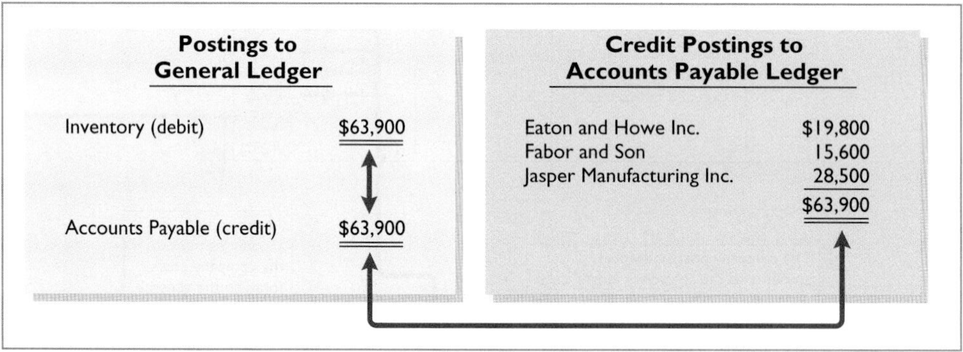

EXPANDING THE PURCHASES JOURNAL

Some companies expand the purchases journal to include all types of purchases on account, not just merchandise. Instead of one column for inventory and accounts payable, they use a multiple-column format. This format usually includes a credit column for Accounts Payable and debit columns for purchases of Inventory, Supplies, and Other Accounts. Illustration 7-15 shows a multi-column purchases journal for Hanover Co. The posting procedures are similar to those shown earlier for posting the cash receipts journal. *For homework problems, assume the use of a single-column purchases journal unless instructed otherwise.*

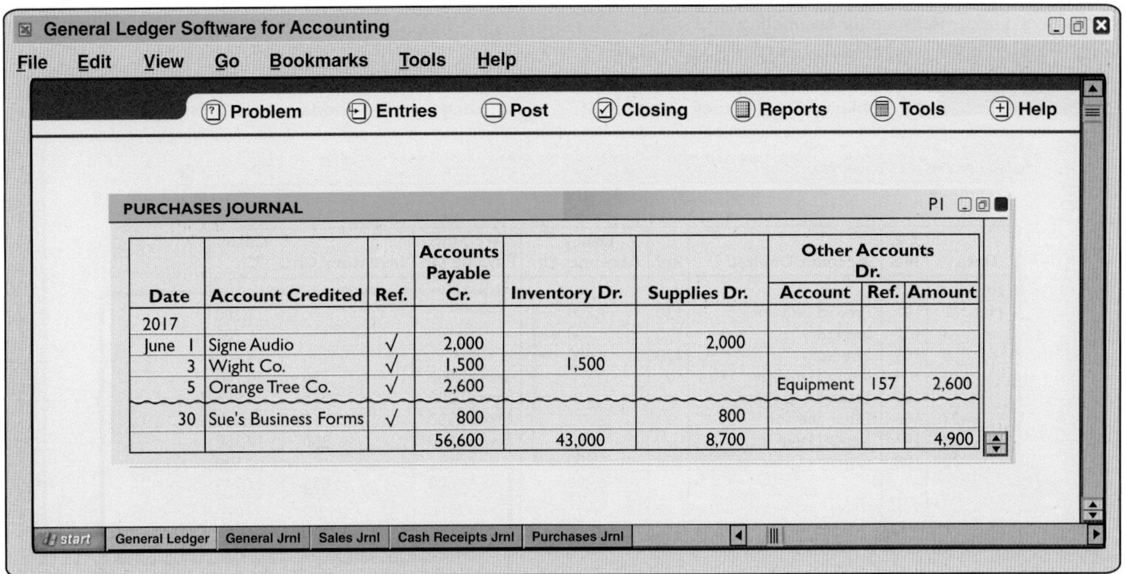

Date	Account Credited	Ref.	Accounts Payable Cr.	Inventory Dr.	Supplies Dr.	Other Accounts Dr.		
						Account	Ref.	Amount
2017								
June 1	Signe Audio	√	2,000		2,000			
3	Wight Co.	√	1,500	1,500				
5	Orange Tree Co.	√	2,600			Equipment	157	2,600
30	Sue's Business Forms	√	800		800			
			56,600	43,000	8,700			4,900

Illustration 7-15
Multi-column purchases journal

Cash Payments Journal

In a **cash payments (cash disbursements) journal**, companies record all disbursements of cash. Entries are made from prenumbered checks. Because companies make cash payments for various purposes, the cash payments journal has multiple columns. Illustration 7-16 (page 264) shows a four-column journal.

JOURNALIZING CASH PAYMENTS TRANSACTIONS

The procedures for journalizing transactions in this journal are similar to those for the cash receipts journal. Karns records each transaction on one line, and for each line there must be equal debit and credit amounts. The entries in the cash payments journal in Illustration 7-16 are based on the following transactions for Karns Wholesale Supply.

May 1 Issued check No. 101 for $1,200 for the annual premium on a fire insurance policy.
3 Issued check No. 102 for $100 in payment of freight when terms were FOB shipping point.
8 Issued check No. 103 for $4,400 for the purchase of merchandise.
10 Sent check No. 104 for $10,780 to Jasper Manufacturing Inc. in payment of May 6 invoice for $11,000 less a 2% discount.
19 Mailed check No. 105 for $6,984 to Eaton and Howe Inc. in payment of May 10 invoice for $7,200 less a 3% discount.
23 Sent check No. 106 for $6,831 to Fabor and Son in payment of May 14 invoice for $6,900 less a 1% discount.
28 Sent check No. 107 for $17,150 to Jasper Manufacturing Inc. in payment of May 19 invoice for $17,500 less a 2% discount.
30 Issued check No. 108 for $500 to D. A. Karns as a cash withdrawal for personal use.

Note that whenever Karns enters an amount in the Other Accounts column, it must identify a specific general ledger account in the Account Debited column. The entries for checks No. 101, 102, 103, and 108 illustrate this situation. Similarly, Karns must identify a subsidiary account in the Account Debited column whenever it enters an amount in the Accounts Payable column. See, for example, the entry for check No. 104.

After Karns journalizes the cash payments journal, it totals the columns. The totals are then balanced to prove the equality of debits and credits.

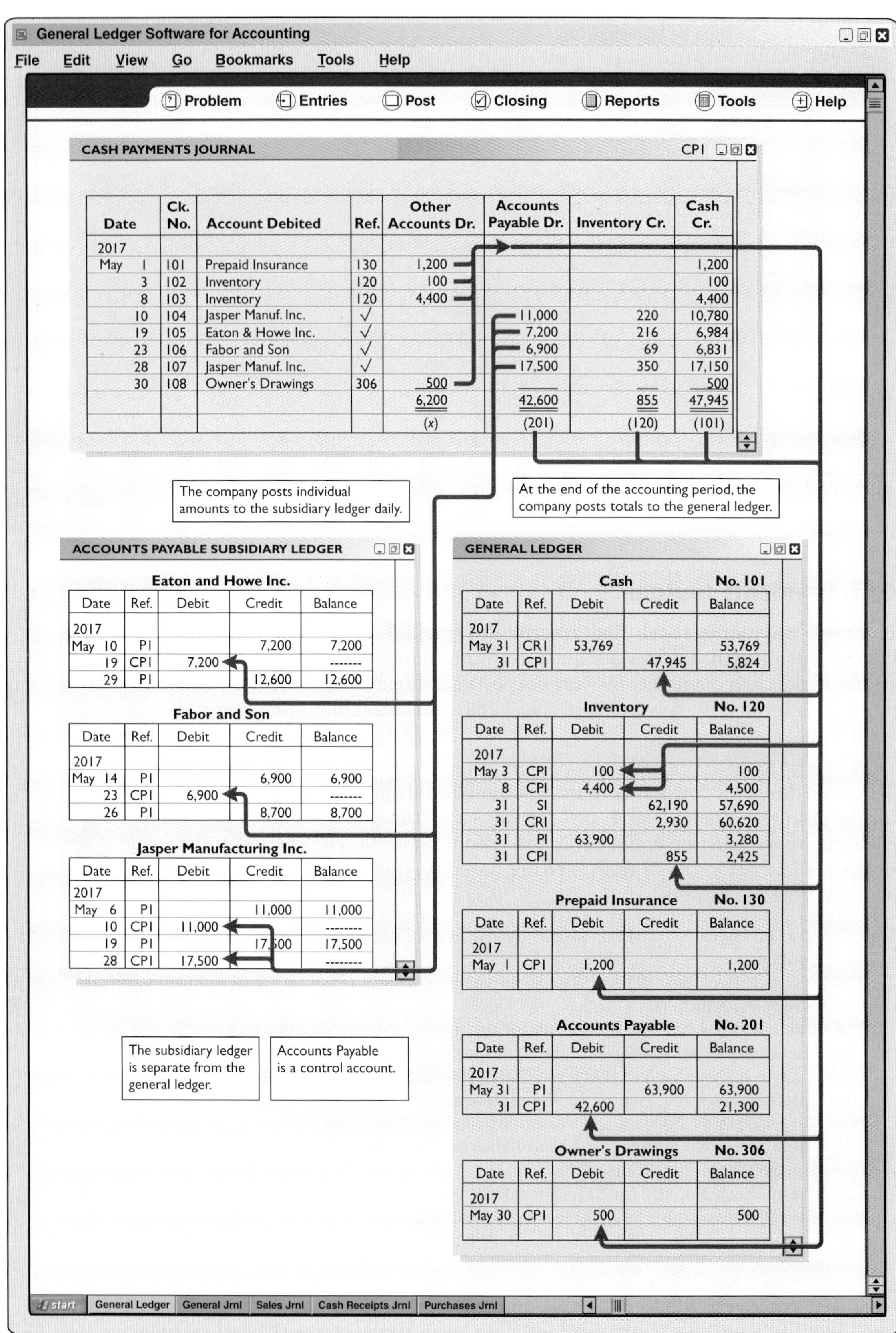

CASH PAYMENTS JOURNAL CP1

Date	Ck. No.	Account Debited	Ref.	Other Accounts Dr.	Accounts Payable Dr.	Inventory Cr.	Cash Cr.
2017							
May 1	101	Prepaid Insurance	130	1,200			1,200
3	102	Inventory	120	100			100
8	103	Inventory	120	4,400			4,400
10	104	Jasper Manuf. Inc.	√		11,000	220	10,780
19	105	Eaton & Howe Inc.	√		7,200	216	6,984
23	106	Fabor and Son	√		6,900	69	6,831
28	107	Jasper Manuf. Inc.	√		17,500	350	17,150
30	108	Owner's Drawings	306	500			500
				6,200	42,600	855	47,945
				(x)	(201)	(120)	(101)

ACCOUNTS PAYABLE SUBSIDIARY LEDGER

Eaton and Howe Inc.

Date	Ref.	Debit	Credit	Balance
2017				
May 10	P1		7,200	7,200
19	CP1	7,200		-------
29	P1		12,600	12,600

Fabor and Son

Date	Ref.	Debit	Credit	Balance
2017				
May 14	P1		6,900	6,900
23	CP1	6,900		-------
26	P1		8,700	8,700

Jasper Manufacturing Inc.

Date	Ref.	Debit	Credit	Balance
2017				
May 6	P1		11,000	11,000
10	CP1	11,000		--------
19	P1		17,500	17,500
28	CP1	17,500		--------

GENERAL LEDGER

Cash No. 101

Date	Ref.	Debit	Credit	Balance
2017				
May 31	CR1	53,769		53,769
31	CP1		47,945	5,824

Inventory No. 120

Date	Ref.	Debit	Credit	Balance
2017				
May 3	CP1	100		100
8	CP1	4,400		4,500
31	S1		62,190	57,690
31	CR1		2,930	60,620
31	P1	63,900		3,280
31	CP1		855	2,425

Prepaid Insurance No. 130

Date	Ref.	Debit	Credit	Balance
2017				
May 1	CP1	1,200		1,200

Accounts Payable No. 201

Date	Ref.	Debit	Credit	Balance
2017				
May 31	P1		63,900	63,900
31	CP1	42,600		21,300

Owner's Drawings No. 306

Date	Ref.	Debit	Credit	Balance
2017				
May 30	CP1	500		500

Illustration 7-16
Journalizing and posting the cash payments journal

POSTING THE CASH PAYMENTS JOURNAL

The procedures for posting the cash payments journal are similar to those for the cash receipts journal. Karns posts the amounts recorded in the Accounts Payable column individually to the subsidiary ledger and in total to the control account. It posts Inventory and Cash only in total at the end of the month. Transactions in the Other Accounts column are posted individually to the appropriate account(s) affected. The company does not post totals for the Other Accounts column.

Illustration 7-16 shows the posting of the cash payments journal. Note that Karns uses the symbol **CP** as the posting reference. After postings are completed, the company proves the equality of the debit and credit balances in the general ledger. In addition, the control account balances should agree with the subsidiary ledger total balance. Illustration 7-17 shows the agreement of these balances.

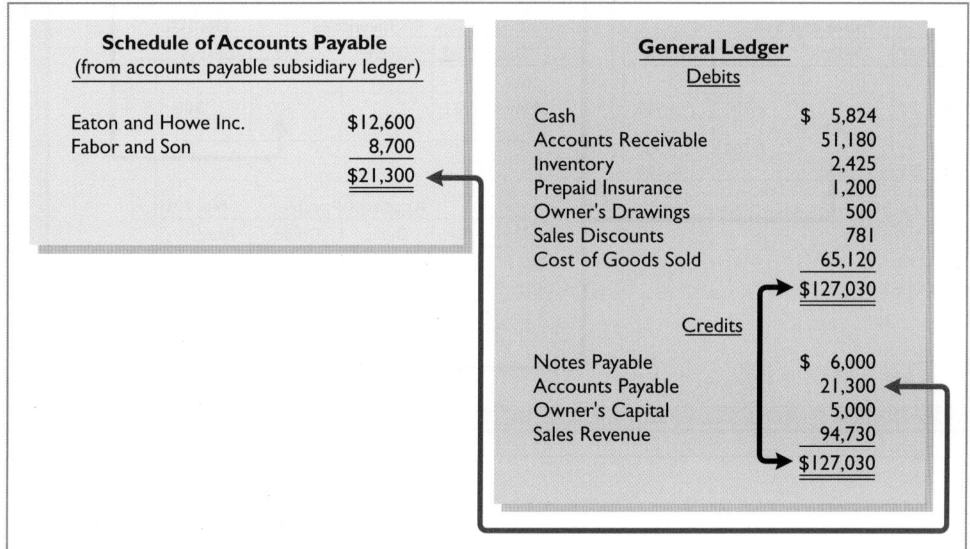

Schedule of Accounts Payable
(from accounts payable subsidiary ledger)

Eaton and Howe Inc.	$12,600
Fabor and Son	8,700
	$21,300

General Ledger

Debits	
Cash	$ 5,824
Accounts Receivable	51,180
Inventory	2,425
Prepaid Insurance	1,200
Owner's Drawings	500
Sales Discounts	781
Cost of Goods Sold	65,120
	$127,030

Credits	
Notes Payable	$ 6,000
Accounts Payable	21,300
Owner's Capital	5,000
Sales Revenue	94,730
	$127,030

Illustration 7-17
Proving the ledgers after postings from the sales, cash receipts, purchases, and cash payments journals

Effects of Special Journals on the General Journal

Special journals for sales, purchases, and cash substantially reduce the number of entries that companies make in the general journal. **Only transactions that cannot be entered in a special journal are recorded in the general journal.** For example, a company may use the general journal to record such transactions as granting of credit to a customer for a sales return or allowance, granting of credit from a supplier for purchases returned, acceptance of a note receivable from a customer, and purchase of equipment by issuing a note payable. Also, **correcting, adjusting, and closing entries are made in the general journal**.

The general journal has columns for date, account title and explanation, reference, and debit and credit amounts. When control and subsidiary accounts are not involved, the procedures for journalizing and posting of transactions are the same as those described in earlier chapters. When control and subsidiary accounts are involved, companies make two changes from the earlier procedures:

1. In **journalizing**, they identify both the control and the subsidiary accounts.
2. In **posting**, there must be a **dual posting**: once to the control account and once to the subsidiary account.

To illustrate, assume that on May 31, Karns Wholesale Supply returns $500 of merchandise for credit to Fabor and Son. Illustration 7-18 shows the entry in the general journal and the posting of the entry.

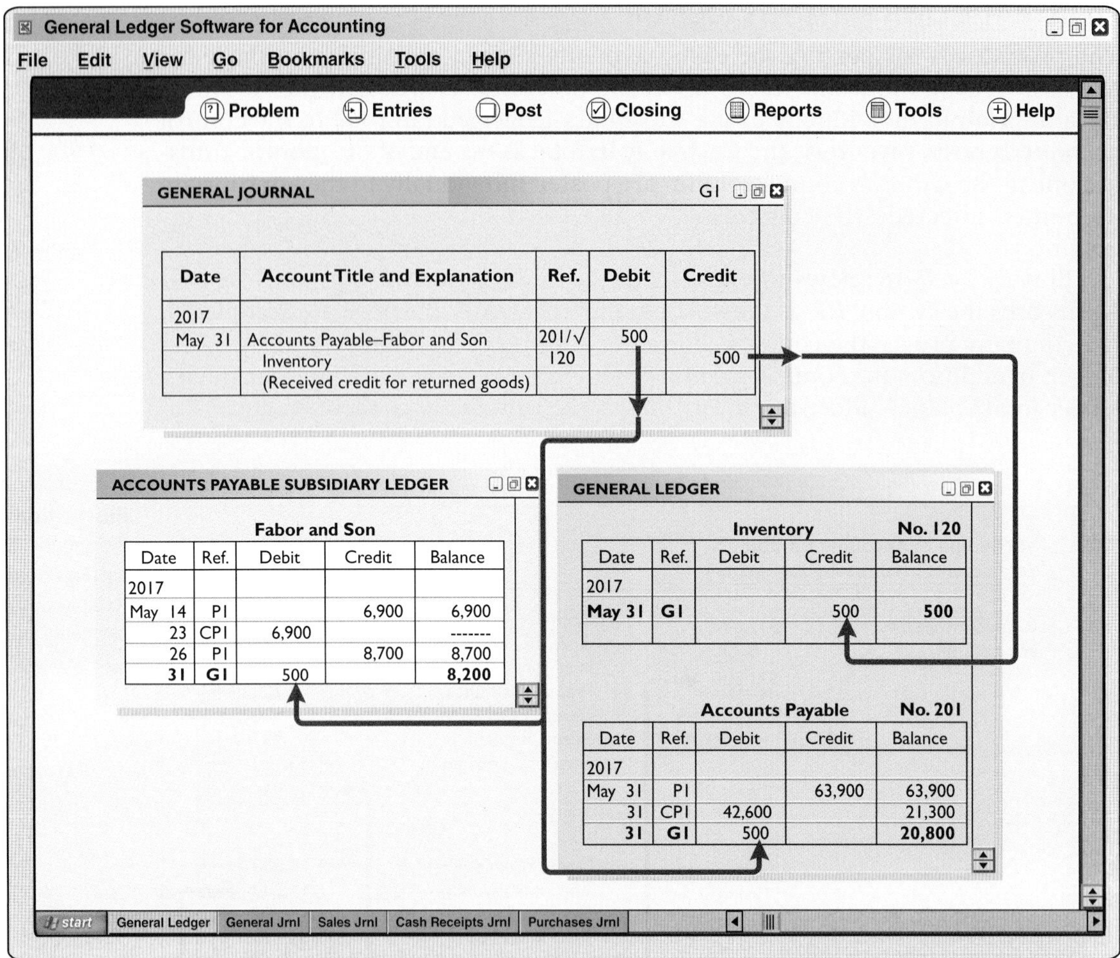

GENERAL JOURNAL — G1

Date	Account Title and Explanation	Ref.	Debit	Credit
2017				
May 31	Accounts Payable–Fabor and Son	201/√	500	
	Inventory	120		500
	(Received credit for returned goods)			

ACCOUNTS PAYABLE SUBSIDIARY LEDGER

Fabor and Son

Date	Ref.	Debit	Credit	Balance
2017				
May 14	P1		6,900	6,900
23	CP1	6,900		-------
26	P1		8,700	8,700
31	**G1**	500		**8,200**

GENERAL LEDGER

Inventory — No. 120

Date	Ref.	Debit	Credit	Balance
2017				
May 31	**G1**		500	**500**

Accounts Payable — No. 201

Date	Ref.	Debit	Credit	Balance
2017				
May 31	P1		63,900	63,900
31	CP1	42,600		21,300
31	**G1**	500		**20,800**

Illustration 7-18
Journalizing and posting the general journal

Note that the general journal indicates two accounts (Accounts Payable, and Fabor and Son) for the debit, and two postings ("201/✓") in the reference column. One debit is posted to the control account and another debit is posted to the creditor's account in the subsidiary ledger. If Karns receives cash instead of credit on this return, then it would record the transaction in the cash receipts journal.

Cyber Security: A Final Comment

Have you ever been hacked? With the increasing use of cell phones, tablets, and other social media outlets, a real risk exists that your confidential information may be stolen and used illegally. Companies, individuals, and even nations have all been victims of **cybercrime**—a crime that involves the Internet, a computer system, or computer technology.

For companies, cybercrime is clearly a major threat as the hacking of employees' or customers' records related to cybercrime can cost millions of dollars. Unfortunately, the numbers of security breaches are increasing. A security breach at Target, for example, cost the company a minimum of $20 million, the CEO lost his job, and sales plummeted.

Here are three reasons for the rise in the successful hacks of corporate computer records.

1. Companies and their employees continue to increase their activity on the Internet, primarily due to the use of mobile devices and cloud computing.

2. Companies today collect and store unprecedented amounts of personal data on customers and employees.
3. Companies often take measures to protect themselves from cyber security attacks but then fail to check if employees are carrying out the proper security guidelines.

Note that cyber security risks extend far beyond company operations and compliance. Many hackers target highly sensitive intellectual information or other strategic assets. Illustration 7-19 highlights the type of hackers and their motives, targets, and impacts.

Illustration 7-19
Profiles of hackers

Malicious Actors	Motives	Targets	Impacts
Nation-state	• Economic, political, and/or military advantage	• Trade secrets • Sensitive business information • Emerging technologies • Critical infrastructure	• Loss of competitive advantage • Disruption to critical infrastructure
Organized crime	• Immediate financial gain • Collect information for future financial gains	• Financial/payment systems • Personally identifiable information • Payment card information • Protected health information	• Costly regulatory inquiries and penalties • Consumer and shareholder lawsuits • Loss of consumer confidence
Hacktivists	• Influence political and/or social change • Pressure businesses to change their practices	• Corporate secrets • Sensitive business information • Information related to key executives, employees, customers, and business partners	• Disruption of business activities • Harm to brand and reputation • Loss of consumer confidence
Insiders	• Personal advantage, monetary gain • Professional revenge • Patriotism	• Sales, deals, market strategies • Corporate secrets, intellectual property • Business operations • Personnel information	• Trade secret disclosure • Operational disruption • Harm to brand and reputation • National security impact

Source: PriceWaterhouseCoopers, "Answering Your Cybersecurity Questions" (January 2014).

Companies now recognize that cyber security systems that protect confidential data must be implemented. It follows that companies (and nations and individuals) must continually verify that their cyber security defenses are sound and uncompromised.

REVIEW AND PRACTICE

LEARNING OBJECTIVES REVIEW

1 **Explain the basic concepts of an accounting information system.** The basic principles in developing an accounting information system are cost-effectiveness, useful output, and flexibility. Most companies use a computerized accounting system. Smaller companies use entry-level software such as QuickBooks® or Sage 50. Larger companies use custom-made software packages, which often integrate all aspects of the organization.

2 **Describe the nature and purpose of a subsidiary ledger.** A subsidiary ledger is a group of accounts with a common characteristic. It facilitates the recording process by freeing the general ledger from details of individual balances.

3 **Record transactions in special journals.** Companies use special journals to group similar types of transactions. In a special journal, generally only one line is used to record a complete transaction.

GLOSSARY REVIEW

Accounting information system A system that collects and processes transaction data and communicates financial information to decision-makers.

Accounts payable (creditors') subsidiary ledger A subsidiary ledger that collects transaction data of individual creditors.

Accounts receivable (customers') subsidiary ledger A subsidiary ledger that collects transaction data of individual customers.

Cash payments (cash disbursements) journal A special journal that records all disbursements of cash.

Cash receipts journal A special journal that records all cash received.

Control account An account in the general ledger that summarizes subsidiary ledger data.

Cybercrime A crime that involves the Internet, a computer system, or computer technology.

Manual accounting system A system in which someone performs each of the steps in the accounting cycle by hand.

Purchases journal A special journal that records all purchases of merchandise on account.

Sales journal A special journal that records all sales of merchandise on account.

Special journals Journals that record similar types of transactions, such as all credit sales.

Subsidiary ledger A group of accounts with a common characteristic.

PRACTICE EXERCISES

Post various journals to control and subsidiary accounts.

(LO 2, 3)

1. On June 1, the balance of the Accounts Receivable control account in the general ledger of Rath Company was $13,620. The customers' subsidiary ledger contained account balances as follows: Wilson $2,000, Sanchez $3,140, Roberts $2,560, and Marks $5,920. At the end of June, the various journals contained the following information.

Sales journal: Sales to Roberts $900, to Wilson $1,400, to Hardy $1,500, and to Marks $1,200.
Cash receipts journal: Cash received from Roberts $1,610, from Marks $2,600, from Hardy $580, from Sanchez $2,100, and from Wilson $1,540.
General journal: An allowance is granted to Marks $325.

Instructions

(a) Set up control and subsidiary accounts and enter the beginning balances. Do not construct the journals.
(b) Post the various journals. Post the items as individual items or as totals, whichever would be the appropriate procedure. (No sales discounts given.)
(c) Prepare a schedule of accounts receivable and prove the agreement of the control account with the subsidiary ledger at June 30, 2017.

Solution

1. (a) and (b)

GENERAL LEDGER

Accounts Receivable

Date	Explanation	Ref.	Debit	Credit	Balance
June 1	Balance	✓			13,620
		S	5,000		18,620
		CR		8,430	10,190
		G		325	9,865

ACCOUNTS RECEIVABLE SUBSIDIARY LEDGER

Hardy

Date	Explanation	Ref.	Debit	Credit	Balance
June 1					0
		S	1,500		1,500
		CR		580	920

Marks

Date	Explanation	Ref.	Debit	Credit	Balance
June 1	Balance	✓			5,920
		S	1,200		7,120
		CR		2,600	4,520
		G		325	4,195

Roberts

Date	Explanation	Ref.	Debit	Credit	Balance
June 1	Balance	✓			2,560
		S	900		3,460
		CR		1,610	1,850

Sanchez

Date	Explanation	Ref.	Debit	Credit	Balance
June 1	Balance	✓			3,140
		CR		2,100	1,040

Wilson

Date	Explanation	Ref.	Debit	Credit	Balance
June 1	Balance	✓			2,000
		S	1,400		3,400
		CR		1,540	1,860

(c)

RATH COMPANY
Schedule of Accounts Receivable
As of June 30, 2017

Hardy	$ 920
Marks	4,195
Roberts	1,850
Sanchez	1,040
Wilson	1,860
Total	$9,865
Accounts Receivable	$9,865

2. Below are some typical transactions incurred by Brimmer Company.

Indicate use of special journals.

(LO 3)

1. Received credit for merchandise purchased on credit.
2. Payment of employee wages.
3. Sales discount taken on goods sold.
4. Income summary closed to owner's capital.
5. Purchase of office supplies for cash.
6. Depreciation on building.
7. Purchase of merchandise on account.
8. Return of merchandise sold for credit.

9. Payment of creditors on account.
10. Collection on account from customers.
11. Sale of merchandise on account.
12. Sale of land for cash.
13. Sale of merchandise for cash.

Instructions

For each transaction, indicate whether it would normally be recorded in a cash receipts journal, cash payments journal, sales journal, single-column purchases journal, or general journal.

Solution

2. 1. General journal
   2. Cash payments journal
   3. Cash receipts journal
   4. General journal
   5. Cash payments journal
   6. General journal
   7. Purchases journal
   8. General journal
   9. Cash payments journal
   10. Cash receipts journal
   11. Sales journal
   12. Cash receipts journal
   13. Cash receipts journal

PRACTICE PROBLEM

Journalize transactions in cash receipts journal and explain posting procedure.

(LO 3)

Cassandra Wilson Company uses a six-column cash receipts journal with the following columns.

Cash (Dr.)	Other Accounts (Cr.)
Sales Discounts (Dr.)	Cost of Goods Sold (Dr.) and Inventory (Cr.)
Accounts Receivable (Cr.)	
Sales Revenue (Cr.)	

Cash receipts transactions for the month of July 2017 are as follows.

July	3	Cash sales total $5,800 (cost, $3,480).
	5	Received a check for $6,370 from Jeltz Company in payment of an invoice dated June 26 for $6,500, terms 2/10, n/30.
	9	Cassandra Wilson, the proprietor, made an additional investment of $5,000 in cash in the business.
	10	Cash sales total $12,519 (cost, $7,511).
	12	Received a check for $7,275 from R. Eliot & Co. in payment of a $7,500 invoice dated July 3, terms 3/10, n/30.
	15	Received an advance of $700 cash for future services.
	20	Cash sales total $15,472 (cost, $9,283).
	22	Received a check for $5,880 from Beck Company in payment of $6,000 invoice dated July 13, terms 2/10, n/30.
	29	Cash sales total $17,660 (cost, $10,596).
	31	Received cash of $200 for interest earned for July.

Instructions

(a) Journalize the transactions in the cash receipts journal.

(b) Contrast the posting of the Accounts Receivable and Other Accounts columns.

Solution

(a)

CASSANDRA WILSON COMPANY
Cash Receipts Journal
CR1

Date	Account Credited	Ref.	Cash Dr.	Sales Discounts Dr.	Accounts Receivable Cr.	Sales Revenue Cr.	Other Accounts Cr.	Cost of Goods Sold Dr. Inventory Cr.
2017								
7/3			5,800			5,800		3,480
5	Jeltz Company		6,370	130	6,500			
9	Owner's Capital		5,000				5,000	
10			12,519			12,519		7,511
12	R. Eliot & Co.		7,275	225	7,500			
15	Unearned Service Revenue		700				700	
20			15,472			15,472		9,283
22	Beck Company		5,880	120	6,000			
29			17,660			17,660		10,596
31	Interest Revenue		200				200	
			76,876	475	20,000	51,451	5,900	30,870

(b) The Accounts Receivable column total is posted as a credit to Accounts Receivable. The individual amounts are credited to the customers' accounts identified in the Account Credited column, which are maintained in the accounts receivable subsidiary ledger. The amounts in the Other Accounts column are posted individually. They are credited to the account titles identified in the Account Credited column.

EXERCISES

E7-1 Nex Company uses both special journals and a general journal as described in this chapter. On June 30, after all monthly postings had been completed, the Accounts Receivable control account in the general ledger had a debit balance of $340,000; the Accounts Payable control account had a credit balance of $77,000.

Determine control account balances, and explain posting of special journals.

(LO 2, 3)

The July transactions recorded in the special journals are summarized below. No entries affecting accounts receivable and accounts payable were recorded in the general journal for July.

Sales journal	Total sales $161,400
Purchases journal	Total purchases $66,400
Cash receipts journal	Accounts receivable column total $131,000
Cash payments journal	Accounts payable column total $47,500

Instructions

(a) What is the balance of the Accounts Receivable control account after the monthly postings on July 31?

(b) What is the balance of the Accounts Payable control account after the monthly postings on July 31?

(c) To what account(s) is the column total of $161,400 in the sales journal posted?

(d) To what account(s) is the accounts receivable column total of $131,000 in the cash receipts journal posted?

E7-2 Presented below is the subsidiary accounts receivable account of Jill Longley.

Explain postings to subsidiary ledger.

(LO 2)

Date	Ref.	Debit	Credit	Balance
2017				
Sept. 2	S31	61,000		61,000
9	G4		14,000	47,000
27	CR8		47,000	—

Instructions

Write a memo to Sara Fogelman, chief financial officer, that explains each transaction.

Post various journals to control and subsidiary accounts.

(LO 2, 3)

E7-3 On September 1, the balance of the Accounts Receivable control account in the general ledger of Montgomery Company was $10,960. The customers' subsidiary ledger contained account balances as follows: Hurley $1,440, Andino $2,640, Fowler $2,060, and Sogard $4,820. At the end of September, the various journals contained the following information.

Sales journal: Sales to Sogard $800, to Hurley $1,260, to Giambi $1,330, and to Fowler $1,600.
Cash receipts journal: Cash received from Fowler $1,310, from Sogard $3,300, from Giambi $380, from Andino $1,800, and from Hurley $1,240.
General journal: An allowance is granted to Sogard $220.

Instructions

(a) Set up control and subsidiary accounts and enter the beginning balances. Do not construct the journals.
(b) Post the various journals. Post the items as individual items or as totals, whichever would be the appropriate procedure. (No sales discounts given.)
(c) Prepare a schedule of accounts receivable and prove the agreement of the controlling account with the subsidiary ledger at September 30, 2017.

Determine control and subsidiary ledger balances for accounts receivable.

(LO 2)

E7-4 Kieschnick Company has a balance in its Accounts Receivable control account of $10,000 on January 1, 2017. The subsidiary ledger contains three accounts: Bixler Company, balance $4,000; Cuddyer Company, balance $2,500; and Freeze Company. During January, the following receivable-related transactions occurred.

	Credit Sales	Collections	Returns
Bixler Company	$9,000	$8,000	$ -0-
Cuddyer Company	7,000	2,500	3,000
Freeze Company	8,500	9,000	-0-

Instructions

(a) What is the January 1 balance in the Freeze Company subsidiary account?
(b) What is the January 31 balance in the control account?
(c) Compute the balances in the subsidiary accounts at the end of the month.
(d) Which January transaction would not be recorded in a special journal?

Determine control and subsidiary ledger balances for accounts payable.

(LO 2)

E7-5 Pennington Company has a balance in its Accounts Payable control account of $9,250 on January 1, 2017. The subsidiary ledger contains three accounts: Hale Company, balance $3,000; Janish Company, balance $1,875; and Valdez Company. During January, the following payable-related transactions occurred.

	Purchases	Payments	Returns
Hale Company	$6,750	$6,000	$ -0-
Janish Company	5,250	1,875	2,250
Valdez Company	6,375	6,750	-0-

Instructions

(a) What is the January 1 balance in the Valdez Company subsidiary account?
(b) What is the January 31 balance in the control account?
(c) Compute the balances in the subsidiary accounts at the end of the month.
(d) Which January transaction would not be recorded in a special journal?

Record transactions in sales and purchases journal.

(LO 3)

E7-6 Gomes Company uses special journals and a general journal. The following transactions occurred during September 2017.

Sept. 2	Sold merchandise on account to H. Drew, invoice no. 101, $620, terms n/30. The cost of the merchandise sold was $420.
10	Purchased merchandise on account from A. Pagan $650, terms 2/10, n/30.
12	Purchased office equipment on account from R. Cairo $6,500.
21	Sold merchandise on account to G. Holliday, invoice no. 102 for $800, terms 2/10, n/30. The cost of the merchandise sold was $480.
25	Purchased merchandise on account from D. Downs $860, terms n/30.
27	Sold merchandise to S. Miller for $700 cash. The cost of the merchandise sold was $400.

Instructions

(a) Prepare a sales journal (see Illustration 7-7) and a single-column purchases journal (see Illustration 7-13). (Use page 1 for each journal.)

(b) Record the transaction(s) for September that should be journalized in the sales journal and the purchases journal.

E7-7 R. Santiago Co. uses special journals and a general journal. The following transactions occurred during May 2017.

Record transactions in cash receipts and cash payments journal.

(LO 3)

May	1	R. Santiago invested $40,000 cash in the business.
	2	Sold merchandise to Lawrie Co. for $6,300 cash. The cost of the merchandise sold was $4,200.
	3	Purchased merchandise for $7,700 from J. Moskos using check no. 101.
	14	Paid salary to H. Rivera $700 by issuing check no. 102.
	16	Sold merchandise on account to K. Stanton for $900, terms n/30. The cost of the merchandise sold was $630.
	22	A check of $9,000 is received from M. Mangini in full for invoice 101; no discount given.

Instructions

(a) Prepare a multiple-column cash receipts journal (see Illustration 7-9) and a multiple-column cash payments journal (see Illustration 7-16). (Use page 1 for each journal.)

(b) Record the transaction(s) for May that should be journalized in the cash receipts journal and cash payments journal.

E7-8 Francisco Company uses the columnar cash journals illustrated in the textbook. In April, the following selected cash transactions occurred.

Explain journalizing in cash journals.

(LO 3)

1. Made a refund to a customer as an allowance for damaged goods.
2. Received collection from customer within the 3% discount period.
3. Purchased merchandise for cash.
4. Paid a creditor within the 3% discount period.
5. Received collection from customer after the 3% discount period had expired.
6. Paid freight on merchandise purchased.
7. Paid cash for office equipment.
8. Received cash refund from supplier for merchandise returned.
9. Withdrew cash for personal use of owner.
10. Made cash sales.

Instructions

Indicate (a) the journal, and (b) the columns in the journal that should be used in recording each transaction.

E7-9 Hasselback Company has the following selected transactions during March.

Journalize transactions in general journal and explain postings.

(LO 3)

Mar.	2	Purchased equipment costing $7,400 from Bole Company on account.
	5	Received credit of $410 from Carwell Company for merchandise damaged in shipment to Hasselback.
	7	Issued credit of $400 to Dempsey Company for merchandise the customer returned. The returned merchandise had a cost of $260.

Hasselback Company uses a one-column purchases journal, a sales journal, the columnar cash journals used in the text, and a general journal.

Instructions

(a) Journalize the transactions in the general journal.

(b) In a brief memo to the president of Hasselback Company, explain the postings to the control and subsidiary accounts from each type of journal.

E7-10 Below are some typical transactions incurred by Ricketts Company.

Indicate journalizing in special journals.

(LO 3)

1. Payment of creditors on account.
2. Return of merchandise sold for credit.
3. Collection on account from customers.
4. Sale of land for cash.

5. Sale of merchandise on account.
6. Sale of merchandise for cash.
7. Received credit for merchandise purchased on credit.
8. Sales discount taken on goods sold.
9. Payment of employee wages.
10. Income summary closed to owner's capital.
11. Depreciation on building.
12. Purchase of office supplies for cash.
13. Purchase of merchandise on account.

Instructions

For each transaction, indicate whether it would normally be recorded in a cash receipts journal, cash payments journal, sales journal, single-column purchases journal, or general journal.

Explain posting to control account and subsidiary ledger.
(LO 2, 3)

E7-11 The general ledger of Hensley Company contained the following Accounts Payable control account (in T-account form). Also shown is the related subsidiary ledger.

GENERAL LEDGER

Accounts Payable

Feb. 15	General journal	1,400	Feb. 1	Balance	26,025
28	?	?	5	General journal	265
			11	General journal	550
			28	Purchases	13,400
			Feb. 28	Balance	10,500

ACCOUNTS PAYABLE LEDGER

Benton

	Feb. 28 Bal. 4,600

Parks

	Feb. 28 Bal. ?

Dooley

	Feb. 28 Bal. 2,300

Instructions

(a) Indicate the missing posting reference and amount in the control account, and the missing ending balance in the subsidiary ledger.
(b) Indicate the amounts in the control account that were dual-posted (i.e., posted to the control account and the subsidiary accounts).

Prepare purchases and general journals.
(LO 2, 3)

E7-12 Selected accounts from the ledgers of Youngblood Company at July 31 showed the following.

GENERAL LEDGER

Equipment No. 157

Date	Explanation	Ref.	Debit	Credit	Balance
July 1		G1	3,900		3,900

Accounts Payable No. 201

Date	Explanation	Ref.	Debit	Credit	Balance
July 1		G1		3,900	3,900
15		G1		400	4,300
18		G1	100		4,200
25		G1	200		4,000
31		P1		9,300	13,300

Inventory No. 120

Date	Explanation	Ref.	Debit	Credit	Balance
July 15		G1	400		400
18		G1		100	300
25		G1		200	100
31		P1	9,300		9,400

ACCOUNTS PAYABLE LEDGER

Flaherty Equipment Co.

Date	Explanation	Ref.	Debit	Credit	Balance
July 1		G1		3,900	3,900

Weller Co.

Date	Explanation	Ref.	Debit	Credit	Balance
July 14		P1		1,100	1,100
25		G1	200		900

Marsh Co.

Date	Explanation	Ref.	Debit	Credit	Balance
July 3		P1		2,400	2,400
20		P1		1,700	4,100

Yates Co.

Date	Explanation	Ref.	Debit	Credit	Balance
July 12		P1		500	500
21		P1		600	1,100

Lange Corp

Date	Explanation	Ref.	Debit	Credit	Balance
July 17		P1		1,400	1,400
18		G1	100		1,300
29		P1		1,600	2,900

Bernardo Inc.

Date	Explanation	Ref.	Debit	Credit	Balance
July 15		G1		400	400

Instructions

From the data prepare:

(a) The single-column purchases journal for July.

(b) The general journal entries for July.

Determine correct posting amount to control account.

(LO 2, 3)

E7-13 Tresh Products uses both special journals and a general journal as described in this chapter. Tresh also posts customers' accounts in the accounts receivable subsidiary ledger. The postings for the most recent month are included in the subsidiary T-accounts below.

Estes

	Debit	Credit
Bal.	340	250
	200	

Gehrke

	Debit	Credit
Bal.	150	150
	290	

Truong

	Debit	Credit
Bal.	–0–	145
	145	

Weiser

	Debit	Credit
Bal.	120	120
	190	
	150	

Instructions

Determine the correct amount of the end-of-month posting from the sales journal to the Accounts Receivable control account.

Compute balances in various accounts.

(LO 3)

E7-14 Selected account balances for Hulse Company at January 1, 2017, are presented below.

Accounts Payable	$14,000
Accounts Receivable	22,000
Cash	17,000
Inventory	13,500

Hulse's sales journal for January shows a total of $110,000 in the selling price column, and its one-column purchases journal for January shows a total of $77,000.

The column totals in Hulse's cash receipts journal are Cash Dr. $61,000, Sales Discounts Dr. $1,100, Accounts Receivable Cr. $45,000, Sales Revenue Cr. $6,000, and Other Accounts Cr. $11,100.

The column totals in Hulse's cash payments journal for January are Cash Cr. $55,000, Inventory Cr. $1,000, Accounts Payable Dr. $46,000, and Other Accounts Dr. $10,000. Hulse's total cost of goods sold for January is $63,600.

Accounts Payable, Accounts Receivable, Cash, Inventory, and Sales Revenue are not involved in the Other Accounts column in either the cash receipts or cash payments journal, and are not involved in any general journal entries.

Instructions

Compute the January 31 balance for Hulse in the following accounts.

(a) Accounts Payable.
(b) Accounts Receivable.
(c) Cash.
(d) Inventory.
(e) Sales Revenue.

PROBLEMS

Journalize transactions in cash receipts journal; post to control account and subsidiary ledger.
(LO 2, 3)

P7-1A Kozma Company's chart of accounts includes the following selected accounts.

101	Cash	401	Sales Revenue
112	Accounts Receivable	414	Sales Discounts
120	Inventory	505	Cost of Goods Sold
301	Owner's Capital		

On April 1, the accounts receivable ledger of Kozma Company showed the following balances: Morrow $1,550, Rose $1,200, Jennings Co. $2,900, and Dent $2,200. The April transactions involving the receipt of cash were as follows.

Apr. 1	The owner, T. Kozma, invested additional cash in the business $7,200.
4	Received check for payment of account from Dent less 2% cash discount.
5	Received check for $920 in payment of invoice no. 307 from Jennings Co.
8	Made cash sales of merchandise totaling $7,245. The cost of the merchandise sold was $4,347.
10	Received check for $600 in payment of invoice no. 309 from Morrow.
11	Received cash refund from a supplier for damaged merchandise $740.
23	Received check for $1,000 in payment of invoice no. 310 from Jennings Co.
29	Received check for payment of account from Rose (no cash discount allowed).

Instructions

(a) Balancing totals $25,452

(a) Journalize the transactions above in a six-column cash receipts journal with columns for Cash Dr., Sales Discounts Dr., Accounts Receivable Cr., Sales Revenue Cr., Other Accounts Cr., and Cost of Goods Sold Dr./Inventory Cr. Foot and cross-foot the journal.
(b) Insert the beginning balances in the Accounts Receivable control and subsidiary accounts, and post the April transactions to these accounts.
(c) Prove the agreement of the control account and subsidiary account balances.

(c) Accounts Receivable $1,930

Journalize transactions in cash payments journal; post to control account and subsidiary ledgers.
(LO 2, 3)

P7-2A Reineke Company's chart of accounts includes the following selected accounts.

101	Cash	201	Accounts Payable
120	Inventory	306	Owner's Drawings
130	Prepaid Insurance	505	Cost of Goods Sold
157	Equipment		

On October 1, the accounts payable ledger of Reineke Company showed the following balances: Uggla Company $2,700, Orr Co. $2,500, Rosenthal Co. $1,800, and Clevenger Company $3,700. The October transactions involving the payment of cash were as follows.

Oct. 1	Purchased merchandise, check no. 63, $300.
3	Purchased equipment, check no. 64, $800.
5	Paid Uggla Company balance due of $2,700, less 2% discount, check no. 65, $2,646.
10	Purchased merchandise, check no. 66, $2,550.
15	Paid Rosenthal Co. balance due of $1,800, check no. 67.
16	C. Reineke, the owner, pays his personal insurance premium of $400, check no. 68.
19	Paid Orr Co. in full for invoice no. 610, $2,000 less 2% cash discount, check no. 69, $1,960.
29	Paid Clevenger Company in full for invoice no. 264, $2,500, check no. 70.

Instructions

(a) Balancing totals $13,050

(a) Journalize the transactions above in a four-column cash payments journal with columns for Other Accounts Dr., Accounts Payable Dr., Inventory Cr., and Cash Cr. Foot and cross-foot the journal.

(b) Insert the beginning balances in the Accounts Payable control and subsidiary accounts, and post the October transactions to these accounts.
(c) Prove the agreement of the control account and the subsidiary account balances.

(c) Accounts Payable $1,700

P7-3A The chart of accounts of LR Company includes the following selected accounts.

Journalize transactions in multi-column purchases journal and sales journal; post to the general and subsidiary ledgers.

(LO 2, 3)

112 Accounts Receivable	401 Sales Revenue
120 Inventory	412 Sales Returns and Allowances
126 Supplies	505 Cost of Goods Sold
157 Equipment	610 Advertising Expense
201 Accounts Payable	

In July, the following transactions were completed. All purchases and sales were on account. The cost of all merchandise sold was 70% of the sales price.

July 1 Purchased merchandise from Eby Company $8,000.
2 Received freight bill from Shaw Shipping on Eby purchase $400.
3 Made sales to Fort Company $1,300 and to Hefner Bros. $1,500.
5 Purchased merchandise from Getz Company $3,200.
8 Received credit on merchandise returned to Getz Company $300.
13 Purchased store supplies from Dayne Supply $720.
15 Purchased merchandise from Eby Company $3,600 and from Bosco Company $4,300.
16 Made sales to Aybar Company $3,450 and to Hefner Bros. $1,870.
18 Received bill for advertising from Welton Advertisements $600.
21 Sales were made to Fort Company $310 and to Duncan Company $2,800.
22 Granted allowance to Fort Company for merchandise damaged in shipment $40.
24 Purchased merchandise from Getz Company $3,000.
26 Purchased equipment from Dayne Supply $900.
28 Received freight bill from Shaw Shipping on Getz purchase of July 24, $380.
30 Sales were made to Aybar Company $5,600.

Instructions

(a) Journalize the transactions above in a purchases journal, a sales journal, and a general journal. The purchases journal should have the following column headings: Date, Account Credited (Debited), Ref., Accounts Payable Cr., Inventory Dr., and Other Accounts Dr.
(b) Post to both the general and subsidiary ledger accounts. (Assume that all accounts have zero beginning balances.)
(c) Prove the agreement of the control and subsidiary accounts.

(a) Purchases journal—Accounts Payable $25,100
Sales journal—Sales Revenue $16,830
(c) Accounts Receivable $16,790
Accounts Payable $24,800

P7-4A Selected accounts from the chart of accounts of Mercer Company are shown below.

Journalize transactions in special journals.

(LO 2, 3)

101 Cash	401 Sales Revenue
112 Accounts Receivable	412 Sales Returns and Allowances
120 Inventory	414 Sales Discounts
126 Supplies	505 Cost of Goods Sold
157 Equipment	726 Salaries and Wages Expense
201 Accounts Payable	

The cost of all merchandise sold was 60% of the sales price. During January, Mercer completed the following transactions.

Jan. 3 Purchased merchandise on account from Gallagher Co. $9,000.
4 Purchased supplies for cash $80.
4 Sold merchandise on account to Wheeler $5,250, invoice no. 371, terms 1/10, n/30.
5 Returned $300 worth of damaged goods purchased on account from Gallagher Co. on January 3.
6 Made cash sales for the week totaling $3,150.
8 Purchased merchandise on account from Phegley Co. $4,500.
9 Sold merchandise on account to Linton Corp. $5,400, invoice no. 372, terms 1/10, n/30.
11 Purchased merchandise on account from Cora Co. $3,700.

13 Paid in full Gallagher Co. on account less a 2% discount.
13 Made cash sales for the week totaling $6,260.
15 Received payment from Linton Corp. for invoice no. 372.
15 Paid semi-monthly salaries of $14,300 to employees.
17 Received payment from Wheeler for invoice no. 371.
17 Sold merchandise on account to Delaney Co. $1,200, invoice no. 373, terms 1/10, n/30.
19 Purchased equipment on account from Dozier Corp. $5,500.
20 Cash sales for the week totaled $3,200.
20 Paid in full Phegley Co. on account less a 2% discount.
23 Purchased merchandise on account from Gallagher Co. $7,800.
24 Purchased merchandise on account from Atchison Corp. $5,100.
27 Made cash sales for the week totaling $4,230.
30 Received payment from Delaney Co. for invoice no. 373.
31 Paid semi-monthly salaries of $13,200 to employees.
31 Sold merchandise on account to Wheeler $9,330, invoice no. 374, terms 1/10, n/30.

Mercer Company uses the following journals.

1. Sales journal.
2. Single-column purchases journal.
3. Cash receipts journal with columns for Cash Dr., Sales Discounts Dr., Accounts Receivable Cr., Sales Revenue Cr., Other Accounts Cr., and Cost of Goods Sold Dr./Inventory Cr.
4. Cash payments journal with columns for Other Accounts Dr., Accounts Payable Dr., Inventory Cr., and Cash Cr.
5. General journal.

(a) Sales journal $21,180
Purchases journal $30,100
Cash receipts journal balancing total $38,794
Cash payments journal balancing total $40,780

Instructions

Using the selected accounts provided:

(a) Record the January transactions in the appropriate journal noted.
(b) Foot and cross-foot all special journals.
(c) Show how postings would be made by placing ledger account numbers and checkmarks as needed in the journals. (Actual posting to ledger accounts is not required.)

Journalize in sales and cash receipts journals; post; prepare a trial balance; prove control to subsidiary; prepare adjusting entries; prepare an adjusted trial balance.

(LO 2, 3)

P7-5A Presented below are the purchases and cash payments journals for Fornelli Co. for its first month of operations.

PURCHASES JOURNAL P1

Date	Account Credited	Ref.	Inventory Dr. Accounts Payable Cr.
July 4	N. Alvarado		6,800
5	F. Rees		8,100
11	J. Gallup		5,920
13	C. Werly		15,300
20	M. Mangus		7,900
			44,020

CASH PAYMENTS JOURNAL CP1

Date	Account Debited	Ref.	Other Accounts Dr.	Accounts Payable Dr.	Inventory Cr.	Cash Cr.
July 4	Supplies		600			600
10	F. Rees			8,100	81	8,019
11	Prepaid Rent		6,000			6,000
15	N. Alvarado			6,800		6,800
19	Owner's Drawings		2,500			2,500
21	C. Werly			15,300	153	15,147
			9,100	30,200	234	39,066

In addition, the following transactions have not been journalized for July. The cost of all merchandise sold was 65% of the sales price.

July	1	The founder, N. Fornelli, invests $80,000 in cash.
	6	Sell merchandise on account to Dow Co. $6,200 terms 1/10, n/30.
	7	Make cash sales totaling $8,000.
	8	Sell merchandise on account to S. Goebel $4,600, terms 1/10, n/30.
	10	Sell merchandise on account to W. Leiss $4,900, terms 1/10, n/30.
	13	Receive payment in full from S. Goebel.
	16	Receive payment in full from W. Leiss.
	20	Receive payment in full from Dow Co.
	21	Sell merchandise on account to H. Kenney $5,000, terms 1/10, n/30.
	29	Returned damaged goods to N. Alvarado and received cash refund of $420.

Instructions

(a) Open the following accounts in the general ledger.

101 Cash	306 Owner's Drawings
112 Accounts Receivable	401 Sales Revenue
120 Inventory	414 Sales Discounts
126 Supplies	505 Cost of Goods Sold
131 Prepaid Rent	631 Supplies Expense
201 Accounts Payable	729 Rent Expense
301 Owner's Capital	

(b) Journalize the transactions that have not been journalized in the sales journal and the cash receipts journal (see Illustration 7-9).

(c) Post to the accounts receivable and accounts payable subsidiary ledgers. Follow the sequence of transactions as shown in the problem.

(d) Post the individual entries and totals to the general ledger.

(e) Prepare a trial balance at July 31, 2017.

(f) Determine whether the subsidiary ledgers agree with the control accounts in the general ledger.

(g) The following adjustments at the end of July are necessary.
   (1) A count of supplies indicates that $140 is still on hand.
   (2) Recognize rent expense for July, $500.
   Prepare the necessary entries in the general journal. Post the entries to the general ledger.

(h) Prepare an adjusted trial balance at July 31, 2017.

(b) Sales journal total $20,700
Cash receipts journal balancing totals $104,120
(e) Totals $122,520
(f) Accounts Receivable $5,000
Accounts Payable $13,820

(h) Totals $122,520

P7-6A The post-closing trial balance for Horner Co. is shown below.

Journalize in special journals; post; prepare a trial balance.

(LO 2, 3)

GLS

HORNER CO.
Post-Closing Trial Balance
December 31, 2017

	Debit	Credit
Cash	$ 41,500	
Accounts Receivable	15,000	
Notes Receivable	45,000	
Inventory	23,000	
Equipment	6,450	
Accumulated Depreciation—Equipment		$ 1,500
Accounts Payable		43,000
Owner's Capital		86,450
	$130,950	$130,950

The subsidiary ledgers contain the following information: (1) accounts receivable—B. Hannigan $2,500, I. Kirk $7,500, and T. Hodges $5,000; (2) accounts payable—T. Igawa $12,000, D. Danford $18,000, and K. Thayer $13,000. The cost of all merchandise sold was 60% of the sales price.

The transactions for January 2018 are as follows.

Jan. 3 Sell merchandise to M. Ziesmer $8,000, terms 2/10, n/30.
5 Purchase merchandise from E. Pheatt $2,000, terms 2/10, n/30.
7 Receive a check from T. Hodges $3,500.
11 Pay freight on merchandise purchased $300.
12 Pay rent of $1,000 for January.
13 Receive payment in full from M. Ziesmer.
14 Post all entries to the subsidiary ledgers. Issued credit of $300 to B. Hannigan for returned merchandise.
15 Send K. Thayer a check for $12,870 in full payment of account, discount $130.
17 Purchase merchandise from G. Roland $1,600, terms 2/10, n/30.
18 Pay sales salaries of $2,800 and office salaries $2,000.
20 Give D. Danford a 60-day note for $18,000 in full payment of account payable.
23 Total cash sales amount to $9,100.
24 Post all entries to the subsidiary ledgers. Sell merchandise on account to I. Kirk $7,400, terms 1/10, n/30.
27 Send E. Pheatt a check for $950.
29 Receive payment on a note of $40,000 from B. Stout.
30 Post all entries to the subsidiary ledgers. Return merchandise of $300 to G. Roland for credit.

Instructions

(a) Open general and subsidiary ledger accounts for the following.

101 Cash
112 Accounts Receivable
115 Notes Receivable
120 Inventory
157 Equipment
158 Accumulated Depreciation—Equipment
200 Notes Payable
201 Accounts Payable
301 Owner's Capital
401 Sales Revenue
412 Sales Returns and Allowances
414 Sales Discounts
505 Cost of Goods Sold
726 Salaries and Wages Expense
729 Rent Expense

(b) Sales journal $15,400
Purchases journal $3,600
Cash receipts journal (balancing) $66,060
Cash payments journal (balancing) $20,050
(d) Totals $144,800
(e) Accounts Receivable $18,600
Accounts Payable $14,350

(b) Record the January transactions in a sales journal, a single-column purchases journal, a cash receipts journal (see Illustration 7-9), a cash payments journal (see Illustration 7-16), and a general journal.
(c) Post the appropriate amounts to the general ledger.
(d) Prepare a trial balance at January 31, 2018.
(e) Determine whether the subsidiary ledgers agree with controlling accounts in the general ledger.

COMPREHENSIVE PROBLEMS: CHAPTERS 3 TO 7

CP7-1 (Perpetual Method) Jeter Co. uses a perpetual inventory system and both an accounts receivable and an accounts payable subsidiary ledger. Balances related to both the general ledger and the subsidiary ledgers for Jeter are indicated in the working papers presented below. Also following are a series of transactions for Jeter Co. for the month of January. Credit sales terms are 2/10, n/30. The cost of all merchandise sold was 60% of the sales price.

GENERAL LEDGER

Account Number	Account Title	January 1 Opening Balance
101	Cash	$35,750
112	Accounts Receivable	13,000
115	Notes Receivable	39,000
120	Inventory	18,000
126	Supplies	1,000
130	Prepaid Insurance	2,000
157	Equipment	6,450
158	Accumulated Depreciation—Equip.	1,500
201	Accounts Payable	35,000
301	Owner's Capital	78,700

Schedule of Accounts Receivable (from accounts receivable subsidiary ledger)	
Customer	**January 1 Opening Balance**
R. Beltre	$1,500
B. Santos	7,500
S. Mahay	4,000

Schedule of Accounts Payable (from accounts payable subsidiary ledger)	
Creditor	**January 1 Opening Balance**
S. Meek	$ 9,000
R. Moses	15,000
D. Saito	11,000

Jan. 3 Sell merchandise on account to B. Corpas $3,600, invoice no. 510, and to J. Revere $1,800, invoice no. 511.

5 Purchase merchandise from S. Gamel $5,000 and D. Posey $2,200, terms n/30.

7 Receive checks from S. Mahay $4,000 and B. Santos $2,000 after discount period has lapsed.

8 Pay freight on merchandise purchased $235.

9 Send checks to S. Meek for $9,000 less 2% cash discount, and to D. Saito for $11,000 less 1% cash discount.

9 Issue credit of $300 to J. Revere for merchandise returned.

10 Daily cash sales from January 1 to January 10 total $15,500. Make one journal entry for these sales.

11 Sell merchandise on account to R. Beltre $1,600, invoice no. 512, and to S. Mahay $900, invoice no. 513.

12 Pay rent of $1,000 for January.

13 Receive payment in full from B. Corpas and J. Revere less cash discounts.

15 Withdraw $800 cash by M. Jeter for personal use.

15 Post all entries to the subsidiary ledgers.

16 Purchase merchandise from D. Saito $15,000, terms 1/10, n/30; S. Meek $14,200, terms 2/10, n/30; and S. Gamel $1,500, terms n/30.

17 Pay $400 cash for office supplies.

18 Return $200 of merchandise to S. Meek and receive credit.

20 Daily cash sales from January 11 to January 20 total $20,100. Make one journal entry for these sales.

21 Issue $15,000 note, maturing in 90 days, to R. Moses in payment of balance due.

21 Receive payment in full from S. Mahay less cash discount.

22 Sell merchandise on account to B. Corpas $2,700, invoice no. 514, and to R. Beltre $2,300, invoice no. 515.

22 Post all entries to the subsidiary ledgers.

23 Send checks to D. Saito and S. Meek for full payment less cash discounts.

25 Sell merchandise on account to B. Santos $3,500, invoice no. 516, and to J. Revere $6,100, invoice no. 517.

27 Purchase merchandise from D. Saito $14,500, terms 1/10, n/30; D. Posey $3,200, terms n/30; and S. Gamel $5,400, terms n/30.

27 Post all entries to the subsidiary ledgers.

28 Pay $200 cash for office supplies.

31 Daily cash sales from January 21 to January 31 total $21,300. Make one journal entry for these sales.

31 Pay sales salaries $4,300 and office salaries $3,800.

Instructions

(a) Record the January transactions in a sales journal, a single-column purchases journal, a cash receipts journal as shown in Illustration 7-9, a cash payments journal as shown in Illustration 7-16, and a two-column general journal.

(b) Post the journals to the general ledger.

(c) Prepare a trial balance at January 31, 2017, in the trial balance columns of the worksheet. Complete the worksheet using the following additional information.

(1) Office supplies at January 31 total $900.

(2) Insurance coverage expires on October 31, 2017.

(3) Annual depreciation on the equipment is $1,500.

(4) Interest of $50 has accrued on the note payable.

(d) Prepare a multiple-step income statement and an owner's equity statement for January and a classified balance sheet at the end of January.

(e) Prepare and post adjusting and closing entries.

(f) Prepare a post-closing trial balance, and determine whether the subsidiary ledgers agree with the control accounts in the general ledger.

CP7-2 (Periodic Inventory) McBride Company has the following opening account balances in its general and subsidiary ledgers on January 1 and uses the periodic inventory system. All accounts have normal debit and credit balances.

GENERAL LEDGER

Account Number	Account Title	January 1 Opening Balance
101	Cash	$33,750
112	Accounts Receivable	13,000
115	Notes Receivable	39,000
120	Inventory	20,000
126	Supplies	1,000
130	Prepaid Insurance	2,000
157	Equipment	6,450
158	Accumulated Depreciation—Equip.	1,500
201	Accounts Payable	35,000
301	Owner's Capital	78,700

Schedule of Accounts Receivable
(from accounts receivable subsidiary ledger)

Customer	January 1 Opening Balance
R. Kotsay	$1,500
B. Boxberger	7,500
S. Andrus	4,000

Schedule of Accounts Payable
(from accounts payable subsidiary ledger)

Creditor	January 1 Opening Balance
S. Otero	$ 9,000
R. Rasmus	15,000
D. Baroni	11,000

In addition, the following transactions have not been journalized for January 2017.

Jan. 3 Sell merchandise on account to B. Berg $3,600, invoice no. 510, and J. Lutz $1,800, invoice no. 511.

5 Purchase merchandise on account from S. Colt $5,000 and D. Kahn $2,700.

7 Receive checks for $4,000 from S. Andrus and $2,000 from B. Boxberger.

8 Pay freight on merchandise purchased $180.

9 Send checks to S. Otero for $9,000 and D. Baroni for $11,000.

9 Issue credit of $300 to J. Lutz for merchandise returned.

10 Cash sales from January 1 to January 10 total $15,500. Make one journal entry for these sales.

11 Sell merchandise on account to R. Kotsay for $2,900, invoice no. 512, and to S. Andrus $900, invoice no. 513.
Post all entries to the subsidiary ledgers.

12 Pay rent of $1,000 for January.

13 Receive payment in full from B. Berg and J. Lutz.

15 Withdraw $800 cash by I. McBride for personal use.

16 Purchase merchandise on account from D. Baroni for $12,000, from S. Otero for $13,900, and from S. Colt for $1,500.

17 Pay $400 cash for supplies.

18 Return $200 of merchandise to S. Otero and receive credit.

20 Cash sales from January 11 to January 20 total $17,500. Make one journal entry for these sales.

21 Issue $15,000 note to R. Rasmus in payment of balance due.

21 Receive payment in full from S. Andrus.
Post all entries to the subsidiary ledgers.

22 Sell merchandise on account to B. Berg for $3,700, invoice no. 514, and to R. Kotsay for $800, invoice no. 515.

23 Send checks to D. Baroni and S. Otero in full payment.

25 Sell merchandise on account to B. Boxberger for $3,500, invoice no. 516, and to J. Lutz for $6,100, invoice no. 517.

27 Purchase merchandise on account from D. Baroni for $12,500, from D. Kahn for $1,200, and from S. Colt for $2,800.
28 Pay $200 cash for office supplies.
31 Cash sales from January 21 to January 31 total $22,920. Make one journal entry for these sales.
31 Pay sales salaries of $4,300 and office salaries of $3,600.

Instructions

(a) Record the January transactions in the appropriate journal—sales, purchases, cash receipts, cash payments, and general.
(b) Post the journals to the general and subsidiary ledgers. Add and number new accounts in an orderly fashion as needed.
(c) Prepare a trial balance at January 31, 2017, using a worksheet. Complete the worksheet using the following additional information.
   (1) Supplies at January 31 total $700.
   (2) Insurance coverage expires on October 31, 2017.
   (3) Annual depreciation on the equipment is $1,500.
   (4) Interest of $30 has accrued on the note payable.
   (5) Inventory at January 31 is $15,000.
(d) Prepare a multiple-step income statement and an owner's equity statement for January and a classified balance sheet at the end of January.
(e) Prepare and post the adjusting and closing entries.
(f) Prepare a post-closing trial balance, and determine whether the subsidiary ledgers agree with the control accounts in the general ledger.

BROADENING YOUR PERSPECTIVE

FINANCIAL REPORTING AND ANALYSIS

Real-World Focus

BYP7-1 **Intuit** provides some of the leading accounting software packages. Information related to its products is found at its website.

Address: **http://quickbooks.intuit.com** or go to **www.wiley.com/college/weygandt**

Instructions

Look under product and services for the product QuickBooks for Accountants. Be ready to discuss its new features with the class.

CRITICAL THINKING

Decision-Making Across the Organization

BYP7-2 Ermler & Trump is a wholesaler of small appliances and parts. Ermler & Trump is operated by two owners, Jack Ermler and Andrea Trump. In addition, the company has one employee, a repair specialist, who is on a fixed salary. Revenues are earned through the sale of appliances to retailers (approximately 75% of total revenues), appliance parts to do-it-yourselfers (10%), and the repair of appliances brought to the store (15%). Appliance sales are made on both a credit and cash basis. Customers are billed on prenumbered sales invoices. Credit terms are always net/30 days. All parts sales and repair work are cash only.

Merchandise is purchased on account from the manufacturers of both the appliances and the parts. Practically all suppliers offer cash discounts for prompt payments, and it is company policy to take all discounts. Most cash payments are made by check. Checks are most frequently issued to suppliers, to trucking companies for freight on merchandise purchases, and to newspapers, radio, and TV stations for advertising. All advertising bills are paid as received. Jack and Andrea each make a monthly drawing in cash for personal living expenses. The salaried repairman is paid twice monthly. Ermler & Trump currently has a manual accounting system.

Instructions
With the class divided into groups, answer the following.

(a) Identify the special journals that Ermler & Trump should have in its manual accounting system. List the column headings appropriate for each of the special journals.
(b) What control and subsidiary accounts should be included in Ermler & Trump's manual accounting system? Why?

Communication Activity

BYP7-3 Jill Locey, a classmate, has a part-time bookkeeping job. She is concerned about the inefficiencies in journalizing and posting transactions. Ben Newell is the owner of the company where Jill works. In response to numerous complaints from Jill and others, Ben hired two additional bookkeepers a month ago. However, the inefficiencies have continued at an even higher rate. The accounting information system for the company has only a general journal and a general ledger. Ben refuses to install a computerized accounting system.

Instructions
Now that Jill is an expert in manual accounting information systems, she decides to send a letter to Ben Newell explaining (1) why the additional personnel did not help and (2) what changes should be made to improve the efficiency of the accounting department. Write the letter that you think Jill should send.

Ethics Case

BYP7-4 Wiemers Products Company operates three divisions, each with its own manufacturing plant and marketing/sales force. The corporate headquarters and central accounting office are in Wiemers, and the plants are in Freeport, Rockport, and Bayport, all within 50 miles of Wiemers. Corporate management treats each division as an independent profit center and encourages competition among them. They each have similar but different product lines. As a competitive incentive, bonuses are awarded each year to the employees of the fastest-growing and most-profitable division.

Indy Grover is the manager of Wiemers's centralized computerized accounting operation that enters the sales transactions and maintains the accounts receivable for all three divisions. Indy came up in the accounting ranks from the Bayport division where his wife, several relatives, and many friends still work.

As sales documents are entered into the computer, the originating division is identified by code. Most sales documents (95%) are coded, but some (5%) are not coded or are coded incorrectly. As the manager, Indy has instructed the data-entry personnel to assign the Bayport code to all uncoded and incorrectly coded sales documents. This is done, he says, "in order to expedite processing and to keep the computer files current since they are updated daily." All receivables and cash collections for all three divisions are handled by Wiemers as one subsidiary accounts receivable ledger.

Instructions
(a) Who are the stakeholders in this situation?
(b) What are the ethical issues in this case?
(c) How might the system be improved to prevent this situation?

All About You

BYP7-5 In this chapter, you learned about a basic manual accounting information system. Computerized accounting systems range from the very basic and inexpensive to the very elaborate and expensive. However, even the most sophisticated systems are based on the fundamental structures and relationships that you learned in this chapter.

Instructions
Go to the book's companion site, **www.wiley.com/college/weygandt**, and review the demonstration that is provided for the general ledger software package that is used with this textbook. Prepare a brief explanation of how the general ledger system works—that is, how it is used and what information it provides.

A Look at IFRS

LEARNING OBJECTIVE 4 **Compare accounting information systems under GAAP and IFRS.**

As discussed in Chapter 1, IFRS is growing in acceptance around the world. For example, recent statistics indicate a substantial number of the Global Fortune 500 companies use IFRS. And the chairman of the IASB predicts that IFRS adoption will grow from its current level of 115 countries to nearly 150 countries in the near future.

When countries accept IFRS for use as accepted accounting policies, companies need guidance to ensure that their first IFRS financial statements contain high-quality information. Specifically, *IFRS 1* requires that information in a company's first IFRS statements (1) be transparent, (2) provide a suitable starting point, and (3) have a cost that does not exceed the benefits.

Relevant Facts

Following are the key similarities and differences between GAAP and IFRS related to accounting information systems.

Similarities

- The basic concepts related to an accounting information system are the same under GAAP and IFRS.
- The use of subsidiary ledgers and control accounts, as well as the system used for recording transactions, are the same under GAAP and IFRS.

Differences

- Many companies will be going through a substantial conversion process to switch from their current reporting standards to IFRS.
- Upon first-time adoption of IFRS, a company must present at least one year of comparative information under IFRS.

Looking to the Future

The basic recording process shown in this textbook is followed by companies around the globe. It is unlikely to change in the future. The definitional structure of assets, liabilities, equity, revenues, and expenses may change over time as the IASB and FASB evaluate their overall conceptual framework for establishing accounting standards. In addition, high-quality international accounting requires both high-quality accounting standards and high-quality auditing. Similar to the convergence of GAAP and IFRS, there is a movement to improve international auditing standards.

Chapter 8 Fraud, Internal Control, and Cash

For many years, Barriques in Madison, Wisconsin, has been named the city's favorite coffeehouse. Barriques not only does a booming business in coffee but also has wonderful baked goods, delicious sandwiches, and a fine selection of wines.

"Our customer base ranges from college students to neighborhood residents as well as visitors to our capital city," says bookkeeper Kerry Stoppleworth, who joined the company shortly after it was founded in 1998. "We are unique because we have customers who come in early on their way to work for a cup of coffee and then will stop back after work to pick up a bottle of wine for dinner. We stay very busy throughout all three parts of the day."

Like most businesses where purchases are low-cost and high-volume, cash control has to be simple. "We use a computerized point-of-sale (POS) system to keep track of our inventory and allow us to efficiently ring through an order for a customer," explains Stoppleworth. "You can either scan a barcode for an item or enter in a code for items that don't have a barcode such as cups of coffee or bakery items." The POS system also automatically tracks sales by department and maintains an electronic journal of all the sales transactions that occur during the day.

"There are two POS stations at each store, and throughout the day any of the staff may operate them," says Stoppleworth. At the end of the day, each POS station is reconciled separately. The staff counts the cash in the drawer and enters this amount into the closing totals in the POS system. The POS system then compares the cash and credit amounts, less the cash being carried forward to the next day (the float), to the shift total in the electronic journal. If there are discrepancies, a recount is done and the journal is reviewed transaction by transaction to identify the problem. The staff then creates a deposit ticket for the cash less the float and puts this in a drop safe with the electronic journal summary report for the manager to review and take to the bank the next day. Ultimately, the bookkeeper reviews all of these documents as well as the deposit receipt that the bank produces to make sure they are all in agreement.

As Stoppleworth concludes, "We keep the closing process and accounting simple so that our staff can concentrate on taking care of our customers and making great coffee and food."

LEARNING OBJECTIVES

1. **Discuss fraud and the principles of internal control.**
2. **Apply internal control principles to cash.**
3. **Identify the control features of a bank account.**
4. **Explain the reporting of cash.**

LEARNING OBJECTIVE 1 **Discuss fraud and the principles of internal control.**

The chapter opening story describes many of the internal control procedures used by **Barriques**. These procedures are necessary to discourage employees from fraudulent activities.

Fraud

A **fraud** is a dishonest act by an employee that results in personal benefit to the employee at a cost to the employer. Examples of fraud reported in the financial press include the following.

- A bookkeeper in a small company diverted $750,000 of bill payments to a personal bank account over a three-year period.
- A shipping clerk with 28 years of service shipped $125,000 of merchandise to himself.
- A computer operator embezzled $21 million from **Wells Fargo Bank** over a two-year period.
- A church treasurer "borrowed" $150,000 of church funds to finance a friend's business dealings.

Why does fraud occur? The three main factors that contribute to fraudulent activity are depicted by the **fraud triangle** in Illustration 8-1 (in the margin).

The most important element of the fraud triangle is **opportunity**. For an employee to commit fraud, the workplace environment must provide opportunities that an employee can take advantage of. Opportunities occur when the workplace lacks sufficient controls to deter and detect fraud. For example, inadequate monitoring of employee actions can create opportunities for theft and can embolden employees because they believe they will not be caught.

Opportunity

Financial Pressure | Rationalization

Illustration 8-1
Fraud triangle

A second factor that contributes to fraud is **financial pressure**. Employees sometimes commit fraud because of personal financial problems caused by too much debt. Or, they might commit fraud because they want to lead a lifestyle that they cannot afford on their current salary.

The third factor that contributes to fraud is **rationalization**. In order to justify their fraud, employees rationalize their dishonest actions. For example, employees sometimes justify fraud because they believe they are underpaid while the employer is making lots of money. Employees feel justified in stealing because they believe they deserve to be paid more.

The Sarbanes-Oxley Act

What can be done to prevent or to detect fraud? After numerous corporate scandals came to light in the early 2000s, Congress addressed this issue by passing the **Sarbanes-Oxley Act (SOX)**. Under SOX, all publicly traded U.S. corporations are required to maintain an adequate system of internal control. Corporate executives and boards of directors must ensure that these controls are reliable and effective. In addition, independent outside auditors must attest to the adequacy of the internal control system. Companies that fail to comply are subject to fines, and company officers can be imprisoned. SOX also created the Public Company Accounting Oversight Board (PCAOB) to establish auditing standards and regulate auditor activity.

One poll found that 60% of investors believe that SOX helps safeguard their stock investments. Many say they would be unlikely to invest in a company that fails to follow SOX requirements. Although some corporate executives have criticized the time and expense involved in following the SOX requirements, SOX appears to be working well. For example, the chief accounting officer of **Eli Lily** noted that SOX triggered a comprehensive review of how the company documents its controls. This review uncovered redundancies and pointed out controls that needed to be added. In short, it added up to time and money well spent.

Internal Control

Internal control is a process designed to provide reasonable assurance regarding the achievement of objectives related to operations, reporting, and compliance. In more detail, it consists of all the related methods and measures adopted within an organization to safeguard assets, enhance the reliability of accounting records, increase efficiency of operations, and ensure compliance with laws and regulations. Internal control systems have five primary components as listed below.[1]

- **A control environment.** It is the responsibility of top management to make it clear that the organization values integrity and that unethical activity will not be tolerated. This component is often referred to as the "tone at the top."
- **Risk assessment.** Companies must identify and analyze the various factors that create risk for the business and must determine how to manage these risks.
- **Control activities.** To reduce the occurrence of fraud, management must design policies and procedures to address the specific risks faced by the company.
- **Information and communication.** The internal control system must capture and communicate all pertinent information both down and up the organization, as well as communicate information to appropriate external parties.
- **Monitoring.** Internal control systems must be monitored periodically for their adequacy. Significant deficiencies need to be reported to top management and/or the board of directors.

Principles of Internal Control Activities

Each of the five components of an internal control system is important. Here, we will focus on one component, the control activities. The reason? These activities are the backbone of the company's efforts to address the risks it faces, such as fraud. The specific control activities used by a company will vary, depending on management's assessment of the risks faced. This assessment is heavily influenced by the size and nature of the company.

The six principles of control activities are as follows.

- Establishment of responsibility
- Segregation of duties
- Documentation procedures
- Physical controls
- Independent internal verification
- Human resource controls

We explain these principles in the following sections. You should recognize that they apply to most companies and are relevant to both manual and computerized accounting systems.

---

[1]The Committee of Sponsoring Organizations of the Treadway Commission, "Internal Control—Integrated Framework," *www.coso.org/documents/990025P_executive_summary_final_May20_e.pdf.*

ESTABLISHMENT OF RESPONSIBILITY

An essential principle of internal control is to assign responsibility to specific employees. **Control is most effective when only one person is responsible for a given task.**

To illustrate, assume that the cash on hand at the end of the day in a **Safeway** supermarket is $10 short of the cash entered in the cash register. If only one person has operated the register, the shift manager can quickly determine responsibility for the shortage. If two or more individuals have worked the register, it may be impossible to determine who is responsible for the error.

Many retailers solve this problem by having registers with multiple drawers. This makes it possible for more than one person to operate a register but still allows identification of a particular employee with a specific drawer. Only the signed-in cashier has access to his or her drawer.

Establishing responsibility often requires limiting access only to authorized personnel, and then identifying those personnel. For example, the automated systems used by many companies have mechanisms such as identifying passcodes that keep track of who made a journal entry, who entered a sale, or who went into an inventory storeroom at a particular time. Use of identifying passcodes enables the company to establish responsibility by identifying the particular employee who carried out the activity.

Transfer of cash drawers

ANATOMY OF A FRAUD

Maureen Frugali was a training supervisor for claims processing at Colossal Healthcare. As a standard part of the claims-processing training program, Maureen created fictitious claims for use by trainees. These fictitious claims were then sent to the accounts payable department. After the training claims had been processed, she was to notify Accounts Payable of all fictitious claims, so that they would not be paid. However, she did not inform Accounts Payable about every fictitious claim. She created some fictitious claims for entities that she controlled (that is, she would receive the payment), and she let Accounts Payable pay her.

Total take: $11 million

THE MISSING CONTROL

Establishment of responsibility. The healthcare company did not adequately restrict the responsibility for authorizing and approving claims transactions. The training supervisor should not have been authorized to create claims in the company's "live" system.

Source: Adapted from Wells, *Fraud Casebook* (2007), pp. 61–70.

SEGREGATION OF DUTIES

Segregation of duties is indispensable in an internal control system. There are two common applications of this principle:

1. Different individuals should be responsible for related activities.
2. The responsibility for recordkeeping for an asset should be separate from the physical custody of that asset.

The rationale for segregation of duties is this: **The work of one employee should, without a duplication of effort, provide a reliable basis for evaluating the work of another employee.** For example, the personnel that design and program computerized systems should not be assigned duties related to day-to-day use of the system. Otherwise, they could design the system to benefit them personally and conceal the fraud through day-to-day use.

SEGREGATION OF RELATED ACTIVITIES **Making one individual responsible for related activities increases the potential for errors and irregularities.** Instead, companies should, for example, assign related **purchasing activities** to different individuals. Related purchasing activities include ordering merchandise, order approval, receiving goods, authorizing payment, and paying for goods or services. Various frauds are possible when one person handles related purchasing activities:

- If a purchasing agent is allowed to order goods without obtaining supervisory approval, the likelihood of the purchasing agent receiving kickbacks from suppliers increases.
- If an employee who orders goods also handles the invoice and receipt of the goods, as well as payment authorization, he or she might authorize payment for a fictitious invoice.

These abuses are less likely to occur when companies divide the purchasing tasks.

Similarly, companies should assign related **sales activities** to different individuals. Related selling activities include making a sale, shipping (or delivering) the goods to the customer, billing the customer, and receiving payment. Various frauds are possible when one person handles related sales activities:

- If a salesperson can make a sale without obtaining supervisory approval, he or she might make sales at unauthorized prices to increase sales commissions.
- A shipping clerk who also has access to accounting records could ship goods to himself.
- A billing clerk who handles billing and receipt could understate the amount billed for sales made to friends and relatives.

These abuses are less likely to occur when companies divide the sales tasks. The salespeople make the sale, the shipping department ships the goods on the basis of the sales order, and the billing department prepares the sales invoice after comparing the sales order with the report of goods shipped.

ANATOMY OF A FRAUD

Lawrence Fairbanks, the assistant vice-chancellor of communications at Aesop University, was allowed to make purchases of under $2,500 for his department without external approval. Unfortunately, he also sometimes bought items for himself, such as expensive antiques and other collectibles. How did he do it? He replaced the vendor invoices he received with fake vendor invoices that he created. The fake invoices had descriptions that were more consistent with the communications department's purchases. He submitted these fake invoices to the accounting department as the basis for their journal entries and to the accounts payable department as the basis for payment.

Total take: $475,000

THE MISSING CONTROL

Segregation of duties. The university had not properly segregated related purchasing activities. Lawrence was ordering items, receiving the items, and receiving the invoice. By receiving the invoice, he had control over the documents that were used to account for the purchase and thus was able to substitute a fake invoice.

Source: Adapted from Wells, *Fraud Casebook* (2007), pp. 3–15.

SEGREGATION OF RECORDKEEPING FROM PHYSICAL CUSTODY The accountant should have neither physical custody of the asset nor access to it. Likewise, the custodian of the asset should not maintain or have access to the accounting records. **The custodian of the asset is not likely to convert the asset to personal use when one employee maintains the record of the asset, and a different employee has physical custody of the asset.** The separation of accounting responsibility from the custody of assets is especially important for cash and inventories because these assets are very vulnerable to fraud.

ANATOMY OF A FRAUD

Angela Bauer was an accounts payable clerk for Aggasiz Construction Company. Angela prepared and issued checks to vendors and reconciled bank statements. She perpetrated a fraud in this way: She wrote checks for costs that the company had not actually incurred (e.g., fake taxes). A supervisor then approved and signed the checks. Before issuing the check, though, Angela would "white-out" the payee line on the check and change it to personal accounts that she controlled. She was able to conceal the theft because she also reconciled the bank account. That is, nobody else ever saw that the checks had been altered.

Total take: $570,000

THE MISSING CONTROL

Segregation of duties. Aggasiz Construction Company did not properly segregate recordkeeping from physical custody. Angela had physical custody of the checks, which essentially was control of the cash. She also had recordkeeping responsibility because she prepared the bank reconciliation.

Source: Adapted from Wells, *Fraud Casebook* (2007), pp. 100–107.

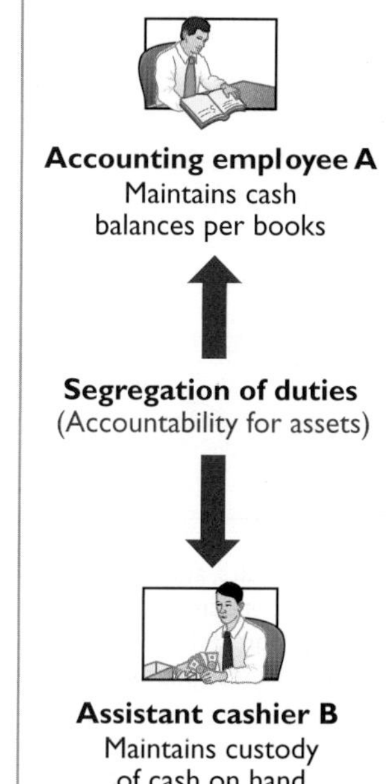

DOCUMENTATION PROCEDURES

Documents provide evidence that transactions and events have occurred. For example, Barriques' point-of-sale terminals are networked with the company's computing and accounting records, which results in direct documentation.

Similarly, a shipping document indicates that the goods have been shipped, and a sales invoice indicates that the company has billed the customer for the goods. By requiring signatures (or initials) on the documents, the company can identify the individual(s) responsible for the transaction or event. Companies should document transactions when they occur.

Companies should establish procedures for documents. First, whenever possible, companies should use **prenumbered documents, and all documents should be accounted for**. Prenumbering helps to prevent a transaction from being recorded more than once, or conversely, from not being recorded at all. Second, the control system should require that employees **promptly forward source documents for accounting entries to the accounting department. This control measure helps to ensure timely recording of the transaction** and contributes directly to the accuracy and reliability of the accounting records.

Prenumbered invoices

ANATOMY OF A FRAUD

To support their reimbursement requests for travel costs incurred, employees at Mod Fashions Corporation's design center were required to submit receipts. The receipts could include the detailed bill provided for a meal, the credit card receipt provided when the credit card payment is made, or a copy of the employee's monthly credit card bill that listed the item. A number of the designers who frequently traveled together came up with a fraud scheme: They submitted claims for the same expenses. For example, if they had a meal together that cost $200, one person submitted the detailed meal bill, another submitted the credit card receipt, and a third submitted a monthly credit card bill showing the meal as a line item. Thus, all three received a $200 reimbursement.

Total take: $75,000

THE MISSING CONTROL

Documentation procedures. Mod Fashions should require the original, detailed receipt. It should not accept photocopies, and it should not accept credit card statements. In addition, documentation procedures could be further improved by requiring the use of a corporate credit card (rather than a personal credit card) for all business expenses.

Source: Adapted from Wells, *Fraud Casebook* (2007), pp. 79–90.

PHYSICAL CONTROLS

Use of physical controls is essential. **Physical controls** relate to the safeguarding of assets and enhance the accuracy and reliability of the accounting records. Illustration 8-2 shows examples of these controls.

Illustration 8-2
Physical controls

Physical Controls

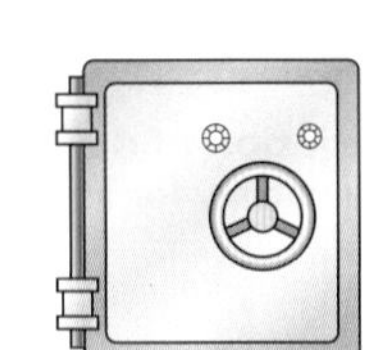

Safes, vaults, and safety deposit boxes for cash and business papers

Locked warehouses and storage cabinets for inventories and records

Computer facilities with pass key access or fingerprint or eyeball scans

Alarms to prevent break-ins

Television monitors and garment sensors to deter theft

Time clocks for recording time worked

ANATOMY OF A FRAUD

At Centerstone Health, a large insurance company, the mailroom each day received insurance applications from prospective customers. Mailroom employees scanned the applications into electronic documents before the applications were processed. Once the applications were scanned, they could be accessed online by authorized employees.

Insurance agents at Centerstone Health earn commissions based upon successful applications. The sales agent's name is listed on the application. However, roughly 15% of the applications are from customers who did not work with a sales agent. Two friends—Alex, an employee in recordkeeping, and Parviz, a sales agent—thought up a way to perpetrate a fraud. Alex identified scanned applications that did not list a sales agent. After business hours, he entered the mailroom and found the hard-copy applications that did not show a sales agent. He wrote in Parviz's name as the sales agent and then rescanned the application for processing. Parviz received the commission, which the friends then split.

Total take: $240,000

THE MISSING CONTROL

Physical controls. Centerstone Health lacked two basic physical controls that could have prevented this fraud. First, the mailroom should have been locked during non-business hours, and access during business hours should have been tightly controlled. Second, the scanned applications supposedly could be accessed only by authorized employees using their passwords. However, the password for each employee was the same as the employee's user ID. Since employee user-ID numbers were available to all other employees, all employees knew all other employees' passwords. Unauthorized employees could access the scanned applications. Thus, Alex could enter the system using another employee's password and access the scanned applications.

Source: Adapted from Wells, *Fraud Casebook* (2007), pp. 316–326.

INDEPENDENT INTERNAL VERIFICATION

Most internal control systems provide for **independent internal verification**. This principle involves the review of data prepared by employees. To obtain maximum benefit from independent internal verification:

1. Companies should verify records periodically or on a surprise basis.
2. An employee who is independent of the personnel responsible for the information should make the verification.

3. Discrepancies and exceptions should be reported to a management level that can take appropriate corrective action.

Independent internal verification is especially useful in comparing recorded accountability with existing assets. The reconciliation of the electronic journal with the cash in the point-of-sale terminal at **Barriques** is an example of this internal control principle. Other common examples are the reconciliation of a company's cash balance per books with the cash balance per bank, and the verification of the perpetual inventory records through a count of physical inventory. Illustration 8-3 shows the relationship between this principle and the segregation of duties principle.

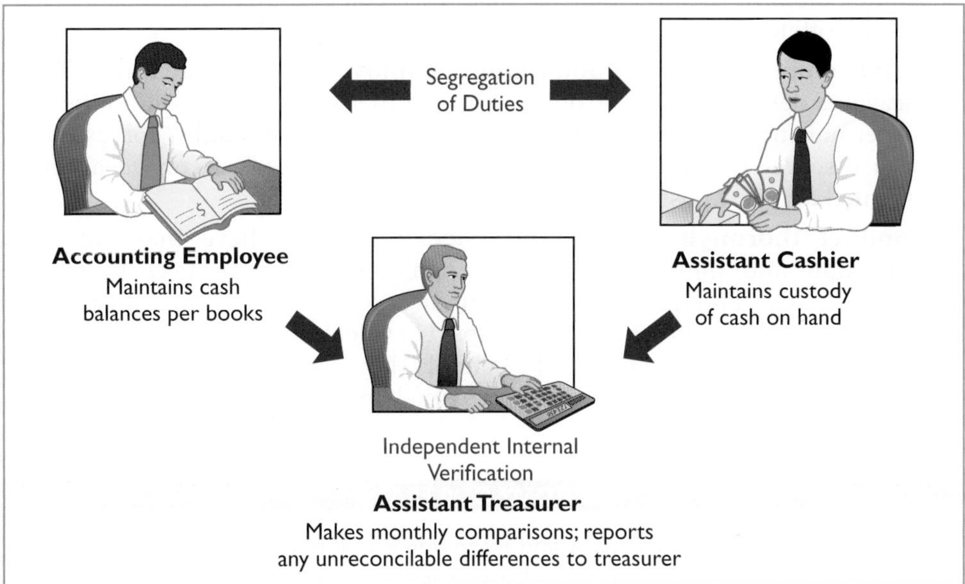

Illustration 8-3
Comparison of segregation of duties principle with independent internal verification principle

ANATOMY OF A FRAUD

Bobbi Jean Donnelly, the office manager for Mod Fashions Corporation's design center, was responsible for preparing the design center budget and reviewing expense reports submitted by design center employees. Her desire to upgrade her wardrobe got the better of her, and she enacted a fraud that involved filing expense-reimbursement requests for her own personal clothing purchases. Bobbi Jean was able to conceal the fraud because she was responsible for reviewing all expense reports, including her own. In addition, she sometimes was given ultimate responsibility for signing off on the expense reports when her boss was "too busy." Also, because she controlled the budget, when she submitted her expenses, she coded them to budget items that she knew were running under budget, so that they would not catch anyone's attention.

Total take: $275,000

THE MISSING CONTROL

Independent internal verification. Bobbi Jean's boss should have verified her expense reports. When asked what he thought her expenses for a year were, the boss said about $10,000. At $115,000 per year, her actual expenses were more than 10 times what would have been expected. However, because he was "too busy" to verify her expense reports or to review the budget, he never noticed.

Source: Adapted from Wells, *Fraud Casebook* (2007), pp. 79–90.

Large companies often assign independent internal verification to internal auditors. **Internal auditors** are company employees who continuously evaluate the effectiveness of the company's internal control systems. They review the activities of departments and individuals to determine whether prescribed internal controls are being followed. They also recommend improvements when needed. For example, WorldCom was at one time the second largest U.S. telecommunications company. The fraud that caused its bankruptcy (the largest ever when it occurred) involved billions of dollars. It was uncovered by an internal auditor.

HUMAN RESOURCE CONTROLS

Human resource control activities include the following.

1. **Bond employees who handle cash. Bonding** involves obtaining insurance protection against theft by employees. It contributes to the safeguarding of cash in two ways. First, the insurance company carefully screens all individuals before adding them to the policy and may reject risky applicants. Second, bonded employees know that the insurance company will vigorously prosecute all offenders.
2. **Rotate employees' duties and require employees to take vacations.** These measures deter employees from attempting thefts since they will not be able to permanently conceal their improper actions. Many banks, for example, have discovered employee thefts when the employee was on vacation or assigned to a new position.
3. **Conduct thorough background checks.** Many believe that the most important and inexpensive measure any business can take to reduce employee theft and fraud is for the human resources department to conduct thorough background checks. Two tips: (1) Check to see whether job applicants actually graduated from the schools they list. (2) Never use telephone numbers for previous employers provided by the applicant. Always look them up yourself.

ANATOMY OF A FRAUD

Ellen Lowry was the desk manager and Josephine Rodriguez was the head of housekeeping at the Excelsior Inn, a luxury hotel. The two best friends were so dedicated to their jobs that they never took vacations, and they frequently filled in for other employees. In fact, Ms. Rodriguez, whose job as head of housekeeping did not include cleaning rooms, often cleaned rooms herself, "just to help the staff keep up." These two "dedicated" employees, working as a team, found a way to earn a little more cash. Ellen, the desk manager, provided significant discounts to guests who paid with cash. She kept the cash and did not register the guest in the hotel's computerized system. Instead, she took the room out of circulation "due to routine maintenance." Because the room did not show up as being used, it did not receive a normal housekeeping assignment. Instead, Josephine, the head of housekeeping, cleaned the rooms during the guests' stay.

Total take: $95,000

THE MISSING CONTROL

Human resource controls. Ellen, the desk manager, had been fired by a previous employer after being accused of fraud. If the Excelsior Inn had conducted a thorough background check, it would not have hired her. The hotel fraud was detected when Ellen missed work for a few days due to illness. A system of mandatory vacations and rotating days off would have increased the chances of detecting the fraud before it became so large.

Source: Adapted from Wells, *Fraud Casebook* (2007), pp. 145–155.

Limitations of Internal Control

Companies generally design their systems of internal control to provide **reasonable assurance** of proper safeguarding of assets and reliability of the accounting records. The concept of reasonable assurance rests on the premise that the costs of establishing control procedures should not exceed their expected benefit.

To illustrate, consider shoplifting losses in retail stores. Stores could eliminate such losses by having a security guard stop and search customers as they leave the store. But store managers have concluded that the negative effects of such a procedure cannot be justified. Instead, they have attempted to control shoplifting losses by less costly procedures. They post signs saying, "We reserve the right to inspect all packages" and "All shoplifters will be prosecuted." They use hidden cameras and store detectives to monitor customer activity, and they install sensor equipment at exits.

The **human element** is an important factor in every system of internal control. A good system can become ineffective as a result of employee fatigue, carelessness, or indifference. For example, a receiving clerk may not bother to count goods received and may just "fudge" the counts. Occasionally, two or more individuals may work together to get around prescribed controls. Such **collusion** can significantly reduce the effectiveness of a system, eliminating the protection offered by segregation of duties. No system of internal control is perfect.

The **size of the business** also may impose limitations on internal control. Small companies often find it difficult to segregate duties or to provide for independent internal verification. A study by the Association of Certified Fraud Examiners (*Report to the Nation on Occupational Fraud and Abuse*) indicates that businesses with fewer than 100 employees are most at risk for employee theft. In fact, 29% of frauds occurred at companies with fewer than 100 employees. The median loss at small companies was $154,000, which was close to the median fraud at companies with more than 10,000 employees ($160,000). A $154,000 loss can threaten the very existence of a small company.

LEARNING OBJECTIVE 2

Apply internal control principles to cash.

Cash is the one asset that is readily convertible into any other type of asset. It also is easily concealed and transported, and is highly desired. Because of these characteristics, **cash is the asset most susceptible to fraudulent activities**. In addition, because of the large volume of cash transactions, numerous errors may occur in executing and recording them. To safeguard cash and to ensure the accuracy of the accounting records for cash, effective internal control over cash is critical.

Cash Receipts Controls

Illustration 8-4 shows how the internal control principles explained earlier apply to cash receipts transactions. As you might expect, companies vary considerably in how they apply these principles. To illustrate internal control over cash receipts, we will examine control activities for a retail store with both over-the-counter and mail receipts.

OVER-THE-COUNTER RECEIPTS

In retail businesses, control of over-the-counter receipts centers on cash registers that are visible to customers. A cash sale is entered in a cash register (or point-of-sale terminal), with the amount clearly visible to the customer. This activity prevents the sales clerk from entering a lower amount and pocketing the difference. The customer receives an itemized cash register receipt slip and is expected to count the change received. (One weakness at **Barriques** in the chapter opening story is that customers are only given a receipt if requested.) The cash register's tape is locked in the register until a supervisor removes it. This tape accumulates the daily transactions and totals.

At the end of the clerk's shift, the clerk counts the cash and sends the cash and the count to the cashier. The cashier counts the cash, prepares a deposit slip, and

Cash Receipts Controls

Establishment of Responsibility
Only designated personnel are authorized to handle cash receipts (cashiers)

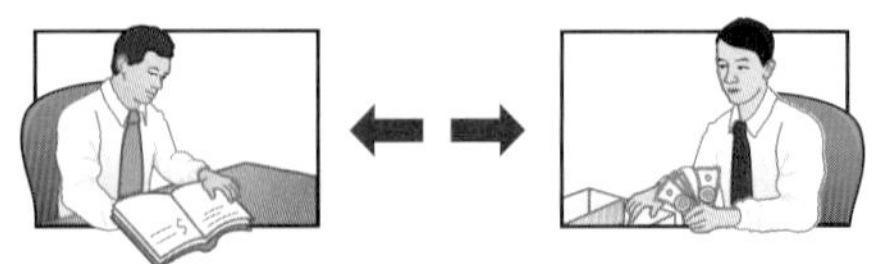

Segregation of Duties
Different individuals receive cash, record cash receipts, and hold the cash

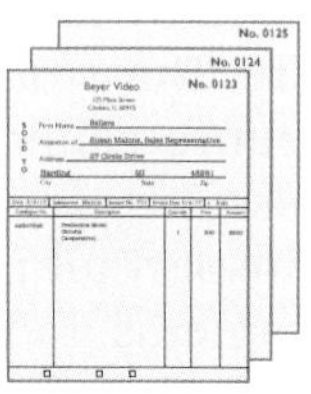

Documentation Procedures
Use remittance advice (mail receipts), cash register tapes or computer records, and deposit slips

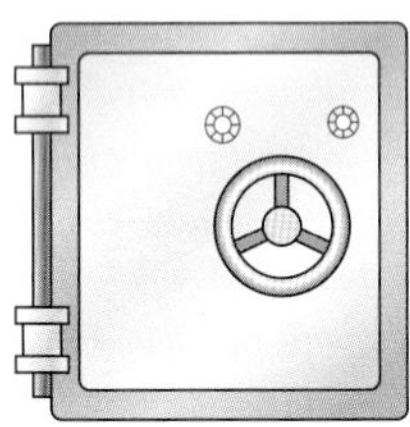

Physical Controls
Store cash in safes and bank vaults; limit access to storage areas; use cash registers

Independent Internal Verification
Supervisors count cash receipts daily; assistant treasurer compares total receipts to bank deposits daily

Human Resource Controls
Bond personnel who handle cash; require employees to take vacations; conduct background checks

Illustration 8-4
Application of internal control principles to cash receipts

deposits the cash at the bank. The cashier also sends a duplicate of the deposit slip to the accounting department to indicate cash received. The supervisor removes the cash register tape and sends it to the accounting department as the basis for a journal entry to record the cash received. (For point-of-sale systems, the accounting department receives information on daily transactions and totals through the computer network.) Illustration 8-5 summarizes this process.

This system for handling cash receipts uses an important internal control principle—segregation of recordkeeping from physical custody. The supervisor has access to the cash register tape but **not** to the cash. The clerk and the cashier have access to the cash but **not** to the register tape. In addition, the cash register tape provides documentation and enables independent internal verification. Use of these three principles of internal control (segregation of recordkeeping from physical custody, documentation, and independent internal verification) provides an effective system of internal control. Any attempt at fraudulent activity should be detected unless there is collusion among the employees.

In some instances, the amount deposited at the bank will not agree with the cash recorded in the accounting records based on the cash register tape. These differences often result because the clerk hands incorrect change back to the retail customer. In this case, the difference between the actual cash and the amount reported on the cash register tape is reported in a Cash Over and Short account. For example, suppose that the cash register tape indicated sales of \$6,956.20 but the amount of cash was only \$6,946.10. A cash shortfall of \$10.10 exists. To account for this cash shortfall and related cash, the company makes the following entry.

A	=	L	+	OE
+6,946.10				
				−10.10
				+6,956.20

Cash Flows
+6,946.10

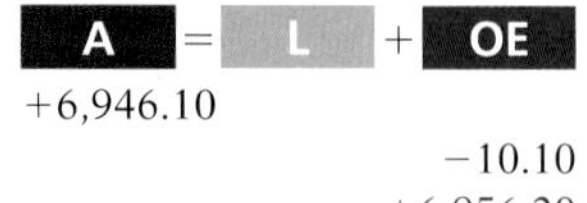

Cash	6,946.10	
Cash Over and Short	10.10	
Sales Revenue		6,956.20
(To record cash shortfall)		

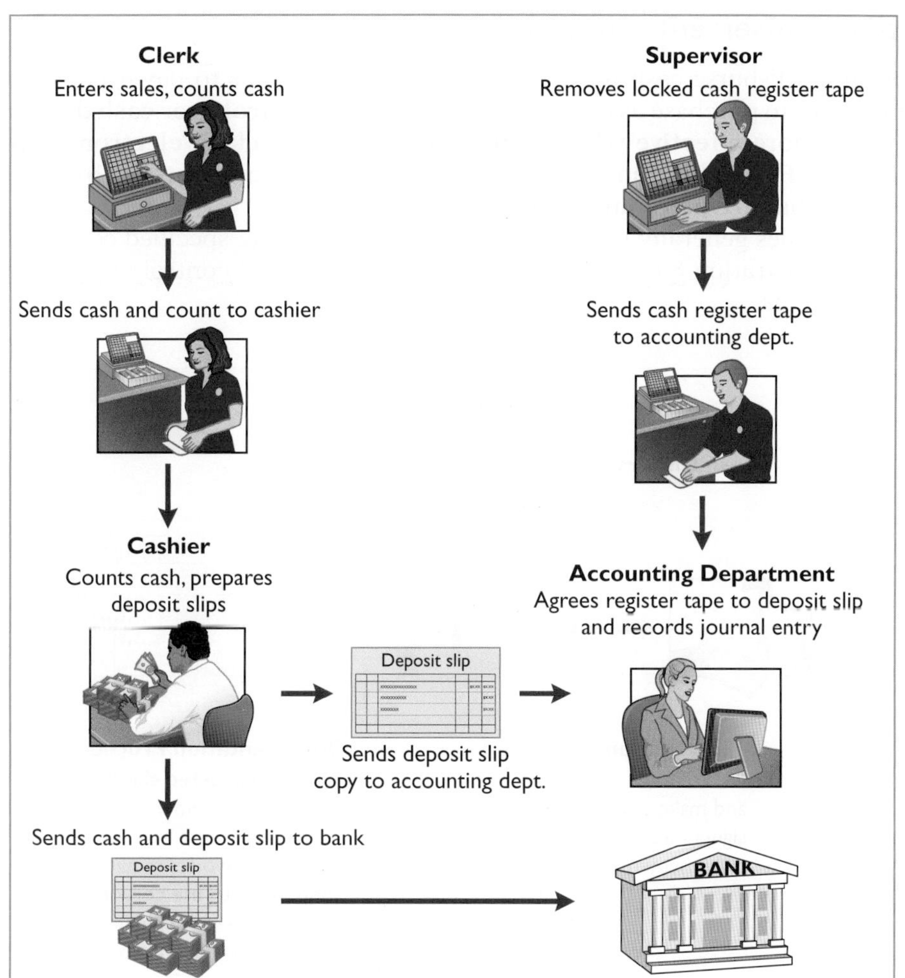

Illustration 8-5
Control of over-the-counter receipts

Cash Over and Short is an income statement item. It is reported as miscellaneous expense when there is a cash shortfall, and as miscellaneous revenue when there is an overage. Clearly, the amount should be small. Any material amounts in this account should be investigated.

MAIL RECEIPTS

All mail receipts should be opened in the presence of at least two mail clerks. These receipts are generally in the form of checks. A mail clerk should endorse each check "For Deposit Only." This restrictive endorsement reduces the likelihood that someone could divert the check to personal use. Banks will not give an individual cash when presented with a check that has this type of endorsement.

The mail clerks prepare, in triplicate, a list of the checks received each day. This list shows the name of the check issuer, the purpose of the payment, and the amount of the check. Each mail clerk signs the list to establish responsibility for the data. The original copy of the list, along with the checks, is then sent to the cashier's department. A copy of the list is sent to the accounting department for recording in the accounting records. The clerks also keep a copy.

This process provides excellent internal control for the company. By employing two clerks, the chance of fraud is reduced. Each clerk knows he or she is being observed by the other clerk(s). To engage in fraud, they would have to collude. The customers who submit payments also provide control because they will contact the company with a complaint if they are not properly credited for payment. Because the cashier has access to cash but not the records, and the accounting department has access to records but not cash, neither can engage in undetected fraud.

Cash Disbursements Controls

Companies disburse cash for a variety of reasons, such as to pay expenses and liabilities or to purchase assets. **Generally, internal control over cash disbursements is more effective when companies pay by check or electronic funds transfer (EFT) rather than by cash.** One exception is **payments for incidental amounts that are paid out of petty cash.**[2]

Companies generally issue checks only after following specified control procedures. Illustration 8-6 shows how principles of internal control apply to cash disbursements.

Cash Disbursements Controls

Establishment of Responsibility
Only designated personnel are authorized to sign checks (treasurer) and approve vendors

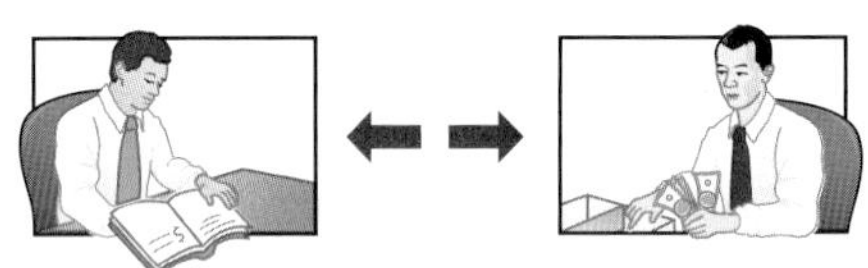

Segregation of Duties
Different individuals approve and make payments; check-signers do not record disbursements

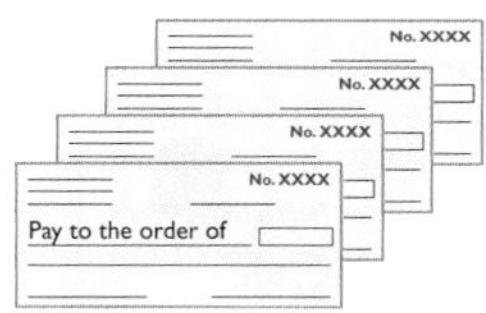

Documentation Procedures
Use prenumbered checks and account for them in sequence; each check must have an approved invoice; require employees to use corporate credit cards for reimbursable expenses; stamp invoices "paid"

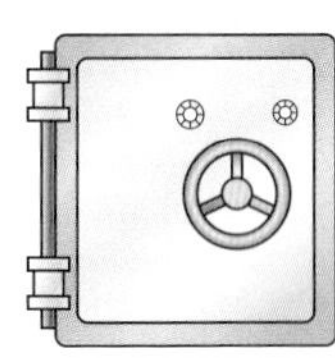

Physical Controls
Store blank checks in safes, with limited access; print check amounts by machine in indelible ink

Independent Internal Verification
Compare checks to invoices; reconcile bank statement monthly

Human Resource Controls
Bond personnel who handle cash; require employees to take vacations; conduct background checks

Illustration 8-6
Application of internal control principles to cash disbursements

VOUCHER SYSTEM CONTROLS

Most medium and large companies use vouchers as part of their internal control over cash disbursements. A **voucher system** is a network of approvals by authorized individuals, acting independently, to ensure that all disbursements by check are proper.

The system begins with the authorization to incur a cost or expense. It ends with the issuance of a check for the liability incurred. A **voucher** is an authorization

[2]We explain the operation of a petty cash fund on pages 299–301.

form prepared for each expenditure. Companies require vouchers for all types of cash disbursements except those from petty cash.

The starting point in preparing a voucher is to fill in the appropriate information about the liability on the face of the voucher. The vendor's invoice provides most of the needed information. Then, an employee in accounts payable records the voucher (in a journal called a **voucher register**) and files it according to the date on which it is to be paid. The company issues and sends a check on that date, and stamps the voucher "paid." The paid voucher is sent to the accounting department for recording (in a journal called the **check register**). A voucher system involves two journal entries, one to record the liability when the voucher is issued and a second to pay the liability that relates to the voucher.

The use of a voucher system, whether done manually or electronically, improves internal control over cash disbursements. First, the authorization process inherent in a voucher system establishes responsibility. Each individual has the responsibility to review the underlying documentation to ensure that it is correct. In addition, the voucher system keeps track of the documents that back up each transaction. By keeping these documents in one place, a supervisor can independently verify the authenticity of each transaction. Consider, for example, the case of Aesop University presented on page 290. Aesop did not use a voucher system for transactions under $2,500. As a consequence, there was no independent verification of the documents, which enabled the employee to submit fake invoices to hide his unauthorized purchases.

Petty Cash Fund

As you just learned, better internal control over cash disbursements is possible when companies make payments by check. However, using checks to pay small amounts is both impractical and a nuisance. For instance, a company would not want to write checks to pay for postage due, working lunches, or taxi fares. A common way of handling such payments, while maintaining satisfactory control, is to use a **petty cash fund** to pay relatively small amounts. The operation of a petty cash fund, often called an **imprest system**, involves (1) establishing the fund, (2) making payments from the fund, and (3) replenishing the fund.[3]

ESTABLISHING THE PETTY CASH FUND

Two essential steps in establishing a petty cash fund are (1) appointing a petty cash custodian who will be responsible for the fund, and (2) determining the size of the fund. Ordinarily, a company expects the amount in the fund to cover anticipated disbursements for a three- to four-week period.

To establish the fund, a company issues a check payable to the petty cash custodian for the stipulated amount. For example, if Laird Company decides to establish a $100 fund on March 1, the general journal entry is:

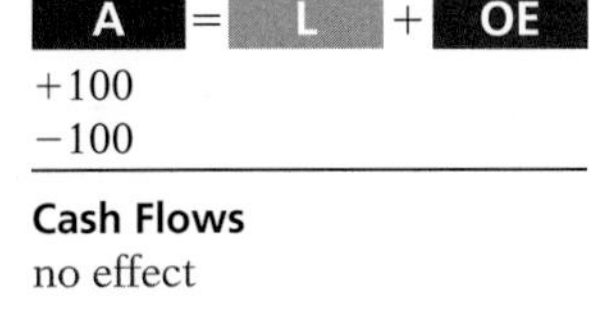

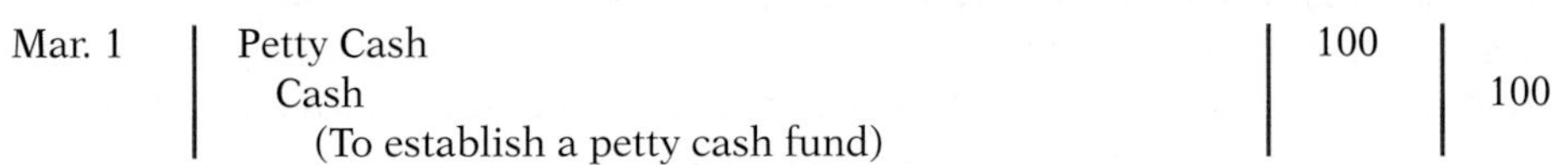

Mar. 1	Petty Cash	100	
	Cash		100
	(To establish a petty cash fund)		

The fund custodian cashes the check and places the proceeds in a locked petty cash box or drawer. Most petty cash funds are established on a fixed-amount basis. The company will make no additional entries to the Petty Cash account unless management changes the stipulated amount of the fund. For example, if Laird Company decides on July 1 to increase the size of the fund to $250, it would debit Petty Cash $150 and credit Cash $150.

[3]The term "imprest" means an advance of money for a designated purpose.

MAKING PAYMENTS FROM THE PETTY CASH FUND

The petty cash custodian has the authority to make payments from the fund that conform to prescribed management policies. Usually, management limits the size of expenditures that come from petty cash. Likewise, it may not permit use of the fund for certain types of transactions (such as making short-term loans to employees).

Each payment from the fund must be documented on a prenumbered petty cash receipt (or petty cash voucher), as shown in Illustration 8-7. The signatures of both the fund custodian and the person receiving payment are required on the receipt. If other supporting documents such as a freight bill or invoice are available, they should be attached to the petty cash receipt.

Illustration 8-7
Petty cash receipt

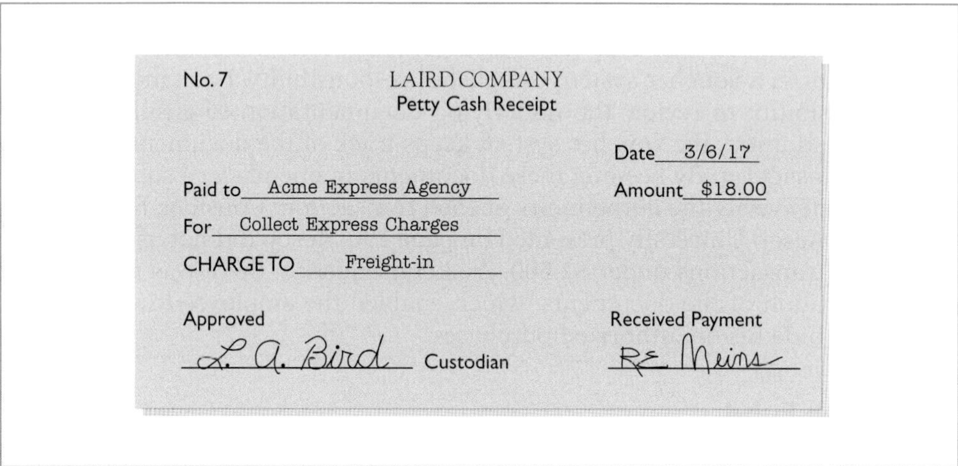
No. 7
LAIRD COMPANY
Petty Cash Receipt

Date 3/6/17
Paid to Acme Express Agency
Amount $18.00
For Collect Express Charges
CHARGE TO Freight-in
Approved
L. A. Bird Custodian
Received Payment
R. E. Mains

The petty cash custodian keeps the receipts in the petty cash box until the fund is replenished. The sum of the petty cash receipts and the money in the fund should equal the established total at all times. Management can (and should) make surprise counts at any time to determine whether the fund is being maintained correctly.

The company does not make an accounting entry to record a payment when it is made from petty cash. It is considered both inexpedient and unnecessary to do so. Instead, the company recognizes the accounting effects of each payment when it replenishes the fund.

REPLENISHING THE PETTY CASH FUND

When the money in the petty cash fund reaches a minimum level, the company replenishes the fund. The petty cash custodian initiates a request for reimbursement. The individual prepares a schedule (or summary) of the payments that have been made and sends the schedule, supported by petty cash receipts and other documentation, to the treasurer's office. The treasurer's office examines the receipts and supporting documents to verify that proper payments from the fund were made. The treasurer then approves the request and issues a check to restore the fund to its established amount. At the same time, all supporting documentation is stamped "paid" so that it cannot be submitted again for payment.

To illustrate, assume that on March 15 Laird's petty cash custodian requests a check for $87. The fund contains $13 cash and petty cash receipts for postage $44, freight-out $38, and miscellaneous expenses $5. The general journal entry to record the check is as follows.

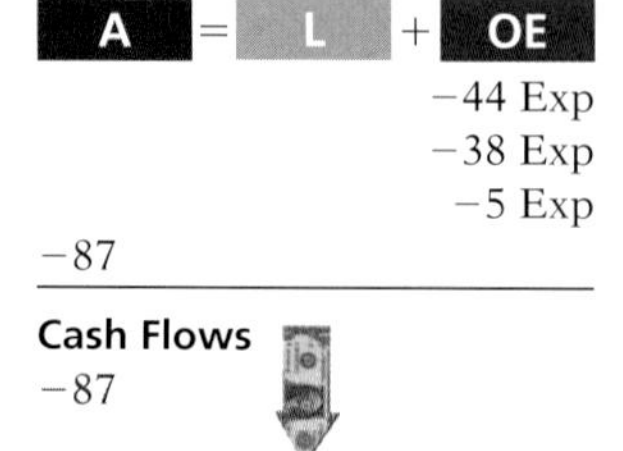

Mar. 15	Postage Expense	44	
	Freight-Out	38	
	Miscellaneous Expense	5	
	Cash		87
	(To replenish petty cash fund)		

Note that the reimbursement entry does not affect the Petty Cash account. Replenishment changes the composition of the fund by replacing the petty cash receipts with cash. It does not change the balance in the fund.

Occasionally, in replenishing a petty cash fund, the company may need to recognize a cash shortage or overage. This results when the total of the cash plus receipts in the petty cash box does not equal the established amount of the petty cash fund. To illustrate, assume that Laird's petty cash custodian has only \$12 in cash in the fund plus the receipts as listed. The request for reimbursement would therefore be for \$88, and Laird would make the following entry.

Mar. 15	Postage Expense	44	
	Freight-Out	38	
	Miscellaneous Expense	5	
	Cash Over and Short	1	
	Cash		88
	(To replenish petty cash fund)		

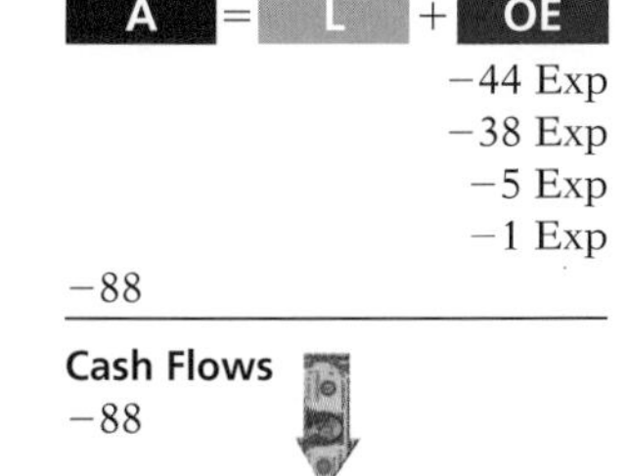

Conversely, if the custodian has \$14 in cash, the reimbursement request would be for \$86. The company would credit Cash Over and Short for \$1 (overage). A company reports a debit balance in Cash Over and Short in the income statement as miscellaneous expense. It reports a credit balance in the account as miscellaneous revenue. The company closes Cash Over and Short to Income Summary at the end of the year.

Companies should replenish a petty cash fund at the end of the accounting period, regardless of the cash in the fund. Replenishment at this time is necessary in order to recognize the effects of the petty cash payments on the financial statements.

Identify the control features of a bank account.

The use of a bank contributes significantly to good internal control over cash. A company can safeguard its cash by using a bank as a depository and as a clearinghouse for checks received and written. Use of a bank minimizes the amount of currency that a company must keep on hand. Also, use of a bank facilitates the control of cash because it creates a double record of all bank transactions—one by the company and the other by the bank. The asset account Cash maintained by the company should have the same balance as the bank's liability account for that company. A **bank reconciliation** compares the bank's balance with the company's balance and explains any differences to make them agree.

Many companies have more than one bank account. For efficiency of operations and better control, national retailers like **Wal-Mart Stores, Inc.** and **Target** may have regional bank accounts. Large companies, with tens of thousands of employees, may have a payroll bank account, as well as one or more general bank accounts. Also, a company may maintain several bank accounts in order to have more than one source for short-term loans when needed.

Making Bank Deposits

An authorized employee, such as the head cashier, should make a company's bank deposits. Each deposit must be documented by a deposit slip (ticket), as shown in Illustration 8-8 (page 302).

Deposit slips are prepared in duplicate. The bank retains the original; the depositor keeps the duplicate, machine-stamped by the bank to establish its authenticity.

Illustration 8-8
Deposit slip

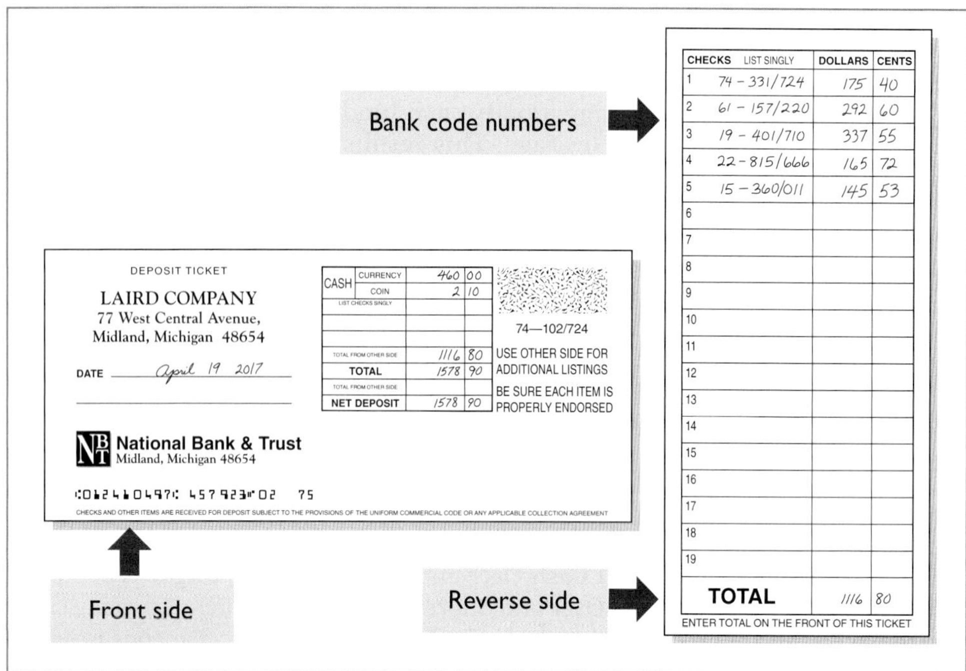

DEPOSIT TICKET
LAIRD COMPANY
77 West Central Avenue,
Midland, Michigan 48654

DATE April 19 2017

CASH		
CURRENCY	460	00
COIN	2	10
LIST CHECKS SINGLY		
TOTAL FROM OTHER SIDE	1116	80
TOTAL	1578	90
TOTAL FROM OTHER SIDE		
NET DEPOSIT	1578	90

74—102/724
USE OTHER SIDE FOR ADDITIONAL LISTINGS
BE SURE EACH ITEM IS PROPERLY ENDORSED

National Bank & Trust
Midland, Michigan 48654

⑆0624⑆0497⑆ 457923⑈02 75

CHECKS AND OTHER ITEMS ARE RECEIVED FOR DEPOSIT SUBJECT TO THE PROVISIONS OF THE UNIFORM COMMERCIAL CODE OR ANY APPLICABLE COLLECTION AGREEMENT

	CHECKS LIST SINGLY	DOLLARS	CENTS
1	74 - 331/724	175	40
2	61 - 157/220	292	60
3	19 - 401/710	337	55
4	22 - 815/666	165	72
5	15 - 360/011	145	53
6			
7			
8			
9			
10			
11			
12			
13			
14			
15			
16			
17			
18			
19			
	TOTAL	1116	80

ENTER TOTAL ON THE FRONT OF THIS TICKET

Writing Checks

A **check** is a written order signed by the depositor directing the bank to pay a specified sum of money to a designated recipient. There are three parties to a check: (1) the **maker** (or drawer) who issues the check, (2) the **bank** (or payer) on which the check is drawn, and (3) the **payee** to whom the check is payable. A check is a **negotiable instrument** that one party can transfer to another party by endorsement. Each check should be accompanied by an explanation of its purpose. In many companies, a remittance advice attached to the check, as shown in Illustration 8-9, explains the check's purpose.

Illustration 8-9
Check with remittance advice

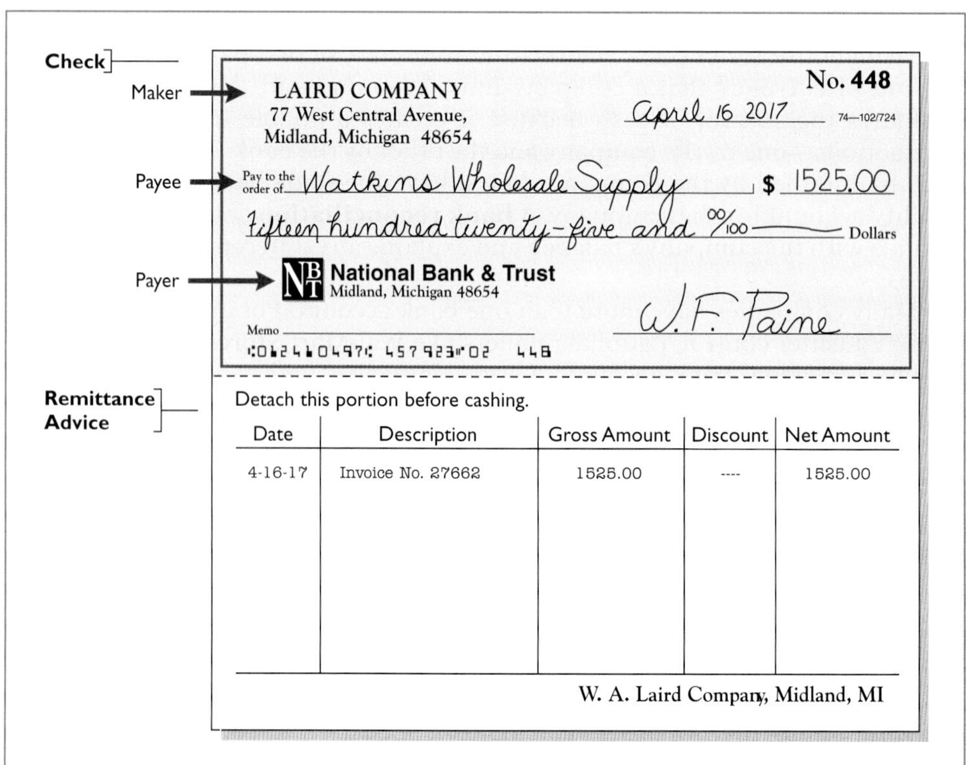

No. **448**
LAIRD COMPANY
77 West Central Avenue,
Midland, Michigan 48654

April 16 2017 74—102/724

Pay to the order of Watkins Wholesale Supply $ 1525.00
Fifteen hundred twenty-five and 00/100 Dollars

National Bank & Trust
Midland, Michigan 48654

Memo
W. F. Paine

⑆0624⑆0497⑆ 457923⑈02 448

Detach this portion before cashing.

Date	Description	Gross Amount	Discount	Net Amount
4-16-17	Invoice No. 27662	1525.00	----	1525.00

W. A. Laird Company, Midland, MI

It is important to know the balance in the checking account at all times. To keep the balance current, the depositor should enter each deposit and check on running-balance memo forms (or online statements) provided by the bank or on the check stubs in the checkbook.

Bank Statements

If you have a personal checking account, you are probably familiar with bank statements. A **bank statement** shows the depositor's bank transactions and balances.[4] Each month, a depositor receives a statement from the bank. Illustration 8-10 presents a typical bank statement for Laird Company. It shows (1) checks paid and other debits (such as debit card transactions or direct withdrawals for bill payments) that reduce the balance in the depositor's account, (2) deposits and other credits that increase the balance in the depositor's account, and (3) the account balance after each day's transactions.

Illustration 8-10
Bank statement

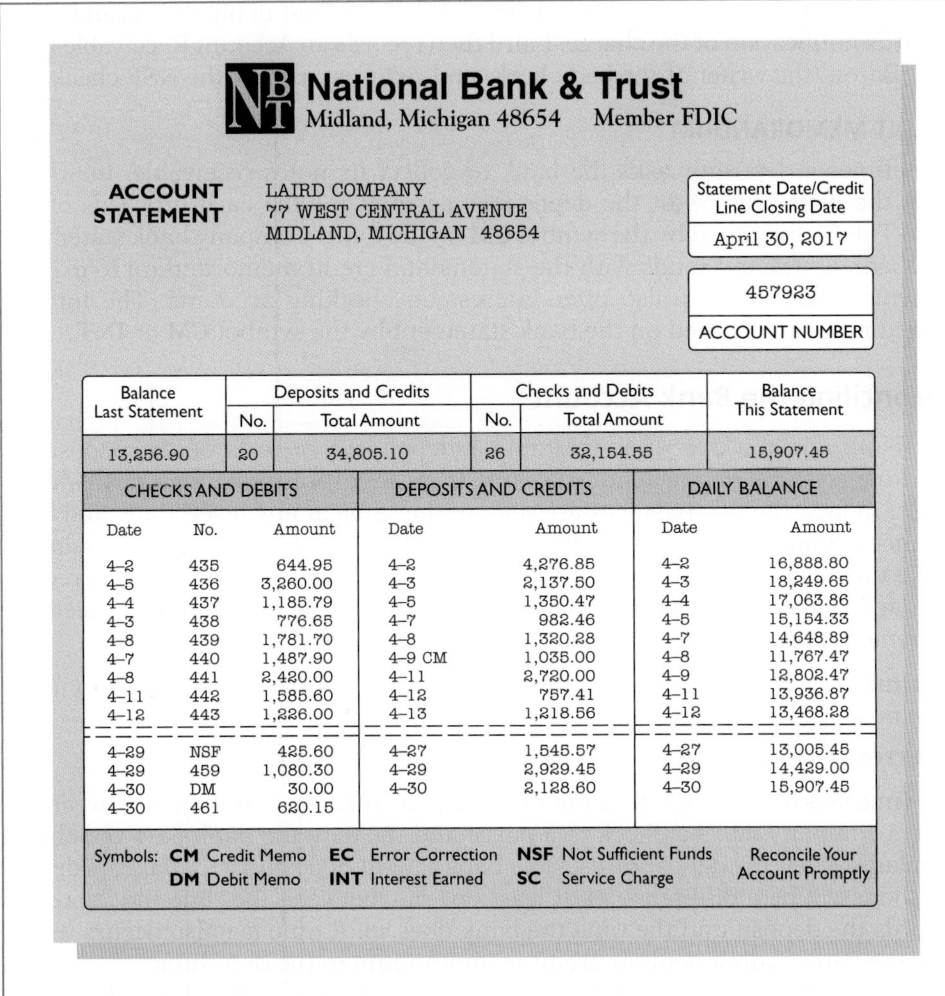

NBT National Bank & Trust
Midland, Michigan 48654 Member FDIC

ACCOUNT STATEMENT
LAIRD COMPANY
77 WEST CENTRAL AVENUE
MIDLAND, MICHIGAN 48654

Statement Date/Credit Line Closing Date: April 30, 2017

457923
ACCOUNT NUMBER

Balance Last Statement	Deposits and Credits		Checks and Debits		Balance This Statement
	No.	Total Amount	No.	Total Amount	
13,256.90	20	34,805.10	26	32,154.55	15,907.45

CHECKS AND DEBITS			DEPOSITS AND CREDITS		DAILY BALANCE	
Date	No.	Amount	Date	Amount	Date	Amount
4-2	435	644.95	4-2	4,276.85	4-2	16,888.80
4-5	436	3,260.00	4-3	2,137.50	4-3	18,249.65
4-4	437	1,185.79	4-5	1,350.47	4-4	17,063.86
4-3	438	776.65	4-7	982.46	4-5	15,154.33
4-8	439	1,781.70	4-8	1,320.28	4-7	14,648.89
4-7	440	1,487.90	4-9 CM	1,035.00	4-8	11,767.47
4-8	441	2,420.00	4-11	2,720.00	4-9	12,802.47
4-11	442	1,585.60	4-12	757.41	4-11	13,936.87
4-12	443	1,226.00	4-13	1,218.56	4-12	13,468.28
4-29	NSF	425.60	4-27	1,545.57	4-27	13,005.45
4-29	459	1,080.30	4-29	2,929.45	4-29	14,429.00
4-30	DM	30.00	4-30	2,128.60	4-30	15,907.45
4-30	461	620.15				

Symbols: **CM** Credit Memo **EC** Error Correction **NSF** Not Sufficient Funds **DM** Debit Memo **INT** Interest Earned **SC** Service Charge

Reconcile Your Account Promptly

The bank statement lists in numerical sequence all "paid" checks, along with the date the check was paid and its amount. Upon paying a check, the bank stamps the check "paid"; a paid check is sometimes referred to as a **canceled** check. On the statement, the bank also includes memoranda explaining other debits and credits it made to the depositor's account.

---

[4]Our presentation assumes that the depositor makes all adjustments at the end of the month. In practice, a company may also make journal entries during the month as it reviews information from the bank regarding its account.

DEBIT MEMORANDUM

Some banks charge a monthly fee for their services. Often, they charge this fee only when the average monthly balance in a checking account falls below a specified amount. They identify the fee, called a **bank service charge**, on the bank statement by a symbol such as **SC**. The bank also sends with the statement a debit memorandum explaining the charge noted on the statement. Other debit memoranda may also be issued for other bank services such as the cost of printing checks, issuing traveler's checks, and wiring funds to other locations. The symbol **DM** is often used for such charges.

Banks also use a debit memorandum when a deposited check from a customer "bounces" because of insufficient funds. For example, assume that J. R. Baron, a customer of Laird Company, sends a check for $425.60 to Laird Company for services performed. Unfortunately, Baron does not have sufficient funds at its bank to pay for these services. In such a case, Baron's bank marks the check **NSF** (not sufficient funds) and returns it to Laird's (the depositor's) bank. Laird's bank then debits Laird's account, as shown by the symbol NSF on the bank statement in Illustration 8-10. The bank sends the NSF check and debit memorandum to Laird as notification of the charge. Laird then records an Account Receivable from J. R. Baron (the writer of the bad check) and reduces cash for the NSF check.

CREDIT MEMORANDUM

Sometimes a depositor asks the bank to collect its notes receivable. In such a case, the bank will credit the depositor's account for the cash proceeds of the note. This is illustrated by the symbol **CM** on the Laird Company bank statement. The bank issues and sends with the statement a credit memorandum to explain the entry. Many banks also offer interest on checking accounts. The interest earned may be indicated on the bank statement by the symbol **CM** or **INT**.

Reconciling the Bank Account

The bank and the depositor maintain independent records of the depositor's checking account. People tend to assume that the respective balances will always agree. In fact, the two balances are seldom the same at any given time, and both balances differ from the "correct" or "true" balance. Therefore, it is necessary to make the balance per books and the balance per bank agree with the correct or true amount—a process called **reconciling the bank account**. The need for agreement has two causes:

1. **Time lags** that prevent one of the parties from recording the transaction in the same period as the other party.
2. **Errors** by either party in recording transactions.

Time lags occur frequently. For example, several days may elapse between the time a company mails a check to a payee and the date the bank pays the check. Similarly, when the depositor uses the bank's night depository to make its deposits, there will be a difference of at least one day between the time the depositor records the deposit and the time the bank does so. A time lag also occurs whenever the bank mails a debit or credit memorandum to the depositor.

The incidence of errors depends on the effectiveness of the internal controls maintained by the company and the bank. Bank errors are infrequent. However, either party could accidentally record a $450 check as $45 or $540. In addition, the bank might mistakenly charge a check drawn by C. D. Berg to the account of C. D. Burg.

RECONCILIATION PROCEDURE

The bank reconciliation should be prepared by an employee who has no other responsibilities pertaining to cash. If a company fails to follow this internal control principle of independent internal verification, cash embezzlements may go unnoticed. For example, a cashier who prepares the reconciliation can embezzle cash and conceal the embezzlement by misstating the reconciliation. Thus, the bank accounts would reconcile, and the embezzlement would not be detected.

In reconciling the bank account, it is customary to reconcile the balance per books and balance per bank to their adjusted (correct or true) cash balances. The starting point in preparing the reconciliation is to enter the balance per bank statement and balance per books on the reconciliation schedule. The company then makes various adjustments, as shown in Illustration 8-11.

Illustration 8-11
Bank reconciliation adjustments

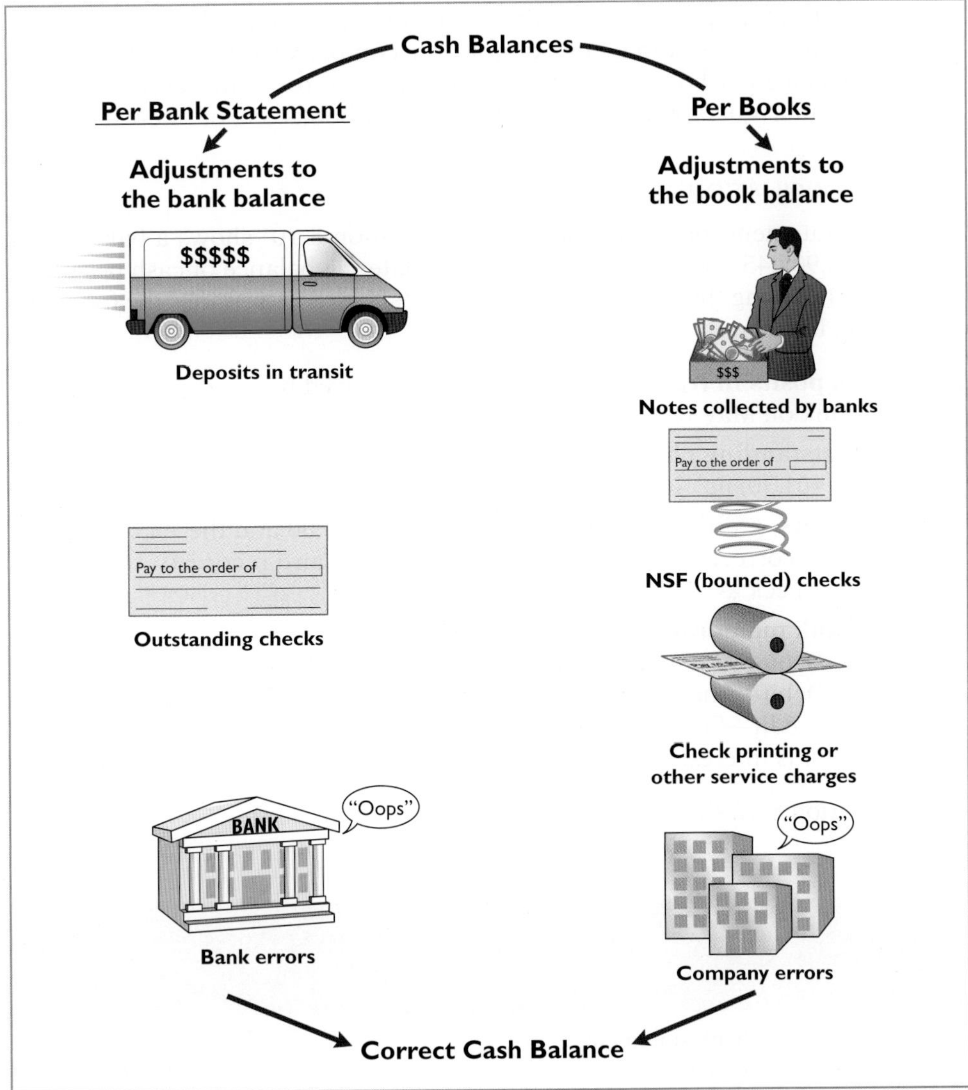

The following steps should reveal all the reconciling items that cause the difference between the two balances.

Step 1. Deposits in transit. Compare the individual deposits listed on the bank statement with deposits in transit from the preceding bank reconciliation and with the deposits per company records or duplicate deposit slips. Deposits recorded by the depositor that have not been recorded by the bank are the **deposits in transit**. Add these deposits to the balance per bank.

Step 2. Outstanding checks. Compare the paid checks shown on the bank statement with (a) checks outstanding from the previous bank reconciliation, and (b) checks issued by the company as recorded in the cash payments journal (or in the check register in your personal checkbook). Issued checks recorded by the company but that have not yet been paid by the bank are **outstanding checks**. Deduct outstanding checks from the balance per bank.

Step 3. Errors. Note any errors discovered in the foregoing steps and list them in the appropriate section of the reconciliation schedule. For example, if the company mistakenly recorded as $169 a paid check correctly written for $196, it would deduct the error of $27 from the balance per books. All errors made by the depositor are reconciling items in determining the adjusted cash balance per books. In contrast, all errors made by the bank are reconciling items in determining the adjusted cash balance per bank.

Step 4. Bank memoranda. Trace bank memoranda to the depositor's records. List in the appropriate section of the reconciliation schedule any unrecorded memoranda. For example, the company would deduct from the balance per books a $5 debit memorandum for bank service charges. Similarly, it would add to the balance per books $32 of interest earned.

BANK RECONCILIATION ILLUSTRATED

The bank statement for Laird Company (Illustration 8-10) shows a balance per bank of $15,907.45 on April 30, 2017. On this date the balance of cash per books is $11,589.45. Using the four reconciliation steps, Laird determines the following reconciling items.

Step 1.	**Deposits in transit:** April 30 deposit (received by bank on May 1).	$2,201.40
Step 2.	**Outstanding checks:** No. 453, $3,000.00; no. 457, $1,401.30; no. 460, $1,502.70.	5,904.00
Step 3.	**Errors:** Laird wrote check no. 443 for $1,226.00 and the bank correctly paid that amount. However, Laird recorded the check as $1,262.00.	36.00
Step 4.	**Bank memoranda:**	
	a. Debit—NSF check from J. R. Baron for $425.60.	425.60
	b. Debit—Charge for printing company checks $30.00.	30.00
	c. Credit—Collection of note receivable for $1,000 plus interest earned $50, less bank collection fee $15.00.	1,035.00

Illustration 8-12 shows Laird's bank reconciliation.

Illustration 8-12
Bank reconciliation

LAIRD COMPANY
Bank Reconciliation
April 30, 2017

Cash balance per bank statement		$ 15,907.45
Add: Deposits in transit		2,201.40
		18,108.85
Less: Outstanding checks		
No. 453	$3,000.00	
No. 457	1,401.30	
No. 460	1,502.70	5,904.00
Adjusted cash balance per bank		**$12,204.85**
Cash balance per books		$ 11,589.45
Add: Collection of note receivable $1,000, plus interest earned $50, less collection fee $15	$1,035.00	
Error in recording check no. 443	36.00	1,071.00
		12,660.45
Less: NSF check	425.60	
Bank service charge	30.00	455.60
Adjusted cash balance per books		**$12,204.85**

Terminology
The terms *adjusted cash balance, true cash balance,* and *correct cash balance* are used interchangeably.

ENTRIES FROM BANK RECONCILIATION

The company records each reconciling item used to determine the **adjusted cash balance per books. If the company does not journalize and post these items, the Cash account will not show the correct balance.** Laird Company would make the following entries on April 30.

COLLECTION OF NOTE RECEIVABLE This entry involves four accounts. Assuming that the interest of $50 has not been accrued and the collection fee is charged to Miscellaneous Expense, the entry is:

Apr. 30	Cash	1,035.00	
	Miscellaneous Expense	15.00	
	Notes Receivable		1,000.00
	Interest Revenue		50.00
	(To record collection of note receivable by bank)		

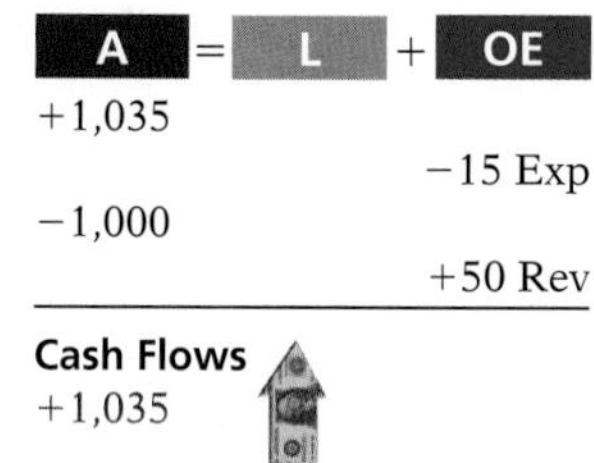

BOOK ERROR The cash disbursements journal shows that check no. 443 was a payment on account to Andrea Company, a supplier. The correcting entry is:

Apr. 30	Cash	36.00	
	Accounts Payable—Andrea Company		36.00
	(To correct error in recording check no. 443)		

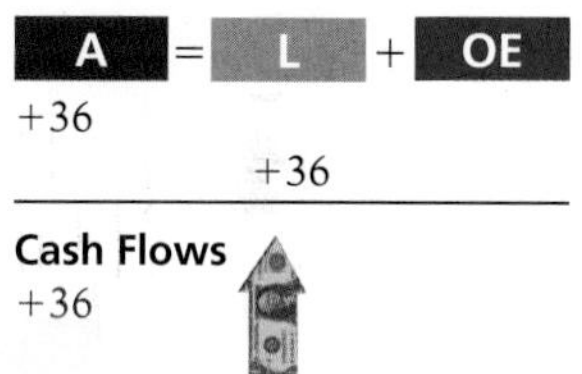

NSF CHECK As indicated earlier, an NSF check becomes an account receivable to the depositor. The entry is:

Apr. 30	Accounts Receivable—J. R. Baron	425.60	
	Cash		425.60
	(To record NSF check)		

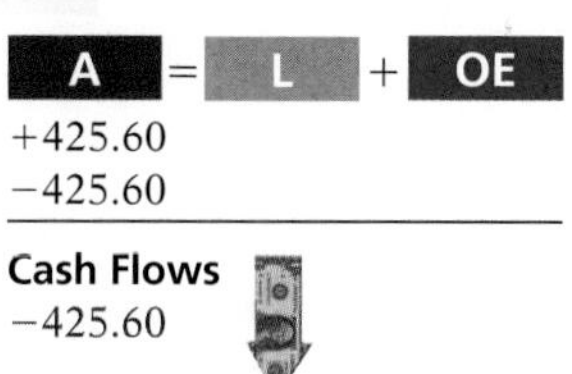

BANK SERVICE CHARGES Depositors debit check printing charges (DM) and other bank service charges (SC) to Miscellaneous Expense because they are usually nominal in amount. The entry is:

Apr. 30	Miscellaneous Expense	30.00	
	Cash		30.00
	(To record charge for printing company checks)		

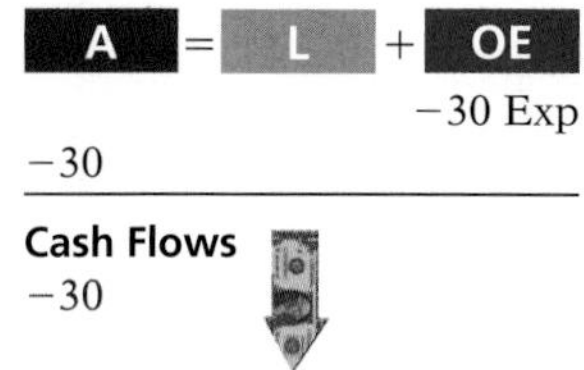

Instead of making four separate entries, Laird could combine them into one compound entry.

After Laird has posted the entries, the Cash account will show the following.

Cash

Apr. 30 Bal.	11,589.45	Apr. 30	425.60
30	1,035.00	30	30.00
30	36.00		
Apr. 30 Bal.	**12,204.85**		

Illustration 8-13 Adjusted balance in Cash account

The adjusted cash balance in the ledger should agree with the adjusted cash balance per books in the bank reconciliation in Illustration 8-12 (page 306).

What entries does the bank make? If the company discovers any bank errors in preparing the reconciliation, it should notify the bank. The bank then can make the necessary corrections in its records. The bank does not make any entries for deposits in transit or outstanding checks. Only when these items reach the bank will the bank record these items.

Electronic Funds Transfer (EFT) System

It is not surprising that companies and banks have developed approaches to transfer funds among parties without the use of paper (deposit tickets, checks, etc.). Such procedures, called **electronic funds transfers (EFT)**, are disbursement systems that use wire, telephone, or computers to transfer cash balances from one location to another. Use of EFT is quite common. For example, many employees receive no formal payroll checks from their employers. Instead, employers send electronic payroll data to the appropriate banks. Also, individuals and companies now frequently make regular payments such as those for house, car, and utilities by EFT.

EFT transactions normally result in better internal control since no cash or checks are handled by company employees. This does not mean that opportunities for fraud are eliminated. In fact, the same basic principles related to internal control apply to EFT transfers. For example, without proper segregation of duties and authorizations, an employee might be able to redirect electronic payments into a personal bank account and conceal the theft with fraudulent accounting entries.

Explain the reporting of cash.

Cash consists of coins, currency (paper money), checks, money orders, and money on hand or on deposit in a bank or similar depository. Companies report cash in two different statements: the balance sheet and the statement of cash flows. The balance sheet reports the amount of cash available at a given point in time. The statement of cash flows shows the sources and uses of cash during a period of time. The statement of cash flows was introduced in Chapter 1 and will be discussed in much detail in Chapter 17. In this section, we discuss some important points regarding the presentation of cash in the balance sheet.

When presented in a balance sheet, cash on hand, cash in banks, and petty cash are often combined and reported simply as **Cash**. Because it is the most liquid asset owned by the company, cash is listed first in the current assets section of the balance sheet.

Cash Equivalents

Many companies use the designation "Cash and cash equivalents" in reporting cash. (See Illustration 8-14 for an example.) **Cash equivalents** are short-term, highly liquid investments that are both:

1. Readily convertible to known amounts of cash, and
2. So near their maturity that their market value is relatively insensitive to changes in interest rates. Generally, only investments with original maturities of three months or less qualify under this definition.

Examples of cash equivalents are Treasury bills, commercial paper (short-term corporate notes), and money market funds. All typically are purchased with cash that is in excess of immediate needs.

Occasionally, a company will have a net negative balance in its bank account. In this case, the company should report the negative balance among current liabilities. For example, farm equipment manufacturer **Ag-Chem** recently reported "Checks outstanding in excess of cash balances" of $2,145,000 among its current liabilities.

Illustration 8-14
Balance sheet presentation of cash

Real World

DELTA AIR LINES, INC. Balance Sheet (partial) December 31, 2013 (in millions)	
Assets	
Current assets	
Cash and cash equivalents	**$2,844**
Short-term investments	959
Restricted cash	**122**

Restricted Cash

A company may have **restricted cash**, cash that is not available for general use but rather is restricted for a special purpose. For example, landfill companies are often required to maintain a fund of restricted cash to ensure they will have adequate resources to cover closing and clean-up costs at the end of a landfill site's useful life. **McKesson Corp.** recently reported restricted cash of $962 million to be paid out as the result of investor lawsuits.

Cash restricted in use should be reported separately on the balance sheet as restricted cash. If the company expects to use the restricted cash within the next year, it reports the amount as a current asset. When this is not the case, it reports the restricted funds as a noncurrent asset.

Illustration 8-14 shows restricted cash reported in the financial statements of **Delta Air Lines**. The company is required to maintain restricted cash as collateral to support insurance obligations related to workers' compensation claims. Delta does not have access to these funds for general use, and so it must report them separately, rather than as part of cash and cash equivalents.

REVIEW AND PRACTICE

LEARNING OBJECTIVES REVIEW

1 Discuss fraud and the principles of internal control. A fraud is a dishonest act by an employee that results in personal benefit to the employee at a cost to the employer. The fraud triangle refers to the three factors that contribute to fraudulent activity by employees: opportunity, financial pressure, and rationalization. Internal control consists of all the related methods and measures adopted within an organization to safeguard its assets, enhance the reliability of its accounting records, increase efficiency of operations, and ensure compliance with laws and regulations.

The principles of internal control are establishment of responsibility, segregation of duties, documentation procedures, physical controls, independent internal verification, and human resource controls such as bonding and requiring employees to take vacations.

2 Apply internal control principles to cash. Internal controls over cash receipts include (a) designating specific personnel to handle cash; (b) assigning different individuals to receive cash, record cash, and maintain custody of cash; (c) using remittance advices for mail receipts, cash register tapes for over-the-counter receipts, and deposit slips for bank deposits; (d) using company safes and bank vaults to store cash with access limited to authorized personnel, and using cash registers in executing over-the-counter receipts; (e) making independent daily counts of register receipts and daily comparison of total receipts with total deposits; and (f) bonding personnel that handle cash and requiring them to take vacations.

Internal controls over cash disbursements include (a) having specific individuals such as the treasurer authorized to sign checks and approve vendors; (b) assigning different individuals to approve items for payment, make the payment, and record the payment; (c) using prenumbered checks and accounting for all checks, with each check supported by an approved invoice; (d) storing blank checks in a safe or vault with access restricted to authorized personnel, and using a check-writing machine to imprint amounts on checks; (e) comparing each check with the approved invoice before issuing the check, and making monthly reconciliations of bank and book balances;

and (f) bonding personnel who handle cash, requiring employees to take vacations, and conducting background checks.

Companies operate a petty cash fund to pay relatively small amounts of cash. They must establish the fund, make payments from the fund, and replenish the fund when the cash in the fund reaches a minimum level.

3 **Identify the control features of a bank account.** A bank account contributes to good internal control by providing physical controls for the storage of cash. It minimizes the amount of currency that a company must keep on hand, and it creates a double record of a depositor's bank transactions. It is customary to reconcile the balance per books and balance per bank to their adjusted balances. The steps in the reconciling process are to determine deposits in transit, outstanding checks, errors by the depositor or the bank, and unrecorded bank memoranda.

4 **Explain the reporting of cash.** Companies list cash first in the current assets section of the balance sheet. In some cases, they report cash together with cash equivalents. Cash restricted for a special purpose is reported separately as a current asset or as a noncurrent asset, depending on when the cash is expected to be used.

GLOSSARY REVIEW

Bank reconciliation The process of comparing the bank's balance of an account with the company's balance and explaining any differences to make them agree.

Bank service charge A fee charged by a bank for the use of its services.

Bank statement A monthly statement from the bank that shows the depositor's bank transactions and balances.

Bonding Obtaining insurance protection against theft by employees.

Cash Resources that consist of coins, currency, checks, money orders, and money on hand or on deposit in a bank or similar depository.

Cash equivalents Short-term, highly liquid investments that can be converted to a specific amount of cash.

Check A written order signed by a bank depositor, directing the bank to pay a specified sum of money to a designated recipient.

Deposits in transit Deposits recorded by the depositor but not yet recorded by the bank.

Electronic funds transfer (EFT) A disbursement system that uses wire, telephone, or computers to transfer funds from one location to another.

Fraud A dishonest act by an employee that results in personal benefit to the employee at a cost to the employer.

Fraud triangle The three factors that contribute to fraudulent activity by employees: opportunity, financial pressure, and rationalization.

Internal auditors Company employees who continuously evaluate the effectiveness of the company's internal control system.

Internal control A process designed to provide reasonable assurance regarding the achievement of objectives related to operations, reporting, and compliance.

NSF check A check that is not paid by a bank because of insufficient funds in a customer's bank account.

Outstanding checks Checks issued and recorded by a company but not yet paid by the bank.

Petty cash fund A cash fund used to pay relatively small amounts.

Restricted cash Cash that must be used for a special purpose.

Sarbanes-Oxley Act (SOX) Regulations passed by Congress to try to reduce unethical corporate behavior.

Voucher An authorization form prepared for each payment in a voucher system.

Voucher system A network of approvals by authorized individuals acting independently to ensure that all disbursements by check are proper.

PRACTICE EXERCISES

Indicate good or weak internal control procedures.
(LO 1, 2)

1. Listed below are five procedures followed by Viel Company.

1. Total cash receipts are compared to bank deposits daily by Vonda Marshall, who receives cash over the counter.
2. Employees write down hours worked and turn in the sheet to the cashier's office.
3. As a cost-saving measure, employees do not take vacations.
4. Only the sales manager can approve credit sales.
5. Three different employees are assigned one task each related to inventory: ship goods to customers, bill customers, and receive payment from customers.

Instructions

Indicate whether each procedure is an example of good internal control or of weak internal control. If it is an example of good internal control, indicate which internal control principle is being followed. If it is an example of weak internal control, indicate which internal control principles is violated. Use the table below.

Procedure	IC Good or Weak?	Related Internal Control Principle
1.		
2.		
3.		
4.		
5.		

Solution

1.

Procedure	IC Good or Weak?	Related Internal Control Principle
1.	Weak	Independent internal verification
2.	Weak	Physical controls
3.	Weak	Human resource controls
4.	Good	Establishment of responsibility
5.	Good	Segregation of duties

Prepare bank reconciliation and adjusting entries.

(LO 3)

2. The information below relates to the Cash account in the ledger of Hillfarms Company.

Balance June 1—$9,947; Cash deposited—$37,120.
Balance June 30—$10,094; Checks written—$36,973.

The June bank statement shows a balance of $9,525 on June 30 and the following memoranda.

Credits		Debits	
Collection of $850 note plus interest $34	$884	NSF check: R. Doll	$245
Interest earned on checking accounts	$26	Safety deposit box rent	$35

At June 30, deposits in transit were $2,581, and outstanding checks totaled $1,382.

Instructions

(a) Prepare the bank reconciliation at June 30.

(b) Prepare the adjusting entries at June 30, assuming (1) the NFS check was from a customer on account, and (2) no interest had been accrued on the note.

Solution

2. (a)

HILLFARMS COMPANY
Bank Reconciliation
June 30

Cash balance per bank statement		$ 9,525
Add: Deposits in transit		2,581
		12,106
Less: Outstanding checks		1,382
Adjusted cash balance per bank		$10,724
Cash balance per books		$10,094
Add: Collection of note receivable ($850 + $34)	$884	
Interest earned	26	910
		11,004
Less: NSF check	245	
Safety deposit box rent	35	280
Adjusted cash balance per books		$10,724

(b)

Date	Account	Debit	Credit
June 30	Cash	884	
	Notes Receivable		850
	Interest Revenue		34
30	Cash	26	
	Interest Revenue		26

30	Miscellaneous Expense	35	
	Cash		35
30	Accounts Receivable (R. Doll)	245	
	Cash		245

PRACTICE PROBLEM

Prepare bank reconciliation and journalize entries.

(LO 3)

Poorten Company's bank statement for May 2017 shows the following data.

Balance 5/1	$12,650	Balance 5/31	$14,280
Debit memorandum:		Credit memorandum:	
NSF check	$175	Collection of note receivable	$505

The cash balance per books at May 31 is $13,319. Your review of the data reveals the following.

1. The NSF check was from Copple Co., a customer.
2. The note collected by the bank was a $500, 3-month, 12% note. The bank charged a $10 collection fee. No interest has been accrued.
3. Outstanding checks at May 31 total $2,410.
4. Deposits in transit at May 31 total $1,752.
5. A Poorten Company check for $352, dated May 10, cleared the bank on May 25. The company recorded this check, which was a payment on account, for $325.

Instructions

(a) Prepare a bank reconciliation at May 31.

(b) Journalize the entries required by the reconciliation.

Solution

(a)

POORTEN COMPANY
Bank Reconciliation
May 31, 2017

Cash balance per bank statement		$14,280
Add: Deposits in transit		1,752
		16,032
Less: Outstanding checks		2,410
Adjusted cash balance per bank		$13,622
Cash balance per books		$13,319
Add: Collection of note receivable $500, plus $15 interest, less collection fee $10		505
		13,824
Less: NSF check	$175	
Error in recording check	27	202
Adjusted cash balance per books		$13,622

(b)

May 31	Cash	505	
	Miscellaneous Expense	10	
	Notes Receivable		500
	Interest Revenue		15
	(To record collection of note by bank)		
31	Accounts Receivable—Copple Co.	175	
	Cash		175
	(To record NSF check from Copple Co.)		
31	Accounts Payable	27	
	Cash		27
	(To correct error in recording check)		

EXERCISES

E8-1 Eve Herschel is the owner of Herschel's Pizza. Herschel's is operated strictly on a carryout basis. Customers pick up their orders at a counter where a clerk exchanges the pizza for cash. While at the counter, the customer can see other employees making the pizzas and the large ovens in which the pizzas are baked.

Identify the principles of internal control.

(LO 1)

Instructions
Identify the six principles of internal control and give an example of each principle that you might observe when picking up your pizza. (*Note:* It may not be possible to observe all the principles.)

E8-2 The following control procedures are used at Torres Company for over-the-counter cash receipts.

Identify internal control weaknesses over cash receipts and suggest improvements.

(LO 1, 2)

1. To minimize the risk of robbery, cash in excess of $100 is stored in an unlocked attaché case in the stock room until it is deposited in the bank.
2. All over-the-counter receipts are processed by three clerks who use a cash register with a single cash drawer.
3. The company accountant makes the bank deposit and then records the day's receipts.
4. At the end of each day, the total receipts are counted by the cashier on duty and reconciled to the cash register total.
5. Cashiers are experienced; they are not bonded.

Instructions
(a) For each procedure, explain the weakness in internal control, and identify the control principle that is violated.
(b) For each weakness, suggest a change in procedure that will result in good internal control.

E8-3 The following control procedures are used in Mendy Lang's Boutique Shoppe for cash disbursements.

Identify internal control weaknesses over cash disbursements and suggest improvements.

(LO 1, 2)

1. The company accountant prepares the bank reconciliation and reports any discrepancies to the owner.
2. The store manager personally approves all payments before signing and issuing checks.
3. Each week, 100 company checks are left in an unmarked envelope on a shelf behind the cash register.
4. After payment, bills are filed in a paid invoice folder.
5. The company checks are unnumbered.

Instructions
(a) For each procedure, explain the weakness in internal control, and identify the internal control principle that is violated.
(b) For each weakness, suggest a change in the procedure that will result in good internal control.

E8-4 At Danner Company, checks are not prenumbered because both the purchasing agent and the treasurer are authorized to issue checks. Each signer has access to unissued checks kept in an unlocked file cabinet. The purchasing agent pays all bills pertaining to goods purchased for resale. Prior to payment, the purchasing agent determines that the goods have been received and verifies the mathematical accuracy of the vendor's invoice. After payment, the invoice is filed by the vendor name, and the purchasing agent records the payment in the cash disbursements journal. The treasurer pays all other bills following approval by authorized employees. After payment, the treasurer stamps all bills PAID, files them by payment date, and records the checks in the cash disbursements journal. Danner Company maintains one checking account that is reconciled by the treasurer.

Identify internal control weaknesses for cash disbursements and suggest improvements.

(LO 2)

Instructions
(a) List the weaknesses in internal control over cash disbursements.
(b) Write a memo to the company treasurer indicating your recommendations for improvement.

Indicate whether procedure is good or weak internal control.
(LO 1, 2)

E8-5 Listed below are five procedures followed by Eikenberry Company.

1. Several individuals operate the cash register using the same register drawer.
2. A monthly bank reconciliation is prepared by someone who has no other cash responsibilities.
3. Joe Cockrell writes checks and also records cash payment journal entries.
4. One individual orders inventory, while a different individual authorizes payments.
5. Unnumbered sales invoices from credit sales are forwarded to the accounting department every four weeks for recording.

Instructions
Indicate whether each procedure is an example of good internal control or of weak internal control. If it is an example of good internal control, indicate which internal control principle is being followed. If it is an example of weak internal control, indicate which internal control principle is violated. Use the table below.

Procedure	IC Good or Weak?	Related Internal Control Principle
1.		
2.		
3.		
4.		
5.		

Indicate whether procedure is good or weak internal control.
(LO 1, 2)

E8-6 Listed below are five procedures followed by Gilmore Company.

1. Employees are required to take vacations.
2. Any member of the sales department can approve credit sales.
3. Paul Jaggard ships goods to customers, bills customers, and receives payment from customers.
4. Total cash receipts are compared to bank deposits daily by someone who has no other cash responsibilities.
5. Time clocks are used for recording time worked by employees.

Instructions
Indicate whether each procedure is an example of good internal control or of weak internal control. If it is an example of good internal control, indicate which internal control principle is being followed. If it is an example of weak internal control, indicate which internal control principle is violated. Use the table below.

Procedure	IC Good or Weak?	Related Internal Control Principle
1.		
2.		
3.		
4.		
5.		

Prepare journal entries for a petty cash fund.
(LO 2)

E8-7 Setterstrom Company established a petty cash fund on May 1, cashing a check for \$100. The company reimbursed the fund on June 1 and July 1 with the following results.

June 1: Cash in fund \$1.75. Receipts: delivery expense \$31.25, postage expense \$39.00, and miscellaneous expense \$25.00.
July 1: Cash in fund \$3.25. Receipts: delivery expense \$21.00, entertainment expense \$51.00, and miscellaneous expense \$24.75.

On July 10, Setterstrom increased the fund from \$100 to \$130.

Instructions
Prepare journal entries for Setterstrom Company for May 1, June 1, July 1, and July 10.

Prepare journal entries for a petty cash fund.
(LO 2)

E8-8 Horvath Company uses an imprest petty cash system. The fund was established on March 1 with a balance of \$100. During March, the following petty cash receipts were found in the petty cash box.

Date	Receipt No.	For	Amount
3/5	1	Stamp Inventory	$39
7	2	Freight-Out	21
9	3	Miscellaneous Expense	6
11	4	Travel Expense	24
14	5	Miscellaneous Expense	5

The fund was replenished on March 15 when the fund contained $2 in cash. On March 20, the amount in the fund was increased to $175.

Instructions
Journalize the entries in March that pertain to the operation of the petty cash fund.

E8-9 Don Wyatt is unable to reconcile the bank balance at January 31. Don's reconciliation is as follows.

Prepare bank reconciliation and adjusting entries.

(LO 3)

Cash balance per bank	$3,560.20
Add: NSF check	490.00
Less: Bank service charge	25.00
Adjusted balance per bank	$4,025.20
Cash balance per books	$3,875.20
Less: Deposits in transit	530.00
Add: Outstanding checks	730.00
Adjusted balance per books	$4,075.20

Instructions
(a) Prepare a correct bank reconciliation.
(b) Journalize the entries required by the reconciliation.

E8-10 On April 30, the bank reconciliation of Westbrook Company shows three outstanding checks: no. 254, $650; no. 255, $620; and no. 257, $410. The May bank statement and the May cash payments journal show the following.

Determine outstanding checks.

(LO 3)

Bank Statement			Cash Payments Journal		
Checks Paid			Checks Issued		
Date	Check No.	Amount	Date	Check No.	Amount
5/4	254	$650	5/2	258	$159
5/2	257	410	5/5	259	275
5/17	258	159	5/10	260	890
5/12	259	275	5/15	261	500
5/20	261	500	5/22	262	750
5/29	263	480	5/24	263	480
5/30	262	750	5/29	264	560

Instructions
Using Step 2 in the reconciliation procedure, list the outstanding checks at May 31.

E8-11 The following information pertains to Crane Video Company.

Prepare bank reconciliation and adjusting entries.

(LO 3)

1. Cash balance per bank, July 31, $7,263.
2. July bank service charge not recorded by the depositor $28.
3. Cash balance per books, July 31, $7,284.
4. Deposits in transit, July 31, $1,300.
5. Bank collected $700 note for Crane in July, plus interest $36, less fee $20. The collection has not been recorded by Crane, and no interest has been accrued.
6. Outstanding checks, July 31, $591.

Instructions

(a) Prepare a bank reconciliation at July 31.
(b) Journalize the adjusting entries at July 31 on the books of Crane Video Company.

Prepare bank reconciliation and adjusting entries.
(LO 3)

E8-12 The information below relates to the Cash account in the ledger of Minton Company.

Balance September 1—$17,150; Cash deposited—$64,000.
Balance September 30—$17,404; Checks written—$63,746.

The September bank statement shows a balance of $16,422 on September 30 and the following memoranda.

Credits		Debits	
Collection of $2,500 note plus interest $30	$2,530	NSF check: Richard Nance	$425
Interest earned on checking account	$45	Safety deposit box rent	$65

At September 30, deposits in transit were $5,450, and outstanding checks totaled $2,383.

Instructions

(a) Prepare the bank reconciliation at September 30.
(b) Prepare the adjusting entries at September 30, assuming (1) the NSF check was from a customer on account, and (2) no interest had been accrued on the note.

Compute deposits in transit and outstanding checks for two bank reconciliations.
(LO 3)

E8-13 The cash records of Dawes Company show the following four situations.

1. The June 30 bank reconciliation indicated that deposits in transit total $920. During July, the general ledger account Cash shows deposits of $15,750, but the bank statement indicates that only $15,600 in deposits were received during the month.
2. The June 30 bank reconciliation also reported outstanding checks of $680. During the month of July, Dawes Company's books show that $17,200 of checks were issued. The bank statement showed that $16,400 of checks cleared the bank in July.
3. In September, deposits per the bank statement totaled $26,700, deposits per books were $26,400, and deposits in transit at September 30 were $2,100.
4. In September, cash disbursements per books were $23,700, checks clearing the bank were $25,000, and outstanding checks at September 30 were $2,100.

There were no bank debit or credit memoranda. No errors were made by either the bank or Dawes Company.

Instructions

Answer the following questions.

(a) In situation (1), what were the deposits in transit at July 31?
(b) In situation (2), what were the outstanding checks at July 31?
(c) In situation (3), what were the deposits in transit at August 31?
(d) In situation (4), what were the outstanding checks at August 31?

Show presentation of cash in financial statements.
(LO 4)

E8-14 Wynn Company has recorded the following items in its financial records.

Cash in bank	$ 42,000
Cash in plant expansion fund	100,000
Cash on hand	12,000
Highly liquid investments	34,000
Petty cash	500
Receivables from customers	89,000
Stock investments	61,000

The highly liquid investments had maturities of 3 months or less when they were purchased. The stock investments will be sold in the next 6 to 12 months. The plant expansion project will begin in 3 years.

Instructions

(a) What amount should Wynn report as "Cash and cash equivalents" on its balance sheet?
(b) Where should the items not included in part (a) be reported on the balance sheet?

PROBLEMS

Identify internal control principles over cash disbursements.

(LO 1, 2)

P8-1A Bolz Office Supply Company recently changed its system of internal control over cash disbursements. The system includes the following features.

Instead of being unnumbered and manually prepared, all checks must now be prenumbered and prepared by using the new accounts payable software purchased by the company. Before a check can be issued, each invoice must have the approval of Kathy Moon, the purchasing agent, and Robin Self, the receiving department supervisor. Checks must be signed by either Jennifer Edwards, the treasurer, or Rich Woodruff, the assistant treasurer. Before signing a check, the signer is expected to compare the amount of the check with the amount on the invoice.

After signing a check, the signer stamps the invoice PAID and inserts within the stamp, the date, check number, and amount of the check. The "paid" invoice is then sent to the accounting department for recording.

Blank checks are stored in a safe in the treasurer's office. The combination to the safe is known only by the treasurer and assistant treasurer. Each month, the bank statement is reconciled with the bank balance per books by the assistant chief accountant. All employees who handle or account for cash are bonded.

Instructions

Identify the internal control principles and their application to cash disbursements of Bolz Office Supply Company.

Journalize and post petty cash fund transactions.

(LO 2)

P8-2A Forney Company maintains a petty cash fund for small expenditures. The following transactions occurred over a 2-month period.

July 1 Established petty cash fund by writing a check on Scranton Bank for $200.

15 Replenished the petty cash fund by writing a check for $196.00. On this date the fund consisted of $4.00 in cash and the following petty cash receipts: freight-out $92.00, postage expense $42.40, entertainment expense $46.60, and miscellaneous expense $11.20.

31 Replenished the petty cash fund by writing a check for $192.00. At this date, the fund consisted of $8.00 in cash and the following petty cash receipts: freight-out $82.10, charitable contributions expense $45.00, postage expense $25.50, and miscellaneous expense $39.40.

Aug. 15 Replenished the petty cash fund by writing a check for $187.00. On this date, the fund consisted of $13.00 in cash and the following petty cash receipts: freight-out $77.60, entertainment expense $43.00, postage expense $33.00, and miscellaneous expense $37.00.

16 Increased the amount of the petty cash fund to $300 by writing a check for $100.

31 Replenished the petty cash fund by writing a check for $284.00. On this date, the fund consisted of $16 in cash and the following petty cash receipts: postage expense $140.00, travel expense $95.60, and freight-out $47.10.

Instructions

(a) Journalize the petty cash transactions.

(b) Post to the Petty Cash account.

(c) What internal control features exist in a petty cash fund?

(a) July 15, Cash short $3.80

(b) Aug. 31 balance $300

Prepare a bank reconciliation and adjusting entries.

(LO 3)

P8-3A On May 31, 2017, Reber Company had a cash balance per books of $6,781.50. The bank statement from New York State Bank on that date showed a balance of $6,404.60. A comparison of the statement with the Cash account revealed the following facts.

1. The statement included a debit memo of $40 for the printing of additional company checks.
2. Cash sales of $836.15 on May 12 were deposited in the bank. The cash receipts journal entry and the deposit slip were incorrectly made for $886.15. The bank credited Reber Company for the correct amount.
3. Outstanding checks at May 31 totaled $576.25. Deposits in transit were $2,416.15.

4. On May 18, the company issued check No. 1181 for $685 to Lynda Carsen on account. The check, which cleared the bank in May, was incorrectly journalized and posted by Reber Company for $658.
5. A $3,000 note receivable was collected by the bank for Reber Company on May 31 plus $80 interest. The bank charged a collection fee of $20. No interest has been accrued on the note.
6. Included with the cancelled checks was a check issued by Stiner Company to Ted Cress for $800 that was incorrectly charged to Reber Company by the bank.
7. On May 31, the bank statement showed an NSF charge of $680 for a check issued by Sue Allison, a customer, to Reber Company on account.

Instructions

(a) Prepare the bank reconciliation at May 31, 2017.
(b) Prepare the necessary adjusting entries for Reber Company at May 31, 2017.

(a) Adjusted cash balance per bank $9,044.50

Prepare a bank reconciliation and adjusting entries from detailed data.

(LO 3)

P8-4A The bank portion of the bank reconciliation for Langer Company at November 30, 2017, was as follows.

LANGER COMPANY
Bank Reconciliation
November 30, 2017

Cash balance per bank			$14,367.90
Add: Deposits in transit			2,530.20
			16,898.10
Less: Outstanding checks			
	Check Number	Check Amount	
	3451	$2,260.40	
	3470	720.10	
	3471	844.50	
	3472	1,426.80	
	3474	1,050.00	6,301.80
Adjusted cash balance per bank			$10,596.30

The adjusted cash balance per bank agreed with the cash balance per books at November 30.

The December bank statement showed the following checks and deposits.

Bank Statement

Checks			Deposits	
Date	**Number**	**Amount**	**Date**	**Amount**
12-1	3451	$ 2,260.40	12-1	$ 2,530.20
12-2	3471	844.50	12-4	1,211.60
12-7	3472	1,426.80	12-8	2,365.10
12-4	3475	1,640.70	12-16	2,672.70
12-8	3476	1,300.00	12-21	2,945.00
12-10	3477	2,130.00	12-26	2,567.30
12-15	3479	3,080.00	12-29	2,836.00
12-27	3480	600.00	12-30	1,025.00
12-30	3482	475.50	Total	$18,152.90
12-29	3483	1,140.00		
12-31	3485	540.80		
	Total	$15,438.70		

The cash records per books for December showed the following.

Cash Payments Journal

Date	Number	Amount	Date	Number	Amount
12-1	3475	$1,640.70	12-20	3482	$ 475.50
12-2	3476	1,300.00	12-22	3483	1,140.00
12-2	3477	2,130.00	12-23	3484	798.00
12-4	3478	621.30	12-24	3485	450.80
12-8	3479	3,080.00	12-30	3486	889.50
12-10	3480	600.00	Total		$13,933.20
12-17	3481	807.40			

Cash Receipts Journal

Date	Amount
12-3	$ 1,211.60
12-7	2,365.10
12-15	2,672.70
12-20	2,954.00
12-25	2,567.30
12-28	2,836.00
12-30	1,025.00
12-31	1,690.40
Total	$17,322.10

The bank statement contained two memoranda:

1. A credit of $5,145 for the collection of a $5,000 note for Langer Company plus interest of $160 and less a collection fee of $15. Langer Company has not accrued any interest on the note.
2. A debit of $572.80 for an NSF check written by L. Rees, a customer. At December 31, the check had not been redeposited in the bank.

At December 31, the cash balance per books was $12,485.20, and the cash balance per the bank statement was $20,154.30. The bank did not make any errors, but two errors were made by Langer Company.

Instructions

(a) Using the four steps in the reconciliation procedure, prepare a bank reconciliation at December 31.

(a) Adjusted balance per books $16,958.40

(b) Prepare the adjusting entries based on the reconciliation. (*Hint:* The correction of any errors pertaining to recording checks should be made to Accounts Payable. The correction of any errors relating to recording cash receipts should be made to Accounts Receivable.)

Prepare a bank reconciliation and adjusting entries.

(LO 3)

P8-5A Rodriguez Company maintains a checking account at the Imura Bank. At July 31, selected data from the ledger balance and the bank statement are shown below.

Cash in Bank

	Per Books	Per Bank
Balance, July 1	$17,600	$15,800
July receipts	81,400	
July credits		83,470
July disbursements	77,150	
July debits		74,756
Balance, July 31	$21,850	$24,514

Analysis of the bank data reveals that the credits consist of $79,000 of July deposits and a credit memorandum of $4,470 for the collection of a $4,400 note plus interest revenue of $70. The July debits per bank consist of checks cleared $74,700 and a debit memorandum of $56 for printing additional company checks.

You also discover the following errors involving July checks. (1) A check for $230 to a creditor on account that cleared the bank in July was journalized and posted as $320. (2) A salary check to an employee for $255 was recorded by the bank for $155.

The June 30 bank reconciliation contained only two reconciling items: deposits in transit $8,000 and outstanding checks of $6,200.

Instructions

(a) Prepare a bank reconciliation at July 31, 2017.

(a) Adjusted balance per books $26,354

(b) Journalize the adjusting entries to be made by Rodriguez Company. Assume that interest on the note has not been accrued.

Identify internal control weaknesses in cash receipts and cash disbursements.

(LO 1, 2)

P8-6A Rondelli Middle School wants to raise money for a new sound system for its auditorium. The primary fund-raising event is a dance at which the famous disc jockey D.J. Sound will play classic and not-so-classic dance tunes. Matt Ballester, the music and theater instructor, has been given the responsibility for coordinating the fund-raising efforts. This is Matt's first experience with fund-raising. He decides to put the eighth-grade choir in charge of the event; he will be a relatively passive observer.

Matt had 500 unnumbered tickets printed for the dance. He left the tickets in a box on his desk and told the choir students to take as many tickets as they thought they could sell for $5 each. In order to ensure that no extra tickets would be floating around, he told them to dispose of any unsold tickets. When the students received payment for the tickets, they were to bring the cash back to Matt and he would put it in a locked box in his desk drawer.

Some of the students were responsible for decorating the gymnasium for the dance. Matt gave each of them a key to the money box and told them that if they took money out to purchase materials, they should put a note in the box saying how much they took and what it was used for. After 2 weeks the money box appeared to be getting full, so Matt asked Jeff Kenney to count the money, prepare a deposit slip, and deposit the money in a bank account Matt had opened.

The day of the dance, Matt wrote a check from the account to pay the DJ. D.J. Sound, however, said that he accepted only cash and did not give receipts. So Matt took $200 out of the cash box and gave it to D.J. At the dance, Matt had Sam Copper working at the entrance to the gymnasium, collecting tickets from students, and selling tickets to those who had not prepurchased them. Matt estimated that 400 students attended the dance.

The following day, Matt closed out the bank account, which had $250 in it, and gave that amount plus the $180 in the cash box to Principal Finke. Principal Finke seemed surprised that, after generating roughly $2,000 in sales, the dance netted only $430 in cash. Matt did not know how to respond.

Instructions

Identify as many internal control weaknesses as you can in this scenario, and suggest how each could be addressed.

COMPREHENSIVE PROBLEM

CP8 On December 1, 2017, Fullerton Company had the following account balances.

	Debit		Credit
Cash	$18,200	Accumulated Depreciation—	
Notes Receivable	2,200	Equipment	$ 3,000
Accounts Receivable	7,500	Accounts Payable	6,100
Inventory	16,000	Owner's Capital	64,400
Prepaid Insurance	1,600		$73,500
Equipment	28,000		
	$73,500		

During December, the company completed the following transactions.

Dec. 7 Received $3,600 cash from customers in payment of account (no discount allowed).
12 Purchased merchandise on account from Vance Co. $12,000, terms 1/10, n/30.
17 Sold merchandise on account $16,000, terms 2/10, n/30. The cost of the merchandise sold was $10,000.
19 Paid salaries $2,200.
22 Paid Vance Co. in full, less discount.
26 Received collections in full, less discounts, from customers billed on December 17.
31 Received $2,700 cash from customers in payment of account (no discount allowed).

Adjustment data:

1. Depreciation $200 per month.
2. Insurance expired $400.

Instructions

(a) Journalize the December transactions. (Assume a perpetual inventory system.)

(b) Enter the December 1 balances in the ledger T-accounts and post the December transactions. Use Cost of Goods Sold, Depreciation Expense, Insurance Expense, Salaries and Wages Expense, Sales Revenue, and Sales Discounts.

(c) The statement from Jackson County Bank on December 31 showed a balance of $26,130. A comparison of the bank statement with the Cash account revealed the following facts.
  1. The bank collected a note receivable of $2,200 for Fullerton Company on December 15.
  2. The December 31 receipts were deposited in a night deposit vault on December 31. These deposits were recorded by the bank in January.
  3. Checks outstanding on December 31 totaled $1,210.
  4. On December 31, the bank statement showed an NSF charge of $680 for a check received by the company from L. Bryan, a customer, on account.

  Prepare a bank reconciliation as of December 31 based on the available information. (*Hint:* The cash balance per books is $26,100. This can be proven by finding the balance in the Cash account from parts (a) and (b).)

(d) Journalize the adjusting entries resulting from the bank reconciliation and adjustment data.
(e) Post the adjusting entries to the ledger T-accounts.
(f) Prepare an adjusted trial balance.
(g) Prepare an income statement for December and a classified balance sheet at December 31.

BROADENING YOUR PERSPECTIVE

FINANCIAL REPORTING AND ANALYSIS

Financial Reporting Problem: Apple Inc.

BYP8-1 The financial statements of Apple Inc. are presented in Appendix A at the end of this textbook. Instructions for accessing and using the company's complete annual report, including the notes to the financial statements, are also provided in Appendix A.

Instructions

(a) What comments, if any, are made about cash in the report of the independent registered public accounting firm?
(b) What data about cash and cash equivalents are shown in the consolidated balance sheet?
(c) In its notes to Consolidated Financial Statements, how does Apple define cash equivalents?
(d) In management's Annual Report on Internal Control over Financial Reporting (Item 9A), what does Apple's management say about internal control?

Comparative Analysis Problem: PepsiCo, Inc. vs. The Coca-Cola Company

BYP8-2 PepsiCo's financial statements are presented in Appendix B. Financial statements of The Coca-Cola Company are presented in Appendix C. Instructions for accessing and using the complete annual reports of PepsiCo and Coca-Cola, including the notes to the financial statements, are also provided in Appendices B and C, respectively.

Instructions

(a) Based on the information contained in these financial statements, determine each of the following for each company:
  (1) Cash and cash equivalents balance at December 28, 2013, for PepsiCo and at December 31, 2013, for Coca-Cola.
  (2) Increase (decrease) in cash and cash equivalents from 2012 to 2013.
  (3) Cash provided by operating activities during the year ended December 2013 (from statement of cash flows).
(b) What conclusions concerning the management of cash can be drawn from these data?

Comparative Analysis Problem: Amazon.com, Inc. vs. Wal-Mart Stores, Inc.

BYP8-3 Amazon.com, Inc.'s financial statements are presented in Appendix D. Financial statements of Wal-Mart Stores, Inc. are presented in Appendix E. Instructions for accessing and using the complete annual reports of Amazon and Wal-Mart, including the notes to the financial statements, are also provided in Appendices D and E, respectively.

Instructions

(a) Based on the information contained in these financial statements, determine each of the following for each company:

(1) Cash and cash equivalents balance at December 31, 2013, for Amazon and at January 31, 2014, for Wal-Mart.

(2) Increase (decrease) in cash and cash equivalents from 2012 to 2013.

(3) Net cash provided by operating activities during the year ended December 31, 2013, for Amazon and January 31, 2014, for Wal-Mart from statement of cash flows.

(b) What conclusions concerning the management of cash can be drawn from these data?

Real-World Focus

BYP8-4 All organizations should have systems of internal control. Universities are no exception. This site discusses the basics of internal control in a university setting.

Address: **www.bc.edu/offices/audit/controls**, or go to **www.wiley.com/college/weygandt**

Steps: Go to the site shown above.

Instructions

The home page of this site provides links to pages that answer critical questions. Use these links to answer the following questions.

(a) In a university setting, who has responsibility for evaluating the adequacy of the system of internal control?

(b) What do reconciliations ensure in the university setting? Who should review the reconciliation?

(c) What are some examples of physical controls?

(d) What are two ways to accomplish inventory counts?

CRITICAL THINKING

Decision-Making Across the Organization

BYP8-5 The board of trustees of a local church is concerned about the internal accounting controls for the offering collections made at weekly services. The trustees ask you to serve on a three-person audit team with the internal auditor of a local college and a CPA who has just joined the church.

At a meeting of the audit team and the board of trustees you learn the following.

1. The church's board of trustees has delegated responsibility for the financial management and audit of the financial records to the finance committee. This group prepares the annual budget and approves major disbursements. It is not involved in collections or recordkeeping. No audit has been made in recent years because the same trusted employee has kept church records and served as financial secretary for 15 years. The church does not carry any fidelity insurance.
2. The collection at the weekly service is taken by a team of ushers who volunteer to serve one month. The ushers take the collection plates to a basement office at the rear of the church. They hand their plates to the head usher and return to the church service. After all plates have been turned in, the head usher counts the cash received. The head usher then places the cash in the church safe along with a notation of the amount counted. The head usher volunteers to serve for 3 months.
3. The next morning the financial secretary opens the safe and recounts the collection. The secretary withholds \$150–\$200 in cash, depending on the cash expenditures expected for the week, and deposits the remainder of the collections in the bank. To facilitate the deposit, church members who contribute by check are asked to make their checks payable to "Cash."
4. Each month, the financial secretary reconciles the bank statement and submits a copy of the reconciliation to the board of trustees. The reconciliations have rarely contained any bank errors and have never shown any errors per books.

Instructions

With the class divided into groups, answer the following.

(a) Indicate the weaknesses in internal accounting control over the handling of collections.

(b) List the improvements in internal control procedures that you plan to make at the next meeting of the audit team for (1) the ushers, (2) the head usher, (3) the financial secretary, and (4) the finance committee.
(c) What church policies should be changed to improve internal control?

Communication Activity

BYP8-6 As a new auditor for the CPA firm of Eaton, Quayle, and Hale, you have been assigned to review the internal controls over mail cash receipts of Pritchard Company. Your review reveals the following. Checks are promptly endorsed "For Deposit Only," but no list of the checks is prepared by the person opening the mail. The mail is opened either by the cashier or by the employee who maintains the accounts receivable records. Mail receipts are deposited in the bank weekly by the cashier.

Instructions
Write a letter to Danny Peak, owner of Pritchard Company, explaining the weaknesses in internal control and your recommendations for improving the system.

Ethics Case

BYP8-7 You are the assistant controller in charge of general ledger accounting at Linbarger Bottling Company. Your company has a large loan from an insurance company. The loan agreement requires that the company's cash account balance be maintained at $200,000 or more, as reported monthly.

At June 30, the cash balance is $80,000, which you report to Lisa Infante, the financial vice president. Lisa excitedly instructs you to keep the cash receipts book open for one additional day for purposes of the June 30 report to the insurance company. Lisa says, "If we don't get that cash balance over $200,000, we'll default on our loan agreement. They could close us down, put us all out of our jobs!" Lisa continues, "I talked to Oconto Distributors (one of Linbarger's largest customers) this morning. They said they sent us a check for $150,000 yesterday. We should receive it tomorrow. If we include just that one check in our cash balance, we'll be in the clear. It's in the mail!"

Instructions
(a) Who will suffer negative effects if you do not comply with Lisa Infante's instructions? Who will suffer if you do comply?
(b) What are the ethical considerations in this case?
(c) What alternatives do you have?

All About You

BYP8-8 The print and electronic media are full of stories about potential security risks that may arise from your computer or smartphone. It is important to keep in mind, however, that there are also many other ways that your identity can be stolen. The federal government provides many resources to help protect you from identity thieves.

Instructions
Go to **http://onguardonline.gov/idtheft.html**, click **Video and Media**, and then click on **ID Theft Faceoff**. Complete the quiz provided there.

FASB Codification Activity

BYP8-9 If your school has a subscription to the FASB Codification, go to **http://aaahq.org/ascLogin.cfm** to log in and prepare responses to the following.

(a) How is cash defined in the Codification?
(b) How are cash equivalents defined in the Codification?
(c) What are the disclosure requirements related to cash and cash equivalents?

A Look at IFRS

LEARNING OBJECTIVE 5 **Compare the accounting for fraud, internal control, and cash under GAAP and IFRS.**

Fraud can occur anywhere. Because the three main factors that contribute to fraud are universal in nature, the principles of internal control activities are used globally by companies. While Sarbanes-Oxley (SOX) does not apply to international companies, most large international companies have internal controls similar to those indicated in the chapter. IFRS and GAAP are also very similar in accounting for cash. *IAS No. 1 (revised),* "Presentation of Financial Statements," is the only standard that discusses issues specifically related to cash.

Relevant Facts

Following are the key similarities and differences between GAAP and IFRS related to fraud, internal control, and cash.

Similarities

- The fraud triangle discussed in this chapter is applicable to all international companies. Some of the major frauds on an international basis are Parmalat (Italy), Royal Ahold (the Netherlands), and Satyam Computer Services (India).
- Rising economic crime poses a growing threat to companies, with nearly one-third of all organizations worldwide being victims of fraud in a recent 12-month period.
- Accounting scandals both in the United States and internationally have re-ignited the debate over the relative merits of GAAP, which takes a "rules-based" approach to accounting, versus IFRS, which takes a "principles-based" approach. The FASB announced that it intends to introduce more principles-based standards.
- On a lighter note, at one time the Ig Nobel Prize in Economics went to the CEOs of those companies involved in the corporate accounting scandals of that year for "adapting the mathematical concept of imaginary numbers for use in the business world." A parody of the Nobel Prizes, the Ig Nobel Prizes (read Ignoble, as not noble) are given each year in early October for 10 achievements that "first make people laugh, and then make them think." Organized by the scientific humor magazine *Annals of Improbable Research* (*AIR*), they are presented by a group that includes genuine Nobel laureates at a ceremony at Harvard University's Sanders Theater. (See **en.wikipedia.org/wiki/Ig_Nobel_Prize**.)
- The accounting and internal control procedures related to cash are essentially the same under both IFRS and this textbook. In addition, the definition used for cash equivalents is the same.
- Most companies report cash and cash equivalents together under IFRS, as shown in this textbook. In addition, IFRS follows the same accounting policies related to the reporting of restricted cash.

Differences

- The SOX internal control standards apply only to companies listed on U.S. exchanges. There is continuing debate over whether foreign issuers should have to comply with this extra layer of regulation.

Looking to the Future

Ethics has become a very important aspect of reporting. Different cultures have different perspectives on bribery and other questionable activities, and consequently penalties for engaging in such activities vary considerably across countries.

High-quality international accounting requires both high-quality accounting standards and high-quality auditing. Similar to the convergence of GAAP and IFRS, there is movement to improve international auditing standards. The International Auditing and Assurance Standards Board (IAASB) functions as an independent standard-setting body. It works to establish high-quality auditing and assurance and quality-control standards throughout the world. Whether the IAASB adopts internal control provisions similar to those in SOX remains to be seen. You can follow developments in the international audit arena at **http://www.ifac.org/iaasb/**.

IFRS Practice

IFRS Self-Test Questions

1. Non-U.S companies that follow IFRS:
(a) do not normally use the principles of internal control activities described in this textbook.
(b) often offset cash with accounts payable on the balance sheet.
(c) are not required to follow SOX.
(d) None of the above.

2. The Sarbanes-Oxley Act applies to:
(a) all U.S. companies listed on U.S. exchanges.
(b) all companies that list stock on any stock exchange in any country.
(c) all European companies listed on European exchanges.
(d) Both (a) and (c).

3. High-quality international accounting requires both high-quality accounting standards and:
(a) a reconsideration of SOX to make it less onerous.
(b) high-quality auditing standards.
(c) government intervention to ensure that the public interest is protected.
(d) the development of new principles of internal control activities.

IFRS Exercise

IFRS8-1 Some people argue that the internal control requirements of the Sarbanes-Oxley Act (SOX) put U.S. companies at a competitive disadvantage to companies outside the United States. Discuss the competitive implications (both pros and cons) of SOX.

International Financial Reporting Problem: Louis Vuitton

IFRS8–2 The financial statements of Louis Vuitton are presented in Appendix F. Instructions for accessing and using the company's complete annual report, including the notes to its financial statements, are also provided in Appendix F.

Instructions
Using the notes to the company's financial statements, what are Louis Vuitton's accounting policies related to cash and cash equivalents?

Answers to IFRS Self-Test Questions

1. c **2.** a **3.** b

Chapter 9 Accounting for Receivables

"Sometimes you have to know when to be very tough, and sometimes you can give them a bit of a break," said Vivi Su. She wasn't talking about her children but about the customers of a subsidiary of former pharmaceutical company Whitehall-Robins, where she worked as supervisor of credit and collections.

For example, while the company's regular terms were 1/15, n/30 (1% discount if paid within 15 days), a customer might have asked for and received a few days of grace and still got the discount. Or a customer might have placed orders above its credit limit, in which case, depending on its payment history and the circumstances, Ms. Su might have authorized shipment of the goods anyway.

"It's not about drawing a line in the sand, and that's all," she explained. "You want a good relationship with your customers—but you also need to bring in the money."

"The money," in Whitehall-Robins' case, amounted to some $170 million in sales a year. Nearly all of it came in through the credit accounts Ms. Su managed. The process started with the decision to grant a customer an account in the first place. The sales rep gave the customer a credit application. "My department reviews this application very carefully; a customer needs to supply three good references, and we also run a check with a credit firm like Equifax. If we accept them, then based on their size and history, we assign a credit limit," Ms. Su explained.

Once accounts were established, "I get an aging report every single day," said Ms. Su. "The rule of thumb is that we should always have at least 85% of receivables current—meaning they were billed less than 30 days ago," she continued. "But we try to do even better than that—I like to see 90%."

At 15 days overdue, Whitehall-Robins phoned the client. After 45 days, Ms. Su noted, "I send a letter. Then a second notice is sent in writing. After the third and final notice, the client has 10 days to pay, and then I hand it over to a collection agency, and it's out of my hands."

Ms. Su's boss, Terry Norton, recorded an estimate for bad debts every year, based on a percentage of receivables. The percentage depended on the current aging history. He also calculated and monitored the company's accounts receivable turnover, which the company reported in its financial statements.

Ms. Su knew that she and Mr. Norton were crucial to the profitability of Whitehall-Robins. "Receivables are generally the second-largest asset of any company (after its capital assets)," she pointed out. "So it's no wonder we keep a very close eye on them."

LEARNING OBJECTIVES

1. **Explain how companies recognize accounts receivable.**
2. **Describe how companies value accounts receivable and record their disposition.**
3. **Explain how companies recognize notes receivable.**
4. **Describe how companies value notes receivable, record their disposition, and present and analyze receivables.**

LEARNING OBJECTIVE 1

Explain how companies recognize accounts receivable.

Types of Receivables

The term **receivables** refers to amounts due from individuals and companies. Receivables are claims that are expected to be collected in cash. The management of receivables is a very important activity for any company that sells goods or services on credit.

Receivables are important because they represent one of a company's most liquid assets. For many companies, receivables are also one of the largest assets. For example, receivables represent 13.7% of the current assets of pharmaceutical giant **Rite Aid**. Illustration 9-1 lists receivables as a percentage of total assets for five other well-known companies in a recent year.

Illustration 9-1
Receivables as a percentage of assets

Company	Receivables as a Percentage of Total Assets
Ford Motor Company	43.2%
General Electric	41.5
Minnesota Mining and Manufacturing Company (3M)	12.7
DuPont Co.	11.7
Intel Corporation	3.9

The relative significance of a company's receivables as a percentage of its assets depends on various factors: its industry, the time of year, whether it extends long-term financing, and its credit policies. To reflect important differences among receivables, they are frequently classified as (1) accounts receivable, (2) notes receivable, and (3) other receivables.

Accounts receivable are amounts customers owe on account. They result from the sale of goods and services. Companies generally expect to collect accounts receivable within 30 to 60 days. They are usually the most significant type of claim held by a company.

Notes receivable are a written promise (as evidenced by a formal instrument) for amounts to be received. The note normally requires the collection of interest and extends for time periods of 60–90 days or longer. Notes and accounts receivable that result from sales transactions are often called **trade receivables**.

Other receivables include nontrade receivables such as interest receivable, loans to company officers, advances to employees, and income taxes refundable. These do not generally result from the operations of the business. Therefore, they are generally classified and reported as separate items in the balance sheet.

Recognizing Accounts Receivable

Recognizing accounts receivable is relatively straightforward. A service organization records a receivable when it performs service on account. A merchandiser records accounts receivable at the point of sale of merchandise on account. When a merchandiser sells goods, it increases (debits) Accounts Receivable and increases (credits) Sales Revenue.

The seller may offer terms that encourage early payment by providing a discount. Sales returns also reduce receivables. The buyer might find some of the goods unacceptable and choose to return the unwanted goods.

To review, assume that Jordache Co. on July 1, 2017, sells merchandise on account to Polo Company for $1,000, terms 2/10, n/30. On July 5, Polo returns merchandise with a sales price of $100 to Jordache Co. On July 11, Jordache receives payment from Polo Company for the balance due. The journal entries to record these transactions on the books of Jordache Co. are as follows. **(Cost of goods sold entries are omitted.)**

July 1	Accounts Receivable—Polo Company	1,000	
	Sales Revenue		1,000
	(To record sales on account)		
July 5	Sales Returns and Allowances	100	
	Accounts Receivable—Polo Company		100
	(To record merchandise returned)		
July 11	Cash ($900 − $18)	882	
	Sales Discounts ($900 × 0.02)	18	
	Accounts Receivable—Polo Company		900
	(To record collection of accounts receivable)		

Some retailers issue their own credit cards. When you use a retailer's credit card (**JCPenney**, for example), the retailer charges interest on the balance due if not paid within a specified period (usually 25–30 days).

To illustrate, assume that you use your JCPenney Company credit card to purchase clothing with a sales price of $300 on June 1, 2017. JCPenney will increase (debit) Accounts Receivable for $300 and increase (credit) Sales Revenue for $300 (cost of goods sold entry omitted) as follows.

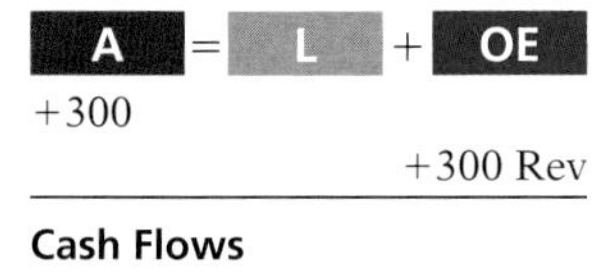

June 1	Accounts Receivable	300	
	Sales Revenue		300
	(To record sale of merchandise)		

Assuming that you owe $300 at the end of the month and JCPenney charges 1.5% per month on the balance due, the adjusting entry that JCPenney makes to record interest revenue of $4.50 ($300 × 1.5%) on June 30 is as follows.

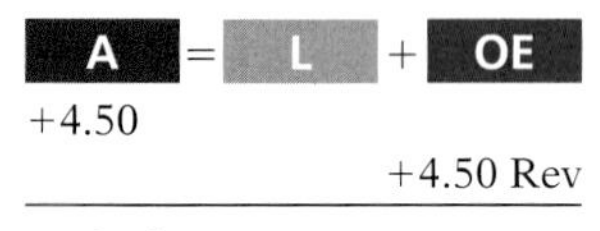

June 30	Accounts Receivable	4.50	
	Interest Revenue		4.50
	(To record interest on amount due)		

Interest revenue is often substantial for many retailers.

ANATOMY OF A FRAUD

Tasanee was the accounts receivable clerk for a large nonprofit foundation that provided performance and exhibition space for the performing and visual arts. Her responsibilities included activities normally assigned to an accounts receivable clerk, such as recording revenues from various sources (donations, facility rental fees, ticket revenue, and bar receipts). However, she was also responsible for handling all cash and checks from the time they were received until the time she deposited them, as well as preparing the bank reconciliation. Tasanee took advantage of her situation by falsifying bank deposits and bank reconciliations so that she could steal cash from the bar receipts. Since nobody else logged the donations or matched the donation receipts to pledges prior to Tasanee receiving them, she was able to offset the cash that was stolen against donations that she received but didn't record. Her crime was made easier by the fact that her boss, the company's controller, only did a very superficial review of the bank reconciliation and thus didn't notice that some numbers had been cut out from other documents and taped onto the bank reconciliation.

Total take: $1.5 million

THE MISSING CONTROLS

Segregation of duties. The foundation should not have allowed an accounts receivable clerk, whose job was to record receivables, to also handle cash, record cash, make deposits, and especially prepare the bank reconciliation.

Independent internal verification. The controller was supposed to perform a thorough review of the bank reconciliation. Because he did not, he was terminated from his position.

Source: Adapted from Wells, *Fraud Casebook* (2007), pp. 183–194.

LEARNING OBJECTIVE 

Describe how companies value accounts receivable and record their disposition.

Valuing Accounts Receivable

Once companies record receivables in the accounts, the next question is: How should they report receivables in the financial statements? Companies report accounts receivable on the balance sheet as an asset. But determining the **amount** to report is sometimes difficult because some receivables will become uncollectible.

Each customer must satisfy the credit requirements of the seller before the credit sale is approved. Inevitably, though, some accounts receivable become uncollectible. For example, a customer may not be able to pay because of a decline in its sales revenue due to a downturn in the economy. Similarly, individuals may be laid off from their jobs or faced with unexpected hospital bills. Companies record credit losses as **Bad Debt Expense** (or Uncollectible Accounts Expense). Such losses are a normal and necessary risk of doing business on a credit basis.

Terminology
You will sometimes see *Bad Debt Expense* called *Uncollectible Accounts Expense.*

When U.S. home prices fell, home foreclosures rose, and the economy slowed as a result of the financial crises of 2008, lenders experienced huge increases in their bad debt expense. For example, during one quarter **Wachovia** (a large U.S. bank now owned by **Wells Fargo**) increased bad debt expense from $108 million to $408 million. Similarly, **American Express** increased its bad debt expense by 70%.

Two methods are used in accounting for uncollectible accounts: (1) the direct write-off method and (2) the allowance method. The following sections explain these methods.

DIRECT WRITE-OFF METHOD FOR UNCOLLECTIBLE ACCOUNTS

Under the **direct write-off method**, when a company determines a particular account to be uncollectible, it charges the loss to Bad Debt Expense. Assume, for example, that Warden Co. writes off as uncollectible M. E. Doran's $200 balance on December 12. Warden's entry is as follows.

Dec. 12	Bad Debt Expense	200	
	Accounts Receivable—M. E. Doran		200
	(To record write-off of M. E. Doran account)		

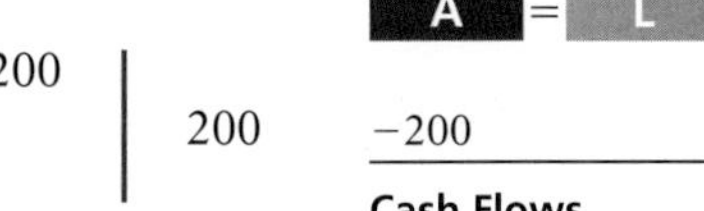

Cash Flows
no effect

Under this method, Bad Debt Expense will show only **actual losses** from uncollectibles. The company will report accounts receivable at its gross amount.

Although this method is simple, its use can reduce the usefulness of both the income statement and balance sheet. Consider the following example. Assume that in 2017, Quick Buck Computer Company decided it could increase its revenues by offering computers to college students without requiring any money down and with no credit-approval process. On campuses across the country, it distributed one million computers with a selling price of $800 each. This increased Quick Buck's revenues and receivables by $800 million. The promotion was a huge success! The 2017 balance sheet and income statement looked great. Unfortunately, during 2018, nearly 40% of the customers defaulted on their loans. This made the 2018 income statement and balance sheet look terrible. Illustration 9-2 shows the effect of these events on the financial statements if the direct write-off method is used.

Illustration 9-2
Effects of direct write-off method

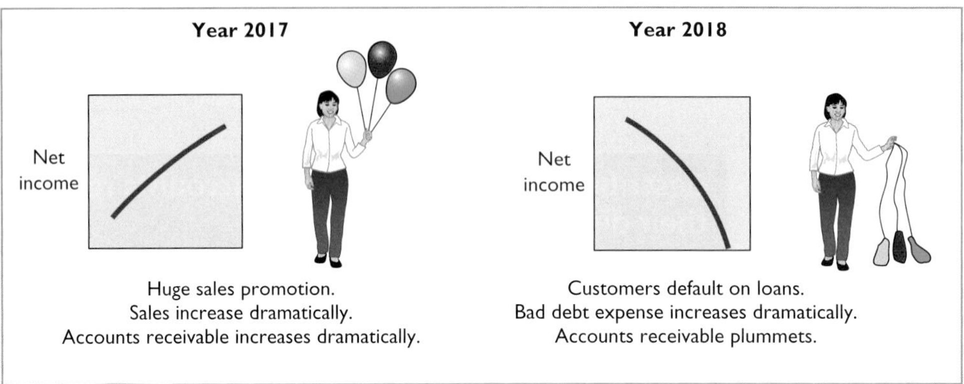

Under the direct write-off method, companies often record bad debt expense in a period different from the period in which they record the revenue. The method does not attempt to match bad debt expense to sales revenue in the income statement. Nor does the direct write-off method show accounts receivable in the balance sheet at the amount the company actually expects to receive. **Consequently, unless bad debt losses are insignificant, the direct write-off method is not acceptable for financial reporting purposes.**

ALLOWANCE METHOD FOR UNCOLLECTIBLE ACCOUNTS

The **allowance method** of accounting for bad debts involves estimating uncollectible accounts at the end of each period. This provides better matching on the income statement. It also ensures that companies state receivables on the balance sheet at their cash (net) realizable value. **Cash (net) realizable value** is the net amount the company expects to receive in cash. It excludes amounts that the company estimates it will not collect. Thus, this method reduces receivables in the balance sheet by the amount of estimated uncollectible receivables.

GAAP requires the allowance method for financial reporting purposes when bad debts are material in amount. This method has three essential features:

1. Companies **estimate** uncollectible accounts receivable. They match this estimated expense **against revenues** in the same accounting period in which they record the revenues.
2. Companies debit estimated uncollectibles to Bad Debt Expense and credit them to Allowance for Doubtful Accounts through an adjusting entry at the end of each period. Allowance for Doubtful Accounts is a contra account to Accounts Receivable.
3. When companies write off a specific account, they debit actual uncollectibles to Allowance for Doubtful Accounts and credit that amount to Accounts Receivable.

RECORDING ESTIMATED UNCOLLECTIBLES To illustrate the allowance method, assume that Hampson Furniture has credit sales of $1,200,000 in 2017. Of this amount, $200,000 remains uncollected at December 31. The credit manager estimates that $12,000 of these sales will be uncollectible. The adjusting entry to record the estimated uncollectibles increases (debits) Bad Debt Expense and increases (credits) Allowance for Doubtful Accounts, as follows.

Dec. 31	Bad Debt Expense	12,000	
	Allowance for Doubtful Accounts		12,000
	(To record estimate of uncollectible accounts)		

A = L + OE
−12,000 | −12,000 Exp
Cash Flows
no effect

Hampson reports Bad Debt Expense in the income statement as an operating expense (usually as a selling expense). Thus, the estimated uncollectibles are matched with sales in 2017. Hampson records the expense in the same year it made the sales.

Allowance for Doubtful Accounts shows the estimated amount of claims on customers that the company expects will become uncollectible in the future. Companies use a contra account instead of a direct credit to Accounts Receivable because they do not know which customers will not pay. The credit balance in the allowance account will absorb the specific write-offs when they occur. As Illustration 9-3 shows, the company deducts the allowance account from accounts receivable in the current assets section of the balance sheet.

Illustration 9-3
Presentation of allowance for doubtful accounts

HAMPSON FURNITURE Balance Sheet (partial)		
Current assets		
Cash		$ 14,800
Accounts receivable	**$200,000**	
Less: Allowance for doubtful accounts	**12,000**	**188,000**
Inventory		310,000
Supplies		25,000
Total current assets		$537,800

The amount of $188,000 in Illustration 9-3 represents the expected **cash realizable value** of the accounts receivable at the statement date. **Companies do not close Allowance for Doubtful Accounts at the end of the fiscal year.**

RECORDING THE WRITE-OFF OF AN UNCOLLECTIBLE ACCOUNT As described in the chapter opening story, companies use various methods of collecting past-due accounts, such as letters, calls, and legal action. When they have exhausted all means of collecting a past-due account and collection appears impossible, the company writes off the account. In the credit card industry, for example, it is standard practice to write off accounts that are 210 days past due. To prevent premature or unauthorized write-offs, authorized management personnel should formally approve each write-off. To maintain segregation of duties, the employee authorized to write off accounts should not have daily responsibilities related to cash or receivables.

To illustrate a receivables write-off, assume that the financial vice president of Hampson Furniture authorizes a write-off of the $500 balance owed by R. A. Ware on March 1, 2018. The entry to record the write-off is as follows.

Mar. 1	Allowance for Doubtful Accounts	500	
	Accounts Receivable—R. A. Ware		500
	(Write-off of R. A. Ware account)		

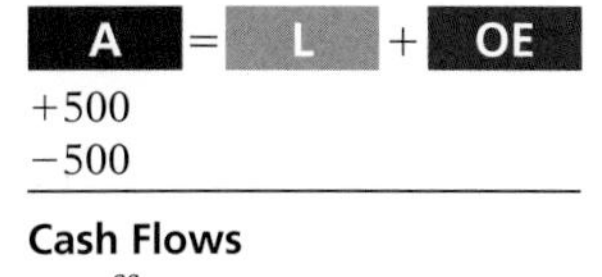

Bad Debt Expense does not increase when the write-off occurs. **Under the allowance method, companies debit every bad debt write-off to the allowance account rather than to Bad Debt Expense.** A debit to Bad Debt Expense would be incorrect because the company has already recognized the expense when it made the adjusting entry for estimated bad debts. Instead, the entry to record the write-off of an uncollectible account reduces both Accounts Receivable and Allowance for Doubtful Accounts. After posting, the general ledger accounts appear as shown in Illustration 9-4 (page 332).

Illustration 9-4
General ledger balances after write-off

Accounts Receivable			
Jan. 1 Bal.	200,000	Mar. 1	**500**
Mar. 1 Bal.	199,500		

Allowance for Doubtful Accounts			
Mar. 1	**500**	Jan. 1 Bal.	12,000
		Mar. 1 Bal.	11,500

A write-off affects **only balance sheet accounts**—not income statement accounts. The write-off of the account reduces both Accounts Receivable and Allowance for Doubtful Accounts. Cash realizable value in the balance sheet, therefore, remains the same, as Illustration 9-5 shows.

Illustration 9-5
Cash realizable value comparison

	Before Write-Off	**After Write-Off**
Accounts receivable	$ 200,000	$ 199,500
Allowance for doubtful accounts	12,000	11,500
Cash realizable value	**$188,000**	**$188,000**

RECOVERY OF AN UNCOLLECTIBLE ACCOUNT Occasionally, a company collects from a customer after it has written off the account as uncollectible. The company makes two entries to record the recovery of a bad debt. (1) It reverses the entry made in writing off the account. This reinstates the customer's account. (2) It journalizes the collection in the usual manner.

To illustrate, assume that on July 1, R. A. Ware pays the $500 amount that Hampson had written off on March 1. Hampson makes the following entries.

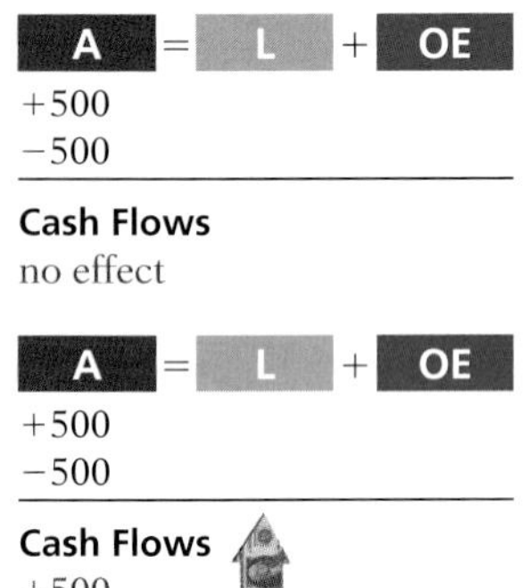

(1)

July 1	Accounts Receivable—R. A. Ware	500	
	Allowance for Doubtful Accounts		500
	(To reverse write-off of R. A. Ware account)		

(2)

July 1	Cash	500	
	Accounts Receivable—R. A. Ware		500
	(To record collection from R. A. Ware)		

Note that the recovery of a bad debt, like the write-off of a bad debt, affects **only balance sheet accounts**. The net effect of the two entries above is a debit to Cash and a credit to Allowance for Doubtful Accounts for $500. Accounts Receivable and Allowance for Doubtful Accounts both increase in entry (1) for two reasons. First, the company made an error in judgment when it wrote off the account receivable. Second, after R. A. Ware did pay, Accounts Receivable in the general ledger and Ware's account in the subsidiary ledger should show the collection for possible future credit purposes.

ESTIMATING THE ALLOWANCE For Hampson Furniture in Illustration 9-3, the amount of the expected uncollectibles was given. However, in "real life," companies must estimate that amount when they use the allowance method. Two bases are used to determine this amount: **(1) percentage of sales** and **(2) percentage of receivables**. Both bases are generally accepted. The choice is a management decision. It depends on the relative emphasis that management wishes to give to expenses and revenues on the one hand or to cash realizable value of the accounts receivable on the other. The choice is whether to emphasize income statement or balance sheet relationships. Illustration 9-6 compares the two bases.

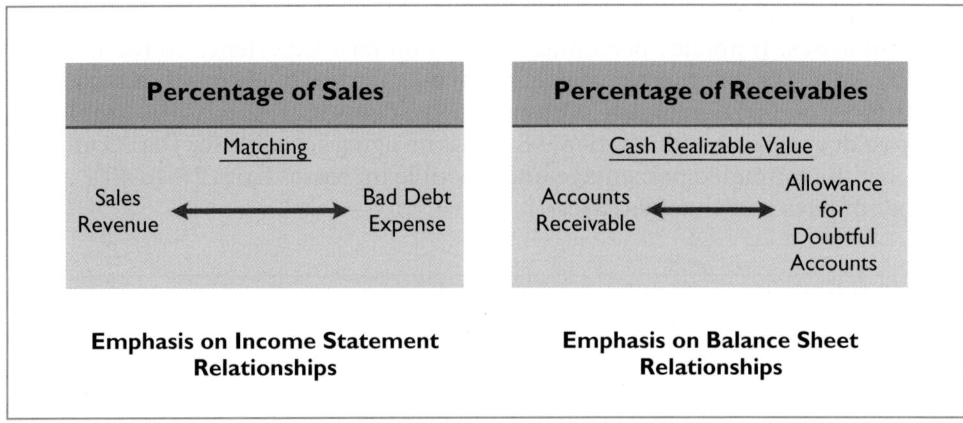

Illustration 9-6
Comparison of bases for estimating uncollectibles

The percentage-of-sales basis results in a better matching of expenses with revenues—an income statement viewpoint. The percentage-of-receivables basis produces the better estimate of cash realizable value—a balance sheet viewpoint. Under both bases, the company must determine its past experience with bad debt losses.

Percentage-of-Sales In the **percentage-of-sales basis**, management estimates what percentage of credit sales will be uncollectible. This percentage is based on past experience and anticipated credit policy.

The company applies this percentage to either total credit sales or net credit sales of the current year. To illustrate, assume that Gonzalez Company elects to use the percentage-of-sales basis. It concludes that 1% of net credit sales will become uncollectible. If net credit sales for 2017 are $800,000, the estimated bad debt expense is $8,000 (1% × $800,000). The adjusting entry is as follows.

Date	Account	Debit	Credit
Dec. 31	Bad Debt Expense	8,000	
	Allowance for Doubtful Accounts		8,000
	(To record estimated bad debts for year)		

A	=	L	+	OE
				−8,000 Exp
−8,000				

Cash Flows
no effect

After the adjusting entry is posted, assuming the allowance account already has a credit balance of $1,723, the accounts of Gonzalez Company will show the following.

Illustration 9-7
Bad debt accounts after posting

Bad Debt Expense		Allowance for Doubtful Accounts	
Dec. 31 Adj. **8,000**			Jan. 1 Bal. 1,723
			Dec. 31 Adj. **8,000**
			Dec. 31 Bal. 9,723

This basis of estimating uncollectibles emphasizes the matching of expenses with revenues. As a result, Bad Debt Expense will show a direct percentage relationship to the sales base on which it is computed. **When the company makes the adjusting entry, it disregards the existing balance in Allowance for Doubtful Accounts.** The adjusted balance in this account should be a reasonable approximation of the realizable value of the receivables. If actual write-offs differ significantly from the amount estimated, the company should modify the percentage for future years.

Percentage-of-Receivables Under the **percentage-of-receivables basis**, management estimates what percentage of receivables will result in losses from uncollectible accounts. The company prepares an **aging schedule**, in which it classifies customer balances by the length of time they have been unpaid. Because of its emphasis on time, the analysis is often called **aging the accounts receivable**. In the chapter opening story, **Whitehall-Robins** prepared an aging report daily.

After the company arranges the accounts by age, it determines the expected bad debt losses. It applies percentages based on past experience to the totals in each category. The longer a receivable is past due, the less likely it is to be collected. Thus, the estimated percentage of uncollectible debts increases as the number of days past due increases. Illustration 9-8 shows an aging schedule for Dart Company. Note that the estimated percentage uncollectible increases from 2% to 40% as the number of days past due increases.

Illustration 9-8
Aging schedule

Worksheet.xls

	A	B	C	D	E	F	G
1				Number of Days Past Due			
2			Not				
3	Customer	Total	Yet Due	1–30	31–60	61–90	Over 90
4	T. E. Adert	$ 600		$ 300		$ 200	$ 100
5	R. C. Bortz	300	$ 300				
6	B. A. Carl	450		200	$ 250		
7	O. L. Diker	700	500			200	
8	T. O. Ebbet	600			300		300
9	Others	36,950	26,200	5,200	2,450	1,600	1,500
10		$39,600	$27,000	$5,700	$3,000	$2,000	$1,900
11	Estimated Percentage Uncollectible		2%	4%	10%	20%	40%
12	Total Estimated Bad Debts	$ 2,228	$ 540	$ 228	$ 300	$ 400	$ 760
13							

Total estimated bad debts for Dart Company ($2,228) represent the amount of existing customer claims the company expects will become uncollectible in the future. This amount represents the **required balance** in Allowance for Doubtful Accounts at the balance sheet date. **The amount of the bad debt adjusting entry is the difference between the required balance and the existing balance in the allowance account.** If the trial balance shows Allowance for Doubtful Accounts with a credit balance of $528, the company will make an adjusting entry for $1,700 ($2,228 − $528), as shown here.

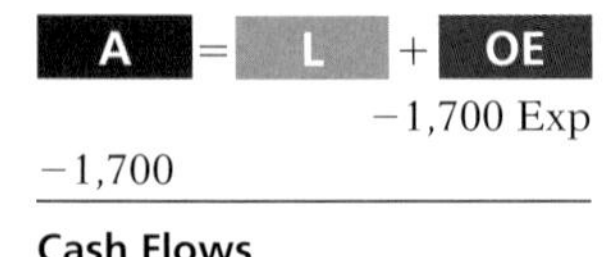

Cash Flows
no effect

Dec. 31	Bad Debt Expense	1,700	
	Allowance for Doubtful Accounts		1,700
	(To adjust allowance account to total estimated uncollectibles)		

After Dart posts its adjusting entry, its accounts will appear as follows.

Illustration 9-9
Bad debt accounts after posting

Bad Debt Expense		Allowance for Doubtful Accounts	
Dec. 31 Adj. **1,700**			Bal. 528
			Dec. 31 Adj. **1,700**
			Bal. 2,228

Allowance for Doubtful Accounts	
Dec. 31 **Unadj.** Bal. 500	Dec. 31 **Adj.** 2,728
	Dec. 31 Bal. 2,228

Occasionally, the allowance account will have a **debit balance** prior to adjustment. This occurs when write-offs during the year have exceeded previous provisions for bad debts. In such a case, the company **adds the debit balance to the required balance** when it makes the adjusting entry. Thus, if there had been a $500 debit balance in the allowance account before adjustment, the adjusting entry would have been for $2,728 ($2,228 + $500) to arrive at a credit balance of $2,228 (see T-account in margin). The percentage-of-receivables basis will normally result in the better approximation of cash realizable value.

Disposing of Accounts Receivable

In the normal course of events, companies collect accounts receivable in cash and remove the receivables from the books. However, as credit sales and receivables have grown in significance, the "normal course of events" has changed. Companies now frequently sell their receivables to another company for cash, thereby shortening the cash-to-cash operating cycle.

Companies sell receivables for two major reasons. First, **they may be the only reasonable source of cash**. When money is tight, companies may not be able to borrow money in the usual credit markets. Or if money is available, the cost of borrowing may be prohibitive.

A second reason for selling receivables is that **billing and collection are often time-consuming and costly**. It is often easier for a retailer to sell the receivables to another party with expertise in billing and collection matters. Credit card companies such as MasterCard, Visa, and Discover specialize in billing and collecting accounts receivable.

SALE OF RECEIVABLES

A common sale of receivables is a sale to a factor. A **factor** is a finance company or bank that buys receivables from businesses and then collects the payments directly from the customers. Factoring is a multibillion dollar business.

Factoring arrangements vary widely. Typically, the factor charges a commission to the company that is selling the receivables. This fee ranges from 1–3% of the amount of receivables purchased. To illustrate, assume that Hendredon Furniture factors $600,000 of receivables to Federal Factors. Federal Factors assesses a service charge of 2% of the amount of receivables sold. The journal entry to record the sale by Hendredon Furniture on April 2, 2017, is as follows.

Apr. 2	Cash	588,000	
	Service Charge Expense (2% × $600,000)	12,000	
	Accounts Receivable		600,000
	(To record the sale of accounts receivable)		

A	=	L	+	OE
+588,000				
				−12,000 Exp
−600,000				

Cash Flows
+588,000

If Hendredon often sells its receivables, it records the service charge expense as a selling expense. If the company infrequently sells receivables, it may report this amount in the "Other expenses and losses" section of the income statement.

CREDIT CARD SALES

Over one billion credit cards are in use in the United States—more than three credit cards for every man, woman, and child in this country. Visa, MasterCard, and American Express are the national credit cards that most individuals use. Three parties are involved when national credit cards are used in retail sales: (1) the credit card issuer, who is independent of the retailer; (2) the retailer; and (3) the customer. A retailer's acceptance of a national credit card is another form of selling (factoring) the receivable.

Illustration 9-10 (page 336) shows the major advantages of national credit cards to the retailer. In exchange for these advantages, the retailer pays the credit card issuer a fee of 2–6% of the invoice price for its services.

Illustration 9-10
Advantages of credit cards to the retailer

ACCOUNTING FOR CREDIT CARD SALES The retailer generally considers sales from the use of national credit card sales as **cash sales**. The retailer must pay to the bank that issues the card a fee for processing the transactions. The retailer records the credit card slips in a similar manner as checks deposited from a cash sale.

To illustrate, Anita Ferreri purchases $1,000 of compact discs for her restaurant from Karen Kerr Music Co., using her Visa First Bank Card. First Bank charges a service fee of 3%. The entry to record this transaction by Karen Kerr Music on March 22, 2017, is as follows.

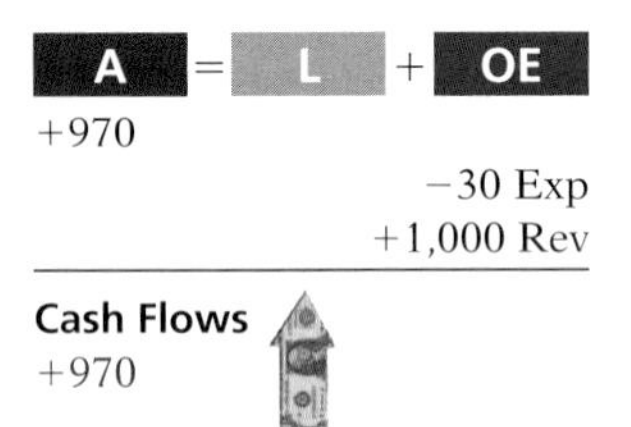

Mar. 22	Cash	970	
	Service Charge Expense	30	
	Sales Revenue		1,000
	(To record Visa credit card sales)		

LEARNING OBJECTIVE 3

Explain how companies recognize notes receivable.

Companies may also grant credit in exchange for a formal credit instrument known as a promissory note. A **promissory note** is a written promise to pay a specified amount of money on demand or at a definite time. Promissory notes may be used (1) when individuals and companies lend or borrow money, (2) when the amount of the transaction and the credit period exceed normal limits, or (3) in settlement of accounts receivable.

In a promissory note, the party making the promise to pay is called the **maker**. The party to whom payment is to be made is called the **payee**. The note may specifically identify the payee by name or may designate the payee simply as the bearer of the note.

In the note shown in Illustration 9-11, Calhoun Company is the maker and Wilma Company is the payee. To Wilma Company, the promissory note is a note receivable. To Calhoun Company, it is a note payable.

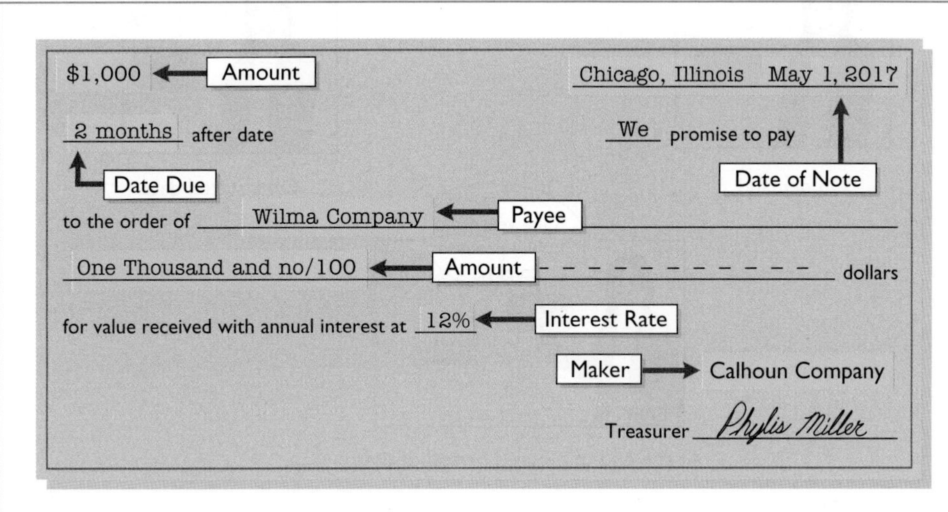

Illustration 9-11
Promissory note

Notes receivable give the holder a stronger legal claim to assets than do accounts receivable. Like accounts receivable, notes receivable can be readily sold to another party. Promissory notes are negotiable instruments (as are checks), which means that they can be transferred to another party by endorsement.

Companies frequently accept notes receivable from customers who need to extend the payment of an outstanding account receivable. They often require such notes from high-risk customers. In some industries (such as the pleasure and sport boat industry), all credit sales are supported by notes. The majority of notes, however, originate from loans.

The basic issues in accounting for notes receivable are the same as those for accounts receivable. On the following pages, we look at these issues. Before we do, however, we need to consider two issues that do not apply to accounts receivable: determining the maturity date and computing interest.

Determining the Maturity Date

When the life of a note is expressed in terms of months, you find the date when it matures by counting the months from the date of issue. For example, the maturity date of a three-month note dated May 1 is August 1. A note drawn on the last day of a month matures on the last day of a subsequent month. That is, a July 31 note due in two months matures on September 30.

When the due date is stated in terms of days, you need to count the exact number of days to determine the maturity date. In counting, **omit the date the note is issued but include the due date**. For example, the maturity date of a 60-day note dated July 17 is September 15, computed as follows.

Illustration 9-12
Computation of maturity date

Term of note		60 days
July (31−17)	14	
August	31	45
Maturity date: September		**15**

Illustration 9-13 shows three ways of stating the maturity date of a promissory note.

Illustration 9-13
Maturity date of different notes

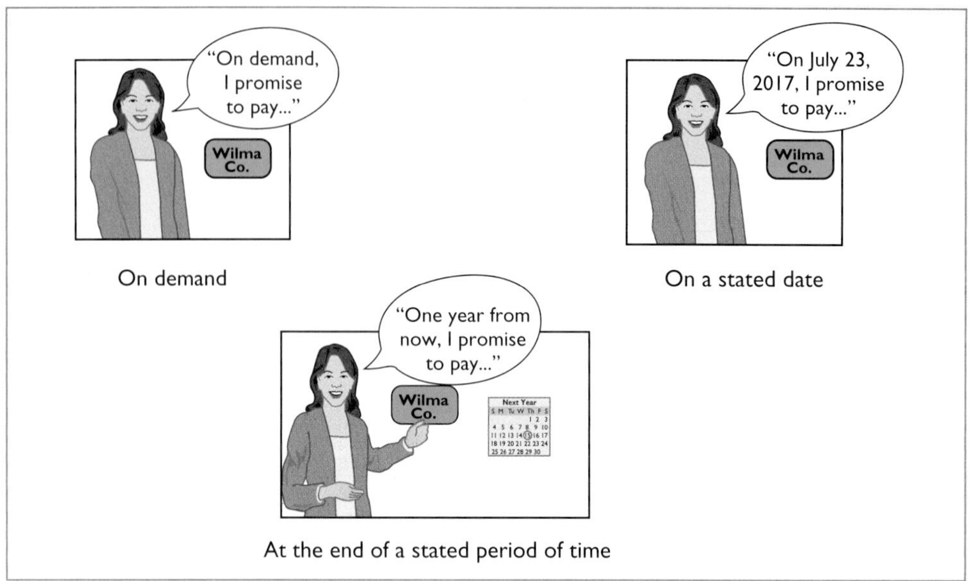

Computing Interest

Illustration 9-14 gives the basic formula for computing interest on an interest-bearing note.

Illustration 9-14
Formula for computing interest

Face Value of Note	×	Annual Interest Rate	×	Time in Terms of One Year	=	Interest

The interest rate specified in a note is an **annual** rate of interest. The time factor in the formula in Illustration 9-14 expresses the fraction of a year that the note is outstanding. When the maturity date is stated in days, the time factor is often the number of days divided by 360. When counting days, omit the date that the note is issued but include the due date. When the due date is stated in months, the time factor is the number of months divided by 12. Illustration 9-15 shows computation of interest for various time periods.

Illustration 9-15
Computation of interest

Terms of Note	**Interest Computation**
	Face × Rate × Time = Interest
$ 730, 12%, 120 days	$ 730 × 12% × **120/360** = $ 29.20
$1,000, 9%, 6 months	$1,000 × 9% × **6/12** = $ 45.00
$2,000, 6%, 1 year	$2,000 × 6% × **1/1** = $120.00

There are different ways to calculate interest. For example, the computation in Illustration 9-15 assumes 360 days for the length of the year. Most financial instruments use 365 days to compute interest. *For homework problems, assume 360 days to simplify computations.*

Recognizing Notes Receivable

To illustrate the basic entry for notes receivable, we will use Calhoun Company's $1,000, two-month, 12% promissory note dated May 1. Assuming that Calhoun Company wrote the note to settle an open account, Wilma Company makes the following entry for the receipt of the note.

May 1	Notes Receivable	1,000	
	Accounts Receivable—Calhoun Company		1,000
	(To record acceptance of Calhoun Company note)		

A	=	L	+	OE
+1,000				
−1,000				

Cash Flows
no effect

The company records the note receivable at its **face value**, the amount shown on the face of the note. No interest revenue is reported when the note is accepted because the revenue recognition principle does not recognize revenue until the performance obligation is satisfied. Interest is earned (accrued) as time passes.

If a company lends money using a note, the entry is a debit to Notes Receivable and a credit to Cash in the amount of the loan.

Describe how companies value notes receivable, record their disposition, and present and analyze receivables.

Valuing Notes Receivable

Valuing short-term notes receivable is the same as valuing accounts receivable. Like accounts receivable, companies report short-term notes receivable at their **cash (net) realizable value**. The notes receivable allowance account is Allowance for Doubtful Accounts. The estimations involved in determining cash realizable value and in recording bad debt expense and the related allowance are done similarly to accounts receivable.

Disposing of Notes Receivable

Notes may be held to their maturity date, at which time the face value plus accrued interest is due. In some situations, the maker of the note defaults, and the payee must make an appropriate adjustment. In other situations, similar to accounts receivable, the holder of the note speeds up the conversion to cash by selling the receivables (as described later in this chapter).

HONOR OF NOTES RECEIVABLE

A note is **honored** when its maker pays in full at its maturity date. For each interest-bearing note, the **amount due at maturity** is the face value of the note plus interest for the length of time specified on the note.

To illustrate, assume that Wolder Co. lends Higley Co. $10,000 on June 1, accepting a five-month, 9% interest note. In this situation, interest is $375 ($\$10,000 \times 9\% \times \frac{5}{12}$). The amount due, **the maturity value**, is $10,375 ($10,000 + $375). To obtain payment, Wolder (the payee) must present the note either to Higley Co. (the maker) or to the maker's agent, such as a bank. If Wolder presents the note to Higley Co. on November 1, the maturity date, Wolder's entry to record the collection is as follows.

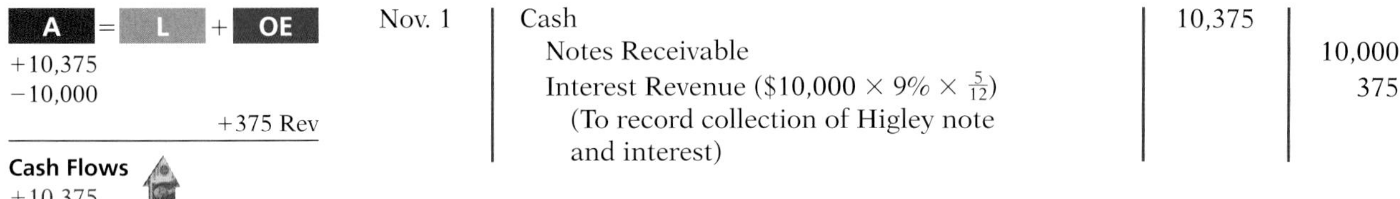

A	=	L	+	OE
+10,375				
−10,000				
				+375 Rev

Cash Flows
+10,375

Nov. 1	Cash	10,375	
	Notes Receivable		10,000
	Interest Revenue ($10,000 × 9% × $\frac{5}{12}$)		375
	(To record collection of Higley note and interest)		

ACCRUAL OF INTEREST RECEIVABLE

Suppose instead that Wolder Co. prepares financial statements as of September 30. The timeline in Illustration 9-16 presents this situation.

Illustration 9-16
Timeline of interest earned

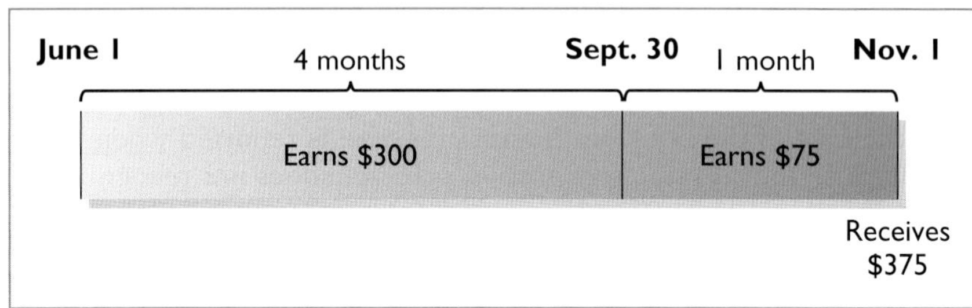

To reflect interest earned but not yet received, Wolder must accrue interest on September 30. In this case, the adjusting entry by Wolder is for four months of interest, or $300, as shown below.

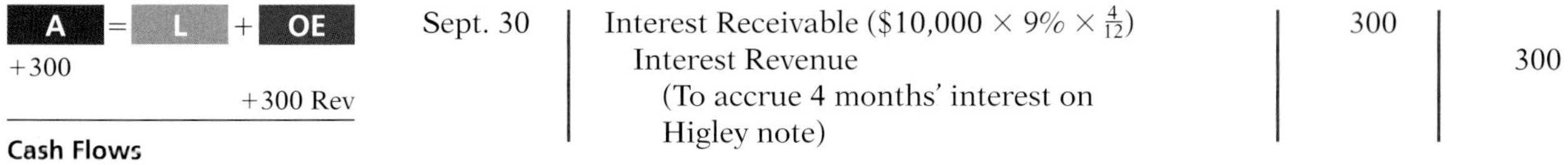

A	=	L	+	OE
+300				
				+300 Rev

Cash Flows
no effect

Sept. 30	Interest Receivable ($10,000 × 9% × $\frac{4}{12}$)	300	
	Interest Revenue		300
	(To accrue 4 months' interest on Higley note)		

At the note's maturity on November 1, Wolder receives $10,375. This amount represents repayment of the $10,000 note as well as five months of interest, or $375, as shown below. The $375 comprises the $300 Interest Receivable accrued on September 30 plus $75 earned during October. Wolder's entry to record the honoring of the Higley note on November 1 is as follows.

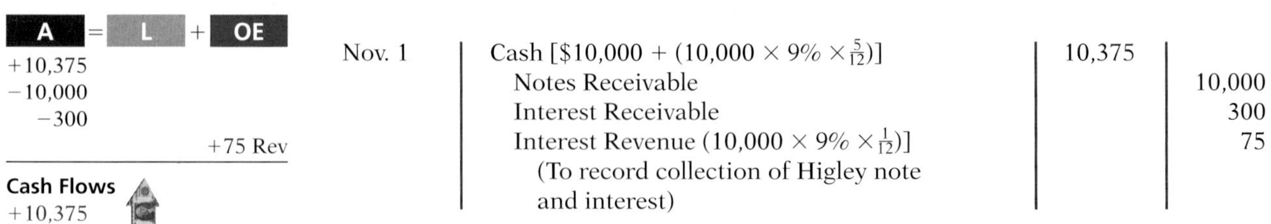

A	=	L	+	OE
+10,375				
−10,000				
−300				
				+75 Rev

Cash Flows
+10,375

Nov. 1	Cash [$10,000 + (10,000 × 9% × $\frac{5}{12}$)]	10,375	
	Notes Receivable		10,000
	Interest Receivable		300
	Interest Revenue (10,000 × 9% × $\frac{1}{12}$)]		75
	(To record collection of Higley note and interest)		

In this case, Wolder credits Interest Receivable because the receivable was established in the adjusting entry on September 30.

DISHONOR OF NOTES RECEIVABLE

A **dishonored (defaulted) note** is a note that is not paid in full at maturity. A dishonored note receivable is no longer negotiable. However, the payee still has a claim against the maker of the note for both the note and the interest. Therefore, the note holder usually transfers the Notes Receivable account to an Accounts Receivable account.

To illustrate, assume that Higley Co. on November 1 indicates that it cannot pay at the present time. The entry to record the dishonor of the note depends on whether Wolder Co. expects eventual collection. If it does expect eventual collection, Wolder Co. debits the amount due (face value and interest) on the note to Accounts Receivable. It would make the following entry at the time the note is dishonored (assuming no previous accrual of interest).

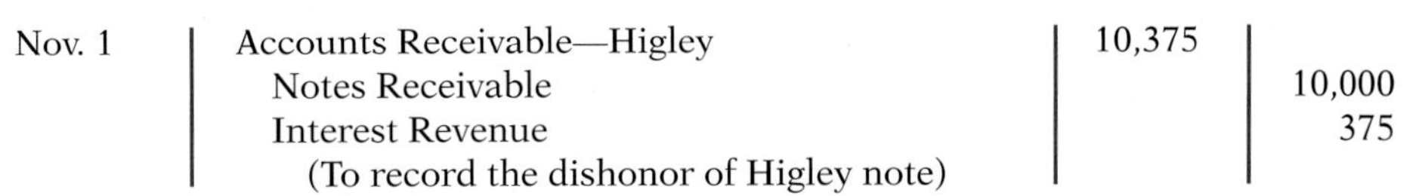

Nov. 1	Accounts Receivable—Higley	10,375	
	Notes Receivable		10,000
	Interest Revenue		375
	(To record the dishonor of Higley note)		

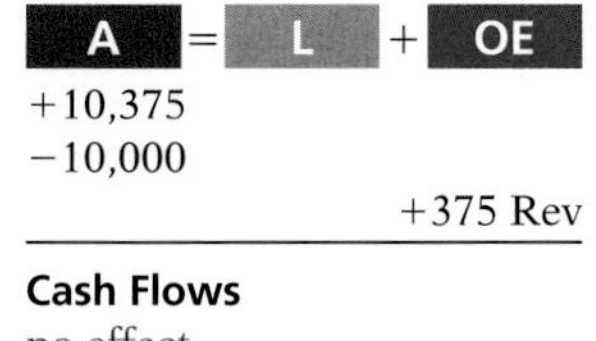

If instead on November 1 there is no hope of collection, the note holder would write off the face value of the note by debiting Allowance for Doubtful Accounts. No interest revenue would be recorded because collection will not occur.

SALE OF NOTES RECEIVABLE

The accounting for the sale of notes receivable is recorded similarly to the sale of accounts receivable. The accounting entries for the sale of notes receivable are left for a more advanced course.

Statement Presentation and Analysis

PRESENTATION

Companies should identify in the balance sheet or in the notes to the financial statements each of the major types of receivables. Short-term receivables appear in the current assets section of the balance sheet. Short-term investments appear before short-term receivables because these investments are more liquid (nearer to cash). Companies report both the gross amount of receivables and the allowance for doubtful accounts.

In a multiple-step income statement, companies report bad debt expense and service charge expense as selling expenses in the operating expenses section. Interest revenue appears under "Other revenues and gains" in the nonoperating activities section of the income statement.

ANALYSIS

Investors and corporate managers compute financial ratios to evaluate the liquidity of a company's accounts receivable. They use the **accounts receivable turnover** to assess the liquidity of the receivables. This ratio measures the number of times, on average, the company collects accounts receivable during the period. It is computed by dividing net credit sales (net sales less cash sales) by the average net accounts receivable during the year. Unless seasonal factors are significant, average net accounts receivable outstanding can be computed from the beginning and ending balances of net accounts receivable.

For example, in 2013 **Cisco Systems** had net sales of $38,029 million for the year. It had a beginning accounts receivable (net) balance of $4,369 million and an ending accounts receivable (net) balance of $5,470 million. Assuming that Cisco's sales were all on credit, its accounts receivable turnover is computed as follows.

Net Credit Sales	÷	Average Net Accounts Receivable	=	Accounts Receivable Turnover
$38,029	÷	$\frac{\$4,369 + \$5,470}{2}$	=	**7.7 times**

Illustration 9-17
Accounts receivable turnover and computation

The result indicates an accounts receivable turnover of 7.7 times per year. The higher the turnover, the more liquid the company's receivables.

A variant of the accounts receivable turnover that makes the liquidity even more evident is its conversion into an **average collection period** in terms of days. This is done by dividing the accounts receivable turnover into 365 days. For example, Cisco's turnover of 7.7 times is divided into 365 days, as shown in Illustration 9-18, to obtain approximately 47 days. This means that it takes Cisco 47 days to collect its accounts receivable.

Illustration 9-18
Average collection period for receivables formula and computation

Days in Year	÷	Accounts Receivable Turnover	=	Average Collection Period in Days
365 days	÷	7.7 times	=	**47 days**

Companies frequently use the average collection period to assess the effectiveness of a company's credit and collection policies. The general rule is that the collection period should not greatly exceed the credit term period (that is, the time allowed for payment).

REVIEW AND PRACTICE

LEARNING OBJECTIVES REVIEW

1 Explain how companies recognize accounts receivable. Receivables are frequently classified as (1) accounts, (2) notes, and (3) other. Accounts receivable are amounts customers owe on account. Notes receivable are claims for which lenders issue formal instruments of credit as proof of the debt. Other receivables include nontrade receivables such as interest receivable, loans to company officers, advances to employees, and income taxes refundable.

Companies record accounts receivable when they perform a service on account or at the point of sale of merchandise on account. Accounts receivable are reduced by sales returns and allowances. Cash discounts reduce the amount received on accounts receivable. When interest is charged on a past due receivable, the company adds this interest to the accounts receivable balance and recognizes it as interest revenue.

2 Describe how companies value accounts receivable and record their disposition. There are two methods of accounting for uncollectible accounts: the allowance method and the direct write-off method. Companies may use either the percentage-of-sales or the percentage-of-receivables basis to estimate uncollectible accounts using the allowance method. The percentage-of-sales basis emphasizes the expense recognition (matching) principle. The percentage-of-receivables basis emphasizes the cash realizable value of the accounts receivable. An aging schedule is often used with this basis.

When a company collects an account receivable, it credits Accounts Receivable. When a company sells (factors) an account receivable, a service charge expense reduces the amount received.

3 Explain how companies recognize notes receivable. For a note stated in months, the maturity date is found by counting the months from the date of issue. For a note stated in days, the number of days is counted, omitting the issue date and counting the due date. The formula for computing interest is Face value × Interest rate × Time.

Companies record notes receivable at face value. In some cases, it is necessary to accrue interest prior to maturity. In this case, companies debit Interest Receivable and credit Interest Revenue.

4 Describe how companies value notes receivable, record their disposition, and present and analyze receivables. As with accounts receivable, companies report notes receivable at their cash (net) realizable value. The notes receivable allowance account is Allowance for Doubtful Accounts. The computation and estimations involved in valuing notes receivable at cash realizable value, and in recording the proper amount of bad debt expense and the related allowance, are similar to those for accounts receivable.

Notes can be held to maturity. At that time the face value plus accrued interest is due, and the note is removed from the accounts. In many cases, the holder of the note speeds up the conversion by selling the receivable to another party (a factor). In some situations, the maker of the note dishonors the note (defaults), in which case the company transfers the note and accrued interest to an account receivable or writes off the note.

Companies should identify in the balance sheet or in the notes to the financial statements each major type of receivable. Short-term receivables are considered current assets. Companies report the gross amount of receivables and the allowance for doubtful accounts. They report bad debt and service charge expenses in the multiple-step income statement as operating (selling) expenses. Interest revenue appears under other revenues and gains in the nonoperating activities section of the statement. Managers and investors evaluate accounts receivable for liquidity by computing a turnover ratio and an average collection period.

GLOSSARY REVIEW

Accounts receivable Amounts owed by customers on account.

Accounts receivable turnover A measure of the liquidity of accounts receivable; computed by dividing net credit sales by average net accounts receivable.

Aging the accounts receivable The analysis of customer balances by the length of time they have been unpaid.

Allowance method A method of accounting for bad debts that involves estimating uncollectible accounts at the end of each period.

Average collection period The average amount of time that a receivable is outstanding; calculated by dividing 365 days by the accounts receivable turnover.

Bad Debt Expense An expense account to record uncollectible receivables.

Cash (net) realizable value The net amount a company expects to receive in cash.

Direct write-off method A method of accounting for bad debts that involves expensing accounts at the time they are determined to be uncollectible.

Dishonored (defaulted) note A note that is not paid in full at maturity.

Factor A finance company or bank that buys receivables from businesses and then collects the payments directly from the customers.

Maker The party in a promissory note who is making the promise to pay.

Notes receivable Written promise (as evidenced by a formal instrument) for amounts to be received.

Other receivables Various forms of nontrade receivables, such as interest receivable and income taxes refundable.

Payee The party to whom payment of a promissory note is to be made.

Percentage-of-receivables basis Management estimates what percentage of receivables will result in losses from uncollectible accounts.

Percentage-of-sales basis Management estimates what percentage of credit sales will be uncollectible.

Promissory note A written promise to pay a specified amount of money on demand or at a definite time.

Receivables Amounts due from individuals and other companies.

Trade receivables Notes and accounts receivable that result from sales transactions.

PRACTICE EXERCISES

Journalize entries to record allowance for doubtful accounts using two different bases.

(LO 2)

1. The ledger of Nuro Company at the end of the current year shows Accounts Receivable $180,000, Sales Revenue $1,800,000, and Sales Returns and Allowances $60,000.

Instructions

(a) If Nuro uses the direct write-off method to account for uncollectible accounts, journalize the adjusting entry at December 31, assuming Nuro determines that Willie's $2,900 balance is uncollectible.

(b) If Allowance for Doubtful Accounts has a credit balance of $4,300 in the trial balance, journalize the adjusting entry at December 31, assuming bad debts are expected to be (1) 1 % of net sales, and (2) 10% of accounts receivable.

(c) If Allowance for Doubtful Accounts has a debit balance of $410 in the trial balance, journalize the adjusting entry at December 31, assuming bad debts are expected to be (1) 0.75% of net sales and (2) 6% of accounts receivable.

Solution

1. (a)	Dec. 31	Bad Debt Expense Accounts Receivable—Willie's	2,900	 2,900
(b) (1)	Dec. 31	Bad Debt Expense [($1,800,000 − $60,000) × 1%] Allowance for Doubtful Accounts	 17,400	 17,400
(2)	Dec. 31	Bad Debt Expense Allowance for Doubtful Accounts [($180,000 × 10%) − $4,300]	13,700	 13,700
(c) (1)	Dec. 31	Bad Debt Expense [($1,800,000 − $60,000) × 0.75%] Allowance for Doubtful Accounts	 13,050	 13,050
(2)	Dec. 31	Bad Debt Expense Allowance for Doubtful Accounts [($180,000 × 6%) + $410]	11,210	 11,210

Journalize entries for notes receivable transactions.

(LO 3, 4)

2. Sargeant Supply Co. has the following transactions related to notes receivable during the last 2 months of 2017.

Nov. 1 Loaned $20,000 cash to Mary Hawkins on a 1-year, 12% note.
Dec. 11 Sold goods to Eminem, Inc., receiving a $9,000. 90-day, 8% note.
16 Received a $8,000, 6-month, 9% note in exchange for Rick DeLong's outstanding accounts receivable.
31 Accrued interest revenue on all notes receivable.

Instructions

(a) Journalize the transactions for Sargeant Supply Co.

(b) Record the collection of the Hawkins note at its maturity in 2018.

Solution

2. (a)

	2017		
Nov. 1	Notes Receivable Cash	20,000	 20,000
Dec. 11	Notes Receivable Sales Revenue	9,000	 9,000
16	Notes Receivable Accounts Receivable—DeLong	8,000	 8,000
31	Interest Receivable Interest Revenue*	470	 470

*Calculation of interest revenue:

Hawkins' note:	$20,000 × 12% × 2/12 =	$400
Eminem's note:	9,000 × 8% × 20/360 =	40
DeLong's note:	8,000 × 9% × 15/360 =	30
Total accrued interest		$470

(b)

	2018		
Nov. 1	Cash Interest Receivable Interest Revenue** Notes Receivable	22,400	 400 2,000 20,000

**($20,000 × 12% × 10/12)

PRACTICE PROBLEM

Prepare entries for various receivables transactions.

(LO 1, 2, 3, 4)

The following selected transactions relate to Dylan Company.

Mar. 1 Sold $20,000 of merchandise to Potter Company, terms 2/10, n/30.
11 Received payment in full from Potter Company for balance due on existing accounts receivable.
12 Accepted Juno Company's $20,000, 6-month, 12% note for balance due.

13	Made Dylan Company credit card sales for $13,200.
15	Made Visa credit card sales totaling $6,700. A 3% service fee is charged by Visa.
Apr. 11	Sold accounts receivable of $8,000 to Harcot Factor. Harcot Factor assesses a service charge of 2% of the amount of receivables sold.
13	Received collections of $8,200 on Dylan Company credit card sales and added finance charges of 1.5% to the remaining balances.
May 10	Wrote off as uncollectible $16,000 of accounts receivable. Dylan uses the percentage-of-sales basis to estimate bad debts.
June 30	Credit sales recorded during the first 6 months total $2,000,000. The bad debt percentage is 1% of credit sales. At June 30, the balance in the allowance account is $3,500 before adjustment.
July 16	One of the accounts receivable written off in May was from J. Simon, who pays the amount due, $4,000, in full.

Instructions

Prepare the journal entries for the transactions. (Ignore entries for cost of goods sold.)

Solution

Mar. 1	Accounts Receivable—Potter	20,000	
	Sales Revenue		20,000
	(To record sales on account)		
11	Cash	19,600	
	Sales Discounts (2% × $20,000)	400	
	Accounts Receivable—Potter		20,000
	(To record collection of accounts receivable)		
12	Notes Receivable	20,000	
	Accounts Receivable—Juno		20,000
	(To record acceptance of Juno Company note)		
13	Accounts Receivable	13,200	
	Sales Revenue		13,200
	(To record company credit card sales)		
15	Cash	6,499	
	Service Charge Expense (3% × $6,700)	201	
	Sales Revenue		6,700
	(To record credit card sales)		
Apr. 11	Cash	7,840	
	Service Charge Expense (2% × $8,000)	160	
	Accounts Receivable		8,000
	(To record sale of receivables to factor)		
13	Cash	8,200	
	Accounts Receivable		8,200
	(To record collection of accounts receivable)		
	Accounts Receivable [($13,200 − $8,200) × 1.5%]	75	
	Interest Revenue		75
	(To record interest on amount due)		
May 10	Allowance for Doubtful Accounts	16,000	
	Accounts Receivable		16,000
	(To record write-off of accounts receivable)		
June 30	Bad Debt Expense ($2,000,000 × 1%)	20,000	
	Allowance for Doubtful Accounts		20,000
	(To record estimate of uncollectible accounts)		
July 16	Accounts Receivable—J. Simon	4,000	
	Allowance for Doubtful Accounts		4,000
	(To reverse write-off of accounts receivable)		
	Cash	4,000	
	Accounts Receivable—J. Simon		4,000
	(To record collection of accounts receivable)		

EXERCISES

Journalize entries related to accounts receivable.

(LO 1)

E9-1 Presented below are selected transactions of Molina Company. Molina sells in large quantities to other companies and also sells its product in a small retail outlet.

March	1	Sold merchandise on account to Dodson Company for $5,000, terms 2/10, n/30.
	3	Dodson Company returned merchandise worth $500 to Molina.
	9	Molina collected the amount due from Dodson Company from the March 1 sale.
	15	Molina sold merchandise for $400 in its retail outlet. The customer used his Molina credit card.
	31	Molina added 1.5% monthly interest to the customer's credit card balance.

Instructions

Prepare journal entries for the transactions above.

Journalize entries for recognizing accounts receivable.

(LO 1)

E9-2 Presented below are two independent situations.

(a) On January 6, Brumbaugh Co. sells merchandise on account to Pryor Inc. for $7,000, terms 2/10, n/30. On January 16, Pryor Inc. pays the amount due. Prepare the entries on Brumbaugh's books to record the sale and related collection.

(b) On January 10, Andrew Farley uses his Paltrow Co. credit card to purchase merchandise from Paltrow Co. for $9,000. On February 10, Farley is billed for the amount due of $9,000. On February 12, Farley pays $5,000 on the balance due. On March 10, Farley is billed for the amount due, including interest at 1% per month on the unpaid balance as of February 12. Prepare the entries on Paltrow Co.'s books related to the transactions that occurred on January 10, February 12, and March 10.

Journalize entries to record allowance for doubtful accounts using two different bases.

(LO 2)

E9-3 The ledger of Costello Company at the end of the current year shows Accounts Receivable $110,000, Sales Revenue $840,000, and Sales Returns and Allowances $20,000.

Instructions

(a) If Costello uses the direct write-off method to account for uncollectible accounts, journalize the adjusting entry at December 31, assuming Costello determines that L. Dole's $1,400 balance is uncollectible.

(b) If Allowance for Doubtful Accounts has a credit balance of $2,100 in the trial balance, journalize the adjusting entry at December 31, assuming bad debts are expected to be (1) 1% of net sales, and (2) 10% of accounts receivable.

(c) If Allowance for Doubtful Accounts has a debit balance of $200 in the trial balance, journalize the adjusting entry at December 31, assuming bad debts are expected to be (1) 0.75% of net sales and (2) 6% of accounts receivable.

Determine bad debt expense; prepare the adjusting entry for bad debt expense.

(LO 2)

E9-4 Menge Company has accounts receivable of $93,100 at March 31. Credit terms are 2/10, n/30. At March 31, Allowance for Doubtful Accounts has a credit balance of $1,200 prior to adjustment. The company uses the percentage-of-receivables basis for estimating uncollectible accounts. The company's estimate of bad debts is shown below.

Age of Accounts	Balance, March 31	Estimated Percentage Uncollectible
1–30 days	$60,000	2.0%
31–60 days	17,600	5.0%
61–90 days	8,500	20.0%
Over 90 days	7,000	50.0%
	$93,100	

Instructions

(a) Determine the total estimated uncollectibles.

(b) Prepare the adjusting entry at March 31 to record bad debt expense.

Journalize write-off and recovery.

(LO 2)

E9-5 At December 31, 2016, Finzelberg Company had a credit balance of $15,000 in Allowance for Doubtful Accounts. During 2017, Finzelberg wrote off accounts totaling $11,000.

One of those accounts ($1,800) was later collected. At December 31, 2017, an aging schedule indicated that the balance in Allowance for Doubtful Accounts should be $19,000.

Instructions
Prepare journal entries to record the 2017 transactions of Finzelberg Company.

E9-6 On December 31, 2017, Ling Co. estimated that 2% of its net sales of $450,000 will become uncollectible. The company recorded this amount as an addition to Allowance for Doubtful Accounts. On May 11, 2018, Ling Co. determined that the Jeff Shoemaker account was uncollectible and wrote off $1,100. On June 12, 2018, Shoemaker paid the amount previously written off.

Journalize percentage of sales basis, write-off, recovery.

(LO 2)

Instructions
Prepare the journal entries on December 31, 2017, May 11, 2018, and June 12, 2018.

E9-7 Presented below are two independent situations.

Journalize entries for the sale of accounts receivable.

(LO 2)

(a) On March 3, Kitselman Appliances sells $650,000 of its receivables to Ervay Factors Inc. Ervay Factors assesses a finance charge of 3% of the amount of receivables sold. Prepare the entry on Kitselman Appliances' books to record the sale of the receivables.
(b) On May 10, Fillmore Company sold merchandise for $3,000 and accepted the customer's America Bank MasterCard. America Bank charges a 4% service charge for credit card sales. Prepare the entry on Fillmore Company's books to record the sale of merchandise.

E9-8 Presented below are two independent situations.

Journalize entries for credit card sales.

(LO 2)

(a) On April 2, Jennifer Elston uses her JCPenney Company credit card to purchase merchandise from a JCPenney store for $1,500. On May 1, Elston is billed for the $1,500 amount due. Elston pays $500 on the balance due on May 3. Elston receives a bill dated June 1 for the amount due, including interest at 1.0% per month on the unpaid balance as of May 3. Prepare the entries on JCPenney Co.'s books related to the transactions that occurred on April 2, May 3, and June 1.
(b) On July 4, Spangler's Restaurant accepts a Visa card for a $200 dinner bill. Visa charges a 2% service fee. Prepare the entry on Spangler's books related to this transaction.

E9-9 Colaw Stores accepts both its own and national credit cards. During the year, the following selected summary transactions occurred.

Journalize credit card sales, and indicate the statement presentation of financing charges and service charge expense.

(LO 2)

Jan.	15	Made Colaw credit card sales totaling $18,000. (There were no balances prior to January 15.)
	20	Made Visa credit card sales (service charge fee 2%) totaling $4,500.
Feb.	10	Collected $10,000 on Colaw credit card sales.
	15	Added finance charges of 1.5% to Colaw credit card account balances.

Instructions
Journalize the transactions for Colaw Stores.

E9-10 Elburn Supply Co. has the following transactions related to notes receivable during the last 2 months of 2017. The company does not make entries to accrue interest except at December 31.

Journalize entries for notes receivable transactions.

(LO 3)

Nov.	1	Loaned $30,000 cash to Manny Lopez on a 12 month, 10% note.
Dec.	11	Sold goods to Ralph Kremer, Inc., receiving a $6,750, 90-day, 8% note.
	16	Received a $4,000, 180 day, 9% note in exchange for Joe Fernetti's outstanding accounts receivable.
	31	Accrued interest revenue on all notes receivable.

Instructions
(a) Journalize the transactions for Elburn Supply Co.
(b) Record the collection of the Lopez note at its maturity in 2018.

E9-11 Record the following transactions for Redeker Co. in the general journal.

Journalize entries for notes receivable.

(LO 3)

2017

May	1	Received a $9,000, 12-month, 10% note in exchange for Mark Chamber's outstanding accounts receivable.
Dec.	31	Accrued interest on the Chamber note.
Dec.	31	Closed the interest revenue account.

2018

May 1 Received principal plus interest on the Chamber note. (No interest has been accrued in 2018.)

Prepare entries for note receivable transactions.
(LO 3, 4)

E9-12 Vandiver Company had the following select transactions.

Apr. 1, 2017	Accepted Goodwin Company's 12-month, 12% note in settlement of a $30,000 account receivable.
July 1, 2017	Loaned $25,000 cash to Thomas Slocombe on a 9-month, 10% note.
Dec. 31, 2017	Accrued interest on all notes receivable.
Apr. 1, 2018	Received principal plus interest on the Goodwin note.
Apr. 1, 2018	Thomas Slocombe dishonored its note; Vandiver expects it will eventually collect.

Instructions
Prepare journal entries to record the transactions. Vandiver prepares adjusting entries once a year on December 31.

Journalize entries for dishonor of notes receivable.
(LO 3, 4)

E9-13 On May 2, McLain Company lends $9,000 to Chang, Inc., issuing a 6-month, 9% note. At the maturity date, November 2, Chang indicates that it cannot pay.

Instructions
(a) Prepare the entry to record the issuance of the note.
(b) Prepare the entry to record the dishonor of the note, assuming that McLain Company expects collection will occur.
(c) Prepare the entry to record the dishonor of the note, assuming that McLain Company does not expect collection in the future.

Compute accounts receivable turnover and average collection period.
(LO 4)

E9-14 Kerwick Company had accounts receivable of $100,000 on January 1, 2017. The only transactions that affected accounts receivable during 2017 were net credit sales of $1,000,000, cash collections of $920,000, and accounts written off of $30,000.

Instructions
(a) Compute the ending balance of accounts receivable.
(b) Compute the accounts receivable turnover for 2017.
(c) Compute the average collection period in days.

PROBLEMS

Prepare journal entries related to bad debt expense.
(LO 1, 2, 4)

P9-1A At December 31, 2016, House Co. reported the following information on its balance sheet.

Accounts receivable	$960,000
Less: Allowance for doubtful accounts	80,000

During 2017, the company had the following transactions related to receivables.

1. Sales on account	$3,700,000
2. Sales returns and allowances	50,000
3. Collections of accounts receivable	2,810,000
4. Write-offs of accounts receivable deemed uncollectible	90,000
5. Recovery of bad debts previously written off as uncollectible	29,000

Instructions
(a) Prepare the journal entries to record each of these five transactions. Assume that no cash discounts were taken on the collections of accounts receivable.
(b) Enter the January 1, 2017, balances in Accounts Receivable and Allowance for Doubtful Accounts, post the entries to the two accounts (use T-accounts), and determine the balances.
(c) Prepare the journal entry to record bad debt expense for 2017, assuming that an aging of accounts receivable indicates that expected bad debts are $115,000.
(d) Compute the accounts receivable turnover for 2017 assuming the expected bad debt information provided in (c).

(b) Accounts receivable $1,710,000 ADA $19,000
(c) Bad debt expense $96,000

Compute bad debt amounts.
(LO 2)

P9-2A Information related to Mingenback Company for 2017 is summarized below.

Total credit sales	$2,500,000
Accounts receivable at December 31	875,000
Bad debts written off	33,000

Instructions

(a) What amount of bad debt expense will Mingenback Company report if it uses the direct write-off method of accounting for bad debts?

(b) Assume that Mingenback Company estimates its bad debt expense to be 2% of credit sales. What amount of bad debt expense will Mingenback record if it has an Allowance for Doubtful Accounts credit balance of $4,000?

(c) Assume that Mingenback Company estimates its bad debt expense based on 6% of accounts receivable. What amount of bad debt expense will Mingenback record if it has an Allowance for Doubtful Accounts credit balance of $3,000?

(d) Assume the same facts as in (c), except that there is a $3,000 debit balance in Allowance for Doubtful Accounts. What amount of bad debt expense will Mingenback record?

(e) What is the weakness of the direct write-off method of reporting bad debt expense?

P9-3A Presented below is an aging schedule for Halleran Company.

Journalize entries to record transactions related to bad debts.

(LO 2)

Worksheet.xls

	A	B	C	D	E	F	G
1				Number of Days Past Due			
2			Not				
3	Customer	Total	Yet Due	1–30	31–60	61–90	Over 90
4	Anders	$ 22,000		$10,000	$12,000		
5	Blake	40,000	$ 40,000				
6	Coulson	57,000	16,000	6,000		$35,000	
7	Deleon	34,000					$34,000
8	Others	132,000	96,000	16,000	14,000		6,000
9		$285,000	$152,000	$32,000	$26,000	$35,000	$40,000
10	Estimated Percentage Uncollectible		3%	6%	13%	25%	50%
11	Total Estimated Bad Debts	$ 38,610	$ 4,560	$ 1,920	$ 3,380	$ 8,750	$20,000
12							

At December 31, 2017, the unadjusted balance in Allowance for Doubtful Accounts is a credit of $12,000.

Instructions

(a) Journalize and post the adjusting entry for bad debts at December 31, 2017.

(b) Journalize and post to the allowance account the following events and transactions in the year 2018.

(1) On March 31, a $1,000 customer balance originating in 2017 is judged uncollectible.

(2) On May 31, a check for $1,000 is received from the customer whose account was written off as uncollectible on March 31.

(c) Journalize the adjusting entry for bad debts on December 31, 2018, assuming that the unadjusted balance in Allowance for Doubtful Accounts is a debit of $800 and the aging schedule indicates that total estimated bad debts will be $31,600.

(a) Bad debt expense $26,610

(c) Bad debt expense $32,400

P9-4A Rigney Inc. uses the allowance method to estimate uncollectible accounts receivable. The company produced the following aging of the accounts receivable at year-end.

Journalize transactions related to bad debts.

(LO 2)

Worksheet.xls

	A	B	C	D	E	F	G
1			Number of Days Outstanding				
2							
3		Total	0–30	31–60	61–90	91–120	Over 120
4	Accounts receivable	200,000	77,000	46,000	39,000	23,000	15,000
5	% uncollectible		1%	4%	5%	8%	20%
6	Estimated bad debts						
7							

Instructions

(a) Tot. est. bad debts $9,400

(a) Calculate the total estimated bad debts based on the above information.
(b) Prepare the year-end adjusting journal entry to record the bad debts using the aged uncollectible accounts receivable determined in (a). Assume the current balance in Allowance for Doubtful Accounts is a $8,000 debit.
(c) Of the above accounts, $5,000 is determined to be specifically uncollectible. Prepare the journal entry to write off the uncollectible account.
(d) The company collects $5,000 subsequently on a specific account that had previously been determined to be uncollectible in (c). Prepare the journal entry(ies) necessary to restore the account and record the cash collection.
(e) Comment on how your answers to (a)–(d) would change if Rigney Inc. used 4% of **total** accounts receivable rather than aging the accounts receivable. What are the advantages to the company of aging the accounts receivable rather than applying a percentage to total accounts receivable?

Journalize entries to record transactions related to bad debts.

(LO 2)

P9-5A At December 31, 2017, the trial balance of Darby Company contained the following amounts before adjustment.

	Debit	Credit
Accounts Receivable	$385,000	
Allowance for Doubtful Accounts		$ 1,000
Sales Revenue		970,000

Instructions

(a) Based on the information given, which method of accounting for bad debts is Darby Company using—the direct write-off method or the allowance method? How can you tell?
(b) Prepare the adjusting entry at December 31, 2017, for bad debt expense under each of the following independent assumptions.
   (1) An aging schedule indicates that $11,750 of accounts receivable will be uncollectible.
   (2) The company estimates that 1% of sales will be uncollectible.

(b) (2) $9,700

(c) Repeat part (b) assuming that instead of a credit balance there is a $1,000 debit balance in Allowance for Doubtful Accounts.
(d) During the next month, January 2018, a $3,000 account receivable is written off as uncollectible. Prepare the journal entry to record the write-off.
(e) Repeat part (d) assuming that Darby uses the direct write-off method instead of the allowance method in accounting for uncollectible accounts receivable.
(f) What type of account is Allowance for Doubtful Accounts? How does it affect how accounts receivable is reported on the balance sheet at the end of the accounting period?

Prepare entries for various notes receivable transactions.

(LO 1, 2, 3, 4)

P9-6A Farwell Company closes its books monthly. On September 30, selected ledger account balances are:

Notes Receivable	$37,000
Interest Receivable	183

Notes Receivable include the following.

Date	Maker	Face	Term	Interest
Aug. 16	K. Goza Inc.	$12,000	60 days	8%
Aug. 25	Holt Co.	9,000	60 days	7%
Sept. 30	Noblitt Corp.	16,000	6 months	9%

Interest is computed using a 360-day year. During October, the following transactions were completed.

Oct. 7	Made sales of $6,900 on Farwell credit cards.
12	Made sales of $900 on MasterCard credit cards. The credit card service charge is 3%.
15	Added $460 to Farwell customer balances for finance charges on unpaid balances.
15	Received payment in full from K. Goza Inc. on the amount due.
24	Received notice that the Holt note has been dishonored. (Assume that Holt is expected to pay in the future.)

Instructions

(a) Journalize the October transactions and the October 31 adjusting entry for accrued interest receivable.

(b) Enter the balances at October 1 in the receivable accounts. Post the entries to all of the receivable accounts. There was no opening balance in accounts receivable. (b) Accounts receivable $16,465

(c) Show the balance sheet presentation of the receivable accounts at October 31. (c) Total receivables $32,585

P9-7A On January 1, 2017, Harter Company had Accounts Receivable $139,000, Notes Receivable $25,000, and Allowance for Doubtful Accounts $13,200. The note receivable is from Willingham Company. It is a 4-month, 9% note dated December 31, 2016. Harter Company prepares financial statements annually at December 31. During the year, the following selected transactions occurred.

Prepare entries for various receivable transactions.

(LO 1, 2, 3, 4)

Jan. 5	Sold $20,000 of merchandise to Sheldon Company, terms n/15.
20	Accepted Sheldon Company's $20,000, 3-month, 8% note for balance due.
Feb. 18	Sold $8,000 of merchandise to Patwary Company and accepted Patwary's $8,000, 6-month, 9% note for the amount due.
Apr. 20	Collected Sheldon Company note in full.
30	Received payment in full from Willingham Company on the amount due.
May 25	Accepted Potter Inc.'s $6,000, 3-month, 7% note in settlement of a past-due balance on account.
Aug. 18	Received payment in full from Patwary Company on note due.
25	The Potter Inc. note was dishonored. Potter Inc. is not bankrupt; future payment is anticipated.
Sept. 1	Sold $12,000 of merchandise to Stanbrough Company and accepted a $12,000, 6-month, 10% note for the amount due.

Instructions

Journalize the transactions.

COMPREHENSIVE PROBLEM

CP9 Winter Company's balance sheet at December 31, 2016, is presented below.

WINTER COMPANY
Balance Sheet
December 31, 2016

Cash	$13,100	Accounts payable	$ 8,750
Accounts receivable	19,780	Owner's capital	32,730
Allowance for doubtful accounts	(800)		$41,480
Inventory	9,400		
	$41,480		

During January 2017, the following transactions occurred. Winter uses the perpetual inventory method.

Jan. 1	Winter accepted a 4-month, 8% note from Merando Company in payment of Merando's $1,200 account.
3	Winter wrote off as uncollectible the accounts of Inwood Corporation ($450) and Goza Company ($280).
8	Winter purchased $17,200 of inventory on account.
11	Winter sold for $28,000 on account inventory that cost $19,600.
15	Winter sold inventory that cost $700 to Mark Lauber for $1,000. Lauber charged this amount on his Visa First Bank card. The service fee charged Winter by First Bank is 3%.
17	Winter collected $22,900 from customers on account.
21	Winter paid $14,300 on accounts payable.
24	Winter received payment in full ($280) from Goza Company on the account written off on January 3.
27	Winter purchased supplies for $1,400 cash.
31	Winter paid other operating expenses, $3,718.

Adjustment data:

1. Interest is recorded for the month on the note from January 1.
2. Bad debts are expected to be 6% of the January 31, 2017, accounts receivable.
3. A count of supplies on January 31, 2017, reveals that $560 remains unused.

Instructions

(You may want to set up T-accounts to determine ending balances.)

(a) Prepare journal entries for the transactions listed above and adjusting entries. (Include entries for cost of goods sold using the perpetual system.)

(b) Totals $74,765

(b) Prepare an adjusted trial balance at January 31, 2017.

(c) Tot. assets $47,473

(c) Prepare an income statement and an owner's equity statement for the month ending January 31, 2017, and a classified balance sheet as of January 31, 2017.

BROADENING YOUR PERSPECTIVE

FINANCIAL REPORTING AND ANALYSIS

Financial Reporting Problem: RLF Company

BYP9-1 RLF Company sells office equipment and supplies to many organizations in the city and surrounding area on contract terms of 2/10, n/30. In the past, over 75% of the credit customers have taken advantage of the discount by paying within 10 days of the invoice date.

The number of customers taking the full 30 days to pay has increased within the last year. Current indications are that less than 60% of the customers are now taking the discount. Bad debts as a percentage of gross credit sales have risen from the 2.5% provided in past years to about 4.5% in the current year.

The company's Finance Committee has requested more information on the collections of accounts receivable. The controller responded to this request with the report reproduced below.

RLF COMPANY
Accounts Receivable Collections
May 31, 2017

The fact that some credit accounts will prove uncollectible is normal. Annual bad debt write-offs have been 2.5% of gross credit sales over the past 5 years. During the last fiscal year, this percentage increased to slightly less than 4.5%. The current Accounts Receivable balance is $1,400,000. The condition of this balance in terms of age and probability of collection is as follows.

Proportion of Total	Age Categories	Probability of Collection
60%	not yet due	98%
22%	less than 30 days past due	96%
9%	30 to 60 days past due	94%
5%	61 to 120 days past due	91%
$2\frac{1}{2}$%	121 to 180 days past due	75%
$1\frac{1}{2}$%	over 180 days past due	30%

Allowance for Doubtful Accounts had a credit balance of $29,500 on June 1, 2016. RLF has provided for a monthly bad debt expense accrual during the current fiscal year based on the assumption that 4.5% of gross credit sales will be uncollectible. Total gross credit sales for the 2016–2017 fiscal year amounted to $2,900,000. Write-offs of bad accounts during the year totaled $102,000.

Instructions

(a) Prepare an accounts receivable aging schedule for RLF Company using the age categories identified in the controller's report to the Finance Committee showing the following.
   (1) The amount of accounts receivable outstanding for each age category and in total.
   (2) The estimated amount that is uncollectible for each category and in total.

(b) Compute the amount of the year-end adjustment necessary to bring Allowance for Doubtful Accounts to the balance indicated by the age analysis. Then prepare the necessary journal entry to adjust the accounting records.

(c) In a recessionary environment with tight credit and high interest rates:
   (1) Identify steps RLF Company might consider to improve the accounts receivable situation.
   (2) Then evaluate each step identified in terms of the risks and costs involved.

Comparative Analysis Problem: PepsiCo, Inc. vs. The Coca-Cola Company

BYP9-2 PepsiCo, Inc.'s financial statements are presented in Appendix B. Financial statements of The Coca-Cola Company are presented in Appendix C. Instructions for accessing and using the complete annual reports of PepsiCo and Coca-Cola, including the notes to the financial statements, are also provided in Appendices B and C, respectively.

Instructions

(a) Based on the information in these financial statements, compute the following 2013 ratios for each company. (Assume all sales are credit sales and that PepsiCo's receivables on its balance sheet are all trade receivables.)
   (1) Accounts receivable turnover.
   (2) Average collection period for receivables.
(b) What conclusions about managing accounts receivable can you draw from these data?

Comparative Analysis Problem: Amazon.com, Inc. vs. Wal-Mart Stores, Inc.

BYP9-3 Amazon.com, Inc.'s financial statements are presented in Appendix D. Financial statements of Wal-Mart Stores, Inc. are presented in Appendix E. Instructions for accessing and using the complete annual reports of Amazon and Wal-Mart, including the notes to the financial statements, are also provided in Appendices D and E, respectively.

Instructions

(a) Based on the information in these financial statements, compute the following ratios for each company (for the most recent year shown). (Assume all sales are credit sales.)
   (1) Accounts receivable turnover.
   (2) Average collection period for receivables.
(b) What conclusions about managing accounts receivable can you draw from these data?

Real-World Focus

BYP9-4 Purpose: To learn more about factoring.

Address: **www.comcapfactoring.com**, or go to **www.wiley.com/college/weygandt**

Steps: Go to the website, click on **Invoice Factoring**, and answer the following questions.
(a) What are some of the benefits of factoring?
(b) What is the range of the percentages of the typical discount rate?
(c) If a company factors its receivables, what percentage of the value of the receivables can it expect to receive from the factor in the form of cash, and how quickly will it receive the cash?

CRITICAL THINKING

Decision-Making Across the Organization

BYP9-5 Carol and Sam Foyle own Campus Fashions. From its inception Campus Fashions has sold merchandise on either a cash or credit basis, but no credit cards have been accepted. During the past several months, the Foyles have begun to question their sales policies. First, they have lost some sales because of refusing to accept credit cards. Second, representatives of two metropolitan banks have been persuasive in almost convincing them to accept their national credit cards. One bank, City National Bank, has stated that its credit card fee is 4%.

The Foyles decide that they should determine the cost of carrying their own credit sales. From the accounting records of the past 3 years, they accumulate the following data.

	2018	2017	2016
Net credit sales	$500,000	$550,000	$400,000
Collection agency fees for slow-paying customers	2,450	2,500	2,300
Salary of part-time accounts receivable clerk	4,100	4,100	4,100

Uncollectible account expense is 1.6% of net credit sales, billing and mailing costs 0.5%, and credit investigation fee on new customers is 0.15%.

Carol and Sam also determine that the average accounts receivable balance outstanding during the year is 5% of net credit sales. The Foyles estimate that they could earn an average of 8% annually on cash invested in other business opportunities.

Instructions

With the class divided into groups, answer the following.

(a) Prepare a table showing, for each year, total credit and collection expenses in dollars and as a percentage of net credit sales.

(b) Determine the net credit and collection expense in dollars and as a percentage of sales after considering the revenue not earned from other investment opportunities.

(c) Discuss both the financial and nonfinancial factors that are relevant to the decision.

Communication Activity

BYP9-6 Jill Epp, a friend of yours, overheard a discussion at work about changes her employer wants to make in accounting for uncollectible accounts. Jill knows little about accounting, and she asks you to help make sense of what she heard. Specifically, she asks you to explain the differences between the percentage-of-sales, percentage-of-receivables, and the direct write-off methods for uncollectible accounts.

Instructions

In a letter of one page (or less), explain to Jill the three methods of accounting for uncollectibles. Be sure to discuss differences among these methods.

Ethics Case

BYP9-7 The controller of Diaz Co. believes that the yearly allowance for doubtful accounts for Diaz Co. should be 2% of net credit sales. The president of Diaz Co., nervous that the owners might expect the company to sustain its 10% growth rate, suggests that the controller increase the allowance for doubtful accounts to 4%. The president thinks that the lower net income, which reflects a 6% growth rate, will be a more sustainable rate for Diaz Co.

Instructions

(a) Who are the stakeholders in this case?

(b) Does the president's request pose an ethical dilemma for the controller?

(c) Should the controller be concerned with Diaz Co.'s growth rate? Explain your answer.

FASB Codification Activity

BYP9-8 If your school has a subscription to the FASB Codification, go to **http://aaahq.org/ascLogin.cfm** to log in and prepare responses to the following.

(a) How are receivables defined in the Codification?

(b) What are the conditions under which losses from uncollectible receivables (Bad Debt Expense) should be reported?

A Look at IFRS

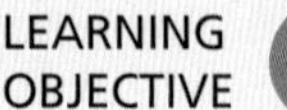

Compare the accounting for receivables under GAAP and IFRS.

The basic accounting and reporting issues related to the recognition, measurement, and disposition of receivables are essentially the same between IFRS and GAAP.

Key Points

Following are the key similarities and differences between GAAP and IFRS as related to the accounting for receivables.

Similarities

- The recording of receivables, recognition of sales returns and allowances and sales discounts, and the allowance method to record bad debts are the same between IFRS and GAAP.

- Both IFRS and GAAP often use the term impairment to indicate that a receivable may not be collected.
- The FASB and IASB have worked to implement fair value measurement (the amount they currently could be sold for) for financial instruments, such as receivables. Both Boards have faced bitter opposition from various factions.

Differences

- Although IFRS implies that receivables with different characteristics should be reported separately, there is no standard that mandates this segregation.
- IFRS and GAAP differ in the criteria used to determine how to record a factoring transaction. IFRS uses a combination approach focused on risks and rewards and loss of control. GAAP uses loss of control as the primary criterion. In addition, IFRS permits partial derecognition of receivables; GAAP does not.

Looking to the Future

The question of recording fair values for financial instruments will continue to be an important issue to resolve as the Boards work toward convergence. Both the IASB and the FASB have indicated that they believe that financial statements would be more transparent and understandable if companies recorded and reported all financial instruments at fair value.

IFRS Practice

IFRS Self-Test Questions

1. Which of the following statements is **false**?
   (a) Receivables include equity securities purchased by the company.
   (b) Receivables include credit card receivables.
   (c) Receivables include amounts owed by employees as a result of company loans to employees.
   (d) Receivables include amounts resulting from transactions with customers.
2. Under IFRS:
   (a) the entry to record estimated uncollected accounts is the same as GAAP.
   (b) it is always acceptable to use the direct write-off method.
   (c) all financial instruments are recorded at fair value.
   (d) None of the above.

International Financial Reporting Problem: Louis Vuitton

IFRS9-1 The financial statements of Louis Vuitton are presented in Appendix F. Instructions for accessing and using the company's complete annual report, including the notes to its financial statements, are also provided in Appendix F.

Instructions
Use the company's annual report to answer the following questions.

(a) What is the accounting policy related to accounting for trade accounts receivable?
(b) According to the notes to the financial statements, what accounted for the difference between gross trade accounts receivable and net accounts receivable?
(c) According to the notes to the financial statements, what was the major reason why the balance in receivables increased relative to the previous year?
(d) Using information in the notes to the financial statements, determine what percentage the provision for impairment of receivables was as a percentage of total trade receivables for 2013 and 2012. How did the ratio change from 2012 to 2013, and what does this suggest about the company's receivables?

Answers to IFRS Self-Test Questions

1. a **2.** a

Chapter 10 Plant Assets, Natural Resources, and Intangible Assets

It's spring break. Your plane has landed, you've finally found your bags, and you're dying to hit the beach—but first you need a "vehicular unit" to get you there. As you turn away from baggage claim, you see a long row of rental agency booths. Many are names that you know—Hertz, Avis, and Budget. But a booth at the far end catches your eye—Rent-A-Wreck. Now there's a company making a clear statement!

Any company that relies on equipment to generate revenues must make decisions about what kind of equipment to buy, how long to keep it, and how vigorously to maintain it. Rent-A-Wreck has decided to rent used rather than new cars and trucks. It rents these vehicles across the United States, Europe, and Asia. While the big-name agencies push vehicles with that "new car smell," Rent-A-Wreck competes on price.

Rent-A-Wreck's message is simple: Rent a used car and save some cash. It's not a message that appeals to everyone. If you're a marketing executive wanting to impress a big client, you probably don't want to pull up in a Rent-A-Wreck car. But if you want to get from point A to point B for the minimum cash per mile, then Rent-A-Wreck is playing your tune. The company's message seems to be getting across to the right clientele. Revenues have increased significantly.

When you rent a car from Rent-A-Wreck, you are renting from an independent businessperson. This owner has paid a "franchise fee" for the right to use the Rent-A-Wreck name. In order to gain a franchise, he or she must meet financial and other criteria, and must agree to run the rental agency according to rules prescribed by Rent-A-Wreck. Some of these rules require that each franchise maintain its cars in a reasonable fashion. This ensures that, though you won't be cruising down Daytona Beach's Atlantic Avenue in a Mercedes convertible, you can be reasonably assured that you won't be calling a towtruck.

LEARNING OBJECTIVES

1. Explain the accounting for plant asset expenditures.
2. Apply depreciation methods to plant assets.
3. Explain how to account for the disposal of plant assets.
4. Describe how to account for natural resources and intangible assets.

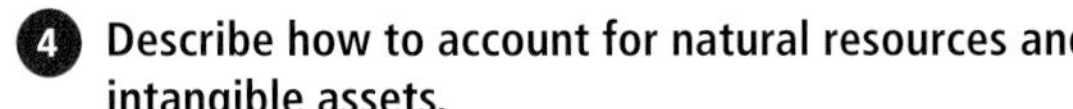

LEARNING OBJECTIVE 1 Explain the accounting for plant asset expenditures.

Plant assets are resources that have three characteristics. They have a physical substance (a definite size and shape), are used in the operations of a business, and are not intended for sale to customers. They are also called **property, plant, and equipment**; **plant and equipment**; and **fixed assets**. These assets are expected to be of use to the company for a number of years. Except for land, plant assets decline in service potential over their useful lives.

Because plant assets play a key role in ongoing operations, companies keep plant assets in good operating condition. They also replace worn-out or outdated plant assets, and expand productive resources as needed. Many companies have substantial investments in plant assets. Illustration 10-1 shows the percentages of plant assets in relation to total assets of companies in a number of industries.

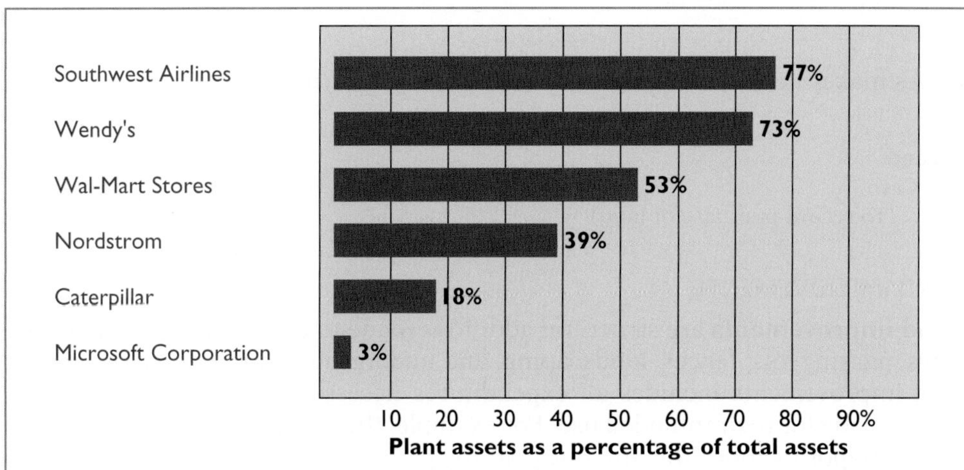

Illustration 10-1
Percentages of plant assets in relation to total assets

Determining the Cost of Plant Assets

The historical cost principle requires that companies record plant assets at cost. Thus, Rent-A-Wreck records its vehicles at cost. **Cost consists of all expenditures necessary to acquire the asset and make it ready for its intended use.** For example, the cost of factory machinery includes the purchase price, freight costs paid by the purchaser, and installation costs. Once cost is established, the company uses that amount as the basis of accounting for the plant asset over its useful life.

In the following sections, we explain the application of the historical cost principle to each of the major classes of plant assets.

LAND

Companies often use **land** as a building site for a manufacturing plant or office building. The cost of land includes (1) the cash purchase price, (2) closing costs such as title and attorney's fees, (3) real estate brokers' commissions, and (4) accrued property taxes and other liens assumed by the purchaser. For example, if the cash price is $50,000 and the purchaser agrees to pay accrued taxes of $5,000, the cost of the land is $55,000.

Companies record as debits (increases) to the Land account all necessary costs incurred to make land **ready for its intended use**. When a company acquires vacant land, these costs include expenditures for clearing, draining, filling, and grading. Sometimes the land has a building on it that must be removed before construction of a new building. In this case, the company debits to the Land account all demolition and removal costs, less any proceeds from salvaged materials.

To illustrate, assume that Hayes Company acquires real estate at a cash cost of $100,000. The property contains an old warehouse that is razed at a net cost of $6,000 ($7,500 in costs less $1,500 proceeds from salvaged materials). Additional expenditures are the attorney's fee, $1,000, and the real estate broker's commission, $8,000. The cost of the land is $115,000, computed as shown in Illustration 10-2.

Illustration 10-2
Computation of cost of land

Land	
Cash price of property	$ 100,000
Net removal cost of warehouse ($7,500 − $1,500)	6,000
Attorney's fee	1,000
Real estate broker's commission	8,000
Cost of land	**$115,000**

Hayes makes the following entry to record the acquisition of the land.

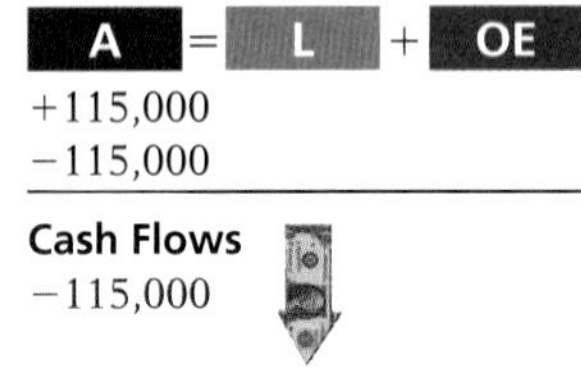

	Debit	Credit
Land	115,000	
Cash		115,000
(To record purchase of land)		

LAND IMPROVEMENTS

Land improvements are structural additions made to land. Examples are driveways, parking lots, fences, landscaping, and underground sprinklers. The cost of land improvements includes all expenditures necessary to make the improvements ready for their intended use. For example, the cost of a new parking lot for Home Depot includes the amount paid for paving, fencing, and lighting. Thus, Home Depot debits to Land Improvements the total of all of these costs.

Land improvements have limited useful lives, and their maintenance and replacement are the responsibility of the company. As a result, companies expense (depreciate) the cost of land improvements over their useful lives.

BUILDINGS

Buildings are facilities used in operations, such as stores, offices, factories, warehouses, and airplane hangars. Companies debit to the Buildings account all necessary expenditures related to the purchase or construction of a building. When a building is **purchased**, such costs include the purchase price, closing costs (attorney's fees, title insurance, etc.), and real estate broker's commission. Costs to make the building ready for its intended use include expenditures for remodeling and replacing or repairing the roof, floors, electrical wiring, and plumbing. When a new building is **constructed**, cost consists of the contract price plus payments for architects' fees, building permits, and excavation costs.

In addition, companies charge certain interest costs to the Buildings account. Interest costs incurred to finance the project are included in the cost of the building when a significant period of time is required to get the building ready for use. In these circumstances, interest costs are considered as necessary as materials and labor. However, the inclusion of interest costs in the cost of a constructed building is **limited to the construction period**. When construction has been completed, the company records subsequent interest payments on funds borrowed to finance the construction as debits (increases) to Interest Expense.

EQUIPMENT

Equipment includes assets used in operations, such as store check-out counters, office furniture, factory machinery, delivery trucks, and airplanes. The cost of equipment, such as Rent-A-Wreck vehicles, consists of the cash purchase price, sales taxes, freight charges, and insurance during transit paid by the purchaser. It also includes expenditures required in assembling, installing, and testing the unit. However, Rent-A-Wreck does not include motor vehicle licenses and accident insurance on company vehicles in the cost of equipment. These costs represent annual recurring expenditures and do not benefit future periods. Thus, they are treated as **expenses** as they are incurred.

To illustrate, assume Merten Company purchases factory machinery at a cash price of $50,000. Related expenditures are for sales taxes $3,000, insurance during shipping $500, and installation and testing $1,000. The cost of the factory machinery is $54,500, as computed in Illustration 10-3.

Illustration 10-3
Computation of cost of factory machinery

Factory Machinery	
Cash price	$ 50,000
Sales taxes	3,000
Insurance during shipping	500
Installation and testing	1,000
Cost of factory machinery	**$54,500**

Merten makes the following summary entry to record the purchase and related expenditures.

	Debit	Credit
Equipment	54,500	
Cash		54,500
(To record purchase of factory machinery)		

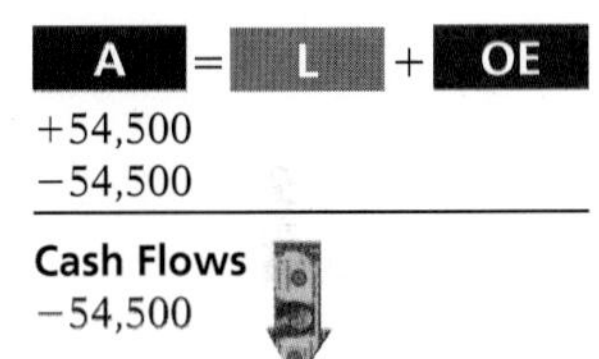

For another example, assume that Lenard Company purchases a delivery truck at a cash price of $22,000. Related expenditures consist of sales taxes $1,320, painting and lettering $500, motor vehicle license $80, and a three-year accident insurance policy $1,600. The cost of the delivery truck is $23,820, computed as follows.

Illustration 10-4
Computation of cost of delivery truck

Delivery Truck	
Cash price	$ 22,000
Sales taxes	1,320
Painting and lettering	500
Cost of delivery truck	**$23,820**

Lenard treats the cost of the motor vehicle license as an expense and the cost of the insurance policy as a prepaid asset. Thus, Lenard makes the following entry to record the purchase of the truck and related expenditures:

	Debit	Credit
Equipment	23,820	
License Expense	80	
Prepaid Insurance	1,600	
Cash		25,500
(To record purchase of delivery truck and related expenditures)		

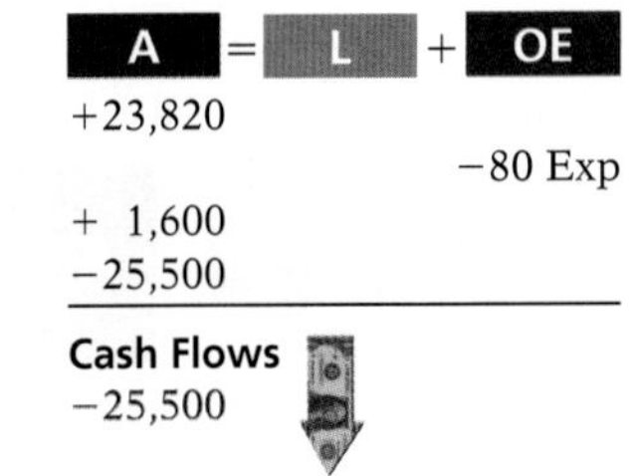

Expenditures During Useful Life

During the useful life of a plant asset, a company may incur costs for ordinary repairs, additions, or improvements. **Ordinary repairs** are expenditures to **maintain** the operating efficiency and productive life of the unit. They usually are small amounts that occur frequently. Examples are motor tune-ups and oil changes, the painting of buildings, and the replacing of worn-out gears on machinery. Companies record such repairs as debits to Maintenance and Repairs Expense as they are incurred. Because they are immediately charged as an expense against revenues, these costs are often referred to as **revenue expenditures**.

In contrast, **additions and improvements** are costs incurred to **increase** the operating efficiency, productive capacity, or useful life of a plant asset. They are usually material in amount and occur infrequently. Additions and improvements increase the company's investment in productive facilities. Companies generally debit these amounts to the plant asset affected. They are often referred to as **capital expenditures**.

Companies must use good judgment in deciding between a revenue expenditure and capital expenditure. For example, assume that Rodriguez Co. purchases a number of wastepaper baskets. The proper accounting would appear to be to capitalize and then depreciate these wastepaper baskets over their useful life. However, Rodriguez will generally expense these wastepaper baskets immediately. This practice is justified on the basis of **materiality**. Materiality refers to the impact of an item's size on a company's financial operations. The **materiality concept** states that if an item would not make a difference in decision-making, the company does not have to follow GAAP in reporting that item.

ANATOMY OF A FRAUD

Bernie Ebbers was the founder and CEO of the phone company WorldCom. The company engaged in a series of increasingly large, debt-financed acquisitions of other companies. These acquisitions made the company grow quickly, which made the stock price increase dramatically. However, because the acquired companies all had different accounting systems, WorldCom's financial records were a mess. When WorldCom's performance started to flatten out, Bernie coerced WorldCom's accountants to engage in a number of fraudulent activities to make net income look better than it really was and thus prop up the stock price. One of these frauds involved treating $7 billion of line costs as capital expenditures. The line costs, which were rental fees paid to other phone companies to use their phone lines, had always been properly expensed in previous years. Capitalization delayed expense recognition to future periods and thus boosted current-period profits.

Total take: $7 billion

THE MISSING CONTROLS

Documentation procedures. The company's accounting system was a disorganized collection of non-integrated systems, which resulted from a series of corporate acquisitions. Top management took advantage of this disorganization to conceal its fraudulent activities.

Independent internal verification. A fraud of this size should have been detected by a routine comparison of the actual physical assets with the list of physical assets shown in the accounting records.

LEARNING OBJECTIVE 2

Apply depreciation methods to plant assets.

As explained in Chapter 3, **depreciation is the process of allocating to expense the cost of a plant asset over its useful (service) life in a rational and systematic manner**. Cost allocation enables companies to properly match expenses with revenues in accordance with the expense recognition principle, as shown in Illustration 10-5.

It is important to understand that **depreciation is a process of cost allocation. It is not a process of asset valuation.** No attempt is made to measure the change in an asset's fair value during ownership. So, the **book value** (cost less accumulated depreciation) of a plant asset may be quite different from its fair value. In fact, if an asset is fully depreciated, it can have a zero book value but still have a fair value.

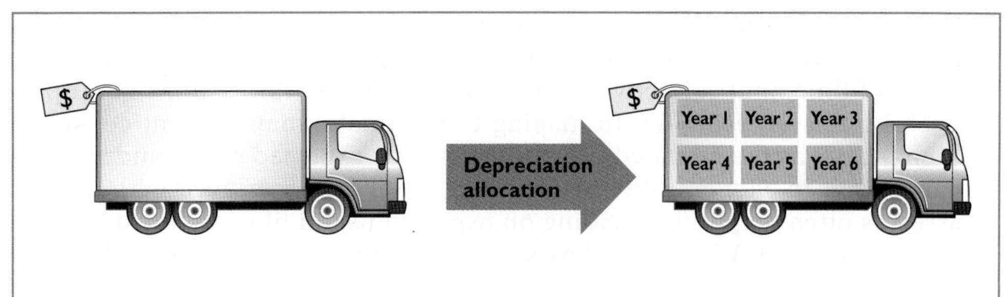

Illustration 10-5
Depreciation as a cost allocation concept

Depreciation applies to three classes of plant assets: land improvements, buildings, and equipment. Each asset in these classes is considered to be a **depreciable asset**. Why? Because the usefulness to the company and revenue-producing ability of each asset will decline over the asset's useful life. Depreciation **does not apply to land** because its usefulness and revenue-producing ability generally remain intact over time. In fact, in many cases, the usefulness of land is greater over time because of the scarcity of good land sites. Thus, **land is not a depreciable asset**.

During a depreciable asset's useful life, its revenue-producing ability declines because of **wear and tear**. A delivery truck that has been driven 100,000 miles will be less useful to a company than one driven only 800 miles.

Revenue-producing ability may also decline because of obsolescence. **Obsolescence** is the process of becoming out of date before the asset physically wears out. For example, major airlines moved from Chicago's Midway Airport to Chicago-O'Hare International Airport because Midway's runways were too short for jumbo jets. Similarly, many companies replace their computers long before they originally planned to do so because improvements in new computing technology make the old computers obsolete.

Recognizing depreciation on an asset does not result in an accumulation of cash for replacement of the asset. The balance in Accumulated Depreciation represents the total amount of the asset's cost that the company has charged to expense. It is not a cash fund.

Note that the concept of depreciation is consistent with the going concern assumption. The **going concern assumption** states that the company will continue in operation for the foreseeable future. If a company does not use a going concern assumption, then plant assets should be stated at their fair value. In that case, depreciation of these assets is not needed.

Factors in Computing Depreciation

Three factors affect the computation of depreciation, as shown in Illustration 10-6.

1. **Cost.** Earlier, we explained the issues affecting the cost of a depreciable asset. Recall that companies record plant assets at cost, in accordance with the historical cost principle.

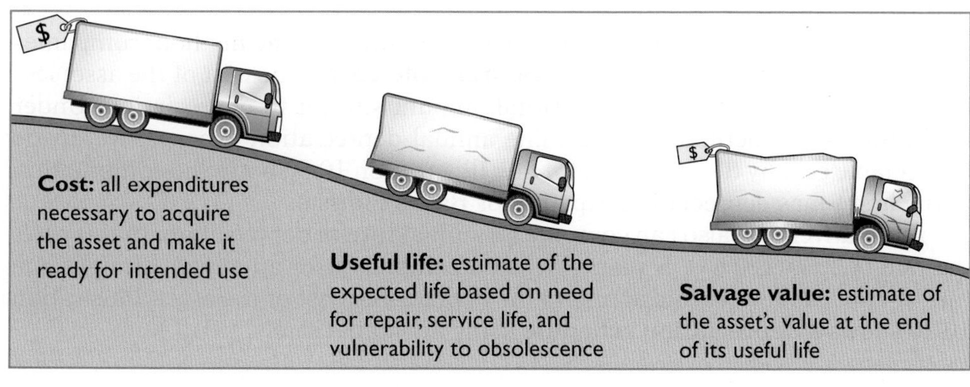

Illustration 10-6
Three factors in computing depreciation

2. **Useful life. Useful life** is an estimate of the expected productive life, also called service life, of the asset for its owner. Useful life may be expressed in terms of time, units of activity (such as machine hours), or units of output. Useful life is an estimate. In making the estimate, management considers such factors as the intended use of the asset, its expected repair and maintenance, and its vulnerability to obsolescence. Past experience with similar assets is often helpful in deciding on expected useful life. We might reasonably expect Rent-A-Wreck and Avis to use different estimated useful lives for their vehicles.

Terminology
Another term sometimes used for salvage value is *residual value*.

3. **Salvage value. Salvage value** is an estimate of the asset's value at the end of its useful life. This value may be based on the asset's worth as scrap or on its expected trade-in value. Like useful life, salvage value is an estimate. In making the estimate, management considers how it plans to dispose of the asset and its experience with similar assets.

Depreciation Methods

Depreciation is generally computed using one of the following methods:

1. Straight-line
2. Units-of-activity
3. Declining-balance

Each method is acceptable under generally accepted accounting principles. Management selects the method(s) it believes to be appropriate. The objective is to select the method that best measures an asset's contribution to revenue over its useful life. Once a company chooses a method, it should apply it consistently over the useful life of the asset. Consistency enhances the comparability of financial statements. Depreciation affects the balance sheet through accumulated depreciation and the income statement through depreciation expense.

We will compare the three depreciation methods using the following data for a small delivery truck purchased by Barb's Florists on January 1, 2017.

Illustration 10-7
Delivery truck data

Cost	\$13,000
Expected salvage value	\$ 1,000
Estimated useful life in years	5
Estimated useful life in miles	100,000

Illustration 10-8 (in the margin) shows the use of the primary depreciation methods in a sample of the largest companies in the United States.

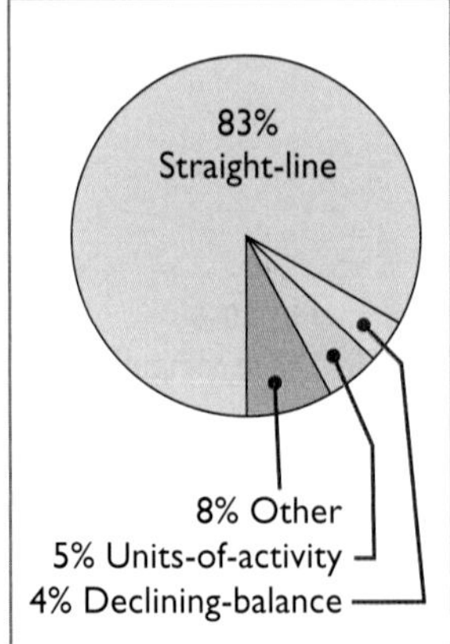

Illustration 10-8
Use of depreciation methods in large U.S. companies

STRAIGHT-LINE METHOD

Under the **straight-line method**, companies expense the same amount of depreciation for each year of the asset's useful life. It is measured solely by the passage of time.

To compute depreciation expense under the straight-line method, companies need to determine depreciable cost. **Depreciable cost** is the cost of the asset less its salvage value. It represents the total amount subject to depreciation. Under the straight-line method, to determine annual depreciation expense, we divide depreciable cost by the asset's useful life. Illustration 10-9 shows the computation of the first year's depreciation expense for Barb's Florists.

Alternatively, we also can compute an annual **rate** of depreciation. In this case, the rate is 20% (100% ÷ 5 years). When a company uses an annual straight-line rate, it applies the percentage rate to the depreciable cost of the asset. Illustration 10-10 shows a **depreciation schedule** using an annual rate.

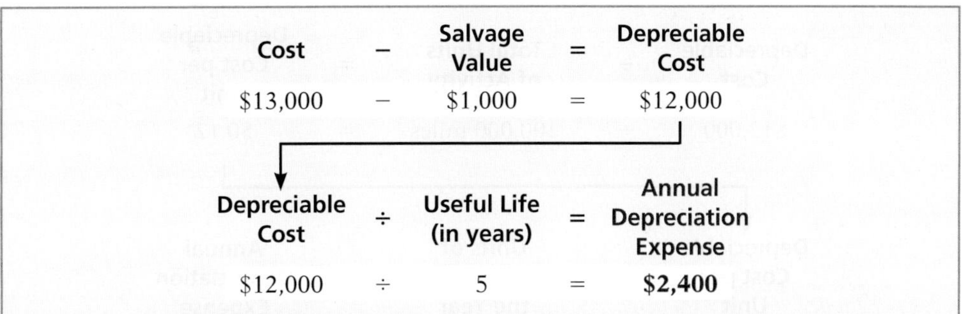

Illustration 10-9
Formula for straight-line method

Illustration 10-10
Straight-line depreciation schedule

BARB'S FLORISTS

	Computation				Annual	End of Year	
Year	**Depreciable Cost**	×	**Depreciation Rate**	=	**Depreciation Expense**	**Accumulated Depreciation**	**Book Value**
2017	$12,000		20%		**$2,400**	$ 2,400	$10,600*
2018	12,000		20		**2,400**	4,800	8,200
2019	12,000		20		**2,400**	7,200	5,800
2020	12,000		20		**2,400**	9,600	3,400
2021	12,000		20		**2,400**	12,000	**1,000**

*Book value = Cost − Accumulated depreciation = ($13,000 − $2,400).

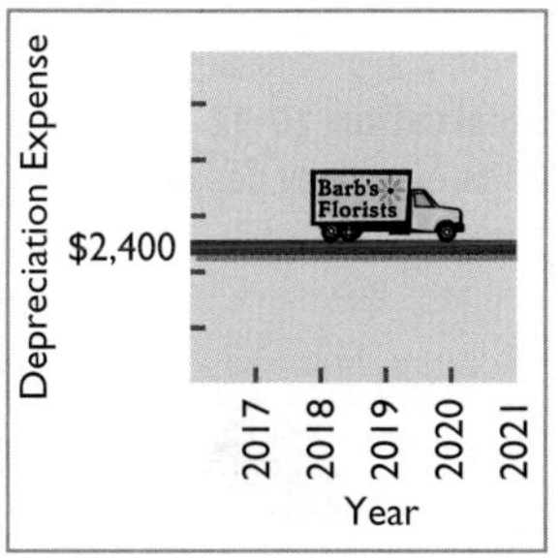

Note that the depreciation expense of $2,400 is the same each year. The book value (computed as cost minus accumulated depreciation) at the end of the useful life is equal to the expected $1,000 salvage value.

What happens to these computations for an asset purchased **during** the year, rather than on January 1? In that case, it is necessary to **prorate the annual depreciation** on a time basis. If Barb's Florists had purchased the delivery truck on April 1, 2017, the company would own the truck for nine months of the first year (April–December). Thus, depreciation for 2017 would be $1,800 ($12,000 × 20% × 9/12 of a year).

The straight-line method predominates in practice. Such large companies as **Campbell Soup**, **Marriott**, and **General Mills** use the straight-line method. It is simple to apply, and it matches expenses with revenues when the use of the asset is reasonably uniform throughout the service life.

UNITS-OF-ACTIVITY METHOD

Under the **units-of-activity method**, useful life is expressed in terms of the total units of production or use expected from the asset, rather than as a time period. The units-of-activity method is ideally suited to factory machinery. Manufacturing companies can measure production in units of output or in machine hours. This method can also be used for such assets as delivery equipment (miles driven) and airplanes (hours in use). The units-of-activity method is generally not suitable for buildings or furniture because depreciation for these assets is more a function of time than of use.

Terminology
Another term often used is the *units-of-production method.*

To use this method, companies estimate the total units of activity for the entire useful life, and then divide these units into depreciable cost. The resulting number represents the depreciable cost per unit. The depreciable cost per unit is then applied to the units of activity during the year to determine the annual depreciation expense.

To illustrate, assume that Barb's Florists drives its delivery truck 15,000 miles in the first year. Illustration 10-11 (page 364) shows the units-of-activity formula and the computation of the first year's depreciation expense.

Illustration 10-11
Formula for units-of-activity method

Depreciable Cost	÷	Total Units of Activity	=	Depreciable Cost per Unit
$12,000	÷	100,000 miles	=	$0.12

Depreciable Cost per Unit	×	Units of Activity during the Year	=	Annual Depreciation Expense
$0.12	×	15,000 miles	=	**$1,800**

The units-of-activity depreciation schedule, using assumed mileage, is as follows.

Illustration 10-12
Units-of-activity depreciation schedule

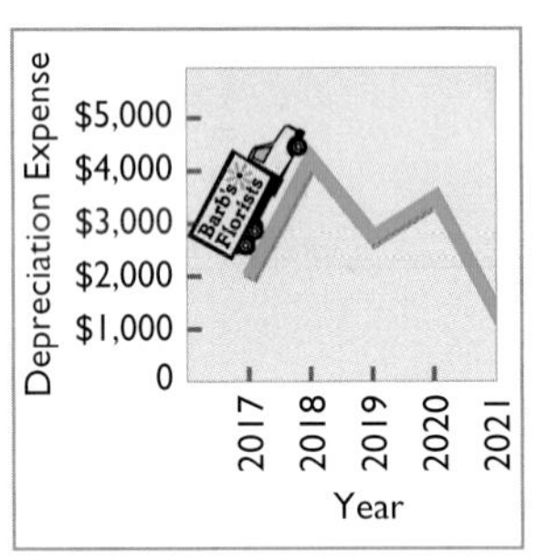

BARB'S FLORISTS

	Computation				Annual	End of Year	
Year	**Units of Activity**	×	**Depreciable Cost/Unit**	=	**Depreciation Expense**	**Accumulated Depreciation**	**Book Value**
2017	15,000		$0.12		**$1,800**	$ 1,800	$11,200*
2018	30,000		0.12		**3,600**	5,400	7,600
2019	20,000		0.12		**2,400**	7,800	5,200
2020	25,000		0.12		**3,000**	10,800	2,200
2021	10,000		0.12		**1,200**	12,000	**1,000**

*($13,000 − $1,800).

This method is easy to apply for assets purchased mid-year. In such a case, the company computes the depreciation using the productivity of the asset for the partial year.

The units-of-activity method is not nearly as popular as the straight-line method (see Illustration 10-8, page 362) primarily because it is often difficult for companies to reasonably estimate total activity. However, some very large companies, such as **Chevron** and **Boise Cascade** (a forestry company), do use this method. When the productivity of an asset varies significantly from one period to another, the units-of-activity method results in the best matching of expenses with revenues.

DECLINING-BALANCE METHOD

The **declining-balance method** produces a decreasing annual depreciation expense over the asset's useful life. The method is so named because the periodic depreciation is based on a **declining book value** (cost less accumulated depreciation) of the asset. With this method, companies compute annual depreciation expense by multiplying the book value at the beginning of the year by the declining-balance depreciation rate. **The depreciation rate remains constant from year to year, but the book value to which the rate is applied declines each year.**

At the beginning of the first year, book value is the cost of the asset. This is because the balance in accumulated depreciation at the beginning of the asset's useful life is zero. In subsequent years, book value is the difference between cost and accumulated depreciation to date. Unlike the other depreciation methods, the declining-balance method does not use depreciable cost in computing annual depreciation expense. That is, **it ignores salvage value in determining the amount to which the declining-balance rate is applied**. Salvage value, however, does limit the total depreciation that can be taken. Depreciation stops when the asset's book value equals expected salvage value.

A common declining-balance rate is double the straight-line rate. The method is often called the **double-declining-balance method**. If Barb's Florists uses the double-declining-balance method, it uses a depreciation rate of 40% (2 × the straight-line rate of 20%). Illustration 10-13 shows the declining-balance formula and the computation of the first year's depreciation on the delivery truck.

Book Value at Beginning of Year	×	Declining-Balance Rate	=	Annual Depreciation Expense
$13,000	×	40%	=	**$5,200**

Illustration 10-13
Formula for declining-balance method

The depreciation schedule under this method is as follows.

BARB'S FLORISTS

	Computation				Annual	End of Year	
Year	**Book Value Beginning of Year**	×	**Depreciation Rate**	=	**Depreciation Expense**	**Accumulated Depreciation**	**Book Value**
2017	$13,000		40%		**$5,200**	$ 5,200	$7,800
2018	7,800		40		**3,120**	8,320	4,680
2019	4,680		40		**1,872**	10,192	2,808
2020	2,808		40		**1,123**	11,315	1,685
2021	1,685		40		**685***	12,000	**1,000**

*Computation of $674 ($1,685 × 40%) is adjusted to $685 in order for book value to equal salvage value.

Illustration 10-14
Double-declining-balance depreciation schedule

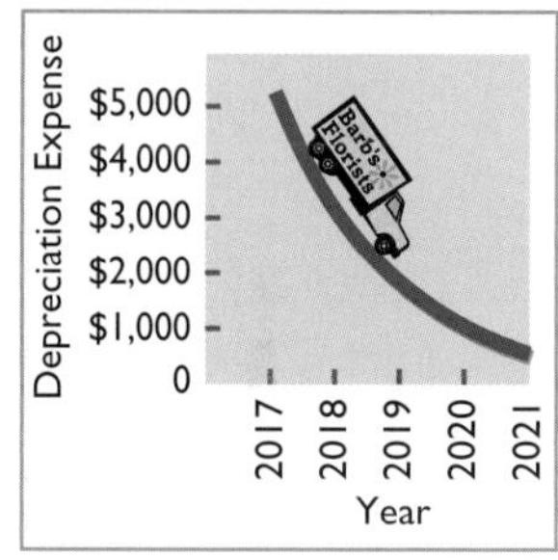

The delivery equipment is 69% depreciated ($8,320 ÷ $12,000) at the end of the second year. Under the straight-line method, the truck would be depreciated 40% ($4,800 ÷ $12,000) at that time. Because the declining-balance method produces higher depreciation expense in the early years than in the later years, it is considered an **accelerated-depreciation method**. The declining-balance method is compatible with the expense recognition principle. It matches the higher depreciation expense in early years with the higher benefits received in these years. It also recognizes lower depreciation expense in later years, when the asset's contribution to revenue is less. Some assets lose usefulness rapidly because of obsolescence. In these cases, the declining-balance method provides the most appropriate depreciation amount.

When a company purchases an asset during the year, it must prorate the first year's declining-balance depreciation on a time basis. For example, if Barb's Florists had purchased the truck on April 1, 2017, depreciation for 2017 would become $3,900 ($13,000 × 40% × 9/12). The book value at the beginning of 2018 is then $9,100 ($13,000 − $3,900), and the 2018 depreciation is $3,640 ($9,100 × 40%). Subsequent computations would follow from those amounts.

COMPARISON OF METHODS

Illustration 10-15 compares annual and total depreciation expense under each of the three methods for Barb's Florists.

Year	Straight-Line	Units-of-Activity	Declining-Balance
2017	$ 2,400	$ 1,800	$ 5,200
2018	2,400	3,600	3,120
2019	2,400	2,400	1,872
2020	2,400	3,000	1,123
2021	2,400	1,200	685
	$12,000	**$12,000**	**$12,000**

Illustration 10-15
Comparison of depreciation methods

Annual depreciation varies considerably among the methods, but **total depreciation expense is the same ($12,000) for the five-year period** under all three methods. Each method is acceptable in accounting because each recognizes in a rational and systematic manner the decline in service potential of the asset. Illustration 10-16 graphs the depreciation expense pattern under each method.

Illustration 10-16
Patterns of depreciation

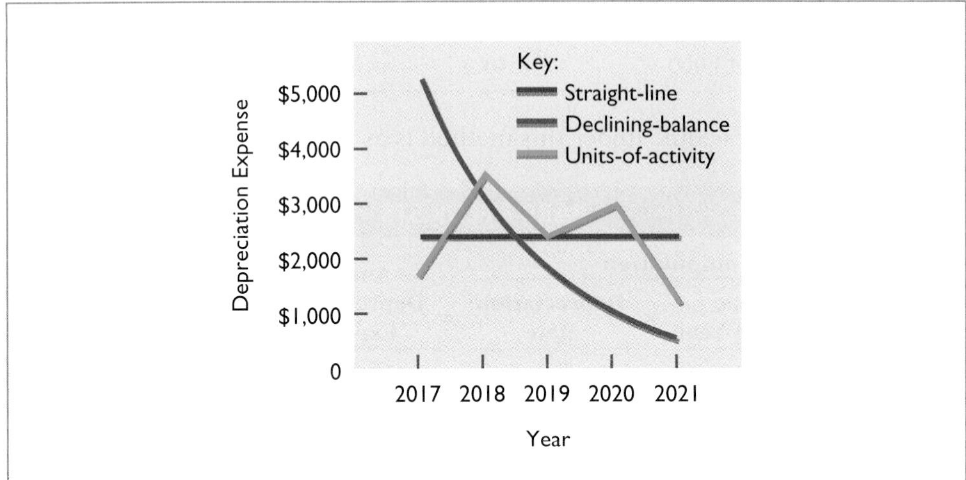

Depreciation and Income Taxes

The Internal Revenue Service (IRS) allows taxpayers to deduct depreciation expense when they compute taxable income. However, the IRS does not require taxpayers to use the same depreciation method on the tax return that is used in preparing financial statements.

Many corporations use straight-line in their financial statements to maximize net income. At the same time, they use a special accelerated-depreciation method on their tax returns to minimize their income taxes. Taxpayers must use on their tax returns either the straight-line method or a special accelerated-depreciation method called the **Modified Accelerated Cost Recovery System** (MACRS).

Revising Periodic Depreciation

Depreciation is one example of the use of estimation in the accounting process. Management should periodically review annual depreciation expense. If wear and tear or obsolescence indicate that annual depreciation estimates are inadequate or excessive, the company should change the amount of depreciation expense.

When a change in an estimate is required, the company makes the change in **current and future years. It does not change depreciation in prior periods.** The rationale is that continual restatement of prior periods would adversely affect confidence in financial statements.

To determine the new annual depreciation expense, the company first computes the asset's depreciable cost at the time of the revision. It then allocates the revised depreciable cost to the remaining useful life.

To illustrate, assume that Barb's Florists decides on January 1, 2020, to extend the useful life of the truck one year (a total life of six years) and increase its salvage value to $2,200. The company has used the straight-line method to depreciate the asset to date. Depreciation per year was $2,400 [($13,000 − $1,000) ÷ 5]. Accumulated depreciation after three years (2017–2019) is $7,200 ($2,400 × 3), and book value is $5,800 ($13,000 − $7,200). The new annual depreciation is $1,200, computed as shown in Illustration 10-17.

Illustration 10-17
Revised depreciation computation

Book value, 1/1/20	$ 5,800	
Less: Salvage value	2,200	
Depreciable cost	$ 3,600	
Remaining useful life	3 years	(2020–2022)
Revised annual depreciation ($3,600 ÷ 3)	**$ 1,200**	

Barb's Florists makes no entry for the change in estimate. On December 31, 2020, during the preparation of adjusting entries, it records depreciation expense of $1,200. Companies must describe in the financial statements significant changes in estimates.

LEARNING OBJECTIVE 3

Explain how to account for the disposal of plant assets.

Companies dispose of plant assets that are no longer useful to them. Illustration 10-18 shows the three ways in which companies make plant asset disposals.

Illustration 10-18
Methods of plant asset disposal

Whatever the disposal method, the company must determine the book value of the plant asset at the disposal date to determine the gain or loss. Recall that the book value is the difference between the cost of the plant asset and the accumulated depreciation to date. If the disposal does not occur on the first day of the year, the company must record depreciation for the fraction of the year to the date of disposal. The company then eliminates the book value by reducing (debiting) Accumulated Depreciation for the total depreciation associated with that asset to the date of disposal and reducing (crediting) the asset account for the cost of the asset.

In this chapter, we examine the accounting for the retirement and sale of plant assets. In the appendix to the chapter, we discuss and illustrate the accounting for exchanges of plant assets.

Retirement of Plant Assets

To illustrate the retirement of plant assets, assume that Hobart Company retires its computer printers, which cost $32,000. The accumulated depreciation on these printers is $32,000. The equipment, therefore, is fully depreciated (zero book value). The entry to record this retirement is as follows.

Accumulated Depreciation—Equipment	32,000	
Equipment		32,000
(To record retirement of fully depreciated equipment)		

A	=	L	+	OE
+32,000				
−32,000				

Cash Flows
no effect

What happens if a fully depreciated plant asset is still useful to the company? In this case, the asset and its accumulated depreciation continue to be reported on the balance sheet, without further depreciation adjustment, until the company retires the asset. Reporting the asset and related accumulated depreciation on the balance sheet informs the financial statement reader that the asset is still in use. Once fully depreciated, no additional depreciation should be taken, even if an asset is still being used. In no situation can the accumulated depreciation on a plant asset exceed its cost.

If a company retires a plant asset before it is fully depreciated and no cash is received for scrap or salvage value, a loss on disposal occurs. For example, assume that Sunset Company discards delivery equipment that cost $18,000 and has accumulated depreciation of $14,000. The entry is as follows.

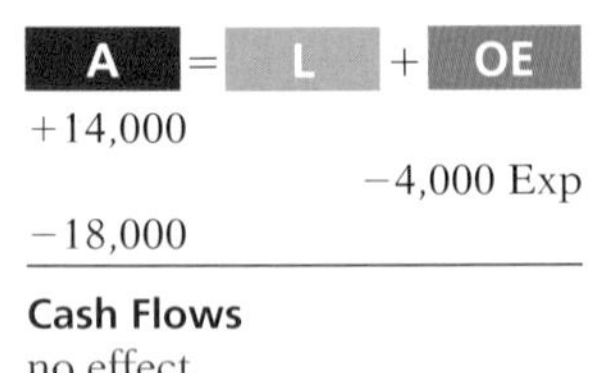

	Debit	Credit
Accumulated Depreciation—Equipment	14,000	
Loss on Disposal of Plant Assets	4,000	
Equipment		18,000
(To record retirement of delivery equipment at a loss)		

Companies report a loss on disposal of plant assets in the "Other expenses and losses" section of the income statement.

Sale of Plant Assets

In a disposal by sale, the company compares the book value of the asset with the proceeds received from the sale. If the proceeds of the sale **exceed** the book value of the plant asset, **a gain on disposal occurs**. If the proceeds of the sale **are less than** the book value of the plant asset sold, **a loss on disposal occurs**.

Only by coincidence will the book value and the fair value of the asset be the same when the asset is sold. Gains and losses on sales of plant assets are therefore quite common. For example, Delta Airlines reported a $94,343,000 gain on the sale of five Boeing B727-200 aircraft and five Lockheed L-1011-1 aircraft.

GAIN ON SALE

To illustrate a gain on sale of plant assets, assume that on July 1, 2017, Wright Company sells office furniture for $16,000 cash. The office furniture originally cost $60,000. As of January 1, 2017, it had accumulated depreciation of $41,000. Depreciation for the first six months of 2017 is $8,000. Wright records depreciation expense and updates accumulated depreciation to July 1 with the following entry.

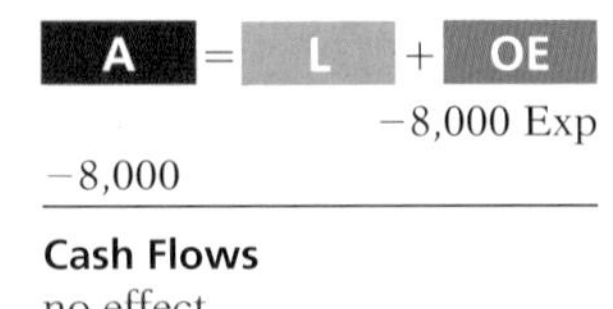

Date	Account	Debit	Credit
July 1	Depreciation Expense	8,000	
	Accumulated Depreciation—Equipment		8,000
	(To record depreciation expense for the first 6 months of 2017)		

After the accumulated depreciation balance is updated, the company computes the gain or loss. The gain or loss is the difference between the proceeds from the sale and the book value at the date of disposal. Illustration 10-19 shows this computation for Wright Company, which has a gain on disposal of $5,000.

Illustration 10-19
Computation of gain on disposal

Cost of office furniture	$60,000
Less: Accumulated depreciation ($41,000 + $8,000)	49,000
Book value at date of disposal	11,000
Proceeds from sale	16,000
Gain on disposal of plant asset	**$ 5,000**

Wright records the sale and the gain on disposal of the plant asset as follows.

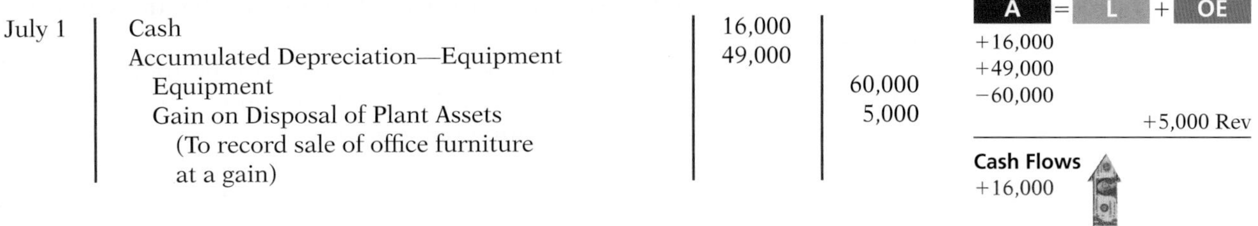

Date	Account	Debit	Credit
July 1	Cash	16,000	
	Accumulated Depreciation—Equipment	49,000	
	Equipment		60,000
	Gain on Disposal of Plant Assets		5,000
	(To record sale of office furniture at a gain)		

Companies report a gain on disposal of plant assets in the "Other revenues and gains" section of the income statement.

LOSS ON SALE

Assume that instead of selling the office furniture for $16,000, Wright sells it for $9,000. In this case, Wright computes a loss of $2,000 as follows.

Illustration 10-20
Computation of loss on disposal

Cost of office furniture	$60,000
Less: Accumulated depreciation	49,000
Book value at date of disposal	11,000
Proceeds from sale	9,000
Loss on disposal of plant asset	**$ 2,000**

Wright records the sale and the loss on disposal of the plant asset as follows.

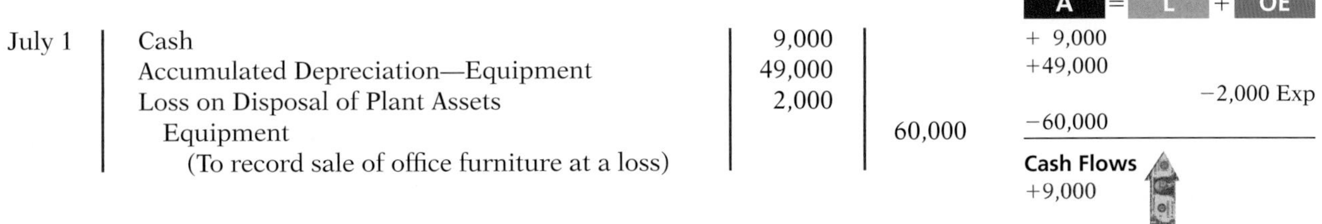

Date	Account	Debit	Credit
July 1	Cash	9,000	
	Accumulated Depreciation—Equipment	49,000	
	Loss on Disposal of Plant Assets	2,000	
	Equipment		60,000
	(To record sale of office furniture at a loss)		

Companies report a loss on disposal of plant assets in the "Other expenses and losses" section of the income statement.

Natural Resources

Natural resources consist of standing timber and underground deposits of oil, gas, and minerals. These long-lived productive assets have two distinguishing characteristics: (1) they are physically extracted in operations (such as mining, cutting, or pumping), and (2) they are replaceable only by an act of nature.

The acquisition cost of a natural resource is the price needed to acquire the resource **and** prepare it for its intended use. For an already-discovered resource, such as an existing coal mine, cost is the price paid for the property.

Depletion

The allocation of the cost of natural resources in a rational and systematic manner over the resource's useful life is called **depletion**. (That is, depletion is to natural resources as depreciation is to plant assets.) **Companies generally use the units-of-activity method** (learned earlier in the chapter) **to compute depletion**. The reason is that **depletion generally is a function of the units extracted during the year**.

Under the units-of-activity method, companies divide the total cost of the natural resource minus salvage value by the number of units estimated to be in the resource. The result is a **depletion cost per unit**. To compute depletion, the cost per unit is then multiplied by the number of units extracted.

To illustrate, assume that Lane Coal Company invests $5 million in a mine estimated to have 1 million tons of coal and no salvage value. Illustration 10-21 shows the computation of the depletion cost per unit.

Illustration 10-21
Computation of depletion cost per unit

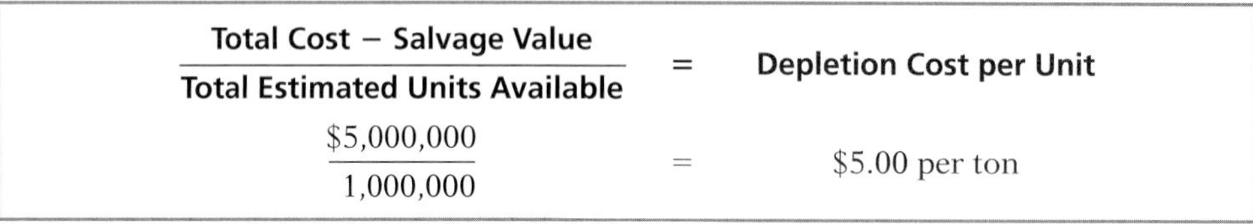

If Lane extracts 250,000 tons in the first year, then the depletion for the year is $1,250,000 (250,000 tons × $5). It records the depletion as follows.

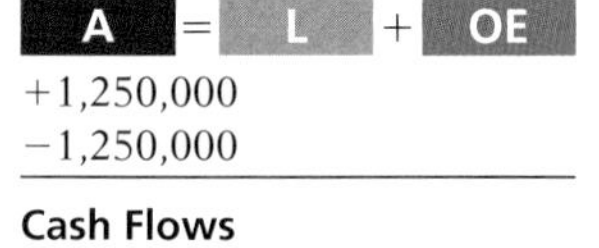

Inventory (coal)	1,250,000	
Accumulated Depletion		1,250,000

Lane debits Inventory for the total depletion for the year and credits Accumulated Depletion to reduce the carrying value of the natural resource. Accumulated Depletion is a contra asset similar to Accumulated Depreciation. Lane credits Inventory when it sells the inventory and debits Cost of Goods Sold. The amount not sold remains in inventory and is reported in the current assets section of the balance sheet.

Some companies do not use an Accumulated Depletion account. In such cases, the company credits the amount of depletion directly to the natural resources account.

Intangible Assets

Intangible assets are rights, privileges, and competitive advantages that result from the ownership of long-lived assets that do not possess physical substance. Evidence of intangibles may exist in the form of contracts or licenses. Intangibles may arise from the following sources:

1. Government grants, such as patents, copyrights, licenses, trademarks, and trade names.
2. Acquisition of another business, in which the purchase price includes a payment for **goodwill**.
3. Private monopolistic arrangements arising from contractual agreements, such as franchises and leases.

Some widely known intangibles are **Microsoft's** patents, **McDonald's** franchises, **Apple**'s trade name iPod, J.K. Rowling's copyrights on the *Harry Potter* books, and the trademark **Rent-A-Wreck** in the chapter opening story.

Accounting for Intangible Assets

Companies record intangible assets at cost. Intangibles are categorized as having either a limited life or an indefinite life. If an intangible has a **limited life**, the company allocates its cost over the asset's useful life using a process similar to depreciation. The process of allocating the cost of intangibles is referred to as

amortization. The cost of intangible assets with **indefinite lives should not be amortized**.

To record amortization of an intangible asset, a company increases (debits) Amortization Expense, and decreases (credits) the specific intangible asset. (Unlike depreciation, no contra account, such as Accumulated Amortization, is usually used.)

Intangible assets are typically amortized on a straight-line basis. For example, the legal life of a patent is 20 years. Companies **amortize the cost of a patent over its 20-year life or its useful life, whichever is shorter**. To illustrate the computation of patent amortization, assume that National Labs purchases a patent at a cost of $60,000. If National estimates the useful life of the patent to be eight years, the annual amortization expense is $7,500 ($60,000 ÷ 8). National records the annual amortization as follows.

Dec. 31	Amortization Expense	7,500	
	Patents		7,500
	(To record patent amortization)		

A	=	L	+	OE
				−7,500 Exp
−7,500				

Cash Flows
no effect

Companies classify Amortization Expense as an operating expense in the income statement.

There is a difference between intangible assets and plant assets in determining cost. For plant assets, cost includes both the purchase price of the asset and the costs incurred in designing and constructing the asset. In contrast, the initial cost for an intangible asset includes **only the purchase price**. Companies expense any costs incurred in developing an intangible asset.

PATENTS

A **patent** is an exclusive right issued by the U.S. Patent Office that enables the recipient to manufacture, sell, or otherwise control an invention for a period of 20 years from the date of the grant. A patent is nonrenewable. But, companies can extend the legal life of a patent by obtaining new patents for improvements or other changes in the basic design. **The initial cost of a patent is the cash or cash equivalent price paid to acquire the patent.**

The saying, "A patent is only as good as the money you're prepared to spend defending it," is very true. Many patents are subject to litigation by competitors. Any legal costs an owner incurs in successfully defending a patent in an infringement suit are considered necessary to establish the patent's validity. **The owner adds those costs to the Patents account and amortizes them over the remaining life of the patent.**

The patent holder amortizes the cost of a patent over its 20-year legal life or its useful life, whichever is shorter. Companies consider obsolescence and inadequacy in determining useful life. These factors may cause a patent to become economically ineffective before the end of its legal life.

COPYRIGHTS

The federal government grants **copyrights**, which give the owner the exclusive right to reproduce and sell an artistic or published work. Copyrights extend for the life of the creator plus 70 years. The cost of a copyright is the **cost of acquiring and defending it**. The cost may be only the small fee paid to the U.S. Copyright Office. Or, it may amount to much more if an infringement suit is involved.

The useful life of a copyright generally is significantly shorter than its legal life. Therefore, copyrights usually are amortized over a relatively short period of time.

TRADEMARKS AND TRADE NAMES

A **trademark** or **trade name** is a word, phrase, jingle, or symbol that identifies a particular enterprise or product. Trade names like Wheaties, Monopoly, Big Mac, Kleenex, Coca-Cola, and Jeep create immediate product identification. They also generally enhance the sale of the product. The creator or original user may obtain exclusive legal right to the trademark or trade name by registering it with the U.S. Patent Office. Such registration provides 20 years of protection. The registration may be renewed indefinitely as long as the trademark or trade name is in use.

If a company purchases the trademark or trade name, its cost is the purchase price. If a company develops and maintains the trademark or trade name, any costs related to these activities are expensed as incurred. Because trademarks and trade names have indefinite lives, they are not amortized.

FRANCHISES

When you fill up your tank at the corner **Shell** station, eat lunch at **Subway**, or rent a car from **Rent-A-Wreck**, you are dealing with franchises. A **franchise** is a contractual arrangement between a franchisor and a franchisee. The franchisor grants the franchisee the right to sell certain products, perform specific services, or use certain trademarks or trade names, usually within a designated geographic area.

Another type of franchise is a **license**. A license granted by a governmental body permits a company to use public property in performing its services. Examples are the use of city streets for a bus line or taxi service, the use of public land for telephone and electric lines, and the use of airwaves for radio or TV broadcasting. In a recent license agreement, **FOX**, **CBS**, and **NBC** agreed to pay $27.9 billion for the right to broadcast **NFL** football games over an eight-year period. Franchises and licenses may by granted for a definite period of time, an indefinite period, or perpetually.

When a company can identify costs with the purchase of a franchise or license, it should recognize an intangible asset. Companies should amortize the cost of a limited-life franchise (or license) over its useful life. If the life is indefinite, the cost is not amortized. Annual payments made under a franchise agreement are recorded as **operating expenses** in the period in which they are incurred.

GOODWILL

Usually, the largest intangible asset that appears on a company's balance sheet is goodwill. **Goodwill** represents the value of all favorable attributes that relate to a company that are not attributable to any other specific asset. These include exceptional management, desirable location, good customer relations, skilled employees, high-quality products, and harmonious relations with labor unions. Goodwill is unique. Unlike assets such as investments and plant assets, which can be sold **individually** in the marketplace, goodwill can be identified only with the business **as a whole**.

If goodwill can be identified only with the business as a whole, how can its amount be determined? One could try to put a dollar value on the factors listed above (exceptional management, desirable location, and so on). But, the results would be very subjective, and such subjective valuations would not contribute to the reliability of financial statements. **Therefore, companies record goodwill only when an entire business is purchased. In that case, goodwill is the excess of cost over the fair value of the net assets (assets less liabilities) acquired.**

In recording the purchase of a business, the company debits (increases) the identifiable acquired assets, credits liabilities at their fair values, credits cash for the purchase price, and records the difference as goodwill. **Goodwill is not amortized** because it is considered to have an indefinite life. Companies report goodwill in the balance sheet under intangible assets.

Research and Development Costs

Research and development costs are expenditures that may lead to patents, copyrights, new processes, and new products. Many companies spend considerable sums of money on research and development (R&D). For example, in a recent year, **IBM** spent over $5.1 billion on R&D.

Research and development costs present accounting problems. For one thing, it is sometimes difficult to assign the costs to specific projects. Also, there are uncertainties in identifying the extent and timing of future benefits. As a result, companies usually record R&D costs **as an expense when incurred**, whether the research and development is successful or not.

To illustrate, assume that Laser Scanner Company spent $3 million on R&D that resulted in two highly successful patents. It spent $20,000 on legal fees for the patents. The company would add the lawyers' fees to the Patents account. The R&D costs, however, cannot be included in the cost of the patents. Instead, the company would record the R&D costs as an expense when incurred.

Many disagree with this accounting approach. They argue that expensing R&D costs leads to understated assets and net income. Others, however, argue that capitalizing these costs will lead to highly speculative assets on the balance sheet. Who is right is difficult to determine.

Discuss how plant assets, natural resources, and intangible assets are reported and analyzed.

Presentation

Usually, companies combine plant assets and natural resources under "Property, plant, and equipment" in the balance sheet. They show intangibles separately. Companies disclose either in the balance sheet or the notes the balances of the major classes of assets, such as land, buildings, and equipment, and accumulated depreciation by major classes or in total. In addition, they should describe the depreciation and amortization methods that were used, as well as disclose the amount of depreciation and amortization expense for the period.

Illustration 10-22 shows a typical financial statement presentation of property, plant, and equipment and intangibles for **The Procter & Gamble Company (P&G)** in its 2013 balance sheet. The notes to P&G's financial statements present greater details about the accounting for its long-term tangible and intangible assets.

Illustration 10-22
P&G's presentation of property, plant, and equipment, and intangible assets

Real World

THE PROCTER & GAMBLE COMPANY
Balance Sheet (partial)
(in millions)

	June 30	
	2013	**2012**
Property, plant, and equipment		
Buildings	$ 7,829	$ 7,324
Machinery and equipment	34,305	32,029
Land	878	880
	43,012	40,233
Accumulated depreciation	(21,346)	(19,856)
Net property, plant, and equipment	21,666	20,377
Goodwill and other intangible assets		
Goodwill	55,188	53,773
Trademarks and other intangible assets, net	31,572	30,988
Net goodwill and other intangible assets	$86,760	$84,761

Illustration 10-23 (page 374) shows another comprehensive presentation of property, plant, and equipment from the balance sheet of **Owens-Illinois**. The notes to the financial statements of Owens-Illinois identify the major classes of property,

Illustration 10-23
Owens-Illinois' presentation of property, plant, and equipment, and intangible assets

Real World

OWENS-ILLINOIS, INC.
Balance Sheet (partial)
(in millions)

Property, plant, and equipment			
Timberlands, at cost, less accumulated depletion		$ 95.4	
Buildings and equipment, at cost	$2,207.1		
Less: Accumulated depreciation	1,229.0	978.1	
Total property, plant, and equipment			$1,073.5
Intangibles			
Patents			410.0
Total			$1,483.5

plant, and equipment. They also indicate that depreciation and amortization are by the straight-line method, and depletion is by the units-of-activity method.

Analysis

Using ratios, we can analyze how efficiently a company uses its assets to generate sales. The **asset turnover** analyzes the productivity of a company's assets. It tells us how many dollars of sales a company generates for each dollar invested in assets. This ratio is computed by dividing net sales by average total assets for the period. Illustration 10-24 shows the computation of the asset turnover for The Procter & Gamble Company. P&G's net sales for 2013 were $84,167 million. Its total ending assets were $139,263 million, and beginning assets were $132,244 million.

Illustration 10-24
Asset turnover formula and computation

Net Sales	÷	Average Total Assets	=	Asset Turnover
$84,167	÷	$\frac{\$132,244 + \$139,263}{2}$	=	**0.62 times**

Thus, each dollar invested in assets produced $0.62 in sales for P&G. If a company is using its assets efficiently, each dollar of assets will create a high amount of sales. This ratio varies greatly among different industries—from those that are asset-intensive (utilities) to those that are not (services).

LEARNING OBJECTIVE *6

APPENDIX 10A: Explain how to account for the exchange of plant assets.

Ordinarily, companies record a gain or loss on the exchange of plant assets. The rationale for recognizing a gain or loss is that most exchanges have **commercial substance**. An exchange has commercial substance if the future cash flows change as a result of the exchange.

To illustrate, Ramos Co. exchanges some of its equipment for land held by Brodhead Inc. It is likely that the timing and amount of the cash flows arising from the land will differ significantly from the cash flows arising from the equipment. As a result, both Ramos and Brodhead are in different economic positions. Therefore, **the exchange has commercial substance**, and the companies recognize a gain or loss in the exchange. Because most exchanges have commercial substance (even when similar assets are exchanged), we illustrate only this type of situation for both a loss and a gain.

Loss Treatment

To illustrate an exchange that results in a loss, assume that Roland Company exchanged a set of used trucks plus cash for a new semi-truck. The used trucks have a combined book value of $42,000 (cost $64,000 less $22,000 accumulated depreciation). Roland's purchasing agent, experienced in the secondhand market, indicates that the used trucks have a fair value of $26,000. In addition to the trucks, Roland must pay $17,000 for the semi-truck. Roland computes the cost of the semi-truck as follows.

Illustration 10A-1
Cost of semi-truck

Fair value of used trucks	$26,000
Cash paid	17,000
Cost of semi-truck	$43,000

Roland incurs a loss on disposal of plant assets of $16,000 on this exchange. The reason is that the book value of the used trucks is greater than the fair value of these trucks. The computation is as follows.

Illustration 10A-2
Computation of loss on disposal

Book value of used trucks ($64,000 − $22,000)	$ 42,000
Fair value of used trucks	26,000
Loss on disposal of plant assets	**$16,000**

In recording an exchange at a loss, three steps are required: (1) eliminate the book value of the asset given up, (2) record the cost of the asset acquired, and (3) recognize the loss on disposal of plant assets. Roland Company thus records the exchange on the loss as follows.

Equipment (new)	43,000	
Accumulated Depreciation—Equipment	22,000	
Loss on Disposal of Plant Assets	16,000	
Equipment (old)		64,000
Cash		17,000
(To record exchange of used trucks for semi-truck)		

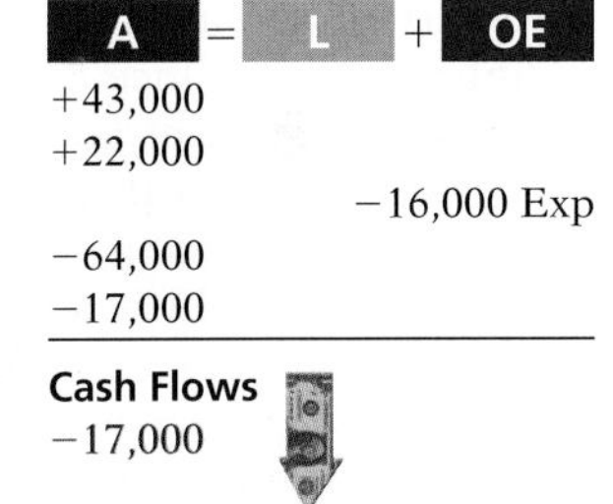

Gain Treatment

To illustrate a gain situation, assume that Mark Express Delivery decides to exchange its old delivery equipment plus cash of $3,000 for new delivery equipment. The book value of the old delivery equipment is $12,000 (cost $40,000 less accumulated depreciation $28,000). The fair value of the old delivery equipment is $19,000.

The cost of the new asset is the fair value of the old asset exchanged plus any cash paid (or other consideration given up). The cost of the new delivery equipment is $22,000, computed as follows.

Illustration 10A-3
Cost of new delivery equipment

Fair value of old delivery equipment	$ 19,000
Cash paid	3,000
Cost of new delivery equipment	**$22,000**

A gain results when the fair value of the old delivery equipment is greater than its book value. For Mark Express, there is a gain of $7,000 on disposal of plant assets, computed as follows.

Illustration 10A-4
Computation of gain on disposal

Fair value of old delivery equipment	$19,000
Book value of old delivery equipment ($40,000 − $28,000)	12,000
Gain on disposal of plant assets	**$ 7,000**

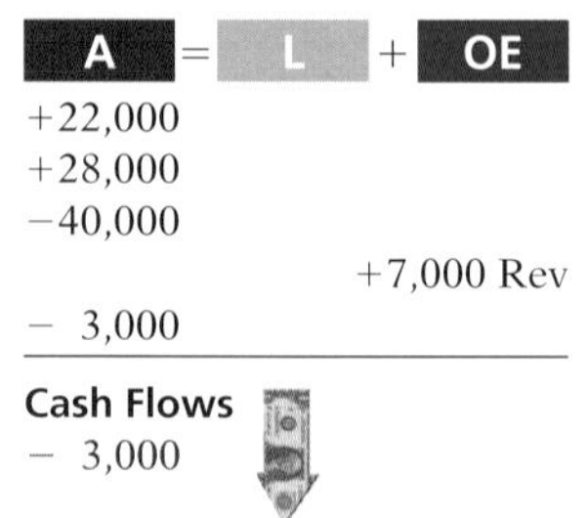

Mark Express Delivery records the exchange as follows.

Equipment (new)	22,000	
Accumulated Depreciation—Equipment (old)	28,000	
Equipment (old)		40,000
Gain on Disposal of Plant Assets		7,000
Cash		3,000
(To record exchange of old delivery equipment for new delivery equipment)		

In recording an exchange at a gain, the following three steps are involved: (1) eliminate the book value of the asset given up, (2) record the cost of the asset acquired, and (3) recognize the gain on disposal of plant assets. Accounting for exchanges of plant assets becomes more complex if the transaction does not have commercial substance. This issue is discussed in more advanced accounting classes.

REVIEW AND PRACTICE

LEARNING OBJECTIVES REVIEW

1 Explain the accounting for plant asset expenditures. The cost of plant assets includes all expenditures necessary to acquire the asset and make it ready for its intended use. Once cost is established, the company uses that amount as the basis of accounting for the plant assets over its useful life.

Companies incur revenue expenditures to maintain the operating efficiency and productive life of an asset. They debit these expenditures to Maintenance and Repairs Expense as incurred. Capital expenditures increase the operating efficiency, productive capacity, or expected useful life of the asset. Companies generally debit these expenditures to the plant asset affected.

2 Apply depreciation methods to plant assets. Depreciation is the allocation of the cost of a plant asset to expense over its useful (service) life in a rational and systematic manner. Depreciation is not a process of valuation, nor is it a process that results in an accumulation of cash.

Three depreciation methods are:

Method	Effect on Annual Depreciation	Formula
Straight-line	Constant amount	Depreciable cost ÷ Useful life (in years)
Units-of-activity	Varying amount	Depreciable cost per unit × Units of activity during the year
Declining-balance	Decreasing amount	Book value at beginning of year × Declining-balance rate

Companies make revisions of periodic depreciation in present and future periods, not retroactively. They determine the new annual depreciation by dividing the depreciable cost at the time of the revision by the remaining useful life.

3 Explain how to account for the disposal of plant assets. The accounting for disposal of a plant asset through retirement or sale is as follows. (a) Eliminate the book value of the plant asset at the date of disposal. (b) Record cash proceeds, if any. (c) Account for the difference between the book value and the cash proceeds as a gain or loss on disposal.

4 Describe how to account for natural resources and intangible assets. Companies compute depletion cost per unit by dividing the total cost of the natural resource minus salvage value by the number of units estimated to be in the resource. They then multiply the depletion cost per unit by the number of units extracted.

The process of allocating the cost of an intangible asset is referred to as amortization. The cost of intangible assets with indefinite lives is not amortized. Companies normally use the straight-line method for amortizing intangible assets.

5 Discuss how plant assets, natural resources, and intangible assets are reported and analyzed. Companies usually combine plant assets and natural resources under property, plant, and equipment. They show intangibles separately under intangible assets. Either within the balance sheet or in the notes, companies should disclose the balances of the major classes of assets, such as land, buildings, and equipment, and accumulated depreciation by major classes or in total. They also should describe the depreciation and amortization methods used, and should disclose the amount of depreciation and amortization expense for the period. The asset turnover measures the productivity of a company's assets in generating sales.

*6 **Explain how to account for the exchange of plant assets.** Ordinarily, companies record a gain or loss on the exchange of plant assets. The rationale for recognizing a gain or loss is that most exchanges have commercial substance. An exchange has commercial substance if the future cash flows change as a result of the exchange.

GLOSSARY REVIEW

Accelerated-depreciation method Depreciation method that produces higher depreciation expense in the early years than in the later years.

Additions and improvements Costs incurred to increase the operating efficiency, productive capacity, or useful life of a plant asset.

Amortization The allocation of the cost of an intangible asset to expense over its useful life in a systematic and rational manner.

Asset turnover A measure of how efficiently a company uses its assets to generate sales; calculated as net sales divided by average total assets.

Capital expenditures Expenditures that increase the company's investment in productive facilities.

Copyrights Exclusive grant from the federal government that allows the owner to reproduce and sell an artistic or published work.

Declining-balance method Depreciation method that applies a constant rate to the declining book value of the asset and produces a decreasing annual depreciation expense over the useful life of the asset.

Depletion The allocation of the cost of a natural resource to expense in a rational and systematic manner over the resource's useful life.

Depreciable cost The cost of a plant asset less its salvage value.

Depreciation The process of allocating to expense the cost of a plant asset over its useful (service) life in a rational and systematic manner.

Franchise (license) A contractual arrangement under which the franchisor grants the franchisee the right to sell certain products, perform specific services, or use certain trademarks or trade names, usually within a designated geographic area.

Going concern assumption States that the company will continue in operation for the foreseeable future.

Goodwill The value of all favorable attributes that relate to a company that is not attributable to any other specific asset.

Intangible assets Rights, privileges, and competitive advantages that result from the ownership of long-lived assets that do not possess physical substance.

Materiality concept If an item would not make a difference in decision-making, a company does not have to follow GAAP in reporting it.

Natural resources Assets that consist of standing timber and underground deposits of oil, gas, and minerals.

Ordinary repairs Expenditures to maintain the operating efficiency and productive life of the unit.

Patent An exclusive right issued by the U.S. Patent Office that enables the recipient to manufacture, sell, or otherwise control an invention for a period of 20 years from the date of the grant.

Plant assets Tangible resources that are used in the operations of the business and are not intended for sale to customers.

Research and development (R&D) costs Expenditures that may lead to patents, copyrights, new processes, or new products.

Revenue expenditures Expenditures that are immediately charged against revenues as an expense.

Salvage value An estimate of an asset's value at the end of its useful life.

Straight-line method Depreciation method in which periodic depreciation is the same for each year of the asset's useful life.

Trademark (trade name) A word, phrase, jingle, or symbol that identifies a particular enterprise or product.

Units-of-activity method Depreciation method in which useful life is expressed in terms of the total units of production or use expected from an asset.

Useful life An estimate of the expected productive life, also called service life, of an asset.

PRACTICE EXERCISES

Determine depreciation for partial periods

(LO 2)

1. Numo Company purchased a new machine on October 1, 2017, at a cost of $145,000. The company estimated that the machine will have a salvage value of $25,000. The machine is expected to be used for 20,000 working hours during its 5-year life.

Instructions

Compute the depreciation expense under the following methods for the year indicated.

(a) Straight-line for 2017.

(b) Units-of-activity for 2017, assuming machine usage was 3,400 hours.

(c) Declining-balance using double the straight-line rate for 2017 and 2018.

Solution

1. (a) Straight-line method:

$$\left(\frac{\$145{,}000 - \$25{,}000}{5}\right) = \$24{,}000 \text{ per year}$$

2017 depreciation = \$24,000 × 3/12 = \$6,000

(b) Units-of-activity method:

$$\left(\frac{\$145{,}000 - \$25{,}000}{20{,}000}\right) = \$6.00 \text{ per hour}$$

2017 depreciation = 3,400 hours × \$6.00 = \$20,400

(c) Declining-balance method:

2017 depreciation = \$145,000 × 40% × 3/12 = \$14,500

Book value January 1, 2018 = \$145,000 − \$14,500 = \$130,500

2018 depreciation = \$130,500 × 40% = \$52,200

Prepare entries to set up appropriate accounts for different intangibles; amortize intangible assets.

(LO 4)

2. Henning Company, organized in 2017, has the following transactions related to intangible assets.

1/2/17	Purchased patent (7-year life)	\$840,000
4/1/17	Goodwill purchased (indefinite life)	450,000
7/1/17	10-year franchise: expiration date 7/1/2027	330,000
9/1/17	Research and development costs	210,000

Instructions

Prepare the necessary entries to record these intangibles. All costs incurred were for cash. Make the adjusting entries as of December 31, 2017, recording any necessary amortization and reflecting all balances accurately as of that date.

Solution

2.

Date	Account	Debit	Credit
1/2/17	Patents	840,000	
	Cash		840,000
4/1/17	Goodwill	450,000	
	Cash		450,000
	(Part of the entry to record purchase of another company)		
7/1/17	Franchises	330,000	
	Cash		330,000
9/1/17	Research and Development Expense	210,000	
	Cash		210,000
12/31/17	Amortization Expense		
	(\$840,000 ÷ 7) + [(\$330,000 ÷ 10) × 1/2]	136,500	
	Patents		120,000
	Franchises		16,500

Ending balances, 12/31/17:

Patents = \$720,000 (\$840,000 − \$120,000)

Goodwill = \$450,000

Franchises = \$313,500 (\$330,000 − \$16,500)

R&D expense = \$210,000

PRACTICE PROBLEMS

1. DuPage Company purchases a factory machine at a cost of $18,000 on January 1, 2017. DuPage expects the machine to have a salvage value of $2,000 at the end of its 4-year useful life.

During its useful life, the machine is expected to be used 160,000 hours. Actual annual hourly use was 2017, 40,000; 2018, 60,000; 2019, 35,000; and 2020, 25,000.

Instructions

Prepare depreciation schedules for the following methods: (a) straight-line, (b) units-of-activity, and (c) declining-balance using double the straight-line rate.

Solution

1. (a)

Straight-Line Method

	Computation					End of Year	
Year	Depreciable Cost*	×	Depreciation Rate	=	Annual Depreciation Expense	Accumulated Depreciation	Book Value
2017	$16,000		25%		$4,000	$ 4,000	$14,000**
2018	16,000		25%		4,000	8,000	10,000
2019	16,000		25%		4,000	12,000	6,000
2020	16,000		25%		4,000	16,000	2,000

*$18,000 − $2,000.
**$18,000 − $4,000.

(b)

Units-of-Activity Method

	Computation					End of Year	
Year	Units of Activity	×	Depreciable Cost/Unit	=	Annual Depreciation Expense	Accumulated Depreciation	Book Value
2017	40,000		$0.10*		$4,000	$ 4,000	$14,000
2018	60,000		0.10		6,000	10,000	8,000
2019	35,000		0.10		3,500	13,500	4,500
2020	25,000		0.10		2,500	16,000	2,000

*($18,000 − $2,000) ÷ 160,000.

(c)

Declining-Balance Method

	Computation					End of Year	
Year	Book Value Beginning of Year	×	Depreciation Rate*	=	Annual Depreciation Expense	Accumulated Depreciation	Book Value
2017	$18,000		50%		$9,000	$ 9,000	$9,000
2018	9,000		50%		4,500	13,500	4,500
2019	4,500		50%		2,250	15,750	2,250
2020	2,250		50%		250**	16,000	2,000

*¼ × 2.
**Adjusted to $250 because ending book value should not be less than expected salvage value.

Record disposal of plant asset. (LO 3)

2. On January 1, 2017, Skyline Limousine Co. purchased a limo at an acquisition cost of $28,000. The vehicle has been depreciated by the straight-line method using a 4-year service life and a $4,000 salvage value. The company's fiscal year ends on December 31.

Instructions

Prepare the journal entry or entries to record the disposal of the limousine assuming that it was:

(a) Retired and scrapped with no salvage value on January 1, 2021.

(b) Sold for $5,000 on July 1, 2020.

Solution

2. (a) 1/1/21	Accumulated Depreciation—Equipment	24,000	
	Loss on Disposal of Plant Assets	4,000	
	Equipment		28,000
	(To record retirement of limousine)		
(b) 7/1/20	Depreciation Expense*	3,000	
	Accumulated Depreciation—Equipment		3,000
	(To record depreciation to date of disposal)		
	Cash	5,000	
	Accumulated Depreciation—Equipment**	21,000	
	Loss on Disposal of Plant Assets	2,000	
	Equipment		28,000
	(To record sale of limousine)		

*[($28,000 − $4,000) ÷ 4] × $\frac{1}{2}$.

**[($28,000 − $4,000) ÷ 4] × 3 = $18,000; $18,000 + $3,000.

EXERCISES

Determine cost of plant acquisitions.

(LO 1)

E10-1 The following expenditures relating to plant assets were made by Prather Company during the first 2 months of 2017.

1. Paid $5,000 of accrued taxes at time plant site was acquired.
2. Paid $200 insurance to cover possible accident loss on new factory machinery while the machinery was in transit.
3. Paid $850 sales taxes on new delivery truck.
4. Paid $17,500 for parking lots and driveways on new plant site.
5. Paid $250 to have company name and advertising slogan painted on new delivery truck.
6. Paid $8,000 for installation of new factory machinery.
7. Paid $900 for one-year accident insurance policy on new delivery truck.
8. Paid $75 motor vehicle license fee on the new truck.

Instructions

(a) Explain the application of the historical cost principle in determining the acquisition cost of plant assets.

(b) List the numbers of the foregoing transactions, and opposite each indicate the account title to which each expenditure should be debited.

Determine property, plant, and equipment costs.

(LO 1)

E10-2 Benedict Company incurred the following costs.

1. Sales tax on factory machinery purchased	$ 5,000
2. Painting of and lettering on truck immediately upon purchase	700
3. Installation and testing of factory machinery	2,000
4. Real estate broker's commission on land purchased	3,500
5. Insurance premium paid for first year's insurance on new truck	880
6. Cost of landscaping on property purchased	7,200
7. Cost of paving parking lot for new building constructed	17,900
8. Cost of clearing, draining, and filling land	13,300
9. Architect's fees on self-constructed building	10,000

Instructions

Indicate to which account Benedict would debit each of the costs.

Determine acquisition costs of land.

(LO 1)

E10-3 On March 1, 2017, Westmorlan Company acquired real estate on which it planned to construct a small office building. The company paid $75,000 in cash. An old warehouse on the property was razed at a cost of $8,600; the salvaged materials were sold for $1,700. Additional expenditures before construction began included $1,100 attorney's fee for work concerning the land purchase, $5,000 real estate broker's fee, $7,800 architect's fee, and $14,000 to put in driveways and a parking lot.

Instructions

(a) Determine the amount to be reported as the cost of the land.

(b) For each cost not used in part (a), indicate the account to be debited.

E10-4 Tom Parkey has prepared the following list of statements about depreciation.

Understand depreciation concepts.

(LO 2)

1. Depreciation is a process of asset valuation, not cost allocation.
2. Depreciation provides for the proper matching of expenses with revenues.
3. The book value of a plant asset should approximate its fair value.
4. Depreciation applies to three classes of plant assets: land, buildings, and equipment.
5. Depreciation does not apply to a building because its usefulness and revenue-producing ability generally remain intact over time.
6. The revenue-producing ability of a depreciable asset will decline due to wear and tear and to obsolescence.
7. Recognizing depreciation on an asset results in an accumulation of cash for replacement of the asset.
8. The balance in accumulated depreciation represents the total cost that has been charged to expense.
9. Depreciation expense and accumulated depreciation are reported on the income statement.
10. Four factors affect the computation of depreciation: cost, useful life, salvage value, and residual value.

Instructions

Identify each statement as true or false. If false, indicate how to correct the statement.

E10-5 Yello Bus Lines uses the units-of-activity method in depreciating its buses. One bus was purchased on January 1, 2017, at a cost of $148,000. Over its 4-year useful life, the bus is expected to be driven 100,000 miles. Salvage value is expected to be $8,000.

Compute depreciation under units-of-activity method.

(LO 2)

Instructions

(a) Compute the depreciable cost per unit.

(b) Prepare a depreciation schedule assuming actual mileage was: 2017, 26,000; 2018, 32,000; 2019, 25,000; and 2020, 17,000.

E10-6 Rottino Company purchased a new machine on October 1, 2017, at a cost of $150,000. The company estimated that the machine will have a salvage value of $12,000. The machine is expected to be used for 10,000 working hours during its 5-year life.

Determine depreciation for partial periods.

(LO 2)

Instructions

Compute the depreciation expense under the following methods for the year indicated.

(a) Straight-line for 2017.

(b) Units-of-activity for 2017, assuming machine usage was 1,700 hours.

(c) Declining-balance using double the straight-line rate for 2017 and 2018.

E10-7 Linton Company purchased a delivery truck for $34,000 on January 1, 2017. The truck has an expected salvage value of $2,000, and is expected to be driven 100,000 miles over its estimated useful life of 8 years. Actual miles driven were 15,000 in 2017 and 12,000 in 2018.

Compute depreciation using different methods.

(LO 2)

Instructions

(a) Compute depreciation expense for 2017 and 2018 using (1) the straight-line method, (2) the units-of-activity method, and (3) the double-declining-balance method.

(b) Assume that Linton uses the straight-line method.
   (1) Prepare the journal entry to record 2017 depreciation.
   (2) Show how the truck would be reported in the December 31, 2017, balance sheet.

E10-8 Terry Wade, the new controller of Hellickson Company, has reviewed the expected useful lives and salvage values of selected depreciable assets at the beginning of 2017. His findings are as follows.

Compute revised annual depreciation.

(LO 2)

Type of Asset	Date Acquired	Cost	Accumulated Depreciation 1/1/17	Useful Life in Years		Salvage Value	
				Old	Proposed	Old	Proposed
Building	1/1/11	$800,000	$114,000	40	50	$40,000	$26,000
Warehouse	1/1/12	100,000	19,000	25	20	5,000	6,000

All assets are depreciated by the straight-line method. Hellickson Company uses a calendar year in preparing annual financial statements. After discussion, management has agreed to accept Terry's proposed changes.

Instructions

(a) Compute the revised annual depreciation on each asset in 2017. (Show computations.)
(b) Prepare the entry (or entries) to record depreciation on the building in 2017.

Journalize entries for disposal of plant assets.
(LO 3)

E10-9 Presented below are selected transactions at Ridge Company for 2017.

Jan. 1 Retired a piece of machinery that was purchased on January 1, 2007. The machine cost $62,000 on that date. It had a useful life of 10 years with no salvage value.

June 30 Sold a computer that was purchased on January 1, 2014. The computer cost $45,000. It had a useful life of 5 years with no salvage value. The computer was sold for $14,000.

Dec. 31 Discarded a delivery truck that was purchased on January 1, 2013. The truck cost $33,000. It was depreciated based on a 6-year useful life with a $3,000 salvage value.

Instructions

Journalize all entries required on the above dates, including entries to update depreciation, where applicable, on assets disposed of. Ridge Company uses straight-line depreciation. (Assume depreciation is up to date as of December 31, 2016.)

Journalize entries for disposal of equipment.
(LO 3)

E10-10 Pryce Company owns equipment that cost $65,000 when purchased on January 1, 2014. It has been depreciated using the straight-line method based on estimated salvage value of $5,000 and an estimated useful life of 5 years.

Instructions

Prepare Pryce Company's journal entries to record the sale of the equipment in these four independent situations.

(a) Sold for $31,000 on January 1, 2017.
(b) Sold for $31,000 on May 1, 2017.
(c) Sold for $11,000 on January 1, 2017.
(d) Sold for $11,000 on October 1, 2017.

Journalize entries for natural resources depletion.
(LO 4)

E10-11 On July 1, 2017, Friedman Inc. invested $720,000 in a mine estimated to have 900,000 tons of ore of uniform grade. During the last 6 months of 2017, 100,000 tons of ore were mined.

Instructions

(a) Prepare the journal entry to record depletion.
(b) Assume that the 100,000 tons of ore were mined, but only 80,000 units were sold. How are the costs applicable to the 20,000 unsold units reported?

Prepare adjusting entries for amortization.
(LO 4)

E10-12 The following are selected 2017 transactions of Pedigo Corporation.

Jan. 1 Purchased a small company and recorded goodwill of $150,000. Its useful life is indefinite.

May 1 Purchased for $75,000 a patent with an estimated useful life of 5 years and a legal life of 20 years.

Instructions

Prepare necessary adjusting entries at December 31 to record amortization required by the events above.

Prepare entries to set up appropriate accounts for different intangibles; amortize intangible assets.
(LO 4)

E10-13 Gill Company, organized in 2017, has the following transactions related to intangible assets.

1/2/17	Purchased patent (7-year life)	$595,000
4/1/17	Goodwill purchased (indefinite life)	360,000
7/1/17	10-year franchise; expiration date 7/1/2027	480,000
9/1/17	Research and development costs	185,000

Instructions

Prepare the necessary entries to record these intangibles. All costs incurred were for cash. Make the adjusting entries as of December 31, 2017, recording any necessary amortization and reflecting all balances accurately as of that date.

E10-14 During 2017, Paola Corporation reported net sales of $3,500,000 and net income of $1,500,000. Its balance sheet reported average total assets of $1,400,000.

Calculate asset turnover.
(LO 5)

Instructions
Calculate the asset turnover.

***E10-15** Presented below are two independent transactions. Both transactions have commercial substance.

Journalize entries for exchanges.
(LO 6)

1. Mercy Co. exchanged old trucks (cost $64,000 less $22,000 accumulated depreciation) plus cash of $17,000 for new trucks. The old trucks had a fair value of $38,000.
2. Pence Inc. trades its used machine (cost $12,000 less $4,000 accumulated depreciation) for a new machine. In addition to exchanging the old machine (which had a fair value of $11,000), Pence also paid cash of $3,000.

Instructions
(a) Prepare the entry to record the exchange of assets by Mercy Co.
(b) Prepare the entry to record the exchange of assets by Pence Inc.

***E10-16** Rizzo's Delivery Company and Overland's Express Delivery exchanged delivery trucks on January 1, 2017. Rizzo's truck cost $22,000. It has accumulated depreciation of $15,000 and a fair value of $3,000. Overland's truck cost $10,000. It has accumulated depreciation of $8,000 and a fair value of $3,000. The transaction has commercial substance.

Journalize entries for the exchange of plant assets.
(LO 6)

Instructions
(a) Journalize the exchange for Rizzo's Delivery Company.
(b) Journalize the exchange for Overland's Express Delivery.

PROBLEMS

P10-1A Venable Company was organized on January 1. During the first year of operations, the following plant asset expenditures and receipts were recorded in random order.

Determine acquisition costs of land and building.
(LO 1)

XLS

Debit

1. Cost of filling and grading the land	$ 4,000
2. Full payment to building contractor	690,000
3. Real estate taxes on land paid for the current year	5,000
4. Cost of real estate purchased as a plant site (land $100,000 and building $45,000)	145,000
5. Excavation costs for new building	35,000
6. Architect's fees on building plans	10,000
7. Accrued real estate taxes paid at time of purchase of real estate	2,000
8. Cost of parking lots and driveways	14,000
9. Cost of demolishing building to make land suitable for construction of new building	25,000
	$930,000

Credit

10. Proceeds from salvage of demolished building	$ 3,500

Instructions
Analyze the foregoing transactions using the following column headings. Insert the number of each transaction in the Item space, and insert the amounts in the appropriate columns. For amounts entered in the Other Accounts column, also indicate the account titles.

Totals
Land $172,500
Buildings $735,000

Item	Land	Buildings	Other Accounts

P10-2A In recent years, Avery Transportation purchased three used buses. Because of frequent turnover in the accounting department, a different accountant selected the depreciation method for each bus, and various methods were selected. Information concerning the buses is summarized as follows.

Compute depreciation under different methods.
(LO 2)

Bus	Acquired	Cost	Salvage Value	Useful Life in Years	Depreciation Method
1	1/1/15	$ 96,000	$ 6,000	5	Straight-line
2	1/1/15	110,000	10,000	4	Declining-balance
3	1/1/16	92,000	8,000	5	Units-of-activity

For the declining-balance method, the company uses the double-declining rate. For the units-of-activity method, total miles are expected to be 120,000. Actual miles of use in the first 3 years were 2016, 24,000; 2017, 34,000; and 2018, 30,000.

Instructions

(a) Bus 2, 2016, $82,500

(a) Compute the amount of accumulated depreciation on each bus at December 31, 2017.
(b) If Bus 2 was purchased on April 1 instead of January 1, what is the depreciation expense for this bus in (1) 2015 and (2) 2016?

Compute depreciation under different methods.

(LO 2)

P10-3A On January 1, 2017, Evers Company purchased the following two machines for use in its production process.

Machine A: The cash price of this machine was $48,000. Related expenditures included: sales tax $1,700, shipping costs $150, insurance during shipping $80, installation and testing costs $70, and $100 of oil and lubricants to be used with the machinery during its first year of operations. Evers estimates that the useful life of the machine is 5 years with a $5,000 salvage value remaining at the end of that time period. Assume that the straight-line method of depreciation is used.

Machine B: The recorded cost of this machine was $180,000. Evers estimates that the useful life of the machine is 4 years with a $10,000 salvage value remaining at the end of that time period.

Instructions

(a) Prepare the following for Machine A.
 (1) The journal entry to record its purchase on January 1, 2017.
 (2) The journal entry to record annual depreciation at December 31, 2017.
(b) Calculate the amount of depreciation expense that Evers should record for Machine B each year of its useful life under the following assumptions.
 (1) Evers uses the straight-line method of depreciation.
 (2) Evers uses the declining-balance method. The rate used is twice the straight-line rate.
 (3) Evers uses the units-of-activity method and estimates that the useful life of the machine is 125,000 units. Actual usage is as follows: 2017, 45,000 units; 2018, 35,000 units; 2019, 25,000 units; 2020, 20,000 units.
(c) Which method used to calculate depreciation on Machine B reports the highest amount of depreciation expense in year 1 (2017)? The highest amount in year 4 (2020)? The highest total amount over the 4-year period?

(b) (2) 2017 DDB depreciation $90,000

P10-4A At the beginning of 2015, Mazzaro Company acquired equipment costing $120,000. It was estimated that this equipment would have a useful life of 6 years and a salvage value of $12,000 at that time. The straight-line method of depreciation was considered the most appropriate to use with this type of equipment. Depreciation is to be recorded at the end of each year.

During 2017 (the third year of the equipment's life), the company's engineers reconsidered their expectations, and estimated that the equipment's useful life would probably be 7 years (in total) instead of 6 years. The estimated salvage value was not changed at that time. However, during 2020 the estimated salvage value was reduced to $5,000.

Instructions

Indicate how much depreciation expense should be recorded each year for this equipment, by completing the following table.

Year	Depreciation Expense	Accumulated Depreciation
2015		
2016		
2017		
2018		
2019		
2020		
2021		

2021 depreciation expense $17,900

P10-5A At December 31, 2017, Grand Company reported the following as plant assets.

Journalize a series of equipment transactions related to purchase, sale, retirement, and depreciation.

(LO 2, 3, 5)

Land		$ 4,000,000
Buildings	$28,500,000	
Less: Accumulated depreciation—buildings	12,100,000	16,400,000
Equipment	48,000,000	
Less: Accumulated depreciation—equipment	5,000,000	43,000,000
Total plant assets		$63,400,000

During 2018, the following selected cash transactions occurred.

April 1	Purchased land for $2,130,000.
May 1	Sold equipment that cost $750,000 when purchased on January 1, 2014. The equipment was sold for $450,000.
June 1	Sold land purchased on June 1, 2008 for $1,500,000. The land cost $400,000.
July 1	Purchased equipment for $2,500,000.
Dec. 31	Retired equipment that cost $500,000 when purchased on December 31, 2008. The company received no proceeds related to salvage.

Instructions

(a) Journalize the above transactions. The company uses straight-line depreciation for buildings and equipment. The buildings are estimated to have a 50-year life and no salvage value. The equipment is estimated to have a 10-year useful life and no salvage value. Update depreciation on assets disposed of at the time of sale or retirement.

(b) Record adjusting entries for depreciation for 2018.

(c) Prepare the plant assets section of Grand's balance sheet at December 31, 2018.

(b) Depreciation Expense—Buildings $570,000; Equipment $4,800,000

(c) Total plant assets $61,760,000

P10-6A Ceda Co. has equipment that cost $80,000 and that has been depreciated $50,000.

Record disposals.

(LO 3)

Instructions

Record the disposal under the following assumptions.

(a) It was scrapped as having no value.

(b) It was sold for $21,000.

(c) It was sold for $31,000.

(b) $9,000 loss

P10-7A The intangible assets section of Sappelt Company at December 31, 2017, is presented below.

Prepare entries to record transactions related to acquisition and amortization of intangibles; prepare the intangible assets section.

(LO 4, 5)

Patents ($70,000 cost less $7,000 amortization)	$63,000
Franchises ($48,000 cost less $19,200 amortization)	28,800
Total	$91,800

The patent was acquired in January 2017 and has a useful life of 10 years. The franchise was acquired in January 2014 and also has a useful life of 10 years. The following cash transactions may have affected intangible assets during 2018.

Jan. 2	Paid $27,000 legal costs to successfully defend the patent against infringement by another company.
Jan.–June	Developed a new product, incurring $140,000 in research and development costs. A patent was granted for the product on July 1. Its useful life is equal to its legal life.
Sept. 1	Paid $50,000 to an extremely large defensive lineman to appear in commercials advertising the company's products. The commercials will air in September and October.
Oct. 1	Acquired a franchise for $140,000. The franchise has a useful life of 50 years.

Instructions

(a) Prepare journal entries to record the transactions above.

(b) Prepare journal entries to record the 2018 amortization expense.

(c) Prepare the intangible assets section of the balance sheet at December 31, 2018.

(b) Amortization Expense (patents) $10,000
Amortization Expense (franchises) $5,500

(c) Total intangible assets $243,300

P10-8A Due to rapid turnover in the accounting department, a number of transactions involving intangible assets were improperly recorded by Goins Company in 2017.

Prepare entries to correct errors made in recording and amortizing intangible assets.

(LO 4)

1. Goins developed a new manufacturing process, incurring research and development costs of $136,000. The company also purchased a patent for $60,000. In early January,

Goins capitalized $196,000 as the cost of the patents. Patent amortization expense of $19,600 was recorded based on a 10-year useful life.

2. On July 1, 2017, Goins purchased a small company and as a result acquired goodwill of $92,000. Goins recorded a half-year's amortization in 2017, based on a 50-year life ($920 amortization). The goodwill has an indefinite life.

1. R&D Exp. $136,000

Instructions

Prepare all journal entries necessary to correct any errors made during 2017. Assume the books have not yet been closed for 2017.

Calculate and comment on asset turnover.

(LO 5)

P10-9A LaPorta Company and Lott Corporation, two corporations of roughly the same size, are both involved in the manufacture of in-line skates. Each company depreciates its plant assets using the straight-line approach. An investigation of their financial statements reveals the following information.

	LaPorta Co.	Lott Corp.
Net income	$ 800,000	$1,000,000
Sales revenue	1,300,000	1,180,000
Average total assets	2,500,000	2,000,000
Average plant assets	1,800,000	1,000,000

Instructions

(a) For each company, calculate the asset turnover.

(b) Based on your calculations in part (a), comment on the relative effectiveness of the two companies in using their assets to generate sales and produce net income.

COMPREHENSIVE PROBLEM: CHAPTERS 3 TO 10

CP10 Hassellhouf Company's trial balance at December 31, 2017, is presented below. All 2017 transactions have been recorded except for the items described as unrecorded transactions.

	Debit	Credit
Cash	$ 28,000	
Accounts Receivable	36,800	
Notes Receivable	10,000	
Interest Receivable	–0–	
Inventory	36,200	
Prepaid Insurance	3,600	
Land	20,000	
Buildings	150,000	
Equipment	60,000	
Patents	9,000	
Allowance for Doubtful Accounts		$ 500
Accumulated Depreciation—Buildings		50,000
Accumulated Depreciation—Equipment		24,000
Accounts Payable		27,300
Salaries and Wages Payable		–0–
Unearned Rent Revenue		6,000
Notes Payable (due in 2018)		11,000
Interest Payable		–0–
Notes Payable (due after 2018)		30,000
Owner's Capital		113,600
Owner's Drawings	12,000	
Sales Revenue		905,000
Interest Revenue		–0–
Rent Revenue		–0–
Gain on Disposal of Plant Assets		–0–
Bad Debt Expense	–0–	
Cost of Goods Sold	630,000	

Depreciation Expense	-0-	
Insurance Expense	-0-	
Interest Expense	-0-	
Other Operating Expenses	61,800	
Amortization Expense	-0-	
Salaries and Wages Expense	110,000	
Total	$1,167,400	$1,167,400

Unrecorded transactions:

1. On May 1, 2017, Hasselhouf purchased equipment for $21,200 plus sales taxes of $1,600 (all paid in cash).
2. On July 1, 2017, Hasselhouf sold for $3,500 equipment which originally cost $5,000. Accumulated depreciation on this equipment at January 1, 2017, was $1,800; 2017 depreciation prior to the sale of the equipment was $450.
3. On December 31, 2017, Hasselhouf sold on account $9,000 of inventory that cost $6,300.
4. Hasselhouf estimates that uncollectible accounts receivable at year-end is $3,500.
5. The note receivable is a one-year, 8% note dated April 1, 2017. No interest has been recorded.
6. The balance in prepaid insurance represents payment of a $3,600 6-month premium on September 1, 2017.
7. The building is being depreciated using the straight-line method over 30 years. The salvage value is $30,000.
8. The equipment owned prior to this year is being depreciated using the straight-line method over 5 years. The salvage value is 10% of cost.
9. The equipment purchased on May 1, 2017, is being depreciated using the straight-line method over 5 years, with a salvage value of $1,800.
10. The patent was acquired on January 1, 2017, and has a useful life of 10 years from that date.
11. Unpaid salaries and wages at December 31, 2017, total $5,200.
12. The unearned rent revenue of $6,000 was received on December 1, 2017, for 3 months' rent.
13. Both the short-term and long-term notes payable are dated January 1, 2017, and carry a 9% interest rate. All interest is payable in the next 12 months.

Instructions

(a) Prepare journal entries for the transactions listed above.
(b) Prepare an updated December 31, 2017, trial balance.
(c) Prepare a 2017 income statement and an owner's equity statement.
(d) Prepare a December 31, 2017, classified balance sheet.

(b) Totals $1,205,040
(d) Total assets $259,200

BROADENING YOUR PERSPECTIVE

FINANCIAL REPORTING AND ANALYSIS

Financial Reporting Problem: Apple Inc.

BYP10-1 The financial statements of **Apple Inc.** are presented in Appendix A. Instructions for accessing and using the company's complete annual report, including the notes to the financial statements, are also provided in Appendix A.

Instructions

Refer to Apple's financial statements and answer the following questions.

(a) What was the total cost and book value of property, plant, and equipment at September 28, 2013?
(b) What was the amount of depreciation and amortization expense for each of the three years 2011–2013?
(c) Using the statement of cash flows, what is the amount of capital spending in 2013 and 2012?
(d) Where does the company disclose its intangible assets, and what types of intangibles did it have at September 28, 2013?

Comparative Analysis Problem: PepsiCo, Inc. vs. The Coca-Cola Company

BYP10-2 PepsiCo, Inc.'s financial statements are presented in Appendix B. Financial statements of The Coca-Cola Company are presented in Appendix C. Instructions for accessing and using the complete annual reports of PepsiCo and Coca-Cola, including the notes to the financial statements, are also provided in Appendices B and C, respectively.

Instructions

(a) Compute the asset turnover for each company for 2013.
(b) What conclusions concerning the efficiency of assets can be drawn from these data?

Comparative Analysis Problem: Amazon.com, Inc. vs. Wal-Mart Stores, Inc.

BYP10-3 Amazon.com, Inc.'s financial statements are presented in Appendix D. Financial statements of Wal-Mart Stores, Inc. are presented in Appendix E. Instructions for accessing and using the complete annual reports of Amazon and Wal-Mart, including the notes to the financial statements, are also provided in Appendices D and E, respectively.

Instructions

(a) Compute the asset turnover for each company for 2013.
(b) What conclusions concerning the efficiency of assets can be drawn from these data?

Real-World Focus

BYP10-4 A company's annual report identifies the amount of its plant assets and the depreciation method used.

Address: **www.annualreports.com**, or go to **www.wiley.com/college/weygandt**

Steps

1. Select a particular company.
2. Search by company name.
3. Follow instructions below.

Instructions

Answer the following questions.

(a) What is the name of the company?
(b) What is the Internet address of the annual report?
(c) At fiscal year-end, what is the net amount of its plant assets?
(d) What is the accumulated depreciation?
(e) Which method of depreciation does the company use?

CRITICAL THINKING

Decision-Making Across the Organization

BYP10-5 Pinson Company and Estes Company are two proprietorships that are similar in many respects. One difference is that Pinson Company uses the straight-line method and Estes Company uses the declining-balance method at double the straight-line rate. On January 2, 2015, both companies acquired the depreciable assets shown below.

Asset	Cost	Salvage Value	Useful Life
Buildings	$360,000	$20,000	40 years
Equipment	130,000	10,000	10 years

Including the appropriate depreciation charges, annual net income for the companies in the years 2015, 2016, and 2017 and total income for the 3 years were as follows.

	2015	2016	2017	Total
Pinson Company	$84,000	$88,400	$90,000	$262,400
Estes Company	68,000	76,000	85,000	229,000

At December 31, 2017, the balance sheets of the two companies are similar except that Estes Company has more cash than Pinson Company.

Lynda Peace is interested in buying one of the companies. She comes to you for advice.

Instructions
With the class divided into groups, answer the following.

(a) Determine the annual and total depreciation recorded by each company during the 3 years.
(b) Assuming that Estes Company also uses the straight-line method of depreciation instead of the declining-balance method as in (a), prepare comparative income data for the 3 years.
(c) Which company should Lynda Peace buy? Why?

Communication Activity

BYP10-6 The following was published with the financial statements to **American Exploration Company.**

AMERICAN EXPLORATION COMPANY
Notes to the Financial Statements

Property, Plant, and Equipment—The Company accounts for its oil and gas exploration and production activities using the successful efforts method of accounting. Under this method, acquisition costs for proved and unproved properties are capitalized when incurred.... The costs of drilling exploratory wells are capitalized pending determination of whether each well has discovered proved reserves. If proved reserves are not discovered, such drilling costs are charged to expense.... Depletion of the cost of producing oil and gas properties is computed on the units-of-activity method.

Instructions
Write a brief memo to your instructor discussing American Exploration Company's note regarding property, plant, and equipment. Your memo should address what is meant by the "successful efforts method" and "units-of-activity method."

Ethics Case

BYP10-7 Turner Container Company is suffering declining sales of its principal product, nonbiodegradeable plastic cartons. The president, Robert Griffin, instructs his controller, Alexis Landrum, to lengthen asset lives to reduce depreciation expense. A processing line of automated plastic extruding equipment, purchased for $3.5 million in January 2017, was originally estimated to have a useful life of 8 years and a salvage value of $300,000. Depreciation has been recorded for 2 years on that basis. Robert wants the estimated life changed to 12 years total, and the straight-line method continued. Alexis is hesitant to make the change, believing it is unethical to increase net income in this manner. Robert says, "Hey, the life is only an estimate, and I've heard that our competition uses a 12-year life on their production equipment."

Instructions
(a) Who are the stakeholders in this situation?
(b) Is the change in asset life unethical, or is it simply a good business practice by an astute president?
(c) What is the effect of Robert Griffin's proposed change on income before taxes in the year of change?

All About You

BYP10-8 The story at the beginning of the chapter discussed the company **Rent-A-Wreck**. Note that the trade name Rent-A-Wreck is a very important asset to the company, as it creates immediate product identification. As indicated in the chapter, companies invest substantial sums to ensure that their product is well-known to the consumer. Test your knowledge of who owns some famous brands and their impact on the financial statements.

Instructions
(a) Provide an answer to the four multiple-choice questions below.
 (1) Which company owns both Taco Bell and Pizza Hut?
  (a) McDonald's. (c) Yum Brands.
  (b) CKE. (d) Wendy's.

(2) Dairy Queen belongs to:
(a) Breyer. (c) GE.
(b) Berkshire Hathaway. (d) The Coca-Cola Company.
(3) Philip Morris, the cigarette maker, is owned by:
(a) Altria. (c) Boeing.
(b) GE. (d) ExxonMobil.
(4) AOL, a major Internet provider, belongs to:
(a) Microsoft. (c) NBC.
(b) Cisco. (d) Time Warner.

(b) How do you think the value of these brands is reported on the appropriate company's balance sheet?

FASB Codification Activity

BYP10-9 If your school has a subscription to the FASB Codification, go to **http://aaahq.org/ascLogin.cfm** to log in and prepare responses to the following.

(a) What does it mean to capitalize an item?
(b) What is the definition provided for an intangible asset?
(c) Your great-uncle, who is a CPA, is impressed that you are taking an accounting class. Based on his experience, he believes that depreciation is something that companies do based on past practice, not on the basis of authoritative guidance. Provide the authoritative literature to support the practice of fixed-asset depreciation.

A Look at IFRS

LEARNING OBJECTIVE  7

Compare the accounting for long-lived assets under GAAP and IFRS.

IFRS follows most of the same principles as GAAP in the accounting for property, plant, and equipment. There are, however, some significant differences in the implementation. IFRS allows the use of revaluation of property, plant, and equipment, and it also requires the use of component depreciation. In addition, there are some significant differences in the accounting for both intangible assets and impairments.

Key Points

The following are the key similarities and differences between GAAP and IFRS as related to the recording process for long-lived assets.

Similarities

- The definition for plant assets for both IFRS and GAAP is essentially the same.
- Both IFRS and GAAP follow the historical cost principle when accounting for property, plant, and equipment at date of acquisition. Cost consists of all expenditures necessary to acquire the asset and make it ready for its intended use.
- Under both IFRS and GAAP, interest costs incurred during construction are capitalized. Recently, IFRS converged to GAAP requirements in this area.
- IFRS also views depreciation as an allocation of cost over an asset's useful life. IFRS permits the same depreciation methods (e.g., straight-line, accelerated, and units-of-activity) as GAAP.
- Under both GAAP and IFRS, changes in the depreciation method used and changes in useful life are handled in current and future periods. Prior periods are not affected. GAAP recently conformed to international standards in the accounting for changes in depreciation methods.

- The accounting for subsequent expenditures (such as ordinary repairs and additions) are essentially the same under IFRS and GAAP.
- The accounting for plant asset disposals is essentially the same under IFRS and GAAP.
- Initial costs to acquire natural resources are essentially the same under IFRS and GAAP.
- The definition of intangible assets is essentially the same under IFRS and GAAP.
- The accounting for exchanges of nonmonetary assets has recently converged between IFRS and GAAP. GAAP now requires that gains on exchanges of nonmonetary assets be recognized if the exchange has commercial substance. This is the same framework used in IFRS.

Differences

- IFRS uses the term **residual value** rather than salvage value to refer to an owner's estimate of an asset's value at the end of its useful life for that owner.
- IFRS allows companies to revalue plant assets to fair value at the reporting date. Companies that choose to use the revaluation framework must follow revaluation procedures. If revaluation is used, it must be applied to all assets in a class of assets. Assets that are experiencing rapid price changes must be revalued on an annual basis, otherwise less frequent revaluation is acceptable.
- IFRS requires component depreciation. **Component depreciation** specifies that any significant parts of a depreciable asset that have different estimated useful lives should be separately depreciated. Component depreciation is allowed under GAAP but is seldom used.
- As in GAAP, under IFRS the costs associated with research and development are segregated into the two components. Costs in the research phase are always expensed under both IFRS and GAAP. Under IFRS, however, costs in the development phase are capitalized as Development Costs once technological feasibility is achieved.
- IFRS permits revaluation of intangible assets (except for goodwill). GAAP prohibits revaluation of intangible assets.

Looking to the Future

The IASB and FASB have identified a project that would consider expanded recognition of internally generated intangible assets. IFRS permits more recognition of intangibles compared to GAAP.

IFRS Practice

IFRS Self-Test Questions

1. Which of the following statements is **correct**?
   (a) Both IFRS and GAAP permit revaluation of property, plant, and equipment and intangible assets (except for goodwill).
   (b) IFRS permits revaluation of property, plant, and equipment and intangible assets (except for goodwill).
   (c) Both IFRS and GAAP permit revaluation of property, plant, and equipment but not intangible assets.
   (d) GAAP permits revaluation of property, plant, and equipment but not intangible assets.
2. Research and development costs are:
   (a) expensed under GAAP.
   (b) expensed under IFRS.
   (c) expensed under both GAAP and IFRS.
   (d) None of the above.

IFRS Exercises

IFRS10-1 What is component depreciation, and when must it be used?

IFRS10-2 What is revaluation of plant assets? When should revaluation be applied?

IFRS10-3 Some product development expenditures are recorded as development expenses and others as development costs. Explain the difference between these accounts and how a company decides which classification is appropriate.

International Financial Statement Analysis: Louis Vuitton

IFRS10-4 The financial statements of Louis Vuitton are presented in Appendix F. Instructions for accessing and using the company's complete annual report, including the notes to its financial statements, are also provided in Appendix F.

Instructions

Use the company's annual report to answer the following questions.

(a) According to the notes to the financial statements, what method or methods does the company use to depreciate "property, plant, and equipment?" What rate(s) does it use to depreciate property, plant, and equipment?

(b) Using the notes to the financial statements, identify the brands and trade names that are most significant to the company.

(c) Using the notes to the financial statements, determine (1) the balance in Accumulated Amortization and Impairment for intangible assets (other the goodwill), and (2) the balance in Accumulated Depreciation for property, plant, and equipment. (Round your amounts to the nearest thousand.)

Answers to IFRS Self-Test Questions

1. b **2.** a

Chapter 11 Current Liabilities and Payroll Accounting

What would you do if you had a great idea for a new product but couldn't come up with the cash to get the business off the ground? Small businesses often cannot attract investors. Nor can they obtain traditional debt financing through bank loans or bond issuances. Instead, they often resort to unusual, and costly, forms of nontraditional financing.

Such was the case for Wilbert Murdock. Murdock grew up in a New York housing project and always had great ambitions. His entrepreneurial spirit led him into some business ventures that failed: a medical diagnostic tool, a device to eliminate carpal tunnel syndrome, custom-designed sneakers, and a device to keep people from falling asleep while driving.

Another idea was computerized golf clubs that analyze a golfer's swing and provide immediate feedback. Murdock saw great potential in the idea. Many golfers are willing to shell out considerable sums of money for devices that might improve their game. But Murdock had no cash to develop his product, and banks and other lenders had shied away. Rather than give up, Murdock resorted to credit cards—in a big way. He quickly owed $25,000 to credit card companies.

While funding a business with credit cards might sound unusual, it isn't. A recent study found that one-third of businesses with fewer than 20 employees financed at least part of their operations with credit cards. As Murdock explained, credit cards are an appealing way to finance a start-up because "credit-card companies don't care how the money is spent." However, they do care how they are paid. And so Murdock faced high interest charges and a barrage of credit card collection letters.

Murdock's debt forced him to sacrifice nearly everything in order to keep his business afloat. His car stopped running, he barely had enough money to buy food, and he lived and worked out of a dimly lit apartment in his mother's basement. Through it all he tried to maintain a positive spirit, joking that, if he becomes successful, he might some day get to appear in an American Express commercial.

Source: Rodney Ho, "Banking on Plastic: To Finance a Dream, Many Entrepreneurs Binge on Credit Cards," *Wall Street Journal* (March 9, 1998), p. A1.

LEARNING OBJECTIVES

1. **Explain how to account for current liabilities.**
2. **Discuss how current liabilities are reported and analyzed.**
3. **Explain how to account for payroll.**

LEARNING OBJECTIVE 1 Explain how to account for current liabilities.

What Is a Current Liability?

You have learned that liabilities are defined as "creditors' claims on total assets" and as "existing debts and obligations." Companies must settle or pay these claims, debts, and obligations at some time in the future by transferring assets or services. The future date on which they are due or payable (the maturity date) is a significant feature of liabilities.

As explained in Chapter 4, a **current liability** is a debt that a company expects to pay within one year or the operating cycle, whichever is longer. Debts that do not meet this criterion are **long-term liabilities.**

Financial statement users want to know whether a company's obligations are current or long-term. A company that has more current liabilities than current assets often lacks liquidity, or short-term debt-paying ability. In addition, users want to know the types of liabilities a company has. If a company declares bankruptcy, a specific, predetermined order of payment to creditors exists. Thus, the amount and type of liabilities are of critical importance.

The different types of current liabilities include notes payable, accounts payable, unearned revenues, and accrued liabilities such as taxes, salaries and wages, and interest payable. In the sections that follow, we discuss common types of current liabilities.

Notes Payable

Companies record obligations in the form of written notes as **notes payable.** Notes payable are often used instead of accounts payable because they give the lender formal proof of the obligation in case legal remedies are needed to collect the debt. Companies frequently issue notes payable to meet short-term financing needs. Notes payable usually require the borrower to pay interest.

Notes are issued for varying periods of time. **Those due for payment within one year of the balance sheet date are usually classified as current liabilities.**

To illustrate the accounting for notes payable, assume that First National Bank agrees to lend $100,000 on September 1, 2017, if Cole Williams Co. signs a $100,000, 12%, four-month note maturing on January 1. When a company issues an interest-bearing note, the amount of assets it receives upon issuance of the note generally equals the note's face value. Cole Williams therefore will receive $100,000 cash and will make the following journal entry.

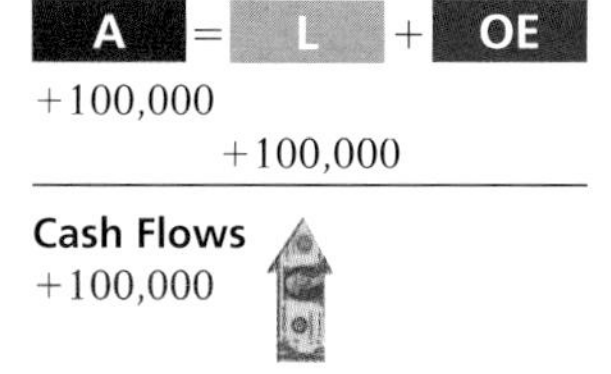

Sept. 1	Cash	100,000	
	Notes Payable		100,000
	(To record issuance of 12%, 4-month note to First National Bank)		

Interest accrues over the life of the note, and the company must periodically record that accrual. If Cole Williams prepares financial statements annually, it makes an adjusting entry at December 31 to recognize interest expense and interest payable of $4,000 ($100,000 × 12% × 4/12). Illustration 11-1 shows the formula for computing interest and its application to Cole Williams' note.

Illustration 11-1
Formula for computing interest

Face Value of Note	×	Annual Interest Rate	×	Time in Terms of One Year	=	Interest
$100,000	×	12%	×	4/12	=	**$4,000**

Cole Williams makes an adjusting entry as follows.

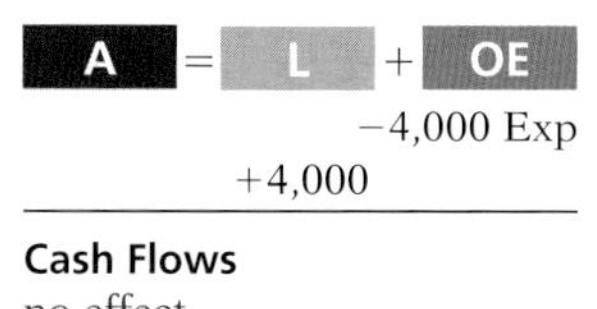

Dec. 31	Interest Expense	4,000	
	Interest Payable		4,000
	(To accrue interest for 4 months on First National Bank note)		

In the December 31 financial statements, the current liabilities section of the balance sheet will show notes payable $100,000 and interest payable $4,000. In addition, the company will report interest expense of $4,000 under "Other expenses and losses" in the income statement. If Cole Williams prepared financial statements monthly, the adjusting entry at the end of each month would be $1,000 ($100,000 × 12% × 1/12).

At maturity (January 1, 2018), Cole Williams must pay the face value of the note ($100,000) plus $4,000 interest ($100,000 × 12% × 4/12). It records payment of the note and accrued interest as follows.

Jan. 1	Notes Payable	100,000	
	Interest Payable	4,000	
	Cash		104,000
	(To record payment of First National Bank interest-bearing note and accrued interest at maturity)		

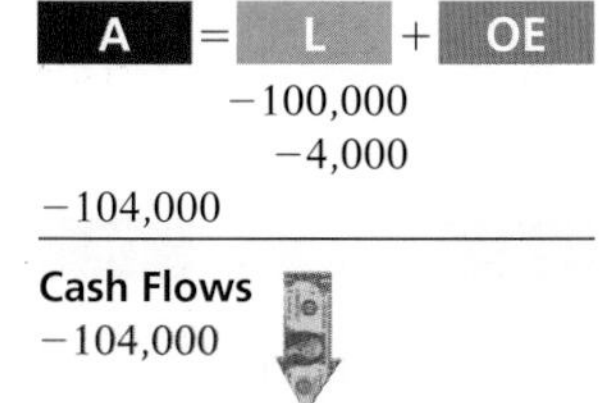

Sales Taxes Payable

Many of the products we purchase at retail stores are subject to sales taxes. Many states also are now collecting sales taxes on purchases made on the Internet as well. Sales taxes are expressed as a percentage of the sales price. The selling company collects the tax from the customer when the sale occurs. Periodically (usually monthly), the retailer remits the collections to the state's department of revenue. Collecting sales taxes is important. For example, the State of New York recently sued **Sprint Corporation** for $300 million for its alleged failure to collect sales taxes on phone calls.

Under most state sales tax laws, the selling company must enter separately in the cash register the amount of the sale and the amount of the sales tax collected. (Gasoline sales are a major exception.) The company then uses the cash register readings to credit Sales Revenue and Sales Taxes Payable. For example, if the March 25 cash register reading for Cooley Grocery shows sales of $10,000 and sales taxes of $600 (sales tax rate of 6%), the journal entry is as follows.

Mar. 25	Cash	10,600	
	Sales Revenue		10,000
	Sales Taxes Payable		600
	(To record daily sales and sales taxes)		

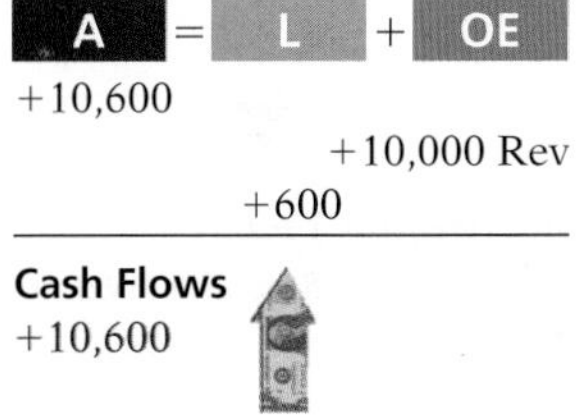

When the company remits the taxes to the taxing agency, it debits Sales Taxes Payable and credits Cash. The company does not report sales taxes as an expense. It simply forwards to the government the amount paid by the customers. Thus, Cooley Grocery serves only as a **collection agent** for the taxing authority.

Sometimes companies do not enter sales taxes separately in the cash register. To determine the amount of sales in such cases, divide total receipts by 100% plus the sales tax percentage. For example, assume that Cooley Grocery enters total receipts of $10,600. The receipts from the sales are equal to the sales price (100%) plus the tax percentage (6% of sales), or 1.06 times the sales total. We can compute the sales amount as follows.

$$\$10,600 \div 1.06 = \$10,000$$

Thus, we can find the sales tax amount of $600 by either (1) subtracting sales from total receipts ($10,600 − $10,000) or (2) multiplying sales by the sales tax rate ($10,000 × 6%).

Unearned Revenues

A magazine publisher, such as **Sports Illustrated**, receives customers' checks when they order magazines. An airline company, such as **American Airlines**, often receives cash when it sells tickets for future flights. Season tickets for concerts, sporting events, and theater programs are also paid for in advance. How do companies account for unearned revenues that are received before goods are delivered or services are performed?

1. When a company receives the advance payment, it debits Cash and credits a current liability account identifying the source of the unearned revenue.
2. When the company recognizes revenue, it debits an unearned revenue account and credits a revenue account.

To illustrate, assume that Superior University sells 10,000 season football tickets at $50 each for its five-game home schedule. The university makes the following entry for the sale of season tickets.

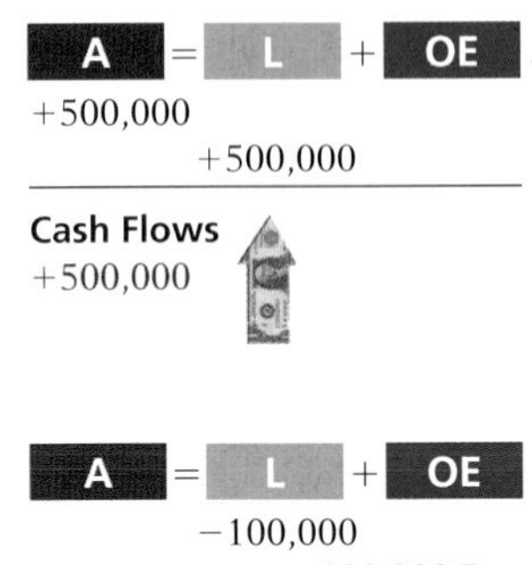

Aug. 6	Cash	500,000	
	Unearned Ticket Revenue		500,000
	(To record sale of 10,000 season tickets)		

As each game is completed, Superior records the recognition of revenue with the following entry.

A = L + OE
−100,000
+100,000 Rev
Cash Flows
no effect

Sept. 7	Unearned Ticket Revenue	100,000	
	Ticket Revenue		100,000
	(To record football ticket revenue)		

The account Unearned Ticket Revenue represents unearned revenue, and Superior reports it as a current liability. As the school recognizes revenue, it reclassifies the amount from unearned revenue to Ticket Revenue. Unearned revenue is material for some companies. In the airline industry, for example, tickets sold for future flights represent almost 50% of total current liabilities. At **United Air Lines**, unearned ticket revenue is its largest current liability, recently amounting to over $1 billion.

Illustration 11-2 shows specific unearned revenue and revenue accounts used in selected types of businesses.

Illustration 11-2
Unearned revenue and revenue accounts

Type of Business	Account Title: Unearned Revenue	Account Title: Revenue
Airline	Unearned Ticket Revenue	Ticket Revenue
Magazine publisher	Unearned Subscription Revenue	Subscription Revenue
Hotel	Unearned Rent Revenue	Rent Revenue

Current Maturities of Long-Term Debt

Companies often have a portion of long-term debt that comes due in the current year. That amount is considered a current liability. As an example, assume that Wendy Construction issues a five-year, interest-bearing $25,000 note on January 1, 2016. This note specifies that each January 1, starting January 1, 2017, Wendy should pay $5,000 of the note. When the company prepares financial statements on December 31, 2016, it should report $5,000 as a current liability and $20,000 as a long-term liability. (The $5,000 amount is the portion of the note that is due to be paid within the next 12 months.) Companies often identify current maturities of long-term debt on the balance sheet as **long-term debt due within one year**. In a recent year, **General Motors** had $724 million of such debt.

It is not necessary to prepare an adjusting entry to recognize the current maturity of long-term debt. At the balance sheet date, all obligations due within one year are classified as current, and all other obligations as long-term.

LEARNING OBJECTIVE 2 **Discuss how current liabilities are reported and analyzed.**

Reporting Uncertainty

With notes payable, interest payable, accounts payable, and sales taxes payable, we know that an obligation to make a payment exists. But, suppose that your company is involved in a dispute with the Internal Revenue Service (IRS) over the amount of its income tax liability. Should you report the disputed amount as a liability on the balance sheet? Or, suppose your company is involved in a lawsuit which, if you lose, might result in bankruptcy. How should you report this major contingency? The answers to these questions are difficult because these liabilities are dependent—contingent—upon some future event. In other words, a **contingent liability** is a potential liability that may become an actual liability in the future.

How should companies report contingent liabilities? They use the following guidelines:

1. If the contingency is **probable** (if it is likely to occur) **and** the amount can be **reasonably estimated**, the liability should be recorded in the accounts.
2. If the contingency is only **reasonably possible** (if it could happen), then it needs to be disclosed only in the notes that accompany the financial statements.
3. If the contingency is **remote** (if it is unlikely to occur), it need not be recorded or disclosed.

REPORTING A CONTINGENT LIABILITY

Product warranties are an example of a contingent liability that companies should record in the accounts. Warranty contracts result in future costs that companies may incur in replacing defective units or repairing malfunctioning units. Generally, a manufacturer, such as Stanley Black & Decker, knows that it will incur some warranty costs. From prior experience with the product, the company usually can reasonably estimate the anticipated cost of servicing (honoring) the warranty.

The accounting for warranty costs is based on the expense recognition principle. **The estimated cost of honoring product warranty contracts should be recognized as an expense in the period in which the sale occurs.** To illustrate, assume that in 2017 Denson Manufacturing Company sells 10,000 washers and dryers at an average price of $600 each. The selling price includes a one-year warranty on parts. Denson expects that 500 units (5%) will be defective and that warranty repair costs will average $80 per unit. In 2017, the company honors warranty contracts on 300 units, at a total cost of $24,000.

At December 31, it is necessary to accrue the estimated warranty costs on the 2017 sales. Denson computes the estimated warranty liability as follows.

Number of units sold	10,000
Estimated rate of defective units	× 5%
Total estimated defective units	500
Average warranty repair cost	× $80
Estimated warranty liability	**$40,000**

Illustration 11-3
Computation of estimated warranty liability

The company makes the following adjusting entry.

Dec. 31	Warranty Expense	40,000	
	Warranty Liability		40,000
	(To accrue estimated warranty costs)		

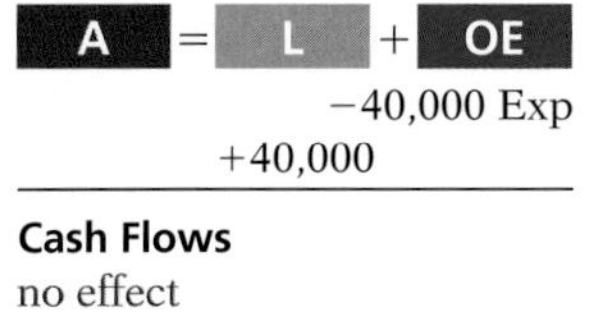

Denson records those repair costs incurred in 2017 to honor warranty contracts on 2017 sales as shown below.

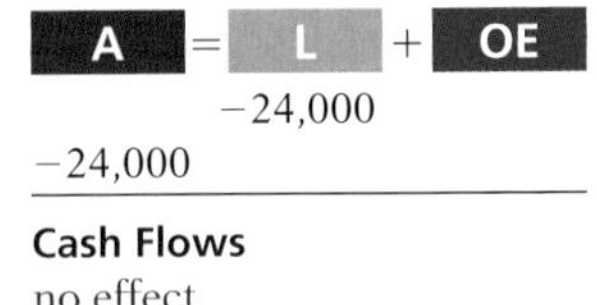

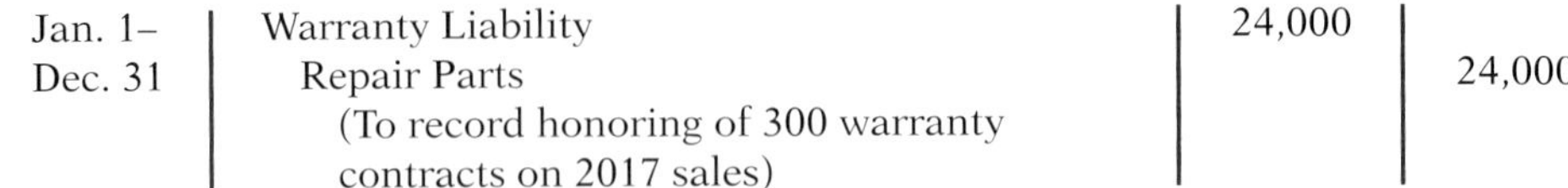

Jan. 1– Dec. 31	Warranty Liability	24,000	
	Repair Parts		24,000
	(To record honoring of 300 warranty contracts on 2017 sales)		

Cash Flows
no effect

The company reports warranty expense of $40,000 under selling expenses in the income statement. It classifies warranty liability of $16,000 ($40,000 – $24,000) as a current liability on the balance sheet, assuming the warranty is estimated to be honored in the next year.

In the following year, Denson should debit to Warranty Liability all expenses incurred in honoring warranty contracts on 2017 sales. To illustrate, assume that the company replaces 20 defective units in January 2018, at an average cost of $80 in parts and labor. The summary entry for the month of January 2018 is as follows.

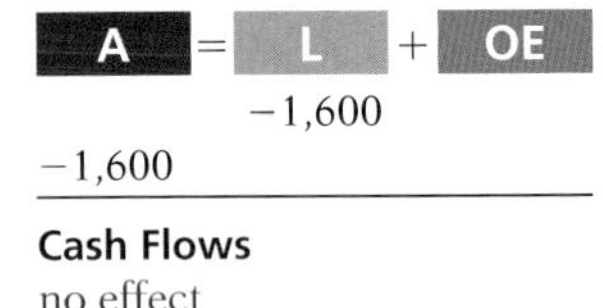

Jan. 31	Warranty Liability	1,600	
	Repair Parts		1,600
	(To record honoring of 20 warranty contracts on 2017 sales)		

Cash Flows
no effect

Reporting of Current Liabilities

Current liabilities are the first category under liabilities on the balance sheet. Each of the principal types of current liabilities is listed separately. In addition, companies disclose the terms of notes payable and other key information about the individual items in the notes to the financial statements.

Companies seldom list current liabilities in the order of liquidity. The reason is that varying maturity dates may exist for specific obligations such as notes payable. As a matter of custom, many companies show notes payable first and then accounts payable, regardless of amount. The current maturity of long-term debt is often shown last in the current liabilities section. Illustration 11-4 provides

Illustration 11-4
Balance sheet reporting of current liabilities

EVAN COMPANY
Balance Sheet
December 31, 2017

Assets	
Current assets	$ 500,000
Property, plant, and equipment (net)	150,000
Other long-term assets	520,000
Total assets	$1,170,000
Liabilities and Owner's Equity	
Current liabilities	
Notes payable	**$ 40,000**
Accounts payable	**110,000**
Unearned revenue	**30,000**
Salaries and wages payable	**90,000**
Warranty liability	**25,000**
Current maturities of long-term debt	**65,000**
Total current liabilities	**360,000**
Noncurrent liabilities	620,000
Total liabilities	980,000
Owner's equity	190,000
Total liabilities and owner's equity	$1,170,000

an excerpt from Evan Company's balance sheet, which is a common order of presentation among companies.

Analysis of Current Liabilities

Use of current and noncurrent classifications makes it possible to analyze a company's liquidity. **Liquidity** refers to the ability to pay maturing obligations and meet unexpected needs for cash. The relationship of current assets to current liabilities is critical in analyzing liquidity. We can express this relationship as a dollar amount (working capital) and as a ratio (the current ratio).

The excess of current assets over current liabilities is **working capital.** Illustration 11-5 shows the formula for the computation of Evan Company's working capital.

Current Assets	−	Current Liabilities	=	Working Capital
$500,000	−	$360,000	=	$140,000

Illustration 11-5
Working capital formula and computation

As an absolute dollar amount, working capital offers limited informational value. For example, $1 million of working capital may be more than needed for a small company but inadequate for a large corporation. Also, $1 million of working capital may be adequate for a company at one time but inadequate at another time.

The **current ratio** permits us to compare the liquidity of different-sized companies and of a single company at different times. The current ratio is calculated as current assets divided by current liabilities. Illustration 11-6 shows the formula for this ratio, along with its computation using Evan's current asset and current liability data.

Current Assets	÷	Current Liabilities	=	Current Ratio
$500,000	÷	$360,000	=	1.39:1

Illustration 11-6
Current ratio formula and computation

Historically, companies and analysts considered a current ratio of 2:1 to be the standard for a good credit rating. In recent years, however, many healthy companies have maintained ratios well below 2:1 by improving management of their current assets and liabilities. Evan's ratio of 1.39:1 is adequate but certainly below the standard of 2:1.

Explain how to account for payroll.

Payroll and related fringe benefits often make up a large percentage of current liabilities. Employee compensation is often the most significant expense that a company incurs. For example, **Costco** recently reported total employees of 103,000 and labor and fringe benefits costs which approximated 70% of the company's total cost of operations.

Payroll accounting involves more than paying employees' wages. Companies are required by law to maintain payroll records for each employee, to file and pay payroll taxes, and to comply with state and federal tax laws related to employee compensation.

The term "payroll" **pertains to both salaries and wages of employees**. Managerial, administrative, and sales personnel are generally paid **salaries**. Salaries are often expressed in terms of a specified amount per month or per year rather than an hourly rate. Store clerks, factory employees, and manual laborers are normally paid **wages**. Wages are based on a rate per hour or on a piecework basis (such as per unit of product). Frequently, people use the terms "salaries" and "wages" interchangeably.

The term "payroll" **does not apply to payments made for services of professionals** such as certified public accountants, attorneys, and architects. Such professionals are independent contractors rather than salaried employees. Payments to them are called **fees**. This distinction is important because government regulations relating to the payment and reporting of payroll taxes apply only to employees.

Determining the Payroll

Determining the payroll involves computing three amounts: (1) gross earnings, (2) payroll deductions, and (3) net pay.

GROSS EARNINGS

Gross earnings is the total compensation earned by an employee. It consists of wages or salaries, plus any bonuses and commissions.

Companies determine total **wages** for an employee by multiplying the hours worked by the hourly rate of pay. In addition to the hourly pay rate, most companies are required by law to pay hourly workers a minimum of 1½ times the regular hourly rate for overtime work in excess of eight hours per day or 40 hours per week. In addition, many employers pay overtime rates for work done at night, on weekends, and on holidays.

For example, assume that Michael Jordan, an employee of Academy Company, worked 44 hours for the weekly pay period ending January 14. His regular wage is $12 per hour. For any hours in excess of 40, the company pays at one-and-a-half times the regular rate. Academy computes Jordan's gross earnings (total wages) as follows.

Illustration 11-7
Computation of total wages

Type of Pay	Hours	×	Rate	=	Gross Earnings
Regular	40	×	$12	=	$480
Overtime	4	×	18	=	72
Total wages					**$552**

This computation assumes that Jordan receives 1½ times his regular hourly rate ($\$12 \times 1.5$) for his overtime hours. Union contracts often require that overtime rates be as much as twice the regular rates.

An employee's **salary** is generally based on a monthly or yearly rate. The company then prorates these rates to its payroll periods (e.g., biweekly or monthly). Most executive and administrative positions are salaried. Federal law does not require overtime pay for employees in such positions.

Many companies have **bonus** agreements for employees. One survey found that over 94% of the largest U.S. manufacturing companies offer annual bonuses to key executives. Bonus arrangements may be based on such factors as increased sales or net income. Companies may pay bonuses in cash and/or by granting employees the opportunity to acquire shares of company stock at favorable prices (called stock option plans).

PAYROLL DEDUCTIONS

As anyone who has received a paycheck knows, gross earnings are usually very different from the amount actually received. The difference is due to **payroll deductions**.

Payroll deductions may be mandatory or voluntary. **Mandatory deductions are required by law and consist of FICA taxes and income taxes.** Voluntary deductions are at the option of the employee. Illustration 11-8 summarizes common types of payroll deductions. Such deductions do not result in payroll tax expense to the employer. The employer is merely a collection agent, and subsequently transfers the deducted amounts to the government and designated recipients.

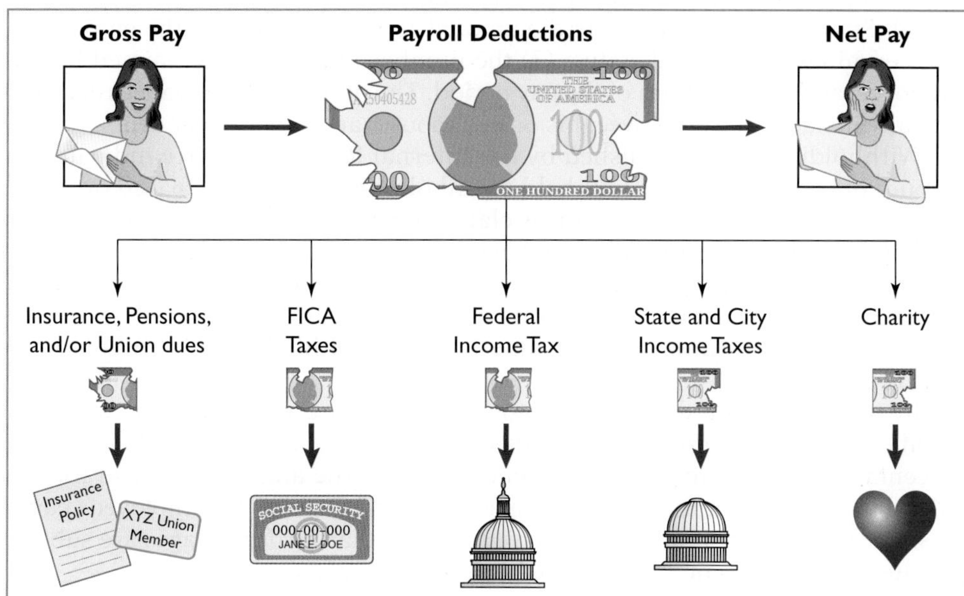

Illustration 11-8
Payroll deductions

FICA TAXES In 1937, Congress enacted the Federal Insurance Contribution Act (FICA). **FICA taxes are designed to provide workers with supplemental retirement, employment disability, and medical benefits.** In 1965, Congress extended benefits to include Medicare for individuals over 65 years of age. The benefits are financed by a tax levied on employees' earnings.

FICA taxes consist of a Social Security tax and a Medicare tax. They are paid by both employee and employer. The FICA tax rate is 7.65% (6.2% Social Security tax up to $117,000 plus 1.45% Medicare tax) of salary and wages for each employee.[1] In addition, the Medicare tax of 1.45% continues for an employee's salary and wages in excess of $117,000. These tax rate and tax base requirements are shown in Illustration 11-9.

Illustration 11-9
FICA tax rate and tax base

Social Security taxes	
Employee and employer	**6.2%** on salary and wages up to **$117,000**
Medicare taxes	
Employee and employer	**1.45%** on all salary and wages without limitation

To illustrate the computation of FICA taxes, assume that Mario Ruez has total wages for the year of $100,000. In this case, Mario pays FICA taxes of $7,650

[1]The $117,000 limit is based upon 2014 guidelines set by the Social Security Administration.

($100,000 × 7.65%). If Mario has total wages of $124,000, Mario pays FICA taxes of $9,052, as shown in Illustration 11-10.

Illustration 11-10
FICA tax computation

Social Security tax	($117,000 × 6.2%)	$ 7,254
Medicare tax	($124,000 × 1.45%)	1,798
Total FICA taxes		**$9,052**

Mario's employer is also required to pay $9,052.

INCOME TAXES Under the U.S. pay-as-you-go system of federal income taxes, employers are required to withhold income taxes from employees each pay period. Four variables determine the amount to be withheld: (1) the employee's gross earnings, (2) marital status, (3) the number of allowances claimed by the employee, and (4) the length of the pay period. The number of allowances claimed typically includes the employee, his or her spouse, and other dependents.

Withholding tables furnished by the Internal Revenue Service indicate the amount of income tax to be withheld. Withholding amounts are based on gross wages and the number of allowances claimed. Separate tables are provided for weekly, biweekly, semimonthly, and monthly pay periods. Illustration 11-11 shows the withholding tax table for Michael Jordan (assuming he earns $552 per week, is married, and claims two allowances). For a weekly salary of $552 with two allowances, the income tax to be withheld is $24 (highlighted in red).

In addition, most states (and some cities) require **employers** to withhold income taxes from employees' earnings. As a rule, the amounts withheld are a percentage (specified in the state revenue code) of the amount withheld for the federal income tax. Or they may be a specified percentage of the employee's earnings. For the sake of simplicity, we have assumed that Jordan's wages are subject to state income taxes of 2%, or $11.04 (2% × $552) per week.

Illustration 11-11
Withholding tax table

MARRIED Persons — **WEEKLY** Payroll Period
(For Wages Paid through December 2017)

If the wages are —		And the number of withholding allowances claimed is —										
At least	But less than	0	1	2	3	4	5	6	7	8	9	10
		The amount of income tax to be withheld is —										
500	**510**	34	27	19	11	4	0	0	0	0	0	0
510	**520**	35	28	20	12	5	0	0	0	0	0	0
520	**530**	37	29	21	13	6	0	0	0	0	0	0
530	**540**	38	30	22	14	7	0	0	0	0	0	0
540	**550**	40	31	23	15	8	0	0	0	0	0	0
550	**560**	41	32	24	16	9	1	0	0	0	0	0
560	**570**	43	33	25	17	10	2	0	0	0	0	0
570	**580**	44	34	26	18	11	3	0	0	0	0	0
580	**590**	46	35	27	19	12	4	0	0	0	0	0
590	**600**	47	36	28	20	13	5	0	0	0	0	0
600	**610**	49	38	29	21	14	6	0	0	0	0	0
610	**620**	50	39	30	22	15	7	0	0	0	0	0
620	**630**	52	41	31	23	16	8	1	0	0	0	0
630	**640**	53	42	32	24	17	9	2	0	0	0	0
640	**650**	55	44	33	25	18	10	3	0	0	0	0
650	**660**	56	45	34	26	19	11	4	0	0	0	0
660	**670**	58	47	35	27	20	12	5	0	0	0	0
670	**680**	59	48	37	28	21	13	6	0	0	0	0
680	**690**	61	50	38	29	22	14	7	0	0	0	0
690	**700**	62	51	40	30	23	15	8	0	0	0	0

There is no limit on the amount of gross earnings subject to income tax withholdings. In fact, under our progressive system of taxation, the higher the earnings, the higher the percentage of income withheld for taxes.

OTHER DEDUCTIONS Employees may voluntarily authorize withholdings for charitable organizations, retirement, and other purposes. All voluntary deductions from gross earnings should be authorized in writing by the employee. The authorization(s) may be made individually or as part of a group plan. Deductions for charitable organizations, such as the United Fund, or for financial arrangements, such as U.S. savings bonds and repayment of loans from company credit unions, are made individually. Deductions for union dues, health and life insurance, and pension plans are often made on a group basis. We assume that Jordan has weekly voluntary deductions of $10 for the United Fund and $5 for union dues.

NET PAY

Academy Company determines **net pay** by subtracting payroll deductions from gross earnings. Illustration 11-12 shows the computation of Jordan's net pay for the pay period.

Terminology
Net pay is also called *take-home pay.*

Illustration 11-12
Computation of net pay

Gross earnings		$ 552.00
Payroll deductions:		
FICA taxes	$42.23	
Federal income taxes	24.00	
State income taxes	11.04	
United Fund	10.00	
Union dues	5.00	92.27
Net pay		**$459.73**

Assuming that Michael Jordan's wages for each week during the year are $552, total wages for the year are $28,704 (52 × $552). Thus, all of Jordan's wages are subject to FICA tax during the year. In comparison, let's assume that Jordan's department head earns $3,000 per week, or $156,000 for the year. Since only the first $117,000 is subject to Social Security taxes, the maximum FICA withholdings on the department head's earnings would be $9,516 [($117,000 × 6.20%) + ($156,000 × 1.45%)].

Recording the Payroll

Recording the payroll involves maintaining payroll department records, recognizing payroll expenses and liabilities, and recording payment of the payroll.

MAINTAINING PAYROLL DEPARTMENT RECORDS

To comply with state and federal laws, an employer must keep a cumulative record of each employee's gross earnings, deductions, and net pay during the year. The record that provides this information is the **employee earnings record**. Illustration 11-13 (page 404) shows Michael Jordan's employee earnings record.

Companies keep a separate earnings record for each employee and update these records after each pay period. The employer uses the cumulative payroll data on the earnings record to (1) determine when an employee has earned the maximum earnings subject to FICA taxes, (2) file state and federal payroll tax returns (as explained later), and (3) provide each employee with a statement of gross earnings and tax withholdings for the year. Illustration 11-17 (page 409) shows this statement.

In addition to employee earnings records, many companies find it useful to prepare a **payroll register**. This record accumulates the gross earnings, deductions, and net pay by employee for each pay period. Illustration 11-14 (page 404)

Academy Company.xls

Home | Insert | Page Layout | Formulas | Data | Review | View

P18 *fx*

ACADEMY COMPANY
Employee Earnings Record
For the Year 2017

Name	Michael Jordan	**Address**	2345 Mifflin Ave.
Social Security Number	329-35-9547		Hampton, Michigan 48292
Date of Birth	December 24, 1994	**Telephone**	555-238-9051
Date Employed	September 1, 2015	**Date Employment Ended**	
Sex	Male	**Exemptions**	2
Single ______	**Married** x		

		Gross Earnings				Deductions						Payment	
2017 Period Ending	**Total Hours**	**Regular**	**Overtime**	**Total**	**Cumulative**	**FICA**	**Fed. Inc. Tax**	**State Inc. Tax**	**United Fund**	**Union Dues**	**Total**	**Net Amount**	**Check No.**
1/7	42	480.00	36.00	516.00	516.00	39.47	20.00	10.32	10.00	5.00	84.79	431.21	974
1/14	**44**	**480.00**	**72.00**	**552.00**	**1,068.00**	**42.23**	**24.00**	**11.04**	**10.00**	**5.00**	**92.27**	**459.73**	**1028**
1/21	43	480.00	54.00	534.00	1,602.00	40.85	22.00	10.68	10.00	5.00	88.53	445.47	1077
1/28	42	480.00	36.00	516.00	2,118.00	39.47	20.00	10.32	10.00	5.00	84.79	431.21	1133
Jan. Total		1,920.00	198.00	2,118.00		162.02	86.00	42.36	40.00	20.00	350.38	1,767.62	

Illustration 11-13
Employee earnings record

Illustration 11-14
Payroll register

Academy Company.xls

Home | Insert | Page Layout | Formulas | Data | Review | View

P18 *fx*

ACADEMY COMPANY
Payroll Register
For the Week Ending January 14, 2017

Row	Employee	Total Hours	Earnings: Regular	Earnings: Over-time	Earnings: Gross	Deductions: FICA	Deductions: Federal Income Tax	Deductions: State Income Tax	Deductions: United Fund	Deductions: Union Dues	Deductions: Total	Paid: Net Pay	Paid: Check No.	Account Debited: Salaries and Wages Expense
10	Arnold, Patricia	40	580.00		580.00	44.37	61.00	11.60	15.00		131.97	448.03	998	580.00
11	Canton, Matthew	40	590.00		590.00	45.14	63.00	11.80	20.00		139.94	450.06	999	590.00
21	Mueller, William	40	530.00		530.00	40.55	54.00	10.60	11.00		116.15	413.85	1000	530.00
22	Bennett, Robin	42	480.00	36.00	516.00	39.47	35.00	10.32	18.00	5.00	107.79	408.21	1025	516.00
23	**Jordan, Michael**	**44**	**480.00**	**72.00**	**552.00**	**42.23**	**24.00**	**11.04**	**10.00**	**5.00**	**92.27**	**459.73**	**1028**	**552.00**
29	Milroy, Lee	43	480.00	54.00	534.00	40.85	46.00	10.68	10.00	5.00	112.53	421.47	1029	534.00
31	Total		16,200.00	1,010.00	17,210.00	1,316.57	3,490.00	344.20	421.50	115.00	5,687.27	11,522.73		17,210.00

presents Academy Company's payroll register. It provides the documentation for preparing a paycheck for each employee. For example, it shows the data for Michael Jordan in the wages section. In this example, Academy's total weekly payroll is $17,210, as shown in the salaries and wages expense column (column N, row 31).

Note that this record is a listing of each employee's payroll data for the pay period. In some companies, a payroll register is a journal or book of original entry. Postings are made from it directly to ledger accounts. In other companies, the payroll register is a memorandum record that provides the data for a general journal entry and subsequent posting to the ledger accounts. Academy follows the latter procedure.

RECOGNIZING PAYROLL EXPENSES AND LIABILITIES

From the payroll register in Illustration 11-14, Academy Company makes a journal entry to record the payroll. For the week ending January 14, the entry is as follows.

Jan. 14	Salaries and Wages Expense	17,210.00	
	FICA Taxes Payable		1,316.57
	Federal Income Taxes Payable		3,490.00
	State Income Taxes Payable		344.20
	United Fund Payable		421.50
	Union Dues Payable		115.00
	Salaries and Wages Payable		11,522.73
	(To record payroll for the week ending January 14)		

A	=	L	+	OE
				−17,210.00 Exp
		+1,316.57		
		+3,490.00		
		+344.20		
		+421.50		
		+115.00		
		+11,522.73		

Cash Flows
no effect

The company credits specific liability accounts for the mandatory and voluntary deductions made during the pay period. In the example, Academy debits Salaries and Wages Expense for the gross earnings of its employees. The amount credited to Salaries and Wages Payable is the sum of the individual checks the employees will receive.

RECORDING PAYMENT OF THE PAYROLL

A company makes payments by check (or electronic funds transfer) either from its regular bank account or a payroll bank account. Each paycheck is usually accompanied by a detachable **statement of earnings** document. This shows the employee's gross earnings, payroll deductions, and net pay, both for the period and for the year-to-date. Academy Company uses its regular bank account for payroll checks. Illustration 11-15 (page 406) shows the paycheck and statement of earnings for Michael Jordan.

Following payment of the payroll, the company enters the check numbers in the payroll register. Academy records payment of the payroll as follows.

Jan. 14	Salaries and Wages Payable	11,522.73	
	Cash		11,522.73
	(To record payment of payroll)		

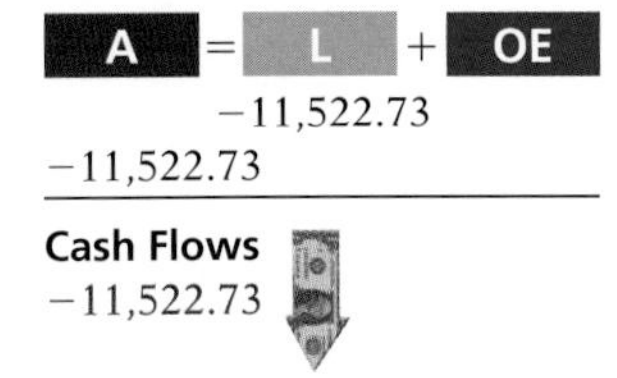

A	=	L	+	OE
		−11,522.73		
−11,522.73				

Cash Flows
−11,522.73

Many medium- and large-size companies use a payroll processing center that performs payroll recordkeeping services. Companies send the center payroll information about employee pay rates and hours worked. The center maintains the payroll records and prepares the payroll checks. In most cases, it costs less to process the payroll through the center (outsource) than if the company did so internally.

Illustration 11-15
Paycheck and statement of earnings

AC — ACADEMY COMPANY, 19 Center St., Hampton, MI 48291 — No. 1028

January 14, 2017 — 62–1113/610

Pay to the order of Michael Jordan $ 459.73

Four Hundred Fifty-nine and 73/100 Dollars

City Bank & Trust
P.O. Box 3000
Hampton, MI 48291

For Payroll — Randall E. Barnes

003244771 1028

DETACH AND RETAIN THIS PORTION FOR YOUR RECORDS

NAME				SOC. SEC. NO.		EMPL. NUMBER	NO. EXEMP	PAY PERIOD ENDING
Michael Jordan				329-35-9547			2	1/14/17
REG. HRS.	O.T. HRS.	OTH. HRS. (1)	OTH. HRS. (2)	REG. EARNINGS	O.T. EARNINGS	OTH. EARNINGS (1)	OTH. EARNINGS (2)	GROSS
40	4			480.00	72.00			$552.00
FED. W/H TAX	FICA	STATE TAX	LOCAL TAX	OTHER DEDUCTIONS (1)	(2)	(3)	(4)	NET PAY
24.00	42.23	11.04		10.00	5.00			459.73

YEAR TO DATE

FED. W/H TAX	FICA	STATE TAX	LOCAL TAX	OTHER DEDUCTIONS (1)	(2)	(3)	(4)	NET PAY
44.00	81.70	21.36		20.00	10.00			$890.94

Employer Payroll Taxes

Payroll tax expense for businesses results from three taxes that governmental agencies levy **on employers**. These taxes are (1) FICA, (2) federal unemployment tax, and (3) state unemployment tax. These taxes plus such items as paid vacations and pensions (discussed in the appendix to this chapter) are collectively referred to as **fringe benefits**. As indicated earlier, the cost of fringe benefits in many companies is substantial.

FICA TAXES

Each employee must pay FICA taxes. In addition, employers must match each employee's FICA contribution. This means the employer must remit to the federal government 12.4% of each employee's first $117,000 of taxable earnings, plus 2.9% of each employee's earnings, regardless of amount. The matching contribution results in **payroll tax expense** to the employer. The employer's tax is subject to the same rate and maximum earnings as the employee's. The company uses the same account, FICA Taxes Payable, to record both the employee's and the employer's FICA contributions. For the January 14 payroll, Academy Company's FICA tax contribution is $1,316.57 ($17,210.00 × 7.65%).

FEDERAL UNEMPLOYMENT TAXES

The Federal Unemployment Tax Act (FUTA) is another feature of the federal Social Security program. **Federal unemployment taxes** provide benefits for a limited period of time to employees who lose their jobs through no fault of their own. The FUTA tax rate is currently 6.2% of taxable wages. The taxable wage base is the first $7,000 of wages paid to each employee in a calendar year. Employers who pay the state unemployment tax on a timely basis will receive an offset credit of up to 5.4%. Therefore, the net federal tax rate is generally 0.8% (6.2% − 5.4%). This rate would equate to a maximum of $56 of federal tax per employee per year (0.8% × $7,000). State tax rates are based on state law.

The **employer** bears the entire federal unemployment tax. There is no deduction or withholding from employees. Companies use the account Federal Unemployment Taxes Payable to recognize this liability. The federal unemployment tax for Academy Company for the January 14 payroll is $137.68 ($17,210.00 × 0.8%).

STATE UNEMPLOYMENT TAXES

All states have unemployment compensation programs under state unemployment tax acts (SUTA). Like federal unemployment taxes, **state unemployment taxes** provide benefits to employees who lose their jobs. These taxes are levied on employers.[2] The basic rate is usually 5.4% on the first $7,000 of wages paid to an employee during the year. The state adjusts the basic rate according to the employer's experience rating. Companies with a history of stable employment may pay less than 5.4%. Companies with a history of unstable employment may pay more than the basic rate. Regardless of the rate paid, the company's credit on the federal unemployment tax is still 5.4%.

Companies use the account State Unemployment Taxes Payable for this liability. The state unemployment tax for Academy Company for the January 14 payroll is $929.34 ($17,210.00 × 5.4%). Illustration 11-16 summarizes the types of employer payroll taxes.

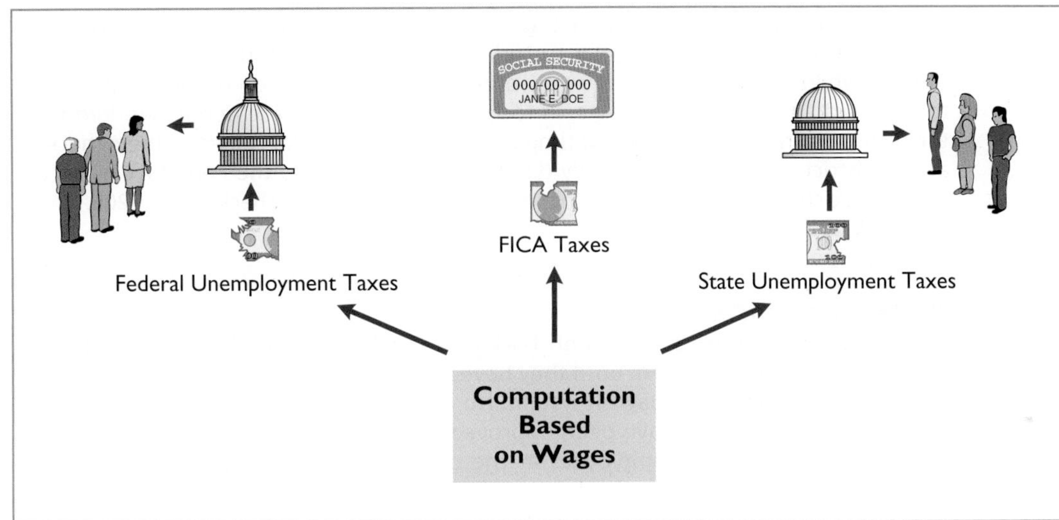

Illustration 11-16
Employer payroll taxes

RECORDING EMPLOYER PAYROLL TAXES

Companies usually record employer payroll taxes at the same time they record the payroll. The entire amount of gross pay ($17,210.00) shown in the payroll register in Illustration 11-14 is subject to each of the three taxes mentioned above. Accordingly, Academy records the payroll tax expense associated with the January 14 payroll with the following entry.

Jan. 14	Payroll Tax Expense	2,383.59	
	FICA Taxes Payable		1,316.57
	Federal Unemployment Taxes Payable		137.68
	State Unemployment Taxes Payable		929.34
	(To record employer's payroll taxes on January 14 payroll)		

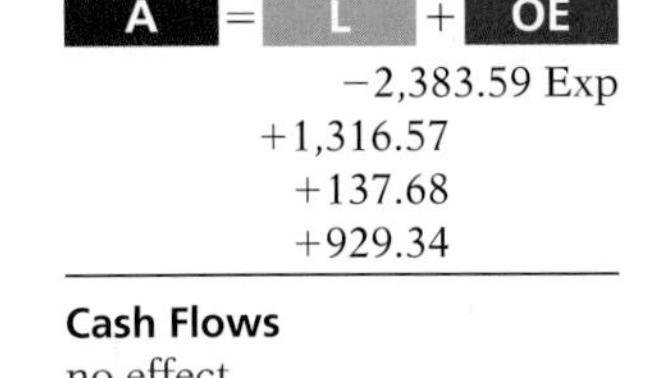

Note that Academy uses separate liability accounts instead of a single credit to Payroll Taxes Payable. Why? Because these liabilities are payable to different taxing authorities at different dates. Companies classify the liability accounts in the balance sheet as current liabilities since they will be paid within the next year. They classify Payroll Tax Expense on the income statement as an operating expense.

[2]In a few states, the employee is also required to make a contribution. *In this textbook, including the homework, we will assume that the tax is only on the employer.*

Filing and Remitting Payroll Taxes

Preparation of payroll tax returns is the responsibility of the payroll department. The treasurer's department makes the tax payment. Much of the information for the returns is obtained from employee earnings records.

For purposes of reporting and remitting to the IRS, the company combines the FICA taxes and federal income taxes that it withheld. **Companies must report the taxes quarterly**, no later than one month following the close of each quarter. The remitting requirements depend on the amount of taxes withheld and the length of the pay period. Companies remit funds through deposits in either a Federal Reserve bank or an authorized commercial bank.

Companies generally file and remit federal unemployment taxes **annually** on or before January 31 of the subsequent year. Earlier payments are required when the tax exceeds a specified amount. Companies usually must file and pay state unemployment taxes by the **end of the month following each quarter**. When payroll taxes are paid, companies debit payroll liability accounts, and credit Cash.

ANATOMY OF A FRAUD

Art was a custodial supervisor for a large school district. The district was supposed to employ between 35 and 40 regular custodians, as well as 3 or 4 substitute custodians to fill in when regular custodians were absent. Instead, in addition to the regular custodians, Art "hired" 77 substitutes. In fact, almost none of these people worked for the district. Instead, Art submitted time cards for these people, collected their checks at the district office, and personally distributed the checks to the "employees." If a substitute's check was for $1,200, that person would cash the check, keep $200, and pay Art $1,000.

Total take: $150,000

THE MISSING CONTROLS

Human resource controls. Thorough background checks should be performed. No employees should begin work until they have been approved by the Board of Education and entered into the payroll system. No employees should be entered into the payroll system until they have been approved by a supervisor. All paychecks should be distributed directly to employees at the official school locations by designated employees.

Independent internal verification. Budgets should be reviewed monthly to identify situations where actual costs significantly exceed budgeted amounts.

Source: Adapted from Wells, *Fraud Casebook* (2007), pp. 164–171.

Employers also must provide each employee with a **Wage and Tax Statement (Form W-2)** by January 31 following the end of a calendar year. This statement shows gross earnings, FICA taxes withheld, and income taxes withheld for the year. The required W-2 form for Michael Jordan, using assumed annual data, is shown in Illustration 11-17. The employer must send a copy of each employee's Wage and Tax Statement (Form W-2) to the Social Security Administration. This agency subsequently furnishes the Internal Revenue Service with the income data required.

Internal Control for Payroll

Chapter 8 introduced internal control. As applied to payrolls, the objectives of internal control are (1) to safeguard company assets against unauthorized payments of payrolls, and (2) to ensure the accuracy and reliability of the accounting records pertaining to payrolls.

Irregularities often result if internal control is lax. Frauds involving payroll include overstating hours, using unauthorized pay rates, adding fictitious employees to the payroll, continuing terminated employees on the payroll, and

22222	Void ☐	a Employee's social security number 329-35-9547	For Official Use Only ► OMB No. 1545-0008

b Employer identification number (EIN) 36-2167852	1 Wages, tips, other compensation 26,300.00	2 Federal income tax withheld 2,248.00
c Employer's name, address, and ZIP code Academy Company 19 Center St. Hampton, MI 48291	3 Social security wages 26,300.00	4 Social security tax withheld 1,630.60
	5 Medicare wages and tips 26,300.00	6 Medicare tax withheld 381.35
	7 Social security tips	8 Allocated tips
d Control number	9 Advance EIC payment	10 Dependent care benefits
e Employee's first name and initial: Michael · Last name: Jordan · Suff.	11 Nonqualified plans	12a See instructions for box 12 (Code)
2345 Mifflin Ave. Hampton, MI 48292	13 Statutory employee ☐ Retirement plan ☐ Third-party sick pay ☐	12b (Code)
	14 Other	12c (Code)
f Employee's address and ZIP code		12d (Code)

15 State	Employer's state ID number	16 State wages, tips, etc.	17 State income tax	18 Local wages, tips, etc.	19 Local income tax	20 Locality name
MI	423-1466-3	26,300.00	526.00			

Form **W-2** **Wage and Tax Statement** **2017**

Department of the Treasury—Internal Revenue Service

For Privacy Act and Paperwork Reduction Act Notice, see back of Copy D.

Copy A For Social Security Administration — Send this entire page with Form W-3 to the Social Security Administration; photocopies are **not** acceptable.

Cat. No. 10134D

Illustration 11-17
W-2 form

distributing duplicate payroll checks. Moreover, inaccurate records will result in incorrect paychecks, financial statements, and payroll tax returns.

Payroll activities involve four functions: hiring employees, timekeeping, preparing the payroll, and paying the payroll. For effective internal control, companies should assign these four functions to different departments or individuals. Illustration 11-18 highlights these functions and illustrates their internal control features.

Illustration 11-18
Internal control for payroll

Payroll Function

Hiring Employees

Internal control feature: Human Resources department documents and authorizes employment.

Fraud prevented: Fictitious employees are not added to payroll.

Timekeeping

Internal control feature: Supervisors monitor hours worked through time cards and time reports.

Fraud prevented: Employee not paid for hours not worked.

Payroll Function

Preparing the Payroll

Internal control feature: Two (or more) employees verify payroll amounts; supervisor approves.

Fraud prevented: Payroll calculations are accurate and relevant.

Paying the Payroll

Internal control feature: Treasurer signs and distributes prenumbered checks.

Fraud prevented: Checks are not lost, misappropriated, or unavailable for proof of payment; endorsed check provides proof of payment.

LEARNING OBJECTIVE *4

APPENDIX 11A: Discuss additional fringe benefits associated with employee compensation.

In addition to the traditional payroll-tax fringe benefits (Social Security taxes, Medicare taxes, and state and federal unemployment taxes), employers incur other substantial fringe benefit costs. Two of the most important are paid absences and postretirement benefits.

Paid Absences

Employees often are given rights to receive compensation for absences when they meet certain conditions of employment. The compensation may be for paid vacations, sick pay benefits, and paid holidays. When the payment for such absences is **probable** and the amount can be **reasonably estimated**, the company should accrue a liability for paid future absences. When the amount cannot be reasonably estimated, the company should instead disclose the potential liability. Ordinarily, vacation pay is the only paid absence that is accrued. The other types of paid absences are only disclosed.

To illustrate, assume that Academy Company employees are entitled to one day's vacation for each month worked. If 30 employees earn an average of $110 per day in a given month, the accrual for vacation benefits in one month is $3,300. Academy records the liability at the end of the month by the following adjusting entry.

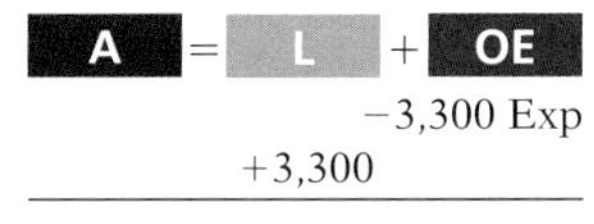

A	=	L	+	OE
		+3,300		−3,300 Exp

Cash Flows
no effect

Jan. 31	Vacation Benefits Expense	3,300	
	Vacation Benefits Payable		3,300
	(To accrue vacation benefits expense)		

This accrual is required by the expense recognition principle. Academy would report Vacation Benefits Expense as an operating expense in the income statement, and Vacation Benefits Payable as a current liability in the balance sheet.

Later, when Academy pays vacation benefits, it debits Vacation Benefits Payable and credits Cash. For example, if employees take 10 days of vacation in July, the entry is as follows.

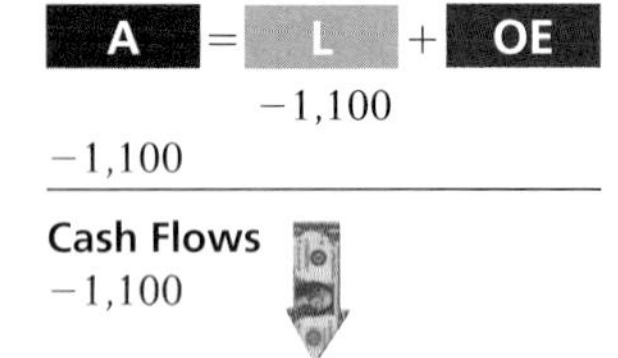

A	=	L	+	OE
−1,100		−1,100		

Cash Flows
−1,100

July 31	Vacation Benefits Payable	1,100	
	Cash		1,100
	(To record payment of vacation benefits)		

The magnitude of unpaid absences has gained employers' attention. Consider the case of an assistant superintendent of schools who worked for 20 years and rarely took a vacation or sick day. A month or so before she retired, the school district discovered that she was due nearly $30,000 in accrued benefits. Yet the school district had never accrued the liability.

Postretirement Benefits

Postretirement benefits are benefits that employers provide to retired employees for (1) pensions and (2) healthcare and life insurance. Companies account for both types of postretirement benefits on the accrual basis. The cost of postretirement benefits is getting steep. For example, states and localities must deal with a $1 trillion deficit in public employees' retirement benefit funds. This shortfall amounts to more than $8,800 for every household in the nation.

Average Americans have debt of approximately $10,000 (not counting the mortgage on their home) and little in the way of savings. What will happen at retirement for these people? The picture is not pretty—people are living longer, the future of Social Security is unclear, and companies are cutting back on post-retirement benefits. This situation may lead to one of the great social and moral dilemmas this country faces in the next 40 years. The more you know about post-retirement benefits, the better you will understand the issues involved in this dilemma.

POSTRETIREMENT HEALTHCARE AND LIFE INSURANCE BENEFITS

Providing medical and related healthcare benefits for retirees was at one time an inexpensive and highly effective way of generating employee goodwill. This practice has now turned into one of corporate America's most worrisome financial problems. Runaway medical costs, early retirement, and increased longevity are sending the liability for retiree health plans through the roof.

Companies estimate and expense postretirement costs during the working years of the employee because the company benefits from the employee's services during this period. However, the company rarely sets up funds to meet the cost of the future benefits. It follows a pay-as-you-go basis for these costs. The major reason is that the company does not receive a tax deduction until it actually pays the medical bill.

PENSION PLANS

A **pension plan** is an agreement whereby an employer provides benefits (payments) to employees after they retire. The need for good accounting for pension plans becomes apparent when we consider the size of existing pension funds. Over 50 million workers currently participate in pension plans in the United States. Most pension plans are subject to the provisions of ERISA (Employee Retirement Income Security Act), a law enacted to curb abuses in the administration and funding of such plans.

Three parties are generally involved in a pension plan. The **employer** (company) sponsors the pension plan. The **plan administrator** receives the contributions from the employer, invests the pension assets, and makes the benefit payments to the **pension recipients** (retired employees). Illustration 11A-1 indicates the flow of cash among the three parties involved in a pension plan.

An employer-financed pension is part of the employees' compensation. ERISA establishes the minimum contribution that a company must make each year toward employee pensions. The most popular type of pension plan used is the 401(k) plan. A 401(k) plan works as follows. As an employee, you can contribute up to a certain percentage of your pay into a 401(k) plan, and your employer will match a percentage of your contribution. These contributions are then generally invested in stocks and bonds through mutual funds. These funds will grow without being taxed and can be withdrawn beginning at age 59-1/2. If you must access the funds earlier, you may be able to do so, but a penalty usually occurs along with a payment of tax on the proceeds. Any time

Illustration 11A-1
Parties in a pension plan

you have the opportunity to be involved in a 401(k) plan, you should avail yourself of this benefit!

Companies record pension costs as an expense while the employees are working because that is when the company receives benefits from the employees' services. Generally, the pension expense is reported as an operating expense in the company's income statement. Frequently, the amount contributed by the company to the pension plan is different from the amount of the pension expense. A **liability** is recognized when the pension expense to date is **more than** the company's contributions to date. An **asset** is recognized when the pension expense to date is **less than** the company's contributions to date. Further consideration of the accounting for pension plans is left for more advanced courses.

The two most common types of pension arrangements for providing benefits to employees after they retire are defined-contribution plans and defined-benefit plans.

DEFINED-CONTRIBUTION PLAN In a **defined-contribution plan**, the plan defines the employer's contribution but not the benefit that the employee will receive at retirement. That is, the employer agrees to contribute a certain sum each period based on a formula. A 401(k) plan is typically a defined-contribution plan.

The accounting for a defined-contribution plan is straightforward. The employer simply makes a contribution each year based on the formula established in the plan. As a result, the employer's obligation is easily determined. It follows that the company reports **the amount of the contribution required each period as pension expense. The employer reports a liability only if it has not made the contribution in full.**

To illustrate, assume that Alba Office Interiors has a defined-contribution plan in which it contributes $200,000 each year to the pension fund for its employees. The entry to record this transaction is:

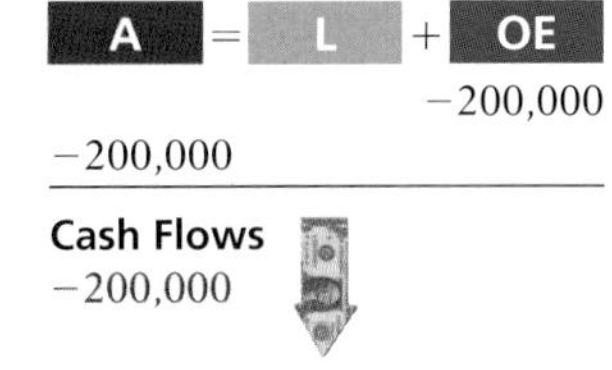

Pension Expense	200,000	
Cash		200,000
(To record pension expense and contribution to pension fund)		

To the extent that Alba did not contribute the $200,000 defined contribution, it would record a liability. Pension payments to retired employees are made from the pension fund by the plan administrator.

DEFINED-BENEFIT PLAN In a **defined-benefit plan**, the **benefits** that the employee will receive at the time of retirement are defined by the terms of the plan. Benefits are typically calculated using a formula that considers an employee's compensation level when he or she nears retirement and the employee's years of service. Because the benefits in this plan are defined in terms of uncertain future variables, an appropriate funding pattern is established to ensure that enough funds are available at retirement to meet the benefits promised. This funding level depends on a number of factors such as employee turnover, length of service, mortality, compensation levels, and investment earnings. **The proper accounting for these plans is complex and is considered in more advanced accounting courses.**

POSTRETIREMENT BENEFITS AS LONG-TERM LIABILITIES

While part of the liability associated with (1) postretirement healthcare and life insurance benefits and (2) pension plans is generally a current liability, the greater portion of these liabilities extends many years into the future. Therefore, many companies are required to report significant amounts as long-term liabilities for postretirement benefits.

REVIEW AND PRACTICE

LEARNING OBJECTIVES REVIEW

1 Explain how to account for current liabilities. A current liability is a debt that a company expects to pay within one year or the operating cycle, whichever is longer. The major types of current liabilities are notes payable, accounts payable, sales taxes payable, unearned revenues, and accrued liabilities such as taxes, salaries and wages, and interest payable.

When a promissory note is interest-bearing, the amount of assets received upon the issuance of the note is generally equal to the face value of the note. Interest expense accrues over the life of the note. At maturity, the amount paid equals the face value of the note plus accrued interest.

Companies record sales taxes payable at the time the related sales occur. The company serves as a collection agent for the taxing authority. Sales taxes are not an expense to the company. Companies initially record unearned revenues in an Unearned Revenue account. As a company recognizes revenue, a transfer from unearned revenue to revenue occurs. Companies report the current maturities of long-term debt as a current liability in the balance sheet.

2 Discuss how current liabilities are reported and analyzed. With notes payable, interest payable, accounts payable, and sales taxes payable, an obligation to make a payment exists. In some cases, it is difficult to determine whether a liability exists. These situations are called contingent liabilities. If the contingency is **probable** (likely to occur) and the amount is reasonably estimable, the company should record the liability in the accounts. If the contingency is only **reasonably possible** (it could happen), then it should be disclosed only in the notes to the financial statements. If the possibility that the contingency will happen is **remote** (unlikely to occur), it need not be recorded or disclosed.

Companies should report the nature and amount of each current liability in the balance sheet or in schedules in the notes accompanying the statements. The liquidity of a company may be analyzed by computing working capital and the current ratio.

3 Explain how to account for payroll. The computation of the payroll involves gross earnings, payroll deductions, and net pay. In recording the payroll, companies debit Salaries and Wages Expense for gross earnings, credit individual tax and other liability accounts for payroll deductions, and credit Salaries and Wages Payable for net pay. When the payroll is paid, companies debit Salaries and Wages Payable and credit Cash.

Employer payroll taxes consist of FICA, federal unemployment taxes, and state unemployment taxes. The taxes are usually accrued at the time the company records the payroll, by debiting Payroll Tax Expense and crediting separate liability accounts for each type of tax.

The objectives of internal control for payroll are (1) to safeguard company assets against unauthorized payments of payrolls, and (2) to ensure the accuracy of the accounting records pertaining to payrolls.

***4 Discuss additional fringe benefits associated with employee compensation.** Additional fringe benefits associated with wages are paid absences (paid vacations, sick pay benefits, and paid holidays), and postretirement benefits (pensions, healthcare, and life insurance).

GLOSSARY REVIEW

Bonus Compensation to management and other personnel, based on factors such as increased sales or the amount of net income.

Contingent liability A potential liability that may become an actual liability in the future.

Current ratio A measure of a company's liquidity; computed as current assets divided by current liabilities.

***Defined-benefit plan** A pension plan in which the benefits that the employee will receive at retirement are defined by the terms of the plan.

***Defined-contribution plan** A pension plan in which the employer's contribution to the plan is defined by the terms of the plan.

Employee earnings record A cumulative record of each employee's gross earnings, deductions, and net pay during the year.

Federal unemployment taxes Taxes imposed on the employer by the federal government that provide benefits for a limited time period to employees who lose their jobs through no fault of their own.

Fees Payments made for the services of professionals.

FICA taxes Taxes designed to provide workers with supplemental retirement, employment disability, and medical benefits.

Gross earnings Total compensation earned by an employee.

Net pay Gross earnings less payroll deductions.

Notes payable Obligations in the form of written notes.

Payroll deductions Deductions from gross earnings to determine the amount of a paycheck.

Payroll register A payroll record that accumulates the gross earnings, deductions, and net pay by employee for each pay period.

***Pension plan** An agreement whereby an employer provides benefits to employees after they retire.

***Postretirement benefits** Payments by employers to retired employees for healthcare, life insurance, and pensions.

Salaries Employee pay based on a specified amount rather than an hourly rate.

Statement of earnings A document attached to a paycheck that indicates the employee's gross earnings, payroll deductions, and net pay.

State unemployment taxes Taxes imposed on the employer by states that provide benefits to employees who lose their jobs.

Wage and Tax Statement (Form W-2) A form showing gross earnings, FICA taxes withheld, and income taxes withheld, prepared annually by an employer for each employee.

Wages Amounts paid to employees based on a rate per hour or on a piecework basis.

Working capital A measure of a company's liquidity; computed as current assets minus current liabilities.

PRACTICE EXERCISES

Prepare entries for interest-bearing notes.

(LO 1)

1. On June 1, Streamsong Company borrows $150,000 from First Bank on a 6-month, $150,000, 8% note.

Instructions

(a) Prepare the entry on June 1.

(b) Prepare the adjusting entry on June 30.

(c) Prepare the entry at maturity (December 1), assuming monthly adjusting entries have been made through November 30.

(d) What was the total financing cost (interest expense)?

Solution

1. (a) June 1	Cash	150,000	
	Notes Payable		150,000
(b) June 30	Interest Expense	1,000	
	Interest Payable		
	($150,000 × 8% × 1/12)		1,000
(c) Dec. 1	Notes Payable	150,000	
	Interest Payable		
	($150,000 × 8% × 6/12)	6,000	
	Cash		156,000
(d) $6,000			

Prepare current liabilities section of the balance sheet and evaluate liquidity.

(LO 2)

2. Fun App Company has the following liability accounts after posting adjusting entries: Accounts Payable $77,000, Unearned Ticket Revenue $36,000, Warranty Liability $25,000, Interest Payable $10,000, Mortgage Payable $150,000, Notes Payable $100,000, and Sales Taxes Payable $14,000. Assume the company's operating cycle is less than 1 year, ticket revenue will be recognized within 1 year, warranty costs are expected to be incurred within 1 year, and the notes mature in 3 years.

Instructions

(a) Prepare the current liabilities section of the balance sheet, assuming $40,000 of the mortgage is payable next year.

(b) Comment on Fun App Company's liquidity, assuming total current assets are $350,000.

Solution

2. (a)

FUN APP COMPANY Partial Balance Sheet	
Current liabilities	
Long-term debt due within one year	$ 40,000
Accounts payable	77,000
Unearned ticket revenue	36,000
Warranty liability	25,000
Sales taxes payable	14,000
Interest payable	10,000
Total current liabilities	$202,000

(b) Fun App Company's working capital is $148,000 ($350,000 − $202,000), and its current ratio is 1.73:1 ($350,000 ÷ $202,000). Although a current ratio of 2:1 has been considered the standard for a good credit rating, many companies operate successfully with a current ratio well below 2:1.

3. Erin Berge's regular hourly wage rate is $18, and she receives a wage of 1½ times the regular hourly rate for work in excess of 40 hours. During a March weekly pay period, Erin worked 42 hours. Her gross earnings prior to the current week were $6,000. Erin is married and claims three withholding allowances. Her only voluntary deduction is for group hospitalization insurance at $20 per week. Assume federal income tax withheld is $76.

Compute net pay and record pay for one employee.

(LO 3)

Instructions

(a) Compute the following amounts for Erin's wages for the current week.
   (1) Gross earnings.
   (2) FICA taxes (based on a 7.65% rate).
   (3) State income taxes withheld (based on a 3% rate).
   (4) Net pay.

(b) Record Erin's pay.

Solution

3. (a) (1) Regular 40 hours × $18 = $720
   Overtime 2 hours × $27 = 54
   Gross earnings $774

   (2) FICA taxes: ($774 × 7.65%) = $59.21
   (3) State income taxes: ($774 × 3%) = $23.22
   (4) Net Pay: ($774.00 − $59.21 − $76.00 − $23.22 −$20.00) = $595.57

(b)

Account	Debit	Credit
Salaries and Wages Expense	774.00	
FICA Taxes Payable		59.21
Federal Income Taxes Payable		76.00
State Income Taxes Payable		23.22
Health Insurance Payable		20.00
Salaries and Wages Payable		595.57

PRACTICE PROBLEM

Indiana Jones Company had the following selected transactions.

Feb. 1 Signs a $50,000, 6-month, 9%-interest-bearing note payable to CitiBank and receives $50,000 in cash.

10 Cash register sales total $43,200, which includes an 8% sales tax.

28 The payroll for the month consists of salaries and wages of $50,000. All wages are subject to 7.65% FICA taxes. A total of $8,900 federal income taxes are withheld. The salaries are paid on March 1.

28 The company develops the following adjustment data.

1. Interest expense of $375 has been incurred on the note.
2. Employer payroll taxes include 7.65% FICA taxes, a 5.4% state unemployment tax, and a 0.8% federal unemployment tax.
3. Some sales were made under warranty. Of the units sold under warranty, 350 are expected to become defective. Repair costs are estimated to be $40 per unit.

Instructions

(a) Journalize the February transactions.

(b) Journalize the adjusting entries at February 28.

Solution

Date	Account	Debit	Credit
(a) Feb. 1	Cash	50,000	
	Notes Payable		50,000
	(Issued 6-month, 9%-interest-bearing note to CitiBank)		
10	Cash	43,200	
	Sales Revenue ($43,200 ÷ 1.08)		40,000
	Sales Taxes Payable ($40,000 × 8%)		3,200
	(To record sales revenue and sales taxes payable)		
28	Salaries and Wages Expense	50,000	
	FICA Taxes Payable (7.65% × $50,000)		3,825
	Federal Income Taxes Payable		8,900
	Salaries and Wages Payable		37,275
	(To record February salaries)		
(b) Feb. 28	Interest Expense	375	
	Interest Payable		375
	(To record accrued interest for February)		
28	Payroll Tax Expense	6,925	
	FICA Taxes Payable		3,825
	Federal Unemployment Taxes Payable (0.8% × $50,000)		400
	State Unemployment Taxes Payable (5.4% × $50,000)		2,700
	(To record employer's payroll taxes on February payroll)		
28	Warranty Expense (350 × $40)	14,000	
	Warranty Liability		14,000
	(To record estimated warranty liability)		

EXERCISES

Prepare entries for interest-bearing notes.

(LO 1)

E11-1 C.S. Lewis Company had the following transactions involving notes payable.

July 1, 2017	Borrows $50,000 from First National Bank by signing a 9-month, 8% note.
Nov. 1, 2017	Borrows $60,000 from Lyon County State Bank by signing a 3-month, 6% note.
Dec. 31, 2017	Prepares adjusting entries.
Feb. 1, 2018	Pays principal and interest to Lyon County State Bank.
Apr. 1, 2018	Pays principal and interest to First National Bank.

Instructions

Prepare journal entries for each of the transactions.

E11-2 On June 1, Merando Company borrows $90,000 from First Bank on a 6-month, $90,000, 8% note.

Prepare entries for interest-bearing notes.

(LO 1)

Instructions

(a) Prepare the entry on June 1.
(b) Prepare the adjusting entry on June 30.
(c) Prepare the entry at maturity (December 1), assuming monthly adjusting entries have been made through November 30.
(d) What was the total financing cost (interest expense)?

E11-3 In performing accounting services for small businesses, you encounter the following situations pertaining to cash sales.

Journalize sales and related taxes.

(LO 1)

1. Poole Company enters sales and sales taxes separately on its cash register. On April 10, the register totals are sales $30,000 and sales taxes $1,500.
2. Waterman Company does not segregate sales and sales taxes. Its register total for April 15 is $25,680, which includes a 7% sales tax.

Instructions

Prepare the entry to record the sales transactions and related taxes for each client.

E11-4 Moreno Company publishes a monthly sports magazine, *Fishing Preview*. Subscriptions to the magazine cost $20 per year. During November 2017, Moreno sells 15,000 subscriptions beginning with the December issue. Moreno prepares financial statements quarterly and recognizes subscription revenue at the end of the quarter. The company uses the accounts Unearned Subscription Revenue and Subscription Revenue.

Journalize unearned subscription revenue.

(LO 1)

Instructions

(a) Prepare the entry in November for the receipt of the subscriptions.
(b) Prepare the adjusting entry at December 31, 2017, to record sales revenue recognized in December 2017.
(c) Prepare the adjusting entry at March 31, 2018, to record sales revenue recognized in the first quarter of 2018.

E11-5 Betancourt Company sells automatic can openers under a 75-day warranty for defective merchandise. Based on past experience, Betancourt estimates that 3% of the units sold will become defective during the warranty period. Management estimates that the average cost of replacing or repairing a defective unit is $15. The units sold and units defective that occurred during the last 2 months of 2017 are as follows.

Record estimated liability and expense for warranties.

(LO 2)

Month	Units Sold	Units Defective Prior to December 31
November	30,000	600
December	32,000	400

Instructions

(a) Prepare the journal entries to record the estimated liability for warranties and the costs incurred in honoring 1,000 warranty claims. (Assume actual costs of $15,000.)
(b) Determine the estimated warranty liability at December 31 for the units sold in November and December.
(c) Give the entry to record the honoring of 500 warranty contracts in January at an average cost of $15.

E11-6 Gallardo Co. is involved in a lawsuit as a result of an accident that took place September 5, 2017. The lawsuit was filed on November 1, 2017, and claims damages of $1,000,000.

Record and disclose contingent liabilities.

(LO 2)

Instructions

(a) At December 31, 2017, Gallardo's attorneys feel it is remote that Gallardo will lose the lawsuit. How should the company account for the effects of the lawsuit?
(b) Assume instead that at December 31, 2017, Gallardo's attorneys feel it is probable that Gallardo will lose the lawsuit and be required to pay $1,000,000. How should the company account for this lawsuit?
(c) Assume instead that at December 31, 2017, Gallardo's attorneys feel it is reasonably possible that Gallardo could lose the lawsuit and be required to pay $1,000,000. How should the company account for this lawsuit?

Prepare the current liabilities section of the balance sheet.

(LO 2)

E11-7 Younger Online Company has the following liability accounts after posting adjusting entries: Accounts Payable $73,000, Unearned Ticket Revenue $24,000, Warranty Liability $18,000, Interest Payable $8,000, Mortgage Payable $120,000, Notes Payable $80,000, and Sales Taxes Payable $10,000. Assume the company's operating cycle is less than 1 year, ticket revenue will be recognized within 1 year, warranty costs are expected to be incurred within 1 year, and the notes mature in 3 years.

Instructions

(a) Prepare the current liabilities section of the balance sheet, assuming $30,000 of the mortgage is payable next year.

(b) Comment on Younger Online Company's liquidity, assuming total current assets are $300,000.

Calculate current ratio and working capital before and after paying accounts payable.

(LO 2)

E11-8 Suppose the following financial data were reported by **3M Company** for 2016 and 2017 (dollars in millions).

3M COMPANY
Balance Sheets (partial)

	2017	**2016**
Current assets		
Cash and cash equivalents	$ 3,040	$1,849
Accounts receivable, net	3,250	3,195
Inventories	2,639	3,013
Other current assets	1,866	1,541
Total current assets	$10,795	$9,598
Current liabilities	$ 4,897	$5,839

Instructions

(a) Calculate the current ratio and working capital for 3M for 2016 and 2017.

(b) Suppose that at the end of 2017, 3M management used $200 million cash to pay off $200 million of accounts payable. How would its current ratio and working capital have changed?

Compute net pay and record pay for one employee.

(LO 3)

E11-9 Maria Garza's regular hourly wage rate is $16, and she receives a wage of 1½ times the regular hourly rate for work in excess of 40 hours. During a March weekly pay period, Maria worked 42 hours. Her gross earnings prior to the current week were $6,000. Maria is married and claims three withholding allowances. Her only voluntary deduction is for group hospitalization insurance at $25 per week.

Instructions

(a) Compute the following amounts for Maria's wages for the current week.
   (1) Gross earnings.
   (2) FICA taxes. (Assume a 7.65% rate on maximum of $117,000.)
   (3) Federal income taxes withheld. (Use the withholding table in the text, page 402.)
   (4) State income taxes withheld. (Assume a 2.0% rate.)
   (5) Net pay.

(b) Record Maria's pay.

Compute maximum FICA deductions.

(LO 3)

E11-10 Employee earnings records for Slaymaker Company reveal the following gross earnings for four employees through the pay period of December 15.

J. Seligman	$93,500	L. Marshall	$115,100
R. Eby	$113,600	T. Olson	$120,000

For the pay period ending December 31, each employee's gross earnings is $4,500. The FICA tax rate is 7.65% on gross earnings of $117,000.

Instructions

Compute the FICA withholdings that should be made for each employee for the December 31 pay period. (Show computations.)

E11-11 Ramirez Company has the following data for the weekly payroll ending January 31.

Prepare payroll register and record payroll and payroll tax expense.

(LO 3)

	Hours							Federal	
Employee	M	T	W	T	F	S	Hourly Rate	Income Tax Withholding	Health Insurance
L. Helton	8	8	9	8	10	3	$12	$34	$10
R. Kenseth	8	8	8	8	8	2	14	37	25
D. Tavaras	9	10	8	8	9	0	15	58	25

Employees are paid 1½ times the regular hourly rate for all hours worked in excess of 40 hours per week. FICA taxes are 7.65% on the first $117,000 of gross earnings. Ramirez Company is subject to 5.4% state unemployment taxes and 0.8% federal unemployment taxes on the first $7,000 of gross earnings.

Instructions

(a) Prepare the payroll register for the weekly payroll.
(b) Prepare the journal entries to record the payroll and Ramirez's payroll tax expense.

E11-12 Selected data from a February payroll register for Sutton Company are presented below. Some amounts are intentionally omitted.

Compute missing payroll amounts and record payroll.

(LO 3)

Gross earnings:		State income taxes	$ (3)
Regular	$9,100	Union dues	100
Overtime	(1)	Total deductions	(4)
Total	(2)	Net pay	$7,595
Deductions:		Account debited:	
FICA taxes	$ 765	Salaries and wages expense	(5)
Federal income taxes	1,140		

FICA taxes are 7.65%. State income taxes are 4% of gross earnings.

Instructions

(a) Fill in the missing amounts.
(b) Journalize the February payroll and the payment of the payroll.

E11-13 According to a payroll register summary of Frederickson Company, the amount of employees' gross pay in December was $850,000, of which $80,000 was not subject to Social Security taxes of 6.2% and $750,000 was not subject to state and federal unemployment taxes.

Determine employer's payroll taxes; record payroll tax expense.

(LO 3)

Instructions

(a) Determine the employer's payroll tax expense for the month, using the following rates: FICA 7.65%, state unemployment 5.4%, and federal unemployment 0.8%.
(b) Prepare the journal entry to record December payroll tax expense.

***E11-14** Mayberry Company has two fringe benefit plans for its employees:

Prepare adjusting entries for fringe benefits.

(LO 4)

1. It grants employees 2 days' vacation for each month worked. Ten employees worked the entire month of March at an average daily wage of $140 per employee.
2. In its pension plan, the company recognizes 10% of gross earnings as a pension expense. Gross earnings in March were $40,000. No contribution has been made to the pension fund.

Instructions

Prepare the adjusting entries at March 31.

***E11-15** Podsednik Corporation has 20 employees who each earn $140 a day. The following information is available.

Prepare journal entries for fringe benefits.

(LO 4)

1. At December 31, Podsednik recorded vacation benefits. Each employee earned 5 vacation days during the year.
2. At December 31, Podsednik recorded pension expense of $100,000, and made a contribution of $70,000 to the pension plan.
3. In January, 18 employees used one vacation day each.

Instructions

Prepare Podsednik's journal entries to record these transactions.

PROBLEMS

Prepare current liability entries, adjusting entries, and current liabilities section.

(LO 1, 2)

P11-1A On January 1, 2017, the ledger of Accardo Company contains the following liability accounts.

Accounts Payable	$52,000
Sales Taxes Payable	7,700
Unearned Service Revenue	16,000

During January, the following selected transactions occurred.

Jan. 5 Sold merchandise for cash totaling $20,520, which includes 8% sales taxes.
12 Performed services for customers who had made advance payments of $10,000. (Credit Service Revenue.)
14 Paid state revenue department for sales taxes collected in December 2016 ($7,700).
20 Sold 900 units of a new product on credit at $50 per unit, plus 8% sales tax. This new product is subject to a 1-year warranty.
21 Borrowed $27,000 from Girard Bank on a 3-month, 8%, $27,000 note.
25 Sold merchandise for cash totaling $12,420, which includes 8% sales taxes.

Instructions

(a) Journalize the January transactions.

(b) Journalize the adjusting entries at January 31 for (1) the outstanding notes payable, and (2) estimated warranty liability, assuming warranty costs are expected to equal 7% of sales of the new product. (*Hint:* Use one-third of a month for the Girard Bank note.)

(c) Current liability total $94,250

(c) Prepare the current liabilities section of the balance sheet at January 31, 2017. Assume no change in accounts payable.

Journalize and post note transactions; show balance sheet presentation.

(LO 1)

P11-2A The following are selected transactions of Blanco Company. Blanco prepares financial statements **quarterly**.

Jan. 2 Purchased merchandise on account from Nunez Company, $30,000, terms 2/10, n/30. (Blanco uses the perpetual inventory system.)
Feb. 1 Issued a 9%, 2-month, $30,000 note to Nunez in payment of account.
Mar. 31 Accrued interest for 2 months on Nunez note.
Apr. 1 Paid face value and interest on Nunez note.
July 1 Purchased equipment from Marson Equipment paying $11,000 in cash and signing a 10%, 3-month, $60,000 note.
Sept. 30 Accrued interest for 3 months on Marson note.
Oct. 1 Paid face value and interest on Marson note.
Dec. 1 Borrowed $24,000 from the Paola Bank by issuing a 3-month, 8% note with a face value of $24,000.
Dec. 31 Recognized interest expense for 1 month on Paola Bank note.

Instructions

(a) Prepare journal entries for the listed transactions and events.

(b) Post to the accounts Notes Payable, Interest Payable, and Interest Expense.

(c) Show the balance sheet presentation of notes and interest payable at December 31.

(d) $2,110

(d) What is total interest expense for the year?

Prepare payroll register and payroll entries.

(LO 3)

P11-3A Mann Hardware has four employees who are paid on an hourly basis plus time-and-a-half for all hours worked in excess of 40 a week. Payroll data for the week ended March 15, 2017, are presented below.

Employee	Hours Worked	Hourly Rate	Federal Income Tax Withholdings	United Fund
Ben Abel	40	$15.00	$?	$5.00
Rita Hager	42	16.00	?	5.00
Jack Never	44	13.00	60.00	8.00
Sue Perez	46	13.00	61.00	5.00

Abel and Hager are married. They claim 0 and 4 withholding allowances, respectively. The following tax rates are applicable: FICA 7.65%, state income taxes 3%, state unemployment taxes 5.4%, and federal unemployment 0.8%.

Instructions

(a) Prepare a payroll register for the weekly payroll. (Use the wage-bracket withholding table in the text for federal income tax withholdings.)

(a) Net pay $2,039.30

(b) Journalize the payroll on March 15, 2017, and the accrual of employer payroll taxes.

(b) Payroll tax expense $349.43

(c) Journalize the payment of the payroll on March 16, 2017.

(d) Journalize the deposit in a Federal Reserve bank on March 31, 2017, of the FICA and federal income taxes payable to the government.

(d) Cash paid $578.02

P11-4A The following payroll liability accounts are included in the ledger of Harmon Company on January 1, 2017.

Journalize payroll transactions and adjusting entries.

(LO 3, 4)

FICA Taxes Payable	$ 760.00
Federal Income Taxes Payable	1,204.60
State Income Taxes Payable	108.95
Federal Unemployment Taxes Payable	288.95
State Unemployment Taxes Payable	1,954.40
Union Dues Payable	870.00
U.S. Savings Bonds Payable	360.00

In January, the following transactions occurred.

Jan. 10	Sent check for $870.00 to union treasurer for union dues.
12	Remitted check for $1,964.60 to the Federal Reserve bank for FICA taxes and federal income taxes withheld.
15	Purchased U.S. Savings Bonds for employees by writing check for $360.00.
17	Paid state income taxes withheld from employees.
20	Paid federal and state unemployment taxes.
31	Completed monthly payroll register, which shows salaries and wages $58,000, FICA taxes withheld $4,437, federal income taxes payable $2,158, state income taxes payable $454, union dues payable $400, United Fund contributions payable $1,888, and net pay $48,663.
31	Prepared payroll checks for the net pay and distributed checks to employees.

At January 31, the company also makes the following accrued adjustments pertaining to employee compensation.

1. Employer payroll taxes: FICA taxes 7.65%, federal unemployment taxes 0.8%, and state unemployment taxes 5.4%.

*2. Vacation pay: 6% of gross earnings.

Instructions

(a) Journalize the January transactions.

(b) Journalize the adjustments pertaining to employee compensation at January 31.

(b) Payroll tax expense $8,033; Vacation benefits expense $3,480

P11-5A For the year ended December 31, 2017, Denkinger Electrical Repair Company reports the following summary payroll data.

Prepare entries for payroll and payroll taxes; prepare W-2 data.

(LO 3)

Gross earnings:	
Administrative salaries	$200,000
Electricians' wages	370,000
Total	$570,000
Deductions:	
FICA taxes	$ 38,645
Federal income taxes withheld	174,400
State income taxes withheld (3%)	17,100
United Fund contributions payable	27,500
Health insurance premiums	17,200
Total	$274,845

Denkinger Company's payroll taxes are Social Security tax 6.2%, Medicare tax 1.45%, state unemployment 2.5% (due to a stable employment record), and 0.8% federal unemployment. Gross earnings subject to Social Security taxes of 6.2% total $490,000, and gross earnings subject to unemployment taxes total $135,000.

(a) Salaries and wages payable $295,155
(b) Payroll tax expense $43,100

Instructions

(a) Prepare a summary journal entry at December 31 for the full year's payroll.
(b) Journalize the adjusting entry at December 31 to record the employer's payroll taxes.
(c) The W-2 Wage and Tax Statement requires the following dollar data.

Wages, Tips, Other Compensation	Federal Income Tax Withheld	State Income Tax Withheld	FICA Wages	FICA Tax Withheld

Complete the required data for the following employees.

Employee	Gross Earnings	Federal Income Tax Withheld
Maria Sandoval	$59,000	$28,500
Jennifer Mingenback	26,000	10,200

COMPREHENSIVE PROBLEM

CP11 Morgan Company's balance sheet at December 31, 2016, is presented below.

MORGAN COMPANY
Balance Sheet
December 31, 2016

Cash	$ 30,000	Accounts Payable	$ 13,750
Inventory	30,750	Interest Payable	250
Prepaid Insurance	6,000	Notes Payable	50,000
Equipment	38,000	Owner's Capital	40,750
	$104,750		$104,750

During January 2017, the following transactions occurred. (Morgan Company uses the perpetual inventory system.)

1. Morgan paid $250 interest on the note payable on January 1, 2017. The note is due December 31, 2018.
2. Morgan purchased $261,100 of inventory on account.
3. Morgan sold for $440,000 cash, inventory which cost $265,000. Morgan also collected $28,600 in sales taxes.
4. Morgan paid $230,000 in accounts payable.
5. Morgan paid $17,000 in sales taxes to the state.
6. Paid other operating expenses of $30,000.
7. On January 31, 2017, the payroll for the month consists of salaries and wages of $60,000. All salaries and wages are subject to 7.65% FICA taxes. A total of $8,900 federal income taxes are withheld. The salaries and wages are paid on February 1.

Adjustment data:

8. Interest expense of $250 has been incurred on the notes payable.
9. The insurance for the year 2017 was prepaid on December 31, 2016.
10. The equipment was acquired on December 31, 2016, and will be depreciated on a straight-line basis over 5 years with a $2,000 salvage value.
11. Employer's payroll taxes include 7.65% FICA taxes, a 5.4% state unemployment tax, and an 0.8% federal unemployment tax.

Instructions

(You may need to set up T-accounts to determine ending balances.)

(a) Prepare journal entries for the transactions listed above and the adjusting entries.
(b) Prepare an adjusted trial balance at January 31, 2017.
(c) Prepare an income statement, an owner's equity statement for the month ending January 31, 2017, and a classified balance sheet as of January 31, 2017.

BROADENING YOUR PERSPECTIVE

FINANCIAL REPORTING AND ANALYSIS

Financial Reporting Problem: Apple Inc.

BYP11-1 The financial statements of Apple Inc. are presented in Appendix A. Instructions for accessing and using the company's complete annual report, including the notes to the financial statements, are also provided in Appendix A.

Instructions

Refer to Apple's financial statements and answer the following questions about current and contingent liabilities and payroll costs.

(a) What were Apple's total current liabilities at September 28, 2013? What was the increase/decrease in Apple's total current liabilities from the prior year?

(b) In Apple's Note 10, the company explains the nature of its contingencies. Under what conditions does Apple recognize (record and report) liabilities for contingencies?

(c) What were the components of total current liabilities on September 28, 2013?

Comparative Analysis Problem: PepsiCo, Inc. vs. The Coca-Cola Company

BYP11-2 PepsiCo, Inc.'s financial statements are presented in Appendix B. Financial statements of The Coca-Cola Company are presented in Appendix C. Instructions for accessing and using the complete annual reports of PepsiCo and Coca-Cola, including the notes to the financial statements, are also provided in Appendices B and C, respectively.

Instructions

(a) At December 28, 2013, what was PepsiCo's largest current liability account? What were its total current liabilities? At December 31, 2013, what was Coca-Cola's largest current liability account? What were its total current liabilities?

(b) Based on information contained in those financial statements, compute the following 2013 values for each company:
(1) Working capital.
(2) Current ratio.

(c) What conclusions concerning the relative liquidity of these companies can be drawn from these data?

Comparative Analysis Problem: Amazon.com, Inc. vs. Wal-Mart Stores, Inc.

BYP11-3 Amazon.com Inc.'s financial statements are presented in Appendix D. Financial statements of Wal-Mart Stores, Inc. are presented in Appendix E. Instructions for accessing and using the complete annual reports of Amazon and Wal-Mart, including the notes to the financial statements, are also provided in Appendices D and E, respectively.

Instructions

(a) At December 31, 2013, what was Amazon's largest current liability account? What were its total current liabilities? At January 31, 2014, what was Wal-Mart's largest current liability account? What were its total current liabilities?

(b) Based on information in these financial statements, compute the following 2013 values for Amazon and 2014 values for Wal-Mart:
(1) Working capital.
(2) Current ratio.

(c) What conclusions concerning the relative liquidity of these companies can be drawn from these data?

Real-World Focus

BYP11-4 The Internal Revenue Service provides considerable information over the Internet. The following site answers payroll tax questions faced by employers.

Address: **www.irs.ustreas.gov/formspubs/index.html**, or go to **www.wiley.com/college/weygandt**

Steps

1. Go to the site shown above.
2. Choose **View Online, Tax Publications**.
3. Choose **Publication 15, Circular E, Employer's Tax Guide**.

Instructions

Answer each of the following questions.

(a) How does the government define "employees"?
(b) What are the special rules for Social Security and Medicare regarding children who are employed by their parents?
(c) How can an employee obtain a Social Security card if he or she doesn't have one?
(d) Must employees report to their employer tips received from customers? If so, how?
(e) Where should the employer deposit Social Security taxes withheld or contributed?

CRITICAL THINKING

Decision-Making Across the Organization

BYP11-5 Cunningham Processing Company performs word-processing services for business clients and students in a university community. The work for business clients is fairly steady throughout the year. The work for students peaks significantly in December and May as a result of term papers, research project reports, and dissertations.

Two years ago, the company attempted to meet the peak demand by hiring part-time help. This led to numerous errors and much customer dissatisfaction. A year ago, the company hired four experienced employees on a permanent basis in place of part-time help. This proved to be much better in terms of productivity and customer satisfaction. But, it has caused an increase in annual payroll costs and a significant decline in annual net income.

Recently, Melissa Braun, a sales representative of Banister Services Inc., has made a proposal to the company. Under her plan, Banister will provide up to four experienced workers at a daily rate of $80 per person for an 8-hour workday. Banister workers are not available on an hourly basis. Cunningham would have to pay only the daily rate for the workers used.

The owner of Cunningham Processing, Carol Holt, asks you, as the company's accountant, to prepare a report on the expenses that are pertinent to the decision. If the Banister plan is adopted, Carol will terminate the employment of two permanent employees and will keep two permanent employees. At the moment, each employee earns an annual income of $22,000. Cunningham pays 7.65% FICA taxes, 0.8% federal unemployment taxes, and 5.4% state unemployment taxes. The unemployment taxes apply to only the first $7,000 of gross earnings. In addition, Cunningham pays $40 per month for each employee for medical and dental insurance. Carol indicates that if the Banister Services plan is accepted, her needs for temporary workers will be as follows.

Months	Number of Employees	Working Days per Month
January–March	2	20
April–May	3	25
June–October	2	18
November–December	3	23

Instructions

With the class divided into groups, answer the following.

(a) Prepare a report showing the comparative payroll expense of continuing to employ permanent workers compared to adopting the Banister Services Inc. plan.
(b) What other factors should Carol consider before finalizing her decision?

Communication Activity

BYP11-6 Mike Falcon, president of the Brownlee Company, has recently hired a number of additional employees. He recognizes that additional payroll taxes will be due as a result of this hiring, and that the company will serve as the collection agent for other taxes.

Instructions

In a memorandum to Mike Falcon, explain each of the taxes, and identify the taxes that result in payroll tax expense to Brownlee Company.

Ethics Case

BYP11-7 Robert Eberle owns and manages Robert's Restaurant, a 24-hour restaurant near the city's medical complex. Robert employs 9 full-time employees and 16 part-time employees. He pays all of

the full-time employees by check, the amounts of which are determined by Robert's public accountant, Anne Farr. Robert pays all of his part-time employees in currency. He computes their wages and withdraws the cash directly from his cash register.

Anne has repeatedly urged Robert to pay all employees by check. But as Robert has told his competitor and friend, Danny Gall, who owns the Greasy Diner, "My part-time employees prefer the currency over a check. Also, I don't withhold or pay any taxes or worker's compensation insurance on those cash wages because they go totally unrecorded and unnoticed."

Instructions

(a) Who are the stakeholders in this situation?
(b) What are the legal and ethical considerations regarding Robert's handling of his payroll?
(c) Anne Farr is aware of Robert's payment of the part-time payroll in currency. What are her ethical responsibilities in this case?
(d) What internal control principle is violated in this payroll process?

All About You

BYP11-8 Medical costs are substantial and rising. But will they be the most substantial expense over your lifetime? Not likely. Will it be housing or food? Again, not likely. The answer is taxes. On average, Americans work 107 days to afford their taxes. Companies, too, have large tax burdens. They look very hard at tax issues in deciding where to build their plants and where to locate their administrative headquarters.

Instructions

(a) Determine what your state income taxes are if your taxable income is $60,000 and you file as a single taxpayer in the state in which you live.
(b) Assume that you own a home worth $200,000 in your community and the tax rate is 2.1%. Compute the property taxes you would pay.
(c) Assume that the total gasoline bill for your automobile is $1,200 a year (300 gallons at $4 per gallon). What are the amounts of state and federal taxes that you pay on the $1,200?
(d) Assume that your purchases for the year total $9,000. Of this amount, $5,000 was for food and prescription drugs. What is the amount of sales tax you would pay on these purchases? (Many states do not levy a sales tax on food or prescription drugs. Does yours?)
(e) Determine what your Social Security taxes are if your income is $60,000.
(f) Determine what your federal income taxes are if your taxable income is $60,000 and you file as a single taxpayer.
(g) Determine your total taxes paid based on the above calculations, and determine the percentage of income that you would pay in taxes based on the following formula: Total taxes paid ÷ Total income.

FASB Codification Activity

BYP11-9 If your school has a subscription to the FASB Codification, go to **http://aaahq.org/ascLogin.cfm** to log in and prepare responses to the following.

(a) What is the definition of current liabilities?
(b) What is the definition of a contingent liability?
(c) What guidance does the Codification provide for the disclosure of contingent liabilities?

A Look at IFRS

LEARNING OBJECTIVE  5 **Compare the accounting for payroll under GAAP and IFRS.**

IFRS and GAAP have similar definitions of liabilities. The general recording procedures for payroll are similar, although differences occur depending on the types of benefits that are provided in different countries. For example, companies in other countries often have different forms of pensions, unemployment benefits, welfare payments, and so on.

Key Points

Following are the key similarities and differences between GAAP and IFRS related to current liabilities and payroll.

Similarities

- The basic definition of a liability under GAAP and IFRS is very similar. In a more technical way, liabilities are defined by the IASB as a present obligation of the entity arising from past events, the settlement of which is expected to result in an outflow from the entity of resources embodying economic benefits.
- The accounting for current liabilities such as notes payable, unearned revenue, and payroll taxes payable are similar between IFRS and GAAP.
- Under IFRS, liabilities are classified as current if they are expected to be paid within 12 months.

Differences

- Companies using IFRS sometimes show liabilities before assets. Also, they will sometimes show long-term liabilities before current liabilities.
- Under IFRS, companies sometimes will net current liabilities against current assets to show working capital on the face of the statement of financial position.
- Under GAAP, some contingent liabilities are recorded in the financial statements, others are disclosed, and in some cases no disclosure is required. Unlike GAAP, IFRS reserves the use of the term **contingent liability** to refer only to possible obligations that are **not** recognized in the financial statements but may be disclosed if certain criteria are met.
- For those items that GAAP would treat as recordable contingent liabilities, IFRS instead uses the term provisions. **Provisions** are defined as liabilities of uncertain timing or amount. Examples of provisions would be provisions for warranties, employee vacation pay, or anticipated losses. Under IFRS, the measurement of a provision related to an uncertain obligation is based on the best estimate of the expenditure required to settle the obligation.

Looking to the Future

The FASB and IASB are currently involved in two projects, each of which has implications for the accounting for liabilities. One project is investigating approaches to differentiate between debt and equity instruments. The other project, the elements phase of the conceptual framework project, will evaluate the definitions of the fundamental building blocks of accounting. The results of these projects could change the classification of many debt and equity securities.

IFRS Practice

IFRS Self-Test Questions

1. Which of the following is **false**?
   (a) Under IFRS, current liabilities must always be presented before noncurrent liabilities.
   (b) Under IFRS, an item is a current liability if it will be paid within the next 12 months.
   (c) Under IFRS, current liabilities are sometimes netted against current assets on the statement of financial position.
   (d) Under IFRS, a liability is only recognized if it is a present obligation.
2. Under IFRS, a contingent liability is:
   (a) disclosed in the notes if certain criteria are met.
   (b) reported on the face of the financial statements if certain criteria are met.
   (c) the same as a provision.
   (d) not covered by IFRS.
3. Under IFRS, obligations related to warranties are considered:
   (a) contingent liabilities.
   (b) provisions.
   (c) possible obligations.
   (d) None of these.
4. The joint projects of the FASB and IASB could potentially:
   (a) change the definition of liabilities.
   (b) change the definition of equity.
   (c) change the definition of assets.
   (d) All of the above.

IFRS Exercises

IFRS11-1 Define a provision and give an example.

IFRS11-2 Briefly describe some of the similarities and differences between GAAP and IFRS with respect to the accounting for liabilities.

International Financial Statement Analysis: Louis Vuitton

IFRS11-3 The financial statements of Louis Vuitton are presented in Appendix F. Instructions for accessing and using the company's complete annual report, including the notes to the financial statements, are also provided in Appendix F.

Instructions

(a) What were the total current liabilities for the company as of December 31, 2013? What portion of these current liabilities related to provisions?

(b) What is the company's accounting policies related to provisions?

Answers to IFRS Self-Test Questions

1. a **2.** a **3.** b **4.** d

Chapter 12 Accounting for Partnerships

In 1990, Cliff Chenfeld and Craig Balsam gave up the razors, ties, and six-figure salaries they had become accustomed to as New York lawyers. Instead, they set up a partnership, Razor & Tie Music, in Cliff's living room. Ten years later, it became the only record company in the country that had achieved success in selling music both on television and in stores. Razor & Tie's entertaining and effective TV commercials have yielded unprecedented sales for multi-artist music compilations. At the same time, its hot retail label has been behind some of the most recent original, progressive releases from artists such as Norma Jean, For Today, Chelsea Grin, and Starset.

Razor & Tie got its start with its first TV release, *Those Fabulous '70s* (100,000 copies sold), followed by *Disco Fever* (over 300,000 sold). After restoring the respectability of the oft-maligned music of the 1970s, the partners forged into the musical '80s with the same zeal that elicited success with their first releases. In 1993, Razor & Tie released *Totally '80s*, a collection of Top-10 singles from the 1980s that has sold over 450,000 units.

In 1995, Razor & Tie broke into the contemporary music world with *Living in the '90s*, the most successful record in the history of the company. Featuring a number of songs that were still hits on the radio at the time the package initially aired, *Living in the '90s* was a blockbuster. It received Gold certification in less than nine months and rewrote the rules on direct-response albums. For the first time, contemporary music was available through an album offered only through direct-response spots.

In fact, Razor & Tie is now a vertically integrated business that includes a music company with major label distribution, a music publishing business, a media buying company, a home video company, a direct marketing operation, and a growing database of entertainment consumers.

Razor & Tie has carved out a sizable piece of the market through the complementary talents of the two partners. Their imagination and savvy, along with exciting new releases planned for the coming years, ensure Razor & Tie's continued growth.

LEARNING OBJECTIVES

1. **Discuss and account for the formation of a partnership.**
2. **Explain how to account for net income or net loss of a partnership.**
3. **Explain how to account for the liquidation of a partnership.**

LEARNING OBJECTIVE 1

Discuss and account for the formation of a partnership.

A **partnership** is an association of two or more persons to carry on as co-owners of a business for profit. Partnerships are sometimes used in small retail, service, or manufacturing companies. Accountants, lawyers, and doctors also find it desirable to form partnerships with other professionals in the field.

Characteristics of Partnerships

Partnerships are fairly easy to form. People form partnerships simply by a verbal agreement or more formally by written agreement. We explain the principal characteristics of partnerships in the following sections.

ASSOCIATION OF INDIVIDUALS

A partnership is a legal entity. A partnership can own property (land, buildings, equipment) and can sue or be sued. **A partnership also is an accounting entity.** Thus, the personal assets, liabilities, and transactions of the partners are excluded from the accounting records of the partnership, just as they are in a proprietorship.

The net income of a partnership is not taxed as a separate entity. But, a partnership must file an information tax return showing partnership net income and each partner's share of that net income. Each partner's share is taxable at **personal tax rates**, regardless of the amount of net income each withdraws from the business during the year.

Association of Individuals

MUTUAL AGENCY

Mutual agency means that each partner acts on behalf of the partnership when engaging in partnership business. The act of any partner is binding on all other partners. This is true even when partners act beyond the scope of their authority, so long as the act appears to be appropriate for the partnership. For example, a partner of a grocery store who purchases a delivery truck creates a binding contract in the name of the partnership, even if the partnership agreement denies this authority. On the other hand, if a partner in a law firm purchased a snowmobile for the partnership, such an act would not be binding on the partnership. The purchase is clearly outside the scope of partnership business.

Mutual Agency

LIMITED LIFE

Corporations have unlimited life. Partnerships do not. A partnership may be ended voluntarily at any time through the acceptance of a new partner or the withdrawal of a partner. It may be ended involuntarily by the death or incapacity of a partner. **Partnership dissolution** occurs whenever a partner withdraws or a new partner is admitted. Dissolution does not necessarily mean that the business ends. If the continuing partners agree, operations can continue without interruption by forming a new partnership.

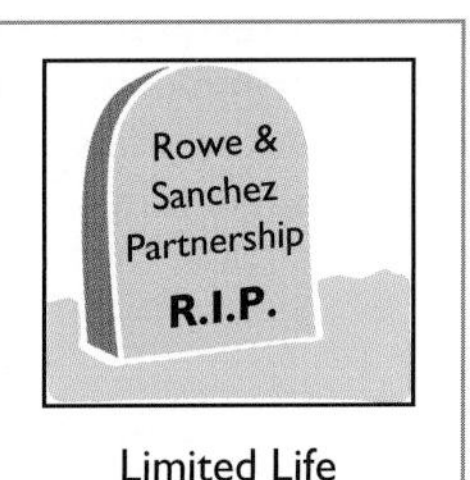

Limited Life

UNLIMITED LIABILITY

Each partner is **personally and individually liable** for all partnership liabilities. Creditors' claims attach first to partnership assets. If these are insufficient, the claims then attach to the personal resources of any partner, irrespective of that partner's equity in the partnership. Because each partner is responsible for all the debts of the partnership, each partner is said to have **unlimited liability**.

Unlimited Liability

CO-OWNERSHIP OF PROPERTY

Partners jointly own partnership assets. If the partnership is dissolved, each partner has a claim on total assets equal to the balance in his or her respective capital account. This claim does not attach to **specific assets** that an individual partner

Co-Ownership of Property

contributed to the firm. Similarly, if a partner invests a building in the partnership valued at $100,000 and the building is later sold at a gain of $20,000, the partners all share in the gain.

Partnership net income (or net loss) is also co-owned. **If the partnership contract does not specify to the contrary, all net income or net loss is shared equally by the partners.** As you will see later, though, partners may agree to unequal sharing of net income or net loss.

Organizations with Partnership Characteristics

If you are starting a business with a friend and each of you has little capital and your business is not risky, you probably want to use a partnership. As indicated above, the partnership is easy to establish and its cost is minimal. These types of partnerships are often called **regular partnerships**. However if your business is risky—say, roof repair or performing some type of professional service—you will want to limit your liability and not use a regular partnership. As a result, special forms of business organizations with partnership characteristics are now often used to provide protection from unlimited liability for people who wish to work together in some activity.

The special partnership forms are limited partnerships, limited liability partnerships, and limited liability companies. These special forms use the same accounting procedures as those described for a regular partnership. In addition, for taxation purposes, all the profits and losses pass through these organizations (similar to the regular partnership) to the owners, who report their share of partnership net income or losses on their personal tax returns.

LIMITED PARTNERSHIPS

In a **limited partnership**, one or more partners have **unlimited liability** and one or more partners have **limited liability** for the debts of the firm. Those with unlimited liability are **general partners**. Those with limited liability are **limited partners**. Limited partners are responsible for the debts of the partnership up to the limit of their investment in the firm.

The words "Limited Partnership," "Ltd.," or "LP" identify this type of organization. For the privilege of limited liability, the limited partner usually accepts less compensation than a general partner and exercises less influence in the affairs of the firm. If the limited partners get involved in management, they risk their liability protection.

International Note 

Much of the funding for successful new U.S. businesses comes from "venture capital" firms, which are organized as limited partnerships. To develop its own venture capital industry, China has taken steps to model its partnership laws to allow for limited partnerships like those in the United States.

LIMITED LIABILITY PARTNERSHIP

Most states allow professionals such as lawyers, doctors, and accountants to form a **limited liability partnership** or "LLP." The LLP is designed to protect innocent partners from malpractice or negligence claims resulting from the acts of another partner. LLPs generally carry large insurance policies as protection against malpractice suits. These professional partnerships vary in size from a medical partnership of three to five doctors, to 150 to 200 partners in a large law firm, to more than 2,000 partners in an international accounting firm.

LIMITED LIABILITY COMPANIES

A hybrid form of business organization with certain features like a corporation and others like a limited partnership is the **limited liability company** or "LLC." An LLC usually has a limited life. The owners, called **members**, have limited liability like owners of a corporation. Whereas limited partners do not actively participate in the management of a limited partnership (LP), the members of a limited liability company (LLC) can assume an active management role. For income tax purposes, the IRS usually classifies an LLC as a partnership.

Illustration 12-1
Different forms of organizations with partnership characteristics

	Major Advantages	Major Disadvantages
Regular Partnership General Partners	Simple and inexpensive to create and operate.	Owners (partners) personally liable for business debts.
Limited Partnership General Partner, Limited Partners	Limited partners have limited personal liability for business debts as long as they do not participate in management. General partners can raise cash without involving outside investors in management of business.	General partners personally liable for business debts. More expensive to create than regular partnership. Suitable mainly for companies that invest in real estate.
Limited Liability Partnership	Mostly of interest to partners in old-line professions such as law, medicine, and accounting. Owners (partners) are not personally liable for the malpractice of other partners.	Unlike a limited liability company, owners (partners) remain personally liable for many types of obligations owed to business creditors, lenders, and landlords. Often limited to a short list of professions.
Limited Liability Company	Owners have limited personal liability for business debts even if they participate in management.	More expensive to create than regular partnership.

Source: www.nolo.com.

Illustration 12-1 summarizes different forms of organizations that have partnership characteristics.

Advantages and Disadvantages of Partnerships

Why do people choose partnerships? One major advantage of a partnership is to combine the skills and resources of two or more individuals. In addition, partnerships are easily formed and are relatively free from government regulations and restrictions. A partnership does not have to contend with the "red tape" that a corporation must face. Also, partners generally can make decisions quickly on substantive business matters without having to consult a board of directors.

On the other hand, partnerships also have some major disadvantages. **Unlimited liability** is particularly troublesome. Many individuals fear they may lose not only their initial investment but also their personal assets if those assets are needed to pay partnership creditors.

Illustration 12-2 (page 432) summarizes the advantages and disadvantages of the regular partnership form of business organization. As indicated previously, different types of partnership forms have evolved to reduce some of the disadvantages.

Illustration 12-2
Advantages and disadvantages of a partnership

Advantages	Disadvantages
Combining skills and resources of two or more individuals	Mutual agency
Ease of formation	Limited life
Freedom from governmental regulations and restrictions	Unlimited liability
Ease of decision-making	

The Partnership Agreement

Ideally, the agreement of two or more individuals to form a partnership should be expressed in a written contract, called the **partnership agreement** or **articles of co-partnership**. The partnership agreement contains such basic information as the name and principal location of the firm, the purpose of the business, and date of inception. In addition, it should specify relationships among the partners, such as:

1. Names and capital contributions of partners.
2. Rights and duties of partners.
3. Basis for sharing net income or net loss.
4. Provision for withdrawals of assets.
5. Procedures for submitting disputes to arbitration.
6. Procedures for the withdrawal or addition of a partner.
7. Rights and duties of surviving partners in the event of a partner's death.

We cannot overemphasize the importance of a written contract. The agreement should attempt to anticipate all possible situations, contingencies, and disagreements. The help of a lawyer is highly desirable in preparing the agreement.

Accounting for a Partnership Formation

We now turn to the basic accounting for partnerships. The major accounting issues relate to forming the partnership, dividing income or loss, and preparing financial statements.

When forming a partnership, each partner's initial investment in a partnership is entered in the partnership records. The partnership should record these investments at the **fair value of the assets at the date of their transfer to the partnership**. All partners must agree to the values assigned.

To illustrate, assume that A. Rolfe and T. Shea combine their proprietorships to start a partnership named U.S. Software. The firm will specialize in developing financial modeling software. Rolfe and Shea have the following assets prior to the formation of the partnership.

Illustration 12-3
Book and fair values of assets invested

*Items under **owners' equity (OE)** in the accounting equation analyses are not labeled in this partnership chapter. Nearly all affect partners' **capital** accounts.*

	Book Value		Fair Value	
	A. Rolfe	T. Shea	A. Rolfe	T. Shea
Cash	$ 8,000	$ 9,000	**$ 8,000**	**$ 9,000**
Equipment	5,000		**4,000**	
Accumulated depreciation—equipment	(2,000)			
Accounts receivable		4,000		**4,000**
Allowance for doubtful accounts		(700)		**(1,000)**
	$11,000	$12,300	**$12,000**	**$12,000**

The partnership records the investments as follows.

A	=	L	+	OE
+8,000				
+4,000				
				+12,000

Cash Flows
+8,000

Investment of A. Rolfe

	Debit	Credit
Cash	8,000	
Equipment	4,000	
A. Rolfe, Capital		12,000
(To record investment of Rolfe)		

Investment of T. Shea

Cash	9,000	
Accounts Receivable	4,000	
Allowance for Doubtful Accounts		1,000
T. Shea, Capital		12,000
(To record investment of Shea)		

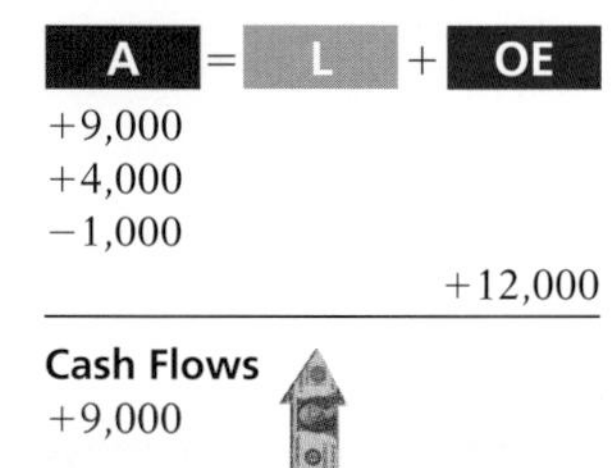

Note that the partnership records neither the original cost of the equipment ($5,000) nor its book value ($5,000 − $2,000). It records the equipment at its fair value, $4,000. The partnership does not carry forward any accumulated depreciation from the books of previous entities (in this case, the two proprietorships).

In contrast, the gross claims on customers ($4,000) are carried forward to the partnership. The partnership adjusts the allowance for doubtful accounts to $1,000, to arrive at a cash (net) realizable value of $3,000. A partnership may start with an allowance for doubtful accounts because it will continue to collect existing accounts receivable, some of which are expected to be uncollectible. In addition, this procedure maintains the control and subsidiary relationship between Accounts Receivable and the accounts receivable subsidiary ledger.

After formation of the partnership, the accounting for transactions is similar to any other type of business organization. For example, the partners record all transactions with outside parties, such as the purchase or sale of inventory and the payment or receipt of cash, the same as would a sole proprietor.

The steps in the accounting cycle described in Chapter 4 for a proprietorship also apply to a partnership. For example, the partnership prepares a trial balance and journalizes and posts adjusting entries. A worksheet may be used. There are minor differences in journalizing and posting closing entries and in preparing financial statements, as we explain in the following sections. The differences occur because there is more than one owner.

Explain how to account for net income or net loss of a partnership.

Dividing Net Income or Net Loss

Partners equally share partnership net income or net loss unless the partnership contract indicates otherwise. The same basis of division usually applies to both net income and net loss. It is customary to refer to this basis as the **income ratio**, the **income and loss ratio**, or the **profit and loss (P&L) ratio**. Because of its wide acceptance, we use the term **income ratio** to identify the basis for dividing net income and net loss. The partnership recognizes a partner's share of net income or net loss in the accounts through closing entries.

CLOSING ENTRIES

As in the case of a proprietorship, a partnership must make four entries in preparing closing entries. The entries are:

1. Debit each revenue account for its balance, and credit Income Summary for total revenues.
2. Debit Income Summary for total expenses, and credit each expense account for its balance.
3. Debit Income Summary for its balance, and credit each partner's capital account for his or her share of net income. Or, credit Income Summary, and debit each partner's capital account for his or her share of net loss.
4. Debit each partner's capital account for the balance in that partner's drawings account, and credit each partner's drawings account for the same amount.

The first two entries are the same as in a proprietorship. The last two entries are different because (1) there are two or more owners' capital and drawings accounts, and (2) it is necessary to divide net income (or net loss) among the partners.

To illustrate the last two closing entries, assume that AB Company has net income of $32,000 for 2017. The partners, L. Arbor and D. Barnett, share net income and net loss equally. Drawings for the year were Arbor $8,000 and Barnett $6,000. The last two closing entries are as follows.

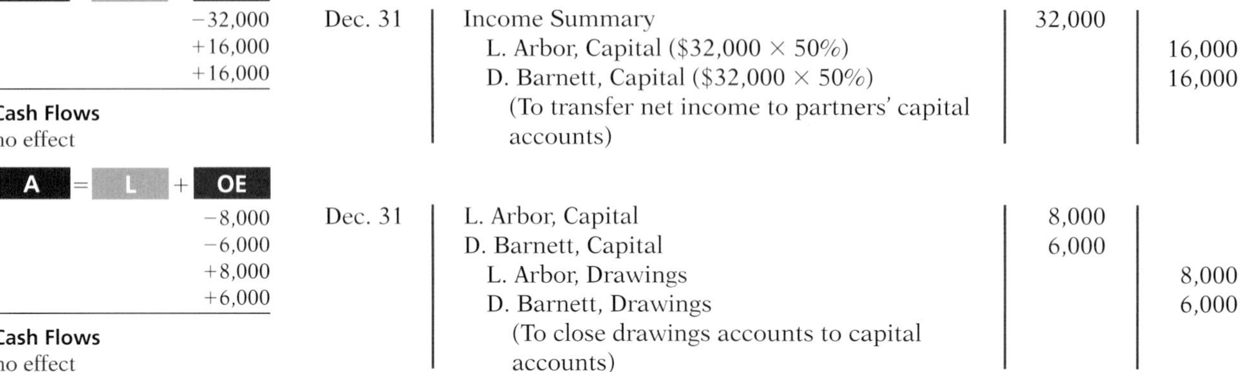

Date	Account	Debit	Credit
Dec. 31	Income Summary	32,000	
	L. Arbor, Capital ($32,000 × 50%)		16,000
	D. Barnett, Capital ($32,000 × 50%)		16,000
	(To transfer net income to partners' capital accounts)		
Dec. 31	L. Arbor, Capital	8,000	
	D. Barnett, Capital	6,000	
	L. Arbor, Drawings		8,000
	D. Barnett, Drawings		6,000
	(To close drawings accounts to capital accounts)		

Assume that the beginning capital balance is $47,000 for Arbor and $36,000 for Barnett. After posting the closing entries, the capital and drawings accounts will appear as shown in Illustration 12-4.

Illustration 12-4
Partners' capital and drawings accounts after closing

L. Arbor, Capital

12/31 **Clos.**	**8,000**	1/1	Bal.	47,000
		12/31	**Clos.**	**16,000**
		12/31	Bal.	55,000

D. Barnett, Capital

12/31 **Clos.**	**6,000**	1/1	Bal.	36,000
		12/31	**Clos.**	**16,000**
		12/31	Bal.	46,000

L. Arbor, Drawings

12/31 Bal.	8,000	12/31 **Clos.**	**8,000**

D. Barnett, Drawings

12/31 Bal.	6,000	12/31 **Clos.**	**6,000**

As in a proprietorship, the partners' capital accounts are permanent accounts. Their drawings accounts are temporary accounts. Normally, the capital accounts will have credit balances, and the drawings accounts will have debit balances. Drawings accounts are debited when partners withdraw cash or other assets from the partnership for personal use.

INCOME RATIOS

As noted earlier, the partnership agreement should specify the basis for sharing net income or net loss. The following are typical income ratios.

1. A fixed ratio, expressed as a proportion (6:4), a percentage (70% and 30%), or a fraction (2/3 and 1/3).
2. A ratio based either on capital balances at the beginning of the year or on average capital balances during the year.
3. Salaries to partners and the remainder on a fixed ratio.
4. Interest on partners' capital balances and the remainder on a fixed ratio.
5. Salaries to partners, interest on partners' capital, and the remainder on a fixed ratio.

The objective is to settle on a basis that will equitably reflect the partners' capital investment and service to the partnership.

A **fixed ratio** is easy to apply, and it may be an equitable basis in some circumstances. Assume, for example, that Hughes and Lane are partners. Each contributes the same amount of capital, but Hughes expects to work full-time in the partnership and Lane expects to work only half-time. Accordingly, the partners agree to a fixed ratio of 2/3 to Hughes and 1/3 to Lane.

A **ratio based on capital balances** may be appropriate when the funds invested in the partnership are considered the critical factor. Capital ratios may also be equitable when the partners hire a manager to run the business and do not plan to take an active role in daily operations.

The three remaining ratios (items 3, 4, and 5) give specific recognition to differences among partners. These ratios provide salary allowances for time worked and interest allowances for capital invested. Then, the partnership allocates any remaining net income or net loss on a fixed ratio.

Salaries to partners and interest on partners' capital are not expenses of the partnership. Therefore, these items do not enter into the matching of expenses with revenues and the determination of net income or net loss. For a partnership, as for other entities, salaries and wages expense pertains to the cost of services performed by employees. Likewise, interest expense relates to the cost of borrowing from creditors. But partners, as owners, are not considered either **employees** or **creditors**. When the partnership agreement permits the partners to make monthly withdrawals of cash based on their "salary," the partnership debits these withdrawals to the partner's drawings account.

SALARIES, INTEREST, AND REMAINDER ON A FIXED RATIO

Under income ratio (5) in the list above, the partnership must apply salaries and interest **before** it allocates the remainder on the specified fixed ratio. **This is true even if the provisions exceed net income. It is also true even if the partnership has suffered a net loss for the year.** The partnership's income statement should show, below net income, detailed information concerning the division of net income or net loss.

To illustrate, assume that Sara King and Ray Lee are co-partners in the Kingslee Company. The partnership agreement provides for (1) salary allowances of $8,400 to King and $6,000 to Lee, (2) interest allowances of 10% on capital balances at the beginning of the year, and (3) the remaining income to be divided equally. Capital balances on January 1 were King $28,000, and Lee $24,000. In 2017, partnership net income is $22,000. The division of net income is as shown in Illustration 12-5.

Illustration 12-5
Division of net income schedule

KINGSLEE COMPANY
Division of Net Income
For the Year Ended December 31, 2017

Net income	$ 22,000		
Division of Net Income			
	Sara King	**Ray Lee**	**Total**
Salary allowance	$ 8,400	$6,000	$14,400
Interest allowance on partners' capital			
Sara King ($28,000 × 10%)	2,800		
Ray Lee ($24,000 × 10%)		2,400	
Total interest allowance			5,200
Total salaries and interest	11,200	8,400	19,600
Remaining income, $2,400 ($22,000 – $19,600)			
Sara King ($2,400 × 50%)	1,200		
Ray Lee ($2,400 × 50%)		1,200	
Total remainder			2,400
Total division of net income	**$12,400**	**$9,600**	**$22,000**

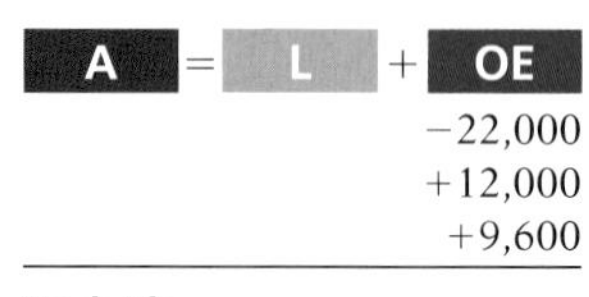

Cash Flows
no effect

Kingslee records the division of net income as follows.

Dec. 31	Income Summary	22,000	
	Sara King, Capital		12,400
	Ray Lee, Capital		9,600
	(To close net income to partners' capital)		

Now let's look at a situation in which the salary and interest allowances **exceed** net income. Assume that Kingslee Company's net income is only $18,000. In this case, the salary and interest allowances will create a deficiency of $1,600 ($18,000 − $19,600). The computations of the allowances are the same as those in the preceding example. Beginning with total salaries and interest, we complete the division of net income as shown in Illustration 12-6.

Illustration 12-6
Division of net income—income deficiency

	Sara King	Ray Lee	Total
Total salaries and interest	$11,200	$8,400	$19,600
Remaining deficiency ($1,600)			
($18,000 − $19,600)			
Sara King ($1,600 × 50%)	(800)		
Ray Lee ($1,600 × 50%)		(800)	
Total remainder			(1,600)
Total division	**$10,400**	**$7,600**	**$18,000**

Partnership Financial Statements

The financial statements of a partnership are similar to those of a proprietorship. The differences are due to the number of owners involved. The income statement for a partnership is identical to the income statement for a proprietorship except for the division of net income, as shown earlier.

The owners' equity statement for a partnership is called the **partners' capital statement**. It explains the changes in each partner's capital account and in total partnership capital during the year. Illustration 12-7 shows the partners' capital statement for Kingslee Company. It is based on the division of $22,000 of net income in Illustration 12-5 (page 435). The statement includes assumed data for the additional investment and drawings. The partnership prepares the partners' capital statement from the income statement and the partners' capital and drawings accounts.

Illustration 12-7
Partners' capital statement

KINGSLEE COMPANY
Partners' Capital Statement
For the Year Ended December 31, 2017

	Sara King	Ray Lee	Total
Capital, January 1	$28,000	$24,000	$52,000
Add: Additional investment	2,000		2,000
Net income	12,400	9,600	22,000
	42,400	33,600	76,000
Less: Drawings	7,000	5,000	12,000
Capital, December 31	**$35,400**	**$28,600**	**$64,000**

The balance sheet for a partnership is the same as for a proprietorship except for the owners' equity section. For a partnership, the balance sheet shows the capital balances of each partner. Illustration 12-8 shows the owners' equity section for Kingslee Company.

Illustration 12-8
Owners' equity section of a partnership balance sheet

KINGSLEE COMPANY Balance Sheet (partial) December 31, 2017		
Total liabilities (assumed amount)		$115,000
Owners' equity		
Sara King, capital	$35,400	
Ray Lee, capital	28,600	
Total owners' equity		64,000
Total liabilities and owners' equity		$179,000

LEARNING OBJECTIVE 3

Explain how to account for the liquidation of a partnership.

Liquidation of a business involves selling the assets of the firm, paying liabilities, and distributing any remaining assets. Liquidation may result from the sale of the business by mutual agreement of the partners, from the death of a partner, or from bankruptcy. **Partnership liquidation** ends both the legal and economic life of the entity.

From an accounting standpoint, the partnership should complete the accounting cycle for the final operating period prior to liquidation. This includes preparing adjusting entries and financial statements. It also involves preparing closing entries and a post-closing trial balance. Thus, only balance sheet accounts should be open as the liquidation process begins.

In liquidation, the sale of noncash assets for cash is called **realization**. Any difference between book value and the cash proceeds is called the **gain or loss on realization**. To liquidate a partnership, it is necessary to:

1. Sell noncash assets for cash and recognize a gain or loss on realization.
2. Allocate gain/loss on realization to the partners based on their income ratios.
3. Pay partnership liabilities in cash.
4. Distribute remaining cash to partners on the basis of their **capital balances**.

Each of the steps must be performed in sequence. The partnership must pay creditors **before** partners receive any cash distributions. Also, an accounting entry must record each step.

When a partnership is liquidated, all partners may have credit balances in their capital accounts. This situation is called **no capital deficiency**. Or, one or more partners may have a debit balance in the capital account. This situation is termed a **capital deficiency**. To illustrate each of these conditions, assume that Ace Company is liquidated when its ledger shows the following assets, liabilities, and owners' equity accounts.

Illustration 12-9
Account balances prior to liquidation

Assets		Liabilities and Owners' Equity	
Cash	$ 5,000	Notes Payable	$15,000
Accounts Receivable	15,000	Accounts Payable	16,000
Inventory	18,000	R. Arnet, Capital	15,000
Equipment	35,000	P. Carey, Capital	17,800
Accum. Depr.—Equipment	(8,000)	W. Eaton, Capital	1,200
	$65,000		$65,000

No Capital Deficiency

The partners of Ace Company agree to liquidate the partnership on the following terms. (1) The partnership will sell its noncash assets to Jackson Enterprises for

$75,000 cash. (2) The partnership will pay its partnership liabilities. The income ratios of the partners are 3:2:1, respectively. The steps in the liquidation process are as follows.

1. Ace sells the noncash assets (accounts receivable, inventory, and equipment) for $75,000. The book value of these assets is $60,000 ($15,000 + $18,000 + $35,000 − $8,000). Thus, Ace realizes a gain of $15,000 on the sale. The entry is:

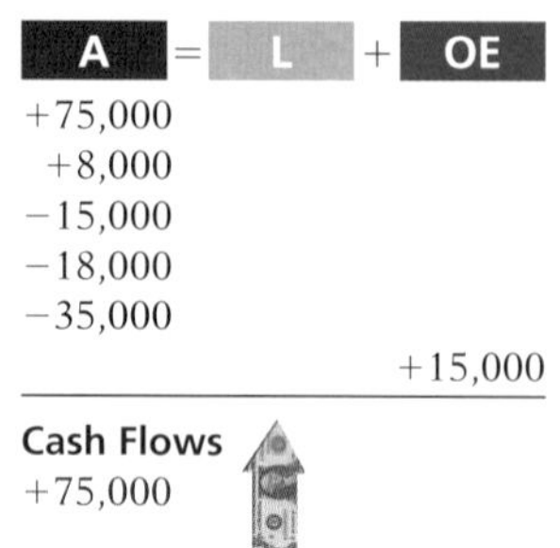

(1)

Cash	75,000	
Accumulated Depreciation–Equipment	8,000	
Accounts Receivable		15,000
Inventory		18,000
Equipment		35,000
Gain on Realization		15,000
(To record realization of noncash assets)		

2. Ace allocates the $15,000 gain on realization to the partners based on their income ratios, which are 3:2:1. The entry is:

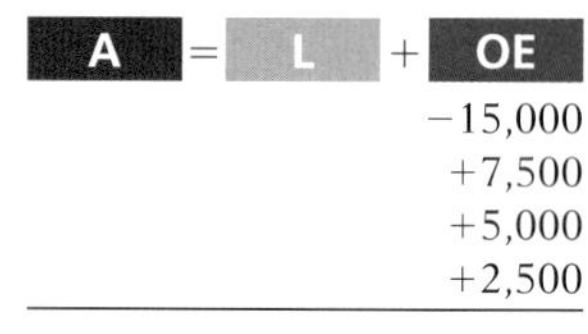

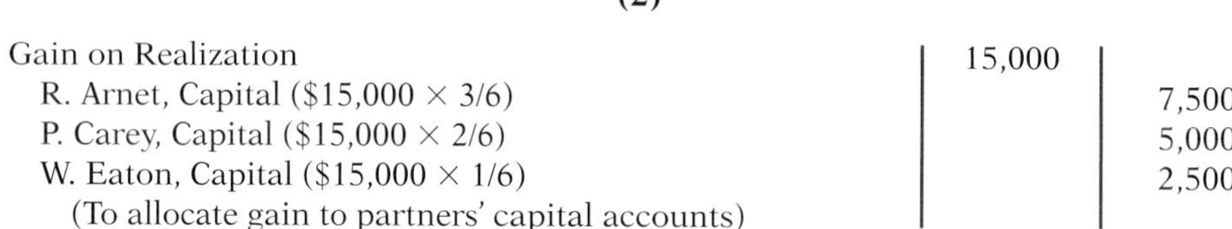

(2)

Gain on Realization	15,000	
R. Arnet, Capital ($15,000 × 3/6)		7,500
P. Carey, Capital ($15,000 × 2/6)		5,000
W. Eaton, Capital ($15,000 × 1/6)		2,500
(To allocate gain to partners' capital accounts)		

3. Partnership liabilities consist of Notes Payable $15,000 and Accounts Payable $16,000. Ace pays creditors in full by a cash payment of $31,000. The entry is:

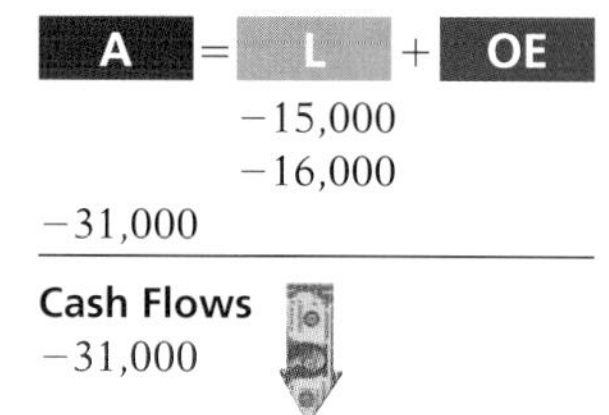

(3)

Notes Payable	15,000	
Accounts Payable	16,000	
Cash		31,000
(To record payment of partnership liabilities)		

4. Ace distributes the remaining cash to the partners on the basis of **their capital balances**. After posting the entries in the first three steps, all partnership accounts, including Gain on Realization, will have zero balances except for four accounts: Cash $49,000; R. Arnet, Capital $22,500; P. Carey, Capital $22,800; and W. Eaton, Capital $3,700, as shown below.

Illustration 12-10
Ledger balances before distribution of cash

Cash	
Bal. 5,000	(3) 31,000
(1) 75,000	
Bal. 49,000	

R. Arnet, Capital	
	Bal. 15,000
	(2) 7,500
	Bal. 22,500

P. Carey, Capital	
	Bal. 17,800
	(2) 5,000
	Bal. 22,800

W. Eaton, Capital	
	Bal. 1,200
	(2) 2,500
	Bal. 3,700

Ace records the distribution of cash as follows.

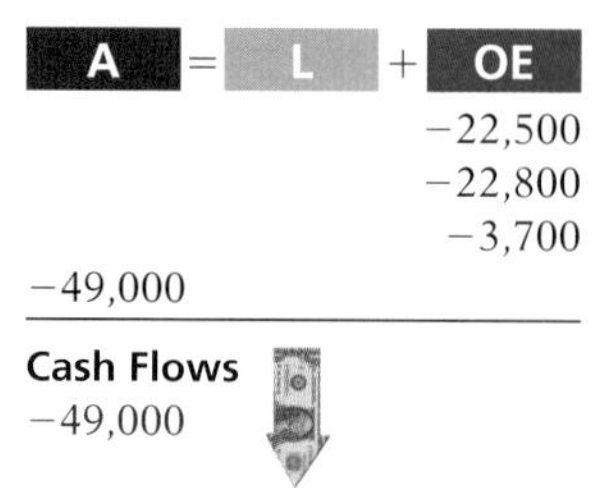

(4)

R. Arnet, Capital	22,500	
P. Carey, Capital	22,800	
W. Eaton, Capital	3,700	
Cash		49,000
(To record distribution of cash to partners)		

After posting this entry, all partnership accounts will have zero balances.

A word of caution: **Partnerships should not distribute remaining cash to partners on the basis of their income-sharing ratios.** On this basis, Arnet would receive three-sixths, or $24,500, which would produce an erroneous debit balance of $2,000. The income ratio is the proper basis for allocating net income or loss. **It is not a proper basis for making the final distribution of cash to the partners.**

Terminology
The schedule of cash payments is sometimes called a *safe cash payments schedule*.

SCHEDULE OF CASH PAYMENTS

The **schedule of cash payments** shows the distribution of cash to the partners in a partnership liquidation. The schedule of cash payments is organized around the basic accounting equation. Illustration 12-11 shows the schedule for Ace Company. The numbers in parentheses in column B refer to the four required steps in the liquidation of a partnership. They also identify the accounting entries that Ace must make. The cash payments schedule is especially useful when the liquidation process extends over a period of time.

Illustration 12-11
Schedule of cash payments, no capital deficiency

ACE Company.xls

Home Insert Page Layout Formulas Data Review View

P18 fx

ACE COMPANY
Schedule of Cash Payments

Item		Cash	+	Noncash Assets	=	Liabilities	+	R. Arnet, Capital	+	P. Carey, Capital	+	W. Eaton, Capital
Balances before liquidation		5,000	+	60,000	=	31,000	+	15,000	+	17,800	+	1,200
Sale of noncash assets and allocation of gain	(1)&(2)	75,000	+	(60,000)	=			7,500	+	5,000	+	2,500
New balances		80,000	+	-0-	=	31,000	+	22,500	+	22,800	+	3,700
Pay liabilities		(31,000)			=	(31,000)						
New balances	(3)	49,000	+	-0-	=	-0-	+	22,500	+	22,800	+	3,700
Cash distribution to partners	(4)	(49,000)			=			(22,500)	+	(22,800)	+	(3,700)
Final balances		-0-		-0-		-0-		-0-		-0-		-0-

Capital Deficiency

A capital deficiency may result from recurring net losses, excessive drawings, or losses from realization suffered during liquidation. To illustrate, assume that Ace Company is on the brink of bankruptcy. The partners decide to liquidate by having a "going-out-of-business" sale. They sell merchandise at substantial discounts, and sell the equipment at auction. Cash proceeds from these sales and collections from customers total only $42,000. Thus, the loss from liquidation is $18,000 ($60,000 − $42,000). The steps in the liquidation process are as follows.

1. The entry for the realization of noncash assets is:

(1)

	Debit	Credit
Cash	42,000	
Accumulated Depreciation—Equipment	8,000	
Loss on Realization	18,000	
Accounts Receivable		15,000
Inventory		18,000
Equipment		35,000
(To record realization of noncash assets)		

A	=	L	+	OE
+42,000				
+8,000				
				−18,000
−15,000				
−18,000				
−35,000				

Cash Flows
+42,000

2. Ace allocates the loss on realization to the partners on the basis of their income ratios. The entry is:

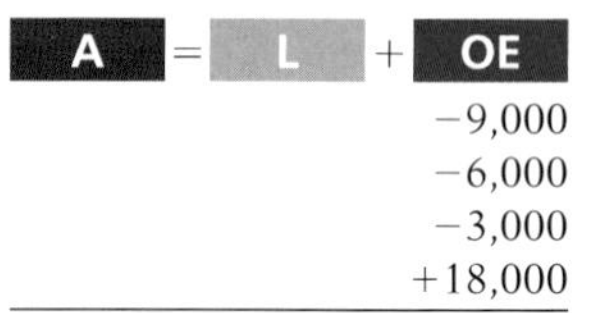

Cash Flows
no effect

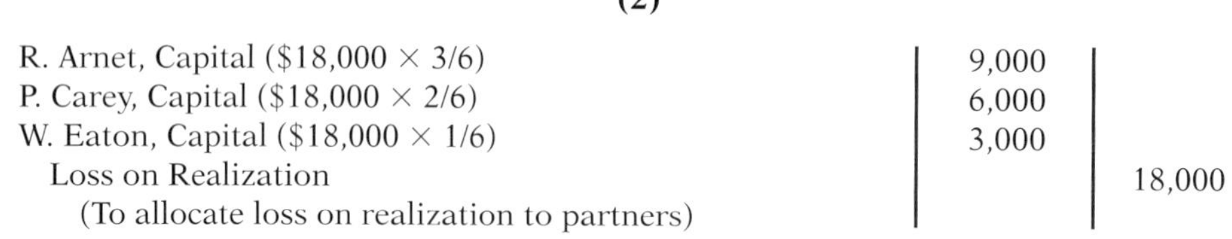

(2)		
R. Arnet, Capital ($18,000 × 3/6)	9,000	
P. Carey, Capital ($18,000 × 2/6)	6,000	
W. Eaton, Capital ($18,000 × 1/6)	3,000	
Loss on Realization		18,000
(To allocate loss on realization to partners)		

3. Ace pays the partnership liabilities. This entry is the same as the previous one.

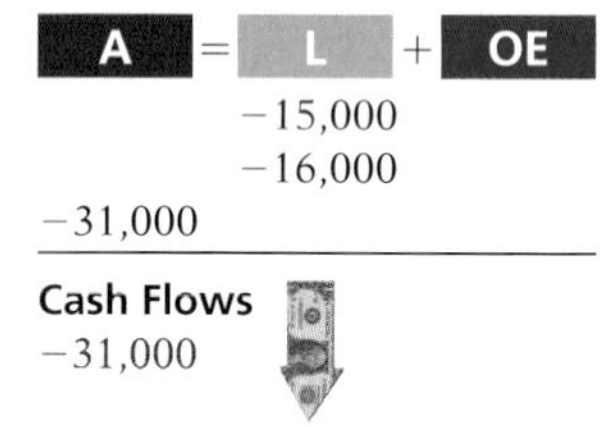

Cash Flows
−31,000

(3)		
Notes Payable	15,000	
Accounts Payable	16,000	
Cash		31,000
(To record payment of partnership liabilities)		

4. After posting the three entries, two accounts will have debit balances—Cash $16,000 and W. Eaton, Capital $1,800. Two accounts will have credit balances—R. Arnet, Capital $6,000 and P. Carey, Capital $11,800. All four accounts are shown below.

Cash		R. Arnet, Capital		P. Carey, Capital		W. Eaton, Capital	
Bal. 5,000	(3) 31,000	(2) 9,000	Bal. 15,000	(2) 6,000	Bal. 17,800	(2) 3,000	Bal. 1,200
(1) 42,000			**Bal. 6,000**		**Bal. 11,800**	**Bal. 1,800**	
Bal. 16,000							

Illustration 12-12
Ledger balances before distribution of cash

Eaton has a capital deficiency of $1,800 and so owes the partnership $1,800. Arnet and Carey have a legally enforceable claim for that amount against Eaton's personal assets. Note that the distribution of cash is still made on the basis of capital balances. But, the amount will vary depending on how Eaton settles the deficiency. Two alternatives are presented in the following sections.

PAYMENT OF DEFICIENCY

If the partner with the capital deficiency pays the amount owed the partnership, the deficiency is eliminated. To illustrate, assume that Eaton pays $1,800 to the partnership. The entry is:

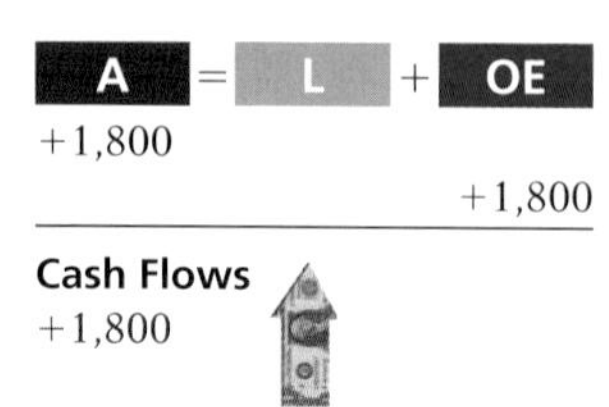

Cash Flows
+1,800

(a)		
Cash	1,800	
W. Eaton, Capital		1,800
(To record payment of capital deficiency by Eaton)		

Illustration 12-13
Ledger balances after paying capital deficiency

After posting this entry, account balances are as follows.

Cash		R. Arnet, Capital		P. Carey, Capital		W. Eaton, Capital	
Bal. 5,000	(3) 31,000	(2) 9,000	Bal. 15,000	(2) 6,000	Bal. 17,800	(2) 3,000	Bal. 1,200
(1) 42,000			**Bal. 6,000**		**Bal. 11,800**		(a) 1,800
(a) 1,800							**Bal. -0-**
Bal. 17,800							

The cash balance of $17,800 is now equal to the credit balances in the capital accounts (Arnet $6,000 + Carey $11,800). Ace now distributes cash on the basis of these balances. The entry is:

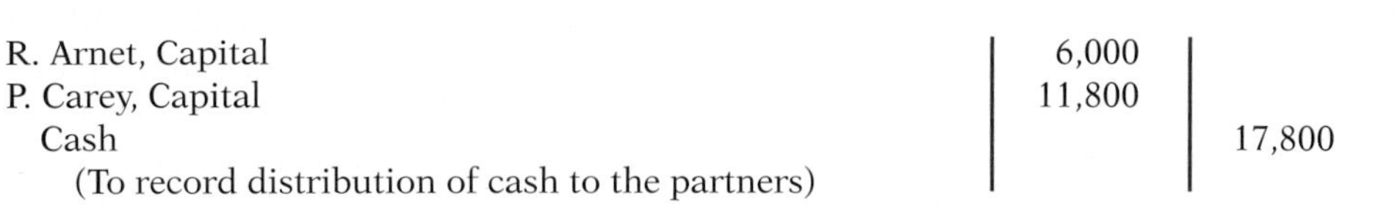

R. Arnet, Capital	6,000	
P. Carey, Capital	11,800	
Cash		17,800
(To record distribution of cash to the partners)		

A	=	L	+	OE
				−6,000
				−11,800
−17,800				

Cash Flows
−17,800

After posting this entry, all accounts will have zero balances.

NONPAYMENT OF DEFICIENCY

If a partner with a capital deficiency is unable to pay the amount owed to the partnership, the partners with credit balances must absorb the loss. The partnership allocates the loss on the basis of the income ratios that exist between the partners with credit balances.

The income ratios of Arnet and Carey are 3:2, or 3/5 and 2/5, respectively. Thus, Ace would make the following entry to remove Eaton's capital deficiency.

(a)

R. Arnet, Capital ($1,800 × 3/5)	1,080	
P. Carey, Capital ($1,800 × 2/5)	720	
W. Eaton, Capital		1,800
(To record write-off of capital deficiency)		

A	=	L	+	OE
				−1,080
				−720
				+1,800

Cash Flows
no effect

After posting this entry, the cash and capital accounts will have the following balances.

Cash		R. Arnet, Capital		P. Carey, Capital		W. Eaton, Capital	
Bal. 5,000	(3) 31,000	(2) 9,000	Bal. 15,000	(2) 6,000	Bal. 17,800	(2) 3,000	Bal. 1,200
(1) 42,000		(a) 1,080		(a) 720			(a) 1,800
Bal. 16,000			**Bal. 4,920**		**Bal. 11,080**		**Bal. –0–**

Illustration 12-14
Ledger balances after nonpayment of capital deficiency

The cash balance ($16,000) now equals the sum of the credit balances in the capital accounts (Arnet $4,920 + Carey $11,080). Ace records the distribution of cash as:

R. Arnet, Capital	4,920	
P. Carey, Capital	11,080	
Cash		16,000
(To record distribution of cash to the partners)		

A	=	L	+	OE
				−4,920
				−11,080
−16,000				

Cash Flows
−16,000

After posting this entry, all accounts will have zero balances.

LEARNING OBJECTIVE *4

APPENDIX 12A: Prepare journal entries when a partner is either admitted or withdraws.

The chapter explained how the basic accounting for a partnership works. We now look at how to account for a common occurrence in partnerships—the addition or withdrawal of a partner.

Admission of a Partner

The admission of a new partner results in the **legal dissolution** of the existing partnership and the beginning of a new one. From an economic standpoint, however, the admission of a new partner (or partners) may be of minor significance in the continuity of the business. For example, in large public accounting or law firms, partners are admitted annually without any change in operating policies. **To recognize the economic effects, it is necessary only to open a capital account for each new partner.** In the entries illustrated in this appendix, we assume that the accounting records of the predecessor firm will continue to be used by the new partnership.

A new partner may be admitted either by (1) purchasing the interest of one or more existing partners or (2) investing assets in the partnership. The former affects only the capital accounts of the partners who are parties to the transaction. The latter increases both net assets and total capital of the partnership.

PURCHASE OF A PARTNER'S INTEREST

The **admission** of a partner **by purchase of an interest** is a personal transaction between one or more existing partners and the new partner. Each party acts as an individual separate from the partnership entity. The individuals involved negotiate the price paid. It may be equal to or different from the capital equity acquired. The purchase price passes directly from the new partner to the partners who are giving up part or all of their ownership claims.

Any money or other consideration exchanged is the personal property of the participants and **not** the property of the partnership. Upon purchase of an interest, the new partner acquires each selling partner's capital interest and income ratio.

Accounting for the purchase of an interest is straightforward. The partnership records only the changes in partners' capital. **Partners' capital accounts are debited for any ownership claims sold.** At the same time, the new partner's capital account is credited for the capital equity purchased. Total assets, total liabilities, and total capital remain unchanged, as do all individual asset and liability accounts.

To illustrate, assume that L. Carson agrees to pay $10,000 each to C. Ames and D. Barker for $33\frac{1}{3}\%$ (one-third) of their interest in the Ames–Barker partnership. At the time of the admission of Carson, each partner has a $30,000 capital balance. Both partners, therefore, give up $10,000 of their capital equity. The entry to record the admission of Carson is:

	Debit	Credit
C. Ames, Capital	10,000	
D. Barker, Capital	10,000	
L. Carson, Capital		20,000
(To record admission of Carson by purchase)		

The effect of this transaction on net assets and partners' capital is shown below.

Net Assets		C. Ames, Capital		D. Barker, Capital		L. Carson, Capital	
60,000		**10,000**	30,000	**10,000**	30,000		**20,000**
			Bal. 20,000		Bal. 20,000		

Illustration 12A-1
Ledger balances after purchase of a partner's interest

Note that net assets remain unchanged at $60,000, and each partner has a $20,000 capital balance. Ames and Barker continue as partners in the firm, but the capital interest of each has changed. The cash paid by Carson goes directly to the individual partners and not to the partnership.

Regardless of the amount paid by Carson for the one-third interest, the entry is exactly the same. If Carson pays $12,000 each to Ames and Barker for one-third of the partnership, the partnership still makes the entry shown above.

INVESTMENT OF ASSETS IN A PARTNERSHIP

The admission of a partner by an investment of assets is a transaction between the new partner and the partnership. Often referred to simply as **admission by investment**, the transaction **increases both the net assets and total capital of the partnership**.

Assume, for example, that instead of purchasing an interest, Carson invests $30,000 in cash in the Ames-Barker partnership for a 33$^1/_3$% capital interest. In such a case, the entry is:

	Debit	Credit
Cash	30,000	
L. Carson, Capital		30,000
(To record admission of Carson by investment)		

Illustration 12A-2 shows the effects of this transaction on the partnership accounts.

Net Assets		C. Ames, Capital		D. Barker, Capital		L. Carson, Capital	
60,000			30,000		30,000		**30,000**
30,000							
Bal. 90,000							

Illustration 12A-2
Ledger balances after investment of assets

Note that both net assets and total capital have increased by $30,000.

Remember that Carson's one-third capital interest might not result in a one-third income ratio. The new partnership agreement should specify Carson's income ratio, and it may or may not be equal to the one-third capital interest.

The comparison of the net assets and capital balances in Illustration 12A-3 shows the different effects of the purchase of an interest and admission by investment.

Illustration 12A-3
Comparison of purchase of an interest and admission by investment

Purchase of an Interest		Admission by Investment	
Net assets	**$60,000**	**Net assets**	**$90,000**
Capital		Capital	
C. Ames	$20,000	C. Ames	$30,000
D. Barker	20,000	D. Barker	30,000
L. Carson	20,000	L. Carson	30,000
Total capital	**$60,000**	**Total capital**	**$90,000**

When a new partner purchases an interest, the total net assets and total capital of the partnership **do not change**. When a partner is admitted by investment, both the total net assets and the total capital **change** by the amount of the new investment.

In the case of admission by investment, further complications occur when the new partner's investment differs from the capital equity acquired. When those amounts are not the same, the difference is considered a **bonus** either to (1) the existing (old) partners or (2) the new partner.

BONUS TO OLD PARTNERS For both personal and business reasons, the existing partners may be unwilling to admit a new partner without receiving a bonus. In an established firm, existing partners may insist on a bonus as compensation for the work they have put into the company over the years. Two accounting factors underlie the business reason. First, total partners' capital equals the **book value** of the recorded net assets of the partnership. When the new partner is admitted, the fair values of assets such as land and buildings may be higher than their book values. The bonus will help make up the difference between fair value and book value. Second, when the partnership has been profitable, goodwill may exist. But, the partnership balance sheet does not report goodwill. The new partner is usually willing to pay the bonus to become a partner.

A bonus to old partners results when the new partner's investment in the firm is greater than the capital credit on the date of admittance. The bonus results in **an increase in the capital balances of the old partners. The partnership allocates the bonus to them on the basis of their income ratios before the admission of the new partner.** To illustrate, assume that the Bart-Cohen partnership, owned by Sam Bart and Tom Cohen, has total capital of $120,000. Lea Eden acquires a 25% ownership (capital) interest in the partnership by making a cash investment of $80,000. The procedure for determining Eden's capital credit and the bonus to the old partners is as follows.

1. **Determine the total capital of the new partnership.** Add the new partner's investment to the total capital of the old partnership. In this case, the total capital of the new firm is $200,000, computed as follows.

Total capital of existing partnership	$120,000
Investment by new partner, Eden	80,000
Total capital of new partnership	$200,000

2. **Determine the new partner's capital credit.** Multiply the total capital of the new partnership by the new partner's ownership interest. Eden's capital credit is $50,000 ($200,000 × 25%).
3. **Determine the amount of bonus.** Subtract the new partner's capital credit from the new partner's investment. The bonus in this case is $30,000 ($80,000 – $50,000).
4. **Allocate the bonus to the old partners on the basis of their income ratios.** Assuming the ratios are Bart 60%, and Cohen 40%, the allocation is Bart $18,000 ($30,000 × 60%) and Cohen $12,000 ($30,000 × 40%).

The entry to record the admission of Eden is:

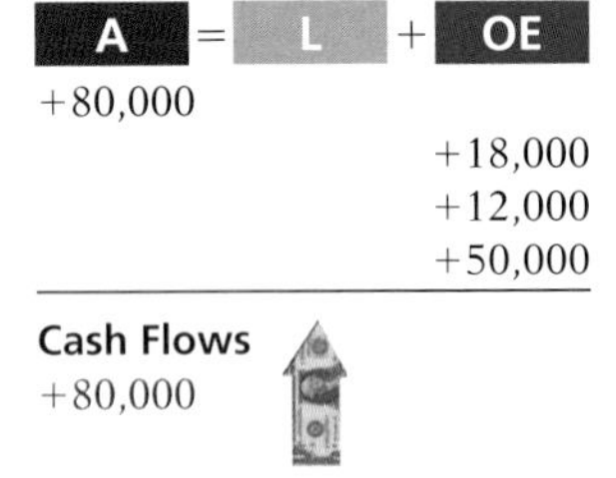

	Debit	Credit
Cash	80,000	
Sam Bart, Capital		18,000
Tom Cohen, Capital		12,000
Lea Eden, Capital		50,000
(To record admission of Eden and bonus to old partners)		

BONUS TO NEW PARTNER A bonus to a new partner results when the new partner's investment in the firm is less than his or her capital credit. This may occur when the new partner possesses special attributes that the partnership wants. For example, the new partner may be able to supply cash that the firm needs for expansion or to meet maturing debts. Or the new partner may be a recognized expert in a relevant field. Thus, an engineering firm may be willing to give a renowned engineer a bonus to join the firm. The partners of a restaurant may offer a bonus to a sports celebrity in order to add the athlete's name to the partnership. A bonus to a new partner may also result when recorded book values on the partnership books are higher than their fair values.

A bonus to a new partner results in a **decrease in the capital balances of the old partners. The amount of the decrease for each partner is based on the income ratios before the admission of the new partner.** To illustrate, assume that Lea Eden invests $20,000 in cash for a 25% ownership interest in the Bart–Cohen partnership. The computations for Eden's capital credit and the bonus are as follows, using the four procedures described in the preceding section.

Illustration 12A-4
Computation of capital credit and bonus to new partner

1. Total capital of Bart–Cohen partnership		$120,000
Investment by new partner, Eden		20,000
Total capital of new partnership		$140,000
2. **Eden's capital credit** (25% × $140,000)		$ 35,000
3. **Bonus to Eden** ($35,000 − $20,000)		$ 15,000
4. Allocation of bonus to old partners:		
Bart ($15,000 × 60%)	$9,000	
Cohen ($15,000 × 40%)	6,000	$ 15,000

The partnership records the admission of Eden as follows.

Cash	20,000	
Sam Bart, Capital	9,000	
Tom Cohen, Capital	6,000	
Lea Eden, Capital		35,000
(To record Eden's admission and bonus)		

A = L + OE
+20,000
−9,000
−6,000
+35,000

Cash Flows
+20,000

Withdrawal of a Partner

Now let's look at the opposite situation–the withdrawal of a partner. A partner may withdraw from a partnership **voluntarily**, by selling his or her equity in the firm. Or, he or she may withdraw **involuntarily**, by reaching mandatory retirement age or by dying. The withdrawal of a partner, like the admission of a partner, legally dissolves the partnership. The legal effects may be recognized by dissolving the firm. However, it is customary to record only the economic effects of the partner's withdrawal, while the firm continues to operate and reorganizes itself legally.

As indicated earlier, the partnership agreement should specify the terms of withdrawal. The withdrawal of a partner may be accomplished by (1) payment from partners' personal assets or (2) payment from partnership assets. The former affects only the partners' capital accounts. The latter decreases total net assets and total capital of the partnership.

PAYMENT FROM PARTNERS' PERSONAL ASSETS

Withdrawal by payment from partners' personal assets is a personal transaction between the partners. **It is the direct opposite of admitting a new partner who purchases a partner's interest.** The remaining partners pay the retiring partner directly from their personal assets. **Partnership assets are not involved in any way, and total capital does not change.** The effect on the partnership is limited to changes in the partners' capital balances.

To illustrate, assume that partners Morz, Nead, and Odom have capital balances of $25,000, $15,000, and $10,000, respectively. Morz and Nead agree to buy out Odom's interest. Each of them agrees to pay Odom $8,000 in exchange for one-half of Odom's total interest of $10,000. The entry to record the withdrawal is:

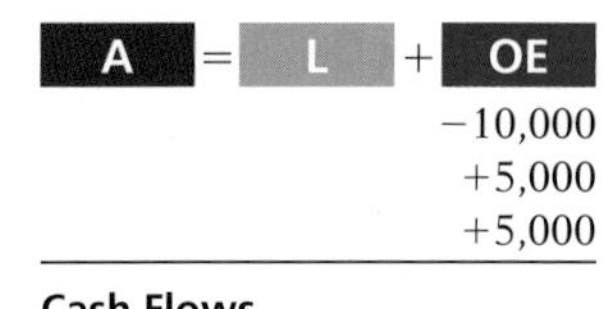

J. Odom, Capital	10,000	
A. Morz, Capital		5,000
M. Nead, Capital		5,000
(To record purchase of Odom's interest)		

Cash Flows
no effect

The effect of this entry on the partnership accounts is shown below.

Illustration 12A-5
Ledger balances after payment from partners' personal assets

Net Assets		A. Morz, Capital		M. Nead, Capital		J. Odom, Capital	
50,000			25,000		15,000	**10,000**	10,000
			5,000		**5,000**		Bal. –0–
			Bal. 30,000		Bal. 20,000		

Note that net assets and total capital remain the same at $50,000.

What about the $16,000 paid to Odom? You've probably noted that it is not recorded. The entry debited Odom's capital only for $10,000, not for the $16,000 that she received. Similarly, both Morz and Nead credit their capital accounts for only $5,000, not for the $8,000 they each paid.

After Odom's withdrawal, Morz and Nead will share net income or net loss equally unless they indicate another income ratio in the partnership agreement.

PAYMENT FROM PARTNERSHIP ASSETS

Withdrawal by payment from partnership assets is a transaction that involves the partnership. **Both partnership net assets and total capital decrease as a result.** Using partnership assets to pay for a withdrawing partner's interest is the **reverse** of admitting a partner through the investment of assets in the partnership.

Many partnership agreements provide that the amount paid should be based on the fair value of the assets at the time of the partner's withdrawal. When this basis is required, some maintain that any differences between recorded asset balances and their fair values should be (1) recorded by an adjusting entry, and (2) allocated to all partners on the basis of their income ratios. This position has serious flaws. Recording the revaluations violates the historical cost principle, which requires that assets be stated at original cost. It also violates the going-concern assumption, which assumes the entity will continue indefinitely. The terms of the partnership contract should not dictate the accounting for this event.

In accounting for a withdrawal by payment from partnership assets, the partnership should not record asset revaluations. Instead, it should consider any difference between the amount paid and the withdrawing partner's capital balance as **a bonus** to the retiring partner or to the remaining partners.

BONUS TO RETIRING PARTNER A partnership may pay a bonus to a retiring partner when:

1. The fair value of partnership assets is more than their book value,
2. There is unrecorded goodwill resulting from the partnership's superior earnings record, or
3. The remaining partners are eager to remove the partner from the firm.

The partnership deducts the bonus from the remaining partners' capital balances on the basis of their income ratios at the time of the withdrawal.

To illustrate, assume that the following capital balances exist in the RST partnership: Roman $50,000, Sand $30,000, and Terk $20,000. The partners share income in the ratio of 3:2:1, respectively. Terk retires from the partnership and receives a cash payment of $25,000 from the firm. The procedure for determining the bonus to the retiring partner and the allocation of the bonus to the remaining partners is as follows.

1. **Determine the amount of the bonus.** Subtract the retiring partner's capital balance from the cash paid by the partnership. The bonus in this case is $5,000 ($25,000 − $20,000).
2. **Allocate the bonus to the remaining partners on the basis of their income ratios.** The ratios of Roman and Sand are 3:2. Thus, the allocation of the $5,000 bonus is: Roman $3,000 ($5,000 × 3/5) and Sand $2,000 ($5,000 × 2/5).

The partnership records the withdrawal of Terk as follows.

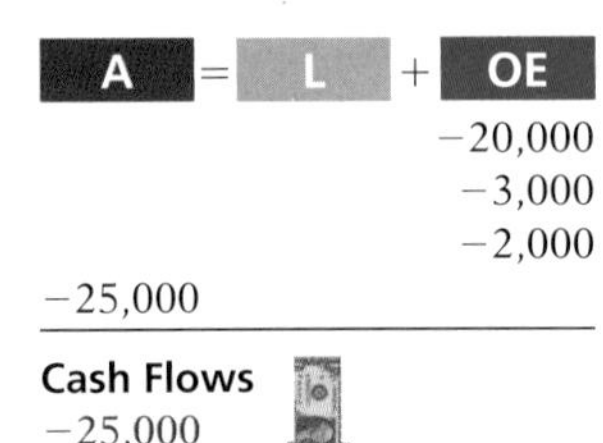

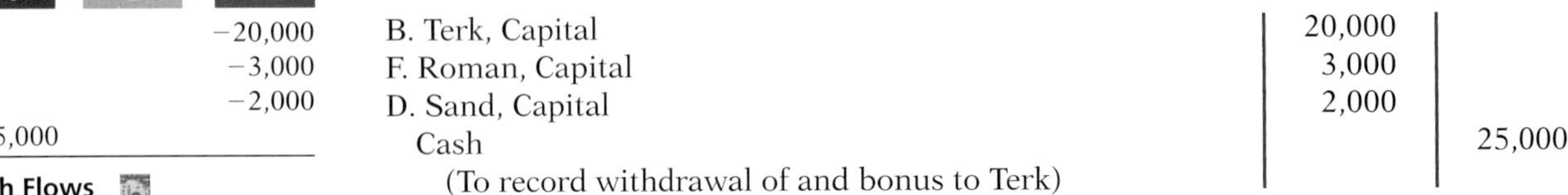

Account	Debit	Credit
B. Terk, Capital	20,000	
F. Roman, Capital	3,000	
D. Sand, Capital	2,000	
Cash		25,000
(To record withdrawal of and bonus to Terk)		

The remaining partners, Roman and Sand, will recover the bonus given to Terk as the partnership sells or uses the undervalued assets.

BONUS TO REMAINING PARTNERS The retiring partner may give a bonus to the remaining partners when:

1. Recorded assets are overvalued.
2. The partnership has a poor earnings record.
3. The partner is eager to leave the partnership.

In such cases, the cash paid to the retiring partner will be less than the retiring partner's capital balance. **The partnership allocates (credits) the bonus to the capital accounts of the remaining partners on the basis of their income ratios.**

To illustrate, assume instead that the partnership pays Terk only $16,000 for her $20,000 equity when she withdraws from the partnership. In that case:

1. The bonus to remaining partners is $4,000 ($20,000 − $16,000).
2. The allocation of the $4,000 bonus is Roman $2,400 ($4,000 × 3/5) and Sand $1,600 ($4,000 × 2/5).

Under these circumstances, the entry to record the withdrawal is as follows.

	Debit	Credit
B. Terk, Capital	20,000	
F. Roman, Capital		2,400
D. Sand, Capital		1,600
Cash		16,000
(To record withdrawal of Terk and bonus to remaining partners)		

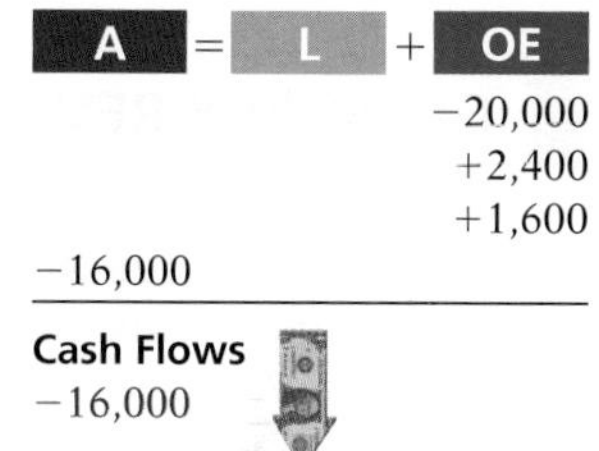

Note that if Sand had withdrawn from the partnership, Roman and Terk would divide any bonus on the basis of their income ratio, which is 3:1 or 75% and 25%.

DEATH OF A PARTNER

The death of a partner dissolves the partnership. However, partnership agreements usually contain a provision for the surviving partners to continue operations. When a partner dies, it usually is necessary to determine the partner's equity at the date of death. This is done by (1) determining the net income or loss for the year to date, (2) closing the books, and (3) preparing financial statements. The partnership agreement may also require an independent audit and a revaluation of assets.

The surviving partners may agree to purchase the deceased partner's equity from their personal assets. Or they may use partnership assets to settle with the deceased partner's estate. In both instances, the entries to record the withdrawal of the partner are similar to those presented earlier.

To facilitate payment from partnership assets, some partnerships obtain life insurance policies on each partner, with the partnership named as the beneficiary. The partnership then uses the proceeds from the insurance policy on the deceased partner to settle with the estate.

REVIEW AND PRACTICE

LEARNING OBJECTIVES REVIEW

1 Discuss and account for the formation of a partnership. The principal characteristics of a partnership are (a) association of individuals, (b) mutual agency, (c) limited life, (d) unlimited liability, and (e) co-ownership of property. When formed, a partnership records each partner's initial investment at the fair value of the assets at the date of their transfer to the partnership.

2 Explain how to account for net income or net loss of a partnership. Partnerships divide net income or net loss on the basis of the income ratio, which may be (a) a fixed ratio, (b) a ratio based on beginning or average capital balances, (c) salaries to partners and the remainder on a fixed ratio, (d) interest on partners' capital and the remainder on a fixed ratio, and (e) salaries to partners, interest on partners' capital, and the remainder on a fixed ratio.

The financial statements of a partnership are similar to those of a proprietorship. The principal differences are as follows. (a) The partnership shows the division of net income on the income statement. (b) The owners' equity statement is called a partners' capital statement. (c) The partnership reports each partner's capital on the balance sheet.

*3 **Explain how to account for the liquidation of a partnership.** When a partnership is liquidated, it is necessary to record the (a) sale of noncash assets, (b) allocation of the gain or loss on realization, (c) payment of partnership liabilities, and (d) distribution of cash to the partners on the basis of their capital balances.

*4 **Prepare journal entries when a partner is either admitted or withdraws.** The entry to record the admittance of a new partner by purchase of a partner's interest affects only partners' capital accounts. The entries to record the admittance by investment of assets in the partnership (a) increase both net assets and total capital and (b) may result in recognition of a bonus to either the old partners or the new partner.

The entry to record a withdrawal from the firm when the partners pay from their personal assets affects only partners' capital accounts. The entry to record a withdrawal when payment is made from partnership assets (a) decreases net assets and total capital and (b) may result in recognizing a bonus either to the retiring partner or the remaining partners.

GLOSSARY REVIEW

***Admission by investment** Admission of a partner by investing assets in the partnership, causing both partnership net assets and total capital to increase.

***Admission by purchase of an interest** Admission of a partner in a personal transaction between one or more existing partners and the new partner; does not change total partnership assets or total capital.

Capital deficiency A debit balance in a partner's capital account after allocation of gain or loss.

General partners Partners who have unlimited liability for the debts of the firm.

Income ratio The basis for dividing net income and net loss in a partnership.

Limited liability company A form of business organization, usually classified as a partnership for tax purposes and usually with limited life, in which partners, who are called members, have limited liability.

Limited liability partnership A partnership of professionals in which partners are given limited liability and the public is protected from malpractice by insurance carried by the partnership.

Limited partners Partners whose liability for the debts of the firm is limited to their investment in the firm.

Limited partnership A partnership in which one or more general partners have unlimited liability and one or more partners have limited liability for the obligations of the firm.

***No capital deficiency** All partners have credit balances after allocation of gain or loss.

Partners' capital statement The owners' equity statement for a partnership which shows the changes in each partner's capital account and in total partnership capital during the year.

Partnership An association of two or more persons to carry on as co-owners of a business for profit.

Partnership agreement A written contract expressing the voluntary agreement of two or more individuals in a partnership.

Partnership dissolution A change in partners due to withdrawal or admission, which does not necessarily terminate the business.

Partnership liquidation An event that ends both the legal and economic life of a partnership.

Schedule of cash payments A schedule showing the distribution of cash to the partners in a partnership liquidation.

***Withdrawal by payment from partners' personal assets** Withdrawal of a partner in a personal transaction between partners; does not change total partnership assets or total capital.

***Withdrawal by payment from partnership assets** Withdrawal of a partner in a transaction involving the partnership, causing both partnership net assets and total capital to decrease.

PRACTICE EXERCISES

Prepare journal entries to record allocation of net income.

(LO 2)

1. M. Gomez (beginning capital $50,000) and I. Inez (beginning capital $80,000) are partners. During 2017 the partnership earned net income of $60,000, and Gomez made drawings of $15,000 while Inez made drawings of $20,000.

Instructions

(a) Assume the partnership income-sharing agreement calls for income to be divided 55% to Gomez and 45% to Inez. Prepare the journal entry to record the allocation of net income.

(b) Assume the partnership income-sharing agreement calls for income to be divided with a salary of $30,000 to Gomez and $20,000 to Inez with the remainder divided 55% to Gomez and 45% to Inez. Prepare the journal entry to record the allocation of net income.

(c) Assume the partnership income-sharing agreement calls for income to be divided with a salary of $40,000 to Gomez and $30,000 to Inez, interest of 10% on beginning capital, and the remainder divided 50%–50%. Prepare the journal entry to record the allocation of net income.

(d) Compute the partners' ending capital balances under the assumption in part (c).

Solution

1. (a) Income Summary	60,000	
M. Gomez, Capital ($60,000 × 55%)		33,000
I. Inez, Capital ($60,000 × 45%)		27,000
(b) Income Summary	60,000	
M. Gomez, Capital [$30,000 + ($10,000 × 55%)]		35,500
I. Inez, Capital [$20,000 + ($10,000 × 45%)]		24,500
(c) Income Summary	60,000	
M. Gomez, Capital [$40,000 + $5,000 − ($23,000 × 50%)]		33,500
I. Inez, Capital [$30,000 + $8,000 − ($23,000 × 50%)]		26,500

(d) Gomez: $50,000 + $33,500 − $15,000 = $68,500

Inez: $80,000 + $26,500 − $20,000 = $86,500

Prepare cash distribution schedule and journalize transactions in a liquidation.

(LO 2, 3)

2. The Braun Company at December 31 has cash $15,000, noncash assets $110,000, liabilities $60,000, and the following capital balances: Ho $40,000 and Li $25,000. The firm is liquidated, and $90,000 in cash is received for the noncash assets. Ho's and Li's income ratios are 60% and 40%, respectively.

Instructions

(a) Prepare a cash distribution schedule.

(b) Prepare the entries to record the following, assuming that The Braun Company decides to liquidate the company.
(1) The sale of noncash assets.
(2) The allocation of the gain or loss on liquidation to the partners.
(3) Payment of creditors.
(4) Distribution of cash to the partners.

Solution

2. (a)

THE BRAUN COMPANY
Schedule of Cash Payments

Item	Cash	+	Noncash Assets	=	Liabilities	+	Ho, Capital	+	Li, Capital
Balances before liquidation	$ 15,000		$110,000		$60,000		$40,000		$25,000
Sale of noncash assets and allocation of gain	90,000		(110,000)				(12,000)		(8,000)
New balances	105,000		0		60,000		28,000		17,000
Pay liabilities	(60,000)				(60,000)				
New balances	45,000		0		0		28,000		17,000
Cash distribution to partners	(45,000)						(28,000)		(17,000)
Final balances	$ 0		$ 0		$ 0		$ 0		$ 0

		Debit	Credit
(b) (1)	Loss of Realization	20,000	
	Cash	90,000	
	Noncash Assets		110,000
(2)	Ho, Capital	12,000	
	Li, Capital	8,000	
	Loss on Realization		20,000
(3)	Accounts Payable	60,000	
	Cash		60,000
(4)	Ho, Capital	28,000	
	Li, Capital	17,000	
	Cash		45,000

PRACTICE PROBLEM

Journalize and prepare a schedule showing distribution of net income.

(LO 2)

On January 1, 2017, the capital balances in Hollingsworth Company are Lois Holly $26,000 and Jim Worth $24,000. In 2017 the partnership reports net income of $30,000. The income ratio provides for salary allowances of $12,000 for Holly and $10,000 to Worth and the remainder to be shared equally. Neither partner had any drawings in 2017.

Instructions

(a) Prepare a schedule showing the distribution of net income in 2017.

(b) Journalize the division of 2017 net income to the partners.

Solution

(a) Net income $30,000

Division of Net Income

	Lois Holly	Jim Worth	Total
Salary allowance	$12,000	$10,000	$22,000
Remaining income $8,000 ($30,000 − $22,000)			
Lois Holly ($8,000 × 50%)	4,000		
Jim Worth ($8,000 × 50%)		4,000	
Total remainder			8,000
Total division of net income	$16,000	$14,000	$30,000

(b) Date	Account	Debit	Credit
12/31/17	Income Summary	30,000	
	Lois Holly, Capital		16,000
	Jim Worth, Capital		14,000
	(To close net income to partners' capital)		

EXERCISES

Identify characteristics of partnership.

(LO 1)

E12-1 Mark Rensing has prepared the following list of statements about partnerships.

1. A partnership is an association of three or more persons to carry on as co-owners of a business for profit.
2. The legal requirements for forming a partnership can be quite burdensome.
3. A partnership is not an entity for financial reporting purposes.
4. The net income of a partnership is taxed as a separate entity.
5. The act of any partner is binding on all other partners, even when partners perform business acts beyond the scope of their authority.
6. Each partner is personally and individually liable for all partnership liabilities.
7. When a partnership is dissolved, the assets legally revert to the original contributor.

8. In a limited partnership, one or more partners have unlimited liability and one or more partners have limited liability for the debts of the firm.
9. Mutual agency is a major advantage of the partnership form of business.

Instructions
Identify each statement as true or false. If false, indicate how to correct the statement.

E12-2 K. Decker, S. Rosen, and E. Toso are forming a partnership. Decker is transferring $50,000 of personal cash to the partnership. Rosen owns land worth $15,000 and a small building worth $80,000, which she transfers to the partnership. Toso transfers to the partnership cash of $9,000, accounts receivable of $32,000, and equipment worth $39,000. The partnership expects to collect $29,000 of the accounts receivable.

Journalize entry for formation of a partnership.

(LO 1)

Instructions
(a) Prepare the journal entries to record each of the partners' investments.
(b) What amount would be reported as total owners' equity immediately after the investments?

E12-3 Suzy Vopat has owned and operated a proprietorship for several years. On January 1, she decides to terminate this business and become a partner in the firm of Vopat and Sigma. Vopat's investment in the partnership consists of $12,000 in cash, and the following assets of the proprietorship: accounts receivable $14,000 less allowance for doubtful accounts of $2,000, and equipment $30,000 less accumulated depreciation of $4,000. It is agreed that the allowance for doubtful accounts should be $3,000 for the partnership. The fair value of the equipment is $23,500.

Journalize entry for formation of a partnership.

(LO 1)

Instructions
Journalize Vopat's admission to the firm of Vopat and Sigma.

E12-4 McGill and Smyth have capital balances on January 1 of $50,000 and $40,000, respectively. The partnership income-sharing agreement provides for (1) annual salaries of $22,000 for McGill and $13,000 for Smyth, (2) interest at 10% on beginning capital balances, and (3) remaining income or loss to be shared 60% by McGill and 40% by Smyth.

Prepare schedule showing distribution of net income and closing entry.

(LO 2)

Instructions
(a) Prepare a schedule showing the distribution of net income, assuming net income is (1) $50,000 and (2) $36,000.
(b) Journalize the allocation of net income in each of the situations above.

E12-5 Coburn (beginning capital, $60,000) and Webb (beginning capital $90,000) are partners. During 2017, the partnership earned net income of $80,000, and Coburn made drawings of $18,000 while Webb made drawings of $24,000.

Prepare journal entries to record allocation of net income.

(LO 2)

Instructions
(a) Assume the partnership income-sharing agreement calls for income to be divided 45% to Coburn and 55% to Webb. Prepare the journal entry to record the allocation of net income.
(b) Assume the partnership income-sharing agreement calls for income to be divided with a salary of $30,000 to Coburn and $25,000 to Webb, with the remainder divided 45% to Coburn and 55% to Webb. Prepare the journal entry to record the allocation of net income.
(c) Assume the partnership income-sharing agreement calls for income to be divided with a salary of $40,000 to Coburn and $35,000 to Webb, interest of 10% on beginning capital, and the remainder divided 50%–50%. Prepare the journal entry to record the allocation of net income.
(d) Compute the partners' ending capital balances under the assumption in part (c).

E12-6 For National Co., beginning capital balances on January 1, 2017, are Nancy Payne $20,000 and Ann Dody $18,000. During the year, drawings were Payne $8,000 and Dody $5,000. Net income was $40,000, and the partners share income equally.

Prepare partners' capital statement and partial balance sheet.

(LO 2)

Instructions
(a) Prepare the partners' capital statement for the year.
(b) Prepare the owners' equity section of the balance sheet at December 31, 2017.

Prepare a classified balance sheet of a partnership.
(LO 2)

E12-7 Terry, Nick, and Frank are forming The Doctor Partnership. Terry is transferring $30,000 of personal cash and equipment worth $25,000 to the partnership. Nick owns land worth $28,000 and a small building worth $75,000, which he transfers to the partnership. There is a long-term mortgage of $20,000 on the land and building, which the partnership assumes. Frank transfers cash of $7,000, accounts receivable of $36,000, supplies worth $3,000, and equipment worth $27,000 to the partnership. The partnership expects to collect $32,000 of the accounts receivable.

Instructions
Prepare a classified balance sheet for the partnership after the partners' investments on December 31, 2017.

Prepare cash payments schedule.
(LO 3)

E12-8 Sedgwick Company at December 31 has cash $20,000, noncash assets $100,000, liabilities $55,000, and the following capital balances: Floyd $45,000 and DeWitt $20,000. The firm is liquidated, and $105,000 in cash is received for the noncash assets. Floyd and DeWitt income ratios are 60% and 40%, respectively.

Instructions
Prepare a schedule of cash payments.

Journalize transactions in a liquidation.
(LO 3)

E12-9 Data for Sedgwick Company are presented in E12-8. Sedgwick Company now decides to liquidate the partnership.

Instructions
Prepare the entries to record:

(a) The sale of noncash assets.
(b) The allocation of the gain or loss on realization to the partners.
(c) Payment of creditors.
(d) Distribution of cash to the partners.

Journalize transactions with a capital deficiency.
(LO 3)

E12-10 Prior to the distribution of cash to the partners, the accounts in the VUP Company are Cash $24,000; Vogel, Capital (Cr.) $17,000; Utech, Capital (Cr.) $15,000; and Pena, Capital (Dr.) $8,000. The income ratios are 5:3:2, respectively. VUP Company decides to liquidate the company.

Instructions
(a) Prepare the entry to record (1) Pena's payment of $8,000 in cash to the partnership and (2) the distribution of cash to the partners with credit balances.
(b) Prepare the entry to record (1) the absorption of Pena's capital deficiency by the other partners and (2) the distribution of cash to the partners with credit balances.

Journalize admission of a new partner by purchase of an interest.
(LO 4)

***E12-11** K. Kolmer, C. Eidman, and C. Ryno share income on a 5:3:2 basis. They have capital balances of $34,000, $26,000, and $21,000, respectively, when Don Jernigan is admitted to the partnership.

Instructions
Prepare the journal entry to record the admission of Don Jernigan under each of the following assumptions.

(a) Purchase of 50% of Kolmer's equity for $19,000.
(b) Purchase of 50% of Eidman's equity for $12,000.
(c) Purchase of $33\frac{1}{3}$% of Ryno's equity for $9,000.

Journalize admission of a new partner by investment.
(LO 4)

***E12-12** S. Pagan and T. Tabor share income on a 6:4 basis. They have capital balances of $100,000 and $60,000, respectively, when W. Wolford is admitted to the partnership.

Instructions
Prepare the journal entry to record the admission of W. Wolford under each of the following assumptions.

(a) Investment of $90,000 cash for a 30% ownership interest with bonuses to the existing partners.
(b) Investment of $50,000 cash for a 30% ownership interest with a bonus to the new partner.

***E12-13** N. Essex, C. Gilmore, and C. Heganbart have capital balances of $50,000, $40,000, and $30,000, respectively. Their income ratios are 4:4:2. Heganbart withdraws from the partnership under each of the following independent conditions.

Journalize withdrawal of a partner with payment from partners' personal assets.

(LO 4)

1. Essex and Gilmore agree to purchase Heganbart's equity by paying $17,000 each from their personal assets. Each purchaser receives 50% of Heganbart's equity.
2. Gilmore agrees to purchase all of Heganbart's equity by paying $22,000 cash from her personal assets.
3. Essex agrees to purchase all of Heganbart's equity by paying $26,000 cash from his personal assets.

Instructions

Journalize the withdrawal of Heganbart under each of the assumptions above.

***E12-14** B. Higgins, J. Mayo, and N. Rice have capital balances of $95,000, $75,000, and $60,000, respectively. They share income or loss on a 5:3:2 basis. Rice withdraws from the partnership under each of the following conditions.

Journalize withdrawal of a partner with payment from partnership assets.

(LO 4)

1. Rice is paid $64,000 in cash from partnership assets, and a bonus is granted to the retiring partner.
2. Rice is paid $52,000 in cash from partnership assets, and bonuses are granted to the remaining partners.

Instructions

Journalize the withdrawal of Rice under each of the assumptions above.

***E12-15** Foss, Albertson, and Espinosa are partners who share profits and losses 50%, 30%, and 20%, respectively. Their capital balances are $100,000, $60,000, and $40,000, respectively.

Journalize withdrawal of a partner with payment from partnership assets.

(LO 4)

Instructions

(a) Assume Garrett joins the partnership by investing $88,000 for a 25% interest with bonuses to the existing partners. Prepare the journal entry to record his investment.

(b) Assume instead that Foss leaves the partnership. Foss is paid $110,000 with a bonus to the retiring partner. Prepare the journal entry to record Foss's withdrawal.

PROBLEMS

P12-1A The post-closing trial balances of two proprietorships on January 1, 2017, are presented below.

Prepare entries for formation of a partnership and a balance sheet.

(LO 1, 2)

	Sorensen Company		Lucas Company	
	Dr.	Cr.	Dr.	Cr.
Cash	$ 14,000		$12,000	
Accounts receivable	17,500		26,000	
Allowance for doubtful accounts		$ 3,000		$ 4,400
Inventory	26,500		18,400	
Equipment	45,000		29,000	
Accumulated depreciation—equipment		24,000		11,000
Notes payable		18,000		15,000
Accounts payable		22,000		31,000
Sorensen, capital		36,000		
Lucas, capital				24,000
	$103,000	$103,000	$85,400	$85,400

Sorensen and Lucas decide to form a partnership, Solu Company, with the following agreed upon valuations for noncash assets.

	Sorensen Company	Lucas Company
Accounts receivable	$17,500	$26,000
Allowance for doubtful accounts	4,500	4,000
Inventory	28,000	20,000
Equipment	25,000	15,000

All cash will be transferred to the partnership, and the partnership will assume all the liabilities of the two proprietorships. Further, it is agreed that Sorensen will invest an additional $5,000 in cash, and Lucas will invest an additional $19,000 in cash.

Instructions

(a) Sorensen, Capital $40,000 Lucas, Capital $23,000

(c) Total assets $173,000

(a) Prepare separate journal entries to record the transfer of each proprietorship's assets and liabilities to the partnership.
(b) Journalize the additional cash investment by each partner.
(c) Prepare a classified balance sheet for the partnership on January 1, 2017.

Journalize divisions of net income and prepare a partners' capital statement.
(LO 2)

P12-2A At the end of its first year of operations on December 31, 2017, NBS Company's accounts show the following.

Partner	Drawings	Capital
Art Niensted	$23,000	$48,000
Greg Bolen	14,000	30,000
Krista Sayler	10,000	25,000

The capital balance represents each partner's initial capital investment. Therefore, net income or net loss for 2017 has not been closed to the partners' capital accounts.

Instructions

(a) (1) Niensted $18,000
(2) Niensted $20,000
(3) Niensted $17,700
(c) Niensted $42,700

(a) Journalize the entry to record the division of net income for the year 2017 under each of the following independent assumptions.
   (1) Net income is $30,000. Income is shared 6:3:1.
   (2) Net income is $40,000. Niensted and Bolen are given salary allowances of $15,000 and $10,000, respectively. The remainder is shared equally.
   (3) Net income is $19,000. Each partner is allowed interest of 10% on beginning capital balances. Niensted is given a $15,000 salary allowance. The remainder is shared equally.
(b) Prepare a schedule showing the division of net income under assumption (3) above.
(c) Prepare a partners' capital statement for the year under assumption (3) above.

Prepare entries with a capital deficiency in liquidation of a partnership.
(LO 3)

P12-3A The partners in Crawford Company decide to liquidate the firm when the balance sheet shows the following.

CRAWFORD COMPANY
Balance Sheet
May 31, 2017

Assets		Liabilities and Owners' Equity	
Cash	$ 27,500	Notes payable	$ 13,500
Accounts receivable	25,000	Accounts payable	27,000
Allowance for doubtful accounts	(1,000)	Salaries and wages payable	4,000
Inventory	34,500	A. Jamison, capital	33,000
Equipment	21,000	S. Moyer, capital	21,000
Accumulated depreciation—equipment	(5,500)	P. Roper, capital	3,000
	$101,500		$101,500

The partners share income and loss 5:3:2. During the process of liquidation, the following transactions were completed in the following sequence.

1. A total of $51,000 was received from converting noncash assets into cash.
2. Gain or loss on realization was allocated to partners.
3. Liabilities were paid in full.
4. P. Roper paid his capital deficiency.
5. Cash was paid to the partners with credit balances.

Instructions

(a) Loss on realization $23,000 Cash paid: to Jamison $21,500; to Moyer $14,100

(a) Prepare the entries to record the transactions.
(b) Post to the cash and capital accounts.
(c) Assume that Roper is unable to pay the capital deficiency.
   (1) Prepare the entry to allocate Roper's debit balance to Jamison and Moyer.
   (2) Prepare the entry to record the final distribution of cash.

***P12-4A** At April 30, partners' capital balances in PDL Company are G. Donley $52,000, C. Lamar $48,000, and J. Pinkston $18,000. The income sharing ratios are 5:4:1, respectively. On May 1, the PDLT Company is formed by admitting J. Terrell to the firm as a partner.

Journalize admission of a partner under different assumptions.

(LO 4)

Instructions

(a) Journalize the admission of Terrell under each of the following independent assumptions.
 (1) Terrell purchases 50% of Pinkston's ownership interest by paying Pinkston $16,000 in cash.
 (2) Terrell purchases 33¹/₃% of Lamar's ownership interest by paying Lamar $15,000 in cash.
 (3) Terrell invests $62,000 for a 30% ownership interest, and bonuses are given to the old partners.
 (4) Terrell invests $42,000 for a 30% ownership interest, which includes a bonus to the new partner.

(b) Lamar's capital balance is $32,000 after admitting Terrell to the partnership by investment. If Lamar's ownership interest is 20% of total partnership capital, what were (1) Terrell's cash investment and (2) the bonus to the new partner?

(a) (1) Terrell $9,000
(2) Terrell $16,000
(3) Terrell $54,000
(4) Terrell $48,000

***P12-5A** On December 31, the capital balances and income ratios in TEP Company are as follows.

Journalize withdrawal of a partner under different assumptions.

(LO 4)

Partner	Capital Balance	Income Ratio
Trayer	$60,000	50%
Emig	40,000	30%
Posada	30,000	20%

Instructions

(a) Journalize the withdrawal of Posada under each of the following assumptions.
 (1) Each of the continuing partners agrees to pay $18,000 in cash from personal funds to purchase Posada's ownership equity. Each receives 50% of Posada's equity.
 (2) Emig agrees to purchase Posada's ownership interest for $25,000 cash.
 (3) Posada is paid $34,000 from partnership assets, which includes a bonus to the retiring partner.
 (4) Posada is paid $22,000 from partnership assets, and bonuses to the remaining partners are recognized.

(b) If Emig's capital balance after Posada's withdrawal is $43,600, what were (1) the total bonus to the remaining partners and (2) the cash paid by the partnership to Posada?

(a) (1) Emig, Capital $15,000
(2) Emig, Capital $30,000
(3) Bonus $4,000
(4) Bonus $8,000

BROADENING YOUR PERSPECTIVE

FINANCIAL REPORTING AND ANALYSIS

Real-World Focus

BYP12-1 This exercise is an introduction to the Big Four accounting firms, all of which are partnerships.

Addresses

Deloitte & Touche	**www.deloitte.com/**
Ernst & Young	**www.ey.com/**
KPMG	**www.us.kpmg.com/**
PricewaterhouseCoopers	**www.pwc.com/**

or go to **www.wiley.com/college/weygandt**

Steps

1. Select a firm that is of interest to you.
2. Go to the firm's homepage.

Instructions

(a) Name two services performed by the firm.
(b) What is the firm's total annual revenue?
(c) How many clients does it service?
(d) How many people are employed by the firm?
(e) How many partners are there in the firm?

Decision-Making Across the Organization

BYP12-2 Stephen Wadson and Mary Shively, two professionals in the finance area, have worked for Morrisen Leasing for a number of years. Morrisen Leasing is a company that leases high-tech medical equipment to hospitals. Stephen and Mary have decided that, with their financial expertise, they might start their own company to perform consulting services for individuals interested in leasing equipment. One form of organization they are considering is a partnership.

If they start a partnership, each individual plans to contribute \$50,000 in cash. In addition, Stephen has a used IBM computer that originally cost \$3,700, which he intends to invest in the partnership. The computer has a present fair value of \$1,500.

Although both Stephen and Mary are financial wizards, they do not know a great deal about how a partnership operates. As a result, they have come to you for advice.

Instructions

With the class divided into groups, answer the following.

(a) What are the major disadvantages of starting a partnership?
(b) What type of document is needed for a partnership, and what should this document contain?
(c) Both Stephen and Mary plan to work full-time in the new partnership. They believe that net income or net loss should be shared equally. However, they are wondering how to provide compensation to Stephen Wadson for his investment of the computer. What would you tell them?
(d) Stephen is not sure how the computer equipment should be reported on his tax return. What would you tell him?
(e) As indicated above, Stephen and Mary have worked together for a number of years. Stephen's skills complement Mary's and vice versa. If one of them dies, it will be very difficult for the other to maintain the business, not to mention the difficulty of paying the deceased partner's estate for his or her partnership interest. What would you advise them to do?

Communication Activity

BYP12-3 You are an expert in the field of forming partnerships. Ronald Hrabik and Meg Percival want to establish a partnership to start "Pasta Shop," and they are going to meet with you to discuss their plans. Prior to the meeting, you will send them a memo discussing the issues they need to consider.

Instructions

Write a memo in good form to be sent to Hrabik and Percival.

Ethics Case

BYP12-4 Alexandra and Kellie operate a beauty salon as partners who share profits and losses equally. The success of their business has exceeded their expectations; the salon is operating quite profitably. Kellie is anxious to maximize profits and schedules appointments from 8 a.m. to 6 p.m. daily, even sacrificing some lunch hours to accommodate regular customers. Alexandra schedules her appointments from 9 a.m. to 5 p.m. and takes long lunch hours. Alexandra regularly makes significantly larger withdrawals of cash than Kellie does, but, she says, "Kellie, you needn't worry, I never make a withdrawal without you knowing about it, so it is properly recorded in my drawings account and charged against my capital at the end of the year." Alexandra's withdrawals to date are double Kellie's.

Instructions

(a) Who are the stakeholders in this situation?
(b) Identify the problems with Alexandra's actions and discuss the ethical considerations involved.
(c) How might the partnership agreement be revised to accommodate the differences in Alexandra's and Kellie's work and withdrawal habits?

All About You

BYP12-5 As this chapter indicates, the partnership form of organization has advantages and disadvantages. The chapter noted that different types of partnerships have been developed to minimize some of these disadvantages. Alternatively, an individual or company can choose the proprietorship or corporate form of organization.

Instructions
Go to two local businesses that are different, such as a restaurant, a retailer, a construction company, or a professional office (dentist, doctor, etc.), and find the answers to the following questions.

(a) What form of organization do you use in your business?
(b) What do you believe are the two major advantages of this form of organization for your business?
(c) What do you believe are the two major disadvantages of this form of organization for your business?
(d) Do you believe that eventually you may choose another form of organization?
(e) Did you have someone help you form this organization (attorney, accountant, relative, etc.)?

As partnership accounting is essentially the same under GAAP and IFRS, there is no A Look at IFRS *section in this chapter.*

Chapter 13 Corporations: Organization and Capital Stock Transactions

What major U.S. corporation got its start 41 years ago with a waffle iron? *Hint:* It doesn't sell food. *Second hint:* Swoosh. *Third hint:* "Just do it." That's right, Nike. In 1971, Nike co-founder Bill Bowerman put a piece of rubber into a kitchen waffle iron, and its trademark sole was born. It seems fair to say that at Nike, "They don't make 'em like they used to."

Nike was co-founded by Bowerman and Phil Knight, a member of Bowerman's University of Oregon track team. Each began in the shoe business independently during the early 1960s. Bowerman got his start by making hand-crafted running shoes for his University of Oregon track team. Knight, after completing graduate school, started a small business importing low-cost, high-quality shoes from Japan. In 1964, the two joined forces, each contributing $500, and formed Blue Ribbon Sports, a partnership that marketed Japanese shoes.

It wasn't until 1971 that the company began manufacturing its own line of shoes. With the new shoes came a new corporate name–Nike–the Greek goddess of victory. It is hard to imagine that the company that now boasts a stable full of world-class athletes as promoters at one time had part-time employees selling shoes out of car trunks at track meets. Nike has achieved its success through relentless innovation combined with unbridled promotion.

By 1980, Nike was sufficiently established and issued its first stock to the public. That same year, it created a stock ownership program for its employees, allowing them to share in the company's success. Since then, Nike has enjoyed phenomenal growth, with 2014 sales reaching $27.8 billion and total dividends paid of $799 million.

Nike is not alone in its quest for the top of the sport shoe world. Reebok used to be Nike's arch rival (get it? "arch"), but then Reebok was acquired by the German company adidas. Now adidas pushes Nike every step of the way.

The shoe market is fickle, with new styles becoming popular almost daily and vast international markets still lying untapped. Whether one of these two giants does eventually take control of the pedi-planet remains to be seen. Meanwhile, the shareholders sit anxiously in the stands as this Olympic-size drama unfolds.

LEARNING OBJECTIVES

1. **Discuss the major characteristics of a corporation.**
2. **Explain how to account for the issuance of common and preferred stock.**
3. **Explain how to account for treasury stock.**
4. **Prepare a stockholders' equity section.**

LEARNING OBJECTIVE 1 **Discuss the major characteristics of a corporation.**

In 1819, Chief Justice John Marshall defined a corporation as "an artificial being, invisible, intangible, and existing only in contemplation of law." This definition is the foundation for the prevailing legal interpretation that a **corporation** is an **entity separate and distinct from its owners**.

A corporation is created by law, and its continued existence depends upon the statutes of the state in which it is incorporated. As a legal entity, a corporation has most of the rights and privileges of a person. The major exceptions relate to privileges that only a living person can exercise, such as the right to vote or to hold public office. A corporation is subject to the same duties and responsibilities as a person. For example, it must abide by the laws, and it must pay taxes.

Two common ways to classify corporations are by **purpose** and by **ownership**. A corporation may be organized for the purpose of making a profit, or it may be not-for-profit. For-profit corporations include such well-known companies as McDonald's, Nike, PepsiCo, and Google. Not-for-profit corporations are organized for charitable, medical, or educational purposes. Examples are the Salvation Army and the American Cancer Society.

Classification by ownership differentiates publicly held and privately held corporations. A **publicly held corporation** may have thousands of stockholders. Its stock is regularly traded on a national securities exchange such as the New York Stock Exchange or NASDAQ. Examples are IBM, Caterpillar, and Apple.

In contrast, a **privately held corporation** usually has only a few stockholders, and does not offer its stock for sale to the general public. Privately held companies are generally much smaller than publicly held companies, although some notable exceptions exist. Cargill Inc., a private corporation that trades in grain and other commodities, is one of the largest companies in the United States.

Terminology
Privately held corporations are also referred to as *closely held corporations.*

Characteristics of a Corporation

In 1964, when Nike's founders Phil Knight and Bill Bowerman were just getting started in the running shoe business, they formed their original organization as a partnership. In 1968, they reorganized the company as a corporation. A number of characteristics distinguish corporations from proprietorships and partnerships. We explain the most important of these characteristics below.

Legal existence separate from owners

SEPARATE LEGAL EXISTENCE

As an entity separate and distinct from its owners, the corporation acts under its own name rather than in the name of its stockholders. Nike may buy, own, and sell property. It may borrow money, and it may enter into legally binding contracts in its own name. It may also sue or be sued, and it pays its own taxes.

In a partnership, the acts of the owners (partners) bind the partnership. In contrast, the acts of its owners (stockholders) do not bind the corporation unless such owners are **agents** of the corporation. For example, if you owned shares of Nike stock, you would not have the right to purchase inventory for the company unless you were designated as an agent of the corporation.

Limited liability of stockholders

LIMITED LIABILITY OF STOCKHOLDERS

Since a corporation is a separate legal entity, creditors have recourse only to corporate assets to satisfy their claims. The liability of stockholders is normally limited to their investment in the corporation. Creditors have no legal claim on the personal assets of the owners unless fraud has occurred. Even in the event of bankruptcy, stockholders' losses are generally limited to their capital investment in the corporation.

TRANSFERABLE OWNERSHIP RIGHTS

Transferable ownership rights

Shares of capital stock give ownership in a corporation. These shares are transferable units. Stockholders may dispose of part or all of their interest in a corporation simply by selling their stock. The transfer of an ownership interest in a partnership requires the consent of each owner. In contrast, the transfer of stock is entirely at the discretion of the stockholder. It does not require the approval of either the corporation or other stockholders.

The transfer of ownership rights between stockholders normally has no effect on the daily operating activities of the corporation. Nor does it affect the corporation's assets, liabilities, and total ownership equity. The transfer of these ownership rights is a transaction between individual owners. The company does not participate in the transfer of these ownership rights after the original sale of the capital stock.

ABILITY TO ACQUIRE CAPITAL

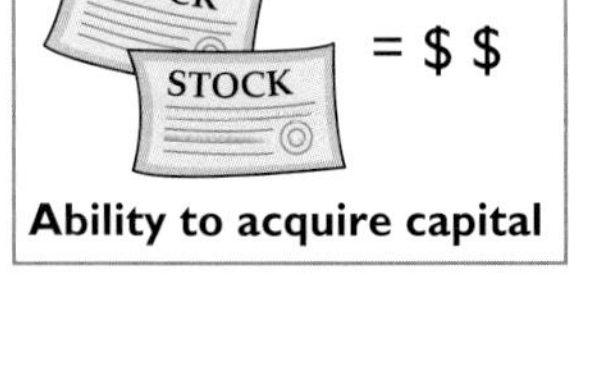

Ability to acquire capital

It is relatively easy for a corporation to obtain capital through the issuance of stock. Buying stock in a corporation is often attractive to an investor because a stockholder has limited liability and shares of stock are readily transferable. Also, numerous individuals can become stockholders by investing relatively small amounts of money.

CONTINUOUS LIFE

Continuous life

The life of a corporation is stated in its charter. The life may be perpetual, or it may be limited to a specific number of years. If it is limited, the company can extend the life through renewal of the charter. Since a corporation is a separate legal entity, its continuance as a going concern is not affected by the withdrawal, death, or incapacity of a stockholder, employee, or officer. As a result, a successful company can have a continuous and perpetual life.

CORPORATION MANAGEMENT

Stockholders legally own the corporation. However, they manage the corporation indirectly through a board of directors they elect. Philip Knight is the chairman of Nike. The board, in turn, formulates the operating policies for the company. The board also selects officers, such as a president and one or more vice presidents, to execute policy and to perform daily management functions. As a result of the Sarbanes-Oxley Act, the board is now required to monitor management's actions more closely. Many feel that the failures of Enron, WorldCom, and more recently MF Global could have been avoided by more diligent boards.

Illustration 13-1 presents a typical organization chart showing the delegation of responsibility. The chief executive officer (CEO) has overall responsibility for managing the business. As the organization chart shows, the CEO delegates responsibility to other officers. The chief accounting officer is the **controller**. The controller's responsibilities include (1) maintaining the accounting records, (2) ensuring an adequate system of internal control, and (3) preparing financial statements, tax returns, and internal reports. The **treasurer** has custody of the corporation's funds and is responsible for maintaining the company's cash position.

The organizational structure of a corporation enables a company to hire professional managers to run the business. On the other hand, the separation of ownership and management often reduces an owner's ability to actively manage the company.

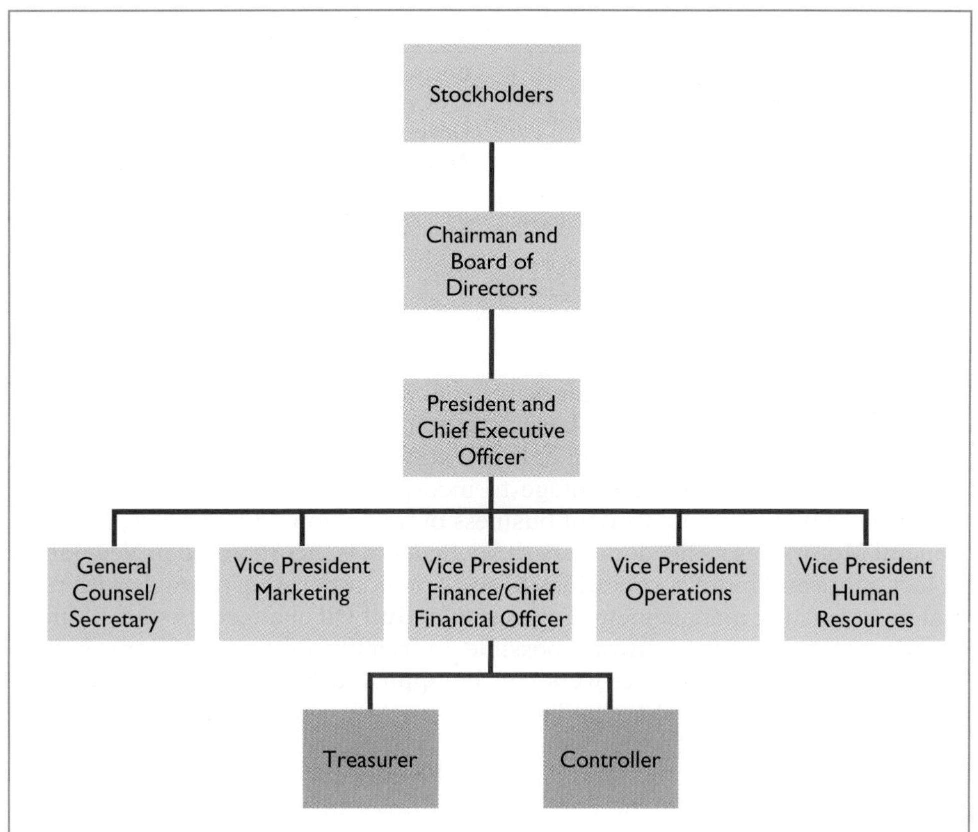

Illustration 13-1
Corporation organization chart

GOVERNMENT REGULATIONS

A corporation is subject to numerous state and federal regulations. For example, state laws usually prescribe the requirements for issuing stock, the distributions of earnings permitted to stockholders, and the acceptable methods for buying back and retiring stock. Federal securities laws govern the sale of capital stock to the general public. Also, most publicly held corporations are required to make extensive disclosure of their financial affairs to the Securities and Exchange Commission (SEC) through quarterly and annual reports (Forms 10Q and 10K). In addition, when a corporation lists its stock on organized securities exchanges, it must comply with the reporting requirements of these exchanges. Government regulations are designed to protect the owners of the corporation.

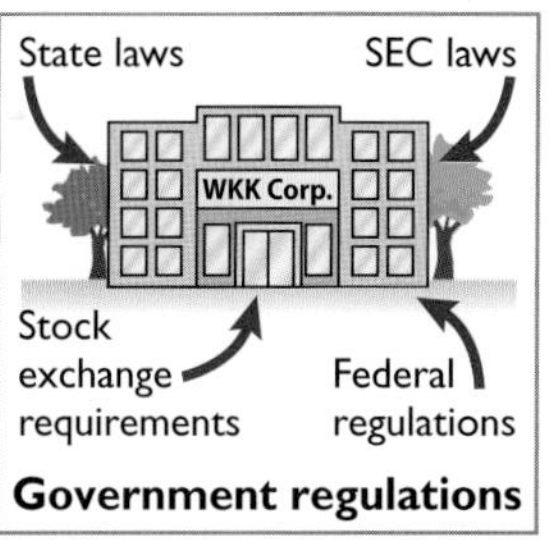

ADDITIONAL TAXES

Owners of proprietorships and partnerships report their share of earnings on their personal income tax returns. The individual owner then pays taxes on this amount. Corporations, on the other hand, must pay federal and state income taxes **as a separate legal entity**. These taxes can be substantial. They can amount to as much as 40% of taxable income.

In addition, stockholders must pay taxes on cash dividends (pro rata distributions of net income). Thus, many argue that the government taxes corporate income **twice (double taxation)**—once at the corporate level and again at the individual level.

In summary, Illustration 13-2 shows the advantages and disadvantages of a corporation compared to a proprietorship and a partnership.

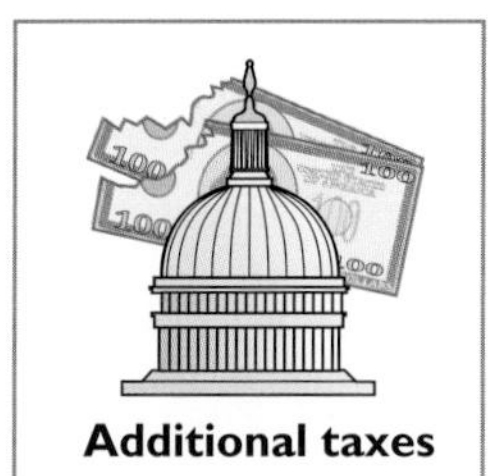

Forming a Corporation

A corporation is formed by grant of a state **charter**. The charter is a document that describes the name and purpose of the corporation, the types and number of shares of stock that are authorized to be issued, the names of the individuals that

Illustration 13-2
Advantages and disadvantages of a corporation

Advantages	Disadvantages
Separate legal existence	Corporation management—separation of ownership and management
Limited liability of stockholders	Government regulations
Transferable ownership rights	Additional taxes
Ability to acquire capital	
Continuous life	
Corporation management—professional managers	

Terminology
The charter is often referred to as the *articles of incorporation.*

formed the company, and the number of shares that these individuals agreed to purchase. Regardless of the number of states in which a corporation has operating divisions, it is incorporated in only one state.

It is to the company's advantage to incorporate in a state whose laws are favorable to the corporate form of business organization. For example, although General Motors has its headquarters in Michigan, it is incorporated in New Jersey. In fact, more and more corporations have been incorporating in states with rules that favor existing management. For example, Gulf Oil changed its state of incorporation to Delaware to thwart possible unfriendly takeovers. There, certain defensive tactics against takeovers can be approved by the board of directors alone, without a vote by shareholders.

Upon receipt of its charter from the state of incorporation, the corporation establishes **by-laws**. The by-laws establish the internal rules and procedures for conducting the affairs of the corporation. Corporations engaged in interstate commerce must also obtain a **license** from each state in which they do business. The license subjects the corporation's operating activities to the general corporation laws of the state.

Costs incurred in the formation of a corporation are called **organization costs**. These costs include legal and state fees, and promotional expenditures involved in the organization of the business. **Corporations expense organization costs as incurred.** Determining the amount and timing of future benefits is so difficult that it is standard procedure to take a conservative approach of expensing these costs immediately.

Stockholder Rights

When chartered, the corporation may begin selling shares of stock. When a corporation has only one class of stock, it is **common stock**. Each share of common stock gives the stockholder the ownership rights pictured in Illustration 13-3. The articles of incorporation or the by-laws state the ownership rights of a share of stock.

Proof of stock ownership is evidenced by a form known as a **stock certificate**. As Illustration 13-4 shows, the face of the certificate shows the name of the corporation, the stockholder's name, the class and special features of the stock, the number of shares owned, and the signatures of authorized corporate officials. Prenumbered certificates facilitate accountability. They may be issued for any quantity of shares.

Stock Issue Considerations

Although Nike incorporated in 1968, it did not sell stock to the public until 1980. At that time, Nike evidently decided it would benefit from the infusion of cash that a public sale would bring. When a corporation decides to issue stock, it must resolve a number of basic questions: How many shares should it authorize for sale? How should it issue the stock? What value should the corporation assign to the stock? We address these questions in the following sections.

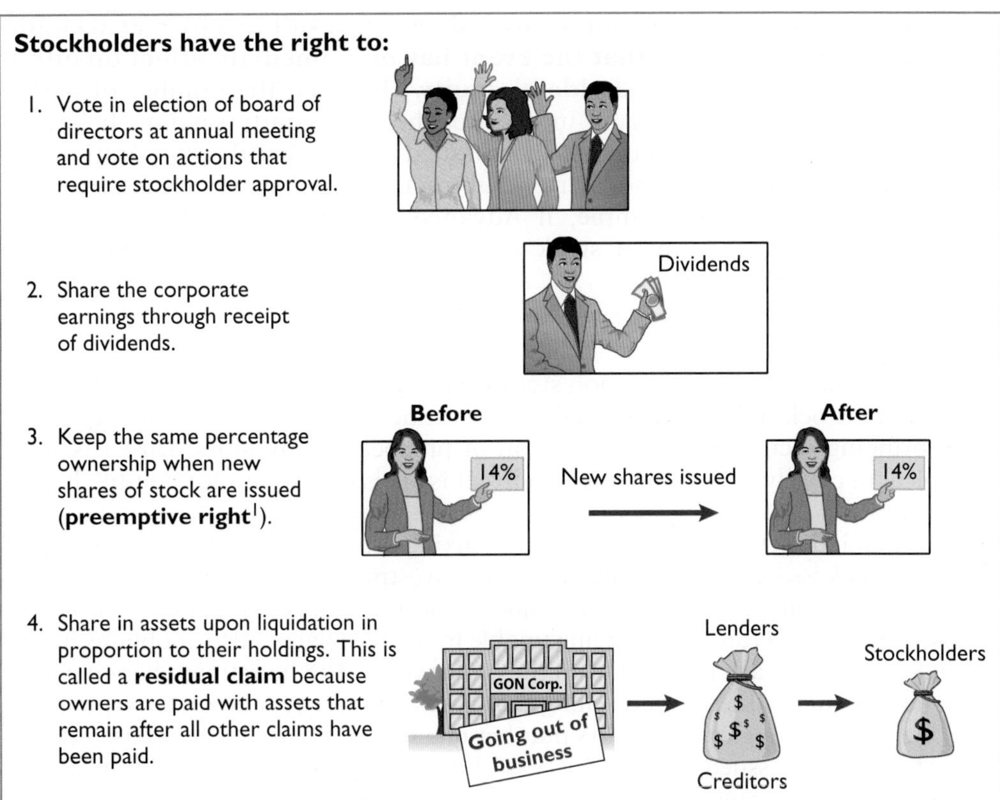

Illustration 13-3
Ownership rights of stockholders

AUTHORIZED STOCK

The charter indicates the amount of stock that a corporation is **authorized** to sell. The total amount of **authorized stock** at the time of incorporation normally anticipates both initial and subsequent capital needs. As a result, the number of shares authorized generally exceeds the number initially sold. If it sells all authorized stock, a corporation must obtain consent of the state to amend its charter before it can issue additional shares.

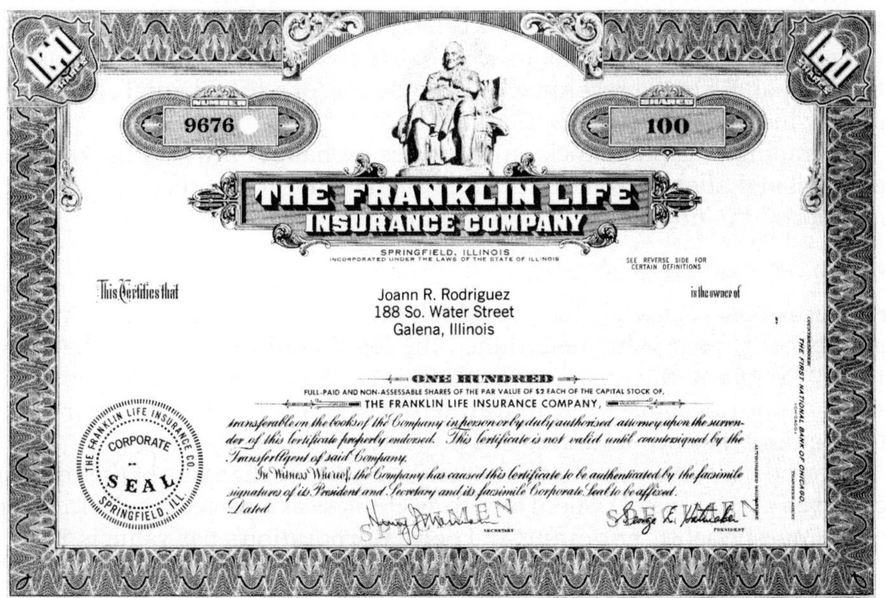

Illustration 13-4
A stock certificate

[1]A number of companies have eliminated the preemptive right because they believe it makes an unnecessary and cumbersome demand on management. For example, by stockholder approval, **IBM** has dropped its preemptive right for stockholders.

Indirect issuance

The authorization of capital stock does not result in a formal accounting entry. The reason is that the event has no immediate effect on either corporate assets or stockholders' equity. However, the number of authorized shares is often reported in the stockholders' equity section. It is then simple to determine the number of unissued shares that the corporation can issue without amending the charter: subtract the total shares issued from the total authorized. For example, if Advanced Micro was authorized to sell 100,000 shares of common stock and issued 80,000 shares, 20,000 shares would remain unissued.

ISSUANCE OF STOCK

A corporation can issue common stock **directly** to investors. Alternatively, it can issue the stock **indirectly** through an investment banking firm that specializes in bringing securities to the attention of prospective investors. Direct issue is typical in closely held companies. Indirect issue is customary for a publicly held corporation.

In an indirect issue, the investment banking firm may agree to **underwrite** the entire stock issue. In this arrangement, the investment banker buys the stock from the corporation at a stipulated price and resells the shares to investors. The corporation thus avoids any risk of being unable to sell the shares. Also, it obtains immediate use of the cash received from the underwriter. The investment banking firm, in turn, assumes the risk of reselling the shares, in return for an underwriting fee.[2] For example, Google (the world's number-one Internet search engine) used underwriters when it issued a highly successful initial public offering, raising $1.67 billion. The underwriters charged a 3% underwriting fee (approximately $50 million) on Google's stock offering.

How does a corporation set the price for a new issue of stock? Among the factors to be considered are (1) the company's anticipated future earnings, (2) its expected dividend rate per share, (3) its current financial position, (4) the current state of the economy, and (5) the current state of the securities market. The calculation can be complex and is properly the subject of a finance course.

MARKET PRICE OF STOCK

The stock of publicly held companies is traded on organized exchanges. The interaction between buyers and sellers determines the prices per share. In general, the prices set by the marketplace tend to follow the trend of a company's earnings and dividends. But, factors beyond a company's control, such as an oil embargo, changes in interest rates, or the outcome of a presidential election, may cause day-to-day fluctuations in market prices.

The trading of capital stock on securities exchanges involves the transfer of **already issued shares** from an existing stockholder to another investor. These transactions have **no impact** on a corporation's stockholders' equity.

PAR AND NO-PAR VALUE STOCKS

Par value stock is capital stock to which the charter has assigned a value per share. Years ago, par value determined the **legal capital** per share that a company must retain in the business for the protection of corporate creditors. That amount was not available for withdrawal by stockholders. Thus, in the past, most states required the corporation to sell its shares at par or above.

However, par value was often immaterial relative to the value of the company's stock—even at the time of issue. Thus, its usefulness as a protective device to creditors was questionable. For example, Loews Corporation's par value is $0.01 per

[2]Alternatively, the investment banking firm may agree only to enter into a **best-efforts contract** with the corporation. In such cases, the banker agrees to sell as many shares as possible at a specified price. The corporation bears the risk of unsold stock. Under a best-efforts arrangement, the banking firm is paid a fee or commission for its services.

share, yet a new issue in 2014 would have sold at a **market price** in the $44 per share range. Thus, par has no relationship with market price. In the vast majority of cases, it is an immaterial amount. As a consequence, today many states do not require a par value. Instead, they use other means to protect creditors.

No-par value stock is capital stock to which the charter has not assigned a value. No-par value stock is fairly common today. For example, Nike and Procter & Gamble both have no-par stock. In many states, the board of directors assigns a **stated value** to no-par shares.

Corporate Capital

Owners' equity is identified by various names: **stockholders' equity, shareholders' equity**, or **corporate capital**. The stockholders' equity section of a corporation's balance sheet consists of two parts: (1) paid-in (contributed) capital and (2) retained earnings (earned capital).

The distinction between **paid-in capital** and **retained earnings** is important from both a legal and a financial point of view. Legally, corporations can make distributions of earnings (declare dividends) out of retained earnings in all states. However, in many states they cannot declare dividends out of paid-in capital. Management, stockholders, and others often look to retained earnings for the continued existence and growth of the corporation.

PAID-IN CAPITAL

Paid-in capital is the total amount of cash and other assets paid in to the corporation by stockholders in exchange for capital stock. As noted earlier, when a corporation has only one class of stock, it is **common stock**.

RETAINED EARNINGS

Retained earnings is net income that a corporation retains for future use. Net income is recorded in Retained Earnings by a closing entry that debits Income Summary and credits Retained Earnings. For example, assuming that net income for Delta Robotics in its first year of operations is $130,000, the closing entry is:

	Debit	Credit
Income Summary	130,000	
Retained Earnings		130,000
(To close Income Summary and transfer net income to Retained Earnings)		

A	=	L	+	SE
				−130,000 Inc
				+130,000 RE

Cash Flows
no effect

If Delta Robotics has a balance of $800,000 in common stock at the end of its first year, its stockholders' equity section is as follows.

Illustration 13-5
Stockholders' equity section

DELTA ROBOTICS Balance Sheet (partial)		
Stockholders' equity		
Paid-in capital		
Common stock	$800,000	
Retained earnings	130,000	
Total stockholders' equity		$930,000

Illustration 13-6 (page 466) compares the owners' equity (stockholders' equity) accounts reported on a balance sheet for a proprietorship, a partnership, and a corporation.

Illustration 13-6
Comparison of owners' equity accounts

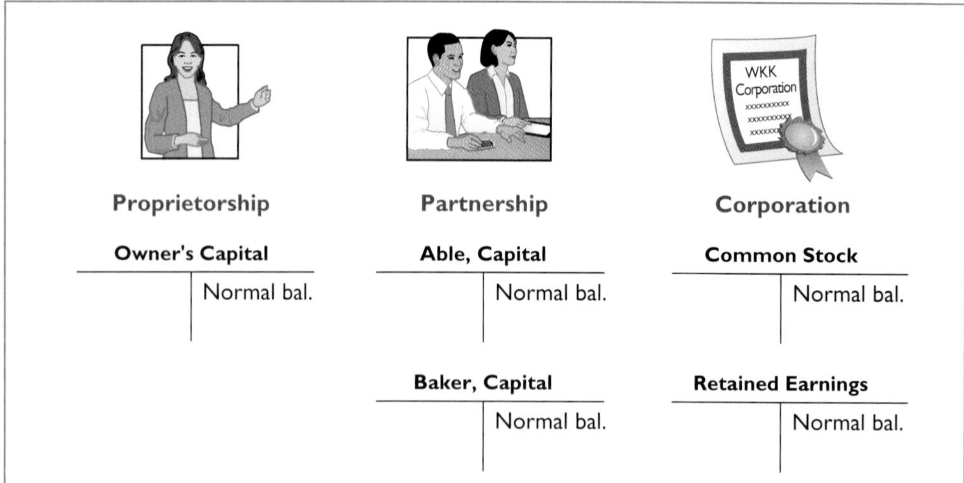

LEARNING OBJECTIVE 2

Explain how to account for the issuance of common and preferred stock.

Let's now look at how to account for issues of common stock. The primary objectives in accounting for the issuance of common stock are (1) to identify the specific sources of paid-in capital, and (2) to maintain the distinction between paid-in capital and retained earnings. **The issuance of common stock affects only paid-in capital accounts.**

Issuing Par Value Common Stock for Cash

As discussed earlier, par value does not indicate a stock's market price. Therefore, the cash proceeds from issuing par value stock may be equal to, greater than, or less than par value. When the company records issuance of common stock for cash, it credits the par value of the shares to Common Stock. It also records in a separate paid-in capital account the portion of the proceeds that is above or below par value.

To illustrate, assume that Hydro-Slide, Inc. issues 1,000 shares of $1 par value common stock at par for cash. The entry to record this transaction is:

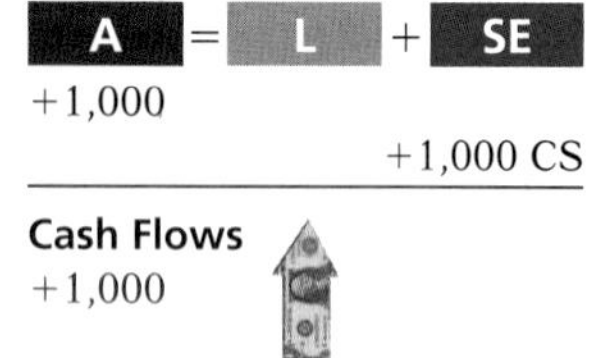

Cash	1,000	
Common Stock		1,000
(To record issuance of 1,000 shares of $1 par common stock at par)		

Now assume that Hydro-Slide issues an additional 1,000 shares of the $1 par value common stock for cash at $5 per share. The amount received above the par value, in this case $4 ($5 − $1), is credited to Paid-in Capital in Excess of Par—Common Stock. The entry is:

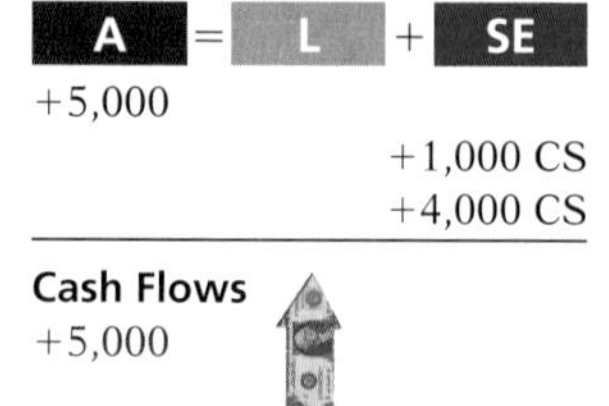

Cash	5,000	
Common Stock		1,000
Paid-in Capital in Excess of Par—Common Stock		4,000
(To record issuance of 1,000 shares of $1 par common stock)		

The total paid-in capital from these two transactions is $6,000, and the legal capital is $2,000. Assuming Hydro-Slide, Inc. has retained earnings of $27,000, Illustration 13-7 shows the company's stockholders' equity section.

HYDRO-SLIDE, INC. Balance Sheet (partial)	
Stockholders' equity	
Paid-in capital	
Common stock	$ 2,000
Paid-in capital in excess of par—common stock	**4,000**
Total paid-in capital	6,000
Retained earnings	27,000
Total stockholders' equity	$33,000

Illustration 13-7
Stockholders' equity—paid-in capital in excess of par

Terminology
Paid-in Capital in Excess of Par is also called *Premium on Stock*.

When a corporation issues stock for less than par value, it debits the account Paid-in Capital in Excess of Par—Common Stock if a credit balance exists in this account. If a credit balance does not exist, then the corporation debits to Retained Earnings the amount less than par. This situation occurs only rarely. Most states do not permit the sale of common stock below par value because stockholders may be held personally liable for the difference between the price paid upon original sale and par value.

Issuing No-Par Common Stock for Cash

When no-par common stock has a stated value, the entries are similar to those illustrated for par value stock. The corporation credits the stated value to Common Stock. Also, when the selling price of no-par stock exceeds stated value, the corporation credits the excess to Paid-in Capital in Excess of Stated Value—Common Stock.

For example, assume that instead of $1 par value stock, Hydro-Slide, Inc. has $5 stated value no-par stock and the company issues 5,000 shares at $8 per share for cash. The entry is as follows.

	Debit	Credit
Cash	40,000	
Common Stock		25,000
Paid-in Capital in Excess of Stated Value—Common Stock		15,000
(To record issue of 5,000 shares of $5 stated value no-par stock)		

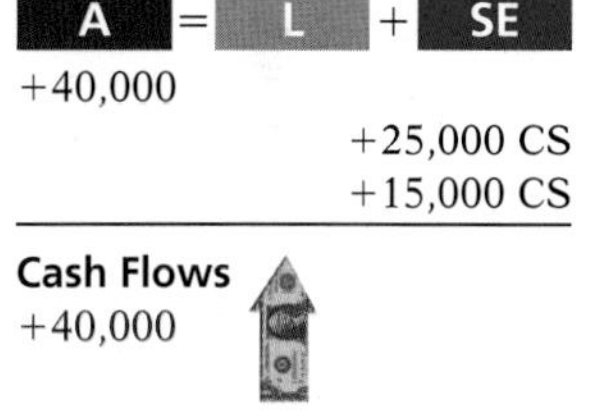

Hydro-Slide, Inc. reports Paid-in Capital in Excess of Stated Value—Common Stock as part of paid-in capital in the stockholders' equity section.

What happens when no-par stock does not have a stated value? In that case, the corporation credits the entire proceeds to Common Stock. Thus, if Hydro-Slide does not assign a stated value to its no-par stock, it records the issuance of the 5,000 shares at $8 per share for cash as follows.

	Debit	Credit
Cash	40,000	
Common Stock		40,000
(To record issue of 5,000 shares of no-par stock)		

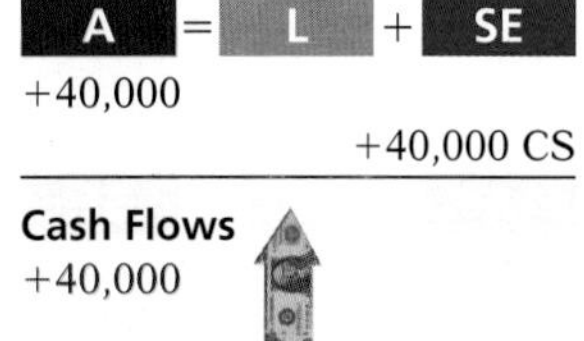

Issuing Common Stock for Services or Noncash Assets

Corporations also may issue stock for services (compensation to attorneys or consultants) or for noncash assets (land, buildings, and equipment). In such cases, what cost should be recognized in the exchange transaction? To comply with the **historical cost principle**, in a noncash transaction **cost is the cash equivalent price**. Thus, **cost is either the fair value of the consideration given up or the fair value of the consideration received**, whichever is more clearly determinable.

To illustrate, assume that attorneys have helped Jordan Company incorporate. They have billed the company $5,000 for their services. They agree to accept 4,000 shares of $1 par value common stock in payment of their bill. At the time of the exchange, there is no established market price for the stock. In this case, the fair value of the consideration received, $5,000, is more clearly evident. Accordingly, Jordan Company makes the following entry.

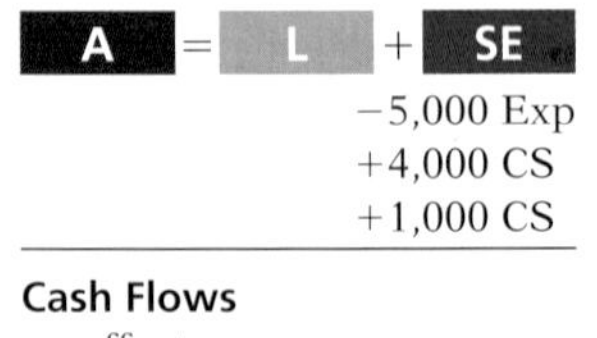

Organization Expense	5,000	
Common Stock		4,000
Paid-in Capital in Excess of Par—Common Stock		1,000
(To record issuance of 4,000 shares of $1 par value stock to attorneys)		

As explained on page 462, organization costs are expensed as incurred.

In contrast, assume that Athletic Research Inc. is an existing publicly held corporation. Its $5 par value stock is actively traded at $8 per share. The company issues 10,000 shares of stock to acquire land recently advertised for sale at $90,000. The most clearly evident value in this noncash transaction is the market price of the consideration given, $80,000. The company records the transaction as follows.

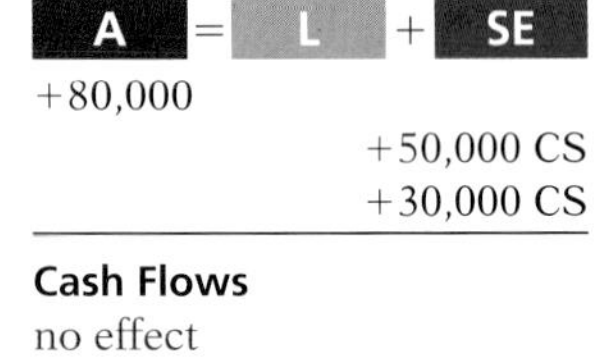

Land	80,000	
Common Stock		50,000
Paid-in Capital in Excess of Par—Common Stock		30,000
(To record issuance of 10,000 shares of $5 par value stock for land)		

As illustrated in these examples, **the par value of the stock is never a factor in determining the cost of the assets or services received in noncash transactions**. This is also true of the stated value of no-par stock.

Accounting for Preferred Stock

To appeal to a larger segment of potential investors, a corporation may issue an additional class of stock, called preferred stock. **Preferred stock** has contractual provisions that give it some preference or priority over common stock. Typically, preferred stockholders have a priority as to (1) distributions of earnings (dividends) and (2) assets in the event of liquidation. However, they generally do not have voting rights.

Like common stock, corporations may issue preferred stock for cash or for noncash assets. The entries for these transactions are similar to the entries for common stock. When a corporation has more than one class of stock, each paid-in capital account title should identify the stock to which it relates. A company might have the following accounts: Preferred Stock, Common Stock, Paid-in Capital in Excess of Par—Preferred Stock, and Paid-in Capital in Excess of Par—Common Stock.

For example, if Stine Corporation issues 10,000 shares of $10 par value preferred stock for $12 cash per share, the entry to record the issuance is as follows.

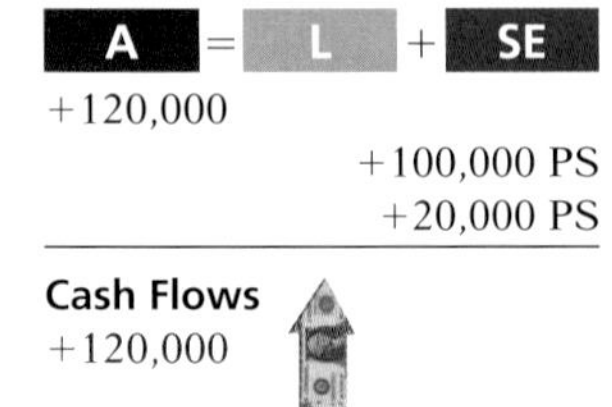

Cash	120,000	
Preferred Stock		100,000
Paid-in Capital in Excess of Par—Preferred Stock		20,000
(To record the issuance of 10,000 shares of $10 par value preferred stock)		

Preferred stock may have either a par value or no-par value. In the stockholders' equity section of the balance sheet, companies list preferred stock first because of its dividend and liquidation preferences over common stock.

LEARNING OBJECTIVE 3

Explain how to account for treasury stock.

Treasury stock is a corporation's own stock that it has issued and subsequently reacquired from shareholders but not retired. A corporation may acquire treasury stock for various reasons:

1. To reissue the shares to officers and employees under bonus and stock compensation plans.
2. To increase trading of the company's stock in the securities market. Companies expect that buying their own stock will signal that management believes the stock is underpriced, which they hope will enhance its market price.
3. To have additional shares available for use in the acquisition of other companies.
4. To reduce the number of shares outstanding and thereby increase earnings per share.

Another infrequent reason for purchasing shares is that management may want to eliminate hostile shareholders by buying them out.

Many corporations have treasury stock. For example, approximately 65% of U.S. companies have treasury stock. In a recent year, **Nike** purchased more than 6 million treasury shares.

Purchase of Treasury Stock

Companies generally account for treasury stock by **the cost method**. This method uses the cost of the shares purchased to value the treasury stock. Under the cost method, the company debits **Treasury Stock** for the **price paid to reacquire the shares**. When the company disposes of the shares, it credits to Treasury Stock **the same amount** it paid to reacquire the shares.

To illustrate, assume that on January 1, 2017, the stockholders' equity section of Mead, Inc. has 400,000 shares authorized and 100,000 shares of $5 par value common stock outstanding (all issued at par value) and Retained Earnings of $200,000. The stockholders' equity section before purchase of treasury stock is as follows.

Illustration 13-8
Stockholders' equity with no treasury stock

MEAD, INC. Balance Sheet (partial)	
Stockholders' equity	
Paid-in capital	
Common stock, $5 par value, 400,000 shares authorized, 100,000 shares issued and outstanding	$500,000
Retained earnings	200,000
Total stockholders' equity	$700,000

On February 1, 2017, Mead acquires 4,000 shares of its stock at $8 per share. The entry is as follows.

		Debit	Credit
Feb. 1	Treasury Stock	32,000	
	Cash		32,000
	(To record purchase of 4,000 shares of treasury stock at $8 per share)		

A	=	L	+	SE
				−32,000 TS
−32,000				

Cash Flows
−32,000

Mead debits Treasury Stock for the cost of the shares purchased ($32,000). Is the original paid-in capital account, Common Stock, affected? No, because the number of issued shares does not change.

In the stockholders' equity section of the balance sheet, Mead deducts treasury stock from total paid-in capital and retained earnings. Treasury Stock is a **contra stockholders' equity account**. Thus, the acquisition of treasury stock reduces stockholders' equity. The stockholders' equity section of Mead, Inc. after purchase of treasury stock is as follows.

Illustration 13-9
Stockholders' equity with treasury stock

MEAD, INC. Balance Sheet (partial)	
Stockholders' equity	
Paid-in capital	
Common stock, $5 par value, 400,000 shares authorized, 100,000 shares issued, and 96,000 shares outstanding	$500,000
Retained earnings	200,000
Total paid-in capital and retained earnings	700,000
Less: Treasury stock (4,000 shares)	**32,000**
Total stockholders' equity	$668,000

Mead discloses in the balance sheet both the number of shares issued (100,000) and the number in the treasury (4,000). The difference is the number of shares of stock outstanding (96,000). The term **outstanding stock** means the number of shares of issued stock that are being held by stockholders.

Some maintain that companies should report treasury stock as an asset because it can be sold for cash. But under this reasoning, companies would also show unissued stock as an asset, which is clearly incorrect. Rather than being an asset, treasury stock reduces stockholder claims on corporate assets. This effect is correctly shown by reporting treasury stock as a deduction from total paid-in capital and retained earnings.

Disposal of Treasury Stock

Treasury stock is usually sold or retired. The accounting for its sale differs when treasury stock is sold above cost than when it is sold below cost.

SALE OF TREASURY STOCK ABOVE COST

If the selling price of the treasury shares is equal to their cost, the company records the sale of the shares by a debit to Cash and a credit to Treasury Stock. When the selling price of the shares is greater than their cost, the company credits the difference to Paid-in Capital from Treasury Stock.

To illustrate, assume that on July 1, Mead, Inc. sells for $10 per share 1,000 of the 4,000 shares of its treasury stock previously acquired at $8 per share. The entry is as follows.

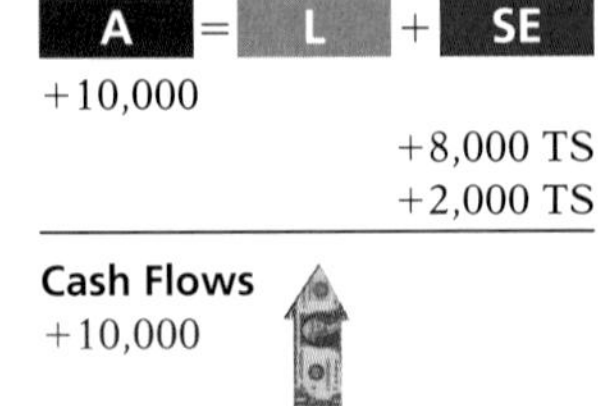

Date	Account	Debit	Credit
July 1	Cash	10,000	
	Treasury Stock		8,000
	Paid-in Capital from Treasury Stock		2,000
	(To record sale of 1,000 shares of treasury stock above cost)		

Mead does not record a $2,000 gain on sale of treasury stock for two reasons. (1) Gains on sales occur when **assets** are sold, and treasury stock is not an asset. (2) A corporation does not realize a gain or suffer a loss from stock transactions with its own stockholders. Thus, companies should **not** include in net income any paid-in capital arising from the sale of treasury stock. Instead, they report Paid-in Capital from Treasury Stock separately on the balance sheet, as a part of paid-in capital.

SALE OF TREASURY STOCK BELOW COST

When a company sells treasury stock below its cost, it usually debits to Paid-in Capital from Treasury Stock the excess of cost over selling price. Thus, if Mead, Inc.

sells an additional 800 shares of treasury stock on October 1 at $7 per share, it makes the following entry.

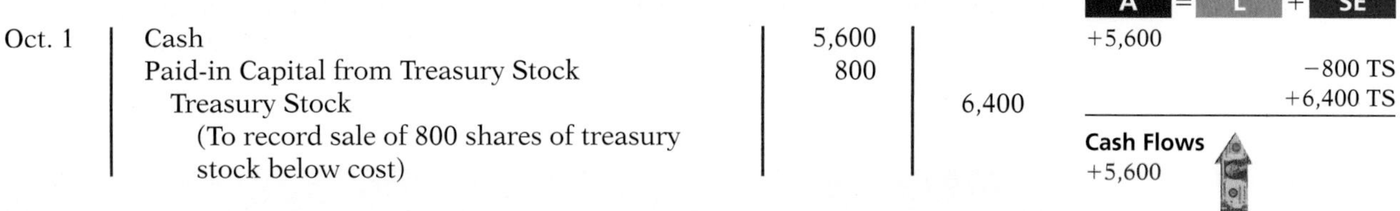

Oct. 1	Cash	5,600	
	Paid-in Capital from Treasury Stock	800	
	Treasury Stock		6,400
	(To record sale of 800 shares of treasury stock below cost)		

A = L + SE
+5,600
−800 TS
+6,400 TS

Cash Flows
+5,600

Observe the following from the two sales entries. (1) Mead credits Treasury Stock at cost in each entry. (2) Mead uses Paid-in Capital from Treasury Stock for the difference between cost and the resale price of the shares. (3) The original paid-in capital account, Common Stock, is not affected. **The sale of treasury stock increases both total assets and total stockholders' equity.**

After posting the foregoing entries, the treasury stock accounts will show the following balances on October 1.

Illustration 13-10
Treasury stock accounts

Treasury Stock				Paid-in Capital from Treasury Stock			
Feb. 1	32,000	July 1	8,000	Oct. 1	800	July 1	2,000
		Oct. 1	6,400			Oct. 1 Bal.	1,200
Oct. 1 Bal.	17,600						

When a company fully depletes the credit balance in Paid-in Capital from Treasury Stock, it debits to Retained Earnings any additional excess of cost over selling price. To illustrate, assume that Mead, Inc. sells its remaining 2,200 shares at $7 per share on December 1. The excess of cost over selling price is $2,200 [2,200 × ($8 − $7)]. In this case, Mead debits $1,200 of the excess to Paid-in Capital from Treasury Stock. It debits the remainder to Retained Earnings. The entry is as follows.

Dec. 1	Cash	15,400	
	Paid-in Capital from Treasury Stock	1,200	
	Retained Earnings	1,000	
	Treasury Stock		17,600
	(To record sale of 2,200 shares of treasury stock at $7 per share)		

A = L + SE
+15,400
−1,200 TS
−1,000 RE
+17,600 TS

Cash Flows
+15,400

Prepare a stockholders' equity section.

Companies report paid-in capital and retained earnings in the stockholders' equity section of the balance sheet. They identify the specific sources of paid-in capital, using the following classifications.

Terminology
Paid-in capital is sometimes called *contributed capital.*

1. **Capital stock.** This category consists of preferred and common stock. Preferred stock appears before common stock because of its preferential rights. Companies report par value, shares authorized, shares issued, and shares outstanding for each class of stock.
2. **Additional paid-in capital.** This category includes the excess of amounts paid in over par or stated value and paid-in capital from treasury stock.

The stockholders' equity section of Connally Inc. in Illustration 13-11 includes most of the accounts discussed in this chapter. The disclosures pertaining to Connally's common stock indicate that the company issued 400,000 shares; 100,000 shares are unissued (500,000 authorized less 400,000 issued); and 390,000 shares are outstanding (400,000 issued less 10,000 shares in treasury).

Illustration 13-11
Stockholders' equity section

CONNALLY INC.
Balance Sheet (partial)

Stockholders' equity		
Paid-in capital		
Capital stock		
9% preferred stock, $100 par value, 10,000 shares authorized, 6,000 shares issued and outstanding		$ 600,000
Common stock, no par, $5 stated value, 500,000 shares authorized, 400,000 shares issued, and 390,000 shares outstanding		2,000,000
Total capital stock		2,600,000
Additional paid-in capital		
In excess of par—preferred stock	$ 30,000	
In excess of stated value—common stock	860,000	
From treasury stock	140,000	
Total additional paid-in capital		1,030,000
Total paid-in capital		3,630,000
Retained earnings		1,058,000
Total paid-in capital and retained earnings		4,688,000
Less: Treasury stock (10,000 common shares) (at cost)		80,000
Total stockholders' equity		$4,608,000

ANATOMY OF A FRAUD

The president, chief operating officer, and chief financial officer of SafeNet, a software encryption company, were each awarded employee stock options by the company's board of directors as part of their compensation package. Stock options enable an employee to buy a company's stock sometime in the future at the price that existed when the stock option was awarded. For example, suppose that you received stock options today, when the stock price of your company was $30. Three years later, if the stock price rose to $100, you could "exercise" your options and buy the stock for $30 per share, thereby making $70 per share. After being awarded their stock options, the three employees changed the award dates in the company's records to dates in the past, when the company's stock was trading at historical lows. For example, using the previous example, they would choose a past date when the stock was selling for $10 per share, rather than the $30 price on the actual award date. In our example, this would increase the profit from exercising the options to $90 per share.

Total take: $1.7 million

THE MISSING CONTROL

Independent internal verification. The company's board of directors should have ensured that the awards were properly administered. For example, the date on the minutes from the board meeting could be compared to the dates that were recorded for the awards. In addition, the dates should again be confirmed upon exercise.

REVIEW AND PRACTICE

LEARNING OBJECTIVES REVIEW

1 Discuss the major characteristics of a corporation. The major characteristics of a corporation are separate legal existence, limited liability of stockholders, transferable ownership rights, ability to acquire capital, continuous life, corporation management, government regulations, and additional taxes.

Paid-in capital is the total amount paid in on capital stock. It is often called contributed capital. Retained earnings is net income retained in a corporation. It is often called earned capital.

2 Explain how to account for the issuance of common and preferred stock. When companies record the issuance of common stock for cash, they credit the par value of the shares to Common Stock. They record in a separate paid-in capital account the portion of the proceeds that is above or below par value. When no-par common stock has a stated value, the entries are similar to those for par value stock. When no-par stock does not have a stated value, companies credit the entire proceeds to Common Stock.

Preferred stock has contractual provisions that give it priority over common stock in certain areas. Typically, preferred stockholders have preferences (1) to dividends and (2) to assets in liquidation. They usually do not have voting rights.

3 Explain how to account for treasury stock. The cost method is generally used in accounting for treasury stock. Under this approach, companies debit Treasury Stock at the price paid to reacquire the shares. They credit the same amount to Treasury Stock when they sell the shares. The difference between the sales price and cost is recorded in stockholders' equity accounts, not in income statement accounts.

4 Prepare a stockholders' equity section. In the stockholders' equity section, companies report paid-in capital and retained earnings and identify specific sources of paid-in capital. Within paid-in capital, two classifications are shown: capital stock and additional paid-in capital. If a corporation has treasury stock, it deducts the cost of treasury stock from total paid-in capital and retained earnings to obtain total stockholders' equity.

GLOSSARY REVIEW

Authorized stock The amount of stock that a corporation is authorized to sell as indicated in its charter.

Charter A document that is issued by the state to set forth important terms and features regarding the creation of a corporation.

Corporation A business organized as a legal entity separate and distinct from its owners under state corporation law.

No-par value stock Capital stock that has not been assigned a value in the corporate charter.

Organization costs Costs incurred in the formation of a corporation.

Outstanding stock Capital stock that has been issued and is being held by stockholders.

Paid-in capital Total amount of cash and other assets paid in to the corporation by stockholders in exchange for capital stock.

Par value stock Capital stock that has been assigned a value per share in the corporate charter.

Preferred stock Capital stock that has some preferences over common stock.

Privately held corporation A corporation that has only a few stockholders and whose stock is not available for sale to the general public.

Publicly held corporation A corporation that may have thousands of stockholders and whose stock is regularly traded on a national securities exchange.

Retained earnings Net income that the corporation retains for future use.

Stated value The amount per share assigned by the board of directors to no-par value stock.

Treasury stock A corporation's own stock that has been issued and subsequently reacquired from shareholders by the corporation but not retired.

PRACTICE EXERCISES

Journalize issuance of common and preferred stock and purchase of treasury stock.

(LO 2, 3)

1. Bostick Co. had the following transactions during the current period.

Mar. 2	Issued 4,000 shares of $1 par value common stock to attorneys in payment of a bill for $35,000 for services performed in helping the company to incorporate.
June 12	Issued 50,000 shares of $1 par value common stock for cash of $360,000.
July 11	Issued 2,000 shares of $100 par value preferred stock for cash at $120 per share.
Nov. 28	Purchased 2,000 shares of treasury stock for $70,000.

Instructions
Journalize the transactions.

Solution

1. Mar. 2	Organization Expense	35,000	
	Common Stock (4,000 × $1)		4,000
	Paid-in Capital in Excess of Par—Common Stock		31,000
June 12	Cash	360,000	
	Common Stock (50,000 × $1)		50,000
	Paid-in Capital in Excess of Par—Common Stock		310,000
July 11	Cash (2,000 × $120)	240,000	
	Preferred Stock (2,000 × $100)		200,000
	Paid-in Capital in Excess of Par—Preferred Stock (2,000 × $20)		40,000
Nov. 28	Treasury Stock	70,000	
	Cash		70,000

Journalize treasury stock transactions.

(LO 3)

2. Star Corporation purchased from its stockholders 5,000 shares of its own previously issued stock for $250,000. It later resold 2,000 shares for $53 per share, then 2,000 more shares for $48 per share, and finally 1,000 shares for $43 per share.

Instructions
Prepare journal entries for the purchase of the treasury stock and the three sales of treasury stock.

Solution

2. Treasury Stock	250,000	
Cash		250,000
Cash (2,000 × $53)	106,000	
Treasury Stock (2,000 × $50)		100,000
Paid-in Capital from Treasury Stock		6,000
Cash (2,000 × $48)	96,000	
Paid-in Capital from Treasury Stock	4,000	
Treasury Stock (2,000 × $50)		100,000
Cash (1,000 × $43)	43,000	
Paid-in Capital from Treasury Stock ($6,000 − $4,000)	2,000	
Retained Earnings	5,000	
Treasury Stock (1,000 × $50)		50,000

PRACTICE PROBLEM

Journalize transactions and prepare stockholders' equity section.

(LO 2, 3, 4)

Rolman Corporation is authorized to issue 1,000,000 shares of $5 par value common stock. In its first year, the company has the following stock transactions.

Jan. 10	Issued 400,000 shares of stock at $8 per share.
July 1	Issued 100,000 shares of stock for land. The land had an asking price of $900,000. The stock is currently selling on a national exchange at $8.25 per share.
Sept. 1	Purchased 10,000 shares of common stock for the treasury at $9 per share.
Dec. 1	Sold 4,000 shares of the treasury stock at $10 per share.

Instructions
(a) Journalize the transactions.
(b) Prepare the stockholders' equity section assuming the company had retained earnings of $200,000 at December 31.

Solution

(a) Jan. 10	Cash	3,200,000	
	Common Stock		2,000,000
	Paid-in Capital in Excess of Par—Common Stock		1,200,000
	(To record issuance of 400,000 shares of $5 par value stock)		
July 1	Land	825,000	
	Common Stock		500,000
	Paid-in Capital in Excess of Par—Common Stock		325,000
	(To record issuance of 100,000 shares of $5 par value stock for land)		
Sept. 1	Treasury Stock	90,000	
	Cash		90,000
	(To record purchase of 10,000 shares of treasury stock at cost)		
Dec. 1	Cash	40,000	
	Treasury Stock		36,000
	Paid-in Capital from Treasury Stock		4,000
	(To record sale of 4,000 shares of treasury stock above cost)		

(b)

ROLMAN CORPORATION
Balance Sheet (partial)

Stockholders' equity		
Paid-in capital		
Capital stock		
Common stock, $5 par value, 1,000,000 shares authorized, 500,000 shares issued, 494,000 shares outstanding		$2,500,000
Additional paid-in capital		
In excess of par—common stock	$1,525,000	
From treasury stock	4,000	
Total additional paid-in capital		1,529,000
Total paid-in capital		4,029,000
Retained earnings		200,000
Total paid-in capital and retained earnings		4,229,000
Less: Treasury stock (6,000 shares)		54,000
Total stockholders' equity		$4,175,000

EXERCISES

E13-1 Andrea has prepared the following list of statements about corporations.

Identify characteristics of a corporation.

(LO 1)

1. A corporation is an entity separate and distinct from its owners.
2. As a legal entity, a corporation has most of the rights and privileges of a person.
3. Most of the largest U.S. corporations are privately held corporations.
4. Corporations may buy, own, and sell property; borrow money; enter into legally binding contracts; and sue and be sued.
5. The net income of a corporation is not taxed as a separate entity.
6. Creditors have a legal claim on the personal assets of the owners of a corporation if the corporation does not pay its debts.
7. The transfer of stock from one owner to another requires the approval of either the corporation or other stockholders.

8. The board of directors of a corporation legally owns the corporation.
9. The chief accounting officer of a corporation is the controller.
10. Corporations are subject to fewer state and federal regulations than partnerships or proprietorships.

Instructions
Identify each statement as true or false. If false, indicate how to correct the statement.

Identify characteristics of a corporation.
(LO 1)

E13-2 Andrea (see E13-1) has studied the information you gave her in that exercise and has come to you with more statements about corporations.

1. Corporation management is both an advantage and a disadvantage of a corporation compared to a proprietorship or a partnership.
2. Limited liability of stockholders, government regulations, and additional taxes are the major disadvantages of a corporation.
3. When a corporation is formed, organization costs are recorded as an asset.
4. Each share of common stock gives the stockholder the ownership rights to vote at stockholder meetings, share in corporate earnings, keep the same percentage ownership when new shares of stock are issued, and share in assets upon liquidation.
5. The number of issued shares is always greater than or equal to the number of authorized shares.
6. A journal entry is required for the authorization of capital stock.
7. Publicly held corporations usually issue stock directly to investors.
8. The trading of capital stock on a securities exchange involves the transfer of already issued shares from an existing stockholder to another investor.
9. The market price of common stock is usually the same as its par value.
10. Retained earnings is the total amount of cash and other assets paid in to the corporation by stockholders in exchange for capital stock.

Instructions
Identify each statement as true or false. If false, indicate how to correct the statement.

Journalize issuance of common stock.
(LO 2)

E13-3 During its first year of operations, Foyle Corporation had the following transactions pertaining to its common stock.

Jan. 10 Issued 70,000 shares for cash at $5 per share.
July 1 Issued 40,000 shares for cash at $7 per share.

Instructions
(a) Journalize the transactions, assuming that the common stock has a par value of $5 per share.
(b) Journalize the transactions, assuming that the common stock is no-par with a stated value of $1 per share.

Journalize issuance of common stock.
(LO 2)

E13-4 Osage Corporation issued 2,000 shares of stock.

Instructions
Prepare the entry for the issuance under the following assumptions.
(a) The stock had a par value of $5 per share and was issued for a total of $52,000.
(b) The stock had a stated value of $5 per share and was issued for a total of $52,000.
(c) The stock had no par or stated value and was issued for a total of $52,000.
(d) The stock had a par value of $5 per share and was issued to attorneys for services during incorporation valued at $52,000.
(e) The stock had a par value of $5 per share and was issued for land worth $52,000.

Journalize issuance of common and preferred stock and purchase of treasury stock.
(LO 2, 3)

E13-5 Quay Co. had the following transactions during the current period.

Mar. 2 Issued 5,000 shares of $5 par value common stock to attorneys in payment of a bill for $30,000 for services performed in helping the company to incorporate.
June 12 Issued 60,000 shares of $5 par value common stock for cash of $375,000.
July 11 Issued 1,000 shares of $100 par value preferred stock for cash at $110 per share.
Nov. 28 Purchased 2,000 shares of treasury stock for $80,000.

Instructions
Journalize the transactions.

E13-6 As an auditor for the CPA firm of Hinkson and Calvert, you encounter the following situations in auditing different clients.

Journalize noncash common stock transactions.

(LO 2)

1. LR Corporation is a closely held corporation whose stock is not publicly traded. On December 5, the corporation acquired land by issuing 5,000 shares of its $20 par value common stock. The owners' asking price for the land was $120,000, and the fair value of the land was $110,000.
2. Vera Corporation is a publicly held corporation whose common stock is traded on the securities markets. On June 1, it acquired land by issuing 20,000 shares of its $10 par value stock. At the time of the exchange, the land was advertised for sale at $250,000. The stock was selling at $11 per share.

Instructions

Prepare the journal entries for each of the situations above.

E13-7 On January 1, 2017, the stockholders' equity section of Newlin Corporation shows common stock ($5 par value) $1,500,000; paid-in capital in excess of par $1,000,000; and retained earnings $1,200,000. During the year, the following treasury stock transactions occurred.

Journalize treasury stock transactions.

(LO 3)

Mar. 1	Purchased 50,000 shares for cash at $15 per share.
July 1	Sold 10,000 treasury shares for cash at $17 per share.
Sept. 1	Sold 8,000 treasury shares for cash at $14 per share.

Instructions

(a) Journalize the treasury stock transactions.
(b) Restate the entry for September 1, assuming the treasury shares were sold at $12 per share.

E13-8 Rinehart Corporation purchased from its stockholders 5,000 shares of its own previously issued stock for $255,000. It later resold 2,000 shares for $54 per share, then 2,000 more shares for $49 per share, and finally 1,000 shares for $43 per share.

Journalize treasury stock transactions.

(LO 3)

Instructions

Prepare journal entries for the purchase of the treasury stock and the three sales of treasury stock.

E13-9 Tran Corporation is authorized to issue both preferred and common stock. The par value of the preferred is $50. During the first year of operations, the company had the following events and transactions pertaining to its preferred stock.

Journalize preferred stock transactions and indicate statement presentation.

(LO 2, 4)

Feb. 1	Issued 20,000 shares for cash at $53 per share.
July 1	Issued 12,000 shares for cash at $57 per share.

Instructions

(a) Journalize the transactions.
(b) Post to the stockholders' equity accounts.
(c) Indicate the financial statement presentation of the related accounts.

E13-10 Gilliam Corporation recently hired a new accountant with extensive experience in accounting for partnerships. Because of the pressure of the new job, the accountant was unable to review his textbooks on the topic of corporation accounting. During the first month, the accountant made the following entries for the corporation's capital stock.

Prepare correct entries for capital stock transactions.

(LO 2, 3)

May 2	Cash	130,000	
	Capital Stock		130,000
	(Issued 10,000 shares of $10 par value common stock at $13 per share)		
10	Cash	600,000	
	Capital Stock		600,000
	(Issued 10,000 shares of $50 par value preferred stock at $60 per share)		

May 15	Capital Stock	15,000	
	Cash		15,000
	(Purchased 1,000 shares of common stock for the treasury at $15 per share)		
31	Cash	8,000	
	Capital Stock		5,000
	Gain on Sale of Stock		3,000
	(Sold 500 shares of treasury stock at $16 per share)		

Instructions

On the basis of the explanation for each entry, prepare the entry that should have been made for the capital stock transactions.

Prepare a stockholders' equity section.

(LO 4)

E13-11 The following stockholders' equity accounts, arranged alphabetically, are in the ledger of Eudaley Corporation at December 31, 2017.

Common Stock ($5 stated value)	$1,500,000
Paid-in Capital in Excess of Par—Preferred Stock	280,000
Paid-in Capital in Excess of Stated Value—Common Stock	900,000
Preferred Stock (8%, $100 par)	500,000
Retained Earnings	1,234,000
Treasury Stock (10,000 common shares)	120,000

Instructions

Prepare the stockholders' equity section of the balance sheet at December 31, 2017.

Answer questions about stockholders' equity section.

(LO 2, 3, 4)

E13-12 The stockholders' equity section of Haley Corporation at December 31 is as follows.

HALEY CORPORATION
Balance Sheet (partial)

Paid-in capital	
Preferred stock, 10,000 shares authorized, 6,000 shares issued and outstanding	$ 300,000
Common stock, no par, 750,000 shares authorized, 600,000 shares issued	1,200,000
Total paid-in capital	1,500,000
Retained earnings	1,858,000
Total paid-in capital and retained earnings	3,358,000
Less: Treasury stock (10,000 common shares)	64,000
Total stockholders' equity	$3,294,000

Instructions

From a review of the stockholders' equity section, as chief accountant, write a memo to the president of the company answering the following questions.

(a) How many shares of common stock are outstanding?
(b) Assuming there is a stated value, what is the stated value of the common stock?
(c) What is the par value of the preferred stock?

Prepare a stockholders' equity section.

(LO 4)

E13-13 The stockholders' equity section of Aluminum Company of America (Alcoa) showed the following (in alphabetical order): additional paid-in capital $6,101, common stock $925, preferred stock $56, retained earnings $7,428, and treasury stock 2,828. All dollar data are in millions.

The preferred stock has 557,740 shares authorized, with a par value of $100. At December 31 of the current year, 557,649 shares of preferred are issued and 546,024 shares are outstanding. There are 1.8 billion shares of $1 par value common stock authorized, of which 924.6 million are issued and 844.8 million are outstanding at December 31.

Instructions
Prepare the stockholders' equity section of the current year, including disclosure of all relevant data.

E13-14 The ledger of Rolling Hills Corporation contains the following accounts: Common Stock, Preferred Stock, Treasury Stock, Paid-in Capital in Excess of Par—Preferred Stock, Paid-in Capital in Excess of Stated Value—Common Stock, Paid-in Capital from Treasury Stock, and Retained Earnings.

Classify stockholders' equity accounts.

(LO 4)

Instructions
Classify each account using the following table headings.

	Paid-in Capital			
Account	**Capital Stock**	**Additional**	**Retained Earnings**	**Other**

PROBLEMS

P13-1A DeLong Corporation was organized on January 1, 2017. It is authorized to issue 10,000 shares of 8%, $100 par value preferred stock, and 500,000 shares of no-par common stock with a stated value of $2 per share. The following stock transactions were completed during the first year.

Journalize stock transactions, post, and prepare paid-in capital section.

(LO 2, 4)

Jan. 10	Issued 80,000 shares of common stock for cash at $4 per share.
Mar. 1	Issued 5,000 shares of preferred stock for cash at $105 per share.
Apr. 1	Issued 24,000 shares of common stock for land. The asking price of the land was $90,000. The fair value of the land was $85,000.
May 1	Issued 80,000 shares of common stock for cash at $4.50 per share.
Aug. 1	Issued 10,000 shares of common stock to attorneys in payment of their bill of $30,000 for services performed in helping the company organize.
Sept. 1	Issued 10,000 shares of common stock for cash at $5 per share.
Nov. 1	Issued 1,000 shares of preferred stock for cash at $109 per share.

Instructions
(a) Journalize the transactions.
(b) Post to the stockholders' equity accounts. (Use J5 as the posting reference.)
(c) Prepare the paid-in capital section of stockholders' equity at December 31, 2017.

(c) Total paid-in capital $1,479,000

P13-2A Fechter Corporation had the following stockholders' equity accounts on January 1, 2017: Common Stock ($5 par) $500,000, Paid-in Capital in Excess of Par—Common Stock $200,000, and Retained Earnings $100,000. In 2017, the company had the following treasury stock transactions.

Journalize and post treasury stock transactions, and prepare stockholders' equity section.

(LO 3, 4)

Mar. 1	Purchased 5,000 shares at $8 per share.
June 1	Sold 1,000 shares at $12 per share.
Sept. 1	Sold 2,000 shares at $10 per share.
Dec. 1	Sold 1,000 shares at $7 per share.

Fechter Corporation uses the cost method of accounting for treasury stock. In 2017, the company reported net income of $30,000.

Instructions
(a) Journalize the treasury stock transactions, and prepare the closing entry at December 31, 2017, for net income.
(b) Open accounts for (1) Paid-in Capital from Treasury Stock, (2) Treasury Stock, and (3) Retained Earnings. Post to these accounts using J10 as the posting reference.
(c) Prepare the stockholders' equity section for Fechter Corporation at December 31, 2017.

(b) Treasury Stock $8,000

(c) Total stockholders' equity $829,000

Journalize and post transactions, and prepare stockholders' equity section.

(LO 1, 2, 3, 4)

P13-3A The stockholders' equity accounts of Castle Corporation on January 1, 2017, were as follows.

Preferred Stock (8%, $50 par, 10,000 shares authorized)	$ 400,000
Common Stock ($1 stated value, 2,000,000 shares authorized)	1,000,000
Paid-in Capital in Excess of Par—Preferred Stock	100,000
Paid-in Capital in Excess of Stated Value—Common Stock	1,450,000
Retained Earnings	1,816,000
Treasury Stock (10,000 common shares)	50,000

During 2017, the corporation had the following transactions and events pertaining to its stockholders' equity.

Feb. 1	Issued 25,000 shares of common stock for $120,000.
Apr. 14	Sold 6,000 shares of treasury stock—common for $33,000.
Sept. 3	Issued 5,000 shares of common stock for a patent valued at $35,000.
Nov. 10	Purchased 1,000 shares of common stock for the treasury at a cost of $6,000.
Dec. 31	Determined that net income for the year was $452,000.

No dividends were declared during the year.

Instructions

(a) Journalize the transactions and the closing entry for net income.

(b) Enter the beginning balances in the accounts, and post the journal entries to the stockholders' equity accounts. (Use J5 for the posting reference.)

(c) Prepare a stockholders' equity section at December 31, 2017.

(c) Total stockholders' equity $5,350,000

Journalize and post stock transactions, and prepare stockholders' equity section.

(LO 1, 2, 4)

P13-4A Peck Corporation is authorized to issue 20,000 shares of $50 par value, 10% preferred stock and 125,000 shares of $5 par value common stock. On January 1, 2017, the ledger contained the following stockholders' equity balances.

Preferred Stock (10,000 shares)	$500,000
Paid-in Capital in Excess of Par—Preferred Stock	75,000
Common Stock (70,000 shares)	350,000
Paid-in Capital in Excess of Par—Common Stock	700,000
Retained Earnings	300,000

During 2017, the following transactions occurred.

Feb. 1	Issued 2,000 shares of preferred stock for land having a fair value of $120,000.
Mar. 1	Issued 1,000 shares of preferred stock for cash at $65 per share.
July 1	Issued 16,000 shares of common stock for cash at $7 per share.
Sept. 1	Issued 400 shares of preferred stock for a patent. The asking price of the patent was $30,000. Market price for the preferred stock was $70 and the fair value for the patent was indeterminable.
Dec. 1	Issued 8,000 shares of common stock for cash at $7.50 per share.
Dec. 31	Net income for the year was $260,000. No dividends were declared.

Instructions

(a) Journalize the transactions and the closing entry for net income.

(b) Enter the beginning balances in the accounts, and post the journal entries to the stockholders' equity accounts. (Use J2 for the posting reference.)

(c) Prepare a stockholders' equity section at December 31, 2017.

(c) Total stockholders' equity $2,570,000

Prepare stockholders' equity section.

(LO 4)

P13-5A The following stockholders' equity accounts arranged alphabetically are in the ledger of Galindo Corporation at December 31, 2017.

Common Stock ($5 stated value)	$2,000,000
Paid-in Capital from Treasury Stock	10,000
Paid-in Capital in Excess of Par—Preferred Stock	679,000
Paid-in Capital in Excess of Stated Value—Common Stock	1,600,000
Preferred Stock (8%, $50 par)	800,000
Retained Earnings	1,748,000
Treasury Stock (10,000 common shares)	130,000

Instructions
Prepare a stockholders' equity section at December 31, 2017.

Total stockholders' equity $6,707,000

P13-6A Irwin Corporation has been authorized to issue 20,000 shares of $100 par value, 10%, preferred stock and 1,000,000 shares of no-par common stock. The corporation assigned a $2.50 stated value to the common stock. At December 31, 2017, the ledger contained the following balances pertaining to stockholders' equity.

Prepare entries for stock transactions and prepare stockholders' equity section.

(LO 2, 3, 4)

Preferred Stock	$ 120,000
Paid-in Capital in Excess of Par—Preferred Stock	20,000
Common Stock	1,000,000
Paid-in Capital in Excess of Stated Value—Common Stock	1,800,000
Treasury Stock (1,000 common shares)	11,000
Paid-in Capital from Treasury Stock	1,500
Retained Earnings	82,000

The preferred stock was issued for land having a fair value of $140,000. All common stock issued was for cash. In November, 1,500 shares of common stock were purchased for the treasury at a per share cost of $11. In December, 500 shares of treasury stock were sold for $14 per share. No dividends were declared in 2017.

Instructions
(a) Prepare the journal entries for the:
 (1) Issuance of preferred stock for land.
 (2) Issuance of common stock for cash.
 (3) Purchase of common treasury stock for cash.
 (4) Sale of treasury stock for cash.
(b) Prepare the stockholders' equity section at December 31, 2017.

(b) Total stockholders' equity $3,012,500

BROADENING YOUR PERSPECTIVE

FINANCIAL REPORTING AND ANALYSIS

Financial Reporting Problem: Apple Inc.

BYP13-1 The stockholders' equity section for Apple Inc. is shown in Appendix A. Instructions for accessing and using the company's complete annual report, including the notes to the financial statements, are also provided in Appendix A.

Instructions
(a) What is the par or stated value per share of Apple's common stock?
(b) What percentage of Apple's authorized common stock was issued at September 28, 2013?

Comparative Analysis Problem: PepsiCo, Inc. vs. The Coca-Cola Company

BYP13-2 PepsiCo, Inc.'s financial statements are presented in Appendix B. Financial statements of The Coca-Cola Company are presented in Appendix C. Instructions for accessing and using the complete annual reports of PepsiCo and Coca-Cola, including the notes to the financial statements, are also provided in Appendices B and C, respectively.

Instructions
(a) What is the par or stated value of Coca-Cola's and PepsiCo's common stock?
(b) What percentage of authorized shares was issued by Coca-Cola at December 31, 2013, and by PepsiCo at December 28, 2013?
(c) How many shares are held as treasury stock by Coca-Cola at December 31, 2013, and by PepsiCo at December 28, 2013?
(d) How many Coca-Cola common shares are outstanding at December 31, 2013? How many PepsiCo shares of common stock are outstanding at December 28, 2013?

Comparative Analysis Problem: Amazon.com, Inc. vs. Wal-Mart Stores, Inc.

BYP13-3 Amazon.com, Inc.'s financial statements are presented in Appendix D. Financial statements of Wal-Mart Stores, Inc. are presented in Appendix E. Instructions for accessing and using the complete annual reports of Amazon and Wal-Mart, including the notes to the financial statements, are also provided in Appendices D and E, respectively. Wal-Mart has 11,000 million shares authorized.

Instructions

(a) What is the par or stated value of Amazon's and Wal-Mart's common stock?
(b) What percentage of authorized shares was issued by Amazon at December 31, 2013, and by Wal-Mart at January 31, 2014?
(c) How many shares are held as treasury stock by Amazon at December 31, 2013, and by Wal-Mart at January 31, 2014?
(d) How many Amazon common shares are outstanding at December 31, 2013? How many Wal-Mart shares of common stock are outstanding at January 31, 2014?

Real-World Focus

BYP13-4 SEC filings of publicly traded companies are available to view online.

Address: **http://biz.yahoo.com/i**, or go to **www.wiley.com/college/weygandt**

Steps

1. Pick a company and type in the company's name.
2. Choose **Quote**.

Instructions

Answer the following questions.

(a) What company did you select?
(b) What is its stock symbol?
(c) What was the stock's trading range today?
(d) What was the stock's trading range for the year?

CRITICAL THINKING

Decision-Making Across the Organization

BYP13-5 The stockholders' meeting for Percival Corporation has been in progress for some time. The chief financial officer for Percival is presently reviewing the company's financial statements and is explaining the items that make up the stockholders' equity section of the balance sheet for the current year. The stockholders' equity section of Percival Corporation at December 31, 2017, is as follows.

PERCIVAL CORPORATION
Balance Sheet (partial)
December 31, 2017

Paid-in capital		
Capital stock		
Preferred stock, authorized 1,000,000 shares, $100 par value, 6,000 shares issued and outstanding		$ 600,000
Common stock, authorized 5,000,000 shares, $1 par value, 3,000,000 shares issued, and 2,700,000 outstanding		3,000,000
Total capital stock		3,600,000
Additional paid-in capital		
In excess of par—preferred stock	$ 50,000	
In excess of par—common stock	25,000,000	
Total additional paid-in capital		25,050,000
Total paid-in capital		28,650,000
Retained earnings		900,000
Total paid-in capital and retained earnings		29,550,000
Less: Treasury stock (300,000 common shares)		9,300,000
Total stockholders' equity		$20,250,000

At the meeting, stockholders have raised a number of questions regarding the stockholders' equity section.

Instructions

With the class divided into groups, answer the following questions as if you were the chief financial officer for Percival Corporation.

(a) "I thought the common stock was presently selling at $29.75, but the company has the stock stated at $1 per share. How can that be?"

(b) "Why is the company buying back its common stock? Furthermore, the treasury stock has a debit balance because it is subtracted from stockholders' equity. Why is treasury stock not reported as an asset if it has a debit balance?"

Communication Activity

BYP13-6 Joe Moyer, your uncle, is an inventor who has decided to incorporate. Uncle Joe knows that you are an accounting major at U.N.O. In a recent letter to you, he ends with the question, "I'm filling out a state incorporation application. Can you tell me the difference in the following terms: (1) authorized stock, (2) issued stock, (3) outstanding stock, and (4) preferred stock?"

Instructions

In a brief note, differentiate for Uncle Joe among the four different stock terms. Write the letter to be friendly, yet professional.

Ethics Case

BYP13-7 The R&D division of Piqua Chemical Corp. has just developed a chemical for sterilizing the vicious Brazilian "killer bees" which are invading Mexico and the southern United States. The president of the company is anxious to get the chemical on the market to boost the company's profits. He believes his job is in jeopardy because of decreasing sales and profits. The company has an opportunity to sell this chemical in Central American countries, where the laws are much more relaxed than in the United States.

The director of Piqua's R&D division strongly recommends further testing in the laboratory for side-effects of this chemical on other insects, birds, animals, plants, and even humans. He cautions the president, "We could be sued from all sides if the chemical has tragic side-effects that we didn't even test for in the labs." The president answers, "We can't wait an additional year for your lab tests. We can avoid losses from such lawsuits by establishing a separate wholly owned corporation to shield Piqua Corp. from such lawsuits. We can't lose any more than our investment in the new corporation, and we'll invest in just the patent covering this chemical. We'll reap the benefits if the chemical works and is safe, and avoid the losses from lawsuits if it's a disaster." The following week, Piqua creates a new wholly owned corporation called Finlay Inc., sells the chemical patent to it for $10, and watches the spraying begin.

Instructions

(a) Who are the stakeholders in this situation?
(b) Are the president's motives and actions ethical?
(c) Can Piqua shield itself against losses of Finlay Inc.?

All About You

BYP13-8 A high percentage of Americans own stock in corporations. As a shareholder in a corporation, you will receive an annual report. One of the goals of this course is for you to learn how to navigate your way around an annual report.

Instructions

Use **Apple**'s 2013 annual report provided in Appendix A to answer the following questions.

(a) What CPA firm performed the audit of Apple's financial statements?
(b) What was the amount of Apple's earnings per share in 2013?
(c) What were net sales in 2013?
(d) How much cash did Apple spend on capital expenditures in 2013?
(e) Over what life does the company depreciate its buildings?
(f) What were the proceeds from issuance of common stock in 2013?

FASB Codification Activity

BYP13-9 If your school has a subscription to the FASB Codification, go to **http://aaahq.org/ascLogin.cfm** to log in and prepare responses to the following.

(a) How is common stock defined?
(b) How is preferred stock defined?
(c) What is the meaning of the term shares?

A Look at IFRS

LEARNING OBJECTIVE 

Compare the accounting for stockholders' equity under GAAP and IFRS.

The accounting for transactions related to stockholders' equity, such as issuance of shares and purchase of treasury stock, are similar under both IFRS and GAAP. Major differences relate to terminology used, introduction of items such as revaluation surplus, and presentation of stockholders' equity information.

Key Points

Following are the key similarities and differences between GAAP and IFRS as related to stockholders' equity.

Similarities

- Aside from terminology used, the accounting transactions for the issuance of shares and the purchase of treasury stocks are similar.
- Like GAAP, IFRS does not allow a company to record gains or losses on purchases of its own shares.

Differences

- Under IFRS, the term **reserves** is used to describe all equity accounts other than those arising from contributed (paid-in) capital. This would include, for example, reserves related to retained earnings, asset revaluations, and fair value differences.
- Many countries have a different mix of investor groups than in the United States. For example, in Germany, financial institutions like banks are not only major creditors of corporations but often are the largest corporate stockholders as well. In the United States, Asia, and the United Kingdom, many companies rely on substantial investment from private investors.
- There are often terminology differences for equity accounts. The following summarizes some of the common differences in terminology.

GAAP	IFRS
Common stock	Share capital—ordinary
Stockholders	Shareholders
Par value	Nominal or face value
Authorized stock	Authorized share capital
Preferred stock	Share capital—preference
Paid-in capital	Issued/allocated share capital
Paid-in capital in excess of par—common stock	Share premium—ordinary
Paid-in capital in excess of par—preferred stock	Share premium—preference
Retained earnings	Retained earnings or retained profits
Retained earnings deficit	Accumulated losses
Accumulated other comprehensive income	General reserve and other reserve accounts

As an example of how similar transactions use different terminology under IFRS, consider the accounting for the issuance of 1,000 shares of $1 par value common stock for $5 per share. Under IFRS, the entry is as follows.

Cash	5,000	
Share Capital—Ordinary		1,000
Share Premium—Ordinary		4,000

- A major difference between IFRS and GAAP relates to the account Revaluation Surplus. Revaluation surplus arises under IFRS because companies are permitted to revalue their property, plant, and equipment to fair value under certain circumstances. This account is part of general reserves under IFRS and is not considered contributed capital.
- IFRS often uses terms such as **retained profits** or **accumulated profit or loss** to describe retained earnings. The term **retained earnings** is also often used.
- Equity is given various descriptions under IFRS, such as shareholders' equity, owners' equity, capital and reserves, and shareholders' funds.

Looking to the Future

As indicated in earlier discussions, the IASB and the FASB are currently working on a project related to financial statement presentation. An important part of this study is to determine whether certain line items, subtotals, and totals should be clearly defined and required to be displayed in the financial statements.

IFRS Practice

IFRS Self-Test Questions

1. Which of the following is **true**?
   (a) In the United States, the primary corporate stockholders are financial institutions.
   (b) Share capital means total assets under IFRS.
   (c) The IASB and FASB are presently studying how financial statement information should be presented.
   (d) The accounting for treasury stock differs extensively between GAAP and IFRS.
2. Under IFRS, the amount of capital received in excess of par value would be credited to:
   (a) Retained Earnings.
   (b) Contributed Capital.
   (c) Share Premium.
   (d) Par value is not used under IFRS.
3. Which of the following is **false**?
   (a) Under GAAP, companies cannot record gains on transactions involving their own shares.
   (b) Under IFRS, companies cannot record gains on transactions involving their own shares.
   (c) Under IFRS, the statement of stockholders' equity is a required statement.
   (d) Under IFRS, a company records a revaluation surplus when it experiences an increase in the price of its common stock.
4. Which of the following does **not** represent a pair of GAAP/IFRS-comparable terms?
   (a) Additional paid-in capital/Share premium.
   (b) Treasury stock/Repurchase reserve.
   (c) Common stock/Share capital.
   (d) Preferred stock/Preference shares.

IFRS Exercises

IFRS13-1 On May 10, Jaurez Corporation issues 1,000 shares of $10 par value ordinary shares for cash at $18 per share. Journalize the issuance of the shares.

IFRS13-2 Meenen Corporation has the following accounts at December 31 (in euros): Share Capital—Ordinary, €10 par, 5,000 shares issued, €50,000; Share Premium—Ordinary €10,000; Retained Earnings €45,000; and Treasury Shares—Ordinary, 500 shares, €11,000. Prepare the equity section of the statement of financial position.

IFRS13-3 Overton Co. had the following transactions during the current period.

Mar. 2	Issued 5,000 shares of $1 par value ordinary shares to attorneys in payment of a bill for $30,000 for services performed in helping the company to incorporate.
June 12	Issued 60,000 shares of $1 par value ordinary shares for cash of $375,000.
July 11	Issued 1,000 shares of $100 par value preference shares for cash at $110 per share.
Nov. 28	Purchased 2,000 treasury shares for $80,000.

Instructions

Journalize the above transactions.

International Financial Reporting Problem: Louis Vuitton

IFRS13-4 The financial statements of Louis Vuitton are presented in Appendix F. Instructions for accessing and using the company's complete annual report, including the notes to its financial statements, are also provided in Appendix F.

Instructions

Use the company's annual report to answer the following questions.

(a) Determine the following amounts at December 31, 2013: (1) total equity, (2) total revaluation reserve, and (3) number of treasury shares.

(b) Examine the equity section of the company's balance sheet. For each of the following, provide the comparable label that would be used under GAAP: (1) share capital, (2) share premium, and (3) net profit, group share.

Answers to IFRS Self-Test Questions

1. c **2.** c **3.** d **4.** b

Chapter 14 Corporations: Dividends, Retained Earnings, and Income Reporting

Van Meter Inc., an electrical-parts distributor in Cedar Rapids, Iowa, is 100% employee-owned. For many years, the company has issued bonuses in the form of shares of company stock to all of its employees. These bonus distributions typically have a value equal to several weeks of pay. Top management always thought that this was a great program. Therefore, it came as quite a surprise a few years ago when an employee stood up at a company-wide meeting and said that he did not see any real value in receiving the company's shares. Instead, he wanted "a few hundred extra bucks for beer and cigarettes."

As it turned out, many of the company's 340 employees felt this way. Rather than end the stock bonus program, however, the company decided to educate its employees on the value of share ownership. The employees are now taught how to determine the worth of their shares, the rights that come with share ownership, and what they can do to help increase the value of those shares.

As part of the education program, management developed a slogan, "Work ten, get five free." The idea is that after working 10 years, an employee's shares would be worth the equivalent of about five years' worth of salary. For example, a person earning a $30,000 salary would earn $300,000 in wages over a 10-year period. During that same 10-year period, it was likely that the value of the employee's shares would accumulate to about $150,000 (five years' worth of salary). This demonstrates in more concrete terms why employees should be excited about share ownership.

A 12-member employee committee has the responsibility of educating new employees about the program. The committee also runs training programs so that employees understand how their cost-saving actions improve the company's results—and its stock price. It appears that the company's education program to encourage employees to act like owners is working. Profitability has increased rapidly, and employee turnover has fallen from 18% to 8%. Given Van Meter's success, many of the 10,000 other employee-owned companies in the United States might want to investigate whether their employees understand the benefits of share ownership.

Source: Adapted from Simona Covel, "How to Get Workers to Think and Act Like Owners," *Wall Street Journal Online* (February 15, 2008).

LEARNING OBJECTIVES

1. **Explain how to account for cash dividends.**
2. **Explain how to account for stock dividends and splits.**
3. **Prepare and analyze a comprehensive stockholders' equity section.**
4. **Describe the form and content of corporation income statements.**

LEARNING OBJECTIVE 1

Explain how to account for cash dividends.

A dividend is a corporation's distribution of cash or stock to its stockholders on a pro rata (proportional to ownership) basis. Pro rata means that if you own 10% of the common shares, you will receive 10% of the dividend. Dividends can take four forms: cash, property, scrip (a promissory note to pay cash), or stock. Cash dividends predominate in practice although companies also declare stock dividends with some frequency. These two forms of dividends are therefore the focus of discussion in this chapter.

Investors are very interested in a company's dividend practices. In the financial press, **dividends are generally reported quarterly as a dollar amount per share**. (Sometimes they are reported on an annual basis.) For example, Nike's **quarterly** dividend rate in the fourth quarter of 2013 was 24 cents per share. The dividend rate for the fourth quarter of 2013 for GE was 22 cents, and for ConAgra Foods it was 25 cents.

Cash Dividends

A **cash dividend** is a pro rata distribution of cash to stockholders. Cash dividends are not paid on treasury shares. For a corporation to pay a cash dividend, it must have the following.

1. **Retained earnings.** The legality of a cash dividend depends on the laws of the state in which the company is incorporated. Payment of cash dividends from retained earnings is legal in all states. In general, cash dividend distributions from only the balance in common stock (legal capital) are illegal.

   A dividend declared out of paid-in capital is termed a **liquidating dividend**. Such a dividend reduces or "liquidates" the amount originally paid in by stockholders. Statutes vary considerably with respect to cash dividends based on paid-in capital in excess of par or stated value. Many states permit such dividends.

2. **Adequate cash.** The legality of a dividend and the ability to pay a dividend are two different things. For example, Nike, with retained earnings of over \$5.6 billion, could legally declare a dividend of at least \$5.6 billion. But Nike's cash balance is only \$3.3 billion.

   Before declaring a cash dividend, a company's board of directors must carefully consider both current and future demands on the company's cash resources. In some cases, current liabilities may make a cash dividend inappropriate. In other cases, a major plant expansion program may warrant only a relatively small dividend.

3. **Declared dividends.** A company does not pay dividends unless its board of directors decides to do so, at which point the board "declares" the dividend. The board of directors has full authority to determine the amount of income to distribute in the form of a dividend and the amount to retain in the business. Dividends do not accrue like interest on a note payable, and they are not a liability until declared.

The amount and timing of a dividend are important issues for management to consider. The payment of a large cash dividend could lead to liquidity problems for the company. On the other hand, a small dividend or a missed dividend may cause unhappiness among stockholders. Many stockholders expect to receive a reasonable cash payment from the company on a periodic basis. Many companies declare and pay cash dividends quarterly. On the other hand, a number of high-growth companies pay no dividends, preferring to conserve cash to finance future capital expenditures.

ENTRIES FOR CASH DIVIDENDS

Three dates are important in connection with dividends: (1) the declaration date, (2) the record date, and (3) the payment date. Normally, there are two to four weeks between each date. Companies make accounting entries on the declaration date and the payment date.

On the **declaration date**, the board of directors formally declares (authorizes) the cash dividend and announces it to stockholders. The declaration of a cash dividend **commits the corporation to a legal obligation**. The company must make an entry to recognize the increase in Cash Dividends and the increase in the liability Dividends Payable.

To illustrate, assume that on December 1, 2017, the directors of Media General declare a 50 cents per share cash dividend on 100,000 shares of $10 par value common stock. The dividend is $50,000 (100,000 × $0.50). The entry to record the declaration is as follows.

Declaration Date

Dec. 1	Cash Dividends	50,000	
	Dividends Payable		50,000
	(To record declaration of cash dividend)		

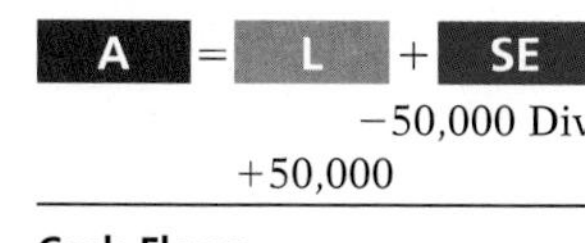

Cash Flows
no effect

Media General debits the account Cash Dividends. Cash dividends decrease retained earnings. We use the specific title Cash Dividends to differentiate it from other types of dividends, such as stock dividends. Dividends Payable is a current liability. It will normally be paid within the next several months. *For homework problems, you should use the Cash Dividends account for recording dividend declarations.*

At the **record date**, the company determines ownership of the outstanding shares for dividend purposes. The stockholders' records maintained by the corporation supply this information. In the interval between the declaration date and the record date, the corporation updates its stock ownership records. For Media General, the record date is December 22. No entry is required on this date because the corporation's liability recognized on the declaration date is unchanged.

Record Date

Dec. 22	No entry		

On the **payment date**, the company makes cash dividend payments to the stockholders of record (as of December 22) and records the payment of the dividend. If January 20 is the payment date for Media General, the entry on that date is as follows.

Payment Date

Jan. 20	Dividends Payable	50,000	
	Cash		50,000
	(To record payment of cash dividend)		

A	=	L	+	SE
		−50,000		
−50,000				

Cash Flows
−50,000

Note that payment of the dividend reduces both current assets and current liabilities. It has no effect on stockholders' equity. The cumulative effect of the declaration and payment of a cash dividend is to **decrease both stockholders' equity and total assets**. Illustration 14-1 (page 490) summarizes the three important dates associated with dividends for Media General.

Illustration 14-1
Key dividend dates

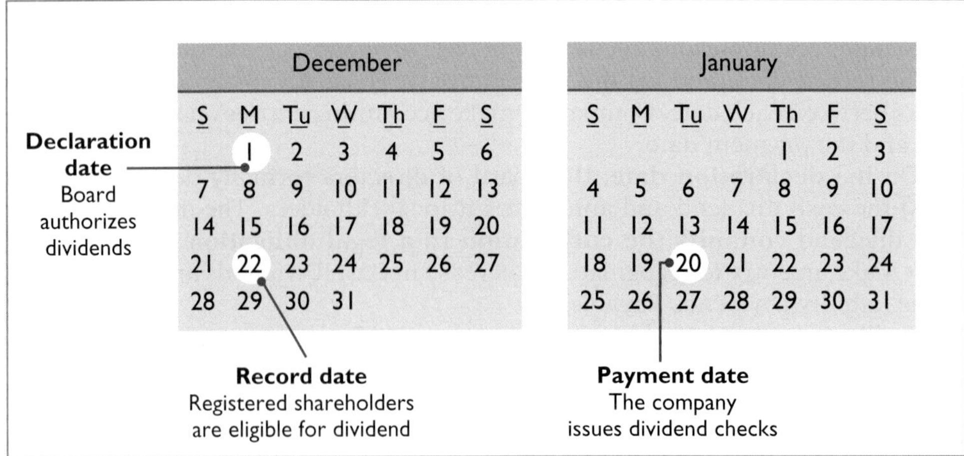

When using a Cash Dividends account, Media General should transfer the balance of that account to Retained Earnings at the end of the year by a closing entry. The entry for Media General at closing is as follows.

Retained Earnings	50,000	
Cash Dividends		50,000
(To close Cash Dividends to Retained Earnings)		

Dividend Preferences

Dividend preferences

Preferred stockholders have the right to receive dividends before common stockholders. For example, if the dividend rate on preferred stock is $5 per share, common shareholders cannot receive any dividends in the current year until preferred stockholders have received $5 per share. The first claim to dividends does not, however, **guarantee** the payment of dividends. Dividends depend on many factors, such as adequate retained earnings and availability of cash. If a company does not pay dividends to preferred stockholders, it cannot pay dividends to common stockholders.

For preferred stock, companies state the per share dividend amount as a percentage of the par value or as a specified amount. For example, Earthlink specifies a 3% dividend on its $100 par value preferred. PepsiCo pays $4.56 per share on its no-par value stock.

Most preferred stocks also have a preference on corporate assets if the corporation fails. This feature provides security for the preferred stockholder. The preference to assets may be for the par value of the shares or for a specified liquidating value. For example, Commonwealth Edison's preferred stock entitles its holders to receive $31.80 per share, plus accrued and unpaid dividends, in the event of liquidation. The liquidation preference establishes the respective claims of creditors and preferred stockholders in litigation involving bankruptcy lawsuits.

CUMULATIVE DIVIDEND

Preferred stock often contains a **cumulative dividend** feature. This feature stipulates that preferred stockholders must be paid both current-year dividends and any unpaid prior-year dividends before common stockholders are paid dividends. When preferred stock is cumulative, preferred dividends not declared in a given period are called **dividends in arrears**.

To illustrate, assume that Scientific Leasing has 5,000 shares of 7%, $100 par value, cumulative preferred stock outstanding. Each $100 share pays a $7 dividend (0.07 × $100). The annual dividend is $35,000 (5,000 × $7 per share). If dividends are two years in arrears, preferred stockholders are entitled to receive the dividends shown in Illustration 14-2.

Dividends in arrears ($35,000 × 2)	$ 70,000
Current-year dividends	35,000
Total preferred dividends	**$105,000**

Illustration 14-2 Computation of total dividends to preferred stock

The company cannot pay dividends to common stockholders until it pays the entire preferred dividend. In other words, companies cannot pay dividends to common stockholders while any preferred dividends are in arrears.

Dividends in arrears are not considered a liability. **No obligation exists until the board of directors formally declares that the corporation will pay a dividend.** However, companies should disclose in the notes to the financial statements the amount of dividends in arrears. Doing so enables investors to assess the potential impact of this commitment on the corporation's financial position.

The investment community does not look favorably on companies that are unable to meet their dividend obligations. As a financial officer noted in discussing one company's failure to pay its cumulative preferred dividend for a period of time, "Not meeting your obligations on something like that is a major black mark on your record."

Payment of a cumulative dividend

Dividend in arrears — Current dividend

Preferred stockholders

ALLOCATING CASH DIVIDENDS BETWEEN PREFERRED AND COMMON STOCK

As indicated, preferred stock has priority over common stock in regard to dividends. Holders of cumulative preferred stock must be paid any unpaid prior-year dividends and their current year's dividend before common stockholders receive dividends.

To illustrate, assume that at December 31, 2017, IBR Inc. has 1,000 shares of 8%, $100 par value cumulative preferred stock. It also has 50,000 shares of $10 par value common stock outstanding. The dividend per share for preferred stock is $8 ($100 par value × 8%). The required annual dividend for preferred stock is therefore $8,000 (1,000 shares × $8). At December 31, 2017, the directors declare a $6,000 cash dividend. In this case, the entire dividend amount goes to preferred stockholders because of their dividend preference. The entry to record the declaration of the dividend is as follows.

Dec. 31	Cash Dividends	6,000	
	Dividends Payable		6,000
	(To record $6 per share cash dividend to preferred stockholders)		

A	=	L	+	SE
				−6,000 Div
		+6,000		

Cash Flows
no effect

Because of the cumulative feature, dividends of $2 ($8 − $6) per share are in arrears on preferred stock for 2017. IBR must pay these dividends to preferred stockholders before it can pay any future dividends to common stockholders. IBR should disclose dividends in arrears in the financial statements.

At December 31, 2018, IBR declares a $50,000 cash dividend. The allocation of the dividend to the two classes of stock is as follows.

Total dividend		$50,000
Allocated to preferred stock		
Dividends in arrears, 2017 (1,000 × $2)	**$2,000**	
2018 dividend (1,000 × $8)	**8,000**	**10,000**
Remainder allocated to common stock		$40,000

Illustration 14-3 Allocating dividends to preferred and common stock

The entry to record the declaration of the dividend is as follows.

Dec. 31	Cash Dividends	50,000	
	Dividends Payable		50,000
	(To record declaration of cash dividends of $10,000 to preferred stock and $40,000 to common stock)		

A	=	L	+	SE
				−50,000 Div
		+50,000		

Cash Flows
no effect

If IBR's preferred stock is not cumulative, preferred stockholders receive only $8,000 in dividends in 2018. Common stockholders receive $42,000.

LEARNING OBJECTIVE 2

Explain how to account for stock dividends and splits.

Stock Dividends

A **stock dividend** is a pro rata (proportional to ownership) distribution of the corporation's own stock to stockholders. Whereas a company pays cash in a cash dividend, a company issues shares of stock in a stock dividend. **A stock dividend results in a decrease in retained earnings and an increase in paid-in capital.** Unlike a cash dividend, a stock dividend does not decrease total stockholders' equity or total assets.

To illustrate, assume that you have a 2% ownership interest in Cetus Inc. That is, you own 20 of its 1,000 shares of common stock. If Cetus declares a 10% stock dividend, it would issue 100 shares (1,000 × 10%) of stock. You would receive two shares (2% × 100). Would your ownership interest change? No, it would remain at 2% (22 ÷ 1,100). **You now own more shares of stock, but your ownership interest has not changed.**

Cetus has disbursed no cash and has assumed no liabilities. What, then, are the purposes and benefits of a stock dividend? Corporations issue stock dividends generally for one or more of the following reasons.

1. To satisfy stockholders' dividend expectations without spending cash.
2. To increase the marketability of the corporation's stock. When the number of shares outstanding increases, the market price per share decreases. Decreasing the market price of the stock makes it easier for smaller investors to purchase the shares.
3. To emphasize that a company has permanently reinvested in the business a portion of stockholders' equity, which therefore is unavailable for cash dividends.

When the dividend is declared, the board of directors determines the size of the stock dividend and the value assigned to each dividend.

Generally, if the company issues a **small stock dividend** (less than 20–25% of the corporation's issued stock), the value assigned to the dividend is the fair value (market price) per share. This treatment is based on the assumption that a small stock dividend will have little effect on the market price of the shares previously outstanding. Thus, many stockholders consider small stock dividends to be distributions of earnings equal to the market price of the shares distributed. If a company issues a **large stock dividend** (greater than 20–25%), the price assigned to the dividend is the par or stated value. Small stock dividends predominate in practice. Thus, we will illustrate only entries for small stock dividends.

ENTRIES FOR STOCK DIVIDENDS

To illustrate the accounting for small stock dividends, assume that Medland Corporation has a balance of $300,000 in retained earnings. It declares a 10% stock dividend on its 50,000 shares of $10 par value common stock. The current market price of its stock is $15 per share. The number of shares to be issued is 5,000 (10% × 50,000). Therefore, the total amount to be debited to Stock Dividends is $75,000 (5,000 × $15). The entry to record the declaration of the stock dividend is as follows.

A	=	L	+	SE
				−75,000 Div
				+50,000 CS
				+25,000 CS

Cash Flows
no effect

	Debit	Credit
Stock Dividends	75,000	
Common Stock Dividends Distributable		50,000
Paid-in Capital in Excess of Par—Common Stock		25,000
(To record declaration of 10% stock dividend)		

Medland debits Stock Dividends for the market price of the stock issued ($15 × 5,000). (Similar to Cash Dividends, Stock Dividends decrease retained earnings.) Medland also credits Common Stock Dividends Distributable for the par value of the dividend shares ($10 × 5,000) and credits Paid-in Capital in Excess of Par—Common Stock for the excess of the market price over par ($5 × 5,000).

Common Stock Dividends Distributable is a **stockholders' equity account.** It is not a liability because assets will not be used to pay the dividend. If the company prepares a balance sheet before it issues the dividend shares, it reports the distributable account under paid-in capital as shown in Illustration 14-4.

Illustration 14-4
Statement presentation of common stock dividends distributable

Paid-in capital	
Common stock	$500,000
Common stock dividends distributable	**50,000**
Paid-in capital in excess of par—common stock	25,000
Total paid-in capital	$575,000

When Medland issues the dividend shares, it debits Common Stock Dividends Distributable and credits Common Stock, as follows.

Common Stock Dividends Distributable	50,000	
Common Stock		50,000
(To record issuance of 5,000 shares in a stock dividend)		

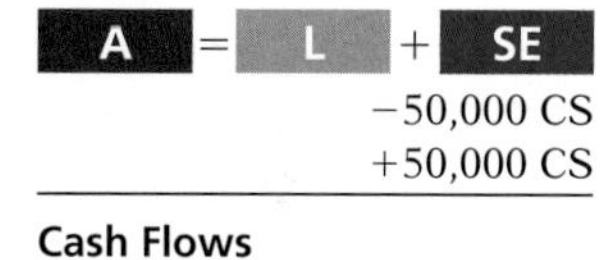

EFFECTS OF STOCK DIVIDENDS

How do stock dividends affect stockholders' equity? They **change the composition of stockholders' equity** because they transfer a portion of retained earnings to paid-in capital. However, **total stockholders' equity remains the same**. Stock dividends also have no effect on the par or stated value per share, but the number of shares outstanding increases. Illustration 14-5 shows these effects for Medland.

Illustration 14-5
Stock dividend effects

	Before Dividend	Change	After Dividend
Stockholders' equity			
Paid-in capital			
Common stock, $10 par	$ 500,000	$ 50,000	$ 550,000
Paid-in capital in excess of par	—	25,000	25,000
Total paid-in capital	500,000	+75,000	575,000
Retained earnings	300,000	−75,000	225,000
Total stockholders' equity	**$800,000**	**$ 0**	**$800,000**
Outstanding shares	**50,000**	**+5,000**	**55,000**
Par value per share	**$10.00**	**$ 0**	**$10.00**

In this example, total paid-in capital increases by $75,000 (50,000 shares × 10% × $15) and retained earnings decreases by the same amount. Note also that total stockholders' equity remains unchanged at $800,000. The number of shares increases by 5,000 (50,000 × 10%).

Stock Splits

A **stock split**, like a stock dividend, involves issuance of additional shares to stockholders according to their percentage ownership. **However, a stock split results in a reduction in the par or stated value per share.** The purpose of a stock split is to increase the marketability of the stock by lowering its market price per share. This, in turn, makes it easier for the corporation to issue additional stock.

The effect of a split on market price is generally **inversely proportional** to the size of the split. For example, after a 2-for-1 stock split, the market price of Nike's stock fell from $111 to approximately $55. The lower market price stimulated market activity. Within one year, the stock was trading above $100 again. Illustration 14-6 shows the effect of a 4-for-1 stock split for stockholders.

Illustration 14-6
Effect of stock split for stockholders

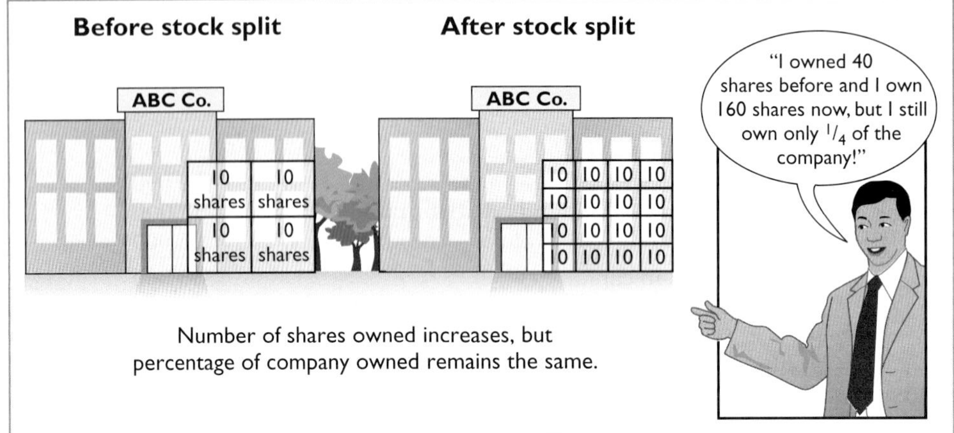

In a stock split, the company increases the number of shares in the same proportion that par or stated value per share decreases. For example, in a 2-for-1 split, the company exchanges one share of $10 par value stock for two shares of $5 par value stock. **A stock split does not have any effect on total paid-in capital, retained earnings, or total stockholders' equity.** However, the number of shares outstanding increases, and par value per share decreases. Illustration 14-7 shows these effects for Medland Corporation, assuming that it splits its 50,000 shares of common stock on a 2-for-1 basis.

Illustration 14-7
Stock split effects

	Before Stock Split	Change	After Stock Split
Stockholders' equity			
Paid-in capital			
Common stock	$ 500,000		$ 500,000
Paid-in capital in excess of par	–0–		–0–
Total paid-in capital	500,000	$ 0	500,000
Retained earnings	300,000	0	300,000
Total stockholders' equity	**$800,000**	**$ 0**	**$800,000**
Outstanding shares	**50,000**	**+50,000**	**100,000**
Par value per share	**$10.00**	**−$5.00**	**$5.00**

A stock split does not affect the balances in any stockholders' equity accounts. Therefore, **a company does not need to journalize a stock split**.

Illustration 14-8 summarizes the differences between stock dividends and stock splits.

Illustration 14-8
Differences between the effects of stock dividends and stock splits

Item	Stock Dividend	Stock Split
Total paid-in capital	Increase	No change
Total retained earnings	Decrease	No change
Total par value (common stock)	Increase	No change
Par value per share	No change	Decrease
Outstanding shares	Increase	Increase
Total stockholders' equity	No change	No change

Prepare and analyze a comprehensive stockholders' equity section.

Retained Earnings

Retained earnings is net income that a company retains in the business. The balance in retained earnings is part of the stockholders' claim on the total assets of the corporation. It does not, however, represent a claim on any specific asset. Nor can the amount of retained earnings be associated with the balance of any asset account. For example, a $100,000 balance in retained earnings does not mean that there should be $100,000 in cash. The reason is that the company may have used the cash resulting from the excess of revenues over expenses to purchase buildings, equipment, and other assets.

To demonstrate that retained earnings and cash may be quite different, Illustration 14-9 shows recent amounts of retained earnings and cash in selected companies.

Illustration 14-9
Retained earnings and cash balances

(in millions)		
Company	**Retained Earnings**	**Cash**
Facebook	$ 3,159	$3,323
Google	61,262	8,989
Nike, Inc.	5,695	3,337
Starbucks	4,130	2,576
Amazon.com	2,190	8,658

Remember from Chapter 13 that when a company has net income, it closes net income to retained earnings. The closing entry is a debit to Income Summary and a credit to Retained Earnings.

When a company has a **net loss** (expenses exceed revenues), it also closes this amount to retained earnings. The closing entry is a debit to Retained Earnings and a credit to Income Summary. To illustrate, assume that Rendle Corporation has a net loss of $400,000 in 2017. The closing entry to record this loss is as follows.

	Debit	Credit
Retained Earnings	400,000	
Income Summary		400,000
(To close net loss to Retained Earnings)		

This closing entry is done even if it results in a debit balance in Retained Earnings. **Companies do not debit net losses to paid-in capital accounts.** To do so would destroy the distinction between paid-in and earned capital. If cumulative losses exceed cumulative income over a company's life, a debit balance in Retained Earnings results. A debit balance in Retained Earnings is identified as a **deficit**. A company reports a deficit as a deduction in the stockholders' equity section, as shown in Illustration 14-10.

Illustration 14-10
Stockholders' equity with deficit

Balance Sheet (partial)	
Stockholders' equity	
Paid-in capital	
Common stock	$800,000
Retained earnings (deficit)	**(50,000)**
Total stockholders' equity	$750,000

RETAINED EARNINGS RESTRICTIONS

The balance in retained earnings is generally available for dividend declarations. In some cases, however, there may be **retained earnings restrictions**. These make a portion of the retained earnings balance currently unavailable for dividends. Restrictions result from one or more of the following causes.

1. **Legal restrictions.** Many states require a corporation to restrict retained earnings for the cost of treasury stock purchased. The restriction keeps intact the corporation's legal capital that is being temporarily held as treasury stock. When the company sells the treasury stock, the restriction is lifted.
2. **Contractual restrictions.** Long-term debt contracts may restrict retained earnings as a condition for the loan. The restriction limits the use of corporate assets for payment of dividends. Thus, it increases the likelihood that the corporation will be able to meet required loan payments.
3. **Voluntary restrictions.** The board of directors may voluntarily create retained earnings restrictions for specific purposes. For example, the board may authorize a restriction for future plant expansion. By reducing the amount of retained earnings available for dividends, the company makes more cash available for the planned expansion.

Companies generally disclose **retained earnings restrictions** in the notes to the financial statements. For example, as shown in Illustration 14-11, Tektronix Inc., a manufacturer of electronic measurement devices, had total retained earnings of $774 million, but the unrestricted portion was only $223.8 million.

Illustration 14-11
Disclosure of restriction

Real World

TEKTRONIX INC.
Notes to the Financial Statements

Certain of the Company's debt agreements require compliance with debt covenants. Management believes that the Company is in compliance with such requirements. The Company had unrestricted retained earnings of $223.8 million after meeting those requirements.

PRIOR PERIOD ADJUSTMENTS

Suppose that a corporation has closed its books and issued financial statements. The corporation then discovers that it made a material error in reporting net income of a prior year. How should the company record this situation in the accounts and report it in the financial statements?

The correction of an error in previously issued financial statements is known as a **prior period adjustment**. The company makes the correction directly to Retained Earnings because the effect of the error is now in this account. The net income for the prior period has been recorded in retained earnings through the journalizing and posting of closing entries.

To illustrate, assume that General Microwave discovers in 2017 that it understated depreciation expense on equipment in 2016 by $300,000 due to computational errors. These errors overstated both net income for 2016 and the current balance in retained earnings. The entry for the prior period adjustment, ignoring all tax effects, is as follows.

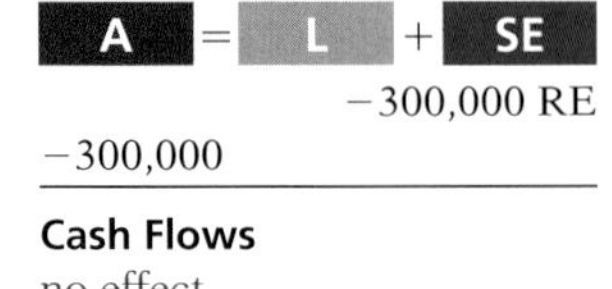

	Debit	Credit
Retained Earnings	300,000	
Accumulated Depreciation—Equipment		300,000
(To adjust for understatement of depreciation in a prior period)		

A debit to an income statement account in 2017 is incorrect because the error pertains to a prior year.

Companies report prior period adjustments in the retained earnings statement. They add (or deduct, as the case may be) these adjustments from the beginning retained earnings balance. This results in an adjusted beginning balance. For example, assuming a beginning balance of $800,000 in retained earnings, General Microwave reports the prior period adjustment as follows.

Illustration 14-12
Statement presentation of prior period adjustments

GENERAL MICROWAVE Retained Earnings Statement (partial)	
Balance, January 1, as reported	$ 800,000
Correction for overstatement of net income in prior period (depreciation error)	**(300,000)**
Balance, January 1, as adjusted	$ 500,000

Again, reporting the correction in the current year's income statement would be incorrect because it applies to a prior year's income statement.

RETAINED EARNINGS STATEMENT

The **retained earnings statement** shows the changes in retained earnings during the year. The company prepares the statement from the Retained Earnings account. Illustration 14-13 shows (in T-account form) transactions that affect retained earnings.

Illustration 14-13
Debits and credits to retained earnings

Retained Earnings	
1. Net loss	1. Net income
2. Prior period adjustments for overstatement of net income	2. Prior period adjustments for understatement of net income
3. Cash dividends and stock dividends	
4. Some disposals of treasury stock	

As indicated, net income increases retained earnings, and a net loss decreases retained earnings. Prior period adjustments may either increase or decrease retained earnings. Both cash dividends and stock dividends decrease retained earnings. The circumstances under which treasury stock transactions decrease retained earnings are explained in Chapter 13, page 471.

A complete retained earnings statement for Graber Inc., based on assumed data, is shown in Illustration 14-14.

Illustration 14-14
Retained earnings statement

GRABER INC. Retained Earnings Statement For the Year Ended December 31, 2017		
Balance, January 1, as reported		$1,050,000
Correction for understatement of net income in prior period (inventory error)		50,000
Balance, January 1, as adjusted		1,100,000
Add: Net income		360,000
		1,460,000
Less: Cash dividends	$100,000	
Stock dividends	200,000	300,000
Balance, December 31		$1,160,000

Statement Presentation and Analysis

PRESENTATION

Illustration 14-15 presents the stockholders' equity section of Graber Inc.'s balance sheet. Note the following: (1) "Common stock dividends distributable" is shown under "Capital stock" in "Paid-in capital" and (2) a note (Note R) discloses a retained earnings restriction.

Illustration 14-15
Comprehensive stockholders' equity section

GRABER INC. Balance Sheet (partial)		
Stockholders' equity		
Paid-in capital		
Capital stock		
9% Preferred stock, $100 par value, cumulative, callable at $120, 10,000 shares authorized, 6,000 shares issued and outstanding		$ 600,000
Common stock, no par, $5 stated value, 500,000 shares authorized, 400,000 shares issued and 390,000 shares outstanding	$2,000,000	
Common stock dividends distributable	**50,000**	2,050,000
Total capital stock		2,650,000
Additional paid-in capital		
In excess of par—preferred stock	30,000	
In excess of stated value—common stock	1,050,000	
Total additional paid-in capital		1,080,000
Total paid-in capital		3,730,000
Retained earnings **(see Note R)**		1,160,000
Total paid-in capital and retained earnings		4,890,000
Less: Treasury stock (10,000 common shares)		80,000
Total stockholders' equity		$4,810,000

Note R: Retained earnings is restricted for the cost of treasury stock, $80,000.

Instead of presenting a detailed stockholders' equity section in the balance sheet and a retained earnings statement, many companies prepare a **stockholders' equity statement**. This statement shows the changes (1) in each stockholders' equity account and (2) in total that occurred during the year. An example of a stockholders' equity statement appears in **Apple**'s financial statements in Appendix A.

ANALYSIS

Investors and analysts can measure profitability from the viewpoint of the common stockholder by the **return on common stockholders' equity**. This ratio, as shown in Illustration 14-16, indicates how many dollars of net income the company earned for each dollar invested by the common stockholders. It is computed by dividing **net income available to common stockholders** (which is net income minus preferred stock dividends) by average common stockholders' equity.

To illustrate, **Walt Disney Company**'s beginning-of-the-year and end-of-the-year common stockholders' equity were $31,820 and $30,753 million, respectively. Its net income was $4,687 million, and no preferred stock was outstanding. The return on common stockholders' equity is computed as follows.

Net Income minus Preferred Dividends	÷	Average Common Stockholders' Equity	=	Return on Common Stockholders' Equity
($4,687 − $0)	÷	$\frac{(\$31,820 + \$30,753)}{2}$	=	**15.0%**

Illustration 14-16
Return on common stockholders' equity and computation

As shown above, if a company has preferred stock, we would deduct the amount of **preferred dividends** from the company's net income to compute income available to common stockholders. Also, the par value of preferred stock is deducted from total stockholders' equity when computing the average common stockholders' equity.

LEARNING OBJECTIVE 4 **Describe the form and content of corporation income statements.**

Income Statement Presentation

Income statements for **corporations are the same as the statements for proprietorships or partnerships except for one thing: the reporting of income taxes**. For income tax purposes, corporations are a separate legal entity. As a result, corporations report **income tax expense** in a separate section of the corporation income statement, before net income. The condensed income statement for Leads Inc. in Illustration 14-17 shows a typical presentation. Note that the corporation reports income before income taxes as one line item and income tax expense as another.

Illustration 14-17
Income statement with income taxes

LEADS INC.
Income Statement
For the Year Ended December 31, 2017

Sales revenue	$800,000
Cost of goods sold	600,000
Gross profit	200,000
Operating expenses	50,000
Income from operations	150,000
Other revenues and gains	10,000
Other expenses and losses	(4,000)
Income before income taxes	**156,000**
Income tax expense	**46,800**
Net income	$109,200

Companies record income tax expense and the related liability for income taxes payable as part of the adjusting process. Using the data for Leads Inc., in Illustration 14-17, the adjusting entry for income tax expense at December 31, 2017, is as follows.

Income Tax Expense	46,800	
Income Taxes Payable		46,800
(To record income taxes for 2017)		

A	=	L	+	SE
				−46,800 Exp
		+46,800		

Cash Flows
no effect

The income statement of **Apple** (in Appendix A) presents another illustration of income taxes.

Income Statement Analysis

The financial press frequently reports earnings data. Stockholders and potential investors widely use these data in evaluating the profitability of a company. A convenient measure of earnings is **earnings per share (EPS)**, which indicates the net income earned by each share of outstanding **common stock**.

EPS AND PREFERRED DIVIDENDS

The existence of preferred dividends slightly complicates the calculation of EPS. When a corporation has both preferred and common stock, we must subtract the current year's preferred dividend from net income, to arrive at **income available to common stockholders**. Illustration 14-18 shows the formula for computing EPS.

Illustration 14-18
Formula for earnings per share

Net Income minus Preferred Dividends	÷	Weighted-Average Common Shares Outstanding	=	Earnings per Share

To illustrate, assume that Rally Inc. reports net income of $211,000 on its 102,500 weighted-average common shares.[1] During the year, it also declares a $6,000 dividend on its preferred stock. Therefore, the amount Rally has available for common stock dividends is $205,000 ($211,000 − $6,000). Earnings per share is $2 ($205,000 ÷ 102,500). If the preferred stock is cumulative, Rally deducts the dividend for the current year, whether or not it is declared. Remember that companies report **earnings per share only for common stock**.

Investors often attempt to link earnings per share to the market price per share of a company's stock.[2] Because of the importance of earnings per share, most companies must report it on the face of the income statement. Generally, companies simply report this amount below net income on the statement. For Rally Inc., the presentation is as follows.

Illustration 14-19
Basic earnings per share disclosure

RALLY INC. Income Statement (partial)	
Net income	$211,000
Earnings per share	**$2.00**

[1]The calculation of the weighted average of common shares outstanding is discussed in advanced accounting courses.

[2]The ratio of the market price per share to the earnings per share is called the **price/earnings (P/E) ratio**. The financial media report this ratio for common stocks listed on major stock exchanges.

REVIEW AND PRACTICE

LEARNING OBJECTIVES REVIEW

1 **Explain how to account for cash dividends.** Companies make entries for cash dividends at the declaration date and at the payment date. At the **declaration date**, the entry is debit Cash Dividends and credit Dividends Payable. At the **payment date**, the entry is debit Dividends Payable and credit Cash.

2 **Explain how to account for stock dividends and splits.** At the declaration date, the entry for a small stock dividend is debit Stock Dividends, credit Paid-in Capital in Excess of Par (or Stated Value)—Common Stock, and credit Common Stock Dividends Distributable.

At the payment date, the entry for a small stock dividend is debit Common Stock Dividends Distributable and credit Common Stock. A stock split reduces the par or stated value per share and increases the number of shares but does not affect balances in stockholders' equity accounts.

3 Prepare and analyze a comprehensive stockholders' equity section. Companies report each of the individual debits and credits to retained earnings in the retained earnings statement. Additions consist of net income and prior period adjustments to correct understatements of prior years' net income. Deductions consist of net loss, prior period adjustments to correct overstatements of prior years' net income, cash and stock dividends, and some disposals of treasury stock.

A comprehensive stockholders' equity section includes all stockholders' equity accounts. It consists of two sections: paid-in capital and retained earnings. It should also include notes to the financial statements that explain any restrictions on retained earnings and any dividends in arrears. One measure of profitability is the return on common stockholders' equity. It is calculated by dividing net income minus preferred stock dividends by average common stockholders' equity.

4 Describe the form and content of corporation income statements. The form and content of corporation income statements are similar to the statements of proprietorships and partnerships with one exception: Corporations must report income taxes or income tax expense in a separate section before net income in the income statement.

Companies compute earnings per share by dividing net income by the weighted-average number of common shares outstanding during the period. When preferred stock dividends exist, they must be deducted from net income in order to calculate EPS.

GLOSSARY REVIEW

Cash dividend A pro rata distribution of cash to stockholders.

Cumulative dividend A feature of preferred stock entitling the stockholder to receive current-year and any unpaid prior-year dividends before common stockholders are paid dividends.

Declaration date The date the board of directors formally declares (authorizes) a dividend and announces it to stockholders.

Deficit A debit balance in retained earnings.

Dividend A corporation's distribution of cash or stock to its stockholders on a pro rata (proportional) basis.

Earnings per share The net income earned by each share of outstanding common stock.

Liquidating dividend A dividend declared out of paid-in capital.

Payment date The date dividends are transferred to stockholders.

Prior period adjustment The correction of an error in previously issued financial statements.

Record date The date when ownership of outstanding shares is determined for dividend purposes.

Retained earnings Net income that a company retains in the business.

Retained earnings restrictions Circumstances that make a portion of retained earnings currently unavailable for dividends.

Retained earnings statement A financial statement that shows the changes in retained earnings during the year.

Return on common stockholders' equity A measure of profitability that shows how many dollars of net income were earned for each dollar invested by the owners; computed as net income minus preferred dividends divided by average common stockholders' equity.

Stock dividend A pro rata distribution to stockholders of the corporation's own stock.

Stockholders' equity statement A statement that shows the changes in each stockholders' equity account and in total stockholders' equity during the year.

Stock split The issuance of additional shares of stock to stockholders according to their percentage ownership. It is accompanied by a reduction in the par or stated value per share.

PRACTICE EXERCISES

Allocate cash dividends to preferred and common stock. (LO 1)

1. At December 31, 2017, Lebron Company distributes $50,000 of cash dividends. Its outstanding common stock has a par value of $400,000, and its 6% preferred stock has a par value of $100,000 at December 31, 2017.

Instructions

(a) Show the allocation of dividends to each class of stock, assuming that the preferred stock dividend is 6% and not cumulative.

(b) Show the allocation of the dividends to each class of stock, assuming the preferred stock dividend of 6% is cumulative and Lebron Company did not pay any dividends on the preferred stock in the preceding 2 years.

(c) Journalize the declaration of the cash dividend at December 31, 2017, assuming the requirements in part (b).

Solution

1. (a)

	2017
Total dividend declaration	$50,000
Allocation to preferred stock (6% × $100,000)	(6,000)
Remainder to common stock	$44,000

(b)

	2017
Total dividend declaration	$50,000
Allocation to preferred stock (6% × $100,000 × 3)	(18,000)
Remainder to common stock	$32,000

(c)

Date	Account	Debit	Credit
Dec. 31	Cash Dividends	50,000	
	Dividends Payable		50,000

Journalize cash dividends; indicate statement presentation.

(LO 1, 3)

2. On January 1, Michelle Corporation had 95,000 shares of no-par common stock issued and outstanding. The stock has a stated value of $5 per share. During the year, the following occurred.

Apr. 1	Issued 55,000 additional shares of common stock for $17 per share.
June 15	Declared a cash dividend of $1 per share to stockholders of record on June 30.
July 10	Paid the $1 cash dividend.
Dec. 1	Issued 2,000 additional shares of common stock for $19 per share.
15	Declared a cash dividend on outstanding shares of $1.20 per share to stockholders of record on December 31.

Instructions

(a) Prepare the entries, if any, on each of the three dividend dates.

(b) How are dividends and dividends payable reported in the financial statements prepared at December 31?

Solution

2. (a)

Date	Account	Debit	Credit
June 15	Cash Dividends (150,000 × $1)	150,000	
	Dividends Payable		150,000
July 10	Dividends Payable	150,000	
	Cash		150,000
Dec. 15	Cash Dividends (152,000 × $1.20)	182,400	
	Dividends Payable		182,400

(b) In the retained earnings statement, dividends of $332,400 will be deducted. In the balance sheet, Dividends Payable of $182,400 will be reported as a current liability.

Prepare a retained earnings statement.

(LO 3)

3. Oswald Company reported retained earnings at December 31, 2016, of $400,000. Oswald had 200,000 shares of common stock outstanding throughout 2017.

The following transactions occurred during 2017.

1. An error was discovered; in 2015, insurance expense was recorded at $90,000, but the correct amount was $60,000.
2. A cash dividend of $0.50 per share was declared and paid.
3. A 5% stock dividend was declared and distributed when the market price per share was $18 per share.
4. Net income was $310,000.

Instruction

Prepare a retained earnings statement for 2017.

Solution

OSWALD COMPANY Retained Earnings Statement For the Year Ended December 31, 2017		
Balance, January 1, as reported		$400,000
Correction for understatement of 2015 net income		30,000
Balance, January 1, as adjusted		430,000
Add: Net income		310,000
		740,000
Less: Cash dividends	$100,000*	
Stock dividends	180,000**	280,000
Balance, December 31		$460,000

*(200,000 × $0.50/sh); **(200,000 × 0.05 × $18/sh)

PRACTICE PROBLEM

Prepare dividend entries and stockholders' equity section.

(LO 1, 2, 3)

On January 1, 2017, Hayslett Corporation had the following stockholders' equity accounts.

Common Stock ($10 par value, 260,000 shares issued and outstanding)	$2,600,000
Paid-in Capital in Excess of Par—Common Stock	1,500,000
Retained Earnings	3,200,000

During the year, the following transactions occurred.

April 1 Declared a $1.50 cash dividend per share to stockholders of record on April 15, payable May 1.
May 1 Paid the dividend declared in April.
June 1 Announced a 2-for-1 stock split. Prior to the split, the market price per share was $24.
Aug. 1 Declared a 10% stock dividend to stockholders of record on August 15, distributable August 31. On August 1, the market price of the stock was $10 per share.
31 Issued the shares for the stock dividend.
Dec. 1 Declared a $1.50 per share dividend to stockholders of record on December 15, payable January 5, 2018.
31 Determined that net income for the year was $600,000.

Instructions

(a) Journalize the transactions and the closing entries for net income, stock dividends, and cash dividends.

(b) Prepare a stockholders' equity section at December 31.

Solution

(a) Apr.	1	Cash Dividends (260,000 × $1.50)	390,000	
		Dividends Payable		390,000
May	1	Dividends Payable	390,000	
		Cash		390,000
June	1	No journal entry needed for stock split		
Aug.	1	Stock Dividends (52,000* × $10)	520,000	
		Common Stock Dividends Distributable (52,000 × $5)		260,000
		Paid-in Capital in Excess of Par—Common Stock (52,000 × $5)		260,000
		*520,000 × .10		
	31	Common Stock Dividends Distributable	260,000	
		Common Stock		260,000

Dec. 1	Cash Dividends (572,000** × $1.50)	858,000	
	Dividends Payable		858,000
	**(260,000 × 2) + 52,000		
31	Income Summary	600,000	
	Retained Earnings		600,000
31	Retained Earnings	1,768,000	
	Stock Dividends		520,000
	Cash Dividends ($390,000 + $858,000)		1,248,000

(b)

HAYSLETT CORPORATION
Balance Sheet (Partial)

Stockholders' equity	
Paid-in capital	
Capital stock	
Common stock, $5 par value, 572,000 shares issued and outstanding	$2,860,000
Paid-in capital in excess of par—common stock	1,760,000
Total paid-in capital	4,620,000
Retained earnings	2,032,000*
Total stockholders' equity	$6,652,000

*$3,200,000 + $600,000 − $390,000 − $520,000 − $858,000

EXERCISES

Journalize cash dividends; indicate statement presentation.

(LO 1)

E14-1 On January 1, Guillen Corporation had 95,000 shares of no-par common stock issued and outstanding. The stock has a stated value of $5 per share. During the year, the following occurred.

Apr. 1	Issued 25,000 additional shares of common stock for $17 per share.
June 15	Declared a cash dividend of $1 per share to stockholders of record on June 30.
July 10	Paid the $1 cash dividend.
Dec. 1	Issued 2,000 additional shares of common stock for $19 per share.
15	Declared a cash dividend on outstanding shares of $1.20 per share to stockholders of record on December 31.

Instructions

(a) Prepare the entries to record these transactions.

(b) How are dividends and dividends payable reported in the financial statements prepared at December 31?

Allocate cash dividends to preferred and common stock.

(LO 1)

E14-2 Knudsen Corporation was organized on January 1, 2016. During its first year, the corporation issued 2,000 shares of $50 par value preferred stock and 100,000 shares of $10 par value common stock. At December 31, the company declared the following cash dividends: 2016, $5,000; 2017, $12,000; and 2018, $28,000.

Instructions

(a) Show the allocation of dividends to each class of stock, assuming the preferred stock dividend is 6% and noncumulative.

(b) Show the allocation of dividends to each class of stock, assuming the preferred stock dividend is 7% and cumulative.

(c) Journalize the declaration of the cash dividend at December 31, 2018, under part (b).

Journalize stock dividends.

(LO 2)

E14-3 On January 1, 2017, Frontier Corporation had $1,000,000 of common stock outstanding that was issued at par. It also had retained earnings of $750,000. The company issued 40,000 shares of common stock at par on July 1 and earned net income of $400,000 for the year.

Instructions

Journalize the declaration of a 15% stock dividend on December 10, 2017, for the following independent assumptions.

(a) Par value is $10, and market price is $18.
(b) Par value is $5, and market price is $20.

Compare effects of a stock dividend and a stock split.

(LO 2)

E14-4 On October 31, the stockholders' equity section of Heins Company consists of common stock $500,000 and retained earnings $900,000. Heins is considering the following two courses of action: (1) declaring a 5% stock dividend on the 50,000, $10 par value shares outstanding, or (2) effecting a 2-for-1 stock split that will reduce par value to $5 per share. The current market price is $14 per share.

Instructions

Prepare a tabular summary of the effects of the alternative actions on the components of stockholders' equity, outstanding shares, and par value per share. Use the following column headings: Before Action, After Stock Dividend, and After Stock Split.

Indicate account balances after a stock dividend.

(LO 2)

E14-5 On October 1, Little Bobby Corporation's stockholders' equity is as follows.

Common stock, $5 par value	$400,000
Paid-in capital in excess of par—common stock	25,000
Retained earnings	155,000
Total stockholders' equity	$580,000

On October 1, Little Bobby declares and distributes a 10% stock dividend when the market price of the stock is $15 per share.

Instructions

(a) Compute the par value per share (1) before the stock dividend and (2) after the stock dividend.
(b) Indicate the balances in the three stockholders' equity accounts after the stock dividend shares have been distributed.

Indicate the effects on stockholders' equity components.

(LO 1, 2, 3)

E14-6 During 2017, Roblez Corporation had the following transactions and events.

1. Declared a cash dividend.
2. Issued par value common stock for cash at par value.
3. Completed a 2-for-1 stock split in which $10 par value stock was changed to $5 par value stock.
4. Declared a small stock dividend when the market price was higher than par value.
5. Made a prior period adjustment for overstatement of net income.
6. Issued the shares of common stock required by the stock dividend declaration in item no. 4 above.
7. Paid the cash dividend in item no. 1 above.
8. Issued par value common stock for cash above par value.

Instructions

Indicate the effect(s) of each of the foregoing items on the subdivisions of stockholders' equity. Present your answer in tabular form with the following columns. Use (I) for increase, (D) for decrease, and (NE) for no effect. Item no. 1 is given as an example.

	Paid-in Capital		
Item	**Capital Stock**	**Additional**	**Retained Earnings**
1	NE	NE	D

Prepare correcting entries for dividends and a stock split.

(LO 2)

E14-7 Before preparing financial statements for the current year, the chief accountant for Toso Company discovered the following errors in the accounts.

1. The declaration and payment of $50,000 cash dividend was recorded as a debit to Interest Expense $50,000 and a credit to Cash $50,000.
2. A 10% stock dividend (1,000 shares) was declared on the $10 par value stock when the market price per share was $18. The only entry made was Stock Dividends (Dr.) $10,000 and Dividend Payable (Cr.) $10,000. The shares have not been issued.
3. A 4-for-1 stock split involving the issue of 400,000 shares of $5 par value common stock for 100,000 shares of $20 par value common stock was recorded as a debit to Retained Earnings $2,000,000 and a credit to Common Stock $2,000,000.

Instructions

Prepare the correcting entries at December 31.

Prepare a retained earnings statement.
(LO 3)

E14-8 On January 1, 2017, Eddy Corporation had retained earnings of $650,000. During the year, Eddy had the following selected transactions.

1. Declared cash dividends $120,000.
2. Corrected overstatement of 2016 net income because of inventory error $40,000.
3. Earned net income $350,000.
4. Declared stock dividends $90,000.

Instructions

Prepare a retained earnings statement for the year.

Prepare a retained earnings statement.
(LO 3)

E14-9 Newland Company reported retained earnings at December 31, 2016, of $310,000. Newland had 200,000 shares of common stock outstanding at the beginning of 2017.

The following transactions occurred during 2017.

1. An error was discovered. In 2015, depreciation expense was recorded at $70,000, but the correct amount was $50,000.
2. A cash dividend of $0.50 per share was declared and paid.
3. A 5% stock dividend was declared and distributed when the market price per share was $15 per share.
4. Net income was $285,000.

Instructions

Prepare a retained earnings statement for 2017.

Prepare a stockholders' equity section.
(LO 3)

E14-10 Dirk Company reported the following balances at December 31, 2016: common stock $500,000, paid-in capital in excess of par value—common stock $100,000, and retained earnings $250,000. During 2017, the following transactions affected stockholders' equity.

1. Issued preferred stock with a par value of $125,000 for $200,000.
2. Purchased treasury stock (common) for $40,000.
3. Earned net income of $180,000.
4. Declared and paid cash dividends of $56,000.

Instructions

Prepare the stockholders' equity section of Dirk Company's December 31, 2017, balance sheet.

Prepare a stockholders' equity section.
(LO 3)

E14-11 The following accounts appear in the ledger of Horner Inc. after the books are closed at December 31.

Common Stock, no par, $1 stated value, 400,000 shares authorized; 300,000 shares issued	$ 300,000
Common Stock Dividends Distributable	30,000
Paid-in Capital in Excess of Stated Value—Common Stock	1,200,000
Preferred Stock, $5 par value, 8%, 40,000 shares authorized; 30,000 shares issued	150,000
Retained Earnings	800,000
Treasury Stock (10,000 common shares)	74,000
Paid-in Capital in Excess of Par—Preferred Stock	344,000

Instructions

Prepare the stockholders' equity section at December 31, assuming retained earnings is restricted for plant expansion in the amount of $100,000.

Prepare an income statement and compute earnings per share.
(LO 4)

E14-12 The following information is available for Norman Corporation for the year ended December 31, 2017: sales revenue $700,000, other revenues and gains $92,000, operating expenses $110,000, cost of goods sold $465,000, other expenses and losses $32,000, and preferred stock dividends $30,000. The company's tax rate was 30%, and it had 50,000 shares outstanding during the entire year.

Instructions

(a) Prepare a corporate income statement.
(b) Calculate earnings per share.

Prepare an income statement and compute return on equity.
(LO 3, 4)

E14-13 In 2017, Pennington Corporation had net sales of $600,000 and cost of goods sold of $360,000. Operating expenses were $153,000, and interest expense was $7,500. The corporation's tax rate is 30%. The corporation declared preferred dividends of $15,000 in 2017, and its average common stockholders' equity during the year was $200,000.

Instructions

(a) Prepare an income statement for Pennington Corporation.
(b) Compute Pennington Corporation's return on common stockholders' equity for 2017.

E14-14 Ringgold Corporation has outstanding at December 31, 2017, 50,000 shares of $20 par value, cumulative, 6% preferred stock and 200,000 shares of $5 par value common stock. All shares were outstanding the entire year. During 2017, Ringgold earned total revenues of $2,000,000 and incurred total expenses (except income taxes) of $1,300,000. Ringgold's income tax rate is 30%.

Compute EPS.

(LO 4)

Instructions

Compute Ringgold's 2017 earnings per share.

E14-15 The following financial information is available for Plummer Corporation.

Calculate ratios to evaluate earnings performance.

(LO 3, 4)

	2017	2016
Average common stockholders' equity	$1,200,000	$900,000
Dividends paid to common stockholders	50,000	30,000
Dividends paid to preferred stockholders	20,000	20,000
Net income	290,000	200,000
Market price of common stock	20	15

The weighted-average number of shares of common stock outstanding was 80,000 for 2016 and 100,000 for 2017.

Instructions

Calculate earnings per share and return on common stockholders' equity for 2017 and 2016.

E14-16 This financial information is available for Klinger Corporation.

Calculate ratios to evaluate earnings performance.

(LO 3, 4)

	2017	2016
Average common stockholders' equity	$1,800,000	$1,900,000
Dividends paid to common stockholders	90,000	70,000
Dividends paid to preferred stockholders	20,000	20,000
Net income	200,000	191,000
Market price of common stock	20	25

The weighted-average number of shares of common stock outstanding was 180,000 for 2016 and 150,000 for 2017.

Instructions

Calculate earnings per share and return on common stockholders' equity for 2017 and 2016.

E14-17 At December 31, 2017, Millwood Corporation has 2,000 shares of $100 par value, 8%, preferred stock outstanding and 100,000 shares of $10 par value common stock issued. Millwood's net income for the year is $241,000.

Compute earnings per share under different assumptions.

(LO 4)

Instructions

Compute the earnings per share of common stock under the following independent situations. (Round to two decimals.)

(a) The dividend to preferred stockholders was declared. There has been no change in the number of shares of common stock outstanding during the year.
(b) The dividend to preferred stockholders was not declared. The preferred stock is cumulative. Millwood held 10,000 shares of common treasury stock throughout the year.

PROBLEMS

P14-1A On January 1, 2017, Geffrey Corporation had the following stockholders' equity accounts.

Prepare dividend entries and stockholders' equity section.

(LO 1, 2, 3)

Common Stock ($20 par value, 60,000 shares issued and outstanding)	$1,200,000
Paid-in Capital in Excess of Par—Common Stock	200,000
Retained Earnings	600,000

During the year, the following transactions occurred.

Feb. 1 Declared a $1 cash dividend per share to stockholders of record on February 15, payable March 1.

Mar. 1 Paid the dividend declared in February.

Apr. 1 Announced a 2-for-1 stock split. Prior to the split, the market price per share was $36.

July 1 Declared a 10% stock dividend to stockholders of record on July 15, distributable July 31. On July 1, the market price of the stock was $13 per share.

31 Issued the shares for the stock dividend.

Dec. 1 Declared a $0.50 per share dividend to stockholders of record on December 15, payable January 5, 2018.

31 Determined that net income for the year was $350,000.

Instructions

(a) Journalize the transactions and the closing entries for net income and dividends.

(b) Enter the beginning balances, and post the entries to the stockholders' equity accounts. (*Note:* Open additional stockholders' equity accounts as needed.)

(c) Prepare a stockholders' equity section at December 31.

(c) Total stockholders' equity $2,224,000

Journalize and post transactions; prepare retained earnings statement and stockholders' equity section.

(LO 1, 2, 3)

P14-2A The stockholders' equity accounts of Karp Company at January 1, 2017, are as follows.

Preferred Stock, 6%, $50 par	$600,000
Common Stock, $5 par	800,000
Paid-in Capital in Excess of Par—Preferred Stock	200,000
Paid-in Capital in Excess of Par—Common Stock	300,000
Retained Earnings	800,000

There were no dividends in arrears on preferred stock. During 2017, the company had the following transactions and events.

July 1 Declared a $0.60 cash dividend per share on common stock.

Aug. 1 Discovered $25,000 understatement of depreciation expense in 2016. (Ignore income taxes.)

Sept. 1 Paid the cash dividend declared on July 1.

Dec. 1 Declared a 15% stock dividend on common stock when the market price of the stock was $18 per share.

15 Declared a 6% cash dividend on preferred stock payable January 15, 2018.

31 Determined that net income for the year was $355,000.

31 Recognized a $200,000 restriction of retained earnings for plant expansion.

Instructions

(a) Journalize the transactions, events, and closing entries for net income and dividends.

(b) Enter the beginning balances in the accounts, and post to the stockholders' equity accounts. (*Note:* Open additional stockholders' equity accounts as needed.)

(c) Prepare a retained earnings statement for the year.

(d) Prepare a stockholders' equity section at December 31, 2017.

(c) Ending balance $566,000
(d) Total stockholders' equity $2,898,000

Prepare retained earnings statement and stockholders' equity section, and compute allocation of dividends and earnings per share.

(LO 1, 2, 3, 4)

P14-3A The post-closing trial balance of Storey Corporation at December 31, 2017, contains the following stockholders' equity accounts.

Preferred Stock (15,000 shares issued)	$ 750,000
Common Stock (250,000 shares issued)	2,500,000
Paid-in Capital in Excess of Par—Preferred Stock	250,000
Paid-in Capital in Excess of Par—Common Stock	400,000
Common Stock Dividends Distributable	250,000
Retained Earnings	1,042,000

A review of the accounting records reveals the following.

1. No errors have been made in recording 2017 transactions or in preparing the closing entry for net income.
2. Preferred stock is $50 par, 6%, and cumulative; 15,000 shares have been outstanding since January 1, 2016.

3. Authorized stock is 20,000 shares of preferred, 500,000 shares of common with a $10 par value.
4. The January 1 balance in Retained Earnings was $1,170,000.
5. On July 1, 20,000 shares of common stock were issued for cash at $16 per share.
6. On September 1, the company discovered an understatement error of $90,000 in computing salaries and wages expense in 2016. The net of tax effect of $63,000 was properly debited directly to Retained Earnings.
7. A cash dividend of $250,000 was declared and properly allocated to preferred and common stock on October 1. No dividends were paid to preferred stockholders in 2016.
8. On December 31, a 10% common stock dividend was declared out of retained earnings on common stock when the market price per share was $16.
9. Net income for the year was $585,000.
10. On December 31, 2017, the directors authorized disclosure of a $200,000 restriction of retained earnings for plant expansion. (Use Note X.)

Instructions

(a) Reproduce the Retained Earnings account (T-account) for 2017.
(b) Prepare a retained earnings statement for 2017.
(c) Prepare a stockholders' equity section at December 31, 2017.
(d) Compute the allocation of the cash dividend to preferred and common stock.

(c) Total stockholders' equity $5,192,000

P14-4A On January 1, 2017, Ven Corporation had the following stockholders' equity accounts.

Prepare the stockholders' equity section, reflecting dividends and stock split.

(LO 1, 2, 3)

Common Stock (no par value, 90,000 shares issued and outstanding)	$1,600,000
Retained Earnings	500,000

During the year, the following transactions occurred.

Feb.	1	Declared a $1 cash dividend per share to stockholders of record on February 15, payable March 1.
Mar.	1	Paid the dividend declared in February.
Apr.	1	Announced a 3-for-1 stock split. Prior to the split, the market price per share was $36.
July	1	Declared a 5% stock dividend to stockholders of record on July 15, distributable July 31. On July 1, the market price of the stock was $16 per share.
	31	Issued the shares for the stock dividend.
Dec.	1	Declared a $0.50 per share dividend to stockholders of record on December 15, payable January 5, 2018.
	31	Determined that net income for the year was $350,000.

Instructions

Prepare the stockholders' equity section of the balance sheet at (a) March 31, (b) June 30, (c) September 30, and (d) December 31, 2017.

(d) Total stockholders' equity $2,218,250

P14-5A On January 1, 2017, Shellenburger Inc. had the following stockholders' equity account balances.

Prepare the stockholders' equity section, reflecting various events.

(LO 1, 2, 3)

Common Stock, no-par value (500,000 shares issued)	$1,500,000
Common Stock Dividends Distributable	200,000
Retained Earnings	600,000

During 2017, the following transactions and events occurred.

1. Issued 50,000 shares of common stock as a result of a 10% stock dividend declared on December 15, 2016.
2. Issued 30,000 shares of common stock for cash at $6 per share.
3. Corrected an error that had understated the net income for 2015 by $70,000.
4. Declared and paid a cash dividend of $80,000.
5. Earned net income of $300,000.

Instructions

Prepare the stockholders' equity section of the balance sheet at December 31, 2017.

Total stockholders' equity $2,770,000

BROADENING YOUR PERSPECTIVE

FINANCIAL REPORTING AND ANALYSIS

Financial Reporting Problem: Apple Inc.

BYP14-1 The financial statements of Apple Inc. are presented in Appendix A. Instructions for accessing and using the company's complete annual report, including the notes to the financial statements, are also provided in Appendix A.

Instructions

Refer to Apple's financial statements and answer the following question.

What amount, if any, did Apple declare in dividends on common stock in the year ended September 28, 2013?

Comparative Analysis Problem: PepsiCo, Inc. vs. The Coca-Cola Company

BYP14-2 PepsiCo's financial statements are presented in Appendix B. Financial statements of The Coca-Cola Company are presented in Appendix C. Instructions for accessing and using the complete annual reports of PepsiCo and Coca-Cola, including the notes to the financial statements, are also provided in Appendices B and C, respectively.

Instructions

(a) Compute earnings per share and return on common stockholders' equity for both companies for 2013. Assume PepsiCo's weighted-average shares were 1,541 million and Coca-Cola's weighted-average shares were 4,568 million. Can these measures be used to compare the profitability of the two companies? Why or why not?

(b) What was the total amount of dividends paid by each company in 2013?

Comparative Analysis Problem: Amazon.com, Inc. vs. Wal-Mart Stores, Inc.

BYP14-3 Amazon.com, Inc.'s financial statements are presented in Appendix D. Financial statements of Wal-Mart Stores, Inc. are presented in Appendix E. Instructions for accessing and using the complete annual reports of Amazon and Wal-Mart, including the notes to the financial statements, are also provided in Appendices D and E, respectively.

Instructions

(a) What are the basic earnings per share for both Amazon and Wal-Mart as of December 31, 2013, and January 31, 2014, respectively?

(b) What was the total amount of dividends, if any, paid by Amazon for the year ending December 31, 2013? What was the total dividends paid by Wal-Mart for the year ending January 31, 2014?

Real-World Focus

BYP14-4 Use the stockholders' equity section of an annual report and identify the major components.

Address: **www.annualreports.com**, or go to **www.wiley.com/college/weygandt**

Steps

1. From the Annual Reports Homepage, choose **Search by Alphabet**, and choose a letter.
2. Select a particular company.
3. Choose Annual Report.
4. Follow instructions below.

Instructions

Answer the following questions.

(a) What is the company's name?

(b) What classes of capital stock has the company issued?

(c) For each class of stock:

(1) How many shares are authorized, issued, and/or outstanding?

(2) What is the par value?

(d) What are the company's retained earnings?

(e) Has the company acquired treasury stock? How many shares?

CRITICAL THINKING

Decision-Making Across the Organization

BYP14-5 The stockholders' equity accounts of Gonzalez, Inc., at January 1, 2017, are as follows.

Preferred Stock, no par, 4,000 shares issued	$400,000
Common Stock, no par, 140,000 shares issued	700,000
Retained Earnings	550,000

During 2017, the company had the following transactions and events.

July	1	Declared a $0.50 cash dividend per share on common stock.
Aug.	1	Discovered a $72,000 overstatement of 2016 depreciation expense. (Ignore income taxes.)
Sept.	1	Paid the cash dividend declared on July 1.
Dec.	1	Declared a 10% stock dividend on common stock when the market price of the stock was $12 per share.
	15	Declared a $6 per share cash dividend on preferred stock, payable January 31, 2018.
	31	Determined that net income for the year was $320,000.

Instructions

With the class divided into groups, answer the following questions.

(a) Prepare a retained earnings statement for the year. There are no preferred dividends in arrears.

(b) Discuss why the overstatement of 2016 depreciation expense is not treated as an adjustment of the current year's income.

(c) Discuss the reasons why a company might decide to issue a stock dividend rather than a cash dividend.

Communication Activity

BYP14-6 In the past year, Gosser Corporation declared a 10% stock dividend, and Jenks, Inc. announced a 2-for-1 stock split. Your parents own 100 shares of each company's $50 par value common stock. During a recent phone call, your parents ask you, as an accounting student, to explain the differences between the two events.

Instructions

Write a letter to your parents that explains the effects of the two events on them as stockholders and the effects of each event on the financial statements of each corporation.

Ethics Case

BYP14-7 Molina Corporation has paid 60 consecutive quarterly cash dividends (15 years). The last 6 months, however, have been a cash drain on the company, as profit margins have been greatly narrowed by increasing competition. With a cash balance sufficient to meet only day-to-day operating needs, the president, Rob Lowery, has decided that a stock dividend instead of a cash dividend should be declared. He tells Molina's financial vice president, Debbie Oler, to issue a press release stating that the company is extending its consecutive dividend record with the issuance of a 5% stock dividend. "Write the press release convincing the stockholders that the stock dividend is just as good as a cash dividend," he orders. "Just watch our stock rise when we announce the stock dividend. It must be a good thing if that happens."

Instructions

(a) Who are the stakeholders in this situation?

(b) Is there anything unethical about Lowery's intentions or actions?

(c) What is the effect of a stock dividend on a corporation's stockholders' equity accounts? Which would you rather receive as a stockholder—a cash dividend or a stock dividend? Why?

All About You

BYP14-8 In this textbook, you learned that in response to the Sarbanes-Oxley Act, many companies have implemented formal ethics codes. Many other organizations also have ethics codes.

Instructions

Obtain the ethics code from an organization that you belong to (e.g., student organization, business school, employer, or a volunteer organization). Evaluate the ethics code based on how clearly it identifies proper and improper behavior. Discuss its strengths, and how it might be improved.

FASB Codification Activity

BYP14-9 If your school has a subscription to the FASB Codification, go to **http://aaahq.org/ascLogin.cfm** to log in and prepare responses to the following.

(a) What is the stock dividend?
(b) What is a stock split?
(c) At what percentage point does the issuance of additional shares qualify as a stock dividend, as opposed to a stock split?

A Look at IFRS

LEARNING OBJECTIVE 5 **Compare the accounting for dividends, retained earnings, and income reporting under GAAP and IFRS.**

The basic accounting for cash and stock dividends is essentially the same under both GAAP and IFRS although IFRS terminology may differ.

Key Points

Following are the key similarities and differences between GAAP and IFRS as related to dividends, retained earnings, and income reporting.

Similarities

- The accounting related to prior period adjustment is essentially the same under IFRS and GAAP.
- The stockholders' equity section is essentially the same under IFRS and GAAP. However, terminology used to describe certain components is often different. These differences are discussed in Chapter 13.
- The income statement using IFRS is called the **statement of comprehensive income**. A statement of comprehensive income is presented in a one- or two-statement format. The single-statement approach includes all items of income and expense, as well as each component of other comprehensive income or loss by its individual characteristic. In the two-statement approach, a traditional income statement is prepared. It is then followed by a statement of comprehensive income, which starts with net income or loss and then adds other comprehensive income or loss items. Regardless of which approach is reported, income tax expense is required to be reported.
- The computations related to earnings per share are essentially the same under IFRS and GAAP.

Differences

- The term **reserves** is used in IFRS to indicate all non–contributed (non–paid-in) capital. Reserves include retained earnings and other comprehensive income items, such as revaluation surplus and unrealized gains or losses on available-for-sale securities.
- IFRS often uses terms such as **retained profits** or **accumulated profit or loss** to describe retained earnings. The term retained earnings is also often used.
- Equity is given various descriptions under IFRS, such as shareholders' equity, owners' equity, capital and reserves, and shareholders' funds.

Looking to the Future

The IASB and the FASB are currently working on a project related to financial statement presentation. An important part of this study is to determine whether certain line items, subtotals, and totals should be clearly defined and required to be displayed in the financial statements. For example, it is likely that the statement of stockholders' equity and its presentation will be examined closely.

Both the IASB and FASB are working toward convergence of any remaining differences related to earnings per share computations. This convergence will deal with highly technical changes beyond the scope of this textbook.

IFRS Practice

IFRS Self-Test Questions

1. The basic accounting for cash dividends and stock dividends:
   (a) is different under IFRS versus GAAP.
   (b) is the same under IFRS and GAAP.
   (c) differs only for the accounting for cash dividends between GAAP and IFRS.
   (d) differs only for the accounting for stock dividends between GAAP and IFRS.
2. Which item is **not** considered part of reserves?
   (a) Unrealized loss on available-for-sale investments.
   (b) Revaluation surplus.
   (c) Retained earnings.
   (d) Issued shares.
3. Under IFRS, a statement of comprehensive income must include:
   (a) accounts payable.
   (b) retained earnings.
   (c) income tax expense.
   (d) preference stock.
4. Which set of terms can be used to describe total stockholders' equity under IFRS?
   (a) Shareholders' equity, capital and reserves, other comprehensive income.
   (b) Capital and reserves, shareholders' equity, shareholders' funds.
   (c) Capital and reserves, retained earnings, shareholders' equity.
   (d) All of the answer choices are correct.
5. Earnings per share computations related to IFRS and GAAP:
   (a) are essentially similar.
   (b) result in an amount referred to as earnings per share.
   (c) must deduct preferred (preference) dividends when computing earnings per share.
   (d) All of the answer choices are correct.

International Financial Reporting Problem: Louis Vuitton

IFRS14-1 The financial statements of Louis Vuitton are presented in Appendix F. Instructions for accessing and using the company's complete annual report, including the notes to its financial statements, are also provided in Appendix F.

Instructions

Use the company's annual report to answer the following questions.

(a) Did the company declare and pay any dividends for the year ended December 31, 2013?
(b) Compute the company's return on ordinary shareholders' equity for the year ended December 31, 2013.
(c) What was Louis Vuitton's earnings per share for the year ended December 31, 2013?

Answers to IFRS Self-Test Questions

1. b **2.** d **3.** c **4.** b **5.** d

Chapter 15 Long-Term Liabilities

Debt can help a company acquire the things it needs to grow, but it is often the very thing that kills a company. A brief history of Maxwell Car Company illustrates the role of debt in the U.S. auto industry. In 1920, Maxwell Car Company was on the brink of financial ruin. Because it was unable to pay its bills, its creditors stepped in and took over. They hired a former General Motors (GM) executive named Walter Chrysler to reorganize the company. By 1925, he had taken over the company and renamed it Chrysler. By 1933, Chrysler was booming, with sales surpassing even those of Ford.

But the next few decades saw Chrysler make a series of blunders. By 1980, with its creditors pounding at the gates, Chrysler was again on the brink of financial ruin.

At that point, Chrysler brought in a former Ford executive named Lee Iacocca to save the company. Iacocca argued that the United States could not afford to let Chrysler fail because of the loss of jobs. He convinced the federal government to grant loan guarantees—promises that if Chrysler failed to pay its creditors, the government would pay them. Iacocca then streamlined operations and brought out some profitable products. Chrysler repaid all of its government-guaranteed loans by 1983, seven years ahead of the scheduled final payment.

To compete in today's global vehicle market, you must be big—really big. So in 1998, Chrysler merged with German automaker Daimler-Benz to form DaimlerChrysler. For a time, this left just two U.S.-based auto manufacturers—GM and Ford. But in 2007, DaimlerChrysler sold 81% of Chrysler to Cerberus, an investment group, to provide much-needed cash infusions to the automaker. In 2009, Daimler turned over its remaining stake to Cerberus. Three days later, Chrysler filed for bankruptcy. But by 2010, it was beginning to show signs of a turnaround.

The car companies are giants. GM and Ford typically rank among the top five U.S. firms in total assets. But GM and Ford accumulated truckloads of debt on their way to getting big. Although debt made it possible to get so big, the Chrysler story, and GM's recent bankruptcy, make it clear that debt can also threaten a company's survival.

LEARNING OBJECTIVES

1. Describe the major characteristics of bonds.
2. Explain how to account for bond transactions.
3. Explain how to account for long-term notes payable.
4. Discuss how long-term liabilities are reported and analyzed.

LEARNING OBJECTIVE 

Describe the major characteristics of bonds.

Long-term liabilities are obligations that a company expects to pay more than one year in the future. In this chapter, we explain the accounting for the principal types of obligations reported in the long-term liabilities section of the balance sheet. These obligations often are in the form of bonds or long-term notes.

Bonds are a form of interest-bearing note payable issued by corporations, universities, and governmental agencies. Bonds, like common stock, are sold in small denominations (usually $1,000 or multiples of $1,000). As a result, bonds attract many investors. When a corporation issues bonds, it is borrowing money. The person who buys the bonds (the bondholder) is investing in bonds.

Types of Bonds

Bonds may have many different features. In the following sections, we describe the types of bonds commonly issued.

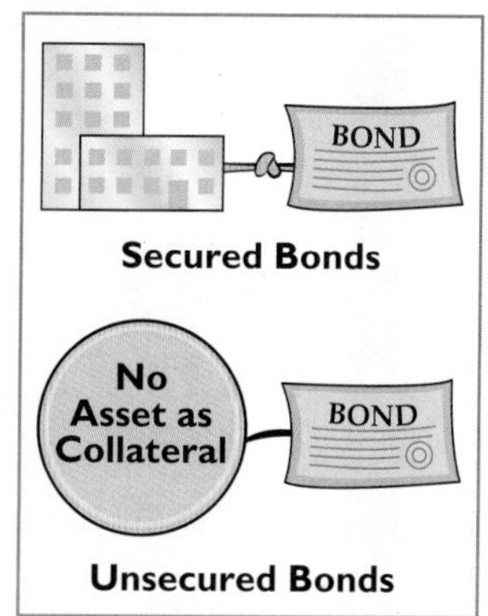

SECURED AND UNSECURED BONDS

Secured bonds have specific assets of the issuer pledged as collateral for the bonds. A bond secured by real estate, for example, is called a **mortgage bond**. A bond secured by specific assets set aside to redeem (retire) the bonds is called a **sinking fund bond**.

Unsecured bonds, also called **debenture bonds**, are issued against the general credit of the borrower. Companies with good credit ratings use these bonds extensively. For example, at one time **DuPont** reported over $2 billion of debenture bonds outstanding.

CONVERTIBLE AND CALLABLE BONDS

Bonds that can be converted into common stock at the bondholder's option are **convertible bonds**. The conversion feature generally is attractive to bond buyers. Bonds that the issuing company can redeem (buy back) at a stated dollar amount prior to maturity are **callable bonds**. A call feature is included in nearly all corporate bond issues.

Issuing Procedures

State laws grant corporations the power to issue bonds. Both the board of directors and stockholders usually must approve bond issues. **In authorizing the bond issue, the board of directors must stipulate the number of bonds to be authorized, total face value, and contractual interest rate.** The total bond authorization often exceeds the number of bonds the company originally issues. This gives the corporation the flexibility to issue more bonds, if needed, to meet future cash requirements.

The **face value** is the amount of principal due at the maturity date. The **maturity date** is the date that the final payment is due to the investor from the issuing company. The **contractual interest rate**, often referred to as the **stated rate**, is the rate used to determine the amount of cash interest the borrower pays and the investor receives. Usually, the contractual rate is stated as an annual rate.

The terms of the bond issue are set forth in a legal document called a **bond indenture**. The indenture shows the terms and summarizes the rights of the bondholders and their trustees, and the obligations of the issuing company. The **trustee** (usually a financial institution) keeps records of each bondholder, maintains custody of unissued bonds, and holds conditional title to pledged property.

In addition, the issuing company arranges for the printing of **bond certificates**. The indenture and the certificate are separate documents. As shown in Illustration 15-1 (page 516), a bond certificate provides the following information: name of the issuer, face value, contractual interest rate, and maturity date. An investment company that specializes in selling securities generally sells the bonds for the issuing company.

Determining the Market Price of a Bond

If you were an investor wanting to purchase a bond, how would you determine how much to pay? To be more specific, assume that Coronet, Inc. issues a

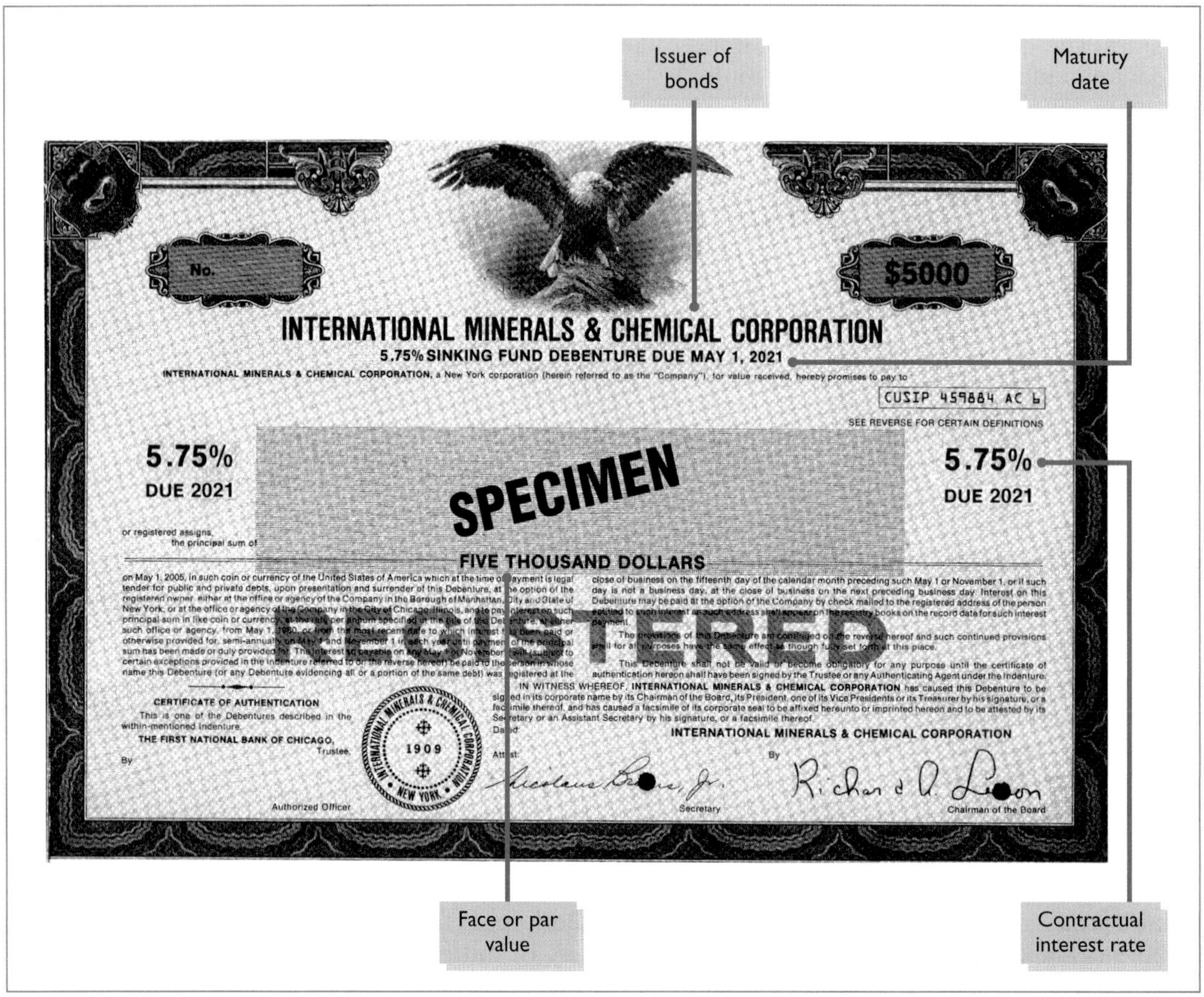

Issuer of bonds

Maturity date

INTERNATIONAL MINERALS & CHEMICAL CORPORATION

5.75% SINKING FUND DEBENTURE DUE MAY 1, 2021

Face or par value

Contractual interest rate

Illustration 15-1
Bond certificate

zero-interest bond (pays no interest) with a face value of $1,000,000 due in 20 years. For this bond, the only cash you receive is a million dollars at the end of 20 years. Would you pay a million dollars for this bond? We hope not! A million dollars received 20 years from now is not the same as a million dollars received today.

Same dollars at different times are not equal.

The term **time value of money** is used to indicate the relationship between time and money—that a dollar received today is worth more than a dollar promised at some time in the future. If you had $1 million today, you would invest it. From that investment, you would earn interest such that at the end of 20 years, you would have much more than $1 million. Thus, if someone is going to pay you $1 million 20 years from now, you would want to find its equivalent today, or its present value. In other words, you would want to determine the value today of the amount to be received in the future after taking into account current interest rates.

The current market price (present value) of a bond is the value at which it should sell in the marketplace. Market price therefore is a function of the three factors that determine present value: (1) the dollar amounts to be received, (2) the length of time until the amounts are received, and (3) the market rate of interest. The **market interest rate** is the rate investors demand for loaning funds.

To illustrate, assume that Acropolis Company on January 1, 2017, issues $100,000 of 9% bonds, due in five years, with interest payable annually at year-end. The purchaser of the bonds would receive the following two types of cash payments: (1) **principal** of $100,000 to be paid at maturity, and (2) five $9,000

interest payments ($100,000 × 9%) over the term of the bonds. Illustration 15-2 shows a time diagram depicting both cash flows.

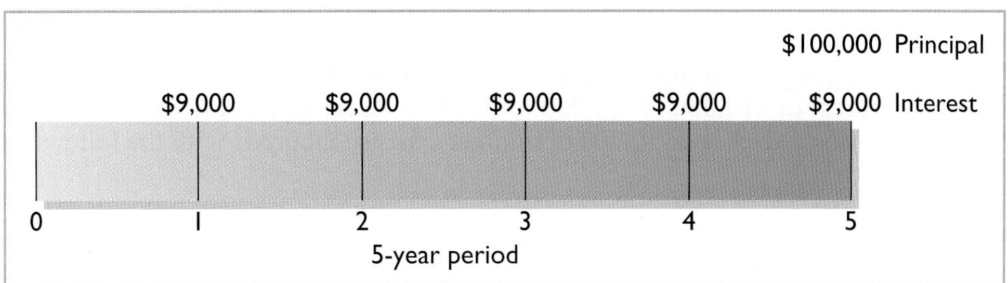

Illustration 15-2
Time diagram depicting cash flows

The current market price of a bond is equal to the present value of all the future cash payments promised by the bond. Illustration 15-3 lists and totals the present values of these amounts, assuming the market rate of interest is 9%.

Illustration 15-3
Computing the market price of bonds

Present value of $100,000 received in 5 years	$ 64,993
Present value of $9,000 received annually for 5 years	35,007
Market price of bonds	**$100,000**

Tables are available to provide the present value numbers to be used, or these values can be determined mathematically or with financial calculators.[1] Appendix G, near the end of the textbook, provides further discussion of the concepts and the mechanics of the time value of money computations.

LEARNING OBJECTIVE 2 **Explain how to account for bond transactions.**

A corporation records bond transactions when it issues (sells) or redeems (buys back) bonds and when bondholders convert bonds into common stock. If bondholders sell their bond investments to other investors, the issuing firm receives no further money on the transaction, **nor does the issuing corporation journalize the transaction** (although it does keep records of the names of bondholders in some cases).

Bonds may be issued at face value, below face value (discount), or above face value (premium). Bond prices for both new issues and existing bonds are quoted as **a percentage of the face value of the bond**. **Face value is usually $1,000.** Thus, a $1,000 bond with a quoted price of 97 means that the selling price of the bond is 97% of face value, or $970.

Issuing Bonds at Face Value

To illustrate the accounting for bonds issued at face value, assume that on January 1, 2017, Candlestick, Inc. issues $100,000, five-year, 10% bonds at 100 (100% of face value). The entry to record the sale is as follows.

Jan. 1	Cash	100,000	
	Bonds Payable		100,000
	(To record sale of bonds at face value)		

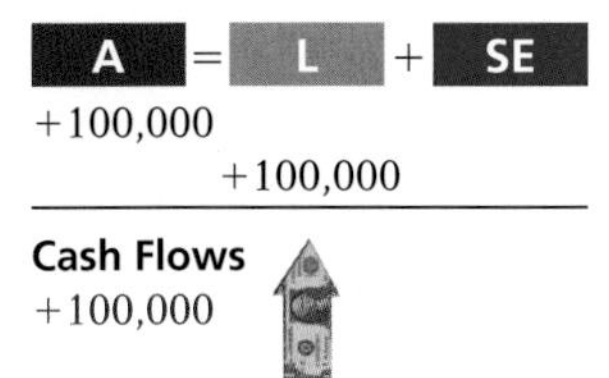

[1]For those knowledgeable in the use of present value tables, the computations in the example shown in Illustration 15-3 are $100,000 × 0.64993 = $64,993, and $9,000 × 3.88965 = 35,007 (rounded).

Candlestick reports bonds payable in the long-term liabilities section of the balance sheet because the maturity date is January 1, 2022 (more than one year away).

Over the term (life) of the bonds, companies make entries to record bond interest. Interest on bonds payable is computed in the same manner as interest on notes payable, as explained in Chapter 11 (page 394). Assume that interest is payable annually on January 1 on the Candlestick bonds. In that case, Candlestick accrues interest of $10,000 ($100,000 × 10%) on December 31. At December 31, Candlestick recognizes the $10,000 of interest expense incurred with the following adjusting entry.

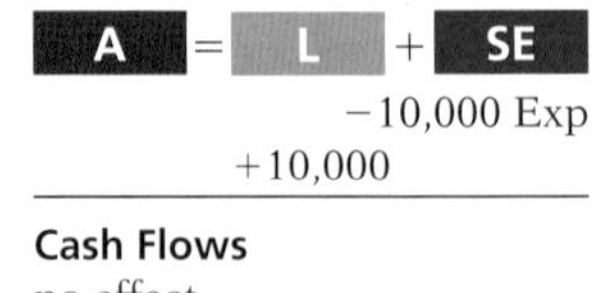

Dec. 31	Interest Expense	10,000	
	Interest Payable		10,000
	(To accrue bond interest)		

The company classifies interest payable as a current liability because it is scheduled for payment within the next year. When Candlestick pays the interest on January 1, 2018, it debits (decreases) Interest Payable and credits (decreases) Cash for $10,000.

Candlestick records the payment on January 1 as follows.

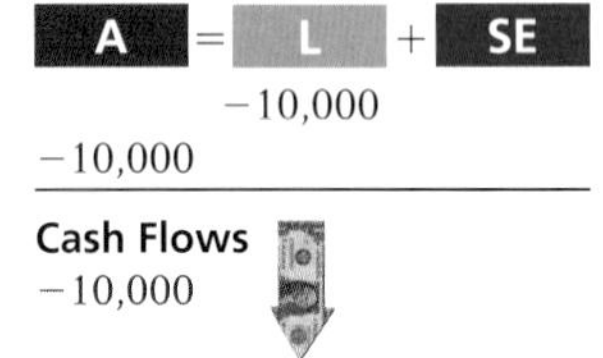

Jan. 1	Interest Payable	10,000	
	Cash		10,000
	(To record payment of bond interest)		

Discount or Premium on Bonds

The previous example assumed that the contractual (stated) interest rate and the market (effective) interest rate paid on the bonds were the same. Recall that the **contractual interest rate** is the rate applied to the face (par) value to arrive at the interest paid in a year. The **market interest rate** is the rate investors demand for loaning funds to the corporation. When the contractual interest rate and the market interest rate are the same, bonds sell **at face value (par value)**.

However, market interest rates change daily. The type of bond issued, the state of the economy, current industry conditions, and the company's performance all affect market interest rates. As a result, contractual and market interest rates often differ. To make bonds salable when the two rates differ, bonds sell below or above face value.

To illustrate, suppose that a company issues 10% bonds at a time when other bonds of similar risk are paying 12%. Investors will not be interested in buying the 10% bonds, so their value will fall below their face value. When a bond is sold for less than its face value, the difference between the face value of a bond and its selling price is called a **discount**. As a result of the decline in the bonds' selling price, the actual interest rate incurred by the company increases to the level of the current market interest rate.

Conversely, if the market rate of interest is **lower than** the contractual interest rate, investors will have to pay more than face value for the bonds. That is, if the market rate of interest is 8% but the contractual interest rate on the bonds is 10%, the price of the bonds will be bid up. When a bond is sold for more than its face value, the difference between the face value and its selling price is called a **premium**. Illustration 15-4 shows these relationships.

Issuance of bonds at an amount different from face value is quite common. By the time a company prints the bond certificates and markets the bonds, it will be a coincidence if the market rate and the contractual rate are the same. Thus, the issuance of bonds at a discount does not mean that the issuer's financial strength is suspect. Conversely, the sale of bonds at a premium does not indicate that the financial strength of the issuer is exceptional.

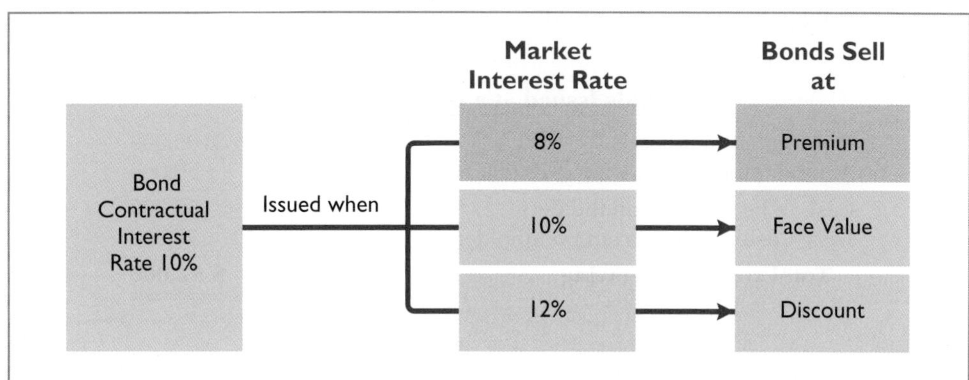

Illustration 15-4
Interest rates and bond prices

Issuing Bonds at a Discount

To illustrate issuance of bonds at a discount, assume that on January 1, 2017, Candlestick, Inc. sells $100,000, five-year, 10% bonds for $98,000 (98% of face value). Interest is payable annually on January 1. The entry to record the issuance is as follows.

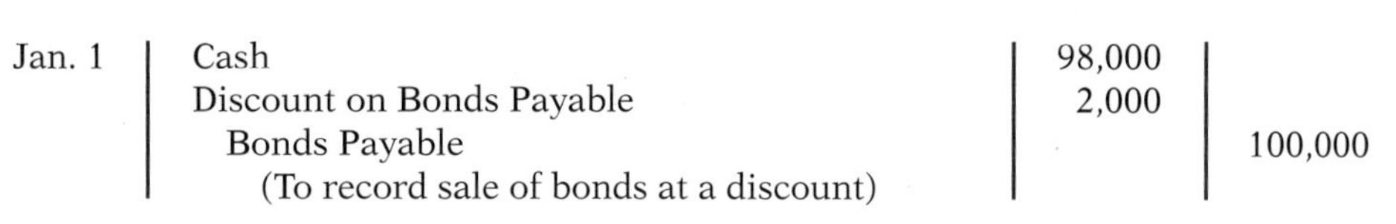

Jan. 1	Cash	98,000	
	Discount on Bonds Payable	2,000	
	Bonds Payable		100,000
	(To record sale of bonds at a discount)		

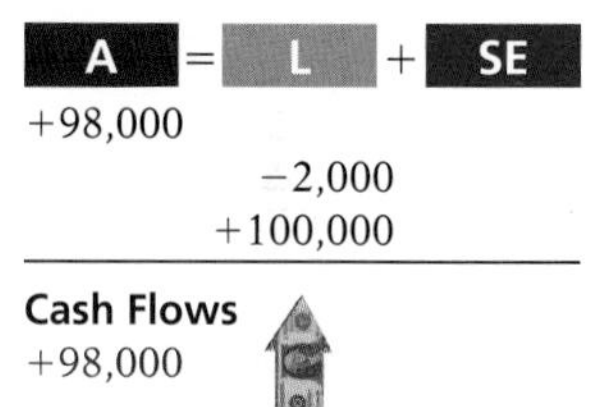

Although Discount on Bonds Payable has a debit balance, **it is not an asset**. Rather, it is a **contra account**. This account is **deducted from bonds payable** on the balance sheet, as shown in Illustration 15-5.

CANDLESTICK, INC.
Balance Sheet (partial)

Long-term liabilities		
Bonds payable	$100,000	
Less: Discount on bonds payable	**2,000**	$98,000

Illustration 15-5
Statement presentation of discount on bonds payable

The $98,000 represents the **carrying (or book) value** of the bonds. On the date of issue, this amount equals the market price of the bonds.

The issuance of bonds below face value—at a discount—causes the total cost of borrowing to differ from the bond interest paid. That is, the issuing corporation must pay not only the contractual interest rate over the term of the bonds but also the face value (rather than the issuance price) at maturity. Therefore, the difference between the issuance price and face value of the bonds—the discount—is an **additional cost of borrowing**. The company records this additional cost as **interest expense** over the life of the bonds. The total cost of borrowing $98,000 for Candlestick, Inc. is therefore $52,000, computed as follows.

Bonds Issued at a Discount

Annual interest payments	
($100,000 × 10% = $10,000; $10,000 × 5)	$ 50,000
Add: Bond discount ($100,000 − $98,000)	2,000
Total cost of borrowing	**$52,000**

Illustration 15-6
Total cost of borrowing—bonds issued at a discount

Alternatively, we can compute the total cost of borrowing as follows.

Illustration 15-7
Alternative computation of total cost of borrowing—bonds issued at a discount

Bonds Issued at a Discount	
Principal at maturity	$100,000
Annual interest payments ($10,000 × 5)	50,000
Cash to be paid to bondholders	150,000
Less: Cash received from bondholders	98,000
Total cost of borrowing	**$ 52,000**

To follow the expense recognition principle, companies allocate bond discount to expense in each period in which the bonds are outstanding. This is referred to as **amortizing the discount**. Amortization of the discount **increases** the amount of interest expense reported each period. That is, after the company amortizes the discount, the amount of interest expense it reports in a period will exceed the contractual amount. As shown in Illustration 15-6, for the bonds issued by Candlestick, Inc., total interest expense will exceed the contractual interest by $2,000 over the life of the bonds.

As the discount is amortized, its balance declines. As a consequence, the carrying value of the bonds will increase, until at maturity the carrying value of the bonds equals their face amount. This is shown in Illustration 15-8. Appendices 15A and 15B at the end of this chapter discuss procedures for amortizing bond discount.

Illustration 15-8
Amortization of bond discount

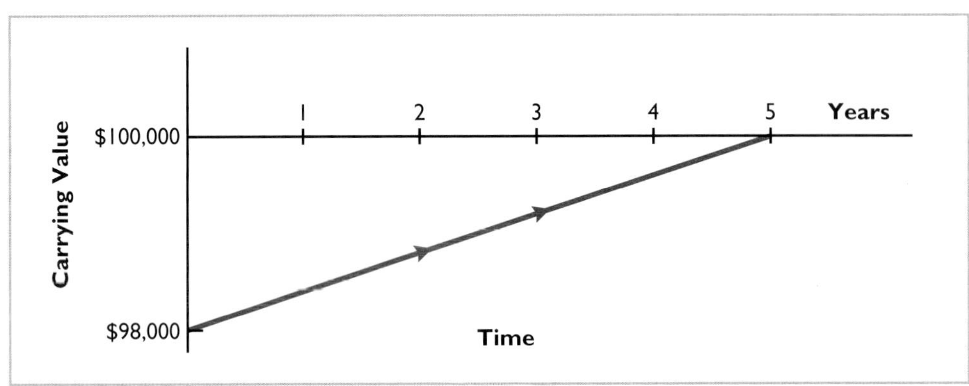

Issuing Bonds at a Premium

To illustrate the issuance of bonds at a premium, we now assume the Candlestick, Inc. bonds described above sell for $102,000 (102% of face value) rather than for $98,000. The entry to record the sale is as follows.

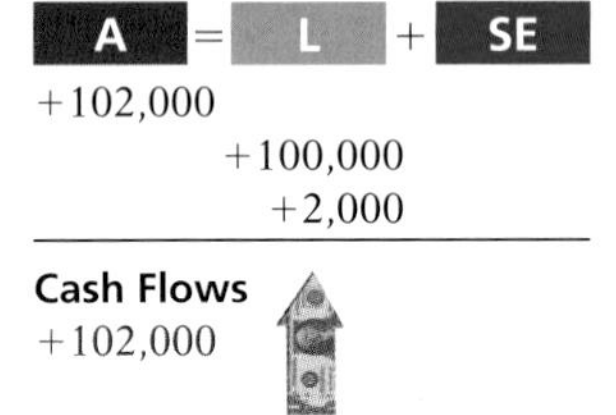

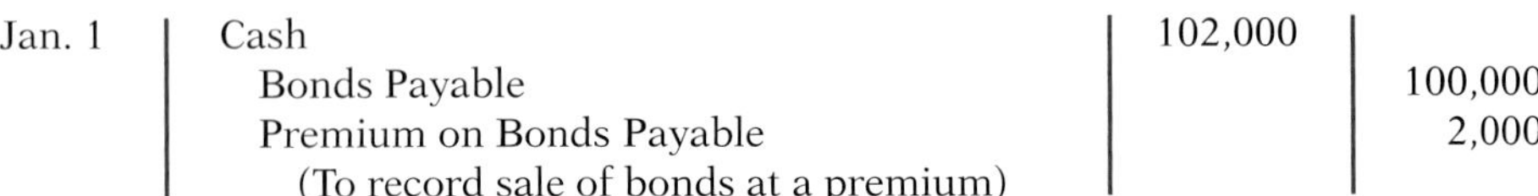

Jan. 1	Cash	102,000	
	Bonds Payable		100,000
	Premium on Bonds Payable		2,000
	(To record sale of bonds at a premium)		

Candlestick adds the premium on bonds payable **to the bonds payable amount** on the balance sheet, as shown in Illustration 15-9.

Illustration 15-9
Statement presentation of bond premium

CANDLESTICK, INC. Balance Sheet (partial)		
Long-term liabilities		
Bonds payable	$100,000	
Add: Premium on bonds payable	**2,000**	**$102,000**

The sale of bonds above face value causes the total cost of borrowing to be **less than the bond interest paid**. The reason: The borrower is not required to pay the bond premium at the maturity date of the bonds. Thus, the bond premium is considered to be **a reduction in the cost of borrowing** that reduces bond interest over the life of the bonds. The total cost of borrowing $102,000 for Candlestick, Inc. is computed as follows.

Illustration 15-10
Total cost of borrowing—bonds issued at a premium

Bonds Issued at a Premium	
Annual interest payments	
($100,000 × 10% = $10,000; $10,000 × 5)	$ 50,000
Less: Bond premium ($102,000 − $100,000)	2,000
Total cost of borrowing	**$48,000**

Alternatively, we can compute the cost of borrowing as follows.

Illustration 15-11
Alternative computation of total cost of borrowing—bonds issued at a premium

Bonds Issued at a Premium	
Principal at maturity	$100,000
Annual interest payments ($10,000 × 5)	50,000
Cash to be paid to bondholders	150,000
Less: Cash received from bondholders	102,000
Total cost of borrowing	**$ 48,000**

Similar to bond discount, companies allocate bond premium to expense in each period in which the bonds are outstanding. This is referred to as **amortizing the premium**. Amortization of the premium **decreases** the amount of interest expense reported each period. That is, after the company amortizes the premium, the amount of interest expense it reports in a period will be less than the contractual amount. As shown in Illustration 15-10, for the bonds issued by Candlestick, Inc., contractual interest will exceed the interest expense by $2,000 over the life of the bonds.

As the premium is amortized, its balance declines. As a consequence, the carrying value of the bonds will decrease, until at maturity the carrying value of the bonds equals their face amount. This is shown in Illustration 15-12. Appendices 15A and 15B at the end of this chapter discuss procedures for amortizing bond premium.

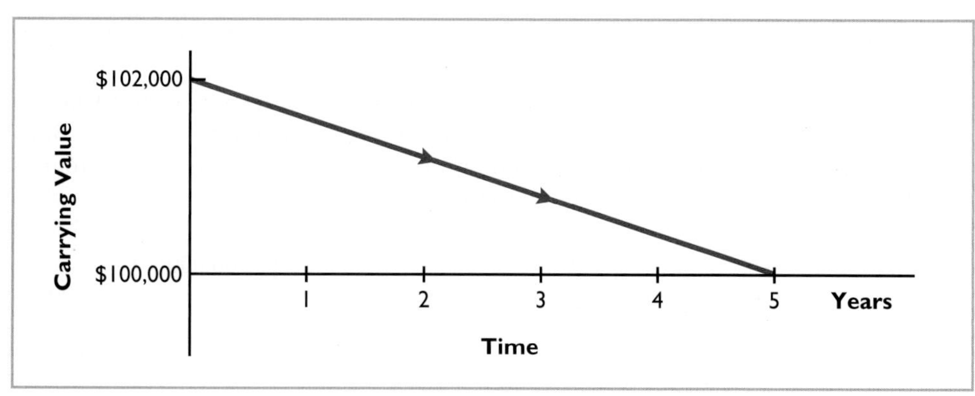

Illustration 15-12
Amortization of bond premium

Redeeming and Converting Bonds

REDEEMING BONDS AT MATURITY

Regardless of the issue price of bonds, the book value of the bonds at maturity will equal their face value. Assuming that the company pays and records separately the interest for the last interest period, Candlestick records the redemption of its bonds at maturity as follows.

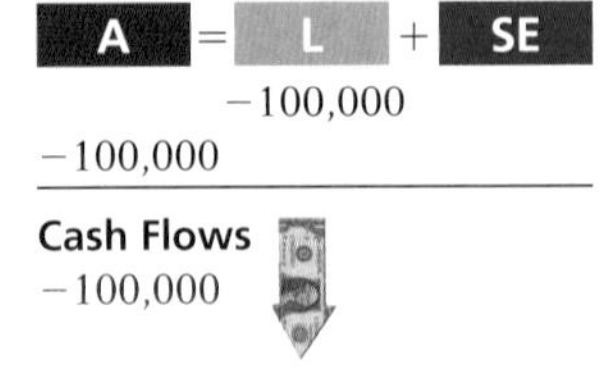

Jan. 1	Bonds Payable	100,000	
	Cash		100,000
	(To record redemption of bonds at maturity)		

REDEEMING BONDS BEFORE MATURITY

Bonds may be redeemed before maturity. A company may decide to redeem bonds before maturity to reduce interest cost and to remove debt from its balance sheet. A company should redeem debt early only if it has sufficient cash resources.

When a company redeems bonds before maturity, it is necessary to (1) eliminate the carrying value of the bonds at the redemption date, (2) record the cash paid, and (3) recognize the gain or loss on redemption. The **carrying value** of the bonds is the face value of the bonds less any remaining bond discount or plus any remaining bond premium at the redemption date.

To illustrate, assume that Candlestick, Inc. has sold its bonds at a premium. At the end of the fourth period, Candlestick redeems these bonds at 103 after paying the annual interest. Assume that the carrying value of the bonds at the redemption date is $100,400 (principal $100,000 and premium $400). Candlestick records the redemption at the end of the fourth interest period (January 1, 2021) as follows.

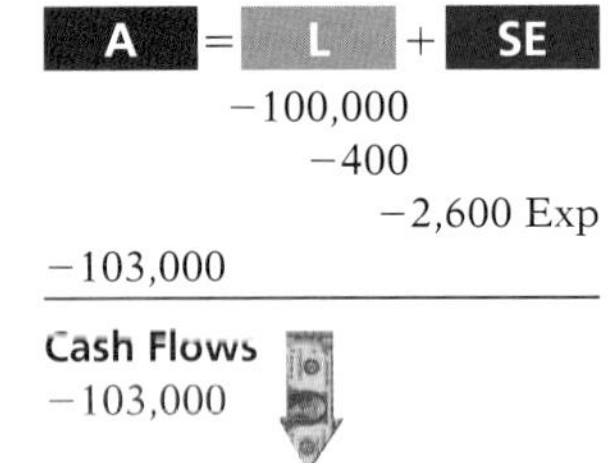

Jan. 1	Bonds Payable	100,000	
	Premium on Bonds Payable	400	
	Loss on Bond Redemption	2,600	
	Cash		103,000
	(To record redemption of bonds at 103)		

Note that the loss of $2,600 is the difference between the cash paid of $103,000 and the carrying value of the bonds of $100,400.

CONVERTING BONDS INTO COMMON STOCK

Convertible bonds have features that are attractive both to bondholders and to the issuer. The conversion often gives bondholders an opportunity to benefit if the market price of the common stock increases substantially. Until conversion, though, the bondholder receives interest on the bond. For the issuer of convertible bonds, the bonds sell at a higher price and pay a lower rate of interest than comparable debt securities without the conversion option. Many corporations, such as Intel, Ford, and Wells Fargo, have convertible bonds outstanding.

When the issuing company records a conversion, the company ignores the current market prices of the bonds and stock. Instead, the company transfers the **carrying value** of the bonds to paid-in capital accounts. **No gain or loss is recognized.**

To illustrate, assume that on July 1, Saunders Associates converts $100,000 bonds sold at face value into 2,000 shares of $10 par value common stock. Both the bonds and the common stock have a market value of $130,000. Saunders makes the following entry to record the conversion.

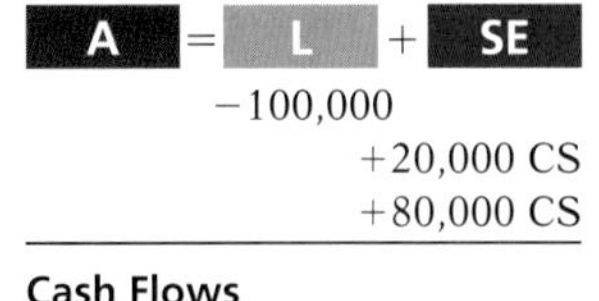

July 1	Bonds Payable	100,000	
	Common Stock		20,000
	Paid-in Capital in Excess of Par—Common Stock		80,000
	(To record bond conversion)		

Note that the company does not consider the current market value of the bonds and stock ($130,000) in making the entry. This method of recording the bond conversion is often referred to as the **carrying (or book) value method**.

LEARNING OBJECTIVE 3 **Explain how to account for long-term notes payable.**

Other common types of long-term obligations are notes payable and lease liabilities. We discuss notes payable next.

Long-Term Notes Payable

The use of notes payable in long-term debt financing is quite common. **Long-term notes payable** are similar to short-term interest-bearing notes payable except that the term of the notes exceeds one year. In periods of unstable interest rates, lenders may tie the interest rate on long-term notes to changes in the market rate for comparable loans.

A long term note may be secured by a **mortgage** that pledges title to specific assets as security for a loan. Individuals widely use **mortgage notes payable** to purchase homes, and many small and some large companies use them to acquire plant assets. At one time, approximately 18% of McDonald's long-term debt related to mortgage notes on land, buildings, and improvements.

Like other long-term notes payable, the mortgage loan terms may stipulate either a **fixed** or an **adjustable** interest rate. The interest rate on a fixed-rate mortgage remains the same over the life of the mortgage. The interest rate on an adjustable-rate mortgage is adjusted periodically to reflect changes in the market rate of interest. Typically, the terms require the borrower to make equal installment payments over the term of the loan. Each payment consists of (1) interest on the unpaid balance of the loan and (2) a reduction of loan principal. While the total amount of the payment remains constant, the interest decreases each period, while the portion applied to the loan principal increases.

Companies initially record mortgage notes payable at face value. They subsequently make entries for each installment payment. To illustrate, assume that Porter Technology Inc. issues a $500,000, 8%, 20-year mortgage note on December 31, 2017, to obtain needed financing for a new research laboratory. The terms provide for annual installment payments of $50,926 (not including real estate taxes and insurance). The installment payment schedule for the first four years is as follows.

Illustration 15-13
Mortgage installment payment schedule

Interest Period	(A) Cash Payment	(B) Interest Expense (D) × 8%	(C) Reduction of Principal (A) − (B)	(D) Principal Balance (D) − (C)
Issue date				$500,000
1	$50,926	$40,000	$10,926	489,074
2	50,926	39,126	11,800	477,274
3	50,926	38,182	12,744	464,530
4	50,926	37,162	13,764	450,766

Porter records the mortgage loan on December 31, 2017, as follows.

A	=	L	+	SE
+500,000				
		+500,000		

Cash Flows
+500,000

Dec. 31	Cash	500,000	
	Mortgage Payable		500,000
	(To record mortgage loan)		

On December 31, 2018, Porter records the first installment payment as follows.

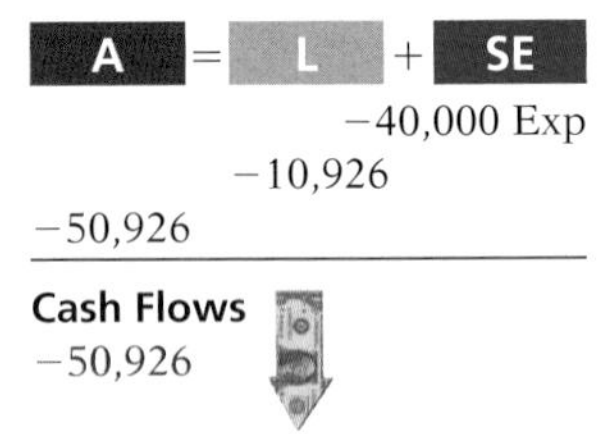

Dec. 31	Interest Expense	40,000	
	Mortgage Payable	10,926	
	Cash		50,926
	(To record annual payment on mortgage)		

In the balance sheet, the company reports the reduction in principal for the next year as a current liability, and it classifies the remaining unpaid principal balance as a long-term liability. At December 31, 2018, the total liability is $489,074. Of that amount, $11,800 is current and $477,274 ($489,074 − $11,800) is long-term.

LEARNING OBJECTIVE 4

Discuss how long-term liabilities are reported and analyzed.

Presentation

Companies report long-term liabilities in a separate section of the balance sheet immediately following current liabilities, as shown in Illustration 15-14. Alternatively, companies may present summary data in the balance sheet, with detailed data (interest rates, maturity dates, conversion privileges, and assets pledged as collateral) shown in a supporting schedule.

Illustration 15-14
Balance sheet presentation of long-term liabilities

LAX CORPORATION Balance Sheet (partial)		
Long-term liabilities		
Bonds payable 10% due in 2022	$1,000,000	
Less: Discount on bonds payable	80,000	$ 920,000
Mortgage payable, 11%, due in 2028 and secured by plant assets		500,000
Lease liability		440,000
Total long-term liabilities		$1,860,000

Companies report the current maturities of long-term debt under current liabilities if they are to be paid within one year or the operating cycle, whichever is longer.

Use of Ratios

Two ratios are helpful in better understanding a company's debt-paying ability and long-term solvency. Long-term creditors and stockholders are interested in a company's long-run solvency. Of particular interest is the company's ability to pay interest as it comes due and to repay the face value of the debt at maturity.

The **debt to assets ratio** measures the percentage of the total assets provided by creditors. It is computed by dividing total liabilities (both current and long-term liabilities) by total assets. To illustrate, we use data from a recent **Kellogg Company** annual report. The company reported total liabilities of $8,925 million, total assets of $11,200 million, interest expense of $295 million, income taxes of $476 million, and net income of $1,208 million. As shown in Illustration 15-15, Kellogg's debt to assets ratio is 79.7%. The higher the percentage of debt to assets, the greater the risk that the company may be unable to meet its maturing obligation.

Total Liabilities	÷	Total Assets	=	Debt to Assets Ratio
$8,925	÷	$11,200	=	**79.7%**

Illustration 15-15
Debt to assets ratio

Times interest earned indicates the company's ability to meet interest payments as they come due. It is computed by dividing the sum of net income, interest expense, and income tax expense by interest expense. As shown in Illustration 15-16, Kellogg's times interest earned is 6.71 times. This interest coverage is considered safe.

Net Income + Interest Expense + Income Tax Expense	÷	Interest Expense	=	Times Interest Earned
$1,208 + $295 + $476	÷	$295	=	**6.71 times**

Illustration 15-16
Times interest earned

Debt and Equity Financing

To obtain large amounts of long-term capital, corporate management has to decide whether to issue additional common stock (equity financing), bonds or notes (debt financing), or a combination of the two. This decision is important to both the company and to investors and creditors. The capital structure of a company provides clues as to the potential profit that can be achieved and the risks taken by the company. Debt financing offers these advantages over common stock, as shown in Illustration 15-17.

Bond Financing	Advantages
Ballot	1. **Stockholder control is not affected.** Bondholders do not have voting rights, so current owners (stockholders) retain full control of the company.
Tax Bill	2. **Tax savings result.** Bond interest is deductible for tax purposes; dividends on stock are not.
Income statement / EPS	3. **Earning per share (EPS) may be higher.** Although bond interest expense reduces net income, earning per share is higher under bond financing because no additional shares of common stock are issued.

Illustration 15-17
Advantages of bond financing over common stock

As Illustration 15-17 shows, one reason to issue bonds is that they do not affect stockholder control. Because bondholders do not have voting rights, owners can raise capital with bonds and still maintain corporate control. In addition, bonds are attractive to corporations because the cost of bond interest is tax-deductible. As a result of this tax treatment, which stock dividends do not offer, bonds may result in lower cost of capital than equity financing.

To illustrate another advantage of bond financing, assume that Microsystems, Inc. is considering two plans for financing the construction of a new $5 million plant. Plan A involves issuance of 200,000 shares of common stock at the current market price of $25 per share. Plan B involves issuance of $5 million, 8% bonds at face value. Income before interest and taxes on the new plant will be $1.5 million. Income taxes are expected to be 30%. Microsystems currently has 100,000 shares of common stock outstanding. Illustration 15-18 (page 526) shows the alternative effects on earnings per share.

Illustration 15-18
Effects on earnings per share—stocks vs. bonds

	Plan A Issue Stock	Plan B Issue Bonds
Income before interest and taxes	$1,500,000	$1,500,000
Interest (8% × $5,000,000)	—	400,000
Income before income taxes	1,500,000	1,100,000
Income tax expense (30%)	450,000	330,000
Net income	$1,050,000	$ 770,000
Outstanding shares	300,000	100,000
Earnings per share	**$3.50**	**$7.70**

Note that net income is $280,000 less ($1,050,000 − $770,000) with long-term debt financing (bonds). However, earnings per share is higher because there are 200,000 fewer shares of common stock outstanding.

A major disadvantage of using debt financing is that a company must pay interest on a periodic basis. In addition, the company must also repay principal at the due date. A company with fluctuating earnings and a relatively weak cash position may have great difficulty making interest payments when earnings are low. Furthermore, when the economy, stock market, or a company's revenues stagnate, debt payments can gobble up cash quickly and limit a company's ability to meet its financial obligations.

Lease Liabilities and Off-Balance-Sheet Financing

A lease is a contractual arrangement between a lessor (owner of the property) and a lessee (renter of the property). It grants the right to use specific property for a period of time in return for cash payments. Leasing is big business. The global leasing market for capital equipment has recently been over $850 billion. This represents approximately one-third of equipment financed in a year. The two most common types of leases are operating leases and capital leases.

OPERATING LEASES

The renting of an apartment and the rental of a car at an airport are examples of **operating leases**. **In an operating lease, the intent is temporary use of the property by the lessee, while the lessor continues to own the property.**

In an operating lease, the lessee records the lease (or rental) payments as an expense. The lessor records the payments as revenue. For example, assume that a sales representative for Western Inc. leases a car from Hertz Car Rental at the Los Angeles airport and that Hertz charges a total of $275. Western, the lessee, records the rental as follows.

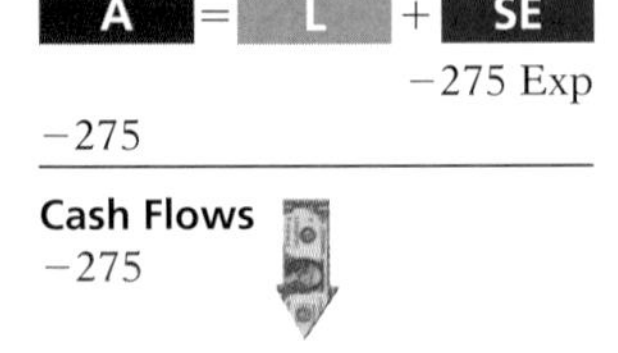

	Debit	Credit
Rent Expense	275	
Cash		275
(To record payment of lease rental charge)		

The lessee may incur other costs during the lease period. For example, in the case above, Western will generally incur costs for gas. Western would report these costs as an expense.

CAPITAL LEASES

In most lease contracts, the lessee makes a periodic payment and records that payment in the income statement as rent expense. In some cases, however, the lease contract transfers to the lessee substantially all the benefits and risks of ownership. Such a lease is in effect a purchase of the property. This type of lease is a **capital lease**. Its name comes from the fact that the company capitalizes the present value of the cash payments for the lease and records that amount as an asset. Illustration 15-19 indicates the major difference between operating and capital leases.

Illustration 15-19
Types of leases

If **any one** of the following conditions exists, the lessee must record a lease **as an asset**—that is, as a capital lease:

1. **The lease transfers ownership of the property to the lessee.** *Rationale:* If during the lease term the lessee receives ownership of the asset, the lessee should report the leased item as an asset on its books.
2. **The lease contains a bargain purchase option.** *Rationale:* If during the term of the lease the lessee can purchase the asset at a price substantially below its fair value, the lessee will exercise this option. Thus, the lessee should report the leased item as an asset on its books.
3. **The lease term is equal to 75% or more of the economic life of the leased property.** *Rationale:* If the lease term is for much of the asset's useful life, the lessee should report the leased item as an asset on its books.
4. **The present value of the lease payments equals or exceeds 90% of the fair value of the leased property.** *Rationale:* If the present value of the lease payments is equal to or almost equal to the fair value of the asset, the lessee has essentially purchased the asset. As a result, the lessee should report the leased item as an asset on its books.

To illustrate, assume that Gonzalez Company decides to lease new equipment. The lease period is four years. The economic life of the leased equipment is estimated to be five years. The present value of the lease payments is $190,000, which is equal to the fair value of the equipment. There is no transfer of ownership during the lease term, nor is there any bargain purchase option.

In this example, Gonzalez has essentially purchased the equipment. Conditions 3 and 4 have been met. First, the lease term is 75% or more of the economic life of the asset. Second, the present value of cash payments is equal to the equipment's fair value. Gonzalez records the transaction as follows.

Leased Asset—Equipment	190,000	
Lease Liability		190,000
(To record leased asset and lease liability)		

A	=	L	+	SE
+190,000				
		+190,000		

Cash Flows
no effect

The lessee reports a leased asset on the balance sheet under plant assets. It reports the lease liability on the balance sheet as a liability. **The portion of the lease liability expected to be paid in the next year is a current liability. The remainder is classified as a long-term liability.**

Most lessees do not like to report leases on their balance sheets. Why? Because the lease liability increases the company's total liabilities. This, in turn, may make it more difficult for the company to obtain needed funds from lenders. As a result, companies attempt to keep leased assets and lease liabilities off the balance sheet by structuring leases so as not to meet any of the four conditions discussed earlier. The practice of keeping liabilities off the balance sheet is referred to as **off-balance-sheet financing**.

LEARNING OBJECTIVE *5

APPENDIX 15A: Apply the straight-line method of amortizing bond discount and bond premium.

Amortizing Bond Discount

To follow the expense recognition principle, companies allocate bond discount to expense in each period in which the bonds are outstanding. The **straight-line method of amortization** allocates the same amount to interest expense in each interest period. The calculation is presented in Illustration 15A-1.

Illustration 15A-1
Formula for straight-line method of bond discount amortization

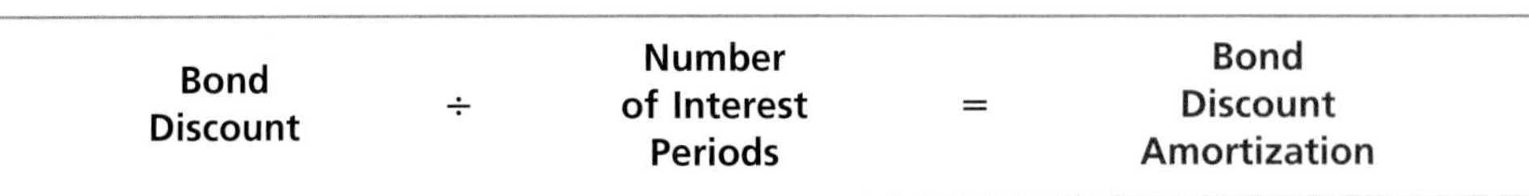

In the Candlestick, Inc. example (page 519), the company sold $100,000, five-year, 10% bonds on January 1, 2017, for $98,000. This resulted in a $2,000 bond discount ($100,000 − $98,000). The bond discount amortization is $400 ($2,000 ÷ 5) for each of the five amortization periods. Candlestick records the first accrual of bond interest and the amortization of bond discount on December 31 as follows.

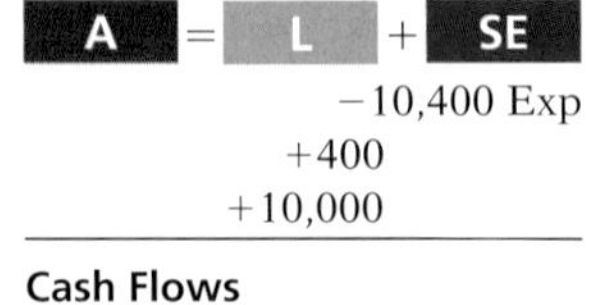

−10,400 Exp
+400
+10,000

Cash Flows
no effect

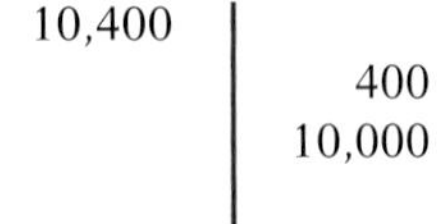

Dec. 31	Interest Expense	10,400	
	Discount on Bonds Payable		400
	Interest Payable		10,000
	(To record accrued bond interest and amortization of bond discount)		

Terminology
The amount in the Discount on Bonds Payable account is often referred to as *Unamortized Discount on Bonds Payable*.

Over the term of the bonds, the balance in Discount on Bonds Payable will decrease annually by the same amount until it has a zero balance at the maturity date of the bonds. Thus, the carrying value of the bonds at maturity will be equal to the face value of the bonds.

Preparing a bond discount amortization schedule, as shown in Illustration 15A-2, is useful to determine interest expense, discount amortization, and the carrying value of the bond. As indicated, the interest expense recorded each period is $10,400. Also note that the carrying value of the bond increases $400 each period until it reaches its face value of $100,000 at the end of period 5.

Candlestick Inc.xls

CANDLESTICK, INC.
Bond Discount Amortization Schedule
Straight-Line Method—Annual Interest Payments
$100,000 of 10%, 5-Year Bonds

Interest Periods	(A) Interest to Be Paid (10% × $100,000)	(B) Interest Expense to Be Recorded (A) + (C)	(C) Discount Amortization ($2,000 ÷ 5)	(D) Unamortized Discount (D) − (C)	(E) Bond Carrying Value ($100,000 − D)
Issue date				$2,000	$ 98,000
1	$10,000	$10,400	$ 400	1,600	98,400
2	10,000	10,400	400	1,200	98,800
3	10,000	10,400	400	800	99,200
4	10,000	10,400	400	400	99,600
5	10,000	10,400	400	0	100,000
	$50,000	$52,000	$2,000		

Column **(A)** remains constant because the face value of the bonds ($100,000) is multiplied by the annual contractual interest rate (10%) each period.
Column **(B)** is computed as the interest paid (Column A) plus the discount amortization (Column C).
Column **(C)** indicates the discount amortization each period.
Column **(D)** decreases each period by the same amount until it reaches zero at maturity.
Column **(E)** increases each period by the amount of discount amortization until it equals the face value at maturity.

Illustration 15A-2
Bond discount amortization schedule

Amortizing Bond Premium

The amortization of bond premium parallels that of bond discount. Illustration 15A-3 presents the formula for determining bond premium amortization under the straight-line method.

Bond Premium	÷	Number of Interest Periods	=	Bond Premium Amortization

Illustration 15A-3
Formula for straight-line method of bond premium amortization

Continuing our example, assume Candlestick, Inc., sells the bonds described above for $102,000, rather than $98,000 (see page 520). This results in a bond premium of $2,000 ($102,000 − $100,000). The premium amortization for each interest period is $400 ($2,000 ÷ 5). Candlestick records the first accrual of interest on December 31 as follows.

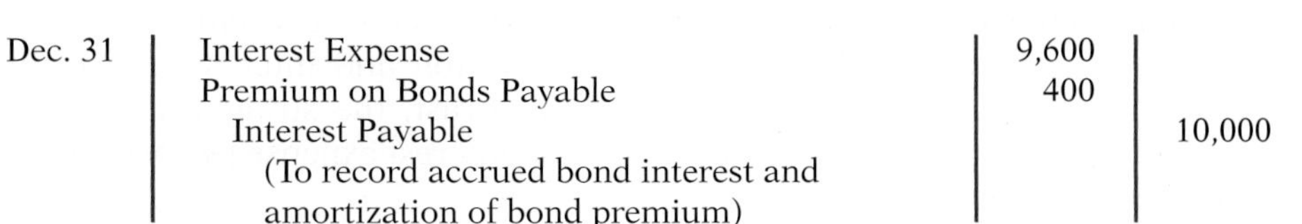

Date	Account	Debit	Credit
Dec. 31	Interest Expense	9,600	
	Premium on Bonds Payable	400	
	Interest Payable		10,000
	(To record accrued bond interest and amortization of bond premium)		

A = L + SE
−9,600 Exp
−400
+10,000

Cash Flows
no effect

A bond premium amortization schedule, as shown in Illustration 15A-4 (page 530), is useful to determine interest expense, premium amortization, and the carrying value of the bond. As indicated, the interest expense Candlestick records each period is $9,600. Note that the carrying value of the bond decreases $400 each period until it reaches its face value of $100,000 at the end of period 5.

Candlestick Inc.xls

CANDLESTICK, INC.
Bond Premium Amortization Schedule
Straight-Line Method—Annual Interest Payments
$100,000 of 10%, 5-Year Bonds

Interest Periods	(A) Interest to Be Paid (10% × $100,000)	(B) Interest Expense to Be Recorded (A) − (C)	(C) Premium Amortization ($2,000 ÷ 5)	(D) Unamortized Premium (D) − (C)	(E) Bond Carrying Value ($100,000 + D)
Issue date				$2,000	$102,000
1	$10,000	$ 9,600	$ 400	1,600	101,600
2	10,000	9,600	400	1,200	101,200
3	10,000	9,600	400	800	100,800
4	10,000	9,600	400	400	100,400
5	10,000	9,600	400	0	100,000
	$50,000	$48,000	$2,000		

Column (A) remains constant because the face value of the bonds ($100,000) is multiplied by the annual contractual interest rate (10%) each period.
Column (B) is computed as the interest paid (Column A) less the premium amortization (Column C).
Column (C) indicates the premium amortization each period.
Column (D) decreases each period by the same amount until it reaches zero at maturity.
Column (E) decreases each period by the amount of premium amortization until it equals the face value at maturity.

Illustration 15A-4
Bond premium amortization schedule

LEARNING OBJECTIVE *6

APPENDIX 15B: Apply the effective-interest method of amortizing bond discount and bond premium.

To follow the expense recognition principle, companies allocate bond discount to expense in each period in which the bonds are outstanding. However, to completely comply with the expense recognition principle, interest expense as a percentage of carrying value should not change over the life of the bonds.

This percentage, referred to as the **effective-interest rate**, is established when the bonds are issued and remains constant in each interest period. Unlike the straight-line method, the effective-interest method of amortization accomplishes this result.

Under the **effective-interest method of amortization**, the amortization of bond discount or bond premium results in periodic interest expense equal to a constant percentage of the carrying value of the bonds. The effective-interest method results in **varying amounts** of amortization and interest expense per period but a **constant percentage rate**. In contrast, the straight-line method results in constant amounts of amortization and interest expense per period but a varying percentage rate.

Companies follow three steps under the effective-interest method:

1. Compute the **bond interest expense** by multiplying the carrying value of the bonds at the beginning of the interest period by the effective-interest rate.
2. Compute the **bond interest paid** (or accrued) by multiplying the face value of the bonds by the contractual interest rate.
3. Compute the **amortization amount** by determining the difference between the amounts computed in steps (1) and (2).

Illustration 15B-1 depicts these steps.

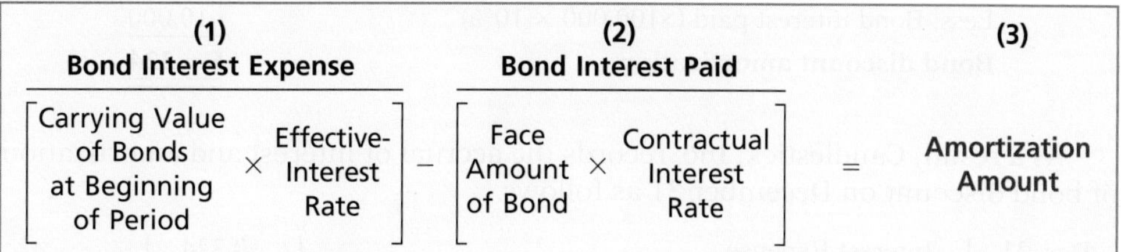

Illustration 15B-1
Computation of amortization using effective-interest method

Both the straight-line and effective-interest methods of amortization result in the same total amount of interest expense over the term of the bonds. Furthermore, interest expense each interest period is generally comparable in amount. However, **when the amounts are materially different, generally accepted accounting principles (GAAP) require use of the effective-interest method.**

Amortizing Bond Discount

In the Candlestick, Inc. example (page 519), the company sold $100,000, five-year, 10% bonds on January 1, 2017, for $98,000. This resulted in a $2,000 bond discount ($100,000 − $98,000). This discount results in an effective-interest rate of approximately 10.5348%. (The effective-interest rate can be computed using the techniques shown in Appendix G near the end of this textbook.)

Preparing a bond discount amortization schedule as shown in Illustration 15B-2 facilitates the recording of interest expense and the discount amortization. Note that interest expense as a percentage of carrying value remains constant at 10.5348%.

Candlestick Inc.xls

CANDLESTICK, INC.
Bond Discount Amortization Schedule
Effective-Interest Method—Annual Interest Payments
10% Bonds Issued at 10.5348%

Interest Periods	(A) Interest to Be Paid (10% × $100,000)	(B) Interest Expense to Be Recorded (10.5348% × Preceding Bond Carrying Value)		(C) Discount Amortization (B) − (A)	(D) Unamortized Discount (D) − (C)	(E) Bond Carrying Value ($100,000 − D)
Issue date					$2,000	$ 98,000
1	$10,000	$10,324	(10.5348% × $98,000)	$ 324	1,676	98,324
2	10,000	10,358	(10.5348% × $98,324)	358	1,318	98,682
3	10,000	10,396	(10.5348% × $98,682)	396	922	99,078
4	10,000	10,438	(10.5348% × $99,078)	438	484	99,516
5	10,000	10,484	(10.5348% × $99,516)	484	–0–	100,000
	$50,000	$52,000		$2,000		

Column (A) remains constant because the face value of the bonds ($100,000) is multiplied by the annual contractual interest rate (10%) each period.
Column (B) is computed as the preceding bond carrying value times the annual effective-interest rate (10.5348%).
Column (C) indicates the discount amortization each period.
Column (D) decreases each period until it reaches zero at maturity.
Column (E) increases each period until it equals face value at maturity.

Illustration 15B-2
Bond discount amortization schedule

For the first interest period, the computations of bond interest expense and the bond discount amortization are as follows.

Illustration 15B-3
Computation of bond discount amortization

Bond interest expense ($98,000 × 10.5348%)	$10,324
Less: Bond interest paid ($100,000 × 10%)	10,000
Bond discount amortization	**$ 324**

As a result, Candlestick, Inc. records the accrual of interest and amortization of bond discount on December 31 as follows.

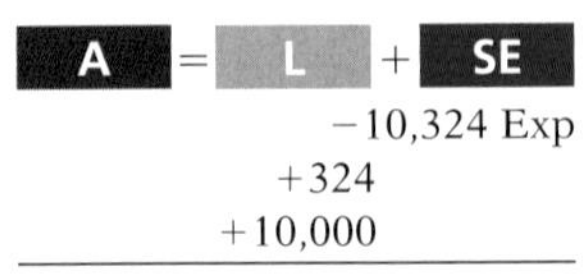

Cash Flows
no effect

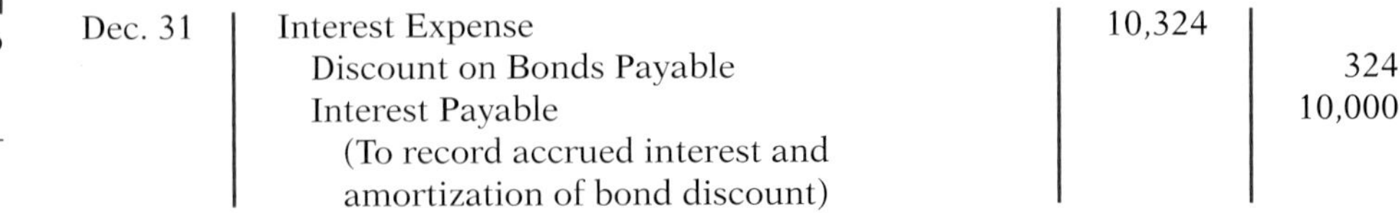

Dec. 31	Interest Expense	10,324	
	Discount on Bonds Payable		324
	Interest Payable		10,000
	(To record accrued interest and amortization of bond discount)		

For the second interest period, bond interest expense will be $10,358 ($98,324 × 10.5348%), and the discount amortization will be $358. At December 31, Candlestick makes the following adjusting entry.

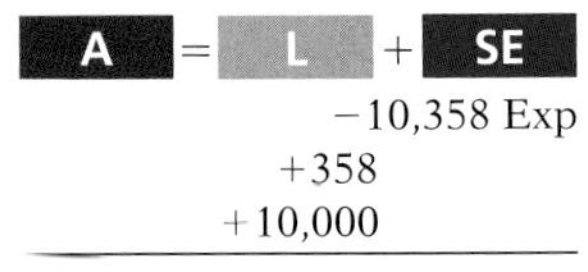

Cash Flows
no effect

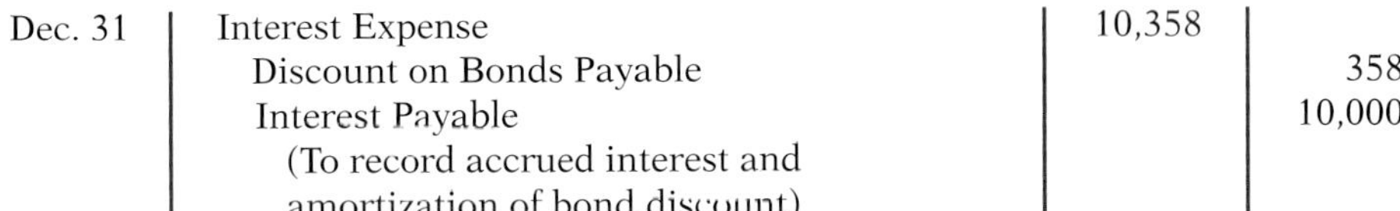

Dec. 31	Interest Expense	10,358	
	Discount on Bonds Payable		358
	Interest Payable		10,000
	(To record accrued interest and amortization of bond discount)		

Amortizing Bond Premium

Continuing our example, assume Candlestick, Inc. sells the bonds described above for $102,000 rather than $98,000 (see page 520). This would result in a bond premium of $2,000 ($102,000 − $100,000). This premium results in an effective-interest rate of approximately 9.4794%. (The effective-interest rate can be solved for using the techniques shown in Appendix G near the end of this textbook.) Illustration 15B-4 shows the bond premium amortization schedule.

Illustration 15B-4
Bond premium amortization schedule

Candlestick Inc.xls

CANDLESTICK, INC.
Bond Premium Amortization Schedule
Effective-Interest Method—Annual Interest Payments
10% Bonds Issued at 9.4794%

Interest Periods	(A) Interest to Be Paid (10% × $100,000)	(B) Interest Expense to Be Recorded (9.4794% × Preceding Bond Carrying Value)	(C) Premium Amortization (A) − (B)	(D) Unamortized Premium (D) − (C)	(E) Bond Carrying Value ($100,000 + D)
Issue date				$2,000	$102,000
1	$10,000	$ 9,669 (9.4794% × $102,000)	$ 331	1,669	101,669
2	10,000	9,638 (9.4794% × $101,669)	362	1,307	101,307
3	10,000	9,603 (9.4794% × $101,307)	397	910	100,910
4	10,000	9,566 (9.4794% × $100,910)	434	476	100,476
5	10,000	9,524* (9.4794% × $100,476)	476*	–0–	100,000
	$50,000	$48,000	$2,000		

Column **(A)** remains constant because the face value of the bonds ($100,000) is multiplied by the contractual interest rate (10%) each period.
Column **(B)** is computed as the carrying value of the bonds times the annual effective-interest rate (9.4794%).
Column **(C)** indicates the premium amortization each period.
Column **(D)** decreases each period until it reaches zero at maturity.
Column **(E)** decreases each period until it equals face value at maturity.

*Rounded to eliminate remaining discount resulting from rounding the effective rate.

For the first interest period, the computations of bond interest expense and the bond premium amortization are as follows.

Bond interest paid ($100,000 × 10%)	$10,000
Less: Bond interest expense ($102,000 × 9.4794%)	9,669
Bond premium amortization	**$ 331**

Illustration 15B-5
Computation of bond premium amortization

Dec. 31	Interest Expense	9,669	
	Premium on Bonds Payable	331	
	Interest Payable		10,000
	(To record accrued interest and amortization of bond premium)		

A	=	L	+	SE
				−9,669 Exp
		−331		
		+10,000		

Cash Flows
no effect

For the second interest period, interest expense will be $9,638, and the premium amortization will be $362. Note that the amount of periodic interest expense decreases over the life of the bond when companies apply the effective-interest method to bonds issued at a premium. The reason is that a constant percentage is applied to a decreasing bond carrying value to compute interest expense. The carrying value is decreasing because of the amortization of the premium.

REVIEW AND PRACTICE

LEARNING OBJECTIVES REVIEW

1 Describe the major characteristics of bonds. Bonds can have many different features and may be secured, unsecured, convertible, or callable. The terms of the bond issue are set forth in a bond indenture, and a bond certificate provides the specific information about the bond itself.

2 Explain how to account for bond transactions. When companies issue bonds, they debit Cash for the cash proceeds and credit Bonds Payable for the face value of the bonds. The account Premium on Bonds Payable shows a bond premium. Discount on Bonds Payable shows a bond discount.

When bondholders redeem bonds at maturity, the issuing company credits Cash and debits Bonds Payable for the face value of the bonds. When bonds are redeemed before maturity, the issuing company (a) eliminates the carrying value of the bonds at the redemption date, (b) records the cash paid, and (c) recognizes the gain or loss on redemption. When bonds are converted to common stock, the issuing company transfers the carrying (or book) value of the bonds to appropriate paid-in capital accounts. No gain or loss is recognized.

3 Explain how to account for long-term notes payable. Each payment consists of (1) interest on the unpaid balance of the loan and (2) a reduction of loan principal. The interest decreases each period, while the portion applied to the loan principal increases.

4 Discuss how long-term liabilities are reported and analyzed. Companies should report the nature and amount of each long-term debt in the balance sheet or in the notes accompanying the financial statements. Companies may sell bonds to investors to raise long-term capital. Bonds offer the following advantages over common stock: (a) stockholder control is not affected, (b) tax savings result, and (c) earnings per share of common stock may be higher.

Stockholders and long-term creditors are interested in a company's long-run solvency. Debt to assets and times interest earned are two ratios that provide information about debt-paying ability and long-run solvency.

A lease grants the right to use specific property for a period of time in return for cash payments. For an operating lease, the lessee (renter) records lease (rental) payments as an expense. For a capital lease, the lessee records the asset and related obligation at the present value of the future lease payments.

***5 Apply the straight-line method of amortizing bond discount and bond premium.** The straight-line method of amortization results in a constant amount of amortization and interest expense per period.

***6 Apply the effective-interest method of amortizing bond discount and bond premium.** The effective-interest method results in varying amounts of amortization and interest expense per period but a constant percentage rate of interest. When the difference between the straight-line and effective-interest method is material, GAAP requires use of the effective-interest method.

GLOSSARY REVIEW

Bond certificate A legal document that indicates the name of the issuer, the face value of the bonds, the contractual interest rate, and maturity date of the bonds.

Bond indenture A legal document that sets forth the terms of the bond issue.

Bonds A form of interest-bearing notes payable issued by corporations, universities, and governmental entities.

Callable bonds Bonds that are subject to redemption (buy back) at a stated dollar amount prior to maturity at the option of the issuer.

Capital lease A contractual arrangement that transfers substantially all the benefits and risks of ownership to the lessee so that the lease is in effect a purchase of the property.

Contractual interest rate Rate used to determine the amount of cash interest the borrower pays and the investor receives.

Convertible bonds Bonds that permit bondholders to convert them into common stock at the bondholders' option.

Debenture bonds Bonds issued against the general credit of the borrower. Also called unsecured bonds.

Debt to assets ratio A solvency measure that indicates the percentage of total assets provided by creditors; computed as total liabilities divided by total assets.

Discount (on a bond) The difference between the face value of a bond and its selling price, when the bond is sold for less than its face value.

***Effective-interest method of amortization** Amortization of bond discount or bond premium which results in periodic interest expense equal to a constant percentage of the carrying value of the bonds.

***Effective-interest rate** Rate established when bonds are issued that maintains a constant value for interest expense as a percentage of bond carrying value in each interest period.

Face value Amount of principal due at the maturity date of the bond.

Long-term liabilities Obligations expected to be paid more than one year in the future.

Market interest rate The rate investors demand for loaning funds to the corporation.

Maturity date The date on which the final payment on the bond is due from the bond issuer to the investor.

Mortgage bond A bond secured by real estate.

Mortgage notes payable A long-term note secured by a mortgage that pledges title to specific assets as security for a loan.

Operating lease A contractual arrangement giving the lessee temporary use of the property, with continued ownership of the property by the lessor.

Premium (on a bond) The difference between the selling price and the face value of a bond, when the bond is sold for more than its face value.

Secured bonds Bonds that have specific assets of the issuer pledged as collateral.

Sinking fund bonds Bonds secured by specific assets set aside to redeem them.

***Straight-line method of amortization** Allocates the same amount to interest expense in each interest period.

Times interest earned A solvency measure that indicates a company's ability to meet interest payments; computed by dividing the sum of net income, interest expense, and income tax expense by interest expense.

Time value of money The relationship between time and money. A dollar received today is worth more than a dollar promised at some time in the future.

Unsecured bonds Bonds issued against the general credit of the borrower. Also called debenture bonds.

PRACTICE EXERCISES

Prepare entries for bonds issued at face value.

(LO 2)

1. North Airlines Company issued $900,000 of 8%, 10-year bonds on January 1, 2017, at face value. Interest is payable annually on January 1.

Instructions

Prepare the journal entries to record the following events.

(a) The issuance of the bonds.

(b) The accrual of interest on December 31.

(c) The payment of interest on January 1, 2018.

(d) The redemption of bonds at maturity, assuming interest for the last interest period has been paid and recorded.

Solution

1. (a)	**January 1, 2017**		
	Cash	900,000	
	Bonds Payable		900,000
(b)	**December 31, 2017**		
	Interest Expense	72,000	
	Interest Payable ($900,000 × 8%)		72,000
(c)	**January 1, 2018**		
	Interest Payable	72,000	
	Cash		72,000
(d)	**January 1, 2027**		
	Bonds Payable	900,000	
	Cash		900,000

2. Hollenbeck Company issued $3,000,000 of bonds on January 1, 2017.

Prepare entries for issuance, retirement, and conversion of bonds.

(LO 2)

Instructions

(a) Prepare the journal entry to record the issuance of the bonds if they are issued at (1) 100, (2) 98, and (3) 103.

(b) Prepare the journal entry to record the retirement of the bonds at maturity, assuming the bonds were issued at 100.

(c) Prepare the journal entry to record the retirement of the bonds before maturity at 98. Assume the balance in Premium on Bonds Payable is $18,000.

(d) Prepare the journal entry to record the conversion of the bonds into 70,000 shares of $1 par value common stock. Assume the bonds were issued at par.

Solution

At 100		
2. (a) (1) Cash ($3,000,000 × 100%)	3,000,000	
Bonds Payable		3,000,000
At 98		
(2) Cash ($3,000,000 × 98%)	2,940,000	
Discount on Bonds Payable	60,000	
Bonds Payable		3,000,000
At 103		
(3) Cash ($3,000,000 × 103%)	3,090,000	
Bonds Payable		3,000,000
Premium on Bonds Payable		90,000
(b) Bonds Payable	3,000,000	
Cash		3,000,000
(c) Bonds Payable	3,000,000	
Premium on Bonds Payable	18,000	
Cash ($3,000,000 × 98%)		2,940,000
Gain on Bond Redemption		78,000
(d) Bonds Payable	3,000,000	
Common Stock (70,000 × $1)		70,000
Paid-in Capital in Excess of Par—Common Stock		2,930,000

3. Clipper Company borrowed $500,000 on December 31, 2017, by issuing a $500,000, 7% mortgage note payable. The terms call for annual installment payments of $80,000 on December 31.

Prepare entries to record mortgage note and installment payments.

(LO 3)

Instructions

(a) Prepare the journal entries to record the mortgage loan and the first two installment payments.

(b) Indicate the amount of mortgage note payable to be reported as a current liability and as a long-term liability at December 31, 2018.

Solution

3. (a)	December 31, 2017		
	Cash	500,000	
	Mortgage Payable		500,000
	December 31, 2018		
	Interest Expense ($500,000 × 7%)	35,000	
	Mortgage Payable	45,000	
	Cash		80,000
	December 31, 2019		
	Interest Expense [($500,000 − $45,000) × 7%]	31,850	
	Mortgage Payable	48,150	
	Cash		80,000

(b) Current: $48,150
Long-term: $406,850 ($500,000 − $45,000 − $48,150)

PRACTICE PROBLEM

Prepare entries to record issuance of bonds and long-term notes, interest accrual, and bond redemption.

(LO 1, 2, 3)

Snyder Software Inc. has successfully developed a new spreadsheet program. To produce and market the program, the company needed $1.9 million of additional financing. On January 1, 2017, Snyder borrowed money as follows.

1. Snyder issued $500,000, 11%, 10-year convertible bonds. The bonds sold at face value and pay annual interest on January 1. Each $1,000 bond is convertible into 30 shares of Snyder's $20 par value common stock.
2. Snyder issued $1 million, 10%, 10-year bonds at face value. Interest is payable on January 1.
3. Snyder also issued a $400,000, 6%, 15-year mortgage payable. The terms provide for annual installment payments of $41,185 on December 31.

Instructions

1. For the convertible bonds, prepare journal entries for:
   (a) The issuance of the bonds on January 1, 2017.
   (b) Interest expense on December 31, 2017.
   (c) The payment of interest on January 1, 2018.
   (d) The conversion of all bonds into common stock on January 1, 2018, when the market price of the common stock was $67 per share.
2. For the 10-year, 10% bonds:
   (a) Journalize the issuance of the bonds on January 1, 2017.
   (b) Prepare the journal entry for interest expense in 2017.
   (c) Prepare the entry for the redemption of the bonds at 101 on January 1, 2020, after paying the interest due on this date.
3. For the mortgage payable:
   (a) Prepare the entry for the issuance of the note on January 1, 2017.
   (b) Prepare a payment schedule for the first four installment payments.
   (c) Indicate the current and noncurrent amounts for the mortgage payable at December 31, 2017.

Solution

1. (a)	**2017**			
	Jan. 1	Cash	500,000	
		Bonds Payable		500,000
		(To record issue of 11%, 10-year convertible bonds at face value)		
(b)	Dec. 31	Interest Expense	55,000	
		Interest Payable ($500,000 × 11%)		55,000
		(To record accrual of annual bond interest)		

(c) **2018**

		Debit	Credit
Jan. 1	Interest Payable	55,000	
	Cash		55,000
	(To record payment of accrued interest)		

(d)

		Debit	Credit
Jan. 1	Bonds Payable	500,000	
	Common Stock		300,000*
	Paid-in Capital in Excess of Par—Common Stock		200,000
	(To record conversion of bonds into common stock)		

*($500,000 ÷ $1,000 = 500 bonds; 500 × 30 = 15,000 shares; 15,000 × $20 = $300,000)

2. (a) **2017**

		Debit	Credit
Jan. 1	Cash	1,000,000	
	Bonds Payable		1,000,000
	(To record issuance of bonds)		

(b) **2017**

		Debit	Credit
Dec. 31	Interest Expense	100,000	
	Interest Payable ($1,000,000 × 10%)		100,000
	(To record accrual of annual interest)		

(c) **2020**

		Debit	Credit
Jan. 1	Bonds Payable	1,000,000	
	Loss on Bond Redemption	10,000*	
	Cash		1,010,000
	(To record redemption of bonds at 101)		

*($1,010,000 − $1,000,000)

3. (a) **2017**

		Debit	Credit
Jan. 1	Cash	400,000	
	Mortgage Payable		400,000
	(To record issuance of mortgage payable)		

(b)

Interest Period	Cash Payment	Interest Expense	Reduction of Principal	Principal Balance
Issue date				$400,000
1	$41,185	$24,000	$17,185	382,815
2	41,185	22,969	18,216	364,599
3	41,185	21,876	19,309	345,290
4	41,185	20,717	20,468	324,822

(c) Current liability: $18,216
Long-term liability: $364,599

EXERCISES

E15-1 Nick Bosch has prepared the following list of statements about bonds.

Evaluate statements about bonds.

(LO 1)

1. Bonds are a form of interest-bearing notes payable.
2. Secured bonds have specific assets of the issuer pledged as collateral for the bonds.
3. Secured bonds are also known as debenture bonds.
4. A conversion feature may be added to bonds to make them more attractive to bond buyers.
5. The rate used to determine the amount of cash interest the borrower pays is called the stated rate.
6. Bond prices are usually quoted as a percentage of the face value of the bond.
7. The present value of a bond is the value at which it should sell in the marketplace.

Instructions
Identify each statement as true or false. If false, indicate how to correct the statement.

Prepare entries for issuance of bonds, and payment and accrual of bond interest.
(LO 2)

E15-2 On January 1, 2017, Klosterman Company issued $500,000, 10%, 10-year bonds at face value. Interest is payable annually on January 1.

Instructions
Prepare journal entries to record the following.

(a) The issuance of the bonds.
(b) The accrual of interest on December 31, 2017.
(c) The payment of interest on January 1, 2018.

Prepare entries for bonds issued at face value.
(LO 2)

E15-3 On January 1, 2017, Forrester Company issued $400,000, 8%, 5-year bonds at face value. Interest is payable annually on January 1.

Instructions
Prepare journal entries to record the following.

(a) The issuance of the bonds.
(b) The accrual of interest on December 31, 2017.
(c) The payment of interest on January 1, 2018.

Prepare entries for bonds issued at face value.
(LO 2)

E15-4 Laudie Company issued $400,000 of 9%, 10-year bonds on January 1, 2017, at face value. Interest is payable annually on January 1, 2018.

Instructions
Prepare the journal entries to record the following events.

(a) The issuance of the bonds.
(b) The accrual of interest on December 31, 2017.
(c) The payment of interest on January 1, 2018.
(d) The redemption of bonds at maturity, assuming interest for the last interest period has been paid and recorded.

Prepare entries for issuance, redemption, and conversion of bonds.
(LO 2)

E15-5 Swisher Company issued $2,000,000 of bonds on January 1, 2017.

Instructions
(a) Prepare the journal entry to record the issuance of the bonds if they are issued at (1) 100, (2) 98, and (3) 103.
(b) Prepare the journal entry to record the redemption of the bonds at maturity, assuming the bonds were issued at 100.
(c) Prepare the journal entry to record the redemption of the bonds before maturity at 98. Assume the balance in Premium on Bonds Payable is $9,000.
(d) Prepare the journal entry to record the conversion of the bonds into 60,000 shares of $10 par value common stock. Assume the bonds were issued at par.

Prepare entries to record issuance of bonds at discount and premium.
(LO 2)

E15-6 Whitmore Company issued $500,000 of 5-year, 8% bonds at 97 on January 1, 2017. The bonds pay interest annually.

Instructions
(a) (1) Prepare the journal entry to record the issuance of the bonds.
(2) Compute the total cost of borrowing for these bonds.
(b) Repeat the requirements from part (a), assuming the bonds were issued at 105.

Prepare entries for bond interest and redemption.
(LO 2)

E15-7 The following section is taken from Ohlman Corp.'s balance sheet at December 31, 2016.

Current liabilities	
Interest payable	$ 112,000
Long-term liabilities	
Bonds payable, 7%, due January 1, 2021	1,600,000

Bond interest is payable annually on January 1. The bonds are callable on any interest date.

Instructions

(a) Journalize the payment of the bond interest on January 1, 2017.
(b) Assume that on January 1, 2017, after paying interest, Ohlman calls bonds having a face value of $600,000. The call price is 103. Record the redemption of the bonds.
(c) Prepare the entry to record the accrual of interest on December 31, 2017.

E15-8 Presented below are three independent situations.

Prepare entries for redemption of bonds and conversion of bonds into common stock.

(LO 2)

1. Longbine Corporation redeemed $130,000 face value, 12% bonds on June 30, 2017, at 102. The carrying value of the bonds at the redemption date was $117,500. The bonds pay annual interest, and the interest payment due on June 30, 2017, has been made and recorded.
2. Tastove Inc. redeemed $150,000 face value, 12.5% bonds on June 30, 2017, at 98. The carrying value of the bonds at the redemption date was $151,000. The bonds pay annual interest, and the interest payment due on June 30, 2017, has been made and recorded.
3. Precision Company has $80,000, 8%, 12-year convertible bonds outstanding. These bonds were sold at face value and pay annual interest on December 31 of each year. The bonds are convertible into 30 shares of Precision $5 par value common stock for each $1,000 worth of bonds. On December 31, 2017, after the bond interest has been paid, $20,000 face value bonds were converted. The market price of Precision common stock was $44 per share on December 31, 2017.

Instructions

For each independent situation above, prepare the appropriate journal entry for the redemption or conversion of the bonds.

E15-9 Jernigan Co. receives $300,000 when it issues a $300,000, 10%, mortgage note payable to finance the construction of a building at December 31, 2017. The terms provide for annual installment payments of $50,000 on December 31.

Prepare entries to record mortgage note and payments.

(LO 3)

Instructions

Prepare the journal entries to record the mortgage loan and the first two payments.

E15-10 Dreiling Company borrowed $300,000 on January 1, 2017, by issuing a $300,000, 8% mortgage note payable. The terms call for annual installment payments of $40,000 on December 31.

Prepare entries to record mortgage note and installment payments.

(LO 3)

Instructions

(a) Prepare the journal entries to record the mortgage loan and the first two installment payments.
(b) Indicate the amount of mortgage note payable to be reported as a current liability and as a long-term liability at December 31, 2017.

E15-11 The adjusted trial balance for Karr Farm Corporation at the end of the current year contained the following accounts.

Prepare long-term liabilities section.

(LO 4)

Interest Payable	$ 9,000
Lease Liability	89,500
Bonds Payable, due 2022	180,000
Premium on Bonds Payable	32,000

Instructions

Prepare the long-term liabilities section of the balance sheet.

E15-12 Gilliland Airlines is considering two alternatives for the financing of a purchase of a fleet of airplanes. These two alternatives are:

Compare two alternatives of financing—issuance of common stock vs. issuance of bonds.

(LO 4)

1. Issue 90,000 shares of common stock at $30 per share. (Cash dividends have not been paid nor is the payment of any contemplated.)
2. Issue 10%, 10-year bonds at face value for $2,700,000.

It is estimated that the company will earn $800,000 before interest and taxes as a result of this purchase. The company has an estimated tax rate of 30% and has 120,000 shares of common stock outstanding prior to the new financing.

Instructions
Determine the effect on net income and earnings per share for these two methods of financing.

Compute debt to assets ratio and times interest earned.
(LO 4)

E15-13 Hatfield Corporation reports the following amounts in its 2017 financial statements:

	At December 31, 2017	For the Year 2017
Total assets	$1,000,000	
Total liabilities	580,000	
Total stockholders' equity	?	
Interest expense		$ 20,000
Income tax expense		100,000
Net income		150,000

Instructions
(a) Compute the December 31, 2017, balance in stockholders' equity.
(b) Compute the debt to assets ratio at December 31, 2017.
(c) Compute times interest earned for 2017.

Prepare entries for operating lease and capital lease.
(LO 4)

E15-14 Presented below are two independent situations.

1. Flinthills Car Rental leased a car to Jayhawk Company for one year. Terms of the operating lease agreement call for monthly payments of $500.
2. On January 1, 2017, Throm Inc. entered into an agreement to lease 20 computers from Drummond Electronics. The terms of the lease agreement require three annual rental payments of $20,000 (including 10% interest) beginning December 31, 2017. The present value of the three rental payments is $49,735. Throm considers this a capital lease.

Instructions
(a) Prepare the appropriate journal entry to be made by Jayhawk Company for the first lease payment.
(b) Prepare the journal entry to record the lease agreement on the books of Throm Inc. on January 1, 2017.

Prepare entries to record issuance of bonds, payment of interest, amortization of premium, and redemption at maturity.
(LO 5)

***E15-15** Adcock Company issued $600,000, 9%, 20-year bonds on January 1, 2017, at 103. Interest is payable annually on January 1. Adcock uses straight-line amortization for bond premium or discount.

Instructions
Prepare the journal entries to record the following.

(a) The issuance of the bonds.
(b) The accrual of interest and the premium amortization on December 31, 2017.
(c) The payment of interest on January 1, 2018.
(d) The redemption of the bonds at maturity, assuming interest for the last interest period has been paid and recorded.

Prepare entries to record issuance of bonds, payment of interest, amortization of discount, and redemption at maturity.
(LO 5)

***E15-16** Gridley Company issued $800,000, 11%, 10-year bonds on December 31, 2016, for $730,000. Interest is payable annually on December 31. Gridley Company uses the straight-line method to amortize bond premium or discount.

Instructions
Prepare the journal entries to record the following.

(a) The issuance of the bonds.
(b) The payment of interest and the discount amortization on December 31, 2017.
(c) The redemption of the bonds at maturity, assuming interest for the last interest period has been paid and recorded.

Prepare entries for issuance of bonds, payment of interest, and amortization of discount using effective-interest method.
(LO 6)

***E15-17** Lorance Corporation issued $400,000, 7%, 20-year bonds on January 1, 2017, for $360,727. This price resulted in an effective-interest rate of 8% on the bonds. Interest is payable annually on January 1. Lorance uses the effective-interest method to amortize bond premium or discount.

Instructions

Prepare the journal entries to record the following. (Round to the nearest dollar.)

(a) The issuance of the bonds.
(b) The accrual of interest and the discount amortization on December 31, 2017.
(c) The payment of interest on January 1, 2018.

***E15-18** LRNA Company issued $380,000, 7%, 10-year bonds on January 1, 2017, for $407,968. This price resulted in an effective-interest rate of 6% on the bonds. Interest is payable annually on January 1. LRNA uses the effective-interest method to amortize bond premium or discount.

Prepare entries for issuance of bonds, payment of interest, and amortization of premium using effective-interest method.

(LO 6)

Instructions

Prepare the journal entries to record the following. (Round to the nearest dollar.)

(a) The issuance of the bonds.
(b) The accrual of interest and the premium amortization on December 31, 2017.
(c) The payment of interest on January 1, 2018.

PROBLEMS

P15-1A On May 1, 2017, Herron Corp. issued $600,000, 9%, 5-year bonds at face value. The bonds were dated May 1, 2017, and pay interest annually on May 1. Financial statements are prepared annually on December 31.

Prepare entries to record issuance of bonds, interest accrual, and bond redemption.

(LO 2, 4)

Instructions

(a) Prepare the journal entry to record the issuance of the bonds.
(b) Prepare the adjusting entry to record the accrual of interest on December 31, 2017.
(c) Show the balance sheet presentation on December 31, 2017.
(d) Prepare the journal entry to record payment of interest on May 1, 2018.
(e) Prepare the adjusting entry to record the accrual of interest on December 31, 2018.
(f) Assume that on January 1, 2019, Herron pays the accrual bond interest and calls the bonds. The call price is 102. Record the payment of interest and redemption of the bonds.

(d) Int. exp. $18,000

P15-2A Kershaw Electric sold $6,000,000, 10%, 10-year bonds on January 1, 2017. The bonds were dated January 1, 2017, and paid interest on January 1. The bonds were sold at 98.

Prepare entries to record issuance of bonds, interest accrual, and bond redemption.

(LO 2, 4)

Instructions

(a) Prepare the journal entry to record the issuance of the bonds on January 1, 2017.
(b) At December 31, 2017, $8,000 of the Discount on Bonds Payable account has been amortized. Show the balance sheet presentation of the long-term liability at December 31, 2017.
(c) On January 1, 2019, when the carrying value of the bonds was $5,896,000, the company redeemed the bonds at 102. Record the redemption of the bonds assuming that interest for the period has already been paid.

(c) Loss $224,000

P15-3A The following section is taken from Mareska's balance sheet at December 31, 2017.

Prepare entries for interest payment, bond redemption, and interest accrual.

(LO 2)

Current liabilities	
Interest payable	$ 40,000
Long-term liabilities	
Bonds payable (8%, due January 1, 2021)	500,000

Interest is payable annually on January 1. The bonds are callable on any annual interest date.

Instructions

(a) Journalize the payment of the bond interest on January 1, 2018.
(b) Assume that on January 1, 2018, after paying interest, Mareska calls bonds having a face value of $200,000. The call price is 103. Record the redemption of the bonds.

(c) Prepare the adjusting entry on December 31, 2018, to accrue the interest on the remaining bonds.

Prepare installment payments schedule and journal entries for a mortgage note payable.
(LO 3, 4)

P15-4A Talkington Electronics issues a $400,000, 8%, 15-year mortgage note on December 31, 2016. The proceeds from the note are to be used in financing a new research laboratory. The terms of the note provide for annual installment payments, exclusive of real estate taxes and insurance, of $59,612. Payments are due on December 31.

Instructions

(b) December 31 debit Mortgage Payable $27,612
(c) Current liability—2017 $29,821

(a) Prepare an installment payments schedule for the first 4 years.
(b) Prepare the entries for (1) the loan and (2) the first installment payment.
(c) Show how the total mortgage liability should be reported on the balance sheet at December 31, 2017.

Analyze three different lease situations and prepare journal entries.
(LO 4)

P15-5A Presented below are three different lease transactions that occurred for Ruggiero Inc. in 2017. Assume that all lease contracts start on January 1, 2017. In no case does Ruggiero receive title to the properties leased during or at the end of the lease term.

	Lessor		
	Judson Delivery	**Hester Co.**	**Gunselman Auto**
Type of property	Computer	Delivery equipment	Automobile
Yearly rental	$ 5,000	$ 4,200	$ 3,700
Lease term	6 years	4 years	2 years
Estimated economic life	7 years	7 years	5 years
Fair value of lease asset	$27,500	$19,000	$11,000
Present value of the lease rental payments	$26,000	$13,000	$ 6,400
Bargain purchase option	None	None	None

Instructions

(a) Which of the leases are operating leases and which are capital leases? Explain.
(b) How should the lease transaction for Hester Co. be recorded in 2017?
(c) How should the lease transaction for Judson Delivery be recorded on January 1, 2017?

Prepare entries to record issuance of bonds, interest accrual, and straight-line amortization for 2 years.
(LO 4, 5)

***P15-6A** Paris Electric sold $3,000,000, 10%, 10-year bonds on January 1, 2017. The bonds were dated January 1 and pay interest annually on January 1. Paris Electric uses the straight-line method to amortize bond premium or discount. The bonds were sold at 104.

Instructions

(b) Amortization $12,000
(d) Premium on bonds payable $96,000

(a) Prepare the journal entry to record the issuance of the bonds on January 1, 2017.
(b) Prepare a bond premium amortization schedule for the first 4 interest periods.
(c) Prepare the journal entries for interest and the amortization of the premium in 2017 and 2018.
(d) Show the balance sheet presentation of the bond liability at December 31, 2018.

Prepare entries to record issuance of bonds, interest, and straight-line amortization of bond premium and discount.
(LO 4, 5)

***P15-7A** Saberhagen Company sold $3,500,000, 8%, 10-year bonds on January 1, 2017. The bonds were dated January 1, 2017 and pay interest annually on January 1. Saberhagen Company uses the straight-line method to amortize bond premium or discount.

(a) Amortization $14,000
(b) Amortization $7,000
(c) Premium on bonds payable $126,000
Discount on bonds payable $63,000

Instructions

(a) Prepare all the necessary journal entries to record the issuance of the bonds and bond interest expense for 2017, assuming that the bonds sold at 104.
(b) Prepare journal entries as in part (a) assuming that the bonds sold at 98.
(c) Show balance sheet presentation for the bonds at December 31, 2017, for both the requirements in (a) and (b).

***P15-8A** The following is taken from the Colaw Company balance sheet.

Prepare entries to record interest payments, straight-line premium amortization, and redemption of bonds.

(LO 5)

COLAW COMPANY
Balance Sheet (partial)
December 31, 2017

Current liabilities		
Interest payable (for 12 months from January 1 to December 31)		$ 210,000
Long-term liabilities		
Bonds payable, 7% due January 1, 2028	$3,000,000	
Add: Premium on bonds payable	200,000	3,200,000

Interest is payable annually on January 1. The bonds are callable on any annual interest date. Colaw uses straight-line amortization for any bond premium or discount. From December 31, 2017, the bonds will be outstanding for an additional 10 years (120 months).

Instructions

(a) Journalize the payment of bond interest on January 1, 2018.
(b) Prepare the entry to amortize bond premium and to accrue the interest due on December 31, 2018.
(c) Assume that on January 1, 2019, after paying interest, Colaw Company calls bonds having a face value of $1,200,000. The call price is 101. Record the redemption of the bonds.
(d) Prepare the adjusting entry at December 31, 2019, to amortize bond premium and to accrue interest on the remaining bonds.

(b) Amortization $20,000

(c) Gain $60,000

(d) Amortization $12,000

***P15-9A** On January 1, 2017, Lock Corporation issued $1,800,000 face value, 5%, 10-year bonds at $1,667,518. This price resulted in an effective-interest rate of 6% on the bonds. Lock uses the efective-interest method to amortize bond premium or discount. The bonds pay annual interest January 1.

Prepare journal entries to record issuance of bonds, payment of interest, and amortization of bond discount using effective-interest method.

(LO 6)

Instructions

(Round all computations to the nearest dollar.)

(a) Prepare the journal entry to record the issuance of the bonds on January 1, 2017.
(b) Prepare an amortization table through December 31, 2019 (three interest periods) for this bond issue.
(c) Prepare the journal entry to record the accrual of interest and the amortization of the discount on December 31, 2017.
(d) Prepare the journal entry to record the payment of interest on January 1, 2018.
(e) Prepare the journal entry to record the accrual of interest and the amortization of the discount on December 31, 2018.

(c) Interest Expense $100,051

***P15-10A** On January 1, 2017, Jade Company issued $2,000,000 face value, 7%, 10-year bonds at $2,147,202. This price resulted in a 6% effective-interest rate on the bonds. Jade uses the effective-interest method to amortize bond premium or discount. The bonds pay annual interest on each January 1.

Prepare journal entries to record issuance of bonds, payment of interest, and effective-interest amortization, and balance sheet presentation.

(LO 4, 6)

Instructions

(a) Prepare the journal entries to record the following transactions.
    (1) The issuance of the bonds on January 1, 2017.
    (2) Accrual of interest and amortization of the premium on December 31, 2017.
    (3) The payment of interest on January 1, 2018.
    (4) Accrual of interest and amortization of the premium on December 31, 2018.
(b) Show the proper long-term liabilities balance sheet presentation for the liability for bonds payable at December 31, 2018.
(c) Provide the answers to the following questions in narrative form.
    (1) What amount of interest expense is reported for 2018?
    (2) Would the bond interest expense reported in 2018 be the same as, greater than, or less than the amount that would be reported if the straight-line method of amortization were used?

(a) (4) Interest Expense $128,162

COMPREHENSIVE PROBLEM: CHAPTERS 13 TO 15

CP15 Quigley Corporation's trial balance at December 31, 2017, is presented below. All 2017 transactions have been recorded except for the items described below.

	Debit	Credit
Cash	$ 25,500	
Accounts Receivable	51,000	
Inventory	22,700	
Land	65,000	
Buildings	95,000	
Equipment	40,000	
Allowance for Doubtful Accounts		$ 450
Accumulated Depreciation—Buildings		30,000
Accumulated Depreciation—Equipment		14,400
Accounts Payable		19,300
Interest Payable		–0–
Dividends Payable		–0–
Unearned Rent Revenue		8,000
Bonds Payable (10%)		50,000
Common Stock ($10 par)		30,000
Paid-in Capital in Excess of Par—Common Stock		6,000
Preferred Stock ($20 par)		–0–
Paid-in Capital in Excess of Par—Preferred Stock		–0–
Retained Earnings		75,050
Treasury Stock	–0–	
Cash Dividends	–0–	
Sales Revenue		570,000
Rent Revenue		–0–
Bad Debt Expense	–0–	
Interest Expense	–0–	
Cost of Goods Sold	400,000	
Depreciation Expense	–0–	
Other Operating Expenses	39,000	
Salaries and Wages Expense	65,000	
Total	$803,200	$803,200

Unrecorded transactions and adjustments:

1. On January 1, 2017, Quigley issued 1,000 shares of $20 par, 6% preferred stock for $22,000.
2. On January 1, 2017, Quigley also issued 1,000 shares of common stock for $23,000.
3. Quigley reacquired 300 shares of its common stock on July 1, 2017, for $49 per share.
4. On December 31, 2017, Quigley declared the annual cash dividend on the preferred stock and a $1.50 per share dividend on the outstanding common stock, all payable on January 15, 2018.
5. Quigley estimates that uncollectible accounts receivable at year-end is $5,100.
6. The building is being depreciated using the straight-line method over 30 years. The salvage value is $5,000.
7. The equipment is being depreciated using the straight-line method over 10 years. The salvage value is $4,000.
8. The unearned rent was collected on October 1, 2017. It was the receipt of 4 months' rent in advance (October 1, 2017 through January 31, 2018).
9. The 10% bonds payable pay interest every January 1. The interest for the 12 months ended December 31, 2017, has not been paid or recorded.

Instructions

(Ignore income taxes.)

(a) Prepare journal entries for the transactions and adjustment listed above.

(b) Total $871,200 (b) Prepare an updated December 31, 2017, trial balance, reflecting the journal entries in (a).

(c) Prepare a multiple-step income statement for the year ending December 31, 2017.

(e) Total assets $273,400 (d) Prepare a retained earnings statement for the year ending December 31, 2017.

(e) Prepare a classified balance sheet as of December 31, 2017.

BROADENING YOUR PERSPECTIVE

FINANCIAL REPORTING AND ANALYSIS

Financial Reporting Problem: Apple Inc.

BYP15-1 The financial statements of Apple Inc. are presented in Appendix A. Instructions for accessing and using the company's complete annual report, including the notes to the financial statements, are also provided in Appendix A.

Instructions

(a) What were Apple's total long-term liabilities at September 28, 2013? What was the increase/decrease in total long-term liabilities from the prior year?

(b) Determine whether Apple redeemed (bought back) any long-term liabilities during the fiscal year ended September 28, 2013.

Comparative Analysis Problem: PepsiCo, Inc. vs. The Coca-Cola Company

BYP15-2 PepsiCo's financial statements are presented in Appendix B. Financial statements of The Coca-Cola Company are presented in Appendix C. Instructions for accessing and using the complete annual reports of PepsiCo and Coca-Cola, including the notes to the financial statements, are also provided in Appendices B and C, respectively.

Instructions

(a) Based on the information contained in these financial statements, compute the following 2013 ratios for each company.
   (1) Debt to assets.
   (2) Times interest earned.

(b) What conclusions concerning the companies' long-run solvency can be drawn from these ratios?

Comparative Analysis Problem: Amazon.com, Inc. vs. Wal-Mart Stores, Inc.

BYP15-3 Amazon.com, Inc.'s financial statements are presented in Appendix D. Financial statements of Wal-Mart Stores, Inc. are presented in Appendix E. Instructions for accessing and using the complete annual reports of Amazon and Wal-Mart, including the notes to the financial statements, are also provided in Appendices D and E, respectively.

Instructions

(a) Based on the information contained in these financial statements, compute the following 2013 ratios for Amazon and 2014 ratios for Wal-Mart.
   (1) Debt to assets.
   (2) Times interest earned.

(b) What conclusions concerning the companies' long-run solvency can be drawn from these ratios?

Real-World Focus

BYP15-4 Bond or debt securities pay a stated rate of interest. This rate of interest is dependent on the risk associated with the investment. Also, bond prices change when the risks associated with those bonds change. Standard & Poor's provides ratings for companies that issue debt securities.

Address: **www.standardandpoors.com/ratings/definitions-and-faqs/en/us**, or go to **www.wiley.com/college/weygandt**

Instructions

Go to the website shown and answer the following questions.

(a) Explain the meaning of an "A" rating. Explain the meaning of a "C" rating.

(b) What types of things can cause a change in a company's credit rating?

(c) Explain the relationship between a company's credit rating and the merit of an investment in that company's bonds.

CRITICAL THINKING

Decision-Making Across the Organization

***BYP15-5** On January 1, 2015, Glover Corporation issued $2,400,000 of 5-year, 8% bonds at 95. The bonds pay interest annually on January 1. By January 1, 2017, the market rate of interest for bonds of risk similar to those of Glover Corporation had risen. As a result, the market value of these bonds was $2,000,000 on January 1, 2017—below their carrying value. Joanna Glover, president of the company, suggests repurchasing all of these bonds in the open market at the $2,000,000 price. To do so, the company will have to issue $2,000,000 (face value) of new 10-year, 11% bonds at par. The president asks you, as controller, "What is the feasibility of my proposed repurchase plan?"

Instructions

With the class divided into groups, answer the following.

(a) What is the carrying value of the outstanding Glover Corporation 5-year bonds on January 1, 2017? (Assume straight-line amortization.)

(b) Prepare the journal entry to redeem the 5-year bonds on January 1, 2017. Prepare the journal entry to issue the new 10-year bonds.

(c) Prepare a short memo to the president in response to her request for advice. List the economic factors that you believe should be considered for her repurchase proposal.

Communication Activity

BYP15-6 Sam Masasi, president of Masasi Corporation, is considering the issuance of bonds to finance an expansion of his business. He has asked you to (1) discuss the advantages of bonds over common stock financing, (2) indicate the types of bonds he might issue, and (3) explain the issuing procedures used in bond transactions.

Instructions

Write a memo to the president, answering his request.

Ethics Case

BYP15-7 Ken Iwig is the president, founder, and majority owner of Olathe Medical Corporation, an emerging medical technology products company. Olathe is in dire need of additional capital to keep operating and to bring several promising products to final development, testing, and production. Ken, as owner of 51% of the outstanding stock, manages the company's operations. He places heavy emphasis on research and development and on long-term growth. The other principal stockholder is Barb Lowery who, as a nonemployee investor, owns 40% of the stock. Barb would like to deemphasize the R&D functions and emphasize the marketing function, to maximize short-run sales and profits from existing products. She believes this strategy would raise the market price of Olathe's stock.

All of Ken's personal capital and borrowing power is tied up in his 51% stock ownership. He knows that any offering of additional shares of stock will dilute his controlling interest because he won't be able to participate in such an issuance. But, Barb has money and would likely buy enough shares to gain control of Olathe. She then would dictate the company's future direction, even if it meant replacing Ken as president and CEO.

The company already has considerable debt. Raising additional debt will be costly, will adversely affect Olathe's credit rating, and will increase the company's reported losses due to the growth in interest expense. Barb and the other minority stockholders express opposition to the assumption of additional debt, fearing the company will be pushed to the brink of bankruptcy. Wanting to maintain his control and to preserve the direction of "his" company, Ken is doing everything to avoid a stock issuance. He is contemplating a large issuance of bonds, even if it means the bonds are issued with a high effective-interest rate.

Instructions

(a) Who are the stakeholders in this situation?

(b) What are the ethical issues in this case?

(c) What would you do if you were Ken?

All About You

BYP15-8 Numerous articles have been written that identify early warning signs that you might be getting into trouble with your personal debt load. You can find many good articles on this topic on the Internet.

Instructions
Find an article that identifies early warning signs of personal debt trouble. Write a summary of the article and bring your summary and the article to class to share.

FASB Codification Activity

BYP15-9 If your school has a subscription to the FASB Codification, go to **http://aaahq.org/ascLogin.cfm** to log in and prepare responses to the following:

(a) What is the definition of long-term obligation?
(b) What guidance does the Codification provide for the disclosure of long-term obligations?

A Look at IFRS

LEARNING OBJECTIVE 7 **Compare the accounting for long-term liabilities under GAAP and IFRS.**

IFRS and GAAP have similar definitions of liabilities but have a different approach for accounting certain long-term liabilities.

Key Points

Following are the key similarities and difference between GAAP and IFRS as related to accounting for long-term liabilities.

Similarities

- As indicated in Chapter 11, in general GAAP and IFRS define liabilities similarly.
- IFRS requires that companies classify liabilities as current or noncurrent on the face of the statement of financial position (balance sheet), except in industries where a **presentation** based on liquidity would be considered to provide more useful information (such as financial institutions). When current liabilities (also called short-term liabilities) are presented, they are generally presented in order of liquidity.
- Under IFRS, liabilities are classified as current if they are expected to be paid within 12 months.
- Similar to GAAP, items are normally reported in order of liquidity. Companies sometimes show liabilities before assets. Also, they will sometimes show noncurrent (long-term) liabilities before current liabilities.
- The basic calculation for bond valuation is the same under GAAP and IFRS. In addition, the accounting for bond liability transactions is essentially the same between GAAP and IFRS.
- IFRS requires use of the effective-interest method for amortization of bond discounts and premiums. GAAP also requires the effective-interest method, except that it allows use of the straight-line method where the difference is not material. Under IFRS, companies do not use a premium or discount account but instead show the bond at its net amount. For example, if a $100,000 bond was issued at 97, under IFRS a company would record:

Cash	97,000	
Bonds Payable		97,000

Differences

- The accounting for convertible bonds differs between IFRS and GAAP. Unlike GAAP, IFRS splits the proceeds from the convertible bond between an equity component and a debt component. The equity conversion rights are reported in equity.

To illustrate, assume that Harris Corp. issues convertible 7% bonds with a face value of $1,000,000 and receives $1,000,000. Comparable bonds without a conversion feature would have required a 9% rate of interest. To determine how much of the proceeds would be allocated to debt and how much to equity, the promised payments of the bond obligation would be discounted at the market rate of 9%. Suppose that this results in a present value of $850,000. The entry to record the issuance would be:

Cash	1,000,000	
Bonds Payable		850,000
Share Premium—Conversion Equity		150,000

- The IFRS leasing standard is *IAS 17*. Both Boards share the same objective of recording leases by lessees and lessors according to their economic substance—that is, according to the definitions of assets and liabilities. However, GAAP for leases is much more "rules-based" with specific bright-line criteria (such as the "90% of fair value" test) to determine if a lease arrangement transfers the risks and rewards of ownership; IFRS is more conceptual in its provisions. Rather than a 90% cut-off, it asks whether the agreement transfers substantially all of the risks and rewards associated with ownership.

Looking to the Future

The FASB and IASB are currently involved in two projects, each of which has implications for the accounting for liabilities. One project is investigating approaches to differentiate between debt and equity instruments. The other project, the elements phase of the conceptual framework project, will evaluate the definitions of the fundamental building blocks of accounting. The results of these projects could change the classification of many debt and equity securities.

In addition to these projects, the FASB and IASB have also identified leasing as one of the most problematic areas of accounting. A joint project is now focused on lessee accounting. One of the first areas studied is, "What are the assets and liabilities to be recognized related to a lease contract?" Should the focus remain on the leased item or the right to use the leased item? This question is tied to the Boards' joint project on the conceptual framework—defining an "asset" and a "liability."

IFRS Practice

IFRS Self-Test Questions

1. The accounting for bonds payable is:
   (a) essentially the same under IFRS and GAAP.
   (b) differs in that GAAP requires use of the straight-line method for amortization of bond premium and discount.
   (c) the same except that market prices may be different because the present value calculations are different between IFRS and GAAP.
   (d) not covered by IFRS.

2. Stevens Corporation issued 5% convertible bonds with a total face value of $3,000,000 for $3,000,000. If the bonds had not had a conversion feature, they would have sold for $2,600,000. Under IFRS, the entry to record the transaction would require a credit to:
   (a) Bonds Payable for $3,000,000.
   (b) Bonds Payable for $400,000.
   (c) Share Premium—Conversion Equity for $400,000.
   (d) Discount on Bonds Payable for $400,000.

3. The leasing standards employed by IFRS:
   (a) rely more heavily on interpretation of the conceptual meaning of assets and liabilities than GAAP.
   (b) are more "rules based" than those of GAAP.
   (c) employ the same "bright-line test" as GAAP.
   (d) are identical to those of GAAP.

4. The joint projects of the FASB and IASB could potentially:
   (a) change the definition of liabilities.
   (b) change the definition of equity.
   (c) change the definition of assets.
   (d) All of the above.

IFRS Exercises

IFRS15-1 Briefly describe some of the similarities and differences between GAAP and IFRS with respect to the accounting for liabilities.

IFRS15-2 Ratzlaff Company issues (in euros) €2 million, 10-year, 8% bonds at 97, with interest payable annually on January 1.

Instructions

(a) Prepare the journal entry to record the sale of these bonds on January 1, 2017.
(b) Assuming instead that the above bonds sold for 104, prepare the journal entry to record the sale of these bonds on January 1, 2017.

IFRS15-3 Archer Company issued (in pounds) £4,000,000 par value, 7% convertible bonds at 99 for cash. The net present value of the debt without the conversion feature is £3,800,000. Prepare the journal entry to record the issuance of the convertible bonds.

International Financial Statement Analysis: Louis Vuitton

IFRS15-4 The financial statements of Louis Vuitton are presented in Appendix F. Instructions for accessing and using the company's complete annual report, including the notes to its financial statements, are also provided in Appendix F.

Instructions

Use the company's annual report to answer the following questions.

(a) According to the notes to the financial statements, what is the composition of long-term gross borrowings?
(b) According to the accounting policy note to the financial statements, how are borrowings measured?
(c) Determine the amount of fixed-rate and adjustable-rate (floating) borrowings (gross) that the company reports.
(d) Identify where non-current liabilities are reported on the company's balance sheet.

Answers to IFRS Self-Test Questions

1. a **2.** c **3.** a **4.** d

Chapter 16 Investments

In a rapidly changing world, you must keep up or suffer the consequences. In business, change requires investment.

A case in point is found in the entertainment industry. Technology is bringing about innovations so quickly that it is nearly impossible to guess which technologies will last and which will soon fade away. For example, will both satellite TV and cable TV survive? Or, will both be replaced by something else?

Consider the publishing industry as well. Will paper newspapers and magazines be replaced completely by online news? If you are a publisher, you have to make your best guess about what the future holds and invest accordingly.

Time Warner Inc. lives at the center of this arena. It is not an environment for the timid, and Time Warner's philosophy is anything but that. Instead, it might be characterized as, "If we can't beat you, we will buy you." Its mantra is "invest, invest, invest." A partial list of Time Warner's holdings gives an idea of its reach:

Magazines: Time, Life, Sports Illustrated, and *Fortune*.

Book publishers: Time-Life Books; Book-of-the-Month Club; Little, Brown & Co; and Sunset Books.

Television and movies: Warner Bros. ("The Big Bang Theory" and "The Mentalist"), HBO, and movies like *The Hobbit: The Battle of the Five Armies* and *Into the Storm*.

Broadcasting: TNT, CNN news, and Turner's library of thousands of classic movies.

Internet: America Online and AOL Anywhere.

Time Warner owns more information and entertainment copyrights and brands than any other company in the world.

Recently, Rupert Murdoch, chairman and CEO of 21st Century Fox, made an unsolicited $80 billion offer to buy the major media conglomerate. Murdoch's bid put "a positive light on Time Warner's assets," says one analyst. Murdoch eventually withdrew his bid, which resulted in driving down Time Warner's stock price. However, analysts expect the stock to eventually rebound as the long-term institutional investors start taking advantage of the lower price.

Source: Gene Marcial, "Why Time Warner Will Deliver Superb Growth and Valuation Despite Murdoch's Surrender," *Forbes* (August 6, 2014).

LEARNING OBJECTIVES

1. **Explain how to account for debt investments.**
2. **Explain how to account for stock investments.**
3. **Discuss how debt and stock investments are reported in financial statements.**

LEARNING OBJECTIVE 1 **Explain how to account for debt investments.**

Why Corporations Invest

Corporations purchase investments in debt or stock securities generally for one of three reasons. First, a corporation may **have excess cash** that it does not need for the immediate purchase of operating assets. For example, many companies experience seasonal fluctuations in sales. A Cape Cod marina has more sales in the spring and summer than in the fall and winter. The reverse is true for an Aspen ski shop. Thus, at the end of an operating cycle, many companies may have cash on hand that is temporarily idle until the start of another operating cycle. These companies may invest the excess funds to earn—through interest and dividends—a greater return than they would get by just holding the funds in the bank. Illustration 16-1 shows the role that temporary investments play in the operating cycle.

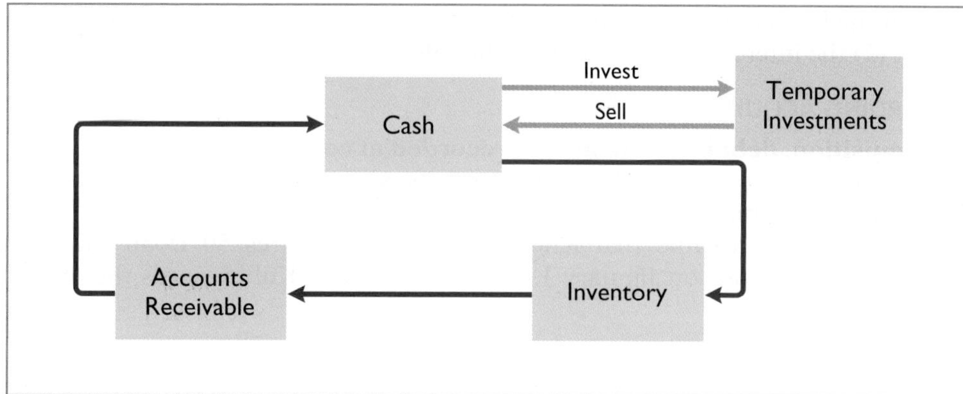

Illustration 16-1
Temporary investments and the operating cycle

A second reason some companies such as banks purchase investments is to generate **earnings from investment income**. Although banks make most of their earnings by lending money, they also generate earnings by investing primarily in debt securities. Banks purchase investment securities because loan demand varies both seasonally and with changes in the economic climate. Thus, when loan demand is low, a bank must find other uses for its cash.

Some companies attempt to generate investment income through speculative investments. That is, they are speculating that the investment will increase in value and thus result in positive returns. Therefore, they invest mostly in the common stock of other corporations.

Third, companies also invest for **strategic reasons**. A company may purchase a noncontrolling interest in another company in a related industry in which it wishes to establish a presence. Or, a company can exercise some influence over one of its customers or suppliers by purchasing a significant, but not controlling, interest in that company. Another option is for a corporation to purchase a controlling interest in another company in order to enter a new industry without incurring the costs and risks associated with starting from scratch.

In summary, businesses invest in other companies for the reasons shown in Illustration 16-2 (page 552).

Illustration 16-2
Why corporations invest

Reason	Typical Investment
To house excess cash until needed	Low-risk, highly liquid, short-term securities such as government-issued securities
To generate earnings	Debt securities (banks and other financial institutions) and stock securities (mutual funds and pension funds)
To meet strategic goals	Stocks of companies in a related industry or in an unrelated industry that the company wishes to enter

Accounting for Debt Investments

Debt investments are investments in government and corporation bonds. In accounting for debt investments, companies make entries to record (1) the acquisition, (2) the interest revenue, and (3) the sale.

RECORDING ACQUISITION OF BONDS

At acquisition, debt investments are recorded at cost. Cost includes all expenditures necessary to acquire these investments, such as the price paid plus brokerage fees (commissions), if any.

For example, assume that Kuhl Corporation acquires 50 Doan Inc. 8%, 10-year, $1,000 bonds on January 1, 2017, for $50,000. Kuhl records the investment as:

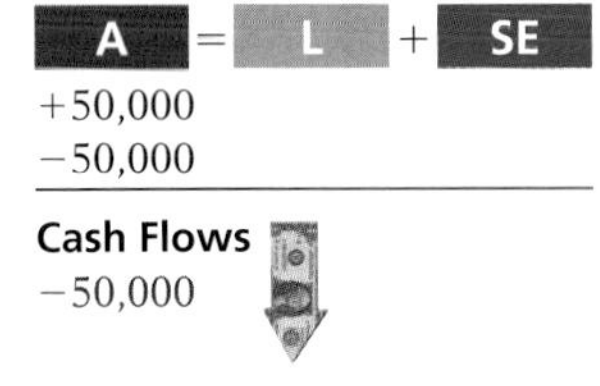

Jan. 1	Debt Investments (50 × $1,000)	50,000	
	Cash		50,000
	(To record purchase of 50 Doan Inc. bonds)		

RECORDING BOND INTEREST

The Doan Inc. bonds pay interest of $4,000 annually on January 1 ($50,000 × 8%). If Kuhl Corporation's fiscal year ends on December 31, it accrues the interest of $4,000 earned since January 1. The adjusting entry is:

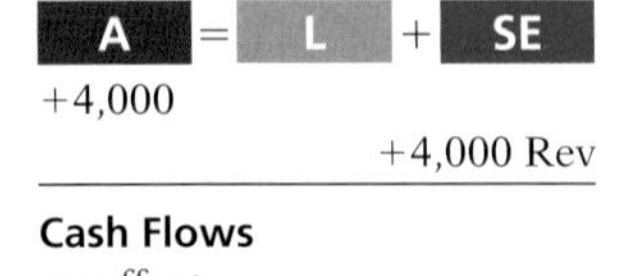

Dec. 31	Interest Receivable	4,000	
	Interest Revenue		4,000
	(To accrue interest on Doan Inc. bonds)		

Kuhl reports Interest Receivable as a current asset in the balance sheet. It reports Interest Revenue under "Other revenues and gains" in the income statement.

Kuhl reports receipt of the interest on January 1 as follows.

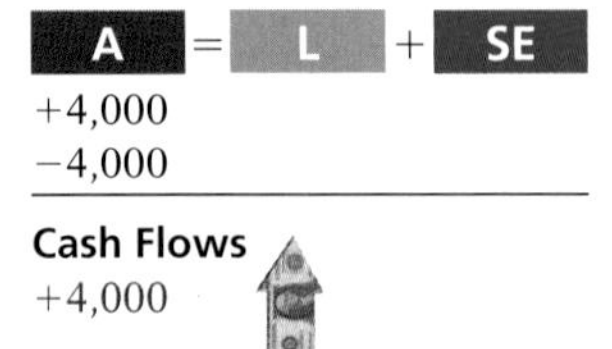

Jan. 1	Cash	4,000	
	Interest Receivable		4,000
	(To record receipt of accrued interest)		

A credit to Interest Revenue at this time is incorrect because the company earned and accrued interest revenue in the **preceding** accounting period.

RECORDING SALE OF BONDS

When Kuhl sells the bonds, it credits the investment account for the cost of the bonds. Kuhl records as a gain or loss any difference between the net proceeds from the sale (sales price less brokerage fees) and the cost of the bonds.

Assume, for example, that Kuhl Corporation receives net proceeds of $54,000 on the sale of the Doan Inc. bonds on January 1, 2018, after receiving the interest due. Since the securities cost $50,000, the company realizes a gain of $4,000. It records the sale as:

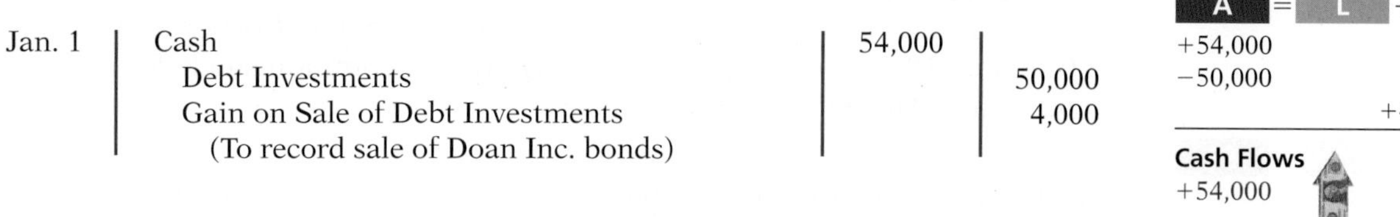

Jan. 1	Cash	54,000	
	Debt Investments		50,000
	Gain on Sale of Debt Investments		4,000
	(To record sale of Doan Inc. bonds)		

A	=	L	+	SE
+54,000				
−50,000				
				+4,000 Rev

Cash Flows
+54,000

Kuhl reports the gain on sale of debt investments under "Other revenues and gains" in the income statement and reports losses under "Other expenses and losses."

LEARNING OBJECTIVE 2 Explain how to account for stock investments.

Stock investments are investments in the capital stock of other corporations. When a company holds stock (and/or debt) of several different corporations, the group of securities is identified as an **investment portfolio**.

The accounting for investments in common stock depends on the extent of the investor's influence over the operating and financial affairs of the issuing corporation (the **investee**). Illustration 16-3 shows the general guidelines.

Illustration 16-3
Accounting guidelines for stock investments

Investor's Ownership Interest in Investee's Common Stock	Presumed Influence on Investee	Accounting Guidelines
Less than 20%	Insignificant	Cost method
Between 20% and 50%	Significant	Equity method
More than 50%	Controlling	Consolidated financial statements

Companies are required to use judgment instead of blindly following the guidelines.[1] We explain the application of each guideline next.

[1]Among the questions that are considered in determining an investor's influence are these: (1) Does the investor have representation on the investee's board? (2) Does the investor participate in the investee's policy-making process? (3) Are there material transactions between the investor and investee? (4) Is the common stock held by other stockholders concentrated or dispersed?

Holdings of Less than 20%

In accounting for stock investments of less than 20%, companies use the cost method. Under the **cost method**, companies record the investment at cost, and recognize revenue only when cash dividends are received.

RECORDING ACQUISITION OF STOCK INVESTMENTS

At acquisition, stock investments are recorded at cost. Cost includes all expenditures necessary to acquire these investments, such as the price paid plus any brokerage fees (commissions), if any.

For example, assume that on July 1, 2017, Sanchez Corporation acquires 1,000 shares (10% ownership) of Beal Corporation common stock. Sanchez pays $40 per share. The entry for the purchase is:

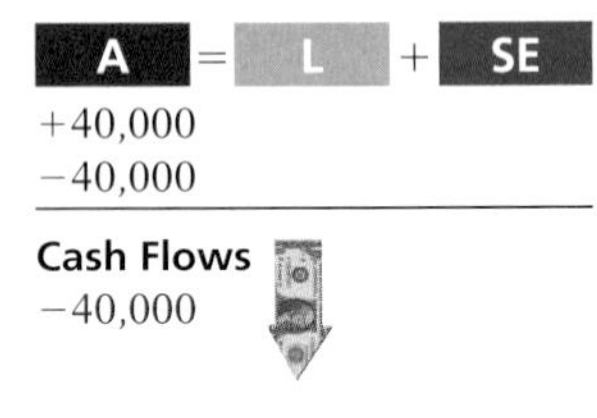

July 1	Stock Investments (1,000 × $40)	40,000	
	Cash		40,000
	(To record purchase of 1,000 shares of Beal Corporation common stock)		

RECORDING DIVIDENDS

During the time Sanchez owns the stock, it makes entries for any cash dividends received. If Sanchez receives a $2 per share dividend on December 31, the entry is:

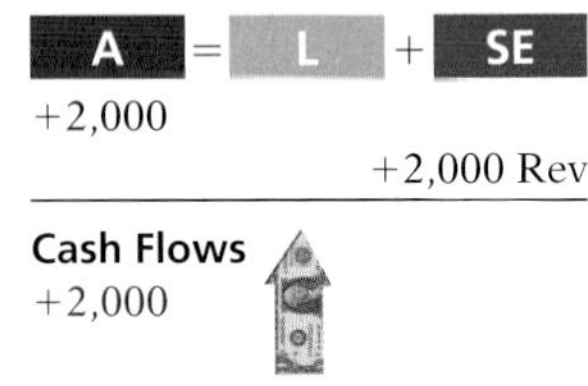

Dec. 31	Cash (1,000 × $2)	2,000	
	Dividend Revenue		2,000
	(To record receipt of a cash dividend)		

Sanchez reports Dividend Revenue under "Other revenues and gains" in the income statement. Unlike interest on notes and bonds, dividends do not accrue. Therefore, companies do not make adjusting entries to accrue dividends.

RECORDING SALE OF STOCK

When a company sells a stock investment, it recognizes as a gain or a loss the difference between the net proceeds from the sale (sales price less brokerage fees) and the cost of the stock.

Assume that Sanchez Corporation receives net proceeds of $39,000 on the sale of its Beal stock on February 10, 2018. Because the stock cost $40,000, Sanchez incurred a loss of $1,000. The entry to record the sale is:

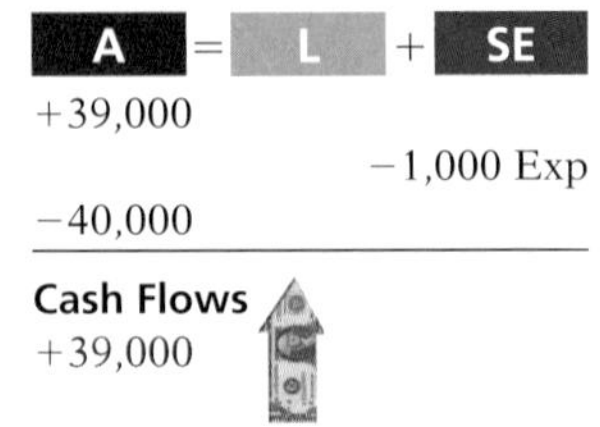

Feb. 10	Cash	39,000	
	Loss on Sale of Stock Investments	1,000	
	Stock Investments		40,000
	(To record sale of Beal common stock)		

Sanchez reports the loss under "Other expenses and losses" in the income statement. It would show a gain on sale under "Other revenues and gains."

Holdings Between 20% and 50%

When an investor company owns only a small portion of the shares of stock of another company, the investor cannot exercise control over the investee. But, when an investor owns between 20% and 50% of the common stock of a corporation, it is presumed that the investor has significant influence over the financial and operating activities of the investee. The investor probably has a representative on the investee's board of directors. Through that representative, the investor may exercise some control over the investee. The investee company in some sense becomes part of the investor company.

For example, even prior to purchasing all of **Turner Broadcasting**, **Time Warner** owned 20% of Turner. Because it exercised significant control over major decisions made by Turner, Time Warner used an approach called the equity method. Under the **equity method**, **the investor records its share of the net income of the investee in the year when it is earned**. An alternative might be to delay recognizing the investor's share of net income until the investee declares a cash dividend. But, that approach would ignore the fact that the investor and investee are, in some sense, one company, making the investor better off by the investee's earned income.

Under the equity method, the investor company initially records the investment in common stock at cost. After that, it **adjusts** the investment account annually to show the investor's equity in the investee. Each year, the investor does the following. (1) It increases (debits) the investment account and increases (credits) revenue for its share of the investee's net income.[2] (2) The investor also decreases (credits) the investment account for the amount of dividends received. The investment account is reduced for dividends received because payment of a dividend decreases the net assets of the investee.

RECORDING ACQUISITION OF STOCK

Assume that Milar Corporation acquires 30% of the common stock of Beck Company for $120,000 on January 1, 2017. The entry to record this transaction is:

Jan. 1	Stock Investments	120,000	
	Cash		120,000
	(To record purchase of Beck common stock)		

A = L + SE
+120,000
−120,000
Cash Flows
−120,000

RECORDING REVENUE AND DIVIDENDS

For 2017, Beck reports net income of $100,000. It declares and pays a $40,000 cash dividend. Milar records (1) its share of Beck's income, $30,000 (30% × $100,000) and (2) the reduction in the investment account for the dividends received, $12,000 ($40,000 × 30%). The entries are:

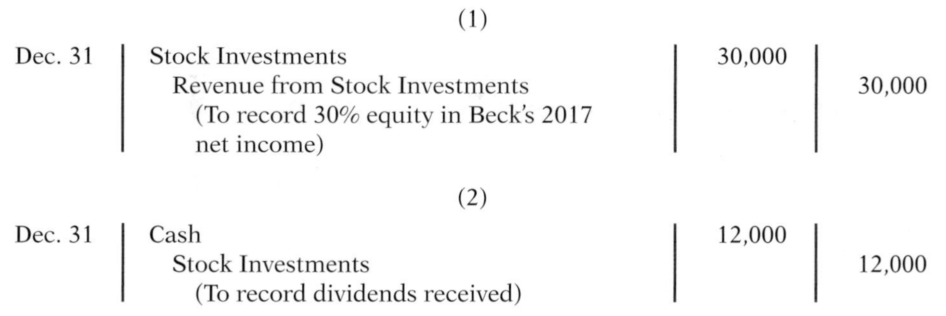

(1)

Dec. 31	Stock Investments	30,000	
	Revenue from Stock Investments		30,000
	(To record 30% equity in Beck's 2017 net income)		

(2)

Dec. 31	Cash	12,000	
	Stock Investments		12,000
	(To record dividends received)		

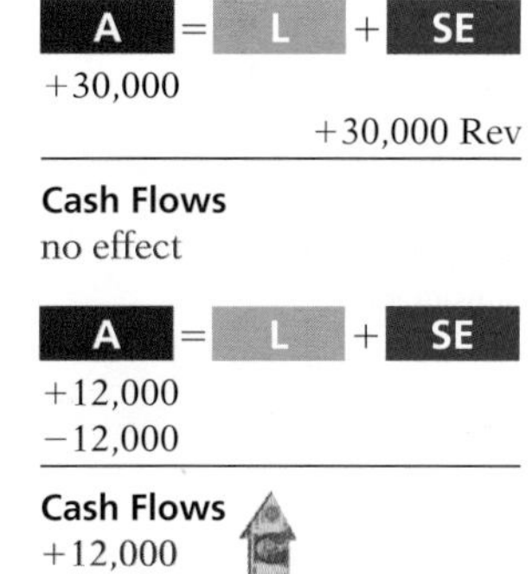

After Milar posts the transactions for the year, its investment and revenue accounts will show the following.

Illustration 16-4
Investment and revenue accounts after posting

Stock Investments				Revenue from Stock Investments	
Jan. 1	120,000	Dec. 31	**12,000**		Dec. 31 **30,000**
Dec. 31	**30,000**				
Dec. 31 Bal.	138,000				

During the year, the investment account increased $18,000. This increase of $18,000 is explained as follows: (1) Milar records a $30,000 increase in revenue

[2]Conversely, the investor increases (debits) a loss account and decreases (credits) the investment account for its share of the investee's net loss.

from its stock investment in Beck, and (2) Milar records a $12,000 decrease due to dividends received from its stock investment in Beck.

Note that the difference between reported revenue under the cost method and reported revenue under the equity method can be significant. For example, Milar would report only $12,000 of dividend revenue (30% × $40,000) if it used the cost method.

Holdings of More than 50%

A company that owns more than 50% of the common stock of another entity is known as the **parent company**. The entity whose stock the parent company owns is called the **subsidiary (affiliated) company**. Because of its stock ownership, the parent company has a **controlling interest** in the subsidiary.

When a company owns more than 50% of the common stock of another company, it usually prepares **consolidated financial statements**. These statements present the total assets and liabilities controlled by the parent company. They also present the total revenues and expenses of the subsidiary companies. Companies prepare consolidated statements **in addition to** the financial statements for the parent and individual subsidiary companies.

As noted earlier, when Time Warner had a 20% investment in Turner, it reported this investment in a single line item—Other Investments. After the merger, Time Warner instead consolidated Turner's results with its own. Under this approach, Time Warner included Turner's individual assets and liabilities with its own. Its plant and equipment were added to Time Warner's plant and equipment, its receivables were added to Time Warner's receivables, and so on.

Consolidated statements are useful to the stockholders, board of directors, and management of the parent company. These statements indicate the magnitude and scope of operations of the companies under common control. For example, regulators and the courts undoubtedly used the consolidated statements of AT&T to determine whether a breakup of the company was in the public interest. Illustration 16-5 lists three companies that prepare consolidated statements and some of the companies they have owned.

Illustration 16-5
Examples of consolidated companies and their subsidiaries

PepsiCo	Cendant	The Disney Company
Frito-Lay	Howard Johnson	Capital Cities/ABC, Inc.
Tropicana	Ramada Inn	Disneyland, Disney World
Quaker Oats	Century 21	Mighty Ducks
Pepsi-Cola	Coldwell Banker	Anaheim Angels
Gatorade	Avis	ESPN

LEARNING OBJECTIVE 

Discuss how debt and stock investments are reported in financial statements.

The value of debt and stock investments may fluctuate greatly during the time they are held. For example, in one 12-month period, the stock price of **Time Warner** hit a high of $58.50 and a low of $9. In light of such price fluctuations, how should companies value investments at the balance sheet date? Valuation could be at cost, at fair value, or at the lower-of-cost-or-market value.

Many people argue that fair value offers the best approach because it represents the expected cash realizable value of securities. **Fair value** is the amount for which a security could be sold in a normal market. Others counter that unless a security is going to be sold soon, the fair value is not relevant because the price of the security will likely change again.

Categories of Securities

For purposes of valuation and reporting at a financial statement date, companies classify **debt investments** into three categories:

1. **Trading securities** are bought and held primarily for sale in the near term to generate income on short-term price differences.
2. **Available-for-sale securities** are held with the intent of selling them sometime in the future.
3. **Held-to-maturity securities** are debt securities that the investor has the intent and ability to hold to maturity.[3]

Stock investments are classified into two categories:

1. **Trading securities** (as defined above).
2. **Available-for-sale securities** (as defined above).

Stock investments have no maturity date. Therefore, they are never classified as held-to-maturity securities.

Illustration 16-6 shows the valuation guidelines for these securities. **These guidelines apply to all debt securities and all stock investments in which the holdings are less than 20%.**

Illustration 16-6
Valuation guidelines for securities

TRADING SECURITIES

Companies hold trading securities with the intention of selling them in a short period (generally less than a month). **Trading** means frequent buying and selling. As indicated in Illustration 16-7, companies adjust trading securities to fair value at the end of each period (an approach referred to as mark-to-market accounting). They report changes from cost as part of net income. The changes are reported as **unrealized gains or losses** because the securities have not been sold. The unrealized gain or loss is the difference between the **total cost** of trading securities and their **total fair value**. Companies classify trading securities as current assets.

Illustration 16-7 shows the cost and fair values for investments Pace Corporation classified as trading securities on December 31, 2017. Pace has an unrealized gain of $7,000 because total fair value of $147,000 is $7,000 greater than total cost of $140,000.

Illustration 16-7
Valuation of trading securities

Trading Securities, December 31, 2017

Investments	Cost	Fair Value	Unrealized Gain (Loss)
Yorkville Company bonds	$ 50,000	$ 48,000	$(2,000)
Kodak Company stock	90,000	99,000	9,000
Total	$140,000	$147,000	**$ 7,000**

[3]This category is provided for completeness. The accounting and valuation issues related to held-to-maturity securities are discussed in more advanced accounting courses.

Pace records fair value and unrealized gain or loss through an adjusting entry at the time it prepares financial statements. In this entry, the company uses a valuation allowance account, Fair Value Adjustment—Trading, to record the difference between the total cost and the total fair value of the securities. The adjusting entry for Pace Corporation is:

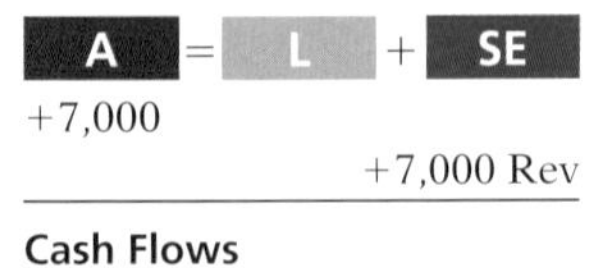

Dec. 31	Fair Value Adjustment—Trading	7,000	
	Unrealized Gain—Income		7,000
	(To record unrealized gain on trading securities)		

The use of a Fair Value Adjustment—Trading account enables Pace to maintain a record of the investment cost. It needs actual cost to determine the gain or loss realized when it sells the securities. Pace adds the debit balance (or subtracts a credit balance) of the Fair Value Adjustment—Trading account to the cost of the investments to arrive at a fair value for the trading securities.

The fair value of the securities is the amount Pace reports on its balance sheet. It reports the unrealized gain in the income statement in the "Other revenues and gains" section. The term "Income" in the account title indicates that the gain affects net income.

If the total cost of the trading securities is greater than total fair value, an unrealized loss has occurred. In such a case, the adjusting entry is a debit to Unrealized Loss—Income and a credit to Fair Value Adjustment—Trading. Companies report the unrealized loss under "Other expenses and losses" in the income statement.

The Fair Value Adjustment—Trading account is carried forward into future accounting periods. The company does not make any entry to the account until the end of each reporting period. At that time, the company adjusts the balance in the account to the difference between cost and fair value. For trading securities, it closes the Unrealized Gain (Loss)—Income account at the end of the reporting period.

AVAILABLE-FOR-SALE SECURITIES

As indicated earlier, companies hold available-for-sale securities with the intent of selling these investments sometime in the future. If the intent is to sell the securities within the next year or operating cycle, the investor classifies the securities as current assets in the balance sheet. Otherwise, it classifies them as long-term assets in the investments section of the balance sheet.

Companies report available-for-sale securities at fair value. The procedure for determining fair value and the unrealized gain or loss for these securities is the same as for trading securities. To illustrate, assume that Ingrao Corporation has two securities that it classifies as available-for-sale. Illustration 16-8 provides information on the cost, fair value, and amount of the unrealized gain or loss on December 31, 2017. There is an unrealized loss of $9,537 because total cost of $293,537 is $9,537 more than total fair value of $284,000.

Illustration 16-8
Valuation of available-for-sale securities

Available-for-Sale Securities, December 31, 2017

Investments	Cost	Fair Value	Unrealized Gain (Loss)
Campbell Soup Corporation 8% bonds	$ 93,537	$103,600	$10,063
Hershey Company stock	200,000	180,400	(19,600)
Total	$293,537	$284,000	**$(9,537)**

Both the adjusting entry and the reporting of the unrealized gain or loss for Ingrao's available-for-sale securities differ from those illustrated for trading securities. The differences result because Ingrao does not expect to sell these securities in the near term. Thus, prior to actual sale it is more likely that changes in fair value may change either unrealized gains or losses. Therefore, Ingrao does not report an unrealized gain or loss in the income statement. Instead, it reports it as a **separate component of stockholders' equity**.

In the adjusting entry, Ingrao identifies the fair value adjustment account with available-for-sale securities, and it identifies the unrealized gain or loss account with stockholders' equity. Ingrao records the unrealized loss of $9,537 as follows.

Dec. 31	Unrealized Gain or Loss—Equity	9,537	
	Fair Value Adjustment—Available-for-Sale		9,537
	(To record unrealized loss on available-for-sale securities)		

A	=	L	+	SE
				−9,537 Exp
−9,537				

Cash Flows
no effect

If total fair value exceeds total cost, Ingrao debits Fair Value Adjustment—Available-for-Sale and credits Unrealized Gain or Loss—Equity.

For available-for-sale securities, the company carries forward the Unrealized Gain or Loss—Equity account to future periods. At each future balance sheet date, Ingrao adjusts the Fair Value Adjustment—Available-for-Sale account and the Unrealized Gain or Loss—Equity account to show the difference between cost and fair value at that time.

Balance Sheet Presentation

In the balance sheet, companies classify investments as either short-term or long-term.

SHORT-TERM INVESTMENTS

Short-term investments (also called **marketable securities**) are securities held by a company that are (1) **readily marketable** and (2) **intended to be converted into cash** within the next year or operating cycle, whichever is longer. Investments that do not meet **both criteria** are classified as **long-term investments**.

READILY MARKETABLE An investment is readily marketable when it can be sold easily whenever the need for cash arises. Short-term paper[4] meets this criterion. It can be readily sold to other investors. Stocks and bonds traded on organized securities exchanges, such as the New York Stock Exchange, are readily marketable. They can be bought and sold daily. In contrast, there may be only a limited market for the securities issued by small corporations, and no market for the securities of a privately held company.

INTENT TO CONVERT Intent to convert means that management intends to sell the investment within the next year or operating cycle, whichever is longer. Generally, this criterion is satisfied when the investment is considered a resource that the investor will use whenever the need for cash arises. For example, a ski resort may invest idle cash during the summer months with the intent to sell the securities to buy supplies and equipment shortly before the winter season. This investment is considered short-term even if lack of snow cancels the next ski season and eliminates the need to convert the securities into cash as intended.

Because of their high liquidity, short-term investments appear immediately below Cash in the "Current assets" section of the balance sheet. They are reported at fair value. For example, Pace Corporation would report its trading securities as shown in Illustration 16-9 (page 560).

[4]**Short-term paper** includes (1) certificates of deposit (CDs) issued by banks, (2) money market certificates issued by banks and savings and loan associations, (3) Treasury bills issued by the U.S. government, and (4) commercial paper (notes) issued by corporations with good credit ratings.

Illustration 16-9
Presentation of short-term investments

PACE CORPORATION Balance Sheet (partial)	
Current assets	
Cash	$ 21,000
Short-term investments, at fair value	147,000

LONG-TERM INVESTMENTS

Companies generally report long-term investments in a separate section of the balance sheet immediately below "Current assets," as shown later in Illustration 16-12. Long-term investments in available-for-sale securities are reported at fair value. Investments in common stock accounted for under the equity method are reported at equity.

Presentation of Realized and Unrealized Gain or Loss

Companies must present in the financial statements gains and losses on investments, whether realized or unrealized. In the income statement, companies report gains and losses in the nonoperating activities section under the categories listed in Illustration 16-10. Interest and dividend revenue are also reported in that section.

Illustration 16-10
Nonoperating items related to investments

Other Revenues and Gains	Other Expenses and Losses
Interest Revenue	Loss on Sale of Investments
Dividend Revenue	Unrealized Loss—Income
Gain on Sale of Investments	
Unrealized Gain—Income	

As indicated earlier, companies report an unrealized gain or loss on available-for-sale securities as a separate component of stockholders' equity. To illustrate, assume that Dawson Inc. has common stock of $3,000,000, retained earnings of $1,500,000, and an unrealized loss on available-for-sale securities of $100,000. Illustration 16-11 shows the balance sheet presentation of the unrealized loss.

Illustration 16-11
Unrealized loss in stockholders' equity section

DAWSON INC. Balance Sheet (partial)	
Stockholders' equity	
Common stock	$3,000,000
Retained earnings	1,500,000
Total paid-in capital and retained earnings	4,500,000
Less: Unrealized loss on available-for-sale securities	**100,000**
Total stockholders' equity	$4,400,000

Note that the presentation of the loss is similar to the presentation of the cost of treasury stock in the stockholders' equity section (it decreases stockholders' equity). An unrealized gain would be added to this section. Reporting the unrealized gain or loss in the stockholders' equity section serves two purposes. (1) It reduces the volatility of net income due to fluctuations in fair value. (2) It informs the financial statement user of the gain or loss that would occur if the securities were sold at fair value.

Companies must report items such as unrealized gains or losses on available-for-sale securities as part of a more inclusive measure called comprehensive income. Unrealized gains and losses on available-for-sale securities therefore

Illustration 16-12
Classified balance sheet

PACE CORPORATION
Balance Sheet
December 31, 2017

Assets			
Current assets			
Cash			$ 21,000
Short-term investments, at fair value			**147,000**
Accounts receivable		$ 84,000	
Less: Allowance for doubtful accounts		4,000	80,000
Inventory, at FIFO cost			43,000
Prepaid insurance			23,000
Total current assets			314,000
Investments			
Investments in stock of less than 20% owned companies, at fair value		**50,000**	
Investment in stock of 20–50% owned company, at equity		**150,000**	
Total investments			200,000
Property, plant, and equipment			
Land		200,000	
Buildings	$800,000		
Less: Accumulated depreciation—buildings	200,000	600,000	
Equipment	180,000		
Less: Accumulated depreciation—equipment	54,000	126,000	
Total property, plant, and equipment			926,000
Intangible assets			
Goodwill			270,000
Total assets			$1,710,000
Liabilities and Stockholders' Equity			
Current liabilities			
Accounts payable			$ 185,000
Federal income taxes payable			60,000
Interest payable			10,000
Total current liabilities			255,000
Long-term liabilities			
Bonds payable, 10%, due 2024		$ 300,000	
Less: Discount on bonds		10,000	
Total long-term liabilities			290,000
Total liabilities			545,000
Stockholders' equity			
Paid-in capital			
Common stock, $10 par value, 200,000 shares authorized, 80,000 shares issued and outstanding		800,000	
Paid-in capital in excess of par—common stock		100,000	
Total paid-in capital		900,000	
Retained earnings (Note 1)		255,000	
Total paid-in capital and retained earnings		1,155,000	
Add: Unrealized gain on available-for-sale securities		**10,000**	
Total stockholders' equity			1,165,000
Total liabilities and stockholders' equity			$1,710,000

Note 1. Retained earnings of $100,000 is restricted for plant expansion.

affect comprehensive income (and stockholders' equity) but are not included in the computation of net income. We discuss comprehensive income more fully in Chapter 18.

Classified Balance Sheet

We have presented many sections of classified balance sheets in this and preceding chapters. The classified balance sheet in Illustration 16-12 (page 561) includes, in one place, key topics from previous chapters: the issuance of par value common stock, restrictions of retained earnings, and issuance of long-term bonds. From this chapter, the statement includes (highlighted in red) short-term and long-term investments. The investments in short-term securities are considered trading securities. The long-term investments in stock of less than 20% owned companies are considered available-for-sale securities. Illustration 16-12 also includes a long-term investment reported at equity and descriptive notations within the statement, such as the cost flow method for valuing inventory and one note to the statement.

REVIEW AND PRACTICE

LEARNING OBJECTIVES REVIEW

1 Explain how to account for debt investments. Companies record investments in debt securities when they purchase bonds, receive or accrue interest, and sell the bonds. They report gains or losses on the sale of bonds in the "Other revenues and gains" or "Other expenses and losses" sections of the income statement.

2 Explain how to account for stock investments. Companies record investments in common stock when they purchase the stock, receive dividends, and sell the stock. When ownership is less than 20%, the cost method is used. When ownership is between 20% and 50%, the equity method should be used. When ownership is more than 50%, companies prepare consolidated financial statements. Consolidated financial statements indicate the magnitude and scope of operations of the companies under common control.

3 Discuss how debt and stock investments are reported in financial statements. Investments in debt securities are classified as trading, available-for-sale, or held-to-maturity securities for valuation and reporting purposes. Stock investments are classified either as trading or available-for-sale securities. Stock investments have no maturity date and therefore are never classified as held-to-maturity securities. Trading securities are reported as current assets at fair value, with changes from cost reported in net income. Available-for-sale securities are also reported at fair value, with the changes from cost reported in stockholders' equity. Available-for-sale securities are classified as short-term or long-term, depending on their expected future sale date.

Short-term investments are securities that are (a) readily marketable and (b) intended to be converted to cash within the next year or operating cycle, whichever is longer. Investments that do not meet both criteria are classified as long-term investments.

GLOSSARY REVIEW

Available-for-sale securities Securities that are held with the intent of selling them sometime in the future.

Consolidated financial statements Financial statements that present the assets and liabilities controlled by the parent company and the total revenues and expenses of the subsidiary companies.

Controlling interest Ownership of more than 50% of the common stock of another entity.

Cost method An accounting method in which the investment in common stock is recorded at cost, and revenue is recognized only when cash dividends are received.

Debt investments Investments in government and corporation bonds.

Equity method An accounting method in which the investment in common stock is initially recorded at cost, and the investment account is then adjusted annually to show the investor's equity in the investee.

Fair value Amount for which a security could be sold in a normal market.

Held-to-maturity securities Debt securities that the investor has the intent and ability to hold to their maturity date.

Investment portfolio A group of stocks and/or debt securities in different corporations held for investment purposes.

Long-term investments Investments that are not readily marketable or that management does not intend to convert into cash within the next year or operating cycle, whichever is longer.

Parent company A company that owns more than 50% of the common stock of another entity.

Short-term investments Investments that are readily marketable and intended to be converted into cash within the next year or operating cycle, whichever is longer.

Stock investments Investments in the capital stock of other corporations.

Subsidiary (affiliated) company A company in which more than 50% of its stock is owned by another company.

Trading securities Securities bought and held primarily for sale in the near term to generate income on short-term price differences.

PRACTICE EXERCISES

Journalize debt investment transactions, accrue interest, and record sale.

(LO 1)

1. Potter Company purchased 50 Quinn Company 6%, 10-year, $1,000 bonds on January 1, 2017, for $50,000. The bonds pay interest annually. On January 1, 2018, after receipt of interest, Potter Company sold 30 of the bonds for $28,100.

Instructions

Prepare the journal entries to record the transactions described above.

Solution

1.		
January 1, 2017		
Debt Investments	50,000	
Cash		50,000
December 31, 2017		
Interest Receivable	3,000	
Interest Revenue ($50,000 × 6%)		3,000
January 1, 2018		
Cash	3,000	
Interest Receivable		3,000
January 1, 2018		
Cash	28,100	
Loss on Sale of Debt Investments	1,900	
Debt Investments (30/50 × $50,000)		30,000

Journalize transactions for investments in stocks.

(LO 2)

2. Lucy Inc. had the following transactions in 2017 pertaining to investments in common stock.

Jan. 1	Purchased 4,000 shares of Morgan Corporation common stock (5%) for $180,000 cash.
July 1	Received a cash dividend of $3 per share.
Dec. 1	Sold 600 shares of Morgan Corporation common stock for $32,000 cash.
Dec. 31	Received a cash dividend of $3 per share.

Instructions

Journalize the transactions.

Solution

2.		
January 1, 2017		
Stock Investments	180,000	
Cash		180,000
July 1, 2017		
Cash (4,000 × $3)	12,000	
Dividend Revenue		12,000

	December 1, 2017	
Cash	32,000	
Stock Investments ($180,000 × 600/4,000)		27,000
Gain on Sale of Stock Investments		5,000
	December 31, 2017	
Cash [($4,000 − $600) × $3]	10,200	
Dividend Revenue		10,200

Prepare adjusting entries for fair value, and indicate statement presentation for two classes of securities.

(LO 3)

3. Remy Company started business on January 1, 2017, and has the following data at December 31, 2017.

Securities	Cost	Fair Value
Trading	$120,000	$132,000
Available-for-sale	100,000	86,000

The available-for-sale securities are held as a long-term investment.

Instructions

(a) Prepare the adjusting entries to report each class of securities at fair value.

(b) Indicate the statement presentation of each class of securities and the related unrealized gain (loss) accounts.

Solution

3. **December 31, 2017**

	Debit	Credit
(a) Fair Value Adjustment—Trading ($132,000 − $120,000)	12,000	
Unrealized Gain—Income		12,000
Unrealized Gain or Loss—Equity ($100,000 − $86,000)	14,000	
Fair Value Adjustment—Available-for-Sale		14,000

(b) **Balance Sheet**

Current assets	
Short-term investments, at fair value	$132,000
Investments	
Investment in stock of less than 20% owned companies, at fair value	86,000
Stockholders' equity	
Less: Unrealized loss on available-for-sale securities	$(14,000)

Income Statement

Other revenues and gains	
Unrealized gain on trading securities	$ 12,000

PRACTICE PROBLEM

Journalize transactions and prepare adjusting entry to record fair value.

(LO 2, 3)

In its first year of operations, DeMarco Company had the following selected transactions in stock investments that are considered trading securities.

June 1 Purchased for cash 600 shares of Sanburg common stock at $24 per share.

July 1 Purchased for cash 800 shares of Cey Corporation common stock at $33 per share.

Sept. 1 Received a $1 per share cash dividend from Cey Corporation.
Nov. 1 Sold 200 shares of Sanburg common stock for cash at $27 per share.
Dec. 15 Received a $0.50 per share cash dividend on Sanburg common stock.

At December 31, the fair values per share were Sanburg $25 and Cey $30.

Instructions

(a) Journalize the transactions.

(b) Prepare the adjusting entry at December 31 to report the securities at fair value.

Solution

Date	Account	Debit	Credit
(a) June 1	Stock Investments	14,400	
	Cash (600 × $24)		14,400
	(To record purchase of 600 shares of Sanburg common stock)		
July 1	Stock Investments	26,400	
	Cash (800 × $33)		26,400
	(To record purchase of 800 shares of Cey common stock)		
Sept. 1	Cash (800 × $1.00)	800	
	Dividend Revenue		800
	(To record receipt of $1 per share cash dividend from Cey Corporation)		
Nov. 1	Cash (200 × $27)	5,400	
	Stock Investments (200 × $24)		4,800
	Gain on Sale of Stock Investments		600
	(To record sale of 200 shares of Sanburg common stock)		
Dec. 15	Cash [(600 − 200) × $0.50]	200	
	Dividend Revenue		200
	(To record receipt of $0.50 per share dividend from Sanburg)		
(b) Dec. 31	Unrealized Loss—Income	2,000	
	Fair Value Adjustment—Trading		2,000
	(To record unrealized loss on trading securities)		

Investment	Cost	Fair Value	Unrealized Gain (Loss)
Sanburg common stock	$ 9,600[a]	$10,000[b]	$ 400
Cey common stock	26,400[c]	24,000[d]	(2,400)
Totals	$36,000	$34,000	$(2,000)

[a]400 × $24; [b]400 × $25; [c]800 × $33; [d]800 × $30

EXERCISES

Understand debt and stock investments. (LO 1)

E16-1 Mr. Taliaferro is studying for an accounting test and has developed the following questions about investments.

1. What are three reasons why companies purchase investments in debt or stock securities?
2. Why would a corporation have excess cash that it does not need for operations?
3. What is the typical investment when investing cash for short periods of time?
4. What are the typical investments when investing cash to generate earnings?
5. Why would a company invest in securities that provide no current cash flows?
6. What is the typical stock investment when investing cash for strategic reasons?

Instructions

Provide answers for Mr. Taliaferro.

Journalize debt investment transactions and accrue interest.

(LO 1)

E16-2 Jenek Corporation had the following transactions pertaining to debt investments.

1. Purchased 50 9%, $1,000 Leeds Co. bonds for $50,000 cash. Interest is payable annually on January 1, 2017.
2. Accrued interest on Leeds Co. bonds on December 31, 2017.
3. Received interest on Leeds Co. bonds on January 1, 2018.
4. Sold 30 Leeds Co. bonds for $33,000 on January 1, 2018.

Instructions
Journalize the transactions.

Journalize debt investment transactions, accrue interest, and record sale.

(LO 1)

E16-3 Flynn Company purchased 70 Rinehart Company 6%, 10-year, $1,000 bonds on January 1, 2017, for $70,000. The bonds pay interest annually on January 1. On January 1, 2018, after receipt of interest, Flynn Company sold 40 of the bonds for $38,500.

Instructions
Prepare the journal entries to record the transactions described above.

Journalize stock investment transactions.

(LO 2)

E16-4 Hulse Company had the following transactions pertaining to stock investments.

Feb. 1 Purchased 600 shares of Wade common stock (2%) for $7,200 cash.
July 1 Received cash dividends of $1 per share on Wade common stock.
Sept. 1 Sold 300 shares of Wade common stock for $4,300.
Dec. 1 Received cash dividends of $1 per share on Wade common stock.

Instructions
(a) Journalize the transactions.
(b) Explain how dividend revenue and the gain (loss) on sale should be reported in the income statement.

Journalize transactions for investments in stocks.

(LO 2)

E16-5 Nosker Inc. had the following transactions pertaining to investments in common stock.

Jan. 1 Purchased 2,500 shares of Escalante Corporation common stock (5%) for $152,000 cash.
July 1 Received a cash dividend of $3 per share.
Dec. 1 Sold 500 shares of Escalante Corporation common stock for $32,000 cash.
Dec. 31 Received a cash dividend of $3 per share.

Instructions
Journalize the transactions.

Journalize transactions for investments in stocks.

(LO 2)

E16-6 On February 1, Rinehart Company purchased 500 shares (2% ownership) of Givens Company common stock for $32 per share. On March 20, Rinehart Company sold 100 shares of Givens stock for $2,900. Rinehart received a dividend of $1.00 per share on April 25. On June 15, Rinehart sold 200 shares of Givens stock for $7,600. On July 28, Rinehart received a dividend of $1.25 per share.

Instructions
Prepare the journal entries to record the transactions described above.

Journalize and post transactions, under the equity method.

(LO 2)

E16-7 On January 1, Zabel Corporation purchased a 25% equity in Helbert Corporation for $180,000. At December 31, Helbert declared and paid a $60,000 cash dividend and reported net income of $200,000.

Instructions
(a) Journalize the transactions.
(b) Determine the amount to be reported as an investment in Helbert stock at December 31.

Journalize entries under cost and equity methods.

(LO 2, 3)

E16-8 Presented below are two independent situations.

1. Gambino Cosmetics acquired 10% of the 200,000 shares of common stock of Nevins Fashion at a total cost of $13 per share on March 18, 2017. On June 30, Nevins declared and paid a $60,000 dividend. On December 31, Nevins reported net income of $122,000 for the year. At December 31, the market price of Nevins Fashion was $15 per share. The stock is classified as available-for-sale.

2. Kanza, Inc., obtained significant influence over Rogan Corporation by buying 40% of Rogan's 30,000 outstanding shares of common stock at a total cost of $9 per share on January 1, 2017. On June 15, Rogan declared and paid a cash dividend of $30,000. On December 31, Rogan reported a net income of $80,000 for the year.

Instructions

Prepare all the necessary journal entries for 2017 for (a) Gambino Cosmetics and (b) Kanza, Inc.

E16-9 Agee Company purchased 70% of the outstanding common stock of Himes Corporation.

Understand the usefulness of consolidated statements.

(LO 2)

Instructions

(a) Explain the relationship between Agee Company and Himes Corporation.
(b) How should Agee account for its investment in Himes?
(c) Why is the accounting treatment described in (b) useful?

E16-10 At December 31, 2017, the trading securities for Storrer, Inc. are as follows.

Prepare adjusting entry to record fair value, and indicate statement presentation.

(LO 3)

Security	Cost	Fair Value
A	$17,500	$16,000
B	12,500	14,000
C	23,000	21,000
	$53,000	$51,000

Instructions

(a) Prepare the adjusting entry at December 31, 2017, to report the securities at fair value.
(b) Show the balance sheet and income statement presentation at December 31, 2017, after adjustment to fair value.

E16-11 Data for investments in stock classified as trading securities are presented in E16-10. Assume instead that the investments are classified as available-for-sale securities. They have the same cost and fair value. The securities are considered to be a long-term investment.

Prepare adjusting entry to record fair value, and indicate statement presentation.

(LO 3)

Instructions

(a) Prepare the adjusting entry at December 31, 2017, to report the securities at fair value.
(b) Show the statement presentation at December 31, 2017, after adjustment to fair value.
(c) E. Kretsinger, a member of the board of directors, does not understand the reporting of the unrealized gains or losses. Write a letter to Ms. Kretsinger explaining the reporting and the purposes that it serves.

E16-12 Uttinger Company has the following data at December 31, 2017.

Prepare adjusting entries for fair value, and indicate statement presentation for two classes of securities.

(LO 3)

Securities	Cost	Fair Value
Trading	$120,000	$126,000
Available-for-sale	100,000	96,000

The available-for-sale securities are held as a long-term investment.

Instructions

(a) Prepare the adjusting entries to report each class of securities at fair value.
(b) Indicate the statement presentation of each class of securities and the related unrealized gain (loss) accounts.

PROBLEMS

P16-1A Vilander Carecenters Inc. provides financing and capital to the healthcare industry, with a particular focus on nursing homes for the elderly. The following selected transactions relate to bonds acquired as an investment by Vilander, whose fiscal year ends on December 31.

Journalize debt investment transactions and show financial statement presentation.

(LO 2, 3)

2017

Jan. 1 Purchased at face value $2,000,000 of Javier Nursing Centers, Inc., 10-year, 8% bonds dated January 1, 2017, directly from Javier.
Dec. 31 Accrual of interest at year-end on the Javier bonds.

(Assume that all intervening transactions and adjustments have been properly recorded and that the number of bonds owned has not changed from December 31, 2017, to December 31, 2019.)

2020

Jan. 1 Received the annual interest on the Javier bonds.
Jan. 1 Sold $1,000,000 Javier bonds at 106.
Dec. 31 Accrual of interest at year-end on the Javier bonds.

(a) Gain on sale of debt investment $60,000

Instructions

(a) Journalize the listed transactions for the years 2017 and 2020.
(b) Assume that the fair value of the bonds at December 31, 2017, was $2,200,000. These bonds are classified as available-for-sale securities. Prepare the adjusting entry to record these bonds at fair value.
(c) Based on your analysis in part (b), show the balance sheet presentation of the bonds and interest receivable at December 31, 2017. Assume the investments are considered long-term. Indicate where any unrealized gain or loss is reported in the financial statements.

Journalize investment transactions, prepare adjusting entry, and show statement presentation.

(LO 2, 3)

GLS

P16-2A In January 2017, the management of Kinzie Company concludes that it has sufficient cash to permit some short-term investments in debt and stock securities. During the year, the following transactions occurred.

Feb. 1 Purchased 600 shares of Muninger common stock for $32,400.
Mar. 1 Purchased 800 shares of Tatman common stock for $20,000.
Apr. 1 Purchased 50 $1,000, 7% Yoakem bonds for $50,000. Interest is payable semiannually on April 1 and October 1.
July 1 Received a cash dividend of $0.60 per share on the Muninger common stock.
Aug. 1 Sold 200 shares of Muninger common stock at $58 per share.
Sept. 1 Received a $1 per share cash dividend on the Tatman common stock.
Oct. 1 Received the semiannual interest on the Yoakem bonds.
Oct. 1 Sold the Yoakem bonds for $49,000.

At December 31, the fair value of the Muninger common stock was $55 per share. The fair value of the Tatman common stock was $24 per share.

(a) Gain on sale of stock investment $800

Instructions

(a) Journalize the transactions and post to the accounts Debt Investments and Stock Investments. (Use the T-account form.)
(b) Prepare the adjusting entry at December 31, 2017, to report the investment securities at fair value. All securities are considered to be trading securities.
(c) Show the balance sheet presentation of investment securities at December 31, 2017.
(d) Identify the income statement accounts and give the statement classification of each account.

Journalize transactions and adjusting entry for stock investments.

(LO 2, 3)

P16-3A On December 31, 2017, Turnball Associates owned the following securities, held as a long-term investment. The securities are not held for influence or control of the investee.

Common Stock	Shares	Cost
Gehring Co.	2,000	$60,000
Wooderson Co.	5,000	45,000
Kitselton Co.	1,500	30,000

On December 31, 2017, the total fair value of the securities was equal to its cost. In 2018, the following transactions occurred.

Aug. 1 Received $0.50 per share cash dividend on Gehring Co. common stock.
Sept. 1 Sold 1,500 shares of Wooderson Co. common stock for cash at $8 per share.

Oct. 1 Sold 800 shares of Gehring Co. common stock for cash at $33 per share.
Nov. 1 Received $1 per share cash dividend on Kitselton Co. common stock.
Dec. 15 Received $0.50 per share cash dividend on Gehring Co. common stock.
31 Received $1 per share annual cash dividend on Wooderson Co. common stock.

At December 31, the fair values per share of the common stocks were: Gehring Co. $32, Wooderson Co. $8, and Kitselton Co. $18.

Instructions

(a) Journalize the 2018 transactions and post to the account Stock Investments. (Use the T-account form.)
(b) Prepare the adjusting entry at December 31, 2018, to show the securities at fair value. The stock should be classified as available-for-sale securities.
(c) Show the balance sheet presentation of the investments at December 31, 2018. At this date, Turnball Associates has common stock $1,500,000 and retained earnings $1,000,000.

(b) Unrealized loss $4,100

P16-4A Heidebrecht Design acquired 20% of the outstanding common stock of Quayle Company on January 1, 2017, by paying $800,000 for the 30,000 shares. Quayle declared and paid $0.30 per share cash dividends on March 15, June 15, September 15, and December 15, 2017. Quayle reported net income of $320,000 for the year. At December 31, 2017, the market price of Quayle common stock was $34 per share.

Prepare entries under the cost and equity methods, and tabulate differences.

(LO 2)

Instructions

(a) Prepare the journal entries for Heidebrecht Design for 2017 assuming Heidebrecht Design cannot exercise significant influence over Quayle. (Use the cost method and assume that Quayle common stock should be classified as a trading security.)
(b) Prepare the journal entries for Heidebrecht Design for 2017, assuming Heidebrecht Design can exercise significant influence over Quayle. Use the equity method.
(c) Indicate the balance sheet and income statement account balances at December 31, 2017, under each method of accounting.

(a) Total dividend revenue $36,000

(b) Revenue from stock investments $64,000

P16-5A The following securities are in Frederick Company's portfolio of long-term available-for-sale securities at December 31, 2017.

Journalize stock investment transactions and show statement presentation.

(LO 2, 3)

	Cost
1,000 shares of Willhite Corporation common stock	$52,000
1,400 shares of Hutcherson Corporation common stock	84,000
1,200 shares of Downing Corporation preferred stock	33,600

On December 31, 2017, the total cost of the portfolio equaled total fair value. Frederick had the following transactions related to the securities during 2018.

Jan. 20 Sold all 1,000 shares of Willhite Corporation common stock at $55 per share.
28 Purchased 400 shares of $70 par value common stock of Liggett Corporation at $78 per share.
30 Received a cash dividend of $1.15 per share on Hutcherson Corp. common stock.
Feb. 8 Received cash dividends of $0.40 per share on Downing Corp. preferred stock.
18 Sold all 1,200 shares of Downing Corp. preferred stock at $27 per share.
July 30 Received a cash dividend of $1.00 per share on Hutcherson Corp. common stock.
Sept. 6 Purchased an additional 900 shares of $10 par value common stock of Liggett Corporation at $82 per share.
Dec. 1 Received a cash dividend of $1.50 per share on Liggett Corporation common stock.

At December 31, 2018, the fair values of the securities were:

Hutcherson Corporation common stock	$64 per share
Liggett Corporation common stock	$72 per share

Instructions

(a) Prepare journal entries to record the transactions.
(b) Post to the investment accounts. (Use T-accounts.)
(c) Prepare the adjusting entry at December 31, 2018 to report the portfolio at fair value.
(d) Show the balance sheet presentation at December 31, 2018, for the investment-related accounts.

(a) Loss on sale of stock investment $1,200

(c) Unrealized loss $5,800

Prepare a balance sheet.
(LO 3)

P16-6A The following data, presented in alphabetical order, are taken from the records of Nieto Corporation.

Accounts payable	$ 260,000
Accounts receivable	140,000
Accumulated depreciation—buildings	180,000
Accumulated depreciation—equipment	52,000
Allowance for doubtful accounts	6,000
Bonds payable (10%, due 2025)	500,000
Buildings	950,000
Cash	62,000
Common stock ($10 par value; 500,000 shares authorized, 150,000 shares issued)	1,500,000
Dividends payable	80,000
Equipment	275,000
Fair value adjustment—available-for-sale securities (Dr)	8,000
Goodwill	200,000
Income taxes payable	120,000
Inventory	170,000
Investment in Mara common stock (30% ownership), at equity	380,000
Investment in Sasse common stock (10% ownership), at cost	278,000
Land	390,000
Notes payable (due 2018)	70,000
Paid-in capital in excess of par—common stock	130,000
Premium on bonds payable	40,000
Prepaid insurance	16,000
Retained earnings	103,000
Short-term investments, at fair value (and cost)	180,000
Unrealized gain—available-for-sale securities	8,000

The investment in Sasse common stock is considered to be a long-term available-for-sale security.

Instructions

Prepare a classified balance sheet at December 31, 2017.

Total assets $2,811,000

COMPREHENSIVE PROBLEM: CHAPTERS 12 TO 16

CP16 Part I Debby Kauffman and her two colleagues, Jamie Hiatt and Ella Rincon, are personal trainers at an upscale health spa/resort in Tampa, Florida. They want to start a health club that specializes in health plans for people in the 50+ age range. The growing population in this age range and strong consumer interest in the health benefits of physical activity have convinced them they can profitably operate their own club. In addition to many other decisions, they need to determine what type of business organization they want. Jamie believes there are more advantages to the corporate form than a partnership, but he hasn't yet convinced Debby and Ella. They have come to you, a small-business consulting specialist, seeking information and advice regarding the choice of starting a partnership versus a corporation.

Instructions

(a) Prepare a memo (dated May 26, 2016) that describes the advantages and disadvantages of both partnerships and corporations. Advise Debby, Jamie, and Ella regarding which organizational form you believe would better serve their purposes. Make sure to include reasons supporting your advice.

Part II After deciding to incorporate, each of the three investors receives 20,000 shares of $2 par common stock on June 12, 2016, in exchange for their co-owned building ($200,000 fair value) and $100,000 total cash they contributed to the business. The next decision that Debby, Jamie, and Ella need to make is how to obtain financing for renovation and equipment. They understand the difference between equity securities and debt securities, but do not understand the tax, net income, and earnings per share consequences of equity versus debt financing on the future of their business.

Instructions

(b) Prepare notes for a discussion with the three entrepreneurs in which you will compare the consequences of using equity versus debt financing. As part of your notes, show the differences in interest and tax expense assuming $1,400,000 is financed with common stock, and then alternatively with debt. Assume that when common stock is used, 140,000 shares will be issued. When debt is used, assume the interest rate on debt is 9%, the tax rate is 32%, and income before interest and taxes is $300,000. (You may want to use an electronic spreadsheet.)

Part III During the discussion about financing, Ella mentions that one of her clients, Timothy Hansen, has approached her about buying a significant interest in the new club. Having an interested investor sways the three to issue equity securities to provide the financing they need. On July 21, 2016, Mr. Hansen buys 90,000 shares at a price of $10 per share.

The club, LifePath Fitness, opens on January 12, 2017, and after a slow start begins to produce the revenue desired by the owners. The owners decide to pay themselves a stock dividend since cash has been less than abundant since they opened their doors. The 10% stock dividend is declared by the owners on July 27, 2017. The market price of the stock is $3 on the declaration date. The date of record is July 31, 2017 (there have been no changes in stock ownership since the initial issuance), and the issue date is August 15, 2017. By the middle of the fourth quarter of 2017, the cash flow of LifePath Fitness has improved to the point that the owners feel ready to pay themselves a cash dividend. They declare a $0.05 cash dividend on December 4, 2017. The record date is December 14, 2017, and the payment date is December 24, 2017.

Instructions

(c) (1) Record all of the transactions related to the common stock of LifePath Fitness during the years 2016 and 2017. (2) Indicate how many shares are issued and outstanding after the stock dividend is issued.

Part IV Since the club opened, a major concern has been the pool facilities. Although the existing pool is adequate, Debby, Jamie, and Ella all desire to make LifePath a cutting-edge facility. Until the end of 2017, financing concerns prevented this improvement. However, because there has been steady growth in clientele, revenue, and income since the third quarter of 2017, the owners have explored possible financing options. They are hesitant to issue stock and change the ownership mix because they have been able to work together as a team with great effectiveness. They have formulated a plan to issue secured term bonds to raise the needed $600,000 for the pool facilities. By the end of December 2017, everything was in place for the bond issue to go ahead. On January 1, 2018, the bonds were issued for $548,000. The bonds pay annual interest of 6% on January 1 of each year. The bonds mature in 10 years, and amortization is computed using the straight-line method.

Instructions

(d) Record (1) the issuance of the secured bonds, (2) the adjusting entry required at December 31, 2018, (3) the interest payment made on January 1, 2019, and (4) the interest accrued on December 31, 2019.

Part V Mr. Hansen's purchase of the stock of LifePath Fitness was done through his business. The stock investment has always been accounted for using the cost method on his firm's books. However, early in 2019 he decided to take his company public. He is preparing an IPO (initial public offering), and he needs to have the firm's financial statements audited. One of the issues to be resolved is to restate the stock investment in LifePath Fitness using the equity method since Mr. Hansen's ownership percentage is greater than 20%.

Instructions

(e) (1) Give the entries that would have been made on Hansen's books if the equity method of accounting for investments had been used from the initial investment through 2018. Assume the following data for LifePath.

	2016	2017	2018
Net income	$30,000	$70,000	$105,000
Total cash dividends	$ 2,100	$20,000	$ 50,000

(2) Compute the balance in the Stock Investment account (as it relates to LifePath Fitness) at the end of 2018.

BROADENING YOUR PERSPECTIVE

FINANCIAL REPORTING AND ANALYSIS

Financial Reporting Problem: Apple Inc.

BYP16-1 The annual report of Apple Inc. is presented in Appendix A. Instructions for accessing and using the company's complete annual report, including the notes to the financial statements, are also provided in Appendix A.

Instructions

(a) Determine the percentage increase for (1) short-term marketable securities from 2012 to 2013, and (2) long-term marketable securities from 2012 to 2013.

(b) Using Apple's consolidated statement of cash flows, determine:

(1) Purchases of marketable securities during the current year.

(2) How much was spent for business acquisitions, net of cash acquired during the current year.

Comparative Analysis Problem: PepsiCo, Inc. vs. The Coca-Cola Company

BYP16-2 PepsiCo's financial statements are presented in Appendix B. Financial statements of The Coca-Cola Company are presented in Appendix C. Instructions for accessing and using the complete annual reports of PepsiCo and Coca-Cola, including the notes to the financial statements, are also provided in Appendices B and C, respectively.

Instructions

(a) Based on the information contained in these financial statements, determine the following for each company.

(1) Net cash used in investing (investment) activities for the current year (from the statement of cash flows).

(2) Cash used for capital expenditures during the current year.

(b) Each of PepsiCo's financial statements is labeled "consolidated." What has been consolidated? That is, from the contents of PepsiCo's annual report, identify by name the corporations that have been consolidated (parent and subsidiaries).

Comparative Analysis Problem: Amazon.com, Inc. vs. Wal-Mart Stores, Inc.

BYP16-3 Amazon.com, Inc.'s financial statements are presented in Appendix D. Financial statements of Wal-Mart Stores, Inc. are presented in Appendix E. Instructions for accessing and using the complete annual reports of Amazon and Wal-Mart, including the notes to the financial statements, are also provided in Appendices D and E, respectively.

Instructions

(a) Based on the information contained in these financial statements, determine the following for each company.

(1) Net cash used for investing (investment) activities for the current year (from the statement of cash flows).

(2) Cash used for business acquisitions, net of cash acquired during the current year.

(b) Each of Amazon's financial statements is labeled "consolidated." What has been consolidated? That is, from the contents of Amazon's annual report, identify by name the corporations that have been consolidated (parent and subsidiaries).

Real-World Focus

BYP16-4 Most publicly traded companies are examined by numerous analysts. These analysts often don't agree about a company's future prospects. In this exercise, you will find analysts' ratings about companies and make comparisons over time and across companies in the same industry. You will also see to what extent the analysts experienced "earnings surprises." Earnings surprises can cause changes in stock prices.

Address: **biz.yahoo.com/i**, or go to **www.wiley.com/college/weygandt**

Steps

1. Choose a company.
2. Use the index to find the company's name.
3. Choose **Research**.

Instructions

(a) How many analysts rated the company?
(b) What percentage rated it a strong buy?
(c) What was the average rating for the week?
(d) Did the average rating improve or decline relative to the previous week?
(e) What was the amount of the earnings surprise percentage during the last quarter?

CRITICAL THINKING

Decision-Making Across the Organization

BYP16-5 At the beginning of the question-and-answer portion of the annual stockholders' meeting of Neosho Corporation, stockholder John Linton asks, "Why did management sell the holdings in JMB Company at a loss when this company has been very profitable during the period Neosho held its stock?"

Since president Tony Cedeno has just concluded his speech on the recent success and bright future of Neosho, he is taken aback by this question and responds, "I remember we paid $1,300,000 for that stock some years ago. I am sure we sold that stock at a much higher price. You must be mistaken."

Linton retorts, "Well, right here in footnote number 7 to the annual report it shows that 240,000 shares, a 30% interest in JMB, were sold on the last day of the year. Also, it states that JMB earned $520,000 this year and paid out $160,000 in cash dividends. Further, a summary statement indicates that in past years, while Neosho held JMB stock, JMB earned $1,240,000 and paid out $440,000 in dividends. Finally, the income statement for this year shows a loss on the sale of JMB stock of $180,000. So, I doubt that I am mistaken."

Red-faced, president Cedeno turns to you.

Instructions

With the class divided into groups, answer the following.

(a) What dollar amount did Neosho receive upon the sale of the JMB stock?
(b) Explain why both stockholder Linton and president Cedeno are correct.

Communication Activity

BYP16-6 Fegan Corporation has purchased two securities for its portfolio. The first is a stock investment in Plummer Corporation, one of its suppliers. Fegan purchased 10% of Plummer with the intention of holding it for a number of years, but has no intention of purchasing more shares. The second investment was a purchase of debt securities. Fegan purchased the debt securities because its analysts believe that changes in market interest rates will cause these securities to increase in value in a short period of time. Fegan intends to sell the securities as soon as they have increased in value.

Instructions

Write a memo to Sam Nichols, the chief financial officer, explaining how to account for each of these investments. Explain what the implications for reported income are from this accounting treatment.

Ethics Case

BYP16-7 Harding Financial Services Company holds a large portfolio of debt and stock securities as an investment. The total fair value of the portfolio at December 31, 2017, is greater than total cost. Some securities have increased in value and others have decreased. Ann Bales, the financial vice president, and Kim Reeble, the controller, are in the process of classifying for the first time the securities in the portfolio.

Bales suggests classifying the securities that have increased in value as trading securities in order to increase net income for the year. She wants to classify the securities that have decreased in value as long-term available-for-sale securities, so that the decreases in value will not affect 2017 net income.

Reeble disagrees. She recommends classifying the securities that have decreased in value as trading securities and those that have increased in value as long-term available-for-sale securities. Reeble argues that the company is having a good earnings year and that recognizing the losses now will help to smooth income for this year. Moreover, for future years, when the company may not be as profitable, the company will have built-in gains.

Instructions

(a) Will classifying the securities as Bales and Reeble suggest actually affect earnings as each says it will?

(b) Is there anything unethical in what Bales and Reeble propose? Who are the stakeholders affected by their proposals?

(c) Assume that Bales and Reeble properly classify the portfolio. At year-end, Bales proposes to sell the securities that will increase 2017 net income, and that Reeble proposes to sell the securities that will decrease 2017 net income. Is this unethical?

All About You

BYP16-8 The Securities and Exchange Commission (SEC) is the primary regulatory agency of U.S. financial markets. Its job is to ensure that the markets remain fair for all investors. The following SEC sites provide useful information for investors.

Address: **www.sec.gov/answers.shtml** and **http://www.sec.gov/investor/tools/quiz.htm**, or go to **www.wiley.com/college/weygandt**.

Instructions

(a) Go to the first SEC site and find the definition of the following terms.
   (i) Ask price.
   (ii) Margin.
   (iii) Prospectus.
   (iv) Index fund.

(b) Go to the second SEC site and take the short quiz.

FASB Codification Activity

BYP16-9 If your school has a subscription to the FASB Codification, go to **http://aaahq.org/ascLogin.cfm** to log in and prepare responses to the following.

(a) What is the definition of a trading security?
(b) What is the definition of an available-for-sale security?
(c) What is definition of a holding gain or loss?

A Look at IFRS

Compare the accounting for investments under GAAP and IFRS.

Until recently, when the IASB issued *IFRS 9*, the accounting and reporting for investments under IFRS and GAAP were for the most part very similar. However, *IFRS 9* introduces a new framework for classifying investments.

Key Points

Following are the similarities and differences between GAAP and IFRS as related to investments.

Similarities

- The basic accounting entries to record the acquisition of debt securities, the receipt of interest, and the sale of debt securities are the same under IFRS and GAAP.
- The basic accounting entries to record the acquisition of stock investments, the receipt of dividends, and the sale of stock securities are the same under IFRS and GAAP.
- Both IFRS and GAAP use the same criteria to determine whether the equity method of accounting should be used—that is, significant influence with a general guide of over 20% ownership, IFRS uses the term **associate investment** rather than equity investment to describe its investment under the equity method.
- Equity investments are generally recorded and reported at fair value under IFRS. Equity investments do not have a fixed interest or principal payment schedule and therefore cannot be accounted for at amortized cost. In general, equity investments are valued at fair value, with all gains and losses reported in income, similar to GAAP.
- Unrealized gains and losses related to available-for-sale securities are reported in other comprehensive income under GAAP and IFRS. These gains and losses that accumulate are then reported in the balance sheet.

Differences

- Under IFRS, both the investor and an associate company should follow the same accounting policies. As a result, in order to prepare financial information, adjustments are made to the associate's policies to conform to the investor's books. GAAP does not have that requirement.
- In general, IFRS requires that companies determine how to measure their financial assets based on two criteria:
  - The company's business model for managing their financial assets; and
  - The contractual cash flow characteristics of the financial asset.

  If a company has (1) a business model whose objective is to hold assets in order to collect contractual cash flows and (2) the contractual terms of the financial asset gives specified dates to cash flows that are solely payments of principal and interest on the principal amount outstanding, then the company should use cost (often referred to as amortized cost).

  For example, assume that **Mitsubishi** purchases a bond investment that it intends to hold to maturity (held-for-collection). Its business model for this type of investment is to collect interest and then principal at maturity. The payment dates for the interest rate and principal are stated on the bond. In this case, Mitsubishi accounts for the investment at cost. If, on the other hand, Mitsubishi purchased the bonds as part of a trading strategy to speculate on interest rate changes (a trading investment), then the debt investment is reported at fair value. As a result, only debt investments such as receivables, loans, and bond investments that meet the two criteria above are recorded at amortized cost. All other debt investments are recorded and reported at fair value.

Looking to the Future

As indicated earlier, the IASB has issued a new revised IFRS which deals with the accounting issues related to investment securities. The FASB is now in the final process of issuing a new standard in this area. It is likely that some differences will continue to exist between the IFRS and the FASB regarding investments.

IFRS Practice

IFRS Self-Test Questions

1. The following asset is **not** considered a financial asset under IFRS:
   (a) trading securities.
   (b) equity securities.
   (c) held-for-collection securities.
   (d) inventories.

2. Under IFRS, the equity method of accounting for long-term investments in common stock should be used when the investor has significant influence over an investee and owns:
   (a) between 20% and 50% of the investee's common stock.
   (b) 30% or more of the investee's common stock.
   (c) more than 50% of the investee's common stock.
   (d) less than 20% of the investee's common stock.
3. Under IFRS, the unrealized loss on trading investments should be reported:
   (a) as part of other comprehensive loss reducing net income.
   (b) on the income statement reducing net income.
   (c) as part of other comprehensive loss not affecting net income.
   (d) directly to stockholders' equity bypassing the income statement.

Answers to IFRS Self-Test Questions

1. d **2.** a **3.** b

Chapter 17 Statement of Cash Flows

Companies must be ready to respond to changes quickly in order to survive and thrive. This requires careful management of cash. One company that managed cash successfully in its early years was Microsoft. During those years, the company paid much of its payroll with stock options (rights to purchase company stock in the future at a given price) instead of cash. This conserved cash and turned more than a thousand of its employees into millionaires.

In recent years, Microsoft has had a different kind of cash problem. Now that it has reached a more "mature" stage in life, it generates so much cash—roughly $1 billion per month—that it cannot always figure out what to do with it. At one time, Microsoft had accumulated $60 billion.

The company said it was accumulating cash to invest in new opportunities, buy other companies, and pay off pending lawsuits. Microsoft's stockholders complained that holding all this cash was putting a drag on the company's profitability. Why? Because Microsoft had the cash invested in very low-yielding government securities. Stockholders felt that the company either should find new investment projects that would bring higher returns, or return some of the cash to stockholders.

Finally, Microsoft announced a plan to return cash to stockholders by paying a special one-time $32 billion dividend. This special dividend was so large that, according to the U.S. Commerce Department, it caused total personal income in the United States to rise by 3.7% in one month—the largest increase ever recorded by the agency. (It also made the holiday season brighter, especially for retailers in the Seattle area.) Microsoft also doubled its regular annual dividend to $3.50 per share. Further, it announced that it would spend another $30 billion buying treasury stock.

Apple also has encountered this cash "problem." Recently, Apple had nearly $100 billion in liquid assets (cash, cash equivalents, and investment securities). The company was generating $37 billion of cash per year from its operating activities but spending only about $7 billion on plant assets and purchases of patents. Shareholders pressured Apple to unload some of this cash. In response, Apple announced that it would begin to pay a quarterly dividend of $2.65 per share and it would buy back up to $10 billion of its stock. Analysts noted that the dividend consumes only $10 billion of cash per year. This leaves Apple wallowing in cash. The rest of us should have such problems.

Source: "Business: An End to Growth? Microsoft's Cash Bonanza," *The Economist* (July 23, 2005), p. 61.

LEARNING OBJECTIVES

1. **Discuss the usefulness and format of the statement of cash flows.**
2. **Prepare a statement of cash flows using the indirect method.**
3. **Analyze the statement of cash flows.**

LEARNING OBJECTIVE 1

Discuss the usefulness and format of the statement of cash flows.

The balance sheet, income statement, and retained earnings statement provide only limited information about a company's cash flows (cash receipts and cash payments). For example, comparative balance sheets show the increase in property, plant, and equipment during the year. But, they do not show how the additions were financed or paid for. The income statement shows net income. But, it does not indicate the amount of cash generated by operating activities. The retained earnings statement shows cash dividends declared but not the cash dividends paid during the year. None of these statements presents a detailed summary of where cash came from and how it was used.

Usefulness of the Statement of Cash Flows

The **statement of cash flows** reports the cash receipts, cash payments, and net change in cash resulting from operating, investing, and financing activities during a period. The information in a statement of cash flows helps investors, creditors, and others assess the following.

1. **The entity's ability to generate future cash flows.** By examining relationships between items in the statement of cash flows, investors can better predict the amounts, timing, and uncertainty of future cash flows than they can from accrual-basis data.
2. **The entity's ability to pay dividends and meet obligations.** If a company does not have adequate cash, it cannot pay employees, settle debts, or pay dividends. Employees, creditors, and stockholders should be particularly interested in this statement because it alone shows the flows of cash in a business.
3. **The reasons for the difference between net income and net cash provided (used) by operating activities.** Net income provides information on the success or failure of a business. However, some financial statement users are critical of accrual-basis net income because it requires many estimates. As a result, users often challenge the reliability of the number. Such is not the case with cash. Many readers of the statement of cash flows want to know the reasons for the difference between net income and net cash provided by operating activities. Then, they can assess for themselves the reliability of the income number.
4. **The cash investing and financing transactions during the period.** By examining a company's investing and financing transactions, a financial statement reader can better understand why assets and liabilities changed during the period.

Classification of Cash Flows

The statement of cash flows classifies cash receipts and cash payments as operating, investing, and financing activities. Transactions and other events characteristic of each kind of activity are as follows.

1. **Operating activities** include the cash effects of transactions that create revenues and expenses. They thus enter into the determination of net income.
2. **Investing activities** include (a) acquiring and disposing of investments and property, plant, and equipment, and (b) lending money and collecting the loans.
3. **Financing activities** include (a) obtaining cash from issuing debt and repaying the amounts borrowed, and (b) obtaining cash from stockholders, repurchasing shares, and paying dividends.

The operating activities category is the most important. It shows the cash provided by company operations. This source of cash is generally considered to be the best measure of a company's ability to generate sufficient cash to continue as a going concern.

Illustration 17-1 lists typical cash receipts and cash payments within each of the three classifications. **Study the list carefully.** It will prove very useful in solving homework exercises and problems.

Illustration 17-1
Typical receipt and payment classifications

TYPES OF CASH INFLOWS AND OUTFLOWS

Operating activities—Income statement items
Cash inflows:
From sale of goods or services.
From interest received and dividends received.
Cash outflows:
To suppliers for inventory.
To employees for wages.
To government for taxes.
To lenders for interest.
To others for expenses.

Operating activities

Investing activities—Changes in investments and long-term assets
Cash inflows:
From sale of property, plant, and equipment.
From sale of investments in debt or equity securities of other entities.
From collection of principal on loans to other entities.
Cash outflows:
To purchase property, plant, and equipment.
To purchase investments in debt or equity securities of other entities.
To make loans to other entities.

Investing activities

Financing activities—Changes in long-term liabilities and stockholders' equity
Cash inflows:
From sale of common stock.
From issuance of debt (bonds and notes).
Cash outflows:
To stockholders as dividends.
To redeem long-term debt or reacquire capital stock (treasury stock).

Financing activities

Note the following general guidelines:

1. Operating activities involve income statement items.
2. Investing activities involve cash flows resulting from changes in investments and long-term asset items.
3. Financing activities involve cash flows resulting from changes in long-term liability and stockholders' equity items.

Companies classify as operating activities some cash flows related to investing or financing activities. For example, receipts of investment revenue (interest and dividends) are classified as operating activities. So are payments of interest to lenders. Why are these considered operating activities? **Because companies report these items in the income statement, where results of operations are shown.**

Significant Noncash Activities

Not all of a company's significant activities involve cash. Examples of significant noncash activities are as follows.

1. Direct issuance of common stock to purchase assets.
2. Conversion of bonds into common stock.
3. Direct issuance of debt to purchase assets.
4. Exchanges of plant assets.

Companies do not report in the body of the statement of cash flows significant financing and investing activities that do not affect cash. Instead, they report these activities in either a **separate schedule** at the bottom of the statement of cash flows or in a **separate note or supplementary schedule** to the financial statements. The reporting of these noncash activities in a separate schedule satisfies the **full disclosure principle**.

In solving homework assignments, you should present significant noncash investing and financing activities in a separate schedule at the bottom of the statement of cash flows (see the last entry in Illustration 17-2 below).

Format of the Statement of Cash Flows

The general format of the statement of cash flows presents the results of the three activities discussed previously—operating, investing, and financing—plus the significant noncash investing and financing activities. Illustration 17-2 shows a widely used form of the statement of cash flows.

Illustration 17-2
Format of statement of cash flows

COMPANY NAME Statement of Cash Flows For the Period Covered		
Cash flows from operating activities		
(List of individual items)	XX	
Net cash provided (used) by operating activities		XXX
Cash flows from investing activities		
(List of individual inflows and outflows)	XX	
Net cash provided (used) by investing activities		XXX
Cash flows from financing activities		
(List of individual inflows and outflows)	XX	
Net cash provided (used) by financing activities		XXX
Net increase (decrease) in cash		XXX
Cash at beginning of period		XXX
Cash at end of period		XXX
Noncash investing and financing activities		
(List of individual noncash transactions)		XXX

The cash flows from operating activities section always appears first, followed by the investing activities section and then the financing activities section. The sum of the operating, investing, and financing sections equals the net increase or decrease in cash for the period. This amount is added to the beginning cash balance to arrive at the ending cash balance—the same amount reported on the balance sheet.

LEARNING OBJECTIVE 2

Prepare a statement of cash flows using the indirect method.

Companies prepare the statement of cash flows differently from the three other basic financial statements. First, it is not prepared from an adjusted trial balance. It requires detailed information concerning the changes in account balances that occurred between two points in time. An adjusted trial balance will not provide the necessary data. Second, the statement of cash flows deals with cash receipts and payments. As a result, the company **adjusts** the effects of the use of accrual accounting **to determine cash flows**.

The information to prepare this statement usually comes from three sources:

- **Comparative balance sheets.** Information in the comparative balance sheets indicates the amount of the changes in assets, liabilities, and stockholders' equities from the beginning to the end of the period.

- **Current income statement.** Information in this statement helps determine the amount of net cash provided or used by operating activities during the period.
- **Additional information.** Such information includes transaction data that are needed to determine how cash was provided or used during the period.

Preparing the statement of cash flows from these data sources involves three major steps, explained in Illustration 17-3.

Illustration 17-3
Three major steps in preparing the statement of cash flows

STEP 1: Determine net cash provided/used by operating activities by converting net income from an accrual basis to a cash basis.

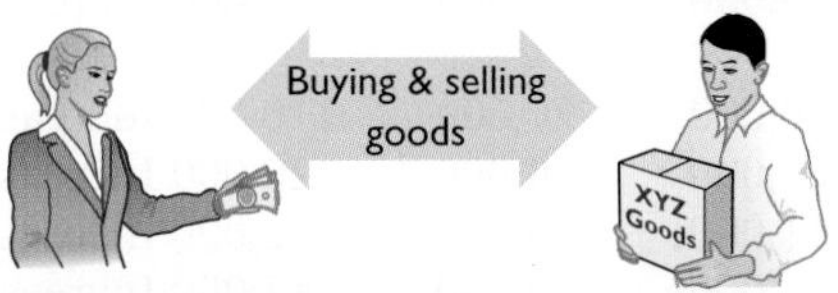

This step involves analyzing not only the current year's income statement but also comparative balance sheets and selected additional data.

STEP 2: Analyze changes in noncurrent asset and liability accounts and record as investing and financing activities, or disclose as noncash transactions.

This step involves analyzing comparative balance sheet data and selected additional information for their effects on cash.

STEP 3: Compare the net change in cash on the statement of cash flows with the change in the Cash account reported on the balance sheet to make sure the amounts agree.

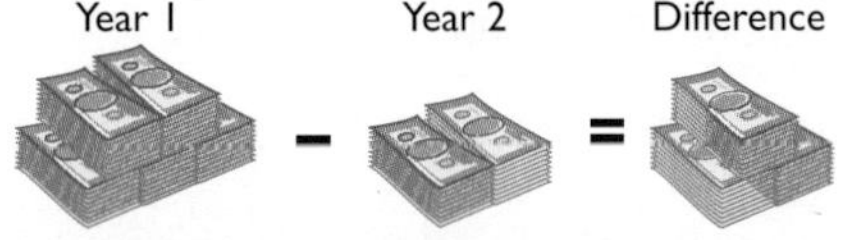

The difference between the beginning and ending cash balances can be easily computed from comparative balance sheets.

Indirect and Direct Methods

In order to perform Step 1, a company **must convert net income from an accrual basis to a cash basis**. This conversion may be done by either of two methods: (1) the indirect method or (2) the direct method. **Both methods arrive at the same amount** for "Net cash provided by operating activities." They differ in **how** they arrive at the amount.

The **indirect method** adjusts net income for items that do not affect cash. A great majority of companies use this method. Companies favor the indirect method for two reasons: (1) it is easier and less costly to prepare, and (2) it focuses on the differences between net income and net cash flow from operating activities.

The **direct method** shows operating cash receipts and payments. It is prepared by adjusting each item in the income statement from the accrual basis to the cash basis. The FASB has expressed a preference for the direct method but allows the use of either method.

The next section illustrates the more popular indirect method. Appendix 17A illustrates the direct method.

Indirect Method—Computer Services Company

To explain how to prepare a statement of cash flows using the indirect method, we use financial information from Computer Services Company. Illustration 17-4 (page 582) presents Computer Services' current- and previous-year balance sheets, its current-year income statement, and related financial information for the current year.

Illustration 17-4
Comparative balance sheets, income statement, and additional information for Computer Services Company

COMPUTER SERVICES COMPANY
Comparative Balance Sheets
December 31

Assets	**2017**	**2016**	**Change in Account Balance Increase/Decrease**
Current assets			
Cash	$ 55,000	$ 33,000	$ 22,000 Increase
Accounts receivable	20,000	30,000	10,000 Decrease
Inventory	15,000	10,000	5,000 Increase
Prepaid expenses	5,000	1,000	4,000 Increase
Property, plant, and equipment			
Land	130,000	20,000	110,000 Increase
Buildings	160,000	40,000	120,000 Increase
Accumulated depreciation—buildings	(11,000)	(5,000)	6,000 Increase
Equipment	27,000	10,000	17,000 Increase
Accumulated depreciation—equipment	(3,000)	(1,000)	2,000 Increase
Total assets	$398,000	$138,000	
Liabilities and Stockholders' Equity			
Current liabilities			
Accounts payable	$ 28,000	$ 12,000	$ 16,000 Increase
Income taxes payable	6,000	8,000	2,000 Decrease
Long-term liabilities			
Bonds payable	130,000	20,000	110,000 Increase
Stockholders' equity			
Common stock	70,000	50,000	20,000 Increase
Retained earnings	164,000	48,000	116,000 Increase
Total liabilities and stockholders' equity	$398,000	$138,000	

COMPUTER SERVICES COMPANY
Income Statement
For the Year Ended December 31, 2017

Sales revenue		$507,000
Cost of goods sold	$150,000	
Operating expenses (excluding depreciation)	111,000	
Depreciation expense	9,000	
Loss on disposal of equipment	3,000	
Interest expense	42,000	315,000
Income before income tax		192,000
Income tax expense		47,000
Net income		$145,000

Additional information for 2017:

1. Depreciation expense comprised $6,000 for building and $3,000 for equipment.
2. The company sold equipment with a book value of $7,000 (cost $8,000, less accumulated depreciation $1,000) for $4,000 cash.
3. Issued $110,000 of long-term bonds in direct exchange for land.
4. A building costing $120,000 was purchased for cash. Equipment costing $25,000 was also purchased for cash.
5. Issued common stock for $20,000 cash.
6. The company declared and paid a $29,000 cash dividend.

We now apply the three steps for preparing a statement of cash flows to the information provided for Computer Services Company.

Step 1: Operating Activities

DETERMINE NET CASH PROVIDED/USED BY OPERATING ACTIVITIES BY CONVERTING NET INCOME FROM AN ACCRUAL BASIS TO A CASH BASIS

To determine net cash provided by operating activities under the indirect method, companies **adjust net income in numerous ways**. A useful starting point is to understand **why** net income must be converted to net cash provided by operating activities.

Under generally accepted accounting principles, most companies use the accrual basis of accounting. This basis requires that companies record revenue when their performance obligation is satisfied and record expenses when incurred. Revenues include credit sales for which the company has not yet collected cash. Expenses incurred include some items that it has not yet paid in cash. Thus, under the accrual basis, net income is not the same as net cash provided by operating activities.

Therefore, under the **indirect method**, companies must adjust net income to convert certain items to the cash basis. The indirect method (or reconciliation method) starts with net income and converts it to net cash provided by operating activities. Illustration 17-5 lists the three types of adjustments.

Illustration 17-5
Three types of adjustments to convert net income to net cash provided by operating activities

Net Income	+/−	Adjustments	=	Net Cash Provided/ Used by Operating Activities
		• **Add back noncash expenses,** such as depreciation expense and amortization expense. • **Deduct gains and add losses** that resulted from investing and financing activities. • **Analyze changes** to noncash current asset and current liability accounts.		

We explain the three types of adjustments in the next three sections.

DEPRECIATION EXPENSE

Computer Services' income statement reports depreciation expense of $9,000. Although depreciation expense reduces net income, it does not reduce cash. In other words, depreciation expense is a noncash charge. The company must add it back to net income to arrive at net cash provided by operating activities. Computer Services reports depreciation expense in the statement of cash flows as shown below.

Illustration 17-6
Adjustment for depreciation

Cash flows from operating activities	
Net income	$145,000
Adjustments to reconcile net income to net cash provided by operating activities:	
Depreciation expense	**9,000**
Net cash provided by operating activities	$154,000

As the first adjustment to net income in the statement of cash flows, companies frequently list depreciation and similar noncash charges such as amortization of intangible assets, depletion expense, and bad debt expense.

LOSS ON DISPOSAL OF EQUIPMENT

Illustration 17-1 states that cash received from the sale (disposal) of plant assets is reported in the investing activities section. Because of this, **companies eliminate**

from net income all gains and losses related to the disposal of plant assets, to arrive at net cash provided by operating activities.

In our example, Computer Services' income statement reports a $3,000 loss on the disposal of equipment (book value $7,000, less $4,000 cash received from disposal of equipment). The company's loss of $3,000 should not be included in the operating activities section of the statement of cash flows. Illustration 17-7 shows that the $3,000 loss is eliminated by adding $3,000 back to net income to arrive at net cash provided by operating activities.

Illustration 17-7
Adjustment for loss on disposal of equipment

Cash flows from operating activities		
Net income		$145,000
Adjustments to reconcile net income to net cash provided by operating activities:		
Depreciation expense	$9,000	
Loss on disposal of equipment	**3,000**	12,000
Net cash provided by operating activities		$157,000

If a gain on disposal occurs, the company deducts the gain from net income in order to determine net cash provided by operating activities. **In the case of either a gain or a loss, companies report as a source of cash in the investing activities section of the statement of cash flows the actual amount of cash received from the sale.**

CHANGES TO NONCASH CURRENT ASSET AND CURRENT LIABILITY ACCOUNTS

A final adjustment in reconciling net income to net cash provided by operating activities involves examining all changes in current asset and current liability accounts. The accrual-accounting process records revenues in the period in which the performance obligation is satisfied and expenses are incurred. For example, Accounts Receivable reflects amounts owed to the company for sales that have been made but for which cash collections have not yet been received. Prepaid Insurance reflects insurance that has been paid for but which has not yet expired (therefore has not been expensed). Similarly, Salaries and Wages Payable reflects salaries and wages expense that has been incurred but has not been paid.

As a result, companies need to adjust net income for these accruals and prepayments to determine net cash provided by operating activities. Thus, they must analyze the change in each current asset and current liability account to determine its impact on net income and cash.

CHANGES IN NONCASH CURRENT ASSETS. The adjustments required for changes in noncash current asset accounts are as follows. **Deduct from net income increases in current asset accounts, and add to net income decreases in current asset accounts, to arrive at net cash provided by operating activities.** We observe these relationships by analyzing the accounts of Computer Services.

DECREASE IN ACCOUNTS RECEIVABLE Computer Services' accounts receivable decreased by $10,000 (from $30,000 to $20,000) during the period. For Computer Services, this means that cash receipts were $10,000 higher than sales revenue. The Accounts Receivable account in Illustration 17-8 shows that Computer Services had $507,000 in sales revenue (as reported on the income statement), but it collected $517,000 in cash.

Illustration 17-8
Analysis of accounts receivable

Accounts Receivable

1/1/17	Balance	30,000	**Receipts from customers**	**517,000**
	Sales revenue	**507,000**		
12/31/17	Balance	20,000		

As shown in Illustration 17-9 (below), to adjust net income to net cash provided by operating activities, the company adds to net income the decrease of $10,000 in accounts receivable. When the Accounts Receivable balance increases, cash receipts are lower than sales revenue earned under the accrual basis. Therefore, the company deducts from net income the amount of the increase in accounts receivable, to arrive at net cash provided by operating activities.

INCREASE IN INVENTORY Computer Services' inventory increased $5,000 (from $10,000 to $15,000) during the period. The change in the Inventory account reflects the difference between the amount of inventory purchased and the amount sold. For Computer Services, this means that the cost of merchandise purchased exceeded the cost of goods sold by $5,000. As a result, cost of goods sold does not reflect $5,000 of cash payments made for merchandise. The company deducts from net income this inventory increase of $5,000 during the period, to arrive at net cash provided by operating activities (see Illustration 17-9). If inventory decreases, the company adds to net income the amount of the change, to arrive at net cash provided by operating activities.

INCREASE IN PREPAID EXPENSES Computer Services' prepaid expenses increased during the period by $4,000. This means that cash paid for expenses is higher than expenses reported on an accrual basis. In other words, the company has made cash payments in the current period but will not charge expenses to income until future periods (as charges to the income statement). To adjust net income to net cash provided by operating activities, the company deducts from net income the $4,000 increase in prepaid expenses (see Illustration 17-9).

Illustration 17-9
Adjustments for changes in current asset accounts

Cash flows from operating activities		
Net income		$145,000
Adjustments to reconcile net income to net cash provided by operating activities:		
Depreciation expense	$ 9,000	
Loss on disposal of equipment	3,000	
Decrease in accounts receivable	**10,000**	
Increase in inventory	**(5,000)**	
Increase in prepaid expenses	**(4,000)**	13,000
Net cash provided by operating activities		$158,000

If prepaid expenses decrease, reported expenses are higher than the expenses paid. Therefore, the company adds to net income the decrease in prepaid expenses, to arrive at net cash provided by operating activities.

CHANGES IN CURRENT LIABILITIES. The adjustments required for changes in current liability accounts are as follows. **Add to net income increases in current liability accounts and deduct from net income decreases in current liability accounts, to arrive at net cash provided by operating activities.**

INCREASE IN ACCOUNTS PAYABLE For Computer Services, Accounts Payable increased by $16,000 (from $12,000 to $28,000) during the period. That means the company received $16,000 more in goods than it actually paid for. As shown in Illustration 17-10, to adjust net income to determine net cash provided by operating activities, the company adds to net income the $16,000 increase in Accounts Payable.

DECREASE IN INCOME TAXES PAYABLE When a company incurs income tax expense but has not yet paid its taxes, it records income taxes payable. A change in the Income Taxes Payable account reflects the difference between income tax expense incurred and income tax actually paid. Computer Services' Income Taxes Payable account decreased by $2,000. That means the $47,000 of income tax expense reported on the income statement was $2,000 less than the amount of taxes paid during the period of $49,000. As shown in Illustration 17-10, to adjust net income to a cash basis, the company must reduce net income by $2,000.

Illustration 17-10
Adjustments for changes in current liability accounts

Cash flows from operating activities		
Net income		$145,000
Adjustments to reconcile net income to net cash provided by operating activities:		
Depreciation expense	$ 9,000	
Loss on disposal of equipment	3,000	
Decrease in accounts receivable	10,000	
Increase in inventory	(5,000)	
Increase in prepaid expenses	(4,000)	
Increase in accounts payable	**16,000**	
Decrease in income taxes payable	**(2,000)**	27,000
Net cash provided by operating activities		$172,000

Illustration 17-10 shows that after starting with net income of $145,000, the sum of all of the adjustments to net income was $27,000. This resulted in net cash provided by operating activities of $172,000.

Summary of Conversion to Net Cash Provided by Operating Activities—Indirect Method

As shown in the previous illustrations, the statement of cash flows prepared by the indirect method starts with net income. It then adds or deducts items to arrive at net cash provided by operating activities. The required adjustments are of three types:

1. Noncash charges such as depreciation and amortization.
2. Gains and losses on the disposal of plant assets.
3. Changes in noncash current asset and current liability accounts.

Illustration 17-11 provides a summary of these changes and required adjustments.

Illustration 17-11
Adjustments required to convert net income to net cash provided by operating activities

		Adjustments Required to Convert Net Income to Net Cash Provided by Operating Activities
Noncash Charges	Depreciation expense	Add
	Amortization expense	Add
Gains and Losses	Loss on disposal of plant assets	Add
	Gain on disposal of plant assets	Deduct
Changes in Current Assets and Current Liabilities	Increase in current asset account	Deduct
	Decrease in current asset account	Add
	Increase in current liability account	Add
	Decrease in current liability account	Deduct

Step 2: Investing and Financing Activities

ANALYZE CHANGES IN NONCURRENT ASSET AND LIABILITY ACCOUNTS AND RECORD AS INVESTING AND FINANCING ACTIVITIES, OR AS NONCASH INVESTING AND FINANCING ACTIVITIES

INCREASE IN LAND As indicated from the change in the Land account and the additional information, Computer Services purchased land of $110,000 by directly exchanging bonds for land. The issuance of bonds payable for land has no effect on cash. But, it is a significant noncash investing and financing activity that merits disclosure in a separate schedule (see Illustration 17-13).

INCREASE IN BUILDINGS As the additional data indicate, Computer Services acquired an office building for $120,000 cash. This is a cash outflow reported in the investing activities section (see Illustration 17-13).

INCREASE IN EQUIPMENT The Equipment account increased $17,000. The additional information explains that this net increase resulted from two transactions: (1) a purchase of equipment of $25,000, and (2) the sale for $4,000 of equipment costing $8,000. These transactions are investing activities. The company should report each transaction separately. Thus, it reports the purchase of equipment as an outflow of cash for $25,000. It reports the sale as an inflow of cash for $4,000. The T-account below shows the reasons for the change in this account during the year.

Illustration 17-12
Analysis of equipment

Equipment				
1/1/17	Balance	10,000	Cost of equipment sold	8,000
	Purchase of equipment	**25,000**		
12/31/17	Balance	27,000		

The following entry shows the details of the equipment sale transaction.

Cash	4,000	
Accumulated Depreciation—Equipment	1,000	
Loss on Disposal of Equipment	3,000	
Equipment		8,000

A	=	L	+	SE
+4,000				
+1,000				
				−3,000 Exp
−8,000				

Cash Flows
+4,000

INCREASE IN BONDS PAYABLE The Bonds Payable account increased $110,000. As indicated in the additional information, the company acquired land from the issuance of these bonds. It reports this noncash transaction in a separate schedule at the bottom of the statement.

INCREASE IN COMMON STOCK The balance sheet reports an increase in Common Stock of $20,000. The additional information section notes that this increase resulted from the issuance of new shares of stock. This is a cash inflow reported in the financing activities section.

INCREASE IN RETAINED EARNINGS Retained earnings increased $116,000 during the year. This increase can be explained by two factors: (1) net income of $145,000 increased retained earnings, and (2) dividends of $29,000 decreased retained earnings. The company adjusts net income to net cash provided by operating activities in the operating activities section. Payment of the dividends (not the declaration) is a **cash outflow that the company reports as a financing activity**.

STATEMENT OF CASH FLOWS—2017

Using the previous information, we can now prepare a statement of cash flows for 2017 for Computer Services Company as shown in Illustration 17-13 (page 588).

Step 3: Net Change in Cash

COMPARE THE NET CHANGE IN CASH ON THE STATEMENT OF CASH FLOWS WITH THE CHANGE IN THE CASH ACCOUNT REPORTED ON THE BALANCE SHEET TO MAKE SURE THE AMOUNTS AGREE

Illustration 17-13 indicates that the net change in cash during the period was an increase of $22,000. This agrees with the change in Cash account reported on the balance sheet in Illustration 17-4 (page 582).

Illustration 17-13
Statement of cash flows, 2017—indirect method

COMPUTER SERVICES COMPANY Statement of Cash Flows—Indirect Method For the Year Ended December 31, 2017		
Cash flows from operating activities		
Net income		$145,000
Adjustments to reconcile net income to net cash provided by operating activities:		
Depreciation expense	$ 9,000	
Loss on disposal of equipment	3,000	
Decrease in accounts receivable	10,000	
Increase in inventory	(5,000)	
Increase in prepaid expenses	(4,000)	
Increase in accounts payable	16,000	
Decrease in income taxes payable	(2,000)	27,000
Net cash provided by operating activities		172,000
Cash flows from investing activities		
Purchase of building	(120,000)	
Purchase of equipment	(25,000)	
Sale of equipment	4,000	
Net cash used by investing activities		(141,000)
Cash flows from financing activities		
Issuance of common stock	20,000	
Payment of cash dividends	(29,000)	
Net cash used by financing activities		(9,000)
Net increase in cash		22,000
Cash at beginning of period		33,000
Cash at end of period		$ 55,000
Noncash investing and financing activities		
Issuance of bonds payable to purchase land		$110,000

LEARNING OBJECTIVE 3

Analyze the statement of cash flows.

Traditionally, investors and creditors used ratios based on accrual accounting. These days, cash-based ratios are gaining increased acceptance among analysts.

Free Cash Flow

In the statement of cash flows, net cash provided by operating activities is intended to indicate the cash-generating capability of a company. Analysts have noted, however, that **net cash provided by operating activities fails to take into account that a company must invest in new fixed assets** just to maintain its current level of operations. Companies also must at least **maintain dividends at current levels** to satisfy investors. The measurement of free cash flow provides additional insight regarding a company's cash-generating ability. **Free cash flow** describes the net cash provided by operating activities after adjustment for capital expenditures and dividends.

Consider the following example. Suppose that MPC produced and sold 10,000 personal computers this year. It reported $100,000 net cash provided by operating activities. In order to maintain production at 10,000 computers, MPC invested $15,000 in equipment. It chose to pay $5,000 in dividends. Its free cash flow was $80,000 ($100,000 − $15,000 − $5,000). The company could use this $80,000 either to purchase new assets to expand the business or to pay an $80,000 dividend and continue to produce 10,000 computers. In practice, free cash flow is often calculated with the formula in Illustration 17-14. (Alternative definitions also exist.)

Free Cash Flow	=	Net Cash Provided by Operating Activities	−	Capital Expenditures	−	Cash Dividends

Illustration 17-14
Free cash flow

Illustration 17-15 provides basic information (in millions) excerpted from the 2013 statement of cash flows of Microsoft Corporation.

Illustration 17-15
Microsoft's cash flow information ($ in millions)

Real World

MICROSOFT CORPORATION
Statement of Cash Flows (partial)
2013

Cash provided by operating activities		$21,863
Cash flows from investing activities		
Additions to property and equipment	$ (4,257)	
Purchases of investments	(75,396)	
Sales of investments	52,464	
Acquisitions of companies	(1,584)	
Maturities of investments	5,130	
Other	(168)	
Cash used by investing activities		(23,811)
Cash paid for dividends		(7,455)

Microsoft's free cash flow is calculated as shown in Illustration 17-16.

Illustration 17-16
Calculation of Microsoft's free cash flow ($ in millions)

Cash provided by operating activities	$21,863
Less: Expenditures on property, plant, and equipment	4,257
Dividends paid	7,455
Free cash flow	**$10,151**

Microsoft generated approximately $10.15 billion of free cash flow. This is a tremendous amount of cash generated in a single year. It is available for the acquisition of new assets, the retirement of stock or debt, or the payment of dividends. Also note that Microsoft's cash from operations of $21.8 billion is nearly identical to its 2013 net income of $21.9 billion. This lends additional credibility to Microsoft's income number as an indicator of potential future performance.

APPENDIX 17A: Prepare a statement of cash flows using the direct method.

To explain and illustrate the direct method for preparing a statement of cash flows, we use the transactions of Computer Services Company for 2017. Illustration 17A-1 (page 590) presents information related to 2017 for the company.

To prepare a statement of cash flows under the direct approach, we apply the three steps outlined in Illustration 17-3 (page 581).

Step 1: Operating Activities

DETERMINE NET CASH PROVIDED/USED BY OPERATING ACTIVITIES BY CONVERTING NET INCOME FROM AN ACCRUAL BASIS TO A CASH BASIS

Under the **direct method**, companies compute net cash provided by operating activities by **adjusting each item in the income statement** from the accrual

Illustration 17A-1
Comparative balance sheets, income statement, and additional information for Computer Services Company

COMPUTER SERVICES COMPANY
Comparative Balance Sheets
December 31

Assets	2017	2016	Change in Account Balance Increase/Decrease
Current assets			
Cash	$ 55,000	$ 33,000	$ 22,000 Increase
Accounts receivable	20,000	30,000	10,000 Decrease
Inventory	15,000	10,000	5,000 Increase
Prepaid expenses	5,000	1,000	4,000 Increase
Property, plant, and equipment			
Land	130,000	20,000	110,000 Increase
Buildings	160,000	40,000	120,000 Increase
Accumulated depreciation—buildings	(11,000)	(5,000)	6,000 Increase
Equipment	27,000	10,000	17,000 Increase
Accumulated depreciation—equipment	(3,000)	(1,000)	2,000 Increase
Total assets	$398,000	$138,000	
Liabilities and Stockholders' Equity			
Current liabilities			
Accounts payable	$ 28,000	$ 12,000	$ 16,000 Increase
Income taxes payable	6,000	8,000	2,000 Decrease
Long-term liabilities			
Bonds payable	130,000	20,000	110,000 Increase
Stockholders' equity			
Common stock	70,000	50,000	20,000 Increase
Retained earnings	164,000	48,000	116,000 Increase
Total liabilities and stockholders' equity	$398,000	$138,000	

COMPUTER SERVICES COMPANY
Income Statement
For the Year Ended December 31, 2017

Sales revenue		$507,000
Cost of goods sold	$150,000	
Operating expenses (excluding depreciation)	111,000	
Depreciation expense	9,000	
Loss on disposal of equipment	3,000	
Interest expense	42,000	315,000
Income before income tax		192,000
Income tax expense		47,000
Net income		$145,000

Additional information for 2017:

1. Depreciation expense comprised $6,000 for building and $3,000 for equipment.
2. The company sold equipment with a book value of $7,000 (cost $8,000, less accumulated depreciation $1,000) for $4,000 cash.
3. Issued $110,000 of long-term bonds in direct exchange for land.
4. A building costing $120,000 was purchased for cash. Equipment costing $25,000 was also purchased for cash.
5. Issued common stock for $20,000 cash.
6. The company declared and paid a $29,000 cash dividend.

basis to the cash basis. To simplify and condense the operating activities section, companies **report only major classes of operating cash receipts and cash payments**. For these major classes, the difference between cash receipts and cash payments is the net cash provided by operating activities. These relationships are as shown in Illustration 17A-2.

Illustration 17A-2
Major classes of cash receipts and payments

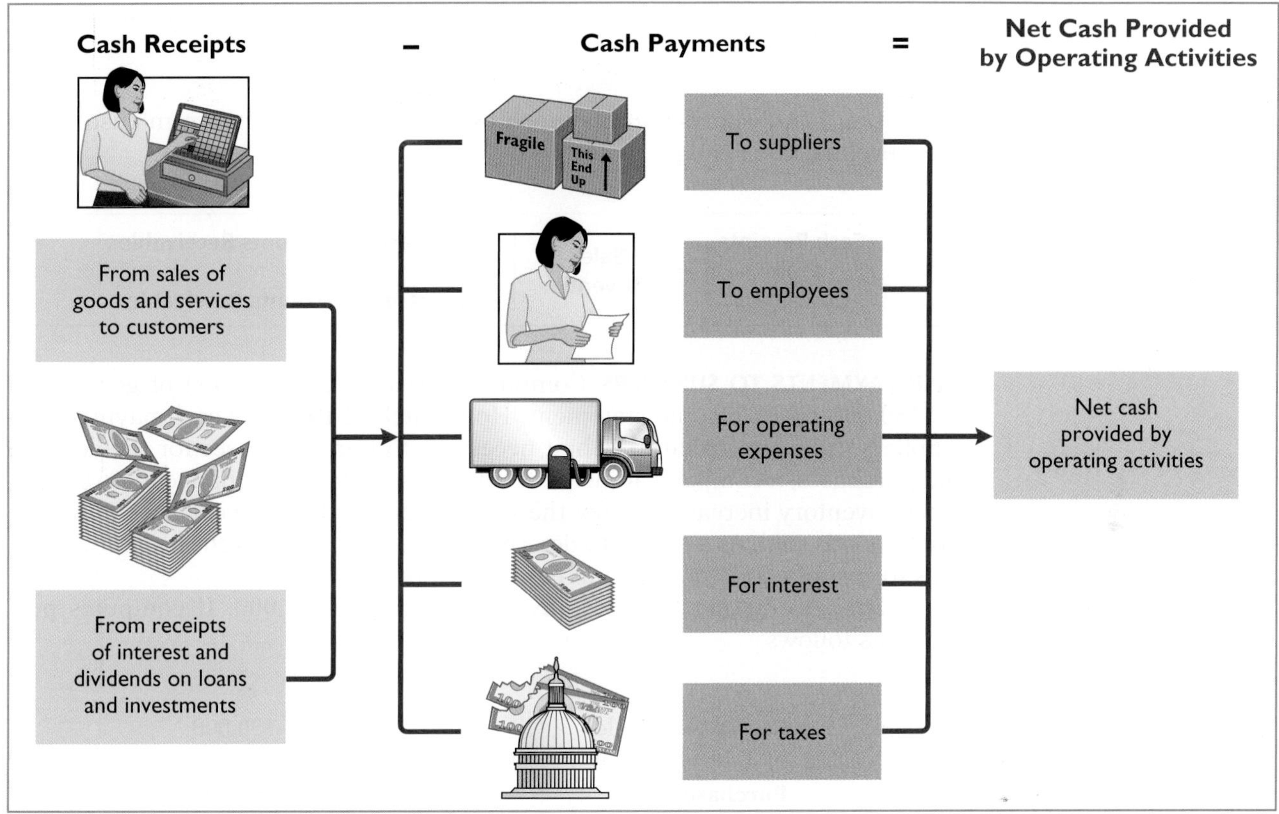

An efficient way to apply the direct method is to analyze the items reported in the income statement in the order in which they are listed. We then determine cash receipts and cash payments related to these revenues and expenses. The following presents the adjustments required to prepare a statement of cash flows for Computer Services Company using the direct approach.

CASH RECEIPTS FROM CUSTOMERS The income statement for Computer Services reported sales revenue from customers of $507,000. How much of that was cash receipts? To answer that, a company considers the change in accounts receivable during the year. When accounts receivable increase during the year, revenues on an accrual basis are higher than cash receipts from customers. Operations led to revenues, but not all of those revenues resulted in cash receipts.

To determine the amount of cash receipts, a company deducts from sales revenue the increase in accounts receivable. On the other hand, there may be a decrease in accounts receivable. That would occur if cash receipts from customers exceeded sales revenue. In that case, a company adds to sales revenue the decrease in accounts receivable. For Computer Services, accounts receivable decreased $10,000. Thus, cash receipts from customers were $517,000, computed as shown in Illustration 17A-3.

Sales revenue	$ 507,000
Add: Decrease in accounts receivable	10,000
Cash receipts from customers	**$517,000**

Illustration 17A-3
Computation of cash receipts from customers

Computer Services can also determine cash receipts from customers from an analysis of the Accounts Receivable account, as shown in Illustration 17A-4.

Illustration 17A-4
Analysis of accounts receivable

Accounts Receivable				
1/1/17	Balance	30,000	**Receipts from customers**	**517,000**
	Sales revenue	507,000		
12/31/17	Balance	20,000		

Illustration 17A-5 shows the relationships among cash receipts from customers, sales revenue, and changes in accounts receivable.

Illustration 17A-5
Formula to compute cash receipts from customers—direct method

Cash Receipts From Customers	=	Sales Revenue	+ Decrease in Accounts Receivable or − Increase in Accounts Receivable

CASH PAYMENTS TO SUPPLIERS Computer Services reported cost of goods sold of $150,000 on its income statement. How much of that was cash payments to suppliers? To answer that, it is first necessary to find purchases for the year. To find purchases, a company adjusts cost of goods sold for the change in inventory. When inventory increases during the year, purchases for the year have exceeded cost of goods sold. As a result, to determine the amount of purchases, a company adds to cost of goods sold the increase in inventory.

In 2017, Computer Services' inventory increased $5,000. It computes purchases as follows.

Illustration 17A-6
Computation of purchases

Cost of goods sold	$ 150,000
Add: Increase in inventory	5,000
Purchases	**$155,000**

Computer Services can also determine purchases from an analysis of the Inventory account, as shown in Illustration 17A-7.

Illustration 17A-7
Analysis of inventory

Inventory				
1/1/17	Balance	10,000	Cost of goods sold	150,000
	Purchases	**155,000**		
12/31/17	Balance	15,000		

After computing purchases, a company can determine cash payments to suppliers. This is done by adjusting purchases for the change in accounts payable. When accounts payable increase during the year, purchases on an accrual basis are higher than they are on a cash basis. As a result, to determine cash payments to suppliers, a company deducts from purchases the increase in accounts payable. On the other hand, if cash payments to suppliers exceed purchases, there will be a decrease in accounts payable. In that case, a company adds to purchases the decrease in accounts payable. For Computer Services, cash payments to suppliers were $139,000, computed as follows.

Illustration 17A-8
Computation of cash payments to suppliers

Purchases	$ 155,000
Deduct: Increase in accounts payable	16,000
Cash payments to suppliers	**$139,000**

Computer Services also can determine cash payments to suppliers from an analysis of the Accounts Payable account, as shown in Illustration 17A-9.

Illustration 17A-9
Analysis of accounts payable

Accounts Payable				
Payments to suppliers	**139,000**	1/1/17	Balance	12,000
			Purchases	155,000
		12/31/17	Balance	28,000

Illustration 17A-10 shows the relationships among cash payments to suppliers, cost of goods sold, changes in inventory, and changes in accounts payable.

Illustration 17A-10
Formula to compute cash payments to suppliers—direct method

Cash Payments to Suppliers	=	Cost of Goods Sold	+ Increase in Inventory or − Decrease in Inventory	+ Decrease in Accounts Payable or − Increase in Accounts Payable

CASH PAYMENTS FOR OPERATING EXPENSES Computer Services reported on its income statement operating expenses of $111,000. How much of that amount was cash paid for operating expenses? To answer that, we need to adjust this amount for any changes in prepaid expenses and accrued expenses payable. For example, if prepaid expenses increased during the year, cash paid for operating expenses is higher than operating expenses reported on the income statement. To convert operating expenses to cash payments for operating expenses, a company adds the increase in prepaid expenses to operating expenses. On the other hand, if prepaid expenses decrease during the year, it deducts the decrease from operating expenses.

Companies must also adjust operating expenses for changes in accrued expenses payable. When accrued expenses payable increase during the year, operating expenses on an accrual basis are higher than they are in a cash basis. As a result, to determine cash payments for operating expenses, a company deducts from operating expenses an increase in accrued expenses payable. On the other hand, a company adds to operating expenses a decrease in accrued expenses payable because cash payments exceed operating expenses.

Computer Services' cash payments for operating expenses were $115,000, computed as follows.

Illustration 17A-11
Computation of cash payments for operating expenses

Operating expenses	$ 111,000
Add: Increase in prepaid expenses	4,000
Cash payments for operating expenses	**$115,000**

Illustration 17A-12 shows the relationships among cash payments for operating expenses, changes in prepaid expenses, and changes in accrued expenses payable.

Illustration 17A-12
Formula to compute cash payments for operating expenses—direct method

Cash Payments for Operating Expenses	=	Operating Expenses	+ Increase in Prepaid Expenses or − Decrease in Prepaid Expenses	+ Decrease in Accrued Expenses Payable or − Increase in Accrued Expenses Payable

DEPRECIATION EXPENSE AND LOSS ON DISPOSAL OF EQUIPMENT Computer Services' depreciation expense in 2017 was $9,000. Depreciation expense is not shown on a statement of cash flows under the direct method because it is a noncash charge. If the amount for operating expenses includes depreciation expense, operating expenses must be reduced by the amount of depreciation to determine cash payments for operating expenses.

The loss on disposal of equipment of $3,000 is also a noncash charge. The loss on disposal of equipment reduces net income, but it does not reduce cash. Thus, the loss on disposal of equipment is not shown on the statement of cash flows under the direct method.

Other charges to expense that do not require the use of cash, such as the amortization of intangible assets, depletion expense, and bad debt expense, are treated in the same manner as depreciation.

CASH PAYMENTS FOR INTEREST Computer Services reported on the income statement interest expense of $42,000. Since the balance sheet did not include an accrual for interest payable for 2016 or 2017, the amount reported as expense is the same as the amount of interest paid.

CASH PAYMENTS FOR INCOME TAXES Computer Services reported income tax expense of $47,000 on the income statement. Income taxes payable, however, decreased $2,000. This decrease means that income taxes paid were more than income taxes reported in the income statement. Cash payments for income taxes were therefore $49,000 as shown below.

Illustration 17A-13
Computation of cash payments for income taxes

Income tax expense	$ 47,000
Add: Decrease in income taxes payable	2,000
Cash payments for income taxes	**$49,000**

Computer Services can also determine cash payments for income taxes from an analysis of the Income Taxes Payable account, as shown in Illustration 17A-14.

Illustration 17A-14
Analysis of income taxes payable

Income Taxes Payable

Cash payments for income taxes	**49,000**	1/1/17	Balance	8,000
			Income tax expense	47,000
		12/31/17	Balance	6,000

Illustration 17A-15 shows the relationships among cash payments for income taxes, income tax expense, and changes in income taxes payable.

Illustration 17A-15
Formula to compute cash payments for income taxes—direct method

Cash Payments for Income Taxes = **Income Tax Expense** { + **Decrease in Income Taxes Payable** or − **Increase in Income Taxes Payable** }

The operating activities section of the statement of cash flows of Computer Services is shown in Illustration 17A-16.

Illustration 17A-16
Operating activities section of the statement of cash flows

Cash flows from operating activities		
Cash receipts from customers		$517,000
Less: Cash payments:		
To suppliers	$139,000	
For operating expenses	115,000	
For interest expense	42,000	
For income taxes	49,000	345,000
Net cash provided by operating activities		$172,000

When a company uses the direct method, it must also provide in a **separate schedule** (not shown here) the net cash flows from operating activities as computed under the indirect method.

Step 2: Investing and Financing Activities

ANALYZE CHANGES IN NONCURRENT ASSET AND LIABILITY ACCOUNTS AND RECORD AS INVESTING AND FINANCING ACTIVITIES, OR DISCLOSE AS NONCASH TRANSACTIONS

INCREASE IN LAND As indicated from the change in the Land account and the additional information, Computer Services purchased land of $110,000 by directly exchanging bonds for land. The exchange of bonds payable for land has no effect on cash. But, it is a significant noncash investing and financing activity that merits disclosure in a separate schedule (see Illustration 17A-18).

INCREASE IN BUILDINGS As the additional data indicate, Computer Services acquired an office building for $120,000 cash. This is a cash outflow reported in the investing activities section (see Illustration 17A-18).

INCREASE IN EQUIPMENT The Equipment account increased $17,000. The additional information explains that this was a net increase that resulted from two transactions: (1) a purchase of equipment of $25,000, and (2) the sale for $4,000 of equipment costing $8,000. These transactions are investing activities. The company should report each transaction separately. The statement in Illustration 17A-18 reports the purchase of equipment as an outflow of cash for $25,000. It reports the sale as an inflow of cash for $4,000. The T-account below shows the reasons for the change in this account during the year.

Illustration 17A-17
Analysis of equipment

Equipment				
1/1/17	Balance	10,000	Cost of equipment sold	8,000
	Purchase of equipment	**25,000**		
12/31/17	Balance	27,000		

The following entry shows the details of the equipment sale transaction.

Cash	4,000	
Accumulated Depreciation—Equipment	1,000	
Loss on Disposal of Equipment	3,000	
Equipment		8,000

A	=	L	+	SE
+4,000				
+1,000				
				−3,000 Exp
−8,000				

Cash Flows
+4,000

INCREASE IN BONDS PAYABLE The Bonds Payable account increased $110,000. As indicated in the additional information, the company acquired land by directly exchanging bonds for land. Illustration 17A-18 reports this noncash transaction in a separate schedule at the bottom of the statement.

INCREASE IN COMMON STOCK The balance sheet reports an increase in Common Stock of $20,000. The additional information section notes that this increase resulted from the issuance of new shares of stock. This is a cash inflow reported in the financing activities section in Illustration 17A-18.

INCREASE IN RETAINED EARNINGS Retained earnings increased $116,000 during the year. This increase can be explained by two factors: (1) net income of $145,000 increased retained earnings, and (2) dividends of $29,000 decreased retained earnings. The company adjusts net income to net cash provided by operating activities in the operating activities section. **Payment** of the dividends (not the declaration) is a **cash outflow that the company reports as a financing activity in Illustration 17A-18**.

STATEMENT OF CASH FLOWS—2017

Illustration 17A-18 shows the statement of cash flows for Computer Services Company.

Illustration 17A-18
Statement of cash flows, 2017—direct method

COMPUTER SERVICES COMPANY Statement of Cash Flows—Direct Method For the Year Ended December 31, 2017		
Cash flows from operating activities		
Cash receipts from customers		$ 517,000
Less: Cash payments:		
To suppliers	$ 139,000	
For operating expenses	115,000	
For income taxes	49,000	
For interest expense	42,000	345,000
Net cash provided by operating activities		172,000
Cash flows from investing activities		
Sale of equipment	4,000	
Purchase of building	(120,000)	
Purchase of equipment	(25,000)	
Net cash used by investing activities		(141,000)
Cash flows from financing activities		
Issuance of common stock	20,000	
Payment of cash dividends	(29,000)	
Net cash used by financing activities		(9,000)
Net increase in cash		22,000
Cash at beginning of period		33,000
Cash at end of period		$ 55,000
Noncash investing and financing activities		
Issuance of bonds payable to purchase land		$ 110,000

Step 3: Net Change in Cash

COMPARE THE NET CHANGE IN CASH ON THE STATEMENT OF CASH FLOWS WITH THE CHANGE IN THE CASH ACCOUNT REPORTED ON THE BALANCE SHEET TO MAKE SURE THE AMOUNTS AGREE

Illustration 17A-18 indicates that the net change in cash during the period was an increase of $22,000. This agrees with the change in balances in the Cash account reported on the balance sheets in Illustration 17A-1 (page 590).

APPENDIX 17B: Use a worksheet to prepare the statement of cash flows using the indirect method.

When preparing a statement of cash flows, companies may need to make numerous adjustments of net income. In such cases, they often use **a worksheet to assemble and classify the data that will appear on the statement**. The worksheet is merely an aid in preparing the statement. Its use is optional. Illustration 17B-1 shows the skeleton format of the worksheet for preparation of the statement of cash flows.

Illustration 17B-1
Format of worksheet

XYZ Company.xls

Home | Insert | Page Layout | Formulas | Data | Review | View

P18 | *fx*

	A	B	C	D	E
1					
2	**XYZ COMPANY**				
3	**Worksheet**				
4	**Statement of Cash Flows For the Year Ended . . .**				
5					
6		End of			End of
7		Last Year	Reconciling Items		Current Year
8	Balance Sheet Accounts	Balances	Debit	Credit	Balances
9	Debit balance accounts	XX	XX	XX	XX
10		XX	XX	XX	XX
11	Totals	XXX			XXX
12	Credit balance accounts	XX	XX	XX	XX
13		XX	XX	XX	XX
14	Totals	XXX			XXX
15					
16	Statement of Cash				
17	Flows Effects				
18	Operating activities				
19	Net income		XX		
20	Adjustments to net income		XX	XX	
21	Investing activities				
22	Receipts and payments		XX	XX	
23	Financing activities				
24	Receipts and payments		XX	XX	
25	Totals		XXX	XXX	
26	Increase (decrease) in cash		(XX)	XX	
27	Totals		XXX	XXX	
28					

The following guidelines are important in preparing a worksheet.

1. In the balance sheet accounts section, **list accounts with debit balances separately from those with credit balances**. This means, for example, that Accumulated Depreciation appears under credit balances and not as a contra account under debit balances. Enter the beginning and ending balances of each account in the appropriate columns. Enter as reconciling items in the two middle columns the transactions that caused the change in the account balance during the year.

   After all reconciling items have been entered, each line pertaining to a balance sheet account should "foot across." That is, the beginning balance plus or minus the reconciling item(s) must equal the ending balance. When this agreement exists for all balance sheet accounts, all changes in account balances have been reconciled.

2. The bottom portion of the worksheet consists of the operating, investing, and financing activities sections. It provides the information necessary to prepare the formal statement of cash flows. **Enter inflows of cash as debits in the reconciling columns. Enter outflows of cash as credits in the reconciling columns.** Thus, in this section, the sale of equipment for cash at book value appears as a debit under investing activities. Similarly, the purchase of land for cash appears as a credit under investing activities.

3. **The reconciling items shown in the worksheet are not entered in any journal or posted to any account.** They do not represent either adjustments or corrections of the balance sheet accounts. They are used only to facilitate the preparation of the statement of cash flows.

Preparing the Worksheet

As in the case of worksheets illustrated in earlier chapters, preparing a worksheet involves a series of prescribed steps. The steps in this case are:

1. Enter in the balance sheet accounts section the balance sheet accounts and their beginning and ending balances.

2. Enter in the reconciling columns of the worksheet the data that explain the changes in the balance sheet accounts other than cash and their effects on the statement of cash flows.
3. Enter on the cash line and at the bottom of the worksheet the increase or decrease in cash. This entry should enable the totals of the reconciling columns to be in agreement.

To illustrate the preparation of a worksheet, we will use the 2017 data for Computer Services Company. Your familiarity with these data (from the chapter) should help you understand the use of a worksheet. For ease of reference, the comparative balance sheets, income statement, and selected data for 2017 are presented in Illustration 17B-2.

DETERMINING THE RECONCILING ITEMS

Companies can use one of several approaches to determine the reconciling items. For example, they can first complete the changes affecting net cash provided by operating activities, and then can determine the effects of financing and investing transactions. Or, they can analyze the balance sheet accounts in the order in which they are listed on the worksheet. We will follow this latter approach for Computer Services, except for cash. As indicated in Step 3, **cash is handled last**.

ACCOUNTS RECEIVABLE The decrease of $10,000 in accounts receivable means that cash collections from sales revenue are higher than the sales revenue reported in the income statement. To convert net income to net cash provided by operating activities, we add the decrease of $10,000 to net income. The entry in the reconciling columns of the worksheet is:

(a)	Operating—Decrease in Accounts Receivable	10,000	
	Accounts Receivable		10,000

INVENTORY Computer Services Company's inventory balance increases $5,000 during the period. The Inventory account reflects the difference between the amount of inventory that the company purchased and the amount that it sold. For Computer Services, this means that the cost of merchandise purchased exceeds the cost of goods sold by $5,000. As a result, cost of goods sold does not reflect $5,000 of cash payments made for merchandise. We deduct this inventory increase of $5,000 during the period from net income to arrive at net cash provided by operating activities. The worksheet entry is:

(b)	Inventory	5,000	
	Operating—Increase in Inventory		5,000

PREPAID EXPENSES An increase of $4,000 in prepaid expenses means that expenses deducted in determining net income are less than expenses that were paid in cash. We deduct the increase of $4,000 from net income in determining net cash provided by operating activities. The worksheet entry is as follows.

(c)	Prepaid Expenses	4,000	
	Operating—Increase in Prepaid Expenses		4,000

LAND The increase in land of $110,000 resulted from a purchase through the issuance of long-term bonds. The company should report this transaction as a significant noncash investing and financing activity. The worksheet entry is:

(d)	Land	110,000	
	Bonds Payable		110,000

Illustration 17B-2
Comparative balance sheets, income statement, and additional information for Computer Services Company

Computer Services Company.xls

COMPUTER SERVICES COMPANY
Comparative Balance Sheets
December 31

Assets	2017	2016	Change in Account Balance Increase/Decrease
Current assets			
Cash	$ 55,000	$ 33,000	$ 22,000 Increase
Accounts receivable	20,000	30,000	10,000 Decrease
Inventory	15,000	10,000	5,000 Increase
Prepaid expenses	5,000	1,000	4,000 Increase
Property, plant, and equipment			
Land	130,000	20,000	110,000 Increase
Buildings	160,000	40,000	120,000 Increase
Accumulated depreciation—buildings	(11,000)	(5,000)	6,000 Increase
Equipment	27,000	10,000	17,000 Increase
Accumulated depreciation—equipment	(3,000)	(1,000)	2,000 Increase
Total assets	$398,000	$138,000	
Liabilities and Stockholders' Equity			
Current liabilities			
Accounts payable	$ 28,000	$ 12,000	$ 16,000 Increase
Income taxes payable	6,000	8,000	2,000 Decrease
Long-term liabilities			
Bonds payable	130,000	20,000	110,000 Increase
Stockholders' equity			
Common stock	70,000	50,000	20,000 Increase
Retained earnings	164,000	48,000	116,000 Increase
Total liabilities and stockholders' equity	$398,000	$138,000	

Computer Services Company.xls

COMPUTER SERVICES COMPANY
Income Statement
For the Year Ended December 31, 2017

Sales revenue		$507,000
Cost of goods sold	$150,000	
Operating expenses (excluding depreciation)	111,000	
Depreciation expense	9,000	
Loss on disposal of equipment	3,000	
Interest expense	42,000	315,000
Income before income tax		192,000
Income tax expense		47,000
Net income		$145,000

Additional information for 2017:

1. Depreciation expense comprised $6,000 for building and $3,000 for equipment.
2. The company sold equipment with a book value of $7,000 (cost $8,000, less accumulated depreciation $1,000) for $4,000 cash.
3. Issued $110,000 of long-term bonds in direct exchange for land.
4. A building costing $120,000 was purchased for cash. Equipment costing $25,000 was also purchased for cash.
5. Issued common stock for $20,000 cash.
6. The company declared and paid a $29,000 cash dividend.

BUILDINGS The cash purchase of a building for $120,000 is an investing activity cash outflow. The entry in the reconciling columns of the worksheet is:

(e)	Buildings	120,000	
	Investing—Purchase of Building		120,000

EQUIPMENT The increase in equipment of $17,000 resulted from a cash purchase of $25,000 and the disposal of equipment costing $8,000. The book value of the equipment was $7,000, the cash proceeds were $4,000, and a loss of $3,000 was recorded. The worksheet entries are:

(f)	Equipment	25,000	
	Investing—Purchase of Equipment		25,000
(g)	Investing—Sale of Equipment	4,000	
	Operating—Loss on Disposal of Equipment	3,000	
	Accumulated Depreciation—Equipment	1,000	
	Equipment		8,000

ACCOUNTS PAYABLE We must add the increase of $16,000 in accounts payable to net income to determine net cash provided by operating activities. The worksheet entry is:

(h)	Operating—Increase in Accounts Payable	16,000	
	Accounts Payable		16,000

INCOME TAXES PAYABLE When a company incurs income tax expense but has not yet paid its taxes, it records income taxes payable. A change in the Income Taxes Payable account reflects the difference between income tax expense incurred and income tax actually paid. Computer Services' Income Taxes Payable account decreases by $2,000. That means the $47,000 of income tax expense reported on the income statement was $2,000 less than the amount of taxes paid during the period of $49,000. To adjust net income to a cash basis, we must reduce net income by $2,000. The worksheet entry is:

(i)	Income Taxes Payable	2,000	
	Operating—Decrease in Income Taxes Payable		2,000

BONDS PAYABLE The increase of $110,000 in this account resulted from the issuance of bonds for land. This is a significant noncash investing and financing activity. Worksheet entry (d) above is the only entry necessary.

COMMON STOCK The balance sheet reports an increase in Common Stock of $20,000. The additional information section notes that this increase resulted from the issuance of new shares of stock. This is a cash inflow reported in the financing section. The worksheet entry is:

(j)	Financing—Issuance of Common Stock	20,000	
	Common Stock		20,000

ACCUMULATED DEPRECIATION—BUILDINGS, AND ACCUMULATED DEPRECIATION—EQUIPMENT Increases in these accounts of $6,000 and $3,000, respectively, resulted from depreciation expense. Depreciation expense is a **noncash charge that we must add to net income** to determine net cash provided by operating activities. The worksheet entries are:

(k)	Operating—Depreciation Expense	6,000	
	Accumulated Depreciation—Buildings		6,000
(l)	Operating—Depreciation Expense	3,000	
	Accumulated Depreciation—Equipment		3,000

RETAINED EARNINGS The $116,000 increase in retained earnings resulted from net income of $145,000 and the declaration and payment of a $29,000 cash dividend. Net income is included in net cash provided by operating activities, and the dividends are a financing activity cash outflow. The entries in the reconciling columns of the worksheet are:

(m)	Operating—Net Income	145,000	
	Retained Earnings		145,000

(n)	Retained Earnings	29,000	
	Financing—Payment of Dividends		29,000

DISPOSITION OF CHANGE IN CASH The firm's cash increased $22,000 in 2017. The final entry on the worksheet, therefore, is:

(o)	Cash	22,000	
	Increase in Cash		22,000

As shown in the worksheet, we enter the increase in cash in the reconciling credit column as a **balancing** amount. This entry should complete the reconciliation of the changes in the balance sheet accounts. Also, it should permit the totals of the reconciling columns to be in agreement. When all changes have been explained and the reconciling columns are in agreement, the reconciling columns are ruled to complete the worksheet. The completed worksheet for Computer Services Company is shown in Illustration 17B-3.

Illustration 17B-3
Completed worksheet—indirect method

Computer Services Company.xls

COMPUTER SERVICES COMPANY
Worksheet
Statement of Cash Flows For the Year Ended December 31, 2017

Balance Sheet Accounts	Balance 12/31/16	Reconciling Items Debit	Reconciling Items Credit	Balance 12/31/17
Debits				
Cash	33,000	(o) 22,000		55,000
Accounts Receivable	30,000		(a) 10,000	20,000
Inventory	10,000	(b) 5,000		15,000
Prepaid Expenses	1,000	(c) 4,000		5,000
Land	20,000	(d) 110,000*		130,000
Buildings	40,000	(e) 120,000		160,000
Equipment	10,000	(f) 25,000	(g) 8,000	27,000
Total	144,000			412,000
Credits				
Accounts Payable	12,000		(h) 16,000	28,000
Income Taxes Payable	8,000	(i) 2,000		6,000
Bonds Payable	20,000		(d) 110,000*	130,000
Accumulated Depreciation—Buildings	5,000		(k) 6,000	11,000
Accumulated Depreciation—Equipment	1,000	(g) 1,000	(l) 3,000	3,000
Common Stock	50,000		(j) 20,000	70,000
Retained Earnings	48,000	(n) 29,000	(m) 145,000	164,000
Total	144,000			412,000
Statement of Cash Flows Effects				
Operating activities				
Net income		(m) 145,000		
Decrease in accounts receivable		(a) 10,000		
Increase in inventory			(b) 5,000	
Increase in prepaid expenses			(c) 4,000	
Increase in accounts payable		(h) 16,000		
Decrease in income taxes payable			(i) 2,000	
Depreciation expense		(k) 6,000		
		(l) 3,000		
Loss on disposal of equipment		(g) 3,000		
Investing activities				
Purchase of building			(e) 120,000	
Purchase of equipment			(f) 25,000	
Sale of equipment		(g) 4,000		
Financing activities				
Issuance of common stock		(j) 20,000		
Payment of dividends			(n) 29,000	
Totals		525,000	503,000	
Increase in cash			(o) 22,000	
Totals		525,000	525,000	

* Significant noncash investing and financing activity.

LEARNING OBJECTIVE *6

APPENDIX 17C: Use the T-account approach to prepare a statement of cash flows.

Many people like to use T-accounts to provide structure to the preparation of a statement of cash flows. The use of T-accounts is based on the accounting equation that you learned in Chapter 1. The basic equation is:

Assets = Liabilities + Equity

Now, let's rewrite the left-hand side as:

Cash + Noncash Assets = Liabilities + Equity

Next, rewrite the equation by subtracting Noncash Assets from each side to isolate Cash on the left-hand side:

Cash = Liabilities + Equity − Noncash Assets

Finally, if we insert the Δ symbol (which means "change in"), we have:

Δ Cash = Δ Liabilities + Δ Equity − Δ Noncash Assets

What this means is that the change in cash is equal to the change in all of the other balance sheet accounts. Another way to think about this is that if we analyze the changes in all of the noncash balance sheet accounts, we will explain the change in the Cash account. This, of course, is exactly what we are trying to do with the statement of cash flows.

To implement this approach, first prepare a large Cash T-account with sections for operating, investing, and financing activities. Then, prepare smaller T-accounts for all of the other noncash balance sheet accounts. Insert the beginning and ending balances for each of these accounts. Once you have done this, then walk through the steps outlined in Illustration 17-3 (page 581). As you walk through the steps, enter debit and credit amounts into the affected accounts. When all of the changes in the T-accounts have been explained, you are done. To demonstrate, we apply this approach to the example of Computer Services Company that is presented in the chapter. Each of the adjustments in Illustration 17C-1 is numbered so you can follow them through the T-accounts.

1. Post net income as a debit to the operating section of the Cash T-account and a credit to Retained Earnings. Make sure to label all adjustments to the Cash T-account. It also helps to number each adjustment so you can trace all of them if you make an error.
2. Post depreciation expense as a debit to the operating section of Cash and a credit to each of the appropriate accumulated depreciation accounts.
3. Post any gains or losses on the sale of property, plant, and equipment. To do this, it is best to first prepare the journal entry that was recorded at the time of the sale and then post each element of the journal entry. For example, for Computer Services the entry was as follows.

Cash	4,000	
Accumulated Depreciation—Equipment	1,000	
Loss on Disposal of Equipment	3,000	
Equipment		8,000

The $4,000 cash entry is a source of cash in the investing section of the Cash account. Accumulated Depreciation—Equipment is debited for $1,000. The Loss on Disposal of Equipment is a debit to the operating section of the Cash T-account. Finally, Equipment is credited for $8,000.

Cash

	Debit	Credit	
Operating			
(1) Net income	145,000	5,000	Inventory (5)
(2) Depreciation expense	9,000	4,000	Prepaid expenses (6)
(3) Loss on equipment	3,000	2,000	Income taxes payable (8)
(4) Accounts receivable	10,000		
(7) Accounts payable	16,000		
Net cash provided by operating activities	172,000		
Investing			
(3) Sold equipment	4,000	120,000	Purchased building (10)
		25,000	Purchased equipment (11)
		141,000	Net cash used by investing activities
Financing			
(12) Issued common stock	20,000	29,000	Dividend paid (13)
		9,000	Net cash used by financing activities
	22,000		

Accounts Receivable		Inventory		Prepaid Expenses		Land	
30,000	10,000 (4)	10,000		1,000		20,000	
		(5) 5,000		(6) 4,000		(9) 110,000	
20,000		15,000		5,000		130,000	

Buildings		Accumulated Depreciation—Buildings		Equipment		Accumulated Depreciation—Equipment	
40,000			5,000	10,000	8,000 (3)	(3) 1,000	1,000
(10) 120,000			6,000 (2)	(11) 25,000			3,000 (2)
160,000			11,000	27,000			3,000

Accounts Payable		Income Taxes Payable		Bonds Payable		Common Stock		Retained Earnings	
	12,000	(8) 2,000	8,000		20,000		50,000	(13) 29,000	48,000
	16,000 (7)				110,000 (9)		20,000 (12)		145,000 (1)
	28,000		6,000		130,000		70,000		164,000

Illustration 17C-1
T-account approach

4–8. Next, post each of the changes to the noncash current asset and current liability accounts. For example, to explain the $10,000 decline in Computer Services' accounts receivable, credit Accounts Receivable for $10,000 and debit the operating section of the Cash T-account for $10,000.

9. Analyze the changes in the noncurrent accounts. Land was purchased by issuing bonds payable. This requires a debit to Land for $110,000 and a credit to Bonds Payable for $110,000. Note that this is a significant noncash event that requires disclosure at the bottom of the statement of cash flows.

10. Buildings is debited for $120,000, and the investing section of the Cash T-account is credited for $120,000 as a use of cash from investing.

11. Equipment is debited for $25,000 and the investing section of the Cash T-account is credited for $25,000 as a use of cash from investing.

12. Common Stock is credited for $20,000 for the issuance of shares of stock, and the financing section of the Cash T-account is debited for $20,000.

13. Retained Earnings is debited to reflect the payment of the $29,000 dividend, and the financing section of the Cash T-account is credited to reflect the use of Cash.

At this point, all of the changes in the noncash accounts have been explained. All that remains is to subtotal each section of the Cash T-account and compare the total change in cash with the change shown on the balance sheet. Once this is done, the information in the Cash T-account can be used to prepare a statement of cash flows.

REVIEW AND PRACTICE

LEARNING OBJECTIVES REVIEW

1 Discuss the usefulness and format of the statement of cash flows. The statement of cash flows provides information about the cash receipts, cash payments, and net change in cash resulting from the operating, investing, and financing activities of a company during the period. Operating activities include the cash effects of transactions that enter into the determination of net income. Investing activities involve cash flows resulting from changes in investments and long-term asset items. Financing activities involve cash flows resulting from changes in long-term liability and stockholders' equity items.

2 Prepare a statement of cash flows using the indirect method. The preparation of a statement of cash flows involves three major steps. (1) Determine net cash provided/used by operating activities by converting net income from an accrual basis to a cash basis. (2) Analyze changes in noncurrent asset and liability accounts and record as investing and financing activities, or disclose as noncash transactions. (3) Compare the net change in cash on the statement of cash flows with the change in the Cash account reported on the balance sheet to make sure the amounts agree.

3 Analyze the statement of cash flows. Free cash flow indicates the amount of cash a company generated during the current year that is available for the payment of additional dividends or for expansion.

***4 Prepare a statement of cash flows using the direct method.** The preparation of the statement of cash flows involves three major steps. (1) Determine net cash provided/used by operating activities by converting net income from an accrual basis to a cash basis. (2) Analyze changes in noncurrent asset and liability accounts and record as investing and financing activities, or disclose as noncash transactions. (3) Compare the net change in cash on the statement of cash flows with the change in the Cash account reported on the balance sheet to make sure the amounts agree. The direct method reports cash receipts less cash payments to arrive at net cash provided by operating activities.

***5 Use a worksheet to prepare the statement of cash flows using the indirect method.** When there are numerous adjustments, a worksheet can be a helpful tool in preparing the statement of cash flows. Key guidelines for using a worksheet are as follows. (1) List accounts with debit balances separately from those with credit balances. (2) In the reconciling columns in the bottom portion of the worksheet, show cash inflows as debits and cash outflows as credits. (3) Do not enter reconciling items in any journal or account, but use them only to help prepare the statement of cash flows.

The steps in preparing the worksheet are as follows. (1) Enter beginning and ending balances of balance sheet accounts. (2) Enter debits and credits in reconciling columns. (3) Enter the increase or decrease in cash in two places as a balancing amount.

***6 Use the T-account approach to prepare a statement of cash flows.** To use T-accounts to prepare the statement of cash flows: (1) prepare a large Cash T-account with sections for operating, investing, and financing activities; (2) prepare smaller T-accounts for all other noncash accounts; (3) insert beginning and ending balances for all accounts; and (4) follows the steps in Illustration 17-3 (page 581), entering debit and credit amounts as needed.

GLOSSARY REVIEW

***Direct method** A method of preparing a statement of cash flows that shows operating cash receipts and payments, making it more consistent with the objective of the statement of cash flows.

Financing activities Cash flow activities that include (a) obtaining cash from issuing debt and repaying the amounts borrowed and (b) obtaining cash from stockholders, repurchasing shares, and paying dividends.

Free cash flow Net cash provided by operating activities adjusted for capital expenditures and dividends paid.

Indirect method A method of preparing a statement of cash flows in which net income is adjusted for items that do not affect cash, to determine net cash provided by operating activities.

Investing activities Cash flow activities that include (a) purchasing and disposing of investments and property, plant, and equipment using cash and (b) lending money and collecting the loans.

Operating activities Cash flow activities that include the cash effects of transactions that create revenues and expenses and thus enter into the determination of net income.

Statement of cash flows A basic financial statement that provides information about the cash receipts, cash payments, and net change in cash during a period, resulting from operating, investing, and financing activities.

PRACTICE EXERCISES

1. Furst Corporation had the following transactions.

Prepare journal entries to determine effect on statement of cash flows.

(LO 2)

1. Paid salaries of $14,000.
2. Issued 1,000 shares of $1 par value common stock for equipment worth $16,000.
3. Sold equipment (cost $10,000, accumulated depreciation $6,000) for $3,000.
4. Sold land (cost $12,000) for $16,000.
5. Issued another 1,000 shares of $1 per value common stock for $18,000.
6. Recorded depreciation of $20,000.

Instructions

For each transaction above, (a) prepare the journal entry, and (b) indicate how it would affect the statement of cash flows. Assume the indirect method.

Solution

		Debit	Credit
1. 1. (a)	Salaries and Wages Expense	14,000	
	Cash		14,000

(b) Salaries and wages expense is not reported separately on the statement of cash flows. It is part of the computation of net income in the income statement and is included in the net income amount on the statement of cash flows.

		Debit	Credit
2. (a)	Equipment	16,000	
	Common Stock		1,000
	Paid-in Capital in Excess of Par—Common Stock		15,000

(b) The issuance of common stock for equipment ($16,000) is reported as a noncash financing and investing activity at the bottom of the statement of cash flows.

		Debit	Credit
3. (a)	Cash	3,000	
	Loss on Disposal of Plant Assets	1,000	
	Accumulated Depreciation—Equipment	6,000	
	Equipment		10,000

(b) The cash receipt ($3,000) is reported in the investing section. The loss ($1,000) is added to net income in the operating section.

		Debit	Credit
4. (a)	Cash	16,000	
	Land		12,000
	Gain on Disposal of Plant Assets		4,000

(b) The cash receipt ($16,000) is reported in the investing section. The gain ($4,000) is deducted from net income in the operating section.

		Debit	Credit
5. (a)	Cash	18,000	
	Common Stock		1,000
	Paid-in Capital in Excess of Par—Common Stock		17,000

(b) The cash receipt ($18,000) is reported in the financing section.

		Debit	Credit
6. (a)	Depreciation Expense	20,000	
	Accumulated Depreciation—Equipment		20,000

(b) Depreciation expense ($20,000) is added to net income in the operating section.

2. Strong Corporation's comparative balance sheets are presented below.

Prepare statement of cash flows and compute free cash flow.

(LO 2, 3)

STRONG CORPORATION
Comparative Balance Sheets
December 31

	2017	2016
Cash	$ 28,200	$ 17,700
Accounts receivable	24,200	22,300
Investments	23,000	16,000
Equipment	60,000	70,000
Accumulated depreciation—equipment	(14,000)	(10,000)
Total	$121,400	$116,000

	2017	2016
Accounts payable	$ 19,600	$ 11,100
Bonds payable	10,000	30,000
Common stock	60,000	45,000
Retained earnings	31,800	29,900
Total	$121,400	$116,000

Additional information:

1. Net income was $28,300. Dividends declared and paid were $26,400.
2. Equipment which cost $10,000 and had accumulated depreciation of $1,200 was sold for $4,300.
3. All other changes in noncurrent account balances had a direct effect on cash flows, except the change in accumulated depreciation.

Instructions

(a) Prepare a statement of cash flows for 2017 using the indirect method.

(b) Compute free cash flow.

Solution

2. (a)

STRONG CORPORATION
Statement of Cash Flows
For the Year Ended December 31, 2017

Cash flows from operating activities		
Net income		$ 28,300
Adjustments to reconcile net income to net cash provided by operating activities:		
Depreciation expense	$ 5,200*	
Loss on sale of equipment	4,500**	
Increase in accounts payable	8,500	
Increase in accounts receivable	(1,900)	16,300
Net cash provided by operating activities		44,600
Cash flows from investing activities		
Sale of equipment	4,300	
Purchase of investments	(7,000)	
Net cash used by investing activities		(2,700)
Cash flows from financing activities		
Issuance of common stock	15,000	
Retirement of bonds	(20,000)	
Payment of dividends	(26,400)	
Net cash used by financing activities		(31,400)
Net increase in cash		10,500
Cash at beginning of period		17,700
Cash at end of period		$ 28,200

*[$14,000 – ($10,000 – $1,200)]; **[$4,300 – ($10,000 – $1,200)]

(b) $44,600 – $0 – $26,400 = $18,200

PRACTICE PROBLEMS

Prepare statement of cash flows using indirect method.
(LO 2)

1. The income statement for the year ended December 31, 2017, for Kosinski Manufacturing Company contains the following condensed information.

KOSINSKI MANUFACTURING COMPANY
Income Statement
For the Year Ended December 31, 2017

Sales revenue		$6,583,000
Operating expenses (excluding depreciation)	$4,920,000	
Depreciation expense	880,000	5,800,000
Income before income taxes		783,000
Income tax expense		353,000
Net income		$ 430,000

Included in operating expenses is a $24,000 loss resulting from the sale of equipment for $270,000 cash. Equipment was purchased at a cost of $750,000.

The following balances are reported on Kosinski's comparative balance sheets at December 31.

KOSINSKI MANUFACTURING COMPANY
Comparative Balance Sheets (partial)

	2017	2016
Cash	$672,000	$130,000
Accounts receivable	775,000	610,000
Inventory	834,000	867,000
Accounts payable	521,000	501,000

Income tax expense of $353,000 represents the amount paid in 2017. Dividends declared and paid in 2017 totaled $200,000.

Instructions

Prepare the statement of cash flows using the indirect method.

Solution

1.

KOSINSKI MANUFACTURING COMPANY
Statement of Cash Flows—Indirect Method
For the Year Ended December 31, 2017

Cash flows from operating activities		
Net income		$ 430,000
Adjustments to reconcile net income to net cash provided by operating activities:		
Depreciation expense	$ 880,000	
Loss on disposal of equipment	24,000	
Increase in accounts receivable	(165,000)	
Decrease in inventory	33,000	
Increase in accounts payable	20,000	792,000
Net cash provided by operating activities		1,222,000
Cash flows from investing activities		
Sale of equipment	270,000	
Purchase of equipment	(750,000)	
Net cash used by investing activities		(480,000)
Cash flows from financing activities		
Payment of cash dividends		(200,000)
Net increase in cash		542,000
Cash at beginning of period		130,000
Cash at end of period		$ 672,000

Prepare statement of cash flows using direct method.
(LO 4)

*2. The income statement for Kosinski Manufacturing Company contains the following condensed information.

KOSINSKI MANUFACTURING COMPANY
Income Statement
For the Year Ended December 31, 2017

Sales revenue		$6,583,000
Operating expenses, excluding depreciation	$4,920,000	
Depreciation expense	880,000	5,800,000
Income before income taxes		783,000
Income tax expense		353,000
Net income		$ 430,000

Included in operating expenses is a $24,000 loss resulting from the sale of equipment for $270,000 cash. Equipment was purchased at a cost of $750,000. The following balances are reported on Kosinski's comparative balance sheet at December 31.

KOSINSKI MANUFACTURING COMPANY
Comparative Balance Sheets (partial)

	2017	2016
Cash	$672,000	$130,000
Accounts receivable	775,000	610,000
Inventory	834,000	867,000
Accounts payable	521,000	501,000

Income tax expense of $353,000 represents the amount paid in 2017. Dividends declared and paid in 2017 totaled $200,000.

Instructions

Prepare the statement of cash flows using the direct method.

Solution

2.

KOSINSKI MANUFACTURING COMPANY
Statement of Cash Flows—Direct Method
For the Year Ended December 31, 2017

Cash flows from operating activities		
Cash collections from customers		$6,418,000*
Cash payments:		
For operating expenses	$4,843,000**	
For income taxes	353,000	5,196,000
Net cash provided by operating activities		1,222,000
Cash flows from investing activities		
Sale of equipment	270,000	
Purchase of equipment	(750,000)	
Net cash used by investing activities		(480,000)
Cash flows from financing activities		
Payment of cash dividends	(200,000)	
Net cash used by financing activities		(200,000)
Net increase in cash		542,000
Cash at beginning of period		130,000
Cash at end of period		$ 672,000

Direct-Method Computations:

*Computation of cash collections from customers:	
Sales revenue	$6,583,000
Deduct: Increase in accounts receivable	(165,000)
Cash collections from customers	$6,418,000
**Computation of cash payments for operating expenses:	
Operating expenses	$4,920,000
Deduct: Loss on disposal of equipment	(24,000)
Deduct: Decrease in inventories	(33,000)
Deduct: Increase in accounts payable	(20,000)
Cash payments for operating expenses	$4,843,000

EXERCISES

Classify transactions by type of activity.

(LO 1)

E17-1 Tabares Corporation had these transactions during 2017.

(a) Issued $50,000 par value common stock for cash.
(b) Purchased a machine for $30,000, giving a long-term note in exchange.
(c) Issued $200,000 par value common stock upon conversion of bonds having a face value of $200,000.
(d) Declared and paid a cash dividend of $18,000.
(e) Sold a long-term investment with a cost of $15,000 for $15,000 cash.
(f) Collected $16,000 of accounts receivable.
(g) Paid $18,000 on accounts payable.

Instructions

Analyze the transactions and indicate whether each transaction resulted in a cash flow from operating activities, investing activities, financing activities, or noncash investing and financing activities.

Classify transactions by type of activity.

(LO 1)

E17-2 An analysis of comparative balance sheets, the current year's income statement, and the general ledger accounts of Wellman Corp. uncovered the following items. Assume all items involve cash unless there is information to the contrary.

(a) Payment of interest on notes payable.
(b) Exchange of land for patent.
(c) Sale of building at book value.
(d) Payment of dividends.
(e) Depreciation.
(f) Receipt of dividends on investment in stock.
(g) Receipt of interest on notes receivable.
(h) Issuance of common stock.
(i) Amortization of patent.
(j) Issuance of bonds for land.
(k) Purchase of land.
(l) Conversion of bonds into common stock.
(m) Sale of land at a loss.
(n) Retirement of bonds.

Instructions

Indicate how each item should be classified in the statement of cash flows using these four major classifications: operating activity (indirect method), investing activity, financing activity, and significant noncash investing and financing activity.

Prepare journal entry and determine effect on cash flows.

(LO 1)

E17-3 Cushenberry Corporation had the following transactions.

1. Sold land (cost $12,000) for $15,000.
2. Issued common stock at par for $20,000.
3. Recorded depreciation on buildings for $17,000.
4. Paid salaries of $9,000.
5. Issued 1,000 shares of $1 par value common stock for equipment worth $8,000.
6. Sold equipment (cost $10,000, accumulated depreciation $7,000) for $1,200.

Instructions
For each transaction above, (a) prepare the journal entry, and (b) indicate how it would affect the statement of cash flows using the indirect method.

Prepare the operating activities section—indirect method.
(LO 2)

E17-4 Gutierrez Company reported net income of $225,000 for 2017. Gutierrez also reported depreciation expense of $45,000 and a loss of $5,000 on the disposal of equipment. The comparative balance sheet shows a decrease in accounts receivable of $15,000 for the year, a $17,000 increase in accounts payable, and a $4,000 decrease in prepaid expenses.

Instructions
Prepare the operating activities section of the statement of cash flows for 2017. Use the indirect method.

Prepare the operating activities section—indirect method.
(LO 2)

E17-5 The current sections of Scoggin Inc.'s balance sheets at December 31, 2016 and 2017, are presented here. Scoggin's net income for 2017 was $153,000. Depreciation expense was $24,000.

	2017	**2016**
Current assets		
Cash	$105,000	$ 99,000
Accounts receivable	110,000	89,000
Inventory	158,000	172,000
Prepaid expenses	27,000	22,000
Total current assets	$400,000	$382,000
Current liabilities		
Accrued expenses payable	$ 15,000	$ 5,000
Accounts payable	85,000	92,000
Total current liabilities	$100,000	$ 97,000

Instructions
Prepare the net cash provided by operating activities section of the company's statement of cash flows for the year ended December 31, 2017, using the indirect method.

Prepare partial statement of cash flows—indirect method.
(LO 2)

E17-6 The three accounts shown below appear in the general ledger of Herrick Corp. during 2017.

Equipment

Date		Debit	Credit	Balance
Jan. 1	Balance			160,000
July 31	Purchase of equipment	70,000		230,000
Sept. 2	Cost of equipment constructed	53,000		283,000
Nov. 10	Cost of equipment sold		49,000	234,000

Accumulated Depreciation—Equipment

Date		Debit	Credit	Balance
Jan. 1	Balance			71,000
Nov. 10	Accumulated depreciation on equipment sold	30,000		41,000
Dec. 31	Depreciation for year		28,000	69,000

Retained Earnings

Date		Debit	Credit	Balance
Jan. 1	Balance			105,000
Aug. 23	Dividends (cash)	14,000		91,000
Dec. 31	Net income		77,000	168,000

Instructions

From the postings in the accounts, indicate how the information is reported on a statement of cash flows using the indirect method. The loss on disposal of equipment was $7,000. (*Hint:* Cost of equipment constructed is reported in the investing activities section as a decrease in cash of $53,000.)

Prepare statement of cash flows and compute free cash flow.

(LO 2, 3)

E17-7 Rojas Corporation's comparative balance sheets are presented below.

ROJAS CORPORATION
Comparative Balance Sheets
December 31

	2017	2016
Cash	$ 14,300	$ 10,700
Accounts receivable	21,200	23,400
Land	20,000	26,000
Buildings	70,000	70,000
Accumulated depreciation—buildings	(15,000)	(10,000)
Total	$110,500	$120,100
Accounts payable	$ 12,370	$ 31,100
Common stock	75,000	69,000
Retained earnings	23,130	20,000
Total	$110,500	$120,100

Additional information:

1. Net income was $22,630. Dividends declared and paid were $19,500.
2. No noncash investing and financing activities occurred during 2017.
3. The land was sold for cash of $4,900.

Instructions

(a) Prepare a statement of cash flows for 2017 using the indirect method.
(b) Compute free cash flow.

Prepare a statement of cash flows—indirect method.

(LO 2)

E17-8 Here are comparative balance sheets for Velo Company.

VELO COMPANY
Comparative Balance Sheets
December 31

Assets	2017	2016
Cash	$ 63,000	$ 22,000
Accounts receivable	85,000	76,000
Inventory	170,000	189,000
Land	75,000	100,000
Equipment	270,000	200,000
Accumulated depreciation—equipment	(66,000)	(32,000)
Total	$597,000	$555,000
Liabilities and Stockholders' Equity		
Accounts payable	$ 39,000	$ 47,000
Bonds payable	150,000	200,000
Common stock ($1 par)	216,000	174,000
Retained earnings	192,000	134,000
Total	$597,000	$555,000

Additional information:

1. Net income for 2017 was $93,000.
2. Cash dividends of $35,000 were declared and paid.
3. Bonds payable amounting to $50,000 were redeemed for cash $50,000.
4. Common stock was issued for $42,000 cash.
5. No equipment was sold during 2017, but land was sold at cost.

Instructions
Prepare a statement of cash flows for 2017 using the indirect method.

Prepare statement of cash flows and compute free cash flow.
(LO 2, 3)

E17-9 Rodriquez Corporation's comparative balance sheets are presented below.

RODRIQUEZ CORPORATION
Comparative Balance Sheets
December 31

	2017	2016
Cash	$ 15,200	$ 17,700
Accounts receivable	25,200	22,300
Investments	20,000	16,000
Equipment	60,000	70,000
Accumulated depreciation—equipment	(14,000)	(10,000)
Total	$106,400	$116,000
Accounts payable	$ 14,600	$ 11,100
Bonds payable	10,000	30,000
Common stock	50,000	45,000
Retained earnings	31,800	29,900
Total	$106,400	$116,000

Additional information:

1. Net income was $18,300. Dividends declared and paid were $16,400.
2. Equipment which cost $10,000 and had accumulated depreciation of $1,200 was sold for $3,300.
3. No noncash investing and financing activities occurred during 2017.

Instructions
(a) Prepare a statement of cash flows for 2017 using the indirect method.
(b) Compute free cash flow.

Compute net cash provided by operating activities—direct method.
(LO 4)

***E17-10** Macgregor Company completed its first year of operations on December 31, 2017. Its initial income statement showed that Macgregor had revenues of $192,000 and operating expenses of $78,000. Accounts receivable and accounts payable at year-end were $60,000 and $23,000, respectively. Assume that accounts payable related to operating expenses. Ignore income taxes.

Instructions
Compute net cash provided by operating activities using the direct method.

Compute cash payments—direct method.
(LO 4)

***E17-11** Suppose a recent income statement for **McDonald's Corporation** shows cost of goods sold $4,852.7 million and operating expenses (including depreciation expense of $1,201 million) $10,671.5 million. The comparative balance sheet for the year shows that inventory increased $18.1 million, prepaid expenses increased $56.3 million, accounts payable (merchandise suppliers) increased $136.9 million, and accrued expenses payable increased $160.9 million.

Instructions
Using the direct method, compute (a) cash payments to suppliers and (b) cash payments for operating expenses.

Compute cash flow from operating activities—direct method.
(LO 4)

***E17-12** The 2017 accounting records of Blocker Transport reveal these transactions and events.

Payment of interest	$ 10,000	Collection of accounts receivable	$182,000
Cash sales	48,000	Payment of salaries and wages	53,000
Receipt of dividend revenue	18,000	Depreciation expense	16,000
Payment of income taxes	12,000	Proceeds from sale of vehicles	12,000
Net income	38,000	Purchase of equipment for cash	22,000
Payment of accounts payable for merchandise	115,000	Loss on disposal of vehicles	3,000
		Payment of dividends	14,000
Payment for land	74,000	Payment of operating expenses	28,000

Instructions

Prepare the cash flows from operating activities section using the direct method. (Not all of the items will be used.)

***E17-13** The following information is taken from the 2017 general ledger of Swisher Company.

Calculate cash flows—direct method.

(LO 4)

Rent	Rent expense	$ 48,000
	Prepaid rent, January 1	5,900
	Prepaid rent, December 31	9,000
Salaries	Salaries and wages expense	$ 54,000
	Salaries and wages payable, January 1	10,000
	Salaries and wages payable, December 31	8,000
Sales	Sales revenue	$175,000
	Accounts receivable, January 1	16,000
	Accounts receivable, December 31	7,000

Instructions

In each case, compute the amount that should be reported in the operating activities section of the statement of cash flows under the direct method.

***E17-14** Comparative balance sheets for International Company are presented below.

Prepare a worksheet.

(LO 5)

INTERNATIONAL COMPANY
Comparative Balance Sheets
December 31

Assets	**2017**	**2016**
Cash	$ 73,000	$ 22,000
Accounts receivable	85,000	76,000
Inventory	180,000	189,000
Land	75,000	100,000
Equipment	250,000	200,000
Accumulated depreciation—equipment	(66,000)	(42,000)
Total	$597,000	$545,000
Liabilities and Stockholders' Equity		
Accounts payable	$ 34,000	$ 47,000
Bonds payable	150,000	200,000
Common stock ($1 par)	214,000	164,000
Retained earnings	199,000	134,000
Total	$597,000	$545,000

Additional information:

1. Net income for 2017 was $135,000.
2. Cash dividends of $70,000 were declared and paid.
3. Bonds payable amounting to $50,000 were redeemed for cash $50,000.
4. Common stock was issued for $50,000 cash.
5. Depreciation expense was $24,000.
6. Sales revenue for the year was $978,000.
7. Land was sold at cost, and equipment was purchased for cash.

Instructions

Prepare a worksheet for a statement of cash flows for 2017 using the indirect method. Enter the reconciling items directly on the worksheet, using letters to cross-reference each entry.

PROBLEMS

Distinguish among operating, investing, and financing activities.

(LO 1)

P17-1A You are provided with the following transactions that took place during a recent fiscal year.

Transaction	Statement of Cash Flows Activity Affected	Cash Inflow, Outflow, or No Effect?
(a) Recorded depreciation expense on the plant assets.		
(b) Recorded and paid interest expense.		
(c) Recorded cash proceeds from a disposal of plant assets.		
(d) Acquired land by issuing common stock.		
(e) Paid a cash dividend to preferred stockholders.		
(f) Paid a cash dividend to common stockholders.		
(g) Recorded cash sales.		
(h) Recorded sales on account.		
(i) Purchased inventory for cash.		
(j) Purchased inventory on account.		

Instructions

Complete the table indicating whether each item (1) affects operating (O) activities, investing (I) activities, financing (F) activities, or is a noncash (NC) transaction reported in a separate schedule, and (2) represents a cash inflow or cash outflow or has no cash flow effect. Assume use of the indirect approach.

Determine cash flow effects of changes in equity accounts.

(LO 2)

P17-2A The following account balances relate to the stockholders' equity accounts of Kerbs Corp. at year-end.

	2017	2016
Common stock, 10,500 and 10,000 shares, respectively, for 2017 and 2016	$170,000	$140,000
Preferred stock, 5,000 shares	125,000	125,000
Retained earnings	300,000	250,000

A small stock dividend was declared and issued in 2017. The market value of the shares was $10,500. Cash dividends were $15,000 in both 2017 and 2016. The common stock has no par or stated value.

Instructions

(a) Net income $75,500

(a) What was the amount of net income reported by Kerbs Corp. in 2017?

(b) Determine the amounts of any cash inflows or outflows related to the common stock and dividend accounts in 2017.

(c) Indicate where each of the cash inflows or outflows identified in (b) would be classified on the statement of cash flows.

Prepare the operating activities section—indirect method.

(LO 2)

P17-3A The income statement of Whitlock Company is presented here.

WHITLOCK COMPANY
Income Statement
For the Year Ended November 30, 2017

Sales revenue		$7,700,000
Cost of goods sold		
Beginning inventory	$1,900,000	
Purchases	4,400,000	
Goods available for sale	6,300,000	
Ending inventory	1,400,000	
Total cost of goods sold		4,900,000
Gross profit		2,800,000
Operating expenses		1,150,000
Net income		$1,650,000

Additional information:

1. Accounts receivable increased $200,000 during the year, and inventory decreased $500,000.
2. Prepaid expenses increased $150,000 during the year.
3. Accounts payable to suppliers of merchandise decreased $340,000 during the year.
4. Accrued expenses payable decreased $100,000 during the year.
5. Operating expenses include depreciation expense of $70,000.

Instructions
Prepare the operating activities section of the statement of cash flows for the year ended November 30, 2017, for Whitlock Company, using the indirect method.

Cash from operations $1,430,000

***P17-4A** Data for Whitlock Company are presented in P17-3A.

Prepare the operating activities section—direct method.

(LO 4)

Instructions
Prepare the operating activities section of the statement of cash flows using the direct method.

Cash from operations $1,430,000

P17-5A Zumbrunn Company's income statement contained the condensed information below.

Prepare the operating activities section—indirect method.

(LO 2)

ZUMBRUNN COMPANY
Income Statement
For the Year Ended December 31, 2017

Service revenue		$970,000
Operating expenses, excluding depreciation	$624,000	
Depreciation expense	60,000	
Loss on disposal of equipment	16,000	700,000
Income before income taxes		270,000
Income tax expense		40,000
Net income		$230,000

Zumbrunn's balance sheet contained the comparative data at December 31, shown below.

	2017	**2016**
Accounts receivable	$75,000	$65,000
Accounts payable	46,000	28,000
Income taxes payable	11,000	7,000

Accounts payable pertain to operating expenses.

Instructions
Prepare the operating activities section of the statement of cash flows using the indirect method.

Cash from operations $318,000

***P17-6A** Data for Zumbrunn Company are presented in P17-5A.

Prepare the operating activities section—direct method.

(LO 4)

Instructions
Prepare the operating activities section of the statement of cash flows using the direct method.

Cash from operations $318,000

P17-7A The following are the financial statements of Nosker Company.

Prepare a statement of cash flows—indirect method, and compute free cash flow.

(LO 2, 3)

NOSKER COMPANY
Comparative Balance Sheets
December 31

Assets	**2017**	**2016**
Cash	$ 38,000	$ 20,000
Accounts receivable	30,000	14,000
Inventory	27,000	20,000
Equipment	60,000	78,000
Accumulated depreciation—equipment	(29,000)	(24,000)
Total	$126,000	$108,000

Liabilities and Stockholders' Equity	2017	2016
Accounts payable	$ 24,000	$ 15,000
Income taxes payable	7,000	8,000
Bonds payable	27,000	33,000
Common stock	18,000	14,000
Retained earnings	50,000	38,000
Total	$126,000	$108,000

NOSKER COMPANY
Income Statement
For the Year Ended December 31, 2017

Sales revenue	$242,000
Cost of goods sold	175,000
Gross profit	67,000
Operating expenses	24,000
Income from operations	43,000
Interest expense	3,000
Income before income taxes	40,000
Income tax expense	8,000
Net income	$ 32,000

Additional data:

1. Dividends declared and paid were $20,000.
2. During the year equipment was sold for $8,500 cash. This equipment cost $18,000 originally and had a book value of $8,500 at the time of sale.
3. All depreciation expense, $14,500, is in the operating expenses.
4. All sales and purchases are on account.

Instructions

(a) Cash from operations $31,500

(a) Prepare a statement of cash flows using the indirect method.
(b) Compute free cash flow.

Prepare a statement of cash flows—direct method, and compute free cash flow.

(LO 3, 4)

***P17-8A** Data for Nosker Company are presented in P17-7A. Further analysis reveals the following.

1. Accounts payable pertain to merchandise suppliers.
2. All operating expenses except for depreciation were paid in cash.

Instructions

(a) Cash from operations $31,500

(a) Prepare a statement of cash flows for Nosker Company using the direct method.
(b) Compute free cash flow.

Prepare a statement of cash flows—indirect method.

(LO 2)

P17-9A Condensed financial data of Cheng Inc. follow.

CHENG INC.
Comparative Balance Sheets
December 31

Assets	2017	2016
Cash	$ 80,800	$ 48,400
Accounts receivable	92,800	33,000
Inventory	117,500	102,850
Prepaid expenses	28,400	26,000
Investments	143,000	114,000
Equipment	270,000	242,500
Accumulated depreciation—equipment	(50,000)	(52,000)
Total	$682,500	$514,750

Liabilities and Stockholders' Equity		
Accounts payable	$112,000	$ 67,300
Accrued expenses payable	16,500	17,000
Bonds payable	110,000	150,000
Common stock	220,000	175,000
Retained earnings	224,000	105,450
Total	$682,500	$514,750

CHENG INC.
Income Statement
For the Year Ended December 31, 2017

Sales revenue		$392,780
Less:		
Cost of goods sold	$135,460	
Operating expenses, excluding depreciation	12,410	
Depreciation expense	46,500	
Income tax expense	27,280	
Interest expense	4,730	
Loss on disposal of plant assets	7,500	233,880
Net income		$158,900

Additional information:

1. New equipment costing $85,000 was purchased for cash during the year.
2. Old equipment having an original cost of $57,500 was sold for $1,500 cash.
3. Bonds matured and were paid off at face value for cash.
4. A cash dividend of $40,350 was declared and paid during the year.

Instructions
Prepare a statement of cash flows using the indirect method.

Cash from operations $180,250

***P17-10A** Data for Cheng Inc. are presented in P17-9A. Further analysis reveals that accounts payable pertain to merchandise creditors.

Prepare a statement of cash flows—direct method.

(LO 4)

Instructions
Prepare a statement of cash flows for Cheng Inc. using the direct method.

Cash from operations $180,250

P17-11A The comparative balance sheets for Rothlisberger Company as of December 31 are presented below.

Prepare a statement of cash flows—indirect method.

(LO 2)

ROTHLISBERGER COMPANY
Comparative Balance Sheets
December 31

Assets	2017	2016
Cash	$ 81,000	$ 45,000
Accounts receivable	41,000	62,000
Inventory	151,450	142,000
Prepaid expenses	15,280	21,000
Land	105,000	130,000
Buildings	200,000	200,000
Accumulated depreciation—buildings	(60,000)	(40,000)
Equipment	221,000	155,000
Accumulated depreciation—equipment	(45,000)	(35,000)
Total	$709,730	$680,000

Liabilities and Stockholders' Equity		
Accounts payable	$ 47,730	$ 40,000
Bonds payable	260,000	300,000
Common stock, $1 par	200,000	160,000
Retained earnings	202,000	180,000
Total	$709,730	$680,000

Additional information:

1. Operating expenses include depreciation expense of $42,000 and charges from prepaid expenses of $5,720.
2. Land was sold for cash at book value.
3. Cash dividends of $20,000 were paid.
4. Net income for 2017 was $42,000.
5. Equipment was purchased for $88,000 cash. In addition, equipment costing $22,000 with a book value of $10,000 was sold for $6,000 cash.
6. Bonds were converted at face value by issuing 40,000 shares of $1 par value common stock.

Cash from operations $113,000

Instructions

Prepare a statement of cash flows for the year ended December 31, 2017, using the indirect method.

Prepare a worksheet—indirect method.

(LO 5)

***P17-12A** Condensed financial data of Oakley Company appear below.

OAKLEY COMPANY
Comparative Balance Sheets
December 31

Assets	**2017**	**2016**
Cash	$ 82,700	$ 47,250
Accounts receivable	90,800	57,000
Inventory	126,900	102,650
Investments	84,500	87,000
Equipment	255,000	205,000
Accumulated depreciation—equipment	(49,500)	(40,000)
	$590,400	$458,900
Liabilities and Stockholders' Equity		
Accounts payable	$ 57,700	$ 48,280
Accrued expenses payable	12,100	18,830
Bonds payable	100,000	70,000
Common stock	250,000	200,000
Retained earnings	170,600	121,790
	$590,400	$458,900

OAKLEY COMPANY
Income Statement
For the Year Ended December 31, 2017

Sales revenue		$297,500
Gain on disposal of equipment		8,750
		306,250
Less:		
Cost of goods sold	$99,460	
Operating expenses (excluding depreciation expense)	14,670	
Depreciation expense	49,700	
Income tax expense	7,270	
Interest expense	2,940	174,040
Net income		$132,210

Additional information:

1. Equipment costing $97,000 was purchased for cash during the year.
2. Investments were sold at cost.
3. Equipment costing $47,000 was sold for $15,550, resulting in gain of $8,750.
4. A cash dividend of $83,400 was declared and paid during the year.

Reconciling items total $610,210

Instructions

Prepare a worksheet for the statement of cash flows using the indirect method. Enter the reconciling items directly in the worksheet columns, using letters to cross-reference each entry.

BROADENING YOUR PERSPECTIVE

FINANCIAL REPORTING AND ANALYSIS

Financial Reporting Problem: Apple Inc.

BYP17-1 The financial statements of Apple Inc. are presented in Appendix A. Instructions for accessing and using the company's complete annual report, including the notes to the financial statements, are also provided in Appendix A.

Instructions

(a) What was the amount of net cash provided by operating activities for the year ended September 28, 2013? For the year ended September 29, 2012?
(b) What was the amount of increase or decrease in cash and cash equivalents for the year ended September 28, 2013? For the year ended September 29, 2012?
(c) Which method of computing net cash provided by operating activities does Apple use?
(d) From your analysis of the 2013 statement of cash flows, did the change in accounts and notes receivable require or provide cash? Did the change in inventories require or provide cash? Did the change in accounts payable and other current liabilities require or provide cash?
(e) What was the net outflow or inflow of cash from investing activities for the year ended September 28, 2013?
(f) What was the amount of income taxes paid in the year ended September 28, 2013?

Comparative Analysis Problem: PepsiCo, Inc. vs. The Coca-Cola Company

BYP17-2 PepsiCo's financial statements are presented in Appendix B. Financial statements of The Coca-Cola Company are presented in Appendix C. Instructions for accessing and using the complete annual reports of PepsiCo and Coca-Cola, including the notes to the financial statements, are also provided in Appendices B and C, respectively.

Instructions

(a) Based on the information contained in these financial statements, compute free cash flow for each company.
(b) What conclusions concerning the management of cash can be drawn from these data?

Comparative Analysis Problem: Amazon.com, Inc. vs. Wal-Mart Stores, Inc.

BYP17-3 Amazon.com, Inc.'s financial statements are presented in Appendix D. Financial statements of Wal-Mart Stores, Inc. are presented in Appendix E. Instructions for accessing and using the complete annual reports for Amazon and Wal-Mart, including the notes to the financial statements, are also provided in Appendices D and E, respectively.

Instructions

(a) Based on the information contained in these financial statements, compute free cash flow for each company.
(b) What conclusions concerning the management of cash can be drawn from these data?

Decision-Making Across the Organization

BYP17-4 Tom Epps and Mary Jones are examining the following statement of cash flows for Guthrie Company for the year ended January 31, 2017.

GUTHRIE COMPANY
Statement of Cash Flows
For the Year Ended January 31, 2017

Sources of cash	
From sales of merchandise	$380,000
From sale of capital stock	420,000
From sale of investment (purchased below)	80,000
From depreciation	55,000
From issuance of note for truck	20,000
From interest on investments	6,000
Total sources of cash	961,000

Uses of cash	
For purchase of fixtures and equipment	330,000
For merchandise purchased for resale	258,000
For operating expenses (including depreciation)	160,000
For purchase of investment	75,000
For purchase of truck by issuance of note	20,000
For purchase of treasury stock	10,000
For interest on note payable	3,000
Total uses of cash	856,000
Net increase in cash	$105,000

Tom claims that Guthrie's statement of cash flows is an excellent portrayal of a superb first year with cash increasing $105,000. Mary replies that it was not a superb first year. Rather, she says, the year was an operating failure, that the statement is presented incorrectly, and that $105,000 is not the actual increase in cash. The cash balance at the beginning of the year was $140,000.

Instructions
With the class divided into groups, answer the following.

(a) Using the data provided, prepare a statement of cash flows in proper form using the indirect method. The only noncash items in the income statement are depreciation and the gain from the sale of the investment.
(b) With whom do you agree, Tom or Mary? Explain your position.

Real-World Focus

BYP17-5 Purpose: Learn about the SEC.

Address: **www.sec.gov/index.htm**, or go to **www.wiley.com/college/weygandt**

From the SEC homepage, choose **About the SEC**.

Instructions
Answer the following questions.

(a) How many enforcement actions does the SEC take each year against securities law violators? What are typical infractions?
(b) After the Depression, Congress passed the Securities Acts of 1933 and 1934 to improve investor confidence in the markets. What two "common sense" notions are these laws based on?
(c) Who was the President of the United States at the time of the creation of the SEC? Who was the first SEC Chairperson?

BYP17-6 Purpose: Use the Internet to view SEC filings.

Address: **biz.yahoo.com/i**, or go to **www.wiley.com/college/weygandt**

Steps:
1. Type in a company name.
2. Choose **Profile**.
3. Choose **SEC Filings**. (This will take you to Yahoo-Edgar Online.)

Instructions
Answer the following questions.

(a) What company did you select?
(b) Which filing is the most recent? What is the date?
(c) What other recent SEC filings are available for your viewing?

CRITICAL THINKING

Communication Activity

BYP17-7 Will Hardin, the owner-president of Computer Services Company, is unfamiliar with the statement of cash flows that you, as his accountant, prepared. He asks for further explanation.

Instructions
Write him a brief memo explaining the form and content of the statement of cash flows as shown in Illustration 17-13 (page 588).

Ethics Case

BYP17-8 Wesley Corp. is a medium-sized wholesaler of automotive parts. It has 10 stockholders who have been paid a total of $1 million in cash dividends for 8 consecutive years. The board's policy requires that, for this dividend to be declared, net cash provided by operating activities as reported in Wesley's current year's statement of cash flows must exceed $1 million. President and CEO Samuel Gunkle's job is secure so long as he produces annual operating cash flows to support the usual dividend.

At the end of the current year, controller Gerald Rondelli presents president Samuel Gunkle with some disappointing news: The net cash provided by operating activities is calculated by the indirect method to be only $970,000. The president says to Gerald, "We must get that amount above $1 million. Isn't there some way to increase operating cash flow by another $30,000?" Gerald answers, "These figures were prepared by my assistant. I'll go back to my office and see what I can do." The president replies, "I know you won't let me down, Gerald."

Upon close scrutiny of the statement of cash flows, Gerald concludes that he can get the operating cash flows above $1 million by reclassifying a $60,000, 2-year note payable listed in the financing activities section as "Proceeds from bank loan—$60,000." He will report the note instead as "Increase in payables—$60,000" and treat it as an adjustment of net income in the operating activities section. He returns to the president, saying, "You can tell the board to declare their usual dividend. Our net cash flow provided by operating activities is $1,030,000." "Good man, Gerald! I knew I could count on you," exults the president.

Instructions

(a) Who are the stakeholders in this situation?
(b) Was there anything unethical about the president's actions? Was there anything unethical about the controller's actions?
(c) Are the board members or anyone else likely to discover the misclassification?

All About You

BYP17-9 In this chapter, you learned that companies prepare a statement of cash flows in order to keep track of their sources and uses of cash and to help them plan for their future cash needs. Planning for your own short- and long-term cash needs is every bit as important as it is for a company.

Instructions

Read the article ("Financial Uh-Oh? No Problem") provided at **www.fool.com/personal-finance/saving/index.aspx**, and answer the following questions. To access this article, it may be necessary to register at no cost.

(a) Describe the three factors that determine how much money you should set aside for short-term needs.
(b) How many months of living expenses does the article suggest to set aside?
(c) Estimate how much you should set aside based upon your current situation. Are you closer to Cliff's scenario or to Prudence's?

FASB Codification Activity

AP **BYP17-10** If your school has a subscription to the FASB Codification, go to **http://aaahq.org/ascLogin.cfm** to log in and prepare responses to the following. Use the Master Glossary to determine the proper definitions.

(a) What are cash equivalents?
(b) What are financing activities?
(c) What are investing activities?
(d) What are operating activities?
(e) What is the primary objective for the statement of cash flow? Is working capital the basis for meeting this objective?
(f) Do companies need to disclose information about investing and financing activities that do not affect cash receipts or cash payments? If so, how should such information be disclosed?

A Look at IFRS

LEARNING OBJECTIVE

Compare the procedures for the statement of cash flows under GAAP and IFRS.

As in GAAP, the statement of cash flows is a required statement for IFRS. In addition, the content and presentation of an IFRS statement of cash flows is similar to the one used for GAAP. However, the disclosure requirements related to the statement of cash flows are more extensive under GAAP. *IAS 7* ("Cash Flow Statements") provides the overall IFRS requirements for cash flow information.

Relevant Facts

Following are the key similarities and differences between GAAP and IFRS as related to the statement of cash flows.

Similarities

- Companies preparing financial statements under IFRS must also prepare a statement of cash flows as an integral part of the financial statements.
- Both IFRS and GAAP require that the statement of cash flows should have three major sections—operating, investing, and financing activities—along with changes in cash and cash equivalents.
- Similar to GAAP, the statement of cash flows can be prepared using either the indirect or direct method under IFRS. In both U.S. and international settings, companies choose for the most part to use the indirect method for reporting net cash flows from operating activities.
- The definition of cash equivalents used in IFRS is similar to that used in GAAP. A major difference is that in certain situations, bank overdrafts are considered part of cash and cash equivalents under IFRS (which is not the case in GAAP). Under GAAP, bank overdrafts are classified as financing activities in the statement of cash flows and are reported as liabilities on the balance sheet.

Differences

- IFRS requires that noncash investing and financing activities be excluded from the statement of cash flows. Instead, these noncash activities should be reported elsewhere. This requirement is interpreted to mean that noncash investing and financing activities should be disclosed in the notes to the financial statements instead of in the financial statements. Under GAAP, companies may present this information on the face of the statement of cash flows.
- One area where there can be substantial differences between IFRS and GAAP relates to the classification of interest, dividends, and taxes. The following table indicates the differences between the two approaches.

Item	IFRS	GAAP
Interest paid	Operating or financing	Operating
Interest received	Operating or investing	Operating
Dividends paid	Operating or financing	Financing
Dividends received	Operating or investing	Operating
Taxes paid	Operating—unless specific identification with financing or investing activity	Operating

- Under IFRS, some companies present the operating section in a single line item, with a full reconciliation provided in the notes to the financial statements. This presentation is not seen under GAAP.

Looking to the Future

Presently, the FASB and the IASB are involved in a joint project on the presentation and organization of information in the financial statements. One interesting approach, revealed in a published proposal from that project, is that in the future the income statement and balance sheet would adopt headings similar to those of the statement of cash flows. That is, the income statement and balance sheet would be broken into operating, investing, and financing sections.

IFRS Practice

IFRS Self-Test Questions

1. Under IFRS, interest paid can be reported as:
   (a) only a financing activity.
   (b) a financing activity or an investing activity.
   (c) a financing activity or an operating activity.
   (d) only an operating activity.
2. IFRS requires that noncash items:
   (a) be reported in the section to which they relate, that is, a noncash investing activity would be reported in the investing section.
   (b) be disclosed in the notes to the financial statements.
   (c) do not need to be reported.
   (d) be treated in a fashion similar to cash equivalents.
3. In the future, it appears likely that:
   (a) the income statement and balance sheet will have headings of operating, investing, and financing, much like the statement of cash flows.
   (b) cash and cash equivalents will be combined in a single line item.
   (c) the IASB will not allow companies to use the direct approach to the statement of cash flows.
   (d) None of the above.
4. Under IFRS:
   (a) taxes are always treated as an operating activity.
   (b) the income statement uses the headings operating, investing, and financing.
   (c) dividends received can be either an operating or investing activity.
   (d) dividends paid can be either an operating or investing activity.
5. Which of the following is **correct**?
   (a) Under IFRS, the statement of cash flows is optional.
   (b) IFRS requires use of the direct approach in preparing the statement of cash flows.
   (c) The majority of companies following GAAP and the majority following IFRS employ the indirect approach to the statement of cash flows.
   (d) Under IFRS, companies offset financing activities against investing activities.

IFRS Exercises

IFRS17-1 Discuss the differences that exist in the treatment of bank overdrafts under GAAP and IFRS.

IFRS17-2 Describe the treatment of each of the following items under IFRS versus GAAP.

(a) Interest paid.
(b) Interest received.
(c) Dividends paid.
(d) Dividends received.

International Financial Reporting Problem: Louis Vuitton

IFRS17-3 The financial statements of Louis Vuitton are presented in Appendix F. Instructions for accessing and using the company's complete annual report, including the notes to its financial statements, are also provided in Appendix F.

Instructions
Use the company's annual report to answer the following questions.

(a) In which section (operating, investing, or financing) does Louis Vuitton report interest paid (finance costs)?
(b) In which section (operating, investing, or financing) does Louis Vuitton report dividends received?
(c) If Louis Vuitton reported under GAAP rather than IFRS, how would its treatment of bank overdrafts differ?

Answers to IFRS Self-Test Questions

1. c **2.** b **3.** a **4.** c **5.** c

Chapter 18 Financial Statement Analysis

A recent issue of *Forbes* magazine listed Warren Buffett as the richest person in the world. His estimated wealth was $62 billion, give or take a few million. How much is $62 billion? If you invested $62 billion in an investment earning just 4%, you could spend $6.8 million per day—every day—forever.

So, how does Buffett spend his money? Basically, he doesn't! He still lives in the same house that he purchased in Omaha, Nebraska, in 1958 for $31,500. He still drives his own car (a Cadillac DTS). And, in case you believe that his kids are riding the road to Easy Street, think again. Buffett has committed to donate virtually all of his money to charity before he dies.

How did Buffett amass this wealth? Through careful investing. He applies the basic techniques he learned in the 1950s from the great value investor Benjamin Graham. Buffett looks for companies that have good long-term potential but are currently underpriced. He invests in companies that have low exposure to debt and that reinvest their earnings for future growth. He does not get caught up in fads or the latest trends.

For example, Buffett sat out on the dot-com mania in the 1990s. When other investors put lots of money into fledgling high-tech firms, Buffett didn't bite because the dot-com companies failed to meet his criteria. He didn't get to enjoy the stock price boom on the way up, but on the other hand, he didn't have to suffer the plummet back down to Earth. When the dot-com bubble burst, everyone else suffered from investment shock. Buffett swooped in and scooped up deals on companies that he had been following for years.

In 2012, when the stock market reached near record highs, Buffett's returns significantly lagged behind the market. Only 26% of his investments at that time were in stock, and he was sitting on $38 billion in cash. One commentator noted that "if the past is any guide, just when Buffett seems to look most like a loser, the party is about to end."

If you think you want to follow Buffett's example and transform your humble nest egg into a mountain of cash, be warned. His techniques have been widely circulated and emulated, but never practiced with the same degree of success. You should probably start by honing your financial analysis skills. A good way for you to begin your career as a successful investor is to master the fundamentals of financial analysis discussed in this chapter.

Source: Jason Zweig, "Buffett Is Out of Step," *Wall Street Journal* (May 7, 2012).

LEARNING OBJECTIVES

1. **Apply horizontal and vertical analysis to financial statements.**
2. **Analyze a company's performance using ratio analysis.**
3. **Apply the concept of sustainable income.**

LEARNING OBJECTIVE 1

Apply horizontal and vertical analysis to financial statements.

Analyzing financial statements involves evaluating three characteristics: a company's liquidity, profitability, and solvency. A **short-term creditor**, such as a bank, is primarily interested in liquidity—the ability of the borrower to pay obligations when they come due. The liquidity of the borrower is extremely important in evaluating the safety of a loan. A **long-term creditor**, such as a bondholder, looks to profitability and solvency measures that indicate the company's ability to survive over a long period of time. Long-term creditors consider such measures as the amount of debt in the company's capital structure and its ability to meet interest payments. Similarly, **stockholders** look at the profitability and solvency of the company. They want to assess the likelihood of dividends and the growth potential of the stock.

Need for Comparative Analysis

Every item reported in a financial statement has significance. When **Macy's, Inc.** reports cash and cash equivalents of $2.3 billion on its balance sheet, we know the company had that amount of cash on the balance sheet date. But, we do not know whether the amount represents an increase over prior years, or whether it is adequate in relation to the company's need for cash. To obtain such information, we need to compare the amount of cash with other financial statement data.

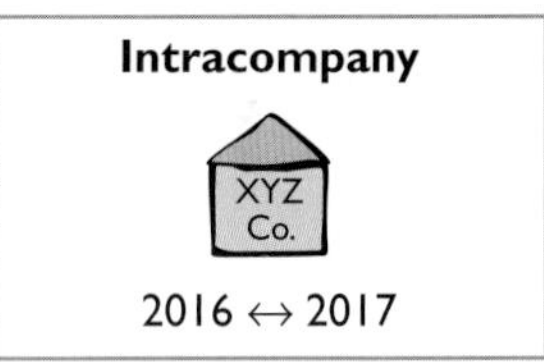

Comparisons can be made on a number of different bases. Three are illustrated in this chapter.

1. **Intracompany basis.** Comparisons within a company are often useful to detect changes in financial relationships and significant trends. For example, a comparison of Macy's current year's cash amount with the prior year's cash amount shows either an increase or a decrease. Likewise, a comparison of Macy's year-end cash amount with the amount of its total assets at year-end shows the proportion of total assets in the form of cash.

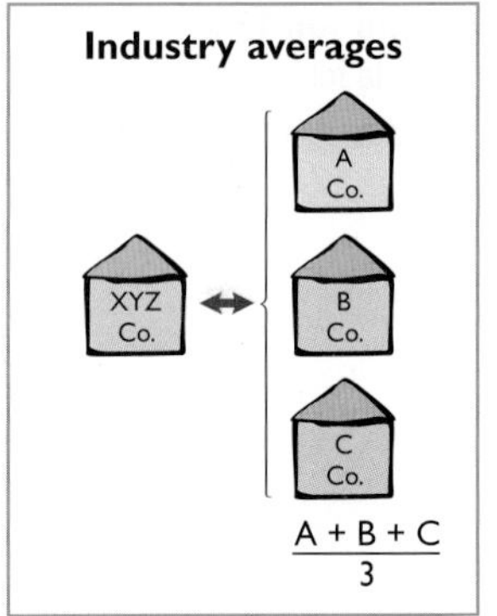

2. **Industry averages.** Comparisons with industry averages provide information about a company's relative position within the industry. For example, financial statement readers can compare Macy's financial data with the averages for its industry compiled by financial rating organizations such as **Dun & Bradstreet**, **Moody's**, and **Standard & Poor's**, or with information provided on the Internet by organizations such as **Yahoo!** on its financial site.

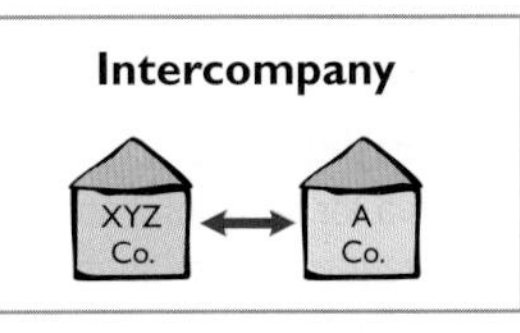

3. **Intercompany basis.** Comparisons with other companies provide insight into a company's competitive position. For example, investors can compare Macy's total sales for the year with the total sales of its competitors in retail, such as **J.C. Penney**.

Tools of Analysis

We use various tools to evaluate the significance of financial statement data. Three commonly used tools are as follows.

- **Horizontal analysis** evaluates a series of financial statement data over a period of time.
- **Vertical analysis** evaluates financial statement data by expressing each item in a financial statement as a percentage of a base amount.
- **Ratio analysis** expresses the relationship among selected items of financial statement data.

Horizontal analysis is used primarily in intracompany comparisons. Two features in published financial statements and annual report information facilitate this type of comparison. First, each of the basic financial statements presents comparative financial data for a minimum of two years. Second, a summary of selected financial data is presented for a series of five to 10 years or more. Vertical analysis is used in both intra- and intercompany comparisons. Ratio analysis is used in all three types of comparisons. In the following sections, we explain and illustrate each of the three types of analysis.

Horizontal Analysis

Horizontal analysis, also called **trend analysis**, is a technique for evaluating a series of financial statement data over a period of time. Its purpose is to determine the increase or decrease that has taken place. This change may be expressed as either an amount or a percentage. For example, Illustration 18-1 shows recent net sales figures of Macy's, Inc.

Illustration 18-1
Macy's, Inc.'s net sales

Real World

MACY'S, INC.
Net Sales (in millions)

2013	2012	2011
$27,931	$27,686	$26,405

If we assume that 2011 is the base year, we can measure all percentage increases or decreases from this base period amount as follows.

Illustration 18-2
Formula for horizontal analysis of changes since base period

$$\text{Change Since Base Period} = \frac{\text{Current Year Amount} - \text{Base Year Amount}}{\text{Base Year Amount}}$$

For example, we can determine that net sales for Macy's increased from 2011 to 2012 approximately 4.9% [($27,686 − $26,405) ÷ $26,405]. Similarly, we can determine that net sales increased from 2011 to 2013 approximately 5.8% [($27,931 − $26,405) ÷ $26,405].

Alternatively, we can express current year sales as a percentage of the base period. We do this by dividing the current year amount by the base year amount, as shown below.

Illustration 18-3
Formula for horizontal analysis of current year in relation to base year

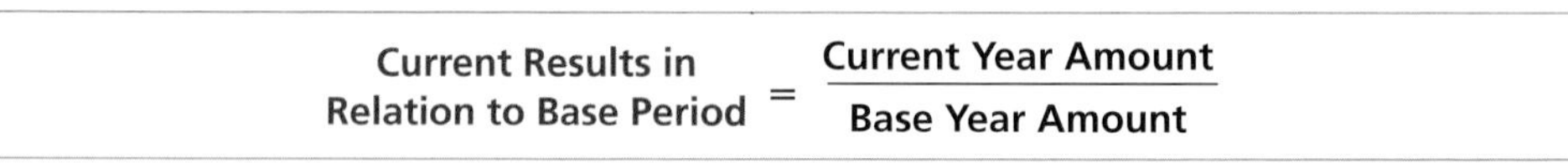

$$\text{Current Results in Relation to Base Period} = \frac{\text{Current Year Amount}}{\text{Base Year Amount}}$$

Illustration 18-4 presents this analysis for Macy's for a three-year period using 2011 as the base period.

Illustration 18-4
Horizontal analysis of Macy's, Inc.'s net sales in relation to base period

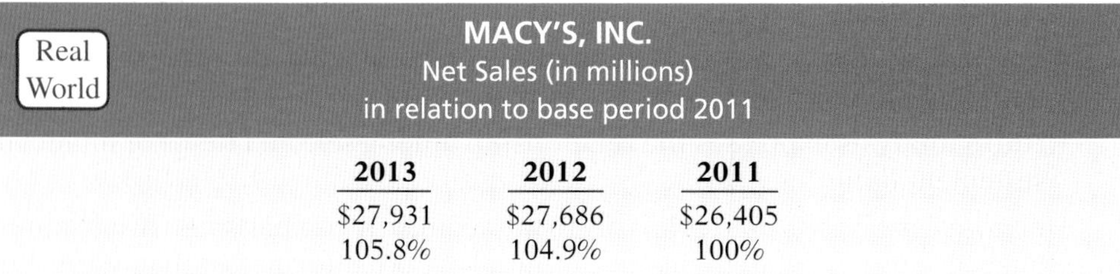

Real World

MACY'S, INC.
Net Sales (in millions)
in relation to base period 2011

2013	2012	2011
$27,931	$27,686	$26,405
105.8%	104.9%	100%

BALANCE SHEET

To further illustrate horizontal analysis, we will use the financial statements of Quality Department Store Inc., a fictional retailer. Illustration 18-5 presents a horizontal analysis of its two-year condensed balance sheets, showing dollar and percentage changes.

Illustration 18-5
Horizontal analysis of balance sheets

QUALITY DEPARTMENT STORE INC.
Condensed Balance Sheets
December 31

			Increase or (Decrease) During 2013	
	2013	**2012**	**Amount**	**Percent**
Assets				
Current assets	$1,020,000	$ 945,000	**$ 75,000**	**7.9%**
Plant assets (net)	800,000	632,500	**167,500**	**26.5%**
Intangible assets	15,000	17,500	**(2,500)**	**(14.3%)**
Total assets	$1,835,000	$1,595,000	**$240,000**	**15.0%**
Liabilities				
Current liabilities	$ 344,500	$ 303,000	**$ 41,500**	**13.7%**
Long-term liabilities	487,500	497,000	**(9,500)**	**(1.9%)**
Total liabilities	832,000	800,000	**32,000**	**4.0%**
Stockholders' Equity				
Common stock, $1 par	275,400	270,000	**5,400**	**2.0%**
Retained earnings	727,600	525,000	**202,600**	**38.6%**
Total stockholders' equity	1,003,000	795,000	**208,000**	**26.2%**
Total liabilities and stockholders' equity	$1,835,000	$1,595,000	**$240,000**	**15.0%**

The comparative balance sheets in Illustration 18-5 show that a number of significant changes have occurred in Quality Department Store's financial structure from 2012 to 2013:

- In the assets section, plant assets (net) increased $167,500, or 26.5%.
- In the liabilities section, current liabilities increased $41,500, or 13.7%.
- In the stockholders' equity section, retained earnings increased $202,600, or 38.6%.

These changes suggest that the company expanded its asset base during 2013 and **financed this expansion primarily by retaining income** rather than assuming additional long-term debt.

INCOME STATEMENT

Illustration 18-6 (page 628) presents a horizontal analysis of the two-year condensed income statements of Quality Department Store Inc. for the years 2013 and 2012. Horizontal analysis of the income statements shows the following changes:

- Net sales increased $260,000, or 14.2% ($260,000 ÷ $1,837,000).
- Cost of goods sold increased $141,000, or 12.4% ($141,000 ÷ $1,140,000).
- Total operating expenses increased $37,000, or 11.6% ($37,000 ÷ $320,000).

Overall, gross profit and net income were up substantially. Gross profit increased 17.1%, and net income, 26.5%. Quality's profit trend appears favorable.

Illustration 18-6
Horizontal analysis of income statements

QUALITY DEPARTMENT STORE INC.
Condensed Income Statements
For the Years Ended December 31

			Increase or (Decrease) During 2013	
	2013	**2012**	**Amount**	**Percent**
Sales revenue	$2,195,000	$1,960,000	$235,000	12.0%
Sales returns and allowances	98,000	123,000	(25,000)	(20.3%)
Net sales	2,097,000	1,837,000	260,000	14.2%
Cost of goods sold	1,281,000	1,140,000	141,000	12.4%
Gross profit	816,000	697,000	119,000	17.1%
Selling expenses	253,000	211,500	41,500	19.6%
Administrative expenses	104,000	108,500	(4,500)	(4.1%)
Total operating expenses	357,000	320,000	37,000	11.6%
Income from operations	459,000	377,000	82,000	21.8%
Other revenues and gains				
Interest and dividends	9,000	11,000	(2,000)	(18.2%)
Other expenses and losses				
Interest expense	36,000	40,500	(4,500)	(11.1%)
Income before income taxes	432,000	347,500	84,500	24.3%
Income tax expense	168,200	139,000	29,200	21.0%
Net income	$ 263,800	$ 208,500	$ 55,300	26.5%

RETAINED EARNINGS STATEMENT

Illustration 18-7 presents a horizontal analysis of Quality Department Store's comparative retained earnings statements. Analyzed horizontally, net income increased $55,300, or 26.5%, whereas dividends on the common stock increased only $1,200, or 2%. We saw in the horizontal analysis of the balance sheet that ending retained earnings increased 38.6%. As indicated earlier, the company retained a significant portion of net income to finance additional plant facilities.

Illustration 18-7
Horizontal analysis of retained earnings statements

QUALITY DEPARTMENT STORE INC.
Retained Earnings Statements
For the Years Ended December 31

			Increase or (Decrease) During 2013	
	2013	**2012**	**Amount**	**Percent**
Retained earnings, Jan. 1	$525,000	$376,500	$148,500	39.4%
Add: Net income	263,800	208,500	55,300	26.5%
	788,800	585,000	203,800	
Deduct: Dividends	61,200	60,000	1,200	2.0%
Retained earnings, Dec. 31	$727,600	$525,000	$202,600	38.6%

Horizontal analysis of changes from period to period is relatively straightforward and is quite useful. But, complications can occur in making the computations. If an item has no value in a base year or preceding year but does have a value in the next year, we cannot compute a percentage change. Similarly, if a negative amount appears in the base or preceding period and a positive amount exists the following year (or vice versa), no percentage change can be computed.

Vertical Analysis

Vertical analysis, also called **common-size analysis**, is a technique that expresses each financial statement item as a percentage of a base amount. On a balance sheet, we might say that current assets are 22% of total assets—total assets being the base amount. Or on an income statement, we might say that selling expenses are 16% of net sales—net sales being the base amount.

BALANCE SHEET

Illustration 18-8 presents the vertical analysis of Quality Department Store Inc.'s comparative balance sheets. The base for the asset items is **total assets**. The base for the liability and stockholders' equity items is **total liabilities and stockholders' equity**.

Illustration 18-8
Vertical analysis of balance sheets

QUALITY DEPARTMENT STORE INC.
Condensed Balance Sheets
December 31

	2013		2012	
	Amount	**Percent**	**Amount**	**Percent**
Assets				
Current assets	$1,020,000	**55.6%**	$ 945,000	**59.2%**
Plant assets (net)	800,000	**43.6%**	632,500	**39.7%**
Intangible assets	15,000	**0.8%**	17,500	**1.1%**
Total assets	$1,835,000	**100.0%**	$1,595,000	**100.0%**
Liabilities				
Current liabilities	$ 344,500	**18.8%**	$ 303,000	**19.0%**
Long-term liabilities	487,500	**26.5%**	497,000	**31.2%**
Total liabilities	832,000	**45.3%**	800,000	**50.2%**
Stockholders' Equity				
Common stock, $1 par	275,400	**15.0%**	270,000	**16.9%**
Retained earnings	727,600	**39.7%**	525,000	**32.9%**
Total stockholders' equity	1,003,000	**54.7%**	795,000	**49.8%**
Total liabilities and stockholders' equity	$1,835,000	**100.0%**	$1,595,000	**100.0%**

Vertical analysis shows the relative size of each category in the balance sheet. It also can show the **percentage change** in the individual asset, liability, and stockholders' equity items. For example, we can see that current assets decreased from 59.2% of total assets in 2012 to 55.6% in 2013 (even though the absolute dollar amount increased $75,000 in that time). Plant assets (net) have increased from 39.7% to 43.6% of total assets. Retained earnings have increased from 32.9% to 39.7% of total liabilities and stockholders' equity. These results reinforce the earlier observations that **Quality Department Store is choosing to finance its growth through retention of earnings rather than through issuing additional debt**.

INCOME STATEMENT

Illustration 18-9 (page 630) shows vertical analysis of Quality Department Store's income statements. Cost of goods sold as a percentage of net sales declined 1%

Illustration 18-9
Vertical analysis of income statements

QUALITY DEPARTMENT STORE INC.
Condensed Income Statements
For the Years Ended December 31

	2013		2012	
	Amount	**Percent**	**Amount**	**Percent**
Sales revenue	$2,195,000	**104.7%**	$1,960,000	**106.7%**
Sales returns and allowances	98,000	**4.7%**	123,000	**6.7%**
Net sales	2,097,000	**100.0%**	1,837,000	**100.0%**
Cost of goods sold	1,281,000	**61.1%**	1,140,000	**62.1%**
Gross profit	816,000	**38.9%**	697,000	**37.9%**
Selling expenses	253,000	**12.0%**	211,500	**11.5%**
Administrative expenses	104,000	**5.0%**	108,500	**5.9%**
Total operating expenses	357,000	**17.0%**	320,000	**17.4%**
Income from operations	459,000	**21.9%**	377,000	**20.5%**
Other revenues and gains				
Interest and dividends	9,000	**0.4%**	11,000	**0.6%**
Other expenses and losses				
Interest expense	36,000	**1.7%**	40,500	**2.2%**
Income before income taxes	432,000	**20.6%**	347,500	**18.9%**
Income tax expense	168,200	**8.0%**	139,000	**7.5%**
Net income	$ 263,800	**12.6%**	$ 208,500	**11.4%**

(62.1% vs. 61.1%), and total operating expenses declined 0.4% (17.4% vs. 17.0%). As a result, it is not surprising to see net income as a percentage of net sales increase from 11.4% to 12.6%. Quality Department Store appears to be a profitable business that is becoming even more successful.

An associated benefit of vertical analysis is that it enables you to compare companies of different sizes. For example, suppose Quality Department Store's main competitor is a Macy's store in a nearby town. Using vertical analysis, we can compare the condensed income statements of Quality Department Store Inc. (a small retail company) with Macy's, Inc.[1] (a giant international retailer), as shown in Illustration 18-10.

Illustration 18-10
Intercompany income statement comparison

Condensed Income Statements
For the Year Ended December 31, 2013
(in thousands)

	Quality Department Store Inc.		Macy's, Inc.	
	Dollars	**Percent**	**Dollars**	**Percent**
Net sales	$2,097	**100.0%**	$27,931,000	**100.0%**
Cost of goods sold	1,281	**61.1%**	16,725,000	**59.9%**
Gross profit	816	**38.9%**	11,206,000	**40.1%**
Selling and administrative expenses	357	**17.0%**	8,440,000	**30.2%**
Income from operations	459	**21.9%**	2,766,000	**9.9%**
Other expenses and revenues (including income taxes)	195	**9.3%**	1,280,000	**4.6%**
Net income	$ 264	**12.6%**	$ 1,486,000	**5.3%**

[1] *2013 Annual Report,* Macy's, Inc. (Cincinnati, Ohio).

Macy's net sales are 13,320 times greater than the net sales of relatively tiny Quality Department Store. But vertical analysis eliminates this difference in size. The percentages show that Quality's and Macy's gross profit rates were comparable at 38.9% and 40.1%, respectively. However, the percentages related to income from operations were significantly different at 21.9% and 9.9%, respectively. This disparity can be attributed to Quality's selling and administrative expense percentage (17%) which is much lower than Macy's (30.2%). Although Macy's earned net income more than 5,629 times larger than Quality's, Macy's net income as a **percentage of each sales dollar** (5.3%) is only 42% of Quality's (12.6%).

LEARNING OBJECTIVE 

Analyze a company's performance using ratio analysis.

Ratio analysis expresses the relationship among selected items of financial statement data. A **ratio** expresses the mathematical relationship between one quantity and another. The relationship is expressed in terms of either a percentage, a rate, or a simple proportion. To illustrate, in 2013 **Nike, Inc.** had current assets of $13,626 million and current liabilities of $3,926 million. We can find the relationship between these two measures by dividing current assets by current liabilities. The alternative means of expression are as follows.

Percentage: Current assets are 347% of current liabilities.
Rate: Current assets are 3.47 times current liabilities.
Proportion: The relationship of current assets to liabilities is 3.47:1.

To analyze the primary financial statements, we can use ratios to evaluate liquidity, profitability, and solvency. Illustration 18-11 describes these classifications.

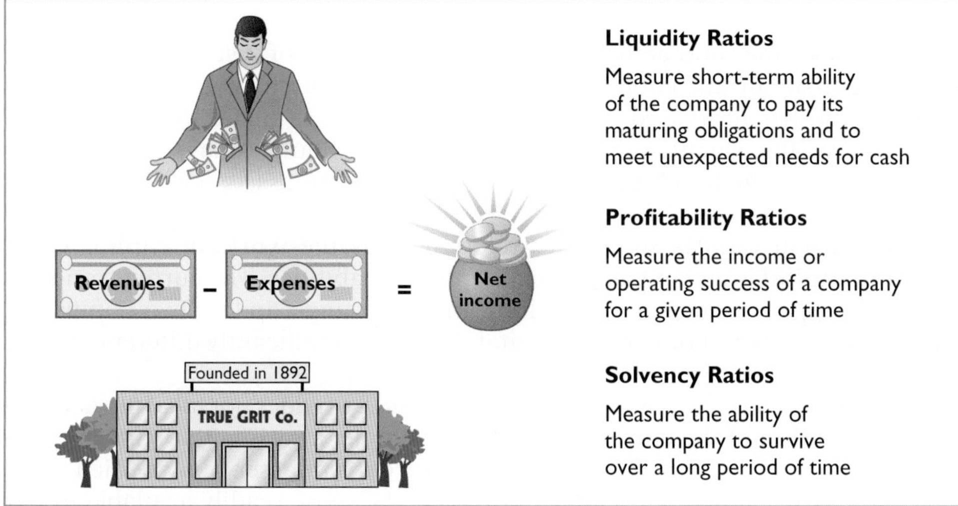

Illustration 18-11
Financial ratio classifications

Ratios can provide clues to underlying conditions that may not be apparent from individual financial statement components. However, a single ratio by itself is not very meaningful. Thus, in the discussion of ratios we will use the following types of comparisons.

1. **Intracompany comparisons** for two years for Quality Department Store.
2. **Industry average comparisons** based on median ratios for department stores.

International Note

As more countries adopt international accounting standards, the ability of analysts to compare companies from different countries should improve. However, international standards are open to widely varying interpretations. In addition, some countries adopt international standards "with modifications." As a consequence, most cross-country comparisons are still not as transparent as within-country comparisons.

3. **Intercompany comparisons** based on Macy's, Inc. as Quality Department Store's principal competitor.

Liquidity Ratios

Liquidity ratios measure the short-term ability of the company to pay its maturing obligations and to meet unexpected needs for cash. Short-term creditors such as bankers and suppliers are particularly interested in assessing liquidity. The ratios we can use to determine the company's short-term debt-paying ability are the current ratio, the acid-test ratio, accounts receivable turnover, and inventory turnover.

1. CURRENT RATIO

The **current ratio** is a widely used measure for evaluating a company's liquidity and short-term debt-paying ability. The ratio is computed by dividing current assets by current liabilities. Illustration 18-12 shows the 2013 and 2012 current ratios for Quality Department Store and 2013 comparative data.

Illustration 18-12
Current ratio

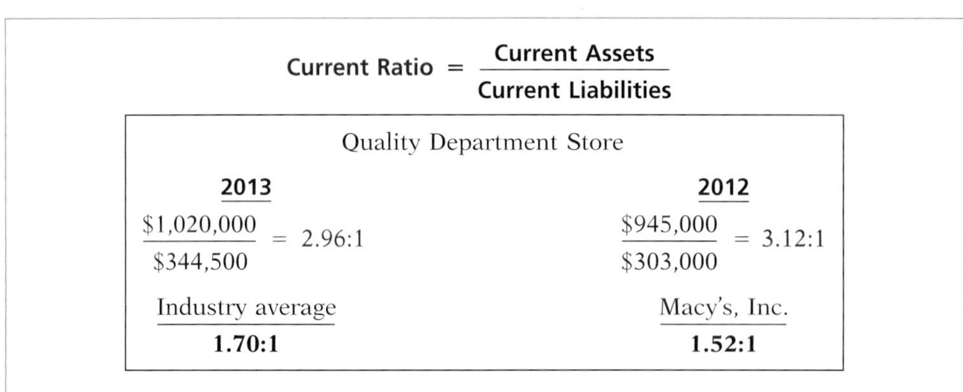

$$\text{Current Ratio} = \frac{\text{Current Assets}}{\text{Current Liabilities}}$$

Quality Department Store

2013	2012
$\frac{\$1{,}020{,}000}{\$344{,}500} = 2.96:1$	$\frac{\$945{,}000}{\$303{,}000} = 3.12:1$
Industry average	Macy's, Inc.
1.70:1	**1.52:1**

What does the ratio actually mean? The 2013 ratio of 2.96:1 means that for every dollar of current liabilities, Quality has $2.96 of current assets. Quality's current ratio has decreased in the current year. But, compared to the industry average of 1.70:1, Quality appears to be reasonably liquid. Macy's has a current ratio of 1.52:1, which indicates it has adequate current assets relative to its current liabilities.

The current ratio is sometimes referred to as the **working capital ratio**. **Working capital** is current assets minus current liabilities. The current ratio is a more dependable indicator of liquidity than working capital. Two companies with the same amount of working capital may have significantly different current ratios.

The current ratio is only one measure of liquidity. It does not take into account the **composition** of the current assets. For example, a satisfactory current ratio does not disclose the fact that a portion of the current assets may be tied up in slow-moving inventory. A dollar of cash would be more readily available to pay the bills than a dollar of slow-moving inventory.

2. ACID-TEST RATIO

The **acid-test (quick) ratio** is a measure of a company's immediate short-term liquidity. We compute this ratio by dividing the sum of cash, short-term investments, and net accounts receivable by current liabilities. Thus, it is an important complement to the current ratio. For example, assume that the current assets of Quality Department Store for 2013 and 2012 consist of the items shown in Illustration 18-13.

Illustration 18-13
Current assets of Quality Department Store

QUALITY DEPARTMENT STORE INC.
Balance Sheet (partial)

	2013	2012
Current assets		
Cash	**$ 100,000**	**$155,000**
Short-term investments	**20,000**	**70,000**
Accounts receivable (net*)	**230,000**	**180,000**
Inventory	620,000	500,000
Prepaid expenses	50,000	40,000
Total current assets	$1,020,000	$ 945,000

*Allowance for doubtful accounts is $10,000 at the end of each year.

Cash, short-term investments, and accounts receivable (net) are highly liquid compared to inventory and prepaid expenses. The inventory may not be readily saleable, and the prepaid expenses may not be transferable to others. Thus, the acid-test ratio measures **immediate** liquidity. The 2013 and 2012 acid-test ratios for Quality Department Store and 2013 comparative data are as follows.

Illustration 18-14
Acid-test ratio

$$\text{Acid-Test Ratio} = \frac{\text{Cash + Short-Term Investments + Accounts Receivable (Net)}}{\text{Current Liabilities}}$$

Quality Department Store

2013	2012
$\frac{\$100{,}000 + \$20{,}000 + \$230{,}000}{\$344{,}500} = 1.02{:}1$	$\frac{\$155{,}000 + \$70{,}000 + \$180{,}000}{\$303{,}000} = 1.34{:}1$
Industry average	Macy's, Inc.
0.70:1	**0.47:1**

The ratio has declined in 2013. Is an acid-test ratio of 1.02:1 adequate? This depends on the industry and the economy. When compared with the industry average of 0.70:1 and Macy's of 0.47:1, Quality's acid-test ratio seems adequate.

3. ACCOUNTS RECEIVABLE TURNOVER

We can measure liquidity by how quickly a company can convert certain assets to cash. How liquid, for example, are the accounts receivable? The ratio used to assess the liquidity of the receivables is the **accounts receivable turnover**. It measures the number of times, on average, the company collects receivables during the period. We compute accounts receivable turnover by dividing net credit sales (net sales less cash sales) by the average net accounts receivable. Unless seasonal factors are significant, average net accounts receivable can be computed from the beginning and ending balances of the net accounts receivable.[2]

Assume that all sales are credit sales. The balance of net accounts receivable at the beginning of 2012 is $200,000. Illustration 18-15 (page 634) shows the accounts receivable turnover for Quality Department Store and 2013 comparative data. Quality's accounts receivable turnover improved in 2013. However, the turnover of 10.2

[2] If seasonal factors are significant, the average accounts receivable balance might be determined by using monthly amounts.

times is substantially lower than Macy's 69.1 times and is also lower than the department store industry's average of 46.4 times.

Illustration 18-15
Accounts receivable turnover

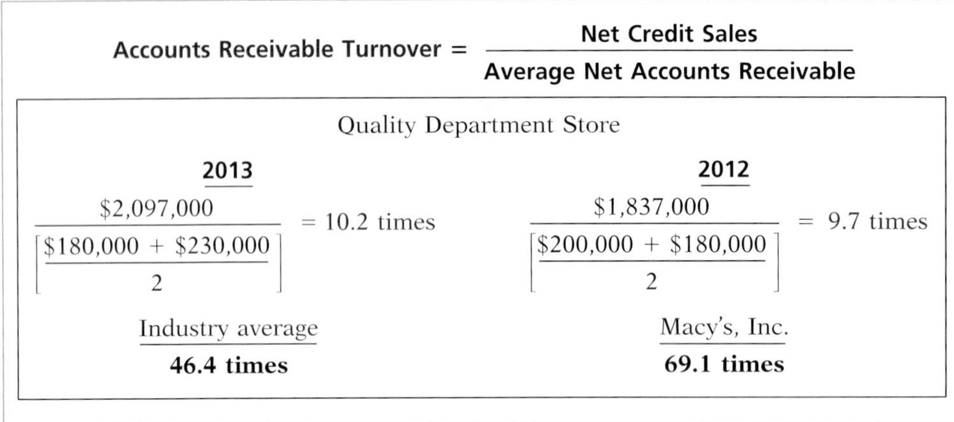

$$\textbf{Accounts Receivable Turnover} = \frac{\textbf{Net Credit Sales}}{\textbf{Average Net Accounts Receivable}}$$

Quality Department Store

2013	2012
$\dfrac{\$2,097,000}{\left[\frac{\$180,000 + \$230,000}{2}\right]} = 10.2$ times	$\dfrac{\$1,837,000}{\left[\frac{\$200,000 + \$180,000}{2}\right]} = 9.7$ times
Industry average	Macy's, Inc.
46.4 times	**69.1 times**

AVERAGE COLLECTION PERIOD A popular variant of the accounts receivable turnover is to convert it to an **average collection period** in terms of days. To do so, we divide the accounts receivable turnover into 365 days. For example, the accounts receivable turnover of 10.2 times divided into 365 days gives an average collection period of approximately 36 days. This means that accounts receivable are collected on average every 36 days, or about every 5 weeks. Analysts frequently use the average collection period to assess the effectiveness of a company's credit and collection policies. The general rule is that the collection period should not greatly exceed the credit term period (the time allowed for payment).

4. INVENTORY TURNOVER

Inventory turnover measures the number of times, on average, the inventory is sold during the period. Its purpose is to measure the liquidity of the inventory. We compute the inventory turnover by dividing cost of goods sold by the average inventory. Unless seasonal factors are significant, we can use the beginning and ending inventory balances to compute average inventory.

Assuming that the inventory balance for Quality Department Store at the beginning of 2012 was $450,000, its inventory turnover and 2013 comparative data are as shown in Illustration 18-16. Quality's inventory turnover declined slightly in 2013. The turnover of 2.3 times is low compared with the industry average of 4.3 and Macy's 3.1. Generally, the faster the inventory turnover, the less cash a company has tied up in inventory and the less chance a company has of inventory obsolescence.

Illustration 18-16
Inventory turnover

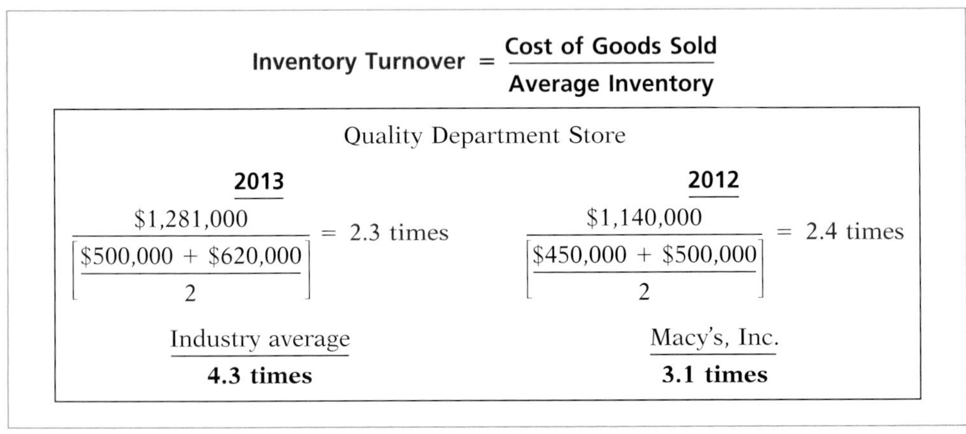

$$\textbf{Inventory Turnover} = \frac{\textbf{Cost of Goods Sold}}{\textbf{Average Inventory}}$$

Quality Department Store

2013	2012
$\dfrac{\$1,281,000}{\left[\frac{\$500,000 + \$620,000}{2}\right]} = 2.3$ times	$\dfrac{\$1,140,000}{\left[\frac{\$450,000 + \$500,000}{2}\right]} = 2.4$ times
Industry average	Macy's, Inc.
4.3 times	**3.1 times**

DAYS IN INVENTORY A variant of inventory turnover is the **days in inventory**. We calculate it by dividing the inventory turnover into 365. For example, Quality's 2013 inventory turnover of 2.3 times divided into 365 is 158.7 days. An average selling time of 158.7 days is also high compared with the industry average of 84.9 days (365 ÷ 4.3) and Macy's 117.7 days (365 ÷ 3.1).

Inventory turnovers vary considerably among industries. For example, grocery store chains have a turnover of 17.1 times and an average selling period of 21 days. In contrast, jewelry stores have an average turnover of 0.80 times and an average selling period of 456 days.

Profitability Ratios

Profitability ratios measure the income or operating success of a company for a given period of time. Income, or the lack of it, affects the company's ability to obtain debt and equity financing. It also affects the company's liquidity position and the company's ability to grow. As a consequence, both creditors and investors are interested in evaluating earning power—profitability. Analysts frequently use profitability as the ultimate test of management's operating effectiveness.

5. PROFIT MARGIN

Profit margin is a measure of the percentage of each dollar of sales that results in net income. We can compute it by dividing net income by net sales. Illustration 18-17 shows Quality Department Store's profit margin and 2013 comparative data.

Terminology
Profit margin is also called the *rate of return on sales.*

Illustration 18-17
Profit margin

$$\textbf{Profit Margin} = \frac{\textbf{Net Income}}{\textbf{Net Sales}}$$

Quality Department Store

2013	2012
$\frac{\$263,800}{\$2,097,000} = 12.6\%$	$\frac{\$208,500}{\$1,837,000} = 11.4\%$
Industry average	Macy's, Inc.
8.0%	**5.3%**

Quality experienced an increase in its profit margin from 2012 to 2013. Its profit margin is unusually high in comparison with the industry average of 8% and Macy's 5.3%.

High-volume (high inventory turnover) businesses, such as grocery stores (**Safeway** or **Kroger**) and discount stores (**Kmart** or **Wal-Mart**), generally experience low profit margins. In contrast, low-volume businesses, such as jewelry stores (**Tiffany & Co.**) or airplane manufacturers (**Boeing Co.**), have high profit margins.

6. ASSET TURNOVER

Asset turnover measures how efficiently a company uses its assets to generate sales. It is determined by dividing net sales by average total assets. The resulting number shows the dollars of sales produced by each dollar invested in assets. Unless seasonal factors are significant, we can use the beginning and ending balance of total assets to determine average total assets. Assuming that total assets at the beginning of 2012 were $1,446,000, the 2013 and 2012 asset turnover for Quality Department Store and 2013 comparative data are shown in Illustration 18-18.

Illustration 18-18
Asset turnover

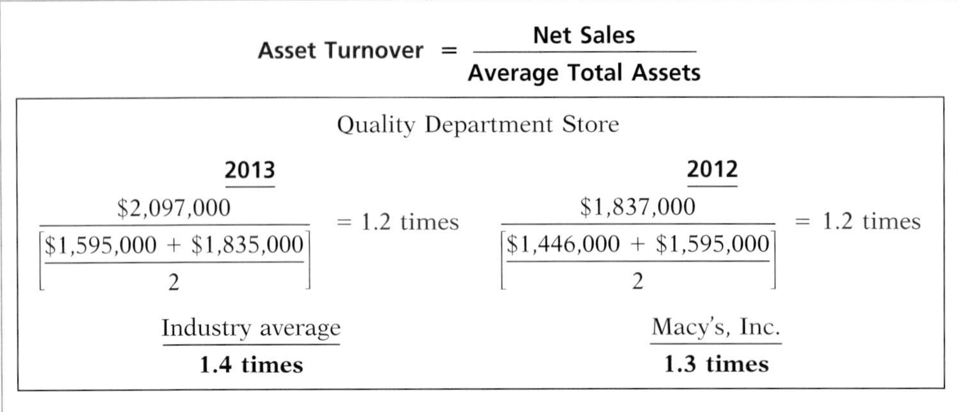

$$\textbf{Asset Turnover} = \frac{\textbf{Net Sales}}{\textbf{Average Total Assets}}$$

Quality Department Store

2013

$$\frac{\$2{,}097{,}000}{\left[\frac{\$1{,}595{,}000 + \$1{,}835{,}000}{2}\right]} = 1.2 \text{ times}$$

2012

$$\frac{\$1{,}837{,}000}{\left[\frac{\$1{,}446{,}000 + \$1{,}595{,}000}{2}\right]} = 1.2 \text{ times}$$

Industry average	Macy's, Inc.
1.4 times	**1.3 times**

Asset turnover shows that in 2013 Quality generated sales of $1.20 for each dollar it had invested in assets. The ratio changed very little from 2012 to 2013. Quality's asset turnover is below the industry average of 1.4 times and Macy's ratio of 1.3 times.

Asset turnovers vary considerably among industries. For example, a large utility company like **Consolidated Edison** (New York) has a ratio of 0.4 times, and the large grocery chain **Kroger Stores** has a ratio of 3.4 times.

7. RETURN ON ASSETS

An overall measure of profitability is **return on assets**. We compute this ratio by dividing net income by average total assets. The 2013 and 2012 return on assets for Quality Department Store and 2013 comparative data are shown below.

Illustration 18-19
Return on assets

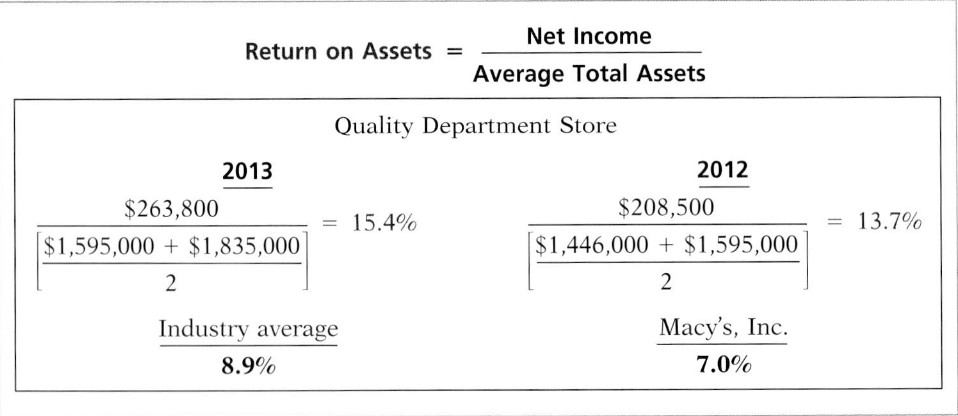

$$\textbf{Return on Assets} = \frac{\textbf{Net Income}}{\textbf{Average Total Assets}}$$

Quality Department Store

2013

$$\frac{\$263{,}800}{\left[\frac{\$1{,}595{,}000 + \$1{,}835{,}000}{2}\right]} = 15.4\%$$

2012

$$\frac{\$208{,}500}{\left[\frac{\$1{,}446{,}000 + \$1{,}595{,}000}{2}\right]} = 13.7\%$$

Industry average	Macy's, Inc.
8.9%	**7.0%**

Quality's return on assets improved from 2012 to 2013. Its return of 15.4% is very high compared with the department store industry average of 8.9% and Macy's 7.0%.

8. RETURN ON COMMON STOCKHOLDERS' EQUITY

Another widely used profitability ratio is **return on common stockholders' equity**. It measures profitability from the common stockholders' viewpoint. This ratio shows how many dollars of net income the company earned for each dollar invested by the owners. We compute it by dividing net income by average common stockholders' equity. Assuming that common stockholders' equity at the beginning of 2012 was $667,000, Illustration 18-20 shows the 2013 and 2012 ratios for Quality Department Store and 2013 comparative data.

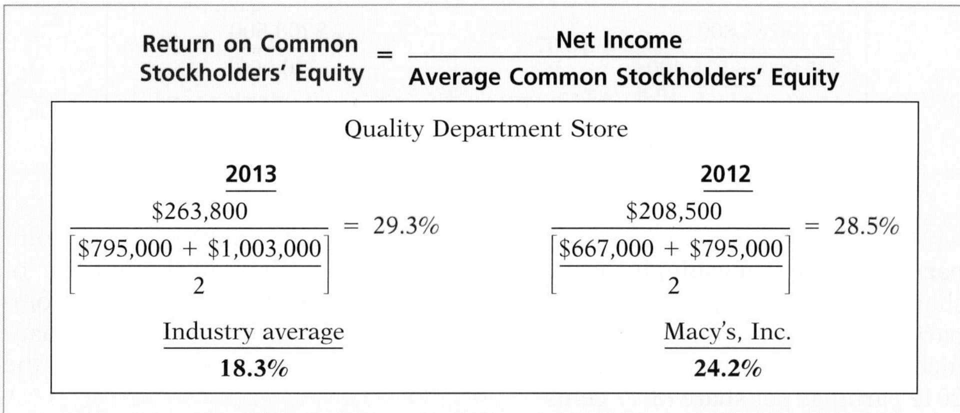

$$\text{Return on Common Stockholders' Equity} = \frac{\text{Net Income}}{\text{Average Common Stockholders' Equity}}$$

Quality Department Store

2013	2012
$\dfrac{\$263{,}800}{\left[\dfrac{\$795{,}000 + \$1{,}003{,}000}{2}\right]} = 29.3\%$	$\dfrac{\$208{,}500}{\left[\dfrac{\$667{,}000 + \$795{,}000}{2}\right]} = 28.5\%$
Industry average	Macy's, Inc.
18.3%	**24.2%**

Illustration 18-20
Return on common stockholders' equity

Quality's rate of return on common stockholders' equity is high at 29.3%, considering an industry average of 18.3% and a rate of 24.2% for Macy's.

WITH PREFERRED STOCK When a company has preferred stock, we must deduct **preferred dividend** requirements from net income to compute income available to common stockholders. Similarly, we deduct the par value of preferred stock (or call price, if applicable) from total stockholders' equity to determine the amount of common stockholders' equity used in this ratio. The ratio then appears as follows.

$$\text{Return on Common Stockholders' Equity} = \frac{\text{Net Income} - \text{Preferred Dividends}}{\text{Average Common Stockholders' Equity}}$$

Illustration 18-21
Return on common stockholders' equity with preferred stock

Note that Quality's rate of return on stockholders' equity (29.3%) is substantially higher than its rate of return on assets (15.4%). The reason is that Quality has made effective use of **leverage**. **Leveraging** or **trading on the equity** at a gain means that the company has borrowed money at a lower rate of interest than it is able to earn by using the borrowed money. Leverage enables Quality to use money supplied by nonowners to increase the return to the owners. A comparison of the rate of return on total assets with the rate of interest paid for borrowed money indicates the profitability of trading on the equity. Quality earns more on its borrowed funds than it has to pay in the form of interest. Thus, the return to stockholders exceeds the return on the assets, due to benefits from the positive leveraging.

9. EARNINGS PER SHARE (EPS)

Earnings per share (EPS) is a measure of the net income earned on each share of common stock. It is computed by dividing net income less preferred dividends by the number of weighted-average common shares outstanding during the year. A measure of net income earned on a per share basis provides a useful perspective for determining profitability. Assuming that there is no change in the number of outstanding shares during 2012 and that the 2013 increase occurred midyear, Illustration 18-22 (page 638) shows the net income per share for Quality Department Store for 2013 and 2012, assuming no preferred dividends.

Illustration 18-22
Earnings per share

$$\text{Earnings per Share} = \frac{\text{Net Income} - \text{Preferred Dividends}}{\text{Weighted-Average Common Shares Outstanding}}$$

Quality Department Store

2013	2012
$\dfrac{\$263,800}{\left[\dfrac{270,000 + 275,400}{2}\right]} = \$0.97$	$\dfrac{\$208,500}{270,000} = \$0.77$

Note that no industry or specific competitive data are presented. Such comparisons are not meaningful because of the wide variations in the number of shares of outstanding stock among companies. The only meaningful EPS comparison is an intracompany trend comparison. Here, Quality's earnings per share increased 20 cents per share in 2013. This represents a 26% increase over the 2012 earnings per share of 77 cents.

The terms "earnings per share" and "net income per share" refer to the amount of net income applicable to each share of **common stock**. Therefore, in computing EPS, if there are preferred dividends declared for the period, we must deduct them from net income to determine income available to the common stockholders.

10. PRICE-EARNINGS RATIO

The **price-earnings (P-E) ratio** is a widely used measure of the ratio of the market price of each share of common stock to the earnings per share. The price-earnings (P-E) ratio reflects investors' assessments of a company's future earnings. We compute it by dividing the market price per share of the stock by earnings per share. Assuming that the market price of Quality Department Store stock is $8 in 2012 and $12 in 2013, the price-earnings ratio computation is computed as shown in Illustration 18-23.

Illustration 18-23
Price-earnings ratio

$$\text{Price-Earnings Ratio} = \frac{\text{Market Price per Share}}{\text{Earnings per Share}}$$

Quality Department Store

2013	2012
$\dfrac{\$12.00}{\$0.97} = 12.4$ times	$\dfrac{\$8.00}{\$0.77} = 10.4$ times
Industry average	Macy's, Inc.
21.3 times	**13.5 times**

In 2013, each share of Quality's stock sold for 12.4 times the amount that the company earned on each share. Quality's price-earnings ratio is lower than the industry average of 21.3 times but much closer to the ratio of 13.5 times for Macy's. For overall comparison to the market, the average price-earnings ratio for the stocks that constitute the Standard and Poor's 500 Index (500 largest U.S. firms) in mid-2014 was approximately 19.6 times.

11. PAYOUT RATIO

The **payout ratio** measures the percentage of earnings distributed in the form of cash dividends. We compute it by dividing cash dividends declared on common stock by net income. Companies that have high growth rates generally have low payout ratios because they reinvest most of their net income into the business. The 2013 and 2012 payout ratios for Quality Department Store are computed as shown in Illustration 18-24.

Illustration 18-24
Payout ratio

$$\textbf{Payout Ratio} = \frac{\textbf{Cash Dividends Declared on Common Stock}}{\textbf{Net Income}}$$

Quality Department Store

2013	2012
$\frac{\$61,200}{\$263,800} = 23.2\%$	$\frac{\$60,000}{\$208,500} = 28.8\%$
Industry average	Macy's, Inc.
16.1%	**24.2%**

Quality's payout ratio is higher than the industry average payout ratio of 16.1%.

Solvency Ratios

Solvency ratios measure the ability of a company to survive over a long period of time. Long-term creditors and stockholders are particularly interested in a company's ability to pay interest as it comes due and to repay the face value of debt at maturity. Debt to assets and times interest earned are two ratios that provide information about debt-paying ability.

12. DEBT TO ASSETS RATIO

The **debt to assets ratio** measures the percentage of the total assets that creditors provide. We compute it by dividing total liabilities (both current and long-term liabilities) by total assets. This ratio indicates the company's degree of leverage. It also provides some indication of the company's ability to withstand losses without impairing the interests of creditors. The higher the percentage of total liabilities to total assets, the greater the risk that the company may be unable to meet its maturing obligations. The 2013 and 2012 ratios for Quality Department Store and 2013 comparative data are as follows.

Illustration 18-25
Debt to assets ratio

$$\textbf{Debt to Assets Ratio} = \frac{\textbf{Total Liabilities}}{\textbf{Total Assets}}$$

Quality Department Store

2013	2012
$\frac{\$832,000}{\$1,835,000} = 45.3\%$	$\frac{\$800,000}{\$1,595,000} = 50.2\%$
Industry average	Macy's, Inc.
34.2%	**71.1%**

A ratio of 45.3% means that creditors have provided 45.3% of Quality Department Store's total assets. Quality's 45.3% is above the industry average of 34.2%. It is considerably below the high 71.1% ratio of Macy's. The lower the ratio, the more equity "buffer" there is available to the creditors. Thus, from the creditors' point of view, a low ratio of debt to assets is usually desirable.

The adequacy of this ratio is often judged in the light of the company's earnings. Generally, companies with relatively stable earnings (such as public utilities) have higher debt to assets ratios than cyclical companies with widely fluctuating earnings (such as many high-tech companies).

13. TIMES INTEREST EARNED

Terminology
Times interest earned is also called *interest coverage*.

Times interest earned provides an indication of the company's ability to meet interest payments as they come due. We compute it by dividing the sum of net income, interest expense, and income tax expense by interest expense. Illustration 18-26 shows the 2013 and 2012 ratios for Quality Department Store and 2013 comparative data. Note that times interest earned uses net income before income tax expense and interest expense. This represents the amount available to cover interest. For Quality Department Store, the 2013 amount is computed by taking net income of $263,800 and adding back the $36,000 of interest expense and the $168,200 of income tax expense.

Illustration 18-26
Times interest earned

$$\text{Times Interest Earned} = \frac{\text{Net Income} + \text{Interest Expense} + \text{Income Tax Expense}}{\text{Interest Expense}}$$

Quality Department Store

2013	2012
$\frac{\$263,800 + \$36,000 + \$168,200}{\$36,000} = 13 \text{ times}$	$\frac{\$208,500 + \$40,500 + \$139,000}{\$40,500} = 9.6 \text{ times}$
Industry average	Macy's, Inc.
16.1 times	**6.9 times**

Quality's interest expense is well covered at 13 times. It is less than the industry average of 16.1 times but significantly exceeds Macy's 6.9 times.

Summary of Ratios

Illustration 18-27 summarizes the ratios discussed in this chapter. The summary includes the formula and purpose or use of each ratio.

Illustration 18-27
Summary of liquidity, profitability, and solvency ratios

Ratio	Formula	Purpose or Use
Liquidity Ratios		
1. Current ratio	$\frac{\text{Current assets}}{\text{Current liabilities}}$	Measures short-term debt-paying ability.
2. Acid-test (quick) ratio	$\frac{\text{Cash} + \text{Short-term investments} + \text{Accounts receivable (net)}}{\text{Current liabilities}}$	Measures immediate short-term liquidity.
3. Accounts receivable turnover	$\frac{\text{Net credit sales}}{\text{Average net accounts receivable}}$	Measures liquidity of accounts receivable.
4. Inventory turnover	$\frac{\text{Cost of goods sold}}{\text{Average inventory}}$	Measures liquidity of inventory.
Profitability Ratios		
5. Profit margin	$\frac{\text{Net income}}{\text{Net sales}}$	Measures net income generated by each dollar of sales.
6. Asset turnover	$\frac{\text{Net sales}}{\text{Average total assets}}$	Measures how efficiently assets are used to generate sales.

Ratio	Formula	Purpose or Use
7. Return on assets	$\dfrac{\text{Net income}}{\text{Average total assets}}$	Measures overall profitability of assets.
8. Return on common stockholders' equity	$\dfrac{\text{Net income} - \text{Preferred dividends}}{\text{Average common stockholders' equity}}$	Measures profitability of owners' investment.
9. Earnings per share (EPS)	$\dfrac{\text{Net income} - \text{Preferred dividends}}{\text{Weighted-average common shares outstanding}}$	Measures net income earned on each share of common stock.
10. Price-earnings (P-E) ratio	$\dfrac{\text{Market price per share}}{\text{Earnings per share}}$	Measures the ratio of the market price per share to earnings per share.
11. Payout ratio	$\dfrac{\text{Cash dividends declared on common stock}}{\text{Net income}}$	Measures percentage of earnings distributed in the form of cash dividends.
Solvency Ratios		
12. Debt to assets ratio	$\dfrac{\text{Total liabilities}}{\text{Total assets}}$	Measures the percentage of total assets provided by creditors.
13. Times interest earned	$\dfrac{\text{Net income} + \text{Interest expense} + \text{Income tax expense}}{\text{Interest expense}}$	Measures ability to meet interest payments as they come due.

LEARNING OBJECTIVE 3

Apply the concept of sustainable income.

The value of a company like **Google** is a function of the amount, timing, and uncertainty of its future cash flows. Google's current and past income statements are particularly useful in helping analysts predict these future cash flows. In using this approach, analysts must make sure that Google's past income numbers reflect its **sustainable income**, that is, do not include unusual (out-of-the-ordinary) revenues, expenses, gains, and losses. **Sustainable income** is, therefore, the most likely level of income to be obtained by a company in the future. Sustainable income differs from actual net income by the amount of unusual revenues, expenses, gains, and losses included in the current year's income. Analysts are interested in sustainable income because it helps them derive an estimate of future earnings without the "noise" of unusual items.

Fortunately, an income statement provides information on sustainable income by separating operating transactions from nonoperating transactions. This statement also highlights intermediate components of income such as income from operations, income before income taxes, and income from continuing operations. In addition, information on unusual items such as gains or losses on discontinued items and components of other comprehensive income are disclosed.

Illustration 18-28 (page 642) presents a statement of comprehensive income for Cruz Company for the year 2017. A statement of comprehensive income includes not only net income but a broader measure of income called comprehensive income. The two major unusual items in this statement are discontinued operations and other comprehensive income (highlighted in red). When estimating future cash flows, analysts must consider the implications of each of these components.

Illustration 18-28
Statement of comprehensive income

CRUZ COMPANY Statement of Comprehensive Income For the Year Ended 2017	
Sales revenue	$900,000
Cost of goods sold	650,000
Gross profit	250,000
Operating expenses	100,000
Income from operations	150,000
Other revenues (expenses) and gains (losses)	20,000
Income before income taxes	170,000
Income tax expense	24,000
Income from continuing operations	146,000
Discontinued operations (net of tax)	**30,000**
Net income	176,000
Other comprehensive income items (net of tax)	**10,000**
Comprehensive income	$186,000

In looking at Illustration 18-28, note that Cruz Company's two major types of unusual items, discontinued operations and other comprehensive income, are reported net of tax. That is, Cruz first calculates income tax expense before income from continuing operations. Then, it calculates income tax expense related to the discontinued operations and other comprehensive income. The general concept is, "Let the tax follow the income or loss." We discuss discontinued operations and other comprehensive income in more detail next.

Discontinued Operations

Discontinued operations refers to the disposal of a **significant component** of a business, such as the elimination of a major class of customers, or an entire activity. For example, to downsize its operations, **General Dynamics Corp.** sold its missile business to **Hughes Aircraft Co.** for $450 million. In its statement of comprehensive income, General Dynamics reported the sale in a separate section entitled "Discontinued operations."

Following the disposal of a significant component, the company should report on its statement both income from continuing operations and income (or loss) from discontinued operations. **The income (loss) from discontinued operations consists of two parts: the income (loss) from operations** and **the gain (loss) on disposal of the component.**

To illustrate, assume that during 2017 Acro Energy Inc. has income before income taxes of $800,000. During 2017, Acro discontinued and sold its unprofitable chemical division. The loss in 2017 from chemical operations (net of $60,000 taxes) was $140,000. The loss on disposal of the chemical division (net of $30,000 taxes) was $70,000. Assuming a 30% tax rate on income, Illustration 18-29 shows Acro's statement of comprehensive income presentation.

Note that the statement uses the caption "Income from continuing operations" and adds a new section "Discontinued operations." **The new section reports both the operating loss and the loss on disposal net of applicable income taxes.** This presentation clearly indicates the separate effects of continuing operations and discontinued operations on net income.

Other Comprehensive Income

Most revenues, expenses, gains, and losses are included in net income. However, certain gains and losses bypass net income. Instead, companies record these items as direct adjustments to stockholders' equity. The FASB requires companies to report not only net income but also other comprehensive income.

Illustration 18-29
Statement presentation of discontinued operations

ACRO ENERGY INC. Statement of Comprehensive Income (partial) For the Year Ended December 31, 2017		
Income before income taxes		$ 800,000
Income tax expense		240,000
Income from continuing operations		560,000
Discontinued operations		
Loss from operation of chemical division, net of $60,000 income tax savings	**$140,000**	
Loss from disposal of chemical division, net of $30,000 income tax savings	**70,000**	**210,000**
Net income		$ 350,000

Other comprehensive income includes all changes in stockholders' equity during a period except those changes resulting from investments by stockholders and distributions to stockholders.

ILLUSTRATION OF OTHER COMPREHENSIVE INCOME

Accounting standards require that companies adjust most investments in stocks and bonds up or down to their market price at the end of each accounting period. For example, assume that during 2017 Stassi Company purchased IBM stock for $10,000 as an investment. At the end of 2017, Stassi was still holding the investment, but the stock's market price was now $8,000. In this case, Stassi is required to reduce the recorded value of its IBM investment by $2,000. The $2,000 difference is an unrealized loss.

Should Stassi include this $2,000 unrealized loss in net income? It depends on whether Stassi classifies the IBM stock as a trading security or an available-for-sale security. A **trading security** is bought and held primarily for sale in the near term to generate income on short-term price differences. Companies report unrealized losses on trading securities in the "Other expenses and losses" section of the income statement. The rationale: It is likely that the company will realize the unrealized loss (or an unrealized gain), so the company should report the loss (gain) as part of net income.

If Stassi did not purchase the investment for trading purposes, it is classified as available-for-sale. **Available-for-sale securities** are held with the intent of selling them sometime in the future. Companies do not include unrealized gains or losses on available-for-sale securities in net income. Instead, they report them as part of "Other comprehensive income." Other comprehensive income is not included in net income. It bypasses net income and is recorded as a direct adjustment to stockholders' equity.

FORMAT

One format for reporting other comprehensive income is to report a statement of comprehensive income. For example, assuming that Stassi Company has a net income of $300,000, the unrealized loss would be reported below net income as follows.

Illustration 18-30
Lower portion of statement of comprehensive income

STASSI CORPORATION Statement of Comprehensive Income (partial) For the Year Ended 2017	
Net income	$ 300,000
Unrealized loss on available-for-sale securities (net of tax)	2,000
Comprehensive income	**$298,000**

Companies also report the unrealized loss on available-for-sale securities as a separate component of stockholders' equity. To illustrate, assume Stassi Corporation has common stock of $3,000,000, retained earnings of $1,500,000, and an unrealized loss on available-for-sale securities of $2,000. Illustration 18-31 shows the balance sheet presentation of the unrealized loss.

Illustration 18-31
Unrealized loss in stockholders' equity section

Balance Sheet (partial)	
Stockholders' equity	
Common stock	$3,000,000
Retained earnings	1,500,000
Total paid-in capital and retained earnings	4,500,000
Less: Unrealized loss on available-for-sale securities	**2,000**
Total stockholders' equity	$4,498,000

Note that the presentation of the loss is similar to the presentation of the cost of treasury stock in the stockholders' equity section. (An unrealized gain would be added in this section of the balance sheet.) Reporting the unrealized gain or loss in the stockholders' equity section serves two important purposes: (1) it reduces the volatility of net income due to fluctuations in fair value, and (2) it informs the financial statement user of the gain or loss that would occur if the company sold the securities at fair value.

COMPLETE STATEMENT OF COMPREHENSIVE INCOME

The statement of comprehensive income for Pace Corporation in Illustration 18-32 presents the types of items found on this statement, such as net sales, cost of goods sold, operating expenses, and income taxes. In addition, it shows how companies report discontinued operations and other comprehensive income (highlighted in red).

Illustration 18-32
Complete statement of comprehensive income

PACE CORPORATION Statement of Comprehensive Income For the Year Ended December 31, 2017		
Net sales		$440,000
Cost of goods sold		260,000
Gross profit		180,000
Operating expenses		110,000
Income from operations		70,000
Other revenues and gains		5,600
Other expenses and losses		9,600
Income before income taxes		66,000
Income tax expense ($66,000 × 30%)		19,800
Income from continuing operations		46,200
Discontinued operations		
Loss from operation of Plastics Division, net of income tax savings $18,000 ($60,000 × 30%)	**$42,000**	
Gain on disposal of Plastics Division, net of $15,000 income taxes ($50,000 × 30%)	**35,000**	**7,000**
Net income		**39,200**
Unrealized gain on available-for-sale securities, net of income taxes ($15,000 × 30%)		**10,500**
Comprehensive income		**$ 49,700**

REVIEW AND PRACTICE

LEARNING OBJECTIVES REVIEW

1 Apply horizontal and vertical analysis to financial statements. There are three bases of comparison: (1) intracompany, which compares an item or financial relationship with other data within a company; (2) industry, which compares company data with industry averages; and (3) intercompany, which compares an item or financial relationship of a company with data of one or more competing companies.

Horizontal analysis is a technique for evaluating a series of data over a period of time to determine the increase or decrease that has taken place, expressed as either an amount or a percentage. Vertical analysis is a technique that expresses each item within a financial statement in terms of a percentage of a relevant total or a base amount.

2 Analyze a company's performance using ratio analysis. The formula and purpose of each ratio is presented in Illustration 18-27 (page 640).

3 Apply the concept of sustainable income. Sustainable income analysis is useful in evaluating a company's performance. Sustainable income is the most likely level of income to be obtained by the company in the future. Discontinued operations and other comprehensive income are presented on the statement of comprehensive income to highlight their unusual nature. Items below income from continuing operations must be presented net of tax.

GLOSSARY REVIEW

Accounts receivable turnover A measure of the liquidity of accounts receivable; computed by dividing net credit sales by average net accounts receivable.

Acid-test (quick) ratio A measure of a company's immediate short-term liquidity; computed by dividing the sum of cash, short-term investments, and net accounts receivable by current liabilities.

Asset turnover A measure of how efficiently a company uses its assets to generate sales; computed by dividing net sales by average total assets.

Current ratio A measure used to evaluate a company's liquidity and short-term debt-paying ability; computed by dividing current assets by current liabilities.

Debt to assets ratio Measures the percentage of assets provided by creditors; computed by dividing total liabilities by total assets.

Discontinued operations The disposal of a significant component of a business.

Earnings per share (EPS) The net income earned on each share of common stock; computed by dividing net income minus preferred dividends (if any) by the number of weighted-average common shares outstanding.

Horizontal analysis A technique for evaluating a series of financial statement data over a period of time, to determine the increase (decrease) that has taken place, expressed as either an amount or a percentage.

Inventory turnover A measure of the liquidity of inventory; computed by dividing cost of goods sold by average inventory.

Leveraging See *Trading on the equity*.

Liquidity ratios Measures of the short-term ability of the company to pay its maturing obligations and to meet unexpected needs for cash.

Other comprehensive income Includes all changes in stockholders' equity during a period except those resulting from investments by stockholders and distributions to stockholders.

Payout ratio Measures the percentage of earnings distributed in the form of cash dividends; computed by dividing cash dividends declared on common stock by net income.

Price-earnings (P-E) ratio Measures the ratio of the market price of each share of common stock to the earnings per share; computed by dividing the market price per share by earnings per share.

Profit margin Measures the percentage of each dollar of sales that results in net income; computed by dividing net income by net sales.

Profitability ratios Measures of the income or operating success of a company for a given period of time.

Ratio An expression of the mathematical relationship between one quantity and another. The relationship may be expressed either as a percentage, a rate, or a simple proportion.

Ratio analysis A technique for evaluating financial statements that expresses the relationship between selected financial statement data.

Return on assets An overall measure of profitability; computed by dividing net income by average total assets.

Return on common stockholders' equity Measures the dollars of net income earned for each dollar invested by the owners; computed by dividing net income minus preferred dividends (if any) by average common stockholders' equity.

Solvency ratios Measures of the ability of the company to survive over a long period of time.

Sustainable income The most likely level of income to be obtained by a company in the future.

Times interest earned Measures a company's ability to meet interest payments as they come due; computed by dividing the sum of net income, interest expense, and income tax expense by interest expense.

Trading on the equity Borrowing money at a lower rate of interest than can be earned by using the borrowed money.

Vertical analysis A technique for evaluating financial statement data that expresses each item within a financial statement as a percentage of a base amount.

PRACTICE EXERCISES

Prepare horizontal and vertical analysis.

(LO 1)

1. The comparative condensed balance sheets of Roadway Corporation are presented below.

ROADWAY CORPORATION
Condensed Balance Sheets
December 31

	2017	2016
Assets		
Current assets	$ 76,000	$ 80,000
Property, plant, and equipment (net)	99,000	90,000
Intangibles	25,000	40,000
Total assets	$200,000	$210,000
Liabilities and stockholders' equity		
Current liabilities	$ 40,800	$ 48,000
Long-term liabilities	143,000	150,000
Stockholders' equity	16,200	12,000
Total liabilities and stockholders' equity	$200,000	$210,000

Instructions

(a) Prepare a horizontal analysis of the balance sheet data for Roadway Corporation using 2016 as a base.

(b) Prepare a vertical analysis of the balance sheet data for Roadway Corporation in columnar form for 2017.

Solution

1. (a)

ROADWAY CORPORATION
Condensed Balance Sheets
December 31

	2017	2016	Increase (Decrease)	Percent Change From 2016
Assets				
Current assets	$ 76,000	$ 80,000	$ (4,000)	(5.0%)
Property, plant, and equipment (net)	99,000	90,000	9,000	10.0%
Intangibles	25,000	40,000	(15,000)	(37.5%)
Total assets	$200,000	$210,000	$(10,000)	(4.8%)
Liabilities and stockholders' equity				
Current liabilities	$ 40,800	$ 48,000	$ (7,200)	(15.0%)
Long-term liabilities	143,000	150,000	(7,000)	(4.7%)
Stockholders' equity	16,200	12,000	4,200	35.0%
Total liabilities and stockholders' equity	$200,000	$210,000	$(10,000)	(4.8%)

(b)

ROADWAY CORPORATION
Condensed Balance Sheet
December 31, 2017

	Amount	Percent
Assets		
Current assets	$ 76,000	38.0%
Property, plant, and equipment (net)	99,000	49.5%
Intangibles	25,000	12.5%
Total assets	$200,000	100.0%
Liabilities and stockholders' equity		
Current liabilities	$ 40,800	20.4%
Long-term liabilities	143,000	71.5%
Stockholders' equity	16,200	8.1%
Total liabilities and stockholders' equity	$200,000	100.0%

2. Rondo Corporation's comparative balance sheets are presented below.

Compute ratios.

(LO 2)

RONDO CORPORATION
Balance Sheets
December 31

	2017	2016
Cash	$ 5,300	$ 3,700
Accounts receivable	21,200	23,400
Inventory	9,000	7,000
Land	20,000	26,000
Buildings	70,000	70,000
Accumulated depreciation—buildings	(15,000)	(10,000)
Total	$110,500	$120,100
Accounts payable	$ 10,370	$ 31,100
Common stock	75,000	69,000
Retained earnings	25,130	20,000
Total	$110,500	$120,100

Rondo's 2017 income statement included net sales of $120,000, cost of goods sold of $70,000, and net income of $14,000.

Instructions

Compute the following ratios for 2017.

(a) Current ratio.
(b) Acid-test ratio.
(c) Accounts receivable turnover.
(d) Inventory turnover.
(e) Profit margin.
(f) Asset turnover.
(g) Return on assets.
(h) Return on common stockholders' equity.
(i) Debt to assets ratio.

Solution

2. (a) ($5,300 + $21,200 + $9,000)/$10,370 = 3.42
(b) ($5,300 + $21,200)/$10,370 = 2.56
(c) $120,000/[($21,200 + $23,400)/2] = 5.38
(d) $70,000/[($9,000 + $7,000)/2] = 8.8
(e) $14,000/$120,000 = 11.7%
(f) $120,000/[($110,500 + $120,100)/2] = 1.04
(g) $14,000/[($110,500 + $120,100)/2] = 12.1%
(h) $14,000/[($100,130 + $89,000)/2] = 14.8%
(i) $10,370/$110,500 = 9.4%

PRACTICE PROBLEM

Prepare a statement of comprehensive income.

(LO 3)

The events and transactions of Dever Corporation for the year ending December 31, 2017, resulted in the following data.

Cost of goods sold	$2,600,000
Net sales	4,400,000
Other expenses and losses	9,600
Other revenues and gains	5,600
Selling and administrative expenses	1,100,000
Income from operations of plastics division	70,000
Gain from disposal of plastics division	500,000
Unrealized loss on available-for-sale securities	60,000

Analysis reveals the following:

1. All items are before the applicable income tax rate of 30%.
2. The plastics division was sold on July 1.
3. All operating data for the plastics division have been segregated.

Instructions

Prepare a statement of comprehensive income for the year.

Solution

DEVER CORPORATION
Statement of Comprehensive Income
For the Year Ended December 31, 2017

Net sales		$4,400,000
Cost of goods sold		2,600,000
Gross profit		1,800,000
Selling and administrative expenses		1,100,000
Income from operations		700,000
Other revenues and gains		5,600
Other expenses and losses		9,600
Income before income taxes		696,000
Income tax expense ($696,000 × 30%)		208,800
Income from continuing operations		487,200
Discontinued operations		
Income from operation of plastics division, net of $21,000 income taxes ($70,000 × 30%)	49,000	
Gain from disposal of plastics division, net of $150,000 income taxes ($500,000 × 30%)	350,000	399,000
Net income		886,200
Unrealized loss on available-for-sale securities, net of $18,000 income tax savings ($60,000 × 30%)		42,000
Comprehensive income		$ 844,200

EXERCISES

Follow the rounding procedures used in the chapter.

Prepare horizontal analysis.

(LO 1)

E18-1 Financial information for Kurzen Inc. is presented below.

	December 31, 2017	December 31, 2016
Current assets	$125,000	$100,000
Plant assets (net)	396,000	330,000
Current liabilities	91,000	70,000
Long-term liabilities	133,000	95,000
Common stock, $1 par	161,000	115,000
Retained earnings	136,000	150,000

Instructions
Prepare a schedule showing a horizontal analysis for 2017 using 2016 as the base year.

E18-2 Operating data for Navarro Corporation are presented below.

Prepare vertical analysis.
(LO 1)

	2017	2016
Net sales	$750,000	$600,000
Cost of goods sold	465,000	390,000
Selling expenses	105,000	66,000
Administrative expenses	60,000	54,000
Income tax expense	36,000	27,000
Net income	84,000	63,000

Instructions
Prepare a schedule showing a vertical analysis for 2017 and 2016.

E18-3 The comparative condensed balance sheets of Gurley Corporation are presented below.

Prepare horizontal and vertical analyses.
(LO 1)

GURLEY CORPORATION
Comparative Condensed Balance Sheets
December 31

	2017	2016
Assets		
Current assets	$ 74,000	$ 80,000
Property, plant, and equipment (net)	99,000	90,000
Intangibles	27,000	40,000
Total assets	$200,000	$210,000
Liabilities and stockholders' equity		
Current liabilities	$ 42,000	$ 48,000
Long-term liabilities	143,000	150,000
Stockholders' equity	15,000	12,000
Total liabilities and stockholders' equity	$200,000	$210,000

Instructions
(a) Prepare a horizontal analysis of the balance sheet data for Gurley Corporation using 2016 as a base.
(b) Prepare a vertical analysis of the balance sheet data for Gurley Corporation in columnar form for 2017.

E18-4 The comparative condensed income statements of Emley Corporation are shown below.

Prepare horizontal and vertical analyses.
(LO 1)

EMLEY CORPORATION
Comparative Condensed Income Statements
For the Years Ended December 31

	2017	2016
Net sales	$660,000	$600,000
Cost of goods sold	483,000	420,000
Gross profit	177,000	180,000
Operating expenses	125,000	120,000
Net income	$ 52,000	$ 60,000

Instructions

(a) Prepare a horizontal analysis of the income statement data for Emley Corporation using 2016 as a base. (Show the amounts of increase or decrease.)
(b) Prepare a vertical analysis of the income statement data for Emley Corporation in columnar form for both years.

Compute liquidity ratios and compare results.
(LO 2)

E18-5 Suppose Nordstrom, Inc., which operates department stores in numerous states, has the following selected financial statement data for a recent year.

NORDSTROM, INC.
Balance Sheet (partial)

(in millions)	End-of-Year	Beginning-of-Year
Cash and cash equivalents	$ 795	$ 72
Accounts receivable (net)	2,035	1,942
Inventory	898	900
Prepaid expenses	88	93
Other current assets	238	210
Total current assets	$4,054	$3,217
Total current liabilities	$2,014	$1,601

For the year, net sales were $8,258 and cost of goods sold was $5,328 (in millions).

Instructions

(a) Compute the four liquidity ratios at the end of the year.
(b) Using the data in the chapter, compare Nordstrom's liquidity with (1) that of Macy's, Inc., and (2) the industry averages for department stores.

Perform current and acid-test ratio analysis.
(LO 2)

E18-6 Keener Incorporated had the following transactions occur involving current assets and current liabilities during February 2017.

Feb. 3 Accounts receivable of $15,000 are collected.
7 Equipment is purchased for $28,000 cash.
11 Paid $3,000 for a 3-year insurance policy.
14 Accounts payable of $12,000 are paid.
18 Cash dividends of $5,000 are declared.

Additional information:

1. As of February 1, 2017, current assets were $110,000, and current liabilities were $50,000.
2. As of February 1, 2017, current assets included $15,000 of inventory and $2,000 of prepaid expenses.

Instructions

(a) Compute the current ratio as of the beginning of the month and after each transaction.
(b) Compute the acid-test ratio as of the beginning of the month and after each transaction.

Compute selected ratios.
(LO 2)

E18-7 Frizell Company has the following comparative balance sheet data.

FRIZELL COMPANY
Balance Sheets
December 31

	2017	2016
Cash	$ 15,000	$ 30,000
Accounts receivable (net)	70,000	60,000
Inventory	60,000	50,000
Plant assets (net)	200,000	180,000
	$345,000	$320,000
Accounts payable	$ 50,000	$ 60,000
Mortgage payable (6%)	100,000	100,000
Common stock, $10 par	140,000	120,000
Retained earnings	55,000	40,000
	$345,000	$320,000

Additional information for 2017:

1. Net income was $25,000.
2. Sales on account were $410,000. Sales returns and allowances were $20,000.
3. Cost of goods sold was $198,000.

Instructions

Compute the following ratios at December 31, 2017.

(a) Current ratio.
(b) Acid-test ratio.
(c) Accounts receivable turnover.
(d) Inventory turnover.

E18-8 Selected comparative statement data for Queen Products Company are presented below. All balance sheet data are as of December 31.

Compute selected ratios.

(LO 2)

	2017	2016
Net sales	$750,000	$720,000
Cost of goods sold	480,000	440,000
Interest expense	7,000	5,000
Net income	45,000	42,000
Accounts receivable	120,000	100,000
Inventory	85,000	75,000
Total assets	580,000	500,000
Total common stockholders' equity	430,000	325,000

Instructions

Compute the following ratios for 2017.

(a) Profit margin.
(b) Asset turnover.
(c) Return on assets.
(d) Return on common stockholders' equity.

E18-9 The income statement for Sutherland, Inc., appears below.

Compute selected ratios.

(LO 2)

SUTHERLAND, INC.
Income Statement
For the Year Ended December 31, 2017

Net sales	$400,000
Cost of goods sold	230,000
Gross profit	170,000
Expenses (including $16,000 interest and $24,000 income taxes)	105,000
Net income	$ 65,000

Additional information:

1. The weighted-average common shares outstanding in 2017 were 30,000 shares.
2. The market price of Sutherland, Inc. stock was $13 in 2017.
3. Cash dividends of $26,000 were paid, $5,000 of which were to preferred stockholders.

Instructions

Compute the following ratios for 2017.

(a) Earnings per share.
(b) Price-earnings ratio.
(c) Payout ratio.
(d) Times interest earned.

E18-10 Lingenfelter Corporation experienced a fire on December 31, 2017, in which its financial records were partially destroyed. It has been able to salvage some of the records and has ascertained the following balances.

Compute amounts from ratios.

(LO 2)

	December 31, 2017	December 31, 2016
Cash	$ 30,000	$ 10,000
Accounts receivable (net)	72,500	126,000
Inventory	200,000	180,000
Accounts payable	50,000	90,000
Notes payable	30,000	60,000
Common stock, $100 par	400,000	400,000
Retained earnings	113,500	101,000

Additional information:

1. The inventory turnover is 4.5 times.
2. The return on common stockholders' equity is 16%. The company had no additional paid-in capital.
3. The accounts receivable turnover is 8.8 times.
4. The return on assets is 12.5%.
5. Total assets at December 31, 2016, were $655,000.

Instructions

Compute the following for Lingenfelter Corporation.

(a) Cost of goods sold for 2017.
(b) Net sales (credit) for 2017.
(c) Net income for 2017.
(d) Total assets at December 31, 2017.

Compute ratios.

(LO 2)

E18-11 Wiemers Corporation's comparative balance sheets are presented below.

WIEMERS CORPORATION
Balance Sheets
December 31

	2017	2016
Cash	$ 4,300	$ 3,700
Accounts receivable (net)	21,200	23,400
Inventory	10,000	7,000
Land	20,000	26,000
Buildings	70,000	70,000
Accumulated depreciation—buildings	(15,000)	(10,000)
Total	$110,500	$120,100
Accounts payable	$ 12,370	$ 31,100
Common stock	75,000	69,000
Retained earnings	23,130	20,000
Total	$110,500	$120,100

Wiemers's 2017 income statement included net sales of $100,000, cost of goods sold of $60,000, and net income of $15,000.

Instructions

Compute the following ratios for 2017.

(a) Current ratio.
(b) Acid-test ratio.
(c) Accounts receivable turnover.
(d) Inventory turnover.
(e) Profit margin.
(f) Asset turnover.
(g) Return on assets.
(h) Return on common stockholders' equity.
(i) Debt to assets ratio.

Prepare a correct statement of comprehensive income.

(LO 3)

E18-12 For its fiscal year ending October 31, 2017, Haas Corporation reports the following partial data shown below.

Income before income taxes	$540,000
Income tax expense (20% × $420,000)	84,000
Income from continuing operations	456,000
Loss on discontinued operations	120,000
Net income	$336,000

The loss on discontinued operations comprised a $50,000 loss from operations and a $70,000 loss from disposal. The income tax rate is 20% on all items.

Instructions

(a) Prepare a correct statement of comprehensive income beginning with income before income taxes.
(b) Explain in memo form why the income statement data are misleading.

Prepare statement of comprehensive income.

(LO 3)

E18-13 Trayer Corporation has income from continuing operations of $290,000 for the year ended December 31, 2017. It also has the following items (before considering income taxes).

1. An unrealized loss of $80,000 on available-for-sale securities.
2. A gain of $30,000 on the discontinuance of a division (comprising a $10,000 loss from operations and a $40,000 gain on disposal).
3. A correction of an error in last year's financial statements that resulted in a $20,000 understatement of 2016 net income.

Assume all items are subject to income taxes at a 20% tax rate.

Instructions
Prepare a statement of comprehensive income, beginning with income from continuing operations.

PROBLEMS

Follow the rounding procedures used in the chapter.

P18-1 Comparative statement data for Farris Company and Ratzlaff Company, two competitors, appear below. All balance sheet data are as of December 31, 2017, and December 31, 2016.

Prepare vertical analysis and comment on profitability.

(LO 1, 2)

	Farris Company		Ratzlaff Company	
	2017	**2016**	**2017**	**2016**
Net sales	$1,549,035		$339,038	
Cost of goods sold	1,080,490		241,000	
Operating expenses	302,275		79,000	
Interest expense	8,980		2,252	
Income tax expense	54,500		6,650	
Current assets	325,975	$312,410	83,336	$ 79,467
Plant assets (net)	521,310	500,000	139,728	125,812
Current liabilities	65,325	75,815	35,348	30,281
Long-term liabilities	108,500	90,000	29,620	25,000
Common stock, $10 par	500,000	500,000	120,000	120,000
Retained earnings	173,460	146,595	38,096	29,998

Instructions
(a) Prepare a vertical analysis of the 2017 income statement data for Farris Company and Ratzlaff Company in columnar form.
(b) Comment on the relative profitability of the companies by computing the return on assets and the return on common stockholders' equity for both companies.

P18-2 The comparative statements of Painter Tool Company are presented below and on page 654.

Compute ratios from balance sheet and income statement.

(LO 2)

PAINTER TOOL COMPANY
Income Statement
For the Years Ended December 31

	2017	2016
Net sales	$1,818,500	$1,750,500
Cost of goods sold	1,011,500	996,000
Gross profit	807,000	754,500
Selling and administrative expenses	499,000	479,000
Income from operations	308,000	275,500
Other expenses and losses		
Interest expense	18,000	14,000
Income before income taxes	290,000	261,500
Income tax expense	87,000	77,000
Net income	$ 203,000	$ 184,500

PAINTER TOOL COMPANY
Balance Sheets
December 31

Assets	**2017**	**2016**
Current assets		
Cash	$ 60,100	$ 64,200
Short-term investments	69,000	50,000
Accounts receivable (net)	107,800	102,800
Inventory	133,000	115,500
Total current assets	369,900	332,500
Plant assets (net)	600,300	520,300
Total assets	$970,200	$852,800
Liabilities and Stockholders' Equity		
Current liabilities		
Accounts payable	$160,000	$145,400
Income taxes payable	43,500	42,000
Total current liabilities	203,500	187,400
Bonds payable	200,000	200,000
Total liabilities	403,500	387,400
Stockholders' equity		
Common stock ($5 par)	280,000	300,000
Retained earnings	286,700	165,400
Total stockholders' equity	566,700	465,400
Total liabilities and stockholders' equity	$970,200	$852,800

All sales were on account.

Instructions

Compute the following ratios for 2017. (Weighted-average common shares in 2017 were 57,000.)

(a) Earnings per share.
(b) Return on common stockholders' equity.
(c) Return on assets.
(d) Current ratio.
(e) Acid-test ratio.
(f) Accounts receivable turnover.
(g) Inventory turnover.
(h) Times interest earned.
(i) Asset turnover.
(j) Debt to assets ratio.

Perform ratio analysis, and evaluate financial position and operating results.

(LO 2)

P18-3 Condensed balance sheet and income statement data for Landwehr Corporation appear below and on page 655.

LANDWEHR CORPORATION
Balance Sheets
December 31

	2018	**2017**	**2016**
Cash	$ 25,000	$ 20,000	$ 18,000
Accounts receivable (net)	50,000	45,000	48,000
Other current assets	90,000	95,000	64,000
Investments	75,000	70,000	45,000
Plant and equipment (net)	400,000	370,000	358,000
	$640,000	$600,000	$533,000
Current liabilities	$ 75,000	$ 80,000	$ 70,000
Long-term debt	80,000	85,000	50,000
Common stock, $10 par	340,000	310,000	300,000
Retained earnings	145,000	125,000	113,000
	$640,000	$600,000	$533,000

LANDWEHR CORPORATION
Income Statement
For the Years Ended December 31

	2018	2017
Sales revenue	$740,000	$700,000
Less: Sales returns and allowances	40,000	50,000
Net sales	700,000	650,000
Cost of goods sold	420,000	400,000
Gross profit	280,000	250,000
Operating expenses (including income taxes)	235,000	220,000
Net income	$ 45,000	$ 30,000

Additional information:

1. The market price of Landwehr's common stock was $4.00, $5.00, and $8.00 for 2016, 2017, and 2018, respectively.
2. All dividends were paid in cash.

Instructions

(a) Compute the following ratios for 2017 and 2018.
  (1) Profit margin.
  (2) Asset turnover.
  (3) Earnings per share. (Weighted-average common shares in 2018 were 32,000 and in 2017 were 31,000.)
  (4) Price-earnings ratio.
  (5) Payout ratio.
  (6) Debt to assets ratio.

(b) Based on the ratios calculated, discuss briefly the improvement or lack thereof in financial position and operating results from 2017 to 2018 of Landwehr Corporation.

P18-4 Financial information for Messersmith Company is presented below and on page 656.

Compute ratios, and comment on overall liquidity and profitability.

(LO 2)

MESSERSMITH COMPANY
Balance Sheets
December 31

Assets	2017	2016
Cash	$ 70,000	$ 65,000
Short-term investments	52,000	40,000
Accounts receivable (net)	98,000	80,000
Inventory	125,000	135,000
Prepaid expenses	29,000	23,000
Land	130,000	130,000
Building and equipment (net)	180,000	175,000
	$684,000	$648,000

Liabilities and Stockholders' Equity		
Notes payable	$100,000	$100,000
Accounts payable	48,000	42,000
Accrued liabilities	50,000	40,000
Bonds payable, due 2020	150,000	150,000
Common stock, $10 par	200,000	200,000
Retained earnings	136,000	116,000
	$684,000	$648,000

MESSERSMITH COMPANY
Income Statement
For the Years Ended December 31

	2017	2016
Net sales	$850,000	$790,000
Cost of goods sold	620,000	575,000
Gross profit	230,000	215,000
Operating expenses	187,000	173,000
Net income	$ 43,000	$ 42,000

Additional information:

1. Inventory at the beginning of 2016 was $118,000.
2. Total assets at the beginning of 2016 were $630,000.
3. No common stock transactions occurred during 2016 or 2017.
4. All sales were on account. Accounts receivable, net at the beginning of 2016, were $88,000.
5. Notes payable are classified as current liabilities.

Instructions

(a) Indicate, by using ratios, the change in liquidity and profitability of Messersmith Company from 2016 to 2017. (*Note:* Not all profitability ratios can be computed.)

(b) Given below are three independent situations and a ratio that may be affected. For each situation, compute the affected ratio (1) as of December 31, 2017, and (2) as of December 31, 2018, after giving effect to the situation. Net income for 2018 was $50,000. Total assets on December 31, 2018, were $700,000.

Situation	Ratio
(1) 18,000 shares of common stock were sold at par on July 1, 2018.	Return on common stockholders' equity
(2) All of the notes payable were paid in 2018. The only change in liabilities was that the notes payable were paid.	Debt to assets ratio
(3) Market price of common stock was $9 on December 31, 2017, and $12.80 on December 31, 2018.	Price-earnings ratio

Compute selected ratios, and compare liquidity, profitability, and solvency for two companies.

(LO 2)

P18-5 Selected financial data of **Target Corporation** and **Wal-Mart Stores, Inc.** for a recent year are presented here (in millions).

	Target Corporation	Wal-Mart Stores, Inc.
	Income Statement Data for Year	
Net sales	$61,471	$374,526
Cost of goods sold	41,895	286,515
Selling and administrative expenses	16,200	70,847
Interest expense	647	1,798
Other income (expense)	1,896	4,273
Income tax expense	1,776	6,908
Net income	$ 2,849	$ 12,731
	Balance Sheet Data (End of Year)	
Current assets	$18,906	$ 47,585
Noncurrent assets	25,654	115,929
Total assets	$44,560	$163,514
Current liabilities	$11,782	$ 58,454
Long-term debt	17,471	40,452
Total stockholders' equity	15,307	64,608
Total liabilities and stockholders' equity	$44,560	$163,514

	Target Corporation	Wal-Mart Stores, Inc.
	Beginning-of-Year Balances	
Total assets	$37,349	$151,587
Total stockholders' equity	15,633	61,573
Current liabilities	11,117	52,148
Total liabilities	21,716	90,014
	Other Data	
Average net accounts receivable	$ 7,124	$ 3,247
Average inventory	6,517	34,433
Net cash provided by operating activities	4,125	20,354

Instructions

(a) For each company, compute the following ratios.

(1) Current ratio.
(2) Accounts receivable turnover.
(3) Average collection period.
(4) Inventory turnover.
(5) Days in inventory.
(6) Profit margin.
(7) Asset turnover.
(8) Return on assets.
(9) Return on common stockholders' equity.
(10) Debt to assets ratio.
(11) Times interest earned.

(b) Compare the liquidity, profitability, and solvency of the two companies.

P18-6 The comparative statements of Corbin Company are presented below and on page 658.

Compute numerous ratios.

(LO 2)

CORBIN COMPANY
Income Statement
For the Years Ended December 31

	2017	2016
Net sales (all on account)	$595,000	$520,000
Expenses		
Cost of goods sold	415,000	354,000
Selling and administrative	120,800	114,800
Interest expense	7,800	6,000
Income tax expense	15,000	14,000
Total expenses	558,600	488,800
Net income	$ 36,400	$ 31,200

CORBIN COMPANY
Balance Sheets
December 31

Assets	2017	2016
Current assets		
Cash	$ 21,000	$ 18,000
Short-term investments	18,000	15,000
Accounts receivable (net)	91,000	74,000
Inventory	85,000	70,000
Total current assets	215,000	177,000
Plant assets (net)	423,000	383,000
Total assets	$638,000	$560,000

Liabilities and Stockholders' Equity	2017	2016
Current liabilities		
Accounts payable	$122,000	$110,000
Income taxes payable	23,000	20,000
Total current liabilities	145,000	130,000
Long-term liabilities		
Bonds payable	120,000	80,000
Total liabilities	265,000	210,000
Stockholders' equity		
Common stock ($5 par)	150,000	150,000
Retained earnings	223,000	200,000
Total stockholders' equity	373,000	350,000
Total liabilities and stockholders' equity	$638,000	$560,000

Additional data:

The common stock recently sold at $19.50 per share.

Instructions

Compute the following ratios for 2017.

(a) Current ratio.
(b) Acid-test ratio.
(c) Accounts receivable turnover.
(d) Inventory turnover.
(e) Profit margin.
(f) Asset turnover.
(g) Return on assets.
(h) Return on common stockholders' equity.
(i) Earnings per share.
(j) Price-earnings ratio.
(k) Payout ratio.
(l) Debt to assets ratio.
(m) Times interest earned.

Compute missing information given a set of ratios.

(LO 2)

P18-7 An incomplete income statement and an incomplete comparative balance sheet of Deines Corporation are presented below and on page 659.

DEINES CORPORATION
Income Statement
For the Year Ended December 31, 2017

Net sales	$11,000,000
Cost of goods sold	?
Gross profit	?
Operating expenses	1,665,000
Income from operations	?
Other expenses and losses	
Interest expense	?
Income before income taxes	?
Income tax expense	560,000
Net income	$?

DEINES CORPORATION
Balance Sheets
December 31

Assets	2017	2016
Current assets		
Cash	$ 450,000	$ 375,000
Accounts receivable (net)	?	950,000
Inventory	?	1,720,000
Total current assets	?	3,045,000
Plant assets (net)	4,620,000	3,955,000
Total assets	$?	$7,000,000

Liabilities and Stockholders' Equity	2017	2016
Current liabilities	$?	$ 825,000
Long-term notes payable	?	2,800,000
Total liabilities	?	3,625,000
Common stock, $1 par	3,000,000	3,000,000
Retained earnings	400,000	375,000
Total stockholders' equity	3,400,000	3,375,000
Total liabilities and stockholders' equity	$?	$7,000,000

Additional information:

1. The accounts receivable turnover for 2017 is 10 times.
2. All sales are on account.
3. The profit margin for 2017 is 14.5%.
4. Return on assets is 22% for 2017.
5. The current ratio on December 31, 2017, is 3.0.
6. The inventory turnover for 2017 is 4.8 times.

Instructions

Compute the missing information given the ratios above. Show computations. (*Note:* Start with one ratio and derive as much information as possible from it before trying another ratio. List all missing amounts under the ratio used to find the information.)

P18-8 Terwilliger Corporation owns a number of cruise ships and a chain of hotels. The hotels, which have not been profitable, were discontinued on September 1, 2017. The 2017 operating results for the company were as follows.

Prepare a statement of comprehensive income.

(LO 3)

Operating revenues	$12,850,000
Operating expenses	8,700,000
Operating income	$ 4,150,000

Analysis discloses that these data include the operating results of the hotel chain, which were operating revenues $1,500,000 and operating expenses $2,400,000. The hotels were sold at a gain of $200,000 before taxes. This gain is not included in the operating results. During the year, Terwilliger had an unrealized loss on its available-for-sale securities of $600,000 before taxes, which is not included in the operating results. In 2017, the company had other revenues and gains of $100,000, which are not included in the operating results. The corporation is in the 30% income tax bracket.

Instructions

Prepare a statement of comprehensive income.

P18-9 The ledger of Jaime Corporation at December 31, 2017, contains the following summary data.

Prepare a statement of comprehensive income.

(LO 3)

Net sales	$1,700,000	Cost of goods sold	$1,100,000
Selling expenses	120,000	Administrative expenses	150,000
Other revenues and gains	20,000	Other expenses and losses	28,000

Your analysis reveals the following additional information that is not included in the above data.

1. The entire Puzzles Division was discontinued on August 31. The income from operation for this division before income taxes was $20,000. The Puzzles Division was sold at a loss of $90,000 before income taxes.
2. The company had an unrealized gain on available-for-sale securities of $120,000 before income taxes for the year.
3. The income tax rate on all items is 25%.

Instructions

Prepare a statement of comprehensive income for the year ended December 31, 2017.

BROADENING YOUR PERSPECTIVE

FINANCIAL REPORTING AND ANALYSIS

Financial Reporting Problem: Apple Inc.

BYP18-1 Your parents are considering investing in **Apple Inc.** common stock. They ask you, as an accounting expert, to make an analysis of the company for them. Apple's financial statements are presented in Appendix A. Instructions for accessing and using the company's complete annual report, including the notes to the financial statements, are also provided in Appendix A.

Instructions

(Follow the approach in the chapter for rounding numbers.)

(a) Make a 3-year trend analysis, using 2011 as the base year, of (1) net sales and (2) net income. Comment on the significance of the trend results.

(b) Compute for 2013 and 2012 the (1) profit margin, (2) asset turnover, (3) return on assets, and (4) return on common stockholders' equity. How would you evaluate Apple's profitability? Total assets at September 24, 2011, were \$116,371 and total stockholders' equity at September 24, 2011, was \$76,615.

(c) Compute for 2013 and 2012 the (1) debt to assets ratio and (2) times interest earned. How would you evaluate Apple's long-term solvency?

(d) What information outside the annual report may also be useful to your parents in making a decision about Apple?

Comparative Analysis Problem: PepsiCo, Inc. vs. The Coca-Cola Company

BYP18-2 PepsiCo's financial statements are presented in Appendix B. Financial statements of **The Coca-Cola Company** are presented in Appendix C. Instructions for accessing and using the complete annual reports of PepsiCo and Coca-Cola, including the notes to the financial statements, are also provided in Appendices B and C, respectively.

Instructions

(a) Based on the information contained in these financial statements, determine each of the following for each company.
   (1) The percentage increase (decrease) in (i) net sales and (ii) net income from 2012 to 2013.
   (2) The percentage increase in (i) total assets and (ii) total common stockholders' (shareholders') equity from 2012 to 2013.
   (3) The basic earnings per share and price-earnings ratio for 2013. (For both PepsiCo and Coca-Cola, use the basic earnings per share.) Coca-Cola's common stock had a market price of \$41.31 at the end of fiscal-year 2013, and PepsiCo's common stock had a market price of \$82.71.

(b) What conclusions concerning the two companies can be drawn from these data?

Comparative Analysis Problem: Amazon.com, Inc. vs. Wal-Mart Stores, Inc.

BYP18-3 Amazon.com, Inc.'s financial statements are presented in Appendix D. Financial statements of **Wal-Mart Stores, Inc.** are presented in Appendix E. Instructions for accessing and using the complete annual reports of Amazon and Wal-Mart, including the notes to be financial statements, are also provided in Appendices D and E, respectively.

Instructions

(a) Based on the information contained in these financial statements, determine each of the following for each company.
   (1) The percentage increase (decrease) in (i) net sales and (ii) net income from 2012 to 2013.
   (2) The percentage increase in (i) total assets and (ii) total common stockholders' (shareholders') equity from 2012 to 2013.
   (3) The basic earnings per share and price-earnings ratio for 2013. (For both Amazon and Wal-Mart, use the basic earnings per share.) Amazon's common stock had a market price of \$398.79 at the end of fiscal-year 2013, and Wal-Mart's common stock had a market price of \$74.68.

(b) What conclusions concerning the two companies can be drawn from these data?

Decision-Making Across the Organization

BYP18-4 As the CPA for Gandara Manufacturing Inc., you have been asked to develop some key ratios from the comparative financial statements. This information is to be used to convince creditors that the company is solvent and will continue as a going concern. The data requested and the computations developed from the financial statements follow.

	2017	2016
Current ratio	3.1 times	2.1 times
Acid-test ratio	.8 times	1.4 times
Asset turnover	2.8 times	2.2 times
Net income	Up 32%	Down 8%
Earnings per share	$3.30	$2.50

Instructions

With the class divided into groups, complete the following.

Gandara Manufacturing Inc. asks you to prepare a list of brief comments stating how each of these items supports the solvency and going-concern potential of the business. The company wishes to use these comments to support its presentation of data to its creditors. You are to prepare the comments as requested, giving the implications and the limitations of each item separately. Then prepare a collective inference that may be drawn from the individual items about Gandara's solvency and going-concern potential.

Real-World Focus

BYP18-5 The Management Discussion and Analysis section of an annual report addresses corporate performance for the year and sometimes uses financial ratios to support its claims.

Address: **www.ibm.com/investor/tools/index.phtml**, or go to **www.wiley.com/college/weygandt**

Steps

1. Choose **How to read annual reports** (in the Guides section).
2. Choose **Anatomy**.

Instructions

Using the information from the above site, answer the following questions.

(a) What are the optional elements that are often included in an annual report?
(b) What are the elements of an annual report that are required by the SEC?
(c) Describe the contents of the Management Discussion.
(d) Describe the contents of the Auditors' Report.
(e) Describe the contents of the Selected Financial Data.

CRITICAL THINKING

Communication Activity

BYP18-6 Abby Landis is the CEO of Pletcher's Electronics. Landis is an expert engineer but a novice in accounting. She asks you to explain the bases for comparison in analyzing Pletcher's financial statements.

Instructions

Write a letter to Abby Landis that explains the bases for comparison.

Ethics Case

BYP18-7 Dave Schonhardt, president of Schonhardt Industries, wishes to issue a press release to bolster his company's image and maybe even its stock price, which has been gradually falling. As controller, you have been asked to provide a list of 20 financial ratios along with some other operating statistics relative to Schonhardt Industries' first quarter financials and operations.

Two days after you provide the ratios and data requested, Steven Verlin, the public relations director of Schonhardt, asks you to prove the accuracy of the financial and operating data contained in the press release written by the president and edited by Steven. In the press release, the president highlights the sales increase of 25% over last year's first quarter and the positive change in the current ratio from 1.5:1 last year to 3:1 this year. He also emphasizes that production was up 50% over the prior year's first quarter.

You note that the press release contains only positive or improved ratios and none of the negative or deteriorated ratios. For instance, no mention is made that the debt to assets ratio has increased from 35% to 55%, that inventories are up 89%, and that while the current ratio improved, the acid-test ratio fell from 1:1 to 0.5:1. Nor is there any mention that the reported profit for the quarter would have been a loss had not the estimated lives of Schonhardt's plant and machinery been increased by 30%. Steven emphasizes, "The prez wants this release by early this afternoon."

Instructions

(a) Who are the stakeholders in this situation?
(b) Is there anything unethical in president Schonhardt's actions?
(c) Should you as controller remain silent? Does Steven have any responsibility?

All About You

BYP18-8 In this chapter, you learned how to use many tools for performing a financial analysis of a company. When making personal investments, however, it is most likely that you won't be buying stocks and bonds in individual companies. Instead, when most people want to invest in stock, they buy mutual funds. By investing in a mutual fund, you reduce your risk because the fund diversifies by buying the stock of a variety of different companies, bonds, and other investments, depending on the stated goals of the fund.

Before you invest in a fund, you will need to decide what type of fund you want. For example, do you want a fund that has the potential of high growth (but also high risk), or are you looking for lower risk and a steady stream of income? Do you want a fund that invests only in U.S. companies, or do you want one that invests globally? Many resources are available to help you with these types of decisions.

Instructions

Go to **http://web.archive.org/web/20050210200843/http://www.cnb1.com/invallocmdl.htm** and complete the investment allocation questionnaire. Add up your total points to determine the type of investment fund that would be appropriate for you.

FASB Codification Activity

BYP18-9 If your school has a subscription to the FASB Codification, go to **http://aaahq.org/ascLogin.cfm** to log in and prepare responses to the following. Use the Master Glossary for determining the proper definitions.

(a) Discontinued operations.
(b) Comprehensive income.

A Look at IFRS

LEARNING OBJECTIVE 4 **Compare financial statement analysis and income statement presentation under GAAP and IFRS.**

The tools of financial statement analysis, covered in the first section of this chapter, are the same throughout the world. Techniques such as vertical and horizontal analysis, for example, are tools used by analysts regardless of whether GAAP- or IFRS-related financial statements are being evaluated. In addition, the ratios provided in the textbook are the same ones that are used internationally.

The latter part of this chapter relates to the income statement and irregular items. As in GAAP, the income statement is a required statement under IFRS. In addition, the content and presentation of an IFRS income statement is similar to the one used for GAAP.

Relevant Facts

Following are the key similarities between GAAP and IFRS as related to financial statement analysis and income statement presentation. There are no significant differences between the two standards.

- The tools of financial statement analysis covered in this chapter are universal and therefore no significant differences exist in the analysis methods used.

- The basic objectives of the income statement are the same under both GAAP and IFRS. A very important objective is to ensure that users of the income statement can evaluate the sustainable income of the company.
- The basic accounting for discontinued operations is the same under IFRS and GAAP.
- The accounting for changes in accounting principles and changes in accounting estimates are the same for both GAAP and IFRS.
- Both GAAP and IFRS follow the same approach in reporting comprehensive income.

Looking to the Future

The FASB and the IASB are working on a project that would rework the structure of financial statements. Recently, the IASB decided to require a statement of comprehensive income, similar to what was required under GAAP.

IFRS Practice

IFRS Self-Test Questions

1. The basic tools of financial analysis are the same under both GAAP and IFRS **except** that:
   (a) horizontal analysis cannot be done because the format of the statements is sometimes different.
   (b) analysis is different because vertical analysis cannot be done under IFRS.
   (c) the current ratio cannot be computed because current liabilities are often reported before current assets in IFRS statements of position.
   (d) None of the above.
2. Presentation of comprehensive income must be reported under IFRS in:
   (a) the statement of stockholders' equity.
   (b) the income statement ending with net income.
   (c) the notes to the financial statements.
   (d) a statement of comprehensive income.
3. In preparing its income statement for 2017, Parmalane assembles the following information.

Sales revenue	$500,000
Cost of goods sold	300,000
Operating expenses	40,000
Loss on discontinued operations	20,000

   Ignoring income taxes, what is Parmalane's income from continuing operations for 2017 under IFRS?
   (a) $260,000.
   (b) $250,000
   (c) $240,000.
   (d) $160,000.

International Financial Reporting Problem: Louis Vuitton

IFRS18-1 The financial statements of **Louis Vuitton** are presented in Appendix F. Instructions for accessing and using the company's complete annual report, including the notes to its financial statements, are also provided in Appendix F.

Instructions
Use the company's **2013 annual report** to answer the following questions.

(a) What was the company's profit margin for 2013? Has it increased or decreased from 2011?
(b) What was the company's operating profit for 2013?
(c) The company reported comprehensive income of €4,255 billion in 2013. What are the other comprehensive gains and losses recorded in 2013?

Answers to IFRS Self-Test Questions
1. d **2.** d **3.** d

Chapter 19 Managerial Accounting

Mike Cichanowski grew up on the Mississippi River in Winona, Minnesota. At a young age, he learned to paddle a canoe so he could explore the river. Before long, Mike began crafting his own canoes from bent wood and fiberglass in his dad's garage. Then, when his canoe-making shop outgrew the garage, he moved it into an old warehouse. When that was going to be torn down, Mike came to a critical juncture in his life. He took out a bank loan and built his own small shop, giving birth to the company Wenonah Canoe.

Wenonah Canoe soon became known as a pioneer in developing techniques to get the most out of new materials such as plastics, composites, and carbon fibers—maximizing strength while minimizing weight.

In the 1990s, as kayaking became popular, Mike made another critical decision when he acquired Current Designs, a premier Canadian kayak manufacturer. This venture allowed Wenonah to branch out with new product lines while providing Current Designs with much-needed capacity expansion and manufacturing expertise. Mike moved Current Designs' headquarters to Minnesota and made a big (and potentially risky) investment in a new production facility. Today, the company's 90 employees produce about 12,000 canoes and kayaks per year. These are sold across the country and around the world.

Mike will tell you that business success is "a three-legged stool." The first leg is the knowledge and commitment to make a great product. Wenonah's canoes and Current Designs' kayaks are widely regarded as among the very best. The second leg is the ability to sell your product. Mike's company started off making great canoes, but it took a little longer to figure out how to sell them. The third leg is not something that most of you would immediately associate with entrepreneurial success. It is what goes on behind the scenes—accounting. Good accounting information is absolutely critical to the countless decisions, big and small, that ensure the survival and growth of the company.

Bottom line: No matter how good your product is, and no matter how many units you sell, if you don't have a firm grip on your numbers, you are up a creek without a paddle.

Source: www.wenonah.com.

LEARNING OBJECTIVES

1. **Identify the features of managerial accounting and the functions of management.**
2. **Describe the classes of manufacturing costs and the differences between product and period costs.**
3. **Demonstrate how to compute cost of goods manufactured and prepare financial statements for a manufacturer.**
4. **Discuss trends in managerial accounting.**

LEARNING OBJECTIVE 1

Identify the features of managerial accounting and the functions of management.

Managerial accounting provides economic and financial information for managers and other internal users. The skills that you learn in this course will be vital to your future success in business. You don't believe us? Let's look at some examples of some of the crucial activities of employees at **Current Designs** and where those activities are addressed in this textbook.

In order to know whether it is making a profit, Current Designs needs accurate information about the cost of each kayak (Chapters 20 and 21). To be profitable, Current Designs adjusts the number of kayaks it produces in response to changes in economic conditions and consumer tastes. It needs to understand how changes in the number of kayaks it produces impact its production costs and profitability (Chapter 22). Further, Current Designs' managers often consider alternative courses of action. For example, should the company accept a special order from a customer, produce a particular kayak component internally or outsource it, or continue or discontinue a particular product line (Chapter 26)?

In order to plan for the future, Current Designs prepares budgets (Chapter 23), and it then compares its budgeted numbers with its actual results to evaluate performance and identify areas that need to change (Chapters 24 and 25). Finally, it sometimes needs to make substantial investment decisions, such as the building of a new plant or the purchase of new equipment (Chapter 26).

Someday, you are going to face decisions just like these. You may end up in sales, marketing, management, production, or finance. You may work for a company that provides medical care, produces software, or serves up mouth-watering meals. No matter what your position is and no matter what your product, the skills you acquire in this class will increase your chances of business success. Put another way, in business you can either guess or you can make an informed decision. As a CEO of **Microsoft** once noted: "If you're supposed to be making money in business and supposed to be satisfying customers and building market share, there are numbers that characterize those things. And if somebody can't speak to me quantitatively about it, then I'm nervous." This course gives you the skills you need to quantify information so you can make informed business decisions.

Comparing Managerial and Financial Accounting

There are both similarities and differences between managerial and financial accounting. First, each field of accounting deals with the economic events of a business. For example, *determining* the unit cost of manufacturing a product is part of managerial accounting. *Reporting* the total cost of goods manufactured and sold is part of financial accounting. In addition, both managerial and financial accounting require that a company's economic events be quantified and communicated to interested parties. Illustration 19-1 (page 666) summarizes the principal differences between financial accounting and managerial accounting.

Management Functions

Managers' activities and responsibilities can be classified into three broad functions:

1. Planning
2. Directing
3. Controlling

Feature	Financial Accounting	Managerial Accounting
Primary Users of Reports	External users: stockholders, creditors, and regulators.	Internal users: officers and managers.
Types and Frequency of Reports	Financial statements. Quarterly and annually.	Internal reports. As frequently as needed.
Purpose of Reports	General-purpose.	Special-purpose for specific decisions.
Content of Reports	Pertains to business as a whole. Highly aggregated (condensed). Limited to double-entry accounting and cost data. Generally accepted accounting principles.	Pertains to subunits of the business. Very detailed. Extends beyond double-entry accounting to any relevant data. Standard is relevance to decisions.
Verification Process	Audited by CPA.	No independent audits.

Illustration 19-1
Differences between financial and managerial accounting

In performing these functions, managers make decisions that have a significant impact on the organization.

Planning requires managers to look ahead and to establish objectives. These objectives are often diverse: maximizing short-term profits and market share, maintaining a commitment to environmental protection, and contributing to social programs. For example, **Hewlett-Packard**, in an attempt to gain a stronger foothold in the computer industry, greatly reduced its prices to compete with **Dell**. A key objective of management is to **add value** to the business under its control. Value is usually measured by the price of the company's stock and by the potential selling price of the company.

Directing involves coordinating a company's diverse activities and human resources to produce a smooth-running operation. This function relates to implementing planned objectives and providing necessary incentives to motivate employees. For example, manufacturers such as **Campbell Soup Company**, **General Motors**, and **Dell** need to coordinate purchasing, manufacturing, warehousing, and selling. Service corporations such as **American Airlines**, **Federal Express**, and **AT&T** coordinate scheduling, sales, service, and acquisitions of equipment and supplies. Directing also involves selecting executives, appointing managers and supervisors, and hiring and training employees.

The third management function, **controlling**, is the process of keeping the company's activities on track. In controlling operations, managers determine whether planned goals are met. When there are deviations from targeted objectives, managers decide what changes are needed to get back on track. Scandals at companies like **Enron**, **Lucent**, and **Xerox** attest to the fact that companies need adequate controls to ensure that the company develops and distributes accurate information.

How do managers achieve control? A smart manager in a very small operation can make personal observations, ask good questions, and know how to evaluate the answers. But using this approach in a larger organization would result in chaos. Imagine the president of **Current Designs** attempting to determine whether the company is meeting its planned objectives without some record of what has happened and what is expected to occur. Thus, large businesses typically use a formal system of evaluation. These systems include such features as budgets, responsibility centers, and performance evaluation reports—all of which are features of managerial accounting.

Decision-making is not a separate management function. Rather, it is the outcome of the exercise of good judgment in planning, directing, and controlling.

Organizational Structure

Most companies prepare **organization charts** to show the interrelationships of activities and the delegation of authority and responsibility within the company. Illustration 19-2 shows a typical organization chart.

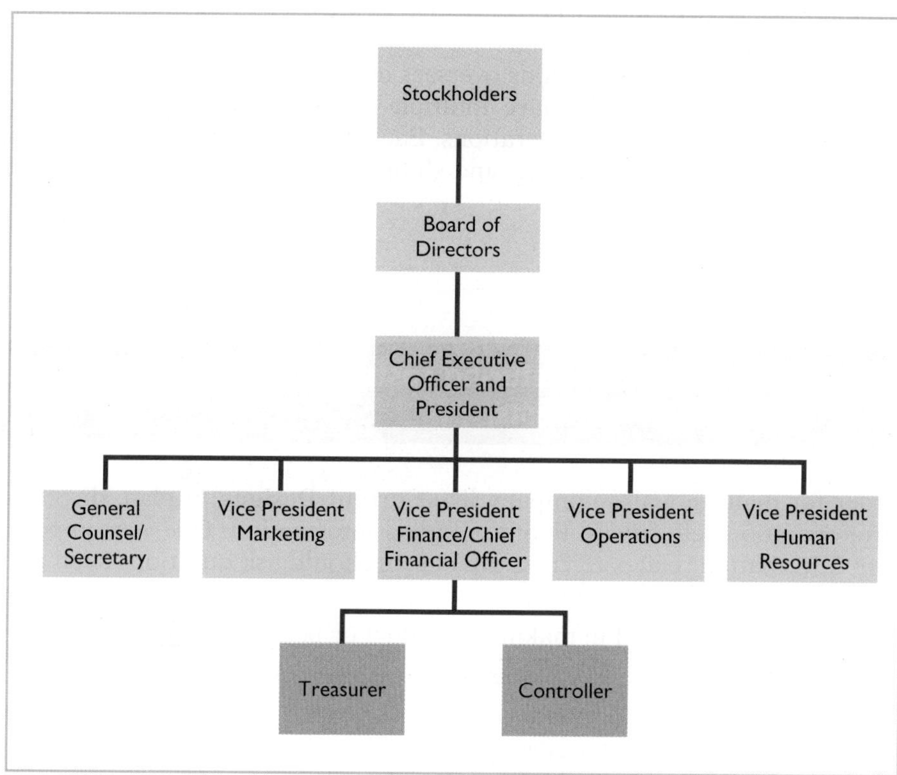

Illustration 19-2
A typical corporate organization chart

Stockholders own the corporation, but they manage it indirectly through a **board of directors** they elect. The board formulates the operating policies for the company or organization. The board also selects officers, such as a president and one or more vice presidents, to execute policy and to perform daily management functions.

The **chief executive officer (CEO)** has overall responsibility for managing the business. As the organization chart in Illustration 19-2 shows, the CEO delegates responsibilities to other officers.

Responsibilities within the company are frequently classified as either line or staff positions. Employees with **line positions** are directly involved in the company's primary revenue-generating operating activities. Examples of line positions include the vice president of operations, vice president of marketing, plant managers, supervisors, and production personnel. Employees with **staff positions** are involved in activities that support the efforts of the line employees. In a company like General Electric or Facebook, employees in finance, legal, and human resources have staff positions. While activities of staff employees are vital to the company, these employees are nonetheless there to serve the line employees who engage in the company's primary operations.

The **chief financial officer (CFO)** is responsible for all of the accounting and finance issues the company faces. The CFO is supported by the **controller** and the **treasurer**. The controller's responsibilities include (1) maintaining the accounting records, (2) ensuring an adequate system of internal control, and (3) preparing financial statements, tax returns, and internal reports. The treasurer has custody of the corporation's funds and is responsible for maintaining the company's cash position.

Also serving the CFO is the internal audit staff. The staff's responsibilities include reviewing the reliability and integrity of financial information provided by the controller and treasurer. Staff members also ensure that internal control systems are functioning properly to safeguard corporate assets. In addition, they investigate compliance with policies and regulations. In many companies, these staff members also determine whether resources are used in the most economical and efficient fashion.

The vice president of operations oversees employees with line positions. For example, the company might have multiple plant managers, each of whom reports to the vice president of operations. Each plant also has department managers, such as fabricating, painting, and shipping, each of whom reports to the plant manager.

LEARNING OBJECTIVE 2

Describe the classes of manufacturing costs and the differences between product and period costs.

In order for managers at a company like **Current Designs** to plan, direct, and control operations effectively, they need good information. One very important type of information relates to costs. Managers should ask questions such as the following.

1. What costs are involved in making a product or performing a service?
2. If we decrease production volume, will costs decrease?
3. What impact will automation have on total costs?
4. How can we best control costs?

To answer these questions, managers obtain and analyze reliable and relevant cost information. The first step is to understand the various cost categories that companies use.

Manufacturing Costs

Manufacturing consists of activities and processes that convert raw materials into finished goods. Contrast this type of operation with merchandising, which sells products in the form in which they are purchased. Manufacturing costs are classified as direct materials, direct labor, and manufacturing overhead.

DIRECT MATERIALS

To obtain the materials that will be converted into the finished product, the manufacturer purchases raw materials. **Raw materials** are the basic materials and parts used in the manufacturing process.

Direct Materials

Raw materials that can be physically and directly associated with the finished product during the manufacturing process are **direct materials**. Examples include flour in the baking of bread, syrup in the bottling of soft drinks, and steel in the making of automobiles. A primary direct material of many Current Designs' kayaks is polyethylene powder. Some of its high-performance kayaks use Kevlar®.

Some raw materials cannot be easily associated with the finished product. These are called indirect materials. **Indirect materials** have one of two characteristics. (1) They do not physically become part of the finished product (such as polishing compounds used by Current Designs for the finishing touches on kayaks). Or, (2) they are impractical to trace to the finished product because their physical association with the finished product is too small in terms of cost (such as cotter pins and lock washers). Companies account for indirect materials as part of **manufacturing overhead**.

DIRECT LABOR

The work of factory employees that can be physically and directly associated with converting raw materials into finished goods is **direct labor**. Bottlers at **Coca-Cola**, bakers at **Sara Lee**, and equipment operators at **Current Designs** are employees whose activities are usually classified as direct labor. **Indirect labor** refers to the work of employees that has no physical association with the finished product or for which it is impractical to trace costs to the goods produced. Examples include wages of factory maintenance people, factory time-keepers, and factory supervisors. Like indirect materials, companies classify indirect labor as **manufacturing overhead**.

Direct Labor

MANUFACTURING OVERHEAD

Manufacturing overhead consists of costs that are indirectly associated with the manufacture of the finished product. Overhead costs also include manufacturing costs that cannot be classified as direct materials or direct labor. Manufacturing overhead includes indirect materials, indirect labor, depreciation on factory buildings and machines, and insurance, taxes, and maintenance on factory facilities.

$ $
Manufacturing Overhead

One study of manufactured goods found the following magnitudes of the three different product costs as a percentage of the total product cost: direct materials 54%, direct labor 13%, and manufacturing overhead 33%. Note that the direct labor component is the smallest. This component of product cost is dropping substantially because of automation. Companies are working hard to increase productivity by decreasing labor. In some companies, direct labor has become as little as 5% of the total cost.

Terminology
Some companies use terms such as *factory overhead, indirect manufacturing costs*, and *burden* instead of manufacturing overhead.

Allocating direct materials and direct labor costs to specific products is fairly straightforward. Good recordkeeping can tell a company how much plastic it used in making each type of gear, or how many hours of factory labor it took to assemble a part. But allocating overhead costs to specific products presents problems. How much of the purchasing agent's salary is attributable to the hundreds of different products made in the same plant? What about the grease that keeps the machines humming, or the computers that make sure paychecks come out on time? Boiled down to its simplest form, the question becomes: Which products cause the incurrence of which costs? In subsequent chapters, we show various methods of allocating overhead to products.

Product Versus Period Costs

Each of the manufacturing cost components—direct materials, direct labor, and manufacturing overhead—are product costs. As the term suggests, **product costs** are costs that are a necessary and integral part of producing the finished product. Companies record product costs, when incurred, as inventory. These costs do not become expenses until the company sells the finished goods inventory. At that point, the company records the expense as cost of goods sold.

Terminology
Product costs are also called *inventoriable costs.*

Period costs are costs that are matched with the revenue of a specific time period rather than included as part of the cost of a salable product. These are nonmanufacturing costs. Period costs include selling and administrative expenses. In order to determine net income, companies deduct these costs from revenues in the period in which they are incurred.

Illustration 19-3 summarizes these relationships and cost terms. Our main concern in this chapter is with product costs.

Illustration 19-3
Product versus period costs

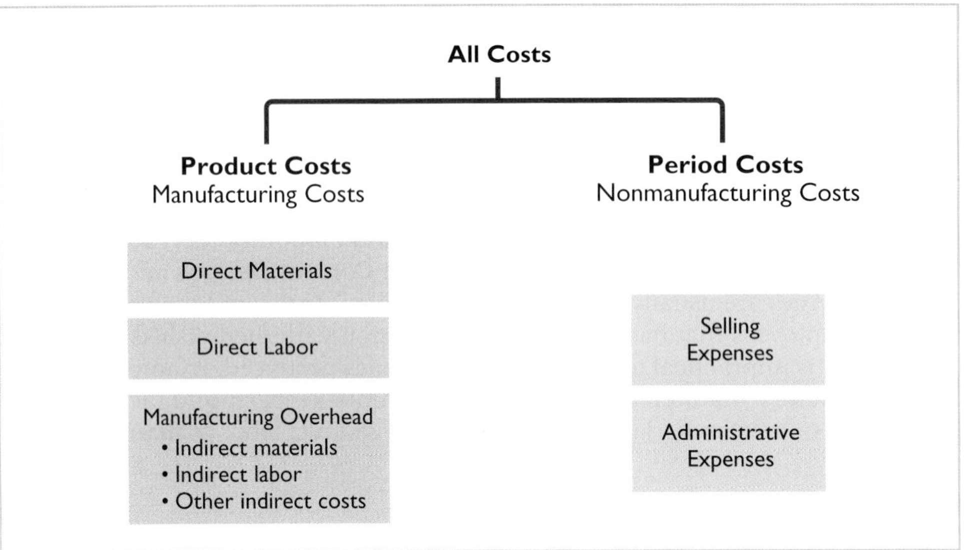

Illustration of Cost Concepts

To improve your understanding of cost concepts, we illustrate them here through an extended example. Suppose you started your own snowboard factory, Terrain Park Boards. Think that's impossible? **Burton Snowboards** was started by Jake Burton Carpenter, when he was only 23 years old. Jake initially experimented with 100 different prototype designs before settling on a final design. Then Jake, along with two relatives and a friend, started making 50 boards per day in Londonderry, Vermont. Unfortunately, while they made a lot of boards in their first year, they were only able to sell 300 of them. To get by during those early years, Jake taught tennis and tended bar to pay the bills.

Here are some of the costs that your snowboard factory would incur.

1. The materials cost of each snowboard (wood cores, fiberglass, resins, metal screw holes, metal edges, and ink) is $30.
2. The labor costs (for example, to trim and shape each board using jig saws and band saws) are $40.
3. Depreciation on the factory building and equipment (for example, presses, grinding machines, and lacquer machines) used to make the snowboards is $25,000 per year.
4. Property taxes on the factory building (where the snowboards are made) are $6,000 per year.
5. Advertising costs (mostly online and catalogue) are $60,000 per year.
6. Sales commissions related to snowboard sales are $20 per snowboard.
7. Salaries for factory maintenance employees are $45,000 per year.
8. The salary of the plant manager is $70,000.
9. The cost of shipping is $8 per snowboard.

Illustration 19-4 shows how Terrain Park Boards would assign these manufacturing and selling costs to the various categories.

Total manufacturing costs are the sum of the **product costs—**direct materials, direct labor, and manufacturing overhead—incurred in the current period. If Terrain Park Boards produces 10,000 snowboards the first year, the total manufacturing costs would be $846,000, as shown in Illustration 19-5.

Illustration 19-4
Assignment of costs to cost categories

Terrain Park Boards

Cost Item	Product Costs: Direct Materials	Product Costs: Direct Labor	Product Costs: Manufacturing Overhead	Period Costs
1. Material cost ($30 per board)	X			
2. Labor costs ($40 per board)		X		
3. Depreciation on factory equipment ($25,000 per year)			X	
4. Property taxes on factory building ($6,000 per year)			X	
5. Advertising costs ($60,000 per year)				X
6. Sales commissions ($20 per board)				X
7. Maintenance salaries (factory facilities, $45,000 per year)			X	
8. Salary of plant manager ($70,000 per year)			X	
9. Cost of shipping boards ($8 per board)				X

Illustration 19-5
Computation of total manufacturing costs

Cost Number and Item	Manufacturing Cost
1. Material cost ($30 × 10,000)	$300,000
2. Labor cost ($40 × 10,000)	400,000
3. Depreciation on factory equipment	25,000
4. Property taxes on factory building	6,000
7. Maintenance salaries (factory facilities)	45,000
8. Salary of plant manager	70,000
Total manufacturing costs	**$846,000**

Once it knows the total manufacturing costs, Terrain Park Boards can compute the manufacturing cost per unit. Assuming 10,000 units, the cost to produce one snowboard is $84.60 ($846,000 ÷ 10,000 units).

In subsequent chapters, we use extensively the cost concepts discussed in this chapter. So study Illustration 19-4 carefully. If you do not understand any of these classifications, go back and reread the appropriate section.

LEARNING OBJECTIVE 

Demonstrate how to compute cost of goods manufactured and prepare financial statements for a manufacturer.

The financial statements of a manufacturer are very similar to those of a merchandiser. For example, you will find many of the same sections and same accounts in the financial statements of **Procter & Gamble** that you find in the financial statements of **Dick's Sporting Goods**. The principal differences between their financial statements occur in two places: the cost of goods sold section in the income statement and the current assets section in the balance sheet.

Income Statement

Under a periodic inventory system, the income statements of a merchandiser and a manufacturer differ in the cost of goods sold section. Merchandisers compute cost of goods sold by adding the beginning inventory to the **cost of goods purchased** and subtracting the ending inventory. Manufacturers compute cost of goods sold by adding the beginning finished goods inventory to the **cost of goods manufactured** and subtracting the ending finished goods inventory. Illustration 19-6 shows these different methods.

Illustration 19-6
Cost of goods sold components

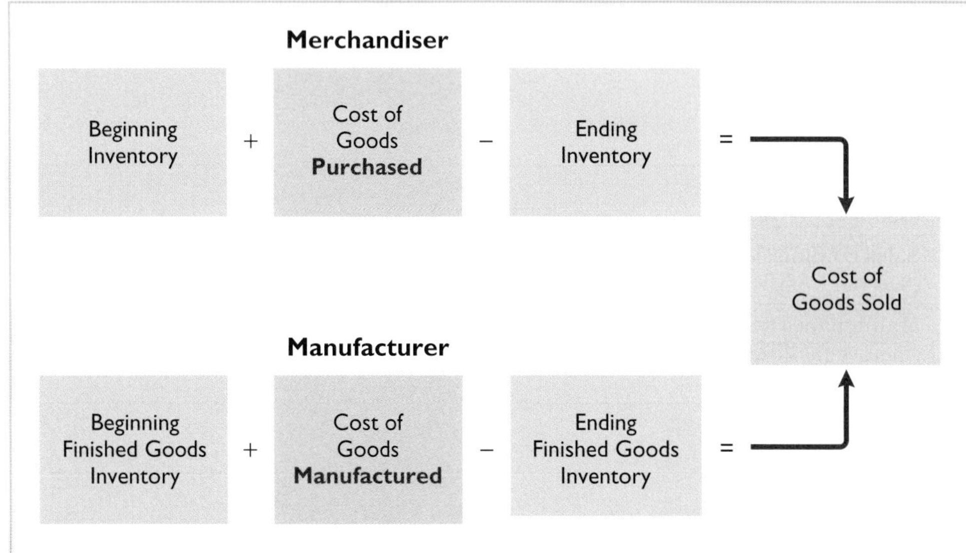

A number of accounts are involved in determining the cost of goods manufactured. To eliminate excessive detail, income statements typically show only the total cost of goods manufactured. A separate statement, called a Cost of Goods Manufactured Schedule, presents the details. (See the discussion on page 673 and Illustration 19-9.)

Illustration 19-7 shows the different presentations of the cost of goods sold sections for merchandising and manufacturing companies. The other sections of an income statement are similar for merchandisers and manufacturers.

Illustration 19-7
Cost of goods sold sections of merchandising and manufacturing income statements

MERCHANDISING COMPANY Income Statement (partial) For the Year Ended December 31, 2017		MANUFACTURING COMPANY Income Statement (partial) For the Year Ended December 31, 2017	
Cost of goods sold		Cost of goods sold	
Inventory, Jan. 1	**$ 70,000**	**Finished goods inventory, Jan. 1**	**$ 90,000**
Cost of goods purchased	**650,000**	**Cost of goods manufactured (see Illustration 19-9)**	**370,000**
Cost of goods available for sale	720,000	Cost of goods available for sale	460,000
Less: Inventory, Dec. 31	**400,000**	**Less: Finished goods inventory, Dec. 31**	**80,000**
Cost of goods sold	$ 320,000	Cost of goods sold	$ 380,000

Cost of Goods Manufactured

An example may help show how companies determine the cost of goods manufactured. Assume that on January 1, **Current Designs** has a number of kayaks in various stages of production. In total, these partially completed units are called **beginning work in process inventory**. The costs the company assigns to beginning work in process inventory are based on the **manufacturing costs incurred in the prior period**.

Current Designs first incurs manufacturing costs in the current year to complete the work that was in process on January 1. It then incurs manufacturing costs for production of new orders. The sum of the direct materials costs, direct labor costs, and manufacturing overhead incurred in the current year is the **total manufacturing costs** for the current period.

We now have two cost amounts: (1) the cost of the beginning work in process and (2) the total manufacturing costs for the current period. The sum of these costs is the **total cost of work in process** for the year.

At the end of the year, Current Designs may have some kayaks that are only partially completed. The costs of these units become the cost of the **ending work in process inventory**. To find the **cost of goods manufactured**, we subtract this cost from the total cost of work in process. Illustration 19-8 shows the formula for determining the cost of goods manufactured.

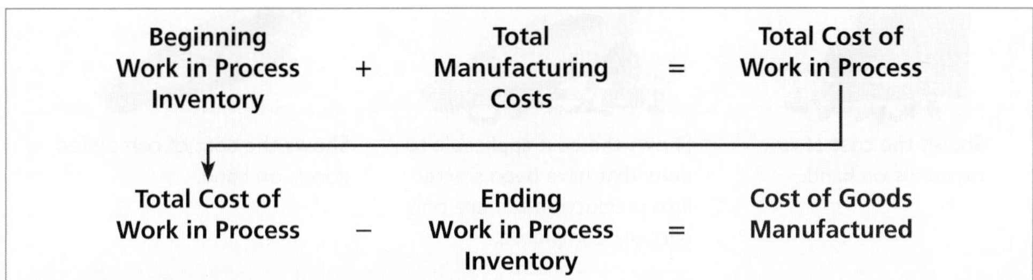

Illustration 19-8
Cost of goods manufactured formula

Cost of Goods Manufactured Schedule

The **cost of goods manufactured schedule** reports cost elements used in calculating cost of goods manufactured. Illustration 19-9 shows the schedule for

Illustration 19-9
Cost of goods manufactured schedule

CURRENT DESIGNS
Cost of Goods Manufactured Schedule
For the Year Ended December 31, 2017

Work in process, January 1			**$ 18,400**
Direct materials			
Raw materials inventory, January 1	$ 16,700		
Raw materials purchases	152,500		
Total raw materials available for use	169,200		
Less: Raw materials inventory, December 31	22,800		
Direct materials used		$146,400	
Direct labor		175,600	
Manufacturing overhead			
Indirect labor	14,300		
Factory repairs	12,600		
Factory utilities	10,100		
Factory depreciation	9,440		
Factory insurance	8,360		
Total manufacturing overhead		54,800	
Total manufacturing costs			**376,800**
Total cost of work in process			395,200
Less: Work in process, December 31			**25,200**
Cost of goods manufactured			**$370,000**

Current Designs (using assumed data). The schedule presents detailed data for direct materials and for manufacturing overhead.

Review Illustration 19-8 and then examine the cost of goods manufactured schedule in Illustration 19-9. You should be able to distinguish between "Total manufacturing costs" and "Cost of goods manufactured." The difference is the effect of the change in work in process during the period.

Balance Sheet

The balance sheet for a merchandising company shows just one category of inventory. In contrast, the balance sheet for a manufacturer may have three inventory accounts, as shown in Illustration 19-10 for Current Designs' kayak inventory.

Illustration 19-10
Inventory accounts for a manufacturer

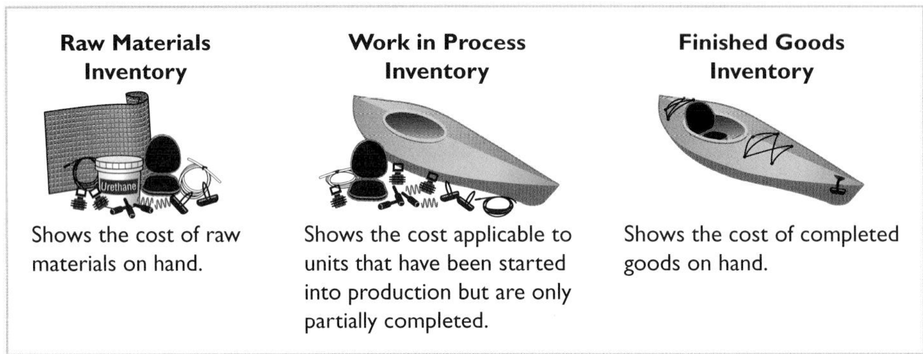

Finished Goods Inventory is to a manufacturer what Inventory is to a merchandiser. Each of these classifications represents the goods that the company has available for sale. The current assets sections presented in Illustration 19-11 contrast the presentations of inventories for merchandising and manufacturing companies. The remainder of the balance sheet is similar for the two types of companies.

Illustration 19-11
Current assets sections of merchandising and manufacturing balance sheets

MERCHANDISING COMPANY Balance Sheet December 31, 2017	
Current assets	
Cash	$100,000
Accounts receivable (net)	210,000
Inventory	**400,000**
Prepaid expenses	22,000
Total current assets	$732,000

MANUFACTURING COMPANY Balance Sheet December 31, 2017		
Current assets		
Cash		$180,000
Accounts receivable (net)		210,000
Inventory		
Finished goods	**$80,000**	
Work in process	**25,200**	
Raw materials	**22,800**	**128,000**
Prepaid expenses		18,000
Total current assets		$536,000

Each step in the accounting cycle for a merchandiser applies to a manufacturer. For example, prior to preparing financial statements, manufacturers make adjusting entries. The adjusting entries are essentially the same as those of a merchandiser. The closing entries are also similar for manufacturers and merchandisers.

LEARNING OBJECTIVE 4 **Discuss trends in managerial accounting.**

The business environment never stands still. Regulations are always changing, global competition continues to intensify, and technology is a source of constant upheaval. In this rapidly changing world, managerial accounting needs to continue to innovate in order to provide managers with the information they need.

Service Industries

Much of the U.S. economy has shifted toward an emphasis on services. Today, more than 50% of U.S. workers are employed by service companies. Airlines, marketing agencies, cable companies, and governmental agencies are just a few examples of service companies. How do service companies differ from manufacturing companies? One difference is that services are consumed immediately. For example, when a restaurant produces a meal, that meal is not put in inventory but is instead consumed immediately. An airline uses special equipment to provide its product, but again, the output of that equipment is consumed immediately by the customer in the form of a flight. And a marketing agency performs services for its clients that are immediately consumed by the customer in the form of a marketing plan. For a manufacturing company, like **Boeing**, there is often a long lead time before its airplane is used or consumed by the customer.

This chapter's examples featured manufacturing companies because accounting for the manufacturing environment requires the use of the broadest range of accounts. That is, the accounts used by service companies represent a subset of those used by manufacturers because service companies are not producing inventory. Neither the restaurant, the airline, or the marketing agency discussed above produces an inventoriable product. However, just like a manufacturer, each needs to keep track of the costs of its services in order to know whether it is generating a profit. A successful restaurateur needs to know the cost of each offering on the menu, an airline needs to know the cost of flight service to each destination, and a marketing agency needs to know the cost to develop a marketing plan. Thus, the techniques shown in this chapter, to accumulate manufacturing costs to determine manufacturing inventory, are equally useful for determining the costs of performing services.

For example, let's consider the costs that **Hewlett-Packard (HP)** might incur on a consulting engagement. A significant portion of its costs would be salaries of consulting personnel. It might also incur travel costs, materials, software costs, and depreciation charges on equipment. In the same way that it needs to keep track of the cost of manufacturing its computers and printers, HP needs to know what its costs are on each consulting job. It could prepare a cost of services performed schedule similar to the cost of goods manufactured schedule in Illustration 19-9 (page 673). The structure would be essentially the same as the cost of goods manufactured schedule, but section headings would be reflective of the costs of the particular service organization.

Many of the examples we present in subsequent chapters will be based on service companies. To highlight the relevance of the techniques used in this course for service companies, we have placed a service company icon (see margin) next to those items in the text and end-of-chapter materials that relate to nonmanufacturing companies.

Focus on the Value Chain

The **value chain** refers to all business processes associated with providing a product or performing a service. Illustration 19-12 (page 676) depicts the value chain for a manufacturer. Many of the most significant business innovations in recent years have resulted either directly, or indirectly, from a focus on the value

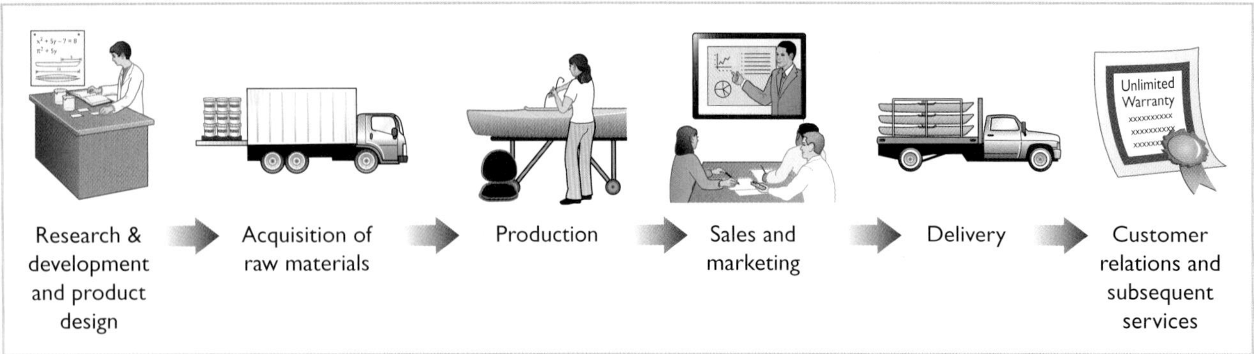

Illustration 19-12
A manufacturer's value chain

chain. For example, so-called **lean manufacturing**, originally pioneered by Japanese automobile manufacturer Toyota but now widely practiced, reviews all business processes in an effort to increase productivity and eliminate waste, all while continually trying to improve quality.

Just-in-time (JIT) inventory methods, which have significantly lowered inventory levels and costs for many companies, are one innovation that resulted from the focus on the value chain. Under the JIT inventory method, goods are manufactured or purchased just in time for sale. For example, Dell can produce and deliver a custom computer within 48 hours of a customer's order. However, JIT also necessitates increased emphasis on product quality. Because JIT companies do not have excess inventory on hand, they cannot afford to stop production because of defects or machine breakdowns. If they stop production, deliveries will be delayed and customers will be unhappy. For example, a design flaw in an Intel computer chip was estimated to cost the company $1 billion in repairs and reduced revenue. As a consequence, many companies now focus on **total quality management (TQM)** to reduce defects in finished products, with the goal of zero defects. The TQM philosophy has been employed by some of the most successful businesses to improve all aspects of the value chain.

Another innovation, the **theory of constraints**, involves identification of "bottlenecks"—constraints within the value chain that limit a company's profitability. Once a major constraint has been identified and eliminated, the company moves on to fix the next most significant constraint. General Motors found that by eliminating bottlenecks, it improved its use of overtime labor while meeting customer demand.

Technology has played a big role in the focus on the value chain and the implementation of lean manufacturing. For example, **enterprise resource planning (ERP) systems**, such as those provided by SAP, provide a comprehensive, centralized, integrated source of information to manage all major business processes—from purchasing, to manufacturing, to sales, to human resources. ERP systems have, in some large companies, replaced as many as 200 individual software packages. In addition, the focus on improving efficiency in the value chain has also resulted in adoption of automated manufacturing processes. Many companies now use computer-integrated manufacturing. These systems often reduce the reliance on manual labor by using robotic equipment. This increases overhead costs as a percentage of total product costs.

As overhead costs increased because of factory automation, the accuracy of overhead cost allocation to specific products became more important. Managerial accounting devised an approach, called **activity-based costing (ABC)**, which allocates overhead based on each product's use of particular activities in making the product. In addition to providing more accurate product costing, ABC also can contribute to increased efficiency in the value chain. For example, suppose one of a company's overhead pools is allocated based on the number of setups that each product requires. If a particular product's cost is high because it is allocated a lot of overhead due to a high number of setups, management will be motivated to try to reduce the number of setups and thus reduce its overhead allocation. ABC is discussed further in Chapter 21.

Balanced Scorecard

As companies implement various business practice innovations, managers sometimes focus too enthusiastically on the latest innovation, to the detriment of other areas of the business. For example, by focusing on total quality management, companies sometimes lose sight of cost/benefit considerations. Similarly, in focusing on reducing inventory levels through just-in-time inventory methods, companies sometimes lose sales due to inventory shortages. The **balanced scorecard** corrects for this limited perspective: This approach uses both financial and nonfinancial measures to evaluate all aspects of a company's operations in an integrated fashion. The performance measures are linked in a cause-and-effect fashion to ensure that they all tie to the company's overall objectives. For example, to increase return on assets, the company could try to increase sales. To increase sales, the company could try to increase customer satisfaction. To increase customer satisfaction, the company could try to reduce product defects. Finally, to reduce product defects, the company could increase employee training. The balanced scorecard, which is discussed further in Chapter 25, is now used by many companies, including **Hilton Hotels**, **Wal-Mart Stores, Inc.**, and **HP**.

Business Ethics

All employees within an organization are expected to act ethically in their business activities. Given the importance of ethical behavior to corporations and their owners (stockholders), an increasing number of organizations provide codes of business ethics for their employees.

CREATING PROPER INCENTIVES

Companies like **Amazon.com**, **IBM**, and **Nike** use complex systems to monitor, control, and evaluate the actions of managers. Unfortunately, these systems and controls sometimes unwittingly create incentives for managers to take unethical actions. For example, because budgets are also used as an evaluation tool, some managers try to "game" the budgeting process by underestimating their division's predicted performance so that it will be easier to meet their performance targets. On the other hand, if budgets are set at unattainable levels, managers sometimes take unethical actions to meet the targets in order to receive higher compensation or, in some cases, to keep their jobs.

For example, at one time, airline manufacturer **Boeing** was plagued by a series of scandals including charges of over-billing, corporate espionage, and illegal conflicts of interest. Some long-time employees of Boeing blamed the decline in ethics on a change in the corporate culture that took place after Boeing merged with **McDonnell Douglas**. They suggested that evaluation systems implemented after the merger to evaluate employee performance gave employees the impression that they needed to succeed no matter what actions were required to do so.

As another example, manufacturing companies need to establish production goals for their processes. Again, if controls are not effective and realistic, problems develop. To illustrate, **Schering-Plough**, a pharmaceutical manufacturer, found that employees were so concerned with meeting production quantity standards that they failed to monitor the quality of the product, and as a result the dosages were often wrong.

CODE OF ETHICAL STANDARDS

In response to corporate scandals, the U.S. Congress enacted the **Sarbanes-Oxley Act (SOX)** to help prevent lapses in internal control. One result of SOX was to clarify top management's responsibility for the company's financial statements. CEOs and

CFOs are now required to certify that financial statements give a fair presentation of the company's operating results and its financial condition. In addition, top managers must certify that the company maintains an adequate system of internal controls to safeguard the company's assets and ensure accurate financial reports.

Another result of SOX is that companies now pay more attention to the composition of the board of directors. In particular, the audit committee of the board of directors must be comprised entirely of independent members (that is, non-employees) and must contain at least one financial expert. Finally, the law substantially increases the penalties for misconduct.

To provide guidance for managerial accountants, the Institute of Management Accountants (IMA) has developed a code of ethical standards, entitled *IMA Statement of Ethical Professional Practice*. Management accountants should not commit acts in violation of these standards. Nor should they condone such acts by others within their organizations. We include the IMA code of ethical standards in Appendix H. Throughout the textbook, we will address various ethical issues managers face.

Corporate Social Responsibility

The balanced scorecard attempts to take a broader, more inclusive view of corporate profitability measures. Many companies, however, have begun to evaluate not just corporate profitability but also **corporate social responsibility**. In addition to profitability, corporate social responsibility considers a company's efforts to employ sustainable business practices with regard to its employees, society, and the environment. This is sometimes referred to as the **triple bottom line** because it evaluates a company's performance with regard to **people, planet, and profit**. Recent reports indicate that over 50% of the 500 largest U.S. companies provide sustainability reports. Make no mistake, these companies are still striving to maximize profits—in a competitive world, they won't survive long if they don't. In fact, you might recognize a few of the names on a recent Forbes.com list of the 100 most sustainable companies in the world. Are you surprised that **General Electric**, **adidas**, **Toyota**, **Coca-Cola**, or **Starbucks** made the list? These companies have learned that with a long-term, sustainable approach, they can maximize profits while also acting in the best interest of their employees, their communities, and the environment.

Sustainable business practices present numerous issues for management and managerial accountants. First, companies need to decide what items need to be measured, generally those that are of utmost importance to its stakeholders. For example, a particular company might be most concerned with minimizing water pollution or maximizing employee safety. Then, for each item identified, the company determines measurable attributes that provide relevant information regarding the company's performance with regard to that item, such as the amount of waste released into public waterways or the number of accidents per 1,000 hours worked. Finally, the company needs to consider the materiality of the item, the cost of measuring these attributes, and the reliability of the measurements. If the company uses this information to make decisions, then accuracy is critical. Of particular concern is whether the measurements can be verified by an outside third party.

Unlike financial reporting, which is overseen by the Financial Accounting Standards Board, the reporting of sustainable business practices currently has no agreed-upon standard-setter. A number of organizations have, however, published guidelines. The guidelines published by the **Global Reporting Initiative** are among the most widely recognized and followed. Illustration 19-13 provides a list of major categories provided by the Global Reporting Initiative for sustainability reporting and a sample of aspects that companies might consider within each category.

Economic	Environmental	Social: Labor Practices and Decent Work	Social: Human Rights	Social: Society	Social: Product Responsibility
Economic performance Market presence Indirect economic impacts Procurement practices	Energy Biodiversity Effluents and waste Compliance	Occupational health and safety Training and education Diversity and equal opportunity Labor practices grievance mechanisms	Non-discrimination Child labor Indigenous rights Supplier human rights assessment	Anti-corruption Anti-competitive behavior Supplier assessment for impacts on society Grievance mechanisms for impacts on society	Customer health and safety Product and service labeling Marketing communi-cations Customer privacy

Source: Global Reporting Initiative, *G4 Sustainability Reporting Guidelines,* p. 9. The full report is available at *www.globalreporting.org.*

Illustration 19-13
Sample categories in Global Reporting Initiative guidelines

REVIEW AND PRACTICE

LEARNING OBJECTIVES REVIEW

1 Identify the features of managerial accounting and the functions of management. The *primary users* of managerial accounting reports, issued as frequently as needed, are internal users, who are officers, department heads, managers, and supervisors in the company. The purpose of these reports is to provide special-purpose information for a particular user for a specific decision. The content of managerial accounting reports pertains to subunits of the business. It may be very detailed, and may extend beyond the double-entry accounting system. The reporting standard is relevance to the decision being made. No independent audits are required in managerial accounting.

The functions of management are planning, directing, and controlling. Planning requires management to look ahead and to establish objectives. Directing involves coordinating the diverse activities and human resources of a company to produce a smooth-running operation. Controlling is the process of keeping the activities on track.

2 Describe the classes of manufacturing costs and the differences between product and period costs. Manufacturing costs are typically classified as either (1) direct materials, (2) direct labor, or (3) manufacturing overhead. Raw materials that can be physically and directly associated with the finished product during the manufacturing process are called direct materials. The work of factory employees that can be physically and directly associated with converting raw materials into finished goods is considered direct labor. Manufacturing overhead consists of costs that are indirectly associated with the manufacture of the finished product.

Product costs are costs that are a necessary and integral part of producing the finished product. Product costs are also called inventoriable costs. These costs do not become expenses until the company sells the finished goods inventory. Period costs are costs that are identified with a specific time period rather than with a salable product. These costs relate to nonmanufacturing costs and therefore are not inventoriable costs.

3 Demonstrate how to compute cost of goods manufactured and prepare financial statements for a manufacturer. Companies add the cost of the beginning work in process to the total manufacturing costs for the current year to arrive at the total cost of work in process for the year. They then subtract the ending work in process from the total cost of work in process to arrive at the cost of goods manufactured.

The difference between a merchandising and a manufacturing income statement is in the cost of goods sold section. A manufacturing cost of goods sold section shows beginning and ending finished goods inventories and the cost of goods manufactured.

The difference between a merchandising and a manufacturing balance sheet is in the current assets section. The current assets section of a manufacturing company's balance sheet presents three inventory accounts: finished goods inventory, work in process inventory, and raw materials inventory.

4 **Discuss trends in managerial accounting.** Managerial accounting has experienced many changes in recent years, including a shift toward service companies as well as an emphasis on ethical behavior. Improved practices include a focus on managing the value chain through techniques such as just-in-time inventory, total quality management, activity-based costing, and theory of constraints. The balanced scorecard is now used by many companies in order to attain a more comprehensive view of the company's operations. Finally, companies are now evaluating their performance with regard to their corporate social responsibility.

GLOSSARY REVIEW

Activity-based costing (ABC) A method of allocating overhead based on each product's use of activities in making the product.

Balanced scorecard A performance-measurement approach that uses both financial and nonfinancial measures, tied to company objectives, to evaluate a company's operations in an integrated fashion.

Board of directors The group of officials elected by the stockholders of a corporation to formulate operating policies and select officers who will manage the company.

Chief executive officer (CEO) Corporate officer who has overall responsibility for managing the business and delegates responsibilities to other corporate officers.

Chief financial officer (CFO) Corporate officer who is responsible for all of the accounting and finance issues of the company.

Controller Financial officer responsible for a company's accounting records, system of internal control, and preparation of financial statements, tax returns, and internal reports.

Corporate social responsibility The efforts of a company to employ sustainable business practices with regard to its employees, society, and the environment.

Cost of goods manufactured Total cost of work in process less the cost of the ending work in process inventory.

Direct labor The work of factory employees that can be physically and directly associated with converting raw materials into finished goods.

Direct materials Raw materials that can be physically and directly associated with manufacturing the finished product.

Enterprise resource planning (ERP) system Software that provides a comprehensive, centralized, integrated source of information used to manage all major business processes.

Indirect labor Work of factory employees that has no physical association with the finished product or for which it is impractical to trace the costs to the goods produced.

Indirect materials Raw materials that do not physically become part of the finished product or for which it is impractical to trace to the finished product because their physical association with the finished product is too small.

Just-in-time (JIT) inventory Inventory system in which goods are manufactured or purchased just in time for sale.

Line positions Jobs that are directly involved in a company's primary revenue-generating operating activities.

Managerial accounting A field of accounting that provides economic and financial information for managers and other internal users.

Manufacturing overhead Manufacturing costs that are indirectly associated with the manufacture of the finished product.

Period costs Costs that are matched with the revenue of a specific time period and charged to expense as incurred.

Product costs Costs that are a necessary and integral part of producing the finished product.

Sarbanes-Oxley Act (SOX) Law passed by Congress intended to reduce unethical corporate behavior.

Staff positions Jobs that support the efforts of line employees.

Theory of constraints A specific approach used to identify and manage constraints in order to achieve the company's goals.

Total cost of work in process Cost of the beginning work in process plus total manufacturing costs for the current period.

Total manufacturing costs The sum of direct materials, direct labor, and manufacturing overhead incurred in the current period.

Total quality management (TQM) Systems implemented to reduce defects in finished products with the goal of achieving zero defects.

Treasurer Financial officer responsible for custody of a company's funds and for maintaining its cash position.

Triple bottom line The evaluation of a company's social responsibility performance with regard to people, planet, and profit.

Value chain All business processes associated with providing a product or performing a service.

PRACTICE EXERCISES

1. Fredricks Company reports the following costs and expenses in May.

Determine the total amount of various types of costs.

(LO 2)

Factory utilities	$ 15,600	Direct labor	$89,100
Depreciation on factory equipment	12,650	Sales salaries	46,400
Depreciation on delivery trucks	8,800	Property taxes on factory building	2,500
Indirect factory labor	48,900	Repairs to office equipment	2,300
Indirect materials	80,800	Factory repairs	2,000
Direct materials used	137,600	Advertising	18,000
Factory manager's salary	13,000	Office supplies used	5,640

Instructions

From the information, determine the total amount of:

(a) Manufacturing overhead.

(b) Product costs.

(c) Period costs.

Solution

1. (a)	Factory utilities	$ 15,600
	Depreciation on factory equipment	12,650
	Indirect factory labor	48,900
	Indirect materials	80,800
	Factory manager's salary	13,000
	Property taxes on factory building	2,500
	Factory repairs	2,000
	Manufacturing overhead	$175,450
(b)	Direct materials	$137,600
	Direct labor	89,100
	Manufacturing overhead	175,450
	Product costs	$402,150
(c)	Depreciation on delivery trucks	$ 8,800
	Sales salaries	46,400
	Repairs to office equipment	2,300
	Advertising	18,000
	Office supplies used	5,640
	Period costs	$ 81,140

2. Tommi Corporation incurred the following costs while manufacturing its product.

Compute cost of goods manufactured and sold.

(LO 3)

Materials used in product	$120,000	Advertising expense	$45,000
Depreciation on plant	60,000	Property taxes on plant	19,000
Property taxes on store	7,500	Delivery expense	21,000
Labor costs of assembly-line workers	110,000	Sales commissions	35,000
Factory supplies used	25,000	Salaries paid to sales clerks	50,000

Work-in-process inventory was $10,000 at January 1 and $14,000 at December 31. Finished goods inventory was $60,500 at January 1 and $50,600 at December 31.

Instructions

(a) Compute cost of goods manufactured.

(b) Compute cost of goods sold.

Solution

2. (a)	Work-in-process, 1/1			$ 10,000
	Direct materials used		$120,000	
	Direct labor		110,000	
	Manufacturing overhead			
	Depreciation on plant	$60,000		
	Factory supplies used	25,000		
	Property taxes on plant	19,000		
	Total manufacturing overhead		104,000	
	Total manufacturing costs			334,000
	Total cost of work-in-process			344,000
	Less: Ending work-in-process			14,000
	Cost of goods manufactured			$330,000
(b)	Finished goods, 1/1			$ 60,500
	Cost of goods manufactured			330,000
	Cost of goods available for sale			390,500
	Less: Finished goods, 12/31			50,600
	Cost of goods sold			$339,900

PRACTICE PROBLEM

Prepare a cost of goods manufactured schedule, an income statement, and a partial balance sheet.

(LO 3)

Superior Company has the following cost and expense data for the year ending December 31, 2017.

Raw materials, 1/1/17	$ 30,000	Insurance, factory	$ 14,000
Raw materials, 12/31/17	20,000	Property taxes, factory building	6,000
Raw materials purchases	205,000	Sales revenue	1,500,000
Indirect materials	15,000	Delivery expenses	100,000
Work in process, 1/1/17	80,000	Sales commissions	150,000
Work in process, 12/31/17	50,000	Indirect labor	90,000
Finished goods, 1/1/17	110,000	Factory machinery rent	40,000
Finished goods, 12/31/17	120,000	Factory utilities	65,000
Direct labor	350,000	Depreciation, factory building	24,000
Factory manager's salary	35,000	Administrative expenses	300,000

Instructions

(a) Prepare a cost of goods manufactured schedule for Superior Company for 2017.

(b) Prepare an income statement for Superior Company for 2017.

(c) Assume that Superior Company's accounting records show the balances of the following current asset accounts: Cash $17,000, Accounts Receivable (net) $120,000, Prepaid Expenses $13,000, and Short-Term Investments $26,000. Prepare the current assets section of the balance sheet for Superior Company as of December 31, 2017.

Solution

(a)

SUPERIOR COMPANY
Cost of Goods Manufactured Schedule
For the Year Ended December 31, 2017

Work in process, 1/1			$ 80,000
Direct materials			
Raw materials inventory, 1/1	$ 30,000		
Raw materials purchases	205,000		
Total raw materials available for use	235,000		
Less: Raw materials inventory, 12/31	20,000		
Direct materials used		$215,000	
Direct labor		350,000	

Manufacturing overhead			
Indirect labor	90,000		
Factory utilities	65,000		
Factory machinery rent	40,000		
Factory manager's salary	35,000		
Depreciation, factory building	24,000		
Indirect materials	15,000		
Insurance, factory	14,000		
Property taxes, factory building	6,000		
Total manufacturing overhead		289,000	
Total manufacturing costs			854,000
Total cost of work in process			934,000
Less: Work in process, 12/31			50,000
Cost of goods manufactured			$ 884,000

(b)

SUPERIOR COMPANY
Income Statement
For the Year Ended December 31, 2017

Sales revenue		$1,500,000
Cost of goods sold		
Finished goods inventory, January 1	$110,000	
Cost of goods manufactured	884,000	
Cost of goods available for sale	994,000	
Less: Finished goods inventory, December 31	120,000	
Cost of goods sold		874,000
Gross profit		626,000
Operating expenses		
Administrative expenses	300,000	
Sales commissions	150,000	
Delivery expenses	100,000	
Total operating expenses		550,000
Net income		$ 76,000

(c)

SUPERIOR COMPANY
Balance Sheet (partial)
December 31, 2017

Current assets		
Cash		$ 17,000
Short-term investments		26,000
Accounts receivable (net)		120,000
Inventory		
Finished goods	$120,000	
Work in process	50,000	
Raw materials	20,000	190,000
Prepaid expenses		13,000
Total current assets		$366,000

EXERCISES

E19-1 Justin Bleeber has prepared the following list of statements about managerial accounting, financial accounting, and the functions of management.

Identify distinguishing features of managerial accounting.

(LO 1)

1. Financial accounting focuses on providing information to internal users.
2. Staff positions are directly involved in the company's primary revenue-generating activities.
3. Preparation of budgets is part of financial accounting.
4. Managerial accounting applies only to merchandising and manufacturing companies.

5. Both managerial accounting and financial accounting deal with many of the same economic events.
6. Managerial accounting reports are prepared only quarterly and annually.
7. Financial accounting reports are general-purpose reports.
8. Managerial accounting reports pertain to subunits of the business.
9. Managerial accounting reports must comply with generally accepted accounting principles.
10. The company treasurer reports directly to the vice president of operations.

Instructions

Identify each statement as true or false. If false, indicate how to correct the statement.

Classify costs into three classes of manufacturing costs.

(LO 2)

E19-2 Presented below is a list of costs and expenses usually incurred by Barnum Corporation, a manufacturer of furniture, in its factory.

1. Salaries for assembly line inspectors.
2. Insurance on factory machines.
3. Property taxes on the factory building.
4. Factory repairs.
5. Upholstery used in manufacturing furniture.
6. Wages paid to assembly line workers.
7. Factory machinery depreciation.
8. Glue, nails, paint, and other small parts used in production.
9. Factory supervisors' salaries.
10. Wood used in manufacturing furniture.

Instructions

Classify the above items into the following categories: (a) direct materials, (b) direct labor, and (c) manufacturing overhead.

Identify types of cost and explain their accounting.

(LO 2)

E19-3 Trak Corporation incurred the following costs while manufacturing its bicycles.

Bicycle components	$100,000	Advertising expense	$45,000
Depreciation on plant	60,000	Property taxes on plant	14,000
Property taxes on store	7,500	Delivery expense	21,000
Labor costs of assembly-line workers	110,000	Sales commissions	35,000
Factory supplies used	13,000	Salaries paid to sales clerks	50,000

Instructions

(a) Identify each of the above costs as direct materials, direct labor, manufacturing overhead, or period costs.

(b) Explain the basic difference in accounting for product costs and period costs.

Determine the total amount of various types of costs.

(LO 2)

E19-4 Knight Company reports the following costs and expenses in May.

Factory utilities	$ 15,500	Direct labor	$69,100
Depreciation on factory equipment	12,650	Sales salaries	46,400
Depreciation on delivery trucks	3,800	Property taxes on factory building	2,500
Indirect factory labor	48,900	Repairs to office equipment	1,300
Indirect materials	80,800	Factory repairs	2,000
Direct materials used	137,600	Advertising	15,000
Factory manager's salary	8,000	Office supplies used	2,640

Instructions

From the information, determine the total amount of:

(a) Manufacturing overhead.

(b) Product costs.

(c) Period costs.

Classify various costs into different cost categories.

(LO 2)

E19-5 Gala Company is a manufacturer of laptop computers. Various costs and expenses associated with its operations are as follows.

1. Property taxes on the factory building.
2. Production superintendents' salaries.
3. Memory boards and chips used in assembling computers.
4. Depreciation on the factory equipment.

5. Salaries for assembly-line quality control inspectors.
6. Sales commissions paid to sell laptop computers.
7. Electrical components used in assembling computers.
8. Wages of workers assembling laptop computers.
9. Soldering materials used on factory assembly lines.
10. Salaries for the night security guards for the factory building.

The company intends to classify these costs and expenses into the following categories: (a) direct materials, (b) direct labor, (c) manufacturing overhead, and (d) period costs.

Instructions
List the items (1) through (10). For each item, indicate the cost category to which it belongs.

Classify various costs into different cost categories.
(LO 2)

E19-6 The administrators of Crawford County's Memorial Hospital are interested in identifying the various costs and expenses that are incurred in producing a patient's X-ray. A list of such costs and expenses is presented below.

1. Salaries for the X-ray machine technicians.
2. Wages for the hospital janitorial personnel.
3. Film costs for the X-ray machines.
4. Property taxes on the hospital building.
5. Salary of the X-ray technicians' supervisor.
6. Electricity costs for the X-ray department.
7. Maintenance and repairs on the X-ray machines.
8. X-ray department supplies.
9. Depreciation on the X-ray department equipment.
10. Depreciation on the hospital building.

The administrators want these costs and expenses classified as (a) direct materials, (b) direct labor, or (c) service overhead.

Instructions
List the items (1) through (10). For each item, indicate the cost category to which the item belongs.

Classify various costs into different cost categories.
(LO 2)

E19-7 National Express reports the following costs and expenses in June 2017 for its delivery service.

Indirect materials	$ 6,400	Drivers' salaries	$16,000
Depreciation on delivery equipment	11,200	Advertising	4,600
Dispatcher's salary	5,000	Delivery equipment repairs	300
Property taxes on office building	870	Office supplies	650
CEO's salary	12,000	Office utilities	990
Gas and oil for delivery trucks	2,200	Repairs on office equipment	180

Instructions
Determine the total amount of (a) delivery service (product) costs and (b) period costs.

Compute cost of goods manufactured and sold.
(LO 3)

E19-8 Lopez Corporation incurred the following costs while manufacturing its product.

Materials used in product	$120,000	Advertising expense	$45,000
Depreciation on plant	60,000	Property taxes on plant	14,000
Property taxes on store	7,500	Delivery expense	21,000
Labor costs of assembly-line workers	110,000	Sales commissions	35,000
Factory supplies used	23,000	Salaries paid to sales clerks	50,000

Work in process inventory was $12,000 at January 1 and $15,500 at December 31. Finished goods inventory was $60,000 at January 1 and $45,600 at December 31.

Instructions
(a) Compute cost of goods manufactured.
(b) Compute cost of goods sold.

Determine missing amounts in cost of goods manufactured schedule.
(LO 3)

E19-9 An incomplete cost of goods manufactured schedule is presented below.

HOBBIT COMPANY
Cost of Goods Manufactured Schedule
For the Year Ended December 31, 2017

Work in process (1/1)			$210,000
Direct materials			
Raw materials inventory (1/1)	$?		
Add: Raw materials purchases	158,000		
Total raw materials available for use	?		
Less: Raw materials inventory (12/31)	22,500		
Direct materials used		$180,000	
Direct labor		?	
Manufacturing overhead			
Indirect labor	18,000		
Factory depreciation	36,000		
Factory utilities	68,000		
Total overhead		122,000	
Total manufacturing costs			?
Total cost of work in process			?
Less: Work in process (12/31)			81,000
Cost of goods manufactured			$540,000

Instructions
Complete the cost of goods manufactured schedule for Hobbit Company.

Determine the missing amount of different cost items.
(LO 3)

E19-10 Manufacturing cost data for Copa Company are presented below.

	Case A	Case B	Case C
Direct materials used	$ (a)	$68,400	$130,000
Direct labor	57,000	86,000	(g)
Manufacturing overhead	46,500	81,600	102,000
Total manufacturing costs	195,650	(d)	253,700
Work in process 1/1/17	(b)	16,500	(h)
Total cost of work in process	221,500	(e)	337,000
Work in process 12/31/17	(c)	11,000	70,000
Cost of goods manufactured	185,275	(f)	(i)

Instructions
Indicate the missing amount for each letter (a) through (i).

Determine the missing amount of different cost items, and prepare a condensed cost of goods manufactured schedule.
(LO 3)

E19-11 Incomplete manufacturing cost data for Horizon Company for 2017 are presented as follows for four different situations.

	Direct Materials Used	Direct Labor Used	Manufacturing Overhead	Total Manufacturing Costs	Work in Process 1/1	Work in Process 12/31	Cost of Goods Manufactured
(1)	$117,000	$140,000	$ 87,000	$ (a)	$33,000	$ (b)	$360,000
(2)	(c)	200,000	132,000	450,000	(d)	40,000	470,000
(3)	80,000	100,000	(e)	265,000	60,000	80,000	(f)
(4)	70,000	(g)	75,000	288,000	45,000	(h)	270,000

Instructions
(a) Indicate the missing amount for each letter.
(b) Prepare a condensed cost of goods manufactured schedule for situation (1) for the year ended December 31, 2017.

Prepare a cost of goods manufactured schedule and a partial income statement.
(LO 3)

E19-12 Cepeda Corporation has the following cost records for June 2017.

Indirect factory labor	$ 4,500	Factory utilities	$ 400
Direct materials used	20,000	Depreciation, factory equipment	1,400
Work in process, 6/1/17	3,000	Direct labor	40,000
Work in process, 6/30/17	3,800	Maintenance, factory equipment	1,800
Finished goods, 6/1/17	5,000	Indirect materials	2,200
Finished goods, 6/30/17	7,500	Factory manager's salary	3,000

Instructions

(a) Prepare a cost of goods manufactured schedule for June 2017.
(b) Prepare an income statement through gross profit for June 2017 assuming sales revenue is $92,100.

E19-13 Keisha Tombert, the bookkeeper for Washington Consulting, a political consulting firm, has recently completed a managerial accounting course at her local college. One of the topics covered in the course was the cost of goods manufactured schedule. Keisha wondered if such a schedule could be prepared for her firm. She realized that, as a service-oriented company, it would have no work in process inventory to consider.

Classify various costs into different categories and prepare cost of services performed schedule.

(LO 2, 3)

Listed below are the costs her firm incurred for the month ended August 31, 2017.

Supplies used on consulting contracts	$ 1,700
Supplies used in the administrative offices	1,500
Depreciation on equipment used for contract work	900
Depreciation used on administrative office equipment	1,050
Salaries of professionals working on contracts	15,600
Salaries of administrative office personnel	7,700
Janitorial services for professional offices	700
Janitorial services for administrative offices	500
Insurance on contract operations	800
Insurance on administrative operations	900
Utilities for contract operations	1,400
Utilities for administrative offices	1,300

Instructions

(a) Prepare a schedule of cost of contract services performed (similar to a cost of goods manufactured schedule) for the month.
(b) For those costs not included in (a), explain how they would be classified and reported in the financial statements.

E19-14 The following information is available for Aikman Company.

Prepare a cost of goods manufactured schedule and a partial income statement.

(LO 3)

	January 1, 2017	2017	December 31, 2017
Raw materials inventory	$21,000		$30,000
Work in process inventory	13,500		17,200
Finished goods inventory	27,000		21,000
Materials purchased		$150,000	
Direct labor		220,000	
Manufacturing overhead		180,000	
Sales revenue		910,000	

Instructions

(a) Compute cost of goods manufactured.
(b) Prepare an income statement through gross profit.
(c) Show the presentation of the ending inventories on the December 31, 2017, balance sheet.
(d) How would the income statement and balance sheet of a merchandising company be different from Aikman's financial statements?

E19-15 University Company produces collegiate apparel. From its accounting records, it prepares the following schedule and financial statements on a yearly basis.

Indicate in which schedule or financial statement(s) different cost items will appear.

(LO 3)

(a) Cost of goods manufactured schedule.
(b) Income statement.
(c) Balance sheet.

The following items are found in its ledger and accompanying data.

1. Direct labor
2. Raw materials inventory, 1/1
3. Work in process inventory, 12/31
4. Finished goods inventory, 1/1
5. Indirect labor
6. Depreciation on factory machinery
7. Work in process, 1/1

8. Finished goods inventory, 12/31
9. Factory maintenance salaries
10. Cost of goods manufactured
11. Depreciation on delivery equipment
12. Cost of goods available for sale
13. Direct materials used
14. Heat and electricity for factory
15. Repairs to roof of factory building
16. Cost of raw materials purchases

Instructions

List the items (1)–(16). For each item, indicate by using the appropriate letter or letters, the schedule and/or financial statement(s) in which the item will appear.

Prepare a cost of goods manufactured schedule, and present the ending inventories on the balance sheet.

(LO 3)

E19-16 An analysis of the accounts of Roberts Company reveals the following manufacturing cost data for the month ended June 30, 2017.

Inventory	Beginning	Ending
Raw materials	$9,000	$13,100
Work in process	5,000	7,000
Finished goods	9,000	8,000

Costs incurred: raw materials purchases $54,000, direct labor $47,000, manufacturing overhead $19,900. The specific overhead costs were: indirect labor $5,500, factory insurance $4,000, machinery depreciation $4,000, machinery repairs $1,800, factory utilities $3,100, and miscellaneous factory costs $1,500. Assume that all raw materials used were direct materials.

Instructions

(a) Prepare the cost of goods manufactured schedule for the month ended June 30, 2017.
(b) Show the presentation of the ending inventories on the June 30, 2017, balance sheet.

Determine the amount of cost to appear in various accounts, and indicate in which financial statements these accounts would appear.

(LO 3)

E19-17 McQueen Motor Company manufactures automobiles. During September 2017, the company purchased 5,000 head lamps at a cost of $15 per lamp. McQueen withdrew 4,650 lamps from the warehouse during the month. Fifty of these lamps were used to replace the head lamps in autos used by traveling sales staff. The remaining 4,600 lamps were put in autos manufactured during the month.

Of the autos put into production during September 2017, 90% were completed and transferred to the company's storage lot. Of the cars completed during the month, 70% were sold by September 30.

Instructions

(a) Determine the cost of head lamps that would appear in each of the following accounts at September 30, 2017: Raw Materials, Work in Process, Finished Goods, Cost of Goods Sold, and Selling Expenses.
(b) Write a short memo to the chief accountant, indicating whether and where each of the accounts in (a) would appear on the income statement or on the balance sheet at September 30, 2017.

Identify various managerial accounting practices.

(LO 4)

E19-18 The following is a list of terms related to managerial accounting practices.

1. Activity-based costing.
2. Just-in-time inventory.
3. Balanced scorecard.
4. Value chain.

Instructions

Match each of the terms with the statement below that best describes the term.

(a) ______ A performance-measurement technique that attempts to consider and evaluate all aspects of performance using financial and nonfinancial measures in an integrated fashion.
(b) ______ The group of activities associated with providing a product or performing a service.
(c) ______ An approach used to reduce the cost associated with handling and holding inventory by reducing the amount of inventory on hand.
(d) ______ A method used to allocate overhead to products based on each product's use of the activities that cause the incurrence of the overhead cost.

PROBLEMS

P19-1A Ohno Company specializes in manufacturing a unique model of bicycle helmet. The model is well accepted by consumers, and the company has enough orders to keep the factory production at 10,000 helmets per month (80% of its full capacity). Ohno's monthly manufacturing cost and other expense data are as follows.

Classify manufacturing costs into different categories and compute the unit cost

(LO 2)

Rent on factory equipment	$11,000
Insurance on factory building	1,500
Raw materials (plastics, polystyrene, etc.)	75,000
Utility costs for factory	900
Supplies for general office	300
Wages for assembly line workers	58,000
Depreciation on office equipment	800
Miscellaneous materials (glue, thread, etc.)	1,100
Factory manager's salary	5,700
Property taxes on factory building	400
Advertising for helmets	14,000
Sales commissions	10,000
Depreciation on factory building	1,500

Instructions

(a) Prepare an answer sheet with the following column headings.

	Product Costs			
Cost Item	Direct Materials	Direct Labor	Manufacturing Overhead	Period Costs

Enter each cost item on your answer sheet, placing the dollar amount under the appropriate headings. Total the dollar amounts in each of the columns.

(b) Compute the cost to produce one helmet.

(a) DM $75,000
DL $58,000
MO $22,100
PC $25,100

P19-2A Bell Company, a manufacturer of audio systems, started its production in October 2017. For the preceding 3 years, Bell had been a retailer of audio systems. After a thorough survey of audio system markets, Bell decided to turn its retail store into an audio equipment factory.

Classify manufacturing costs into different categories and compute the unit cost.

(LO 2)

Raw materials cost for an audio system will total $74 per unit. Workers on the production lines are on average paid $12 per hour. An audio system usually takes 5 hours to complete. In addition, the rent on the equipment used to assemble audio systems amounts to $4,900 per month. Indirect materials cost $5 per system. A supervisor was hired to oversee production; her monthly salary is $3,000.

Factory janitorial costs are $1,300 monthly. Advertising costs for the audio system will be $9,500 per month. The factory building depreciation expense is $7,800 per year. Property taxes on the factory building will be $9,000 per year.

Instructions

(a) Prepare an answer sheet with the following column headings.

	Product Costs			
Cost Item	Direct Materials	Direct Labor	Manufacturing Overhead	Period Costs

Assuming that Bell manufactures, on average, 1,500 audio systems per month, enter each cost item on your answer sheet, placing the dollar amount per month under the appropriate headings. Total the dollar amounts in each of the columns.

(b) Compute the cost to produce one audio system.

(a) DM $111,000
DL $ 90,000
MO $ 18,100
PC $ 9,500

P19-3A Incomplete manufacturing costs, expenses, and selling data for two different cases are as follows.

Indicate the missing amount of different cost items, and prepare a condensed cost of goods manufactured schedule, an income statement, and a partial balance sheet.

(LO 3)

	Case	
	1	2
Direct materials used	$ 9,600	$ (g)
Direct labor	5,000	8,000
Manufacturing overhead	8,000	4,000
Total manufacturing costs	(a)	16,000
Beginning work in process inventory	1,000	(h)

	Case 1	Case 2
Ending work in process inventory	(b)	3,000
Sales revenue	24,500	(i)
Sales discounts	2,500	1,400
Cost of goods manufactured	17,000	24,000
Beginning finished goods inventory	(c)	3,300
Goods available for sale	22,000	(j)
Cost of goods sold	(d)	(k)
Ending finished goods inventory	3,400	2,500
Gross profit	(e)	7,000
Operating expenses	2,500	(l)
Net income	(f)	5,000

Instructions

(b) Ending WIP $ 6,600
(c) Current assets $29,000

(a) Indicate the missing amount for each letter.
(b) Prepare a condensed cost of goods manufactured schedule for Case 1.
(c) Prepare an income statement and the current assets section of the balance sheet for Case 1. Assume that in Case 1 the other items in the current assets section are as follows: Cash $3,000, Receivables (net) $15,000, Raw Materials $600, and Prepaid Expenses $400.

Prepare a cost of goods manufactured schedule, a partial income statement, and a partial balance sheet.

(LO 3)

P19-4A The following data were taken from the records of Clarkson Company for the fiscal year ended June 30, 2017.

Raw Materials Inventory 7/1/16	$ 48,000	Factory Insurance	$ 4,600
Raw Materials Inventory 6/30/17	39,600	Factory Machinery Depreciation	16,000
Finished Goods Inventory 7/1/16	96,000	Factory Utilities	27,600
Finished Goods Inventory 6/30/17	75,900	Office Utilities Expense	8,650
Work in Process Inventory 7/1/16	19,800	Sales Revenue	534,000
Work in Process Inventory 6/30/17	18,600	Sales Discounts	4,200
Direct Labor	139,250	Plant Manager's Salary	58,000
Indirect Labor	24,460	Factory Property Taxes	9,600
Accounts Receivable	27,000	Factory Repairs	1,400
		Raw Materials Purchases	96,400
		Cash	32,000

Instructions

(a) CGM $386,910
(b) Gross profit $122,790
(c) Current assets $193,100

(a) Prepare a cost of goods manufactured schedule. (Assume all raw materials used were direct materials.)
(b) Prepare an income statement through gross profit.
(c) Prepare the current assets section of the balance sheet at June 30, 2017.

Prepare a cost of goods manufactured schedule and a correct income statement.

(LO 3)

P19-5A Empire Company is a manufacturer of smart phones. Its controller resigned in October 2017. An inexperienced assistant accountant has prepared the following income statement for the month of October 2017.

EMPIRE COMPANY
Income Statement
For the Month Ended October 31, 2017

Sales revenue		$780,000
Less: Operating expenses		
Raw materials purchases	$264,000	
Direct labor cost	190,000	
Advertising expense	90,000	
Selling and administrative salaries	75,000	
Rent on factory facilities	60,000	
Depreciation on sales equipment	45,000	
Depreciation on factory equipment	31,000	
Indirect labor cost	28,000	
Utilities expense	12,000	
Insurance expense	8,000	803,000
Net loss		$ (23,000)

Prior to October 2017, the company had been profitable every month. The company's president is concerned about the accuracy of the income statement. As her friend, you have been asked to review the income statement and make necessary corrections. After examining other manufacturing cost data, you have acquired additional information as follows.

1. Inventory balances at the beginning and end of October were:

	October 1	October 31
Raw materials	$18,000	$29,000
Work in process	20,000	14,000
Finished goods	30,000	50,000

2. Only 75% of the utilities expense and 60% of the insurance expense apply to factory operations. The remaining amounts should be charged to selling and administrative activities.

Instructions

(a) Prepare a schedule of cost of goods manufactured for October 2017. (a) CGM $581,800

(b) Prepare a correct income statement for October 2017. (b) NI $ 2,000

BROADENING YOUR PERSPECTIVE

MANAGEMENT DECISION-MAKING

Decision-Making Across the Organization

BYP19-1 Wendall Company specializes in producing fashion outfits. On July 31, 2017, a tornado touched down at its factory and general office. The inventories in the warehouse and the factory were completely destroyed as was the general office nearby. Next morning, through a careful search of the disaster site, however, Bill Francis, the company's controller, and Elizabeth Walton, the cost accountant, were able to recover a small part of manufacturing cost data for the current month.

"What a horrible experience," sighed Bill "And the worst part is that we may not have enough records to use in filing an insurance claim."

"It was terrible," replied Elizabeth. "However, I managed to recover some of the manufacturing cost data that I was working on yesterday afternoon. The data indicate that our direct labor cost in July totaled $250,000 and that we had purchased $365,000 of raw materials. Also, I recall that the amount of raw materials used for July was $350,000. But I'm not sure this information will help. The rest of our records are blown away."

"Well, not exactly," said Bill. "I was working on the year-to-date income statement when the tornado warning was announced. My recollection is that our sales in July were $1,240,000 and our gross profit ratio has been 40% of sales. Also, I can remember that our cost of goods available for sale was $770,000 for July."

"Maybe we can work something out from this information!" exclaimed Elizabeth. "My experience tells me that our manufacturing overhead is usually 60% of direct labor."

"Hey, look what I just found," cried Elizabeth. "It's a copy of this June's balance sheet, and it shows that our inventories as of June 30 are Finished goods $38,000, Work in process $25,000, and Raw materials $19,000."

"Super," yelled Bill. "Let's go work something out."

In order to file an insurance claim, Wendall Company needs to determine the amount of its inventories as of July 31, 2017, the date of the tornado touchdown.

Instructions

With the class divided into groups, determine the amount of cost in the Raw Materials, Work in Process, and Finished Goods inventory accounts as of the date of the tornado touchdown.

Managerial Analysis

BYP19-2 Tenrack is a fairly large manufacturing company located in the southern United States. The company manufactures tennis rackets, tennis balls, tennis clothing, and tennis shoes, all bearing the company's distinctive logo, a large green question mark on a white flocked tennis ball. The company's sales have been increasing over the past 10 years.

The tennis racket division has recently implemented several advanced manufacturing techniques. Robot arms hold the tennis rackets in place while glue dries, and machine vision systems check for defects. The engineering and design team uses computerized drafting and testing of new products. The following managers work in the tennis racket division:

Jason Dennis, Sales Manager (supervises all sales representatives)
Peggy Groneman, Technical Specialist (supervises computer programmers)
Dave Marley, Cost Accounting Manager (supervises cost accountants)
Kevin Carson, Production Supervisor (supervises all manufacturing employees)
Sally Renner, Engineer (supervises all new-product design teams)

Instructions

(a) What are the primary information needs of each manager?
(b) Which, if any, financial accounting report(s) is each likely to use?
(c) Name one special-purpose management accounting report that could be designed for each manager. Include the name of the report, the information it would contain, and how frequently it should be issued.

Real-World Focus

BYP19-3 The Institute of Management Accountants (IMA) is an organization dedicated to excellence in the practice of management accounting and financial management.

Address: **www.imanet.org**, or go to **www.wiley.com/college/weygandt**

Instructions

At the IMA's home page, locate the answers to the following questions.

(a) How many members does the IMA have, and what are their job titles?
(b) What are some of the benefits of joining the IMA as a student?
(c) Use the chapter locator function to locate the IMA chapter nearest you, and find the name of the chapter president.

CRITICAL THINKING

Communication Activity

BYP19-4 Refer to P19-5A and add the following requirement.

Prepare a letter to the president of the company, Shelly Phillips, describing the changes you made. Explain clearly why net income is different after the changes. Keep the following points in mind as you compose your letter.

1. This is a letter to the president of a company, who is your friend. The style should be generally formal, but you may relax some requirements. For example, you may call the president by her first name.
2. Executives are very busy. Your letter should tell the president your main results first (for example, the amount of net income).
3. You should include brief explanations so that the president can understand the changes you made in the calculations.

Ethics Case

BYP19-5 Steve Morgan, controller for Newton Industries, was reviewing production cost reports for the year. One amount in these reports continued to bother him—advertising. During the year, the company had instituted an expensive advertising campaign to sell some of its slower-moving products. It was still too early to tell whether the advertising campaign was successful.

There had been much internal debate as how to report advertising cost. The vice president of finance argued that advertising costs should be reported as a cost of production, just like direct materials and direct labor. He therefore recommended that this cost be identified as manufacturing overhead and reported as part of inventory costs until sold. Others disagreed. Morgan believed that this cost should be reported as an expense of the current period, so as not to overstate net income. Others argued that it should be reported as prepaid advertising and reported as a current asset.

The president finally had to decide the issue. He argued that these costs should be reported as inventory. His arguments were practical ones. He noted that the company was experiencing financial difficulty and expensing this amount in the current period might jeopardize a planned bond offering. Also, by reporting the advertising costs as inventory rather than as prepaid advertising, less attention would be directed to it by the financial community.

Instructions

(a) Who are the stakeholders in this situation?
(b) What are the ethical issues involved in this situation?
(c) What would you do if you were Steve Morgan?

All About You

BYP19-6 The primary purpose of managerial accounting is to provide information useful for management decisions. Many of the managerial accounting techniques that you learn in this course will be useful for decisions you make in your everyday life.

Instructions

For each of the following managerial accounting techniques, read the definition provided and then provide an example of a personal situation that would benefit from use of this technique.

(a) Break-even point (page 768).
(b) Budget (page 794).
(c) Balanced scorecard (page 677).
(d) Capital budgeting (page 912).

Considering Your Costs and Benefits

BYP19-7 As noted in this chapter, because of global competition, companies have become increasingly focused on reducing costs. To reduce costs and remain competitive, many companies are turning to outsourcing. Outsourcing means hiring an outside supplier to provide elements of a product or service rather than producing them internally.

Suppose you are the managing partner in a CPA firm with 30 full-time staff. Larger firms in your community have begun to outsource basic tax-return preparation work to India. Should you outsource your basic tax-return work to India as well? You estimate that you would have to lay off six staff members if you outsource the work. The basic arguments for and against are as follows.

YES: The wages paid to Indian accountants are very low relative to U.S. wages. You will not be able to compete unless you outsource.

NO: Tax-return data is highly sensitive. Many customers will be upset to learn that their data is being emailed around the world.

Instructions

Write a response indicating your position regarding this situation. Provide support for your view.

Chapter 20 Job Order Costing

Have you ever had the chance to tour a movie studio? There's a lot going on! Lots of equipment and lots of people with a variety of talents. Running a film studio, whether as an independent company or part of a major corporation, is a complex and risky business. Consider Disney, which has produced such classics as *Snow White and the Seven Dwarfs* and such colossal successes as *Frozen*. The movie studio has, however, also seen its share of losses. Disney's *Lone Ranger* movie brought in revenues of $260 million, but its production and marketing costs were a combined $375 million—a loss of $115 million.

Every time Disney or another movie studio makes a new movie, it is creating a unique product. Ideally, each new movie should be able to stand on its own, that is, the film should generate revenues that exceed its costs. And in order to know whether a particular movie is profitable, the studio must keep track of all of the costs incurred to make and market the film. These costs include such items as salaries of the writers, actors, director, producer, and production team (e.g., film crew); licensing costs; depreciation on equipment; music; studio rental; and marketing and distribution costs. If you've ever watched the credits at the end of a movie, you know the list goes on and on.

The movie studio isn't the only one with an interest in knowing a particular project's profitability. Many of the people involved in making the movie, such as the screenwriters, actors, and producers, have at least part of their compensation tied to its profitability. As such, complaints about inaccurate accounting are common in the movie industry.

In particular, a few well-known and widely attended movies reported low profits, or even losses, once the accountants got done with them. How can this be? The issue is that a large portion of a movie's costs are overhead costs that can't be directly traced to a film, such as depreciation of film equipment and sets, facility maintenance costs, and executives' salaries. Actors and others often suggest that these overhead costs are overallocated to their movie and therefore negatively affect their compensation.

To reduce the risk of financial flops, many of the big studios now focus on making sequels of previous hits. This might explain why, shortly after losing money on the *Lone Ranger*, Disney announced plans to make *The Avengers 2*—a much safer bet.

LEARNING OBJECTIVES

1. **Describe cost systems and the flow of costs in a job order system.**
2. **Use a job cost sheet to assign costs to work in process.**
3. **Demonstrate how to determine and use the predetermined overhead rate.**
4. **Prepare entries for manufacturing and service jobs completed and sold.**
5. **Distinguish between under- and overapplied manufacturing overhead.**

LEARNING OBJECTIVE 1

Describe cost systems and the flow of costs in a job order system.

Cost accounting involves measuring, recording, and reporting product costs. Companies determine both the total cost and the unit cost of each product. The accuracy of the product cost information is critical to the success of the company. Companies use this information to determine which products to produce, what prices to charge, and how many units to produce. Accurate product cost information is also vital for effective evaluation of employee performance.

A **cost accounting system** consists of accounts for the various manufacturing costs. These accounts are fully integrated into the general ledger of a company. An important feature of a cost accounting system is the use of **a perpetual inventory system**. Such a system **provides immediate, up-to-date information on the cost of a product**.

There are two basic types of cost accounting systems: (1) a process cost system and (2) a job order cost system. Although cost accounting systems differ widely from company to company, most involve one of these two traditional product costing systems.

Process Cost System

A company uses a **process cost system** when it manufactures a large volume of similar products. Production is continuous. Examples of a process cost system are the manufacture of cereal by **Kellogg**, the refining of petroleum by **ExxonMobil**, and the production of ice cream by **Ben & Jerry's**. Process costing accumulates product-related costs **for a period of time** (such as a week or a month) instead of assigning costs to specific products or job orders. In process costing, companies assign the costs to departments or processes for the specified period of time. Illustration 20-1 shows examples of the use of a process cost system. We will discuss the process cost system further in Chapter 21.

Illustration 20-1
Process cost system

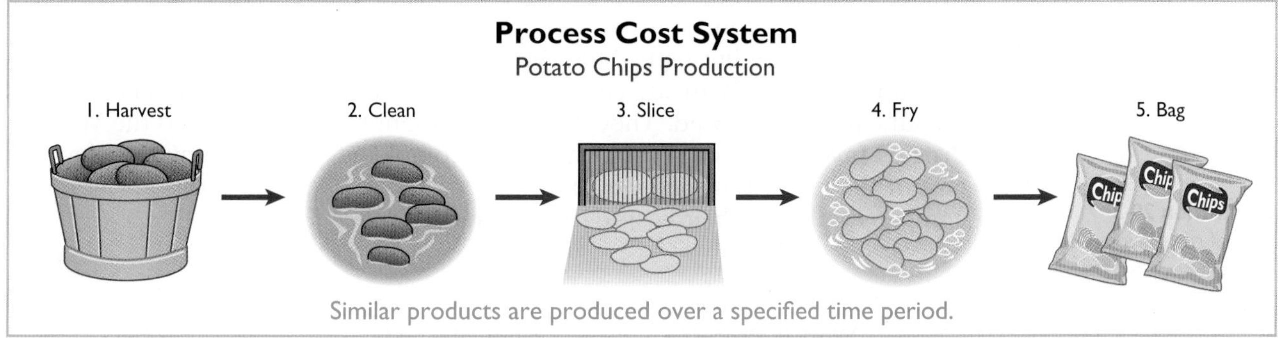

Job Order Cost System

Under a **job order cost system**, the company assigns costs to each **job** or to each **batch** of goods. An example of a job is the manufacture of a jet by **Boeing**, the production of a movie by **Disney**, or the making of a fire truck by **American LaFrance**. An example of a batch is the printing of 225 wedding invitations by a local print shop, or the printing of a weekly issue of *Fortune* magazine by a high-tech printer such as **Quad Graphics**.

An important feature of job order costing is that each job or batch has its own distinguishing characteristics. For example, each house is custom built, each consulting engagement by a CPA firm is unique, and each printing job is different. **The objective is to compute the cost per job.** At each point in manufacturing a product or performing a service, the company can identify the job and its associated costs. A job order cost system measures costs for each completed job, rather than for set time periods. Illustration 20-2 shows the recording of costs in a job order cost system for Disney as it produced two different films at the same time: an animated film and an action thriller.

Illustration 20-2
Job order cost system for Disney

Can a company use both types of cost systems? Yes. For example, General Motors uses process cost accounting for its standard model cars, such as Malibus and Corvettes, and job order cost accounting for a custom-made limousine for the President of the United States.

The objective of both cost accounting systems is to provide unit cost information for product pricing, cost control, inventory valuation, and financial statement presentation.

Job Order Cost Flow

The flow of costs (direct materials, direct labor, and manufacturing overhead) in job order cost accounting parallels the physical flow of the materials as they are converted into finished goods. As shown in Illustration 20-3, companies first **accumulate** manufacturing costs in the form of raw materials, factory labor, or manufacturing overhead. They then **assign** manufacturing costs to the Work in Process Inventory account. When a job is completed, the company transfers the cost of the job to Finished Goods Inventory. Later when the goods are sold, the company transfers their cost to Cost of Goods Sold.

Illustration 20-3
Flow of costs in job order costing

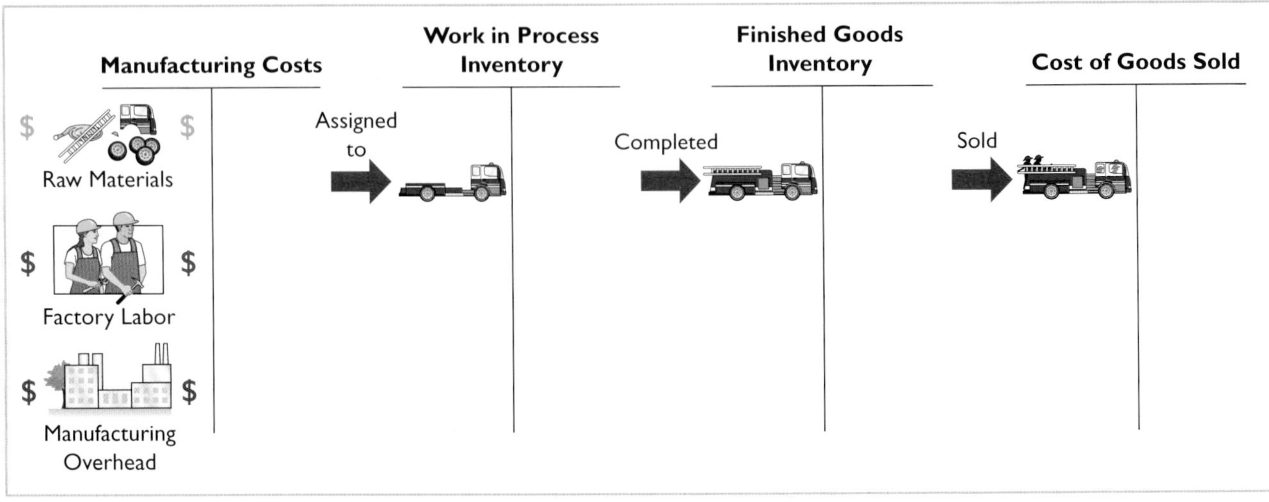

Illustration 20-3 provides a basic overview of the flow of costs in a manufacturing setting for production of a fire truck. A more detailed presentation of the flow of costs is summarized near the end of this chapter in Illustration 20-15. There are two major steps in the flow of costs: (1) *accumulating* the manufacturing costs incurred, and (2) *assigning* the accumulated costs to the work done. The following discussion shows that the company accumulates manufacturing costs incurred by debits to Raw Materials Inventory, Factory Labor, and Manufacturing Overhead. When the company incurs these costs, it does not attempt to associate the costs with specific jobs. The company makes additional entries to assign manufacturing costs incurred to specific jobs. In the remainder of this chapter, we will use a case study to explain how a job order cost system operates.

Accumulating Manufacturing Costs

To illustrate a job order cost system, we will use the January transactions of Wallace Company, which makes custom electronic sensors for corporate safety applications (such as fire and carbon monoxide) and security applications (such as theft and corporate espionage).

RAW MATERIALS COSTS

When Wallace receives the raw materials it has purchased, **it debits the cost of the materials to Raw Materials Inventory**. The company debits this account for the invoice cost of the raw materials and freight costs chargeable to the purchaser. It credits the account for purchase discounts taken and purchase returns and allowances. Wallace makes **no effort at this point to associate the cost of materials with specific jobs or orders.**

To illustrate, assume that Wallace purchases 2,000 lithium batteries (Stock No. AA2746) at $5 per unit ($10,000) and 800 electronic modules (Stock No. AA2850) at $40 per unit ($32,000) for a total cost of $42,000 ($10,000 + $32,000). The entry to record this purchase on January 4 is:

(1)[1]

Jan. 4	Raw Materials Inventory	42,000	
	Accounts Payable		42,000
	(Purchase of raw materials on account)		

Raw Materials Inventory

42,000	

At this point, Raw Materials Inventory has a balance of $42,000, as shown in the T-account in the margin. As we will explain later in the chapter, the company subsequently assigns direct raw materials inventory to work in process and indirect raw materials inventory to manufacturing overhead.

FACTORY LABOR COSTS

Some of a company's employees are involved in the manufacturing process, while others are not. As discussed in Chapter 19, wages and salaries of nonmanufacturing employees are expensed as period costs (e.g., Salaries and Wages Expense). Costs related to manufacturing employees are accumulated in Factory Labor to ensure their treatment as product costs. Factory labor consists of three costs: (1) gross earnings of factory workers, (2) employer payroll taxes on these earnings, and (3) fringe benefits (such as sick pay, pensions, and vacation pay) incurred by the employer. **Companies debit labor costs to Factory Labor as they incur those costs.**

[1]The numbers placed above the entries for Wallace Company are used for reference purposes in the summary provided in Illustration 20-15.

To illustrate, assume that Wallace incurs $32,000 of factory labor costs. Of that amount, $27,000 relates to wages payable and $5,000 relates to payroll taxes payable in February. The entry to record factory labor for the month is:

Factory Labor	
32,000	

(2)

Jan. 31	Factory Labor	32,000	
	Factory Wages Payable		27,000
	Employer Payroll Taxes Payable		5,000
	(To record factory labor costs)		

At this point, Factory Labor has a balance of $32,000, as shown in the T-account in the margin. The company subsequently assigns direct factory labor to work in process and indirect factory labor to manufacturing overhead.

MANUFACTURING OVERHEAD COSTS

A company has many types of overhead costs. If these overhead costs, such as property taxes, depreciation, insurance, and repairs, relate to overhead costs of a nonmanufacturing facility, such as an office building, then these costs are expensed as period costs (e.g., Property Tax Expense, Depreciation Expense, Insurance Expense, and Maintenance and Repairs Expense). If the costs relate to the manufacturing process, then they are accumulated in Manufacturing Overhead to ensure their treatment as product costs.

Using assumed data, the summary entry for manufacturing overhead in Wallace Company is:

Manufacturing Overhead	
13,800	

(3)

Jan. 31	Manufacturing Overhead	13,800	
	Utilities Payable		4,800
	Prepaid Insurance		2,000
	Accounts Payable (for repairs)		2,600
	Accumulated Depreciation		3,000
	Property Taxes Payable		1,400
	(To record overhead costs)		

At this point, Manufacturing Overhead has a balance of $13,800, as shown in the T-account in the margin. The company subsequently assigns manufacturing overhead to work in process.

Use a job cost sheet to assign costs to work in process.

Assigning manufacturing costs to work in process results in the following entries.

1. **Debits** made to Work in Process Inventory.
2. **Credits** made to Raw Materials Inventory, Factory Labor, and Manufacturing Overhead.

An essential accounting record in assigning costs to jobs is a **job cost sheet**, as shown in Illustration 20-4. A **job cost sheet** is a form used to record the costs chargeable to a specific job and to determine the total and unit costs of the completed job.

Companies keep a separate job cost sheet for each job. The job cost sheets constitute the subsidiary ledger for the Work in Process Inventory account. A **subsidiary ledger** consists of individual records for each individual item—in this case, each job. The Work in Process account is referred to as a **control account**

Illustration 20-4
Job cost sheet

Job Cost Sheet

Job No. ______ Quantity ______
Item ______ Date Requested ______
For ______ Date Completed ______

Date	Direct Materials	Direct Labor	Manufacturing Overhead

Cost of completed job	
Direct materials	$ ______
Direct labor	______
Manufacturing overhead	______
Total cost	$ ______
Unit cost (total dollars ÷ quantity)	$ ______

because it summarizes the detailed data regarding specific jobs contained in the job cost sheets. **Each entry to Work in Process Inventory must be accompanied by a corresponding posting to one or more job cost sheets.**

Raw Materials Costs

Companies assign raw materials costs to jobs when their materials storeroom issues the materials in response to requests. Requests for issuing raw materials are made on a prenumbered **materials requisition slip**. The materials issued may be used directly on a job, or they may be considered indirect materials. As Illustration 20-5 shows, the requisition should indicate the quantity and type of materials withdrawn and the account to be charged. The company will charge direct materials to Work in Process Inventory, and indirect materials to Manufacturing Overhead.

Illustration 20-5
Materials requisition slip

Wallace Company
Materials Requisition Slip

Deliver to: Assembly Department Req. No. R247
Charge to: Work in Process–Job No. 101 Date: 1/6/17

Quantity	Description	Stock No.	Cost per Unit	Total
200	Lithium batteries	AA2746	$5.00	$1,000

Requested by *Bruce Howart* Received by *Herb Crowley*
Approved by *Kap Shin* Costed by *Heather Remmers*

The company may use any of the inventory costing methods (FIFO, LIFO, or average-cost) in costing the requisitions **to the individual job cost sheets**.

Periodically, the company journalizes the requisitions. For example, if Wallace uses $24,000 of direct materials and $6,000 of indirect materials in January, the entry is:

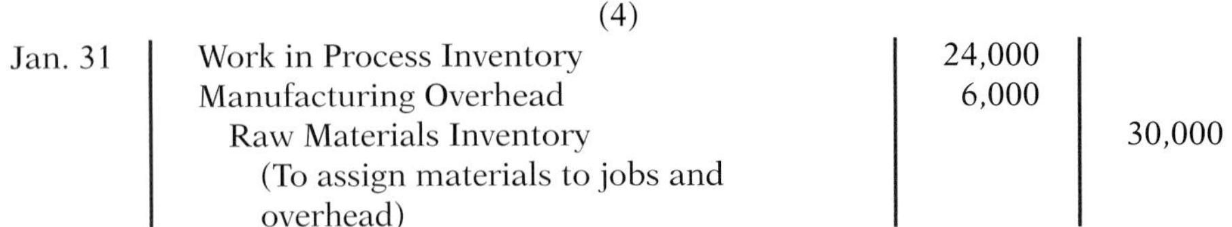

(4)

Date	Account	Debit	Credit
Jan. 31	Work in Process Inventory	24,000	
	Manufacturing Overhead	6,000	
	Raw Materials Inventory		30,000
	(To assign materials to jobs and overhead)		

This entry reduces Raw Materials Inventory by $30,000, increases Work in Process Inventory by $24,000, and increases Manufacturing Overhead by $6,000, as shown below.

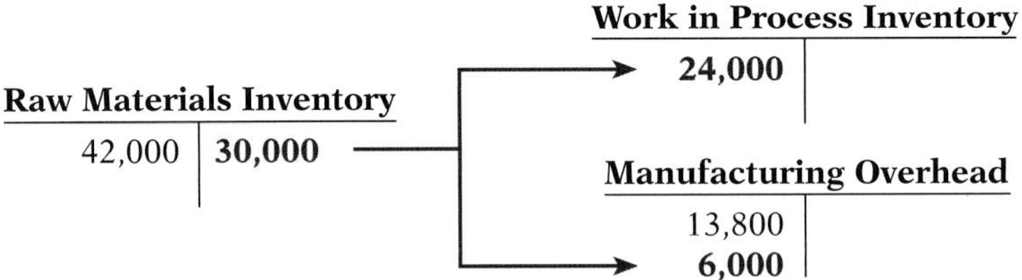

Illustration 20-6 shows the posting of requisition slip R247 to Job No. 101 and other assumed postings to the job cost sheets for materials. The requisition slips provide the basis for total direct materials costs of $12,000 for Job No. 101, $7,000 for Job No. 102, and $5,000 for Job No. 103. After the company has completed all postings, the sum of the direct materials columns of the job cost sheets (the subsidiary

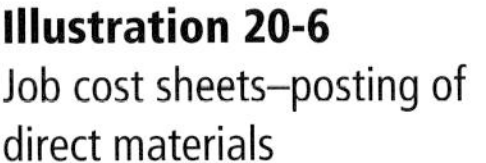

Illustration 20-6
Job cost sheets–posting of direct materials

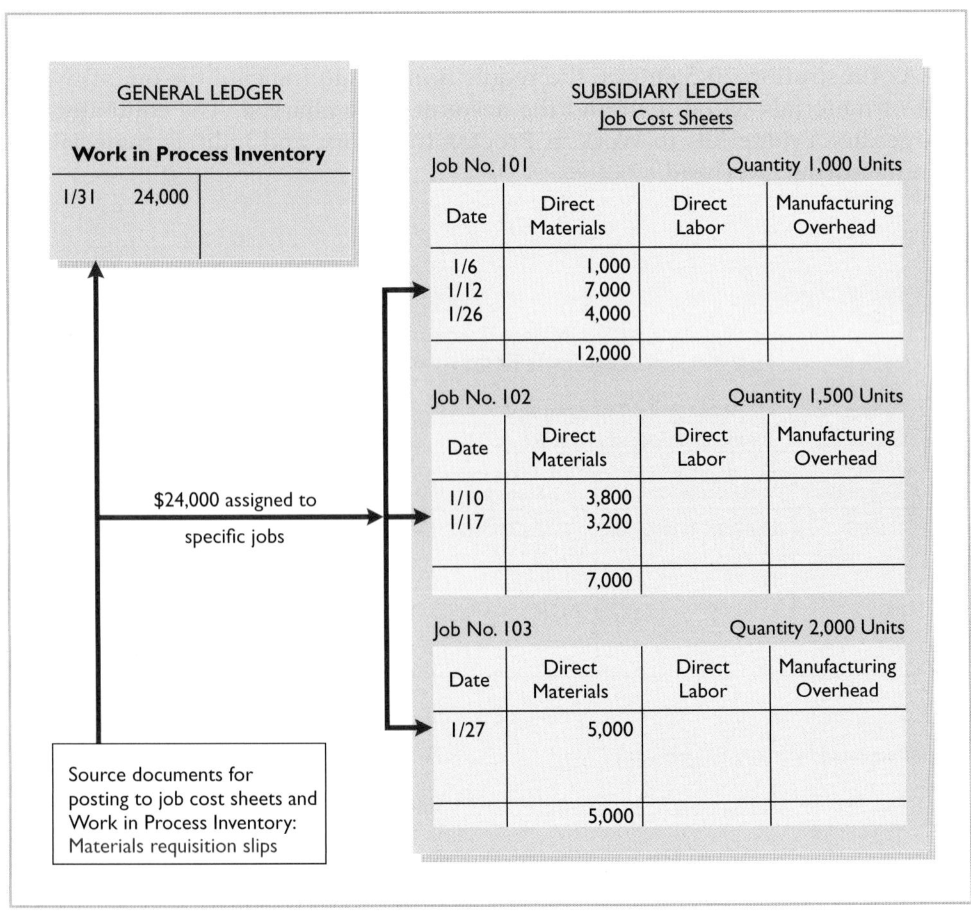

account amounts of $12,000, $7,000, and $5,000) should equal the direct materials debited to Work in Process Inventory (the control account amount of $24,000).

Factory Labor Costs

Companies assign factory labor costs to jobs on the basis of time tickets prepared when the work is performed. The **time ticket** indicates the employee, the hours worked, the account and job to be charged, and the total labor cost. Many companies accumulate these data through the use of bar coding and scanning devices. When they start and end work, employees scan bar codes on their identification badges and bar codes associated with each job they work on. When direct labor is involved, the time ticket must indicate the job number, as shown in Illustration 20-7. The employee's supervisor should approve all time tickets.

Illustration 20-7
Time ticket

Wallace Company
Time Ticket

Date: 1/6/17
Employee: John Nash — Employee No. 124
Charge to: Work in Process — Job No. 101

Time			Hourly Rate	Total Cost
Start	Stop	Total Hours		
0800	1200	4	10.00	40.00

Approved by Bob Kadler — Costed by M Chen

The time tickets are later sent to the payroll department, which applies the employee's hourly wage rate and computes the total labor cost. Finally, the company journalizes the time tickets. It debits the account Work in Process Inventory for direct labor and debits Manufacturing Overhead for indirect labor. For example, if the $32,000 total factory labor cost consists of $28,000 of direct labor and $4,000 of indirect labor, the entry is:

	(5)		
Jan. 31	Work in Process Inventory	28,000	
	Manufacturing Overhead	4,000	
	Factory Labor		32,000
	(To assign labor to jobs and overhead)		

As a result of this entry, Factory Labor is reduced by $32,000 so it has a zero balance, and labor costs are assigned to the appropriate manufacturing accounts. The entry increases Work in Process Inventory by $28,000 and increases Manufacturing Overhead by $4,000, as shown below.

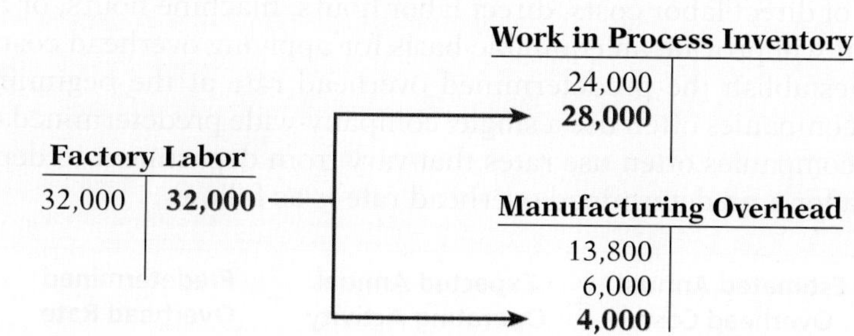

Let's assume that the labor costs chargeable to Wallace's three jobs are $15,000, $9,000, and $4,000. Illustration 20-8 shows the Work in Process Inventory and job cost sheets after posting. As in the case of direct materials, the postings to the direct labor columns of the job cost sheets should equal the posting of direct labor to Work in Process Inventory.

Illustration 20-8
Job cost sheets—direct labor

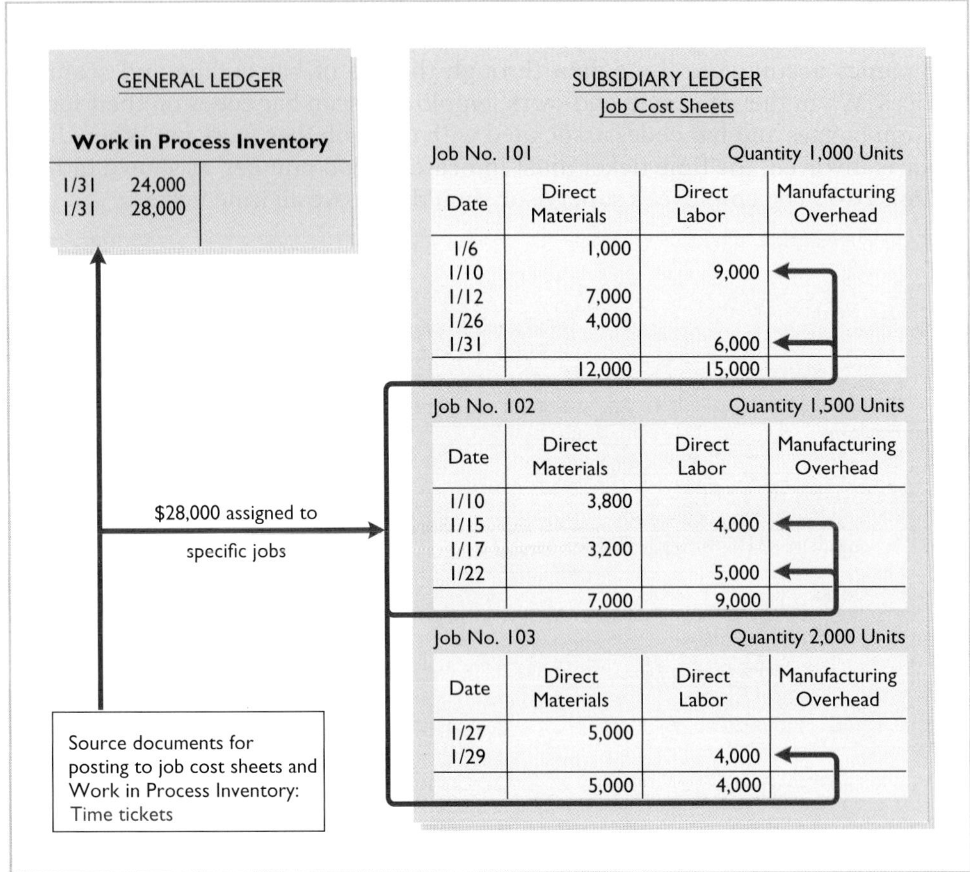

LEARNING OBJECTIVE 

Demonstrate how to determine and use the predetermined overhead rate.

Companies charge the actual costs of direct materials and direct labor to specific jobs. In contrast, manufacturing **overhead** relates to production operations **as a whole**. As a result, overhead costs cannot be assigned to specific jobs on the basis of actual costs incurred. Instead, companies assign manufacturing overhead to work in process and to specific jobs **on an estimated basis through the use of a predetermined overhead rate**.

The **predetermined overhead rate** is based on the relationship between estimated annual overhead costs and expected annual operating activity, expressed in terms of a common **activity base**. The company may state the activity in terms of direct labor costs, direct labor hours, machine hours, or any other measure that will provide an equitable basis for applying overhead costs to jobs. Companies establish the predetermined overhead rate at the beginning of the year. Small companies often use a single, company-wide predetermined overhead rate. Large companies often use rates that vary from department to department. The formula for a predetermined overhead rate is as follows.

Illustration 20-9
Formula for predetermined overhead rate

Estimated Annual Overhead Costs	÷	Expected Annual Operating Activity	=	Predetermined Overhead Rate

Overhead relates to production operations as a whole. To know what "the whole" is, the logical thing is to wait until the end of the year's operations. At that time, the company knows all of its costs for the period. As a practical matter, though, managers cannot wait until the end of the year. To price products effectively as they are completed, managers need information about product costs of specific jobs completed during the year. Using a predetermined overhead rate enables a cost to be determined for the job immediately. Illustration 20-10 indicates how manufacturing overhead is assigned to work in process.

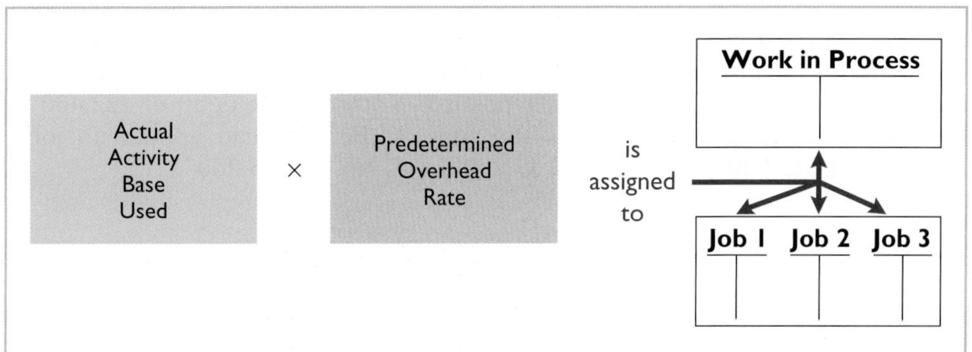

Illustration 20-10
Using predetermined overhead rates

Wallace Company uses direct labor cost as the activity base. Assuming that the company expects annual overhead costs to be $280,000 and direct labor costs for the year to be $350,000, the overhead rate is 80%, computed as follows.

Estimated Annual Overhead Costs	÷	Expected Direct Labor Cost	=	Predetermined Overhead Rate
$280,000	÷	$350,000	=	80%

Illustration 20-11
Calculation of predetermined overhead rate

This means that for every dollar of direct labor, Wallace will assign 80 cents of manufacturing overhead to a job. The use of a predetermined overhead rate enables the company to determine the approximate total cost of each job **when it completes the job**.

Historically, companies used direct labor costs or direct labor hours as the activity base. The reason was the relatively high correlation between direct labor and manufacturing overhead. Today, more companies are using **machine hours as the activity base, due to increased reliance on automation in manufacturing operations**. Or, as mentioned in Chapter 19 (and discussed in Chapter 21), many companies now use activity-based costing to more accurately allocate overhead costs based on the activities that give rise to the costs.

A company may use more than one activity base. For example, if a job is manufactured in more than one factory department, each department may have its own overhead rate. In chapter opening story, **Disney** might use two bases in assigning overhead to film jobs: direct materials dollars for indirect materials, and direct labor hours for such costs as insurance and supervisor salaries.

Wallace Company applies manufacturing overhead to work in process when it assigns direct labor costs. It also applies manufacturing overhead to specific jobs at the same time. For January, Wallace applied overhead of $22,400 in response to its assignment of $28,000 of direct labor costs (direct labor cost of $28,000 × 80%). The following entry records this application.

(6)

Date	Account	Debit	Credit
Jan. 31	Work in Process Inventory	22,400	
	Manufacturing Overhead		22,400
	(To assign overhead to jobs)		

This entry reduces the balance in Manufacturing Overhead and increases Work in Process Inventory by $22,400, as shown below.

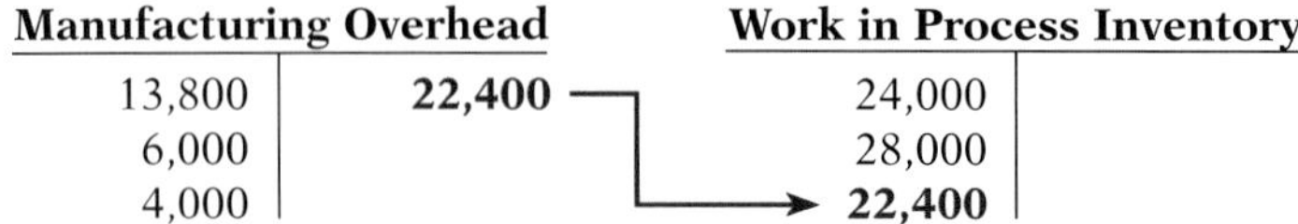

The overhead that Wallace applies to each job will be 80% of the direct labor cost of the job for the month. Illustration 20-12 shows the Work in Process Inventory account and the job cost sheets after posting. Note that the debit of $22,400 to Work in Process Inventory equals the sum of the overhead applied to jobs: Job No. 101 $12,000 + Job No. 102 $7,200 + Job No. 103 $3,200.

Illustration 20-12
Job cost sheets–manufacturing overhead applied

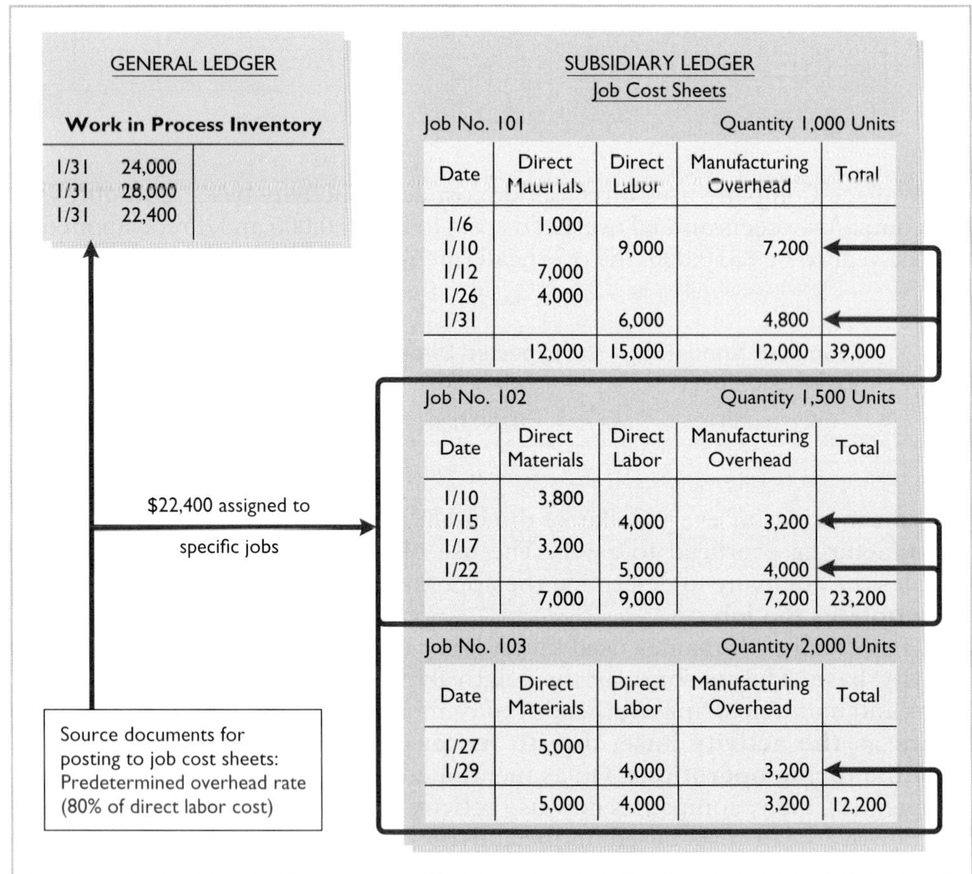

At the end of each month, the **balance in Work in Process Inventory should equal the sum of the costs shown on the job cost sheets of unfinished jobs**. Illustration 20-13 presents proof of the agreement of the control and subsidiary accounts in Wallace. (It assumes that all jobs are still in process.)

Illustration 20-13
Proof of job cost sheets to work in process inventory

Work in Process Inventory

Date	Debit	Credit
Jan. 31	24,000	
31	28,000	
31	22,400	
	74,400	

Job Cost Sheets

No. 101	$ 39,000
102	23,200
103	12,200
	$74,400

LEARNING OBJECTIVE 

Prepare entries for manufacturing and service jobs completed and sold.

Assigning Costs to Finished Goods

When a job is completed, Wallace Company summarizes the costs and completes the lower portion of the applicable job cost sheet. For example, if we assume that Wallace completes Job No. 101, a batch of electronic sensors, on January 31, the job cost sheet appears as shown in Illustration 20-14.

Illustration 20-14
Completed job cost sheet

Job Cost Sheet

Job No.	101	Quantity	1,000
Item	Electronic Sensors	Date Requested	January 5
For	Tanner Company	Date Completed	January 31

Date	Direct Materials	Direct Labor	Manufacturing Overhead
1/6	$ 1,000		
1/10		$ 9,000	$ 7,200
1/12	7,000		
1/26	4,000		
1/31		6,000	4,800
	$12,000	$15,000	$12,000

Cost of completed job	
Direct materials	$ 12,000
Direct labor	15,000
Manufacturing overhead	12,000
Total cost	$ 39,000
Unit cost ($39,000 ÷ 1,000)	$ 39.00

When a job is finished, Wallace makes an entry to transfer its total cost to finished goods inventory. The entry is as follows.

(7)

Jan. 31	Finished Goods Inventory	39,000	
	Work in Process Inventory		39,000
	(To record completion of Job No. 101)		

This entry increases Finished Goods Inventory and reduces Work in Process Inventory by $39,000, as shown in the T-accounts below.

Work in Process Inventory			Finished Goods Inventory	
24,000	**39,000**	→	**39,000**	
28,000				
22,400				

Finished Goods Inventory is a control account. It controls individual finished goods records in a finished goods subsidiary ledger.

Assigning Costs to Cost of Goods Sold

Companies recognize cost of goods sold when each sale occurs. To illustrate the entries a company makes when it sells a completed job, assume that on January 31

Wallace Company sells on account Job No. 101. The job cost $39,000, and it sold for $50,000. The entries to record the sale and recognize cost of goods sold are:

(8)

Jan. 31	Accounts Receivable	50,000	
	Sales Revenue		50,000
	(To record sale of Job No. 101)		
31	Cost of Goods Sold	39,000	
	Finished Goods Inventory		39,000
	(To record cost of Job No. 101)		

This entry increases Cost of Goods Sold and reduces Finished Goods Inventory by $39,000, as shown in the T-accounts below.

Finished Goods Inventory			Cost of Goods Sold	
39,000	**39,000**	→	**39,000**	

Summary of Job Order Cost Flows

Illustration 20-15 shows a completed flowchart for a job order cost accounting system. All postings are keyed to entries 1–8 in the example presented in the previous pages for Wallace Company.

Illustration 20-15
Flow of costs in a job order cost system

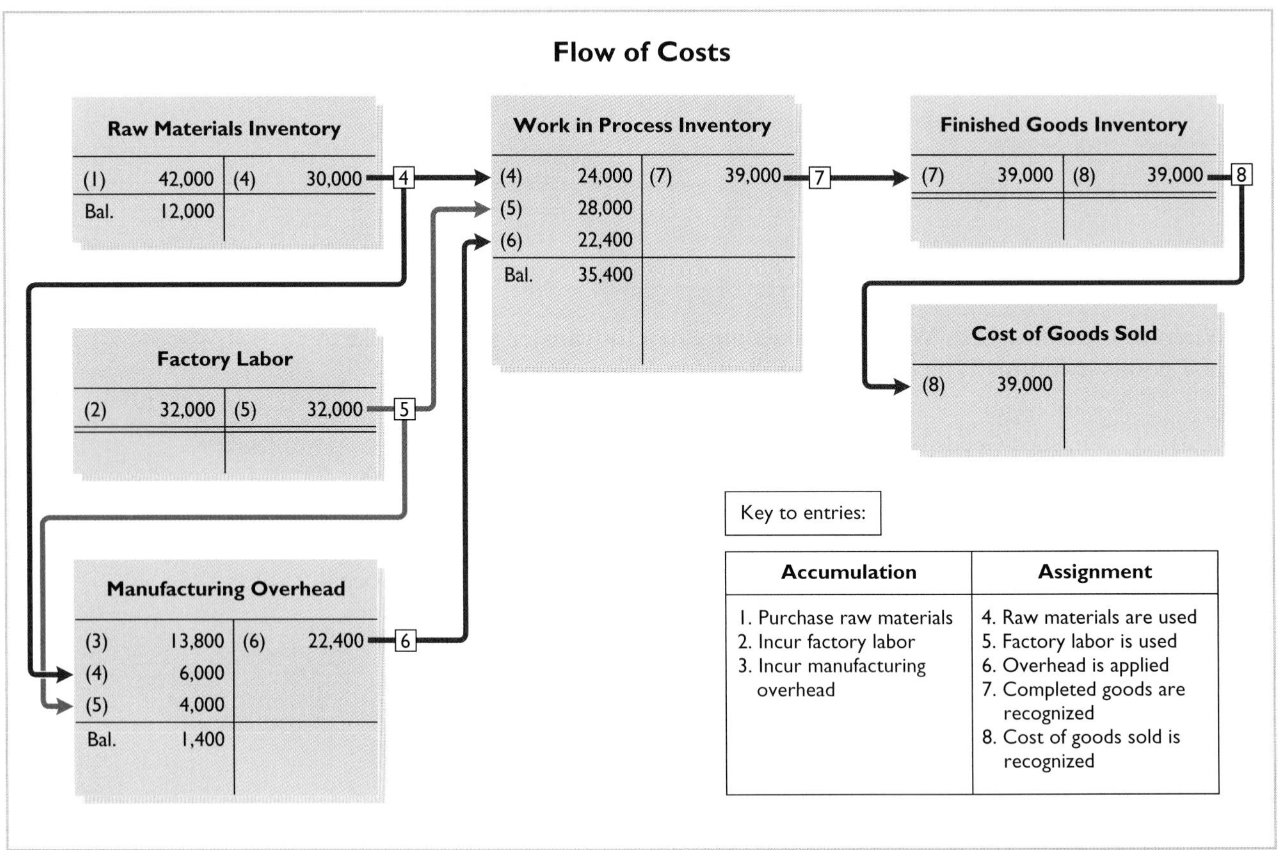

The cost flows in the diagram can be categorized as one of four types:

- **Accumulation.** The company first accumulates costs by (1) purchasing raw materials, (2) incurring labor costs, and (3) incurring manufacturing overhead costs.

- **Assignment to jobs.** Once the company has incurred manufacturing costs, it must assign them to specific jobs. For example, as it uses raw materials on specific jobs (4), the company assigns them to work in process or treats them as manufacturing overhead if the raw materials cannot be associated with a specific job. Similarly, the company either assigns factory labor (5) to work in process or treats it as manufacturing overhead if the factory labor cannot be associated with a specific job. Finally the company assigns manufacturing overhead (6) to work in process using a *predetermined overhead rate*. This deserves emphasis: **Do not assign overhead using actual overhead costs but instead use a predetermined rate.**
- **Completed jobs.** As jobs are completed (7), the company transfers the cost of the completed job out of work in process inventory into finished goods inventory.
- **When goods are sold.** As specific items are sold (8), the company transfers their cost out of finished goods inventory into cost of goods sold.

Illustration 20-16 summarizes the flow of documents in a job order cost system.

Illustration 20-16
Flow of documents in a job order cost system

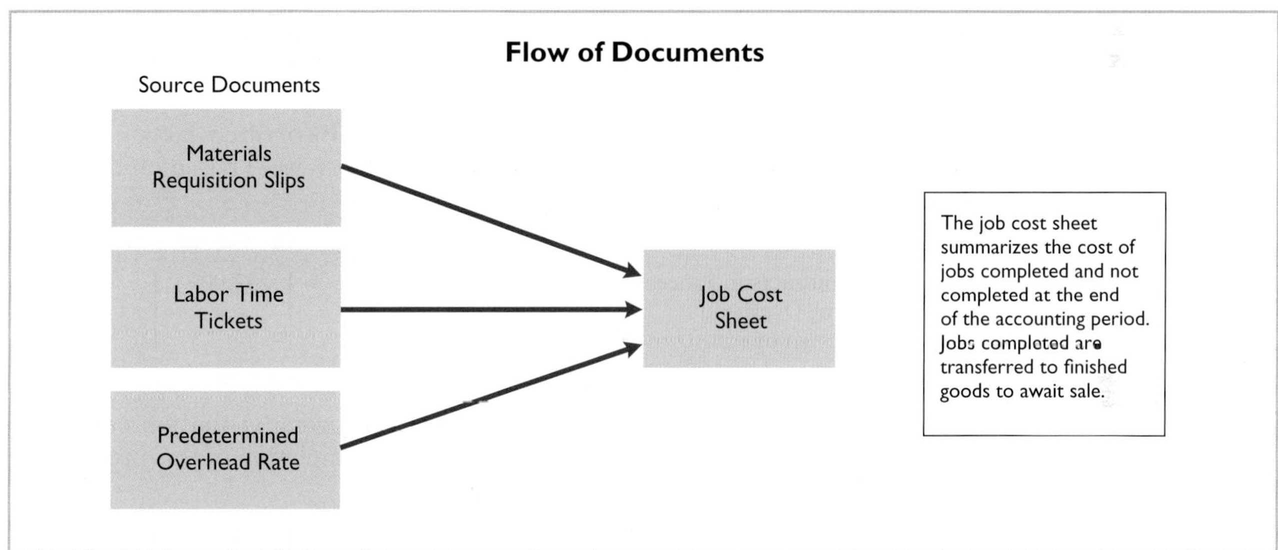

Job Order Costing for Service Companies

Our extended job order costing example focuses on a manufacturer so that you see the flow of costs through the inventory accounts. It is important to understand, however, that job order costing is also commonly used by service companies. While service companies do not have inventory, the techniques of job order costing are still quite useful in many service-industry environments. Consider, for example, the **Mayo Clinic** (healthcare), **PriceWaterhouseCoopers** (accounting), and **Goldman Sachs** (investment banking). These companies need to keep track of the cost of jobs performed for specific customers to evaluate the profitability of medical treatments, audits, or investment banking engagements.

Many service organizations bill their customers using cost-plus contracts. Cost-plus contracts mean that the customer's bill is the sum of the costs incurred on the job, plus a profit amount that is calculated as a percentage of the costs incurred. In order to minimize conflict with customers and reduce potential contract disputes, service companies that use cost-plus contracts must maintain accurate and up-to-date costing records. Up-to-date cost records enable a service company to immediately notify a customer of cost overruns due to customer requests for changes to the original plan or unexpected complications. Timely recordkeeping allows the contractor and customer to consider alternatives before it is too late.

A service company that uses a job order cost system does not have inventory accounts. It does, however, use an account similar to Work in Process Inventory, referred to here as Service Contracts in Process, to record job costs prior to completion. To illustrate the journal entries for a service company under a job order cost system, consider the following transactions for Dorm Decor, an interior design company. The entry to record the assignment of $9,000 of supplies to projects ($7,000 direct and $2,000 indirect) is:

Service Contracts in Process	7,000	
Operating Overhead	2,000	
Supplies		9,000
(To assign supplies to projects)		

The entry to record the assignment of service salaries and wages of $100,000 ($84,000 direct and $16,000 indirect) is:

Service Contracts in Process	84,000	
Operating Overhead	16,000	
Service Salaries and Wages		100,000
(To assign personnel costs to projects)		

Dorm Decor applies operating overhead at a rate of 50% of direct labor costs. The entry to record the application of overhead ($84,000 × 50%) based on the direct labor costs is:

Service Contracts in Process	42,000	
Operating Overhead		42,000
(To assign operating overhead to projects)		

Upon completion of a design project (for State University) the job cost sheet shows a total cost of $34,000. The entry to record completion of this project is:

Cost of Completed Service Contracts	34,000	
Service Contracts in Process		34,000
(To record completion of State University project)		

Job cost sheets for a service company keep track of materials, labor, and overhead used on a particular job similar to a manufacturer. Several exercises at the end of this chapter apply job order costing to service companies.

Advantages and Disadvantages of Job Order Costing

Job order costing is more precise in the assignment of costs to projects than process costing. For example, assume that a construction company, Juan Company, builds 10 custom homes a year at a total cost of $2,000,000. One way to determine the cost of the homes is to divide the total construction cost incurred during the year by the number of homes produced during the year. For Juan Company, an average cost of $200,000 ($2,000,000 ÷ 10) is computed. If the homes are nearly identical, then this approach is adequate for purposes of determining profit per home. But if the homes vary in terms of size, style, and material types, using the average cost of $200,000 to determine profit per home is inappropriate. Instead, Juan Company should use a job order cost system to determine the specific cost incurred to build each home and the amount of profit made on each. Thus, job order costing provides more useful information for determining the profitability of particular projects and for estimating costs when preparing bids on future jobs.

However, job order costing requires a significant amount of data entry. For Juan Company, it is much easier to simply keep track of total costs incurred during the year than it is to keep track of the costs incurred on each job (home built). Recording this information is time-consuming, and if the data is not entered accurately, then the product costs are incorrect. In recent years, technological advances, such as bar-coding devices for both labor costs and materials, have increased the accuracy and reduced the effort needed to record costs on specific jobs. These innovations expand the opportunities to apply job order costing in a wider variety of business settings, thus improving management's ability to control costs and make better informed decisions.

A common problem of all costing systems is how to allocate overhead to the finished product. Overhead often represents more than 50% of a product's cost, and this cost is often difficult to allocate meaningfully to the product. How, for example, is the salary of a project manager at Juan Company allocated to the various homes, which may differ in size, style, and cost of materials used? The accuracy of the job order cost system is largely dependent on the accuracy of the overhead allocation process. Even if the company does a good job of keeping track of the specific amounts of materials and labor used on each job, if the overhead costs are not allocated to individual jobs in a meaningful way, the product costing information is not useful. We address this issue in Chapter 21.

Distinguish between under- and overapplied manufacturing overhead.

At the end of a period, companies prepare financial statements that present aggregate data on all jobs manufactured and sold. The cost of goods manufactured schedule in job order costing is the same as in Chapter 19 with one exception: **The schedule shows manufacturing overhead applied, rather than actual overhead costs. The company adds this amount to direct materials and direct labor to determine total manufacturing costs.**

Companies prepare the cost of goods manufactured schedule directly from the Work in Process Inventory account. Illustration 20-17 shows a condensed schedule for Wallace Company for January.

Illustration 20-17
Cost of goods manufactured schedule

WALLACE COMPANY Cost of Goods Manufactured Schedule For the Month Ending January 31, 2017		
Work in process, January 1		$ -0-
Direct materials used	$ 24,000	
Direct labor	28,000	
Manufacturing overhead applied	**22,400**	
Total manufacturing costs		74,400
Total cost of work in process		74,400
Less: Work in process, January 31		35,400
Cost of goods manufactured		$39,000

Note that the cost of goods manufactured ($39,000) agrees with the amount transferred from Work in Process Inventory to Finished Goods Inventory in journal entry No. 7 in Illustration 20-15 (page 706).

The income statement and balance sheet are the same as those illustrated in Chapter 19. For example, Illustration 20-18 shows the partial income statement for Wallace for the month of January.

Illustration 20-18
Partial income statement

WALLACE COMPANY Income Statement (partial) For the Month Ending January 31, 2017		
Sales revenue		$50,000
Cost of goods sold		
Finished goods inventory, January 1	$ –0–	
Cost of goods manufactured (see Illustration 20-17)	**39,000**	
Cost of goods available for sale	39,000	
Less: Finished goods inventory, January 31	–0–	
Cost of goods sold		39,000
Gross profit		$11,000

Under- or Overapplied Manufacturing Overhead

Recall that overhead is applied based on an estimate of total annual overhead costs. This estimate will rarely be exactly equal to actual overhead incurred. Therefore, at the end of the year, after overhead has been applied to specific jobs, the Manufacturing Overhead account will likely have a remaining balance.

When Manufacturing Overhead has a **debit balance**, overhead is said to be underapplied. **Underapplied overhead** means that the overhead assigned to work in process is less than the overhead incurred. Conversely, when manufacturing overhead has a **credit balance**, overhead is overapplied. **Overapplied overhead** means that the overhead assigned to work in process is greater than the overhead incurred. Illustration 20-19 shows these concepts.

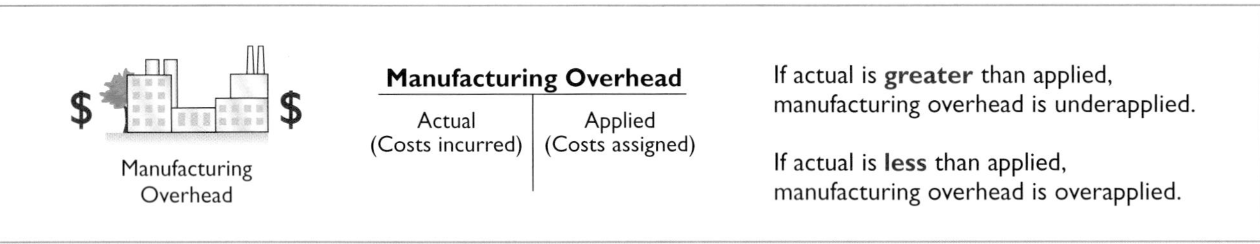

Illustration 20-19
Under- and overapplied overhead

YEAR-END BALANCE

At the end of the year, all manufacturing overhead transactions are complete. There is no further opportunity for offsetting events to occur. At this point, Wallace Company eliminates any balance in Manufacturing Overhead by an adjusting entry. It considers under- or overapplied overhead to be an **adjustment to cost of goods sold**. Thus, Wallace **debits underapplied overhead to Cost of Goods Sold**. It **credits overapplied overhead to Cost of Goods Sold**.

To illustrate, assume that Wallace has a $2,500 credit balance in Manufacturing Overhead at December 31. The adjusting entry for the overapplied overhead is:

Dec. 31	Manufacturing Overhead	2,500	
	Cost of Goods Sold		2,500
	(To transfer overapplied overhead to cost of goods sold)		

After Wallace posts this entry, Manufacturing Overhead has a zero balance. In preparing an income statement for the year, Wallace reports cost of goods sold **after adjusting it** for either under- or overapplied overhead.

Conceptually, some argue that under- or overapplied overhead at the end of the year should be allocated among ending work in process, finished goods, and cost of goods sold. The discussion of this possible allocation approach is left to more advanced courses.

REVIEW AND PRACTICE

LEARNING OBJECTIVES REVIEW

1 Describe cost systems and the flow of costs in a job order system. Cost accounting involves the procedures for measuring, recording, and reporting product costs. From the data accumulated, companies determine the total cost and the unit cost of each product. The two basic types of cost accounting systems are process cost and job order cost.

In job order costing, companies first accumulate manufacturing costs in three accounts: Raw Materials Inventory, Factory Labor, and Manufacturing Overhead. They then assign the accumulated costs to Work in Process Inventory and eventually to Finished Goods Inventory and Cost of Goods Sold.

2 Use a job cost sheet to assign costs to work in process. A job cost sheet is a form used to record the costs chargeable to a specific job and to determine the total and unit costs of the completed job. Job cost sheets constitute the subsidiary ledger for the Work in Process Inventory control account.

3 Demonstrate how to determine and use the predetermined overhead rate. The predetermined overhead rate is based on the relationship between estimated annual overhead costs and expected annual operating activity. This is expressed in terms of a common activity base, such as direct labor cost. Companies use this rate to assign overhead costs to work in process and to specific jobs.

4 Prepare entries for manufacturing and service jobs completed and sold. When jobs are completed, companies debit the cost to Finished Goods Inventory and credit it to Work in Process Inventory. When a job is sold, the entries are (a) debit Cash or Accounts Receivable and credit Sales Revenue for the selling price, and (b) debit Cost of Goods Sold and credit Finished Goods Inventory for the cost of the goods.

5 Distinguish between under- and overapplied manufacturing overhead. Underapplied manufacturing overhead indicates that the overhead assigned to work in process is less than the overhead incurred. Overapplied overhead indicates that the overhead assigned to work in process is greater than the overhead incurred.

GLOSSARY REVIEW

Cost accounting An area of accounting that involves measuring, recording, and reporting product costs.

Cost accounting system Manufacturing-cost accounts that are fully integrated into the general ledger of a company.

Job cost sheet A form used to record the costs chargeable to a specific job and to determine the total and unit costs of the completed job.

Job order cost system A cost accounting system in which costs are assigned to each job or batch.

Materials requisition slip A document authorizing the issuance of raw materials from the storeroom to production.

Overapplied overhead A situation in which overhead assigned to work in process is greater than the overhead incurred.

Predetermined overhead rate A rate based on the relationship between estimated annual overhead costs and expected annual operating activity, expressed in terms of a common activity base.

Process cost system A cost accounting system used when a company manufactures a large volume of similar products.

Time ticket A document that indicates the employee, the hours worked, the account and job to be charged, and the total labor cost.

Underapplied overhead A situation in which overhead assigned to work in process is less than the overhead incurred.

PRACTICE EXERCISES

Analyze a job cost sheet and prepare entries for manufacturing costs.

(LO 1, 2, 3, 4)

1. A job order cost sheet for Michaels Company is shown below.

Job No. 92			**For 2,000 Units**
Date	Direct Materials	Direct Labor	Manufacturing Overhead
Beg. bal. Jan. 1	3,925	6,000	4,200
8	6,000		
12		8,500	6,375
25	2,000		
27		4,000	3,000
	11,925	18,500	13,575

Cost of completed job:	
Direct materials	$11,925
Direct labor	18,500
Manufacturing overhead	13,575
Total cost	$44,000
Unit cost ($44,000 ÷ 2,000)	$ 22.00

Instructions

(a) Answer the following questions.
   (1) What was the balance in Work in Process Inventory on January 1 if this was the only unfinished job?
   (2) If manufacturing overhead is applied on the basis of direct labor cost, what overhead rate was used in each year?

(b) Prepare summary entries at January 31 to record the current year's transactions pertaining to Job No. 92.

Solution

1. (a) 1. $14,125, or ($3,925 + $6,000 + $4,200).
   2. Last year 70%, or ($4,200 ÷ $6,000); this year 75% (either $6,375 ÷ $8,500 or $3,000 ÷ $4,000).

(b) Jan. 31	Work in Process Inventory	8,000	
	Raw Materials Inventory		8,000
	($6,000 + $2,000)		
31	Work in Process Inventory	12,500	
	Factory Labor		12,500
	($8,500 + $4,000)		
31	Work in Process Inventory	9,375	
	Manufacturing Overhead		9,375
	($6,375 + $3,000)		
31	Finished Goods Inventory	44,000	
	Work in Process Inventory		44,000

Compute the overhead rate and under- or overapplied overhead.

(LO 3, 5)

2. Kwik Kopy Company applies operating overhead to photocopying jobs on the basis of machine hours used. Overhead costs are expected to total $290,000 for the year, and machine usage is estimated at 125,000 hours.

For the year, $295,000 of overhead costs are incurred and 130,000 hours are used.

Instructions

(a) Compute the service overhead rate for the year.

(b) What is the amount of under- or overapplied overhead at December 31?

(c) Assuming the under- or overapplied overhead for the year is not allocated to inventory accounts, prepare the adjusting entry to assign the amount to cost of jobs finished.

Solution

2. (a) \$2.32 per machine hour (\$290,000 ÷ 125,000).
   (b) (\$295,000) − (\$2.32 × 130,000 machine hours)
   \$295,000 − \$301,600 = \$6,600 overapplied
   (c)

Operating Overhead	6,600	
Cost of Goods Sold		6,600

PRACTICE PROBLEM

Compute predetermined overhead rate, apply overhead, and calculate under- or overapplied overhead.

(LO 3, 5)

Cardella Company applies overhead on the basis of direct labor costs. The company estimates annual overhead costs will be \$760,000 and annual direct labor costs will be \$950,000. During February, Cardella works on two jobs: A16 and B17. Summary data concerning these jobs are as follows.

Manufacturing Costs Incurred

Purchased \$54,000 of raw materials on account.
Factory labor \$76,000, plus \$4,000 employer payroll taxes.
Manufacturing overhead exclusive of indirect materials and indirect labor \$59,800.

Assignment of Costs

Direct materials: Job A16 \$27,000, Job B17 \$21,000
Indirect materials: \$3,000
Direct labor: Job A16 \$52,000, Job B17 \$26,000
Indirect labor: \$2,000

The company completed Job A16 and sold it on account for \$150,000. Job B17 was only partially completed.

Instructions

(a) Compute the predetermined overhead rate.
(b) Journalize the February transactions in the sequence followed in the chapter.
(c) What was the amount of under- or overapplied manufacturing overhead?

Solution

(a) Estimated annual overhead costs	÷	Expected annual operating activity	=	Predetermined overhead rate
\$760,000	÷	\$950,000	=	80%

(b)

Date	Account	Debit	Credit
	(1)		
Feb. 28	Raw Materials Inventory	54,000	
	Accounts Payable		54,000
	(Purchase of raw materials on account)		
	(2)		
28	Factory Labor	80,000	
	Factory Wages Payable		76,000
	Employer Payroll Taxes Payable		4,000
	(To record factory labor costs)		
	(3)		
28	Manufacturing Overhead	59,800	
	Accounts Payable, Accumulated Depreciation, and Prepaid Insurance		59,800
	(To record overhead costs)		
	(4)		
28	Work in Process Inventory	48,000	
	Manufacturing Overhead	3,000	
	Raw Materials Inventory		51,000
	(To assign raw materials to production)		

Date	Account Titles and Explanation	Debit	Credit
	(5)		
28	Work in Process Inventory	78,000	
	Manufacturing Overhead	2,000	
	Factory Labor		80,000
	(To assign factory labor to production)		
	(6)		
28	Work in Process Inventory	62,400	
	Manufacturing Overhead		62,400
	(To assign overhead to jobs—80% × $78,000)		
	(7)		
28	Finished Goods Inventory	120,600	
	Work in Process Inventory		120,600
	(To record completion of Job A16: direct materials $27,000, direct labor $52,000, and manufacturing overhead $41,600)		
	(8)		
28	Accounts Receivable	150,000	
	Sales Revenue		150,000
	(To record sale of Job A16)		
28	Cost of Goods Sold	120,600	
	Finished Goods Inventory		120,600
	(To record cost of sale for Job A16)		

(c) Manufacturing Overhead has a debit balance of $2,400 as shown below.

Manufacturing Overhead

(3)	59,800	(6)	62,400
(4)	3,000		
(5)	2,000		
Bal.	2,400		

Thus, manufacturing overhead is underapplied for the month.

EXERCISES

Prepare entries for factory labor.

(LO 1, 2)

E20-1 The gross earnings of the factory workers for Larkin Company during the month of January are $76,000. The employer's payroll taxes for the factory payroll are $8,000. The fringe benefits to be paid by the employer on this payroll are $6,000. Of the total accumulated cost of factory labor, 85% is related to direct labor and 15% is attributable to indirect labor.

Instructions

(a) Prepare the entry to record the factory labor costs for the month of January.
(b) Prepare the entry to assign factory labor to production.

Prepare journal entries for manufacturing costs.

(LO 1, 2, 3, 4)

E20-2 Stine Company uses a job order cost system. On May 1, the company has a balance in Work in Process Inventory of $3,500 and two jobs in process: Job No. 429 $2,000, and Job No. 430 $1,500. During May, a summary of source documents reveals the following.

Job Number	Materials Requisition Slips		Labor Time Tickets	
429	$2,500		$1,900	
430	3,500		3,000	
431	4,400	$10,400	7,600	$12,500
General use		800		1,200
		$11,200		$13,700

Stine Company applies manufacturing overhead to jobs at an overhead rate of 60% of direct labor cost. Job No. 429 is completed during the month.

Instructions

(a) Prepare summary journal entries to record (1) the requisition slips, (2) the time tickets, (3) the assignment of manufacturing overhead to jobs, and (4) the completion of Job No. 429.

(b) Post the entries to Work in Process Inventory, and prove the agreement of the control account with the job cost sheets. (Use a T-account.)

E20-3 A job order cost sheet for Ryan Company is shown below.

Analyze a job cost sheet and prepare entries for manufacturing costs.

(LO 1, 2, 3, 4)

Job No. 92			**For 2,000 Units**
Date	Direct Materials	Direct Labor	Manufacturing Overhead
Beg. bal. Jan. 1	5,000	6,000	4,200
8	6,000		
12		8,000	6,400
25	2,000		
27		4,000	3,200
	13,000	18,000	13,800
Cost of completed job:			
Direct materials			$13,000
Direct labor			18,000
Manufacturing overhead			13,800
Total cost			$44,800
Unit cost ($44,800 ÷ 2,000)			$22.40

Instructions

(a) On the basis of the foregoing data, answer the following questions.

(1) What was the balance in Work in Process Inventory on January 1 if this was the only unfinished job?

(2) If manufacturing overhead is applied on the basis of direct labor cost, what overhead rate was used in each year?

(b) Prepare summary entries at January 31 to record the current year's transactions pertaining to Job No. 92.

E20-4 Manufacturing cost data for Orlando Company, which uses a job order cost system, are presented below.

Analyze costs of manufacturing and determine missing amounts.

(LO 1, 5)

	Case A	**Case B**	**Case C**
Direct materials used	$ (a)	$ 83,000	$ 63,150
Direct labor	50,000	140,000	(h)
Manufacturing overhead applied	42,500	(d)	(i)
Total manufacturing costs	145,650	(e)	213,000
Work in process 1/1/17	(b)	15,500	18,000
Total cost of work in process	201,500	(f)	(j)
Work in process 12/31/17	(c)	11,800	(k)
Cost of goods manufactured	192,300	(g)	222,000

Instructions

Indicate the missing amount for each letter. Assume that in all cases manufacturing overhead is applied on the basis of direct labor cost and the rate is the same.

E20-5 Ikerd Company applies manufacturing overhead to jobs on the basis of machine hours used. Overhead costs are expected to total $300,000 for the year, and machine usage is estimated at 125,000 hours.

For the year, $322,000 of overhead costs are incurred and 130,000 hours are used.

Compute the manufacturing overhead rate and under- or overapplied overhead.

(LO 3, 5)

Instructions

(a) Compute the manufacturing overhead rate for the year.

(b) What is the amount of under- or overapplied overhead at December 31?

(c) Prepare the adjusting entry to assign the under- or overapplied overhead for the year to cost of goods sold.

Analyze job cost sheet and prepare entry for completed job.

(LO 1, 2, 3, 4)

E20-6 A job cost sheet of Sandoval Company is given below.

Job Cost Sheet

JOB NO. 469 — Quantity 2,500
ITEM White Lion Cages — Date Requested 7/2
FOR Todd Company — Date Completed 7/31

Date	Direct Materials	Direct Labor	Manufacturing Overhead
7/10	700		
12	900		
15		440	550
22		380	475
24	1,600		
27	1,500		
31		540	675

Cost of completed job:	
Direct materials	_____
Direct labor	_____
Manufacturing overhead	_____
Total cost	_____
Unit cost	_____

Instructions

(a) Answer the following questions.
  (1) What are the source documents for direct materials, direct labor, and manufacturing overhead costs assigned to this job?
  (2) What is the predetermined manufacturing overhead rate?
  (3) What are the total cost and the unit cost of the completed job? (Round unit cost to nearest cent.)

(b) Prepare the entry to record the completion of the job.

Prepare entries for manufacturing and nonmanufacturing costs.

(LO 1, 2, 3, 4)

E20-7 Crawford Corporation incurred the following transactions.

1. Purchased raw materials on account $46,300.
2. Raw materials of $36,000 were requisitioned to the factory. An analysis of the materials requisition slips indicated that $6,800 was classified as indirect materials.
3. Factory labor costs incurred were $59,900, of which $51,000 pertained to factory wages payable and $8,900 pertained to employer payroll taxes payable.
4. Time tickets indicated that $54,000 was direct labor and $5,900 was indirect labor.
5. Manufacturing overhead costs incurred on account were $80,500.
6. Depreciation on the company's office building was $8,100.
7. Manufacturing overhead was applied at the rate of 150% of direct labor cost.
8. Goods costing $88,000 were completed and transferred to finished goods.
9. Finished goods costing $75,000 to manufacture were sold on account for $103,000.

Instructions

Journalize the transactions. (Omit explanations.)

Prepare entries for manufacturing and nonmanufacturing costs.

(LO 1, 2, 3, 4)

E20-8 Enos Printing Corp. uses a job order cost system. The following data summarize the operations related to the first quarter's production.

1. Materials purchased on account $192,000, and factory wages incurred $87,300.
2. Materials requisitioned and factory labor used by job:

Job Number	Materials	Factory Labor
A20	$ 35,240	$18,000
A21	42,920	22,000
A22	36,100	15,000
A23	39,270	25,000
General factory use	4,470	7,300
	$158,000	$87,300

3. Manufacturing overhead costs incurred on account $49,500.
4. Depreciation on factory equipment $14,550.
5. Depreciation on the company's office building was $14,300.
6. Manufacturing overhead rate is 90% of direct labor cost.
7. Jobs completed during the quarter: A20, A21, and A23.

Instructions
Prepare entries to record the operations summarized above. (Prepare a schedule showing the individual cost elements and total cost for each job in item 7.)

Prepare a cost of goods manufactured schedule and partial financial statements.

(LO 1, 5)

E20-9 At May 31, 2017, the accounts of Lopez Company show the following.

1. May 1 inventories—finished goods $12,600, work in process $14,700, and raw materials $8,200.
2. May 31 inventories—finished goods $9,500, work in process $15,900, and raw materials $7,100.
3. Debit postings to work in process were direct materials $62,400, direct labor $50,000, and manufacturing overhead applied $40,000.
4. Sales revenue totaled $215,000.

Instructions
(a) Prepare a condensed cost of goods manufactured schedule.
(b) Prepare an income statement for May through gross profit.
(c) Indicate the balance sheet presentation of the manufacturing inventories at May 31, 2017.

Compute work in process and finished goods from job cost sheets.

(LO 2, 4)

E20-10 Tierney Company begins operations on April 1. Information from job cost sheets shows the following.

	Manufacturing Costs Assigned			
Job Number	**April**	**May**	**June**	**Month Completed**
10	$5,200	$4,400		May
11	4,100	3,900	$2,000	June
12	1,200			April
13		4,700	4,500	June
14		5,900	3,600	Not complete

Job 12 was completed in April. Job 10 was completed in May. Jobs 11 and 13 were completed in June. Each job was sold for 25% above its cost in the month following completion.

Instructions
(a) What is the balance in Work in Process Inventory at the end of each month?
(b) What is the balance in Finished Goods Inventory at the end of each month?
(c) What is the gross profit for May, June, and July?

Prepare entries for costs of services provided.

(LO 1, 3, 4)

E20-11 The following are the job cost related accounts for the law firm of Colaw Associates and their manufacturing equivalents:

Law Firm Accounts	Manufacturing Firm Accounts
Supplies	Raw Materials
Salaries and Wages Payable	Factory Wages Payable
Operating Overhead	Manufacturing Overhead
Service Contracts in Process	Work in Process
Cost of Completed Service Contracts	Cost of Goods Sold

Cost data for the month of March follow.

1. Purchased supplies on account $1,800.
2. Issued supplies $1,200 (60% direct and 40% indirect).
3. Assigned labor costs based on time cards for the month which indicated labor costs of $70,000 (80% direct and 20% indirect).
4. Operating overhead costs incurred for cash totaled $40,000.
5. Operating overhead is applied at a rate of 90% of direct labor cost.
6. Work completed totaled $75,000.

Instructions

(a) Journalize the transactions for March. (Omit explanations.)
(b) Determine the balance of the Service Contracts in Process account. (Use a T-account.)

Determine cost of jobs and ending balance in work in process and overhead accounts.

(LO 2, 3, 4)

E20-12 Don Lieberman and Associates, a CPA firm, uses job order costing to capture the costs of its audit jobs. There were no audit jobs in process at the beginning of November. Listed below are data concerning the three audit jobs conducted during November.

	Lynn	Brian	Mike
Direct materials	$600	$400	$200
Auditor labor costs	$5,400	$6,600	$3,375
Auditor hours	72	88	45

Overhead costs are applied to jobs on the basis of auditor hours, and the predetermined overhead rate is $50 per auditor hour. The Lynn job is the only incomplete job at the end of November. Actual overhead for the month was $11,000.

Instructions

(a) Determine the cost of each job.
(b) Indicate the balance of the Service Contracts in Process account at the end of November.
(c) Calculate the ending balance of the Operating Overhead account for November.

Determine predetermined overhead rate, apply overhead, and determine whether balance under- or overapplied.

(LO 3, 5)

E20-13 Tombert Decorating uses a job order cost system to collect the costs of its interior decorating business. Each client's consultation is treated as a separate job. Overhead is applied to each job based on the number of decorator hours incurred. Listed below are data for the current year.

Estimated overhead	$960,000
Actual overhead	$982,800
Estimated decorator hours	40,000
Actual decorator hours	40,500

The company uses Operating Overhead in place of Manufacturing Overhead.

Instructions

(a) Compute the predetermined overhead rate.
(b) Prepare the entry to apply the overhead for the year.
(c) Determine whether the overhead was under- or overapplied and by how much.

PROBLEMS

Prepare entries in a job order cost system and job cost sheets.

(LO 1, 2, 3, 4, 5)

P20-1A Lott Company uses a job order cost system and applies overhead to production on the basis of direct labor costs. On January 1, 2017, Job 50 was the only job in process. The costs incurred prior to January 1 on this job were as follows: direct materials $20,000, direct labor $12,000, and manufacturing overhead $16,000. As of January 1, Job 49 had been completed at a cost of $90,000 and was part of finished goods inventory. There was a $15,000 balance in the Raw Materials Inventory account.

During the month of January, Lott Company began production on Jobs 51 and 52, and completed Jobs 50 and 51. Jobs 49 and 50 were also sold on account during the month for $122,000 and $158,000, respectively. The following additional events occurred during the month.

1. Purchased additional raw materials of $90,000 on account.
2. Incurred factory labor costs of $70,000. Of this amount $16,000 related to employer payroll taxes.
3. Incurred manufacturing overhead costs as follows: indirect materials $17,000, indirect labor $20,000, depreciation expense on equipment $12,000, and various other manufacturing overhead costs on account $16,000.
4. Assigned direct materials and direct labor to jobs as follows.

Job No.	Direct Materials	Direct Labor
50	$10,000	$ 5,000
51	39,000	25,000
52	30,000	20,000

Instructions

(a) Calculate the predetermined overhead rate for 2017, assuming Lott Company estimates total manufacturing overhead costs of $840,000, direct labor costs of $700,000, and direct labor hours of 20,000 for the year.

(b) Open job cost sheets for Jobs 50, 51, and 52. Enter the January 1 balances on the job cost sheet for Job 50.

(c) Prepare the journal entries to record the purchase of raw materials, the factory labor costs incurred, and the manufacturing overhead costs incurred during the month of January.

(d) Prepare the journal entries to record the assignment of direct materials, direct labor, and manufacturing overhead costs to production. In assigning manufacturing overhead costs, use the overhead rate calculated in (a). Post all costs to the job cost sheets as necessary.

(e) Total the job cost sheets for any job(s) completed during the month. Prepare the journal entry (or entries) to record the completion of any job(s) during the month.

(e) Job 50, $69,000
Job 51, $94,000

(f) Prepare the journal entry (or entries) to record the sale of any job(s) during the month.

(g) What is the balance in the Finished Goods Inventory account at the end of the month? What does this balance consist of?

(h) What is the amount of over- or underapplied overhead?

Prepare entries in a job order cost system and partial income statement.

(LO 1, 2, 3, 4, 5)

P20-2A For the year ended December 31, 2017, the job cost sheets of Cinta Company contained the following data.

Job Number	Explanation	Direct Materials	Direct Labor	Manufacturing Overhead	Total Costs
7640	Balance 1/1	$25,000	$24,000	$28,800	$ 77,800
	Current year's costs	30,000	36,000	43,200	109,200
7641	Balance 1/1	11,000	18,000	21,600	50,600
	Current year's costs	43,000	48,000	57,600	148,600
7642	Current year's costs	58,000	55,000	66,000	179,000

Other data:

1. Raw materials inventory totaled $15,000 on January 1. During the year, $140,000 of raw materials were purchased on account.
2. Finished goods on January 1 consisted of Job No. 7638 for $87,000 and Job No. 7639 for $92,000.
3. Job No. 7640 and Job No. 7641 were completed during the year.
4. Job Nos. 7638, 7639, and 7641 were sold on account for $530,000.
5. Manufacturing overhead incurred on account totaled $120,000.
6. Other manufacturing overhead consisted of indirect materials $14,000, indirect labor $18,000, and depreciation on factory machinery $8,000.

Instructions

(a) Prove the agreement of Work in Process Inventory with job cost sheets pertaining to unfinished work. (*Hint:* Use a single T-account for Work in Process Inventory.) Calculate each of the following, then post each to the T-account: (1) beginning balance, (2) direct materials, (3) direct labor, (4) manufacturing overhead, and (5) completed jobs.

(a) $179,000; Job 7642: $179,000

(b) Prepare the adjusting entry for manufacturing overhead, assuming the balance is allocated entirely to Cost of Goods Sold.

(b) Amount = $6,800

(c) Determine the gross profit to be reported for 2017.

(c) $158,600

Prepare entries in a job order cost system and cost of goods manufactured schedule.

(LO 1, 2, 3, 4, 5)

P20-3A Case Inc. is a construction company specializing in custom patios. The patios are constructed of concrete, brick, fiberglass, and lumber, depending upon customer preference. On June 1, 2017, the general ledger for Case Inc. contains the following data.

Raw Materials Inventory	$4,200	Manufacturing Overhead Applied	$32,640
Work in Process Inventory	$5,540	Manufacturing Overhead Incurred	$31,650

Subsidiary data for Work in Process Inventory on June 1 are as follows.

Job Cost Sheets

Cost Element	Customer Job		
	Rodgers	**Stevens**	**Linton**
Direct materials	$ 600	$ 800	$ 900
Direct labor	320	540	580
Manufacturing overhead	400	675	725
	$1,320	$2,015	$2,205

During June, raw materials purchased on account were $4,900, and all wages were paid. Additional overhead costs consisted of depreciation on equipment $900 and miscellaneous costs of $400 incurred on account.

A summary of materials requisition slips and time tickets for June shows the following.

Customer Job	Materials Requisition Slips	Time Tickets
Rodgers	$ 800	$ 850
Koss	2,000	800
Stevens	500	360
Linton	1,300	1,200
Rodgers	300	390
	4,900	3,600
General use	1,500	1,200
	$6,400	$4,800

Overhead was charged to jobs at the same rate of $1.25 per dollar of direct labor cost. The patios for customers Rodgers, Stevens, and Linton were completed during June and sold for a total of $18,900. Each customer paid in full.

Instructions

(a) Journalize the June transactions: (1) for purchase of raw materials, factory labor costs incurred, and manufacturing overhead costs incurred; (2) assignment of direct materials, labor, and overhead to production; and (3) completion of jobs and sale of goods.

(b) Post the entries to Work in Process Inventory.

(c) Reconcile the balance in Work in Process Inventory with the costs of unfinished jobs.

(d) Prepare a cost of goods manufactured schedule for June.

(d) Cost of goods manufactured $14,740

Compute predetermined overhead rates, apply overhead, and calculate under- or overapplied overhead.

(LO 3, 5)

P20-4A Agassi Company uses a job order cost system in each of its three manufacturing departments. Manufacturing overhead is applied to jobs on the basis of direct labor cost in Department D, direct labor hours in Department E, and machine hours in Department K.

In establishing the predetermined overhead rates for 2017, the following estimates were made for the year.

	Department		
	D	**E**	**K**
Manufacturing overhead	$1,200,000	$1,500,000	$900,000
Direct labor costs	$1,500,000	$1,250,000	$450,000
Direct labor hours	100,000	125,000	40,000
Machine hours	400,000	500,000	120,000

During January, the job cost sheets showed the following costs and production data.

	Department		
	D	**E**	**K**
Direct materials used	$140,000	$126,000	$78,000
Direct labor costs	$120,000	$110,000	$37,500
Manufacturing overhead incurred	$ 99,000	$124,000	$79,000
Direct labor hours	8,000	11,000	3,500
Machine hours	34,000	45,000	10,400

Instructions

(a) Compute the predetermined overhead rate for each department.

(b) Compute the total manufacturing costs assigned to jobs in January in each department.

(c) Compute the under- or overapplied overhead for each department at January 31.

(a) 80%, $12, $7.50
(b) $356,000, $368,000, $193,500
(c) $3,000, $(8,000), $1,000

P20-5A Phillips Corporation's fiscal year ends on November 30. The following accounts are found in its job order cost accounting system for the first month of the new fiscal year.

Analyze manufacturing accounts and determine missing amounts.

(LO 1, 2, 3, 4, 5)

Raw Materials Inventory

Dec. 1	Beginning balance	(a)	Dec. 31	Requisitions	16,850
31	Purchases	17,225			
Dec. 31	Ending balance	7,975			

Work in Process Inventory

Dec. 1	Beginning balance	(b)	Dec. 31	Jobs completed	(f)
31	Direct materials	(c)			
31	Direct labor	8,400			
31	Overhead	(d)			
Dec. 31	Ending balance	(e)			

Finished Goods Inventory

Dec. 1	Beginning balance	(g)	Dec. 31	Cost of goods sold	(i)
31	Completed jobs	(h)			
Dec. 31	Ending balance	(j)			

Factory Labor

Dec. 31	Factory wages	12,025	Dec. 31	Wages assigned	(k)

Manufacturing Overhead

Dec. 31	Indirect materials	2,900	Dec. 31	Overhead applied	(m)
31	Indirect labor	(l)			
31	Other overhead	1,245			

Other data:

1. On December 1, two jobs were in process: Job No. 154 and Job No. 155. These jobs had combined direct materials costs of $9,750 and direct labor costs of $15,000. Overhead was applied at a rate that was 75% of direct labor cost.
2. During December, Job Nos. 156, 157, and 158 were started. On December 31, Job No. 158 was unfinished. This job had charges for direct materials $3,800 and direct labor $4,800, plus manufacturing overhead. All jobs, except for Job No. 158, were completed in December.
3. On December 1, Job No. 153 was in the finished goods warehouse. It had a total cost of $5,000. On December 31, Job No. 157 was the only job finished that was not sold. It had a cost of $4,000.
4. Manufacturing overhead was $1,470 underapplied in December.

Instructions

List the letters (a) through (m) and indicate the amount pertaining to each letter.

(c) $13,950
(f) $52,450
(i) $53,450

COMPREHENSIVE CASE

Greetings Inc., a nationally recognized retailer of greeting cards and small gift items, decides to employ Internet technology to expand its sales opportunities. For this case, you will employ traditional job order costing techniques and then evaluate the resulting product costs.

Go to the book's companion website, at **www.wiley.com/college/weygandt**, *for complete case details and instructions.*

BROADENING YOUR PERSPECTIVE

MANAGEMENT DECISION-MAKING

Decision-Making Across the Organization

BYP20-1 Khan Products Company uses a job order cost system. For a number of months, there has been an ongoing rift between the sales department and the production department concerning a special-order product, TC-1. TC-1 is a seasonal product that is manufactured in batches of 1,000 units. TC-1 is sold at cost plus a markup of 40% of cost.

The sales department is unhappy because fluctuating unit production costs significantly affect selling prices. Sales personnel complain that this has caused excessive customer complaints and the loss of considerable orders for TC-1.

The production department maintains that each job order must be fully costed on the basis of the costs incurred during the period in which the goods are produced. Production personnel maintain that the only real solution is for the sales department to increase sales in the slack periods.

Andrea Parley, president of the company, asks you as the company accountant to collect quarterly data for the past year on TC-1. From the cost accounting system, you accumulate the following production quantity and cost data.

	Quarter			
Costs	**1**	**2**	**3**	**4**
Direct materials	$100,000	$220,000	$ 80,000	$200,000
Direct labor	60,000	132,000	48,000	120,000
Manufacturing overhead	105,000	153,000	97,000	125,000
Total	$265,000	$505,000	$225,000	$445,000
Production in batches	5	11	4	10
Unit cost (per batch)	$ 53,000	$ 45,909	$ 56,250	$ 44,500

Instructions

With the class divided into groups, answer the following questions.

(a) What manufacturing cost element is responsible for the fluctuating unit costs? Why?
(b) What is your recommended solution to the problem of fluctuating unit cost?
(c) Restate the quarterly data on the basis of your recommended solution.

Managerial Analysis

BYP20-2 In the course of routine checking of all journal entries prior to preparing year-end reports, Betty Eller discovered several strange entries. She recalled that the president's son Joe had come in to help out during an especially busy time and that he had recorded some journal entries. She was relieved that there were only a few of his entries, and even more relieved that he had included rather lengthy explanations. The entries Joe made were:

(1)

	Debit	Credit
Work in Process Inventory	25,000	
Cash		25,000

(This is for materials put into process. I can't find the record that we paid for these, so I'm crediting Cash because I know we'll have to pay for them sooner or later.)

(2)

	Debit	Credit
Manufacturing Overhead	12,000	
Cash		12,000

(This is for bonuses paid to salespeople. I know they're part of overhead, and I can't find an account called "Non-Factory Overhead" or "Other Overhead" so I'm putting it in Manufacturing Overhead. I have the check stubs, so I know we paid these.)

(3)

Wages Expense	120,000	
Cash		120,000

(This is for the factory workers' wages. I have a note that employer payroll taxes are $18,000. I still think that's part of wages expense and that we'll have to pay it all in cash sooner or later, so I credited Cash for the wages and the taxes.)

(4)

Work in Process Inventory	3,000	
Raw Materials Inventory		3,000

(This is for the glue used in the factory. I know we used this to make the products, even though we didn't use very much on any one of the products. I got it out of inventory, so I credited an inventory account.)

Instructions

(a) How should Joe have recorded each of the four events?
(b) If an entry was not corrected, which financial statements (income statement or balance sheet) would be affected? What balances would be overstated or understated?

Real-World Focus

BYP20-3 The Institute of Management Accountants sponsors a certification for management accountants, allowing them to obtain the title of Certified Management Accountant.

Address: **www.imanet.org**, or go to **www.wiley.com/college/weygandt**

Steps

1. Go to the site shown above.
2. Choose **CMA Certification**, then **Become a CMA**, and then **How to Get Started**. Answer part (a) below.
3. Choose **CMA Resource Center** and then **Continuing Education for CMAs**. Answer part (b) below.

Instructions

(a) What is the experience qualification requirement?
(b) How many hours of continuing education are required, and what types of courses qualify?

CRITICAL THINKING

Communication Activity

BYP20-4 You are the management accountant for Williams Company. Your company does custom carpentry work and uses a job order cost system. Williams sends detailed job cost sheets to its customers, along with an invoice. The job cost sheets show the date materials were used, the dollar cost of materials, and the hours and cost of labor. A predetermined overhead application rate is used, and the total overhead applied is also listed.

Nancy Kopay is a customer who recently had custom cabinets installed. Along with her check in payment for the work done, she included a letter. She thanked the company for including the detailed cost information but questioned why overhead was estimated. She stated that she would be interested in knowing exactly what costs were included in overhead, and she thought that other customers would, too.

Instructions

Prepare a letter to Ms. Kopay (address: 123 Cedar Lane, Altoona, KS 66651) and tell her why you did not send her information on exact costs of overhead included in her job. Respond to her suggestion that you provide this information.

Ethics Case

BYP20-5 LRF Printing provides printing services to many different corporate clients. Although LRF bids most jobs, some jobs, particularly new ones, are negotiated on a "cost-plus" basis. Cost-plus means that the buyer is willing to pay the actual cost plus a return (profit) on these costs to LRF.

Alice Reiley, controller for LRF, has recently returned from a meeting where LRF's president stated that he wanted her to find a way to charge more costs to any project that was on a cost-plus basis. The president noted that the company needed more profits to meet its stated goals this period. By charging more costs to the cost-plus projects and therefore fewer costs to the jobs that were bid, the company should be able to increase its profit for the current year.

Alice knew why the president wanted to take this action. Rumors were that he was looking for a new position and if the company reported strong profits, the president's opportunities would be enhanced. Alice also recognized that she could probably increase the cost of certain jobs by changing the basis used to allocate manufacturing overhead.

Instructions

(a) Who are the stakeholders in this situation?
(b) What are the ethical issues in this situation?
(c) What would you do if you were Alice Reiley?

All About You

BYP20-6 Many of you will work for a small business. Some of you will even own your own business. In order to operate a small business, you will need a good understanding of managerial accounting, as well as many other skills. Much information is available to assist people who are interested in starting a new business. A great place to start is the website provided by the Small Business Administration, which is an agency of the federal government whose purpose is to support small businesses.

Instructions

Go to **www.sba.gov/smallbusinessplanner/index.html** and in the Small Business Planner, Plan Your Business link, review the material under "Get Ready." Answer the following questions.

(a) What are some of the characteristics required of a small business owner?
(b) What are the top 10 reasons given for business failure?

Considering Your Costs and Benefits

BYP20-7 After graduating, you might decide to start a small business. As discussed in this chapter, owners of any business need to know how to calculate the cost of their products. In fact, many small businesses fail because they don't accurately calculate their product costs, so they don't know if they are making a profit or losing money—until it's too late.

Suppose that you decide to start a landscape business. You use an old pickup truck that you've fully paid for. You store the truck and other equipment in your parents' barn, and you store trees and shrubs on their land. Your parents will not charge you for the use of these facilities for the first two years, but beginning in the third year they will charge a reasonable rent. Your mother helps you by answering phone calls and providing customers with information. She doesn't charge you for this service, but she plans on doing it for only your first two years in business. In pricing your services, should you include charges for the truck, the barn, the land, and your mother's services when calculating your product cost? The basic arguments for and against are as follows.

YES: If you don't include charges for these costs, your costs are understated and your profitability is overstated.

NO: At this point, you are not actually incurring costs related to these activities; therefore, you shouldn't record charges.

Instructions

Write a response indicating your position regarding this situation. Provide support for your view.

Chapter 21 Process Costing

It isn't easy for a small company to get a foothold in the bottled beverage business. The giants, The Coca-Cola Company and PepsiCo Inc., vigilantly defend their turf, constantly watching for new trends and opportunities. It is nearly impossible to get shelf space in stores, and consumer tastes can change faster than a bottle of soda can lose its fizz. But Jones Soda Co., headquartered in Seattle, has overcome these and other obstacles to make a name for itself. Its corporate motto is, "Run with the little guy . . . create some change."

The company started as a Canadian distributor of other companies' beverages. Soon, it decided to make its own products under the corporate name Urban Juice and Soda Company. Eventually, its name changed to Jones Soda—the name of its most popular product. From the very start, Jones Soda was different. It sold soda from machines placed in tattoo parlors and piercing shops, and it sponsored a punk rock band as well as surfers and snowboarders. At one time, the company's product was the official drink at the Seattle Seahawks' stadium and was served on Alaskan Airlines.

Today, Jones Soda makes a wide variety of products: soda-flavored candy, energy drinks, and product-promoting gear that includes t-shirts, sweatshirts, caps, shorts, and calendars. Its most profitable product is still its multi-flavored, pure cane soda with its creative labeling. If you've seen Jones Soda on a store shelf, then you know that it appears to have an infinite variety of labels. The bottle labels are actually created by customers and submitted on the company's website. (To see some of the best labels from the past, see the Gallery at *www.jonessoda.com*.) If you would like some soda with a custom label of your own, you can design and submit a label and order a 12-pack.

Because Jones Soda has a dizzying array of product variations, keeping track of costs is of vital importance. Recently, management developed a reorganization plan that involved cost-cutting from top to bottom and eliminating unprofitable products. No matter how good your products are, if you don't keep your costs under control, you are likely to fail. Jones Soda's managers need accurate cost information regarding each primary product and each variation to ensure profitability. So while its marketing approach differs dramatically from the giants, Jones Soda needs the same kind of cost information as the big guys.

LEARNING OBJECTIVES

1. **Discuss the uses of a process cost system and how it compares to a job order system.**
2. **Explain the flow of costs in a process cost system and the journal entries to assign manufacturing costs.**
3. **Compute equivalent units.**
4. **Complete the four steps to prepare a production cost report.**
5. **Explain just-in-time (JIT) processing and activity-based costing (ABC).**

LEARNING OBJECTIVE 

Discuss the uses of a process cost system and how it compares to a job order system.

Uses of Process Cost Systems

Companies use **process cost systems** to apply costs to similar products that are mass-produced in a continuous fashion. **Jones Soda Co.** uses a process cost system: Production of the soda, once it begins, continues until the soda emerges. The processing is the same for the entire run—with precisely the same amount of materials, labor, and overhead. Each finished bottle of soda is indistinguishable from another.

A company such as **USX** uses process costing in the manufacturing of steel. **Kellogg** and **General Mills** use process costing for cereal production; **ExxonMobil** uses process costing for its oil refining. **Sherwin Williams** uses process costing for its paint products. At a bottling company like Jones Soda, the manufacturing process begins with the blending of ingredients. Next, automated machinery moves the bottles into position and fills them. The production process then caps, packages, and forwards the bottles to the finished goods warehouse. Illustration 21-1 shows this process.

Illustration 21-1
Manufacturing processes

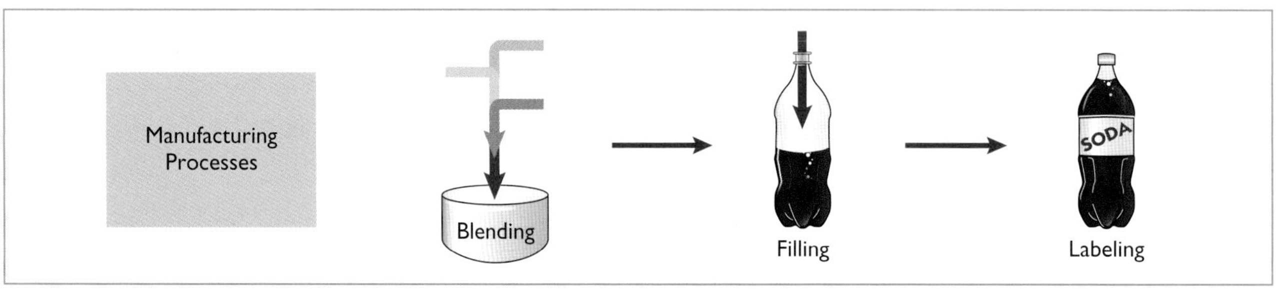

For Jones Soda, as well as the other companies just mentioned, once production begins, it continues until the finished product emerges. Each unit of finished product is like every other unit.

In comparison, a job order cost system assigns costs to a *specific job*. Examples are the construction of a customized home, the making of a movie, or the manufacturing of a specialized machine. Illustration 21-2 provides examples of companies that primarily use either a process cost system or a job order cost system.

Illustration 21-2
Process cost and job order cost companies and products

Process Cost System		Job Order Cost System	
Company	**Product**	**Company**	**Product**
Jones Soda, PepsiCo	Soft drinks	Young & Rubicam, J. Walter Thompson	Advertising
ExxonMobil, Royal Dutch Shell	Oil	Disney, Warner Brothers	Movies
Intel, Advanced Micro Devices	Computer chips	Center Ice Consultants, Ice Pro	Ice rinks
Dow Chemical, DuPont	Chemicals	Kaiser, Mayo Clinic	Patient health care

Process Costing for Service Companies

When considering service companies, you might initially think of specific, nonroutine tasks, such as rebuilding an automobile engine, consulting on a business acquisition, or defending a major lawsuit. However, many service companies perform repetitive, routine work. For example, **Jiffy Lube** regularly performs oil changes. **H&R Block** focuses on the routine aspects of basic tax practice. Service companies that perform individualized, nonroutine services will probably benefit from using a job order cost system. Those that perform routine, repetitive services will probably be better off with a process cost system.

Similarities and Differences Between Job Order Cost and Process Cost Systems

In a job order cost system, companies assign costs to each job. In a process cost system, companies track costs through a series of connected manufacturing processes or departments, rather than by individual jobs. Thus, companies use process cost systems when they produce a large volume of uniform or relatively homogeneous products. Illustration 21-3 shows the basic flow of costs in these two systems.

Illustration 21-3
Job order cost and process cost flow

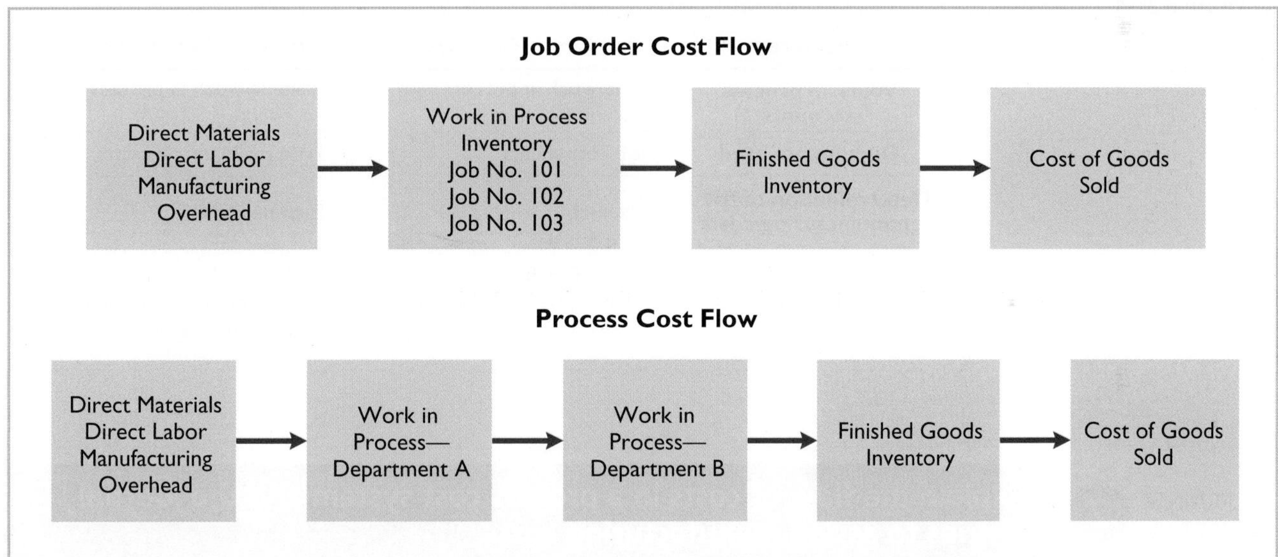

The following analysis highlights the basic similarities and differences between these two systems.

SIMILARITIES

Job order cost and process cost systems are similar in three ways:

1. **The manufacturing cost elements.** Both costing systems track three manufacturing cost elements—direct materials, direct labor, and manufacturing overhead.
2. **The accumulation of the costs of materials, labor, and overhead.** Both costing systems debit raw materials to Raw Materials Inventory, factory labor to Factory Labor, and manufacturing overhead costs to Manufacturing Overhead.
3. **The flow of costs.** As noted above, both systems accumulate all manufacturing costs by debits to Raw Materials Inventory, Factory Labor, and Manufacturing Overhead. Both systems then assign these costs to the same accounts—Work in Process, Finished Goods Inventory, and Cost of Goods Sold. **The methods of assigning costs, however, differ significantly.** These differences are explained and illustrated later in the chapter.

DIFFERENCES

The differences between a job order cost and a process cost system are as follows.

1. **The number of work in process accounts used.** A job order cost system uses only one work in process account. A process cost system uses multiple work in process accounts.
2. **Documents used to track costs.** A job order cost system charges costs to individual jobs and summarizes them in a job cost sheet. A process cost system summarizes costs in a production cost report for each department.
3. **The point at which costs are totaled.** A job order cost system totals costs when the job is completed. A process cost system totals costs at the end of a period of time.
4. **Unit cost computations.** In a job order cost system, the unit cost is the total cost per job divided by the units produced. In a process cost system, the unit cost is total manufacturing costs for the period divided by the equivalent units produced during the period.

Illustration 21-4 summarizes the major differences between a job order cost and a process cost system.

Illustration 21-4
Job order versus process cost systems

Feature	Job Order Cost System	Process Cost System
Work in process accounts	One work in process account	Multiple work in process accounts
Documents used	Job cost sheets	Production cost reports
Determination of total manufacturing costs	Each job	Each period
Unit-cost computations	Cost of each job ÷ Units produced for the job	Total manufacturing costs ÷ Equivalent units produced during the period

LEARNING OBJECTIVE 2

Explain the flow of costs in a process cost system and the journal entries to assign manufacturing costs.

Process Cost Flow

Illustration 21-5 shows the flow of costs in the process cost system for Tyler Company. Tyler manufactures roller blade and skateboard wheels that it sells to manufacturers and retail outlets. Manufacturing consists of two processes: machining and assembly. The Machining Department shapes, hones, and drills the raw materials. The Assembly Department assembles and packages the parts.

Illustration 21-5
Flow of costs in process cost system

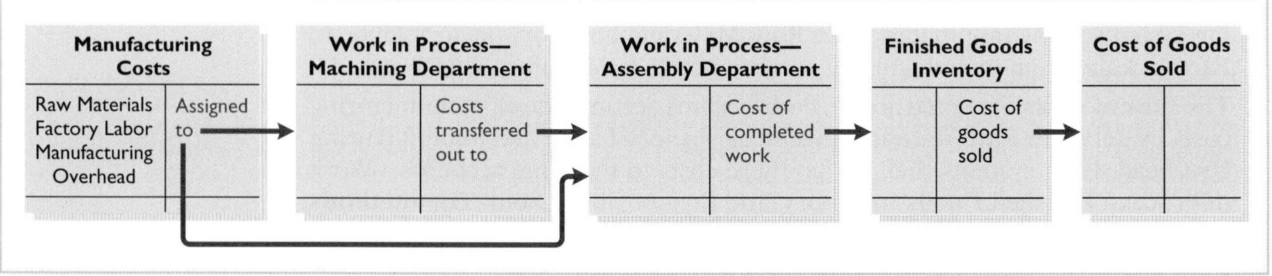

As the flow of costs indicates, the company can add materials, labor, and manufacturing overhead in both the Machining and Assembly Departments. When it finishes its work, the Machining Department transfers the partially completed units to the Assembly Department. The Assembly Department finishes the goods and then transfers them to the finished goods inventory. Upon sale, Tyler removes the goods from the finished goods inventory. Within each department, a similar set of activities is performed on each unit processed.

Assigning Manufacturing Costs—Journal Entries

As indicated, the accumulation of the costs of materials, labor, and manufacturing overhead is the same in a process cost system as in a job order cost system. That is, both systems follow these procedures:

- Companies debit all raw materials to Raw Materials Inventory at the time of purchase.
- They debit all factory labor to Factory Labor as the labor costs are incurred.
- They debit overhead costs to Manufacturing Overhead as these costs are incurred.

However, the assignment of the three manufacturing cost elements to Work in Process in a process cost system is different from a job order cost system. Here we'll look at how companies assign these manufacturing cost elements in a process cost system.

MATERIALS COSTS

All raw materials issued for production are a materials cost to the producing department. A process cost system may use materials requisition slips, but **it generally requires fewer requisitions than in a job order cost system. The materials are used for processes rather than for specific jobs** and therefore typically are for larger quantities.

At the beginning of the first process, a company usually adds most of the materials needed for production. However, other materials may be added at various points. For example, in the manufacture of **Hershey** candy bars, the chocolate and other ingredients are added at the beginning of the first process, and the wrappers and cartons are added at the end of the packaging process. Tyler Company adds materials at the beginning of each process. Tyler makes the following entry to record the materials used.

Work in Process—Machining	XXXX	
Work in Process—Assembly	XXXX	
Raw Materials Inventory		XXXX
(To record materials used)		

Ice cream maker **Ben & Jerry's** adds materials in three departments: milk and flavoring in the mixing department, extras such as cherries and dark chocolate in the prepping department, and cardboard containers in the pinting (packaging) department.

FACTORY LABOR COSTS

In a process cost system, as in a job order cost system, companies may use time tickets to determine the cost of labor assignable to production departments. Since they assign labor costs to a process rather than a job, they can obtain, from the payroll register or departmental payroll summaries, the labor cost chargeable to a process.

Labor costs for the Machining Department include the wages of employees who shape, hone, and drill the raw materials. The entry to assign labor costs to machining and assembly for Tyler Company is:

Work in Process—Machining	XXXX	
Work in Process—Assembly	XXXX	
Factory Labor		XXXX
(To assign factory labor to production)		

MANUFACTURING OVERHEAD COSTS

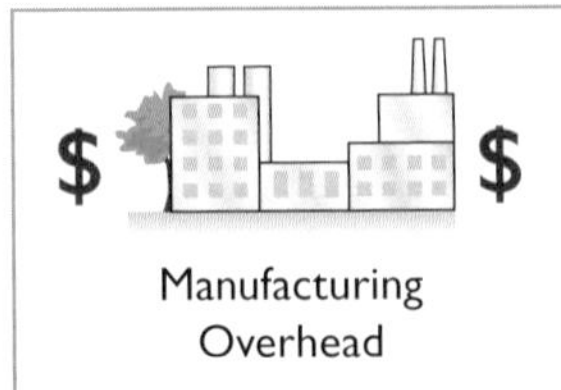

The objective in assigning overhead in a process cost system is to allocate the overhead costs to the production departments on an objective and equitable basis. That basis is the activity that "drives" or causes the costs. A primary driver of overhead costs in continuous manufacturing operations is **machine time used**, not direct labor. Thus, companies **widely use machine hours** in allocating manufacturing overhead costs using predetermined overhead rates. Tyler Company's entry to allocate overhead to the two processes is:

Work in Process—Machining	XXXX	
Work in Process—Assembly	XXXX	
Manufacturing Overhead		XXXX
(To assign overhead to production)		

TRANSFER TO NEXT DEPARTMENT

At the end of the month, Tyler Company needs an entry to record the cost of the goods transferred out of the Machining Department. In this case, the transfer is to the Assembly Department, and Tyler makes the following entry.

Work in Process—Assembly	XXXXX	
Work in Process—Machining		XXXXX
(To record transfer of units to the Assembly Department)		

TRANSFER TO FINISHED GOODS

When the Assembly Department completes the units, it transfers them to the finished goods warehouse. The entry for this transfer is as follows.

Finished Goods Inventory	XXXXX	
Work in Process—Assembly		XXXXX
(To record transfer of units to finished goods)		

TRANSFER TO COST OF GOODS SOLD

When Tyler Company sells the finished goods, it records the cost of goods sold as follows.

Cost of Goods Sold	XXXXX	
Finished Goods Inventory		XXXXX
(To record cost of units sold)		

LEARNING OBJECTIVE 3

Compute equivalent units.

Suppose you have a work-study job in the office of your college's president, and she asks you to compute the cost of instruction per full-time equivalent student at your college. The college's vice president for finance provides the following information.

Costs:	
Total cost of instruction	$9,000,000
Student population:	
Full-time students	900
Part-time students	1,000

Illustration 21-6
Information for full-time student example

Part-time students take 60% of the classes of a full-time student during the year. To compute the number of full-time equivalent students per year, you would make the following computation.

Full-Time Students	+	Equivalent Units of Part-Time Students	=	Full-Time Equivalent Students
900	+	(1,000 × 60%)	=	1,500

Illustration 21-7
Full-time equivalent unit computation

The cost of instruction per full-time equivalent student is therefore the total cost of instruction ($9,000,000) divided by the number of full-time equivalent students (1,500), which is $6,000 ($9,000,000 ÷ 1,500).

A process cost system uses the same idea, called equivalent units of production. **Equivalent units of production** measure the work done during the period, expressed in fully completed units. Companies use this measure to determine the cost per unit of completed product.

Weighted-Average Method

The formula to compute equivalent units of production is as follows.

Units Completed and Transferred Out	+	Equivalent Units of Ending Work in Process	=	Equivalent Units of Production

Illustration 21-8
Equivalent units of production formula

To better understand this concept of equivalent units, consider the following two separate examples.

Example 1. In a specific period, the entire output of Sullivan Company's Blending Department consists of ending work in process of 4,000 units which are 60% complete as to materials, labor, and overhead. The equivalent units of production for the Blending Department are therefore 2,400 units (4,000 × 60%).

Example 2. The output of Kori Company's Packaging Department during the period consists of 10,000 units completed and transferred out, and 5,000 units in ending work in process which are 70% completed. The equivalent units of production are therefore 13,500 [10,000 + (5,000 × 70%)].

This method of computing equivalent units is referred to as the **weighted-average method**. It considers the degree of completion (weighting) of the units completed and transferred out and the ending work in process.

Refinements on the Weighted-Average Method

Kellogg Company has produced Eggo® Waffles since 1970. Three departments produce these waffles: Mixing, Baking, and Freezing/Packaging. The Mixing Department combines dry ingredients, including flour, salt, and baking powder, with liquid ingredients, including eggs and vegetable oil, to make waffle batter. Illustration 21-9 provides information related to the Mixing Department at the end of June.

Illustration 21-9
Information for Mixing Department

MIXING DEPARTMENT			
		Percentage Complete	
	Physical Units	Materials	Conversion Costs
Work in process, June 1	100,000	100%	70%
Started into production	800,000		
Total units	900,000		
Units transferred out	700,000		
Work in process, June 30	200,000	100%	60%
Total units	900,000		

Illustration 21-9 indicates that the beginning work in process is 100% complete as to materials cost and 70% complete as to conversion costs. **Conversion costs are the sum of labor costs and overhead costs.** In other words, Kellogg adds both the dry and liquid ingredients (materials) at the beginning of the waffle-making process, and the conversion costs (labor and overhead) related to the mixing of these ingredients are incurred uniformly and are 70% complete. The ending work in process is 100% complete as to materials cost and 60% complete as to conversion costs.

We then use the Mixing Department information to determine equivalent units. **In computing equivalent units, the beginning work in process is not part of the equivalent-units-of-production formula.** The units transferred out to the Baking Department are fully complete as to both materials and conversion costs. The ending work in process is fully complete as to materials, but only 60% complete as to conversion costs. We therefore need to make **two equivalent unit computations**: one for materials, and the other for conversion costs. Illustration 21-10 shows these computations.

Illustration 21-10
Computation of equivalent units—Mixing Department

MIXING DEPARTMENT		
	Equivalent Units	
	Materials	Conversion Costs
Units transferred out	700,000	700,000
Work in process, June 30		
200,000 × 100%	200,000	
200,000 × 60%		120,000
Total equivalent units	900,000	820,000

We can refine the earlier formula used to compute equivalent units of production (Illustration 21-8, page 731) to show the computations for materials and for conversion costs, as follows.

Illustration 21-11
Refined equivalent units of production formula

Units Completed and Transferred Out—Materials	+	Equivalent Units of Ending Work in Process—Materials	=	Equivalent Units of Production—Materials
Units Completed and Transferred Out—Conversion Costs	+	Equivalent Units of Ending Work in Process—Conversion Costs	=	Equivalent Units of Production—Conversion Costs

LEARNING OBJECTIVE 4

Complete the four steps to prepare a production cost report.

As mentioned earlier, companies prepare a production cost report for each department. A **production cost report** is the key document that management uses to understand the activities in a department; it shows the production quantity and cost data related to that department. For example, in producing Eggo® Waffles, **Kellogg Company** uses three production cost reports: Mixing, Baking, and Freezing/Packaging. Illustration 21-12 shows the flow of costs to make an Eggo® Waffle and the related production cost reports for each department.

Illustration 21-12
Flow of costs in making Eggo® Waffles

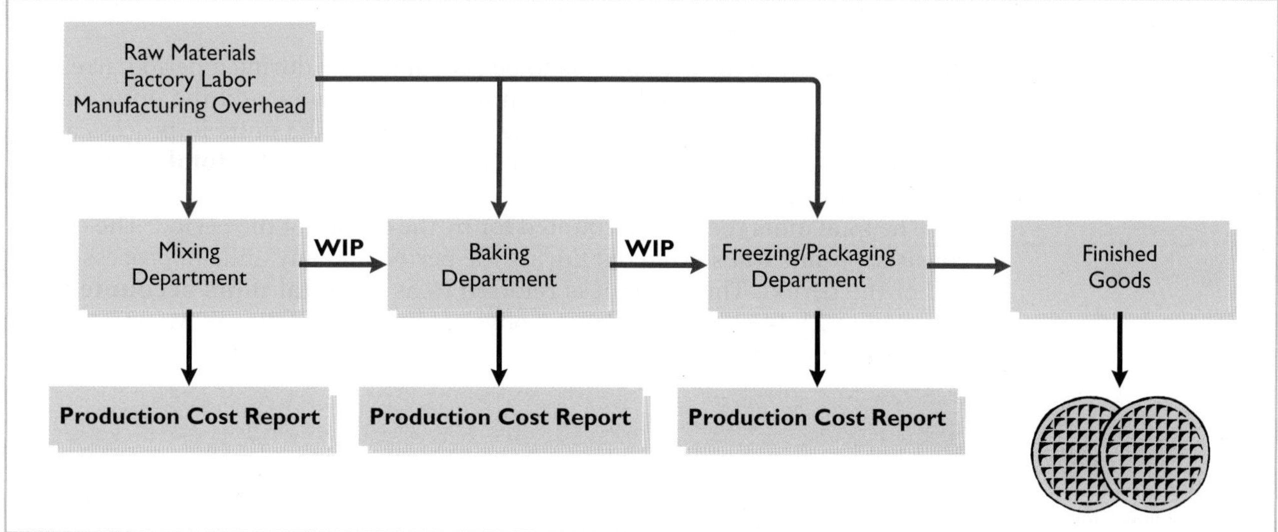

In order to complete a production cost report, the company must perform four steps, which as a whole make up the process cost system.

1. Compute the physical unit flow.
2. Compute the equivalent units of production.
3. Compute unit production costs.
4. Prepare a cost reconciliation schedule.

Illustration 21-13 shows assumed data for the Mixing Department at **Kellogg Company** for the month of June. We will use this information to complete a production cost report for the Mixing Department.

Illustration 21-13
Unit and cost data—Mixing Department

MIXING DEPARTMENT	
Units	
Work in process, June 1	100,000
Direct materials: 100% complete	
Conversion costs: 70% complete	
Units started into production during June	800,000
Units completed and transferred out to Baking Department	700,000
Work in process, June 30	200,000
Direct materials: 100% complete	
Conversion costs: 60% complete	

Illustration 21-13
(cont'd.)

Costs	
Work in process, June 1	
Direct materials: 100% complete	$ 50,000
Conversion costs: 70% complete	35,000
Cost of work in process, June 1	$ 85,000
Costs incurred during production in June	
Direct materials	$400,000
Conversion costs	170,000
Costs incurred in June	$570,000

Compute the Physical Unit Flow (Step 1)

Physical units are the actual units to be accounted for during a period, irrespective of any work performed. To keep track of these units, add the units started (or transferred) into production during the period to the units in process at the beginning of the period. This amount is referred to as the **total units to be accounted for**.

The total units then are accounted for by the output of the period. The output consists of units transferred out during the period and any units in process at the end of the period. This amount is referred to as the **total units accounted for**. Illustration 21-14 shows the flow of physical units for Kellogg's Mixing Department for the month of June.

Illustration 21-14
Physical unit flow—Mixing Department

MIXING DEPARTMENT	
	Physical Units
Units to be accounted for	
Work in process, June 1	100,000
Started (transferred) into production	800,000
Total units	**900,000**
Units accounted for	
Completed and transferred out	700,000
Work in process, June 30	200,000
Total units	**900,000**

The records indicate that the Mixing Department must account for 900,000 units. Of this sum, 700,000 units were transferred to the Baking Department and 200,000 units were still in process.

Compute the Equivalent Units of Production (Step 2)

Once the physical flow of the units is established, Kellogg must measure the Mixing Department's productivity in terms of equivalent units of production. The Mixing Department adds materials at the beginning of the process, and it incurs conversion costs uniformly during the process. Thus, we need two computations of equivalent units: one for materials and one for conversion costs. The equivalent unit computation is as follows.

Illustration 21-15
Computation of equivalent units—Mixing Department

	Equivalent Units	
	Materials	**Conversion Costs**
Units transferred out	700,000	700,000
Work in process, June 30		
200,000 × 100%	200,000	
200,000 × 60%		120,000
Total equivalent units	**900,000**	**820,000**

Compute Unit Production Costs (Step 3)

Armed with the knowledge of the equivalent units of production, we can now compute the unit production costs. **Unit production costs** are costs expressed in terms of equivalent units of production. When equivalent units of production are different for materials and conversion costs, we compute three unit costs: (1) materials, (2) conversion, and (3) total manufacturing.

The computation of total materials cost related to Eggo® Waffles is as follows.

Illustration 21-16
Total materials cost computation

Work in process, June 1	
Direct materials cost	$ 50,000
Costs added to production during June	
Direct materials cost	400,000
Total materials cost	**$450,000**

The computation of unit materials cost is as follows.

Illustration 21-17
Unit materials cost computation

Total Materials Cost	÷	Equivalent Units of Materials	=	Unit Materials Cost
$450,000	÷	900,000	=	$0.50

Illustration 21-18 shows the computation of total conversion costs.

Illustration 21-18
Total conversion costs computation

Work in process, June 1	
Conversion costs	$ 35,000
Costs added to production during June	
Conversion costs	170,000
Total conversion costs	**$205,000**

The computation of unit conversion cost is as follows.

Illustration 21-19
Unit conversion cost computation

Total Conversion Costs	÷	Equivalent Units of Conversion Costs	=	Unit Conversion Cost
$205,000	÷	820,000	=	$0.25

Total manufacturing cost per unit is therefore computed as shown in Illustration 21-20 (page 736).

Illustration 21-20
Total manufacturing cost per unit

Unit Materials Cost	+	Unit Conversion Cost	=	Total Manufacturing Cost per Unit
$0.50	+	$0.25	=	$0.75

Prepare a Cost Reconciliation Schedule (Step 4)

We are now ready to determine the cost of goods transferred out of the Mixing Department to the Baking Department and the costs in ending work in process. Kellogg charged total costs of $655,000 to the Mixing Department in June, calculated as follows.

Illustration 21-21
Costs charged to Mixing Department

Costs to be accounted for	
Work in process, June 1	$ 85,000
Started into production	570,000
Total costs	**$655,000**

The company then prepares a cost reconciliation schedule to assign these costs to (a) units transferred out to the Baking Department and (b) ending work in process.

Illustration 21-22
Cost reconciliation schedule—Mixing Department

MIXING DEPARTMENT
Cost Reconciliation Schedule

Costs accounted for		
Transferred out (700,000 × $0.75)		$ 525,000
Work in process, June 30		
Materials (200,000 × $0.50)	$100,000	
Conversion costs (120,000 × $0.25)	30,000	130,000
Total costs		**$655,000**

Kellogg uses the total manufacturing cost per unit, $0.75, in costing the **units completed** and transferred to the Baking Department. In contrast, the unit cost of materials and the unit cost of conversion are needed in costing **units in process**. The **cost reconciliation schedule** shows that the **total costs accounted for** (Illustration 21-22) equal the **total costs to be accounted for** (Illustration 21-21).

Preparing the Production Cost Report

At this point, Kellogg is ready to prepare the production cost report for the Mixing Department. As indicated earlier, this report is an internal document for management that shows production quantity and cost data for a production department. Illustration 21-23 shows the completed production cost report for the Mixing Department and identifies the four steps used in preparing it.

Production cost reports provide a basis for evaluating the productivity of a department. In addition, managers can use the cost data to assess whether unit costs and total costs are reasonable. By comparing the quantity and cost data with predetermined goals, top management can also judge whether current performance is meeting planned objectives.

Illustration 21-23
Production cost report

Mixing Department.xls

	A	B	C	D	E
1	**MIXING DEPARTMENT**				
2	**Production Cost Report**				
3	**For the Month Ended June 30, 2017**				
4			**Equivalent Units**		
5		Physical Units	Materials	Conversion Costs	
6	**Quantities**				
7	Units to be accounted for	Step 1		Step 2	
8	Work in process, June 1	100,000			
9	Started into production	800,000			
10	Total units	900,000			
11	Units accounted for				
12	Transferred out	700,000	700,000	700,000	
13	Work in process, June 30	200,000	200,000	120,000	(200,000 × 60%)
14	Total units	900,000	900,000	820,000	
15	**Costs**				
16	Unit costs Step 3		Materials	Conversion Costs	Total
17	Total cost	(a)	$450,000	$205,000	$655,000
18	Equivalent units	(b)	900,000	820,000	
19	Unit costs [(a) ÷ (b)]		$0.50	$0.25	$0.75
20	Costs to be accounted for				
21	Work in process, June 1				$ 85,000
22	Started into production				570,000
23	Total costs				$655,000
24	**Cost Reconciliation Schedule** Step 4				
25	Costs accounted for				
26	Transferred out (700,000 × $0.75)				$525,000
27	Work in process, June 30				
28	Materials (200,000 × $0.50)			$100,000	
29	Conversion costs (120,000 × $0.25)			30,000	130,000
30	Total costs				$655,000
31					

Costing Systems—Final Comments

Companies often use a combination of a process cost and a job order cost system. Called **operations costing**, this hybrid system is similar to process costing in its assumption that standardized methods are used to manufacture the product. At the same time, the product may have some customized, individual features that require the use of a job order cost system.

Consider, for example, **Ford Motor Company**. Each vehicle at a given plant goes through the same assembly line, but Ford uses different materials (such as seat coverings, paint, and tinted glass) for different vehicles. Similarly, **Kellogg's** Pop-Tarts® toaster pastries go through numerous standardized processes—mixing, filling, baking, frosting, and packaging. The pastry dough, though, comes in different flavors—plain, chocolate, and graham—and fillings include Smucker's® real fruit, chocolate fudge, vanilla creme, brown sugar cinnamon, and s'mores.

A cost-benefit trade-off occurs as a company decides which costing system to use. A job order cost system, for example, provides detailed information related to the cost of the product. Because each job has its own distinguishing characteristics, the system can provide an accurate cost per job. This information is useful in controlling costs and pricing products. However, the cost of implementing a job order cost system is often expensive because of the accounting costs involved.

On the other hand, for a company like **Intel**, is there a benefit in knowing whether the cost of the one-hundredth computer chip produced is different from the one-thousandth chip produced? Probably not. An average cost of the product will suffice for control and pricing purposes.

In summary, when deciding to use one of these systems or a combination system, a company must weigh the costs of implementing the system against the benefits from the additional information provided.

LEARNING OBJECTIVE  **Explain just-in-time (JIT) processing and activity-based costing (ABC).**

Just-in-Time Processing

Traditionally, continuous process manufacturing has been based on a **just-in-case** philosophy: Inventories of raw materials are maintained *just in case* some items are of poor quality or a key supplier is shut down by a strike. Similarly, subassembly parts are manufactured and stored *just in case* they are needed later in the manufacturing process. Finished goods are completed and stored *just in case* unexpected and rush customer orders are received. This philosophy often results in a "**push approach**," in which raw materials and subassembly parts are pushed through each process. Traditional processing often results in the buildup of extensive manufacturing inventories.

Primarily in response to foreign competition, many U.S. firms have switched to **just-in-time (JIT) processing**. JIT manufacturing is dedicated to having the right amount of materials, parts, or products just as they are needed. JIT first hit the United States in the early 1980s when automobile companies adopted it to compete with foreign automakers. Many companies, including **Dell**, **Caterpillar**, and **Harley-Davidson**, now successfully use JIT. Under JIT processing, companies receive raw materials **just in time** for use in production, they complete subassembly parts **just in time** for use in finished goods, and they complete finished goods **just in time** to be sold. Illustration 21-24 shows the sequence of activities in just-in-time processing.

Illustration 21-24
Just-in-time processing

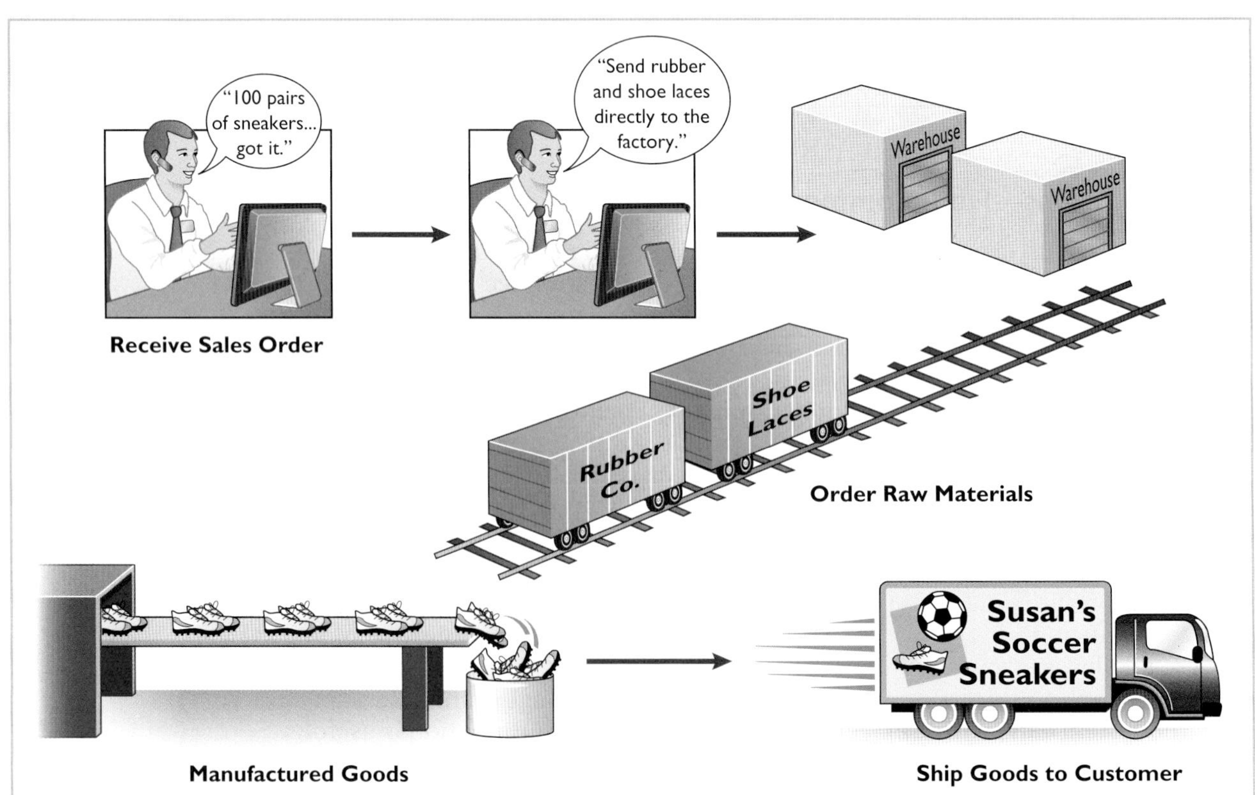

OBJECTIVE OF JIT PROCESSING

A primary objective of JIT is to eliminate all manufacturing inventories. Inventories have an adverse effect on net income because they tie up funds and storage space that could be put to more productive uses. JIT strives to eliminate inventories by using a "**pull approach**" in manufacturing. This approach begins with the customer placing an order with the company, which starts the process of pulling the product through the manufacturing process. A computer at the final workstation sends a signal to the preceding workstation. This signal indicates the exact materials (parts and subassemblies) needed to complete the production of a specified product for a specified time period, such as an eight-hour shift. The next-preceding process, in turn, sends its signal to other processes back up the line. The goal is a smooth continuous flow in the manufacturing process, with no buildup of inventories at any point.

ELEMENTS OF JIT PROCESSING

There are three important elements in JIT processing:

1. **Dependable suppliers.** Suppliers must be willing to deliver on short notice exact quantities of raw materials according to precise quality specifications (even including multiple deliveries within the same day). Suppliers must also be willing to deliver the raw materials at specified workstations rather than at a central receiving department. This type of purchasing requires constant and direct communication. Such communication is facilitated by an online computer linkage between the company and its suppliers.
2. **A multiskilled work force.** Under JIT, machines are often strategically grouped into work cells or workstations. Much of the work is automated. As a result, one worker may operate and maintain several different types of machines.
3. **A total quality control system.** The company must establish total quality control throughout the manufacturing operations. Total quality control means **no defects**. Since the pull approach signals only required quantities, any defects at any workstation will shut down operations at subsequent workstations. Total quality control requires continuous monitoring by both line employees and supervisors at each workstation.

BENEFITS OF JIT PROCESSING

The major benefits of implementing JIT processing are as follows.

1. Significant reduction or elimination of manufacturing inventories.
2. Enhanced product quality.
3. Reduction or elimination of rework costs and inventory storage costs.
4. Production cost savings from the improved flow of goods through the processes.

The effects in many cases have been dramatic. For example, after using JIT for two years, a major division of **Hewlett-Packard** found that work in process inventories (in dollars) were down 82%, scrap/rework costs were down 30%, space utilization improved by 40%, and labor efficiency improved 50%. As indicated, JIT not only reduces inventory but also enables a company to manufacture a better product faster and with less waste.

One of the major accounting benefits of JIT is the elimination of separate raw materials and work in process inventory accounts. These accounts are replaced by **one account**, Raw and In-Process Inventory. All materials and conversion costs are charged to this account. The reduction (or elimination) of in-process inventories results in a simpler computation of equivalent units of production.

Activity-Based Costing

Activity-based costing (ABC) focuses on the activities required to produce a product or perform a service. An ABC system is similar to conventional costing systems in accounting for direct materials and direct labor, but it differs in regard to manufacturing overhead.

A conventional cost system uses a **single unit-level** basis to allocate overhead costs to products. The basis may be direct labor or machine hours used to manufacture the product. The assumption in this approach is that as volume of units produced increases, so does the cost of overhead. However, in recent years the amount of direct labor used in many industries has greatly **decreased**, and total overhead costs resulting from depreciation on expensive equipment and machinery, utilities, repairs, and maintenance have significantly **increased**.

In ABC, the cost of a product is equal to the sum of the costs of all activities performed to manufacture it. ABC recognizes that to have accurate and meaningful cost data, **more than one basis** of allocating activity costs to products is needed.

In selecting the allocation basis, ABC seeks to identify the **cost drivers** that measure the activities performed on the product. A **cost driver** may be any factor or activity that has a direct cause–effect relationship with the resources consumed. Examples of activities and possible cost drivers are as follows.

Illustration 21-25
Activities and cost drivers in ABC

Activity	Cost Driver
Ordering raw materials	Ordering hours; number of orders
Receiving raw materials	Receiving hours; number of shipments
Materials handling	Number of requisitions; weight of materials; handling hours
Production scheduling	Number of orders
Machine setups	Setup hours; number of setups
Machining (fabricating, assembling, etc.)	Machine hours
Quality control inspections	Number of inspections
Factory supervision	Number of employees

Two important assumptions must be met in order to obtain accurate product costs under ABC:

1. All overhead costs related to the activity must be driven by the cost driver used to assign costs to products.
2. All overhead costs related to the activity should respond proportionally to changes in the activity level of the cost driver.

For example, if there is little or no correlation between changes in the cost driver and consumption of the overhead cost, inaccurate product costs are inevitable. An example of the use of ABC is illustrated in the appendix at the end of this chapter.

Activity-based costing may be used with either a job order or a process cost accounting system. The primary benefit of ABC is more accurate and meaningful product costing. Also, improved cost data about an activity can lead to reduced costs for the activity. In sum, ABC makes managers realize that it is **activities**, and not products, that determine the profitability of a company—a realization that should lead to better management decisions.

APPENDIX 21A: Apply activity-based costing to a manufacturer.

In this appendix, we present a simple case example that compares activity-based costing with traditional costing. It illustrates how ABC eliminates the distortion that can occur in traditional overhead cost allocation. As you study this example, you should understand that ABC does not *replace* an existing job order or process cost system. What ABC does is to segregate overhead into various cost pools in an effort to provide more accurate cost information. As a result, ABC supplements—rather than replaces—these cost systems.

Assume that Atlas Company produces two abdominal fitness products—the Ab Bench and the Ab Coaster. Each year, the company produces 25,000 Ab Benches but only 5,000 Ab Coasters. Each unit produced requires one hour of direct labor, for a total of 30,000 labor hours (25,000 + 5,000). The direct labor cost is $12 per unit for each product. The direct materials cost per unit is $40 for the Ab Bench and $30 for the Ab Coaster.

Atlas also expects to incur annual manufacturing overhead costs of $900,000. Atlas allocates overhead using a single predetermined overhead rate based on the 30,000 direct labor hours it expects to use. Thus, the predetermined overhead rate is $30 per direct labor hour ($900,000 / 30,000 direct labor hours).

Since both products require one direct labor hour per unit, both products are allocated overhead costs of $30 per unit under traditional costing. Illustration 21A-1 shows the total unit costs for the Ab Bench and the Ab Coaster.

Illustration 21A-1
Total unit costs—traditional costing

Atlas Company.xls

ATLAS COMPANY		
Manufacturing Costs	Ab Bench	Ab Coaster
Direct materials	$40	$30
Direct labor	12	12
Overhead	30	30
Total direct cost per unit	$82	$72

With this information, we can now calculate unit costs under ABC for the Ab Bench and the Ab Coaster. Activity-based costing involves the following four steps.

1. **Identify and classify the activities** involved in the manufacture of specific products and **assign overhead to cost pools**.
2. **Identify the cost driver** that has a strong correlation to the costs accumulated in each cost pool.
3. **Compute the activity-based overhead rate** for each cost pool.
4. **Allocate overhead costs to products** using the overhead rates determined for each cost pool.

Identify and Classify Activities and Assign Overhead to Cost Pools (Step 1)

Activity-based costing starts with an analysis of the activities needed to manufacture a product or perform a service. This analysis should identify all resource-consuming activities. It requires documenting every activity undertaken to accomplish a task. Atlas Company identifies five activity cost pools: manufacturing, setups, purchase ordering, product development, and property and plant.

Next, the company assigns overhead costs directly to the appropriate activity cost pool. For example, Atlas assigns all overhead costs directly associated with machine setups (such as salaries, supplies, and depreciation) to the setup cost pool. Illustration 21A-2 shows the five cost pools, along with the estimated overhead assigned to each cost pool.

Illustration 21A-2
Activity cost pools and estimated overhead

Atlas Company.xls

	A	B	C
1	ATLAS COMPANY		
2	Activity Cost Pools	Estimated Overhead	
3	Manufacturing		$500,000
4	Setups		100,000
5	Purchase ordering		50,000
6	Product development		200,000
7	Property and plant		50,000
8	Total		$900,000
9			

Identify Cost Drivers (Step 2)

After costs are assigned to the activity cost pools, the company must identify the cost drivers for each cost pool. The cost driver must accurately measure the actual consumption of the activity by the various products. To achieve accurate costing, a **high degree of correlation** must exist between the cost driver and the actual consumption of the overhead costs in the cost pool.

Illustration 21A-3 shows the cost drivers that Atlas Company identifies and their total expected use per activity cost pool.

Illustration 21A-3
Cost drivers and their expected use

Activity Cost Pools	Cost Drivers	Expected Use of Cost Drivers per Activity
Manufacturing	Machine hours	50,000 machine hours
Setups	Number of setups	2,000 setups
Purchase ordering	Number of purchase orders	2,500 purchase orders
Product development	Products developed	2 products developed
Property and plant	Square footage	25,000 square feet

Availability and ease of obtaining data relating to the cost driver is an important factor that must be considered in its selection.

Compute Activity-Based Overhead Rates (Step 3)

Next, the company computes an **activity-based overhead rate** per cost driver by dividing the estimated overhead per activity by the number of cost drivers expected to be used per activity. Illustration 21A-4 shows the formula for this computation.

Illustration 21A-4
Formula for computing activity-based overhead rate

$$\frac{\textbf{Estimated Overhead per Activity}}{\textbf{Expected Use of Cost Drivers per Activity}} = \textbf{Activity-Based Overhead Rate}$$

Atlas Company computes its activity-based overhead rates by using the estimated overhead per activity cost pool, shown in Illustration 21A-2, and the expected use of cost drivers per activity, shown in Illustration 21A-3. These computations are presented in Illustration 21A-5.

Illustration 21A-5
Computation of activity-based overhead rates

	A	B	C	D	E	F
1	ATLAS COMPANY					
2	Activity Cost Pools	Estimated Overhead	÷	Expected Use of Cost Drivers per Activity	=	Activity-Based Overhead Rates
3	Manufacturing	$500,000		50,000 machine hours		$10 per machine hour
4	Setups	100,000		2,000 setups		$50 per setup
5	Purchase ordering	50,000		2,500 purchase orders		$20 per order
6	Product development	200,000		2 products developed		$100,000 per product
7	Plant and property	50,000		25,000 square feet		$2 per square foot
8	Total	$900,000				
9						

Allocate Overhead Costs to Products (Step 4)

In allocating overhead costs, the company must know the expected use of cost drivers **for each product**. Because of its low volume and higher number of components, the Ab Coaster requires more setups and purchase orders than the Ab Bench. Illustration 21A-6 shows the expected use of cost drivers per product for each of Atlas Company's products.

Illustration 21A-6
Expected use of cost drivers per product

Activity Cost Pools	Cost Drivers	Expected Use of Cost Drivers per Activity	Expected Use of Cost Drivers per Product: Ab Bench	Ab Coaster
Manufacturing	Machine hours	50,000 machine hours	30,000	20,000
Setups	Number of setups	2,000 setups	500	1,500
Purchase ordering	Number of purchase orders	2,500 purchase orders	750	1,750
Product development	Products developed	2 products developed	1	1
Property and plant	Square feet	25,000 square feet	10,000	15,000

To allocate overhead costs to each product, Atlas multiplies the activity-based overhead rates per cost driver (Illustration 21A-5) by the number of cost drivers expected to be used per product (Illustration 21A-6). Illustration 21A-7 shows the overhead cost allocated to each product.

Illustration 21A-7
Allocation of activity cost pools to products

	A	B	C	D	E	F	G	H	I	J	K	L
1	ATLAS COMPANY											
2		Ab Bench						Ab Coaster				
3	Activity Cost Pools	Expected Use of Cost Drivers per Product	×	Activity-Based Overhead Rates	=	Cost Allocated		Expected Use of Cost Drivers per Product	×	Activity-Based Overhead Rates	=	Cost Allocated
4	Manufacturing	30,000		$10		$300,000		20,000		$10		$200,000
5	Setups	500		$50		25,000		1,500		$50		75,000
6	Purchase ordering	750		$20		15,000		1,750		$20		35,000
7	Product development	1		$100,000		100,000		1		$100,000		100,000
8	Property and plant	10,000		$2.00		20,000		15,000		$2.00		30,000
9	Total costs allocated (a)					$460,000						$440,000
10	Units produced (b)					25,000						5,000
11	Overhead cost per unit [(a)÷(b)], rounded					$18.40						$88.00
12												

Under ABC, the overhead cost per unit is $18.40 for the Ab Bench and $88.00 for the Ab Coaster. We see next how this per unit amount substantially differs from that computed under a traditional costing system.

Comparing Unit Costs

Illustration 21A-8 compares the unit costs for Atlas Company's Ab Bench and Ab Coaster under traditional costing and ABC.

Illustration 21A-8
Comparison of unit product costs

	Ab Bench		Ab Coaster	
Manufacturing Costs	**Traditional Costing**	**ABC**	**Traditional Costing**	**ABC**
Direct materials	$40.00	$40.00	$30.00	$ 30.00
Direct labor	12.00	12.00	12.00	12.00
Overhead	30.00	18.40	30.00	88.00
Total direct cost per unit	**$82.00**	**$70.40**	**$72.00**	**$130.00**
	Overstated $11.60		**Understated $58.00**	

The comparison shows that unit costs under traditional costing are different and often misleading. Traditional costing overstates the cost of producing the Ab Bench by $11.60 per unit and understates the cost of producing the Ab Coaster by $58 per unit. These differences are attributable to how Atlas allocates manufacturing overhead across the two systems. Thus, ABC helps Atlas avoid some negative consequences of a traditional costing system, such as overpricing its Ab Benches and thereby possibly losing market share to competitors. Atlas has also been sacrificing profitability by underpricing the Ab Coaster.

Benefits of ABC

The primary benefit of ABC is **more accurate product costing**. Here's why:

1. **ABC leads to more cost pools** being used to assign overhead costs to products. Instead of one plantwide pool (or even departmental pools) and a single cost driver, companies use numerous activity cost pools with more relevant cost drivers. Costs are assigned more directly on the basis of the cost drivers used to produce each product.
2. **ABC leads to enhanced control over overhead costs.** Under ABC, companies can trace many overhead costs directly to activities—allowing some indirect costs to be identified as direct costs. Thus, managers have become more aware of their responsibility to control the activities that generate those costs.
3. **ABC leads to better management decisions.** More accurate product costing should contribute to setting selling prices that can help achieve desired product profitability levels. In addition, more accurate cost data could be helpful in deciding whether to make or buy a product part or component, and sometimes even whether to eliminate a product.

Activity-based costing does not change the amount of overhead costs. What it does do is allocate those overhead costs in a more accurate manner. Furthermore, if the scorekeeping is more realistic and more accurate, managers should be able to better understand cost behavior and overall profitability.

Limitations of ABC

Although ABC systems often provide better product cost data than traditional volume-based systems, there are limitations:

1. **ABC can be expensive to use.** The increased cost of identifying multiple activities and applying numerous cost drivers discourages many companies

from using ABC. Activity-based costing systems are more complex than traditional costing systems—sometimes significantly more complex. So companies must ask, is the cost of implementation greater than the benefit of greater accuracy? Sometimes it may be. For some companies, there may be no need to consider ABC at all because their existing system is sufficient. If the costs of ABC outweigh the benefits, then the company should not implement ABC.

2. **Some arbitrary allocations continue.** Even though more overhead costs can be assigned directly to products through ABC's multiple activity cost pools, certain overhead costs remain to be allocated by means of some arbitrary volume-based cost driver such as labor or machine hours.

REVIEW AND PRACTICE

LEARNING OBJECTIVES REVIEW

1 Discuss the uses of a process cost system and how it compares to a job order system. Companies that mass-produce similar products in a continuous fashion use process cost systems. Once production begins, it continues until the finished product emerges. Each unit of finished product is indistinguishable from every other unit.

Job order cost systems are similar to process cost systems in three ways. (1) Both systems track the same cost elements—direct materials, direct labor, and manufacturing overhead. (2) Both accumulate costs in the same accounts—Raw Materials Inventory, Factory Labor, and Manufacturing Overhead. (3) Both assign accumulated costs to the same accounts—Work in Process, Finished Goods Inventory, and Cost of Goods Sold. However, the method of assigning costs differs significantly.

There are four main differences between the two cost systems. (1) A process cost system uses separate accounts for each department or manufacturing process, rather than only one work in process account used in a job order cost system. (2) A process cost system summarizes costs in a production cost report for each department. A job order cost system charges costs to individual jobs and summarizes them in a job cost sheet. (3) Costs are totaled at the end of a time period in a process cost system but at the completion of a job in a job order cost system. (4) A process cost system calculates unit cost as Total manufacturing costs for the period ÷ Units produced during the period. A job order cost system calculates unit cost as Total cost per job ÷ Units produced.

2 Explain the flow of costs in a process cost system and the journal entries to assign manufacturing costs. A process cost system assigns manufacturing costs for raw materials, labor, and overhead to work in process accounts for various departments or manufacturing processes. It transfers the costs of partially completed units from one department to another as those units move through the manufacturing process. The system transfers the costs of completed work to Finished Goods Inventory. Finally, when inventory is sold, the system transfers the costs to Cost of Goods Sold.

Entries to assign the costs of raw materials, labor, and overhead consist of a credit to Raw Materials Inventory, Factory Labor, and Manufacturing Overhead, and a debit to Work in Process for each department. Entries to record the cost of goods transferred to another department are a credit to Work in Process for the department whose work is finished and a debit to the department to which the goods are transferred. The entry to record units completed and transferred to the warehouse is a credit to Work in Process for the department whose work is finished and a debit to Finished Goods Inventory. The entry to record the sale of goods is a credit to Finished Goods Inventory and a debit to Cost of Goods Sold.

3 Compute equivalent units. Equivalent units of production measure work done during a period, expressed in fully completed units. Companies use this measure to determine the cost per unit of completed product. Equivalent units are the sum of units completed and transferred out plus equivalent units of ending work in process.

4 Complete the four steps to prepare a production cost report. The four steps to complete a production cost report are as follows. (1) Compute the physical unit flow—that is, the total units to be accounted for. (2) Compute the equivalent units of production. (3) Compute the unit production costs, expressed in terms of equivalent units of production. (4) Prepare a cost reconciliation schedule, which shows that the total costs accounted for equal the total costs to be accounted for.

The production cost report contains both quantity and cost data for a production department. There are four sections in the report: (1) number of physical units, (2) equivalent units determination, (3) unit costs, and (4) cost reconciliation schedule.

5 Explain just-in-time (JIT) processing and activity-based costing (ABC). JIT is a manufacturing technique dedicated to producing the right products at the right time as needed. One of the principal accounting effects is that a Raw and In-Process Inventory account replaces both the raw materials and work in process inventory accounts. ABC is a method of product costing that focuses on the activities performed to produce products. It assigns the cost of the activities to products by using cost drivers that measure the activities performed. The primary objective of ABC is accurate and meaningful product costs.

*6 **Apply activity-based costing to a manufacturer.** In applying ABC, it is necessary to compute the overhead rate for each activity by dividing total expected overhead by the total expected usage of the cost driver. The overhead cost for each activity is then assigned to products on the basis of each product's use of the cost driver.

GLOSSARY REVIEW

Activity-based costing (ABC) A costing system that focuses on the activities required to produce a product or perform a service.

Conversion costs The sum of labor costs and overhead costs.

Cost driver Any factor or activity that has a direct cause-effect relationship with the resources consumed.

Cost reconciliation schedule A schedule that shows that the total costs accounted for equal the total costs to be accounted for.

Equivalent units of production A measure of the work done during the period, expressed in fully completed units.

Just-in-time (JIT) processing A processing system dedicated to having the right amount of materials, parts, or products arrive as they are needed, thereby reducing the amount of inventory.

Operations costing A combination of a process cost and a job order cost system in which products are manufactured primarily by standardized methods, with some customization.

Physical units Actual units to be accounted for during a period, irrespective of any work performed.

Process cost system An accounting system used to apply costs to similar products that are mass-produced in a continuous fashion.

Production cost report An internal report for management that shows both production quantity and cost data for a production department.

Total units (costs) accounted for The sum of the units (costs) transferred out during the period plus the units (costs) in process at the end of the period.

Total units (costs) to be accounted for The sum of the units (costs) started (or transferred) into production during the period plus the units (costs) in process at the beginning of the period.

Unit production costs Costs expressed in terms of equivalent units of production.

Weighted-average method Method of computing equivalent units of production which considers the degree of completion (weighting) of the units completed and transferred out and the ending work in process.

PRACTICE EXERCISES

Journalize transactions.
(LO 2)

1. Armando Company manufactures pizza sauce through two production departments: Cooking and Canning. In each process, materials and conversion costs are incurred evenly throughout the process. For the month of April, the work in process accounts show the following debits.

	Cooking	Canning
Beginning work in process	$ -0-	$ 4,000
Materials	25,000	8,000
Labor	8,500	7,500
Overhead	29,000	25,800
Costs transferred in		55,000

Instructions

Journalize the April transactions.

Solution

1. (a) April	30	Work in Process—Cooking	25,000	
		Work in Process—Canning	8,000	
		Raw Materials Inventory		33,000
	30	Work in Process—Cooking	8,500	
		Work in Process—Canning	7,500	
		Factory Labor		16,000
	30	Work in Process—Cooking	29,000	
		Work in Process—Canning	25,800	
		Manufacturing Overhead		54,800
	30	Work in Process—Canning	55,000	
		Work in Process—Cooking		55,000

2. The Sanding Department of Jo Furniture Company has the following production and manufacturing cost data for March 2017, the first month of operation.

Prepare a production cost report.

(LO 3, 4)

Production: 11,000 units finished and transferred out; 4,000 units started that are 100% complete as to materials and 25% complete as to conversion costs.
Manufacturing costs: Materials $48,000; labor $42,000; and overhead $36,000.

Instructions

Prepare a production cost report.

Solution

2.

JO FURNITURE COMPANY
Sanding Department
Production Cost Report
For the Month Ended March 31, 2017

		Equivalent Units		
Quantities	**Physical Units**	**Materials**	**Conversion Costs**	
Units to be accounted for				
Work in process, March 1	0			
Started into production	15,000			
Total units	15,000			
Units accounted for				
Transferred out	11,000	11,000	11,000	
Work in process, March 31	4,000	4,000	1,000	(4,000 × 25%)
Total units	15,000	15,000	12,000	

Costs		**Materials**	**Conversion Costs**	**Total**
Unit costs				
Costs in March		$48,000	$78,000*	$126,000
Equivalent units		15,000	12,000	
Unit costs [(a) ÷ (b)]		$3.20	$6.50	$9.70
Costs to be accounted for				
Work in process, March 1				$ 0
Started into production				126,000
Total costs				$126,000
Cost Reconciliation Schedule				
Costs accounted for				
Transferred out (11,000 × $9.70)				$106,700
Work in process, March 31				
Materials (4,000 × $3.20)			$12,800	
Conversion costs (1,000 × $6.50)			6,500	19,300
Total costs				$126,000

*$42,000 + $36,000

PRACTICE PROBLEM

Karlene Industries produces plastic ice cube trays in two processes: heating and stamping. All materials are added at the beginning of the Heating Department process. Karlene uses the weighted-average method to compute equivalent units.

Prepare a production cost report and journalize.

(LO 3, 4)

On November 1, the Heating Department had in process 1,000 trays that were 70% complete. During November, it started into production 12,000 trays. On November 30, 2017, 2,000 trays that were 60% complete were in process.

The following cost information for the Heating Department was also available.

Work in process, November 1:		Costs incurred in November:	
Materials	$ 640	Material	$3,000
Conversion costs	360	Labor	2,300
Cost of work in process, Nov. 1	$1,000	Overhead	4,050

Instructions

(a) Prepare a production cost report for the Heating Department for the month of November 2017, using the weighted-average method.

(b) Journalize the transfer of costs to the Stamping Department.

Solution

(a)

KARLENE INDUSTRIES
Heating Department
Production Cost Report
For the Month Ended November 30, 2017

		Equivalent Units	
	Physical Units	**Materials**	**Conversion Costs**
Quantities	Step 1	Step 2	
Units to be accounted for			
Work in process, November 1	1,000		
Started into production	12,000		
Total units	13,000		
Units accounted for			
Transferred out	11,000	11,000	11,000
Work in process, November 30	2,000	2,000	1,200
Total units	13,000	13,000	12,200

Costs				
Unit costs Step 3		**Materials**	**Conversion Costs**	**Total**
Total cost	(a)	$ 3,640*	$ 6,710**	$10,350
Equivalent units	(b)	13,000	12,200	
Unit costs [(a) ÷ (b)]		$0.28	$0.55	$0.83
Costs to be accounted for				
Work in process, November 1				$ 1,000
Started into production				9,350
Total costs				$10,350

*$640 + $3,000

**$360 + $2,300 + $4,050

Cost Reconciliation Schedule Step 4		
Costs accounted for		
Transferred out (11,000 × $0.83)		$ 9,130
Work in process, November 30		
Materials (2,000 × $0.28)	$560	
Conversion costs (1,200 × $0.55)	660	1,220
Total costs		$10,350

(b)	Debit	Credit
Work in Process—Stamping	9,130	
Work in Process—Heating		9,130
(To record transfer of units to the Stamping Department)		

EXERCISES

Understand process cost accounting.

(LO 1)

E21-1 Robert Wilkins has prepared the following list of statements about process cost accounting.

1. Process cost systems are used to apply costs to similar products that are mass-produced in a continuous fashion.
2. A process cost system is used when each finished unit is indistinguishable from another.
3. Companies that produce soft drinks, movies, and computer chips would all use process cost accounting.
4. In a process cost system, costs are tracked by individual jobs.
5. Job order costing and process costing track different manufacturing cost elements.
6. Both job order costing and process costing account for direct materials, direct labor, and manufacturing overhead.

7. Costs flow through the accounts in the same basic way for both job order costing and process costing.
8. In a process cost system, only one work in process account is used.
9. In a process cost system, costs are summarized in a job cost sheet.
10. In a process cost system, the unit cost is total manufacturing costs for the period divided by the equivalent units produced during the period.

Instructions

Identify each statement as true or false. If false, indicate how to correct the statement.

Journalize transactions.

(LO 2)

E21-2 Harrelson Company manufactures pizza sauce through two production departments: Cooking and Canning. In each process, materials and conversion costs are incurred evenly throughout the process. For the month of April, the work in process accounts show the following debits.

	Cooking	Canning
Beginning work in process	$ –0–	$ 4,000
Materials	21,000	9,000
Labor	8,500	7,000
Overhead	31,500	25,800
Costs transferred in		53,000

Instructions

Journalize the April transactions.

Answer questions on costs and production.

(LO 2, 3, 4)

E21-3 The ledger of American Company has the following work in process account.

Work in Process—Painting

5/1	Balance	3,590	5/31	Transferred out	?
5/31	Materials	5,160			
5/31	Labor	2,530			
5/31	Overhead	1,380			
5/31	Balance	?			

Production records show that there were 400 units in the beginning inventory, 30% complete, 1,600 units started, and 1,700 units transferred out. The beginning work in process had materials cost of $2,040 and conversion costs of $1,550. The units in ending inventory were 40% complete. Materials are entered at the beginning of the painting process.

Instructions

(a) How many units are in process at May 31?
(b) What is the unit materials cost for May?
(c) What is the unit conversion cost for May?
(d) What is the total cost of units transferred out in May?
(e) What is the cost of the May 31 inventory?

Journalize transactions for two processes.

(LO 2)

E21-4 Schrager Company has two production departments: Cutting and Assembly. July 1 inventories are Raw Materials $4,200, Work in Process—Cutting $2,900, Work in Process—Assembly $10,600, and Finished Goods $31,000. During July, the following transactions occurred.

1. Purchased $62,500 of raw materials on account.
2. Incurred $60,000 of factory labor. (Credit Wages Payable.)
3. Incurred $70,000 of manufacturing overhead; $40,000 was paid and the remainder is unpaid.
4. Requisitioned materials for Cutting $15,700 and Assembly $8,900.
5. Used factory labor for Cutting $33,000 and Assembly $27,000.
6. Applied overhead at the rate of $18 per machine hour. Machine hours were Cutting 1,680 and Assembly 1,720.
7. Transferred goods costing $67,600 from the Cutting Department to the Assembly Department.
8. Transferred goods costing $134,900 from Assembly to Finished Goods.
9. Sold goods costing $150,000 for $200,000 on account.

Instructions

Journalize the transactions. (Omit explanations.)

Compute physical units and equivalent units of production.

(LO 3, 4)

E21-5 In Shady Company, materials are entered at the beginning of each process. Work in process inventories, with the percentage of work done on conversion costs, and production data for its Sterilizing Department in selected months during 2017 are as follows.

	Beginning Work in Process			Ending Work in Process	
Month	**Units**	**Conversion Cost%**	**Units Transferred Out**	**Units**	**Conversion Cost%**
January	–0–	—	11,000	2,000	60
March	–0–	—	12,000	3,000	30
May	–0–	—	14,000	7,000	80
July	–0–	—	10,000	1,500	40

Instructions

(a) Compute the physical units for January and May.

(b) Compute the equivalent units of production for (1) materials and (2) conversion costs for each month.

Determine equivalent units, unit costs, and assignment of costs.

(LO 3, 4)

E21-6 The Cutting Department of Cassel Company has the following production and cost data for July.

Production	Costs	
1. Transferred out 12,000 units.	Beginning work in process	$ –0–
2. Started 3,000 units that are 60% complete as to conversion costs and 100% complete as to materials at July 31.	Materials	45,000
	Labor	16,200
	Manufacturing overhead	18,300

Materials are entered at the beginning of the process. Conversion costs are incurred uniformly during the process.

Instructions

(a) Determine the equivalent units of production for (1) materials and (2) conversion costs.

(b) Compute unit costs and prepare a cost reconciliation schedule.

Prepare a production cost report.

(LO 3, 4)

XLS

E21-7 The Sanding Department of Quik Furniture Company has the following production and manufacturing cost data for March 2017, the first month of operation.

Production: 7,000 units finished and transferred out; 3,000 units started that are 100% complete as to materials and 20% complete as to conversion costs.

Manufacturing costs: Materials $33,000; labor $21,000; and overhead $36,000.

Instructions

Prepare a production cost report.

Determine equivalent units, unit costs, and assignment of costs.

(LO 3, 4)

E21-8 The Blending Department of Luongo Company has the following cost and production data for the month of April.

Costs:	
Work in process, April 1	
Direct materials: 100% complete	$100,000
Conversion costs: 20% complete	70,000
Cost of work in process, April 1	$170,000
Costs incurred during production in April	
Direct materials	$ 800,000
Conversion costs	365,000
Costs incurred in April	$1,165,000

Units transferred out totaled 17,000. Ending work in process was 1,000 units that are 100% complete as to materials and 40% complete as to conversion costs.

Instructions

(a) Compute the equivalent units of production for (1) materials and (2) conversion costs for the month of April.
(b) Compute the unit costs for the month.
(c) Determine the costs to be assigned to the units transferred out and in ending work in process.

Determine equivalent units, unit costs, and assignment of costs.

(LO 3, 4)

E21-9 Baden Company has gathered the following information.

Units in beginning work in process	–0–
Units started into production	36,000
Units in ending work in process	6,000
Percent complete in ending work in process:	
Conversion costs	40%
Materials	100%
Costs incurred:	
Direct materials	$72,000
Direct labor	$61,000
Overhead	$101,000

Instructions

(a) Compute equivalent units of production for materials and for conversion costs.
(b) Determine the unit costs of production.
(c) Show the assignment of costs to units transferred out and in process.

Determine equivalent units, unit costs, and assignment of costs.

(LO 3, 4)

E21-10 Overton Company has gathered the following information.

Units in beginning work in process	20,000
Units started into production	164,000
Units in ending work in process	24,000
Percent complete in ending work in process:	
Conversion costs	60%
Materials	100%
Costs incurred:	
Direct materials	$101,200
Direct labor	$164,800
Overhead	$184,000

Instructions

(a) Compute equivalent units of production for materials and for conversion costs.
(b) Determine the unit costs of production.
(c) Show the assignment of costs to units transferred out and in process.

Compute equivalent units, unit costs, and costs assigned.

(LO 3, 4)

E21-11 The Polishing Department of Major Company has the following production and manufacturing cost data for September. Materials are entered at the beginning of the process.

Production: Beginning inventory 1,600 units that are 100% complete as to materials and 30% complete as to conversion costs; units started during the period are 42,900; ending inventory of 5,000 units 10% complete as to conversion costs.

Manufacturing costs: Beginning inventory costs, comprising $20,000 of materials and $43,180 of conversion costs; materials costs added in Polishing during the month, $175,800; labor and overhead applied in Polishing during the month, $125,680 and $257,140, respectively.

Instructions

(a) Compute the equivalent units of production for materials and conversion costs for the month of September.
(b) Compute the unit costs for materials and conversion costs for the month.
(c) Determine the costs to be assigned to the units transferred out and in process.

Explain the production cost report.

(LO 4)

E21-12 David Skaros has recently been promoted to production manager. He has just started to receive various managerial reports, including the production cost report that you prepared. It showed that his department had 2,000 equivalent units in ending inventory. His department has had a history of not keeping enough inventory on hand to meet demand. He has come to you, very angry, and wants to know why you credited him with only 2,000 units when he knows he had at least twice that many on hand.

Instructions

Explain to him why his production cost report showed only 2,000 equivalent units in ending inventory. Write an informal memo. Be kind and explain very clearly why he is mistaken.

Prepare a production cost report.
(LO 3, 4)

E21-13 The Welding Department of Healthy Company has the following production and manufacturing cost data for February 2017. All materials are added at the beginning of the process.

Manufacturing Costs			**Production Data**	
Beginning work in process			Beginning work in process	15,000 units
Materials	$18,000			1/10 complete
Conversion costs	14,175	$ 32,175	Units transferred out	55,000
Materials		180,000	Units started	51,000
Labor		67,380	Ending work in process	11,000 units
Overhead		61,445		1/5 complete

Instructions

Prepare a production cost report for the Welding Department for the month of February.

Compute physical units and equivalent units of production.
(LO 3, 4)

E21-14 Remington Inc. is contemplating the use of process costing to track the costs of its operations. The operation consists of three segments (departments): Receiving, Shipping, and Delivery. Containers are received at Remington's docks and sorted according to the ship they will be carried on. The containers are loaded onto a ship, which carries them to the appropriate port of destination. The containers are then off-loaded and delivered to the Receiving Department.

Remington wants to begin using process costing in the Shipping Department. Direct materials represent the fuel costs to run the ship, and "Containers in transit" represents work in process. Listed below is information about the Shipping Department's first month's activity.

Containers in transit, April 1	0
Containers loaded	1,200
Containers in transit, April 30	350, 40% of direct materials and 20% of conversion costs

Instructions

(a) Determine the physical flow of containers for the month.
(b) Calculate the equivalent units for direct materials and conversion costs.

Determine equivalent units, unit costs, and assignment of costs.
(LO 3, 4)

E21-15 Santana Mortgage Company uses a process cost system to accumulate costs in its Application Department. When an application is completed, it is forwarded to the Loan Department for final processing. The following processing and cost data pertain to September.

1. Applications in process on September 1: 100.
2. Applications started in September: 1,000.
3. Completed applications during September: 800.
4. Applications still in process at September 30: 100% complete as to materials (forms) and 60% complete as to conversion costs.

Beginning WIP:	
Direct materials	$ 1,000
Conversion costs	3,960
September costs:	
Direct materials	$ 4,500
Direct labor	12,000
Overhead	9,520

Materials are the forms used in the application process, and these costs are incurred at the beginning of the process. Conversion costs are incurred uniformly during the process.

Instructions

(a) Determine the equivalent units of service (production) for materials and conversion costs.
(b) Compute the unit costs and prepare a cost reconciliation schedule.

Compute overhead rates and assign overhead using ABC.
(LO 6)

***E21-16** Major Instrument, Inc. manufactures two products: missile range instruments and space pressure gauges. During April, 50 range instruments and 300 pressure gauges were produced, and overhead costs of $94,500 were estimated. An analysis of estimated overhead costs reveals the following activities.

Activities	Cost Drivers	Total Cost
1. Materials handling	Number of requisitions	$40,000
2. Machine setups	Number of setups	27,500
3. Quality inspections	Number of inspections	27,000
		$94,500

The cost driver volume for each product was as follows.

Cost Drivers	Instruments	Gauges	Total
Number of requisitions	400	600	1,000
Number of setups	200	300	500
Number of inspections	200	400	600

Instructions

(a) Determine the overhead rate for each activity.

(b) Assign the manufacturing overhead costs for April to the two products using activity-based costing.

(c) Write a memorandum to the president of Major Instrument explaining the benefits of activity-based costing.

***E21-17** Kowalski Company manufactures a number of specialized machine parts. Part Compo-24 uses $35 of direct materials and $15 of direct labor per unit. Kowalski's estimated manufacturing overhead is as follows.

Compute product cost using traditional costing and ABC.

(LO 6)

Materials handling	$150,000
Machining	180,000
Factory supervision	138,000
Total	$468,000

Overhead is applied based on direct labor costs, which were estimated at $200,000.

Kowalski is considering adopting activity-based costing. The cost drivers are estimated at:

Activity	Cost Driver	Expected Use
Materials handling	Weight of materials	50,000 pounds
Machining	Machine hours	20,000 hours
Factory supervision	Direct labor hours	12,000 hours

Instructions

(a) Compute the cost of 1,000 units of Compo-24 using the current traditional costing system.

(b) Compute the cost of 1,000 units of Compo-24 using the proposed activity-based costing system. Assume the 1,000 units use 2,500 pounds of materials, 500 machine hours, and 1,000 direct labor hours.

PROBLEMS

P21-1A Fire Out Company manufactures its product, Vitadrink, through two manufacturing processes: Mixing and Packaging. All materials are entered at the beginning of each process. On October 1, 2017, inventories consisted of Raw Materials $26,000, Work in Process—Mixing $0, Work in Process—Packaging $250,000, and Finished Goods $289,000. The beginning inventory for Packaging consisted of 10,000 units that were 50% complete as to conversion costs and fully complete as to materials. During October, 50,000 units were started into production in the Mixing Department and the following transactions were completed.

Journalize transactions.

(LO 2)

1. Purchased $300,000 of raw materials on account.
2. Issued raw materials for production: Mixing $210,000 and Packaging $45,000.
3. Incurred labor costs of $278,900.
4. Used factory labor: Mixing $182,500 and Packaging $96,400.
5. Incurred $810,000 of manufacturing overhead on account.
6. Applied manufacturing overhead on the basis of $23 per machine hour. Machine hours were 28,000 in Mixing and 6,000 in Packaging.
7. Transferred 45,000 units from Mixing to Packaging at a cost of $979,000.
8. Transferred 53,000 units from Packaging to Finished Goods at a cost of $1,315,000.
9. Sold goods costing $1,604,000 for $2,500,000 on account.

Instructions

Journalize the October transactions.

Complete four steps necessary to prepare a production cost report.

(LO 3, 4)

P21-2A Rosenthal Company manufactures bowling balls through two processes: Molding and Packaging. In the Molding Department, the urethane, rubber, plastics, and other materials are molded into bowling balls. In the Packaging Department, the balls are placed in cartons and sent to the finished goods warehouse. All materials are entered at the beginning of each process. Labor and manufacturing overhead are incurred uniformly throughout each process. Production and cost data for the Molding Department during June 2017 are presented below.

Production Data	June
Beginning work in process units	–0–
Units started into production	22,000
Ending work in process units	2,000
Percent complete—ending inventory	40%

Cost Data	
Materials	$198,000
Labor	53,600
Overhead	112,800
Total	$364,400

(c) Materials $9.00
CC $8.00
(d) Transferred out $340,000
WIP $ 24,400

Instructions

(a) Prepare a schedule showing physical units of production.
(b) Determine the equivalent units of production for materials and conversion costs.
(c) Compute the unit costs of production.
(d) Determine the costs to be assigned to the units transferred out and in process for June.
(e) Prepare a production cost report for the Molding Department for the month of June.

Complete four steps necessary to prepare a production cost report.

(LO 3, 4)

P21-3A Thakin Industries Inc. manufactures dorm furniture in separate processes. In each process, materials are entered at the beginning, and conversion costs are incurred uniformly. Production and cost data for the first process in making two products in two different manufacturing plants are as follows.

	Cutting Department	
	Plant 1	Plant 2
Production Data—July	**T12-Tables**	**C10-Chairs**
Work in process units, July 1	–0–	–0–
Units started into production	20,000	18,000
Work in process units, July 31	3,000	500
Work in process percent complete	60	80
Cost Data—July		
Work in process, July 1	$ –0–	$ –0–
Materials	380,000	288,000
Labor	234,400	110,000
Overhead	104,000	104,800
Total	$718,400	$502,800

(a) (3) T12:
Materials $19
CC $18
(4) T12:
Transferred out $629,000
WIP $ 89,400

Instructions

(a) For each plant:
 (1) Compute the physical units of production.
 (2) Compute equivalent units of production for materials and for conversion costs.
 (3) Determine the unit costs of production.
 (4) Show the assignment of costs to units transferred out and in process.
(b) Prepare the production cost report for Plant 1 for July 2017.

Assign costs and prepare production cost report.

(LO 3, 4)

P21-4A Rivera Company has several processing departments. Costs charged to the Assembly Department for November 2017 totaled $2,280,000 as follows.

Work in process, November 1		
Materials	$79,000	
Conversion costs	48,150	$ 127,150
Materials added		1,589,000
Labor		225,920
Overhead		337,930

Production records show that 35,000 units were in beginning work in process 30% complete as to conversion costs, 660,000 units were started into production, and 25,000 units were in ending work in process 40% complete as to conversion costs. Materials are entered at the beginning of each process.

Instructions

(a) Determine the equivalent units of production and the unit production costs for the Assembly Department.

(b) Determine the assignment of costs to goods transferred out and in process.

(c) Prepare a production cost report for the Assembly Department.

(b) Transferred out $2,211,000
WIP $ 69,000

P21-5A Polk Company manufactures basketballs. Materials are added at the beginning of the production process and conversion costs are incurred uniformly. Production and cost data for the month of July 2017 are as follows.

Determine equivalent units and unit costs and assign costs.

(LO 3, 4)

Production Data—Basketballs	Units	Percentage Complete
Work in process units, July 1	500	60%
Units started into production	1,000	
Work in process units, July 31	600	40%

Cost Data—Basketballs		
Work in process, July 1		
Materials	$750	
Conversion costs	600	$1,350
Direct materials		2,400
Direct labor		1,580
Manufacturing overhead		1,240

Instructions

(a) Calculate the following.

(1) The equivalent units of production for materials and conversion costs.

(2) The unit costs of production for materials and conversion costs.

(3) The assignment of costs to units transferred out and in process at the end of the accounting period.

(b) Prepare a production cost report for the month of July for the basketballs.

(a) (2) Materials $2.10
(3) Transferred out $4,590
WIP $1,980

P21-6A Hamilton Processing Company uses a weighted-average process cost system and manufactures a single product—an industrial carpet shampoo and cleaner used by many universities. The manufacturing activity for the month of October has just been completed. A partially completed production cost report for the month of October for the Mixing and Cooking Department is shown below.

Compute equivalent units and complete production cost report.

(LO 3, 4)

HAMILTON PROCESSING COMPANY
Mixing and Cooking Department
Production Cost Report
For the Month Ended October 31

		Equivalent Units	
Quantities	**Physical Units**	**Materials**	**Conversion Costs**
Units to be accounted for			
Work in process, October 1 (all materials, 70% conversion costs)	20,000		
Started into production	150,000		
Total units	170,000		
Units accounted for			
Transferred out	120,000	?	?
Work in process, October 31 (60% materials, 40% conversion costs)	50,000	?	?
Total units accounted for	170,000	?	?

Costs

Unit costs	Materials		Conversion Costs		Total
Total cost	$240,000		$105,000		$345,000
Equivalent units	?		?		
Unit costs	$?	+	$?	=	$?
Costs to be accounted for					
Work in process, October 1					$ 30,000
Started into production					315,000
Total costs					$345,000

Cost Reconciliation Schedule

Costs accounted for		
Transferred out		$?
Work in process, October 31		
Materials	$?	
Conversion costs	?	?
Total costs		$?

(a) Materials $1.60
(b) Transferred out $282,000
WIP $ 63,000

Instructions

(a) Prepare a schedule that shows how the equivalent units were computed so that you can complete the "Quantities: Units accounted for" equivalent units section shown in the production cost report, and compute October unit costs.

(b) Complete the "Cost Reconciliation Schedule" part of the production cost report.

Assign overhead to products using ABC and evaluate decision.

(LO 6)

***P21-7A** Schultz Electronics manufactures two large-screen television models: the Royale which sells for $1,600, and a new model, the Majestic, which sells for $1,300. The production cost computed per unit under traditional costing for each model in 2017 was as follows.

Traditional Costing	Royale	Majestic
Direct materials	$ 700	$420
Direct labor ($20 per hour)	120	100
Manufacturing overhead ($38 per DLH)	228	190
Total per unit cost	$1,048	$710

In 2017, Schultz manufactured 25,000 units of the Royale and 10,000 units of the Majestic. The overhead rate of $38 per direct labor hour was determined by dividing total expected manufacturing overhead of $7,600,000 by the total direct labor hours (200,000) for the two models.

Under traditional costing, the gross profit on the models was Royale $552 or ($1,600 − $1,048), and Majestic $590 or ($1,300 − $710). Because of this difference, management is considering phasing out the Royale model and increasing the production of the Majestic model.

Before finalizing its decision, management asks Schultz's controller to prepare an analysis using activity-based costing (ABC). The controller accumulates the following information about overhead for the year ended December 31, 2017.

Activities	Cost Drivers	Estimated Overhead	Expected Use of Cost Drivers	Activity-Based Overhead Rate
Purchasing	Number of orders	$1,200,000	40,000	$30/order
Machine setups	Number of setups	900,000	18,000	$50/setup
Machining	Machine hours	4,800,000	120,000	$40/hour
Quality control	Number of inspections	700,000	28,000	$25/inspection

The cost drivers used for each product were:

Cost Drivers	Royale	Majestic	Total
Purchase orders	17,000	23,000	40,000
Machine setups	5,000	13,000	18,000
Machine hours	75,000	45,000	120,000
Inspections	11,000	17,000	28,000

Instructions

(a) Assign the total 2017 manufacturing overhead costs to the two products using activity-based costing (ABC) and determine the overhead cost per unit.

(b) What was the cost per unit and gross profit of each model using ABC?

(c) Are management's future plans for the two models sound? Explain.

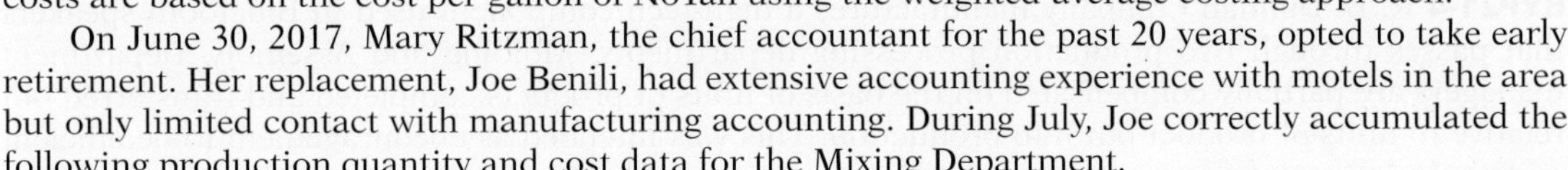

MANAGEMENT DECISION-MAKING

Decision-Making Across the Organization

BYP21-1 Florida Beach Company manufactures sunscreen, called NoTan, in 11-ounce plastic bottles. NoTan is sold in a competitive market. As a result, management is very cost-conscious. NoTan is manufactured through two processes: mixing and filling. Materials are entered at the beginning of each process, and labor and manufacturing overhead occur uniformly throughout each process. Unit costs are based on the cost per gallon of NoTan using the weighted-average costing approach.

On June 30, 2017, Mary Ritzman, the chief accountant for the past 20 years, opted to take early retirement. Her replacement, Joe Benili, had extensive accounting experience with motels in the area but only limited contact with manufacturing accounting. During July, Joe correctly accumulated the following production quantity and cost data for the Mixing Department.

Production quantities: Work in process, July 1, 8,000 gallons 75% complete; started into production 100,000 gallons; work in process, July 31, 5,000 gallons 20% complete. Materials are added at the beginning of the process.

Production costs: Beginning work in process $88,000, comprising $21,000 of materials costs and $67,000 of conversion costs; incurred in July: materials $573,000, conversion costs $765,000.

Joe then prepared a production cost report on the basis of physical units started into production. His report showed a production cost of $14.26 per gallon of NoTan. The management of Florida Beach was surprised at the high unit cost. The president comes to you, as Mary's top assistant, to review Joe's report and prepare a correct report if necessary.

Instructions

With the class divided into groups, answer the following questions.

(a) Show how Joe arrived at the unit cost of $14.26 per gallon of NoTan.

(b) What error(s) did Joe make in preparing his production cost report?

(c) Prepare a correct production cost report for July.

Managerial Analysis

BYP21-2 Harris Furniture Company manufactures living room furniture through two departments: Framing and Upholstering. Materials are entered at the beginning of each process. For May, the following cost data are obtained from the two work in process accounts.

	Framing	**Upholstering**
Work in process, May 1	$ -0-	$?
Materials	450,000	?
Conversion costs	261,000	330,000
Costs transferred in	-0-	600,000
Costs transferred out	600,000	?
Work in process, May 31	111,000	?

Instructions

Answer the following questions.

(a) If 3,000 sofas were started into production on May 1 and 2,500 sofas were transferred to Upholstering, what was the unit cost of materials for May in the Framing Department?

(b) Using the data in (a) above, what was the per unit conversion cost of the sofas transferred to Upholstering?

(c) Continuing the assumptions in (a) above, what is the percentage of completion of the units in process at May 31 in the Framing Department?

Real-World Focus

BYP21-3 Paintball is now played around the world. The process of making paintballs is actually quite similar to the process used to make certain medical pills. In fact, paintballs were previously often made at the same factories that made pharmaceuticals.

Address: Go to **www.youtube.com/watch?v=2hKrv60PJKE#t=129** to access the video.

Instructions
View the video at the site listed above and then answer the following questions.

(a) Describe in sequence the primary steps used to manufacture paintballs.
(b) Explain the costs incurred by the company that would fall into each of the following categories: materials, labor, and overhead. Of these categories, which do you think would be the greatest cost in making paintballs?
(c) Discuss whether a paintball manufacturer would use job order costing or process costing.

CRITICAL THINKING

Ethics Case

BYP21-4 R. B. Dillman Company manufactures a high-tech component used in Bluetooth speakers that passes through two production processing departments, Molding and Assembly. Department managers are partially compensated on the basis of units of products completed and transferred out relative to units of product put into production. This was intended as encouragement to be efficient and to minimize waste.

Jan Wooten is the department head in the Molding Department, and Tony Ferneti is her quality control inspector. During the month of June, Jan had three new employees who were not yet technically skilled. As a result, many of the units produced in June had minor molding defects. In order to maintain the department's normal high rate of completion, Jan told Tony to pass through inspection and on to the Assembly Department all units that had defects nondetectable to the human eye. "Company and industry tolerances on this product are too high anyway," says Jan. "Less than 2% of the units we produce are subjected in the market to the stress tolerance we've designed into them. The odds of those 2% being any of this month's units are even less. Anyway, we're saving the company money."

Instructions
(a) Who are the potential stakeholders involved in this situation?
(b) What alternatives does Tony have in this situation? What might the company do to prevent this situation from occurring?

Considering People, Planet, and Profit

BYP21-5 In a recent year, an oil refinery in Texas City, Texas, on the Houston Ship Channel exploded. The explosion killed 14 people and sent a plume of smoke hundreds of feet into the air. The blast started as a fire in the section of the plant that increased the octane of the gasoline that was produced at the refinery. The Houston Ship Channel is the main waterway that allows commerce to flow from the Gulf of Mexico into Houston.

The Texas Commission on Environmental Quality expressed concern about the release of nitrogen oxides, benzene, and other known carcinogens as a result of the blast. Neighbors of the plant complained that the plant had been emitting carcinogens for years and that the regulators had ignored their complaints about emissions and unsafe working conditions.

Instructions
Answer the following questions.

(a) Outline the costs that the company now faces as a result of the accident.
(b) How could the company have reduced the costs associated with the accident?

Chapter 22 Cost-Volume-Profit

It wasn't that Jeff Bezos didn't have a good job. He was a vice president at a Wall Street firm. But, he quit his job, moved to Seattle, and started an online retailer, which he named Amazon.com. Like any good entrepreneur, Jeff strove to keep his initial investment small. Operations were run out of his garage. And, to avoid the need for a warehouse, he took orders for books and had them shipped from other distributors' warehouses.

By its fourth month, Amazon was selling 100 books a day. In its first full year, it had $15.7 million in sales. The next year, sales increased eightfold. Two years later, sales were $1.6 billion.

Although its sales growth was impressive, Amazon's ability to lose money was equally amazing. One analyst nicknamed it *Amazon.bomb*, while another, predicting its demise, called it *Amazon.toast*. Why was it losing money? The company used every available dollar to reinvest in itself. It built massive warehouses and bought increasingly sophisticated (and expensive) computers and equipment to improve its distribution system. This desire to grow as fast as possible was captured in a T-shirt slogan at its company picnic, which read "Eat another hot dog, get big fast." This buying binge was increasing the company's fixed costs at a rate that exceeded its sales growth. Skeptics predicted that Amazon would soon run out of cash. It didn't.

In the fourth quarter of 2010 (only 15 years after its world headquarters was located in a garage), Amazon reported quarterly revenues of $12.95 billion and quarterly income of $416 million. But, even as it announced record profits, its share price fell by 9%. Why? Because although the company was predicting that its sales revenue in the next quarter would increase by at least 28%, it predicted that its operating profit would fall by at least 2% and perhaps by as much as 34%. The company made no apologies. It explained that it was in the process of expanding from 39 distribution centers to 52. As Amazon's finance chief noted, "You're not as productive on those assets for some time. I'm very pleased with the investments we're making and we've shown over our history that we've been able to make great returns on the capital we invest in." In other words, eat another hot dog.

Sources: Christine Frey and John Cook, "How Amazon.com Survived, Thrived and Turned a Profit," *Seattle Post* (January 28, 2008); and Stu Woo, "Sticker Shock Over Amazon Growth," *Wall Street Journal Online* (January 28, 2011).

LEARNING OBJECTIVES

1. **Explain variable, fixed, and mixed costs and the relevant range.**
2. **Apply the high-low method to determine the components of mixed costs.**
3. **Prepare a CVP income statement to determine contribution margin.**
4. **Compute the break-even point using three approaches.**
5. **Determine the sales required to earn target net income and determine margin of safety.**
6. **Use CVP analysis to respond to changes in the business environment.**

LEARNING OBJECTIVE 1

Explain variable, fixed, and mixed costs and the relevant range.

Cost behavior analysis is the study of how specific costs respond to changes in the level of business activity. As you might expect, some costs change, and others remain the same. For example, for an airline company such as **Southwest** or **United**, the longer the flight, the higher the fuel costs. On the other hand, **Massachusetts General Hospital**'s costs to staff the emergency room on any given night are relatively constant regardless of the number of patients treated. A knowledge of cost behavior helps management plan operations and decide between alternative courses of action. Cost behavior analysis applies to all types of entities.

The starting point in cost behavior analysis is measuring the key business activities. Activity levels may be expressed in terms of sales dollars (in a retail company), miles driven (in a trucking company), room occupancy (in a hotel), or dance classes taught (by a dance studio). Many companies use more than one measurement base. A manufacturer, for example, may use direct labor hours or units of output for manufacturing costs, and sales revenue or units sold for selling expenses.

For an activity level to be useful in cost behavior analysis, changes in the level or volume of activity should be correlated with changes in costs. The activity level selected is referred to as the activity (or volume) index. The **activity index** identifies the activity that causes changes in the behavior of costs. With an appropriate activity index, companies can classify the behavior of costs in response to changes in activity levels into three categories: variable, fixed, or mixed.

Variable Costs

Variable costs are costs that vary **in total** directly and proportionately with changes in the activity level. If the level increases 10%, total variable costs will increase 10%. If the level of activity decreases by 25%, variable costs will decrease 25%. Examples of variable costs include direct materials and direct labor for a manufacturer; cost of goods sold, sales commissions, and freight-out for a merchandiser; and gasoline in airline and trucking companies. A variable cost may also be defined as a cost that **remains the same *per unit* at every level of activity**.

To illustrate the behavior of a variable cost, assume that Damon Company manufactures tablet computers that contain $10 cameras. The activity index is the number of tablet computers produced. As Damon manufactures each tablet, the total cost of cameras used increases by $10. As part (a) of Illustration 22-1

Illustration 22-1
Behavior of total and unit variable costs

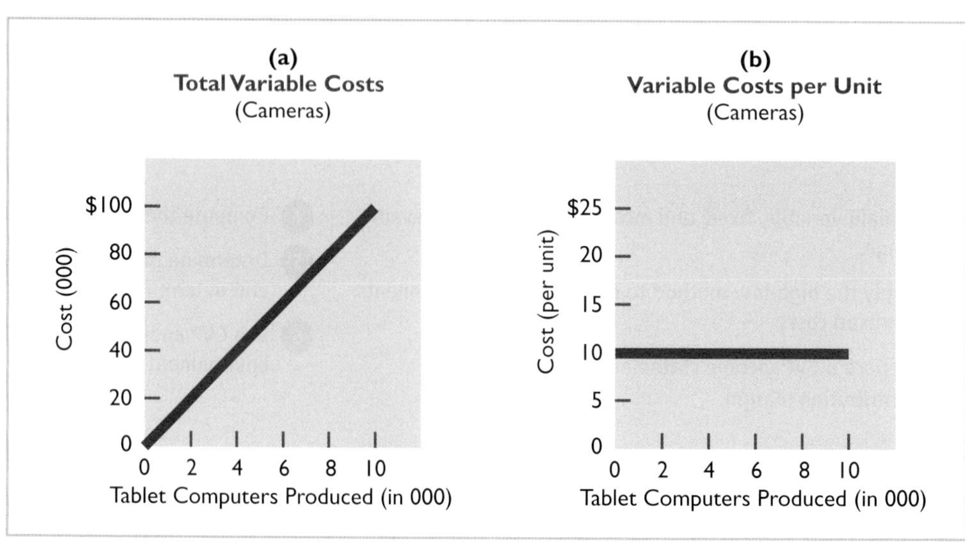

shows, total cost of the cameras will be $20,000 if Damon produces 2,000 tablets, and $100,000 when it produces 10,000 tablets. We also can see that a variable cost remains the same per unit as the level of activity changes. As part (b) of Illustration 22-1 shows, the unit cost of $10 for the cameras is the same whether Damon produces 2,000 or 10,000 tablets.

Companies that rely heavily on labor to manufacture a product, such as **Nike** or **Reebok**, or to perform a service, such as **Hilton** or **Marriott**, are likely to have many variable costs. In contrast, companies that use a high proportion of machinery and equipment in producing revenue, such as **AT&T** or **Duke Energy Co.**, may have few variable costs.

Fixed Costs

Fixed costs are costs that **remain the same in total** regardless of changes in the activity level. Examples include property taxes, insurance, rent, supervisory salaries, and depreciation on buildings and equipment. Because total fixed costs remain constant as activity changes, it follows that **fixed costs *per unit* vary inversely with activity: As volume increases, unit cost declines, and vice versa**.

To illustrate the behavior of fixed costs, assume that Damon Company leases its productive facilities at a cost of $10,000 per month. Total fixed costs of the facilities will remain constant at every level of activity, as part (a) of Illustration 22-2 shows. But, **on a per unit basis, the cost of rent will decline as activity increases**, as part (b) of Illustration 22-2 shows. At 2,000 units, the unit cost per tablet computer is $5 ($10,000 ÷ 2,000). When Damon produces 10,000 tablets, the unit cost of the rent is only $1 per tablet ($10,000 ÷ 10,000).

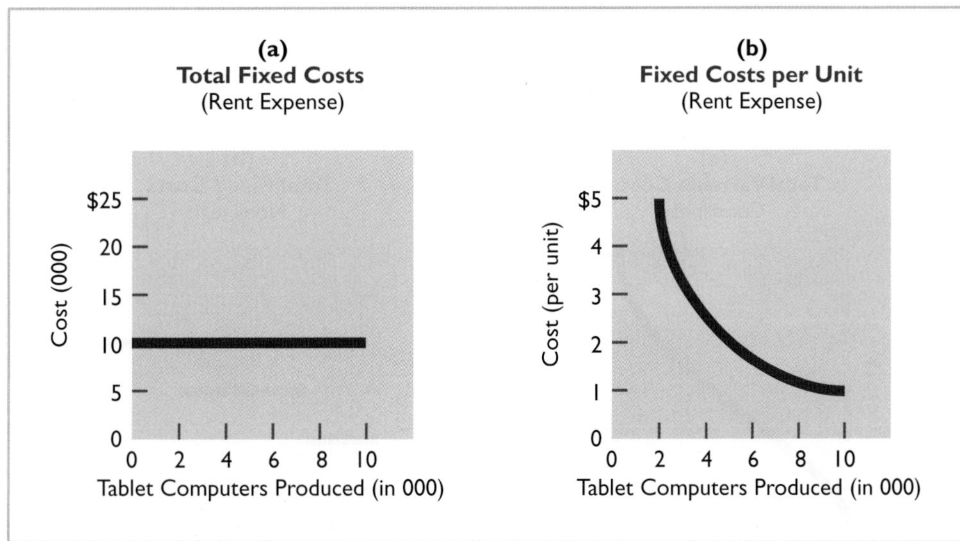

Illustration 22-2
Behavior of total and unit fixed costs

The trend for many manufacturers is to have more fixed costs and fewer variable costs. This trend is the result of increased use of automation and less use of employee labor. As a result, depreciation and lease charges (fixed costs) increase, whereas direct labor costs (variable costs) decrease.

Relevant Range

In Illustration 22-1 part (a) (page 760), a straight line is drawn throughout the entire range of the activity index for total variable costs. In essence, the assumption is that the costs are **linear**. If a relationship is linear (that is, straight-line), then changes in the activity index will result in a direct, proportional change in the variable cost. For example, if the activity level doubles, the cost doubles.

It is now necessary to ask: Is the straight-line relationship realistic? In most business situations, a straight-line relationship **does not exist** for variable costs throughout the entire range of possible activity. At abnormally low levels of activity, it may be impossible to be cost-efficient. Small-scale operations may not allow the company to obtain quantity discounts for raw materials or to use specialized labor. In contrast, at abnormally high levels of activity, labor costs may increase sharply because of overtime pay. Also, at high activity levels, materials costs may jump significantly because of excess spoilage caused by worker fatigue.

As a result, in the real world, the relationship between the behavior of a variable cost and changes in the activity level is often **curvilinear**, as shown in part (a) of Illustration 22-3. In the curved sections of the line, a change in the activity index will not result in a direct, proportional change in the variable cost. That is, a doubling of the activity index will not result in an exact doubling of the variable cost. The variable cost may more than double, or it may be less than double.

Total fixed costs also do not have a straight-line relationship over the entire range of activity. Some fixed costs will not change. But it is possible for management to change other fixed costs. For example, in some instances, salaried employees (fixed) are replaced with freelance workers (variable). Illustration 22-3, part (b), shows an example of the behavior of total fixed costs through all potential levels of activity.

For most companies, operating at almost zero or at 100% capacity is the exception rather than the rule. Instead, companies often operate over a somewhat

Illustration 22-3
Nonlinear behavior of variable and fixed costs

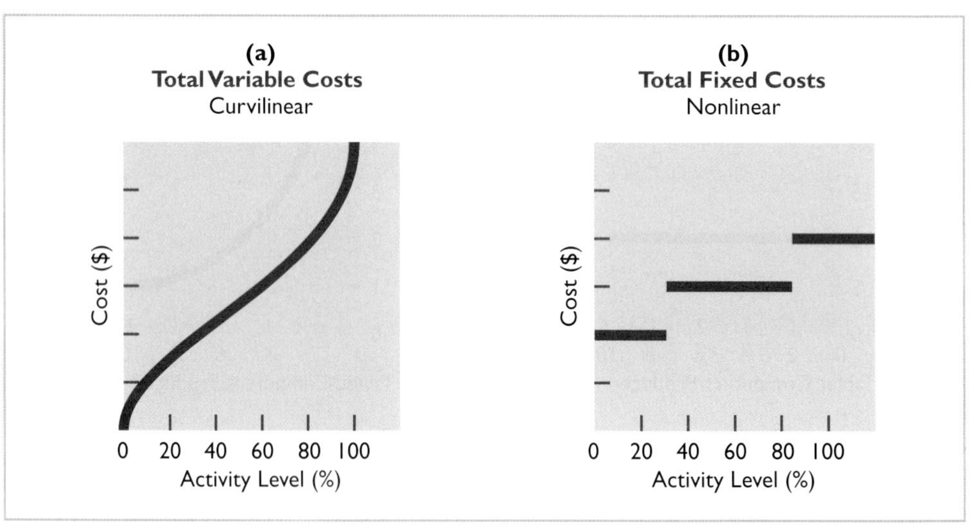

Terminology
The relevant range is also called the *normal* or *practical range*.

narrower range, such as 40–80% of capacity. The range over which a company expects to operate during a year is called the **relevant range** of the activity index. Within the relevant range, as both diagrams in Illustration 22-4 show, a straight-line relationship generally exists for both variable and fixed costs.

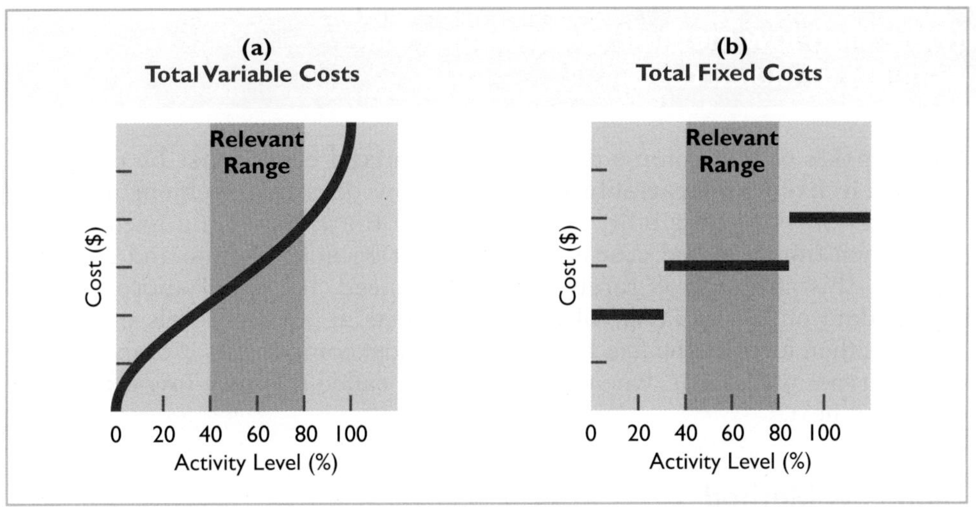

Illustration 22-4
Linear behavior within relevant range

As you can see, although the linear (straight-line) relationship may not be completely realistic, **the linear assumption produces useful data for CVP analysis as long as the level of activity remains within the relevant range.**

Mixed Costs

Mixed costs are costs that contain both a variable- and a fixed-cost element. **Mixed costs, therefore, change in total but not proportionately with changes in the activity level.**

The rental of a U-Haul truck is a good example of a mixed cost. Assume that local rental terms for a 17-foot truck, including insurance, are $50 per day plus 50 cents per mile. When determining the cost of a one-day rental, the per day charge is a fixed cost (with respect to miles driven), whereas the mileage charge is a variable cost. The graphic presentation of the rental cost for a one-day rental is shown in Illustration 22-5.

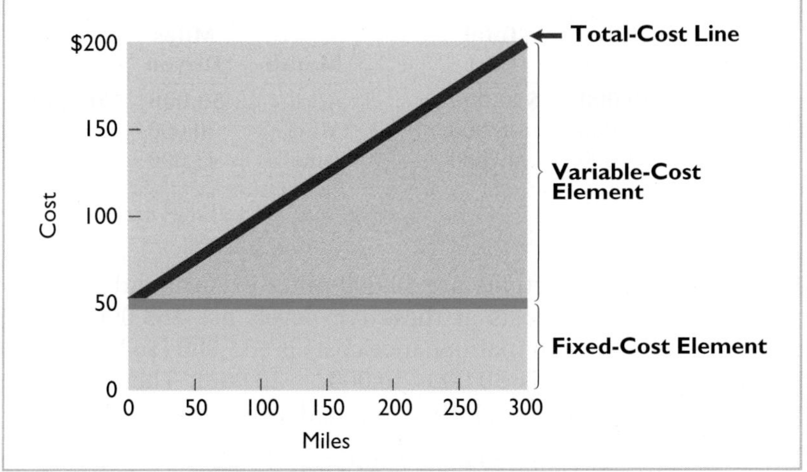

Illustration 22-5
Behavior of a mixed cost

In this case, the fixed-cost element is the cost of having the service available. The variable-cost element is the cost of actually using the service. Utility costs such as for electricity are another example of a mixed cost. Each month the electric bill includes a flat service fee plus a usage charge.

LEARNING OBJECTIVE 

Apply the high-low method to determine the components of mixed costs.

For purposes of cost-volume-profit analysis, **mixed costs must be classified into their fixed and variable elements**. How does management make the classification? One possibility is to determine the variable and fixed components each time a mixed cost is incurred. But because of time and cost constraints, this approach is rarely followed. Instead, the usual approach is to collect data on the behavior of the mixed costs at various levels of activity. Analysts then identify the fixed- and variable-cost components. Companies use various types of analysis. One type of analysis, called the **high-low method**, is discussed next.

High-Low Method

The **high-low method** uses the total costs incurred at the high and low levels of activity to classify mixed costs into fixed and variable components. The difference in costs between the high and low levels represents variable costs, since only the variable-cost element can change as activity levels change.

The steps in computing fixed and variable costs under this method are as follows.

1. Determine variable cost per unit from the following formula.

Illustration 22-6
Formula for variable cost per unit using high-low method

Change in Total Costs	÷	High Minus Low Activity Level	=	Variable Cost per Unit

To illustrate, assume that Metro Transit Company has the following maintenance costs and mileage data for its fleet of buses over a 6-month period.

Illustration 22-7
Assumed maintenance costs and mileage data

Month	Miles Driven	Total Cost	Month	Miles Driven	Total Cost
January	**20,000**	**$30,000**	April	**50,000**	**$63,000**
February	40,000	48,000	May	30,000	42,000
March	35,000	49,000	June	43,000	61,000

The high and low levels of activity are 50,000 miles in April and 20,000 miles in January. The maintenance costs at these two levels are $63,000 and $30,000, respectively. The difference in maintenance costs is $33,000 ($63,000 − $30,000), and the difference in miles is 30,000 (50,000 − 20,000). Therefore, for Metro Transit, variable cost per unit is $1.10, computed as follows.

$$\$33,000 \div 30,000 = \$1.10$$

2. Determine the fixed costs by subtracting the total variable costs at either the high or the low activity level from the total cost at that activity level.

For Metro Transit, the computations are shown in Illustration 22-8.

Illustration 22-8
High-low method computation of fixed costs

Metro Transit.xls

	A	B	C	D
1		**METRO TRANSIT**		
2			Activity Level	
3			High	Low
4	Total cost		$63,000	$30,000
5	Less:	Variable costs		
6		50,000 × $1.10	55,000	
7		20,000 × $1.10		22,000
8	Total fixed costs		$ 8,000	$ 8,000
9				
10				

Maintenance costs are therefore $8,000 per month of fixed costs plus $1.10 per mile of variable costs. This is represented by the following formula:

$$\text{Maintenance costs} = \$8{,}000 + (\$1.10 \times \text{Miles driven})$$

For example, at 45,000 miles, estimated maintenance costs would be $8,000 fixed and $49,500 variable ($1.10 × 45,000) for a total of $57,500.

The graph in Illustration 22-9 plots the 6-month data for Metro Transit Company. The red line drawn in the graph connects the high and low data points, and therefore represents the equation that we just solved using the high-low method. The red, "high-low" line intersects the y-axis at $8,000 (the fixed-cost level), and it rises by $1.10 per unit (the variable cost per unit). Note that a completely different line would result if we chose any two of the other data points. That is, by choosing any two other data points, we would end up with a different estimate of fixed costs and a different variable cost per unit. Thus, from this scatter plot, we can see that while the high-low method is simple, the result is rather arbitrary. A better approach, which uses information from all the data points to estimate fixed and variable costs, is called *regression analysis*. A discussion of regression analysis is provided in a supplement on the book's companion website.

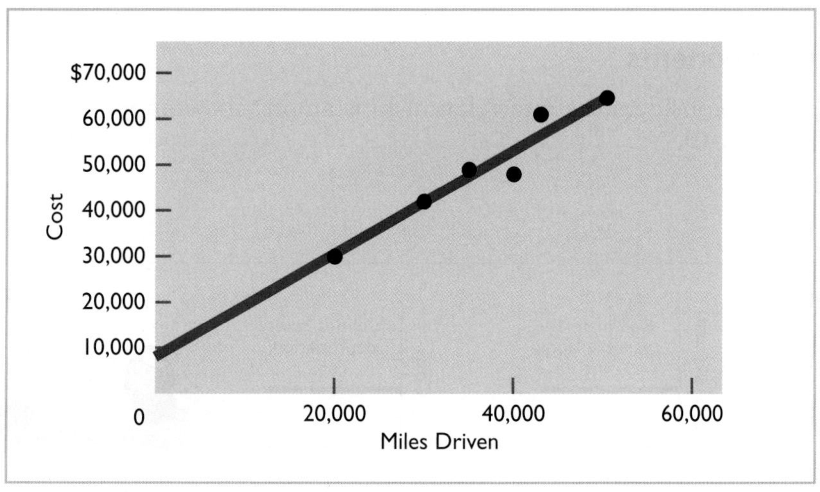

Illustration 22-9
Scatter plot for Metro Transit Company

Importance of Identifying Variable and Fixed Costs

Why is it important to segregate mixed costs into variable and fixed elements? The answer may become apparent if we look at the following four business decisions.

1. If American Airlines is to make a profit when it reduces all domestic fares by 30%, what reduction in costs or increase in passengers will be required?
   Answer: To make a profit when it cuts domestic fares by 30%, American Airlines will have to increase the number of passengers or cut its variable costs for those flights. Its fixed costs will not change.
2. If Ford Motor Company meets workers' demands for higher wages, what increase in sales revenue will be needed to maintain current profit levels?
   Answer: Higher wages at Ford Motor Company will increase the variable costs of manufacturing automobiles. To maintain present profit levels, Ford will have to cut other variable costs or increase the price of its automobiles.
3. If United States Steel Corp.'s program to modernize plant facilities through significant equipment purchases reduces the work force by 50%, what will be the effect on the cost of producing one ton of steel?
   Answer: The modernizing of plant facilities at United States Steel Corp. changes the proportion of fixed and variable costs of producing one ton of steel. Fixed costs increase because of higher depreciation charges, whereas variable costs decrease due to the reduction in the number of steelworkers.
4. What happens if Kellogg's increases its advertising expenses but cannot increase prices because of competitive pressure?
   Answer: Sales volume must be increased to cover the increase in fixed advertising costs.

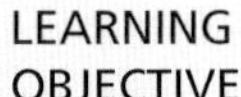

LEARNING OBJECTIVE 3

Prepare a CVP income statement to determine contribution margin.

Cost-volume-profit (CVP) analysis is the study of the effects of changes in costs and volume on a company's profits. CVP analysis is important in profit planning. It also is a critical factor in such management decisions as setting selling prices, determining product mix, and maximizing use of production facilities.

Basic Components

CVP analysis considers the interrelationships among the components shown in Illustration 22-10.

Illustration 22-10
Components of CVP analysis

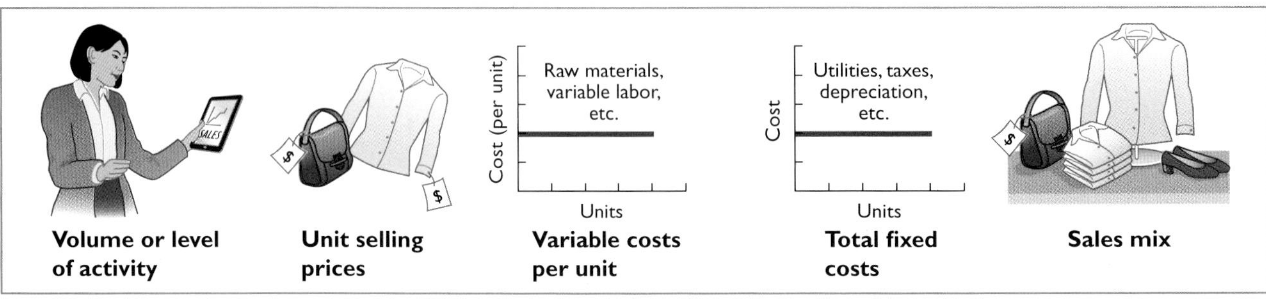

The following assumptions underlie each CVP analysis.

1. The behavior of both costs and revenues is linear throughout the relevant range of the activity index.
2. Costs can be classified accurately as either variable or fixed.
3. Changes in activity are the only factors that affect costs.
4. All units produced are sold.
5. When more than one type of product is sold, the sales mix will remain constant. That is, the percentage that each product represents of total sales will stay the same. Sales mix complicates CVP analysis because different products will have different cost relationships. In this chapter, we assume a single product.

When these assumptions are not valid, the CVP analysis may be inaccurate.

CVP Income Statement

Because CVP is so important for decision-making, management often wants this information reported in a **cost-volume-profit (CVP) income statement** format for internal use. The CVP income statement classifies costs as variable or fixed and computes a contribution margin. **Contribution margin (CM)** is the amount of revenue remaining after deducting variable costs. It is often stated both as a total amount and on a per unit basis.

We will use Vargo Video Company to illustrate a CVP income statement. Vargo Video produces a high-definition digital camcorder with 15× optical zoom and a wide-screen, high-resolution LCD monitor. Relevant data for the camcorders sold by this company in June 2017 are as follows.

Illustration 22-11
Assumed selling and cost data for Vargo Video

Unit selling price of camcorder	$500
Unit variable costs	$300
Total monthly fixed costs	$200,000
Units sold	1,600

The CVP income statement for Vargo therefore would be reported as follows.

Illustration 22-12
CVP income statement, with net income

VARGO VIDEO COMPANY
CVP Income Statement
For the Month Ended June 30, 2017

	Total
Sales (1,600 camcorders)	$ 800,000
Variable costs	480,000
Contribution margin	**320,000**
Fixed costs	200,000
Net income	**$120,000**

A traditional income statement and a CVP income statement both report the same net income of $120,000. However, a traditional income statement does not classify costs as variable or fixed, and therefore it does not report a contribution margin. In addition, sometimes per unit amounts and percentage of sales amounts are shown in separate columns on a CVP income statement to facilitate CVP analysis. *Homework assignments specify which columns to present.*

In the applications of CVP analysis that follow, we assume that the term "cost" includes all costs and expenses related to production and sale of the product. That is, cost includes manufacturing costs plus selling and administrative expenses.

UNIT CONTRIBUTION MARGIN

The formula for **unit contribution margin** and the computation for Vargo Video are as follows.

Illustration 22-13
Formula for unit contribution margin

Unit Selling Price	−	Unit Variable Costs	=	Unit Contribution Margin
$500	−	$300	=	$200

Unit contribution margin indicates that for every camcorder sold, the selling price exceeds the variable costs by $200. Vargo generates $200 per unit sold to cover fixed costs and contribute to net income. Because Vargo has fixed costs of $200,000, it must sell 1,000 camcorders ($200,000 ÷ $200) to cover its fixed costs.

At the point where total contribution margin exactly equals fixed costs, Vargo will report net income of zero. At this point, referred to as the **break-even point**, total costs (variable plus fixed) exactly equal total revenue. Illustration 22-14 shows Vargo's CVP income statement at the point where net income equals zero. It shows a contribution margin of $200,000, and a unit contribution margin of $200 ($500 − $300).

Illustration 22-14
CVP income statement, with zero net income

VARGO VIDEO COMPANY
CVP Income Statement
For the Month Ended June 30, 2017

	Total	Per Unit
Sales (1,000 camcorders)	$ 500,000	$ 500
Variable costs	300,000	300
Contribution margin	**200,000**	**$200**
Fixed costs	200,000	
Net income	**$ -0-**	

It follows that for every camcorder sold above the break-even point of 1,000 units, **net income increases by the amount of the unit contribution margin, $200**. For example, assume that Vargo sold one more camcorder, for a total of 1,001 camcorders sold. In this case, Vargo reports net income of $200, as shown in Illustration 22-15.

Illustration 22-15
CVP income statement, with net income and per unit data

VARGO VIDEO COMPANY
CVP Income Statement
For the Month Ended June 30, 2017

	Total	Per Unit
Sales (1,001 camcorders)	$500,500	$ 500
Variable costs	300,300	300
Contribution margin	**200,200**	**$200**
Fixed costs	200,000	
Net income	**$ 200**	

CONTRIBUTION MARGIN RATIO

Some managers prefer to use a contribution margin ratio in CVP analysis. The contribution margin ratio is the contribution margin expressed as a percentage of sales, as shown in Illustration 22-16.

Illustration 22-16
CVP income statement, with net income and percent of sales data

VARGO VIDEO COMPANY CVP Income Statement For the Month Ended June 30, 2017		
	Total	**Percent of Sales**
Sales (1,001 camcorders)	$500,500	100%
Variable costs	300,300	60
Contribution margin	**200,200**	**40%**
Fixed costs	200,000	
Net income	**$ 200**	

Alternatively, the **contribution margin ratio** can be determined by dividing the unit contribution margin by the unit selling price. For Vargo Video, the ratio is as follows.

Illustration 22-17
Formula for contribution margin ratio

Unit Contribution Margin	÷	Unit Selling Price	=	Contribution Margin Ratio
$200	÷	$500	=	40%

The contribution margin ratio of 40% means that Vargo generates 40 cents of contribution margin with each dollar of sales. That is, $0.40 of each sales dollar (40% × $1) is available to apply to fixed costs and to contribute to net income.

This expression of contribution margin is very helpful in determining the effect of changes in sales on net income. For example, if Vargo's sales increase $100,000, net income will increase $40,000 (40% × $100,000). Thus, by using the contribution margin ratio, managers can quickly determine increases in net income from any change in sales.

We can also see this effect through a CVP income statement. Assume that Vargo's current sales are $500,000 and it wants to know the effect of a $100,000 (200-unit) increase in sales. Vargo prepares a comparative CVP income statement analysis as follows.

Illustration 22-18
Comparative CVP income statements

VARGO VIDEO COMPANY CVP Income Statements For the Month Ended June 30, 2017						
	No Change			**With Change**		
	Total	**Per Unit**	**Percent of Sales**	**Total**	**Per Unit**	**Percent of Sales**
Sales	$500,000	$ 500	100%	$600,000	$ 500	100%
Variable costs	300,000	300	60	360,000	300	60
Contribution margin	**200,000**	**$200**	**40%**	**240,000**	**$200**	**40%**
Fixed costs	200,000			200,000		
Net income	**$ -0-**			**$ 40,000**		

The $40,000 increase in net income can be calculated on either a unit contribution margin basis (200 units × $200 per unit) or using the contribution margin ratio times the increase in sales dollars (40% × $100,000). Note that the unit contribution margin and contribution margin as a percentage of sales remain unchanged by the increase in sales.

Study these CVP income statements carefully. The concepts presented in these statements are used extensively in this and later chapters.

Compute the break-even point using three approaches.

A key relationship in CVP analysis is the level of activity at which total revenues equal total costs (both fixed and variable)—the **break-even point**. At this volume of sales, the company will realize no income but will suffer no loss. The process of finding the break-even point is called **break-even analysis**. Knowledge of the break-even point is useful to management when it considers decisions such as whether to introduce new product lines, change sales prices on established products, or enter new market areas.

The break-even point can be:

1. Computed from a mathematical equation.
2. Computed by using contribution margin.
3. Derived from a cost-volume-profit (CVP) graph.

The break-even point can be expressed either in **sales units** or **sales dollars**.

Mathematical Equation

The first line of Illustration 22-19 shows a common equation used for CVP analysis. When net income is set to zero, this equation can be used to calculate the break-even point.

Illustration 22-19
Basic CVP equation

Required Sales	–	Variable Costs	–	Fixed Costs	=	Net Income
\$500Q	–	\$300Q	–	\$200,000	=	\$0

As shown in Illustration 22-14 (page 768), net income equals zero when the contribution margin (sales minus variable costs) is equal to fixed costs.

To reflect this, Illustration 22-20 rewrites the equation with contribution margin (sales minus variable costs) on the left side, and fixed costs and net income on the right. We can compute the break-even point **in units** by **using unit selling prices** and **unit variable costs**. The computation for Vargo Video is as follows.

Illustration 22-20
Computation of break-even point in units

$$\text{Required Sales} - \text{Variable Costs} - \text{Fixed Costs} = \text{Net Income}$$

$$\$500Q - \$300Q - \$200{,}000 = \$0$$

$$\$500Q - \$300Q = \$200{,}000 + \$0$$

$$\$200Q = \$200{,}000$$

$$Q = \frac{\$200{,}000}{\$200} = \frac{\textbf{Fixed Costs}}{\textbf{Unit Contribution Margin}}$$

$$Q = 1{,}000 \text{ units}$$

where

Q = sales volume in units
\$500 = selling price
\$300 = variable costs per unit
\$200,000 = total fixed costs

Thus, Vargo must sell 1,000 units to break even.

To find the amount of **sales dollars** required to break even, we multiply the units sold at the break-even point times the selling price per unit, as shown below.

1,000 × $500 = $500,000 (break-even sales dollars)

Contribution Margin Technique

Many managers employ the contribution margin to compute the break-even point.

CONTRIBUTION MARGIN IN UNITS

The final step in Illustration 22-20 divides fixed costs by the unit contribution margin (highlighted in red). Thus, rather than walk through all of the steps of the equation approach, we can simply employ this formula shown in Illustration 22-21.

Fixed Costs	÷	Unit Contribution Margin	=	Break-Even Point in Units
$200,000	÷	$200	=	1,000 units

Illustration 22-21
Formula for break-even point in units using unit contribution margin

Why does this formula work? The unit contribution margin is the net amount by which each sale exceeds the variable costs per unit. Every sale generates this much money to pay off fixed costs. Consequently, if we divide fixed costs by the unit contribution margin, we know how many units we need to sell to break even.

CONTRIBUTION MARGIN RATIO

When a company has numerous products, it is not practical to determine the unit contribution margin for each product. In this case, using the contribution margin ratio is very useful for determining the break-even point in total dollars (rather than units). Recall that the contribution margin ratio is the percentage of each dollar of sales that is available to cover fixed costs and generate net income. Therefore, **to determine the sales dollars needed to cover fixed costs**, we divide fixed costs by the contribution margin ratio, as shown in Illustration 22-22.

Fixed Costs	÷	Contribution Margin Ratio	=	Break-Even Point in Dollars
$200,000	÷	40%	=	$500,000

Illustration 22-22
Formula for break-even point in dollars using contribution margin ratio

To apply this formula to Vargo Video, consider that its 40% contribution margin ratio means that for every dollar sold, it generates 40 cents of contribution margin. The question is, how many dollars of sales does Vargo need in order to generate total contribution margin of $200,000 to pay off fixed costs? We divide the fixed costs of $200,000 by the 40 cents of contribution margin generated by each dollar of sales to arrive at $500,000 ($200,000 ÷ 40%). To prove this result, if we generate 40 cents of contribution margin for each dollar of sales, then the total contribution margin generated by $500,000 in sales is $200,000 ($500,000 × 40%).

Graphic Presentation

An effective way to find the break-even point is to prepare a break-even graph. Because this graph also shows costs, volume, and profits, it is referred to as a **cost-volume-profit (CVP) graph**.

As the CVP graph in Illustration 22-23 (page 772) shows, sales volume is recorded along the horizontal axis. This axis should extend to the maximum level of expected sales. Both total revenues (sales) and total costs (fixed plus variable) are recorded on the vertical axis.

Illustration 22-23
CVP graph

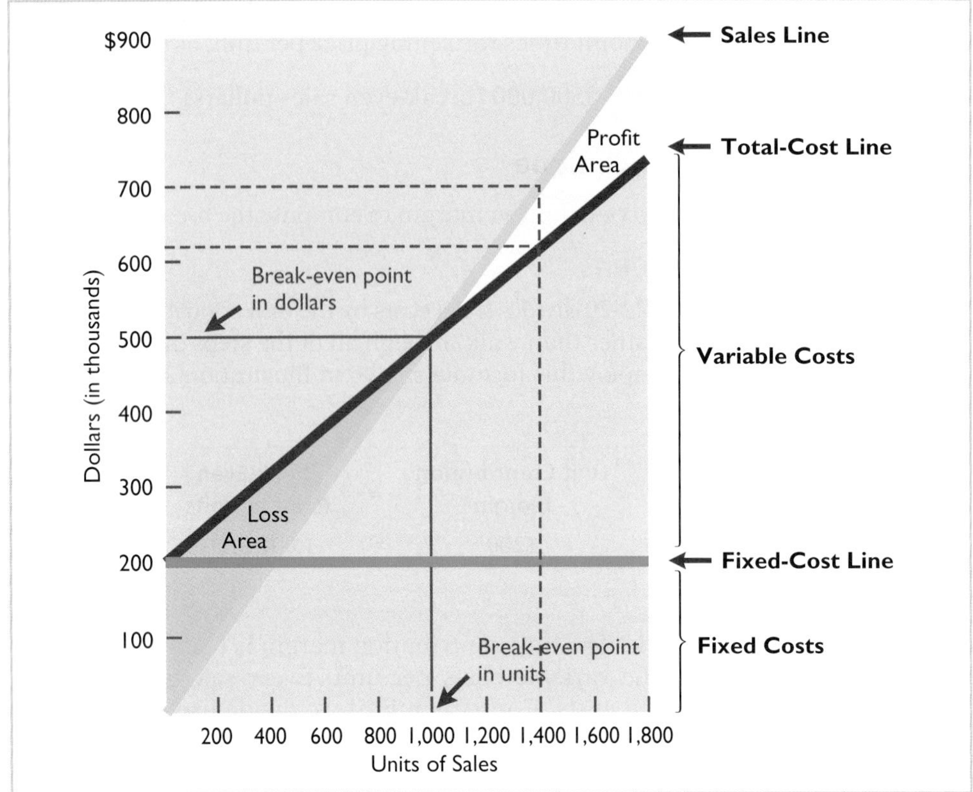

The construction of the graph, using the data for Vargo Video, is as follows.

1. Plot the sales line, starting at the zero activity level. For every camcorder sold, total revenue increases by $500. For example, at 200 units, sales are $100,000. At the upper level of activity (1,800 units), sales are $900,000. The revenue line is assumed to be linear through the full range of activity.
2. Plot the total fixed costs using a horizontal line. For the camcorders, this line is plotted at $200,000. The fixed costs are the same at every level of activity.
3. Plot the total-cost line. This starts at the fixed-cost line at zero activity. It increases by the variable costs at each level of activity. For each camcorder, variable costs are $300. Thus, at 200 units, total variable costs are $60,000 ($300 × 200) and the total cost is $260,000 ($60,000 + $200,000). At 1,800 units, total variable costs are $540,000 ($300 × 1,800) and total cost is $740,000 ($540,000 + $200,000). On the graph, the amount of the variable costs can be derived from the difference between the total-cost and fixed-cost lines at each level of activity.
4. Determine the break-even point from the intersection of the total-cost line and the sales line. The break-even point in dollars is found by drawing a horizontal line from the break-even point to the vertical axis. The break-even point in units is found by drawing a vertical line from the break-even point to the horizontal axis. For the camcorders, the break-even point is $500,000 of sales, or 1,000 units. At this sales level, Vargo will cover costs but make no profit.

The CVP graph also shows both the net income and net loss areas. Thus, the amount of income or loss at each level of sales can be derived from the sales and total-cost lines.

A CVP graph is useful because the effects of a change in any element in the CVP analysis can be quickly seen. For example, a 10% increase in selling price will change the location of the sales line. Likewise, the effects on total costs of wage increases can be quickly observed.

Determine the sales required to earn target net income and determine margin of safety.

Target Net Income

Rather than simply "breaking even," management usually sets an income objective often called **target net income**. It then determines the sales necessary to achieve this specified level of income. Companies determine the sales necessary to achieve target net income by using one of the three approaches discussed earlier.

MATHEMATICAL EQUATION

We know that at the break-even point no profit or loss results for the company. By adding an amount for target net income to the same basic equation, we obtain the following formula for determining required sales.

$$\text{Required Sales} - \text{Variable Costs} - \text{Fixed Costs} = \text{Target Net Income}$$

Illustration 22-24
Formula for required sales to meet target net income

Recall that once the break-even point has been reached so that fixed costs are covered, each additional unit sold increases net income by the amount of the unit contribution margin. We can rewrite the equation with contribution margin (required sales minus variable costs) on the left-hand side, and fixed costs and target net income on the right. Assuming that target net income is $120,000 for Vargo Video, the computation of required sales in units is as shown in Illustration 22-25.

$$\text{Required Sales} - \text{Variable Costs} - \text{Fixed Costs} = \text{Target Net Income}$$

$$\$500Q - \$300Q - \$200{,}000 = \$120{,}000$$

$$\$500Q - \$300Q = \$200{,}000 + \$120{,}000$$

$$\$200Q = \$200{,}000 + \$120{,}000$$

$$Q = \frac{\$200{,}000 + \$120{,}000}{\$200} = \frac{\textbf{Fixed Costs + Target Net Income}}{\textbf{Unit Contribution Margin}}$$

$$Q = 1{,}600$$

where

Q = sales volume
$500 = selling price
$300 = variable costs per unit
$200,000 = total fixed costs
$120,000 = target net income

Illustration 22-25
Computation of required sales

Vargo must sell 1,600 units to achieve target net income of $120,000. The sales dollars required to achieve the target net income is found by multiplying the units sold by the unit selling price [(1,600 × $500) = $800,000].

CONTRIBUTION MARGIN TECHNIQUE

As in the case of break-even sales, we can compute in either units or dollars the sales required to meet target net income. The formula to compute required sales in units for Vargo Video using the unit contribution margin can be seen in the final step of the equation approach in Illustration 22-25 (shown in red). We simply divide the sum of fixed costs and target net income by the unit contribution margin. Illustration 22-26 (page 774) shows this for Vargo.

Illustration 22-26
Formula for required sales in units using unit contribution margin

(Fixed Costs + Target Net Income)	÷	Unit Contribution Margin	=	Required Sales in Units
($200,000 + $120,000)	÷	$200	=	1,600 units

To achieve its desired target net income of $120,000, Vargo must sell 1,600 camcorders.

The formula to compute the required sales in dollars for Vargo using the contribution margin ratio is shown below.

Illustration 22-27
Formula for required sales in dollars using contribution margin ratio

(Fixed Costs + Target Net Income)	÷	Contribution Margin Ratio	=	Required Sales in Dollars
($200,000 + $120,000)	÷	40%	=	$800,000

To achieve its desired target net income of $120,000, Vargo must generate sales of $800,000.

GRAPHIC PRESENTATION

We also can use the CVP graph in Illustration 22-23 (on page 772) to find the sales required to meet target net income. In the profit area of the graph, the distance between the sales line and the total-cost line at any point equals net income. We can find required sales by analyzing the differences between the two lines until the desired net income is found.

For example, suppose Vargo Video sells 1,400 camcorders. Illustration 22-23 shows that a vertical line drawn at 1,400 units intersects the sales line at $700,000 and the total-cost line at $620,000. The difference between the two amounts represents the net income (profit) of $80,000.

Margin of Safety

Margin of safety is the difference between actual or expected sales and sales at the break-even point. It measures the "cushion" that a particular level of sales provides. It tells us how far sales could fall before the company begins operating at a loss. The margin of safety is expressed in dollars or as a ratio.

The formula for stating the **margin of safety in dollars** is actual (or expected) sales minus break-even sales. Assuming that actual (expected) sales for Vargo Video are $750,000, the computation is as follows.

Illustration 22-28
Formula for margin of safety in dollars

Actual (Expected) Sales	−	Break-Even Sales	=	Margin of Safety in Dollars
$750,000	−	$500,000	=	$250,000

Vargo's margin of safety is $250,000. Its sales could fall $250,000 before it operates at a loss.

The **margin of safety ratio** is the margin of safety in dollars divided by actual (or expected) sales. Illustration 22-29 shows the formula and computation for determining the margin of safety ratio.

Illustration 22-29
Formula for margin of safety ratio

Margin of Safety in Dollars	÷	Actual (Expected) Sales	=	Margin of Safety Ratio
$250,000	÷	$750,000	=	33%

This means that the company's sales could fall by 33% before it operates at a loss.

The higher the dollars or the percentage, the greater the margin of safety. Management continuously evaluates the adequacy of the margin of safety in terms of such factors as the vulnerability of the product to competitive pressures and to downturns in the economy.

LEARNING OBJECTIVE 6

Use CVP analysis to respond to changes in the business environment.

When the personal computer was introduced, it sold for $2,500. Today, similar computers sell for much less. When oil prices rise, the break-even point for airline companies such as **American** and **Delta Air Lines** also rise. Because of lower prices for imported steel, the demand for domestic steel dropped significantly. The point should be clear: Business conditions change rapidly, and management must respond intelligently to these changes. CVP analysis can help.

To better understand how CVP analysis works, let's look at three independent situations that might occur at Vargo Video. Each case uses the original camcorder sales and cost data, which were as follows.

Illustration 22-30
Original camcorder sales and cost data

Unit selling price	$500
Unit variable cost	$300
Total fixed costs	$200,000
Break-even sales	$500,000 or 1,000 units

Case I: Offering a Discount

A competitor is offering a 10% discount on the selling price of its camcorders. Management must decide whether to offer a similar discount.

Question: What effect will a 10% discount on selling price have on the break-even point for camcorders?

Answer: A 10% discount on selling price reduces the selling price per unit to $450 [$500 − ($500 × 10%)]. Variable costs per unit remain unchanged at $300. Thus, the unit contribution margin is $150. Assuming no change in fixed costs, break-even sales are 1,333 units, computed as follows.

Illustration 22-31
Computation of break-even sales in units

Fixed Costs	÷	Unit Contribution Margin	=	Break-Even Sales
$200,000	÷	$150	=	1,333 units (rounded)

For Vargo, this change requires monthly sales to increase by 333 units, or 33 1/3%, in order to break even. In reaching a conclusion about offering a 10% discount to customers, management must determine how likely it is to achieve the increased sales. Also, management should estimate the possible loss of sales if the competitor's discount price is not matched.

Case II: Investing in New Equipment

To meet the threat of foreign competition, management invests in new robotic equipment that will lower the amount of direct labor required to make camcorders. The company estimates that total fixed costs will increase 30% and that variable cost per unit will decrease 30%.

Question: What effect will the new equipment have on the sales volume required to break even?

Answer: Total fixed costs become $260,000 [$200,000 + (30% × $200,000)]. The variable cost per unit becomes $210 [$300 − (30% × $300)]. The new break-even point is approximately 897 units, computed as shown in Illustration 22-32.

Illustration 22-32
Computation of break-even sales in units

Fixed Costs	÷	Unit Contribution Margin	=	Break-Even Sales
$260,000	÷	($500 − $210)	=	897 units (rounded)

These changes appear to be advantageous for Vargo. The break-even point is reduced by approximately 10%, or 100 units.

Case III: Determining Required Sales

Vargo's principal supplier of raw materials has just announced a price increase. The higher cost is expected to increase the variable cost of camcorders by $25 per unit. Management decides to hold the line on the selling price of the camcorders. It plans a cost-cutting program that will save $17,500 in fixed costs per month. Vargo is currently realizing monthly net income of $80,000 on sales of 1,400 camcorders.

Question: What increase in units sold will be needed to maintain the same level of net income?

Answer: The variable cost per unit increases to $325 ($300 + $25). Fixed costs are reduced to $182,500 ($200,000 − $17,500). Because of the change in variable cost, the unit contribution margin becomes $175 ($500 − $325). The required number of units sold to achieve the target net income is computed as follows.

Illustration 22-33
Computation of required sales

(Fixed Costs + Target Net Income)	÷	Unit Contribution Margin	=	Required Sales in Units
($182,500 + $80,000)	÷	$175	=	1,500

To achieve the required sales, Vargo Video will have to sell 1,500 camcorders, an increase of 100 units. If this does not seem to be a reasonable expectation, management will either have to make further cost reductions or accept less net income if the selling price remains unchanged.

CVP Income Statement Revisited

Earlier in the chapter, we presented a simple CVP income statement. When companies prepare a CVP income statement, they provide more detail about specific variable and fixed-cost items.

To illustrate a more detailed CVP income statement, we will assume that Vargo Video reaches its target net income of $120,000 (see Illustration 22-25 on page 773). The following information is obtained on the $680,000 of costs that were incurred in June to produce and sell 1,600 units.

Illustration 22-34
Assumed cost and expense data

	Variable	Fixed	Total
Cost of goods sold	$400,000	$120,000	$520,000
Selling expenses	60,000	40,000	100,000
Administrative expenses	20,000	40,000	60,000
	$480,000	$200,000	$680,000

The detailed CVP income statement for Vargo is shown below.

Illustration 22-35
Detailed CVP income statement

VARGO VIDEO COMPANY CVP Income Statement For the Month Ended June 30, 2017			
		Total	**Per Unit**
Sales		$ 800,000	$ 500
Variable expenses			
Cost of goods sold	$400,000		
Selling expenses	60,000		
Administrative expenses	20,000		
Total variable expenses		480,000	300
Contribution margin		**320,000**	**$200**
Fixed expenses			
Cost of goods sold	120,000		
Selling expenses	40,000		
Administrative expenses	40,000		
Total fixed expenses		200,000	
Net income		**$120,000**	

LEARNING OBJECTIVE *7

APPENDIX 22A: Explain the differences between absorption costing and variable costing.

In the earlier chapters, we classified both variable and fixed manufacturing costs as product costs. In job order costing, for example, a job is assigned the costs of direct materials, direct labor, and **both** variable and fixed manufacturing overhead. This costing approach is referred to as **full** or **absorption costing**. It is so named because all manufacturing costs are charged to, or absorbed by, the product. Absorption costing is the approach used for external reporting under generally accepted accounting principles.

An alternative approach is to use **variable costing**. Under variable costing, only direct materials, direct labor, and variable manufacturing overhead costs are considered product costs. Companies recognize fixed manufacturing overhead costs as period costs (expenses) when incurred. The difference between absorption costing and variable costing is shown graphically as follows.

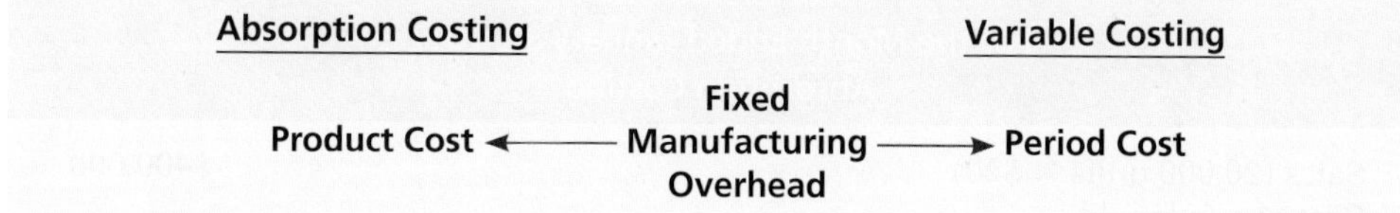

Illustration 22A-1
Difference between absorption costing and variable costing

Under both absorption and variable costing, selling and administrative expenses are period costs.

Companies may not use variable costing for external financial reports because generally accepted accounting principles require that fixed manufacturing overhead be accounted for as a product cost.

Example Comparing Absorption Costing with Variable Costing

To illustrate absorption and variable costing, assume that Premium Products Corporation manufactures a polyurethane sealant, called Fix-It, for car windshields. Relevant data for Fix-It in January 2017, the first month of production, are shown in Illustration 22A-2 (page 778).

Illustration 22A-2
Sealant sales and cost data for Premium Products Corporation

Selling price	$20 per unit.
Units	Produced 30,000; sold 20,000; beginning inventory zero.
Variable unit costs	Manufacturing $9 (direct materials $5, direct labor $3, and variable overhead $1).
	Selling and administrative expenses $2.
Fixed costs	Manufacturing overhead $120,000.
	Selling and administrative expenses $15,000.

The per unit manufacturing cost under each costing approach is computed in Illustration 22A-3.

Illustration 22A-3
Computation of per unit manufacturing cost

Type of Cost	Absorption Costing	Variable Costing
Direct materials	$ 5	$5
Direct labor	3	3
Variable manufacturing overhead	1	1
Fixed manufacturing overhead ($120,000 ÷ 30,000 units produced)	**4**	**0**
Manufacturing cost per unit	**$13**	**$9**

The manufacturing cost per unit is $4 higher ($13 − $9) for absorption costing. This occurs because fixed manufacturing overhead costs are a product cost under absorption costing. Under variable costing, they are, instead, a period cost, and so they are expensed. Based on these data, each unit sold and each unit remaining in inventory is costed under absorption costing at $13 and under variable costing at $9.

ABSORPTION COSTING EXAMPLE

Illustration 22A-4 shows the income statement for Premium Products using absorption costing. It shows that cost of goods manufactured is $390,000, computed by multiplying the 30,000 units produced times the manufacturing cost per unit of $13 (see Illustration 22A-3). Cost of goods sold is $260,000, after subtracting ending inventory of $130,000. Under absorption costing, $40,000 of the fixed overhead (10,000 units × $4) is deferred to a future period as part of the cost of ending inventory.

Illustration 22A-4
Absorption costing income statement

PREMIUM PRODUCTS CORPORATION
Income Statement
For the Month Ended January 31, 2017
Absorption Costing

Sales (20,000 units × $20)		$400,000
Cost of goods sold		
Inventory, January 1	$ -0-	
Cost of goods manufactured (30,000 units × $13)	390,000	
Cost of goods available for sale	390,000	
Less: Inventory, January 31 (10,000 units × $13)	**130,000**	
Cost of goods sold (20,000 units × $13)		260,000
Gross profit		140,000
Variable selling and administrative expenses (20,000 × $2)	40,000	
Fixed selling and administrative expenses	15,000	55,000
Net income		**$ 85,000**

VARIABLE COSTING EXAMPLE

As Illustration 22A-5 shows, companies use the cost-volume-profit format in preparing a variable costing income statement. The variable manufacturing cost of $270,000 is computed by multiplying the 30,000 units produced times variable manufacturing cost of $9 per unit (see Illustration 22A-3). As in absorption costing, both variable and fixed selling and administrative expenses are treated as period costs.

Illustration 22A-5
Variable costing income statement

PREMIUM PRODUCTS CORPORATION Income Statement For the Month Ended January 31, 2017 Variable Costing		
Sales (20,000 units × $20)		$400,000
Variable cost of goods sold		
Inventory, January 1	$ -0-	
Variable cost of goods manufactured (30,000 units × $9)	270,000	
Variable cost of goods available for sale	270,000	
Less: Inventory, January 31 (10,000 units × $9)	**90,000**	
Variable cost of goods sold	180,000	
Variable selling and administrative expenses (20,000 units × $2)	40,000	220,000
Contribution margin		180,000
Fixed manufacturing overhead	120,000	
Fixed selling and administrative expenses	15,000	135,000
Net income		**$ 45,000**

There is one primary difference between variable and absorption costing: Under variable costing, companies charge the fixed manufacturing overhead as an expense in the current period. Fixed manufacturing overhead costs of the current period, therefore, are not deferred to future periods through the ending inventory. As a result, absorption costing will show a **higher net income number** than variable costing **whenever units produced exceed units sold**. This difference can be seen in the income statements in Illustrations 22A-4 and 22A-5. There is a $40,000 difference in the ending inventories ($130,000 under absorption costing versus $90,000 under variable costing). Under absorption costing, $40,000 of the fixed overhead costs (10,000 units × $4) has been deferred to a future period as part of inventory. In contrast, under variable costing, all fixed manufacturing costs are expensed in the current period.

The following relationships apply:

- When units produced exceed units sold, income under absorption costing is *higher* then variable costing.
- When units produced are less than units sold, income under absorption costing is *lower* then variable costing.
- When units produced and sold are the same, net income will be *equal* under the two costing approaches. In this case, there is no increase in ending inventory. So fixed overhead costs of the current period are not deferred to future periods through the ending inventory.

Illustration 22A-6 summarizes the foregoing effects of the two costing approaches from operations.

Illustration 22A-6
Summary of income effects under absorption costing and variable costing

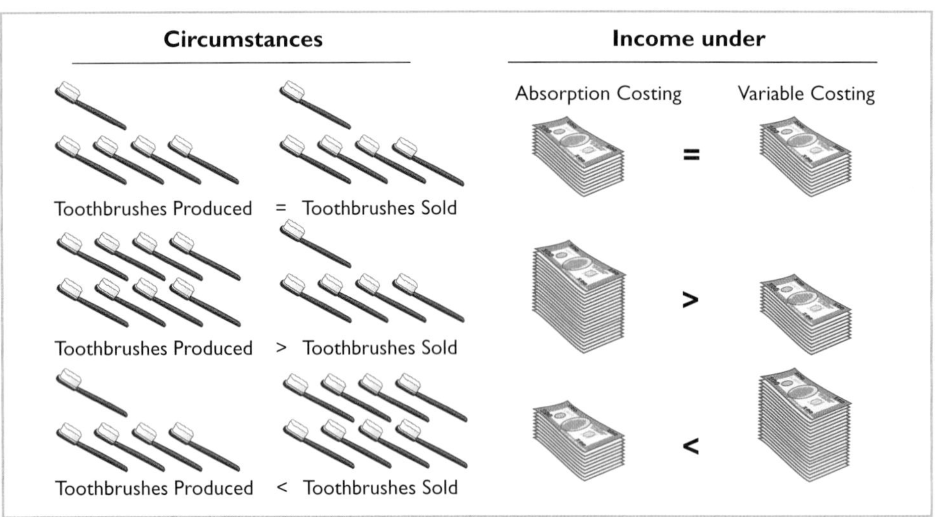

Rationale for Variable Costing

The purpose of fixed manufacturing costs is **to have productive facilities available for use**. A company incurs these costs whether it operates at zero or at 100% of capacity. Thus, proponents of variable costing argue that these costs are period costs and therefore should be expensed when incurred.

Supporters of absorption costing defend the assignment of fixed manufacturing overhead costs to inventory. They say that these costs are as much a cost of getting a product ready for sale as direct materials or direct labor. Accordingly, they contend, these costs should not be matched with revenues until the product is sold.

The use of variable costing is acceptable **only for internal use by management**. It cannot be used in determining product costs in financial statements prepared in accordance with generally accepted accounting principles because it understates inventory costs. To comply with the matching principle, a company must use absorption costing for its work in process and finished goods inventories. Similarly, companies must use absorption costing for income tax purposes.

REVIEW AND PRACTICE

LEARNING OBJECTIVES REVIEW

1 Explain variable, fixed, and mixed costs and the relevant range. Variable costs are costs that vary in total directly and proportionately with changes in the activity index. Fixed costs are costs that remain the same in total regardless of changes in the activity index.

The relevant range is the range of activity in which a company expects to operate during a year. It is important in CVP analysis because the behavior of costs is assumed to be linear throughout the relevant range.

Mixed costs change in total but not proportionately with changes in the activity level. For purposes of CVP analysis, mixed costs must be classified into their fixed and variable elements.

2 Apply the high-low method to determine the components of mixed costs. Determine the variable costs per unit by dividing the change in total costs at the highest and lowest levels of activity by the difference in activity at those levels. Then, determine fixed costs by subtracting total variable costs from the amount of total costs at either the highest or lowest level of activity.

3 Prepare a CVP income statement to determine contribution margin. The five components of CVP analysis are (1) volume or level of activity, (2) unit selling prices, (3) variable costs per unit, (4) total fixed costs, and (5) sales mix. Contribution margin is the amount of revenue remaining after deducting variable costs. It is identified in a CVP income statement, which classifies costs as variable or fixed. It can be expressed as a total amount, as a per unit amount, or as a ratio.

4 Compute the break-even point using three approaches. The break-even point can be (a) computed from a mathematical equation, (b) computed by using a contribution margin technique, and (c) derived from a CVP graph.

5 Determine the sales required to earn target net income and determine margin of safety. The general formula for required sales is Required sales − Variable costs − Fixed costs = Target net income. Two other formulas are (1) Required sales in units = (Fixed costs + Target net income) ÷ Unit contribution margin, and (2) Required sales in dollars = (Fixed costs + Target net income) ÷ Contribution margin ratio.

Margin of safety is the difference between actual or expected sales and sales at the break-even point. The formulas for margin of safety are (1) Actual (expected) sales − Break-even sales = Margin of safety in dollars, and (2) Margin of safety in dollars ÷ Actual (expected) sales = Margin of safety ratio.

6 Use CVP analysis to respond to changes in the business environment. Management uses CVP analysis, such as calculating the break-even point or determining the sales required to earn target net income, to decide how best to respond to changes in the business environment.

***7 Explain the difference between absorption costing and variable costing.** Under absorption costing, fixed manufacturing costs are product costs. Under variable costing, fixed manufacturing costs are period costs.

GLOSSARY REVIEW

***Absorption costing** A costing approach in which all manufacturing costs are charged to the product.

Activity index The activity that causes changes in the behavior of costs.

Break-even point The level of activity at which total revenue equals total costs.

Contribution margin (CM) The amount of revenue remaining after deducting variable costs.

Contribution margin ratio The percentage of each dollar of sales that is available to apply to fixed costs and contribute to net income; calculated as unit contribution margin divided by unit selling price.

Cost behavior analysis The study of how specific costs respond to changes in the level of business activity.

Cost-volume-profit (CVP) analysis The study of the effects of changes in costs and volume on a company's profits.

Cost-volume-profit (CVP) graph A graph showing the relationship between costs, volume, and profits.

Cost-volume-profit (CVP) income statement A statement for internal use that classifies costs as fixed or variable and reports contribution margin in the body of the statement.

Fixed costs Costs that remain the same in total regardless of changes in the activity level.

High-low method A mathematical method that uses the total costs incurred at the high and low levels of activity to classify mixed costs into fixed and variable components.

Margin of safety The difference between actual or expected sales and sales at the break-even point.

Mixed costs Costs that contain both a variable- and a fixed-cost element and change in total but not proportionately with changes in the activity level.

Relevant range The range of the activity index over which the company expects to operate during the year.

Target net income The income objective set by management.

Unit contribution margin The amount of revenue remaining per unit after deducting variable costs; calculated as unit selling price minus unit variable costs.

***Variable costing** A costing approach in which only variable manufacturing costs are product costs, and fixed manufacturing costs are period costs (expenses).

Variable costs Costs that vary in total directly and proportionately with changes in the activity level.

PRACTICE EXERCISES

1. The controller of Teton Industries has collected the following monthly expense data for use in analyzing the cost behavior of maintenance costs.

Determine fixed and variable costs using the high-low method and prepare graph.

(LO 1, 2)

Month	Total Maintenance Costs	Total Machine Hours
January	$2,900	300
February	3,000	400
March	3,600	600
April	4,300	790
May	3,200	500
June	4,500	800

Instructions

(a) Determine the fixed-cost and variable-cost components using the high-low method.

(b) Prepare a graph showing the behavior of maintenance costs, and identify the fixed-cost and variable-cost elements. Use 200 unit increments and $1,000 cost increments.

Solution

1. (a) **Maintenance Costs:**

$$\frac{\$4{,}500 - \$2{,}900}{800 - 300} = \frac{\$1{,}600}{500} = \$3.20 \text{ variable cost per machine hour}$$

	800 Machine Hours	300 Machine Hours
Total costs	$4,500	$2,900
Less: Variable costs		
800 × $3.20	2,560	
300 × $3.20		960
Total fixed costs	$1,940	$1,940

Thus, maintenance costs are $1,940 per month plus $3.20 per machine hour.

(b)

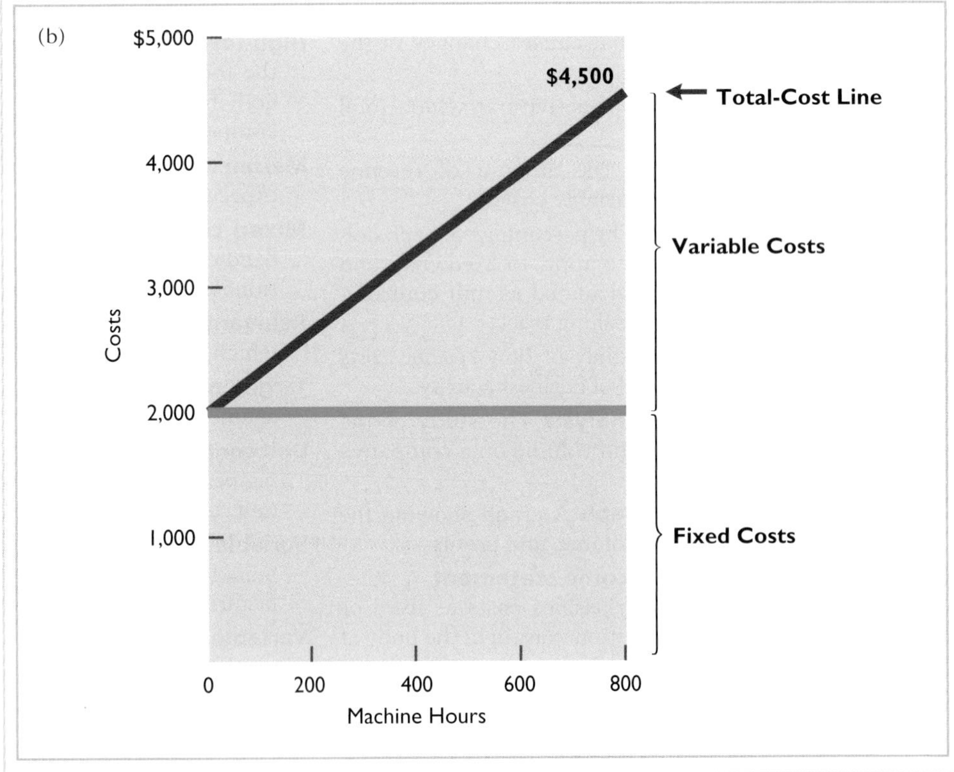

Determine contribution margin ratio, break-even point in dollars, and margin of safety.

(LO 3, 4, 5)

2. Zion Seating Co., a manufacturer of chairs, had the following data for 2017:

Sales	2,400 units
Sales price	$40 per unit
Variable costs	$15 per unit
Fixed costs	$19,500

Instructions

(a) What is the contribution margin ratio?

(b) What is the break-even point in dollars?

(c) What is the margin of safety in units and dollars?

(d) If the company wishes to increase its total dollar contribution margin by 40% in 2018, by how much will it need to increase its sales if all other factors remain constant?

(CGA adapted)

Solution

2. (a) Contribution margin ratio = Unit contribution margin ÷ Unit selling price
($40 − $15) ÷ $40 = 62.5%

(b) Break-even in dollars: $19,500 ÷ 62.5% = $31,200

(c) Margin of safety = (2,400 × $40) − $31,200 = $64,800
$64,800 ÷ $40 = 1,620 in units

(d) Current contribution margin is $40 − $15 = $25
Total contribution margin is $25 × 2,400 = $60,000
40% increase in contribution margin is $60,000 × 40% = $24,000
Total increase in sales required is $24,000 ÷ 62.5% = $38,400

PRACTICE PROBLEM

Mabo Company makes calculators that sell for $20 each. For the coming year, management expects fixed costs to total $220,000 and variable costs to be $9 per unit.

Compute break-even point, contribution margin ratio, margin of safety, and sales for target net income.

(LO 4, 5)

Instructions

(a) Compute break-even point in units using the mathematical equation.
(b) Compute break-even point in dollars using the contribution margin (CM) ratio.
(c) Compute the margin of safety percentage assuming actual sales are $500,000.
(d) Compute the sales required in dollars to earn net income of $165,000.

Solution

(a) Required sales − Variable costs − Fixed costs = Net income
$20Q − $9Q − $220,000 = $0
$11Q = $220,000
Q = 20,000 units

(b) Unit contribution margin = Unit selling price − Unit variable costs
$11 = $20 − $9
Contribution margin ratio = Unit contribution margin ÷ Unit selling price
55% = $11 ÷ $20
Break-even point in dollars = Fixed costs ÷ Contribution margin ratio
= $220,000 ÷ 55%
= $400,000

(c) Margin of safety = $\frac{\text{Actual sales} - \text{Break-even sales}}{\text{Actual sales}}$

= $\frac{\$500{,}000 - \$400{,}000}{\$500{,}000}$

= 20%

(d) Required sales − Variable costs − Fixed costs = Net income
$20Q − $9Q − $220,000 = $165,000
$11Q = $385,000
Q = 35,000 units

35,000 units × $20 = $700,000 required sales

EXERCISES

E22-1 Bonita Company manufactures a single product. Annual production costs incurred in the manufacturing process are shown below for two levels of production.

Define and classify variable, fixed, and mixed costs.

(LO 1)

Production in Units	Costs Incurred			
	5,000		10,000	
Production Costs	**Total Cost**	**Cost/ Unit**	**Total Cost**	**Cost/ Unit**
Direct materials	$8,000	$1.60	$16,000	$1.60
Direct labor	9,500	1.90	19,000	1.90
Utilities	2,000	0.40	3,300	0.33
Rent	4,000	0.80	4,000	0.40
Maintenance	800	0.16	1,400	0.14
Supervisory salaries	1,000	0.20	1,000	0.10

Instructions

(a) Define the terms variable costs, fixed costs, and mixed costs.
(b) Classify each cost above as either variable, fixed, or mixed.

Determine fixed and variable costs using the high-low method and prepare graph.
(LO 1, 2)

E22-2 The controller of Norton Industries has collected the following monthly expense data for use in analyzing the cost behavior of maintenance costs.

Month	Total Maintenance Costs	Total Machine Hours
January	$2,700	300
February	3,000	350
March	3,600	500
April	4,500	690
May	3,200	400
June	5,500	700

Instructions

(a) Determine the fixed- and variable-cost components using the high-low method.
(b) Prepare a graph showing the behavior of maintenance costs, and identify the fixed- and variable-cost elements. Use 100-hour increments and $1,000 cost increments.

Classify variable, fixed, and mixed costs.
(LO 1)

E22-3 Family Furniture Corporation incurred the following costs.

1. Wood used in the production of furniture.
2. Fuel used in delivery trucks.
3. Straight-line depreciation on factory building.
4. Screws used in the production of furniture.
5. Sales staff salaries.
6. Sales commissions.
7. Property taxes.
8. Insurance on buildings.
9. Hourly wages of furniture craftsmen.
10. Salaries of factory supervisors.
11. Utilities expense.
12. Telephone bill.

Instructions

Identify the costs above as variable, fixed, or mixed.

Explain assumptions underlying CVP analysis.
(LO 3)

E22-4 Marty Moser wants Moser Company to use CVP analysis to study the effects of changes in costs and volume on the company. Marty has heard that certain assumptions must be valid in order for CVP analysis to be useful.

Instructions

Prepare a memo to Marty Moser concerning the assumptions that underlie CVP analysis.

E22-5 All That Blooms provides environmentally friendly lawn services for homeowners. Its operating costs are as follows.

Compute break-even point in units and dollars.

(LO 3, 4)

Depreciation	$1,400 per month
Advertising	$200 per month
Insurance	$2,000 per month
Weed and feed materials	$12 per lawn
Direct labor	$10 per lawn
Fuel	$2 per lawn

All That Blooms charges $60 per treatment for the average single-family lawn.

Instructions

Determine the company's break-even point in (a) number of lawns serviced per month and (b) dollars.

E22-6 The Palmer Acres Inn is trying to determine its break-even point during its off-peak season. The inn has 50 rooms that it rents at $60 a night. Operating costs are as follows.

Compute break-even point.

(LO 3, 4)

Salaries	$5,900 per month
Utilities	$1,100 per month
Depreciation	$1,000 per month
Maintenance	$100 per month
Maid service	$14 per room
Other costs	$28 per room

Instructions

Determine the inn's break-even point in (a) number of rented rooms per month and (b) dollars.

E22-7 In the month of March, Style Salon services 560 clients at an average price of $120. During the month, fixed costs were $21,024 and variable costs were 60% of sales.

Compute contribution margin and break-even point.

(LO 3, 4)

Instructions

(a) Determine the contribution margin in dollars, per unit, and as a ratio.
(b) Using the contribution margin technique, compute the break-even point in dollars and in units.

E22-8 Spencer Kars provides shuttle service between four hotels near a medical center and an international airport. Spencer Kars uses two 10-passenger vans to offer 12 round trips per day. A recent month's activity in the form of a cost-volume-profit income statement is shown below.

Compute break-even point.

(LO 3, 4)

Fare revenues (1,500 fares)		$36,000
Variable costs		
Fuel	$ 5,040	
Tolls and parking	3,100	
Maintenance	860	9,000
Contribution margin		27,000
Fixed costs		
Salaries	15,700	
Depreciation	1,300	
Insurance	1,000	18,000
Net income		$ 9,000

Instructions

(a) Calculate the break-even point in (1) dollars and (2) number of fares.
(b) Without calculations, determine the contribution margin at the break-even point.

E22-9 In 2016, Manhoff Company had a break-even point of $350,000 based on a selling price of $5 per unit and fixed costs of $112,000. In 2017, the selling price and the variable costs per unit did not change, but the break-even point increased to $420,000.

Compute variable costs per unit, contribution margin ratio, and increase in fixed costs.

(LO 3, 4)

Instructions

(a) Compute the variable costs per unit and the contribution margin ratio for 2016.
(b) Compute the increase in fixed costs for 2017.

Prepare CVP income statements.
(LO 3, 4)

E22-10 Billings Company has the following information available for September 2017.

Unit selling price of video game consoles	$ 400
Unit variable costs	$ 280
Total fixed costs	$54,000
Units sold	600

Instructions

(a) Compute the unit contribution margin.
(b) Prepare a CVP income statement that shows both total and per unit amounts.
(c) Compute Billings' break-even point in units.
(d) Prepare a CVP income statement for the break-even point that shows both total and per unit amounts.

Compute various components to derive target net income under different assumptions.
(LO 4, 5)

E22-11 Naylor Company had $210,000 of net income in 2016 when the selling price per unit was $150, the variable costs per unit were $90, and the fixed costs were $570,000. Management expects per unit data and total fixed costs to remain the same in 2017. The president of Naylor Company is under pressure from stockholders to increase net income by $52,000 in 2017.

Instructions

(a) Compute the number of units sold in 2016.
(b) Compute the number of units that would have to be sold in 2017 to reach the stockholders' desired profit level.
(c) Assume that Naylor Company sells the same number of units in 2017 as it did in 2016. What would the selling price have to be in order to reach the stockholders' desired profit level?

Compute net income under different alternatives.
(LO 5)

E22-12 Yams Company reports the following operating results for the month of August: sales $400,000 (units 5,000), variable costs $240,000, and fixed costs $90,000. Management is considering the following independent courses of action to increase net income.

1. Increase selling price by 10% with no change in total variable costs or units sold.
2. Reduce variable costs to 55% of sales.

Instructions

Compute the net income to be earned under each alternative. Which course of action will produce the higher net income?

Prepare a CVP graph and compute break-even point and margin of safety.
(LO 4, 5)

E22-13 Glacial Company estimates that variable costs will be 62.5% of sales, and fixed costs will total $600,000. The selling price of the product is $4.

Instructions

(a) Prepare a CVP graph, assuming maximum sales of $3,200,000. (*Note:* Use $400,000 increments for sales and costs and 100,000 increments for units.)
(b) Compute the break-even point in (1) units and (2) dollars.
(c) Assuming actual sales are $2 million, compute the margin of safety in (1) dollars and (2) as a ratio.

Prepare a CVP income statement before and after changes in business environment.
(LO 6)

E22-14 Carey Company had sales in 2016 of $1,560,000 on 60,000 units. Variable costs totaled $900,000, and fixed costs totaled $500,000.

A new raw material is available that will decrease the variable costs per unit by 20% (or $3). However, to process the new raw material, fixed operating costs will increase by $100,000. Management feels that one-half of the decline in the variable costs per unit should be passed on to customers in the form of a sales price reduction. The marketing department expects that this sales price reduction will result in a 5% increase in the number of units sold.

Instructions

Prepare a projected CVP income statement for 2017 (a) assuming the changes have not been made, and (b) assuming that changes are made as described.

Compute manufacturing cost under absorption and variable costing and explain difference.
(LO 7)

***E22-15** Crate Express Co. produces wooden crates used for shipping products by ocean liner. In 2017, Crate Express incurred the following costs.

Wood used in crate production	$54,000
Nails (considered insignificant and a variable expense)	$ 350
Direct labor	$43,000
Utilities for the plant:	
$1,500 each month,	
plus $0.50 for each kilowatt-hour used each month	
Rent expense for the plant for the year	$21,400

Assume Crate Express used an average 500 kilowatt-hours each month over the past year.

Instructions

(a) What is Crate Express's total manufacturing cost if it uses a variable costing approach?
(b) What is Crate Express's total manufacturing cost if it uses an absorption costing approach?
(c) What accounts for the difference in manufacturing costs between these two costing approaches?

***E22-16** Montier Corporation produces one product. Its cost includes direct materials ($10 per unit), direct labor ($8 per unit), variable overhead ($5 per unit), fixed manufacturing ($225,000), and fixed selling and administrative ($30,000). In October 2017, Montier produced 25,000 units and sold 20,000 at $50 each.

Prepare absorption cost and variable cost income statements.

(LO 7)

Instructions

(a) Prepare an absorption costing income statement.
(b) Prepare a variable costing income statement.
(c) Explain the difference in net income in the two income statements.

PROBLEMS

P22-1A Vin Diesel owns the Fredonia Barber Shop. He employs four barbers and pays each a base rate of $1,250 per month. One of the barbers serves as the manager and receives an extra $500 per month. In addition to the base rate, each barber also receives a commission of $4.50 per haircut.

Determine variable and fixed costs, compute break-even point, prepare a CVP graph, and determine net income.

(LO 1, 2, 3, 4)

Other costs are as follows.

Advertising	$200 per month
Rent	$1,100 per month
Barber supplies	$0.30 per haircut
Utilities	$175 per month plus $0.20 per haircut
Magazines	$25 per month

Vin currently charges $10 per haircut.

Instructions

(a) Determine the variable costs per haircut and the total monthly fixed costs.

(a) VC $5

(b) Compute the break-even point in units and dollars.
(c) Prepare a CVP graph, assuming a maximum of 1,800 haircuts in a month. Use increments of 300 haircuts on the horizontal axis and $3,000 on the vertical axis.
(d) Determine net income, assuming 1,600 haircuts are given in a month.

P22-2A Jorge Company bottles and distributes B-Lite, a diet soft drink. The beverage is sold for 50 cents per 16-ounce bottle to retailers, who charge customers 75 cents per bottle. For the year 2017, management estimates the following revenues and costs.

Prepare a CVP income statement, compute break-even point, contribution margin ratio, margin of safety ratio, and sales for target net income.

(LO 3, 4, 5)

Sales	$1,800,000	Selling expenses—variable	$70,000
Direct materials	430,000	Selling expenses—fixed	65,000
Direct labor	360,000	Administrative expenses—variable	20,000
Manufacturing overhead—variable	380,000	Administrative expenses—fixed	60,000
Manufacturing overhead—fixed	280,000		

Instructions

(b) (1) 2,700,000 units
(c) CM ratio 30%

(a) Prepare a CVP income statement for 2017 based on management's estimates. (Show column for total amounts only.)
(b) Compute the break-even point in (1) units and (2) dollars.
(c) Compute the contribution margin ratio and the margin of safety ratio. (Round to nearest full percent.)
(d) Determine the sales dollars required to earn net income of $180,000.

Compute break-even point under alternative courses of action.

(LO 4)

P22-3A Tanek Corp.'s sales slumped badly in 2017. For the first time in its history, it operated at a loss. The company's income statement showed the following results from selling 500,000 units of product: sales $2,500,000, total costs and expenses $2,600,000, and net loss $100,000. Costs and expenses consisted of the amounts shown below.

	Total	**Variable**	**Fixed**
Cost of goods sold	$2,140,000	$1,590,000	$550,000
Selling expenses	250,000	92,000	158,000
Administrative expenses	210,000	68,000	142,000
	$2,600,000	$1,750,000	$850,000

Management is considering the following independent alternatives for 2018.

1. Increase unit selling price 20% with no change in costs, expenses, and sales volume.
2. Change the compensation of salespersons from fixed annual salaries totaling $150,000 to total salaries of $60,000 plus a 5% commission on sales.

Instructions

(b) Alternative 1 $2,023,810

(a) Compute the break-even point in dollars for 2017.
(b) Compute the break-even point in dollars under each of the alternative courses of action. (Round all ratios to nearest full percent.) Which course of action do you recommend?

Compute break-even point and margin of safety ratio, and prepare a CVP income statement before and after changes in business environment.

(LO 3, 4, 5)

P22-4A Mary Willis is the advertising manager for Bargain Shoe Store. She is currently working on a major promotional campaign. Her ideas include the installation of a new lighting system and increased display space that will add $24,000 in fixed costs to the $270,000 currently spent. In addition, Mary is proposing that a 5% price decrease ($40 to $38) will produce a 20% increase in sales volume (20,000 to 24,000). Variable costs will remain at $24 per pair of shoes. Management is impressed with Mary's ideas but concerned about the effects that these changes will have on the break-even point and the margin of safety.

Instructions

(b) Current margin of safety ratio 16%

(a) Compute the current break-even point in units, and compare it to the break-even point in units if Mary's ideas are used.
(b) Compute the margin of safety ratio for current operations and after Mary's changes are introduced. (Round to nearest full percent.)
(c) Prepare a CVP income statement for current operations and after Mary's changes are introduced. (Show column for total amounts only.) Would you make the changes suggested?

Compute contribution margin, fixed costs, break-even point, sales for target net income, and margin of safety ratio.

(LO 3, 4, 5)

P22-5A Viejol Corporation has collected the following information after its first year of sales. Sales were $1,600,000 on 100,000 units, selling expenses $250,000 (40% variable and 60% fixed), direct materials $490,000, direct labor $290,000, administrative expenses $270,000 (20% variable and 80% fixed), and manufacturing overhead $380,000 (70% variable and 30% fixed). Top management has asked you to do a CVP analysis so that it can make plans for the coming year. It has projected that unit sales will increase by 10% next year.

Instructions

(a) Compute (1) the contribution margin for the current year and the projected year, and (2) the fixed costs for the current year. (Assume that fixed costs will remain the same in the projected year.)

(b) Compute the break-even point in units and sales dollars for the current year.
(c) The company has a target net income of $200,000. What is the required sales in dollars for the company to meet its target?
(d) If the company meets its target net income number, by what percentage could its sales fall before it is operating at a loss? That is, what is its margin of safety ratio?

(b) 120,000 units

***P22-6A** Jackson Company produces plastic that is used for injection-molding applications such as gears for small motors. In 2016, the first year of operations, Jackson produced 4,000 tons of plastic and sold 3,500 tons. In 2017, the production and sales results were exactly reversed. In each year, the selling price per ton was $2,000, variable manufacturing costs were 15% of the sales price of units produced, variable selling expenses were 10% of the selling price of units sold, fixed manufacturing costs were $2,800,000, and fixed administrative expenses were $500,000.

Prepare income statements under absorption costing and variable costing for a company with beginning inventory, and reconcile differences.

(LO 7)

Instructions

(a) Prepare income statements for each year using variable costing. (Use the format from Illustration 22A-5.)
(b) Prepare income statements for each year using absorption costing. (Use the format from Illustration 22A-4.)
(c) Reconcile the differences each year in net income under the two costing approaches.
(d) Comment on the effects of production and sales on net income under the two costing approaches.

(a) 2017 $2,700,000

(b) 2017 $2,350,000

BROADENING YOUR PERSPECTIVE

MANAGEMENT DECISION-MAKING

Decision-Making Across the Organization

BYP22-1 Creative Ideas Company has decided to introduce a new product. The new product can be manufactured by either a capital-intensive method or a labor-intensive method. The manufacturing method will not affect the quality of the product. The estimated manufacturing costs by the two methods are as follows.

	Capital-Intensive	Labor-Intensive
Direct materials	$5 per unit	$5.50 per unit
Direct labor	$6 per unit	$8.00 per unit
Variable overhead	$3 per unit	$4.50 per unit
Fixed manufacturing costs	$2,524,000	$1,550,000

Creative Ideas' market research department has recommended an introductory unit sales price of $32. The incremental selling expenses are estimated to be $502,000 annually plus $2 for each unit sold, regardless of manufacturing method.

Instructions

With the class divided into groups, answer the following.

(a) Calculate the estimated break-even point in annual unit sales of the new product if Creative Ideas Company uses the:
 (1) Capital-intensive manufacturing method.
 (2) Labor-intensive manufacturing method.
(b) Determine the annual unit sales volume at which Creative Ideas Company would be indifferent between the two manufacturing methods.
(c) Explain the circumstance under which Creative Ideas should employ each of the two manufacturing methods.

(CMA adapted)

Managerial Analysis

BYP22-2 The condensed income statement for the Peri and Paul partnership for 2017 is as follows.

PERI AND PAUL COMPANY
Income Statement
For the Year Ended December 31, 2017

Sales (240,000 units)		$1,200,000
Cost of goods sold		800,000
Gross profit		400,000
Operating expenses		
Selling	$280,000	
Administrative	150,000	430,000
Net loss		$ (30,000)

A cost behavior analysis indicates that 75% of the cost of goods sold are variable, 42% of the selling expenses are variable, and 40% of the administrative expenses are variable.

Instructions

(Round to nearest unit, dollar, and percentage, where necessary. Use the CVP income statement format in computing profits.)

(a) Compute the break-even point in total sales dollars and in units for 2017.

(b) Peri has proposed a plan to get the partnership "out of the red" and improve its profitability. She feels that the quality of the product could be substantially improved by spending $0.25 more per unit on better raw materials. The selling price per unit could be increased to only $5.25 because of competitive pressures. Peri estimates that sales volume will increase by 25%. What effect would Peri's plan have on the profits and the break-even point in dollars of the partnership? (Round the contribution margin ratio to two decimal places.)

(c) Paul was a marketing major in college. He believes that sales volume can be increased only by intensive advertising and promotional campaigns. He therefore proposed the following plan as an alternative to Peri's: (1) increase variable selling expenses to $0.59 per unit, (2) lower the selling price per unit by $0.25, and (3) increase fixed selling expenses by $40,000. Paul quoted an old marketing research report that said that sales volume would increase by 60% if these changes were made. What effect would Paul's plan have on the profits and the break-even point in dollars of the partnership?

(d) Which plan should be accepted? Explain your answer.

Real-World Focus

BYP22-3 The Coca-Cola Company hardly needs an introduction. A line taken from the cover of a recent annual report says it all: If you measured time in servings of Coca-Cola, "a billion Coca-Cola's ago was yesterday morning." On average, every U.S. citizen drinks 363 8-ounce servings of Coca-Cola products each year. Coca-Cola's primary line of business is the making and selling of syrup to bottlers. These bottlers then sell the finished bottles and cans of Coca-Cola to the consumer.

In the annual report of Coca-Cola, the information shown below was provided.

THE COCA-COLA COMPANY
Management Discussion

Our gross margin declined to 61 percent this year from 62 percent in the prior year, primarily due to costs for materials such as sweeteners and packaging.

The increases [in selling expenses] in the last two years were primarily due to higher marketing expenditures in support of our Company's volume growth.

We measure our sales volume in two ways: (1) gallon shipments of concentrates and syrups and (2) unit cases of finished product (bottles and cans of Coke sold by bottlers).

Instructions

Answer the following questions.

(a) Are sweeteners and packaging a variable cost or a fixed cost? What is the impact on the contribution margin of an increase in the per unit cost of sweeteners or packaging? What are the implications for profitability?

(b) In your opinion, are Coca-Cola's marketing expenditures a fixed cost, variable cost, or mixed cost? Give justification for your answer.
(c) Which of the two measures cited for measuring volume represents the activity index as defined in this chapter? Why might Coca-Cola use two different measures?

BYP22-4 The May 21, 2010, edition of the *Wall Street Journal* includes an article by Jeffrey Trachtenberg entitled "E-Books Rewrite Bookselling."

Instructions
Read the article and answer the following questions.

(a) What aspect of Barnes and Noble's current structure puts it at risk if electronic books become a significant portion of book sales?
(b) What was Barnes and Noble's primary competitive advantage in a "paper book" world? How has this advantage been eliminated by e-books?
(c) What event do the authors say might eventually be viewed as the big turning point for e-books?
(d) What amount does Barnes and Noble earn on a $25 hardcover book? How much would it likely earn on an e-book version of the same title? What implications does this have for Barnes and Noble versus its competitors?
(e) What two mistakes does the author suggest that Barnes and Noble made that left it ill-prepared for an e-book environment?

CRITICAL THINKING

Communication Activity

BYP22-5 Your roommate asks for your help on the following questions about CVP analysis formulas.

(a) How can the mathematical equation for break-even sales show both sales units and sales dollars?
(b) How do the formulas differ for unit contribution margin and contribution margin ratio?
(c) How can contribution margin be used to determine break-even sales in units and in dollars?

Instructions
Write a memo to your roommate stating the relevant formulas and answering each question.

Ethics Case

BYP22-6 Scott Bestor is an accountant for Westfield Company. Early this year, Scott made a highly favorable projection of sales and profits over the next 3 years for Westfield's hot-selling computer PLEX. As a result of the projections Scott presented to senior management, the company decided to expand production in this area. This decision led to dislocations of some plant personnel who were reassigned to one of the company's newer plants in another state. However, no one was fired, and in fact the company expanded its workforce slightly.

Unfortunately, Scott rechecked his projection computations a few months later and found that he had made an error that would have reduced his projections substantially. Luckily, sales of PLEX have exceeded projections so far, and management is satisfied with its decision. Scott, however, is not sure what to do. Should he confess his honest mistake and jeopardize his possible promotion? He suspects that no one will catch the error because PLEX sales have exceeded his projections, and it appears that profits will materialize close to his projections.

Instructions

(a) Who are the stakeholders in this situation?
(b) Identify the ethical issues involved in this situation.
(c) What are the possible alternative actions for Scott? What would you do in Scott's position?

All About You

BYP22-7 Cost-volume-profit analysis can also be used in making personal financial decisions. For example, the purchase of a new car is one of your biggest personal expenditures. It is important that you carefully analyze your options.

Suppose that you are considering the purchase of a hybrid vehicle. Let's assume the following facts. The hybrid will initially cost an additional $4,500 above the cost of a traditional vehicle. The hybrid will get 40 miles per gallon of gas, and the traditional car will get 30 miles per gallon. Also, assume that the cost of gas is $3.60 per gallon.

Instructions

Using the facts above, answer the following questions.

(a) What is the variable gasoline cost of going one mile in the hybrid car? What is the variable cost of going one mile in the traditional car?

(b) Using the information in part (a), if "miles" is your unit of measure, what is the "contribution margin" of the hybrid vehicle relative to the traditional vehicle? That is, express the variable cost savings on a per-mile basis.

(c) How many miles would you have to drive in order to break even on your investment in the hybrid car?

(d) What other factors might you want to consider?

Chapter 23 Budgetary Planning

The best business plans often result from meeting a basic human need. Many people would argue that cupcakes aren't necessarily essential to support life. But if you found out that allergies were going to deprive you forever of cupcakes, you might view baked goods in a whole new light. Such was the dilemma faced by Erin McKenna. When she found that her wheat allergies prevented her from consuming most baked sweets, she decided to open a bakery that met her needs. Her vegan and kosher bakery, BabyCakes NYC, advertises that it is refined-sugar-free, gluten-free, wheat-free, soy-free, dairy-free, and egg-free. So if you're one of the more than 10 million Americans with a food allergy or some other dietary constraint, this is probably the bakery for you.

Those of you that have spent a little time in the kitchen might wonder what kind of ingredients BabyCakes uses. To avoid the gluten in wheat, the company uses Bob's Red Mill rice flour, a garbanzo/fava bean mix, or oat flours. How does BabyCakes get all those great frosting colors without artificial dyes? The company achieves pink with beets, green with chlorophyll, yellow with turmeric, and blue/purple with red cabbage. To eliminate dairy and soy, the bakers use rice and coconut milk. And finally, to accomplish over-the-top deliciousness without refined sugar, BabyCakes uses agave nectar (a sweetener derived from cactus) and evaporated cane juice (often referred to as organic or unrefined sugar).

With cupcakes priced at over $3 per item and a brisk business, you might think that making money is easy for BabyCakes. But all of these specialty ingredients don't come cheap. In addition, BabyCakes' shops are located in Manhattan, Los Angeles, and Orlando, so rent isn't exactly inexpensive either. Despite these costs, Erin's first store made a profit its first year and did even better in later years. To achieve this profitability, Erin relies on careful budgeting. First, she needs to estimate how many items she will sell. Then, she determines her needs for materials, labor, and overhead. Prices for BabyCakes' materials can fluctuate significantly, so Erin needs to update her budget accordingly. Finally, she has to budget for other products such as her cookbooks, baking kits, and T-shirts. Without a budget, Erin's business might not be so sweet.

LEARNING OBJECTIVES

1. **State the essentials of effective budgeting and the components of the master budget.**
2. **Prepare budgets for sales, production, and direct materials.**
3. **Prepare budgets for direct labor, manufacturing overhead, and selling and administrative expenses, and a budgeted income statement.**
4. **Prepare a cash budget and a budgeted balance sheet.**
5. **Apply budgeting principles to nonmanufacturing companies.**

LEARNING OBJECTIVE 1

State the essentials of effective budgeting and the components of the master budget.

One of management's major responsibilities is planning. As explained in Chapter 19, **planning** is the process of establishing company-wide objectives. A successful organization makes both long-term and short-term plans. These plans establish the objectives of the company and the proposed way of accomplishing them.

A **budget** is a formal written statement of management's plans for a specified future time period, expressed in financial terms. It represents the primary method of communicating agreed-upon objectives throughout the organization. Once adopted, a budget becomes an important basis for evaluating performance. It promotes efficiency and serves as a deterrent to waste and inefficiency. We consider the role of budgeting as a **control device** in Chapter 24.

Budgeting and Accounting

Accounting information makes major contributions to the budgeting process. From the accounting records, companies can obtain historical data on revenues, costs, and expenses. These data are helpful in formulating future budget goals.

Normally, accountants have the responsibility for presenting management's budgeting goals in financial terms. In this role, they translate management's plans and communicate the budget to employees throughout the company. They prepare periodic budget reports that provide the basis for measuring performance and comparing actual results with planned objectives. The budget itself and the administration of the budget, however, are entirely management responsibilities.

The Benefits of Budgeting

The primary benefits of budgeting are as follows.

1. It requires all levels of management to **plan ahead** and to formalize goals on a recurring basis.
2. It provides **definite objectives** for evaluating performance at each level of responsibility.
3. It creates an **early warning system** for potential problems so that management can make changes before things get out of hand.
4. It facilitates the **coordination of activities** within the business. It does this by correlating the goals of each segment with overall company objectives. Thus, the company can integrate production and sales promotion with expected sales.
5. It results in greater **management awareness** of the entity's overall operations and the impact on operations of external factors, such as economic trends.
6. It **motivates personnel** throughout the organization to meet planned objectives.

A budget is an aid to management; it is not a *substitute* for management. A budget cannot operate or enforce itself. Companies can realize the benefits of budgeting only when managers carefully administer budgets.

Essentials of Effective Budgeting

Effective budgeting depends on a **sound organizational structure**. In such a structure, authority and responsibility for all phases of operations are clearly defined. Budgets based on **research and analysis** are more likely to result in realistic goals that will contribute to the growth and profitability of a company. And, the effectiveness of a budget program is directly related to its **acceptance by all levels of management**.

Once adopted, the budget is an important tool for evaluating performance. Managers should systematically and periodically review variations between actual and expected results to determine their cause(s). However, individuals should not be held responsible for variations that are beyond their control.

LENGTH OF THE BUDGET PERIOD

The budget period is not necessarily one year in length. **A budget may be prepared for any period of time.** Various factors influence the length of the budget period. These factors include the type of budget, the nature of the organization, the need for periodic appraisal, and prevailing business conditions.

The budget period should be long enough to provide an attainable goal under normal business conditions. Ideally, the time period should minimize the impact of seasonal or cyclical fluctuations. On the other hand, the budget period should not be so long that reliable estimates are impossible.

The **most common budget period is one year**. The annual budget, in turn, is often supplemented by monthly and quarterly budgets. Many companies use **continuous 12-month budgets**. These budgets drop the month just ended and add a future month. One benefit of continuous budgeting is that it keeps management planning a full year ahead.

THE BUDGETING PROCESS

The development of the budget for the coming year generally starts several months before the end of the current year. The budgeting process usually begins with the collection of data from each organizational unit of the company. Past performance is often the starting point from which future budget goals are formulated.

The budget is developed within the framework of a **sales forecast**. This forecast shows potential sales for the industry and the company's expected share of such sales. Sales forecasting involves a consideration of various factors: (1) general economic conditions, (2) industry trends, (3) market research studies, (4) anticipated advertising and promotion, (5) previous market share, (6) changes in prices, and (7) technological developments. The input of sales personnel and top management is essential to the sales forecast.

In small companies like **BabyCakes NYC**, the budgeting process is often informal. In larger companies, a **budget committee** has responsibility for coordinating the preparation of the budget. The committee ordinarily includes the president, treasurer, chief accountant (controller), and management personnel from each of the major areas of the company, such as sales, production, and research. The budget committee serves as a review board where managers can defend their budget goals and requests. Differences are reviewed, modified if necessary, and reconciled. The budget is then put in its final form by the budget committee, approved, and distributed.

BUDGETING AND HUMAN BEHAVIOR

A budget can have a significant impact on human behavior. If done well, it can inspire managers to higher levels of performance. However, if done poorly, budgets can discourage additional effort and pull down the morale of managers. Why do these diverse effects occur? The answer is found in how the budget is developed and administered.

In developing the budget, each level of management should be invited to participate. This "bottom-to-top" approach is referred to as **participative budgeting**. One benefit of participative budgeting is that lower-level managers have more detailed knowledge of their specific area and thus are able to provide more accurate budgetary estimates. Also, when lower-level managers participate in the budgeting process, they are more likely to perceive the resulting budget as fair. The overall goal is to reach agreement on a budget that the managers consider fair and achievable, but which also meets the corporate goals set by top management. When this goal is met, the budget will provide positive motivation for the managers.

In contrast, if managers view the budget as unfair and unrealistic, they may feel discouraged and uncommitted to budget goals. The risk of having unrealistic budgets is generally greater when the budget is developed from top management down to lower management than vice versa. Illustration 23-1 graphically displays the flow of budget data from bottom to top under participative budgeting.

Illustration 23-1
Flow of budget data under participative budgeting

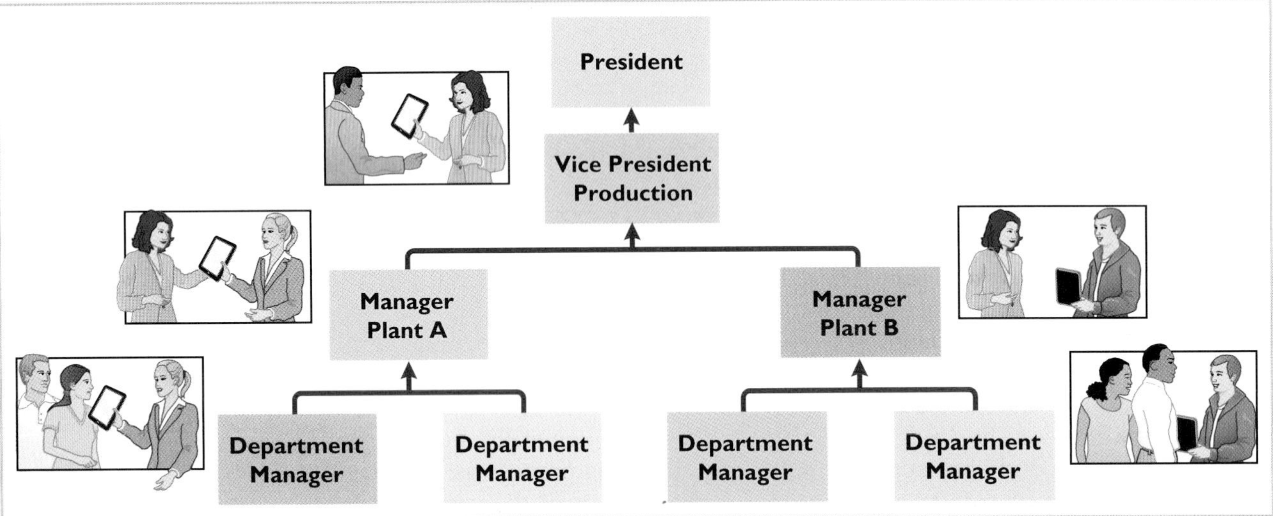

For example, at one time, in an effort to revive its plummeting stock price, Time Warner's top management determined and publicly announced bold new financial goals for the coming year. Unfortunately, these goals were not reached. The next year, the company got a new CEO who said the company would now actually set reasonable goals that it could meet. The new budgets were developed with each operating unit setting what it felt were optimistic but attainable goals. In the words of one manager, using this approach created a sense of teamwork.

Participative budgeting does, however, have potential disadvantages. First, the "give and take" of participative budgeting is time-consuming (and thus more costly). Under a "top-down" approach, the budget is simply developed by top management and then dictated to lower-level managers. A second disadvantage is that participative budgeting can foster budgetary "gaming" through budgetary slack. **Budgetary slack** occurs when managers intentionally underestimate budgeted revenues or overestimate budgeted expenses in order to make it easier to achieve budgetary goals. To minimize budgetary slack, higher-level managers must carefully review and thoroughly question the budget projections provided to them by employees whom they supervise.

For the budget to be effective, top management must completely support the budget. The budget is an important basis for evaluating performance. It also can be used as a positive aid in achieving projected goals. The effect of an evaluation is positive when top management tempers criticism with advice and assistance. In contrast, a manager is likely to respond negatively if top management uses the budget exclusively to assess blame. A budget should not be used as a pressure device to force improved performance. In sum, a budget can be a manager's friend or foe.

BUDGETING AND LONG-RANGE PLANNING

Budgeting and long-range planning are not the same. One important difference is the **time period involved**. The maximum length of a budget is usually one year, and budgets are often prepared for shorter periods of time, such as a month or a quarter. In contrast, long-range planning usually encompasses a period of at least five years.

A second significant difference is in **emphasis**. Budgeting focuses on achieving specific short-term goals, such as meeting annual profit objectives. **Long-range planning**, on the other hand, identifies long-term goals, selects strategies to achieve those goals, and develops policies and plans to implement the strategies. In long-range planning, management also considers anticipated trends in the economic and political environment and how the company should cope with them.

The final difference between budgeting and long-range planning relates to the **amount of detail presented**. Budgets, as you will see in this chapter, can be very detailed. Long-range plans contain considerably less detail. The data in long-range plans are intended more for a review of progress toward long-term goals than as a basis of control for achieving specific results. The primary objective of long-range planning is to develop the best strategy to maximize the company's performance over an extended future period.

The Master Budget

The term "budget" is actually a shorthand term to describe a variety of budget documents. All of these documents are combined into a master budget. The **master budget** is a set of interrelated budgets that constitutes a plan of action for a specified time period.

The master budget contains two classes of budgets. **Operating budgets** are the individual budgets that result in the preparation of the budgeted income statement. These budgets establish goals for the company's sales and production personnel. In contrast, **financial budgets** focus primarily on the cash resources needed to fund expected operations and planned capital expenditures. Financial budgets include the capital expenditure budget, the cash budget, and the budgeted balance sheet.

Illustration 23-2 shows the individual budgets included in a master budget, and the sequence in which they are prepared. The company first develops the operating budgets, beginning with the sales budget. Then, it prepares the financial budgets. We will explain and illustrate each budget shown in Illustration 23-2

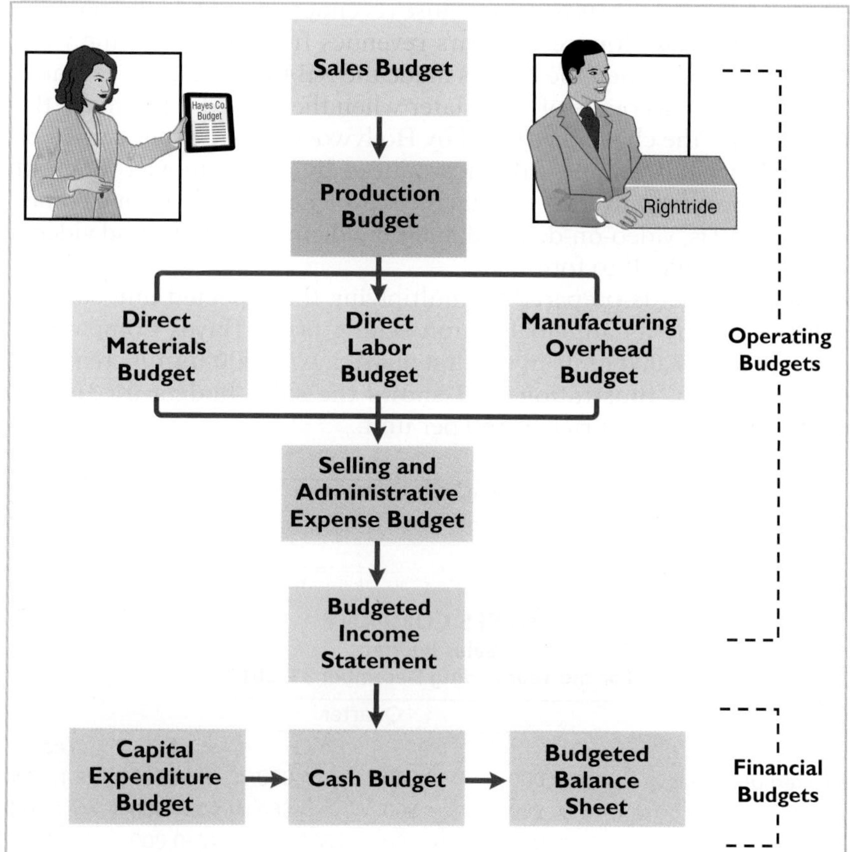

Illustration 23-2
Components of the master budget

except the capital expenditure budget. That budget is discussed under the topic of capital budgeting in Chapter 26.

LEARNING OBJECTIVE  **Prepare budgets for sales, production, and direct materials.**

We use a case study of Hayes Company in preparing the operating budgets. Hayes manufactures and sells a single product, an ergonomically designed bike seat with multiple customizable adjustments, called the Rightride. The budgets are prepared by quarters for the year ending December 31, 2017. Hayes Company begins its annual budgeting process on September 1, 2016, and it completes the budget for 2017 by December 1, 2016. The company begins by preparing the budgets for sales, production, and direct materials.

Sales Budget

As shown in the master budget in Illustration 23-2, **the sales budget is prepared first**. Each of the other budgets depends on the sales budget. The **sales budget** is derived from the sales forecast. It represents management's best estimate of sales revenue for the budget period. An inaccurate sales budget may adversely affect net income. For example, an overly optimistic sales budget may result in excessive inventories that may have to be sold at reduced prices. In contrast, an unduly pessimistic sales budget may result in loss of sales revenue due to inventory shortages.

For example, at one time Amazon.com significantly underestimated demand for its e-book reader, the Kindle. As a consequence, it did not produce enough Kindles and was completely sold out well before the holiday shopping season. Not only did this represent a huge lost opportunity for Amazon, but it exposed the company to potential competitors, who were eager to provide customers with alternatives to the Kindle.

Forecasting sales is challenging. For example, consider the forecasting challenges faced by major sports arenas, whose revenues depend on the success of the home team. Madison Square Garden's revenues from April to June were $193 million during a year when the Knicks made the NBA playoffs. But revenues were only $133.2 million a couple of years later when the team did not make the playoffs. Or, consider the challenges faced by Hollywood movie producers in predicting the complicated revenue stream produced by a new movie. Movie theater ticket sales represent only 20% of total revenue. The bulk of revenue comes from global sales, DVDs, video-on-demand, merchandising products, and videogames, all of which are difficult to forecast.

The sales budget is prepared by multiplying the expected unit sales volume for each product by its anticipated unit selling price. Hayes Company expects sales volume to be 3,000 units in the first quarter, with 500-unit increases in each succeeding quarter. Illustration 23-3 shows the sales budget for the year, by quarter, based on a sales price of $60 per unit.

Illustration 23-3
Sales budget

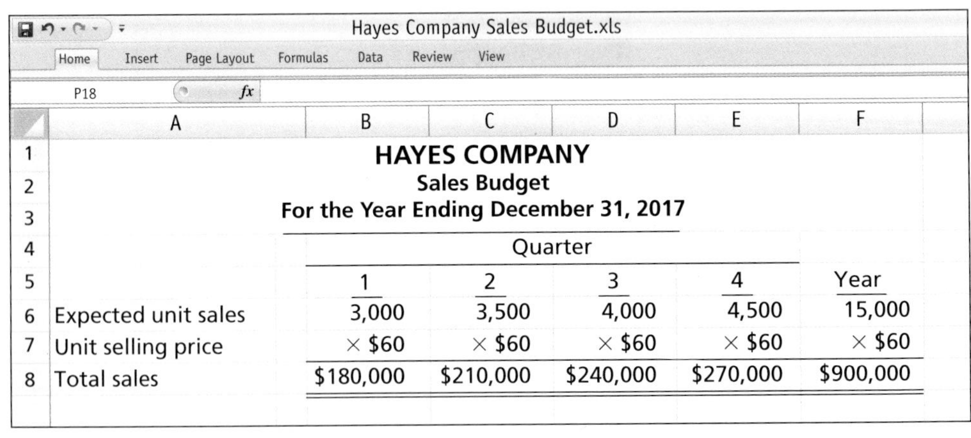

Hayes Company Sales Budget.xls

HAYES COMPANY
Sales Budget
For the Year Ending December 31, 2017

	Quarter 1	Quarter 2	Quarter 3	Quarter 4	Year
Expected unit sales	3,000	3,500	4,000	4,500	15,000
Unit selling price	× $60	× $60	× $60	× $60	× $60
Total sales	$180,000	$210,000	$240,000	$270,000	$900,000

Some companies classify the anticipated sales revenue as cash or credit sales and by geographical regions, territories, or salespersons.

Production Budget

The **production budget** shows the number of units of a product to produce to meet anticipated sales demand. Production requirements are determined from the following formula.[1]

Budgeted Sales Units	+	Desired Ending Finished Goods Units	−	Beginning Finished Goods Units	=	Required Production Units

Illustration 23-4
Production requirements formula

A realistic estimate of ending inventory is essential in scheduling production requirements. Excessive inventories in one quarter may lead to cutbacks in production and employee layoffs in a subsequent quarter. On the other hand, inadequate inventories may result either in added costs for overtime work or in lost sales. Hayes Company believes it can meet future sales requirements by maintaining an ending inventory equal to 20% of the next quarter's budgeted sales volume. For example, the ending finished goods inventory for the first quarter is 700 units (20% × anticipated second-quarter sales of 3,500 units). Illustration 23-5 shows the production budget.

Units of Finished Goods Inventory

Beg. Inv.	Sales
Required Prod. Units	
End. Inv.	

Hayes Company Production Budget.xls

Home Insert Page Layout Formulas Data Review View

P18 fx

HAYES COMPANY
Production Budget
For the Year Ending December 31, 2017

	Quarter 1	2	3	4	Year
Expected unit sales (Illustration 23-3)	3,000	3,500	4,000	4,500	
Add: Desired ending finished goods units[a]	700	800	900	1,000[b]	
Total required units	3,700	4,300	4,900	5,500	
Less: Beginning finished goods units	600[c]	700	800	900	
Required production units	3,100	3,600	4,100	4,600	15,400

[a]20% of next quarter's sales
[b]Expected 2018 first-quarter sales, 5,000 units × 20%
[c]20% of estimated first-quarter 2017 sales units

Units of Finished Goods Inventory

600	3,000
3,100	
700	

Illustration 23-5
Production budget

The production budget, in turn, provides the basis for the budgeted costs for each manufacturing cost element, as explained in the following pages.

Direct Materials Budget

The **direct materials budget** shows both the quantity and cost of direct materials to be purchased. The quantities of direct materials are derived from the following formula.

[1]This formula ignores any work in process inventories, which are assumed to be nonexistent in Hayes Company.

Illustration 23-6
Formula for direct materials quantities

Direct Materials Units Required for Production	+	Desired Ending Direct Materials Units	−	Beginning Direct Materials Units	=	Required Direct Materials Units to Be Purchased

After the company determines the number of units to purchase, it can compute the budgeted cost of direct materials to be purchased. It does so by multiplying the required units of direct materials by the anticipated cost per unit.

Units of Direct Materials

Beg. Inv.	
Direct Materials to Purchase	Direct Materials Required for Prod.
End. Inv.	

The desired ending inventory is again a key component in the budgeting process. For example, inadequate inventories could result in temporary shutdowns of production. Because of its close proximity to suppliers, Hayes Company maintains an ending inventory of raw materials equal to 10% of the next quarter's production requirements. The manufacture of each Rightride requires 2 pounds of raw materials, and the expected cost per pound is $4. Illustration 23-7 shows the direct materials budget. Assume that the desired ending direct materials amount is 1,020 pounds for the fourth quarter of 2017.

Illustration 23-7
Direct materials budget

Units of Direct Materials (1st Qtr.)

620	
6,300	6,200
720	

Hayes Company Direct Materials Budget.xls

HAYES COMPANY
Direct Materials Budget
For the Year Ending December 31, 2017

	Quarter 1	2	3	4	Year
Units to be produced (Illustration 23-5)	3,100	3,600	4,100	4,600	
Direct materials per unit	× 2	× 2	× 2	× 2	
Total pounds needed for production	6,200	7,200	8,200	9,200	
Add: Desired ending direct materials (pounds)[a]	720	820	920	1,020	
Total materials required	6,920	8,020	9,120	10,220	
Less: Beginning direct materials (pounds)	620[b]	720	820	920	
Direct materials purchases	6,300	7,300	8,300	9,300	
Cost per pound	× $4	× $4	× $4	× $4	
Total cost of direct materials purchases	**$25,200**	**$29,200**	**$33,200**	**$37,200**	**$124,800**

[a]10% of next quarter's production requirements
[b]10% of estimated first-quarter pounds needed for production

LEARNING OBJECTIVE 3

Prepare budgets for direct labor, manufacturing overhead, and selling and administrative expenses, and a budgeted income statement.

As shown in Illustration 23-2 (page 797), the operating budgets culminate with preparation of the budgeted income statement. Before we can do that, we need to prepare budgets for direct labor, manufacturing overhead, and selling and administrative expenses.

Direct Labor Budget

Like the direct materials budget, the **direct labor budget** contains the quantity (hours) and cost of direct labor necessary to meet production requirements. The total direct labor cost is derived from the following formula.

Units to Be Produced	×	Direct Labor Hours per Unit	×	Direct Labor Cost per Hour	=	Total Direct Labor Cost

Illustration 23-8
Formula for direct labor cost

Direct labor hours are determined from the production budget. At Hayes Company, two hours of direct labor are required to produce each unit of finished goods. The anticipated hourly wage rate is $10. Illustration 23-9 shows these data.

Hayes Company Direct Labor Budget.xls

	A	B	C	D	E	F	G	H	I	J
1	**HAYES COMPANY**									
2	**Direct Labor Budget**									
3	**For the Year Ending December 31, 2017**									
4			Quarter							
5			1		2		3		4	Year
6	Units to be produced (Illustration 23-5)		3,100		3,600		4,100		4,600	
7	Direct labor time (hours) per unit		× 2		× 2		× 2		× 2	
8	Total required direct labor hours		6,200		7,200		8,200		9,200	
9	Direct labor cost per hour		× $10		× $10		× $10		× $10	
10	**Total direct labor cost**		**$62,000**		**$72,000**		**$82,000**		**$92,000**	**$308,000**
11										

Illustration 23-9
Direct labor budget

The direct labor budget is critical in maintaining a labor force that can meet the expected levels of production.

Manufacturing Overhead Budget

The **manufacturing overhead budget** shows the expected manufacturing overhead costs for the budget period. As Illustration 23-10 shows, **this budget**

Hayes Company Manufacturing Overhead Budget.xls

	A	B	C	D	E	F
1	**HAYES COMPANY**					
2	**Manufacturing Overhead Budget**					
3	**For the Year Ending December 31, 2017**					
4		Quarter				
5		1	2	3	4	Year
6	Variable costs					
7	Indirect materials ($1.00/hour)	$ 6,200	$ 7,200	$ 8,200	$ 9,200	$ 30,800
8	Indirect labor ($1.40/hour)	8,680	10,080	11,480	12,880	43,120
9	Utilities ($0.40/hour)	2,480	2,880	3,280	3,680	12,320
10	Maintenance ($0.20/hour)	1,240	1,440	1,640	1,840	6,160
11	Total variable costs	18,600	21,600	24,600	27,600	92,400
12	Fixed costs					
13	Supervisory salaries	20,000	20,000	20,000	20,000	80,000
14	Depreciation	3,800	3,800	3,800	3,800	15,200
15	Property taxes and insurance	9,000	9,000	9,000	9,000	36,000
16	Maintenance	5,700	5,700	5,700	5,700	22,800
17	Total fixed costs	38,500	38,500	38,500	38,500	154,000
18	**Total manufacturing overhead**	**$57,100**	**$60,100**	**$63,100**	**$66,100**	**$246,400**
19	**Direct labor hours (Illustration 23-9)**	6,200	7,200	8,200	9,200	30,800
20	**Manufacturing overhead rate per direct labor hour ($246,400 ÷ 30,800)**					**$8**
21						

Illustration 23-10
Manufacturing overhead budget

distinguishes between variable and fixed overhead costs. Hayes Company expects variable costs to fluctuate with production volume on the basis of the following rates per direct labor hour: indirect materials \$1.00, indirect labor \$1.40, utilities \$0.40, and maintenance \$0.20. Thus, for the 6,200 direct labor hours to produce 3,100 units, budgeted indirect materials are \$6,200 (6,200 × \$1), and budgeted indirect labor is \$8,680 (6,200 × \$1.40). Hayes also recognizes that some maintenance is fixed. The amounts reported for fixed costs are assumed for our example. The accuracy of budgeted overhead cost estimates can be greatly improved by employing activity-based costing.

At Hayes Company, overhead is applied to production on the basis of direct labor hours. Thus, as Illustration 23-10 shows, the budgeted annual rate is \$8 per hour (\$246,400 ÷ 30,800).

Selling and Administrative Expense Budget

Hayes Company combines its operating expenses into one budget, the **selling and administrative expense budget**. This budget projects anticipated selling and administrative expenses for the budget period. This budget (Illustration 23-11) also classifies expenses as either variable or fixed. In this case, the variable expense rates per unit of sales are sales commissions \$3 and freight-out \$1. Variable expenses per quarter are based on the unit sales from the sales budget (see Illustration 23-3, page 798). For example, Hayes expects sales in the first quarter to be 3,000 units. Thus, sales commissions expense is \$9,000 (3,000 × \$3), and freight-out is \$3,000 (3,000 × \$1). Fixed expenses are based on assumed data.

Illustration 23-11
Selling and administrative expense budget

Hayes Company Manufacturing Selling and Administrative Expense Budget.xls

HAYES COMPANY
Selling and Administrative Expense Budget
For the Year Ending December 31, 2017

	Quarter 1	2	3	4	Year
Budgeted sales in units (Illustration 23-3)	3,000	3,500	4,000	4,500	15,000
Variable expenses					
Sales commissions (\$3 per unit)	\$ 9,000	\$10,500	\$12,000	\$13,500	\$ 45,000
Freight-out (\$1 per unit)	3,000	3,500	4,000	4,500	15,000
Total variable expenses	12,000	14,000	16,000	18,000	60,000
Fixed expenses					
Advertising	5,000	5,000	5,000	5,000	20,000
Sales salaries	15,000	15,000	15,000	15,000	60,000
Office salaries	7,500	7,500	7,500	7,500	30,000
Depreciation	1,000	1,000	1,000	1,000	4,000
Property taxes and insurance	1,500	1,500	1,500	1,500	6,000
Total fixed expenses	30,000	30,000	30,000	30,000	120,000
Total selling and administrative expenses	**\$42,000**	**\$44,000**	**\$46,000**	**\$48,000**	**\$180,000**

Budgeted Income Statement

The **budgeted income statement** is the important end-product of the operating budgets. This budget indicates the expected profitability of operations for the budget period. The budgeted income statement provides the basis for evaluating company performance. Budgeted income statements often act as a call to action. For example, a board member at **XM Satellite Radio Holdings** felt that budgeted costs were too high relative to budgeted revenues. When management refused to cut its marketing and programming costs, the board member resigned. He felt that without the cuts, the company risked financial crisis.

As you would expect, the budgeted income statement is prepared from the various operating budgets. For example, to find the cost of goods sold, Hayes Company must first determine the total unit cost of producing one Rightride, as follows.

Illustration 23-12
Computation of total unit cost

Cost of One Rightride				
Cost Element	**Illustration**	**Quantity**	**Unit Cost**	**Total**
Direct materials	23-7	2 pounds	$ 4.00	$ 8.00
Direct labor	23-9	2 hours	$10.00	20.00
Manufacturing overhead	23-10	2 hours	$ 8.00	16.00
Total unit cost				**$44.00**

Hayes then determines cost of goods sold by multiplying the units sold by the unit cost. Its budgeted cost of goods sold is $660,000 (15,000 × $44). All data for the income statement come from the individual operating budgets except the following: (1) interest expense is expected to be $100, and (2) income taxes are estimated to be $12,000. Illustration 23-13 shows the budgeted multiple-step income statement.

Illustration 23-13
Budgeted multiple-step income statement

HAYES COMPANY
Budgeted Income Statement
For the Year Ending December 31, 2017

Sales (Illustration 23-3)	$900,000
Cost of goods sold (15,000 × $44)	660,000
Gross profit	240,000
Selling and administrative expenses (Illustration 23-11)	180,000
Income from operations	60,000
Interest expense	100
Income before income taxes	59,900
Income tax expense	12,000
Net income	$ 47,900

Prepare a cash budget and a budgeted balance sheet.

As shown in Illustration 23-2 (page 797), the financial budgets consist of the capital expenditure budget, the cash budget, and the budgeted balance sheet. We will discuss the capital expenditure budget in Chapter 26.

Cash Budget

The **cash budget** shows anticipated cash flows. Because cash is so vital, this budget is often considered to be the most important financial budget. The cash budget contains three sections (cash receipts, cash disbursements, and financing) and the beginning and ending cash balances, as shown in Illustration 23-14 (page 804).

Illustration 23-14
Basic form of a cash budget

Any Company Cash Budget.xls

	A	B	C
1	**ANY COMPANY**		
2	**Cash Budget**		
3	Beginning cash balance	$X,XXX	
4	**Add: Cash receipts** (itemized)	X,XXX	
5	Total available cash	X,XXX	
6	**Less: Cash disbursements** (itemized)	X,XXX	
7	Excess (deficiency) of available cash over cash disbursements	X,XXX	
8	**Financing**	X,XXX	
9	Ending cash balance	$X,XXX	

The **cash receipts section** includes expected receipts from the company's principal source(s) of revenue. These are usually cash sales and collections from customers on credit sales. This section also shows anticipated receipts of interest and dividends, and proceeds from planned sales of investments, plant assets, and the company's capital stock.

The **cash disbursements section** shows expected cash payments. Such payments include direct materials, direct labor, manufacturing overhead, and selling and administrative expenses. This section also includes projected payments for income taxes, dividends, investments, and plant assets.

The **financing section** shows expected borrowings and the repayment of the borrowed funds plus interest. Companies need this section when there is a cash deficiency or when the cash balance is below management's minimum required balance.

Data in the cash budget are prepared in sequence. The ending cash balance of one period becomes the beginning cash balance for the next period. Companies obtain data for preparing the cash budget from other budgets and from information provided by management. In practice, cash budgets are often prepared for the year on a monthly basis.

To minimize detail, we will assume that Hayes Company prepares an annual cash budget by quarters. Its cash budget is based on the following assumptions.

1. The January 1, 2017, cash balance is expected to be $38,000. Hayes wishes to maintain a balance of at least $15,000.
2. Sales (Illustration 23-3, page 798): 60% are collected in the quarter sold and 40% are collected in the following quarter. Accounts receivable of $60,000 at December 31, 2016, are expected to be collected in full in the first quarter of 2017.
3. Short-term investment securities are expected to be sold for $2,000 cash in the first quarter.
4. Direct materials (Illustration 23-7, page 800): 50% are paid in the quarter purchased and 50% are paid in the following quarter. Accounts payable of $10,600 at December 31, 2016, are expected to be paid in full in the first quarter of 2017.
5. Direct labor (Illustration 23-9, page 801): 100% is paid in the quarter incurred.
6. Manufacturing overhead (Illustration 23-10, page 801) and selling and administrative expenses (Illustration 23-11, page 802): All items except depreciation are paid in the quarter incurred.
7. Management plans to purchase a truck in the second quarter for $10,000 cash.

Illustration 23-15
Collections from customers

Hayes Company.xls

	A	B	C	D	E	F
1	**HAYES COMPANY**					
2	**Schedule of Expected Collections From Customers**					
3			Collections by Quarter			
4		Sales[a]	1	2	3	4
5	Accounts receivable, 12/31/16		$ 60,000			
6	First quarter	$180,000	108,000[b]	$ 72,000[c]		
7	Second quarter	210,000		126,000	$ 84,000	
8	Third quarter	240,000			144,000	$ 96,000
9	Fourth quarter	270,000				162,000
10	**Total collections**		**$168,000**	**$198,000**	**$228,000**	**$258,000**
11						
12	[a]Per Illustration 23-3; [b]$180,000 × 0.60; [c]$180,000 × 0.40					
13						

8. Hayes makes equal quarterly payments of its estimated $12,000 annual income taxes.
9. Loans are repaid in the earliest quarter in which there is sufficient cash (that is, when the cash on hand exceeds the $15,000 minimum required balance).

In preparing the cash budget, it is useful to prepare schedules for collections from customers (assumption 2) and cash payments for direct materials (assumption 4). These schedules are shown in Illustrations 23-15 and 23-16.

Illustration 23-16
Payments for direct materials

Hayes Company.xls

	A	B	C	D	E	F
1	**HAYES COMPANY**					
2	**Schedule of Expected Payments for Direct Materials**					
3			Payments by Quarter			
4		Purchases[a]	1	2	3	4
5	Accounts payable, 12/31/16		$10,600			
6	First quarter	$25,200	12,600[b]	$12,600[c]		
7	Second quarter	29,200		14,600	$14,600	
8	Third quarter	33,200			16,600	$16,600
9	Fourth quarter	37,200				18,600
10	**Total payments**		**$23,200**	**$27,200**	**$31,200**	**$35,200**
11						
12	[a]Per Illustration 23-7; [b]$25,200 × 0.50; [c]$25,200 × 0.50					
13						

Illustration 23-17 (page 806) shows the cash budget for Hayes Company. The budget indicates that Hayes will need $3,000 of financing in the second quarter to maintain a minimum cash balance of $15,000. Since there is an excess of available cash over disbursements of $22,500 at the end of the third quarter, the borrowing, plus $100 interest, is repaid in this quarter.

Illustration 23-17
Cash budget

Hayes Company Cash Budget.xls

	Assumption	1	2	3	4
HAYES COMPANY					
Cash Budget					
For the Year Ending December 31, 2017					
		Quarter			
Beginning cash balance	1	$ 38,000	$ 25,500	$ 15,000	$ 19,400
Add: Receipts					
Collections from customers	2	168,000	198,000	228,000	258,000
Sale of investment securities	3	2,000	0	0	0
Total receipts		170,000	198,000	228,000	258,000
Total available cash		208,000	223,500	243,000	277,400
Less: Disbursements					
Direct materials	4	23,200	27,200	31,200	35,200
Direct labor	5	62,000	72,000	82,000	92,000
Manufacturing overhead	6	53,300[a]	56,300	59,300	62,300
Selling and administrative expenses	6	41,000[b]	43,000	45,000	47,000
Purchase of truck	7	0	10,000	0	0
Income tax expense	8	3,000	3,000	3,000	3,000
Total disbursements		182,500	211,500	220,500	239,500
Excess (deficiency) of available cash over cash disbursements		25,500	12,000	22,500	37,900
Financing					
Add: Borrowings		0	3,000	0	0
Less: Repayments including interest	9	0	0	3,100	0
Ending cash balance		$ 25,500	$ 15,000	$ 19,400	$ 37,900

[a]$57,100 – $3,800 depreciation
[b]$42,000 – $1,000 depreciation

A cash budget contributes to more effective cash management. It shows managers when additional financing is necessary well before the actual need arises. And, it indicates when excess cash is available for investments or other purposes.

Budgeted Balance Sheet

The **budgeted balance sheet** is a projection of financial position at the end of the budget period. This budget is developed from the budgeted balance sheet for the preceding year and the budgets for the current year. Pertinent data from the budgeted balance sheet at December 31, 2016, are as follows.

Buildings and equipment	$182,000	Common stock	$225,000
Accumulated depreciation	$ 28,800	Retained earnings	$ 46,480

Illustration 23-18 shows Hayes Company's budgeted classified balance sheet at December 31, 2017.

Illustration 23-18
Budgeted classified balance sheet

HAYES COMPANY Budgeted Balance Sheet December 31, 2017		
Assets		
Current assets		
Cash		$ 37,900
Accounts receivable		108,000
Finished goods inventory		44,000
Raw materials inventory		4,080
Total current assets		193,980
Property, plant, and equipment		
Buildings and equipment	$192,000	
Less: Accumulated depreciation	48,000	144,000
Total assets		$337,980
Liabilities and Stockholders' Equity		
Liabilities		
Accounts payable		$ 18,600
Stockholders' equity		
Common stock	$225,000	
Retained earnings	94,380	
Total stockholders' equity		319,380
Total liabilities and stockholders' equity		$337,980

The computations and sources of the amounts are explained below.

Cash: Ending cash balance $37,900, shown in the cash budget (Illustration 23-17, page 806).

Accounts receivable: 40% of fourth-quarter sales $270,000, shown in the schedule of expected collections from customers (Illustration 23-15, page 805).

Finished goods inventory: Desired ending inventory 1,000 units, shown in the production budget (Illustration 23-5, page 799) times the total unit cost $44 (shown in Illustration 23-12, page 803).

Raw materials inventory: Desired ending inventory 1,020 pounds, times the cost per pound $4, shown in the direct materials budget (Illustration 23-7, page 800).

Buildings and equipment: December 31, 2016, balance $182,000, plus purchase of truck for $10,000 (Illustration 23-17, page 806).

Accumulated depreciation: December 31, 2016, balance $28,800, plus $15,200 depreciation shown in manufacturing overhead budget (Illustration 23-10, page 801) and $4,000 depreciation shown in selling and administrative expense budget (Illustration 23-11, page 802).

Accounts payable: 50% of fourth-quarter purchases $37,200, shown in schedule of expected payments for direct materials (Illustration 23-16, page 805).

Common stock: Unchanged from the beginning of the year.

Retained earnings: December 31, 2016, balance $46,480, plus net income $47,900, shown in budgeted income statement (Illustration 23-13, page 803).

After budget data are entered into the computer, Hayes prepares the various budgets (sales, cash, etc.), as well as the budgeted financial statements. Using spreadsheets, management can also perform "what if" (sensitivity) analyses based on different hypothetical assumptions. For example, suppose that sales managers project that sales will be 10% higher in the coming quarter. What impact does this change have on the rest of the budgeting process and the financing needs of the business? The impact of the various assumptions on the budget is quickly determined by the spreadsheet. Armed with these analyses, managers make more informed decisions about the impact of various projects. They also anticipate future problems and business opportunities. As seen in this chapter, budgeting is an excellent use of computer spreadsheets.

LEARNING OBJECTIVE 

Apply budgeting principles to nonmanufacturing companies.

Budgeting is not limited to manufacturers. Budgets are also used by merchandisers, service companies, and not-for-profit organizations.

Merchandisers

As in manufacturing operations, the sales budget for a merchandiser is both the starting point and the key factor in the development of the master budget. The major differences between the master budgets of a merchandiser and a manufacturer are as follows.

1. A merchandiser **uses a merchandise purchases budget instead of a production budget**.
2. A merchandiser **does not use the manufacturing budgets (direct materials, direct labor, and manufacturing overhead)**.

The **merchandise purchases budget** shows the estimated cost of goods to be purchased to meet expected sales. The formula for determining budgeted merchandise purchases is as follows.

Illustration 23-19
Merchandise purchases formula

Budgeted Cost of Goods Sold	+	Desired Ending Merchandise Inventory	−	Beginning Merchandise Inventory	=	Required Merchandise Purchases

To illustrate, assume that the budget committee of Lima Company is preparing the merchandise purchases budget for July 2017. It estimates that budgeted sales will be \$300,000 in July and \$320,000 in August. Cost of goods sold is expected to be 70% of sales—that is, \$210,000 in July (0.70 × \$300,000) and \$224,000 in August (0.70 × \$320,000). The company's desired ending inventory is 30% of the following month's cost of goods sold. Required merchandise purchases for July are \$214,200, computed as follows.

Illustration 23-20
Merchandise purchases budget

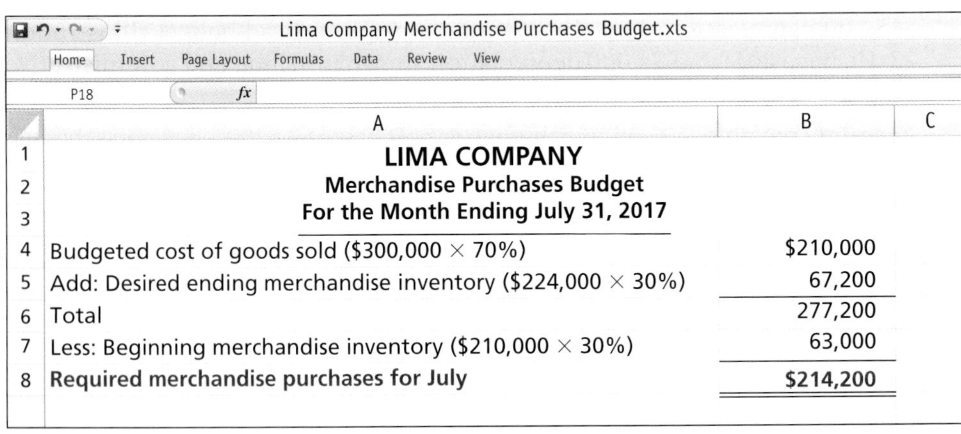

Lima Company Merchandise Purchases Budget.xls

	A	B
1	**LIMA COMPANY**	
2	**Merchandise Purchases Budget**	
3	**For the Month Ending July 31, 2017**	
4	Budgeted cost of goods sold (\$300,000 × 70%)	\$210,000
5	Add: Desired ending merchandise inventory (\$224,000 × 30%)	67,200
6	Total	277,200
7	Less: Beginning merchandise inventory (\$210,000 × 30%)	63,000
8	**Required merchandise purchases for July**	**\$214,200**

When a merchandiser is departmentalized, it prepares separate budgets for each department. For example, a grocery store prepares sales budgets and purchases budgets for each of its major departments, such as meats, dairy, and produce. The store then combines these budgets into a master budget for the store. When a retailer has branch stores, it prepares separate master budgets for each store. Then, it incorporates these budgets into master budgets for the company as a whole.

Departmentalized Budgets

Service Companies

In a service company, such as a public accounting firm, a law office, or a medical practice, the critical factor in budgeting is **coordinating professional staff needs with anticipated services**. If a firm is overstaffed, several problems may result: Labor costs are disproportionately high. Profits are lower because of the additional salaries. Staff turnover sometimes increases because of lack of challenging work. In contrast, if a service company is understaffed, it may lose revenue because existing and prospective client needs for service cannot be met. Also, professional staff may seek other jobs because of excessive work loads.

Suppose that Stephan Lawn and Plowing Service estimates that it will service 300 small lawns, 200 medium lawns, and 100 large lawns during the month of July. It estimates its direct labor needs as 1 hour per small lawn, 1.75 hours for a medium lawn, and 2.75 hours for a large lawn. Its average cost for direct labor is $15 per hour. Stephan prepares a direct labor budget as follows.

Illustration 23-21
Direct labor budget for service company

Stephan Lawn and Plowing Service Direct Labor Budget.xls

Home Insert Page Layout Formulas Data Review View

P18 fx

STEPHAN LAWN AND PLOWING SERVICE
Direct Labor Budget
For the Month Ending July 31, 2017

	Small	Medium	Large	Total
Lawns to be serviced	300	200	100	
Direct labor time (hours) per lawn	× 1	× 1.75	× 2.75	
Total required direct labor hours	300	350	275	
Direct labor cost per hour	× $15	× $15	× $15	
Total direct labor cost	**$4,500**	**$5,250**	**$4,125**	**$13,875**

Service companies can obtain budget data for service revenue from **expected output** or **expected input**. When output is used, it is necessary to determine the expected billings of clients for services performed. In a public accounting firm, for example, output is the sum of its billings in auditing, tax, and consulting services. When input data are used, each professional staff member projects his or her billable time. The firm then applies billing rates to billable time to produce expected service revenue.

Not-for-Profit Organizations

Budgeting is just as important for not-for-profit organizations as for profit-oriented businesses. The budget process, however, is different. In most cases, not-for-profit entities budget **on the basis of cash flows (expenditures and receipts), rather than on a revenue and expense basis**. Further, the starting point in the process is usually expenditures, not receipts. For the not-for-profit entity, management's task generally is to find the receipts needed to support the planned expenditures. The activity index is also likely to be significantly different. For example, in a not-for-profit entity, such as a university, budgeted faculty positions may be based on full-time equivalent students or credit hours expected to be taught in a department.

For some governmental units, voters approve the budget. In other cases, such as state governments and the federal government, legislative approval is required. After the budget is adopted, it must be followed. Overspending is often illegal. In governmental budgets, authorizations tend to be on a line-by-line basis. That is, the budget for a municipality may have a specified authorization for police and fire protection, garbage collection, street paving, and so on. The line-item authorization of governmental budgets significantly limits the amount of discretion management can exercise. The city manager often cannot use savings from one line item, such as street paving, to cover increased spending in another line item, such as snow removal.

REVIEW AND PRACTICE

LEARNING OBJECTIVES REVIEW

1 State the essentials of effective budgeting and the components of the master budget. The primary benefits of budgeting are that it (a) requires management to plan ahead, (b) provides definite objectives for evaluating performance, (c) creates an early warning system for potential problems, (d) facilitates coordination of activities, (e) results in greater management awareness, and (f) motivates personnel to meet planned objectives. The essentials of effective budgeting are (a) sound organizational structure, (b) research and analysis, and (c) acceptance by all levels of management.

The master budget consists of the following budgets: (a) sales, (b) production, (c) direct materials, (d) direct labor, (e) manufacturing overhead, (f) selling and administrative expense, (g) budgeted income statement, (h) capital expenditure budget, (i) cash budget, and (j) budgeted balance sheet.

2 Prepare budgets for sales, production, and direct materials. The sales budget is derived from sales forecasts. The production budget starts with budgeted sales units, adds desired ending finished goods inventory, and subtracts beginning finished goods inventory to arrive at the required number of production units. The direct materials budget starts with the direct materials units (e.g., pounds) required for budgeted production, adds desired ending direct materials units, and subtracts beginning direct materials units to arrive at required direct materials units to be purchased. This amount is multiplied by the direct materials cost (e.g., cost per pound) to arrive at the total cost of direct materials purchases.

3 Prepare budgets for direct labor, manufacturing overhead, and selling and administrative expenses, and a budgeted income statement. The direct labor budget starts with the units to be produced as determined in the production budget. This amount is multiplied by the direct labor hours per unit and the direct labor cost per hour to arrive at the total direct labor cost. The manufacturing overhead budget lists all of the individual types of overhead costs, distinguishing between fixed and variable costs. The selling and administrative expense budget lists all of the individual types of selling and administrative expense items, distinguishing between fixed and variable costs. The budgeted income statement is prepared from the various operating budgets. Cost of goods sold is determined by calculating the budgeted cost to produce one unit, then multiplying this amount by the number of units sold.

4 Prepare a cash budget and a budgeted balance sheet. The cash budget has three sections (receipts, disbursements, and financing) and the beginning and ending cash balances. Receipts and payments sections are determined after preparing separate schedules for collections from customers and payments to suppliers. The budgeted balance sheet is developed from the budgeted balance sheet from the preceding year and the various budgets for the current year.

5 Apply budgeting principles to nonmanufacturing companies. Budgeting may be used by merchandisers for development of a merchandise purchases budget. In service companies, budgeting is a critical factor in coordinating staff needs with anticipated services. In not-for-profit organizations, the starting point in budgeting is usually expenditures, not receipts.

GLOSSARY REVIEW

Budget A formal written statement of management's plans for a specified future time period, expressed in financial terms.

Budgetary slack The amount by which a manager intentionally underestimates budgeted revenues or overestimates budgeted expenses in order to make it easier to achieve budgetary goals.

Budget committee A group responsible for coordinating the preparation of the budget.

Budgeted balance sheet A projection of financial position at the end of the budget period.

Budgeted income statement An estimate of the expected profitability of operations for the budget period.

Cash budget A projection of anticipated cash flows.

Direct labor budget A projection of the quantity and cost of direct labor necessary to meet production requirements.

Direct materials budget An estimate of the quantity and cost of direct materials to be purchased.

Financial budgets Individual budgets that focus primarily on the cash resources needed to fund expected operations and planned capital expenditures.

Long-range planning A formalized process of identifying long-term goals, selecting strategies to achieve those goals, and developing policies and plans to implement the strategies.

Manufacturing overhead budget An estimate of expected manufacturing overhead costs for the budget period.

Master budget A set of interrelated budgets that constitutes a plan of action for a specific time period.

Merchandise purchases budget The estimated cost of goods to be purchased by a merchandiser to meet expected sales.

Operating budgets Individual budgets that result in a budgeted income statement.

Participative budgeting A budgetary approach that starts with input from lower-level managers and works upward so that managers at all levels participate.

Production budget A projection of the units that must be produced to meet anticipated sales.

Sales budget An estimate of expected sales revenue for the budget period.

Sales forecast The projection of potential sales for the industry and the company's expected share of such sales.

Selling and administrative expense budget A projection of anticipated selling and administrative expenses for the budget period.

PRACTICE EXERCISES

Prepare production and direct materials budgets by quarter for 6 months.

(LO 2)

1. On January 1, 2017 the Heche Company budget committee has reached agreement on the following data for the 6 months ending June 30, 2017.

Sales units:	First quarter 5,000; second quarter 6,000; third quarter 7,000
Ending raw materials inventory:	40% of the next quarter's production requirements
Ending finished goods inventory:	30% of the next quarter's expected sales units
Third-quarter 2017 production:	7,500 units

The ending raw materials and finished goods inventories at December 31, 2016, follow the same percentage relationships to production and sales that occur in 2017. Two pounds of raw materials are required to make each unit of finished goods. Raw materials purchased are expected to cost $5 per pound.

Instructions

(a) Prepare a production budget by quarters for the 6-month period ended June 30, 2017.
(b) Prepare a direct materials budget by quarters for the 6-month period ended June 30, 2017.

Solution

1. (a)

Heche Company Production Budget.xls

HECHE COMPANY
Production Budget
For the Six Months Ending June 30, 2017

	Quarter 1	Quarter 2	Six Months
Expected unit sales	5,000	6,000	
Add: Desired ending finished goods units	1,800[(1)]	2,100[(2)]	
Total required units	6,800	8,100	
Less: Beginning finished goods units	1,500[(3)]	1,800	
Required production units	**5,300**	**6,300**	**11,600**

[(1)]30% × 6,000; [(2)]30% × 7,000; [(3)]30% × 5,000

(b)

Heche Company Direct Materials Budget.xls

	A	B	C	D	E	F
1	**HECHE COMPANY**					
2	**Direct Materials Budget**					
3	**For the Six Months Ending June 30, 2017**					
4		Quarter				
5		1		2		Six Months
6	Units to be produced	5,300		6,300		
7	Direct materials per unit	× 2		× 2		
8	Total pounds needed for production	10,600		12,600		
9	Add: Desired ending direct materials (pounds)	5,040[(1)]		6,000[(2)]		
10	Total materials required	15,640		18,600		
11	Less: Beginning direct materials (pounds)	4,240[(3)]		5,040		
12	Direct materials purchase	11,400		13,560		
13	Cost per pound	× $5		× $5		
14	**Total cost of direct materials purchase**	**$57,000**		**$67,800**		**$124,800**
15						
16	(1)40% × 12,600; (2)7,500 × (2 × 40%); (3)40% × 10,600					
17						

Prepare a cash budget for 2 months.

(LO 4)

2. Jake Company expects to have a cash balance of $45,000 on January 1, 2017. Relevant monthly budget data for the first 2 months of 2017 are as follows.

Collections from customers: January $100,000. February $160,000.
Payments for direct materials: January $60,000, February $80,000.
Direct labor: January $30,000, February $45,000. Wages are paid in the month they are incurred.
Manufacturing overhead: January $26,000, February $31,000. These costs include depreciation of $1,000 per month. All other overhead costs are paid as incurred.
Selling and administrative expenses: January $15,000. February $20,000. These costs are exclusive of depreciation. They are paid as incurred.

Sales of marketable securities in January are expected to realize $10,000 in cash. Jake Company has a line of credit at a local bank that enables it to borrow up to $25,000. The company wants to maintain a minimum monthly cash balance of $25,000.

Instructions

Prepare a cash budget for January and February.

Solution

2.

Jake Company Cash Budget.xls

	A	B	C
1	**JAKE COMPANY**		
2	**Cash Budget**		
3	**For the Two Months Ending February 28, 2017**		
4		January	February
5	Beginning cash balance	$ 45,000	$ 25,000
6	Add: Receipts		
7	Collections from customers	100,000	160,000
8	Sale of marketable securities	10,000	0
9	Total receipts	110,000	160,000
10	Total available cash	155,000	185,000
11	Less: Disbursements		
12	Direct materials	60,000	80,000
13	Direct labor	30,000	45,000
14	Manufacturing overhead	25,000	30,000
15	Selling and administrative expenses	15,000	20,000
16	Total disbursements	130,000	175,000
17	Excess (deficiency) of available cash over cash		
18	Disbursements	25,000	10,000
19	Financing		
20	Borrowings	0	15,000
21	Repayments	0	0
22	**Ending cash balance**	$ 25,000	$ 25,000
23			

PRACTICE PROBLEMS

Prepare sales and production budgets. (LO 2)

1. Asheville Company is preparing its master budget for 2017. Relevant data pertaining to its sales and production budgets are as follows.

Sales. Sales for the year are expected to total 2,100,000 units. Quarterly sales, as a percentage of total sales, are 15%, 25%, 35%, and 25%, respectively. The sales price is expected to be $70 per unit for the first three quarters and $75 per unit beginning in the fourth quarter. Sales in the first quarter of 2018 are expected to be 10% higher than the budgeted sales volume for the first quarter of 2017.

Production. Management desires to maintain ending finished goods inventories at 20% of the next quarter's budgeted sales volume.

Instructions

Prepare the sales budget and production budget by quarters for 2017.

Solution

1.

Asheville Company Sales Budget and Production Budget.xls

ASHEVILLE COMPANY
For the Year Ending December 31, 2017
Sales Budget

	Quarter 1	2	3	4	Year
Expected unit sales	315,000	525,000	735,000	525,000	2,100,000
Unit selling price	× $70	× $70	× $70	× $75	
Total sales	$22,050,000	$36,750,000	$51,450,000	$39,375,000	$149,625,000

Production Budget

	1	2	3	4	Year
Expected unit sales	315,000	525,000	735,000	525,000	
Add: Desired ending finished goods units	105,000	147,000	105,000	69,300[a]	
Total required units	420,000	672,000	840,000	594,300	
Less: Beginning finished goods units	63,000[b]	105,000	147,000	105,000	
Required production units	**357,000**	**567,000**	**693,000**	**489,300**	**2,106,300**

[a]Estimated first-quarter 2018 sales volume 315,000 + (315,000 × 10%) = 346,500; 346,500 × 20%

[b]20% of estimated first-quarter 2017 sales units (315,000 × 20%)

Prepare budgeted cost of goods sold, income statement, and balance sheet. (LO 3, 4)

2. Barrett Company has completed all operating budgets other than the income statement for 2017. Selected data from these budgets follow.

Sales: $300,000
Purchases of raw materials: $145,000
Ending inventory of raw materials: $15,000
Direct labor: $40,000
Manufacturing overhead: $73,000, including $3,000 of depreciation expense
Selling and administrative expenses: $36,000 including depreciation expense of $1,000
Interest expense: $1,000
Principal payment on note: $2,000
Dividends declared: $2,000
Income tax rate: 30%

Other information:

Assume that the number of units produced equals the number sold.
Year-end accounts receivable: 4% of 2017 sales.

Year-end accounts payable: 50% of ending inventory of raw materials.
Interest, direct labor, manufacturing overhead, and selling and administrative expenses other than depreciation are paid as incurred.
Dividends declared and income taxes for 2017 will not be paid until 2018.

BARRETT COMPANY
Balance Sheet
December 31, 2016

Assets

Current assets		
Cash		$20,000
Raw materials inventory		10,000
Total current assets		30,000
Property, plant, and equipment		
Equipment	$40,000	
Less: Accumulated depreciation	4,000	36,000
Total assets		$66,000

Liabilities and Stockholders' Equity

Liabilities		
Accounts payable	$ 5,000	
Notes payable	22,000	
Total liabilities		$27,000
Stockholders' equity		
Common stock	25,000	
Retained earnings	14,000	
Total stockholders' equity		39,000
Total liabilities and stockholders' equity		$66,000

Instructions

(a) Calculate budgeted cost of goods sold.

(b) Prepare a budgeted multiple-step income statement for the year ending December 31, 2017.

(c) Prepare a budgeted classified balance sheet as of December 31, 2017.

Solution

2. (a) Beginning raw materials + Purchases − Ending raw materials = Cost of direct materials used ($10,000 + $145,000 − $15,000 = $140,000)
Direct materials used + Direct labor + Manufacturing overhead = Cost of goods sold ($140,000 + $40,000 + $73,000 = $253,000)

(b)

BARRETT COMPANY
Budgeted Income Statement
For the Year Ending December 31, 2017

Sales	$300,000
Cost of goods sold	253,000
Gross profit	47,000
Selling and administrative expenses	36,000
Income from operations	11,000
Interest expense	1,000
Income before income tax expense	10,000
Income tax expense (30%)	3,000
Net income	$ 7,000

(c)

BARRETT COMPANY
Budgeted Balance Sheet
December 31, 2017

Assets

Current assets		
Cash[(1)]		$17,500
Accounts receivable (4% × $300,000)		12,000
Raw materials inventory		15,000
Total current assets		44,500
Property, plant, and equipment		
Equipment	$40,000	
Less: Accumulated depreciation	8,000	32,000
Total assets		$76,500

[(1)]Beginning cash balance		$ 20,000
Add: Collections from customers		
(96% × $300,000 sales)		288,000
Total available cash		308,000
Less: Disbursements		
Direct materials ($5,000 + $145,000 − $7,500)	$142,500	
Direct labor	40,000	
Manufacturing overhead	70,000	
Selling and administrative expenses	35,000	
Total disbursements		287,500
Excess of available cash over cash disbursements		20,500
Financing		
Less: Repayment of principal and interest		3,000
Ending cash balance		$ 17,500

Liabilities and Stockholders' Equity

Liabilities		
Accounts payable (50% × $15,000)	$ 7,500	
Income taxes payable	3,000	
Dividends payable	2,000	
Note payable	20,000	
Total liabilities		$32,500
Stockholders' equity		
Common stock	25,000	
Retained earnings[(2)]	19,000	
Total stockholders' equity		44,000
Total liabilities and stockholders' equity		$76,500

[(2)]Beginning retained earnings + Net income − Dividends declared = Ending retained earnings ($14,000 + $7,000 − $2,000 = $19,000)

EXERCISES

E23-1 Trusler Company has always done some planning for the future, but the company has never prepared a formal budget. Now that the company is growing larger, it is considering preparing a budget.

Explain the concept of budgeting.

(LO 1)

Instructions

Write a memo to Jim Dixon, the president of Trusler Company, in which you define budgeting, identify the budgets that make up the master budget, identify the primary benefits of budgeting, and discuss the essentials of effective budgeting.

Prepare a sales budget for 2 quarters.

(LO 2)

E23-2 Edington Electronics Inc. produces and sells two models of pocket calculators, XQ-103 and XQ-104. The calculators sell for $15 and $25, respectively. Because of the intense competition Edington faces, management budgets sales semiannually. Its projections for the first 2 quarters of 2017 are as follows.

	Unit Sales	
Product	**Quarter 1**	**Quarter 2**
XQ-103	20,000	22,000
XQ-104	12,000	15,000

No changes in selling prices are anticipated.

Instructions

Prepare a sales budget for the 2 quarters ending June 30, 2017. List the products and show for each quarter and for the 6 months, units, selling price, and total sales by product and in total.

Prepare a sales budget for 4 quarters.

(LO 2)

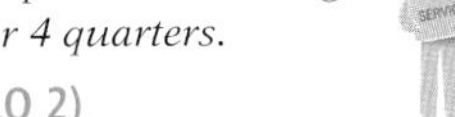

E23-3 Thome and Crede, CPAs, are preparing their service revenue (sales) budget for the coming year (2017). The practice is divided into three departments: auditing, tax, and consulting. Billable hours for each department, by quarter, are as follows.

Department	Quarter 1	Quarter 2	Quarter 3	Quarter 4
Auditing	2,300	1,600	2,000	2,400
Tax	3,000	2,200	2,000	2,500
Consulting	1,500	1,500	1,500	1,500

Average hourly billing rates are auditing $80, tax $90, and consulting $110.

Instructions

Prepare the service revenue (sales) budget for 2017 by listing the departments and showing for each quarter and the year in total, billable hours, billable rate, and total revenue.

Prepare quarterly production budgets.

(LO 2)

E23-4 Turney Company produces and sells automobile batteries, the heavy-duty HD-240. The 2017 sales forecast is as follows.

Quarter	HD-240
1	5,000
2	7,000
3	8,000
4	10,000

The January 1, 2017, inventory of HD-240 is 2,000 units. Management desires an ending inventory each quarter equal to 40% of the next quarter's sales. Sales in the first quarter of 2018 are expected to be 25% higher than sales in the same quarter in 2017.

Instructions

Prepare quarterly production budgets for each quarter and in total for 2017.

Prepare a direct materials purchases budget.

(LO 2)

E23-5 DeWitt Industries has adopted the following production budget for the first 4 months of 2017.

Month	Units	Month	Units
January	10,000	March	5,000
February	8,000	April	4,000

Each unit requires 2 pounds of raw materials costing $3 per pound. On December 31, 2016, the ending raw materials inventory was 4,000 pounds. Management wants to have a raw materials inventory at the end of the month equal to 20% of next month's production requirements.

Instructions

Prepare a direct materials purchases budget by month for the first quarter.

E23-6 On January 1, 2017, the Hardin Company budget committee has reached agreement on the following data for the 6 months ending June 30, 2017.

Prepare production and direct materials budgets by quarters for 6 months.

(LO 2)

Sales units: First quarter 5,000; second quarter 6,000; third quarter 7,000.

Ending raw materials inventory: 40% of the next quarter's production requirements.

Ending finished goods inventory: 25% of the next quarter's expected sales units.

Third-quarter production: 7,200 units.

The ending raw materials and finished goods inventories at December 31, 2016, follow the same percentage relationships to production and sales that occur in 2017. Three pounds of raw materials are required to make each unit of finished goods. Raw materials purchased are expected to cost $4 per pound.

Instructions

(a) Prepare a production budget by quarters for the 6-month period ended June 30, 2017.
(b) Prepare a direct materials budget by quarters for the 6-month period ended June 30, 2017.

E23-7 Rensing Ltd. estimates sales for the second quarter of 2017 will be as follows.

Calculate raw materials purchases in dollars.

(LO 2)

Month	Units
April	2,550
May	2,675
June	2,390

The target ending inventory of finished products is as follows.

March 31	2,000
April 30	2,230
May 31	2,200
June 30	2,310

Two units of material are required for each unit of finished product. Production for July is estimated at 2,700 units to start building inventory for the fall sales period. Rensing's policy is to have an inventory of raw materials at the end of each month equal to 50% of the following month's production requirements.

Raw materials are expected to cost $4 per unit throughout the period.

Instructions

Calculate the May raw materials purchases in dollars.

(CGA adapted)

E23-8 Fuqua Company's sales budget projects unit sales of part 198Z of 10,000 units in January, 12,000 units in February, and 13,000 units in March. Each unit of part 198Z requires 4 pounds of materials, which cost $2 per pound. Fuqua Company desires its ending raw materials inventory to equal 40% of the next month's production requirements, and its ending finished goods inventory to equal 20% of the next month's expected unit sales. These goals were met at December 31, 2016.

Prepare a production and a direct materials budget.

(LO 2)

Instructions

(a) Prepare a production budget for January and February 2017.
(b) Prepare a direct materials budget for January 2017.

E23-9 Rodriguez, Inc., is preparing its direct labor budget for 2017 from the following production budget based on a calendar year.

Prepare a direct labor budget.

(LO 3)

Quarter	Units	Quarter	Units
1	20,000	3	35,000
2	25,000	4	30,000

Each unit requires 1.5 hours of direct labor.

Instructions

Prepare a direct labor budget for 2017. Wage rates are expected to be $16 for the first 2 quarters and $18 for quarters 3 and 4.

E23-10 Lowell Company makes and sells artistic frames for pictures. The controller is responsible for preparing the master budget and has accumulated the following information for 2017.

Prepare production and direct labor budgets.

(LO 2, 3)

	January	February	March	April	May
Estimated unit sales	12,000	14,000	13,000	11,000	11,000
Sales price per unit	$50.00	$47.50	$47.50	$47.50	$47.50
Direct labor hours per unit	2.0	2.0	1.5	1.5	1.5
Wage per direct labor hour	$8.00	$8.00	$8.00	$9.00	$9.00

Lowell has a labor contract that calls for a wage increase to $9.00 per hour on April 1. New labor-saving machinery has been installed and will be fully operational by March 1.

Lowell expects to begin the year with 17,600 frames on hand and has a policy of carrying an end-of-month inventory of 100% of the following month's sales, plus 40% of the second following month's sales.

Instructions
Prepare a production budget and a direct labor budget for Lowell Company by month and for the first quarter of the year. The direct labor budget should include direct labor hours.
(CMA-Canada adapted)

Prepare a manufacturing overhead budget for the year.
(LO 3)

E23-11 Atlanta Company is preparing its manufacturing overhead budget for 2017. Relevant data consist of the following.

Units to be produced (by quarters): 10,000, 12,000, 14,000, 16,000.

Direct labor: time is 1.5 hours per unit.

Variable overhead costs per direct labor hour: indirect materials $0.80; indirect labor $1.20; and maintenance $0.50.

Fixed overhead costs per quarter: supervisory salaries $35,000; depreciation $15,000; and maintenance $12,000.

Instructions
Prepare the manufacturing overhead budget for the year, showing quarterly data.

Prepare a selling and administrative expense budget for 2 quarters.
(LO 3)

E23-12 Kirkland Company combines its operating expenses for budget purposes in a selling and administrative expense budget. For the first 6 months of 2017, the following data are available.

1. Sales: 20,000 units quarter 1; 22,000 units quarter 2.
2. Variable costs per dollar of sales: sales commissions 5%, delivery expense 2%, and advertising 3%.
3. Fixed costs per quarter: sales salaries $12,000, office salaries $8,000, depreciation $4,200, insurance $1,500, utilities $800, and repairs expense $500.
4. Unit selling price: $20.

Instructions
Prepare a selling and administrative expense budget by quarters for the first 6 months of 2017.

Prepare a budgeted income statement for the year.
(LO 3)

E23-13 Fultz Company has accumulated the following budget data for the year 2017.

1. Sales: 30,000 units, unit selling price $85.
2. Cost of one unit of finished goods: direct materials 1 pound at $5 per pound, direct labor 3 hours at $15 per hour, and manufacturing overhead $5 per direct labor hour.
3. Inventories (raw materials only): beginning, 10,000 pounds; ending, 15,000 pounds.
4. Selling and administrative expenses: $170,000; interest expense: $30,000.
5. Income taxes: 30% of income before income taxes.

Instructions
(a) Prepare a schedule showing the computation of cost of goods sold for 2017.
(b) Prepare a budgeted multiple-step income statement for 2017.

Prepare a cash budget for 2 months.
(LO 4)

E23-14 Danner Company expects to have a cash balance of $45,000 on January 1, 2017. Relevant monthly budget data for the first 2 months of 2017 are as follows.

Collections from customers: January $85,000, February $150,000.

Payments for direct materials: January $50,000, February $75,000.

Direct labor: January $30,000, February $45,000. Wages are paid in the month they are incurred.

Manufacturing overhead: January $21,000, February $25,000. These costs include depreciation of $1,500 per month. All other overhead costs are paid as incurred.

Selling and administrative expenses: January $15,000, February $20,000. These costs are exclusive of depreciation. They are paid as incurred.

Sales of marketable securities in January are expected to realize $12,000 in cash. Danner Company has a line of credit at a local bank that enables it to borrow up to $25,000. The company wants to maintain a minimum monthly cash balance of $20,000.

Instructions

Prepare a cash budget for January and February.

Prepare a cash budget.

(LO 4)

E23-15 Deitz Corporation is projecting a cash balance of $30,000 in its December 31, 2016, balance sheet. Deitz's schedule of expected collections from customers for the first quarter of 2017 shows total collections of $185,000. The schedule of expected payments for direct materials for the first quarter of 2017 shows total payments of $43,000. Other information gathered for the first quarter of 2017 is sale of equipment $3,000, direct labor $70,000, manufacturing overhead $35,000, selling and administrative expenses $45,000, and purchase of securities $14,000. Deitz wants to maintain a balance of at least $25,000 cash at the end of each quarter.

Instructions

Prepare a cash budget for the first quarter.

Prepare cash budget for a month.

(LO 4)

E23-16 The controller of Trenshaw Company wants to improve the company's control system by preparing a month-by-month cash budget. The following information is for the month ending July 31, 2017.

June 30, 2017, cash balance	$45,000
Dividends to be declared on July 15*	12,000
Cash expenditures to be paid in July for operating expenses	40,800
Amortization expense in July	4,500
Cash collections to be received in July	90,000
Merchandise purchases to be paid in cash in July	56,200
Equipment to be purchased for cash in July	20,000

*Dividends are payable 30 days after declaration to shareholders of record on the declaration date.

Trenshaw Company wants to keep a minimum cash balance of $25,000.

Instructions

(a) Prepare a cash budget for the month ended July 31, 2017, and indicate how much money, if any, Trenshaw Company will need to borrow to meet its minimum cash requirement.

(b) Explain how cash budgeting can reduce the cost of short-term borrowing.

(CGA adapted)

Prepare schedules of expected collections and payments.

(LO 4)

E23-17 Nieto Company's budgeted sales and direct materials purchases are as follows.

	Budgeted Sales	Budgeted D.M. Purchases
January	$200,000	$30,000
February	220,000	36,000
March	250,000	38,000

Nieto's sales are 30% cash and 70% credit. Credit sales are collected 10% in the month of sale, 50% in the month following sale, and 36% in the second month following sale; 4% are uncollectible. Nieto's purchases are 50% cash and 50% on account. Purchases on account are paid 40% in the month of purchase, and 60% in the month following purchase.

Instructions

(a) Prepare a schedule of expected collections from customers for March.

(b) Prepare a schedule of expected payments for direct materials for March.

Prepare schedules for cash receipts and cash payments, and determine ending balances for balance sheet.

(LO 4)

E23-18 Green Landscaping Inc. is preparing its budget for the first quarter of 2017. The next step in the budgeting process is to prepare a cash receipts schedule and a cash payments schedule. To that end the following information has been collected.

Clients usually pay 60% of their fee in the month that service is performed, 30% the month after, and 10% the second month after receiving service.

Actual service revenue for 2016 and expected service revenues for 2017 are November 2016, $80,000; December 2016, $90,000; January 2017, $100,000; February 2017, $120,000; and March 2017, $140,000.

Purchases of landscaping supplies (direct materials) are paid 60% in the month of purchase and 40% the following month. Actual purchases for 2016 and expected purchases for 2017 are December 2016, $14,000; January 2017, $12,000; February 2017, $15,000; and March 2017, $18,000.

Instructions

(a) Prepare the following schedules for each month in the first quarter of 2017 and for the quarter in total:
  (1) Expected collections from clients.
  (2) Expected payments for landscaping supplies.
(b) Determine the following balances at March 31, 2017:
  (1) Accounts receivable.
  (2) Accounts payable.

Prepare a cash budget for 2 quarters.

(LO 4, 5)

E23-19 Pletcher Dental Clinic is a medium-sized dental service specializing in family dental care. The clinic is currently preparing the master budget for the first 2 quarters of 2017. All that remains in this process is the cash budget. The following information has been collected from other portions of the master budget and elsewhere.

Beginning cash balance	$ 30,000
Required minimum cash balance	25,000
Payment of income taxes (2nd quarter)	4,000
Professional salaries:	
1st quarter	140,000
2nd quarter	140,000
Interest from investments (2nd quarter)	7,000
Overhead costs:	
1st quarter	77,000
2nd quarter	100,000
Selling and administrative costs, including $2,000 depreciation:	
1st quarter	50,000
2nd quarter	70,000
Purchase of equipment (2nd quarter)	50,000
Sale of equipment (1st quarter)	12,000
Collections from patients:	
1st quarter	235,000
2nd quarter	380,000
Interest payments (2nd quarter)	200

Instructions

Prepare a cash budget for each of the first two quarters of 2017.

Prepare a purchases budget and budgeted income statement for a merchandiser.

(LO 5)

E23-20 In May 2017, the budget committee of Grand Stores assembles the following data in preparation of budgeted merchandise purchases for the month of June.

1. Expected sales: June $500,000, July $600,000.
2. Cost of goods sold is expected to be 75% of sales.
3. Desired ending merchandise inventory is 30% of the following (next) month's cost of goods sold.
4. The beginning inventory at June 1 will be the desired amount.

Instructions

(a) Compute the budgeted merchandise purchases for June.
(b) Prepare the budgeted multiple-step income statement for June through gross profit.

E23-21 Emeric and Ellie's Painting Service estimates that it will paint 10 small homes, 5 medium homes, and 2 large homes during the month of June 2017. The company estimates its direct labor needs as 40 hours per small home, 70 hours for a medium home, and 120 hours for a large home. Its average cost for direct labor is $18 per hour.

Prepare a direct labor budget for a service company.

(LO 5)

Instructions

Prepare a direct labor budget for Emeric and Ellie's Painting Service for June 2017.

PROBLEMS

P23-1A Cook Farm Supply Company manufactures and sells a pesticide called Snare. The following data are available for preparing budgets for Snare for the first 2 quarters of 2017.

Prepare budgeted income statement and supporting budgets.

(LO 2, 3)

XLS

1. Sales: quarter 1, 40,000 bags; quarter 2, 56,000 bags. Selling price is $60 per bag.
2. Direct materials: each bag of Snare requires 4 pounds of Gumm at a cost of $3.80 per pound and 6 pounds of Tarr at $1.50 per pound.
3. Desired inventory levels:

Type of Inventory	January 1	April 1	July 1
Snare (bags)	8,000	15,000	18,000
Gumm (pounds)	9,000	10,000	13,000
Tarr (pounds)	14,000	20,000	25,000

4. Direct labor: direct labor time is 15 minutes per bag at an hourly rate of $16 per hour.
5. Selling and administrative expenses are expected to be 15% of sales plus $175,000 per quarter.
6. Interest expense is $100,000.
7. Income taxes are expected to be 30% of income before income taxes.

Your assistant has prepared two budgets: (1) the manufacturing overhead budget shows expected costs to be 125% of direct labor cost, and (2) the direct materials budget for Tarr shows the cost of Tarr purchases to be $297,000 in quarter 1 and $439,500 in quarter 2.

Instructions

Prepare the budgeted multiple-step income statement for the first 6 months and all required operating budgets by quarters. (*Note:* Use variable and fixed in the selling and administrative expense budget.) Do not prepare the manufacturing overhead budget or the direct materials budget for Tarr.

Net income $881,160
Cost per bag $33.20

P23-2A Deleon Inc. is preparing its annual budgets for the year ending December 31, 2017. Accounting assistants furnish the data shown below.

Prepare sales, production, direct materials, direct labor, and income statement budgets.

(LO 2, 3)

	Product JB 50	Product JB 60
Sales budget:		
Anticipated volume in units	400,000	200,000
Unit selling price	$20	$25
Production budget:		
Desired ending finished goods units	30,000	15,000
Beginning finished goods units	25,000	10,000
Direct materials budget:		
Direct materials per unit (pounds)	2	3
Desired ending direct materials pounds	30,000	10,000
Beginning direct materials pounds	40,000	15,000
Cost per pound	$3	$4
Direct labor budget:		
Direct labor time per unit	0.4	0.6
Direct labor rate per hour	$12	$12
Budgeted income statement:		
Total unit cost	$13	$20

An accounting assistant has prepared the detailed manufacturing overhead budget and the selling and administrative expense budget. The latter shows selling expenses of

(a) Total sales $13,000,000
(b) Required production units: JB 50, 405,000 JB 60, 205,000
(c) Total cost of direct materials purchases $4,840,000
(d) Total direct labor cost $3,420,000
(e) Net income $1,295,000

$560,000 for product JB 50 and $360,000 for product JB 60, and administrative expenses of $540,000 for product JB 50 and $340,000 for product JB 60. Interest expense is $150,000 (not allocated to products). Income taxes are expected to be 30%.

Instructions

Prepare the following budgets for the year. Show data for each product. Quarterly budgets should not be prepared.

(a) Sales.
(b) Production.
(c) Direct materials.
(d) Direct labor.
(e) Multiple-step income statement (*Note:* income taxes are not allocated to the products).

Prepare sales and production budgets and compute cost per unit under two plans.

(LO 2)

P23-3A Hill Industries had sales in 2016 of $6,800,000 and gross profit of $1,100,000. Management is considering two alternative budget plans to increase its gross profit in 2017.

Plan A would increase the selling price per unit from $8.00 to $8.40. Sales volume would decrease by 10% from its 2016 level. Plan B would decrease the selling price per unit by $0.50. The marketing department expects that the sales volume would increase by 100,000 units.

At the end of 2016, Hill has 40,000 units of inventory on hand. If Plan A is accepted, the 2017 ending inventory should be equal to 5% of the 2017 sales. If Plan B is accepted, the ending inventory should be equal to 60,000 units. Each unit produced will cost $1.80 in direct labor, $1.40 in direct materials, and $1.20 in variable overhead. The fixed overhead for 2017 should be $1,895,000.

(c) Unit cost: Plan A $6.88 Plan B $6.35
(d) Gross profit: Plan A $1,162,800 Plan B $1,092,500

Instructions

(a) Prepare a sales budget for 2017 under each plan.
(b) Prepare a production budget for 2017 under each plan.
(c) Compute the production cost per unit under each plan. Why is the cost per unit different for each of the two plans? (Round to two decimals.)
(d) Which plan should be accepted? (*Hint:* Compute the gross profit under each plan.)

Prepare cash budget for 2 months.

(LO 4)

P23-4A Colter Company prepares monthly cash budgets. Relevant data from operating budgets for 2017 are as follows.

	January	February
Sales	$360,000	$400,000
Direct materials purchases	120,000	125,000
Direct labor	90,000	100,000
Manufacturing overhead	70,000	75,000
Selling and administrative expenses	79,000	85,000

All sales are on account. Collections are expected to be 50% in the month of sale, 30% in the first month following the sale, and 20% in the second month following the sale. Sixty percent (60%) of direct materials purchases are paid in cash in the month of purchase, and the balance due is paid in the month following the purchase. All other items above are paid in the month incurred except for selling and administrative expenses that include $1,000 of depreciation per month.

Other data:

1. Credit sales: November 2016, $250,000; December 2016, $320,000.
2. Purchases of direct materials: December 2016, $100,000.
3. Other receipts: January—collection of December 31, 2016, notes receivable $15,000; February—proceeds from sale of securities $6,000.
4. Other disbursements: February—payment of $6,000 cash dividend.

The company's cash balance on January 1, 2017, is expected to be $60,000. The company wants to maintain a minimum cash balance of $50,000.

(a) January: collections $326,000 payments $112,000
(b) Ending cash balance: January $51,000 February $50,000

Instructions

(a) Prepare schedules for (1) expected collections from customers and (2) expected payments for direct materials purchases for January and February.
(b) Prepare a cash budget for January and February in columnar form.

P23-5A The budget committee of Suppar Company collects the following data for its San Miguel Store in preparing budgeted income statements for May and June 2017.

Prepare purchases and income statement budgets for a merchandiser.

(LO 5)

1. Sales for May are expected to be $800,000. Sales in June and July are expected to be 5% higher than the preceding month.
2. Cost of goods sold is expected to be 75% of sales.
3. Company policy is to maintain ending merchandise inventory at 10% of the following month's cost of goods sold.
4. Operating expenses are estimated to be as follows:

Sales salaries	$35,000 per month
Advertising	6% of monthly sales
Delivery expense	2% of monthly sales
Sales commissions	5% of monthly sales
Rent expense	$5,000 per month
Depreciation	$800 per month
Utilities	$600 per month
Insurance	$500 per month

5. Interest expense is $2,000 per month. Income taxes are estimated to be 30% of income before income taxes.

Instructions

(a) Prepare the merchandise purchases budget for each month in columnar form.
(b) Prepare budgeted multiple-step income statements for each month in columnar form. Show in the statements the details of cost of goods sold.

(a) Purchases:
May $603,000
June $633,150
(b) Net income:
May $36,470
June $39,830

P23-6A Krause Industries' balance sheet at December 31, 2016, is presented below.

Prepare budgeted cost of goods sold, income statement, retained earnings, and balance sheet.

(LO 3, 4)

KRAUSE INDUSTRIES
Balance Sheet
December 31, 2016

Assets

Current assets		
Cash		$ 7,500
Accounts receivable		73,500
Finished goods inventory (1,500 units)		24,000
Total current assets		105,000
Property, plant, and equipment		
Equipment	$40,000	
Less: Accumulated depredation	10,000	30,000
Total assets		$135,000

Liabilities and Stockholders' Equity

Liabilities		
Notes payable		$ 25,000
Accounts payable		45,000
Total liabilities		70,000
Stockholders' equity		
Common stock	$40,000	
Retained earnings	25,000	
Total stockholders' equity		65,000
Total liabilities and stockholders' equity		$135,000

Budgeted data for the year 2017 include the following.

	2017	
	Quarter 4	Total
Sales budget (8,000 units at $32)	$76,800	$256,000
Direct materials used	17,000	62,500
Direct labor	12,500	50,900
Manufacturing overhead applied	10,000	48,600
Selling and administrative expenses	18,000	75,000

To meet sales requirements and to have 2,500 units of finished goods on hand at December 31, 2017, the production budget shows 9,000 required units of output. The total unit cost of production is expected to be $18. Krause uses the first-in, first-out (FIFO) inventory costing method. Interest expense is expected to be $3,500 for the year. Income taxes are expected to be 40% of income before income taxes. In 2017, the company expects to declare and pay an $8,000 cash dividend.

The company's cash budget shows an expected cash balance of $5,880 at December 31, 2017. All sales and purchases are on account. It is expected that 60% of quarterly sales are collected in cash within the quarter and the remainder is collected in the following quarter. Direct materials purchased from suppliers are paid 50% in the quarter incurred and the remainder in the following quarter. Purchases in the fourth quarter were the same as the materials used. In 2017, the company expects to purchase additional equipment costing $9,000. $4,000 of depreciation expense on equipment is included in the budget data and split equally between manufacturing overhead and selling and administrative expenses. Krause expects to pay $8,000 on the outstanding notes payable balance plus all interest due and payable to December 31 (included in interest expense $3,500, above). Accounts payable at December 31, 2017, includes amounts due suppliers (see above) plus other accounts payable of $7,200. Unpaid income taxes at December 31 will be $5,000.

Instructions

Net income $21,900
Total assets $116,600

Prepare a budgeted statement of cost of goods sold, budgeted multiple-step income statement and retained earnings statement for 2017, and a budgeted classified balance sheet at December 31, 2017.

COMPREHENSIVE CASE

Sweats Galore is a new business venture that will make custom sweatshirts using a silk-screen process. In helping the company's owner, Michael Woods, set up his business, you will have the opportunity to apply your understanding of CVP relationships (Chapter 22) and budgetary planning (Chapter 23).

Go to the book's companion website, at **www.wiley.com/college/weygandt**, *for complete case details and instructions.*

BROADENING YOUR PERSPECTIVE

MANAGEMENT DECISION-MAKING

Decision-Making Across the Organization

BYP23-1 Palmer Corporation operates on a calendar-year basis. It begins the annual budgeting process in late August when the president establishes targets for the total dollar sales and net income before taxes for the next year.

The sales target is given first to the marketing department. The marketing manager formulates a sales budget by product line in both units and dollars. From this budget, sales quotas by product line in units and dollars are established for each of the corporation's sales districts. The marketing manager also estimates the cost of the marketing activities required to support the target sales volume and prepares a tentative marketing expense budget.

The executive vice president uses the sales and profit targets, the sales budget by product line, and the tentative marketing expense budget to determine the dollar amounts that can be devoted to manufacturing and corporate office expense. The executive vice president prepares the budget for corporate expenses. She then forwards to the production department the product-line sales budget in units and the total dollar amount that can be devoted to manufacturing.

The production manager meets with the factory managers to develop a manufacturing plan that will produce the required units when needed within the cost constraints set by the executive vice president. The budgeting process usually comes to a halt at this point because the production department does not consider the financial resources allocated to be adequate.

When this standstill occurs, the vice president of finance, the executive vice president, the marketing manager, and the production manager meet together to determine the final budgets for each of the areas. This normally results in a modest increase in the total amount available for manufacturing costs and cuts in the marketing expense and corporate office expense budgets. The total sales and net income figures proposed by the president are seldom changed. Although the participants are seldom pleased with the compromise, these budgets are final. Each executive then develops a new detailed budget for the operations in his or her area.

None of the areas has achieved its budget in recent years. Sales often run below the target. When budgeted sales are not achieved, each area is expected to cut costs so that the president's profit target can be met. However, the profit target is seldom met because costs are not cut enough. In fact, costs often run above the original budget in all functional areas (marketing, production, and corporate office).

The president is disturbed that Palmer has not been able to meet the sales and profit targets. He hired a consultant with considerable experience with companies in Palmer's industry. The consultant reviewed the budgets for the past 4 years. He concluded that the product line sales budgets were reasonable and that the cost and expense budgets were adequate for the budgeted sales and production levels.

Instructions

With the class divided into groups, answer the following.

(a) Discuss how the budgeting process employed by Palmer Corporation contributes to the failure to achieve the president's sales and profit targets.
(b) Suggest how Palmer Corporation's budgeting process could be revised to correct the problems.
(c) Should the functional areas be expected to cut their costs when sales volume falls below budget? Explain your answer.

(CMA adapted)

Managerial Analysis

BYP23-2 Elliot & Hesse Inc. manufactures ergonomic devices for computer users. Some of its more popular products include anti-glare filters and privacy filters (for computer monitors) and keyboard stands with wrist rests. Over the past 5 years, it experienced rapid growth, with sales of all products increasing 20% to 50% each year.

Last year, some of the primary manufacturers of computers began introducing new products with some of the ergonomic designs, such as anti-glare filters and wrist rests, already built in. As a result, sales of Elliot & Hesse's accessory devices have declined somewhat. The company believes that the privacy filters will probably continue to show growth, but that the other products will probably continue to decline. When the next year's budget was prepared, increases were built into research and development so that replacement products could be developed or the company could expand into some other product line. Some product lines being considered are general-purpose ergonomic devices including back supports, foot rests, and sloped writing pads.

The most recent results have shown that sales decreased more than was expected for the anti-glare filters. As a result, the company may have a shortage of funds. Top management has therefore asked that all expenses be reduced 10% to compensate for these reduced sales. Summary budget information is as follows.

Direct materials	$240,000
Direct labor	110,000
Insurance	50,000
Depreciation	90,000
Machine repairs	30,000
Sales salaries	50,000
Office salaries	80,000
Factory salaries (indirect labor)	50,000
Total	$700,000

Instructions

Using the information above, answer the following questions.

(a) What are the implications of reducing each of the costs? For example, if the company reduces direct materials costs, it may have to do so by purchasing lower-quality materials. This may affect sales in the long run.
(b) Based on your analysis in (a), what do you think is the best way to obtain the $70,000 in cost savings requested? Be specific. Are there any costs that cannot or should not be reduced? Why?

Real-World Focus

BYP23-3 Information regarding many approaches to budgeting can be found online. The following activity investigates the merits of "zero-based" budgeting, as discussed by Michael LaFaive, Director of Fiscal Policy of the Mackinac Center for Public Policy.

Address: **www.mackinac.org/5928**, or go to **www.wiley.com/college/weygandt**

Instructions

Read the article at the website and answer the following questions.

(a) How does zero-based budgeting differ from standard budgeting procedures?
(b) What are some potential advantages of zero-based budgeting?
(c) What are some potential disadvantages of zero-based budgeting?
(d) How often do departments in Oklahoma undergo zero-based budgeting?

CRITICAL THINKING

Communication Activity

BYP23-4 In order to better serve their rural patients, Drs. Joe and Rick Parcells (brothers) began giving safety seminars. Especially popular were their "emergency-preparedness" talks given to farmers. Many people asked whether the "kit" of materials the doctors recommended for common farm emergencies was commercially available.

After checking with several suppliers, the doctors realized that no other company offered the supplies they recommended in their seminars, packaged in the way they described. Their wives, Megan and Sue, agreed to make a test package by ordering supplies from various medical supply companies and assembling them into a "kit" that could be sold at the seminars. When these kits proved a runaway success, the sisters-in-law decided to market them. At the advice of their accountant, they organized this venture as a separate company, called Life Protection Products (LPP), with Megan Parcells as CEO and Sue Parcells as Secretary-Treasurer.

LPP soon started receiving requests for the kits from all over the country, as word spread about their availability. Even without advertising, LPP was able to sell its full inventory every month. However, the company was becoming financially strained. Megan and Sue had about $100,000 in savings, and they invested about half that amount initially. They believed that this venture would allow them to make money. However, at the present time, only about $30,000 of the cash remains, and the company is constantly short of cash.

Megan has come to you for advice. She does not understand why the company is having cash flow problems. She and Sue have not even been withdrawing salaries. However, they have rented a local building and have hired two more full-time workers to help them cope with the increasing demand. They do not think they could handle the demand without this additional help.

Megan is also worried that the cash problems mean that the company may not be able to support itself. She has prepared the cash budget shown below. All seminar customers pay for their products in full at the time of purchase. In addition, several large companies have ordered the kits for use by employees who work in remote sites. They have requested credit terms and have been allowed to pay in the month following the sale. These large purchasers amount to about 25% of the sales at the present time. LPP purchases the materials for the kits about 2 months ahead of time. Megan and Sue are considering slowing the growth of the company by simply purchasing less materials, which will mean selling fewer kits.

The workers are paid weekly. Megan and Sue need about $15,000 cash on hand at the beginning of the month to pay for purchases of raw materials. Right now they have been using cash from their savings, but as noted, only $30,000 is left.

LIFE PROTECTION PRODUCTS
Cash Budget
For the Quarter Ending June 30, 2017

	April	**May**	**June**
Cash balance, beginning	$15,000	$15,000	$15,000
Cash received			
From prior month sales	5,000	7,500	12,500
From current sales	15,000	22,500	37,500
Total cash on hand	35,000	45,000	65,000

	April	May	June
Cash payments			
To employees	3,000	3,000	3,000
For products	25,000	35,000	45,000
Miscellaneous expenses	5,000	6,000	7,000
Postage	1,000	1,000	1,000
Total cash payments	34,000	45,000	56,000
Cash balance	$ 1,000	$ 0	$ 9,000
Borrow from savings	$14,000	$15,000	$ 1,000
Borrow from bank?	$ 0	$ 0	$ 5,000

Instructions

Write a response to Megan Parcells. Explain why LPP is short of cash. Will this company be able to support itself? Explain your answer. Make any recommendations you deem appropriate.

Ethics Case

BYP23-5 You are an accountant in the budgetary, projections, and special projects department of Fernetti Conductor, Inc., a large manufacturing company. The president, Richard Brown, asks you on very short notice to prepare some sales and income projections covering the next 2 years of the company's much heralded new product lines. He wants these projections for a series of speeches he is making while on a 2-week trip to eight East Coast brokerage firms. The president hopes to bolster Fernetti's stock sales and price.

You work 23 hours in 2 days to compile the projections, hand-deliver them to the president, and are swiftly but graciously thanked as he departs. A week later, you find time to go over some of your computations and discover a miscalculation that makes the projections grossly overstated. You quickly inquire about the president's itinerary and learn that he has made half of his speeches and has half yet to make. You are in a quandary as to what to do.

Instructions

(a) What are the consequences of telling the president of your gross miscalculations?
(b) What are the consequences of not telling the president of your gross miscalculations?
(c) What are the ethical considerations to you and the president in this situation?

All About You

BYP23-6 In order to get your personal finances under control, you need to prepare a personal budget. Assume that you have compiled the following information regarding your expected cash flows for a typical month.

Rent payment	$ 500	Miscellaneous costs	$210
Interest income	50	Savings	50
Income tax withheld	300	Eating out	150
Electricity bill	85	Telephone and Internet costs	125
Groceries	100	Student loan payments	375
Wages earned	2,500	Entertainment costs	250
Insurance	100	Transportation costs	150

Instructions

Using the information above, prepare a personal budget. In preparing this budget, use the format found at *http://financialplan.about.com/cs/budgeting/l/blbudget.htm.* Just skip any unused line items.

Considering Your Costs and Benefits

BYP23-7 You might hear people say that they "need to learn to live within a budget." The funny thing is that most people who say this haven't actually prepared a personal budget, nor do they intend to. Instead, what they are referring to is a vaguely defined, poorly specified collection of rough ideas of how much they should spend on various aspects of their lives. However, you can't live within or even outside of something that doesn't exist. With that in mind, let's take a look at one aspect of personal-budget templates.

Many personal-budget worksheet templates that are provided for college students treat student loans as an income source. See, for example, the template provided at *http://financialplan.about.com/cs/budgeting/l/blmocolbud.htm*. Based on your knowledge of accounting, is this correct?

YES: Student loans provide a source of cash, which can be used to pay costs. As the saying goes, "It all spends the same." Therefore, student loans are income.
NO: Student loans must eventually be repaid; therefore, they are not income. As the name suggests, they are loans.

Instructions
Write a response indicating your position regarding this situation. Provide support for your view.

Chapter 24 Budgetary Control and Responsibility Accounting

Perhaps no place in the world has a wider variety of distinctive, high-end accommodations than New York City. It's tough to set yourself apart in the Big Apple, but unique is what the Tribeca Grand Hotel is all about.

When you walk through the doors of this triangular-shaped building, nestled in one of Manhattan's most affluent neighborhoods, you immediately encounter a striking eight-story atrium. Although the hotel was completely renovated, it still maintains its funky mid-century charm. Just consider the always hip Church Bar. Besides serving up cocktails until 2 a.m., Church's also provides food. These are not the run-of-the-mill, chain hotel, borderline edibles. Church's chef is famous for tantalizing delectables such as duck rillettes, sea salt baked branzino, housemade pappardelle, and pumpkin madeleines.

Another thing that really sets the Tribeca Grand apart is its private screening room. As a guest, you can enjoy plush leather seating, state-of-the-art projection, and digital surround sound, all while viewing a cult classic from the hotel's film series. In fact, on Sundays, free screenings are available to guests and non-guests alike on a first-come-first-served basis.

To attract and satisfy a discerning clientele, the Tribeca Grand's management incurs higher and more unpredictable costs than those of your standard hotel. As fun as it might be to run a high-end hotel, management can't be cavalier about spending money. To maintain profitability, management closely monitors costs and revenues to make sure that they track with budgeted amounts. Further, because of unexpected fluctuations (think Hurricane Sandy or a bitterly cold stretch of winter weather), management must sometimes revise forecasts and budgets and adapt quickly. To evaluate performance when things happen that are beyond management's control, the budget needs to be flexible.

LEARNING OBJECTIVES

1. **Describe budgetary control and static budget reports.**
2. **Prepare flexible budget reports.**
3. **Apply responsibility accounting to cost and profit centers.**
4. **Evaluate performance in investment centers.**

Describe budgetary control and static budget reports.

Budgetary Control

One of management's functions is to control company operations. Control consists of the steps taken by management to see that planned objectives are met. We now ask: How do budgets contribute to control of operations?

The use of budgets in controlling operations is known as **budgetary control**. Such control takes place by means of **budget reports** that compare actual results with planned objectives. The use of budget reports is based on the belief that planned objectives lose much of their potential value without some monitoring of progress along the way. Just as your professors give midterm exams to evaluate your progress, top management requires periodic reports on the progress of department managers toward their planned objectives.

Budget reports provide management with feedback on operations. The feedback for a crucial objective, such as having enough cash on hand to pay bills, may be made daily. For other objectives, such as meeting budgeted annual sales and operating expenses, monthly budget reports may suffice. Budget reports are prepared as frequently as needed. From these reports, management analyzes any differences between actual and planned results and determines their causes. Management then takes corrective action, or it decides to modify future plans. Budgetary control involves the activities shown in Illustration 24-1.

Illustration 24-1
Budgetary control activities

Budgetary control works best when a company has a formalized reporting system. The system does the following:

1. Identifies the name of the budget report, such as the sales budget or the manufacturing overhead budget.
2. States the frequency of the report, such as weekly or monthly.
3. Specifies the purpose of the report.
4. Indicates the primary recipient(s) of the report.

Illustration 24-2 provides a partial budgetary control system for a manufacturing company. Note the frequency of the reports and their emphasis on control. For example, there is a daily report on scrap and a weekly report on labor.

Name of Report	Frequency	Purpose	Primary Recipient(s)
Sales	Weekly	Determine whether sales goals are met	Top management and sales manager
Labor	Weekly	Control direct and indirect labor costs	Vice president of production and production department managers
Scrap	Daily	Determine efficient use of materials	Production manager
Departmental overhead costs	Monthly	Control overhead costs	Department manager
Selling expenses	Monthly	Control selling expenses	Sales manager
Income statement	Monthly and quarterly	Determine whether income goals are met	Top management

Illustration 24-2
Budgetary control reporting system

Static Budget Reports

You learned in Chapter 23 that the master budget formalizes management's planned objectives for the coming year. When used in budgetary control, each budget included in the master budget is considered to be static. A **static budget** is a projection of budget data **at one level of activity**. These budgets do not consider data for different levels of activity. As a result, companies always compare actual results with budget data at the activity level that was used in developing the master budget.

EXAMPLES

To illustrate the role of a static budget in budgetary control, we will use selected data prepared for Hayes Company in Chapter 23. Budget and actual sales data for the Rightride product in the first and second quarters of 2017 are as follows.

Illustration 24-3
Budget and actual sales data

Sales	First Quarter	Second Quarter	Total
Budgeted	$180,000	$210,000	$390,000
Actual	179,000	199,500	378,500
Difference	$ 1,000	$ 10,500	$ 11,500

The sales budget report for Hayes' first quarter is shown below. The rightmost column reports the difference between the budgeted and actual amounts.

Illustration 24-4
Sales budget report—first quarter

Hayes Company Sales Budget Report.xls

HAYES COMPANY
Sales Budget Report
For the Quarter Ended March 31, 2017

Product Line	Budget	Actual	Difference Favorable F Unfavorable U
Rightride[a]	$180,000	$179,000	**$1,000 U**

[a]In practice, each product line would be included in the report.

The report shows that sales are $1,000 under budget—an unfavorable result. This difference is less than 1% of budgeted sales ($1,000 ÷ $180,000 = 0.0056). Top management's reaction to unfavorable differences is often influenced by the materiality (significance) of the difference. Since the difference of $1,000 is immaterial in this case, we assume that Hayes management takes no specific corrective action.

Terminology
The difference between budget and actual is sometimes called a *budget variance*.

Illustration 24-5 shows the budget report for the second quarter. It contains one new feature: cumulative year-to-date information. This report indicates that sales for the second quarter are $10,500 below budget. This is 5% of budgeted sales ($10,500 ÷ $210,000). Top management may now conclude that the difference between budgeted and actual sales requires investigation.

Hayes Company Sales Budget Report.xls

	A	B	C	D	E	F	G	H
1				HAYES COMPANY				
2				Sales Budget Report				
3				For the Quarter Ended June 30, 2017				
4			Second Quarter				Year-to-Date	
5				Difference				Difference
6				Favorable F				Favorable F
7	Product Line	Budget	Actual	Unfavorable U		Budget	Actual	Unfavorable U
8	Rightride	$210,000	$199,500	$10,500 U		$390,000	$378,500	$11,500 U
9								

Illustration 24-5
Sales budget report—second quarter

Management's analysis should start by asking the sales manager the cause(s) of the shortfall. Managers should consider the need for corrective action. For example, management may decide to spur sales by offering sales incentives to customers or by increasing the advertising of Rightrides. Or, if management concludes that a downturn in the economy is responsible for the lower sales, it may modify planned sales and profit goals for the remainder of the year.

USES AND LIMITATIONS

From these examples, you can see that a master sales budget is useful in evaluating the performance of a sales manager. It is now necessary to ask: Is the master budget appropriate for evaluating a manager's performance in controlling costs? Recall that in a static budget, data are not modified or adjusted, regardless of changes in activity. It follows, then, that a static budget is appropriate in evaluating a manager's effectiveness in controlling costs when:

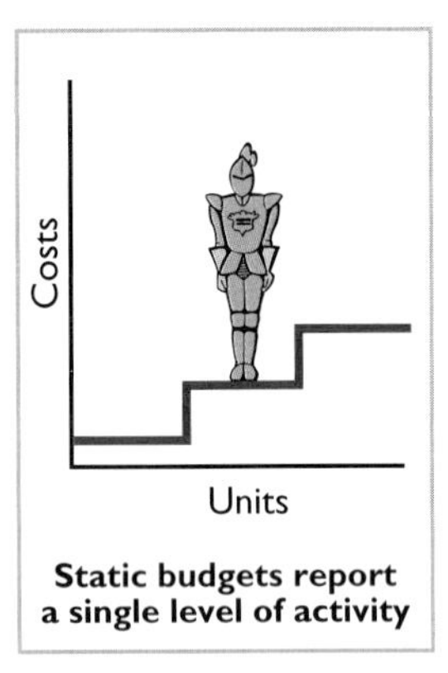

Static budgets report a single level of activity

1. The actual level of activity closely approximates the master budget activity level, and/or
2. The behavior of the costs in response to changes in activity is fixed.

A static budget report is, therefore, appropriate for **fixed manufacturing costs** and for **fixed selling and administrative expenses**. But, as you will see shortly, static budget reports may not be a proper basis for evaluating a manager's performance in controlling variable costs.

LEARNING OBJECTIVE 2

Prepare flexible budget reports.

In contrast to a static budget, which is based on one level of activity, a **flexible budget** projects budget data for various levels of activity. In essence, **the flexible budget is a series of static budgets at different levels of activity**. The flexible budget recognizes that the budgetary process is more useful if it is adaptable to changed operating conditions.

Flexible budgets can be prepared for each of the types of budgets included in the master budget. For example, **Marriott Hotels** can budget revenues and net income on the basis of 60%, 80%, and 100% of room occupancy. Similarly, **American Van Lines** can budget its operating expenses on the basis of various levels of truck-miles driven. **Duke Energy** can budget revenue and net income on the basis of estimated billions of kwh (kilowatt hours) of residential, commercial, and industrial electricity generated. In the following pages, we will illustrate a flexible budget for manufacturing overhead.

Costs

Units

Flexible budgets are static budgets at different activity levels

Why Flexible Budgets?

Assume that you are the manager in charge of manufacturing overhead in the Assembly Department of Barton Robotics. In preparing the manufacturing overhead budget for 2017, you prepare the following static budget based on a production volume of 10,000 units of robotic controls.

Barton Robotics.xls

	A	B
1	**BARTON ROBOTICS**	
2	**Manufacturing Overhead Budget (Static)**	
3	**Assembly Department**	
4	**For the Year Ended December 31, 2017**	
5	Budgeted production in units (robotic controls)	10,000
6		
7	Budgeted costs	
8	Indirect materials	$ 250,000
9	Indirect labor	260,000
10	Utilities	190,000
11	Depreciation	280,000
12	Property taxes	70,000
13	Supervision	50,000
14		**$1,100,000**
15		

Illustration 24-6
Static overhead budget

Fortunately for the company, the demand for robotic controls has increased, and Barton produces and sells 12,000 units during the year rather than 10,000. You are elated! Increased sales means increased profitability, which should mean a bonus or a raise for you and the employees in your department. Unfortunately,

Illustration 24-7
Overhead static budget report

Barton Robotics.xls

	A	B	C	D	E
1	**BARTON ROBOTICS**				
2	**Manufacturing Overhead Static Budget Report**				
3	**For the Year Ended December 31, 2017**				
4				Difference	
5		Budget	Actual	Favorable - F Unfavorable - U	
6	Production in units	10,000	12,000		
7					
8	Costs				
9	Indirect materials	$ 250,000	$ 295,000	**$ 45,000**	U
10	Indirect labor	260,000	312,000	**52,000**	U
11	Utilities	190,000	225,000	**35,000**	U
12	Depreciation	280,000	280,000	**0**	
13	Property taxes	70,000	70,000	**0**	
14	Supervision	50,000	50,000	**0**	
15		$1,100,000	$1,232,000	**$132,000**	U
16					

a comparison of Assembly Department actual and budgeted costs has put you on the spot. The budget report is shown (page 833).

This comparison uses budget data based on the original activity level (10,000 robotic controls). It indicates that the Assembly Department is significantly **over budget** for three of the six overhead costs. There is a total unfavorable difference of \$132,000, which is 12% over budget (\$132,000 ÷ \$1,100,000). Your supervisor is very unhappy. Instead of sharing in the company's success, you may find yourself looking for another job. What went wrong?

When you calm down and carefully examine the manufacturing overhead budget, you identify the problem: The budget data are not relevant! At the time the budget was developed, the company anticipated that only 10,000 units would be produced, **not** 12,000. Comparing actual with budgeted variable costs is meaningless. As production increases, the budget allowances for variable costs should increase proportionately. The variable costs in this example are indirect materials, indirect labor, and utilities.

Analyzing the budget data for these costs at 10,000 units, you arrive at the following per unit results.

Illustration 24-8
Variable costs per unit

Item	Total Cost	Per Unit
Indirect materials	\$250,000	\$25
Indirect labor	260,000	26
Utilities	190,000	19
	\$700,000	\$70

Illustration 24-9 calculates the budgeted variable costs at 12,000 units.

Illustration 24-9
Budgeted variable costs, 12,000 units

Item	Computation	Total
Indirect materials	\$25 × 12,000	\$300,000
Indirect labor	26 × 12,000	312,000
Utilities	19 × 12,000	228,000
		\$840,000

Because fixed costs do not change in total as activity changes, the budgeted amounts for these costs remain the same. Illustration 24-10 shows the budget report based on the flexible budget for **12,000 units** of production. (Compare this with Illustration 24-7.)

This report indicates that the Assembly Department's costs are **under budget**—a favorable difference. Instead of worrying about being fired, you may be in line for a bonus or a raise after all! As this analysis shows, the only appropriate comparison is between actual costs at 12,000 units of production and budgeted costs at 12,000 units. Flexible budget reports provide this comparison.

Developing the Flexible Budget

The flexible budget uses the master budget as its basis. To develop the flexible budget, management uses the following steps.

1. Identify the activity index and the relevant range of activity.
2. Identify the variable costs, and determine the budgeted variable cost per unit of activity for each cost.
3. Identify the fixed costs, and determine the budgeted amount for each cost.
4. Prepare the budget for selected increments of activity within the relevant range.

Illustration 24-10
Overhead flexible budget report

Barton Robotics.xls

	A	B	C	D	E
1	BARTON ROBOTICS				
2	Manufacturing Overhead Flexible Budget Report				
3	For the Year Ended December 31, 2017				
4				Difference	
5		Budget	Actual	Favorable - F Unfavorable - U	
6	Production in units	12,000	12,000		
7					
8	Variable costs				
9	Indirect materials ($25)	$ 300,000	$ 295,000	$5,000	F
10	Indirect labor ($26)	312,000	312,000	0	
11	Utilities ($19)	228,000	225,000	3,000	F
12	Total variable costs	840,000	832,000	8,000	F
13					
14	Fixed costs				
15	Depreciation	280,000	280,000	0	
16	Property taxes	70,000	70,000	0	
17	Supervision	50,000	50,000	0	
18	Total fixed costs	400,000	400,000	0	
19	Total costs	$1,240,000	$1,232,000	$8,000	F
20					

The activity index chosen should significantly influence the costs being budgeted. For manufacturing overhead costs, for example, the activity index is usually the same as the index used in developing the predetermined overhead rate—that is, direct labor hours or machine hours. For selling and administrative expenses, the activity index usually is sales or net sales.

The choice of the increment of activity is largely a matter of judgment. For example, if the relevant range is 8,000 to 12,000 direct labor hours, increments of 1,000 hours may be selected. The flexible budget is then prepared for each increment within the relevant range.

Flexible Budget—A Case Study

To illustrate the flexible budget, we use Fox Company. Fox's management uses a **flexible budget for monthly comparisons** of actual and budgeted manufacturing overhead costs of the Finishing Department. The master budget for the year ending December 31, 2017, shows expected **annual** operating capacity of 120,000 direct labor hours and the following overhead costs.

Illustration 24-11
Master budget data

Variable Costs		Fixed Costs	
Indirect materials	$180,000	Depreciation	$180,000
Indirect labor	240,000	Supervision	120,000
Utilities	60,000	Property taxes	60,000
Total	$480,000	Total	$360,000

The four steps for developing the flexible budget are applied as follows.

STEP 1. Identify the activity index and the relevant range of activity. The activity index is direct labor hours. The relevant range is 8,000–12,000 direct labor hours per **month**.

STEP 2. Identify the variable costs, and determine the budgeted variable cost per unit of activity for each cost. There are three variable costs. The variable cost per unit is found by dividing each total budgeted cost by the direct labor hours used in preparing the annual master budget (120,000 hours). Illustration 24-12 shows the computations for Fox Company.

Illustration 24-12
Computation of variable cost per direct labor hour

Variable Costs	Computation	Variable Cost per Direct Labor Hour
Indirect materials	$180,000 ÷ 120,000	$1.50
Indirect labor	$240,000 ÷ 120,000	2.00
Utilities	$ 60,000 ÷ 120,000	0.50
Total		$4.00

STEP 3. Identify the fixed costs, and determine the budgeted amount for each cost. There are three fixed costs. Since Fox desires **monthly budget data**, it divides each annual budgeted cost by 12 to find the monthly amounts. Therefore, the monthly budgeted fixed costs are depreciation $15,000, supervision $10,000, and property taxes $5,000.

STEP 4. Prepare the budget for selected increments of activity within the relevant range. Management prepares the budget in increments of 1,000 direct labor hours.

Illustration 24-13 shows Fox's flexible budget.

Illustration 24-13
Monthly overhead flexible budget

Fox Company.xls

Home Insert Page Layout Formulas Data Review View

P18 fx

	A	B	C	D	E	F
1	FOX COMPANY					
2	Monthly Manufacturing Overhead Flexible Budget					
3	Finishing Department					
4	For Months During the Year 2017					
5	Activity level					
6	Direct labor hours	8,000	9,000	10,000	11,000	12,000
7	Variable costs					
8	Indirect materials ($1.50)[a]	$12,000[b]	$13,500	$15,000	$16,500	$18,000
9	Indirect labor ($2.00)[a]	16,000[c]	18,000	20,000	22,000	24,000
10	Utilities ($0.50)[a]	4,000[d]	4,500	5,000	5,500	6,000
11	Total variable costs	32,000	36,000	40,000	44,000	48,000
12	Fixed costs					
13	Depreciation	15,000	15,000	15,000	15,000	15,000
14	Supervision	10,000	10,000	10,000	10,000	10,000
15	Property taxes	5,000	5,000	5,000	5,000	5,000
16	Total fixed costs	30,000	30,000	30,000	30,000	30,000
17	Total costs	$62,000	$66,000	$70,000	$74,000	$78,000
18						
19	[a]Cost per direct labor hour; [b]8,000 x $1.50; [c]8,000 x $2.00; [d]8,000 x $0.50					

Fox uses the formula below to determine total budgeted costs at any level of activity.

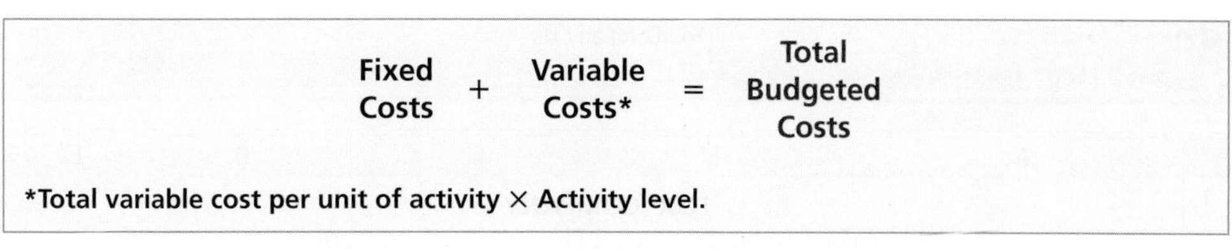

Illustration 24-14
Formula for total budgeted costs

For Fox, fixed costs are $30,000, and total variable cost per direct labor hour is $4 ($1.50 + $2.00 + $0.50). At 9,000 direct labor hours, total budgeted costs are $66,000 [$30,000 + ($4 × 9,000)]. At 8,622 direct labor hours, total budgeted costs are $64,488 [$30,000 + ($4 × 8,622)].

Total budgeted costs can also be shown graphically, as in Illustration 24-15. In the graph, the horizontal axis represents the activity index, and costs are indicated on the vertical axis. The graph highlights two activity levels (10,000 and 12,000). As shown, total budgeted costs at these activity levels are $70,000 [$30,000 + ($4 × 10,000)] and $78,000 [$30,000 + ($4 × 12,000)], respectively.

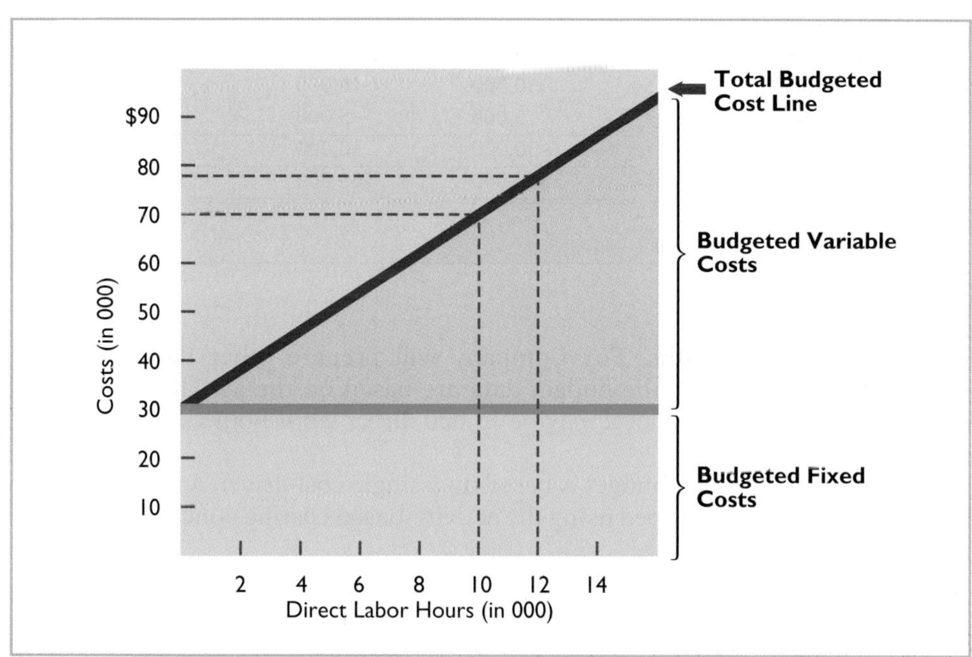

Illustration 24-15
Graphic flexible budget data highlighting 10,000 and 12,000 activity levels

Flexible Budget Reports

Flexible budget reports are another type of internal report. The flexible budget report consists of two sections: (1) production data for a selected activity index, such as direct labor hours, and (2) cost data for variable and fixed costs. The report provides a basis for evaluating a manager's performance in two areas: production control and cost control. Flexible budget reports are widely used in production and service departments.

Illustration 24-16 shows a budget report for the Finishing Department of Fox Company for the month of January. In this month, 9,000 hours are worked. The budget data are therefore based on the flexible budget for 9,000 hours in Illustration 24-13 (page 836). The actual cost data are assumed.

How appropriate is this report in evaluating the Finishing Department manager's performance in controlling overhead costs? The report clearly provides a reliable basis. Both actual and budget costs are based on the activity level worked during January. Since variable costs generally are incurred directly by the department, the difference between the budget allowance for those hours and the actual costs is the responsibility of the department manager.

Illustration 24-16
Overhead flexible budget report

Fox Company.xls

FOX COMPANY				
Manufacturing Overhead Flexible Budget Report				
Finishing Department				
For the Month Ended January 31, 2017				
			Difference	
	Budget at	Actual costs at	Favorable - F	
Direct labor hours (DLH)	9,000 DLH	9,000 DLH	Unfavorable - U	
Variable costs				
Indirect materials ($1.50)[a]	$13,500	$14,000	$ 500	U
Indirect labor ($2.00)[a]	18,000	17,000	1,000	F
Utilities ($0.50)[a]	4,500	4,600	100	U
Total variable costs	36,000	35,600	400	F
Fixed costs				
Depreciation	15,000	15,000	0	
Supervision	10,000	10,000	0	
Property taxes	5,000	5,000	0	
Total fixed costs	30,000	30,000	0	
Total costs	$66,000	$65,600	$ 400	F
[a]Cost per direct labor hour				

In subsequent months, Fox Company will prepare other flexible budget reports. For each month, the budget data are based on the actual activity level attained. In February that level may be 11,000 direct labor hours, in July 10,000, and so on.

Note that this flexible budget is based on a single cost driver. A more accurate budget often can be developed using the activity-based costing concepts explained in Chapter 21.

LEARNING OBJECTIVE 3

Apply responsibility accounting to cost and profit centers.

Like budgeting, responsibility accounting is an important part of management accounting. **Responsibility accounting** involves accumulating and reporting costs (and revenues, where relevant) on the basis of the manager who has the authority to make the day-to-day decisions about the items. Under responsibility accounting, a manager's performance is evaluated on matters directly under that manager's control. Responsibility accounting can be used at every level of management in which the following conditions exist.

1. Costs and revenues can be directly associated with the specific level of management responsibility.
2. The costs and revenues can be controlled by employees at the level of responsibility with which they are associated.
3. Budget data can be developed for evaluating the manager's effectiveness in controlling the costs and revenues.

Illustration 24-17 depicts levels of responsibility for controlling costs.

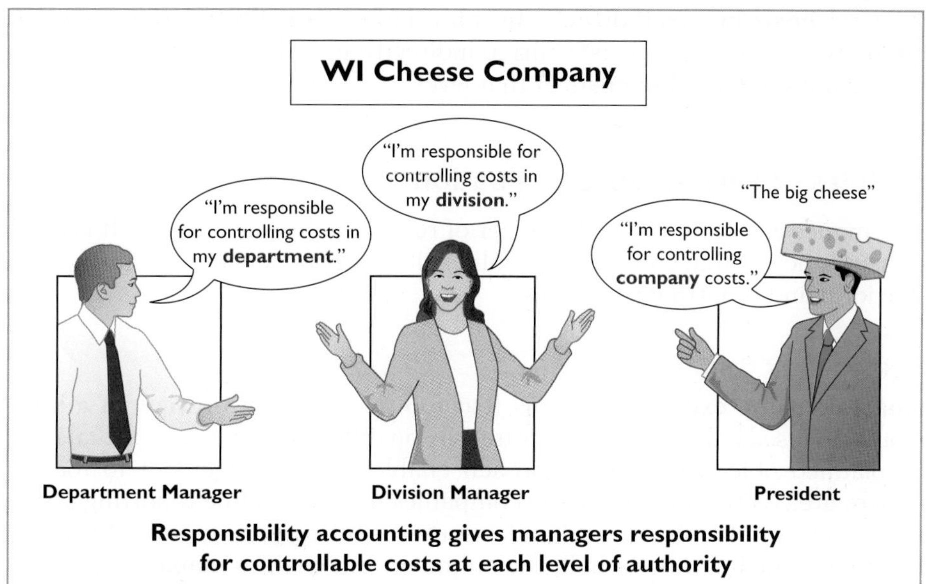

Illustration 24-17
Responsibility for controllable costs at varying levels of management

Under responsibility accounting, any individual who controls a specified set of activities can be a responsibility center. Thus, responsibility accounting may extend from the lowest level of control to the top strata of management. Once responsibility is established, the company first measures and reports the effectiveness of the individual's performance for the specified activity. It then reports that measure upward throughout the organization.

Responsibility accounting is especially valuable in a decentralized company. **Decentralization** means that the control of operations is delegated to many managers throughout the organization. The term **segment** is sometimes used to identify an area of responsibility in decentralized operations. Under responsibility accounting, companies prepare segment reports periodically, such as monthly, quarterly, and annually, to evaluate managers' performance.

Responsibility accounting is an essential part of any effective system of budgetary control. The reporting of costs and revenues under responsibility accounting differs from budgeting in two respects:

1. A distinction is made between controllable and noncontrollable items.
2. Performance reports either emphasize or include only items controllable by the individual manager.

Responsibility accounting applies to both profit and not-for-profit entities. For-profit entities seek to maximize net income. Not-for-profit entities wish to provide services as efficiently as possible.

Controllable Versus Noncontrollable Revenues and Costs

All costs and revenues are controllable at some level of responsibility within a company. This truth underscores the adage by the CEO of any organization that "the buck stops here." Under responsibility accounting, the critical issue is **whether the cost or revenue is controllable at the level of responsibility with which it is associated**. A cost over which a manager has control is called a **controllable cost**. From this definition, it follows that:

1. All costs are controllable by top management because of the broad range of its authority.
2. Fewer costs are controllable as one moves down to each lower level of managerial responsibility because of the manager's decreasing authority.

In general, **costs incurred directly by a level of responsibility are controllable at that level**. In contrast, costs incurred indirectly and allocated to a responsibility level are **noncontrollable costs** at that level.

Principles of Performance Evaluation

Performance evaluation is at the center of responsibility accounting. It is a management function that compares actual results with budget goals. It involves both behavioral and reporting principles.

MANAGEMENT BY EXCEPTION

Management by exception means that top management's review of a budget report is focused either entirely or primarily on differences between actual results and planned objectives. This approach enables top management to focus on problem areas. For example, many companies now use online reporting systems for employees to file their travel and entertainment expense reports. In addition to cutting reporting time in half, the online system enables managers to quickly analyze variances from travel budgets. This cuts down on expense account "padding" such as spending too much on meals or falsifying documents for costs that were never actually incurred.

Management by exception does not mean that top management will investigate every difference. For this approach to be effective, there must be guidelines for identifying an exception. The usual criteria are materiality and controllability.

MATERIALITY Without quantitative guidelines, management would have to investigate every budget difference regardless of the amount. Materiality is usually expressed as a percentage difference from budget. For example, management may set the percentage difference at 5% for important items and 10% for other items. Managers will investigate all differences either over or under budget by the specified percentage. Costs over budget warrant investigation to determine why they were not controlled. Likewise, costs under budget merit investigation to determine whether costs critical to profitability are being curtailed. For example, if maintenance costs are budgeted at $80,000 but only $40,000 is spent, major unexpected breakdowns in productive facilities may occur in the future. Alternatively, as discussed earlier, cost might be under budget due to budgetary slack.

Alternatively, a company may specify a single percentage difference from budget for all items and supplement this guideline with a minimum dollar limit. For example, the exception criteria may be stated at 5% of budget or more than $10,000.

CONTROLLABILITY OF THE ITEM Exception guidelines are more restrictive for controllable items than for items the manager cannot control. In fact, there may be no guidelines for noncontrollable items. For example, a large unfavorable difference between actual and budgeted property tax expense may not be flagged for investigation because the only possible causes are an unexpected increase in the tax rate or in the assessed value of the property. An investigation into the difference would be useless: The manager cannot control either cause.

BEHAVIORAL PRINCIPLES

The human factor is critical in evaluating performance. Behavioral principles include the following.

1. **Managers of responsibility centers should have direct input into the process of establishing budget goals of their area of responsibility.** Without

such input, managers may view the goals as unrealistic or arbitrarily set by top management. Such views adversely affect the managers' motivation to meet the targeted objectives.

2. **The evaluation of performance should be based entirely on matters that are controllable by the manager being evaluated.** Criticism of a manager on matters outside his or her control reduces the effectiveness of the evaluation process. It leads to negative reactions by a manager and to doubts about the fairness of the company's evaluation policies.
3. **Top management should support the evaluation process.** As explained earlier, the evaluation process begins at the lowest level of responsibility and extends upward to the highest level of management. Managers quickly lose faith in the process when top management ignores, overrules, or bypasses established procedures for evaluating a manager's performance.
4. **The evaluation process must allow managers to respond to their evaluations.** Evaluation is not a one-way street. Managers should have the opportunity to defend their performance. Evaluation without feedback is both impersonal and ineffective.
5. **The evaluation should identify both good and poor performance.** Praise for good performance is a powerful motivating factor for a manager. This is especially true when a manager's compensation includes rewards for meeting budget goals.

REPORTING PRINCIPLES

Performance evaluation under responsibility accounting should be based on certain reporting principles. These principles pertain primarily to the internal reports that provide the basis for evaluating performance. Performance reports should:

1. Contain only data that are controllable by the manager of the responsibility center.
2. Provide accurate and reliable budget data to measure performance.
3. Highlight significant differences between actual results and budget goals.
4. Be tailor-made for the intended evaluation.
5. Be prepared at reasonable time intervals.

In recent years, companies have come under increasing pressure from influential shareholder groups to do a better job of linking executive pay to corporate performance. For example, software maker **Siebel Systems** unveiled a new incentive plan after lengthy discussions with the California Public Employees' Retirement System. One unique feature of the plan is that managers' targets will be publicly disclosed at the beginning of each year for investors to evaluate.

Responsibility Reporting System

A **responsibility reporting system** involves the preparation of a report for each level of responsibility in the company's organization chart. To illustrate such a system, we use the partial organization chart and production departments of Francis Chair Company in Illustration 24-18 (page 842).

The responsibility reporting system begins with the lowest level of responsibility for controlling costs and moves upward to each higher level. Illustration 24-19 (page 843) details the connections between levels.

A brief description of the four reports for Francis Chair is as follows.

1. **Report D** is typical of reports that go to department managers. Similar reports are prepared for the managers of the Assembly and Enameling Departments.

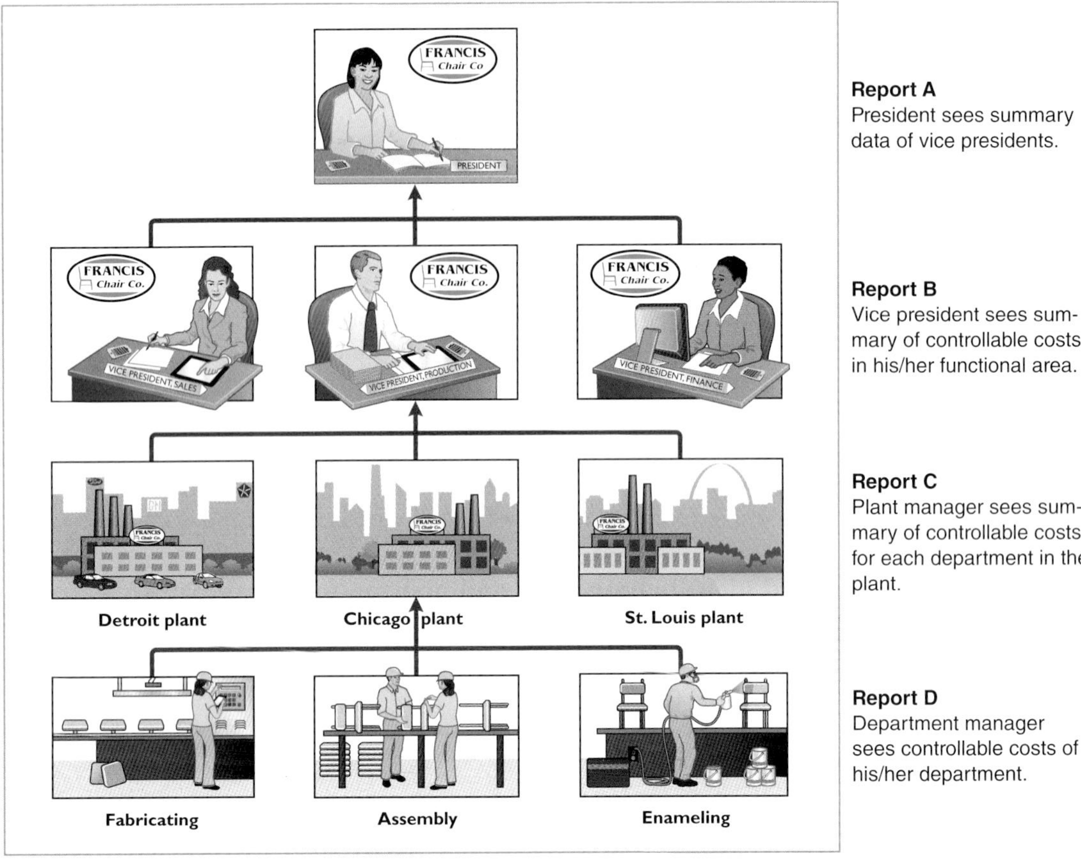

Illustration 24-18
Partial organization chart

2. **Report C** is an example of reports that are sent to plant managers. It shows the costs of the Chicago plant that are controllable at the second level of responsibility. In addition, Report C shows summary data for each department that is controlled by the plant manager. Similar reports are prepared for the Detroit and St. Louis plant managers.
3. **Report B** illustrates the reports at the third level of responsibility. It shows the controllable costs of the vice president of production and summary data on the three assembly plants for which this officer is responsible. Similar reports are prepared for the vice presidents of sales and finance.
4. **Report A** is typical of reports that go to the top level of responsibility—the president. It shows the controllable costs and expenses of this office and summary data on the vice presidents that are accountable to the president.

A responsibility reporting system permits management by exception at each level of responsibility. And, each higher level of responsibility can obtain the detailed report for each lower level of responsibility. For example, the vice president of production in Francis Chair may request the Chicago plant manager's report because this plant is $5,300 over budget.

This type of reporting system also permits comparative evaluations. In Illustration 24-19, the Chicago plant manager can easily rank the department managers' effectiveness in controlling manufacturing costs. Comparative rankings provide further incentive for a manager to control costs.

Types of Responsibility Centers

There are three basic types of responsibility centers: cost centers, profit centers, and investment centers. These classifications indicate the degree of responsibility the manager has for the performance of the center.

Illustration 24-19
Responsibility reporting system

Report A
President sees summary data of vice presidents.

Report A.xls

Report A				
To President			Month: January	
Controllable Costs:	Budget	Actual	Fav/Unfav	
President	$ 150,000	$ 151,500	$ 1,500	U
Vice Presidents:				
Sales	185,000	187,000	2,000	U
Production	**1,179,000**	**1,186,300**	**7,300**	**U**
Finance	100,000	101,000	1,000	U
Total	$1,614,000	$1,625,800	$11,800	U

Report B
Vice president sees summary of controllable costs in his/her functional area.

Report B.xls

Report B				
To Vice President Production			Month: January	
Controllable Costs:	Budget	Actual	Fav/Unfav	
VP Production	$ 125,000	$ 126,000	$ 1,000	U
Assembly Plants:				
Detroit	420,000	418,000	2,000	F
Chicago	**304,000**	**309,300**	**5,300**	**U**
St. Louis	330,000	333,000	3,000	U
Total	**$1,179,000**	**$1,186,300**	**$ 7,300**	**U**

Report C
Plant manager sees summary of controllable costs for each department in the plant.

Report C.xls

Report C				
To Plant Manager-Chicago			Month: January	
Controllable Costs:	Budget	Actual	Fav/Unfav	
Chicago Plant	$110,000	$113,000	$3,000	U
Departments:				
Fabricating	**84,000**	**85,300**	**1,300**	**U**
Enameling	62,000	64,000	2,000	U
Assembly	48,000	47,000	1,000	F
Total	**$304,000**	**$309,300**	**$5,300**	**U**

Report D
Department manager sees controllable costs of his/her department.

Report D.xls

Report D				
To Fabricating Dept. Manager			Month: January	
Controllable Costs:	Budget	Actual	Fav/Unfav	
Direct Materials	$20,000	$20,500	$ 500	U
Direct Labor	40,000	41,000	1,000	U
Overhead	24,000	23,800	200	F
Total	**$84,000**	**$85,300**	**$1,300**	**U**

A **cost center** incurs costs (and expenses) but does not directly generate revenues. Managers of cost centers have the authority to incur costs. They are evaluated on their ability to control costs. **Cost centers are usually either production departments or service departments.** Production departments participate directly in making the product. Service departments provide only support services. In a Ford Motor Company automobile plant, the welding, painting, and assembling departments are production departments. Ford's maintenance, cafeteria, and human resources departments are service departments. All of them are cost centers.

A **profit center** incurs costs (and expenses) and also generates revenues. Managers of profit centers are judged on the profitability of their centers. Examples of profit centers include the individual departments of a retail store, such as clothing, furniture, and automotive products, and branch offices of banks.

Like a profit center, an **investment center** incurs costs (and expenses) and generates revenues. In addition, an investment center has control over decisions regarding the assets available for use. Investment center managers are evaluated on both the profitability of the center and the rate of return earned on the funds invested. Investment centers are often associated with subsidiary companies. Utility Duke Energy has operating divisions such as electric utility, energy trading, and natural gas. Investment center managers control or significantly influence investment decisions related to such matters as plant expansion and entry into new market areas. Illustration 24-20 depicts the three types of responsibility centers.

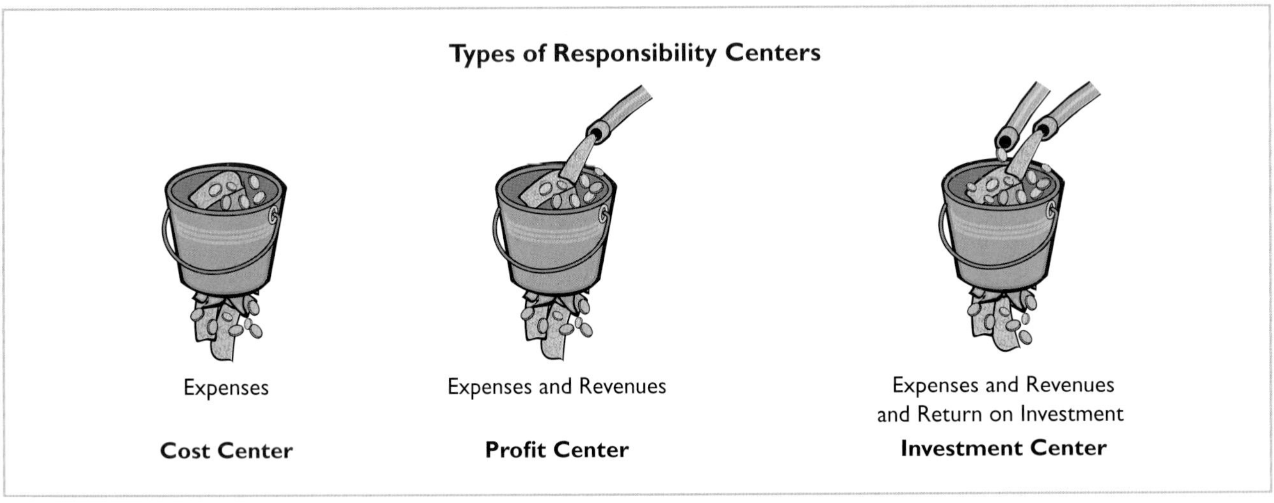

Illustration 24-20
Types of responsibility centers

RESPONSIBILITY ACCOUNTING FOR COST CENTERS

The evaluation of a manager's performance for cost centers is based on his or her ability to meet budgeted goals for controllable costs. **Responsibility reports for cost centers compare actual controllable costs with flexible budget data.**

Illustration 24-21 shows a responsibility report. The report is adapted from the flexible budget report for Fox Company in Illustration 24-16 (page 838). It assumes that the Finishing Department manager is able to control all manufacturing overhead costs except depreciation, property taxes, and his own monthly salary of \$6,000. The remaining \$4,000 (\$10,000 − \$6,000) of supervision costs are assumed to apply to other supervisory personnel within the Finishing Department, whose salaries are controllable by the manager.

Illustration 24-21
Responsibility report for a cost center

	A	B	C	D	E
1	FOX COMPANY				
2	Finishing Department				
3	Responsibility Report				
4	For the Month Ended January 31, 2017				
5				Difference	
6	Controllable Costs	Budget	Actual	Favorable - F Unfavorable - U	
7	Indirect materials	$13,500	$14,000	$ 500	U
8	Indirect labor	18,000	17,000	$1,000	F
9	Utilities	4,500	4,600	100	U
10	Supervision	4,000	4,000	0	
11	Total	$40,000	$39,600	$ 400	F
12					

The report in Illustration 24-21 includes **only controllable costs**, and no distinction is made between variable and fixed costs. The responsibility report continues the concept of management by exception. In this case, top management may request an explanation of the $1,000 favorable difference in indirect labor and/or the $500 unfavorable difference in indirect materials.

RESPONSIBILITY ACCOUNTING FOR PROFIT CENTERS

To evaluate the performance of a profit center manager, upper management needs detailed information about both controllable revenues and controllable costs. The operating revenues earned by a profit center, such as sales, are controllable by the manager. All variable costs (and expenses) incurred by the center are also controllable by the manager because they vary with sales. However, to determine the controllability of fixed costs, it is necessary to distinguish between direct and indirect fixed costs.

DIRECT AND INDIRECT FIXED COSTS A profit center may have both direct and indirect fixed costs. **Direct fixed costs** relate specifically to one center and are incurred for the sole benefit of that center. Examples of such costs include the salaries established by the profit center manager for supervisory personnel and the cost of a timekeeping department for the center's employees. Since these fixed costs can be traced directly to a center, they are also called **traceable costs**. **Most direct fixed costs are controllable by the profit center manager.**

In contrast, **indirect fixed costs** pertain to a company's overall operating activities and are incurred for the benefit of more than one profit center. Management allocates indirect fixed costs to profit centers on some type of equitable basis. For example, property taxes on a building occupied by more than one center may be allocated on the basis of square feet of floor space used by each center. Or, the costs of a company's human resources department may be allocated to profit centers on the basis of the number of employees in each center. Because these fixed costs apply to more than one center, they are also called **common costs**. **Most indirect fixed costs are not controllable by the profit center manager.**

RESPONSIBILITY REPORT The responsibility report for a profit center shows budgeted and actual **controllable revenues and costs**. The report is prepared using the cost-volume-profit income statement explained in Chapter 22. In the report:

1. Controllable fixed costs are deducted from contribution margin.
2. The excess of contribution margin over controllable fixed costs is identified as **controllable margin**.
3. Noncontrollable fixed costs are not reported.

Illustration 24-22 shows the responsibility report for the manager of the Marine Division, a profit center of Mantle Company. For the year, the Marine Division also had $60,000 of indirect fixed costs that were not controllable by the profit center manager.

Illustration 24-22
Responsibility report for profit center

Mantle Company.xls

	MANTLE COMPANY **Marine Division** **Responsibility Report** **For the Year Ended December 31, 2017**			
	Budget	Actual	Difference Favorable - F Unfavorable - U	
Sales	$1,200,000	$1,150,000	$50,000	U
Variable costs				
Cost of goods sold	500,000	490,000	10,000	F
Selling and administrative	160,000	156,000	4,000	F
Total	660,000	646,000	14,000	F
Contribution margin	540,000	504,000	36,000	U
Controllable fixed costs				
Cost of goods sold	100,000	100,000	0	
Selling and administrative	80,000	80,000	0	
Total	180,000	180,000	0	
Controllable margin	$ 360,000	$ 324,000	$36,000	U

Controllable margin is considered to be the best measure of the manager's performance **in controlling revenues and costs**. The report in Illustration 24-22 shows that the manager's performance was below budgeted expectations by 10% ($36,000 ÷ $360,000). Top management would likely investigate the causes of this unfavorable result. Note that the report does not show the Marine Division's noncontrollable fixed costs of $60,000. These costs would be included in a report on the profitability of the profit center.

Management also may choose to see **monthly** responsibility reports for profit centers. In addition, responsibility reports may include cumulative year-to-date results.

LEARNING OBJECTIVE 

Evaluate performance in investment centers.

As explained earlier, an investment center manager can control or significantly influence the investment funds available for use. Thus, the primary basis for evaluating the performance of a manager of an investment center is **return on investment (ROI)**. The return on investment is considered to be a useful performance measurement because it shows the **effectiveness of the manager in utilizing the assets at his or her disposal**.

Return on Investment (ROI)

The formula for computing ROI for an investment center, together with assumed illustrative data, is shown in Illustration 24-23.

Illustration 24-23
ROI formula

Controllable Margin	÷	Average Operating Assets	=	Return on Investment (ROI)
$1,000,000	÷	$5,000,000	=	20%

Both factors in the formula are controllable by the investment center manager. Operating assets consist of current assets and plant assets used in operations by the center and controlled by the manager. Nonoperating assets such as idle plant assets and land held for future use are excluded. Average operating assets are usually based on the cost or book value of the assets at the beginning and end of the year.

Responsibility Report

The scope of the investment center manager's responsibility significantly affects the content of the performance report. Since an investment center is an independent entity for operating purposes, **all fixed costs are controllable by its manager**. For example, the manager is responsible for depreciation on investment center assets. Therefore, more fixed costs are identified as controllable in the performance report for an investment center manager than in a performance report for a profit center manager. The report also shows budgeted and actual ROI below controllable margin.

To illustrate this responsibility report, we will now assume that the Marine Division of Mantle Company is an investment center. It has budgeted and actual average operating assets of $2,000,000. The manager can control $60,000 of fixed costs that were not controllable when the division was a profit center. Illustration 24-24 shows the division's responsibility report.

Illustration 24-24
Responsibility report for investment center

Mantle Company.xls

MANTLE COMPANY
Marine Division
Responsibility Report
For the Year Ended December 31, 2017

	Budget	Actual	Difference Favorable - F Unfavorable - U	
Sales	$ 1,200,000	$ 1,150,000	$ 50,000	U
Variable costs				
Cost of goods sold	500,000	490,000	10,000	F
Selling and administrative	160,000	156,000	4,000	F
Total	660,000	646,000	14,000	F
Contribution margin	540,000	504,000	36,000	U
Controllable fixed costs				
Cost of goods sold	100,000	100,000	0	
Selling and administrative	80,000	80,000	0	
Other fixed costs	60,000	60,000	0	
Total	240,000	240,000	0	
Controllable margin	**$ 300,000**	**$ 264,000**	**$ 36,000**	**U**
Return on investment	**15.0%**	**13.2%**	**1.8%**	**U**
	(a)	(b)	(c)	

(a) $\frac{\$300,000}{\$2,000,000}$ (b) $\frac{\$264,000}{\$2,000,000}$ (c) $\frac{\$36,000}{\$2,000,000}$

The report shows that the manager's performance based on ROI was below budget expectations by 1.8% (15.0% versus 13.2%). Top management would likely want explanations for this unfavorable result.

Judgmental Factors in ROI

The return on investment approach includes two judgmental factors:

1. **Valuation of operating assets.** Operating assets may be valued at acquisition cost, book value, appraised value, or fair value. The first two bases are readily available from the accounting records.
2. **Margin (income) measure.** This measure may be controllable margin, income from operations, or net income.

Each of the alternative values for operating assets can provide a reliable basis for evaluating a manager's performance as long as it is consistently applied between reporting periods. However, the use of income measures other than controllable margin will not result in a valid basis for evaluating the performance of an investment center manager.

Improving ROI

The manager of an investment center can improve ROI by increasing controllable margin, and/or reducing average operating assets. To illustrate, we will use the following assumed data for the Laser Division of Berra Company.

Illustration 24-25
Assumed data for Laser Division

Sales	$2,000,000
Variable costs	1,100,000
Contribution margin (45%)	900,000
Controllable fixed costs	300,000
Controllable margin (a)	$ 600,000
Average operating assets (b)	$5,000,000
Return on investment (a) ÷ (b)	**12%**

INCREASING CONTROLLABLE MARGIN

Controllable margin can be increased by increasing sales or by reducing variable and controllable fixed costs as follows.

1. **Increase sales 10%.** Sales will increase $200,000 ($2,000,000 × 0.10). Assuming no change in the contribution margin percentage of 45%, contribution margin will increase $90,000 ($200,000 × 0.45). Controllable margin will increase by the same amount because controllable fixed costs will not change. Thus, controllable margin becomes $690,000 ($600,000 + $90,000). The new ROI is 13.8%, computed as follows.

Illustration 24-26
ROI computation—increase in sales

$$\text{ROI} = \frac{\text{Controllable margin}}{\text{Average operating assets}} = \frac{\$690{,}000}{\$5{,}000{,}000} = \mathbf{13.8\%}$$

An increase in sales benefits both the investment center and the company if it results in new business. It would not benefit the company if the increase was achieved at the expense of other investment centers.

2. **Decrease variable and fixed costs 10%.** Total costs decrease $140,000 [($1,100,000 + $300,000) × 0.10]. This reduction results in a corresponding increase in controllable margin. Thus, controllable margin becomes $740,000 ($600,000 + $140,000). The new ROI is 14.8%, computed as follows.

$$\text{ROI} = \frac{\text{Controllable margin}}{\text{Average operating assets}} = \frac{\$740{,}000}{\$5{,}000{,}000} = \textbf{14.8\%}$$

Illustration 24-27
ROI computation—decrease in costs

This course of action is clearly beneficial when the reduction in costs is the result of eliminating waste and inefficiency. But, a reduction in costs that results from cutting expenditures on vital activities, such as required maintenance and inspections, is not likely to be acceptable to top management.

REDUCING AVERAGE OPERATING ASSETS

Assume that average operating assets are reduced 10% or \$500,000 (\$5,000,000 × 0.10). Average operating assets become \$4,500,000 (\$5,000,000 − \$500,000). Since controllable margin remains unchanged at \$600,000, the new ROI is 13.3%, computed as follows.

$$\text{ROI} = \frac{\text{Controllable margin}}{\text{Average operating assets}} = \frac{\$600{,}000}{\$4{,}500{,}000} = \textbf{13.3\%}$$

Illustration 24-28
ROI computation-decrease in operating assets

Reductions in operating assets may or may not be prudent. It is beneficial to eliminate overinvestment in inventories and to dispose of excessive plant assets. However, it is unwise to reduce inventories below expected needs or to dispose of essential plant assets.

REVIEW AND PRACTICE

LEARNING OBJECTIVES REVIEW

1 Describe budgetary control and static budget reports. Budgetary control consists of (a) preparing periodic budget reports that compare actual results with planned objectives, (b) analyzing the differences to determine their causes, (c) taking appropriate corrective action, and (d) modifying future plans, if necessary.

Static budget reports are useful in evaluating the progress toward planned sales and profit goals. They are also appropriate in assessing a manager's effectiveness in controlling costs when (a) actual activity closely approximates the master budget activity level, and/or (b) the behavior of the costs in response to changes in activity is fixed.

2 Prepare flexible budget reports. To develop the flexible budget it is necessary to: (a) Identify the activity index and the relevant range of activity. (b) Identify the variable costs, and determine the budgeted variable cost per unit of activity for each cost. (c) Identify the fixed costs, and determine the budgeted amount for each cost. (d) Prepare the budget for selected increments of activity within the relevant range. Flexible budget reports permit an evaluation of a manager's performance in controlling production and costs.

3 Apply responsibility accounting to cost and profit centers. Responsibility accounting involves accumulating and reporting revenues and costs on the basis of the individual manager who has the authority to make the day-to-day decisions about the items. The evaluation of a manager's performance is based on the matters directly under the manager's control. In responsibility accounting, it is necessary to distinguish between controllable and noncontrollable fixed costs and to identify three types of responsibility centers: cost, profit, and investment.

Responsibility reports for cost centers compare actual costs with flexible budget data. The reports show only controllable costs, and no distinction is made between variable and fixed costs. Responsibility reports show contribution margin, controllable fixed costs, and controllable margin for each profit center.

4 Evaluate performance in investment centers. The primary basis for evaluating performance in investment centers is return on investment (ROI). The formula for computing ROI for investment centers is Controllable margin ÷ Average operating assets.

GLOSSARY REVIEW

Budgetary control The use of budgets to control operations.

Controllable cost A cost over which a manager has control.

Controllable margin Contribution margin less controllable fixed costs.

Cost center A responsibility center that incurs costs but does not directly generate revenues.

Decentralization Control of operations is delegated to many managers throughout the organization.

Direct fixed costs Costs that relate specifically to a responsibility center and are incurred for the sole benefit of the center.

Flexible budget A projection of budget data for various levels of activity.

Indirect fixed costs Costs that are incurred for the benefit of more than one profit center.

Investment center A responsibility center that incurs costs, generates revenues, and has control over decisions regarding the assets available for use.

Management by exception The review of budget reports by top management focused entirely or primarily on differences between actual results and planned objectives.

Noncontrollable costs Costs incurred indirectly and allocated to a responsibility center that are not controllable at that level.

Profit center A responsibility center that incurs costs and also generates revenues.

Responsibility accounting A part of management accounting that involves accumulating and reporting revenues and costs on the basis of the manager who has the authority to make the day-to-day decisions about the items.

Responsibility reporting system The preparation of reports for each level of responsibility in the company's organization chart.

Return on investment (ROI) A measure of management's effectiveness in utilizing assets at its disposal in an investment center.

Segment An area of responsibility in decentralized operations.

Static budget A projection of budget data at one level of activity.

PRACTICE EXERCISES

Prepare flexible manufacturing overhead budget.

(LO 2)

1. Felix Company uses a flexible budget for manufacturing overhead based on direct labor hours. Variable manufacturing overhead costs per direct labor hour are as follows.

Indirect labor	$0.70
Indirect materials	0.50
Utilities	0.40

Fixed overhead costs per month are supervision $4,000, depreciation $3,000, and property taxes $800. The company believes it will normally operate in a range of 7,000–10,000 direct labor hours per month.

Instructions

Prepare a monthly flexible manufacturing overhead budget for 2017 for the expected range of activity, using increments of 1,000 direct labor hours.

Solution

1.

FELIX COMPANY
Monthly Flexible Manufacturing Overhead Budget
For the Year 2017

Activity level				
Direct labor hours	7,000	8,000	9,000	10,000
Variable costs				
Indirect labor ($0.70)	$ 4,900	$ 5,600	$ 6,300	$ 7,000
Indirect materials ($0.50)	3,500	4,000	4,500	5,000
Utilities ($0.40)	2,800	3,200	3,600	4,000
Total variable costs ($1.60)	11,200	12,800	14,400	16,000
Fixed costs				
Supervision	4,000	4,000	4,000	4,000
Depreciation	3,000	3,000	3,000	3,000
Property taxes	800	800	800	800
Total fixed costs	7,800	7,800	7,800	7,800
Total costs	$19,000	$20,600	$22,200	$23,800

2. The White Division of Mesin Company reported the following data for the current year.

Compute ROI for current year and for possible future changes.

(LO 4)

Sales	$3,000,000
Variable costs	2,400,000
Controllable fixed costs	400,000
Average operating assets	5,000,000

Top management is unhappy with the investment center's return on investment (ROI). It asks the manager of the White Division to submit plans to improve ROI in the next year. The manager believes it is feasible to consider the following independent courses of action.

1. Increase sales by $300,000 with no change in the contribution margin percentage.
2. Reduce variable costs by $100,000.
3. Reduce average operating assets by 4%.

Instructions

(a) Compute the return on investment (ROI) for the current year.

(b) Using the ROI formula, compute the ROI under each of the proposed courses of action. (Round to one decimal.)

Solution

2. (a) Controllable margin = ($3,000,000 − $2,400,000 − $400,000) = $200,000
ROI = $200,000 ÷ $5,000,000 = 4%

(b) (1) Contribution margin percentage is 20%, or ($600,000 ÷ $3,000,000)
Increase in controllable margin = $300,000 × 20% = $60,000
ROI = ($200,000 + $60,000) ÷ $5,000,000 = 5.2%

(2) ($200,000 + $100,000) ÷ $5,000,000 = 6%

(3) $200,000 ÷ [$5,000,000 − ($5,000,000 × 0.04)] = 4.2%

PRACTICE PROBLEM

Glenda Company uses a flexible budget for manufacturing overhead based on direct labor hours. For 2017, the master overhead budget for the Packaging Department based on 300,000 direct labor hours was as follows.

Prepare flexible budget report.

(LO 2)

Variable Costs		Fixed Costs	
Indirect labor	$360,000	Supervision	$ 60,000
Supplies and lubricants	150,000	Depreciation	24,000
Maintenance	210,000	Property taxes	18,000
Utilities	120,000	Insurance	12,000
	$840,000		$114,000

During July, 24,000 direct labor hours were worked. The company incurred the following variable costs in July: indirect labor $30,200, supplies and lubricants $11,600, maintenance $17,500, and utilities $9,200. Actual fixed overhead costs were the same as monthly budgeted fixed costs.

Instructions

Prepare a flexible budget report for the Packaging Department for July.

Solution

GLENDA COMPANY
Manufacturing Overhead Budget Report (Flexible)
Packaging Department
For the Month Ended July 31, 2017

Direct labor hours (DLH)	Budget 24,000 DLH	Actual Costs 24,000 DLH	Difference Favorable F Unfavorable U
Variable costs			
Indirect labor ($1.20[a])	$28,800	$30,200	$1,400 U
Supplies and lubricants ($0.50[a])	12,000	11,600	400 F
Maintenance ($0.70[a])	16,800	17,500	700 U
Utilities ($0.40[a])	9,600	9,200	400 F
Total variable	67,200	68,500	1,300 U
Fixed costs			
Supervision	$ 5,000[b]	$ 5,000	–0–
Depreciation	2,000[b]	2,000	–0–
Property taxes	1,500[b]	1,500	–0–
Insurance	1,000[b]	1,000	–0–
Total fixed	9,500	9,500	–0–
Total costs	$76,700	$78,000	$1,300 U

[a]($360,000 ÷ 300,000; $150,000 ÷ 300,000; $210,000 ÷ 300,000; $120,000 ÷ 300,000).
[b]Annual cost divided by 12.

EXERCISES

Understand the concept of budgetary control.
(LO 1, 2)

E24-1 Connie Rice has prepared the following list of statements about budgetary control.

1. Budget reports compare actual results with planned objectives.
2. All budget reports are prepared on a weekly basis.
3. Management uses budget reports to analyze differences between actual and planned results and determine their causes.
4. As a result of analyzing budget reports, management may either take corrective action or modify future plans.
5. Budgetary control works best when a company has an informal reporting system.
6. The primary recipients of the sales report are the sales manager and the production supervisor.
7. The primary recipient of the scrap report is the production manager.
8. A static budget is a projection of budget data at one level of activity.
9. Top management's reaction to unfavorable differences is not influenced by the materiality of the difference.
10. A static budget is not appropriate in evaluating a manager's effectiveness in controlling costs unless the actual activity level approximates the static budget activity level or the behavior of the costs is fixed.

Instructions
Identify each statement as true or false. If false, indicate how to correct the statement.

Prepare and evaluate static budget report.
(LO 1)

E24-2 Crede Company budgeted selling expenses of $30,000 in January, $35,000 in February, and $40,000 in March. Actual selling expenses were $31,200 in January, $34,525 in February, and $46,000 in March.

Instructions
(a) Prepare a selling expense report that compares budgeted and actual amounts by month and for the year to date.
(b) What is the purpose of the report prepared in (a), and who would be the primary recipient?
(c) What would be the likely result of management's analysis of the report?

E24-3 Myers Company uses a flexible budget for manufacturing overhead based on direct labor hours. Variable manufacturing overhead costs per direct labor hour are as follows.

Prepare flexible manufacturing overhead budget.

(LO 2)

Indirect labor	$1.00
Indirect materials	0.70
Utilities	0.40

Fixed overhead costs per month are supervision $4,000, depreciation $1,200, and property taxes $800. The company believes it will normally operate in a range of 7,000–10,000 direct labor hours per month.

Instructions

Prepare a monthly manufacturing overhead flexible budget for 2017 for the expected range of activity, using increments of 1,000 direct labor hours.

E24-4 Using the information in E24-3, assume that in July 2017, Myers Company incurs the following manufacturing overhead costs.

Prepare flexible budget reports for manufacturing overhead costs, and comment on findings.

(LO 2)

Variable Costs		**Fixed Costs**	
Indirect labor	$8,800	Supervision	$4,000
Indirect materials	5,800	Depreciation	1,200
Utilities	3,200	Property taxes	800

Instructions

(a) Prepare a flexible budget performance report, assuming that the company worked 9,000 direct labor hours during the month.
(b) Prepare a flexible budget performance report, assuming that the company worked 8,500 direct labor hours during the month.
(c) Comment on your findings.

E24-5 Fallon Company uses flexible budgets to control its selling expenses. Monthly sales are expected to range from $170,000 to $200,000. Variable costs and their percentage relationship to sales are sales commissions 6%, advertising 4%, traveling 3%, and delivery 2%. Fixed selling expenses will consist of sales salaries $35,000, depreciation on delivery equipment $7,000, and insurance on delivery equipment $1,000.

Prepare flexible selling expense budget.

(LO 2)

Instructions

Prepare a monthly flexible budget for each $10,000 increment of sales within the relevant range for the year ending December 31, 2017.

E24-6 The actual selling expenses incurred in March 2017 by Fallon Company are as follows.

Prepare flexible budget reports for selling expenses.

(LO 2)

Variable Expenses		**Fixed Expenses**	
Sales commissions	$11,000	Sales salaries	$35,000
Advertising	6,900	Depreciation	7,000
Travel	5,100	Insurance	1,000
Delivery	3,450		

Instructions

(a) Prepare a flexible budget performance report for March using the budget data in E24-5, assuming that March sales were $170,000.
(b) Prepare a flexible budget performance report, assuming that March sales were $180,000.
(c) Comment on the importance of using flexible budgets in evaluating the performance of the sales manager.

E24-7 Appliance Possible Inc. (AP) is a manufacturer of toaster ovens. To improve control over operations, the president of AP wants to begin using a flexible budgeting system,

Prepare flexible budget report.

(LO 2)

rather than use only the current master budget. The following data are available for AP's expected costs at production levels of 90,000, 100,000, and 110,000 units.

Variable costs	
Manufacturing	$6 per unit
Administrative	$4 per unit
Selling	$3 per unit
Fixed costs	
Manufacturing	$160,000
Administrative	$ 80,000

Instructions

(a) Prepare a flexible budget for each of the possible production levels: 90,000, 100,000, and 110,000 units.

(b) If AP sells the toaster ovens for $16 each, how many units will it have to sell to make a profit of $60,000 before taxes?

(CGA adapted)

Prepare flexible budget report; compare flexible and static budgets.

(LO 1, 2)

E24-8 Rensing Groomers is in the dog-grooming business. Its operating costs are described by the following formulas:

Grooming supplies (variable)	y = $0 + $5x
Direct labor (variable)	y = $0 + $14x
Overhead (mixed)	y = $10,000 + $1x

Milo, the owner, has determined that direct labor is the cost driver for all three categories of costs.

Instructions

(a) Prepare a flexible budget for activity levels of 550, 600, and 700 direct labor hours.

(b) Explain why the flexible budget is more informative than the static budget.

(c) Calculate the total cost per direct labor hour at each of the activity levels specified in part (a).

(d) The groomers at Rensing normally work a total of 650 direct labor hours during each month. Each grooming job normally takes a groomer 1.3 hours. Milo wants to earn a profit equal to 40% of the costs incurred. Determine what he should charge each pet owner for grooming.

(CGA adapted)

Prepare flexible budget report, and answer question.

(LO 1, 2)

E24-9 As sales manager, Joe Batista was given the following static budget report for selling expenses in the Clothing Department of Soria Company for the month of October.

SORIA COMPANY
Clothing Department
Budget Report
For the Month Ended October 31, 2017

	Budget	Actual	Difference Favorable F Unfavorable U
Sales in units	8,000	10,000	2,000 F
Variable expenses			
Sales commissions	$ 2,400	$ 2,600	$ 200 U
Advertising expense	720	850	130 U
Travel expense	3,600	4,100	500 U
Free samples given out	1,600	1,400	200 F
Total variable	8,320	8,950	630 U
Fixed expenses			
Rent	1,500	1,500	–0–
Sales salaries	1,200	1,200	–0–
Office salaries	800	800	–0–
Depreciation—autos (sales staff)	500	500	–0–
Total fixed	4,000	4,000	–0–
Total expenses	$12,320	$12,950	$ 630 U

As a result of this budget report, Joe was called into the president's office and congratulated on his fine sales performance. He was reprimanded, however, for allowing his costs to get out of control. Joe knew something was wrong with the performance report that he had been given. However, he was not sure what to do, and comes to you for advice.

Instructions

(a) Prepare a budget report based on flexible budget data to help Joe.
(b) Should Joe have been reprimanded? Explain.

Prepare flexible budget and responsibility report for manufacturing overhead.

(LO 2, 3)

E24-10 Chubbs Inc.'s manufacturing overhead budget for the first quarter of 2017 contained the following data.

Variable Costs		Fixed Costs	
Indirect materials	$12,000	Supervisory salaries	$36,000
Indirect labor	10,000	Depreciation	7,000
Utilities	8,000	Property taxes and insurance	8,000
Maintenance	6,000	Maintenance	5,000

Actual variable costs were indirect materials $13,500, indirect labor $9,500, utilities $8,700, and maintenance $5,000. Actual fixed costs equaled budgeted costs except for property taxes and insurance, which were $8,300. The actual activity level equaled the budgeted level.

All costs are considered controllable by the production department manager except for depreciation, and property taxes and insurance.

Instructions

(a) Prepare a manufacturing overhead flexible budget report for the first quarter.
(b) Prepare a responsibility report for the first quarter.

Prepare and discuss a responsibility report.

(LO 2, 3)

E24-11 UrLink Company is a newly formed company specializing in high-speed Internet service for home and business. The owner, Lenny Kirkland, had divided the company into two segments: Home Internet Service and Business Internet Service. Each segment is run by its own supervisor, while basic selling and administrative services are shared by both segments.

Lenny has asked you to help him create a performance reporting system that will allow him to measure each segment's performance in terms of its profitability. To that end, the following information has been collected on the Home Internet Service segment for the first quarter of 2017.

	Budget	Actual
Service revenue	$25,000	$26,200
Allocated portion of:		
Building depreciation	11,000	11,000
Advertising	5,000	4,200
Billing	3,500	3,000
Property taxes	1,200	1,000
Material and supplies	1,600	1,200
Supervisory salaries	9,000	9,500
Insurance	4,000	3,900
Wages	3,000	3,250
Gas and oil	2,800	3,400
Equipment depreciation	1,500	1,300

Instructions

(a) Prepare a responsibility report for the first quarter of 2017 for the Home Internet Service segment.
(b) Write a memo to Lenny Kirkland discussing the principles that should be used when preparing performance reports.

State total budgeted cost formulas, and prepare flexible budget graph.

(LO 2)

E24-12 Venetian Company has two production departments, Fabricating and Assembling. At a department managers' meeting, the controller uses flexible budget graphs to explain total budgeted costs. Separate graphs based on direct labor hours are used for each department. The graphs show the following.

1. At zero direct labor hours, the total budgeted cost line and the fixed cost line intersect the vertical axis at $50,000 in the Fabricating Department and $40,000 in the Assembling Department.
2. At normal capacity of 50,000 direct labor hours, the line drawn from the total budgeted cost line intersects the vertical axis at $150,000 in the Fabricating Department, and $120,000 in the Assembling Department.

Instructions

(a) State the total budgeted cost formula for each department.

(b) Compute the total budgeted cost for each department, assuming actual direct labor hours worked were 53,000 and 47,000, in the Fabricating and Assembling Departments, respectively.

(c) Prepare the flexible budget graph for the Fabricating Department, assuming the maximum direct labor hours in the relevant range is 100,000. Use increments of 10,000 direct labor hours on the horizontal axis and increments of $50,000 on the vertical axis.

Prepare reports in a responsibility reporting system.

(LO 3)

E24-13 Fey Company's organization chart includes the president; the vice president of production; three assembly plants—Dallas, Atlanta, and Tucson; and two departments within each plant—Machining and Finishing. Budget and actual manufacturing cost data for July 2017 are as follows.

Finishing Department—Dallas: direct materials $42,500 actual, $44,000 budget; direct labor $83,400 actual, $82,000 budget; manufacturing overhead $51,000 actual, $49,200 budget.

Machining Department—Dallas: total manufacturing costs $220,000 actual, $219,000 budget.

Atlanta Plant: total manufacturing costs $424,000 actual, $420,000 budget.

Tucson Plant: total manufacturing costs $494,200 actual, $496,500 budget.

The Dallas plant manager's office costs were $95,000 actual and $92,000 budget. The vice president of production's office costs were $132,000 actual and $130,000 budget. Office costs are not allocated to departments and plants.

Instructions

Using the format shown in Illustration 24-19 (page 843), prepare the reports in a responsibility system for:

(a) The Finishing Department—Dallas.

(b) The plant manager—Dallas.

(c) The vice president of production.

Prepare a responsibility report for a cost center.

(LO 3)

E24-14 The Mixing Department manager of Malone Company is able to control all overhead costs except rent, property taxes, and salaries. Budgeted monthly overhead costs for the Mixing Department, in alphabetical order, are:

Indirect labor	$12,000	Property taxes	$ 1,000
Indirect materials	7,700	Rent	1,800
Lubricants	1,675	Salaries	10,000
Maintenance	3,500	Utilities	5,000

Actual costs incurred for January 2017 are indirect labor $12,250; indirect materials $10,200; lubricants $1,650; maintenance $3,500; property taxes $1,100; rent $1,800; salaries $10,000; and utilities $6,400.

Instructions

(a) Prepare a responsibility report for January 2017.

(b) What would be the likely result of management's analysis of the report?

E24-15 Horatio Inc. has three divisions which are operated as profit centers. Actual operating data for the divisions listed alphabetically are as follows.

Compute missing amounts in responsibility reports for three profit centers, and prepare a report.

(LO 3)

Operating Data	Women's Shoes	Men's Shoes	Children's Shoes
Contribution margin	$270,000	(3)	$180,000
Controllable fixed costs	100,000	(4)	(5)
Controllable margin	(1)	$ 90,000	95,000
Sales	600,000	450,000	(6)
Variable costs	(2)	320,000	250,000

Instructions

(a) Compute the missing amounts. Show computations.

(b) Prepare a responsibility report for the Women's Shoes Division assuming (1) the data are for the month ended June 30, 2017, and (2) all data equal budget except variable costs which are $5,000 over budget.

E24-16 The Sports Equipment Division of Harrington Company is operated as a profit center. Sales for the division were budgeted for 2017 at $900,000. The only variable costs budgeted for the division were cost of goods sold ($440,000) and selling and administrative ($60,000). Fixed costs were budgeted at $100,000 for cost of goods sold, $90,000 for selling and administrative, and $70,000 for noncontrollable fixed costs. Actual results for these items were:

Prepare a responsibility report for a profit center, and compute ROI.

(LO 3, 4)

Sales	$880,000
Cost of goods sold	
Variable	408,000
Fixed	105,000
Selling and administrative	
Variable	61,000
Fixed	66,000
Noncontrollable fixed	90,000

Instructions

(a) Prepare a responsibility report for the Sports Equipment Division for 2017.

(b) Assume the division is an investment center, and average operating assets were $1,000,000. The noncontrollable fixed costs are controllable at the investment center level. Compute ROI.

E24-17 The South Division of Wiig Company reported the following data for the current year.

Compute ROI for current year and for possible future changes.

(LO 4)

Sales	$3,000,000
Variable costs	1,950,000
Controllable fixed costs	600,000
Average operating assets	5,000,000

Top management is unhappy with the investment center's return on investment (ROI). It asks the manager of the South Division to submit plans to improve ROI in the next year. The manager believes it is feasible to consider the following independent courses of action.

1. Increase sales by $300,000 with no change in the contribution margin percentage.
2. Reduce variable costs by $150,000.
3. Reduce average operating assets by 4%.

Instructions

(a) Compute the return on investment (ROI) for the current year.

(b) Using the ROI formula, compute the ROI under each of the proposed courses of action. (Round to one decimal.)

Prepare a responsibility report for an investment center.

(LO 4)

E24-18 The Dinkle and Frizell Dental Clinic provides both preventive and orthodontic dental services. The two owners, Reese Dinkle and Anita Frizell, operate the clinic as two separate investment centers: Preventive Services and Orthodontic Services. Each of them is in charge of one of the centers: Reese for Preventive Services and Anita for Orthodontic Services. Each month, they prepare an income statement for the two centers to evaluate performance and make decisions about how to improve the operational efficiency and profitability of the clinic.

Recently, they have been concerned about the profitability of the Preventive Services operations. For several months, it has been reporting a loss. The responsibility report for the month of May 2017 is shown below.

	Actual	Difference From Budget
Service revenue	$ 40,000	$1,000 F
Variable costs		
Filling materials	5,000	100 U
Novocain	3,900	100 U
Supplies	1,900	350 F
Dental assistant wages	2,500	–0–
Utilities	500	110 U
Total variable costs	13,800	40 F
Fixed costs		
Allocated portion of receptionist's salary	3,000	200 U
Dentist salary	9,800	400 U
Equipment depreciation	6,000	–0–
Allocated portion of building depreciation	15,000	1,000 U
Total fixed costs	33,800	1,600 U
Operating income (loss)	$ (7,600)	$ 560 U

In addition, the owners know that the investment in operating assets at the beginning of the month was $82,400, and it was $77,600 at the end of the month. They have asked for your assistance in evaluating their current performance reporting system.

Instructions

(a) Prepare a responsibility report for an investment center as illustrated in the chapter.

(b) Write a memo to the owners discussing the deficiencies of their current reporting system.

Prepare missing amounts in responsibility reports for three investment centers.

(LO 4)

E24-19 The Ferrell Transportation Company uses a responsibility reporting system to measure the performance of its three investment centers: Planes, Taxis, and Limos. Segment performance is measured using a system of responsibility reports and return on investment calculations. The allocation of resources within the company and the segment managers' bonuses are based in part on the results shown in these reports.

Recently, the company was the victim of a computer virus that deleted portions of the company's accounting records. This was discovered when the current period's responsibility reports were being prepared. The printout of the actual operating results appeared as follows.

	Planes	Taxis	Limos
Service revenue	$?	$500,000	$?
Variable costs	5,500,000	?	300,000
Contribution margin	?	250,000	480,000
Controllable fixed costs	1,500,000	?	?
Controllable margin	?	80,000	210,000
Average operating assets	25,000,000	?	1,500,000
Return on investment	12%	10%	?

Instructions

Determine the missing pieces of information above.

PROBLEMS

P24-1A Bumblebee Company estimates that 300,000 direct labor hours will be worked during the coming year, 2017, in the Packaging Department. On this basis, the following budgeted manufacturing overhead cost data are computed for the year.

Prepare flexible budget and budget report for manufacturing overhead.

(LO 2)

Fixed Overhead Costs		Variable Overhead Costs	
Supervision	$ 96,000	Indirect labor	$126,000
Depreciation	72,000	Indirect materials	90,000
Insurance	30,000	Repairs	69,000
Rent	24,000	Utilities	72,000
Property taxes	18,000	Lubricants	18,000
	$240,000		$375,000

It is estimated that direct labor hours worked each month will range from 27,000 to 36,000 hours.

During October, 27,000 direct labor hours were worked and the following overhead costs were incurred.

Fixed overhead costs: supervision $8,000, depreciation $6,000, insurance $2,460, rent $2,000, and property taxes $1,500.

Variable overhead costs: indirect labor $12,432, indirect materials $7,680, repairs $6,100, utilities $6,840, and lubricants $1,920.

Instructions

(a) Prepare a monthly manufacturing overhead flexible budget for each increment of 3,000 direct labor hours over the relevant range for the year ending December 31, 2017.

(b) Prepare a flexible budget report for October.

(c) Comment on management's efficiency in controlling manufacturing overhead costs in October.

(a) Total costs: DLH 27,000, $53,750; DLH 36,000, $65,000

(b) Total $1,182 U

P24-2A Zelmer Company manufactures tablecloths. Sales have grown rapidly over the past 2 years. As a result, the president has installed a budgetary control system for 2017. The following data were used in developing the master manufacturing overhead budget for the Ironing Department, which is based on an activity index of direct labor hours.

Prepare flexible budget, budget report, and graph for manufacturing overhead.

(LO 2)

Variable Costs	Rate per Direct Labor Hour	Annual Fixed Costs	
Indirect labor	$0.40	Supervision	$48,000
Indirect materials	0.50	Depreciation	18,000
Factory utilities	0.30	Insurance	12,000
Factory repairs	0.20	Rent	30,000

The master overhead budget was prepared on the expectation that 480,000 direct labor hours will be worked during the year. In June, 41,000 direct labor hours were worked. At that level of activity, actual costs were as shown below.

Variable—per direct labor hour: indirect labor $0.44, indirect materials $0.48, factory utilities $0.32, and factory repairs $0.25.

Fixed: same as budgeted.

Instructions

(a) Prepare a monthly manufacturing overhead flexible budget for the year ending December 31, 2017, assuming production levels range from 35,000 to 50,000 direct labor hours. Use increments of 5,000 direct labor hours.

(b) Prepare a budget report for June comparing actual results with budget data based on the flexible budget.

(c) Were costs effectively controlled? Explain.

(d) State the formula for computing the total budgeted costs for the Ironing Department.

(e) Prepare the flexible budget graph, showing total budgeted costs at 35,000 and 45,000 direct labor hours. Use increments of 5,000 direct labor hours on the horizontal axis and increments of $10,000 on the vertical axis.

(a) Total costs: 35,000 DLH, $58,000; 50,000 DLH, $79,000

(b) Budget $66,400
Actual $70,090

State total budgeted cost formula, and prepare flexible budget reports for 2 time periods.
(LO 1, 2)

P24-3A Ratchet Company uses budgets in controlling costs. The August 2017 budget report for the company's Assembling Department is as follows.

RATCHET COMPANY
Budget Report
Assembling Department
For the Month Ended August 31, 2017

Manufacturing Costs	Budget	Actual	Difference Favorable F Unfavorable U
Variable costs			
Direct materials	$ 48,000	$ 47,000	$1,000 F
Direct labor	54,000	51,200	2,800 F
Indirect materials	24,000	24,200	200 U
Indirect labor	18,000	17,500	500 F
Utilities	15,000	14,900	100 F
Maintenance	12,000	12,400	400 U
Total variable	171,000	167,200	3,800 F
Fixed costs			
Rent	12,000	12,000	–0–
Supervision	17,000	17,000	–0–
Depreciation	6,000	6,000	–0–
Total fixed	35,000	35,000	–0–
Total costs	$206,000	$202,200	$3,800 F

The monthly budget amounts in the report were based on an expected production of 60,000 units per month or 720,000 units per year. The Assembling Department manager is pleased with the report and expects a raise, or at least praise for a job well done. The company president, however, is unhappy with the results for August because only 58,000 units were produced.

Instructions

(a) State the total monthly budgeted cost formula.

(b) Prepare a budget report for August using flexible budget data. Why does this report provide a better basis for evaluating performance than the report based on static budget data?

(b) Budget $200,300

(c) In September, 64,000 units were produced. Prepare the budget report using flexible budget data, assuming (1) each variable cost was 10% higher than its actual cost in August, and (2) fixed costs were the same in September as in August.

(c) Budget $217,400
Actual $218,920

Prepare responsibility report for a profit center.
(LO 3)

P24-4A Clarke Inc. operates the Patio Furniture Division as a profit center. Operating data for this division for the year ended December 31, 2017, are as shown below.

	Budget	Difference from Budget
Sales	$2,500,000	$50,000 F
Cost of goods sold		
Variable	1,300,000	41,000 F
Controllable fixed	200,000	3,000 U
Selling and administrative		
Variable	220,000	6,000 U
Controllable fixed	50,000	2,000 U
Noncontrollable fixed costs	70,000	4,000 U

In addition, Clarke incurs $180,000 of indirect fixed costs that were budgeted at $175,000. 20% of these costs are allocated to the Patio Furniture Division.

Instructions

(a) Prepare a responsibility report for the Patio Furniture Division for the year.

(a) Contribution margin $85,000 F
Controllable margin $80,000 F

(b) Comment on the manager's performance in controlling revenues and costs.

(c) Identify any costs excluded from the responsibility report and explain why they were excluded.

P24-5A Optimus Company manufactures a variety of tools and industrial equipment. The company operates through three divisions. Each division is an investment center. Operating data for the Home Division for the year ended December 31, 2017, and relevant budget data are as follows.

Prepare responsibility report for an investment center, and compute ROI.

(LO 4)

	Actual	Comparison With Budget
Sales	$1,400,000	$100,000 favorable
Variable cost of goods sold	665,000	45,000 unfavorable
Variable selling and administrative expenses	125,000	25,000 unfavorable
Controllable fixed cost of goods sold	170,000	On target
Controllable fixed selling and administrative expenses	80,000	On target

Average operating assets for the year for the Home Division were $2,000,000, which was also the budgeted amount.

Instructions

(a) Prepare a responsibility report (in thousands of dollars) for the Home Division.

(b) Evaluate the manager's performance. Which items will likely be investigated by top management?

(c) Compute the expected ROI in 2017 for the Home Division, assuming the following independent changes to actual data.

(1) Variable cost of goods sold is decreased by 5%.

(2) Average operating assets are decreased by 10%.

(3) Sales are increased by $200,000, and this increase is expected to increase contribution margin by $80,000.

(a) Controllable margin: Budget $330; Actual $360

P24-6A Durham Company uses a responsibility reporting system. It has divisions in Denver, Seattle, and San Diego. Each division has three production departments: Cutting, Shaping, and Finishing. The responsibility for each department rests with a manager who reports to the division production manager. Each division manager reports to the vice president of production. There are also vice presidents for marketing and finance. All vice presidents report to the president.

Prepare reports for cost centers under responsibility accounting, and comment on performance of managers.

(LO 3)

In January 2017, controllable actual and budget manufacturing overhead cost data for the departments and divisions were as shown below.

Manufacturing Overhead	Actual	Budget
Individual costs—Cutting Department—Seattle		
Indirect labor	$ 73,000	$ 70,000
Indirect materials	47,900	46,000
Maintenance	20,500	18,000
Utilities	20,100	17,000
Supervision	22,000	20,000
	$183,500	$171,000
Total costs		
Shaping Department—Seattle	$158,000	$148,000
Finishing Department—Seattle	210,000	205,000
Denver division	678,000	673,000
San Diego division	722,000	715,000

Additional overhead costs were incurred as ollows: Seattle division production manager—actual costs $52,500, budget $51,000; vice president of production—actual costs $65,000, budget $64,000; president—actual costs $76,400, budget $74,200. These expenses are not allocated.

The vice presidents who report to the president, other than the vice president of production, had the following expenses.

Vice President	Actual	Budget
Marketing	$133,600	$130,000
Finance	109,000	104,000

Instructions

(a) Using the format in Illustration 24-19 (page 843), prepare the following responsibility reports.

(1) Manufacturing overhead—Cutting Department manager—Seattle division.

(2) Manufacturing overhead—Seattle division manager.

(a) (1) $12,500 U
(2) $29,000 U

(3) $42,000 U
(4) $52,800 U

(3) Manufacturing overhead—vice president of production.
(4) Manufacturing overhead and expenses—president.

(b) Comment on the comparative performances of:
(1) Department managers in the Seattle division.
(2) Division managers.
(3) Vice presidents.

BROADENING YOUR PERSPECTIVE

MANAGEMENT DECISION-MAKING

Decision-Making Across the Organization

BYP24-1 Green Pastures is a 400-acre farm on the outskirts of the Kentucky Bluegrass, specializing in the boarding of broodmares and their foals. A recent economic downturn in the thoroughbred industry has led to a decline in breeding activities, and it has made the boarding business extremely competitive. To meet the competition, Green Pastures planned in 2017 to entertain clients, advertise more extensively, and absorb expenses formerly paid by clients such as veterinary and blacksmith fees.

The budget report for 2017 is presented below. As shown, the static income statement budget for the year is based on an expected 21,900 boarding days at $25 per mare. The variable expenses per mare per day were budgeted: feed $5, veterinary fees $3, blacksmith fees $0.25, and supplies $0.55. All other budgeted expenses were either semifixed or fixed.

During the year, management decided not to replace a worker who quit in March, but it did issue a new advertising brochure and did more entertaining of clients.[1]

GREEN PASTURES
Static Budget Income Statement
For the Year Ended December 31, 2017

	Actual	Master Budget	Difference
Number of mares	52	60	8 U
Number of boarding days	19,000	21,900	2,900 U
Sales	$380,000	$547,500	$167,500 U
Less: Variable expenses			
Feed	104,390	109,500	5,110 F
Veterinary fees	58,838	65,700	6,862 F
Blacksmith fees	4,984	5,475	491 F
Supplies	10,178	12,045	1,867 F
Total variable expenses	178,390	192,720	14,330 F
Contribution margin	201,610	354,780	153,170 U
Less: Fixed expenses			
Depreciation	40,000	40,000	–0–
Insurance	11,000	11,000	–0–
Utilities	12,000	14,000	2,000 F
Repairs and maintenance	10,000	11,000	1,000 F
Labor	88,000	95,000	7,000 F
Advertisement	12,000	8,000	4,000 U
Entertainment	7,000	5,000	2,000 U
Total fixed expenses	180,000	184,000	4,000 F
Net income	$ 21,610	$170,780	$149,170 U

[1]Data for this case are based on Hans Sprohge and John Talbott, "New Applications for Variance Analysis," *Journal of Accountancy* (AICPA, New York), April 1989, pp. 137–141.

Instructions

With the class divided into groups, answer the following.

(a) Based on the static budget report:
  (1) What was the primary cause(s) of the loss in net income?
  (2) Did management do a good, average, or poor job of controlling expenses?
  (3) Were management's decisions to stay competitive sound?

(b) Prepare a flexible budget report for the year.

(c) Based on the flexible budget report, answer the three questions in part (a) above.

(d) What course of action do you recommend for the management of Green Pastures?

Managerial Analysis

BYP24-2 Lanier Company manufactures expensive watch cases sold as souvenirs. Three of its sales departments are Retail Sales, Wholesale Sales, and Outlet Sales. The Retail Sales Department is a profit center. The Wholesale Sales Department is a cost center. Its managers merely take orders from customers who purchase through the company's wholesale catalog. The Outlet Sales Department is an investment center because each manager is given full responsibility for an outlet store location. The manager can hire and discharge employees, purchase, maintain, and sell equipment, and in general is fairly independent of company control.

Mary Gammel is a manager in the Retail Sales Department. Stephen Flott manages the Wholesale Sales Department. Jose Gomez manages the Golden Gate Club outlet store in San Francisco. The following are the budget responsibility reports for each of the three departments.

	Budget		
	Retail Sales	**Wholesale Sales**	**Outlet Sales**
Sales	$ 750,000	$ 400,000	$200,000
Variable costs			
Cost of goods sold	150,000	100,000	25,000
Advertising	100,000	30,000	5,000
Sales salaries	75,000	15,000	3,000
Printing	10,000	20,000	5,000
Travel	20,000	30,000	2,000
Fixed costs			
Rent	50,000	30,000	10,000
Insurance	5,000	2,000	1,000
Depreciation	75,000	100,000	40,000
Investment in assets	1,000,000	1,200,000	800,000

	Actual Results		
	Retail Sales	**Wholesale Sales**	**Outlet Sales**
Sales	$ 750,000	$ 400,000	$200,000
Variable costs			
Cost of goods sold	192,000	122,000	26,500
Advertising	100,000	30,000	5,000
Sales salaries	75,000	15,000	3,000
Printing	10,000	20,000	5,000
Travel	14,000	21,000	1,500
Fixed costs			
Rent	40,000	50,000	12,300
Insurance	5,000	2,000	1,000
Depreciation	80,000	90,000	56,000
Investment in assets	1,000,000	1,200,000	800,000

Instructions

(a) Determine which of the items should be included in the responsibility report for each of the three managers.

(b) Compare the budgeted measures with the actual results. Decide which results should be called to the attention of each manager.

Real-World Focus

BYP24-3 Computer Associates International, Inc., the world's leading business software company, delivers the end-to-end infrastructure to enable e-business through innovative technology, services, and education. Recently, Computer Associates had 19,000 employees worldwide and revenue of over $6 billion.

The following information is from the company's annual report.

COMPUTER ASSOCIATES INTERNATIONAL, INC.
Management Discussion

The Company has experienced a pattern of business whereby revenue for its third and fourth fiscal quarters reflects an increase over first- and second-quarter revenue. The Company attributes this increase to clients' increased spending at the end of their calendar year budgetary periods and the culmination of its annual sales plan. Since the Company's costs do not increase proportionately with the third- and fourth-quarters' increase in revenue, the higher revenue in these quarters results in greater profit margins and income. Fourth-quarter profitability is traditionally affected by significant new hirings, training, and education expenditures for the succeeding year.

Instructions

(a) Why don't the company's costs increase proportionately as the revenues increase in the third and fourth quarters?

(b) What type of budgeting seems appropriate for the Computer Associates situation?

BYP24-4 There are many useful resources regarding budgeting available on websites. The following activity investigates the results of a comprehensive budgeting study.

Address: **http://www.accountingweb.com/whitepapers/centage_ioma.pdf**, or go to **www.wiley.com/college/weygandt**

Instructions

Go to the address above and then answer the following questions.

(a) What are cited as the two most common "pain points" of budgeting?

(b) What percentage of companies that participated in the survey said that they prepare annual budgets? Of those that prepare budgets, what percentage say that they start the budgeting process by first generating sales projections?

(c) What is the most common amount of time for the annual budgeting process?

(d) When evaluating variances from budgeted amounts, what was the most commonly defined range of acceptable tolerance levels?

(e) The study defines three types of consequences for varying from budgeted amounts. How does it describe "severe" consequences?

CRITICAL THINKING

Communication Activity

BYP24-5 The manufacturing overhead budget for Fleming Company contains the following items.

Variable costs		Fixed costs	
Indirect materials	$22,000	Supervision	$17,000
Indirect labor	12,000	Inspection costs	1,000
Maintenance expense	10,000	Insurance expense	2,000
Manufacturing supplies	6,000	Depreciation	15,000
Total variable	$50,000	Total fixed	$35,000

The budget was based on an estimated 2,000 units being produced. During the past month, 1,500 units were produced, and the following costs incurred.

Variable costs		Fixed costs	
Indirect materials	$22,500	Supervision	$18,400
Indirect labor	13,500	Inspection costs	1,200
Maintenance expense	8,200	Insurance expense	2,200
Manufacturing supplies	5,000	Depreciation	14,700
Total variable	$49,200	Total fixed	$36,500

Instructions

(a) Determine which items would be controllable by Fred Bedner, the production manager.
(b) How much should have been spent during the month for the manufacture of the 1,500 units?
(c) Prepare a flexible manufacturing overhead budget report for Mr. Bedner.
(d) Prepare a responsibility report. Include only the costs that would have been controllable by Mr. Bedner. Assume that the supervision cost above includes Mr. Bedner's salary of $10,000, both at budget and actual. In an attached memo, describe clearly for Mr. Bedner the areas in which his performance needs to be improved.

Ethics Case

BYP24-6 American Products Corporation participates in a highly competitive industry. In order to meet this competition and achieve profit goals, the company has chosen the decentralized form of organization. Each manager of a decentralized investment center is measured on the basis of profit contribution, market penetration, and return on investment. Failure to meet the objectives established by corporate management for these measures has not been acceptable and usually has resulted in demotion or dismissal of an investment center manager.

An anonymous survey of managers in the company revealed that the managers feel the pressure to compromise their personal ethical standards to achieve the corporate objectives. For example, at certain plant locations there was pressure to reduce quality control to a level which could not assure that all unsafe products would be rejected. Also, sales personnel were encouraged to use questionable sales tactics to obtain orders, including gifts and other incentives to purchasing agents.

The chief executive officer is disturbed by the survey findings. In his opinion, such behavior cannot be condoned by the company. He concludes that the company should do something about this problem.

Instructions

(a) Who are the stakeholders (the affected parties) in this situation?
(b) Identify the ethical implications, conflicts, or dilemmas in the above described situation.
(c) What might the company do to reduce the pressures on managers and decrease the ethical conflicts?

(CMA adapted)

All About You

BYP24-7 It is one thing to prepare a personal budget; it is another thing to stick to it. Financial planners have suggested various mechanisms to provide support for enforcing personal budgets. One approach is called "envelope budgeting."

Instructions

Read the article provided at **http://en.wikipedia.org/wiki/Envelope_budgeting**, and answer the following questions.

(a) Summarize the process of envelope budgeting.
(b) Evaluate whether you think you would benefit from envelope budgeting. What do you think are its strengths and weaknesses relative to your situation?

Considering Your Costs and Benefits

BYP24-8 Preparing a personal budget is a great first step toward control over your personal finances. It is especially useful to prepare a budget when you face a big decision. For most people, the biggest decision they will ever make is whether to purchase a house. The percentage of people in the United States who own a home is high compared to many other countries. This is partially the result of U.S. government programs and incentives that encourage home ownership. For example, the interest on a home mortgage is tax-deductible.

Before purchasing a house, you should first consider whether buying it is the best choice for you. Suppose you just graduated from college and are moving to a new community. Should you immediately buy a new home?

YES: If I purchase a home, I am making my housing cost more like a "fixed cost," thus minimizing increases in my future housing costs. Also, I benefit from the appreciation in my home's value. Although recent turbulence in the economy has caused home prices in many communities to decline, I know that over the long term, home prices have increased across the country.

NO: I just moved to a new town, so I don't know the housing market. I am new to my job, so I don't know whether I will like it or my new community. Also, if my job does go well, it is likely that my income will increase in the next few years, so I will able to afford a better house if I wait. Therefore, the flexibility provided by renting is very valuable to me at this point in my life.

Instructions

Write a response indicating your position regarding this situation. Provide support for your view.

Chapter 25 Standard Costs and Balanced Scorecard

When Howard Schultz purchased a small Seattle coffee-roasting business in 1987, he set out to create a new kind of company. He thought the company should sell coffee by the cup in its store, in addition to the bags of roasted beans it already sold. He also saw the store as a place where you could order a beverage, custom-made to your unique tastes, in an environment that would give you the sense that you had escaped, if only momentarily, from the chaos we call life. Finally, Schultz believed that the company would prosper if employees shared in its success.

In a little more than 20 years, Howard Schultz's company, Starbucks, grew from that one store to over 17,000 locations in 54 countries. That is an incredible rate of growth, and it didn't happen by accident. While Starbucks does everything it can to maximize the customer's experience, behind the scenes it needs to control costs. Consider the almost infinite options of beverage combinations and variations at Starbucks. The company must determine the most efficient way to make each beverage, it must communicate these methods in the form of standards to its employees, and it must then evaluate whether those standards are being met.

Schultz's book, *Onward: How Starbucks Fought for Its Life Without Losing Its Soul*, describes a painful period in which Starbucks had to close 600 stores and lay off thousands of employees. However, when a prominent shareholder suggested that the company eliminate its employee healthcare plan, as so many other companies had done, Schultz refused. The healthcare plan represented one of the company's most tangible commitments to employee well-being as well as to corporate social responsibility. Schultz feels strongly that providing health care to the company's employees is an essential part of the standard cost of a cup of Starbucks' coffee.

LEARNING OBJECTIVES

1. **Describe standard costs.**
2. **Determine direct materials variances.**
3. **Determine direct labor and total manufacturing overhead variances.**
4. **Prepare variance reports and balanced scorecards.**

LEARNING OBJECTIVE 

Describe standard costs.

Standards are common in business. Those imposed by government agencies are often called **regulations**. They include the Fair Labor Standards Act, the Equal Employment Opportunity Act, and a multitude of environmental standards. Standards established internally by a company may extend to personnel matters, such as employee absenteeism and ethical codes of conduct, quality control standards for products, and standard costs for goods and services. In managerial accounting, **standard costs** are predetermined unit costs, which companies use as measures of performance.

We focus on manufacturing operations in this chapter. But you should recognize that standard costs also apply to many types of service businesses as well. For example, a fast-food restaurant such as McDonald's knows the price it should pay for pickles, beef, buns, and other ingredients. It also knows how much time it should take an employee to flip hamburgers. If the company pays too much for pickles or if employees take too much time to prepare Big Macs, McDonald's notices the deviations and takes corrective action. Not-for-profit entities, such as universities, charitable organizations, and governmental agencies, also may use standard costs as measures of performance.

Standard costs offer a number of advantages to an organization, as shown in Illustration 25-1. The organization will realize these advantages only when standard costs are carefully established and prudently used. Using standards solely as a way to place blame can have a negative effect on managers and employees. To minimize this effect, many companies offer wage incentives to those who meet the standards.

Illustration 25-1
Advantages of standard costs

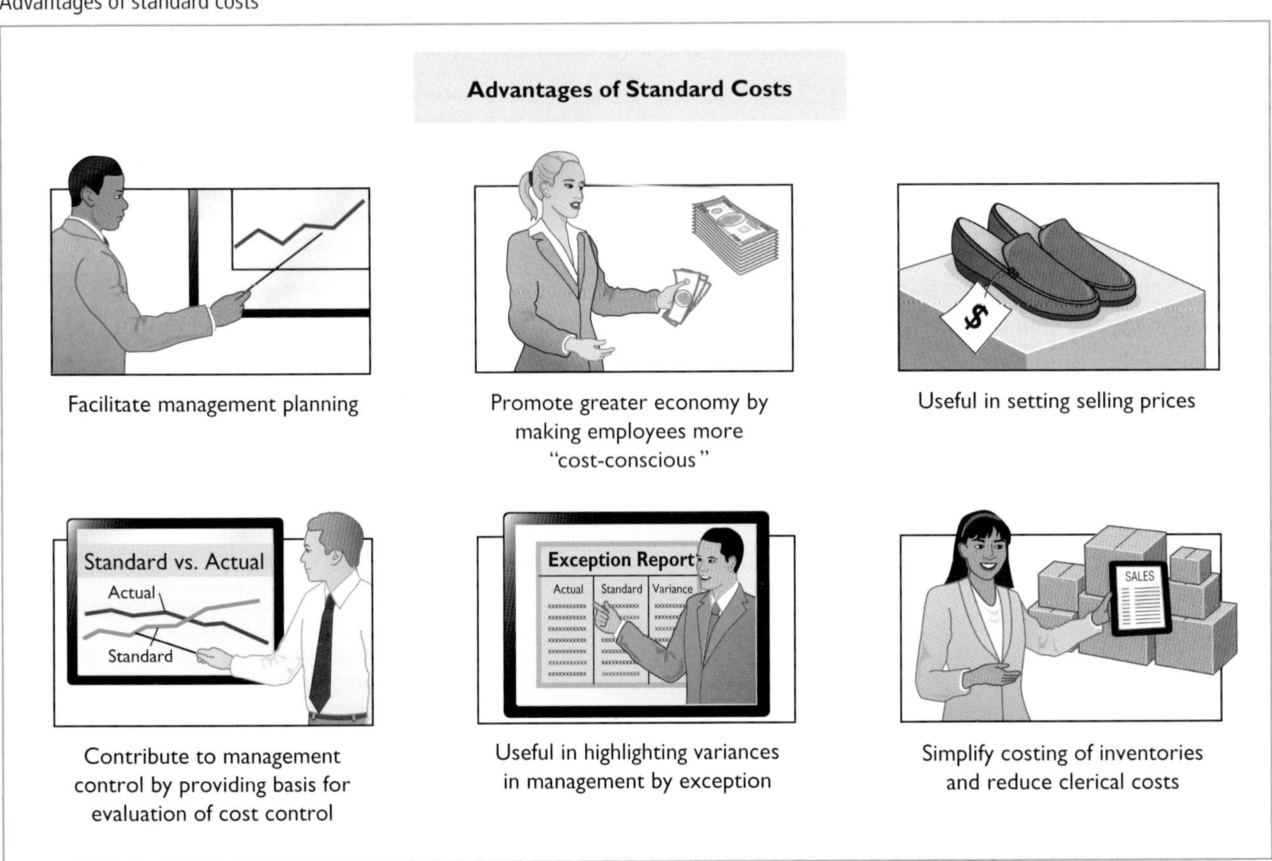

Distinguishing Between Standards and Budgets

Both **standards** and **budgets** are predetermined costs, and both contribute to management planning and control. There is a difference, however, in the way the terms are expressed. A standard is a **unit** amount. A budget is a **total** amount. Thus, it is customary to state that the **standard cost** of direct labor for a unit of product is, say, \$10. If the company produces 5,000 units of the product, the \$50,000 of direct labor is the **budgeted** labor cost. A standard is the budgeted **cost per unit** of product. A standard is therefore concerned with each individual cost component that makes up the entire budget.

There are important accounting differences between budgets and standards. Except in the application of manufacturing overhead to jobs and processes, budget data are not journalized in cost accounting systems. In contrast, as we illustrate in the appendix to this chapter, standard costs may be incorporated into cost accounting systems. Also, a company may report its inventories at standard cost in its financial statements, but it would not report inventories at budgeted costs.

Setting Standard Costs

The setting of standard costs to produce a unit of product is a difficult task. It requires input from all persons who have responsibility for costs and quantities. To determine the standard cost of direct materials, management consults purchasing agents, product managers, quality control engineers, and production supervisors. In setting the standard cost for direct labor, managers obtain pay rate data from the payroll department. Industrial engineers generally determine the labor time requirements. The managerial accountant provides important input for the standard-setting process by accumulating historical cost data and by knowing how costs respond to changes in activity levels.

To be effective in controlling costs, standard costs need to be current at all times. Thus, standards are under continuous review. They should change whenever managers determine that the existing standard is not a good measure of performance. Circumstances that warrant revision of a standard include changed wage rates resulting from a new union contract, a change in product specifications, or the implementation of a new manufacturing method.

IDEAL VERSUS NORMAL STANDARDS

Companies set standards at one of two levels: ideal or normal. **Ideal standards** represent optimum levels of performance under perfect operating conditions. **Normal standards** represent efficient levels of performance that are attainable under expected operating conditions.

Some managers believe ideal standards will stimulate workers to ever-increasing improvement. However, most managers believe that ideal standards lower the morale of the entire workforce because they are difficult, if not impossible, to meet. Very few companies use ideal standards.

Most companies that use standards set them at a normal level. Properly set, normal standards should be **rigorous but attainable**. Normal standards allow for rest periods, machine breakdowns, and other "normal" contingencies in the production process. In the remainder of this chapter, we will assume that standard costs are set at a normal level.

A CASE STUDY

To establish the standard cost of producing a product, it is necessary to establish standards for each manufacturing cost element—direct materials, direct labor, and manufacturing overhead. The standard for each element is derived from the standard price to be paid and the standard quantity to be used.

To illustrate, we use an extended example. Xonic Beverage Company uses standard costs to measure performance at the production facility of its caffeinated energy drink, Xonic Tonic. Xonic produces one-gallon containers of concentrated syrup that it sells to coffee and smoothie shops, and other retail outlets. The syrup is mixed with ice water or ice "slush" before serving. The potency of the beverage varies depending on the amount of concentrated syrup used.

DIRECT MATERIALS The **direct materials price standard** is the cost per unit of direct materials that should be incurred. This standard is based on the purchasing department's best estimate of the **cost of raw materials**. This cost is frequently based on current purchase prices. The price standard also includes an amount for related costs such as receiving, storing, and handling. The materials price standard per pound of material for Xonic Tonic is as follows.

Illustration 25-2
Setting direct materials price standard

Item	Price
Purchase price, net of discounts	$ 2.70
Freight	0.20
Receiving and handling	0.10
Standard direct materials price per pound	**$3.00**

The **direct materials quantity standard** is the quantity of direct materials that should be used per unit of finished goods. This standard is expressed as a physical measure, such as pounds, barrels, or board feet. In setting the standard, management considers both the quality and quantity of materials required to manufacture the product. The standard includes allowances for unavoidable waste and normal spoilage. The standard quantity per unit for Xonic Tonic is shown in Illustration 25-3.

Illustration 25-3
Setting direct materials quantity standard

Item	Quantity (Pounds)
Required materials	3.5
Allowance for waste	0.4
Allowance for spoilage	0.1
Standard direct materials quantity per unit	**4.0**

The standard direct materials cost per unit is the standard direct materials price times the standard direct materials quantity. For Xonic, the standard direct materials cost per gallon of Xonic Tonic is $12.00 ($3 × 4 pounds).

Terminology
The direct labor price standard is also called the *direct labor rate standard.*

DIRECT LABOR The **direct labor price standard** is the rate per hour that should be incurred for direct labor. This standard is based on current wage rates, adjusted for anticipated changes such as cost of living adjustments (COLAs). The price standard also generally includes employer payroll taxes and fringe benefits, such as paid holidays and vacations. For Xonic, the direct labor price standard is as follows.

Illustration 25-4
Setting direct labor price standard

Item	Price
Hourly wage rate	$ 12.50
COLA	0.25
Payroll taxes	0.75
Fringe benefits	1.50
Standard direct labor rate per hour	**$15.00**

Terminology
The direct labor quantity standard is also called the *direct labor efficiency standard.*

The **direct labor quantity standard** is the time that should be required to make one unit of the product. This standard is especially critical in labor-intensive companies. Allowances should be made in this standard for rest periods, cleanup, machine setup, and machine downtime. Illustration 25-5 shows the direct labor quantity standard for Xonic.

Illustration 25-5
Setting direct labor quantity standard

Item	Quantity (Hours)
Actual production time	1.5
Rest periods and cleanup	0.2
Setup and downtime	0.3
Standard direct labor hours per unit	**2.0**

The standard direct labor cost per unit is the standard direct labor rate times the standard direct labor hours. For Xonic, the standard direct labor cost per gallon is $30 ($15 × 2 hours).

Calculating the overhead rate

Overhead ÷ Standard activity index

MANUFACTURING OVERHEAD For manufacturing overhead, companies use a **standard predetermined overhead rate** in setting the standard. This overhead rate is determined by dividing budgeted overhead costs by an expected standard activity index. For example, the index may be standard direct labor hours or standard machine hours.

As discussed in Chapter 21, many companies employ activity-based costing (ABC) to allocate overhead costs. Because ABC uses multiple activity indices to allocate overhead costs, it results in a better correlation between activities and costs incurred than do other methods. As a result, the use of ABC can significantly improve the usefulness of standard costing for management decision-making.

Xonic uses standard direct labor hours as the activity index. The company expects to produce 13,200 gallons of Xonic Tonic during the year at normal capacity. **Normal capacity** is the average activity output that a company should experience over the long run. Since it takes two direct labor hours for each gallon, total standard direct labor hours are 26,400 (13,200 gallons × 2 hours).

At normal capacity of 26,400 direct labor hours, overhead costs are expected to be $132,000. Of that amount, $79,200 are variable and $52,800 are fixed. Illustration 25-6 shows computation of the standard predetermined overhead rates for Xonic.

Illustration 25-6
Computing predetermined overhead rates

Budgeted Overhead Costs	Amount	÷	Standard Direct Labor Hours	=	Overhead Rate per Direct Labor Hour
Variable	$ 79,200		26,400		$3.00
Fixed	52,800		26,400		2.00
Total	$132,000		26,400		**$5.00**

The standard manufacturing overhead cost per unit is the predetermined overhead rate times the activity index quantity standard. For Xonic, which uses direct labor hours as its activity index, the standard manufacturing overhead cost per gallon of Xonic Tonic is $10 ($5 × 2 hours).

TOTAL STANDARD COST PER UNIT After a company has established the standard quantity and price per unit of product, it can determine the total standard cost. The total standard cost per unit is the sum of the standard costs of direct materials, direct labor, and manufacturing overhead. The total standard cost per gallon of Xonic Tonic is $52, as shown on the following standard cost card.

Illustration 25-7
Standard cost per gallon of Xonic Tonic

Product: Xonic Tonic **Unit Measure: Gallon**

Manufacturing Cost Elements	Standard Quantity	×	Standard Price	=	Standard Cost
Direct materials	4 pounds		$ 3.00		$12.00
Direct labor	2 hours		$15.00		30.00
Manufacturing overhead	2 hours		$ 5.00		10.00
					$52.00

The company prepares a standard cost card for each product. This card provides the basis for determining variances from standards.

LEARNING OBJECTIVE 2

Determine direct materials variances.

Analyzing and Reporting Variances

Terminology
In business, the term *variance* is also used to indicate differences between total budgeted and total actual costs.

One of the major management uses of standard costs is to identify variances from standards. **Variances** are the differences between total actual costs and total standard costs.

To illustrate, assume that in producing 1,000 gallons of Xonic Tonic in the month of June, Xonic incurred the following costs.

Illustration 25-8
Actual production costs

Direct materials	$13,020
Direct labor	31,080
Variable overhead	6,500
Fixed overhead	4,400
Total actual costs	$55,000

Companies determine total standard costs by multiplying the units produced by the standard cost per unit. The total standard cost of Xonic Tonic is $52,000 (1,000 gallons × $52). Thus, the total variance is $3,000, as shown below.

Illustration 25-9
Computation of total variance

Actual costs	$55,000
Less: Standard costs	52,000
Total variance	**$ 3,000**

Note that the variance is expressed in total dollars, not on a per unit basis.

When actual costs exceed standard costs, the variance is **unfavorable**. The $3,000 variance in June for Xonic Tonic is unfavorable. An unfavorable variance has a negative connotation. It suggests that the company paid too much for one or more of the manufacturing cost elements or that it used the elements inefficiently.

If actual costs are less than standard costs, the variance is **favorable**. A favorable variance has a positive connotation. It suggests efficiencies in incurring manufacturing costs and in using direct materials, direct labor, and manufacturing overhead.

However, be careful: A favorable variance could be obtained by using inferior materials. In printing wedding invitations, for example, a favorable variance could result from using an inferior grade of paper. Or, a favorable variance might be achieved in installing tires on an automobile assembly line by tightening only half of the lug bolts. A variance is not favorable if the company has sacrificed quality control standards.

To interpret a variance, you must analyze its components. A variance can result from differences related to the cost of materials, labor, or overhead. Illustration 25-10 shows that the total variance is the sum of the materials, labor, and overhead variances.

Materials Variance + Labor Variance + Overhead Variance = Total Variance

Illustration 25-10
Components of total variance

In the following discussion, you will see that the materials variance and the labor variance are the sum of variances resulting from price differences and quantity differences. Illustration 25-11 shows a format for computing the price and quantity variances.

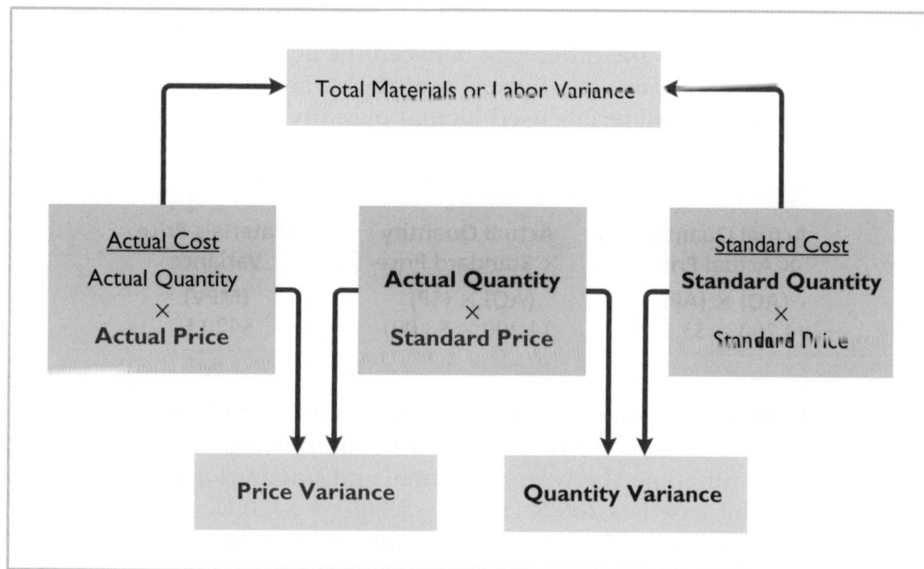

Illustration 25-11
Breakdown of materials or labor variance into price and quantity variances

Note that the left side of the matrix is actual cost (actual quantity times actual price). The right hand is standard cost (standard quantity times standard price). The only additional element you need in order to compute the price and quantity variances is the middle element, the actual quantity at the standard price.

Direct Materials Variances

Part of Xonic's total variance of $3,000 is due to a materials variance. In completing the order for 1,000 gallons of Xonic Tonic, the company used 4,200 pounds of direct materials. The direct materials were purchased at a price of $3.10 per unit. From Illustration 25-3, we know that Xonic's standards require it to use 4 pounds of materials per gallon produced, so it should have only used 4,000 (4 × 1,000) pounds of direct materials to produce 1,000 gallons. Illustration 25-2 shows that the standard cost of each pound of direct materials is $3 instead of the $3.10 actually paid. Illustration 25-12 (page 874) shows that the **total materials variance** is computed as the difference between the amount paid (actual quantity times actual price) and the amount that should have been paid based on standards (standard quantity times standard price of materials).

Illustration 25-12
Formula for total materials variance

Actual Quantity × Actual Price	−	Standard Quantity × Standard Price	=	Total Materials Variance
(AQ) × (AP)		**(SQ) × (SP)**		**(TMV)**
(4,200 × \$3.10)	−	(4,000 × \$3.00)	=	\$1,020 U

Thus, for Xonic, the total materials variance is \$1,020 (\$13,020 − \$12,000) unfavorable.

The total materials variance could be caused by differences in the price paid for the materials or by differences in the amount of materials used. Illustration 25-13 shows that the total materials variance is the sum of the materials price variance and the materials quantity variance.

Illustration 25-13
Components of total materials variance

Materials Price Variance + Materials Quantity Variance = Total Materials Variance

The materials price variance results from a difference between the actual price and the standard price. Illustration 25-14 shows that the **materials price variance** is computed as the difference between the actual amount paid (actual quantity of materials times actual price) and the standard amount that should have been paid for the materials used (actual quantity of materials times standard price).[1]

Illustration 25-14
Formula for materials price variance

Actual Quantity × Actual Price	−	Actual Quantity × Standard Price	=	Materials Price Variance
(AQ) × (AP)		**(AQ) × (SP)**		**(MPV)**
(4,200 × \$3.10)	−	(4,200 × \$3.00)	=	\$420 U

For Xonic, the materials price variance is \$420 (\$13,020 − \$12,600) unfavorable.

The price variance can also be computed by multiplying the actual quantity purchased by the difference between the actual and standard price per unit. The computation in this case is 4,200 × (\$3.10 − \$3.00) = \$420 U.

As seen in Illustration 25-13, the other component of the materials variance is the quantity variance. The quantity variance results from differences between the amount of material actually used and the amount that should have been used. As shown in Illustration 25-15, the **materials quantity variance** is computed as the difference between the standard cost of the actual quantity (actual quantity times standard price) and the standard cost of the amount that should have been used (standard quantity times standard price for materials).

Illustration 25-15
Formula for materials quantity variance

Actual Quantity × Standard Price	−	Standard Quantity × Standard Price	=	Materials Quantity Variance
(AQ) × (SP)		**(SQ) × (SP)**		**(MQV)**
(4,200 × \$3.00)	−	(4,000 × \$3.00)	=	\$600 U

Thus, for Xonic, the materials quantity variance is \$600 (\$12,600 − \$12,000) unfavorable.

[1]Assume that all materials purchased during the period are used in production and that no units remain in inventory at the end of the period.

The quantity variance can also be computed by applying the standard price to the difference between actual and standard quantities used. The computation in this example is $3.00 × (4,200 − 4,000) = $600 U.

The total materials variance of $1,020 U, therefore, consists of the following.

Materials price variance	$ 420 U
Materials quantity variance	600 U
Total materials variance	**$1,020 U**

Illustration 25-16
Summary of materials variances

Companies sometimes use a matrix to analyze a variance. **When the matrix is used, a company computes the amounts using the formulas for each cost element first and then computes the variances.** Illustration 25-17 shows the completed matrix for the direct materials variance for Xonic. The matrix provides a convenient structure for determining each variance.

Illustration 25-17
Matrix for direct materials variances

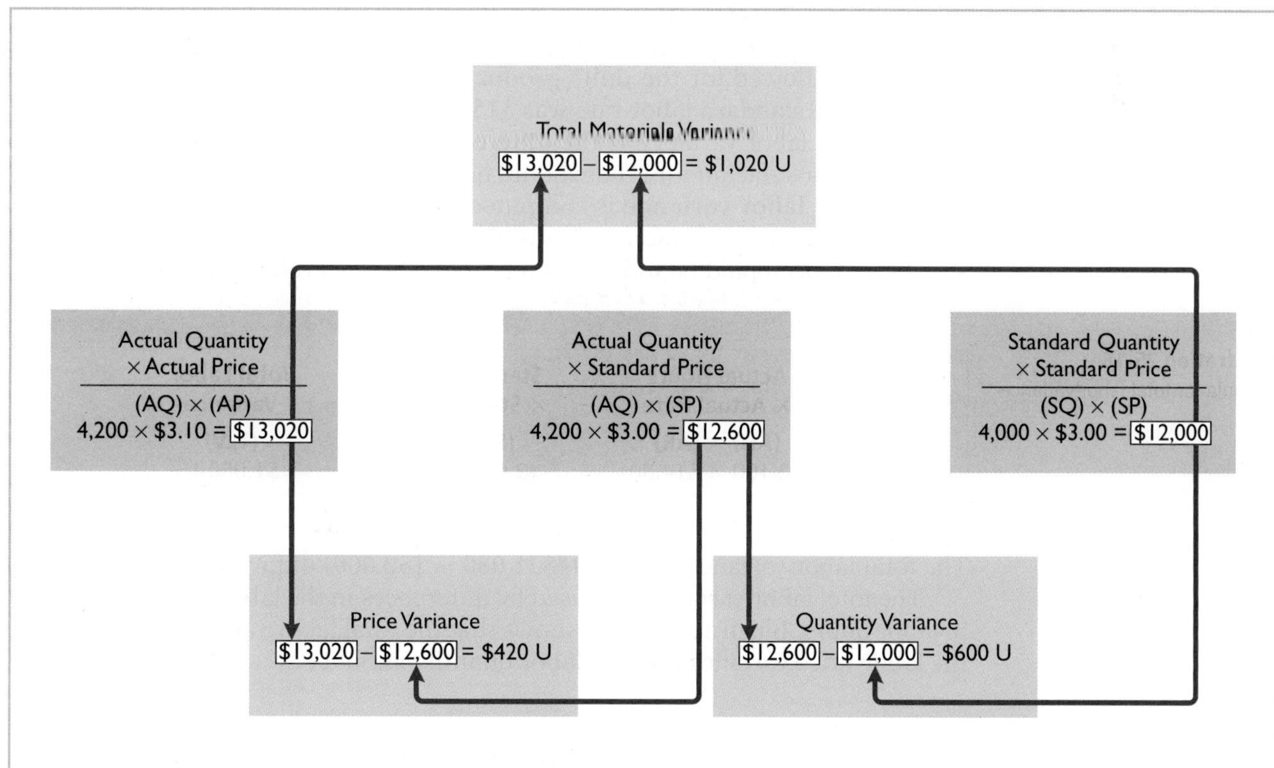

CAUSES OF MATERIALS VARIANCES

What are the causes of a variance? The causes may relate to both internal and external factors. The investigation of a **materials price variance usually begins in the purchasing department**. Many factors affect the price paid for raw materials. These include availability of quantity and cash discounts, the quality of the materials requested, and the delivery method used. To the extent that these factors are considered in setting the price standard, the purchasing department is responsible for any variances.

However, a variance may be beyond the control of the purchasing department. Sometimes, for example, prices may rise faster than expected. Moreover, actions by groups over which the company has no control, such as the OPEC nations' oil price increases, may cause an unfavorable variance. For example,

during a recent year, **Kraft Foods** and **Kellogg Company** both experienced unfavorable materials price variances when the cost of dairy and wheat products jumped unexpectedly. There are also times when a production department may be responsible for the price variance. This may occur when a rush order forces the company to pay a higher price for the materials.

The starting point for determining the cause(s) of a significant **materials quantity variance is in the production department**. If the variances are due to inexperienced workers, faulty machinery, or carelessness, the production department is responsible. However, if the materials obtained by the purchasing department were of inferior quality, then the purchasing department is responsible.

LEARNING OBJECTIVE 3 **Determine direct labor and total manufacturing overhead variances.**

Direct Labor Variances

The process of determining direct labor variances is the same as for determining the direct materials variances. In completing the Xonic Tonic order, the company incurred 2,100 direct labor hours at an average hourly rate of $14.80. The standard hours allowed for the units produced were 2,000 hours (1,000 gallons × 2 hours). The standard labor rate was $15 per hour.

The total labor variance is the difference between the amount actually paid for labor versus the amount that should have been paid. Illustration 25-18 shows that the **total labor variance** is computed as the difference between the amount actually paid for labor (actual hours times actual rate) and the amount that should have been paid (standard hours times standard rate for labor).

Illustration 25-18
Formula for total labor variance

Actual Hours × Actual Rate	−	Standard Hours × Standard Rate	=	Total Labor Variance
(AH) × (AR)		(SH) × (SR)		(TLV)
(2,100 × $14.80)	−	(2,000 × $15.00)	=	$1,080 U

The total labor variance is $1,080 ($31,080 − $30,000) unfavorable.

The total labor variance is caused by differences in the labor rate or difference in labor hours. Illustration 25-19 shows that the total labor variance is the sum of the labor price variance and the labor quantity variance.

Illustration 25-19
Components of total labor variance

Labor Price Variance	+	Labor Quantity Variance	=	Total Labor Variance

The labor price variance results from the difference between the rate paid to workers versus the rate that was supposed to be paid. Illustration 25-20 shows that the **labor price variance** is computed as the difference between the actual amount paid (actual hours times actual rate) and the amount that should have been paid for the number of hours worked (actual hours times standard rate for labor).

Illustration 25-20
Formula for labor price variance

Actual Hours × Actual Rate	−	Actual Hours × Standard Rate	=	Labor Price Variance
(AH) × (AR)		(AH) × (SR)		(LPV)
(2,100 × $14.80)	−	(2,100 × $15.00)	=	$420 F

For Xonic, the labor price variance is $420 ($31,080 − $31,500) favorable.

The labor price variance can also be computed by multiplying actual hours worked by the difference between the actual pay rate and the standard pay rate. The computation in this example is 2,100 × ($15.00 − $14.80) = $420 F.

The other component of the total labor variance is the labor quantity variance. The labor quantity variance results from the difference between the actual number of labor hours and the number of hours that should have been worked for the quantity produced. Illustration 25-21 shows that the **labor quantity variance** is computed as the difference between the amount that should have been paid for the hours worked (actual hours times standard rate) and the amount that should have been paid for the amount of hours that should have been worked (standard hours times standard rate for labor).

Illustration 25-21
Formula for labor quantity variance

Actual Hours × Standard Rate	−	Standard Hours × Standard Rate	=	Labor Quantity Variance
(AH) × (SR)		(SH) × (SR)		(LQV)
(2,100 × $15.00)	−	(2,000 × $15.00)	=	$1,500 U

Thus, for Xonic, the labor quantity variance is $1,500 ($31,500 − $30,000) unfavorable.

The same result can be obtained by multiplying the standard rate by the difference between actual hours worked and standard hours allowed. In this case, the computation is $15.00 × (2,100 − 2,000) = $1,500 U.

The total direct labor variance of $1,080 U, therefore, consists of the following.

Illustration 25-22
Summary of labor variances

Labor price variance	$ 420 F
Labor quantity variance	1,500 U
Total direct labor variance	**$1,080 U**

These results can also be obtained from the matrix in Illustration 25-23.

Illustration 25-23
Matrix for direct labor variances

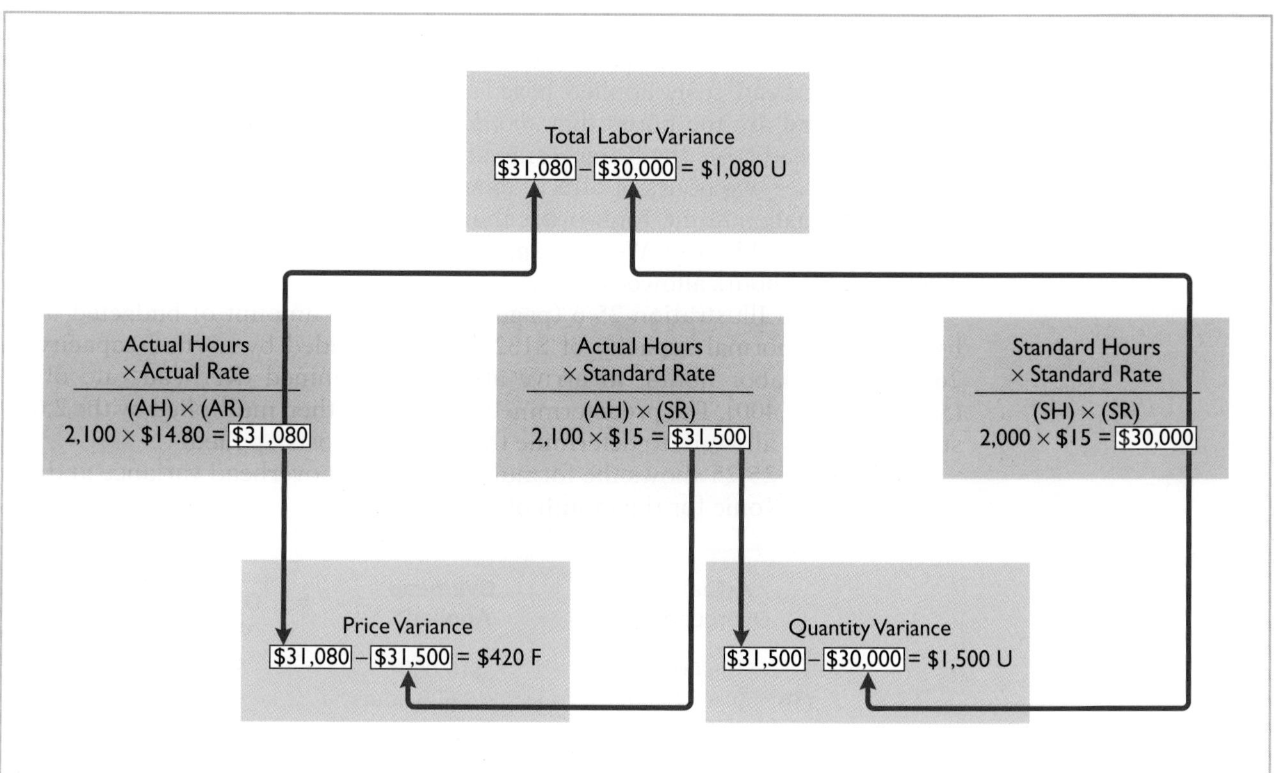

CAUSES OF LABOR VARIANCES

Labor price variances usually result from two factors: (1) paying workers **different wages than expected**, and (2) **misallocation of workers**. In companies where pay rates are determined by union contracts, labor price variances should be infrequent. When workers are not unionized, there is a much higher likelihood of such variances. The responsibility for these variances rests with the manager who authorized the wage change.

Misallocation of the workforce refers to using skilled workers in place of unskilled workers and vice versa. The use of an inexperienced worker instead of an experienced one will result in a favorable price variance because of the lower pay rate of the unskilled worker. An unfavorable price variance would result if a skilled worker were substituted for an inexperienced one. The production department generally is responsible for labor price variances resulting from misallocation of the workforce.

Labor quantity variances relate to the **efficiency of workers**. The cause of a quantity variance generally can be traced to the production department. The causes of an unfavorable variance may be poor training, worker fatigue, faulty machinery, or carelessness. These causes are the responsibility of the **production department**. However, if the excess time is due to inferior materials, the responsibility falls outside the production department.

Manufacturing Overhead Variances

The **total overhead variance** is the difference between the actual overhead costs and overhead costs applied based on standard hours allowed for the amount of goods produced. As indicated in Illustration 25-8 (page 872), Xonic incurred overhead costs of $10,900 to produce 1,000 gallons of Xonic Tonic in June. The computation of the actual overhead comprises a variable and a fixed component. Illustration 25-24 shows this computation.

Illustration 25-24
Actual overhead costs

Variable overhead	$ 6,500
Fixed overhead	4,400
Total actual overhead	**$10,900**

To find the total overhead variance in a standard costing system, we determine the overhead costs applied based on standard hours allowed. **Standard hours allowed** are the hours that *should* have been worked for the units produced. Overhead costs for Xonic Tonic are applied based on direct labor hours. Because it takes two hours of direct labor to produce one gallon of Xonic Tonic, for the 1,000-gallon Xonic Tonic order, the standard hours allowed are 2,000 hours (1,000 gallons × 2 hours). We then apply the predetermined overhead rate to the 2,000 standard hours allowed.

Recall from Illustration 25-6 (page 871) that the amount of budgeted overhead costs at normal capacity of $132,000 was divided by normal capacity of 26,400 direct labor hours, to arrive at a predetermined overhead rate of $5 ($132,000 ÷ 26,400). The predetermined rate of $5 is then multiplied by the 2,000 standard hours allowed, to determine the overhead costs applied.

Illustration 25-25 shows the formula for the total overhead variance and the calculation for Xonic for the month of June.

Illustration 25-25
Formula for total overhead variance

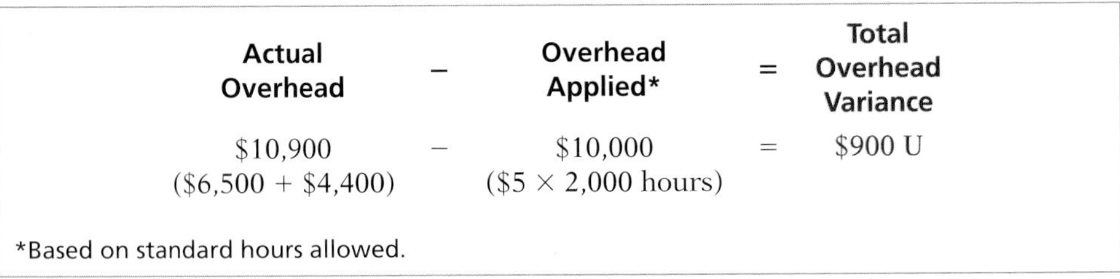

Actual Overhead	−	Overhead Applied*	=	Total Overhead Variance
$10,900 ($6,500 + $4,400)	−	$10,000 ($5 × 2,000 hours)	=	$900 U

*Based on standard hours allowed.

Thus, for Xonic, the total overhead variance is $900 unfavorable.

The overhead variance is generally analyzed through a price and a quantity variance. (These computations are discussed in more detail in advanced courses.) The name usually given to the price variance is the **overhead controllable variance**; the quantity variance is referred to as the **overhead volume variance**. Appendix 25B discusses how the total overhead variance can be broken down into these two variances.

CAUSES OF MANUFACTURING OVERHEAD VARIANCES

One reason for an overhead variance relates to over- or underspending on overhead items. For example, overhead may include indirect labor for which a company paid wages higher than the standard labor price allowed. Or, the price of electricity to run the company's machines increased, and the company did not anticipate this additional cost. Companies should investigate any spending variances to determine whether they will continue in the future. Generally, the responsibility for these variances rests with the production department.

The overhead variance can also result from the inefficient use of overhead. For example, because of poor maintenance, a number of the manufacturing machines are experiencing breakdowns on a consistent basis, leading to reduced production. Or, the flow of materials through the production process is impeded because of a lack of skilled labor to perform the necessary production tasks, due to a lack of planning. In both of these cases, the production department is responsible for the cause of these variances. On the other hand, overhead can also be underutilized because of a lack of sales orders. When the cause is a lack of sales orders, the responsibility rests outside the production department. For example, at one point Chrysler experienced a very significant unfavorable overhead variance because plant capacity was maintained at excessively high levels, due to overly optimistic sales forecasts.

LEARNING OBJECTIVE  **Prepare variance reports and balanced scorecards.**

Reporting Variances

All variances should be reported to appropriate levels of management as soon as possible. The sooner managers are informed, the sooner they can evaluate problems and take corrective action.

The form, content, and frequency of variance reports vary considerably among companies. One approach is to prepare a weekly report for each department that has primary responsibility for cost control. Under this approach, materials price variances are reported to the purchasing department, and all other variances are reported to the production department that did the work. The following report for Xonic, with the materials for the Xonic Tonic order listed first, illustrates this approach.

Illustration 25-26
Materials price variance report

XONIC
Variance Report—Purchasing Department
For Week Ended June 8, 2017

Type of Materials	Quantity Purchased	Actual Price	Standard Price	Price Variance	Explanation
X100	4,200 lbs.	$3.10	$3.00	$ 420 U	Rush order
X142	1,200 units	2.75	2.80	60 F	Quantity discount
A85	600 doz.	5.20	5.10	60 U	Regular supplier on strike
Total price variance				**$420 U**	

The explanation column is completed after consultation with the purchasing department manager.

Variance reports facilitate the principle of "management by exception" explained in Chapter 24. For example, the vice president of purchasing can use the report shown above to evaluate the effectiveness of the purchasing department manager. Or, the vice president of production can use production department variance reports to determine how well each production manager is controlling costs. In using variance reports, top management normally looks for **significant variances**. These may be judged on the basis of some quantitative measure, such as more than 10% of the standard or more than $1,000.

Income Statement Presentation of Variances

In income statements **prepared for management** under a standard cost accounting system, **cost of goods sold is stated at standard cost and the variances are disclosed separately**. Unfavorable variances increase cost of goods sold, while favorable variances decrease cost of goods sold. Illustration 25-27 shows

Illustration 25-27
Variances in income statement for management

XONIC Income Statement For the Month Ended June 30, 2017		
Sales revenue		$70,000
Cost of goods sold (at standard)		52,000
Gross profit (at standard)		18,000
Variances		
Materials price	**$ 420 U**	
Materials quantity	**600 U**	
Labor price	**420 F**	
Labor quantity	**1,500 U**	
Overhead	**900 U**	
Total variance unfavorable		**3,000**
Gross profit (actual)		15,000
Selling and administrative expenses		3,000
Net income		$12,000

the presentation of variances in an income statement. This income statement is based on the production and sale of 1,000 units of Xonic Tonic at $70 per unit. It also assumes selling and administrative costs of $3,000. Observe that each variance is shown, as well as the total net variance. In this example, variations from standard costs reduced net income by $3,000.

Standard costs may be used in financial statements prepared for stockholders and other external users. The costing of inventories at standard costs is in accordance with generally accepted accounting principles when there are no significant differences between actual costs and standard costs. **Hewlett-Packard** and **Jostens, Inc.**, for example, report their inventories at standard costs. However, if there are significant differences between actual and standard costs, the financial statements must report inventories and cost of goods sold at actual costs.

It is also possible to show the variances in an income statement prepared in the variable costing (CVP) format. To do so, it is necessary to analyze the overhead variances into variable and fixed components. This type of analysis is explained in cost accounting textbooks.

Balanced Scorecard

Financial measures (measurement of dollars), such as variance analysis and return on investment (ROI), are useful tools for evaluating performance. However, many companies now supplement these financial measures with nonfinancial measures to better assess performance and anticipate future results. For example, airlines like **Delta** and **United** use capacity utilization as an important measure to understand

and predict future performance. Companies that publish the *New York Times* and the *Chicago Tribune* newspapers use circulation figures as another measure by which to assess performance. **Penske Automotive Group**, the owner of 300 dealerships, rewards executives for meeting employee retention targets. Illustration 25-28 lists some key nonfinancial measures used in various industries.

Illustration 25-28
Nonfinancial measures used in various industries

Industry	Measure
Automobiles	Capacity utilization of plants. Average age of key assets. Impact of strikes. Brand-loyalty statistics.
Computer Systems	Market profile of customer end-products. Number of new products. Employee stock ownership percentages. Number of scientists and technicians used in R&D.
Chemicals	Customer satisfaction data. Factors affecting customer product selection. Number of patents and trademarks held. Customer brand awareness.
Regional Banks	Number of ATMs by state. Number of products used by average customer. Percentage of customer service calls handled by interactive voice response units. Personnel cost per employee. Credit card retention rates.

Source: Financial Accounting Standards Board, *Business Reporting: Insights into Enhancing Voluntary Disclosures* (Norwalk, Conn.: FASB, 2001).

Most companies recognize that both financial and nonfinancial measures can provide useful insights into what is happening in the company. As a result, many companies now use a broad-based measurement approach, called the **balanced scorecard**, to evaluate performance. The **balanced scorecard** incorporates financial and nonfinancial measures in an integrated system that links performance measurement with a company's strategic goals. Nearly 50% of the largest companies in the United States, including **Unilever**, **Chase**, and **Wal-Mart Stores Inc.**, are using the balanced scorecard approach.

The balanced scorecard evaluates company performance from a series of "perspectives." The four most commonly employed perspectives are as follows.

1. The **financial perspective** is the most traditional view of the company. It employs financial measures of performance used by most firms.
2. The **customer perspective** evaluates the company from the viewpoint of those people who buy its products or services. This view compares the company to competitors in terms of price, quality, product innovation, customer service, and other dimensions.
3. The **internal process perspective** evaluates the internal operating processes critical to success. All critical aspects of the value chain—including product development, production, delivery, and after-sale service—are evaluated to ensure that the company is operating effectively and efficiently.
4. The **learning and growth perspective** evaluates how well the company develops and retains its employees. This would include evaluation of such things as employee skills, employee satisfaction, training programs, and information dissemination.

Within each perspective, the balanced scorecard identifies objectives that contribute to attainment of strategic goals. Illustration 25-29 shows examples of objectives within each perspective.

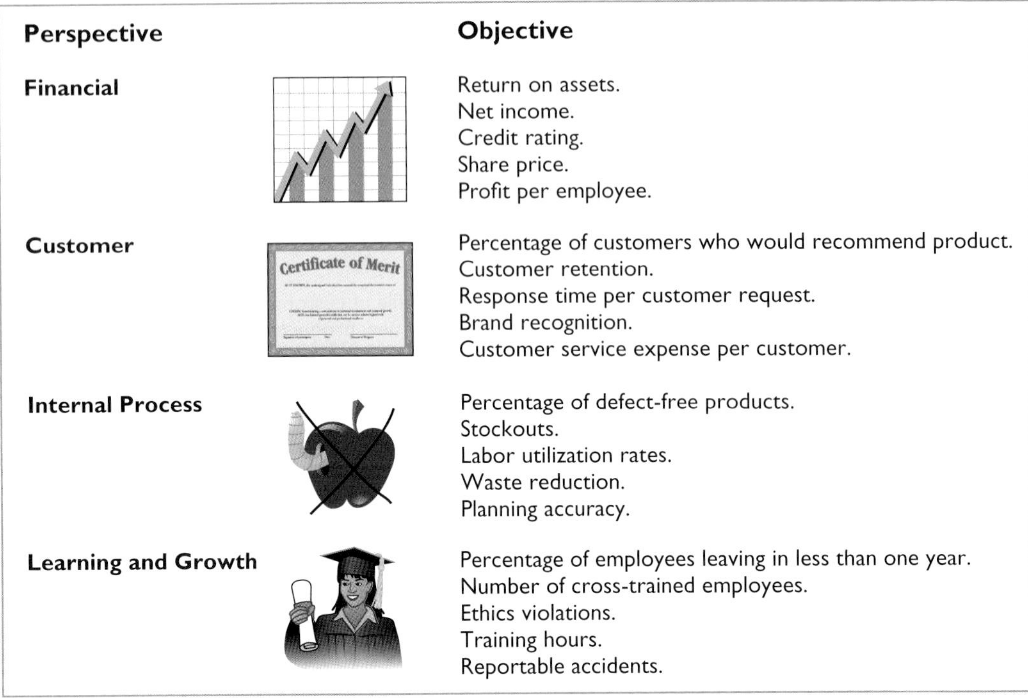

Perspective	Objective
Financial	Return on assets. Net income. Credit rating. Share price. Profit per employee.
Customer	Percentage of customers who would recommend product. Customer retention. Response time per customer request. Brand recognition. Customer service expense per customer.
Internal Process	Percentage of defect-free products. Stockouts. Labor utilization rates. Waste reduction. Planning accuracy.
Learning and Growth	Percentage of employees leaving in less than one year. Number of cross-trained employees. Ethics violations. Training hours. Reportable accidents.

Illustration 25-29
Examples of objectives within the four perspectives of balanced scorecard

The objectives are linked across perspectives in order to tie performance measurement to company goals. The financial-perspective objectives are normally set first, and then objectives are set in the other perspectives in order to accomplish the financial goals.

For example, within the financial perspective, a common goal is to increase profit per dollars invested as measured by ROI. In order to increase ROI, a customer-perspective objective might be to increase customer satisfaction as measured by the percentage of customers who would recommend the product to a friend. In order to increase customer satisfaction, an internal-process-perspective objective might be to increase product quality as measured by the percentage of defect-free units. Finally, in order to increase the percentage of defect-free units, the learning-and-growth-perspective objective might be to reduce factory employee turnover as measured by the percentage of employees leaving in under one year.

Illustration 25-30 illustrates this linkage across perspectives.

Illustration 25-30
Linked process across balanced scorecard perspectives

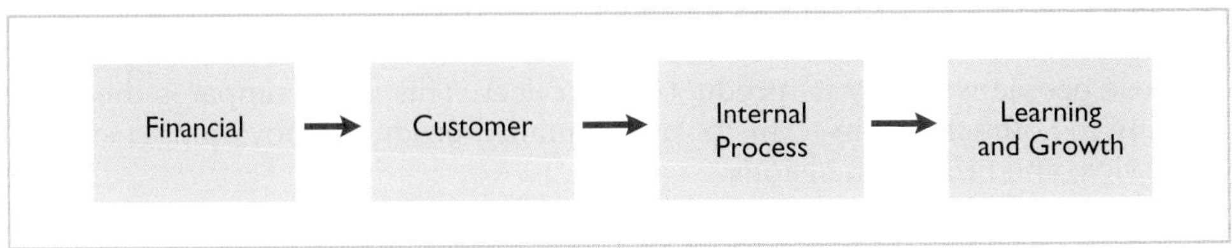

Through this linked process, the company can better understand how to achieve its goals and what measures to use to evaluate performance.

In summary, the balanced scorecard does the following:

1. Employs both **financial and nonfinancial measures**. (For example, ROI is a financial measure; employee turnover is a nonfinancial measure.)

2. **Creates linkages** so that high-level corporate goals can be communicated all the way down to the shop floor.
3. **Provides measurable objectives for nonfinancial measures** such as product quality, rather than vague statements such as "We would like to improve quality."
4. Integrates all of the company's goals into a single performance measurement system, so that **an inappropriate amount of weight will not be placed on any single goal**.

LEARNING OBJECTIVE *5

APPENDIX 25A: Identify the features of a standard cost accounting system.

A **standard cost accounting system** is a double-entry system of accounting. In this system, companies use standard costs in making entries, and they formally recognize variances in the accounts. Companies may use a standard cost system with either job order or process costing.

In this appendix, we will explain and illustrate a **standard cost, job order cost accounting system**. The system is based on two important assumptions:

1. Variances from standards are recognized at the earliest opportunity.
2. The Work in Process account is maintained exclusively on the basis of standard costs.

In practice, there are many variations among standard cost systems. The system described here should prepare you for systems you see in the "real world."

Journal Entries

We will use the transactions of Xonic to illustrate the journal entries. Note as you study the entries that the major difference between the entries here and those for the job order cost accounting system in Chapter 20 is the **variance accounts**.

1. Purchase raw materials on account for $13,020 when the standard cost is $12,600.

Raw Materials Inventory	12,600	
Materials Price Variance	420	
Accounts Payable		13,020
(To record purchase of materials)		

Xonic debits the inventory account for actual quantities at standard cost. This enables the perpetual materials records to show actual quantities. Xonic debits the price variance, which is unfavorable, to Materials Price Variance.

2. Incur direct labor costs of $31,080 when the standard labor cost is $31,500.

Factory Labor	31,500	
Labor Price Variance		420
Factory Wages Payable		31,080
(To record direct labor costs)		

Like the raw materials inventory account, Xonic debits Factory Labor for actual hours worked at the standard hourly rate of pay. In this case, the labor variance is favorable. Thus, Xonic credits Labor Price Variance.

3. Incur actual manufacturing overhead costs of $10,900.

Manufacturing Overhead	10,900	
Accounts Payable/Cash/Acc. Depreciation		10,900
(To record overhead incurred)		

The controllable overhead variance (see Appendix 25B) is not recorded at this time. It depends on standard hours applied to work in process. This amount is not known at the time overhead is incurred.

4. Issue raw materials for production at a cost of $12,600 when the standard cost is $12,000.

Work in Process Inventory	12,000	
Materials Quantity Variance	600	
Raw Materials Inventory		12,600
(To record issuance of raw materials)		

Xonic debits Work in Process Inventory for standard materials quantities used at standard prices. It debits the variance account because the variance is unfavorable. The company credits Raw Materials Inventory for actual quantities at standard prices.

5. Assign factory labor to production at a cost of $31,500 when standard cost is $30,000.

Work in Process Inventory	30,000	
Labor Quantity Variance	1,500	
Factory Labor		31,500
(To assign factory labor to jobs)		

Xonic debits Work in Process Inventory for standard labor hours at standard rates. It debits the unfavorable variance to Labor Quantity Variance. The credit to Factory Labor produces a zero balance in this account.

6. Apply manufacturing overhead to production $10,000.

Work in Process Inventory	10,000	
Manufacturing Overhead		10,000
(To assign overhead to jobs)		

Xonic debits Work in Process Inventory for standard hours allowed multiplied by the standard overhead rate.

7. Transfer completed work to finished goods $52,000.

Finished Goods Inventory	52,000	
Work in Process Inventory		52,000
(To record transfer of completed work to finished goods)		

In this example, both inventory accounts are at standard cost.

8. Sell the 1,000 gallons of Xonic Tonic for $70,000.

Accounts Receivable	70,000	
Cost of Goods Sold	52,000	
Sales		70,000
Finished Goods Inventory		52,000
(To record sale of finished goods and the cost of goods sold)		

The company debits Cost of Goods Sold at standard cost. Gross profit, in turn, is the difference between sales and the standard cost of goods sold.

9. Recognize unfavorable total overhead variance:

Overhead Variance	900	
Manufacturing Overhead		900
(To recognize overhead variances)		

Prior to this entry, a debit balance of $900 existed in Manufacturing Overhead. This entry therefore produces a zero balance in the Manufacturing Overhead account. The information needed for this entry is often not available until the end of the accounting period.

Ledger Accounts

Illustration 25A-1 shows the cost accounts for Xonic after posting the entries. Note that five variance accounts are included in the ledger. The remaining accounts are the same as those illustrated for a job order cost system in Chapter 20, in which only actual costs were used.

Illustration 25A-1
Cost accounts with variances

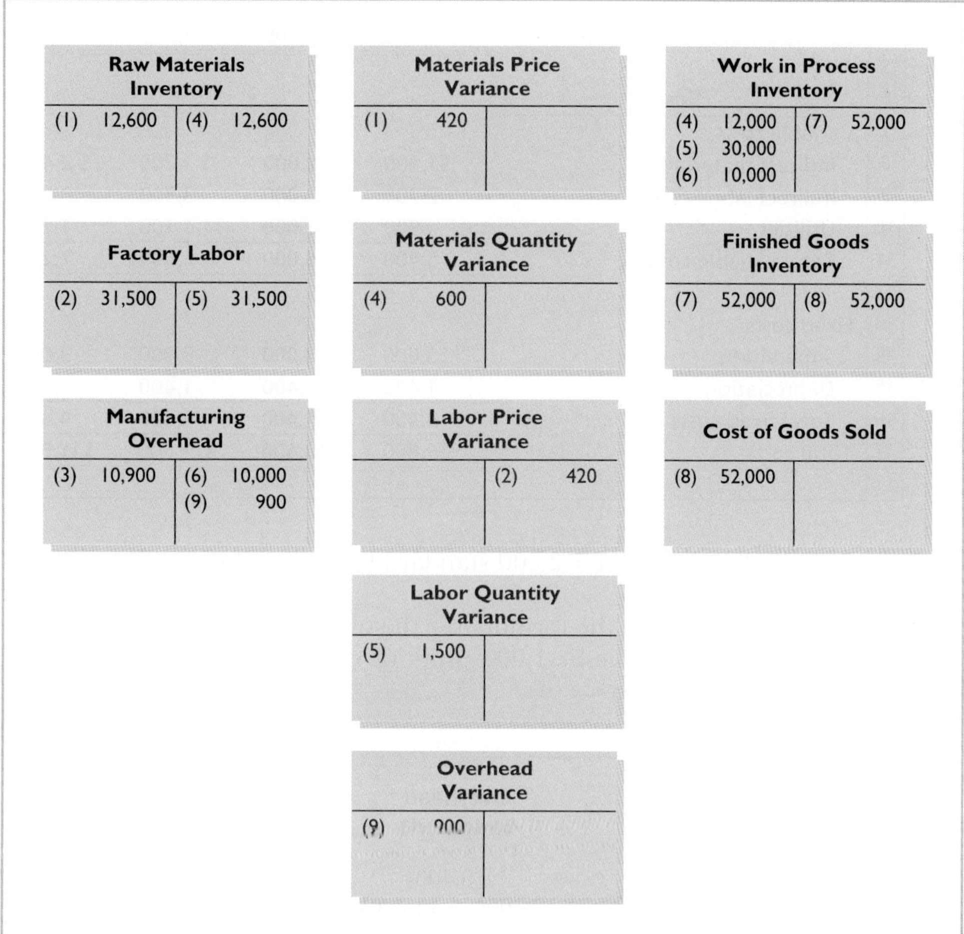

LEARNING OBJECTIVE *6

APPENDIX 25B: Compute overhead controllable and volume variances.

As indicated in the chapter, the total overhead variance is generally analyzed through a price variance and a quantity variance. The name usually given to the price variance is the **overhead controllable variance**; the quantity variance is referred to as the **overhead volume variance**.

Overhead Controllable Variance

The **overhead controllable variance** shows whether overhead costs are effectively controlled. To compute this variance, the company compares actual overhead costs incurred with budgeted costs for the **standard hours allowed**. The budgeted costs are determined from a flexible manufacturing overhead budget. The concepts related to a flexible budget were discussed in Chapter 24.

For Xonic, the budget formula for manufacturing overhead is variable manufacturing overhead cost of $3 per hour of labor plus fixed manufacturing overhead costs of $4,400 ($52,800 ÷ 12, per Illustration 25-6 on page 871). Illustration 25B-1 (page 886) shows the monthly flexible budget for Xonic.

Illustration 25B-1
Flexible budget using standard direct labor hours

A	B	C	D	E
XONIC				
Flexible Manufacturing Overhead Monthly Budget				
Activity Index				
Standard direct labor hours	1,800	2,000	2,200	2,400
Costs				
Variable costs				
Indirect materials	$1,800	$ 2,000	$ 2,200	$ 2,400
Indirect labor	2,700	3,000	3,300	3,600
Utilities	900	1,000	1,100	1,200
Total variable costs	5,400	6,000	6,600	7,200
Fixed costs				
Supervision	3,000	3,000	3,000	3,000
Depreciation	1,400	1,400	1,400	1,400
Total fixed costs	4,400	4,400	4,400	4,400
Total costs	$9,800	$10,400	$11,000	$11,600

As shown, the budgeted costs for 2,000 standard hours are $10,400 ($6,000 variable and $4,400 fixed).

Illustration 25B-2 shows the formula for the overhead controllable variance and the calculation for Xonic at 1,000 units of output (2,000 standard labor hours).

Illustration 25B-2
Formula for overhead controllable variance

Actual Overhead	−	**Overhead Budgeted***	=	**Overhead Controllable Variance**
$10,900 ($6,500 + $4,400)	−	$10,400 ($6,000 + $4,400)	=	$500 U

*Based on standard hours allowed.

The overhead controllable variance for Xonic is $500 unfavorable.

Most controllable variances are associated with variable costs, which are controllable costs. Fixed costs are often known at the time the budget is prepared and are therefore not as likely to deviate from the budgeted amount. In Xonic's case, all of the overhead controllable variance is due to the difference between the actual variable overhead costs ($6,500) and the budgeted variable costs ($6,000).

Management can compare actual and budgeted overhead for each manufacturing overhead cost that contributes to the controllable variance. In addition, management can develop cost and quantity variances for each overhead cost, such as indirect materials and indirect labor.

Overhead Volume Variance

The **overhead volume variance** is the difference between normal capacity hours and standard hours allowed times the fixed overhead rate. The overhead volume variance relates to whether fixed costs were under- or overapplied during the year. For example, the overhead volume variance answers the question of whether Xonic effectively used its fixed costs. If Xonic produces less Xonic Tonic than normal capacity would allow, an unfavorable variance results. Conversely, if

Xonic produces more Xonic Tonic than what is considered normal capacity, a favorable variance results.

The formula for computing the overhead volume variance is as follows.

$$\text{Fixed Overhead Rate} \times \left(\text{Normal Capacity Hours} - \text{Standard Hours Allowed}\right) = \text{Overhead Volume Variance}$$

Illustration 25B-3
Formula for overhead volume variance

To illustrate the fixed overhead rate computation, recall that Xonic budgeted fixed overhead cost for the year of $52,800 (Illustration 25-6 on page 871). At normal capacity, 26,400 standard direct labor hours are required. The fixed overhead rate is therefore $2 per hour ($52,800 ÷ 26,400 hours).

Xonic produced 1,000 units of Xonic Tonic in June. The standard hours allowed for the 1,000 gallons produced in June is 2,000 (1,000 gallons × 2 hours). For Xonic, normal capacity for June is 1,100, so standard direct labor hours for June at normal capacity is 2,200 (26,400 annual hours ÷ 12 months). The computation of the overhead volume variance in this case is as follows.

Fixed Overhead Rate	×	(Normal Capacity Hours	−	Standard Hours Allowed)	=	Overhead Volume Variance
$2	×	(2,200	−	2,000)	=	$400 U

Illustration 25B-4
Computation of overhead volume variance for Xonic

In Xonic's case, a $400 unfavorable volume variance results. The volume variance is unfavorable because Xonic produced only 1,000 gallons rather than the normal capacity of 1,100 gallons in the month of June. As a result, it underapplied fixed overhead for that period.

In computing the overhead variances, it is important to remember the following.

1. Standard hours allowed are used in each of the variances.
2. Budgeted costs for the controllable variance are derived from the flexible budget.
3. The controllable variance generally pertains to variable costs.
4. The volume variance pertains solely to fixed costs.

REVIEW AND PRACTICE

LEARNING OBJECTIVES REVIEW

1 Describe standard costs. Both standards and budgets are predetermined costs. The primary difference is that a standard is a unit amount, whereas a budget is a total amount. A standard may be regarded as the budgeted cost per unit of product.

Standard costs offer a number of advantages. They (a) facilitate management planning, (b) promote greater economy, (c) are useful in setting selling prices, (d) contribute to management control, (e) permit "management by exception," and (f) simplify the costing of inventories and reduce clerical costs.

The direct materials price standard should be based on the delivered cost of raw materials plus an allowance for receiving and handling. The direct materials quantity standard should establish the required quantity plus an allowance for waste and spoilage.

The direct labor price standard should be based on current wage rates and anticipated adjustments such as COLAs. It also generally includes payroll taxes and fringe benefits. Direct labor quantity standards should be based on required production time plus an allowance for rest periods, cleanup, machine setup, and machine downtime.

For manufacturing overhead, a standard predetermined overhead rate is used. It is based on an expected standard activity index such as standard direct labor hours or standard machine hours.

2 Determine direct materials variances. The formulas for the direct materials variances are as follows.

$$\begin{pmatrix}\text{Actual quantity}\\ \times \text{ Actual price}\end{pmatrix} - \begin{pmatrix}\text{Standard quantity}\\ \times \text{ Standard price}\end{pmatrix} = \begin{matrix}\text{Total}\\ \text{materials}\\ \text{variance}\end{matrix}$$

$$\begin{pmatrix}\text{Actual quantity}\\ \times \text{ Actual price}\end{pmatrix} - \begin{pmatrix}\text{Actual quantity}\\ \times \text{ Standard price}\end{pmatrix} = \begin{matrix}\text{Materials}\\ \text{price}\\ \text{variance}\end{matrix}$$

$$\begin{pmatrix}\text{Actual quantity}\\ \times \text{ Standard price}\end{pmatrix} - \begin{pmatrix}\text{Standard quantity}\\ \times \text{ Standard price}\end{pmatrix} = \begin{matrix}\text{Materials}\\ \text{quantity}\\ \text{variance}\end{matrix}$$

3 Determine direct labor and total manufacturing overhead variances. The formulas for the direct labor variances are as follows.

$$\begin{pmatrix}\text{Actual hours}\\ \times \text{ Actual rate}\end{pmatrix} - \begin{pmatrix}\text{Standard hours}\\ \times \text{ Standard rate}\end{pmatrix} = \begin{matrix}\text{Total}\\ \text{labor}\\ \text{variance}\end{matrix}$$

$$\begin{pmatrix}\text{Actual hours}\\ \times \text{ Actual rate}\end{pmatrix} - \begin{pmatrix}\text{Actual hours}\\ \times \text{ Standard rate}\end{pmatrix} = \begin{matrix}\text{Labor}\\ \text{price}\\ \text{variance}\end{matrix}$$

$$\begin{pmatrix}\text{Actual hours}\\ \times \text{ Standard rate}\end{pmatrix} - \begin{pmatrix}\text{Standard hours}\\ \times \text{ Standard rate}\end{pmatrix} = \begin{matrix}\text{Labor}\\ \text{quantity}\\ \text{variance}\end{matrix}$$

The formula for the total manufacturing overhead variance is as follows.

$$\begin{pmatrix}\text{Actual}\\ \text{overhead}\end{pmatrix} - \begin{pmatrix}\text{Overhead}\\ \text{applied at}\\ \text{standard hours}\\ \text{allowed}\end{pmatrix} = \begin{matrix}\text{Total overhead}\\ \text{variance}\end{matrix}$$

4 Prepare variance reports and balanced scorecards. Variances are reported to management in variance reports. The reports facilitate management by exception by highlighting significant differences. Under a standard costing system, an income statement prepared for management will report cost of goods sold at standard cost and then disclose each variance separately.

The balanced scorecard incorporates financial and nonfinancial measures in an integrated system that links performance measurement and a company's strategic goals. It employs four perspectives: financial, customer, internal process, and learning and growth. Objectives are set within each of these perspectives that link to objectives within the other perspectives.

*__5 Identify the features of a standard cost accounting system.__ In a standard cost accounting system, companies journalize and post standard costs, and they maintain separate variance accounts in the ledger.

*__6 Compute overhead controllable and volume variances.__ The total overhead variance is generally analyzed through a price variance and a quantity variance. The name usually given to the price variance is the overhead controllable variance. The quantity variance is referred to as the overhead volume variance.

GLOSSARY REVIEW

Balanced scorecard An approach that incorporates financial and nonfinancial measures in an integrated system that links performance measurement and a company's strategic goals.

Customer perspective A viewpoint employed in the balanced scorecard to evaluate the company from the perspective of those people who buy and use its products or services.

Direct labor price standard The rate per hour that should be incurred for direct labor.

Direct labor quantity standard The time that should be required to make one unit of product.

Direct materials price standard The cost per unit of direct materials that should be incurred.

Direct materials quantity standard The quantity of direct materials that should be used per unit of finished goods.

Financial perspective A viewpoint employed in the balanced scorecard to evaluate a company's performance using financial measures.

Ideal standards Standards based on the optimum level of performance under perfect operating conditions.

Internal process perspective A viewpoint employed in the balanced scorecard to evaluate the effectiveness and efficiency of a company's value chain, including product development, production, delivery, and after-sale service.

Labor price variance The difference between the actual hours times the actual rate and the actual hours times the standard rate for labor.

Labor quantity variance The difference between actual hours times the standard rate and standard hours times the standard rate for labor.

Learning and growth perspective A viewpoint employed in the balanced scorecard to evaluate how well a company develops and retains its employees.

Materials price variance The difference between the actual quantity times the actual price and the actual quantity times the standard price for materials.

Materials quantity variance The difference between the actual quantity times the standard price and the standard quantity times the standard price for materials.

Normal capacity The average activity output that a company should experience over the long run.

Normal standards Standards based on an efficient level of performance that are attainable under expected operating conditions.

***Overhead controllable variance** The difference between actual overhead incurred and overhead budgeted for the standard hours allowed.

***Overhead volume variance** The difference between normal capacity hours and standard hours allowed times the fixed overhead rate.

***Standard cost accounting system** A double-entry system of accounting in which standard costs are used in making entries, and variances are recognized in the accounts.

Standard costs Predetermined unit costs which companies use as measures of performance.

Standard hours allowed The hours that should have been worked for the units produced.

Standard predetermined overhead rate An overhead rate determined by dividing budgeted overhead costs by an expected standard activity index.

Total labor variance The difference between actual hours times the actual rate and standard hours times the standard rate for labor.

Total materials variance The difference between the actual quantity times the actual price and the standard quantity times the standard price of materials.

Total overhead variance The difference between actual overhead costs and overhead costs applied to work done, based on standard hours allowed.

Variance The difference between total actual costs and total standard costs.

PRACTICE EXERCISES

Compute materials and labor variances.

(LO 2, 3)

1. Hector Inc., which produces a single product, has prepared the following standard cost sheet for one unit of the product.

Direct materials (6 pounds at $2.50 per pound)	$15.00
Direct labor (3.1 hours at $12.00 per hour)	$37.20

During the month of April, the company manufactures 250 units and incurs the following actual costs.

Direct materials purchased and used (1,600 pounds)	$4,192
Direct labor (760 hours)	$8,740

Instructions

Compute the total, price, and quantity variances for materials and labor.

Solution

1. Total materials variance:

(AQ × AP)	–	(SQ × SP)		
(1,600 × $2.62*)		(1,500** × $2.50)		
$4,192	–	$3,750	=	$442 U

*$4,192 ÷ 1,600 **250 × 6

Materials price variance:

(AQ × AP)	–	(AQ × SP)		
(1,600 × $2.62)		(1,600 × $2.50)		
$4,192	–	$4,000	=	$192 U

Materials quantity variance:

(AQ × SP)	–	(SQ × SP)		
(1,600 × $2.50)		(1,500 × $2.50)		
$4,000	–	$3,750	=	$250 U

Total labor variance:

(AH × AR)	–	(SH × SR)		
(760 × $11.50*)		(775** × $12.00)		
$8,740	–	$9,300	=	$560 F

*$8,740 ÷ 760 **250 × 3.1

Labor price variance:

(AH × AR)	–	(AH × SR)		
(760 × $11.50)		(760 × $12.00)		
$8,740	–	$9,120	=	$380 F

Labor quantity variance:

(AH × SR)	–	(SH × SR)		
(760 × $12.00)		(775 × $12.00)		
$9,120	–	$9,300	=	$180 F

Compute overhead variances.
(LO 3)

2. Manufacturing overhead data for the production of Product H by Yamato Company are as follows.

Overhead incurred for 35,000 actual direct labor hours worked	$140,000
Overhead rate (variable $3; fixed $1) at normal capacity of 36,000 direct labor hours	$4
Standard hours allowed for work done	34,000

Instructions

Compute the total overhead variance.

Solution

2. Total overhead variance:

Actual Overhead	–	Overhead Applied	=	
$140,000	–	$136,000 (34,000 × $4)	=	$4,000 U

PRACTICE PROBLEM

Compute variances.
(LO 2, 3)

Manlow Company makes a cologne called Allure. The standard cost for one bottle of Allure is as follows.

	Standard					
Manufacturing Cost Elements	**Quantity**	×	**Price**	=	**Cost**
Direct materials	6 oz.	×	$ 0.90	=	$ 5.40
Direct labor	0.5 hrs.	×	$12.00	=	6.00
Manufacturing overhead	0.5 hrs.	×	$ 4.80	=	2.40
					$13.80

During the month, the following transactions occurred in manufacturing 10,000 bottles of Allure.

1. 58,000 ounces of materials were purchased at $1.00 per ounce.
2. All the materials purchased were used to produce the 10,000 bottles of Allure.
3. 4,900 direct labor hours were worked at a total labor cost of $56,350.
4. Variable manufacturing overhead incurred was $15,000 and fixed overhead incurred was $10,400.

The manufacturing overhead rate of $4.80 is based on a normal capacity of 5,200 direct labor hours. The total budget at this capacity is $10,400 fixed and $14,560 variable.

Instructions

(a) Compute the total variance and the variances for direct materials and direct labor elements.

(b) Compute the total variance for manufacturing overhead.

Solution

(a) **Total Variance**

Actual costs incurred	
Direct materials	$ 58,000
Direct labor	56,350
Manufacturing overhead	25,400
	139,750
Standard cost (10,000 × $13.80)	138,000
Total variance	$ 1,750 U

Direct Materials Variances

Total	= $58,000 (58,000 × $1.00)	− $54,000 (60,000* × $0.90)	= $4,000 U
Price	= $58,000 (58,000 × $1.00)	− $52,200 (58,000 × $0.90)	= $5,800 U
Quantity	= $52,200 (58,000 × $0.90)	− $54,000 (60,000 × $0.90)	= $1,800 F

*10,000 × 6

Direct Labor Variances

Total	= $56,350 (4,900 × $11.50*)	− $60,000 (5,000** × $12.00)	= $3,650 F
Price	= $56,350 (4,900 × $11.50)	− $58,800 (4,900 × $12.00)	= $2,450 F
Quantity	= $58,800 (4,900 × $12.00)	− $60,000 (5,000 × $12.00)	= $1,200 F

*56,350 ÷ 4,900; **10,000 × 0.5

(b) **Overhead Variance**

Total	= $25,400 ($15,000 + $10,400)	− $24,000 (5,000 × $4.80)	= $1,400 U

EXERCISES

Compute budget and standard. (LO 1)

E25-1 Parsons Company is planning to produce 2,000 units of product in 2017. Each unit requires 3 pounds of materials at $5 per pound and a half-hour of labor at $16 per hour. The overhead rate is 70% of direct labor.

Instructions

(a) Compute the budgeted amounts for 2017 for direct materials to be used, direct labor, and applied overhead.
(b) Compute the standard cost of one unit of product.
(c) What are the potential advantages to a corporation of using standard costs?

Compute standard materials costs. (LO 1)

E25-2 Hank Itzek manufactures and sells homemade wine, and he wants to develop a standard cost per gallon. The following are required for production of a 50-gallon batch.

3,000 ounces of grape concentrate at $0.06 per ounce
54 pounds of granulated sugar at $0.30 per pound
60 lemons at $0.60 each
50 yeast tablets at $0.25 each
50 nutrient tablets at $0.20 each
2,600 ounces of water at $0.005 per ounce

Hank estimates that 4% of the grape concentrate is wasted, 10% of the sugar is lost, and 25% of the lemons cannot be used.

Instructions

Compute the standard cost of the ingredients for one gallon of wine. (Carry computations to two decimal places.)

Compute standard cost per unit. (LO 1)

E25-3 Stefani Company has gathered the following information about its product.

Direct materials. Each unit of product contains 4.5 pounds of materials. The average waste and spoilage per unit produced under normal conditions is 0.5 pounds. Materials cost $5 per pound, but Stefani always takes the 2% cash discount all of its suppliers offer. Freight costs average $0.25 per pound.

Direct labor. Each unit requires 2 hours of labor. Setup, cleanup, and downtime average 0.4 hours per unit. The average hourly pay rate of Stefani's employees is $12. Payroll taxes and fringe benefits are an additional $3 per hour.

Manufacturing overhead. Overhead is applied at a rate of $7 per direct labor hour.

Instructions

Compute Stefani's total standard cost per unit.

Compute labor cost and labor quantity variance.

(LO 3)

E25-4 Monte Services, Inc. is trying to establish the standard labor cost of a typical oil change. The following data have been collected from time and motion studies conducted over the past month.

Actual time spent on the oil change	1.0 hour
Hourly wage rate	$12
Payroll taxes	10% of wage rate
Setup and downtime	20% of actual labor time
Cleanup and rest periods	30% of actual labor time
Fringe benefits	25% of wage rate

Instructions

(a) Determine the standard direct labor hours per oil change.
(b) Determine the standard direct labor hourly rate.
(c) Determine the standard direct labor cost per oil change.
(d) If an oil change took 1.6 hours at the standard hourly rate, what was the direct labor quantity variance?

Compute materials price and quantity variances.

(LO 2)

E25-5 The standard cost of Product B manufactured by Pharrell Company includes three units of direct materials at $5.00 per unit. During June, 29,000 units of direct materials are purchased at a cost of $4.70 per unit, and 29,000 units of direct materials are used to produce 9,400 units of Product B.

Instructions

(a) Compute the total materials variance and the price and quantity variances.
(b) Repeat (a), assuming the purchase price is $5.15 and the quantity purchased and used is 28,000 units.

Compute labor price and quantity variances.

(LO 3)

E25-6 Lewis Company's standard labor cost of producing one unit of Product DD is 4 hours at the rate of $12.00 per hour. During August, 40,600 hours of labor are incurred at a cost of $12.15 per hour to produce 10,000 units of Product DD.

Instructions

(a) Compute the total labor variance.
(b) Compute the labor price and quantity variances.
(c) Repeat (b), assuming the standard is 4.1 hours of direct labor at $12.25 per hour.

Compute materials and labor variances.

(LO 2, 3)

E25-7 Levine Inc., which produces a single product, has prepared the following standard cost sheet for one unit of the product.

Direct materials (8 pounds at $2.50 per pound)	$20
Direct labor (3 hours at $12.00 per hour)	$36

During the month of April, the company manufactures 230 units and incurs the following actual costs.

Direct materials purchased and used (1,900 pounds)	$5,035
Direct labor (700 hours)	$8,120

Instructions

Compute the total, price, and quantity variances for materials and labor.

Compute the materials and labor variances and list reasons for unfavorable variances.

(LO 2, 3)

E25-8 The following direct materials and direct labor data pertain to the operations of Laurel Company for the month of August.

Costs		Quantities	
Actual labor rate	$13 per hour	Actual hours incurred and used	4,150 hours
Actual materials price	$128 per ton	Actual quantity of materials purchased and used	1,220 tons
Standard labor rate	$12.50 per hour	Standard hours used	4,300 hours
Standard materials price	$130 per ton	Standard quantity of materials used	1,200 tons

Instructions

(a) Compute the total, price, and quantity variances for materials and labor.
(b) Provide two possible explanations for each of the unfavorable variances calculated above, and suggest where responsibility for the unfavorable result might be placed.

Determine amounts from variance report.

(LO 2, 3)

E25-9 You have been given the following information about the production of Usher Co., and are asked to provide the plant manager with information for a meeting with the vice president of operations.

	Standard Cost Card
Direct materials (5 pounds at $4 per pound)	$20.00
Direct labor (0.8 hours at $10)	8.00
Variable overhead (0.8 hours at $3 per hour)	2.40
Fixed overhead (0.8 hours at $7 per hour)	5.60
	$36.00

The following is a variance report for the most recent period of operations.

		Variances	
Costs	**Total Standard Cost**	**Price**	**Quantity**
Direct materials	$410,000	$2,095 F	$9,000 U
Direct labor	180,000	3,840 U	6,000 U

Instructions

(a) How many units were produced during the period?
(b) How many pounds of raw materials were purchased and used during the period?
(c) What was the actual cost per pound of raw materials?
(d) How many actual direct labor hours were worked during the period?
(e) What was the actual rate paid per direct labor hour?

(CGA adapted)

Prepare a variance report for direct labor.

(LO 3, 4)

E25-10 During March 2017, Toby Tool & Die Company worked on four jobs. A review of direct labor costs reveals the following summary data.

Job	Actual		Standard		Total
Number	**Hours**	**Costs**	**Hours**	**Costs**	**Variance**
A257	221	$4,420	225	$4,500	$ 80 F
A258	450	9,450	430	8,600	850 U
A259	300	6,180	300	6,000	180 U
A260	116	2,088	110	2,200	112 F
Total variance					$838 U

Analysis reveals that Job A257 was a repeat job. Job A258 was a rush order that required overtime work at premium rates of pay. Job A259 required a more experienced replacement worker on one shift. Work on Job A260 was done for one day by a new trainee when a regular worker was absent.

Instructions

Prepare a report for the plant supervisor on direct labor cost variances for March. The report should have columns for (1) Job No., (2) Actual Hours, (3) Standard Hours, (4) Quantity Variance, (5) Actual Rate, (6) Standard Rate, (7) Price Variance, and (8) Explanation.

Compute overhead variance.

(LO 3)

E25-11 Manufacturing overhead data for the production of Product H by Shakira Company are as follows.

Overhead incurred for 52,000 actual direct labor hours worked	$263,000
Overhead rate (variable $3; fixed $2) at normal capacity of 54,000 direct labor hours	$5
Standard hours allowed for work done	52,000

Instructions

Compute the total overhead variance.

Compute overhead variances.
(LO 3)

E25-12 Byrd Company produces one product, a putter called GO-Putter. Byrd uses a standard cost system and determines that it should take one hour of direct labor to produce one GO-Putter. The normal production capacity for this putter is 100,000 units per year. The total budgeted overhead at normal capacity is $850,000 comprising $250,000 of variable costs and $600,000 of fixed costs. Byrd applies overhead on the basis of direct labor hours.

During the current year, Byrd produced 95,000 putters, worked 94,000 direct labor hours, and incurred variable overhead costs of $256,000 and fixed overhead costs of $600,000.

Instructions

(a) Compute the predetermined variable overhead rate and the predetermined fixed overhead rate.
(b) Compute the applied overhead for Byrd for the year.
(c) Compute the total overhead variance.

Compute variances for materials.
(LO 2, 3)

E25-13 Ceelo Company purchased (at a cost of $10,200) and used 2,400 pounds of materials during May. Ceelo's standard cost of materials per unit produced is based on 2 pounds per unit at a cost $5 per pound. Production in May was 1,050 units.

Instructions

(a) Compute the total, price, and quantity variances for materials.
(b) Assume Ceelo also had an unfavorable labor quantity variance. What is a possible scenario that would provide one cause for the variances computed in (a) and the unfavorable labor quantity variance?

Prepare a variance report.
(LO 2, 4)

E25-14 Picard Landscaping plants grass seed as the basic landscaping for business campuses. During a recent month, the company worked on three projects (Remington, Chang, and Wyco). The company is interested in controlling the materials costs, namely the grass seed, for these plantings projects.

In order to provide management with useful cost control information, the company uses standard costs and prepares monthly variance reports. Analysis reveals that the purchasing agent mistakenly purchased poor-quality seed for the Remington project. The Chang project, however, received higher-than-standard-quality seed that was on sale. The Wyco project received standard-quality seed. However, the price had increased and a new employee was used to spread the seed.

Shown below are quantity and cost data for each project.

	Actual		Standard		Total
Project	**Quantity**	**Costs**	**Quantity**	**Costs**	**Variance**
Remington	500 lbs.	$1,200	460 lbs.	$1,150	$ 50 U
Chang	400	920	410	1,025	105 F
Wyco	550	1,430	480	1,200	230 U
Total variance					$175 U

Instructions

(a) Prepare a variance report for the purchasing department with the following columns: (1) Project, (2) Actual Pounds Purchased, (3) Actual Price per Pound, (4) Standard Price per Pound, (5) Price Variance, and (6) Explanation.
(b) Prepare a variance report for the production department with the following columns: (1) Project, (2) Actual Pounds, (3) Standard Pounds, (4) Standard Price per Pound, (5) Quantity Variance, and (6) Explanation.

Complete variance report.
(LO 4)

E25-15 Urban Corporation prepared the following variance report.

URBAN CORPORATION
Variance Report—Purchasing Department
For the Week Ended January 9, 2017

Type of Materials	Quantity Purchased	Actual Price	Standard Price	Price Variance	Explanation
Rogue11	? lbs.	$5.20	$5.00	$5,500 ?	Price increase
Storm17	7,000 oz.	?	3.30	1,050 U	Rush order
Beast29	22,000 units	0.40	?	660 F	Bought larger quantity

Instructions

Fill in the appropriate amounts or letters for the question marks in the report.

E25-16 Fisk Company uses a standard cost accounting system. During January, the company reported the following manufacturing variances.

Prepare income statement for management.

(LO 4)

Materials price variance	$1,200 U	Labor quantity variance	$750 U
Materials quantity variance	800 F	Overhead variance	800 U
Labor price variance	550 U		

In addition, 8,000 units of product were sold at $8 per unit. Each unit sold had a standard cost of $5. Selling and administrative expenses were $8,000 for the month.

Instructions

Prepare an income statement for management for the month ended January 31, 2017.

E25-17 The following is a list of terms related to performance evaluation.

Identify performance evaluation terminology.

(LO 1, 4)

1. Balanced scorecard
2. Variance
3. Learning and growth perspective
4. Nonfinancial measures
5. Customer perspective
6. Internal process perspective
7. Ideal standards
8. Normal standards

Instructions

Match each of the following descriptions with one of the terms above.

(a) The difference between total actual costs and total standard costs.
(b) An efficient level of performance that is attainable under expected operating conditions.
(c) An approach that incorporates financial and nonfinancial measures in an integrated system that links performance measurement and a company's strategic goals.
(d) A viewpoint employed in the balanced scorecard to evaluate how well a company develops and retains its employees.
(e) An evaluation tool that is not based on dollars.
(f) A viewpoint employed in the balanced scorecard to evaluate the company from the perspective of those people who buy its products or services.
(g) An optimum level of performance under perfect operating conditions.
(h) A viewpoint employed in the balanced scorecard to evaluate the efficiency and effectiveness of the company's value chain.

E25-18 Indicate which of the four perspectives in the balanced scorecard is most likely associated with the objectives that follow.

Identity balanced scorecard perspectives.

(LO 4)

1. Percentage of repeat customers.
2. Number of suggestions for improvement from employees.
3. Contribution margin.
4. Brand recognition.
5. Number of cross-trained employees.
6. Amount of setup time.

E25-19 Indicate which of the four perspectives in the balanced scorecard is most likely associated with the objectives that follow.

Identify balance scorecard perspectives.

(LO 4)

1. Ethics violations.
2. Credit rating.
3. Customer retention.
4. Stockouts.
5. Reportable accidents.
6. Brand recognition.

***E25-20** Vista Company installed a standard cost system on January 1. Selected transactions for the month of January are as follows.

Journalize entries in a standard cost accounting system.

(LO 5)

1. Purchased 18,000 units of raw materials on account at a cost of $4.50 per unit. Standard cost was $4.40 per unit.
2. Issued 18,000 units of raw materials for jobs that required 17,500 standard units of raw materials.
3. Incurred 15,300 actual hours of direct labor at an actual rate of $5.00 per hour. The standard rate is $5.50 per hour. (Credit Factory Wages Payable.)

4. Performed 15,300 hours of direct labor on jobs when standard hours were 15,400.
5. Applied overhead to jobs at the rate of 100% of direct labor cost for standard hours allowed.

Instructions
Journalize the January transactions.

Answer questions concerning missing entries and balances.
(LO 2, 3, 5)

***E25-21** Lopez Company uses a standard cost accounting system. Some of the ledger accounts have been destroyed in a fire. The controller asks your help in reconstructing some missing entries and balances.

Instructions
Answer the following questions.

(a) Materials Price Variance shows a $2,000 unfavorable balance. Accounts Payable shows $138,000 of raw materials purchases. What was the amount debited to Raw Materials Inventory for raw materials purchased?
(b) Materials Quantity Variance shows a $3,000 favorable balance. Raw Materials Inventory shows a zero balance. What was the amount debited to Work in Process Inventory for direct materials used?
(c) Labor Price Variance shows a $1,500 favorable balance. Factory Labor shows a debit of $145,000 for wages incurred. What was the amount credited to Factory Wages Payable?
(d) Factory Labor shows a credit of $145,000 for direct labor used. Labor Quantity Variance shows a $900 favorable balance. What was the amount debited to Work in Process for direct labor used?
(e) Overhead applied to Work in Process totaled $165,000. If the total overhead variance was $1,200 favorable, what was the amount of overhead costs debited to Manufacturing Overhead?

Journalize entries for materials and labor variances.
(LO 5)

***E25-22** Data for Levine Inc. are given in E25-7.

Instructions
Journalize the entries to record the materials and labor variances.

Compute manufacturing overhead variances and interpret findings.
(LO 6)

***E25-23** The information shown below was taken from the annual manufacturing overhead cost budget of Connick Company.

Variable manufacturing overhead costs	$34,650
Fixed manufacturing overhead costs	$19,800
Normal production level in labor hours	16,500
Normal production level in units	4,125
Standard labor hours per unit	4

During the year, 4,050 units were produced, 16,100 hours were worked, and the actual manufacturing overhead was $55,500. Actual fixed manufacturing overhead costs equaled budgeted fixed manufacturing overhead costs. Overhead is applied on the basis of direct labor hours.

Instructions
(a) Compute the total, fixed, and variable predetermined manufacturing overhead rates.
(b) Compute the total, controllable, and volume overhead variances.
(c) Briefly interpret the overhead controllable and volume variances computed in (b).

Compute overhead variances.
(LO 6)

***E25-24** The loan department of Calgary Bank uses standard costs to determine the overhead cost of processing loan applications. During the current month, a fire occurred, and the accounting records for the department were mostly destroyed. The following data were salvaged from the ashes.

Standard variable overhead rate per hour	$9
Standard hours per application	2
Standard hours allowed	2,000
Standard fixed overhead rate per hour	$6
Actual fixed overhead cost	$12,600
Variable overhead budget based on standard hours allowed	$18,000
Fixed overhead budget	$12,600
Overhead controllable variance	$ 1,200 U

Instructions

(a) Determine the following.
  (1) Total actual overhead cost.
  (2) Actual variable overhead cost.
  (3) Variable overhead costs applied.
  (4) Fixed overhead costs applied.
  (5) Overhead volume variance.
(b) Determine how many loans were processed.

***E25-25** Seacrest Company's overhead rate was based on estimates of $200,000 for overhead costs and 20,000 direct labor hours. Seacrest's standards allow 2 hours of direct labor per unit produced. Production in May was 900 units, and actual overhead incurred in May was $19,500. The overhead budgeted for 1,800 standard direct labor hours is $17,600 ($5,000 fixed and $12,600 variable).

Compute variances.

(LO 6)

Instructions

(a) Compute the total, controllable, and volume variances for overhead.
(b) What are possible causes of the variances computed in part (a)?

PROBLEMS

P25-1A Rogen Corporation manufactures a single product. The standard cost per unit of product is shown below.

Compute variances.

(LO 2, 3)

Direct materials—1 pound plastic at $7.00 per pound	$ 7.00
Direct labor—1.6 hours at $12.00 per hour	19.20
Variable manufacturing overhead	12.00
Fixed manufacturing overhead	4.00
Total standard cost per unit	$42.20

The predetermined manufacturing overhead rate is $10 per direct labor hour ($16.00 ÷ 1.6). It was computed from a master manufacturing overhead budget based on normal production of 8,000 direct labor hours (5,000 units) for the month. The master budget showed total variable costs of $60,000 ($7.50 per hour) and total fixed overhead costs of $20,000 ($2.50 per hour). Actual costs for October in producing 4,800 units were as follows.

Direct materials (5,100 pounds)	$ 36,720
Direct labor (7,400 hours)	92,500
Variable overhead	59,700
Fixed overhead	21,000
Total manufacturing costs	$209,920

The purchasing department buys the quantities of raw materials that are expected to be used in production each month. Raw materials inventories, therefore, can be ignored.

Instructions

(a) Compute all of the materials and labor variances.
(b) Compute the total overhead variance.

(a) MPV $1,020 U

P25-2A Ayala Corporation accumulates the following data relative to jobs started and finished during the month of June 2017.

Compute variances, and prepare income statement.

(LO 2, 3, 4)

XLS

Costs and Production Data	Actual	Standard
Raw materials unit cost	$2.25	$2.10
Raw materials units used	10,600	10,000
Direct labor payroll	$120,960	$120,000
Direct labor hours worked	14,400	15,000
Manufacturing overhead incurred	$189,500	
Manufacturing overhead applied		$193,500
Machine hours expected to be used at normal capacity		42,500
Budgeted fixed overhead for June		$55,250
Variable overhead rate per machine hour		$3.00
Fixed overhead rate per machine hour		$1.30

Overhead is applied on the basis of standard machine hours. Three hours of machine time are required for each direct labor hour. The jobs were sold for $400,000. Selling and administrative expenses were $40,000. Assume that the amount of raw materials purchased equaled the amount used.

Instructions

(a) Compute all of the variances for (1) direct materials and (2) direct labor. (a) LQV $4,800 F

(b) Compute the total overhead variance.

(c) Prepare an income statement for management. (Ignore income taxes.)

P25-3A Rudd Clothiers is a small company that manufactures tall-men's suits. The company has used a standard cost accounting system. In May 2017, 11,250 suits were produced. The following standard and actual cost data applied to the month of May when normal capacity was 14,000 direct labor hours. All materials purchased were used.

Compute and identify significant variances.

(LO 2, 3, 4)

Cost Element	Standard (per unit)	Actual
Direct materials	8 yards at $4.40 per yard	$375,575 for 90,500 yards ($4.15 per yard)
Direct labor	1.2 hours at $13.40 per hour	$200,925 for 14,250 hours ($14.10 per hour)
Overhead	1.2 hours at $6.10 per hour (fixed $3.50; variable $2.60)	$49,000 fixed overhead $37,000 variable overhead

Overhead is applied on the basis of direct labor hours. At normal capacity, budgeted fixed overhead costs were $49,000, and budgeted variable overhead was $36,400.

Instructions

(a) Compute the total, price, and quantity variances for (1) materials and (2) labor. (a) MPV $22,625 F

(b) Compute the total overhead variance.

(c) Which of the materials and labor variances should be investigated if management considers a variance of more than 4% from standard to be significant?

P25-4A Kansas Company uses a standard cost accounting system. In 2017, the company produced 28,000 units. Each unit took several pounds of direct materials and 1.6 standard hours of direct labor at a standard hourly rate of $12.00. Normal capacity was 50,000 direct labor hours. During the year, 117,000 pounds of raw materials were purchased at $0.92 per pound. All materials purchased were used during the year.

Answer questions about variances.

(LO 2, 3)

Instructions

(a) If the materials price variance was $3,510 favorable, what was the standard materials price per pound?

(b) If the materials quantity variance was $4,750 unfavorable, what was the standard materials quantity per unit? (b) 4.0 pounds

(c) What were the standard hours allowed for the units produced?

(d) If the labor quantity variance was $7,200 unfavorable, what were the actual direct labor hours worked?

(e) If the labor price variance was $9,080 favorable, what was the actual rate per hour?

(f) If total budgeted manufacturing overhead was $360,000 at normal capacity, what was the predetermined overhead rate? (f) $7.20 per DLH

(g) What was the standard cost per unit of product?

(h) How much overhead was applied to production during the year?

(i) Using one or more answers above, what were the total costs assigned to work in process?

P25-5A Hart Labs, Inc. provides mad cow disease testing for both state and federal governmental agricultural agencies. Because the company's customers are governmental agencies, prices are strictly regulated. Therefore, Hart Labs must constantly monitor and control its testing costs. Shown below are the standard costs for a typical test.

Compute variances, prepare an income statement, and explain unfavorable variances.

(LO 2, 3, 4)

Direct materials (2 test tubes @ $1.46 per tube)	$ 2.92
Direct labor (1 hour @ $24 per hour)	24.00
Variable overhead (1 hour @ $6 per hour)	6.00
Fixed overhead (1 hour @ $10 per hour)	10.00
Total standard cost per test	$42.92

The lab does not maintain an inventory of test tubes. As a result, the tubes purchased each month are used that month. Actual activity for the month of November 2017, when 1,475 tests were conducted, resulted in the following.

Direct materials (3,050 test tubes)	$ 4,270
Direct labor (1,550 hours)	35,650
Variable overhead	7,400
Fixed overhead	15,000

Monthly budgeted fixed overhead is $14,000. Revenues for the month were $75,000, and selling and administrative expenses were $5,000.

Instructions

(a) Compute the price and quantity variances for direct materials and direct labor. (a) LQV $1,800 U

(b) Compute the total overhead variance.

(c) Prepare an income statement for management.

(d) Provide possible explanations for each unfavorable variance.

***P25-6A** Jorgensen Corporation uses standard costs with its job order cost accounting system. In January, an order (Job No. 12) for 1,900 units of Product B was received. The standard cost of one unit of Product B is as follows.

Journalize and post standard cost entries, and prepare income statement.

(LO 2, 3, 4, 5)

Direct materials	3 pounds at $1.00 per pound	$ 3.00
Direct labor	1 hour at $8.00 per hour	8.00
Overhead	2 hours (variable $4.00 per machine hour; fixed $2.25 per machine hour)	12.50
Standard cost per unit		$23.50

Normal capacity for the month was 4,200 machine hours. During January, the following transactions applicable to Job No. 12 occurred.

1. Purchased 6,200 pounds of raw materials on account at $1.05 per pound.
2. Requisitioned 6,200 pounds of raw materials for Job No. 12.
3. Incurred 2,000 hours of direct labor at a rate of $7.80 per hour.
4. Worked 2,000 hours of direct labor on Job No. 12.
5. Incurred manufacturing overhead on account $25,000.
6. Applied overhead to Job No. 12 on basis of standard machine hours allowed.
7. Completed Job No. 12.
8. Billed customer for Job No. 12 at a selling price of $65,000.

Instructions

(a) Journalize the transactions.

(b) Post to the job order cost accounts.

(c) Prepare the entry to recognize the total overhead variance.

(d) Prepare the January 2017 income statement for management. Assume selling and administrative expenses were $2,000. (d) NI $15,890

***P25-7A** Using the information in P25-1A, compute the overhead controllable variance and the overhead volume variance.

Compute overhead controllable and volume variances.

(LO 6)

***P25-8A** Using the information in P25-2A, compute the overhead controllable variance and the overhead volume variance.

Compute overhead controllable and volume variances.

(LO 6)

***P25-9A** Using the information in P25-3A, compute the overhead controllable variance and the overhead volume variance.

Compute overhead controllable and volume variances.

(LO 6)

***P25-10A** Using the information in P25-5A, compute the overhead controllable variance and the overhead volume variance.

Compute overhead controllable and volume variances.

(LO 6)

BROADENING YOUR PERSPECTIVE

MANAGEMENT DECISION-MAKING

Decision-Making Across the Organization

BYP25-1 Milton Professionals, a management consulting firm, specializes in strategic planning for financial institutions. James Hahn and Sara Norton, partners in the firm, are assembling a new strategic planning model for use by clients. The model is designed for use on most personal computers and replaces a rather lengthy manual model currently marketed by the firm. To market the new model, James and Sara will need to provide clients with an estimate of the number of labor hours and computer time needed to operate the model. The model is currently being test-marketed at five small financial institutions. These financial institutions are listed below, along with the number of combined computer/labor hours used by each institution to run the model one time.

Financial Institutions	Computer/Labor Hours Required
Midland National	25
First State	45
Financial Federal	40
Pacific America	30
Lakeview National	30
Total	170
Average	34

Any company that purchases the new model will need to purchase user manuals for the system. User manuals will be sold to clients in cases of 20, at a cost of $320 per case. One manual must be used each time the model is run because each manual includes a nonreusable computer-accessed password for operating the system. Also required are specialized computer forms that are sold only by Milton. The specialized forms are sold in packages of 250, at a cost of $60 per package. One application of the model requires the use of 50 forms. This amount includes two forms that are generally wasted in each application due to printer alignment errors. The overall cost of the strategic planning model to clients is $12,000. Most clients will use the model four times annually.

Milton must provide its clients with estimates of ongoing costs incurred in operating the new planning model, and would like to do so in the form of standard costs.

Instructions

With the class divided into groups, answer the following.

(a) What factors should be considered in setting a standard for computer/labor hours?
(b) What alternatives for setting a standard for computer/labor hours might be used?
(c) What standard for computer/labor hours would you select? Justify your answer.
(d) Determine the standard materials cost associated with the user manuals and computer forms for each application of the strategic planning model.

Managerial Analysis

***BYP25-2** Ana Carillo and Associates is a medium-sized company located near a large metropolitan area in the Midwest. The company manufactures cabinets of mahogany, oak, and other fine woods for use in expensive homes, restaurants, and hotels. Although some of the work is custom, many of the cabinets are a standard size.

One such non-custom model is called Luxury Base Frame. Normal production is 1,000 units. Each unit has a direct labor hour standard of 5 hours. Overhead is applied to production based on standard direct labor hours. During the most recent month, only 900 units were produced; 4,500 direct labor hours were allowed for standard production, but only 4,000 hours were used. Standard and actual overhead costs were as follows.

	Standard (1,000 units)	Actual (900 units)
Indirect materials	$ 12,000	$ 12,300
Indirect labor	43,000	51,000
(Fixed) Manufacturing supervisors salaries	22,500	22,000
(Fixed) Manufacturing office employees salaries	13,000	12,500
(Fixed) Engineering costs	27,000	25,000
Computer costs	10,000	10,000
Electricity	2,500	2,500
(Fixed) Manufacturing building depreciation	8,000	8,000
(Fixed) Machinery depreciation	3,000	3,000
(Fixed) Trucks and forklift depreciation	1,500	1,500
Small tools	700	1,400
(Fixed) Insurance	500	500
(Fixed) Property taxes	300	300
Total	$144,000	$150,000

Instructions

(a) Determine the overhead application rate.
(b) Determine how much overhead was applied to production.
(c) Calculate the total overhead variance, controllable variance, and volume variance.
(d) Decide which overhead variances should be investigated.
(e) Discuss causes of the overhead variances. What can management do to improve its performance next month?

Real-World Focus

BYP25-3 Glassmaster Company is organized as two divisions and one subsidiary. One division focuses on the manufacture of filaments such as fishing line and sewing thread; the other division manufactures antennas and specialty fiberglass products. Its subsidiary manufactures flexible steel wire controls and molded control panels.

The annual report of Glassmaster provides the following information.

GLASSMASTER COMPANY
Management Discussion

Gross profit margins for the year improved to 20.9% of sales compared to last year's 18.5%. All operations reported improved margins due in large part to improved operating efficiencies as a result of cost reduction measures implemented during the second and third quarters of the fiscal year and increased manufacturing throughout due to higher unit volume sales. Contributing to the improved margins was a favorable materials price variance due to competitive pricing by suppliers as a result of soft demand for petrochemical-based products. This favorable variance is temporary and will begin to reverse itself as stronger worldwide demand for commodity products improves in tandem with the economy. Partially offsetting these positive effects on profit margins were competitive pressures on sales prices of certain product lines. The company responded with pricing strategies designed to maintain and/or increase market share.

Instructions

(a) Is it apparent from the information whether Glassmaster utilizes standard costs?
(b) Do you think the price variance experienced should lead to changes in standard costs for the next fiscal year?

BYP25-4 The Balanced Scorecard Institute *(www.balancedscorecard.org)* is a great resource for information about implementing the balanced scorecard. One item of interest provided at its website is an example of a balanced scorecard for a regional airline.

Address: **http://www.balancedscorecard.org/portals/0/pdf/regional_airline.pdf**, or go to **www.wiley.com/college/weygandt**

Instructions
Go to the address above and answer the following questions.

(a) What are the objectives identified for the airline for each perspective?
(b) What measures are used for the objectives in the customer perspective?
(c) What initiatives are planned to achieve the objective in the learning perspective?

BYP25-5 The December 22, 2009, edition of the *Wall Street Journal* has an article by Kevin Kelliker entitled "In Risky Move, GM to Run Plants Around Clock."

Instructions
Read the article and answer the following questions.

(a) According to the article, what is the normal industry standard for plants to be considered operating at full capacity?
(b) What ideal standard is the company hoping to achieve?
(c) What reasons are given in the article for why most companies do not operate a third shift? How does GM propose to overcome these issues?
(d) What are some potential drawbacks of the midnight shift? What implications does this have for variances from standards?
(e) What potential sales/marketing disadvantage does the third shift create?

CRITICAL THINKING

Communication Activity

BYP25-6 The setting of standards is critical to the effective use of standards in evaluating performance.

Instructions
Explain the following in a memo to your instructor.

(a) The comparative advantages and disadvantages of ideal versus normal standards.
(b) The factors that should be included in setting the price and quantity standards for direct materials, direct labor, and manufacturing overhead.

Ethics Case

BYP25-7 At Symond Company, production workers in the Painting Department are paid on the basis of productivity. The labor time standard for a unit of production is established through periodic time studies conducted by Douglas Management Consultants. In a time study, the actual time required to complete a specific task by a worker is observed. Allowances are then made for preparation time, rest periods, and cleanup time. Bill Carson is one of several veterans in the Painting Department.

Bill is informed by Douglas that he will be used in the time study for the painting of a new product. The findings will be the basis for establishing the labor time standard for the next 6 months. During the test, Bill deliberately slows his normal work pace in an effort to obtain a labor time standard that will be easy to meet. Because it is a new product, the Douglas representative who conducted the test is unaware that Bill did not give the test his best effort.

Instructions
(a) Who was benefited and who was harmed by Bill's actions?
(b) Was Bill ethical in the way he performed the time study test?
(c) What measure(s) might the company take to obtain valid data for setting the labor time standard?

All About You

BYP25-8 From the time you first entered school many years ago, instructors have been measuring and evaluating you by imposing standards. In addition, many of you will pursue professions that administer professional examinations to attain recognized certification. A federal commission presented proposals suggesting all public colleges and universities should require standardized tests to measure their students' learning.

Instructions
Read the article at **www.signonsandiego.com/uniontrib/20060811/news_1n11colleges.html**, and answer the following questions.

(a) What areas of concern did the panel's recommendations address?
(b) What are possible advantages of standard testing?

(c) What are possible disadvantages of standard testing?
(d) Would you be in favor of standardized tests?

Considering Your Costs and Benefits

BYP25-9 Do you think that standard costs are used only in making products like wheel bearings and hamburgers? Think again. Standards influence virtually every aspect of our lives. For example, the next time you call to schedule an appointment with your doctor, ask the receptionist how many minutes the appointment is scheduled for. Doctors are under increasing pressure to see more patients each day, which means the time spent with each patient is shorter. As insurance companies and employers push for reduced medical costs, every facet of medicine has been standardized and analyzed. Doctors, nurses, and other medical staff are evaluated in every part of their operations to ensure maximum efficiency. While keeping medical treatment affordable seems like a worthy goal, what are the potential implications for the quality of health care? Does a focus on the bottom line result in a reduction in the quality of health care?

A simmering debate has centered on a very basic question: To what extent should accountants, through financial measures, influence the type of medical care that you receive? Suppose that your local medical facility is in danger of closing because it has been losing money. Should the facility put in place incentives that provide bonuses to doctors if they meet certain standard-cost targets for the cost of treating specific ailments?

YES: If the facility is in danger of closing, then someone should take steps to change the medical practices to reduce costs. A closed medical facility is of no use to me, my family, or the community.

NO: I don't want an accountant deciding the right medical treatment for me. My family and I deserve the best medical care.

Instructions

Write a response indicating your position regarding this situation. Provide support for your view.

Chapter 26 Incremental Analysis and Capital Budgeting

When you think of new, fast-growing, San Francisco companies, you probably think of fun products like smartphones, social networks, and game apps. You don't tend to think of soap. In fact, given that some of the biggest, most powerful companies in the world dominate the soap market (e.g., Proctor & Gamble, Clorox, and Unilever), starting a new soap company seems like an outrageously bad idea. But that didn't dissuade Adam Lowry and Eric Ryan from giving it a try. The long-time friends and former roommates combined their skills (Adam's chemical engineering and Eric's design and marketing) to start Method Products. Their goal: selling environmentally friendly soaps that actually remove dirt.

Within a year of its formation, the company had products on the shelves at Target stores. Within 5 years, Method was cited by numerous business publications as one of the fastest-growing companies in the country. It was easy—right? Wrong. Running a company is never easy, and given Method's commitment to sustainability, all of its business decisions are just a little more complex than usual. For example, the company wanted to use solar power to charge the batteries for the forklifts used in its factories. No problem, just put solar panels on the buildings. But because Method outsources its manufacturing, it doesn't actually own factory buildings. In fact, the company that does Method's manufacturing doesn't own the buildings either. Solution—Method parked old semi-trailers next to the factories and installed solar panels on those.

Since Method insists on using natural products and sustainable production practices, its production costs are higher than companies that don't adhere to these standards. Adam and Eric insist, however, that this actually benefits them because they have to be far more careful about controlling costs and far more innovative in solving problems. For example, when the cost of the raw materials used for soap production recently jumped by as much as 40%, Method actually viewed it as an opportunity to grab market share. It determined that it could offset the cost increases in other places in its supply chain, thus absorbing the cost much easier than its big competitors.

In these and other instances, Adam and Eric identified their alternative courses of action, determined what was relevant to each choice and what wasn't, and then carefully evaluated the incremental costs of each alternative. When you are small and your competitors have some of the biggest marketing budgets in the world, you can't afford to make very many mistakes.

LEARNING OBJECTIVES

1. **Describe management's decision-making process and incremental analysis.**
2. **Analyze the relevant costs in various decisions involving incremental analysis.**
3. **Contrast annual rate of return and cash payback in capital budgeting.**
4. **Distinguish between the net present value and internal rate of return methods.**

LEARNING OBJECTIVE 

Describe management's decision-making process and incremental analysis.

Making decisions is an important management function. Management's decision-making process does not always follow a set pattern because decisions vary significantly in their scope, urgency, and importance. It is possible, though, to identify some steps that are frequently involved in the process. These steps are shown in Illustration 26-1.

Illustration 26-1
Management's decision-making process

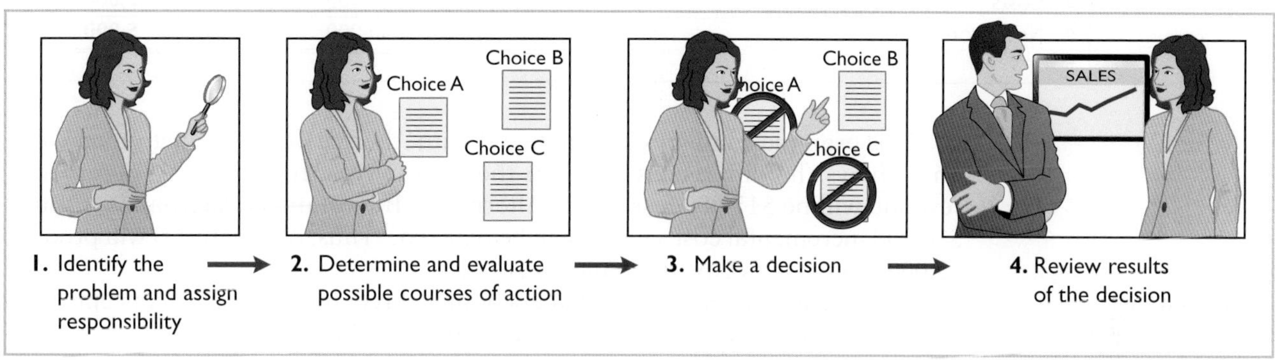

Accounting's contribution to the decision-making process occurs primarily in Steps 2 and 4—evaluating possible courses of action and reviewing results. In Step 2, for each possible course of action, relevant revenue and cost data are provided. These show the expected overall effect on net income. In Step 4, internal reports are prepared that review the actual impact of the decision.

In making business decisions, management ordinarily considers both financial and nonfinancial information. **Financial** information is related to revenues and costs and their effect on the company's overall profitability. **Nonfinancial** information relates to such factors as the effect of the decision on employee turnover, the environment, or the overall image of the company in the community. (These are considerations that we touched on in our Chapter 19 discussion of corporate social responsibility.) Although nonfinancial information can be as important as financial information, we will focus primarily on financial information that is relevant to the decision.

Incremental Analysis Approach

Decisions involve a choice among alternative courses of action. Suppose you face the personal financial decision of whether to purchase or lease a car. The financial data relate to the cost of leasing versus the cost of purchasing. For example, leasing involves periodic lease payments; purchasing requires "up-front" payment of the purchase price. In other words, the financial information relevant to the decision are the data that vary in the future among the possible alternatives. The process used to identify the financial data that change under alternative courses of action is called **incremental analysis**. In some cases, you will find that when you use incremental analysis, both costs **and** revenues vary. In other cases, only costs **or** revenues vary.

Terminology
Incremental analysis is also called *differential analysis* because the analysis focuses on differences.

Just as your decision to buy or lease a car affects your future financial situation, similar decisions, on a larger scale, affect a company's future. Incremental analysis identifies the probable effects of those decisions on future earnings. Such analysis inevitably involves estimates and uncertainty. Gathering data for incremental analyses may involve market analysts, engineers, and accountants. In quantifying the data, the accountant must produce the most reliable information available.

How Incremental Analysis Works

Illustration 26-2
Basic approach in incremental analysis

The basic approach in incremental analysis is illustrated in the following example.

Incremental Analysis.xls

	A	B	C	D
1		Alternative A	Alternative B	Net Income Increase (Decrease)
2	Revenues	$125,000	$110,000	**$ (15,000)**
3	Costs	100,000	80,000	**20,000**
4	Net income	$ 25,000	$ 30,000	**$ 5,000**
5				

This example compares Alternative B with Alternative A. The net income column shows the differences between the alternatives. In this case, incremental revenue will be $15,000 less under Alternative B than under Alternative A. But a $20,000 incremental cost savings will be realized.[1] Thus, Alternative B will produce $5,000 more net income than Alternative A.

In the following pages, you will encounter three important cost concepts used in incremental analysis, as defined and discussed in Illustration 26-3.

Illustration 26-3
Key cost concepts in incremental analysis

- **Relevant cost** In incremental analysis, the only factors to be considered are those costs and revenues that differ across alternatives. Those factors are called **relevant costs**. Costs and revenues that do not differ across alternatives can be ignored when trying to choose between alternatives.

- **Opportunity cost** Often in choosing one course of action, the company must give up the opportunity to benefit from some other course of action. For example, if a machine is used to make one type of product, the benefit of making another type of product with that machine is lost. This lost benefit is referred to as **opportunity cost**.

- **Sunk cost** Costs that have already been incurred and will not be changed or avoided by any present or future decisions are referred to as **sunk costs**. For example, the amount you spent in the past to purchase or repair a laptop should have no bearing on your decision whether to buy a new laptop. **Sunk costs are not relevant costs.**

Incremental analysis sometimes involves changes that at first glance might seem contrary to your intuition. For example, sometimes variable costs **do not change** under the alternative courses of action. Also, sometimes fixed costs

[1]Although income taxes are sometimes important in incremental analysis, they are ignored in the chapter for simplicity's sake.

do change. For example, direct labor, normally a variable cost, is not an incremental cost in deciding between two new factory machines if each asset requires the same amount of direct labor. In contrast, rent expense, normally a fixed cost, is an incremental cost in a decision whether to continue occupancy of a building or to purchase or lease a new building.

It is also important to understand that **the approaches to incremental analysis discussed in this chapter do not take into consideration the time value of money**. That is, amounts to be paid or received in future years are not discounted for the cost of interest. Time value of money is addressed later in this chapter as well as in Appendix G.

Types of Incremental Analysis

A number of different types of decisions involve incremental analysis. The more common types of decisions are whether to:

1. Accept an order at a special price.
2. Make or buy component parts or finished products.
3. Sell products or process them further.
4. Repair, retain, or replace equipment.
5. Eliminate an unprofitable business segment or product.

We consider each of these types of decisions in the following pages.

Analyze the relevant costs in various decisions involving incremental analysis.

Special Price Order

Sometimes a company has an opportunity to obtain additional business if it is willing to make a price concession to a specific customer. To illustrate, assume that Sunbelt Company produces 100,000 Smoothie blenders per month, which is 80% of plant capacity. Variable manufacturing costs are $8 per unit. Fixed manufacturing costs are $400,000, or $4 per unit. The Smoothie blenders are normally sold directly to retailers at $20 each. Sunbelt has an offer from Kensington Co. (a foreign wholesaler) to purchase an additional 2,000 blenders at $11 per unit. Acceptance of the offer would not affect normal sales of the product, and the additional units can be manufactured without increasing plant capacity. What should management do?

If management makes its decision on the basis of the total cost per unit of $12 ($8 variable + $4 fixed), the order would be rejected because costs per unit ($12) exceed revenues per unit ($11) by $1 per unit. However, since the units can be produced within existing plant capacity, the special order **will not increase fixed costs**. Let's identify the relevant data for the decision. First, the variable manufacturing costs increase $16,000 ($8 × 2,000). Second, the expected revenue increases $22,000 ($11 × 2,000). Thus, as shown in Illustration 26-4, Sunbelt increases its net income by $6,000 by accepting this special order.

Illustration 26-4
Incremental analysis—accepting an order at a special price

Incremental Analysis - Accepting an order at a special price.xls

	A	B	C	D
1		Reject Order	Accept Order	Net Income Increase (Decrease)
2	Revenues	$0	$22,000	$ 22,000
3	Costs	0	16,000	(16,000)
4	Net income	$0	$ 6,000	$ 6,000
5				

Two points should be emphasized. First, we assume that sales of the product in other markets **would not be affected by this special order**. If other sales were affected, then Sunbelt would have to consider the lost sales in making the decision. Second, if Sunbelt is operating **at full capacity**, it is likely that the special order would be rejected. Under such circumstances, the company would have to expand plant capacity. In that case, the special order would have to absorb these additional fixed manufacturing costs, as well as the variable manufacturing costs.

Make or Buy

When a manufacturer assembles component parts in producing a finished product, management must decide whether to make or buy the components. The decision to buy parts or services is often referred to as outsourcing. For example, as discussed in the chapter opening story, a company such as **Method Products** may either make or buy the soaps used in its products. Similarly, **Hewlett-Packard Corporation** may make or buy the electronic circuitry, cases, and printer heads for its printers. **Boeing** recently sold some of its commercial aircraft factories in an effort to cut production costs and focus on engineering and final assembly rather than manufacturing. The decision to make or buy components should be made on the basis of incremental analysis.

Baron Company makes motorcycles and scooters. It incurs the following annual costs in producing 25,000 ignition switches for scooters.

Illustration 26-5
Annual product cost data

Direct materials	$ 50,000
Direct labor	75,000
Variable manufacturing overhead	40,000
Fixed manufacturing overhead	60,000
Total manufacturing costs	$225,000
Total cost per unit ($225,000 ÷ 25,000)	**$9.00**

Instead of making its own switches, Baron Company might purchase the ignition switches from Ignition, Inc. at a price of $8 per unit. What should management do?

At first glance, it appears that management should purchase the ignition switches for $8 rather than make them at a cost of $9. However, a review of operations indicates that if the ignition switches are purchased from Ignition, Inc., *all* of Baron's variable costs but only $10,000 of its fixed manufacturing costs will be eliminated (avoided). Thus, $50,000 of the fixed manufacturing costs remain if the ignition switches are purchased. The relevant costs for incremental analysis, therefore, are as shown below.

Illustration 26-6
Incremental analysis—make or buy

Incremental Analysis - Make or buy.xls

Home Insert Page Layout Formulas Data Review View

P18 fx

	A	B	C	D
1		Make	Buy	Net Income Increase (Decrease)
2	Direct materials	$ 50,000	$ 0	$ 50,000
3	Direct labor	75,000	0	75,000
4	Variable manufacturing costs	40,000	0	40,000
5	Fixed manufacturing costs	60,000	50,000	10,000
6	Purchase price (25,000 × $8)	0	200,000	(200,000)
7	Total annual cost	$225,000	$250,000	$ (25,000)
8				

This analysis indicates that Baron Company incurs $25,000 of additional costs by buying the ignition switches rather than making them. Therefore, Baron should continue to make the ignition switches even though the total manufacturing cost is $1 higher per unit than the purchase price. The primary cause of this result is that, even if the company purchases the ignition switches, it will still have fixed costs of $50,000 to absorb.

OPPORTUNITY COST

The foregoing make-or-buy analysis is complete only if it is assumed that the productive capacity used to make the ignition switches cannot be converted to another purpose. If there is an opportunity to use this productive capacity in some other manner, then this opportunity cost must be considered. As indicated earlier, **opportunity cost** is the potential benefit that may be obtained by following an alternative course of action.

To illustrate, assume that through buying the switches, Baron Company can use the released productive capacity to generate additional income of $38,000 from producing a different product. This lost income is an additional cost of continuing to make the switches in the make-or-buy decision. This opportunity cost is therefore added to the "Make" column for comparison. As shown in Illustration 26-7, it is now advantageous to buy the ignition switches. The company's income would increase by $13,000.

Illustration 26-7
Incremental analysis—make or buy, with opportunity cost

Incremental Analysis - Make or buy with opportunity cost.xls

	A	B	C	D
1		Make	Buy	Net Income Increase (Decrease)
2	Total annual cost	$225,000	$250,000	$(25,000)
3	**Opportunity cost**	**38,000**	0	**38,000**
4	Total cost	$263,000	$250,000	$ 13,000
5				

The qualitative factors in this decision include the possible loss of jobs for employees who produce the ignition switches. In addition, management must assess the supplier's ability to satisfy the company's quality control standards at the quoted price per unit.

Sell or Process Further

Many manufacturers have the option of selling products at a given point in the production cycle or continuing to process with the expectation of selling them at a later point at a higher price. For example, a bicycle manufacturer such as **Trek** could sell its bicycles to retailers either unassembled or assembled. A furniture manufacturer such as **Ethan Allen** could sell its dining room sets to furniture stores either unfinished or finished. The sell-or-process-further decision should be made on the basis of incremental analysis. The basic decision rule is: **Process further as long as the incremental revenue from such processing exceeds the incremental processing costs.**

Assume, for example, that Woodmasters Inc. makes tables. It sells unfinished tables for $50. The cost to manufacture an unfinished table is $35, computed as follows.

Illustration 26-8
Per unit cost of unfinished table

Direct materials	$15
Direct labor	10
Variable manufacturing overhead	6
Fixed manufacturing overhead	4
Manufacturing cost per unit	**$35**

Woodmasters currently has unused productive capacity that is expected to continue indefinitely. Some of this capacity could be used to finish the tables and sell them at $60 per unit. For a finished table, direct materials will increase $2 and direct labor costs will increase $4. Variable manufacturing overhead costs will increase by $2.40 (60% of direct labor). No increase is anticipated in fixed manufacturing overhead.

Should the company sell the unfinished tables, or should it process them further? The incremental analysis on a per unit basis is as follows.

Incremental Analysis - Sell or process further.xls

	A	B	C	D
1		Sell Unfinished	Process Further	Net Income Increase (Decrease)
2	Sales price per unit	$50.00	$60.00	$10.00
3	Cost per unit			
4	Direct materials	15.00	17.00	(2.00)
5	Direct labor	10.00	14.00	(4.00)
6	Variable manufacturing overhead	6.00	8.40	(2.40)
7	Fixed manufacturing overhead	4.00	4.00	0.00
8	Total	35.00	43.40	(8.40)
9	Net income per unit	$15.00	$16.60	$ 1.60
10				

Illustration 26-9
Incremental analysis—sell or process further

It would be advantageous for Woodmasters to process the tables further. The incremental revenue of $10.00 from the additional processing is $1.60 higher than the incremental processing costs of $8.40.

Repair, Retain, or Replace Equipment

Management often has to decide whether to continue using an asset, repair, or replace it. For example, **Delta Airlines** must decide whether to replace old jets with new, more fuel-efficient ones. To illustrate, assume that Jeffcoat Company has a factory machine that originally cost $110,000. It has a balance in Accumulated Depreciation of $70,000, so the machine's book value is $40,000. It has a remaining useful life of four years. The company is considering replacing this machine with a new machine. A new machine is available that costs $120,000. It is expected to have zero salvage value at the end of its four-year useful life. If the new machine is acquired, variable manufacturing costs are expected to decrease from $160,000 to $125,000 annually, and the old unit could be sold for $5,000. The incremental analysis for the **four-year period** is as follows.

Illustration 26-10
Incremental analysis—retain or replace equipment

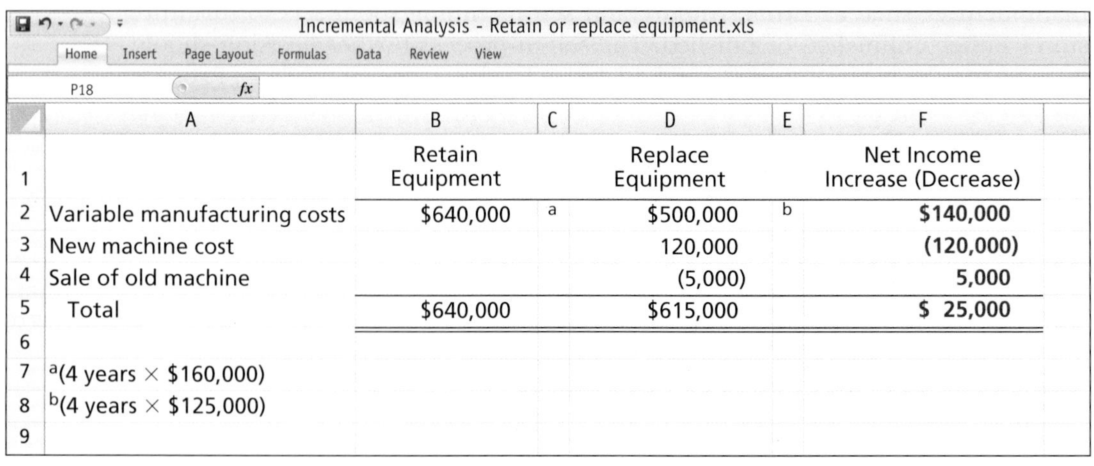

Incremental Analysis - Retain or replace equipment.xls

	A	B	C	D	E	F
1		Retain Equipment		Replace Equipment		Net Income Increase (Decrease)
2	Variable manufacturing costs	$640,000	a	$500,000	b	$140,000
3	New machine cost			120,000		(120,000)
4	Sale of old machine			(5,000)		5,000
5	Total	$640,000		$615,000		$ 25,000
6						
7	[a](4 years × $160,000)					
8	[b](4 years × $125,000)					
9						

In this case, it would be to the company's advantage to replace the equipment. The lower variable manufacturing costs due to replacement more than offset the cost of the new equipment. Note that the $5,000 received from the sale of the old machine is relevant to the decision because it will only be received if the company chooses to replace its equipment. In general, any trade-in allowance or cash disposal value of existing assets is relevant to the decision to retain or replace equipment.

One other point should be mentioned regarding Jeffcoat's decision: **The book value of the old machine does not affect the decision.** Book value is a **sunk cost**, which is a cost that cannot be changed by any present or future decision. **Sunk costs are not relevant in incremental analysis.** In this example, if the asset is retained, book value will be depreciated over its remaining useful life. Or, if the new unit is acquired, book value will be recognized as a loss of the current period. Thus, the effect of book value on cumulative future earnings is the same regardless of the replacement decision.

Eliminate an Unprofitable Segment or Product

Management sometimes must decide whether to eliminate an unprofitable business segment or product. For example, in recent years, many airlines quit servicing certain cities or cut back on the number of flights. **Goodyear** quit producing several brands in the low-end tire market. Again, the key is to **focus on the relevant costs—the data that change under the alternative courses of action**. To illustrate, assume that Venus Company manufactures tennis racquets in three models: Pro, Master, and Champ. Pro and Master are profitable lines. Champ (highlighted in red in the following table) operates at a loss. Condensed income statement data are as follows.

Illustration 26-11
Segment income data

	Pro	Master	Champ	Total
Sales	$800,000	$300,000	**$100,000**	$1,200,000
Variable costs	520,000	210,000	**90,000**	820,000
Contribution margin	280,000	90,000	**10,000**	380,000
Fixed costs	80,000	50,000	**30,000**	160,000
Net income	$200,000	$ 40,000	**$ (20,000)**	$ 220,000

You might think that total net income will increase by $20,000 to $240,000 if the unprofitable Champ line of racquets is eliminated. However, **net income may actually decrease if the Champ line is discontinued**. The reason is that if the fixed costs allocated to the Champ racquets cannot be eliminated, they will have to be absorbed by the other products. To illustrate, assume that the $30,000 of fixed costs applicable to the unprofitable segment are allocated ⅔ to the Pro model and ⅓ to the Master model if the Champ model is eliminated. Fixed costs will increase to $100,000 ($80,000 + $20,000) in the Pro line and to $60,000 ($50,000 + $10,000) in the Master line. The revised income statement is as follows.

Illustration 26-12
Income data after eliminating unprofitable product line

	Pro	Master	Total
Sales	$800,000	$300,000	$1,100,000
Variable costs	520,000	210,000	730,000
Contribution margin	280,000	90,000	370,000
Fixed costs	**100,000**	**60,000**	160,000
Net income	$180,000	$ 30,000	**$ 210,000**

Total net income has decreased $10,000 ($220,000 − $210,000). This result is also obtained in the following incremental analysis of the Champ racquets.

Incremental Analysis - Eliminating an unprofitable segment.xls

	A	B	C	D
1		Continue	Eliminate	Net Income Increase (Decrease)
2	Sales	$100,000	$ 0	**$(100,000)**
3	Variable costs	90,000	0	**90,000**
4	Contribution margin	10,000	0	**(10,000)**
5	Fixed costs	30,000	30,000	**0**
6	Net income	$(20,000)	$(30,000)	**$ (10,000)**
7				

Illustration 26-13
Incremental analysis—eliminating unprofitable segment with no reduction in fixed costs

The loss in net income is attributable to the Champ line's contribution margin ($10,000) that will not be realized if the segment is discontinued.

In deciding on the future status of an unprofitable segment, management should consider the effect of elimination on related product lines. It may be possible for continuing product lines to obtain some or all of the sales lost by the discontinued product line. In some businesses, services or products may be linked—for example, free checking accounts at a bank, or coffee at a donut shop. In addition, management should consider the effect of eliminating the product line on employees who may have to be discharged or retrained.

Contrast annual rate of return and cash payback in capital budgeting.

Capital Budgeting

Individuals make capital expenditures when they buy a new home, car, or television set. Similarly, businesses make capital expenditures when they modernize plant facilities or expand operations. Companies like **Holland America Line** must constantly determine how to invest their resources. As another example, **Dell** announced plans to spend $1 billion on data centers for cloud computing.

In business, as for individuals, the amount of possible capital expenditures usually exceeds the funds available for such expenditures. Thus, the resources available must be allocated (budgeted) among the competing alternatives. The process of making capital expenditure decisions in business is known as **capital budgeting**. Capital budgeting involves choosing among various capital projects to find the one(s) that will maximize a company's return on its financial investment.

Evaluation Process of Capital Budgeting

Many companies follow a carefully prescribed process in capital budgeting. At least once a year, top management requests proposals for projects from each department. A capital budgeting committee screens the proposals and submits its findings to the officers of the company. The officers, in turn, select the projects they believe to be most worthy of funding. They submit this list to the board of directors. Ultimately, the directors approve the capital expenditure budget for the year. Illustration 26-14 shows this process.

The involvement of top management and the board of directors in the process demonstrates the importance of capital budgeting decisions. These decisions often have a significant impact on a company's future profitability. In

1. Project proposals are requested from departments, plants, and authorized personnel.
2. Proposals are screened by a capital budget committee.
3. Officers determine which projects are worthy of funding.
4. Board of directors approves capital budget.

Illustration 26-14
Corporate capital budget authorization process

fact, poor capital budgeting decisions have led to the bankruptcy of some companies.

Accounting data are indispensable in assessing the probable effects of capital expenditures. To provide management with relevant data for capital budgeting decisions, you should be familiar with the quantitative techniques that may be used. The three most common techniques are (1) annual rate of return, (2) cash payback, and (3) discounted cash flow. We demonstrate each of these techniques in the following sections.

To illustrate the three quantitative techniques, assume that Reno Company is considering an investment of $130,000 in new equipment. The new equipment is expected to last 5 years and have zero salvage value at the end of its useful life. Reno uses the straight-line method of depreciation for accounting purposes. The expected annual revenues and costs of the new product that will be produced from the investment are as follows.

Illustration 26-15
Estimated annual net income from capital expenditure

Sales revenue		$200,000
Less: Costs and expenses		
Manufacturing costs (exclusive of depreciation)	$132,000	
Depreciation expenses ($130,000 ÷ 5)	26,000	
Selling and administrative expenses	22,000	180,000
Income before income taxes		20,000
Income tax expense		7,000
Net income		$ 13,000

Annual Rate of Return

The **annual rate of return method** is based directly on accrual accounting data rather than on cash flows. It indicates **the profitability of a capital expenditure** by dividing expected annual net income by the average investment. Illustration 26-16 shows the formula for computing annual rate of return.

$$\text{Expected Annual Net Income} \div \text{Average Investment} = \text{Annual Rate of Return}$$

Illustration 26-16
Annual rate of return formula

Expected annual net income is obtained from the projected income statement. Reno Company's expected annual net income is $13,000. Average investment is derived from the following formula.

$$\frac{\text{Original Investment} + \text{Value at End of Useful Life}}{2} = \text{Average Investment}$$

Illustration 26-17
Formula for computing average investment

The value at the end of useful life is the asset's salvage value, if any. For Reno Company, average investment is $65,000 [($130,000 + $0) ÷ 2]. The expected annual rate of return for Reno's investment in new equipment is therefore 20%, computed as follows.

$$\$13{,}000 \div \$65{,}000 = 20\%$$

Management then compares this annual rate of return with its **required rate of return** for investments of similar risk. The required rate of return is generally based on the company's **cost of capital**. The **cost of capital** is the rate of return that management expects to pay on all borrowed and equity funds. The cost of capital is a company-wide (or sometimes a division-wide) rate; it does not relate to the cost of funding a specific project.

The annual rate of return decision rule is: **A project is acceptable if its rate of return is greater than management's required rate of return. It is unacceptable when the reverse is true.** When companies use the rate of return technique in deciding among several acceptable projects, **the higher the rate of return for a given risk, the more attractive the investment**.

The principal advantages of this method are the simplicity of its calculation and management's familiarity with the accounting terms used in the computation. A major limitation of the annual rate of return method is that it does not consider the time value of money. For example, no consideration is given as to whether cash inflows will occur early or late in the life of the investment. As explained in Appendix G, recognition of the time value of money can make a significant difference between the future value and the discounted present value of an investment. A second disadvantage is that this method relies on accrual accounting numbers rather than expected cash flows.

Cash Payback

The **cash payback technique** identifies the time period required to recover the cost of the capital investment from the net annual cash flow produced by the investment. Illustration 26-18 presents the formula for computing the cash payback period assuming equal annual cash flows.

Illustration 26-18
Cash payback formula

Cost of Capital Investment	÷	Net Annual Cash Flow	=	Cash Payback Period

Net annual cash flow is approximated by taking net income and adding back depreciation expense. Depreciation expense is added back because depreciation on the capital expenditure does not involve an annual outflow of cash. Accordingly, the depreciation deducted in determining net income must be added back to determine net annual cash flows.

In the Reno Company example, net annual cash flow is $39,000, as shown below.

Illustration 26-19
Computation of net annual cash flow

Net income	$ 13,000
Add: Depreciation expense	26,000
Net annual cash flow	**$39,000**

The cash payback period in this example is therefore 3.33 years, computed as follows.

$$\$130{,}000 \div \$39{,}000 = 3.33 \text{ years}$$

Evaluation of the payback period is often related to the expected useful life of the asset. For example, assume that at Reno Company a project is unacceptable if the payback period is longer than 60% of the asset's expected useful life. The 3.33-year payback period in this case is 67% of the project's expected useful life. Thus, the project is unacceptable.

It follows that when the payback method is used to decide among acceptable alternative projects, **the shorter the payback period, the more attractive the investment**. This is true for two reasons. First, the earlier the investment is recovered, the sooner the company can use the cash funds for other purposes. Second, the risk of loss from obsolescence and changed economic conditions is less in a shorter payback period.

The preceding computation of the cash payback period assumes **equal** net annual cash flows in each year of the investment's life. In many cases, this assumption is not valid. In the case of **uneven** net annual cash flows, the company determines the cash payback period when the cumulative net cash flows from the investment equal the cost of the investment.

To illustrate, assume that Chen Company proposes an investment in a new website that is estimated to cost $300,000. Illustration 26-20 shows the proposed investment cost, net annual cash flows, cumulative net cash flows, and the cash payback period.

Illustration 26-20
Net annual cash flow schedule

Year	Investment	Net Annual Cash Flow	Cumulative Net Cash Flow
0	**$300,000**		
1		$ 60,000	$ 60,000
2		90,000	150,000
3		90,000	240,000
4		120,000	360,000
5		100,000	460,000

Cash payback period = 3.5 years

As Illustration 26-20 shows, at the end of year 3, cumulative net cash flow of $240,000 is less than the investment cost of $300,000. However, at the end of year 4, the cumulative net cash flow of $360,000 exceeds the investment cost. The net cash flow needed in year 4 to equal the investment cost is $60,000 ($300,000 − $240,000). Assuming the net cash flow occurs evenly during year 4, we then divide this amount by the net annual cash flow in year 4 ($120,000) to determine the point during the year when the cash payback occurs. Thus, we get 0.50 ($60,000/$120,000), or half of the year, and the cash payback period is 3.5 years.

The cash payback method may be useful as an initial screening tool. It may be the most critical factor in the capital budgeting decision for a company that desires a fast turnaround of its investment because of a weak cash position. Like the annual rate of return, cash payback is relatively easy to compute and understand.

However, cash payback is not ordinarily the only basis for the capital budgeting decision because it **ignores the expected profitability of the project**. To illustrate, assume that Projects A and B have the same payback period, but Project A's useful life is double that of Project B's. Project A's earning power, therefore, is twice as long as Project B's. A further—and major—disadvantage of this technique is that it ignores the time value of money.

LEARNING OBJECTIVE 

Distinguish between the net present value and internal rate of return methods.

The **discounted cash flow technique** is generally recognized as the best conceptual approach to making capital budgeting decisions. This technique considers both the estimated total net cash flows from the investment and the time value of money. The expected total net cash flow consists of the sum of the annual net cash flows plus the estimated liquidation proceeds when the asset is sold for salvage at the end of its useful life. But because liquidation proceeds are generally immaterial, we ignore them in subsequent discussions.

Two methods are used with the discounted cash flow technique: (1) net present value and (2) internal rate of return. **Before we discuss the methods, we recommend that you examine Appendix G if you need a review of present value concepts.**

Net Present Value Method

The **net present value (NPV) method** involves discounting net cash flows to their present value and then comparing that present value with the capital outlay required by the investment. The difference between these two amounts is referred to as **net present value (NPV)**. Company management determines what interest rate to use in discounting the future net cash flows. This rate, often referred to as the **discount rate** or **required rate of return**, is discussed in a later section.

The NVP decision rule is this: **A proposal is acceptable when net present value is zero or positive.** At either of those values, the rate of return on the investment equals or exceeds the required rate of return. When net present value is negative, the project is unacceptable. Illustration 26-21 shows the net present value decision criteria.

Illustration 26-21
Net present value decision criteria

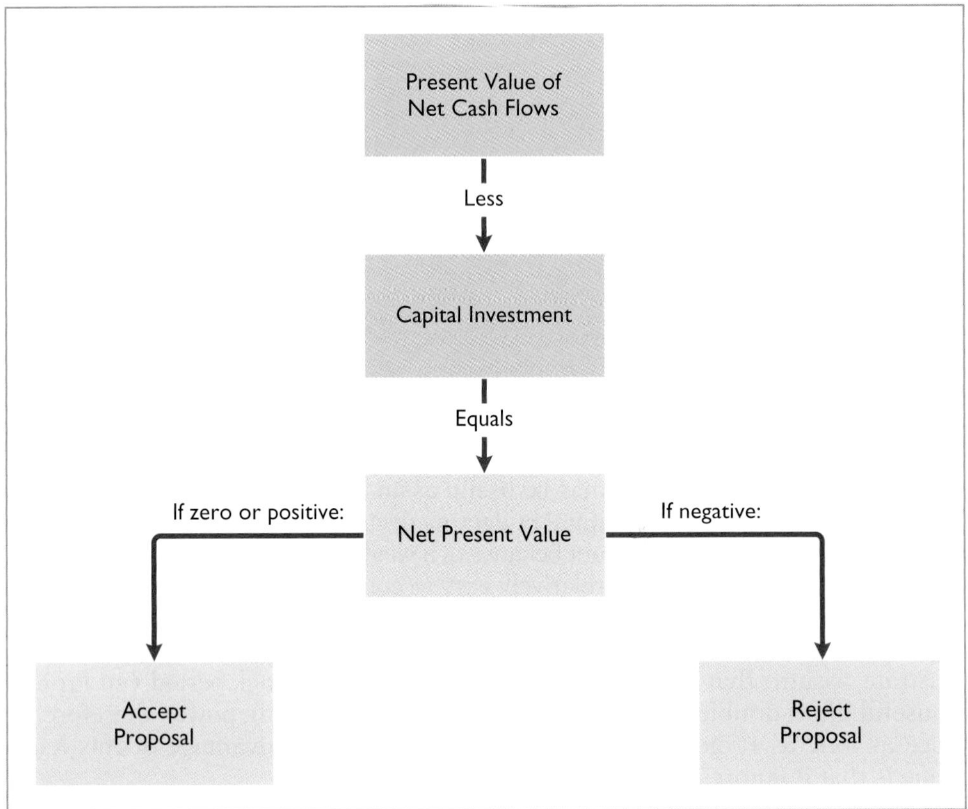

When making a selection among acceptable proposals, **the higher the positive net present value, the more attractive the investment**. The application of this method to two cases is described in the next two sections. In each case, we assume that the investment has no salvage value at the end of its useful life.

EQUAL NET ANNUAL CASH FLOWS

Reno Company's net annual cash flows are $39,000. If we assume this amount is **uniform over the asset's useful life**, we can compute the present value of the net annual cash flows by using the present value of an annuity of 1 for 5 payments (in Table 2, Appendix G). The computation at a rate of return of 12% is as follows.

Illustration 26-22
Present value of net annual cash flows

	Present Value at 12%
Discount factor for 5 periods	3.60478
Present value of net annual cash flows:	
$39,000 × 3.60478	**$140,586**

The analysis of the proposal by the net present value method is shown in Illustration 26-23.

Illustration 26-23
Computation of net present value

	12%
Present value of net annual cash flows	$140,586
Capital investment	130,000
Net present value	**$ 10,586**

The proposed capital expenditure is acceptable at a required rate of return of 12% because the net present value is positive.

UNEQUAL NET ANNUAL CASH FLOWS

When net annual cash flows are unequal, we cannot use annuity tables to calculate their present value. Instead, we use tables showing the **present value of a single future amount for each net annual cash flow**.

To illustrate, assume that Reno Company management expects the same aggregate net annual cash flow ($195,000) over the life of the investment. But because of a declining market demand for the new product over the life of the equipment, the net annual cash flows are higher in the early years and lower in the later years. The present value of the net annual cash flows is calculated as follows using Table 1 in Appendix G.

Illustration 26-24
Computation of present value of unequal annual cash flows

		Discount Factor	Present Value
Year	**Assumed Net Annual Cash Flows**	**12%**	**12%**
	(1)	(2)	(1) × (2)
1	$ 54,000	0.89286	$ 48,214
2	47,000	0.79719	37,468
3	43,000	0.71178	30,607
4	31,000	0.63552	19,701
5	20,000	0.56743	11,349
	$195,000		**$147,339**

Therefore, the analysis of the proposal by the net present value method is as follows.

Illustration 26-25
Analysis of proposal using net present value method

	12%
Present value of net annual cash flows	$147,339
Capital investment	130,000
Net present value	**$ 17,339**

In this example, the present value of the net annual cash flows is greater than the $130,000 capital investment. Thus, the project is acceptable at a 12% required rate of return. The difference between the present values using the 12% rate under equal net annual cash flows ($140,586) and unequal net annual cash flows ($147,339) is due to the pattern of the net cash flows.

Internal Rate of Return Method

The **internal rate of return method** differs from the net present value method in that it finds the **interest yield of the potential investment**. The **internal rate of return (IRR)** is the interest rate that will cause the present value of the proposed capital expenditure to equal the present value of the expected net annual cash flows. Because it recognizes the time value of money, the internal rate of return method is (like the NPV method) a discounted cash flow technique. The determination of the internal rate of return involves two steps.

Step 1. Compute the internal rate of return factor. The formula for this factor is as follows.

Illustration 26-26
Formula for internal rate of return factor

Capital Investment	÷	Net Annual Cash Flow	=	Internal Rate of Return Factor

The computation for Reno Company, assuming equal net annual cash flows,[2] is:

$$\$130{,}000 \div \$39{,}000 = 3.3333$$

Step 2. Use the factor and the present value of an annuity of 1 table to find the internal rate of return. Table 2 of Appendix G is used in this step. The internal rate of return is the discount factor that is closest to the internal rate of return factor for the time period covered by the net annual cash flows.

For Reno Company, the net annual cash flows are expected to continue for 5 years. Thus, it is necessary to read across the period-5 row in Table 2 to find the discount factor. The row for 5 periods is reproduced below for your convenience.

TABLE 2
PRESENT VALUE OF AN ANNUITY OF 1

(*n*) Periods	5%	6%	7%	8%	9%	10%	11%	12%	15%
5	4.32948	4.21236	4.10020	3.99271	3.88965	3.79079	3.69590	3.60478	3.35216

In this case, the closest discount factor to 3.3333 is 3.35216, which represents an interest rate of approximately 15%. The rate of return can be further determined by interpolation, but since we are using estimated net annual cash flows, such precision is seldom required.

Once managers know the internal rate of return, they compare it to the company's required rate of return (the discount rate). The IRR decision rule is as follows: **Accept the project when the internal rate of return is equal to or greater than the required rate of return. Reject the project when the internal rate of return is less than the required rate of return.** Illustration 26-27 on page 919 shows these relationships. Assuming the required rate of return is 10% for Reno Company, the project is acceptable because the 15% internal rate of return is greater than the required rate.

The IRR method is widely used in practice. Most managers find the internal rate of return easy to interpret.

[2]When net annual cash flows are equal, the internal rate of return factor is the same as the cash payback period.

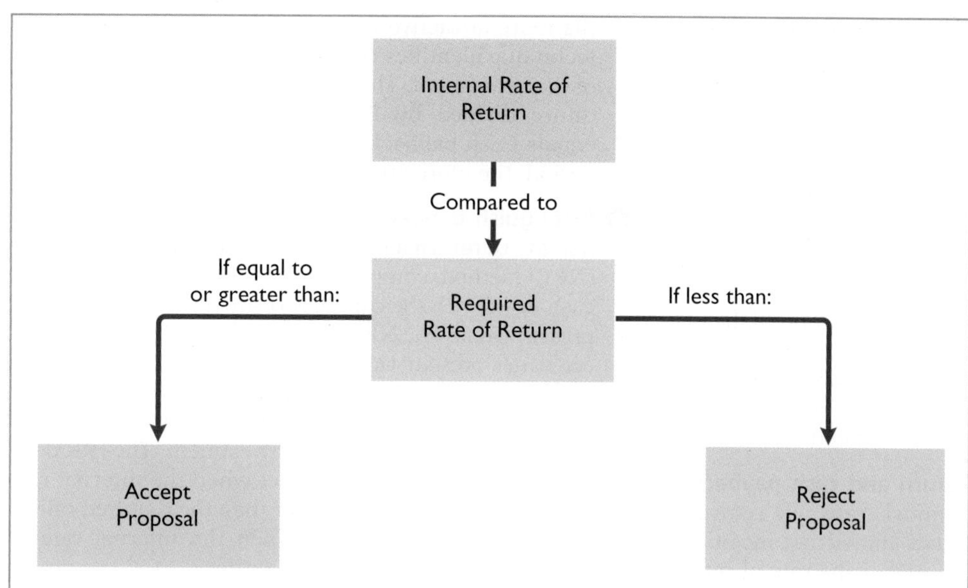

Illustration 26-27
Internal rate of return decision criteria

Comparing Discounted Cash Flow Methods

Illustration 26-28 compares the two discounted cash flow methods—net present value and internal rate of return. When properly used, either method provides management with relevant quantitative data for making capital budgeting decisions.

Illustration 26-28
Comparison of discounted cash flow methods

	Net Present Value	**Internal Rate of Return**
1. Objective	Compute net present value (a dollar amount).	Compute internal rate of return (a percentage).
2. Decision rule	If net present value is zero or positive, accept the proposal. If net present value is negative, reject the proposal.	If internal rate of return is equal to or greater than the required rate of return, accept the proposal. If internal rate of return is less than the required rate of return, reject the proposal.

REVIEW AND PRACTICE

LEARNING OBJECTIVES REVIEW

1 Describe management's decision-making process and incremental analysis. Management's decision-making process consists of (a) identifying the problem and assigning responsibility for the decision, (b) determining and evaluating possible courses of action, (c) making the decision, and (d) reviewing the results of the decision. Incremental analysis identifies financial data that change under alternative courses of action. These data are relevant to the decision because they vary across the possible alternatives.

2 Analyze the relevant costs in various decisions involving incremental analysis. The relevant information in accepting an order at a special price is the difference between the variable manufacturing costs to produce the special order and expected revenues. Any changes in fixed costs, opportunity cost, or other incremental costs or savings (such as additional shipping) should be considered. In a make-or-buy decision, the relevant costs are (a) the variable manufacturing costs that will be saved as well as changes to fixed manufacturing costs, (b) the purchase price, and (c) opportunity cost.

The decision rule for whether to sell or process materials further is: Process further as long as the incremental revenue from processing exceeds the incremental processing costs. The relevant costs to be considered in determining whether equipment should be repaired, retained, or replaced are the effects on variable costs and the cost of the new equipment. Also, any disposal value of the existing asset must be considered.

In deciding whether to eliminate an unprofitable segment or product, the relevant costs are the variable costs that drive the contribution margin, if any, produced by the segment or product. Opportunity cost and reduction of fixed expenses must also be considered.

3 **Contrast annual rate of return and cash payback in capital budgeting.** The annual rate of return is obtained by dividing expected annual net income by the average investment. The higher the rate of return, the more attractive the investment. The cash payback technique identifies the time period to recover the cost of the investment. The formula is Cost of capital expenditure divided by Estimated net annual cash flow equals Cash payback period. The shorter the payback period, the more attractive the investment.

4 **Distinguish between the net present value and internal rate of return methods.** Under the net present value (NPV) method, compare the present value of future net cash flows with the capital investment to determine net present value. The NPV decision rule is: Accept the project if net present value is zero or positive. Reject the investment if net present value is negative.

Under the internal rate of return method, find the interest yield of the potential investment. The IRR decision rule is: Accept the project when the internal rate of return is equal to or greater than the required rate of return. Reject the project when the internal rate of return is less than the required rate.

GLOSSARY REVIEW

Annual rate of return method Determines the profitability of a capital expenditure by dividing expected annual net income by the average investment.

Capital budgeting The process of making capital expenditure decisions in business.

Cash payback technique Identifies the time period required to recover the cost of a capital investment from the net annual cash flow produced by the investment.

Cost of capital The rate of return that management expects to pay on all borrowed and equity funds.

Discounted cash flow technique Considers both the estimated total net cash flows from the investment and the time value of money.

Incremental analysis The process of identifying the financial data that change under alternative courses of action.

Internal rate of return (IRR) The rate that will cause the present value of the proposed capital expenditure to equal the present value of the expected net annual cash flows.

Internal rate of return (IRR) method Finds the interest yield of the potential investment.

Net present value (NPV) The difference that results when the original capital outlay is subtracted from the discounted net cash flows.

Net present value (NPV) method Discounts net cash flows to their present value and then compares that present value to the capital outlay required by the investment.

Opportunity cost The potential benefit that may be obtained from following an alternative course of action.

Relevant costs Those costs and revenues that differ across alternatives.

Required rate of return The rate that is generally based on the company's cost of capital.

Sunk cost A cost that cannot be changed by any present or future decision.

PRACTICE EXERCISES

Use incremental analysis for make-or-buy decision.

(LO 2)

1. Maningly Inc. has been manufacturing its own lampshades for its table lamps. The company is currently operating at 100% of capacity. Variable manufacturing overhead is charged to production at the rate of 50% of direct labor cost. The direct materials and direct labor cost per unit to make the lampshades are $4 and $6, respectively. Normal production is 50,000 table lamps per year.

A supplier offers to make the lampshades at a price of $13.50 per unit. If Maningly accepts the supplier's offer; all variable manufacturing costs will be eliminated, but the $50,000 of fixed manufacturing overhead currently being charged to the lampshades will have to be absorbed by other products.

Instructions

(a) Prepare the incremental analysis for the decision to make or buy the lampshades.

(b) Should Maningly buy the lampshades?

(c) Would your answer be different in (b) if the productive capacity released by not making the lampshades could be used to produce income of $40,000?

Solution

1. (a)

	Make	Buy	Net Income Increase (Decrease)
Direct materials (50,000 × $4.00)	$200,000	$ 0	$ 200,000
Direct labor (50,000 × $6.00)	300,000	0	300,000
Variable manufacturing costs ($300,000 × 50%)	150,000	0	150,000
Fixed manufacturing costs	50,000	50,000	0
Purchase price (50,000 × $13.50)	0	675,000	(675,000)
Total annual cost	$700,000	$725,000	$ (25,000)

(b) No, Maningly should not purchase the lampshades. As indicated by the incremental analysis, it would cost the company $25,000 more to purchase the lampshades.

(c) Yes, by purchasing the lampshades, a total cost saving of $15,000 will result as shown below.

	Make	Buy	Net Income Increase (Decrease)
Total annual cost (from (a))	$700,000	$725,000	$(25,000)
Opportunity cost	40,000	0	40,000
Total cost	$740,000	$725,000	$ 15,000

Use incremental analysis for retaining or replacing equipment.

(LO 2)

2. Tek Enterprises uses a computer to handle its sales invoices. Lately, business has been so good that it takes an extra 3 hours per night, plus every third Saturday, to keep up with the volume of sales invoices. Management is considering updating its computer with a faster model that would eliminate all of the overtime processing.

	Current Machine	New Machine
Original purchase cost	$15,000	$25,000
Accumulated depreciation	6,000	—
Estimated operating costs	25,000	20,000
Useful life	6 years	6 years

If sold now, the current machine would have a salvage value of $5,000. If operated for the remainder of its useful life, the current machine would have zero salvage value. The new machine is expected to have zero salvage value after 6 years.

Instructions

Should the current machine be replaced? (Ignore the time value of money.)

Solution

2.

	Retain Machine	Replace Machine	Net Income Increase (Decrease)
Operating costs	$150,000*	$120,000**	$30,000
New machine cost (depr.)	0	25,000	(25,000)
Salvage value (old)	0	(5,000)	5,000
Total	$150,000	$140,000	$10,000

*$25,000 × 6
**$20,000 × 6

The current machine should be replaced. The incremental analysis shows that net income for the 6-year period will be $10,000 higher by replacing the current machine.

Calculate payback, annual rate of return, and net present value

(LO 3, 4)

3. MCA Corporation is reviewing an investment proposal. The initial cost and estimates of the book value of the investment at the end of each year, the net cash flows for each year, and the net income for each year are presented in the schedule below. All cash flows are assumed to take place at the end of the year. The salvage value of the investment at the end of each year is equal to its book value. There would be no salvage value at the end of the investment's life.

Investment Proposal

Year	Initial Cost and Book Value	Annual Cash Flows	Annual Net Income
0	$105,000		
1	70,000	$45,000	$16,000
2	42,000	40,000	18,000
3	21,000	35,000	20,000
4	7,000	30,000	22,000
5	0	25,000	24,000

MCA Corporation uses a 15% target rate of return for new investment proposals.

Instructions

(a) What is the cash payback period for this proposal?

(b) What is the annual rate of return for the investment?

(c) What is the net present value of the investment?

(CMA-Canada adapted)

Solution

3. (a)

	Year	Amount	Balance
Initial investment	0	$(105,000)	$(105,000)
Less: Cash flow	1	45,000	(60,000)
	2	40,000	(20,000)
	3	35,000	15,000

Payback period = 2 + ($20,000 ÷ $35,000) = 2.57

(b) Average annual net income = ($16,000 + $18,000 + $20,000 + $22,000 + $24,000) ÷ 5 = $20,000
Average investment = ($105,000 + $0) ÷ 2 = $52,500
Annual rate of return = $20,000 ÷ $52,500 = 38.10%

(c)

	Year	Discount Factor, 15%	Amount	Present Value
Net cash flows	1	0.86957	$45,000	$ 39,131
	2	0.75614	40,000	30,246
	3	0.65752	35,000	23,013
	4	0.57175	30,000	17,153
	5	0.49718	25,000	12,430
Present value of cash inflows				121,973
Less: Initial investment				105,000
Net present value				$ 16,973

PRACTICE PROBLEMS

Use incremental analysis for a special order.

(LO 2)

1. Walston Company produces kitchen cabinets for homebuilders across the western United States. The cost of producing 5,000 cabinets is as follows.

Materials	$ 500,000
Labor	250,000
Variable overhead	100,000
Fixed overhead	400,000
Total	$1,250,000

Walston also incurs selling expenses of $20 per cabinet. Wellington Corp. has offered Walston $165 per cabinet for a special order of 1,000 cabinets. The cabinets would be sold to homebuilders in the eastern United States and thus would not conflict with Walston's current sales. Selling expenses per cabinet would be only $5 per cabinet. Walston has available capacity to do the work.

Instructions

(a) Prepare an incremental analysis for the special order.

(b) Should Walston accept the special order? Why or why not?

Solution

1. (a) Relevant costs per unit would be:

Materials	$500,000/5,000 =	$100
Labor	250,000/5,000 =	50
Variable overhead	100,000/5,000 =	20
Selling expenses		5
Total relevant cost per unit		$175

	Reject Order	Accept Order	Net Income Increase (Decrease)
Revenues	$0	$165,000*	$165,000
Costs	0	175,000**	(175,000)
Net income	$0	$ (10,000)	$ (10,000)

*$165 × 1,000; **$175 × 1,000

(b) Walston should reject the offer. The incremental benefit of $165 per cabinet is less than the incremental cost of $175. By accepting the order, Walston's net income would actually decline by $10,000.

Compute annual rate of return, cash payback, and net present value.

(LO 3, 4)

2. Cornfield Company is considering a long-term capital investment project in laser equipment. This will require an investment of $280,000, and it will have a useful life of 5 years. Annual net income is expected to be $16,000 a year. Depreciation is computed by the straight-line method with no salvage value. The company's cost of capital is 10%. (*Hint:* Assume cash flows can be computed by adding back depreciation expense.)

Instructions

(Round all computations to two decimal places unless directed otherwise.)

(a) Compute the cash payback period for the project.

(b) Compute the net present value for the project. (Round to nearest dollar.)

(c) Compute the annual rate of return for the project.

(d) Should the project be accepted? Why?

Solution

2. (a) $280,000 ÷ $72,000 ($16,000 + $56,000) = 3.89 years

(b)

	Present Value at 10%
Discount factor for 5 payments	3.79079
Present value of net cash flows:	
$72,000 × 3.79079	$272,937
Less: Capital investment	280,000
Negative net present value	$ (7,063)

(c) $16,000 ÷ $140,000 ($280,000 ÷ 2) = 11.4%

(d) The annual rate of return of 11.4% is good. However, the cash payback period is 78% of the project's useful life, and net present value is negative. The recommendation is to reject the project.

EXERCISES

Analyze statements about decision-making and incremental analysis.

(LO 1)

E26-1 As a study aid, your classmate Pascal Adams has prepared the following list of statements about decision-making and incremental analysis.

1. The first step in management's decision-making process is, "Determine and evaluate possible courses of action."
2. The final step in management's decision-making process is to actually make the decision.
3. Accounting's contribution to management's decision-making process occurs primarily in evaluating possible courses of action and in reviewing the results.
4. In making business decisions, management ordinarily considers only financial information because it is objectively determined.
5. Decisions involve a choice among alternative courses of action.
6. The process used to identify the financial data that change under alternative courses of action is called incremental analysis.
7. Costs that are the same under all alternative courses of action sometimes affect the decision.
8. When using incremental analysis, some costs will always change under alternative courses of action, but revenues will not.
9. Variable costs will change under alternative courses of action, but fixed costs will not.

Instructions

Identify each statement as true or false. If false, indicate how to correct the statement.

Use incremental analysis for special-order decision.

(LO 2)

E26-2 Gruden Company produces golf discs which it normally sells to retailers for $7 each. The cost of manufacturing 20,000 golf discs is:

Materials	$ 10,000
Labor	30,000
Variable overhead	20,000
Fixed overhead	40,000
Total	$100,000

Gruden also incurs 5% sales commission ($0.35) on each disc sold.

McGee Corporation offers Gruden $4.80 per disc for 5,000 discs. McGee would sell the discs under its own brand name in foreign markets not yet served by Gruden. If Gruden accepts the offer, its fixed overhead will increase from $40,000 to $46,000 due to the purchase of a new imprinting machine. No sales commission will result from the special order.

Instructions

(a) Prepare an incremental analysis for the special order.
(b) Should Gruden accept the special order? Why or why not?
(c) What assumptions underlie the decision made in part (b)?

Use incremental analysis for special-order decision.

(LO 2)

E26-3 Moonbeam Company manufactures toasters. For the first 8 months of 2017, the company reported the following operating results while operating at 75% of plant capacity:

Sales (350,000 units)	$4,375,000
Cost of goods sold	2,600,000
Gross profit	1,775,000
Operating expenses	840,000
Net income	$ 935,000

Cost of goods sold was 70% variable and 30% fixed; operating expenses were 80% variable and 20% fixed.

In September, Moonbeam receives a special order for 15,000 toasters at $7.60 each from Luna Company of Ciudad Juarez. Acceptance of the order would result in an additional $3,000 of shipping costs but no increase in fixed costs.

Instructions

(a) Prepare an incremental analysis for the special order.
(b) Should Moonbeam accept the special order? Why or why not?

Use incremental analysis for make-or-buy decision.

(LO 2)

E26-4 Pottery Ranch Inc. has been manufacturing its own finials for its curtain rods. The company is currently operating at 100% of capacity, and variable manufacturing overhead is charged to production at the rate of 70% of direct labor cost. The direct materials and direct labor cost per unit to make a pair of finials are $4 and $5, respectively. Normal production is 30,000 curtain rods per year.

A supplier offers to make a pair of finials at a price of $12.95 per unit. If Pottery Ranch accepts the supplier's offer, all variable manufacturing costs will be eliminated, but the $45,000 of fixed manufacturing overhead currently being charged to the finials will have to be absorbed by other products.

Instructions

(a) Prepare the incremental analysis for the decision to make or buy the finials.
(b) Should Pottery Ranch buy the finials?
(c) Would your answer be different in (b) if the productive capacity released by not making the finials could be used to produce income of $20,000?

Use incremental analysis for further processing of materials decision.

(LO 2)

E26-5 Anna Garden recently opened her own basketweaving studio. She sells finished baskets in addition to the raw materials needed by customers to weave baskets of their own. Anna has put together a variety of raw material kits, each including materials at various stages of completion. Unfortunately, owing to space limitations, Anna is unable to carry all varieties of kits originally assembled and must choose between two basic packages.

The basic introductory kit includes undyed, uncut reeds (with dye included) for weaving one basket. This basic package costs Anna $16 and sells for $30. The second kit, called Stage 2, includes cut reeds that have already been dyed. With this kit the customer need only soak the reeds and weave the basket. Anna is able to produce the second kit by using the basic materials included in the first kit and adding one hour of her own time, which she values at $18 per hour. Because she is more efficient at cutting and dying reeds than her average customer, Anna is able to make two kits of the dyed reeds, in one hour, from one kit of undyed reeds. The Stage 2 kit sells for $36.

Instructions

Determine whether Anna's basketweaving studio should carry the basic introductory kit with undyed and uncut reeds or the Stage 2 kit with reeds already dyed and cut. Prepare an incremental analysis to support your answer.

Use incremental analysis for retaining or replacing equipment decision.

(LO 2)

E26-6 Johnson Enterprises uses a computer to handle its sales invoices. Lately, business has been so good that it takes an extra 3 hours per night, plus every third Saturday, to keep up with the volume of sales invoices. Management is considering updating its computer with a faster model that would eliminate all of the overtime processing.

	Current Machine	New Machine
Original purchase cost	$15,000	$25,000
Accumulated depreciation	$ 6,000	—
Estimated annual operating costs	$25,000	$20,000
Remaining useful life	5 years	5 years

If sold now, the current machine would have a salvage value of $6,000. If operated for the remainder of its useful life, the current machine would have zero salvage value. The new machine is expected to have zero salvage value after 5 years.

Instructions

Should the current machine be replaced?

Use incremental analysis concerning elimination of division.

E26-7 Veronica Mars, a recent graduate of Bell's accounting program, evaluated the operating performance of Dunn Company's six divisions. Veronica made the following presentation to Dunn's board of directors and suggested the Percy Division be eliminated. "If the Percy Division is eliminated," she said, "our total profits would increase by $26,000."

	The Other Five Divisions	Percy Division	Total
Sales	$1,664,200	$100,000	$1,764,200
Cost of goods sold	978,520	76,000	1,054,520
Gross profit	685,680	24,000	709,680
Operating expenses	527,940	50,000	577,940
Net income	$ 157,740	$ (26,000)	$ 131,740

In the Percy Division, cost of goods sold is $61,000 variable and $15,000 fixed, and operating expenses are $30,000 variable and $20,000 fixed. None of the Percy Division's fixed costs will be eliminated if the division is discontinued.

Instructions

Is Veronica right about eliminating the Percy Division? Prepare a schedule to support your answer.

Use incremental analysis for elimination of a product line.
(LO 2)

E26-8 Cawley Company makes three models of tasers. Information on the three products is given below.

	Tingler	Shocker	Stunner
Sales	$300,000	$500,000	$200,000
Variable expenses	150,000	200,000	145,000
Contribution margin	150,000	300,000	55,000
Fixed expenses	120,000	230,000	95,000
Net income	$ 30,000	$ 70,000	$ (40,000)

Fixed expenses consist of $300,000 of common costs allocated to the three products based on relative sales, and additional fixed expenses of $30,000 (Tingler), $80,000 (Shocker), and $35,000 (Stunner). The common costs will be incurred regardless of how many models are produced. The other fixed expenses would be eliminated if a model is phased out.

James Watt, an executive with the company, feels the Stunner line should be discontinued to increase the company's net income.

Instructions

(a) Compute current net income for Cawley Company.
(b) Compute net income by product line and in total for Cawley Company if the company discontinues the Stunner product line. (*Hint:* Allocate the $300,000 common costs to the two remaining product lines based on their relative sales.)
(c) Should Cawley eliminate the Stunner product line? Why or why not?

Compute cash payback period and net present value.
(LO 3)

E26-9 Doug's Custom Construction Company is considering three new projects, each requiring an equipment investment of $22,000. Each project will last for 3 years and produce the following net annual cash flows.

Year	AA	BB	CC
1	$ 7,000	$10,000	$13,000
2	9,000	10,000	12,000
3	12,000	10,000	11,000
Total	$28,000	$30,000	$36,000

The equipment's salvage value is zero, and Doug uses straight-line depreciation. Doug will not accept any project with a cash payback period over 2 years. Doug's required rate of return is 12%.

Instructions

(a) Compute each project's payback period, indicating the most desirable project and the least desirable project using this method. (Round to two decimals and assume in your computations that cash flows occur evenly throughout the year.)
(b) Compute the net present value of each project. Does your evaluation change? (Round to nearest dollar.)

Compute annual rate of return, cash payback period, and net present value.
(LO 3, 4)

E26-10 Vilas Company is considering a capital investment of $190,000 in additional productive facilities. The new machinery is expected to have a useful life of 5 years with no salvage value. Depreciation is by the straight-line method. During the life of the investment, annual net income and net annual cash flows are expected to be $12,000 and $50,000, respectively. Vilas has a 12% cost of capital rate, which is the required rate of return on the investment.

Instructions

(Round to two decimals.)

(a) Compute (1) the cash payback period and (2) the annual rate of return on the proposed capital expenditure.
(b) Using the discounted cash flow technique, compute the net present value.

Determine internal rate of return.
(LO 4)

E26-11 Iggy Company is considering three capital expenditure projects. Relevant data for the projects are as follows.

Project	Investment	Annual Income	Life of Project
22A	$240,000	$15,500	6 years
23A	270,000	20,600	9 years
24A	280,000	15,700	7 years

Annual income is constant over the life of the project. Each project is expected to have zero salvage value at the end of the project. Iggy Company uses the straight-line method of depreciation.

Instructions

(a) Determine the internal rate of return for each project. Round the internal rate of return factor to three decimals.

(b) If Iggy Company's required rate of return is 10%, which projects are acceptable?

E26-12 Leung Corporation is considering investing in two different projects. It could invest in both, neither, or just one of the projects. The forecasts for the projects are as follows.

Compute net present value and recommend project.

(LO 4)

	Project A	Project B
Capital investment	$200,000	$300,000
Net annual cash flows	$50,000	$65,000
Length of project	5 years	7 years

The required rate of return acceptable to Leung is 9%.

Instructions

(a) Compute the net present value of the two projects.

(b) What capital budgeting decision should Leung make?

(c) Project A could be modified. By spending $25,000 more initially, the net annual cash flows could be increased by $10,000 per year. Would this change Leung's decision?

PROBLEMS

P26-1A ThreePoint Sports Inc. manufactures basketballs for the Women's National Basketball Association (WNBA). For the first 6 months of 2017, the company reported the following operating results while operating at 80% of plant capacity and producing 120,000 units.

Use incremental analysis for special order and identify nonfinancial factors in the decision.

(LO 2)

	Amount
Sales	$4,800,000
Cost of goods sold	3,600,000
Selling and administrative expenses	405,000
Net income	$ 795,000

Fixed costs for the period were cost of goods sold $960,000, and selling and administrative expenses $225,000.

In July, normally a slack manufacturing month, ThreePoint Sports receives a special order for 10,000 basketballs at $28 each from the Greek Basketball Association (GBA). Acceptance of the order would increase variable selling and administrative expenses $0.75 per unit because of shipping costs but would not increase fixed costs and expenses.

Instructions

(a) Prepare an incremental analysis for the special order.

(a) NI increase $37,500

(b) Should ThreePoint Sports Inc. accept the special order? Explain your answer.

(c) What is the minimum selling price on the special order to produce net income of $5.00 per ball?

(d) What nonfinancial factors should management consider in making its decision?

P26-2A The management of Shatner Manufacturing Company is trying to decide whether to continue manufacturing a part or to buy it from an outside supplier. The part, called CISCO, is a component of the company's finished product.

Use incremental analysis related to make or buy, consider opportunity cost, and identify nonfinancial factors.

(LO 2)

The following information was collected from the accounting records and production data for the year ending December 31, 2017.

1. 8,000 units of CISCO were produced in the Machining Department.
2. Variable manufacturing costs applicable to the production of each CISCO unit were: direct materials $4.80, direct labor $4.30, indirect labor $0.43, utilities $0.40.

3. Fixed manufacturing costs applicable to the production of CISCO were:

Cost Item	Direct	Allocated
Depreciation	$2,100	$ 900
Property taxes	500	200
Insurance	900	600
	$3,500	$1,700

All variable manufacturing and direct fixed costs will be eliminated if CISCO is purchased. Allocated costs will have to be absorbed by other production departments.

4. The lowest quotation for 8,000 CISCO units from a supplier is $80,000.
5. If CISCO units are purchased, freight and inspection costs would be $0.35 per unit, and receiving costs totaling $1,300 per year would be incurred by the Machining Department.

Instructions

(a) NI (decrease) $(1,160)

(c) NI increase $1,840

(a) Prepare an incremental analysis for CISCO. Your analysis should have columns for (1) Make CISCO, (2) Buy CISCO, and (3) Net Income Increase/(Decrease).

(b) Based on your analysis, what decision should management make?

(c) Would the decision be different if Shatner Company has the opportunity to produce $3,000 of net income with the facilities currently being used to manufacture CISCO? Show computations.

(d) What nonfinancial factors should management consider in making its decision?

Compute gain or loss, and determine if equipment should be replaced.

(LO 2)

P26-3A Last year (2016), Richter Condos installed a mechanized elevator for its tenants. The owner of the company, Ron Richter, recently returned from an industry equipment exhibition where he watched a computerized elevator demonstrated. He was impressed with the elevator's speed, comfort of ride, and cost efficiency. Upon returning from the exhibition, he asked his purchasing agent to collect price and operating cost data on the new elevator. In addition, he asked the company's accountant to provide him with cost data on the company's elevator. This information is presented below.

	Old Elevator	New Elevator
Purchase price	$120,000	$160,000
Estimated salvage value	0	0
Estimated useful life	5 years	4 years
Depreciation method	Straight-line	Straight-line
Annual operating costs other than depreciation:		
Variable	$ 35,000	$ 10,000
Fixed	23,000	8,500

Annual revenues are $240,000, and selling and administrative expenses are $29,000, regardless of which elevator is used. If the old elevator is replaced now, at the beginning of 2017, Richter Condos will be able to sell it for $25,000.

Instructions

(a) Determine any gain or loss if the old elevator is replaced.

(b) Prepare a 4-year summarized income statement for each of the following assumptions:
   (1) The old elevator is retained.
   (2) The old elevator is replaced.

(b) (2) NI $539,000
(c) NI increase $23,000

(c) Using incremental analysis, determine if the old elevator should be replaced.

(d) Write a memo to Ron Richter explaining why any gain or loss should be ignored in the decision to replace the old elevator.

Prepare incremental analysis concerning elimination of divisions.

(LO 2)

P26-4A Brislin Company has four operating divisions. During the first quarter of 2017, the company reported aggregate income from operations of $213,000 and the following divisional results.

	Division			
	I	II	III	IV
Sales	$250,000	$200,000	$500,000	$450,000
Cost of goods sold	200,000	192,000	300,000	250,000
Selling and administrative expenses	75,000	60,000	60,000	50,000
Income (loss) from operations	$ (25,000)	$ (52,000)	$140,000	$150,000

Analysis reveals the following percentages of variable costs in each division.

	I	II	III	IV
Cost of goods sold	70%	90%	80%	75%
Selling and administrative expenses	40	60	50	60

Discontinuance of any division would save 50% of the fixed costs and expenses for that division.

Top management is very concerned about the unprofitable divisions (I and II). Consensus is that one or both of the divisions should be discontinued.

Instructions

(a) Compute the contribution margin for Divisions I and II.

(a) I $80,000

(b) Prepare an incremental analysis concerning the possible discontinuance of (1) Division I and (2) Division II. What course of action do you recommend for each division?

(c) Prepare a columnar condensed income statement for Brislin Company, assuming Division II is eliminated. (Use the CVP format.) Division II's unavoidable fixed costs are allocated equally to the continuing divisions.

(c) Income III $142,800

(d) Reconcile the total income from operations ($213,000) with the total income from operations without Division II.

P26-5A U3 Company is considering three long-term capital investment proposals. Each investment has a useful life of 5 years. Relevant data on each project are as follows.

Compute annual rate of return, cash payback, and net present value.

(LO 3, 4)

	Project Bono	Project Edge	Project Clayton
Capital investment	$160,000	$175,000	$200,000
Annual net income:			
Year 1	14,000	18,000	27,000
2	14,000	17,000	23,000
3	14,000	16,000	21,000
4	14,000	12,000	13,000
5	14,000	9,000	12,000
Total	$ 70,000	$ 72,000	$ 96,000

Depreciation is computed by the straight-line method with no salvage value. The company's cost of capital is 15%. (Assume that cash flows occur evenly throughout the year.)

Instructions

(a) Compute the cash payback period for each project. (Round to two decimals.)

(b) Compute the net present value for each project. (Round to nearest dollar.)

(b) E $(7,312); C $2,163

(c) Compute the annual rate of return for each project. (Round to two decimals.) (*Hint:* Use average annual net income in your computation.)

(d) Rank the projects on each of the foregoing bases. Which project do you recommend?

P26-6A Lon Timur is an accounting major at a midwestern state university located approximately 60 miles from a major city. Many of the students attending the university are from the metropolitan area and visit their homes regularly on the weekends. Lon, an entrepreneur at heart, realizes that few good commuting alternatives are available for students doing weekend travel. He believes that a weekend commuting service could be organized and run profitably from several suburban and downtown shopping mall locations. Lon has gathered the following investment information.

Compute annual rate of return, cash payback, and net present value.

(LO 3, 4)

1. Five used vans would cost a total of $75,000 to purchase and would have a 3-year useful life with negligible salvage value. Lon plans to use straight-line depreciation.
2. Ten drivers would have to be employed at a total payroll expense of $48,000.
3. Other annual out-of-pocket expenses associated with running the commuter service would include Gasoline $16,000, Maintenance $3,300, Repairs $4,000, Insurance $4,200, and Advertising $2,500.

4. Lon has visited several financial institutions to discuss funding. The best interest rate he has been able to negotiate is 15%. Use this rate for cost of capital.
5. Lon expects each van to make ten round trips weekly and carry an average of six students each trip. The service is expected to operate 30 weeks each year, and each student will be charged $12.00 for a round-trip ticket.

Instructions

(a) (1) $5,000

(b) (1) 2.5 years

(a) Determine the annual (1) net income and (2) net annual cash flows for the commuter service.
(b) Compute (1) the cash payback period and (2) the annual rate of return. (Round to two decimals.)
(c) Compute the net present value of the commuter service. (Round to the nearest dollar.)
(d) What should Lon conclude from these computations?

Compute net present value and internal rate of return.

(LO 3, 4)

P26-7A Brooks Clinic is considering investing in new heart-monitoring equipment. It has two options. Option A would have an initial lower cost but would require a significant expenditure for rebuilding after 4 years. Option B would require no rebuilding expenditure, but its maintenance costs would be higher. Since the Option B machine is of initial higher quality, it is expected to have a salvage value at the end of its useful life. The following estimates were made of the cash flows. The company's cost of capital is 8%.

	Option A	Option B
Initial cost	$160,000	$227,000
Annual cash inflows	$71,000	$80,000
Annual cash outflows	$30,000	$31,000
Cost to rebuild (end of year 4)	$50,000	$0
Salvage value	$0	$8,000
Estimated useful life	7 years	7 years

Instructions

(a) (1) NPV A $16,709
(2) IRR B 12%

(a) Compute the (1) net present value and (2) internal rate of return for each option. (*Hint:* To solve for internal rate of return, experiment with alternative discount rates to arrive at a net present value of zero.)
(b) Which option should be accepted?

COMPREHENSIVE PROBLEM: CHAPTERS 19 TO 26

CP26 You would like to start a business manufacturing a unique model of bicycle helmet. In preparation for an interview with the bank to discuss your financing needs, you need to provide the following information. A number of assumptions are required; clearly note all assumptions that you make.

Instructions

(a) Identify the types of costs that would likely be involved in making this product.
(b) Set up five columns as indicated.

	Product Costs			
Item	Direct Materials	Direct Labor	Manufacturing Overhead	Period Costs

Classify the costs you identified in (a) into the manufacturing cost classifications of product costs (direct materials, direct labor, and manufacturing overhead) and period costs.

(c) Assign hypothetical monthly dollar figures to the costs you identified in (a) and (b).
(d) Assume you have no raw materials or work in process beginning or ending inventories. Prepare a projected cost of goods manufactured schedule for the first month of operations.
(e) Project the number of helmets you expect to produce the first month of operations. Compute the cost to produce one bicycle helmet. Review the result to ensure it is reasonable; if not, return to part (c) and adjust the monthly dollar figures you assigned accordingly.
(f) What type of cost accounting system will you likely use—job order or process costing?
(g) Explain how you would assign costs in either the job order or process costing system you plan to use.
(h) Classify your costs as either variable or fixed costs. For simplicity, assign all costs to either variable or fixed, assuming there are no mixed costs, using the format shown.

Item	Variable Costs	Fixed Costs	Total Costs

(i) Compute the unit variable cost, using the production number you determined in (e).
(j) Project the number of helmets you anticipate selling the first month of operations. Set a unit selling price, and compute both the contribution margin per unit and the contribution margin ratio.
(k) Determine your break-even point in dollars and in units.
(l) Prepare projected operating budgets (sales, production, direct materials, direct labor, manufacturing overhead, selling and administrative expense, and income statement). You will need to make assumptions for each of the following:

Direct materials budget:	Quantity of direct materials required to produce one helmet; cost per unit of quantity; desired ending direct materials (assume none).
Direct labor budget:	Direct labor time required per helmet; direct labor cost per hour.
Budgeted income statement:	Income tax expense is 45% of income from operations.

(m) Prepare a cash budget for the month. Assume the percentage of sales that will be collected from customers is 75%, and the percentage of direct materials that will be paid in the current month is 75%.
(n) Determine a relevant range of activity, using the number of helmets produced as your activity index. Recast your manufacturing overhead budget into a flexible monthly budget for two additional activity levels.
(o) Identify one potential cause of materials, direct labor, and manufacturing overhead variances for your product.
(p) Assume that you wish to purchase production equipment that costs $720,000. Determine the cash payback period, utilizing the monthly cash flow that you computed in part (m) multiplied by 12 months (for simplicity).
(q) Identify any nonfinancial factors that should be considered before commencing your business venture.

COMPREHENSIVE CASES

CC26-1 Auburn Circular Club is planning a major fundraiser that it hopes will become a successful annual event: sponsoring a professional rodeo. For this case, you will encounter many managerial accounting issues that would be common for a start-up business, such as CVP analysis, incremental analysis, and budgetary planning.

CC26-2 For this case, revisit the Greetings Inc. company presented in earlier chapters. The company is now searching for new opportunities for growth. This case will provide you with the opportunity to evaluate a proposal based on initial estimates as well as conduct sensitivity analysis. It also requires evaluation of the underlying assumptions used in the analysis.

CC26-3 Armstrong Helmet Company needs to determine the cost for a given product. For this case, you will have the opportunity to explore cost-volume-profit relationships and prepare a set of budgets.

Go to the book's companion website, **at www.wiley.com/college/weygandt**, *for details and instructions for each of these cases.*

BROADENING YOUR PERSPECTIVE

MANAGEMENT DECISION-MAKING

Decision-Making Across the Organization

BYP26-1 Aurora Company is considering the purchase of a new machine. The invoice price of the machine is $140,000, freight charges are estimated to be $4,000, and installation costs are expected to be $6,000. Salvage value of the new equipment is expected to be zero after a useful life of 5 years. Existing equipment could be retained and used for an additional 5 years if the new machine is not purchased. At that time, the salvage value of the equipment would be zero. If the new machine is purchased now, the existing machine would have to be scrapped. Aurora's accountant, Lisah Huang, has accumulated the following data regarding annual sales and expenses with and without the new machine.

1. Without the new machine, Aurora can sell 12,000 units of product annually at a per unit selling price of $100. If the new machine is purchased, the number of units produced and sold would increase by 10%, and the selling price would remain the same.

2. The new machine is faster than the old machine, and it is more efficient in its usage of materials. With the old machine the gross profit rate will be 25% of sales, whereas the rate will be 30% of sales with the new machine.
3. Annual selling expenses are $180,000 with the current equipment. Because the new equipment would produce a greater number of units to be sold, annual selling expenses are expected to increase by 10% if it is purchased.
4. Annual administrative expenses are expected to be $100,000 with the old machine, and $113,000 with the new machine.
5. The current book value of the existing machine is $36,000. Aurora uses straight-line depreciation.

Instructions

With the class divided into groups, prepare an incremental analysis for the 5 years showing whether Aurora should keep the existing machine or buy the new machine. (Ignore income tax effects.)

Managerial Analysis

BYP26-2 MiniTek manufactures private-label small electronic products, such as alarm clocks, calculators, kitchen timers, stopwatches, and automatic pencil sharpeners. Some of the products are sold as sets, and others are sold individually. Products are studied as to their sales potential, and then cost estimates are made. The Engineering Department develops production plans, and then production begins. The company has generally had very successful product introductions. Only two products introduced by the company have been discontinued.

One of the products currently sold is a multi-alarm clock. The clock has four alarms that can be programmed to sound at various times and for varying lengths of time. The company has experienced a great deal of difficulty in making the circuit boards for the clocks. The production process has never operated smoothly. The product is unprofitable at the present time, primarily because of warranty repairs and product recalls. Two models of the clocks were recalled, for example, because they sometimes caused an electric shock when the alarms were being shut off. The Engineering Department is attempting to revise the manufacturing process, but the revision will take another 6 months at least.

The clocks were very popular when they were introduced, and since they are private-label, the company has not suffered much from the recalls. Presently, the company has a very large order for several items from **Kmart Stores**. The order includes 5,000 of the multi-alarm clocks. When the company suggested that Kmart purchase the clocks from another manufacturer, Kmart threatened to rescind the entire order unless the clocks were included.

The company has therefore investigated the possibility of having another company make the clocks for them. The clocks were bid for the Kmart order based on an estimated $6.90 cost to manufacture:

Circuit board, 1 each @ $2.00	$2.00
Plastic case, 1 each @ $0.80	0.80
Alarms, 4 @ $0.15 each	0.60
Labor, 15 minutes @ $12/hour	3.00
Overhead, $2.00 per labor hour	0.50

MiniTek could purchase clocks to fill the Kmart order for $10 from Trans-Tech Asia, a Korean manufacturer with a very good quality record. Trans-Tech has offered to reduce the price to $7.50 after MiniTek has been a customer for 6 months, placing an order of at least 1,000 units per month. If MiniTek becomes a "preferred customer" by purchasing 15,000 units per year, the price would be reduced still further to $4.50.

Omega Products, a local manufacturer, has also offered to make clocks for MiniTek. They have offered to sell 5,000 clocks for $5 each. However, Omega Products has been in business for only 6 months. They have experienced significant turnover in their labor force, and the local press has reported that the owners may face tax evasion charges soon. The owner of Omega Products is an electronic engineer, however, and the quality of the clocks is likely to be good.

If MiniTek decides to purchase the clocks from either Trans-Tech or Omega, all the costs to manufacture could be avoided, except a total of $1,000 in overhead costs for machine depreciation. The machinery is fairly new, and has no alternate use.

Instructions

(a) What is the difference in profit under each of the alternatives if the clocks are to be sold for $14.50 each to Kmart?

(b) What are the most important nonfinancial factors that MiniTek should consider when making this decision?

(c) What do you think MiniTek should do in regard to the Kmart order? What should it do in regard to continuing to manufacture the multi-alarm clocks? Be prepared to defend your answer.

Real-World Focus

BYP26-3 Founded in 1983 and foreclosed in 1996, **Beverly Hills Fan Company** was located in Woodland Hills, California. With 23 employees and sales of less than $10 million, the company was relatively small. In 1992, management felt that there was potential for growth in the upscale market for ceiling fans and lighting. They were particularly optimistic about growth in Mexican and Canadian markets.

Presented below is information from the president's letter in one of the company's last annual reports.

BEVERLY HILLS FAN COMPANY
President's Letter

An aggressive product development program was initiated during the past year resulting in new ceiling fan models planned for introduction this year. Award winning industrial designer Ron Rezek created several new fan models for the Beverly Hills Fan and L.A. Fan lines, including a new Showroom Collection, designed specifically for the architectural and designer markets. Each of these models has received critical acclaim, and order commitments for this year have been outstanding. Additionally, our Custom Color and special order fans continued to enjoy increasing popularity and sales gains as more and more customers desire fans that match their specific interior decors. Currently, Beverly Hills Fan Company offers a product line of over 100 models of contemporary, traditional, and transitional ceiling fans.

Instructions

(a) What points did the company management need to consider before deciding to offer the special-order fans to customers?
(b) How would have incremental analysis been employed to assist in this decision?

BYP26-4 **Campbell Soup Company** is an international provider of soup products. Management is very interested in continuing to grow the company in its core business, while "spinning off" those businesses that are not part of its core operation.

Address: **www.campbellsoups.com**, or go to **www.wiley.com/college/weygandt**

Steps

1. Go to the home page of Campbell Soup Company at the address shown above.
2. Choose the current annual report

Instructions

Review the financial statements and management's discussion and analysis, and answer the following questions.

(a) What was the total amount of capital expenditures in the current year, and how does this amount compare with the previous year? In your response, note what year you are using.
(b) What interest rate did the company pay on new borrowings in the current year?
(c) Assume that this year's capital expenditures are expected to increase cash flows by $50 million. What is the expected internal rate of return (IRR) for these capital expenditures? (Assume a 10-year period for the cash flows.)

CRITICAL THINKING

Communication Activity

BYP26-5 Refer back to E26-10 to address the following.

Instructions

Prepare a memo to Maria Fierro, your supervisor. Show your calculations from E26-10 (a) and (b). In one or two paragraphs, discuss important nonfinancial considerations. Make any assumptions you believe to be necessary. Make a recommendation based on your analysis.

Ethics Case

BYP26-6 NuComp Company operates in a state where corporate taxes and workers' compensation insurance rates have recently doubled. NuComp's president has just assigned you the task of preparing an economic analysis and making a recommendation relative to moving the entire operation to

Missouri. The president is slightly in favor of such a move because Missouri is his boyhood home and he also owns a fishing lodge there.

You have just completed building your dream house, moved in, and sodded the lawn. Your children are all doing well in school and sports and, along with your spouse, want no part of a move to Missouri. If the company does move, so will you because the town is a one-industry community and you and your spouse will have to move to have employment. Moving when everyone else does will cause you to take a big loss on the sale of your house. The same hardships will be suffered by your coworkers, and the town will be devastated.

In compiling the costs of moving versus not moving, you have latitude in the assumptions you make, the estimates you compute, and the discount rates and time periods you project. You are in a position to influence the decision singlehandedly.

Instructions

(a) Who are the stakeholders in this situation?
(b) What are the ethical issues in this situation?
(c) What would you do in this situation?

All About You

BYP26-7 Managerial accounting techniques can be used in a wide variety of settings. As we have frequently pointed out, you can use them in many personal situations. They also can be useful in trying to find solutions for societal issues that appear to be hard to solve.

Instructions

Read the Fortune article, "The Toughest Customers: How Hardheaded Business Metrics Can Help the Hard-core Homeless," by Cait Murphy, available at *http://money.cnn.com/magazines/fortune/fortune_archive/2006/04/03/8373067/index.htm*. Answer the following questions.

(a) How does the article define "chronic" homelessness?
(b) In what ways does homelessness cost a city money? What are the estimated costs of a chronic homeless person to various cities?
(c) What are the steps suggested to address the problem?
(d) What is the estimated cost of implementing this program in New York? What results have been seen?
(e) In terms of incremental analysis, frame the relevant costs in this situation.

Appendix A Specimen Financial Statements: Apple Inc.

Once each year, a corporation communicates to its stockholders and other interested parties by issuing a complete set of audited financial statements. The **annual report**, as this communication is called, summarizes the financial results of the company's operations for the year and its plans for the future. Many annual reports are attractive, multicolored, glossy public relations pieces, containing pictures of corporate officers and directors as well as photos and descriptions of new products and new buildings. Yet the basic function of every annual report is to report financial information, almost all of which is a product of the corporation's accounting system.

The content and organization of corporate annual reports have become fairly standardized. Excluding the public relations part of the report (pictures, products, etc.), the following are the traditional financial portions of the annual report:

- Financial Highlights
- Letter to the Stockholders
- Management's Discussion and Analysis
- Financial Statements
- Notes to the Financial Statements
- Management's Responsibility for Financial Reporting
- Management's Report on Internal Control Over Financial Reporting
- Report of Independent Registered Public Accounting Firm
- Selected Financial Data

The official SEC filing of the annual report is called a **Form 10-K**, which often omits the public relations pieces found in most standard annual reports. On the following pages, we present **Apple Inc.**'s financial statements taken from the company's 2013 Form 10-K. To access Apple's Form 10-K, including notes to the financial statements, follow these steps:

1. Go to **http://investor.apple.com**.
2. Select the Financial Information tab.
3. Select the 10-K annual report dated September 28, 2013.
4. The Notes to Consolidated Financial Statements begin on page 50.

CONSOLIDATED STATEMENTS OF OPERATIONS

(In millions, except number of shares which are reflected in thousands and per share amounts)

	Years ended		
	September 28, 2013	September 29, 2012	September 24, 2011
Net sales	$ 170,910	$ 156,508	$ 108,249
Cost of sales	106,606	87,846	64,431
Gross margin	64,304	68,662	43,818
Operating expenses:			
Research and development	4,475	3,381	2,429
Selling, general and administrative	10,830	10,040	7,599
Total operating expenses	15,305	13,421	10,028
Operating income	48,999	55,241	33,790
Other income/(expense), net	1,156	522	415
Income before provision for income taxes	50,155	55,763	34,205
Provision for income taxes	13,118	14,030	8,283
Net income	$ 37,037	$ 41,733	$ 25,922
Earnings per share:			
Basic	$ 40.03	$ 44.64	$ 28.05
Diluted	$ 39.75	$ 44.15	$ 27.68
Shares used in computing earnings per share:			
Basic	925,331	934,818	924,258
Diluted	931,662	945,355	936,645
Cash dividends declared per common share	$ 11.40	$ 2.65	$ 0.00

See accompanying Notes to Consolidated Financial Statements.

CONSOLIDATED STATEMENTS OF COMPREHENSIVE INCOME

(In millions)

	Years ended		
	September 28, 2013	September 29, 2012	September 24, 2011
Net income	$37,037	$41,733	$25,922
Other comprehensive income/(loss):			
Change in foreign currency translation, net of tax effects of $35, $13 and $18, respectively	(112)	(15)	(12)
Change in unrecognized gains/losses on derivative instruments:			
Change in fair value of derivatives, net of tax benefit/(expense) of $(351), $73 and $(50), respectively	522	(131)	92
Adjustment for net losses/(gains) realized and included in net income, net of tax expense/(benefit) of $255, $220 and $(250), respectively	(458)	(399)	450
Total change in unrecognized gains/losses on derivative instruments, net of tax	64	(530)	542
Change in unrealized gains/losses on marketable securities:			
Change in fair value of marketable securities, net of tax benefit/(expense) of $458, $(421) and $17, respectively	(791)	715	29
Adjustment for net losses/(gains) realized and included in net income, net of tax expense/(benefit) of $82, $68 and $(40), respectively	(131)	(114)	(70)
Total change in unrealized gains/losses on marketable securities, net of tax	(922)	601	(41)
Total other comprehensive income/(loss)	(970)	56	489
Total comprehensive income	$36,067	$41,789	$26,411

See accompanying Notes to Consolidated Financial Statements.

CONSOLIDATED BALANCE SHEETS

(In millions, except number of shares which are reflected in thousands)

	September 28, 2013	September 29, 2012
ASSETS:		
Current assets:		
Cash and cash equivalents	$ 14,259	$ 10,746
Short-term marketable securities	26,287	18,383
Accounts receivable, less allowances of $99 and $98, respectively	13,102	10,930
Inventories	1,764	791
Deferred tax assets	3,453	2,583
Vendor non-trade receivables	7,539	7,762
Other current assets	6,882	6,458
Total current assets	73,286	57,653
Long-term marketable securities	106,215	92,122
Property, plant and equipment, net	16,597	15,452
Goodwill	1,577	1,135
Acquired intangible assets, net	4,179	4,224
Other assets	5,146	5,478
Total assets	$ 207,000	$ 176,064
LIABILITIES AND SHAREHOLDERS' EQUITY:		
Current liabilities:		
Accounts payable	$ 22,367	$ 21,175
Accrued expenses	13,856	11,414
Deferred revenue	7,435	5,953
Total current liabilities	43,658	38,542
Deferred revenue – non-current	2,625	2,648
Long-term debt	16,960	0
Other non-current liabilities	20,208	16,664
Total liabilities	83,451	57,854
Commitments and contingencies		
Shareholders' equity:		
Common stock, no par value; 1,800,000 shares authorized; 899,213 and 939,208 shares issued and outstanding, respectively	19,764	16,422
Retained earnings	104,256	101,289
Accumulated other comprehensive income/(loss)	(471)	499
Total shareholders' equity	123,549	118,210
Total liabilities and shareholders' equity	$ 207,000	$ 176,064

See accompanying Notes to Consolidated Financial Statements.

CONSOLIDATED STATEMENTS OF SHAREHOLDERS' EQUITY
(In millions, except number of shares which are reflected in thousands)

	Common Stock		Retained Earnings	Accumulated Other Comprehensive Income/(Loss)	Total Shareholders' Equity
	Shares	Amount			
Balances as of September 25, 2010	915,970	$10,668	$ 37,169	$ (46)	$ 47,791
Net income	0	0	25,922	0	25,922
Other comprehensive income/(loss)	0	0	0	489	489
Share-based compensation	0	1,168	0	0	1,168
Common stock issued under stock plans, net of shares withheld for employee taxes	13,307	561	(250)	0	311
Tax benefit from equity awards, including transfer pricing adjustments	0	934	0	0	934
Balances as of September 24, 2011	929,277	13,331	62,841	443	76,615
Net income	0	0	41,733	0	41,733
Other comprehensive income/(loss)	0	0	0	56	56
Dividends and dividend equivalent rights declared	0	0	(2,523)	0	(2,523)
Share-based compensation	0	1,740	0	0	1,740
Common stock issued under stock plans, net of shares withheld for employee taxes	9,931	200	(762)	0	(562)
Tax benefit from equity awards, including transfer pricing adjustments	0	1,151	0	0	1,151
Balances as of September 29, 2012	939,208	16,422	101,289	499	118,210
Net income	0	0	37,037	0	37,037
Other comprehensive income/(loss)	0	0	0	(970)	(970)
Dividends and dividend equivalent rights declared	0	0	(10,676)	0	(10,676)
Repurchase of common stock	(46,976)	0	(22,950)	0	(22,950)
Share-based compensation	0	2,253	0	0	2,253
Common stock issued under stock plans, net of shares withheld for employee taxes	6,981	(143)	(444)	0	(587)
Tax benefit from equity awards, including transfer pricing adjustments	0	1,232	0	0	1,232
Balances as of September 28, 2013	899,213	$19,764	$104,256	$ (471)	$123,549

See accompanying Notes to Consolidated Financial Statements.

CONSOLIDATED STATEMENTS OF CASH FLOWS
(In millions)

	Years ended		
	September 28, 2013	September 29, 2012	September 24, 2011
Cash and cash equivalents, beginning of the year	$ 10,746	$ 9,815	$ 11,261
Operating activities:			
Net income	37,037	41,733	25,922
Adjustments to reconcile net income to cash generated by operating activities:			
Depreciation and amortization	6,757	3,277	1,814
Share-based compensation expense	2,253	1,740	1,168
Deferred income tax expense	1,141	4,405	2,868
Changes in operating assets and liabilities:			
Accounts receivable, net	(2,172)	(5,551)	143
Inventories	(973)	(15)	275
Vendor non-trade receivables	223	(1,414)	(1,934)
Other current and non-current assets	1,080	(3,162)	(1,391)
Accounts payable	2,340	4,467	2,515
Deferred revenue	1,459	2,824	1,654
Other current and non-current liabilities	4,521	2,552	4,495
Cash generated by operating activities	53,666	50,856	37,529
Investing activities:			
Purchases of marketable securities	(148,489)	(151,232)	(102,317)
Proceeds from maturities of marketable securities	20,317	13,035	20,437
Proceeds from sales of marketable securities	104,130	99,770	49,416
Payments made in connection with business acquisitions, net	(496)	(350)	(244)
Payments for acquisition of property, plant and equipment	(8,165)	(8,295)	(4,260)
Payments for acquisition of intangible assets	(911)	(1,107)	(3,192)
Other	(160)	(48)	(259)
Cash used in investing activities	(33,774)	(48,227)	(40,419)
Financing activities:			
Proceeds from issuance of common stock	530	665	831
Excess tax benefits from equity awards	701	1,351	1,133
Taxes paid related to net share settlement of equity awards	(1,082)	(1,226)	(520)
Dividends and dividend equivalent rights paid	(10,564)	(2,488)	0
Repurchase of common stock	(22,860)	0	0
Proceeds from issuance of long-term debt, net	16,896	0	0
Cash generated by/(used in) financing activities	(16,379)	(1,698)	1,444
Increase/(decrease) in cash and cash equivalents	3,513	931	(1,446)
Cash and cash equivalents, end of the year	$ 14,259	$ 10,746	$ 9,815
Supplemental cash flow disclosure:			
Cash paid for income taxes, net	$ 9,128	$ 7,682	$ 3,338

See accompanying Notes to Consolidated Financial Statements.

Appendix B Specimen Financial Statements: PepsiCo, Inc.

PepsiCo, Inc. is a world leader in convenient snacks, foods, and beverages. The following are PepsiCo's financial statements as presented in its 2013 annual report. To access PepsiCo's complete annual report, including notes to the financial statements, follow these steps:

1. Go to **www.pepsico.com**.
2. Select Annual Reports and Proxy Information under the Investors tab.
3. Select the 2013 Annual Report.
4. The Notes to Consolidated Financial Statements begin on page 73.

Consolidated Statement of Income
PepsiCo, Inc. and Subsidiaries
Fiscal years ended December 28, 2013, December 29, 2012 and December 31, 2011
(in millions except per share amounts)

	2013	2012	2011
Net Revenue	**$ 66,415**	$ 65,492	$ 66,504
Cost of sales	**31,243**	31,291	31,593
Selling, general and administrative expenses	**25,357**	24,970	25,145
Amortization of intangible assets	**110**	119	133
Operating Profit	**9,705**	9,112	9,633
Interest expense	**(911)**	(899)	(856)
Interest income and other	**97**	91	57
Income before income taxes	**8,891**	8,304	8,834
Provision for income taxes	**2,104**	2,090	2,372
Net income	**6,787**	6,214	6,462
Less: Net income attributable to noncontrolling interests	**47**	36	19
Net Income Attributable to PepsiCo	**$ 6,740**	$ 6,178	$ 6,443
Net Income Attributable to PepsiCo per Common Share			
Basic	**$ 4.37**	$ 3.96	$ 4.08
Diluted	**$ 4.32**	$ 3.92	$ 4.03
Weighted-average common shares outstanding			
Basic	**1,541**	1,557	1,576
Diluted	**1,560**	1,575	1,597
Cash dividends declared per common share	**$ 2.24**	$ 2.1275	$ 2.025

See accompanying notes to consolidated financial statements.

Consolidated Statement of Comprehensive Income

PepsiCo, Inc. and Subsidiaries
Fiscal years ended December 28, 2013, December 29, 2012 and December 31, 2011
(in millions)

	2013		
	Pre-tax amounts	**Tax amounts**	**After-tax amounts**
Net income			$ 6,787
Other Comprehensive Income			
Currency translation adjustment	$ (1,303)	$ —	(1,303)
Cash flow hedges:			
Reclassification of net losses to net income	45	(17)	28
Net derivative losses	(20)	10	(10)
Pension and retiree medical:			
Net prior service cost	(23)	8	(15)
Net gains	2,540	(895)	1,645
Unrealized gains on securities	57	(28)	29
Other	—	(16)	(16)
Total Other Comprehensive Income	$ 1,296	$ (938)	358
Comprehensive income			7,145
Comprehensive income attributable to noncontrolling interests			(45)
Comprehensive Income Attributable to PepsiCo			$ 7,100

	2012		
	Pre-tax amounts	Tax amounts	After-tax amounts
Net income			$ 6,214
Other Comprehensive Income			
Currency translation adjustment	$ 737	$ —	737
Cash flow hedges:			
Reclassification of net losses to net income	90	(32)	58
Net derivative losses	(50)	10	(40)
Pension and retiree medical:			
Net prior service cost	(32)	12	(20)
Net losses	(41)	(11)	(52)
Unrealized gains on securities	18	—	18
Other	—	36	36
Total Other Comprehensive Income	$ 722	$ 15	737
Comprehensive income			6,951
Comprehensive income attributable to noncontrolling interests			(31)
Comprehensive Income Attributable to PepsiCo			$ 6,920

	2011		
	Pre-tax amounts	Tax amounts	After-tax amounts
Net income			$ 6,462
Other Comprehensive Loss			
Currency translation adjustment	$ (1,464)	$ —	(1,464)
Cash flow hedges:			
Reclassification of net losses to net income	5	4	9
Net derivative losses	(126)	43	(83)
Pension and retiree medical:			
Net prior service cost	(18)	8	(10)
Net losses	(1,468)	501	(967)
Unrealized losses on securities	(27)	19	(8)
Other	(16)	5	(11)
Total Other Comprehensive Loss	$ (3,114)	$ 580	(2,534)
Comprehensive income			3,928
Comprehensive income attributable to noncontrolling interests			(84)
Comprehensive Income Attributable to PepsiCo			$ 3,844

See accompanying notes to consolidated financial statements.

Consolidated Statement of Cash Flows

PepsiCo, Inc. and Subsidiaries
Fiscal years ended December 28, 2013, December 29, 2012 and December 31, 2011
(in millions)

	2013	2012	2011
Operating Activities			
Net income	$ **6,787**	$ 6,214	$ 6,462
Depreciation and amortization	**2,663**	2,689	2,737
Stock-based compensation expense	**303**	278	326
Merger and integration costs	**10**	16	329
Cash payments for merger and integration costs	**(25)**	(83)	(377)
Restructuring and impairment charges	**163**	279	383
Cash payments for restructuring charges	**(133)**	(343)	(31)
Restructuring and other charges related to the transaction with Tingyi	**—**	176	—
Cash payments for restructuring and other charges related to the transaction with Tingyi	**(26)**	(109)	—
Non-cash foreign exchange loss related to Venezuela devaluation	**111**	—	—
Excess tax benefits from share-based payment arrangements	**(117)**	(124)	(70)
Pension and retiree medical plan contributions	**(262)**	(1,865)	(349)
Pension and retiree medical plan expenses	**663**	796	571
Deferred income taxes and other tax charges and credits	**(1,058)**	321	495
Change in accounts and notes receivable	**(88)**	(250)	(666)
Change in inventories	**4**	144	(331)
Change in prepaid expenses and other current assets	**(51)**	89	(27)
Change in accounts payable and other current liabilities	**1,007**	548	520
Change in income taxes payable	**86**	(97)	(340)
Other, net	**(349)**	(200)	(688)
Net Cash Provided by Operating Activities	**9,688**	8,479	8,944
Investing Activities			
Capital spending	**(2,795)**	(2,714)	(3,339)
Sales of property, plant and equipment	**109**	95	84
Acquisition of WBD, net of cash and cash equivalents acquired	**—**	—	(2,428)
Investment in WBD		—	(164)
Cash payments related to the transaction with Tingyi	**(3)**	(306)	—
Other acquisitions and investments in noncontrolled affiliates	**(109)**	(121)	(601)
Divestitures	**133**	(32)	780
Short-term investments, by original maturity			
More than three months – maturities	**—**	—	21
Three months or less, net	**61**	61	45
Other investing, net	**(21)**	12	(16)
Net Cash Used for Investing Activities	**(2,625)**	(3,005)	(5,618)
Financing Activities			
Proceeds from issuances of long-term debt	$ **4,195**	$ 5,999	$ 3,000
Payments of long-term debt	**(3,894)**	(2,449)	(1,596)
Debt repurchase	**—**	—	(771)
Short-term borrowings, by original maturity			
More than three months – proceeds	**23**	549	523
More than three months – payments	**(492)**	(248)	(559)
Three months or less, net	**1,634**	(1,762)	339
Cash dividends paid	**(3,434)**	(3,305)	(3,157)
Share repurchases – common	**(3,001)**	(3,219)	(2,489)
Share repurchases – preferred	**(7)**	(7)	(7)
Proceeds from exercises of stock options	**1,123**	1,122	945
Excess tax benefits from share-based payment arrangements	**117**	124	70
Acquisition of noncontrolling interests	**(20)**	(68)	(1,406)
Other financing	**(33)**	(42)	(27)
Net Cash Used for Financing Activities	**(3,789)**	(3,306)	(5,135)
Effect of exchange rate changes on cash and cash equivalents	**(196)**	62	(67)
Net Increase/(Decrease) in Cash and Cash Equivalents	**3,078**	2,230	(1,876)
Cash and Cash Equivalents, Beginning of Year	**6,297**	4,067	5,943
Cash and Cash Equivalents, End of Year	$ **9,375**	$ 6,297	$ 4,067

See accompanying notes to consolidated financial statements.

Consolidated Balance Sheet

PepsiCo, Inc. and Subsidiaries
December 28, 2013 and December 29, 2012
(in millions except per share amounts)

	2013	2012
ASSETS		
Current Assets		
Cash and cash equivalents	$ 9,375	$ 6,297
Short-term investments	303	322
Accounts and notes receivable, net	6,954	7,041
Inventories	3,409	3,581
Prepaid expenses and other current assets	2,162	1,479
Total Current Assets	22,203	18,720
Property, Plant and Equipment, net	18,575	19,136
Amortizable Intangible Assets, net	1,638	1,781
Goodwill	16,613	16,971
Other nonamortizable intangible assets	14,401	14,744
Nonamortizable Intangible Assets	31,014	31,715
Investments in Noncontrolled Affiliates	1,841	1,633
Other Assets	2,207	1,653
Total Assets	$ 77,478	$ 74,638
LIABILITIES AND EQUITY		
Current Liabilities		
Short-term obligations	$ 5,306	$ 4,815
Accounts payable and other current liabilities	12,533	11,903
Income taxes payable	—	371
Total Current Liabilities	17,839	17,089
Long-Term Debt Obligations	24,333	23,544
Other Liabilities	4,931	6,543
Deferred Income Taxes	5,986	5,063
Total Liabilities	53,089	52,239
Commitments and contingencies		
Preferred Stock, no par value	41	41
Repurchased Preferred Stock	(171)	(164)
PepsiCo Common Shareholders' Equity		
Common stock, par value $1^2/_3$¢ per share (authorized 3,600 shares, issued, net of repurchased common stock at par value: 1,529 and 1,544 shares, respectively)	25	26
Capital in excess of par value	4,095	4,178
Retained earnings	46,420	43,158
Accumulated other comprehensive loss	(5,127)	(5,487)
Repurchased common stock, in excess of par value (337 and 322 shares, respectively)	(21,004)	(19,458)
Total PepsiCo Common Shareholders' Equity	24,409	22,417
Noncontrolling interests	110	105
Total Equity	24,389	22,399
Total Liabilities and Equity	$ 77,478	$ 74,638

See accompanying notes to consolidated financial statements.

Consolidated Statement of Equity

PepsiCo, Inc. and Subsidiaries
Fiscal years ended December 28, 2013, December 29, 2012 and December 31, 2011
(in millions)

	2013		2012		2011	
	Shares	**Amount**	Shares	Amount	Shares	Amount
Preferred Stock	**0.8**	**$ 41**	0.8	$ 41	0.8	$ 41
Repurchased Preferred Stock						
Balance, beginning of year	**(0.6)**	**(164)**	(0.6)	(157)	(0.6)	(150)
Redemptions	—	**(7)**	—	(7)	—	(7)
Balance, end of year	**(0.6)**	**(171)**	(0.6)	(164)	(0.6)	(157)
Common Stock						
Balance, beginning of year	**1,544**	**26**	1,565	26	1,582	26
Repurchased common stock	**(15)**	**(1)**	(21)	—	(17)	—
Balance, end of year	**1,529**	**25**	1,544	26	1,565	26
Capital in Excess of Par Value						
Balance, beginning of year		**4,178**		4,461		4,527
Stock-based compensation expense		**303**		278		326
Stock option exercises/RSUs and PEPUnits converted [(a)]		**(287)**		(431)		(361)
Withholding tax on RSUs converted		**(87)**		(70)		(56)
Other		**(12)**		(60)		25
Balance, end of year		**4,095**		4,178		4,461
Retained Earnings						
Balance, beginning of year		**43,158**		40,316		37,090
Net income attributable to PepsiCo		**6,740**		6,178		6,443
Cash dividends declared – common		**(3,451)**		(3,312)		(3,192)
Cash dividends declared – preferred		**(1)**		(1)		(1)
Cash dividends declared – RSUs		**(26)**		(23)		(24)
Balance, end of year		**46,420**		43,158		40,316
Accumulated Other Comprehensive Loss						
Balance, beginning of year		**(5,487)**		(6,229)		(3,630)
Currency translation adjustment		**(1,301)**		742		(1,529)
Cash flow hedges, net of tax:						
Reclassification of net losses to net income		**28**		58		9
Net derivative losses		**(10)**		(40)		(83)
Pension and retiree medical, net of tax:						
Reclassification of net losses to net income		**230**		421		133
Remeasurement of net liabilities and translation		**1,400**		(493)		(1,110)
Unrealized gains/(losses) on securities, net of tax		**29**		18		(8)
Other		**(16)**		36		(11)
Balance, end of year		**(5,127)**		(5,487)		(6,229)
Repurchased Common Stock						
Balance, beginning of year	**(322)**	**(19,458)**	(301)	(17,870)	(284)	(16,740)
Share repurchases	**(37)**	**(3,000)**	(47)	(3,219)	(39)	(2,489)
Stock option exercises	**20**	**1,301**	24	1,488	20	1,251
Other	**2**	**153**	2	143	2	108
Balance, end of year	**(337)**	**(21,004)**	(322)	(19,458)	(301)	(17,870)
Total PepsiCo Common Shareholders' Equity		**24,409**		22,417		20,704
Noncontrolling Interests						
Balance, beginning of year		**105**		311		312
Net income attributable to noncontrolling interests		**47**		36		19
Distributions to noncontrolling interests, net		**(34)**		(37)		(24)
Currency translation adjustment		**(2)**		(5)		65
Acquisitions and divestitures		**(6)**		(200)		(57)
Other, net		—		—		(4)
Balance, end of year		**110**		105		311
Total Equity		**$ 24,389**		$ 22,399		$ 20,899

(a) Includes total tax benefits of $45 million in 2013, $84 million in 2012 and $43 million in 2011.

See accompanying notes to consolidated financial statements.

Appendix C Specimen Financial Statements: The Coca-Cola Company

The Coca-Cola Company is a global leader in the beverage industry. It offers hundreds of brands, including soft drinks, fruit juices, sports drinks, and other beverages in more than 200 countries. The following are Coca-Cola's financial statements as presented in its 2013 annual report. To access Coca-Cola's complete annual report, including notes to the financial statements, follow these steps:

1. Go to **www.coca-colacompany.com**.
2. Select the Investors link near the bottom of the page, and then select Financial Reports & Information.
3. Select the 2013 Annual Report on Form 10-K.
4. The Notes to Consolidated Financial Statements begin on page 79.

THE COCA-COLA COMPANY AND SUBSIDIARIES

CONSOLIDATED STATEMENTS OF INCOME

Year Ended December 31,	**2013**	2012	2011
(In millions except per share data)			
NET OPERATING REVENUES	**$ 46,854**	$ 48,017	$ 46,542
Cost of goods sold	**18,421**	19,053	18,215
GROSS PROFIT	**28,433**	28,964	28,327
Selling, general and administrative expenses	**17,310**	17,738	17,422
Other operating charges	**895**	447	732
OPERATING INCOME	**10,228**	10,779	10,173
Interest income	**534**	471	483
Interest expense	**463**	397	417
Equity income (loss) — net	**602**	819	690
Other income (loss) — net	**576**	137	529
INCOME BEFORE INCOME TAXES	**11,477**	11,809	11,458
Income taxes	**2,851**	2,723	2,812
CONSOLIDATED NET INCOME	**8,626**	9,086	8,646
Less: Net income attributable to noncontrolling interests	**42**	67	62
NET INCOME ATTRIBUTABLE TO SHAREOWNERS OF THE COCA-COLA COMPANY	**$ 8,584**	$ 9,019	$ 8,584
BASIC NET INCOME PER SHARE[1]	**$ 1.94**	$ 2.00	$ 1.88
DILUTED NET INCOME PER SHARE[1]	**$ 1.90**	$ 1.97	$ 1.85
AVERAGE SHARES OUTSTANDING	**4,434**	4,504	4,568
Effect of dilutive securities	**75**	80	78
AVERAGE SHARES OUTSTANDING ASSUMING DILUTION	**4,509**	4,584	4,646

[1] Calculated based on net income attributable to shareowners of The Coca-Cola Company.

Refer to Notes to Consolidated Financial Statements.

THE COCA-COLA COMPANY AND SUBSIDIARIES

CONSOLIDATED STATEMENTS OF COMPREHENSIVE INCOME

Year Ended December 31,	**2013**	2012	2011
(In millions)			
CONSOLIDATED NET INCOME	**$ 8,626**	$ 9,086	$ 8,646
Other comprehensive income:			
Net foreign currency translation adjustment	**(1,187)**	(182)	(692)
Net gain (loss) on derivatives	**151**	99	145
Net unrealized gain (loss) on available-for-sale securities	**(80)**	178	(7)
Net change in pension and other benefit liabilities	**1,066**	(668)	(763)
TOTAL COMPREHENSIVE INCOME	**8,576**	8,513	7,329
Less: Comprehensive income (loss) attributable to noncontrolling interests	**39**	105	10
TOTAL COMPREHENSIVE INCOME ATTRIBUTABLE TO SHAREOWNERS OF THE COCA-COLA COMPANY	**$ 8,537**	$ 8,408	$ 7,319

Refer to Notes to Consolidated Financial Statements.

THE COCA-COLA COMPANY AND SUBSIDIARIES

CONSOLIDATED BALANCE SHEETS

December 31,	**2013**	2012
(In millions except par value)		
ASSETS		
CURRENT ASSETS		
Cash and cash equivalents	**$ 10,414**	$ 8,442
Short-term investments	**6,707**	5,017
TOTAL CASH, CASH EQUIVALENTS AND SHORT-TERM INVESTMENTS	**17,121**	13,459
Marketable securities	**3,147**	3,092
Trade accounts receivable, less allowances of $61 and $53, respectively	**4,873**	4,759
Inventories	**3,277**	3,264
Prepaid expenses and other assets	**2,886**	2,781
Assets held for sale	**—**	2,973
TOTAL CURRENT ASSETS	**31,304**	30,328
EQUITY METHOD INVESTMENTS	**10,393**	9,216
OTHER INVESTMENTS, PRINCIPALLY BOTTLING COMPANIES	**1,119**	1,232
OTHER ASSETS	**4,661**	3,585
PROPERTY, PLANT AND EQUIPMENT — net	**14,967**	14,476
TRADEMARKS WITH INDEFINITE LIVES	**6,744**	6,527
BOTTLERS' FRANCHISE RIGHTS WITH INDEFINITE LIVES	**7,415**	7,405
GOODWILL	**12,312**	12,255
OTHER INTANGIBLE ASSETS	**1,140**	1,150
TOTAL ASSETS	**$ 90,055**	$ 86,174
LIABILITIES AND EQUITY		
CURRENT LIABILITIES		
Accounts payable and accrued expenses	**$ 9,577**	$ 8,680
Loans and notes payable	**16,901**	16,297
Current maturities of long-term debt	**1,024**	1,577
Accrued income taxes	**309**	471
Liabilities held for sale	**—**	796
TOTAL CURRENT LIABILITIES	**27,811**	27,821
LONG-TERM DEBT	**19,154**	14,736
OTHER LIABILITIES	**3,498**	5,468
DEFERRED INCOME TAXES	**6,152**	4,981
THE COCA-COLA COMPANY SHAREOWNERS' EQUITY		
Common stock, $0.25 par value; Authorized — 11,200 shares; Issued — 7,040 and 7,040 shares, respectively	**1,760**	1,760
Capital surplus	**12,276**	11,379
Reinvested earnings	**61,660**	58,045
Accumulated other comprehensive income (loss)	**(3,432)**	(3,385)
Treasury stock, at cost — 2,638 and 2,571 shares, respectively	**(39,091)**	(35,009)
EQUITY ATTRIBUTABLE TO SHAREOWNERS OF THE COCA-COLA COMPANY	**33,173**	32,790
EQUITY ATTRIBUTABLE TO NONCONTROLLING INTERESTS	**267**	378
TOTAL EQUITY	**33,440**	33,168
TOTAL LIABILITIES AND EQUITY	**$ 90,055**	$ 86,174

Refer to Notes to Consolidated Financial Statements.

THE COCA-COLA COMPANY AND SUBSIDIARIES
CONSOLIDATED STATEMENTS OF CASH FLOWS

Year Ended December 31,	2013	2012	2011
(In millions)			
OPERATING ACTIVITIES			
Consolidated net income	**$ 8,626**	$ 9,086	$ 8,646
Depreciation and amortization	**1,977**	1,982	1,954
Stock-based compensation expense	**227**	259	354
Deferred income taxes	**648**	632	1,035
Equity (income) loss — net of dividends	**(201)**	(426)	(269)
Foreign currency adjustments	**168**	(130)	7
Significant (gains) losses on sales of assets — net	**(670)**	(98)	(220)
Other operating charges	**465**	166	214
Other items	**234**	254	(354)
Net change in operating assets and liabilities	**(932)**	(1,080)	(1,893)
Net cash provided by operating activities	**10,542**	10,645	9,474
INVESTING ACTIVITIES			
Purchases of investments	**(14,782)**	(14,824)	(4,798)
Proceeds from disposals of investments	**12,791**	7,791	5,811
Acquisitions of businesses, equity method investments and nonmarketable securities	**(353)**	(1,486)	(971)
Proceeds from disposals of businesses, equity method investments and nonmarketable securities	**872**	20	398
Purchases of property, plant and equipment	**(2,550)**	(2,780)	(2,920)
Proceeds from disposals of property, plant and equipment	**111**	143	101
Other investing activities	**(303)**	(268)	(145)
Net cash provided by (used in) investing activities	**(4,214)**	(11,404)	(2,524)
FINANCING ACTIVITIES			
Issuances of debt	**43,425**	42,791	27,495
Payments of debt	**(38,714)**	(38,573)	(22,530)
Issuances of stock	**1,328**	1,489	1,569
Purchases of stock for treasury	**(4,832)**	(4,559)	(4,513)
Dividends	**(4,969)**	(4,595)	(4,300)
Other financing activities	**17**	100	45
Net cash provided by (used in) financing activities	**(3,745)**	(3,347)	(2,234)
EFFECT OF EXCHANGE RATE CHANGES ON CASH AND CASH EQUIVALENTS	**(611)**	(255)	(430)
CASH AND CASH EQUIVALENTS			
Net increase (decrease) during the year	**1,972**	(4,361)	4,286
Balance at beginning of year	**8,442**	12,803	8,517
Balance at end of year	**$ 10,414**	$ 8,442	$ 12,803

Refer to Notes to Consolidated Financial Statements.

THE COCA-COLA COMPANY AND SUBSIDIARIES
CONSOLIDATED STATEMENTS OF SHAREOWNERS' EQUITY

Year Ended December 31,	2013	2012	2011
(In millions except per share data)			
EQUITY ATTRIBUTABLE TO SHAREOWNERS OF THE COCA-COLA COMPANY			
NUMBER OF COMMON SHARES OUTSTANDING			
Balance at beginning of year	**4,469**	4,526	4,583
Purchases of treasury stock	**(121)**	(121)	(127)
Treasury stock issued to employees related to stock compensation plans	**54**	64	70
Balance at end of year	**4,402**	4,469	4,526
COMMON STOCK	**$ 1,760**	$ 1,760	$ 1,760
CAPITAL SURPLUS			
Balance at beginning of year	**11,379**	10,332	9,177
Stock issued to employees related to stock compensation plans	**569**	640	724
Tax benefit (charge) from stock compensation plans	**144**	144	79
Stock-based compensation	**227**	259	354
Other activities	**(43)**	4	(2)
Balance at end of year	**12,276**	11,379	10,332
REINVESTED EARNINGS			
Balance at beginning of year	**58,045**	53,621	49,337
Net income attributable to shareowners of The Coca-Cola Company	**8,584**	9,019	8,584
Dividends (per share — $1.12, $1.02 and $0.94 in 2013, 2012 and 2011, respectively)	**(4,969)**	(4,595)	(4,300)
Balance at end of year	**61,660**	58,045	53,621
ACCUMULATED OTHER COMPREHENSIVE INCOME (LOSS)			
Balance at beginning of year	**(3,385)**	(2,774)	(1,509)
Net other comprehensive income (loss)	**(47)**	(611)	(1,265)
Balance at end of year	**(3,432)**	(3,385)	(2,774)
TREASURY STOCK			
Balance at beginning of year	**(35,009)**	(31,304)	(27,762)
Stock issued to employees related to stock compensation plans	**745**	786	830
Purchases of treasury stock	**(4,827)**	(4,491)	(4,372)
Balance at end of year	**(39,091)**	(35,009)	(31,304)
TOTAL EQUITY ATTRIBUTABLE TO SHAREOWNERS OF THE COCA-COLA COMPANY	**$ 33,173**	$ 32,790	$ 31,635
EQUITY ATTRIBUTABLE TO NONCONTROLLING INTERESTS			
Balance at beginning of year	**$ 378**	$ 286	$ 314
Net income attributable to noncontrolling interests	**42**	67	62
Net foreign currency translation adjustment	**(3)**	38	(52)
Dividends paid to noncontrolling interests	**(58)**	(48)	(38)
Acquisition of interests held by noncontrolling owners	**(34)**	(15)	—
Contributions by noncontrolling interests	**6**	—	—
Business combinations	**25**	50	—
Deconsolidation of certain entities	**(89)**	—	—
TOTAL EQUITY ATTRIBUTABLE TO NONCONTROLLING INTERESTS	**$ 267**	$ 378	$ 286

Refer to Notes to Consolidated Financial Statements.

Appendix D Specimen Financial Statements: Amazon.com, Inc.

Amazon.com, Inc. is the world's largest online retailer. It also produces consumer electronics—notably the Kindle e-book reader and the Kindle Fire Tablet computer—and is a major provider of cloud computing services. The following are Amazon's financial statements as presented in the company's 2013 annual report. To access Amazon's complete annual report, including notes to the financial statements, follow these steps:

1. Go to **www.amazon.com**.
2. Select the Investor Relations link at the bottom of the page and then select the 2013 Annual Report under Annual Reports and Proxies.
3. The Notes to Consolidated Financial Statements begin on page 40.

AMAZON.COM, INC.

CONSOLIDATED STATEMENTS OF CASH FLOWS
(in millions)

	Year Ended December 31,		
	2013	2012	2011
CASH AND CASH EQUIVALENTS, BEGINNING OF PERIOD	$ 8,084	$ 5,269	$ 3,777
OPERATING ACTIVITIES:			
Net income (loss)	274	(39)	631
Adjustments to reconcile net income (loss) to net cash from operating activities:			
Depreciation of property and equipment, including internal-use software and website development, and other amortization	3,253	2,159	1,083
Stock-based compensation	1,134	833	557
Other operating expense (income), net	114	154	154
Losses (gains) on sales of marketable securities, net	1	(9)	(4)
Other expense (income), net	166	253	(56)
Deferred income taxes	(156)	(265)	136
Excess tax benefits from stock-based compensation	(78)	(429)	(62)
Changes in operating assets and liabilities:			
Inventories	(1,410)	(999)	(1,777)
Accounts receivable, net and other	(846)	(861)	(866)
Accounts payable	1,888	2,070	2,997
Accrued expenses and other	736	1,038	1,067
Additions to unearned revenue	2,691	1,796	1,064
Amortization of previously unearned revenue	(2,292)	(1,521)	(1,021)
Net cash provided by (used in) operating activities	5,475	4,180	3,903
INVESTING ACTIVITIES:			
Purchases of property and equipment, including internal-use software and website development	(3,444)	(3,785)	(1,811)
Acquisitions, net of cash acquired, and other	(312)	(745)	(705)
Sales and maturities of marketable securities and other investments	2,306	4,237	6,843
Purchases of marketable securities and other investments	(2,826)	(3,302)	(6,257)
Net cash provided by (used in) investing activities	(4,276)	(3,595)	(1,930)
FINANCING ACTIVITIES:			
Excess tax benefits from stock-based compensation	78	429	62
Common stock repurchased	—	(960)	(277)
Proceeds from long-term debt and other	394	3,378	177
Repayments of long-term debt, capital lease, and finance lease obligations	(1,011)	(588)	(444)
Net cash provided by (used in) financing activities	(539)	2,259	(482)
Foreign-currency effect on cash and cash equivalents	(86)	(29)	1
Net increase (decrease) in cash and cash equivalents	574	2,815	1,492
CASH AND CASH EQUIVALENTS, END OF PERIOD	$ 8,658	$ 8,084	$ 5,269
SUPPLEMENTAL CASH FLOW INFORMATION:			
Cash paid for interest on long-term debt	$ 97	$ 31	$ 14
Cash paid for income taxes (net of refunds)	169	112	33
Property and equipment acquired under capital leases	1,867	802	753
Property and equipment acquired under build-to-suit leases	877	29	259

See accompanying notes to consolidated financial statements.

AMAZON.COM, INC.

CONSOLIDATED STATEMENTS OF OPERATIONS
(in millions, except per share data)

	Year Ended December 31,		
	2013	2012	2011
Net product sales	$ 60,903	$ 51,733	$ 42,000
Net services sales	13,549	9,360	6,077
Total net sales	74,452	61,093	48,077
Operating expenses (1):			
Cost of sales	54,181	45,971	37,288
Fulfillment	8,585	6,419	4,576
Marketing	3,133	2,408	1,630
Technology and content	6,565	4,564	2,909
General and administrative	1,129	896	658
Other operating expense (income), net	114	159	154
Total operating expenses	73,707	60,417	47,215
Income from operations	745	676	862
Interest income	38	40	61
Interest expense	(141)	(92)	(65)
Other income (expense), net	(136)	(80)	76
Total non-operating income (expense)	(239)	(132)	72
Income before income taxes	506	544	934
Provision for income taxes	(161)	(428)	(291)
Equity-method investment activity, net of tax	(71)	(155)	(12)
Net income (loss)	$ 274	$ (39)	$ 631
Basic earnings per share	$ 0.60	$ (0.09)	$ 1.39
Diluted earnings per share	$ 0.59	$ (0.09)	$ 1.37
Weighted average shares used in computation of earnings per share:			
Basic	457	453	453
Diluted	465	453	461

(1) Includes stock-based compensation as follows:

	2013	2012	2011
Fulfillment	$ 294	$ 212	$ 133
Marketing	88	61	39
Technology and content	603	434	292
General and administrative	149	126	93

See accompanying notes to consolidated financial statements.

AMAZON.COM, INC.

CONSOLIDATED STATEMENTS OF COMPREHENSIVE INCOME
(in millions)

	Year Ended December 31,		
	2013	2012	2011
Net income (loss)	$ 274	$ (39)	$ 631
Other comprehensive income (loss):			
Foreign currency translation adjustments, net of tax of $(20), $(30), and $20	63	76	(123)
Net change in unrealized gains on available-for-sale securities:			
Unrealized gains (losses), net of tax of $3, $(3), and $1	(10)	8	(1)
Reclassification adjustment for losses (gains) included in “Other income (expense), net,” net of tax of $(1), $3, and $1	1	(7)	(2)
Net unrealized gains (losses) on available-for-sale securities	(9)	1	(3)
Total other comprehensive income (loss)	54	77	(126)
Comprehensive income	$ 328	$ 38	$ 505

See accompanying notes to consolidated financial statements.

AMAZON.COM, INC.

CONSOLIDATED BALANCE SHEETS
(in millions, except per share data)

	December 31, 2013	December 31, 2012
ASSETS		
Current assets:		
Cash and cash equivalents	$ 8,658	$ 8,084
Marketable securities	3,789	3,364
Inventories	7,411	6,031
Accounts receivable, net and other	4,767	3,817
Total current assets	24,625	21,296
Property and equipment, net	10,949	7,060
Goodwill	2,655	2,552
Other assets	1,930	1,647
Total assets	$ 40,159	$ 32,555
LIABILITIES AND STOCKHOLDERS' EQUITY		
Current liabilities:		
Accounts payable	$ 15,133	$ 13,318
Accrued expenses and other	6,688	4,892
Unearned revenue	1,159	792
Total current liabilities	22,980	19,002
Long-term debt	3,191	3,084
Other long-term liabilities	4,242	2,277
Commitments and contingencies		
Stockholders' equity:		
Preferred stock, $0.01 par value:		
Authorized shares — 500		
Issued and outstanding shares — none	—	—
Common stock, $0.01 par value:		
Authorized shares — 5,000		
Issued shares — 483 and 478		
Outstanding shares — 459 and 454	5	5
Treasury stock, at cost	(1,837)	(1,837)
Additional paid-in capital	9,573	8,347
Accumulated other comprehensive loss	(185)	(239)
Retained earnings	2,190	1,916
Total stockholders' equity	9,746	8,192
Total liabilities and stockholders' equity	$ 40,159	$ 32,555

See accompanying notes to consolidated financial statements.

AMAZON.COM, INC.

CONSOLIDATED STATEMENTS OF STOCKHOLDERS' EQUITY
(in millions)

	Common Stock						
	Shares	Amount	Treasury Stock	Additional Paid-In Capital	Accumulated Other Comprehensive Income (Loss)	Retained Earnings	Total Stockholders' Equity
Balance as of January 1, 2011	451	$ 5	$ (600)	$ 6,325	$ (190)	$ 1,324	$ 6,864
Net income	—	—	—	—	—	631	631
Other comprehensive income (loss)	—	—	—	—	(126)	—	(126)
Exercise of common stock options	5	—	—	7	—	—	7
Repurchase of common stock	(1)	—	(277)	—	—	—	(277)
Excess tax benefits from stock-based compensation	—	—	—	62	—	—	62
Stock-based compensation and issuance of employee benefit plan stock	—	—	—	569	—	—	569
Issuance of common stock for acquisition activity	—	—	—	27	—	—	27
Balance as of December 31, 2011	455	5	(877)	6,990	(316)	1,955	7,757
Net income (loss)	—	—	—	—	—	(39)	(39)
Other comprehensive income	—	—	—	—	77	—	77
Exercise of common stock options	4	—	—	8	—	—	8
Repurchase of common stock	(5)	—	(960)	—	—	—	(960)
Excess tax benefits from stock-based compensation	—	—	—	429	—	—	429
Stock-based compensation and issuance of employee benefit plan stock	—	—	—	854	—	—	854
Issuance of common stock for acquisition activity	—	—	—	66	—	—	66
Balance as of December 31, 2012	454	5	(1,837)	8,347	(239)	1,916	8,192
Net income	—	—	—	—	—	274	274
Other comprehensive income	—	—	—	—	54	—	54
Exercise of common stock options	5	—	—	4	—	—	4
Repurchase of common stock	—	—	—	—	—	—	—
Excess tax benefits from stock-based compensation	—	—	—	73	—	—	73
Stock-based compensation and issuance of employee benefit plan stock	—	—	—	1,149	—	—	1,149
Balance as of December 31, 2013	459	$ 5	$ (1,837)	$ 9,573	$ (185)	$ 2,190	$ 9,746

See accompanying notes to consolidated financial statements.

Appendix E Specimen Financial Statements: Wal-Mart Stores, Inc.

The following are **Wal-Mart Stores, Inc.**'s financial statements as presented in the company's 2014 annual report. To access Wal-Mart's complete annual report, including notes to the financial statements, follow these steps:

1. Go to **http://corporate.walmart.com**.
2. Select Annual Reports under the Investors tab.
3. Select the 2014 Annual Report (Wal-Mart's fiscal year ends January 31).
4. The Notes to Consolidated Financial Statements begin on page 40.

Consolidated Statements of Income

	Fiscal Years Ended January 31,		
(Amounts in millions, except per share data)	**2014**	2013	2012
Revenues:			
Net sales	**$473,076**	$465,604	$443,416
Membership and other income	**3,218**	3,047	3,093
Total revenues	**476,294**	468,651	446,509
Costs and expenses:			
Cost of sales	**358,069**	352,297	334,993
Operating, selling, general and administrative expenses	**91,353**	88,629	85,025
Operating income	**26,872**	27,725	26,491
Interest:			
Debt	**2,072**	1,977	2,034
Capital leases	**263**	272	286
Interest income	**(119)**	(186)	(161)
Interest, net	**2,216**	2,063	2,159
Income from continuing operations before income taxes	**24,656**	25,662	24,332
Provision for income taxes:			
Current	**8,619**	7,976	6,722
Deferred	**(514)**	(18)	1,202
Total provision for income taxes	**8,105**	7,958	7,924
Income from continuing operations	**16,551**	17,704	16,408
Income (loss) from discontinued operations, net of income taxes	**144**	52	(21)
Consolidated net income	**16,695**	17,756	16,387
Less consolidated net income attributable to noncontrolling interest	**(673)**	(757)	(688)
Consolidated net income attributable to Walmart	**$ 16,022**	$ 16,999	$ 15,699
Basic net income per common share:			
Basic income per common share from continuing operations attributable to Walmart	**$ 4.87**	$ 5.03	$ 4.55
Basic income (loss) per common share from discontinued operations attributable to Walmart	**0.03**	0.01	(0.01)
Basic net income per common share attributable to Walmart	**$ 4.90**	$ 5.04	$ 4.54
Diluted net income per common share:			
Diluted income per common share from continuing operations attributable to Walmart	**$ 4.85**	$ 5.01	$ 4.53
Diluted income (loss) per common share from discontinued operations attributable to Walmart	**0.03**	0.01	(0.01)
Diluted net income per common share attributable to Walmart	**$ 4.88**	$ 5.02	$ 4.52
Weighted-average common shares outstanding:			
Basic	**3,269**	3,374	3,460
Diluted	**3,283**	3,389	3,474
Dividends declared per common share	**$ 1.88**	$ 1.59	$ 1.46

See accompanying notes.

Consolidated Statements of Comprehensive Income

(Amounts in millions)	Fiscal Years Ended January 31, 2014	2013	2012
Consolidated net income	**$16,695**	$17,756	$16,387
Less consolidated net income attributable to nonredeemable noncontrolling interest	**(606)**	(684)	(627)
Less consolidated net income attributable to redeemable noncontrolling interest	**(67)**	(73)	(61)
Consolidated net income attributable to Walmart	**16,022**	16,999	15,699
Other comprehensive income (loss), net of income taxes			
Currency translation and other	**(3,146)**	1,042	(2,758)
Derivative instruments	**207**	136	(67)
Minimum pension liability	**153**	(166)	43
Other comprehensive income (loss), net of income taxes	**(2,786)**	1,012	(2,782)
Less other comprehensive income (loss) attributable to nonredeemable noncontrolling interest	**311**	(138)	660
Less other comprehensive income (loss) attributable to redeemable noncontrolling interest	**66**	(51)	66
Other comprehensive income (loss) attributable to Walmart	**(2,409)**	823	(2,056)
Comprehensive income, net of income taxes	**13,909**	18,768	13,605
Less comprehensive income (loss) attributable to nonredeemable noncontrolling interest	**(295)**	(822)	33
Less comprehensive income (loss) attributable to redeemable noncontrolling interest	**(1)**	(124)	5
Comprehensive income attributable to Walmart	**$13,613**	$17,822	$13,643

See accompanying notes.

Consolidated Balance Sheets

(Amounts in millions)	As of January 31, 2014	2013
ASSETS		
Current assets:		
Cash and cash equivalents	**$ 7,281**	$ 7,781
Receivables, net	**6,677**	6,768
Inventories	**44,858**	43,803
Prepaid expenses and other	**1,909**	1,551
Current assets of discontinued operations	**460**	37
Total current assets	**61,185**	59,940
Property and equipment:		
Property and equipment	**173,089**	165,825
Less accumulated depreciation	**(57,725)**	(51,896)
Property and equipment, net	**115,364**	113,929
Property under capital leases:		
Property under capital leases	**5,589**	5,899
Less accumulated amortization	**(3,046)**	(3,147)
Property under capital leases, net	**2,543**	2,752
Goodwill	**19,510**	20,497
Other assets and deferred charges	**6,149**	5,987
Total assets	**$204,751**	$203,105
LIABILITIES, REDEEMABLE NONCONTROLLING INTEREST AND EQUITY		
Current liabilities:		
Short-term borrowings	**$ 7,670**	$ 6,805
Accounts payable	**37,415**	38,080
Accrued liabilities	**18,793**	18,808
Accrued income taxes	**966**	2,211
Long-term debt due within one year	**4,103**	5,587
Obligations under capital leases due within one year	**309**	327
Current liabilities of discontinued operations	**89**	—
Total current liabilities	**69,345**	71,818
Long-term debt	**41,771**	38,394
Long-term obligations under capital leases	**2,788**	3,023
Deferred income taxes and other	**8,017**	7,613
Redeemable noncontrolling interest	**1,491**	519
Commitments and contingencies		
Equity:		
Common stock	**323**	332
Capital in excess of par value	**2,362**	3,620
Retained earnings	**76,566**	72,978
Accumulated other comprehensive income (loss)	**(2,996)**	(587)
Total Walmart shareholders' equity	**76,255**	76,343
Nonredeemable noncontrolling interest	**5,084**	5,395
Total equity	**81,339**	81,738
Total liabilities, redeemable noncontrolling interest and equity	**$204,751**	$203,105

See accompanying notes.

Consolidated Statements of Shareholders' Equity

(Amounts in millions)	Common Stock Shares	Common Stock Amount	Capital in Excess of Par Value	Retained Earnings	Accumulated Other Comprehensive Income (Loss)	Total Walmart Shareholders' Equity	Nonredeemable Noncontrolling Interest	Total Equity	Redeemable Noncontrolling Interest
Balances as of February 1, 2011	3,516	$352	$ 3,577	$63,967	$ 646	$68,542	$2,705	$71,247	$ 408
Consolidated net income	—	—	—	15,699	—	15,699	627	16,326	61
Other comprehensive loss, net of income taxes	—	—	—	—	(2,056)	(2,056)	(660)	(2,716)	(66)
Cash dividends declared ($1.46 per share)	—	—	—	(5,048)	—	(5,048)	—	(5,048)	—
Purchase of Company stock	(113)	(11)	(229)	(5,930)	—	(6,170)	—	(6,170)	—
Nonredeemable noncontrolling interest of acquired entity	—	—	—	—	—	—	1,988	1,988	—
Other	15	1	344	3	—	348	(214)	134	1
Balances as of January 31, 2012	3,418	342	3,692	68,691	(1,410)	71,315	4,446	75,761	404
Consolidated net income	—	—	—	16,999	—	16,999	684	17,683	73
Other comprehensive income, net of income taxes	—	—	—	—	823	823	138	961	51
Cash dividends declared ($1.59 per share)	—	—	—	(5,361)	—	(5,361)	—	(5,361)	—
Purchase of Company stock	(115)	(11)	(357)	(7,341)	—	(7,709)	—	(7,709)	—
Nonredeemable noncontrolling interest of acquired entity	—	—	—	—	—	—	469	469	—
Other	11	1	285	(10)	—	276	(342)	(66)	(9)
Balances as of January 31, 2013	**3,314**	**332**	**3,620**	**72,978**	**(587)**	**76,343**	**5,395**	**81,738**	**519**
Consolidated net income	—	—	—	**16,022**	—	**16,022**	**595**	**16,617**	**78**
Other comprehensive loss, net of income taxes	—	—	—	—	**(2,409)**	**(2,409)**	**(311)**	**(2,720)**	**(66)**
Cash dividends declared ($1.88 per share)	—	—	—	**(6,139)**	—	**(6,139)**	—	**(6,139)**	—
Purchase of Company stock	**(87)**	**(9)**	**(294)**	**(6,254)**	—	**(6,557)**	—	**(6,557)**	—
Redemption value adjustment of redeemable noncontrolling interest	—	—	**(1,019)**		—	**(1,019)**	—	**(1,019)**	**1,019**
Other	**6**	—	**55**	**(41)**	—	**14**	**(595)**	**(581)**	**(59)**
Balances as of January 31, 2014	**3,233**	**$323**	**$ 2,362**	**$76,566**	**$(2,996)**	**$76,255**	**$5,084**	**$81,339**	**$1,491**

Consolidated Statements of Cash Flows

	Fiscal Years Ended January 31,		
(Amounts in millions)	**2014**	2013	2012
Cash flows from operating activities:			
Consolidated net income	**$ 16,695**	$ 17,756	$ 16,387
Income (loss) from discontinued operations, net of income taxes	**(144)**	(52)	21
Income from continuing operations	**16,551**	17,704	16,408
Adjustments to reconcile income from continuing operations to net cash provided by operating activities:			
Depreciation and amortization	**8,870**	8,478	8,106
Deferred income taxes	**(279)**	(133)	1,050
Other operating activities	**938**	602	468
Changes in certain assets and liabilities, net of effects of acquisitions:			
Receivables, net	**(566)**	(614)	(796)
Inventories	**(1,667)**	(2,759)	(3,727)
Accounts payable	**531**	1,061	2,687
Accrued liabilities	**103**	271	(935)
Accrued income taxes	**(1,224)**	981	994
Net cash provided by operating activities	**23,257**	25,591	24,255
Cash flows from investing activities:			
Payments for property and equipment	**(13,115)**	(12,898)	(13,510)
Proceeds from the disposal of property and equipment	**727**	532	580
Investments and business acquisitions, net of cash acquired	**(15)**	(316)	(3,548)
Other investing activities	**105**	71	(131)
Net cash used in investing activities	**(12,298)**	(12,611)	(16,609)
Cash flows from financing activities:			
Net change in short-term borrowings	**911**	2,754	3,019
Proceeds from issuance of long-term debt	**7,072**	211	5,050
Payments of long-term debt	**(4,968)**	(1,478)	(4,584)
Dividends paid	**(6,139)**	(5,361)	(5,048)
Dividends paid to and stock purchases of noncontrolling interest	**(722)**	(414)	(526)
Purchase of Company stock	**(6,683)**	(7,600)	(6,298)
Other financing activities	**(488)**	(84)	(71)
Net cash used in financing activities	**(11,017)**	(11,972)	(8,458)
Effect of exchange rates on cash and cash equivalents	**(442)**	223	(33)
Net increase (decrease) in cash and cash equivalents	**(500)**	1,231	(845)
Cash and cash equivalents at beginning of year	**7,781**	6,550	7,395
Cash and cash equivalents at end of year	**$ 7,281**	$ 7,781	$ 6,550
Supplemental disclosure of cash flow information:			
Income taxes paid	**$ 8,641**	$ 7,304	$ 5,899
Interest paid	**2,362**	2,262	2,346

See accompanying notes.

Appendix F

Specimen Financial Statements: Louis Vuitton

Louis Vuitton is a French company and is one of the leading international fashion houses in the world. Louis Vuitton has been named the world's most valuable luxury brand. Note that its financial statements are IFRS-based and are presented in euros (€). To access the company's complete financial statements, follow these steps:

1. Go to **www.lvmh.com/investor-relations**.
2. Select 2013 Annual Report, and then select the Finance tab once the Intro has played.
3. Note that the comments (notes) to the financial statements are placed after each corresponding statement.

CONSOLIDATED BALANCE SHEET

ASSETS *(EUR millions)*	2013	2012[1]	2011[1]
Brands and other intangible assets	11,458	11,510	11,482
Goodwill	9,959	7,806	6,957
Property, plant and equipment	9,602	8,769	8,017
Investments in associates	152	163	170
Non-current available for sale financial assets	7,080	6,004	5,982
Other non-current assets	432	519	478
Deferred tax	909	954	760
NON-CURRENT ASSETS	39,592	35,725	33,846
Inventories and work in progress	8,586	8,080	7,510
Trade accounts receivable	2,189	1,985	1,878
Income taxes	235	201	121
Other current assets	1,851	1,811	1,455
Cash and cash equivalents	3,221	2,196	2,303
CURRENT ASSETS	16,082	14,273	13,267
TOTAL ASSETS	55,674	49,998	47,113

(Continued.)

(Continued.)

LIABILITIES AND EQUITY

(EUR millions)	2013	2012(1)	2011(1)
Share capital	152	152	152
Share premium account	3,849	3,848	3,801
Treasury shares and LVMH-share settled derivatives	(451)	(414)	(485)
Cumulative translation adjustment	(8)	342	431
Revaluation reserves	3,900	2,731	2,637
Other reserves	15,817	14,341	12,770
Net profit, Group share	3,436	3,424	3,065
Equity, Group share	26,695	24,424	22,371
Minority interests	1,028	1,084	1,055
TOTAL EQUITY	27,723	25,508	23,426
Long term borrowings	4,159	3,836	4,132
Provisions	1,755	1,756	1,530
Deferred tax	3,934	3,960	3,925
Other non-current liabilities	6,403	5,456	4,506
NON-CURRENT LIABILITIES	16,251	15,008	14,093
Short term borrowings	4,688	2,976	3,134
Trade accounts payable	3,308	3,134	2,952
Income taxes	382	442	443
Provisions	322	335	349
Other current liabilities	3,000	2,595	2,716
CURRENT LIABILITIES	11,700	9,482	9,594
TOTAL LIABILITIES AND EQUITY	55,674	49,998	47,113

(1) The balance sheets as of December 31, 2012 and 2011 have been restated to reflect the retrospective application as of January 1, 2011 of IAS 19 Employee Benefits as amended.

CONSOLIDATED INCOME STATEMENT

(EUR millions, except for earnings per share)	2013	2012	2011
REVENUE	29,149	28,103	23,659
Cost of sales	(10,055)	(9,917)	(8,092)
GROSS MARGIN	19,094	18,186	15,567
Marketing and selling expenses	(10,849)	(10,101)	(8,360)
General and administrative expenses	(2,224)	(2,164)	(1,944)
PROFIT FROM RECURRING OPERATIONS	6,021	5,921	5,263
Other operating income and expenses	(127)	(182)	(109)
OPERATING PROFIT	5,894	5,739	5,154
Cost of net financial debt	(103)	(140)	(151)
Other financial income and expenses	(96)	126	(91)
NET FINANCIAL INCOME (EXPENSE)	(199)	(14)	(242)
Income taxes	(1,755)	(1,820)	(1,453)
Income (loss) from investments in associates	7	4	6
NET PROFIT BEFORE MINORITY INTERESTS	3,947	3,909	3,465
Minority interests	(511)	(485)	(400)
NET PROFIT, GROUP SHARE	3,436	3,424	3,065
BASIC GROUP SHARE OF NET EARNINGS PER SHARE *(EUR)*	6.87	6.86	6.27
Number of shares on which the calculation is based	500,283,414	499,133,643	488,769,286
DILUTED GROUP SHARE OF NET EARNINGS PER SHARE *(EUR)*	6.83	6.82	6.23
Number of shares on which the calculation is based	503,217,497	502,229,952	492,207,492

CONSOLIDATED STATEMENT OF COMPREHENSIVE GAINS AND LOSSES

(EUR millions)	2013	2012[1]	2011[1]
NET PROFIT BEFORE MINORITY INTERESTS	3,947	3,909	3,465
Translation adjustments	(346)	(99)	190
Tax impact	(48)	(18)	47
	(394)	(117)	237
Change in value of available for sale financial assets	963	(27)	1,634
Amounts transferred to income statement	(16)	(14)	(38)
Tax impact	(35)	(6)	(116)
	912	(47)	1,480
Change in value of hedges of future foreign currency cash flows	304	182	95
Amounts transferred to income statement	(265)	13	(168)
Tax impact	(17)	(50)	21
	22	145	(52)
GAINS AND LOSSES RECOGNIZED IN EQUITY, TRANSFERABLE TO INCOME STATEMENT	540	(19)	1,665
Change in value of vineyard land	369	85	25
Tax impact	(127)	(28)	(11)
	242	57	14
Employee benefit commitments: change in value resulting from actuarial gains and losses	80	(101)	(45)
Tax impact	(22)	29	13
	58	(72)	(32)
GAINS AND LOSSES RECOGNIZED IN EQUITY, NOT TRANSFERABLE TO INCOME STATEMENT	300	(15)	(18)
COMPREHENSIVE INCOME	4,787	3,875	5,112
Minority interests	(532)	(470)	(429)
COMPREHENSIVE INCOME, GROUP SHARE	4,255	3,405	4,683

(1) The consolidated statements of comprehensive gains and losses as of December 31, 2012 and 2011 have been restated to reflect the retrospective application as of January 1, 2011 of IAS 19 Employee Benefits as amended.

CONSOLIDATED CASH FLOW STATEMENT

(EUR millions)	2013	2012	2011
I. OPERATING ACTIVITIES AND OPERATING INVESTMENTS			
Operating profit	5,894	5,739	5,154
Net increase in depreciation, amortization and provisions	1,454	1,299	999
Other computed expenses	(29)	(62)	(45)
Dividends received	86	188	61
Other adjustments	(76)	(51)	(32)
CASH FROM OPERATIONS BEFORE CHANGES IN WORKING CAPITAL	7,329	7,113	6,137
Cost of net financial debt: interest paid	(112)	(154)	(152)
Income taxes paid	(1,979)	(1,970)	(1,544)
NET CASH FROM OPERATING ACTIVITIES BEFORE CHANGES IN WORKING CAPITAL	5,238	4,989	4,441
Change in working capital	(617)	(813)	(534)
NET CASH FROM OPERATING ACTIVITIES	4,621	4,176	3,907
Operating investments	(1,663)	(1,702)	(1,730)
NET CASH FROM OPERATING ACTIVITIES AND OPERATING INVESTMENTS (free cash flow)	2,958	2,474	2,177
II. FINANCIAL INVESTMENTS			
Purchase of non-current available for sale financial assets	(197)	(131)	(518)
Proceeds from sale of non-current available for sale financial assets	38	36	17
Impact of purchase and sale of consolidated investments	(2,158)	(45)	(785)[(1)]
NET CASH FROM (used in) FINANCIAL INVESTMENTS	(2,317)	(140)	(1,286)
III. TRANSACTIONS RELATING TO EQUITY			
Capital increases of LVMH	66	94	94[(1)]
Capital increases of subsidiaries subscribed by minority interests	7	8	3
Acquisition and disposals of treasury shares and LVMH-share settled derivatives	(113)	5	2
Interim and final dividends paid by LVMH	(1,501)	(1,447)	(1,069)
Interim and final dividends paid to minority interests in consolidated subsidiaries	(220)	(314)	(189)
Purchase and proceeds from sale of minority interests	(150)	(206)	(1,413)
NET CASH FROM (used in) TRANSACTIONS RELATING TO EQUITY	(1,911)	(1,860)	(2,572)
CHANGE IN CASH BEFORE FINANCING ACTIVITIES	(1,270)	474	(1,681)
IV. FINANCING ACTIVITIES			
Proceeds from borrowings	3,145	1,068	2,659
Repayment of borrowings	(1,099)	(1,526)	(1,005)
Purchase and proceeds from sale of current available for sale financial assets	101	(67)	6
NET CASH FROM (used in) FINANCING ACTIVITIES	2,147	(525)	1,660
V. EFFECT OF EXCHANGE RATE CHANGES	46	(42)	60
NET INCREASE (decrease) IN CASH AND CASH EQUIVALENTS (I+II+III+IV+V)	923	(93)	39
CASH AND CASH EQUIVALENTS AT BEGINNING OF PERIOD	1,988	2,081	2,042
CASH AND CASH EQUIVALENTS AT END OF PERIOD	2,911	1,988	2,081
Transactions included in the table above, generating no change in cash:			
– acquisition of assets by means of finance leases	7	5	3

(1) Not including the impact of the amount attributable to the acquisition of Bulgari remunerated by the capital increase of LVMH SA as of June 30, 2011, which did not generate any cash flows.

CONSOLIDATED STATEMENT OF CHANGES IN EQUITY

(EUR millions)	*Number of shares*	*Share capital*	*Share premium account*	*Treasury shares and LVMH-share settled derivatives*	*Cumulative translation adjustment*	*Revaluation reserves*				*Net profit and other reserves*	*Total equity*		
						Available for sale financial assets	*Hedges of future foreign currency cash flows*	*Vineyard land*	*Employee benefit commitments*		*Group share*	*Minority interests*	*Total*
AS OF DECEMBER 31, 2012 AFTER RESTATEMENT	508,163,349	152	3,848	(414)	342	1,943	118	758	(88)	17,765	24,424	1,084	25,508
Gains and losses recognized in equity					(350)	912	18	188	51		819	21	840
Net profit										3,436	3,436	511	3,947
COMPREHENSIVE INCOME		-	-	-	(350)	912	18	188	51	3,436	4,255	532	4,787
Stock option plan and similar expenses										31	31	3	34
(Acquisition) disposal of treasury shares and LVMH-share settled derivatives				(103)						(7)	(110)	-	(110)
Exercise of LVMH share subscription options	1,025,418		67								67	-	67
Retirement of LVMH shares	(1,395,106)		(66)	66							-	-	-
Capital increase in subsidiaries											-	8	8
Interim and final dividends paid										(1,500)	(1,500)	(228)	(1,728)
Changes in control of consolidated entities										1	1	50	51
Acquisition and disposal of minority interests' shares										(73)	(73)	(76)	(149)
Purchase commitments for minority interests' shares										(400)	(400)	(345)	(745)
AS OF DECEMBER 31, 2013	507,793,661	152	3,849	(451)	(8)	2,855	136	946	(37)	19,253	26,695	1,028	27,723

Appendix G Time Value of Money

APPENDIX PREVIEW Would you rather receive \$1,000 today or a year from now? You should prefer to receive the \$1,000 today because you can invest the \$1,000 and then earn interest on it. As a result, you will have more than \$1,000 a year from now. What this example illustrates is the concept of the **time value of money**. Everyone prefers to receive money today rather than in the future because of the interest factor.

LEARNING OBJECTIVES

1. **Compute interest and future values.**
   - Nature of interest
   - Future value of a single amount
   - Future value of an annuity
2. **Compute present values.**
   - Present value variables
   - Present value of a single amount
   - Present value of an annuity
   - Time periods and discounting
   - Present value of a long-term note or bond
3. **Compute the present value in capital budgeting situations.**
   - Using alternative discount rates
4. **Use a financial calculator to solve time value of money problems.**
   - Present value of a single sum
   - Present value of an annuity
   - Useful financial calculator applications

LEARNING OBJECTIVE  **Compute interest and future values.**

Nature of Interest

Interest is payment for the use of another person's money. It is the difference between the amount borrowed or invested (called the **principal**) and the amount repaid or collected. The amount of interest to be paid or collected is usually stated as a rate over a specific period of time. The rate of interest is generally stated as an annual rate.

The amount of interest involved in any financing transaction is based on three elements:

1. **Principal (p):** The original amount borrowed or invested.
2. **Interest Rate (i):** An annual percentage of the principal.
3. **Time (n):** The number of periods that the principal is borrowed or invested.

SIMPLE INTEREST

Simple interest is computed on the principal amount only. It is the return on the principal for one period. Simple interest is usually expressed as shown in Illustration G-1.

Illustration G-1
Interest computation

$$\text{Interest} = \underset{p}{\text{Principal}} \times \underset{i}{\text{Rate}} \times \underset{n}{\text{Time}}$$

For example, if you borrowed \$5,000 for 2 years at a simple interest rate of 12% annually, you would pay \$1,200 in total interest, computed as follows.

$$\begin{aligned}\text{Interest} &= p \times i \times n \\ &= \$5{,}000 \times 0.12 \times 2 \\ &= \$1{,}200\end{aligned}$$

COMPOUND INTEREST

Compound interest is computed on principal **and** on any interest earned that has not been paid or withdrawn. It is the return on (or growth of) the principal for two or more time periods. Compounding computes interest not only on the principal but also on the interest earned to date on that principal, assuming the interest is left on deposit.

To illustrate the difference between simple and compound interest, assume that you deposit \$1,000 in Bank Two, where it will earn simple interest of 9% per year, and you deposit another \$1,000 in Citizens Bank, where it will earn compound interest of 9% per year compounded annually. Also assume that in both cases you will not withdraw any cash until three years from the date of deposit. Illustration G-2 shows the computation of interest to be received and the accumulated year-end balances.

Illustration G-2
Simple versus compound interest

Bank Two

Simple Interest Calculation	Simple Interest	Accumulated Year-End Balance
Year 1 \$1,000.00 × 9%	\$ 90.00	\$1,090.00
Year 2 \$1,000.00 × 9%	90.00	\$1,180.00
Year 3 \$1,000.00 × 9%	90.00	\$1,270.00
	\$ 270.00	

Citizens Bank

Compound Interest Calculation	Compound Interest	Accumulated Year-End Balance
Year 1 \$1,000.00 × 9%	\$ 90.00	\$1,090.00
Year 2 \$1,090.00 × 9%	98.10	\$1,188.10
Year 3 \$1,188.10 × 9%	106.93	\$1,295.03
	\$ 295.03	

\$25.03 Difference

Note in Illustration G-2 that simple interest uses the initial principal of \$1,000 to compute the interest in all three years. Compound interest uses the accumulated balance (principal plus interest to date) at each year-end to compute interest in the succeeding year—which explains why your compound interest account is larger.

Obviously, if you had a choice between investing your money at simple interest or at compound interest, you would choose compound interest, all other things—especially risk—being equal. In the example, compounding provides \$25.03 of additional interest income. For practical purposes, compounding assumes that unpaid interest earned becomes a part of the principal, and the accumulated balance at the end of each year becomes the new principal on which interest is earned during the next year.

Illustration G-2 indicates that you should invest your money at the bank that compounds interest. Most business situations use compound interest. Simple interest is generally applicable only to short-term situations of one year or less.

Future Value of a Single Amount

The **future value of a single amount** is the value at a future date of a given amount invested, assuming compound interest. For example, in Illustration G-2, \$1,295.03 is the future value of the \$1,000 investment earning 9% for three years. The \$1,295.03 is determined more easily by using the following formula.

$$FV = p \times (1 + i)^n$$

Illustration G-3
Formula for future value

where:

FV = future value of a single amount
p = principal (or present value; the value today)
i = interest rate for one period
n = number of periods

The \$1,295.03 is computed as follows.

$$\begin{aligned} FV &= p \times (1 + i)^n \\ &= \$1,000 \times (1 + 0.09)^3 \\ &= \$1,000 \times 1.29503 \\ &= \$1,295.03 \end{aligned}$$

The 1.29503 is computed by multiplying (1.09 × 1.09 × 1.09). The amounts in this example can be depicted in the time diagram shown in Illustration G-4.

Illustration G-4
Time diagram

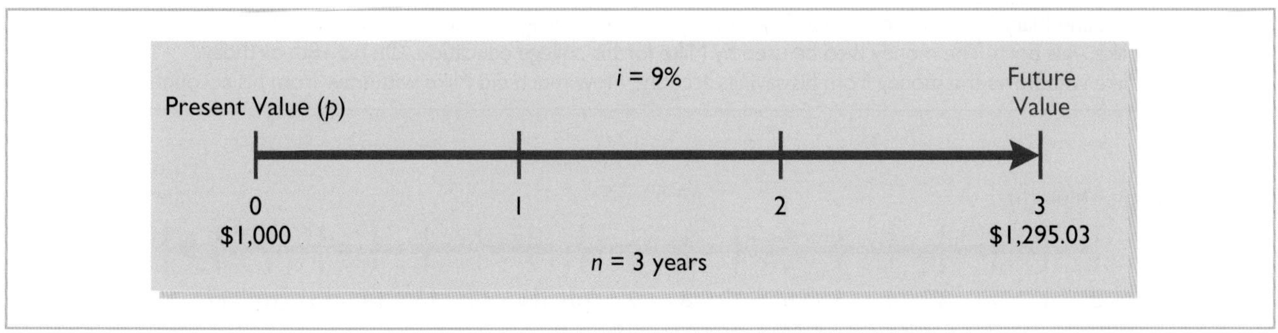

Another method used to compute the future value of a single amount involves a compound interest table. This table shows the future value of 1 for n periods. Table 1 (page G-4) is such a table.

In Table 1, n is the number of compounding periods, the percentages are the periodic interest rates, and the 5-digit decimal numbers in the respective columns are the future value of 1 factors. To use Table 1, you multiply the principal amount by the future value factor for the specified number of periods and interest rate. For example, the future value factor for two periods at 9% is 1.18810. Multiplying this factor by \$1,000 equals \$1,188.10—which is the accumulated balance at the end of year 2 in the Citizens Bank example in Illustration G-2. The \$1,295.03 accumulated balance at the end of the third year is calculated from Table 1 by multiplying the future value factor for three periods (1.29503) by the $1,000.

The demonstration problem in Illustration G-5 shows how to use Table 1.

TABLE 1 Future Value of 1

(*n*) Periods	4%	5%	6%	7%	8%	9%	10%	11%	12%	15%
0	1.00000	1.00000	1.00000	1.00000	1.00000	1.00000	1.00000	1.00000	1.00000	1.00000
1	1.04000	1.05000	1.06000	1.07000	1.08000	1.09000	1.10000	1.11000	1.12000	1.15000
2	1.08160	1.10250	1.12360	1.14490	1.16640	1.18810	1.21000	1.23210	1.25440	1.32250
3	1.12486	1.15763	1.19102	1.22504	1.25971	1.29503	1.33100	1.36763	1.40493	1.52088
4	1.16986	1.21551	1.26248	1.31080	1.36049	1.41158	1.46410	1.51807	1.57352	1.74901
5	1.21665	1.27628	1.33823	1.40255	1.46933	1.53862	1.61051	1.68506	1.76234	2.01136
6	1.26532	1.34010	1.41852	1.50073	1.58687	1.67710	1.77156	1.87041	1.97382	2.31306
7	1.31593	1.40710	1.50363	1.60578	1.71382	1.82804	1.94872	2.07616	2.21068	2.66002
8	1.36857	1.47746	1.59385	1.71819	1.85093	1.99256	2.14359	2.30454	2.47596	3.05902
9	1.42331	1.55133	1.68948	1.83846	1.99900	2.17189	2.35795	2.55803	2.77308	3.51788
10	1.48024	1.62889	1.79085	1.96715	2.15892	2.36736	2.59374	2.83942	3.10585	4.04556
11	1.53945	1.71034	1.89830	2.10485	2.33164	2.58043	2.85312	3.15176	3.47855	4.65239
12	1.60103	1.79586	2.01220	2.25219	2.51817	2.81267	3.13843	3.49845	3.89598	5.35025
13	1.66507	1.88565	2.13293	2.40985	2.71962	3.06581	3.45227	3.88328	4.36349	6.15279
14	1.73168	1.97993	2.26090	2.57853	2.93719	3.34173	3.79750	4.31044	4.88711	7.07571
15	1.80094	2.07893	2.39656	2.75903	3.17217	3.64248	4.17725	4.78459	5.47357	8.13706
16	1.87298	2.18287	2.54035	2.95216	3.42594	3.97031	4.59497	5.31089	6.13039	9.35762
17	1.94790	2.29202	2.69277	3.15882	3.70002	4.32763	5.05447	5.89509	6.86604	10.76126
18	2.02582	2.40662	2.85434	3.37993	3.99602	4.71712	5.55992	6.54355	7.68997	12.37545
19	2.10685	2.52695	3.02560	3.61653	4.31570	5.14166	6.11591	7.26334	8.61276	14.23177
20	2.19112	2.65330	3.20714	3.86968	4.66096	5.60441	6.72750	8.06231	9.64629	16.36654

Illustration G-5
Demonstration problem—
Using Table 1 for *FV* of 1

John and Mary Rich invested $20,000 in a savings account paying 6% interest at the time their son, Mike, was born. The money is to be used by Mike for his college education. On his 18th birthday, Mike withdraws the money from his savings account. How much did Mike withdraw from his account?

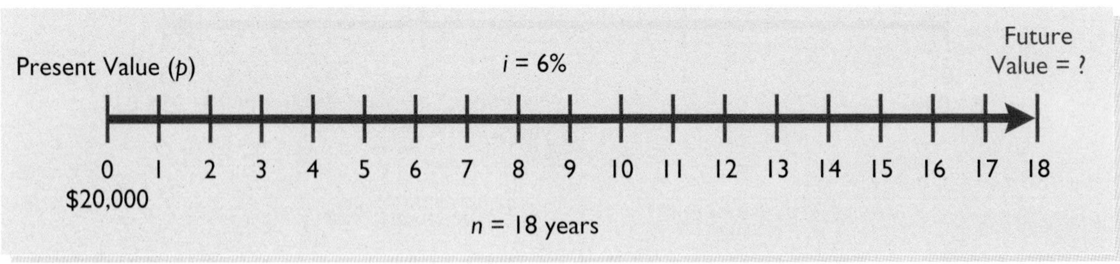

Answer: The future value factor from Table 1 is 2.85434 (18 periods at 6%). The future value of $20,000 earning 6% per year for 18 years is **$57,086.80** ($20,000 × 2.85434).

Future Value of an Annuity

The preceding discussion involved the accumulation of only a single principal sum. Individuals and businesses frequently encounter situations in which a

series of equal dollar amounts are to be paid or received at evenly spaced time intervals (periodically), such as loans or lease (rental) contracts. A series of payments or receipts of equal dollar amounts is referred to as an **annuity**.

The **future value of an annuity** is the sum of all the payments (receipts) plus the accumulated compound interest on them. In computing the future value of an annuity, it is necessary to know (1) the interest rate, (2) the number of payments (receipts), and (3) the amount of the periodic payments (receipts).

To illustrate the computation of the future value of an annuity, assume that you invest $2,000 at the end of each year for three years at 5% interest compounded annually. This situation is depicted in the time diagram in Illustration G-6.

Illustration G-6
Time diagram for a three-year annuity

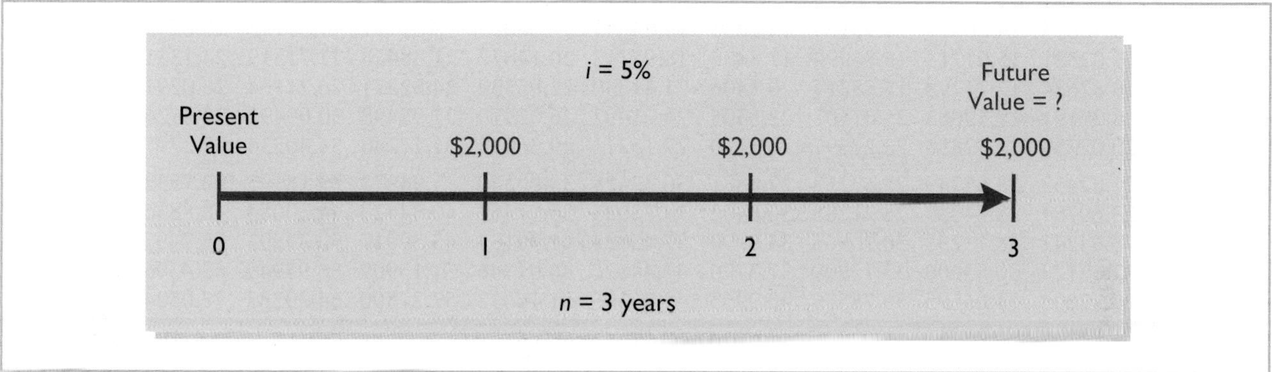

The $2,000 invested at the end of year 1 will earn interest for two years (years 2 and 3), and the $2,000 invested at the end of year 2 will earn interest for one year (year 3). However, the last $2,000 investment (made at the end of year 3) will not earn any interest. Using the future value factors from Table 1, the future value of these periodic payments is computed as shown in Illustration G-7.

Illustration G-7
Future value of periodic payment computation

Invested at End of Year	Number of Compounding Periods	Amount Invested	×	Future Value of 1 Factor at 5%	=	Future Value
1	2	$2,000		1.10250		$ 2,205
2	1	2,000		1.05000		2,100
3	0	2,000		1.00000		2,000
				3.15250		**$6,305**

The first $2,000 investment is multiplied by the future value factor for two periods (1.1025) because two years' interest will accumulate on it (in years 2 and 3). The second $2,000 investment will earn only one year's interest (in year 3) and therefore is multiplied by the future value factor for one year (1.0500). The final $2,000 investment is made at the end of the third year and will not earn any interest. Thus, $n = 0$ and the future value factor is 1.00000. Consequently, the future value of the last $2,000 invested is only $2,000 since it does not accumulate any interest.

Calculating the future value of each individual cash flow is required when the periodic payments or receipts are not equal in each period. However, when the periodic payments (receipts) are **the same in each period**, the future value can be computed by using a future value of an annuity of 1 table. Table 2 (page G-6) is such a table.

TABLE 2 Future Value of an Annuity of 1

(*n*) Payments	4%	5%	6%	7%	8%	9%	10%	11%	12%	15%
1	1.00000	1.00000	1.00000	1.0000	1.00000	1.00000	1.00000	1.00000	1.00000	1.00000
2	2.04000	2.05000	2.06000	2.0700	2.08000	2.09000	2.10000	2.11000	2.12000	2.15000
3	3.12160	3.15250	3.18360	3.2149	3.24640	3.27810	3.31000	3.34210	3.37440	3.47250
4	4.24646	4.31013	4.37462	4.4399	4.50611	4.57313	4.64100	4.70973	4.77933	4.99338
5	5.41632	5.52563	5.63709	5.7507	5.86660	5.98471	6.10510	6.22780	6.35285	6.74238
6	6.63298	6.80191	6.97532	7.1533	7.33592	7.52334	7.71561	7.91286	8.11519	8.75374
7	7.89829	8.14201	8.39384	8.6540	8.92280	9.20044	9.48717	9.78327	10.08901	11.06680
8	9.21423	9.54911	9.89747	10.2598	10.63663	11.02847	11.43589	11.85943	12.29969	13.72682
9	10.58280	11.02656	11.49132	11.9780	12.48756	13.02104	13.57948	14.16397	14.77566	16.78584
10	12.00611	12.57789	13.18079	13.8164	14.48656	15.19293	15.93743	16.72201	17.54874	20.30372
11	13.48635	14.20679	14.97164	15.7836	16.64549	17.56029	18.53117	19.56143	20.65458	24.34928
12	15.02581	15.91713	16.86994	17.8885	18.97713	20.14072	21.38428	22.71319	24.13313	29.00167
13	16.62684	17.71298	18.88214	20.1406	21.49530	22.95339	24.52271	26.21164	28.02911	34.35192
14	18.29191	19.59863	21.01507	22.5505	24.21492	26.01919	27.97498	30.09492	32.39260	40.50471
15	20.02359	21.57856	23.27597	25.1290	27.15211	29.36092	31.77248	34.40536	37.27972	47.58041
16	21.82453	23.65749	25.67253	27.8881	30.32428	33.00340	35.94973	39.18995	42.75328	55.71747
17	23.69751	25.84037	28.21288	30.8402	33.75023	36.97351	40.54470	44.50084	48.88367	65.07509
18	25.64541	28.13238	30.90565	33.9990	37.45024	41.30134	45.59917	50.39593	55.74972	75.83636
19	27.67123	30.53900	33.75999	37.3790	41.44626	46.01846	51.15909	56.93949	63.43968	88.21181
20	29.77808	33.06595	36.78559	40.9955	45.76196	51.16012	57.27500	64.20283	72.05244	102.44358

Table 2 shows the future value of 1 to be received periodically for a given number of payments. It assumes that each payment is made at the **end** of each period. We can see from Table 2 that the future value of an annuity of 1 factor for three payments at 5% is 3.15250. The future value factor is the total of the three individual future value factors as shown in Illustration G-7. Multiplying this amount by the annual investment of $2,000 produces a future value of $6,305.

The demonstration problem in Illustration G-8 shows how to use Table 2.

Illustration G-8
Demonstration problem—Using Table 2 for *FV* of an annuity of 1

John and Char Lewis's daughter, Debra, has just started high school. They decide to start a college fund for her and will invest $2,500 in a savings account at the end of each year she is in high school (4 payments total). The account will earn 6% interest compounded annually. How much will be in the college fund at the time Debra graduates from high school?

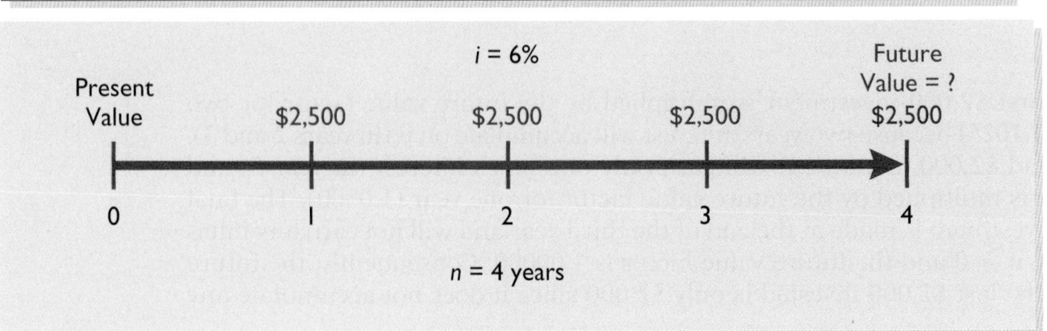

Answer: The future value factor from Table 2 is 4.37462 (4 payments at 6%). The future value of $2,500 invested each year for 4 years at 6% interest is **$10,936.55** ($2,500 × 4.37462).

LEARNING OBJECTIVE 2 **Compute present values.**

Present Value Variables

The **present value** is the value now of a given amount to be paid or received in the future, assuming compound interest. The present value, like the future value, is based on three variables: (1) the dollar amount to be received (future amount), (2) the length of time until the amount is received (number of periods), and (3) the interest rate (the discount rate). The process of determining the present value is referred to as **discounting the future amount**.

Present value computations are used in measuring many items. For example, the present value of principal and interest payments is used to determine the market price of a bond. Determining the amount to be reported for notes payable and lease liabilities also involves present value computations. In addition, capital budgeting and other investment proposals are evaluated using present value computations. Finally, all rate of return and internal rate of return computations involve present value techniques.

Present Value of a Single Amount

To illustrate present value, assume that you want to invest a sum of money today that will provide $1,000 at the end of one year. What amount would you need to invest today to have $1,000 one year from now? If you want a 10% rate of return, the investment or present value is $909.09 ($1,000 ÷ 1.10). The formula for calculating present value is shown in Illustration G-9.

$$\text{Present Value } (PV) = \text{Future Value } (FV) \div (1 + i)^n$$

Illustration G-9
Formula for present value

The computation of $1,000 discounted at 10% for one year is as follows.

$$\begin{aligned} PV &= FV \div (1 + i)^n \\ &= \$1{,}000 \div (1 + 0.10)^1 \\ &= \$1{,}000 \div 1.10 \\ &= \$909.09 \end{aligned}$$

The future amount ($1,000), the discount rate (10%), and the number of periods (1) are known. The variables in this situation are depicted in the time diagram in Illustration G-10.

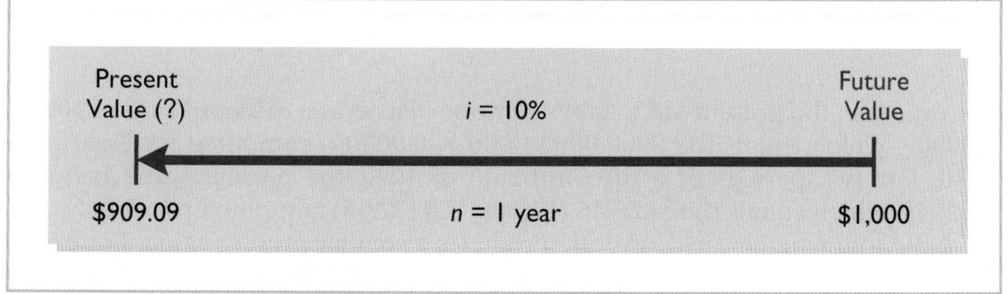

Illustration G-10
Finding present value if discounted for one period

If the single amount of $1,000 is to be received **in two years** and discounted at 10% [$PV = \$1{,}000 \div (1 + 0.10)^2$], its present value is $826.45 [($1,000 ÷ 1.21), depicted in Illustration G-11 (page G-8).

Illustration G-11
Finding present value if discounted for two periods

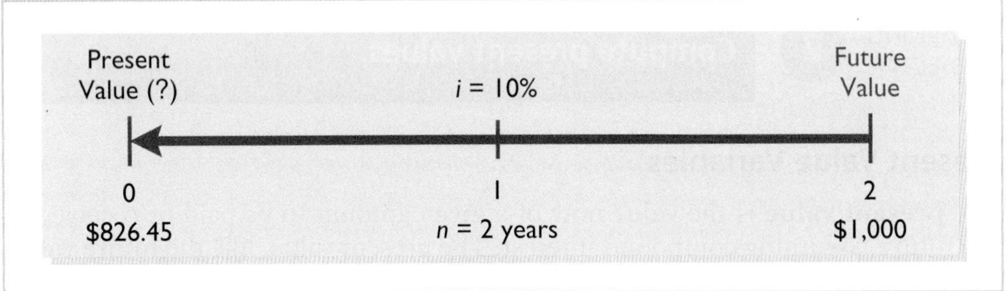

The present value of 1 may also be determined through tables that show the present value of 1 for n periods. In Table 3 (see below), n is the number of discounting periods involved. The percentages are the periodic interest rates or discount rates, and the 5-digit decimal numbers in the respective columns are the present value of 1 factors.

When using Table 3, the future value is multiplied by the present value factor specified at the intersection of the number of periods and the discount rate.

TABLE 3 Present Value of 1

(*n*) Periods	4%	5%	6%	7%	8%	9%	10%	11%	12%	15%
1	0.96154	0.95238	0.94340	0.93458	0.92593	0.91743	0.90909	0.90090	0.89286	0.86957
2	0.92456	0.90703	0.89000	0.87344	0.85734	0.84168	0.82645	0.81162	0.79719	0.75614
3	0.88900	0.86384	0.83962	0.81630	0.79383	0.77218	0.75132	0.73119	0.71178	0.65752
4	0.85480	0.82270	0.79209	0.76290	0.73503	0.70843	0.68301	0.65873	0.63552	0.57175
5	0.82193	0.78353	0.74726	0.71299	0.68058	0.64993	0.62092	0.59345	0.56743	0.49718
6	0.79031	0.74622	0.70496	0.66634	0.63017	0.59627	0.56447	0.53464	0.50663	0.43233
7	0.75992	0.71068	0.66506	0.62275	0.58349	0.54703	0.51316	0.48166	0.45235	0.37594
8	0.73069	0.67684	0.62741	0.58201	0.54027	0.50187	0.46651	0.43393	0.40388	0.32690
9	0.70259	0.64461	0.59190	0.54393	0.50025	0.46043	0.42410	0.39092	0.36061	0.28426
10	0.67556	0.61391	0.55839	0.50835	0.46319	0.42241	0.38554	0.35218	0.32197	0.24719
11	0.64958	0.58468	0.52679	0.47509	0.42888	0.38753	0.35049	0.31728	0.28748	0.21494
12	0.62460	0.55684	0.49697	0.44401	0.39711	0.35554	0.31863	0.28584	0.25668	0.18691
13	0.60057	0.53032	0.46884	0.41496	0.36770	0.32618	0.28966	0.25751	0.22917	0.16253
14	0.57748	0.50507	0.44230	0.38782	0.34046	0.29925	0.26333	0.23199	0.20462	0.14133
15	0.55526	0.48102	0.41727	0.36245	0.31524	0.27454	0.23939	0.20900	0.18270	0.12289
16	0.53391	0.45811	0.39365	0.33873	0.29189	0.25187	0.21763	0.18829	0.16312	0.10687
17	0.51337	0.43630	0.37136	0.31657	0.27027	0.23107	0.19785	0.16963	0.14564	0.09293
18	0.49363	0.41552	0.35034	0.29586	0.25025	0.21199	0.17986	0.15282	0.13004	0.08081
19	0.47464	0.39573	0.33051	0.27615	0.23171	0.19449	0.16351	0.13768	0.11611	0.07027
20	0.45639	0.37689	0.31180	0.25842	0.21455	0.17843	0.14864	0.12403	0.10367	0.06110

For example, the present value factor for one period at a discount rate of 10% is 0.90909, which equals the $909.09 ($1,000 × 0.90909) computed in Illustration G-10. For two periods at a discount rate of 10%, the present value factor is 0.82645, which equals the $826.45 ($1,000 × 0.82645) computed previously.

Note that a higher discount rate produces a smaller present value. For example, using a 15% discount rate, the present value of $1,000 due one year from now is $869.57, versus $909.09 at 10%. Also note that the further removed from the present the future value is, the smaller the present value. For example, using the same discount rate of 10%, the present value of $1,000 due in **five years** is $620.92. The present value of $1,000 due in **one year** is $909.09, a difference of $288.17.

The following two demonstration problems (Illustrations G-12 and G-13) illustrate how to use Table 3.

Illustration G-12
Demonstration problem—Using Table 3 for *PV* of 1

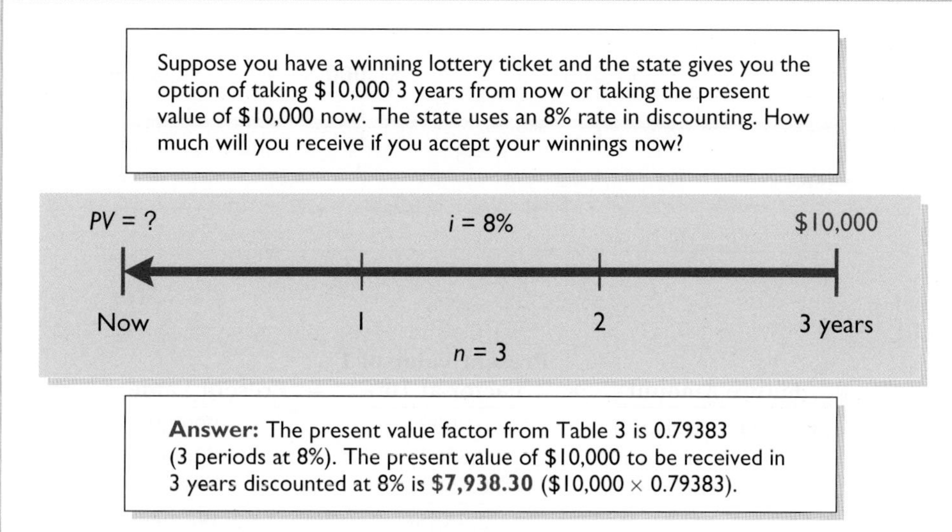

Illustration G-13
Demonstration problem—Using Table 3 for *PV* of 1

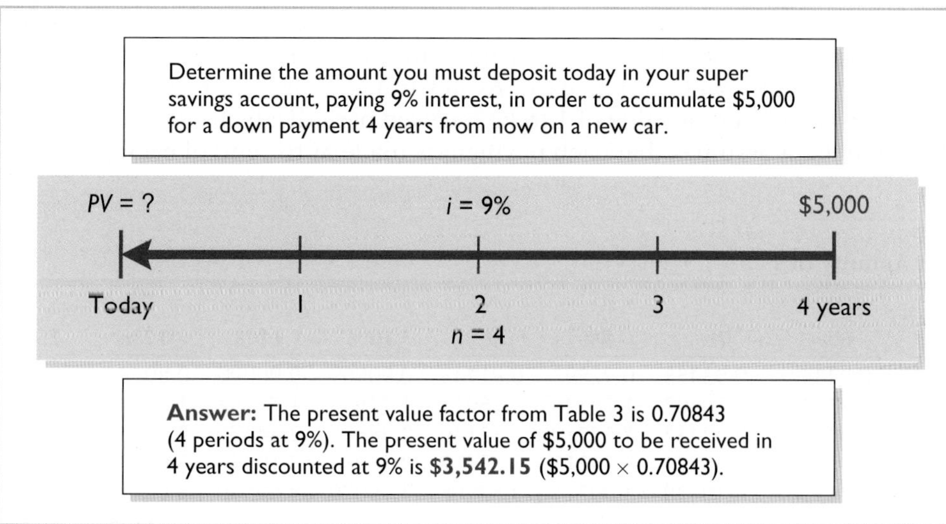

Present Value of an Annuity

The preceding discussion involved the discounting of only a single future amount. Businesses and individuals frequently engage in transactions in which a series of equal dollar amounts are to be received or paid at evenly spaced time intervals (periodically). Examples of a series of periodic receipts or payments are loan agreements, installment sales, mortgage notes, lease (rental) contracts, and pension obligations. As discussed earlier, these periodic receipts or payments are **annuities**.

The **present value of an annuity** is the value now of a series of future receipts or payments, discounted assuming compound interest. In computing the present value of an annuity, it is necessary to know (1) the discount rate, (2) the number of payments (receipts), and (3) the amount of the periodic receipts or payments. To illustrate the computation of the present value of an annuity, assume that you will receive $1,000 cash annually for three years at a time when the discount rate is 10%. This situation is depicted in the time diagram in Illustration G-14. Illustration G-15 shows the computation of its present value in this situation.

Illustration G-14
Time diagram for a three-year annuity

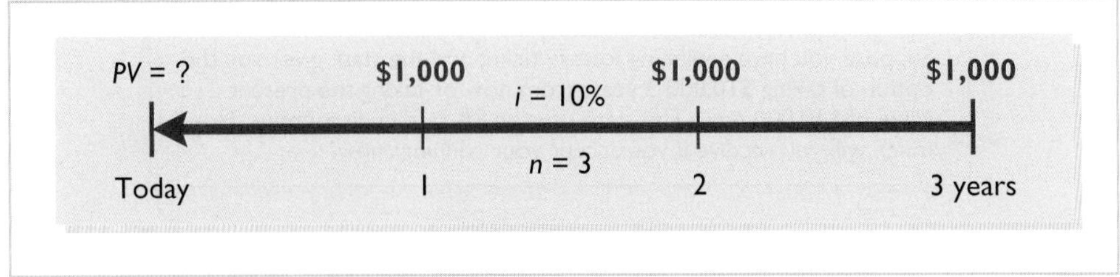

Illustration G-15
Present value of a series of future amounts computation

Future Amount	×	Present Value of 1 Factor at 10%	=	Present Value
$1,000 (1 year away)		0.90909		$ 909.09
1,000 (2 years away)		0.82645		826.45
1,000 (3 years away)		0.75132		751.32
		2.48686		**$2,486.86**

This method of calculation is required when the periodic cash flows are not uniform in each period. However, when the future receipts are the same in each period, an annuity table can be used. As illustrated in Table 4 below, an annuity table shows the present value of 1 to be received periodically for a given number of payments. It assumes that each payment is made at the end of each period.

TABLE 4 Present Value of an Annuity of 1

(n) Payments	4%	5%	6%	7%	8%	9%	10%	11%	12%	15%
1	0.96154	0.95238	0.94340	0.93458	0.92593	0.91743	0.90909	0.90090	0.89286	0.86957
2	1.88609	1.85941	1.83339	1.80802	1.78326	1.75911	1.73554	1.71252	1.69005	1.62571
3	2.77509	2.72325	2.67301	2.62432	2.57710	2.53130	2.48685	2.44371	2.40183	2.28323
4	3.62990	3.54595	3.46511	3.38721	3.31213	3.23972	3.16986	3.10245	3.03735	2.85498
5	4.45182	4.32948	4.21236	4.10020	3.99271	3.88965	3.79079	3.69590	3.60478	3.35216
6	5.24214	5.07569	4.91732	4.76654	4.62288	4.48592	4.35526	4.23054	4.11141	3.78448
7	6.00205	5.78637	5.58238	5.38929	5.20637	5.03295	4.86842	4.71220	4.56376	4.16042
8	6.73274	6.46321	6.20979	5.97130	5.74664	5.53482	5.33493	5.14612	4.96764	4.48732
9	7.43533	7.10782	6.80169	6.51523	6.24689	5.99525	5.75902	5.53705	5.32825	4.77158
10	8.11090	7.72173	7.36009	7.02358	6.71008	6.41766	6.14457	5.88923	5.65022	5.01877
11	8.76048	8.30641	7.88687	7.49867	7.13896	6.80519	6.49506	6.20652	5.93770	5.23371
12	9.38507	8.86325	8.38384	7.94269	7.53608	7.16073	6.81369	6.49236	6.19437	5.42062
13	9.98565	9.39357	8.85268	8.35765	7.90378	7.48690	7.10336	6.74987	6.42355	5.58315
14	10.56312	9.89864	9.29498	8.74547	8.24424	7.78615	7.36669	6.98187	6.62817	5.72448
15	11.11839	10.37966	9.71225	9.10791	8.55948	8.06069	7.60608	7.19087	6.81086	5.84737
16	11.65230	10.83777	10.10590	9.44665	8.85137	8.31256	7.82371	7.37916	6.97399	5.95424
17	12.16567	11.27407	10.47726	9.76322	9.12164	8.54363	8.02155	7.54879	7.11963	6.04716
18	12.65930	11.68959	10.82760	10.05909	9.37189	8.75563	8.20141	7.70162	7.24967	6.12797
19	13.13394	12.08532	11.15812	10.33560	9.60360	8.95012	8.36492	7.83929	7.36578	6.19823
20	13.59033	12.46221	11.46992	10.59401	9.81815	9.12855	8.51356	7.96333	7.46944	6.25933

Table 4 shows that the present value of an annuity of 1 factor for three payments at 10% is 2.48685.[1] This present value factor is the total of the three individual present value factors, as shown in Illustration G-15. Applying this amount to the annual cash flow of $1,000 produces a present value of $2,486.85.

The following demonstration problem (Illustration G-16) illustrates how to use Table 4.

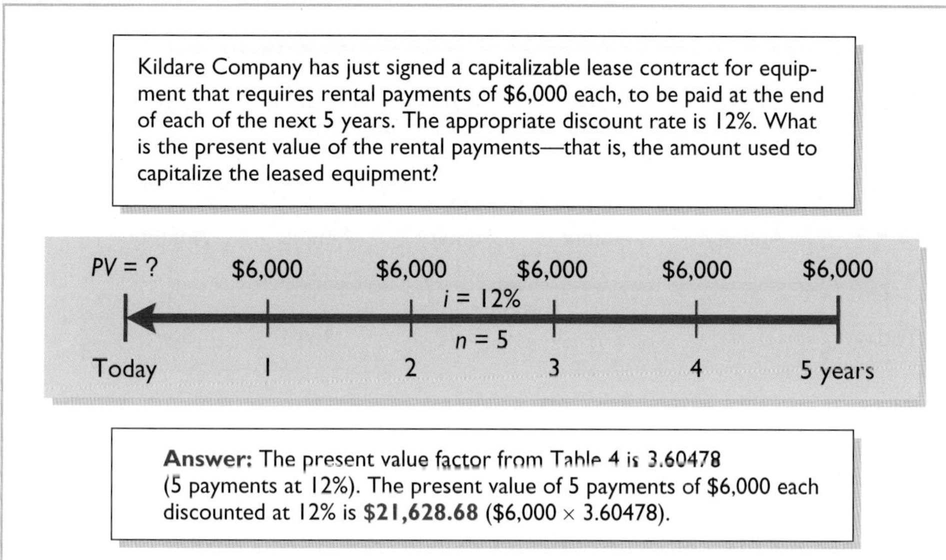

Illustration G-16
Demonstration problem—Using Table 4 for *PV* of an annuity of 1

Time Periods and Discounting

In the preceding calculations, the discounting was done on an annual basis using an annual interest rate. Discounting may also be done over shorter periods of time such as monthly, quarterly, or semiannually.

When the time frame is less than one year, it is necessary to convert the annual interest rate to the applicable time frame. Assume, for example, that the investor in Illustration G-14 received $500 **semiannually** for three years instead of $1,000 annually. In this case, the number of periods becomes six (3 × 2), the discount rate is 5% (10% ÷ 2), the present value factor from Table 4 is 5.07569 (6 periods at 5%), and the present value of the future cash flows is $2,537.85 (5.07569 × $500). This amount is slightly higher than the $2,486.86 computed in Illustration G-15 because interest is computed twice during the same year. That is, during the second half of the year, interest is earned on the first half-year's interest.

Present Value of a Long-Term Note or Bond

The present value (or market price) of a long-term note or bond is a function of three variables: (1) the payment amounts, (2) the length of time until the amounts are paid, and (3) the discount rate. Our example uses a five-year bond issue.

The first variable (dollars to be paid) is made up of two elements: (1) a series of interest payments (an annuity) and (2) the principal amount (a single sum). To

[1]The difference of 0.00001 between 2.48686 and 2.48685 is due to rounding.

compute the present value of the bond, both the interest payments and the principal amount must be discounted—two different computations. The time diagrams for a bond due in five years are shown in Illustration G-17.

Illustration G-17
Time diagrams for the present value of a bond

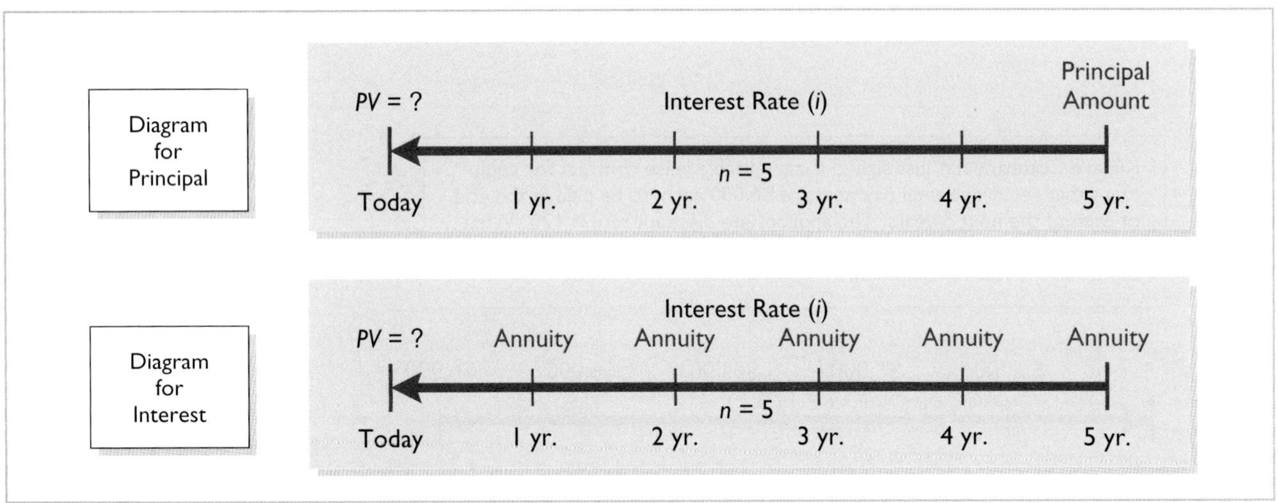

When the investor's market interest rate is equal to the bond's contractual interest rate, the present value of the bonds will equal the face value of the bonds. To illustrate, assume a bond issue of 10%, five-year bonds with a face value of $100,000 with interest payable **semiannually** on January 1 and July 1. If the discount rate is the same as the contractual rate, the bonds will sell at face value. In this case, the investor will receive (1) $100,000 at maturity and (2) a series of ten $5,000 interest payments [($100,000 × 10%) ÷ 2] over the term of the bonds. The length of time is expressed in terms of interest periods—in this case—10, and the discount rate per interest period, 5%. The following time diagram (Illustration G-18) depicts the variables involved in this discounting situation.

Illustration G-18
Time diagram for present value of a 10%, five-year bond paying interest semiannually

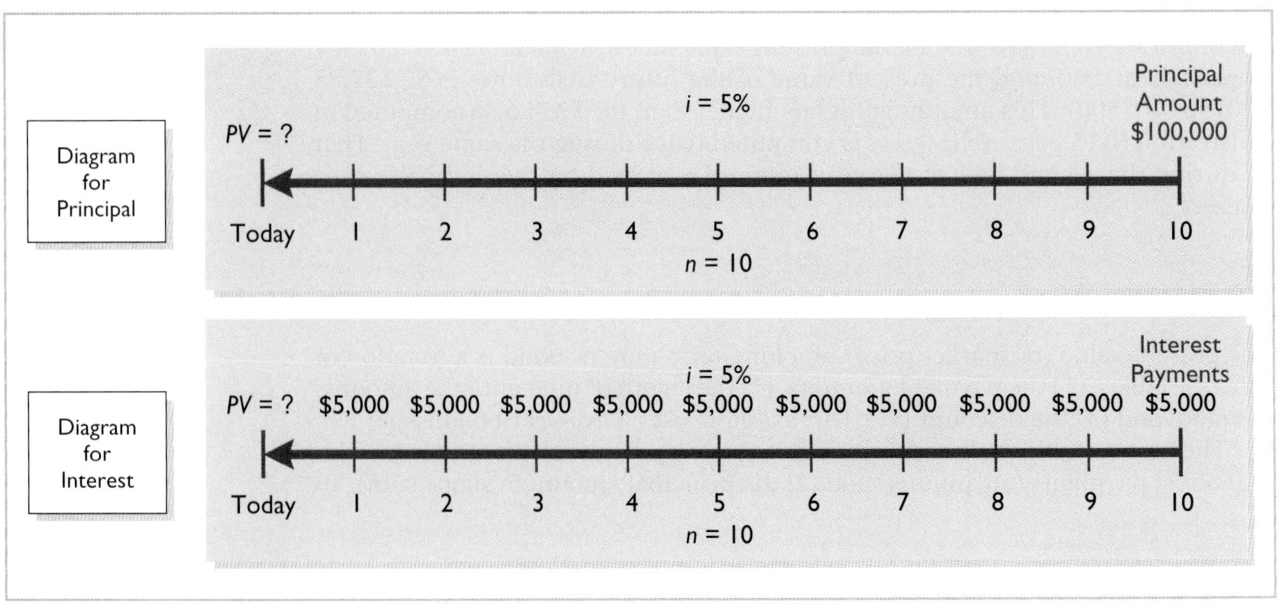

Illustration G-19 shows the computation of the present value of these bonds.

Illustration G-19
Present value of principal and interest—face value

10% Contractual Rate—10% Discount Rate	
Present value of principal to be received at maturity	
$100,000 × *PV* of 1 due in 10 periods at 5%	
$100,000 × 0.61391 (Table 3)	$ 61,391
Present value of interest to be received periodically over the term of the bonds	
$5,000 × *PV* of 1 due periodically for 10 periods at 5%	
$5,000 × 7.72173 (Table 4)	38,609*
Present value of bonds	**$100,000**

*Rounded

Now assume that the investor's required rate of return is 12%, not 10%. The future amounts are again $100,000 and $5,000, respectively, but now a discount rate of 6% (12% ÷ 2) must be used. The present value of the bonds is $92,639, as computed in Illustration G-20.

Illustration G-20
Present value of principal and interest—discount

10% Contractual Rate—12% Discount Rate	
Present value of principal to be received at maturity	
$100,000 × 0.55839 (Table 3)	$ 55,839
Present value of interest to be received periodically over the term of the bonds	
$5,000 × 7.36009 (Table 4)	36,800
Present value of bonds	**$92,639**

Conversely, if the discount rate is 8% and the contractual rate is 10%, the present value of the bonds is $108,111, computed as shown in Illustration G-21.

Illustration G-21
Present value of principal and interest—premium

10% Contractual Rate—8% Discount Rate	
Present value of principal to be received at maturity	
$100,000 × 0.67556 (Table 3)	$ 67,556
Present value of interest to be received periodically over the term of the bonds	
$5,000 × 8.11090 (Table 4)	40,555
Present value of bonds	**$108,111**

The above discussion relied on present value tables in solving present value problems. Calculators may also be used to compute present values without the use of these tables. Many calculators, especially financial calculators, have present value (*PV*) functions that allow you to calculate present values by merely inputting the proper amount, discount rate, periods, and pressing the PV key. We discuss the use of financial calculators in a later section.

LEARNING OBJECTIVE 3

Compute the present value in capital budgeting situations.

The decision to make long-term capital investments is best evaluated using discounting techniques that recognize the time value of money. To do this, many companies calculate the present value of the cash flows involved in a capital investment.

To illustrate, Nagel-Siebert Trucking Company, a cross-country freight carrier in Montgomery, Illinois, is considering adding another truck to its fleet because of a purchasing opportunity. **Navistar Inc.**, Nagel-Siebert's primary supplier of overland rigs, is overstocked and offers to sell its biggest rig for $154,000 cash payable upon delivery. Nagel-Siebert knows that the rig will produce a net cash flow per year of $40,000 for five years (received at the end of each year), at which time it will be sold for an estimated salvage value of $35,000. Nagel-Siebert's discount rate in evaluating capital expenditures is 10%. Should Nagel-Siebert commit to the purchase of this rig?

The cash flows that must be discounted to present value by Nagel-Siebert are as follows.

Cash payable on delivery (today): $154,000.

Net cash flow from operating the rig: $40,000 for 5 years (at the end of each year).

Cash received from sale of rig at the end of 5 years: $35,000.

The time diagrams for the latter two cash flows are shown in Illustration G-22.

Illustration G-22
Time diagrams for Nagel-Siebert Trucking Company

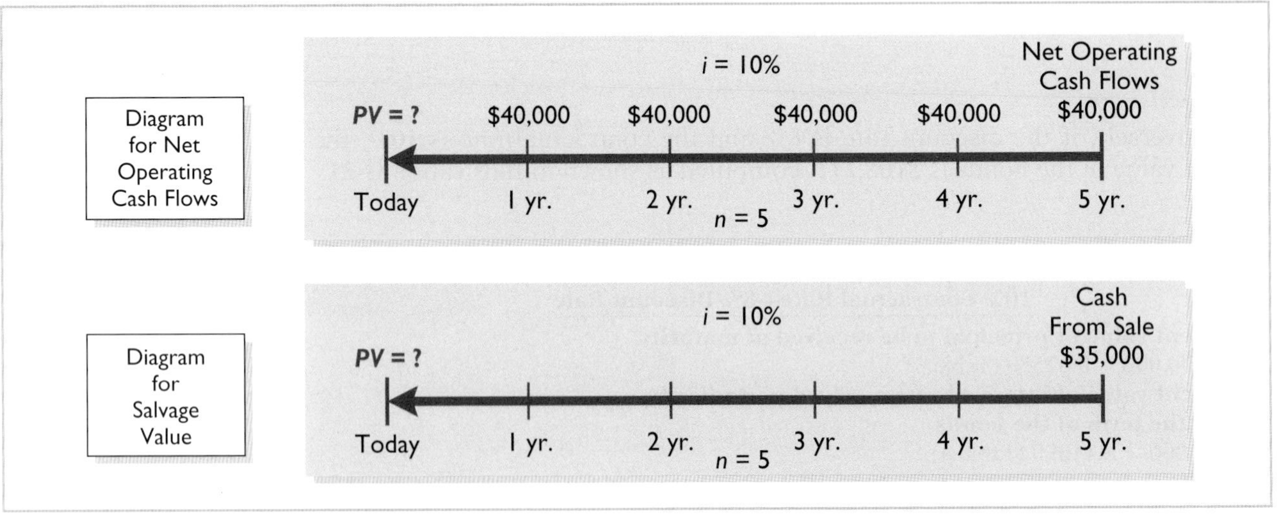

Notice from the diagrams that computing the present value of the net operating cash flows ($40,000 at the end of each year) is **discounting an annuity** (Table 4), while computing the present value of the $35,000 salvage value is **discounting a single sum** (Table 3). The computation of these present values is shown in Illustration G-23.

Illustration G-23
Present value computations at 10%

Present Values Using a 10% Discount Rate	
Present value of net operating cash flows received annually over 5 years	
$40,000 × PV of 1 received annually for 5 years at 10%	
$40,000 × 3.79079 (Table 4)	$ 151,631.60
Present value of salvage value (cash) to be received in 5 years	
$35,000 × PV of 1 received in 5 years at 10%	
$35,000 × 0.62092 (Table 3)	21,732.20
Present value of cash **inflows**	173,363.80
Present value of cash **outflows** (purchase price due today at 10%)	
$154,000 × PV of 1 due today	
$154,000 × 1.00000	(154,000.00)
Net present value	**$ 19,363.80**

Because the present value of the cash receipts (inflows) of $173,363.80 ($151,631.60 + $21,732.20) exceeds the present value of the cash payments (outflows) of $154,000.00, the net present value of $19,363.80 is positive, and **the decision to invest should be accepted**.

Now assume that Nagle-Siebert uses a discount rate of 15%, not 10%, because it wants a greater return on its investments in capital assets. The cash receipts and cash payments by Nagel-Siebert are the same. The present values of these receipts and cash payments discounted at 15% are shown in Illustration G-24.

Illustration G-24
Present value computations at 15%

Present Values Using a 15% Discount Rate	
Present value of net operating cash flows received annually over 5 years at 15%	
$40,000 × 3.35216 (Table 4)	$ 134,086.40
Present value of salvage value (cash) to be received in 5 years at 15%	
$35,000 × 0.49718 (Table 3)	17,401.30
Present value of cash **inflows**	151,487.70
Present value of cash **outflows** (purchase price due today at 15%)	
$154,000 × 1.00000	(154,000.00)
Net present value	**$ (2,512.30)**

Because the present value of the cash payments (outflows) of $154,000.00 exceeds the present value of the cash receipts (inflows) of $151,487.70 ($134,086.40 + $17,401.30), the net present value of $2,512.30 is negative, and **the investment should be rejected**.

The above discussion relied on present value tables in solving present value problems. As we show in the next section, calculators may also be used to compute present values without the use of these tables. Financial calculators have present value (PV) functions that allow you to calculate present values by merely identifying the proper amount, discount rate, periods, and pressing the PV key.

LEARNING OBJECTIVE 

Use a financial calculator to solve time value of money problems.

Business professionals, once they have mastered the underlying time value of money concepts, often use a financial calculator to solve these types of problems. In most cases, they use calculators if interest rates or time periods do not correspond with the information provided in the compound interest tables.

To use financial calculators, you enter the time value of money variables into the calculator. Illustration G-25 shows the five most common keys used to solve time value of money problems.[2]

Illustration G-25
Financial calculator keys

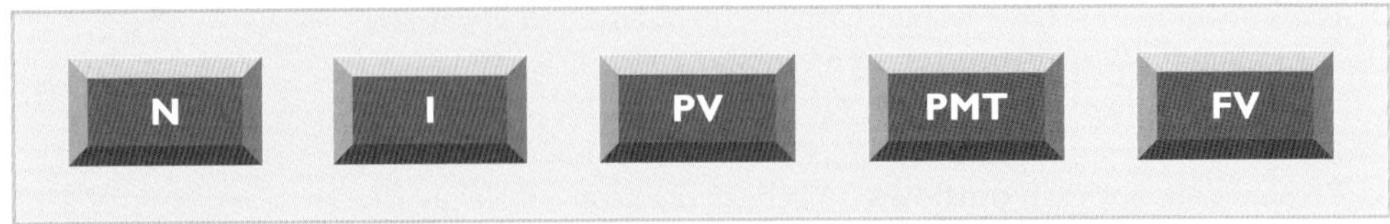

where:

N = number of periods
I = interest rate per period (some calculators use I/YR or i)
PV = present value (occurs at the beginning of the first period)
PMT = payment (all payments are equal, and none are skipped)
FV = future value (occurs at the end of the last period)

In solving time value of money problems in this appendix, you will generally be given three of four variables and will have to solve for the remaining variable. The fifth key (the key not used) is given a value of zero to ensure that this variable is not used in the computation.

Present Value of a Single Sum

To illustrate how to solve a present value problem using a financial calculator, assume that you want to know the present value of $84,253 to be received in five years, discounted at 11% compounded annually. Illustration G-26 depicts this problem.

Illustration G-26
Calculator solution for present value of a single sum

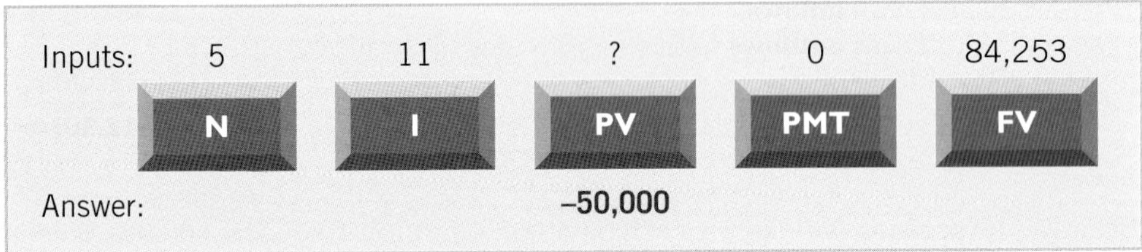

Illustration G-26 shows you the information (inputs) to enter into the calculator: N = 5, I = 11, PMT = 0, and FV = 84,253. You then press PV for the answer: −$50,000. As indicated, the PMT key was given a value of zero because a series of payments did not occur in this problem.

PLUS AND MINUS

The use of plus and minus signs in time value of money problems with a financial calculator can be confusing. Most financial calculators are programmed so that the positive and negative cash flows in any problem offset each other. In the present value problem above, we identified the $84,253 future value initial investment as a positive (inflow); the answer −$50,000 was shown as a negative amount, reflecting a cash outflow. If the 84,253 were entered as a negative, then the final answer would have been reported as a positive 50,000.

Hopefully, the sign convention will not cause confusion. If you understand what is required in a problem, you should be able to interpret a positive or negative amount in determining the solution to a problem.

[2]On many calculators, these keys are actual buttons on the face of the calculator; on others, they appear on the display after the user accesses a present value menu.

COMPOUNDING PERIODS

In the previous problem, we assumed that compounding occurs once a year. Some financial calculators have a default setting, which assumes that compounding occurs 12 times a year. You must determine what default period has been programmed into your calculator and change it as necessary to arrive at the proper compounding period.

ROUNDING

Most financial calculators store and calculate using 12 decimal places. As a result, because compound interest tables generally have factors only up to five decimal places, a slight difference in the final answer can result. In most time value of money problems, the final answer will not include more than two decimal places.

Present Value of an Annuity

To illustrate how to solve a present value of an annuity problem using a financial calculator, assume that you are asked to determine the present value of rental receipts of $6,000 each to be received at the end of each of the next five years, when discounted at 12%, as pictured in Illustration G-27.

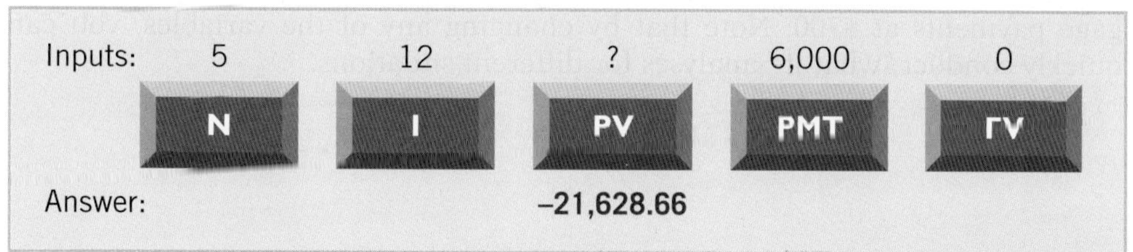

Illustration G-27
Calculator solution for present value of an annuity

In this case, you enter N = 5, I = 12, PMT = 6,000, FV = 0, and then press PV to arrive at the answer of −$21,628.66.

Useful Applications of the Financial Calculator

With a financial calculator, you can solve for any interest rate or for any number of periods in a time value of money problem. Here are some examples of these applications.

AUTO LOAN

Assume you are financing the purchase of a used car with a three-year loan. The loan has a 9.5% stated annual interest rate, compounded monthly. The price of the car is $6,000, and you want to determine the monthly payments, assuming that the payments start one month after the purchase. This problem is pictured in Illustration G-28.

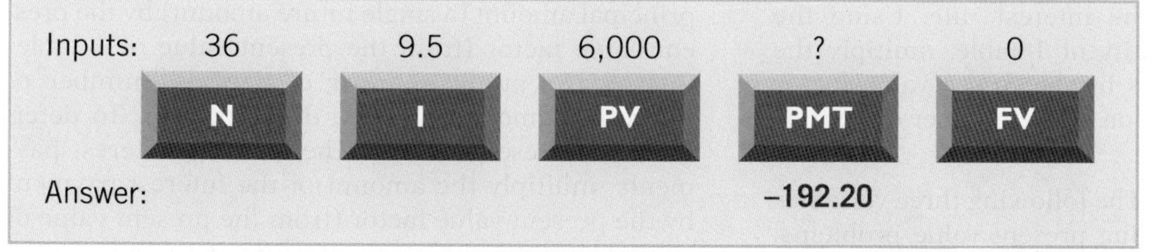

Illustration G-28
Calculator solution for auto loan payments

To solve this problem, you enter N = 36 (12 × 3), I = 9.5, PV = 6,000, FV = 0, and then press PMT. You will find that the monthly payments will be $192.20. Note that the payment key is usually programmed for 12 payments per year. Thus, you must change the default (compounding period) if the payments are other than monthly.

MORTGAGE LOAN AMOUNT

Say you are evaluating financing options for a loan on a house (a mortgage). You decide that the maximum mortgage payment you can afford is $700 per month. The annual interest rate is 8.4%. If you get a mortgage that requires you to make monthly payments over a 15-year period, what is the maximum home loan you can afford? Illustration G-29 depicts this problem.

Illustration G-29
Calculator solution for mortgage amount

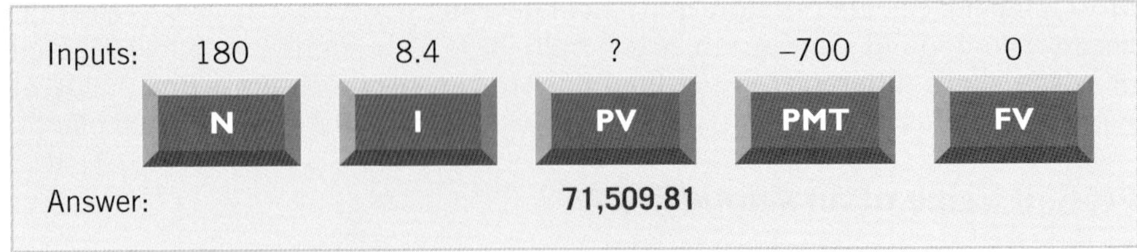

You enter N = 180 (12 × 15 years), I = 8.4, PMT = −700, FV = 0, and press PV. With the payments-per-year key set at 12, you find a present value of $71,509.81—the maximum home loan you can afford, given that you want to keep your mortgage payments at $700. Note that by changing any of the variables, you can quickly conduct "what-if" analyses for different situations.

REVIEW

LEARNING OBJECTIVES REVIEW

1 **Compute interest and future values.** Simple interest is computed on the principal only, while compound interest is computed on the principal and any interest earned that has not been withdrawn.

To solve for future value of a single amount, prepare a time diagram of the problem. Identify the principal amount, the number of compounding periods, and the interest rate. Using the future value of 1 table, multiply the principal amount by the future value factor specified at the intersection of the number of periods and the interest rate.

To solve for future value of an annuity, prepare a time diagram of the problem. Identify the amount of the periodic payments (receipts), the number of payments (receipts), and the interest rate. Using the future value of an annuity of 1 table, multiply the amount of the payments by the future value factor specified at the intersection of the number of periods and the interest rate.

2 **Compute present value.** The following three variables are fundamental to solving present value problems: (1) the future amount, (2) the number of periods, and (3) the interest rate (the discount rate).

To solve for present value of a single amount, prepare a time diagram of the problem. Identify the future amount, the number of discounting periods, and the discount (interest) rate. Using the present value of a single amount table, multiply the future amount by the present value factor specified at the intersection of the number of periods and the discount rate.

To solve for present value of an annuity, prepare a time diagram of the problem. Identify the amount of future periodic receipts or payments (annuities), the number of payments (receipts), and the discount (interest) rate. Using the present value of an annuity of 1 table, multiply the amount of the annuity by the present value factor specified at the intersection of the number of payments and the interest rate.

To compute the present value of notes and bonds, determine the present value of the principal amount and the present value of the interest payments. Multiply the principal amount (a single future amount) by the present value factor (from the present value of 1 table) intersecting at the number of periods (number of interest payments) and the discount rate. To determine the present value of the series of interest payments, multiply the amount of the interest payment by the present value factor (from the present value of an annuity of 1 table) intersecting at the number of periods (number of interest payments) and the discount rate. Add the present value of the principal amount to the present value of the interest payments to arrive at the present value of the note or bond.

3 **Compute the present value in capital budgeting situations.** Compute the present values of all cash

inflows and all cash outflows related to the capital budgeting proposal (an investment-type decision). If the **net** present value is positive, accept the proposal (make the investment). If the **net** present value is negative, reject the proposal (do not make the investment).

4 Use a financial calculator to solve time value of money problems. Financial calculators can be used to solve the same and additional problems as those solved with time value of money tables. Enter into the financial calculator the amounts for all of the known elements of a time value of money problem (periods, interest rate, payments, future or present value), and it solves for the unknown element. Particularly useful situations involve interest rates and compounding periods not presented in the tables.

GLOSSARY REVIEW

Annuity A series of equal dollar amounts to be paid or received at evenly spaced time intervals (periodically).

Compound interest The interest computed on the principal and any interest earned that has not been paid or withdrawn.

Discounting the future amount(s) The process of determining present value.

Future value of an annuity The sum of all the payments (receipts) plus the accumulated compound interest on them.

Future value of a single amount The value at a future date of a given amount invested, assuming compound interest.

Interest Payment for the use of another person's money.

Present value The value now of a given amount to be paid or received in the future, assuming compound interest.

Present value of an annuity The value now of a series of future receipts or payments, discounted assuming compound interest.

Principal The amount borrowed or invested.

Simple interest The interest computed on the principal only.

BRIEF EXERCISES

(Use tables to solve exercises BEG-1 to BEG-23.)

BEG-1 Jozy Altidore invested $6,000 at 5% annual interest, and left the money invested without withdrawing any of the interest for 12 years. At the end of the 12 years, Jozy withdrew the accumulated amount of money. (a) What amount did Jozy withdraw, assuming the investment earns simple interest? (b) What amount did Jozy withdraw, assuming the investment earns interest compounded annually?

Compute the future value of a single amount.

(LO 1)

BEG-2 For each of the following cases, indicate (a) what interest rate columns and (b) what number of periods you would refer to in looking up the future value factor.

Use future value tables.

(LO 1)

(1) In Table 1 (future value of 1):

	Annual Rate	Number of Years Invested	Compounded
Case A	5%	3	Annually
Case B	12%	4	Semiannually

(2) In Table 2 (future value of an annuity of 1):

	Annual Rate	Number of Years Invested	Compounded
Case A	3%	8	Annually
Case B	8%	6	Semiannually

Compute the future value of a single amount.
(LO 1)

BEG-3 Liam Company signed a lease for an office building for a period of 12 years. Under the lease agreement, a security deposit of $9,600 is made. The deposit will be returned at the expiration of the lease with interest compounded at 4% per year. What amount will Liam receive at the time the lease expires?

Compute the future value of an annuity.
(LO 1)

BEG-4 Bates Company issued $1,000,000, 10-year bonds and agreed to make annual sinking fund deposits of $78,000. The deposits are made at the end of each year into an account paying 6% annual interest. What amount will be in the sinking fund at the end of 10 years?

Compute the future value of a single amount and of an annuity.
(LO 1)

BEG-5 Andrew and Emma Garfield invested $8,000 in a savings account paying 5% annual interest when their daughter, Angela, was born. They also deposited $1,000 on each of her birthdays until she was 18 (including her 18th birthday). How much was in the savings account on her 18th birthday (after the last deposit)?

Compute the future value of a single amount.
(LO 1)

BEG-6 Hugh Curtin borrowed $35,000 on July 1, 2017. This amount plus accrued interest at 8% compounded annually is to be repaid on July 1, 2022. How much will Hugh have to repay on July 1, 2022?

Use present value tables.
(LO 2)

BEG-7 For each of the following cases, indicate (a) what interest rate columns and (b) what number of periods you would refer to in looking up the discount rate.

(1) In Table 3 (present value of 1):

	Annual Rate	Number of Years Involved	Discounts per Year
Case A	12%	7	Annually
Case B	8%	11	Annually
Case C	10%	8	Semiannually

(2) In Table 4 (present value of an annuity of 1):

	Annual Rate	Number of Years Involved	Number of Payments Involved	Frequency of Payments
Case A	10%	20	20	Annually
Case B	10%	7	7	Annually
Case C	6%	5	10	Semiannually

Determine present values.
(LO 2)

BEG-8 (a) What is the present value of $25,000 due 9 periods from now, discounted at 10%?
(b) What is the present value of $25,000 to be received at the end of each of 6 periods, discounted at 9%?

Compute the present value of a single amount investment.
(LO 2)

BEG-9 Messi Company is considering an investment that will return a lump sum of $900,000 6 years from now. What amount should Messi Company pay for this investment to earn an 8% return?

Compute the present value of a single amount investment.
(LO 2)

BEG-10 Lloyd Company earns 6% on an investment that will return $450,000 8 years from now. What is the amount Lloyd should invest now to earn this rate of return?

Compute the present value of an annuity investment.
(LO 2)

BEG-11 Robben Company is considering investing in an annuity contract that will return $40,000 annually at the end of each year for 15 years. What amount should Robben Company pay for this investment if it earns an 8% return?

Compute the present value of an annual investment.
(LO 2)

BEG-12 Kaehler Enterprises earns 5% on an investment that pays back $80,000 at the end of each of the next 6 years. What is the amount Kaehler Enterprises invested to earn the 5% rate of return?

Compute the present value of bonds.
(LO 2)

BEG-13 Dempsey Railroad Co. is about to issue $400,000 of 10-year bonds paying an 11% interest rate, with interest payable semiannually. The discount rate for such securities is 10%. How much can Dempsey expect to receive for the sale of these bonds?

BEG-14 Assume the same information as BEG-13 except that the discount rate is 12% instead of 10%. In this case, how much can Dempsey expect to receive from the sale of these bonds?

Compute the present value of bonds.
(LO 2)

BEG-15 Neymar Taco Company receives a $75,000, 6-year note bearing interest of 4% (paid annually) from a customer at a time when the discount rate is 6%. What is the present value of the note received by Neymar?

Compute the present value of a note.
(LO 2)

BEG-16 Gleason Enterprises issued 6%, 8-year, $2,500,000 par value bonds that pay interest semiannually on October 1 and April 1. The bonds are dated April 1, 2017, and are issued on that date. The discount rate of interest for such bonds on April 1, 2017, is 8%. What cash proceeds did Gleason receive from issuance of the bonds?

Compute the present value of bonds.
(LO 2)

BEG-17 Frazier Company issues a 10%, 5-year mortgage note on January 1, 2017, to obtain financing for new equipment. Land is used as collateral for the note. The terms provide for semiannual installment payments of $48,850. What are the cash proceeds received from the issuance of the note?

Compute the present value of a note.
(LO 2)

BEG-18 If Colleen Mooney invests $4,765.50 now and she will receive $12,000 at the end of 12 years, what annual rate of interest will Colleen earn on her investment? (*Hint:* Use Table 3.)

Compute the interest rate on a single amount.
(LO 2)

BEG-19 Tim Howard has been offered the opportunity of investing $36,125 now. The investment will earn 11% per year and at the end of that time will return Tim $75,000. How many years must Tim wait to receive $75,000? (*Hint:* Use Table 3.)

Compute the number of periods of a single amount.
(LO 2)

BEG-20 Joanne Quick made an investment of $10,271.38. From this investment, she will receive $1,200 annually for the next 15 years starting one year from now. What rate of interest will Joanne's investment be earning for her? (*Hint:* Use Table 4.)

Compute the interest rate on an annuity.
(LO 2)

BEG-21 Kevin Morales invests $7,793.83 now for a series of $1,300 annual returns beginning one year from now. Kevin will earn a return of 9% on the initial investment. How many annual payments of $1,300 will Kevin receive? (*Hint:* Use Table 4.)

Compute the number of periods of an annuity.
(LO 2)

BEG-22 Barney Googal owns a garage and is contemplating purchasing a tire retreading machine for $12,820. After estimating costs and revenues, Barney projects a net cash inflow from the retreading machine of $2,700 annually for 7 years. Barney hopes to earn a return of 9% on such investments. What is the present value of the retreading operation? Should Barney Googal purchase the retreading machine?

Compute the present value of a machine for purposes of making a purchase decision.
(LO 3)

BEG-23 Snyder Company is considering purchasing equipment. The equipment will produce the following cash inflows: Year 1, $25,000; Year 2, $30,000; and Year 3, $40,000. Snyder requires a minimum rate of return of 11%. What is the maximum price Snyder should pay for this equipment?

Compute the maximum price to pay for a machine.
(LO 3)

BEG-24 Carly Simon wishes to invest $18,000 on July 1, 2017, and have it accumulate to $50,000 by July 1, 2027. Use a financial calculator to determine at what exact annual rate of interest Carly must invest the $18,000.

Determine interest rate.
(LO 4)

BEG-25 On July 17, 2016, Keith Urban borrowed $42,000 from his grandfather to open a clothing store. Starting July 17, 2017, Keith has to make 10 equal annual payments of $6,500 each to repay the loan. Use a financial calculator to determine what interest rate Keith is paying.

Determine interest rate.
(LO 4)

BEG-26 As the purchaser of a new house, Carrie Underwood has signed a mortgage note to pay the Nashville National Bank and Trust Co. $8,400 every 6 months for 20 years, at the end of which time she will own the house. At the date the mortgage is signed, the purchase price was $198,000 and Underwood made a down payment of $20,000. The first payment will be made 6 months after the date the mortgage is signed. Using a financial calculator, compute the exact rate of interest earned on the mortgage by the bank.

Determine interest rate.
(LO 4)

Various time value of money situations.

(LO 4)

BEG-27 Using a financial calculator, solve for the unknowns in each of the following situations.

(a) On June 1, 2016, Jennifer Lawrence purchases lakefront property from her neighbor, Josh Hutcherson, and agrees to pay the purchase price in seven payments of $16,000 each, the first payment to be payable June 1, 2017. (Assume that interest compounded at an annual rate of 7.35% is implicit in the payments.) What is the purchase price of the property?

(b) On January 1, 2016, Gerrard Corporation purchased 200 of the $1,000 face value, 8% coupon, 10-year bonds of Sterling Inc. The bonds mature on January 1, 2026, and pay interest annually beginning January 1, 2017. Gerrard purchased the bonds to yield 10.65%. How much did Gerrard pay for the bonds?

Various time value of money situations.

(LO 4)

BEG-28 Using a financial calculator, provide a solution to each of the following situations.

(a) Lynn Anglin owes a debt of $42,000 from the purchase of her new sport utility vehicle. The debt bears annual interest of 7.8% compounded monthly. Lynn wishes to pay the debt and interest in equal monthly payments over 8 years, beginning one month hence. What equal monthly payments will pay off the debt and interest?

(b) On January 1, 2017, Roger Molony offers to buy Dave Feeney's used snowmobile for $8,000, payable in five equal annual installments, which are to include 7.25% interest on the unpaid balance and a portion of the principal. If the first payment is to be made on December 31, 2017, how much will each payment be?

Appendix H Standards of Ethical Conduct for Management Accountants

APPENDIX PREVIEW Management accountants have an obligation to the organizations they serve, their profession, the public, and themselves to maintain the highest standards of ethical conduct. In recognition of this obligation, the **Institute of Management Accountants** has published and promoted the following standards of ethical conduct for management accountants.

IMA Statement of Ethical Professional Practice

Members of IMA shall behave ethically. A commitment to ethical professional practice includes: overarching principles that express our values, and standards that guide our conduct.

Principles

IMA's overarching ethical principles include: Honesty, Fairness, Objectivity, and Responsibility. Members shall act in accordance with these principles and shall encourage others within their organizations to adhere to them.

Standards

A member's failure to comply with the following standards may result in disciplinary action.

I. COMPETENCE

Each member has a responsibility to:

1. Maintain an appropriate level of professional expertise by continually developing knowledge and skills.
2. Perform professional duties in accordance with relevant laws, regulations, and technical standards.
3. Provide decision support information and recommendations that are accurate, clear, concise, and timely.
4. Recognize and communicate professional limitations or other constraints that would preclude responsible judgment or successful performance of an activity.

II. CONFIDENTIALITY

Each member has a responsibility to:

1. Keep information confidential except when disclosure is authorized or legally required.
2. Inform all relevant parties regarding appropriate use of confidential information. Monitor subordinates' activities to ensure compliance.
3. Refrain from using confidential information for unethical or illegal advantage.

III. INTEGRITY

Each member has a responsibility to:

1. Mitigate actual conflicts of interest, regularly communicate with business associates to avoid apparent conflicts of interest. Advise all parties of any potential conflicts.
2. Refrain from engaging in any conduct that would prejudice carrying out duties ethically.
3. Abstain from engaging in or supporting any activity that might discredit the profession.

IV. CREDIBILITY

Each member has a responsibility to:

1. Communicate information fairly and objectively.
2. Disclose all relevant information that could reasonably be expected to influence an intended user's understanding of the reports, analyses, or recommendations.
3. Disclose delays or deficiencies in information, timeliness, processing, or internal controls in conformance with organization policy and/or applicable law.

Resolution of Ethical Conflict

In applying the Standards of Ethical Professional Practice, you may encounter problems identifying unethical behavior or resolving an ethical conflict. When faced with ethical issues, you should follow your organization's established policies on the resolution of such conflict. If these policies do not resolve the ethical conflict, you should consider the following courses of action:

1. Discuss the issue with your immediate supervisor except when it appears that the supervisor is involved. In that case, present the issue to the next level. If you cannot achieve a satisfactory resolution, submit the issue to the next management level. If your immediate superior is the chief executive officer or equivalent, the acceptable reviewing authority may be a group such as the audit committee, executive committee, board of directors, board of trustees, or owners. Contact with levels above the immediate superior should be initiated only with your superior's knowledge, assuming he or she is not involved. Communication of such problems to authorities or individuals not employed or engaged by the organization is not considered appropriate, unless you believe there is a clear violation of the law.
2. Clarify relevant ethical issues by initiating a confidential discussion with an IMA Ethics Counselor or other impartial advisor to obtain a better understanding of possible courses of action.
3. Consult your own attorney as to legal obligations and rights concerning the ethical conflict.

Source: Institute of Management Accountants. Reprinted by permission. Go to *www.imanet.org/about_ima/our_mission.aspx* to learn more about the IMA's commitment to ethical professional practices and its available resources, including an Ethics Helpline.

Company Index

Subject Index

C

T

RAPID REVIEW
Chapter Content

ACCOUNTING EQUATION (Chapter 2)

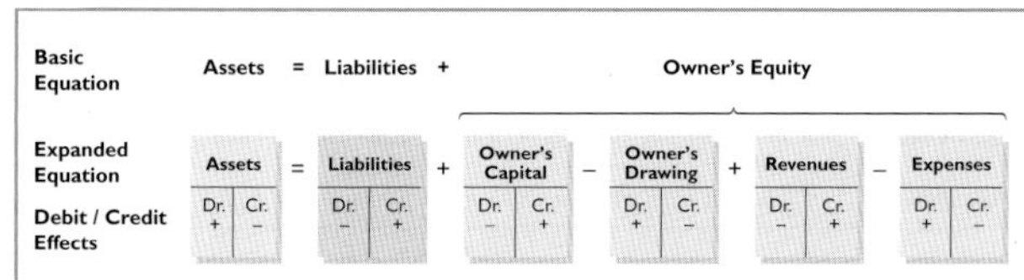

ADJUSTING ENTRIES (Chapter 3)

	Type	Adjusting Entry	
Deferrals	1. Prepaid expenses 2. Unearned revenues	Dr. Expenses Dr. Liabilities	Cr. Assets Cr. Revenues
Accruals	1. Accrued r evenues 2. Accrued expenses	Dr. Assets Dr. Expenses	Cr. Revenues Cr. Liabilities

Note: Each adjusting entry will affect one or more income statement accounts and one or more balance sheet accounts.

Interest Computation

Interest = Face value of note × Annual interest rate × Time in terms of one year

CLOSING ENTRIES (Chapter 4)

Purpose: (1) Update the Owner's Capital account in the ledger by transferring net income (loss) and Owner's Drawings to Owner's Capital. (2) Prepare the temporary accounts (revenue, expense, Owner's Drawings) for the next period's postings by reducing their balances to zero.

Process

1. Debit each revenue account for its balance (assuming normal balances), and credit Income Summary for total revenues.
2. Debit Income Summary for total expenses, and credit each expense account for its balance (assuming normal balances).

   STOP AND CHECK: Does the balance in your Income Summary account equal the net income (loss) reported in the income statement?

3. Debit (credit) Income Summary, and credit (debit) Owner's Capital for the amount of net income (loss).
4. Debit Owner's Capital for the balance in the Owner's Drawings account, and credit Owner's Drawings for the same amount.

   STOP AND CHECK: Does the balance in your Owner's Capital account equal the ending balance reported in the balance sheet and the owner's equity statement? Are all of your temporary account balances zero?

ACCOUNTING CYCLE (Chapter 4)

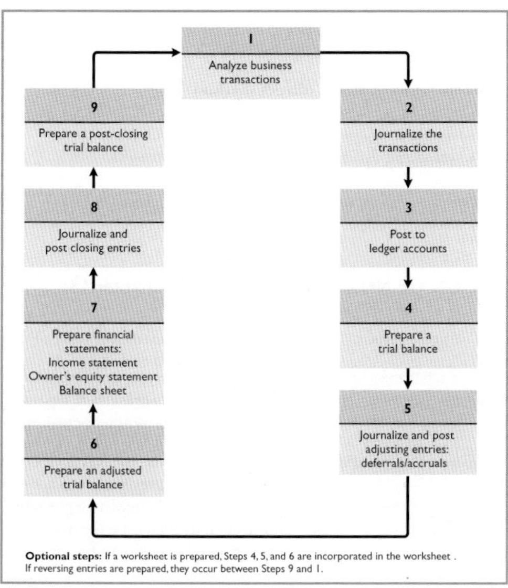

INVENTORY (Chapters 5 and 6)

Ownership

Freight Terms	Ownership of goods on public carrier resides with:	Who pays freight costs:
FOB shipping point	Buyer	Buyer
FOB destination	Seller	Seller

Perpetual vs. Periodic Journal Entries

Event	Perpetual	Periodic*
Purchase of goods	Inventory Cash (A/P)	Purchases Cash (A/P)
Freight (shipping point)	Inventory Cash	Freight-In Cash
Return of goods	Cash (or A/P) Inventory	Cash (or A/P) Purchase Ret. and All.
Sale of goods	Cash (or A/R) Sales Revenue Cost of Goods Sold Inventory	Cash (or A/R) Sales Revenue No entry
Sales returns and allowances	Sales Ret. and All. Accounts Receivable Inventory Cost of Goods Sold	Sales Ret. and All. Accounts Receivable No entry
Sales discounts	Cash Sales Discounts Accounts Receivable	Cash Sales Discounts Accounts Receivable
End of period	No entry	Closing or adjusting entry required

*Covered in appendix.

Cost Flow Methods

- Specific identification
- First-in, first-out (FIFO)
- Weighted-average
- Last-in, first-out (LIFO)

FRAUD, INTERNAL CONTROL, AND CASH (Chapter 8)

The Fraud Triangle

Opportunity

Financial pressure — Rationalization

Principles of Internal Control Activities

- Establishment of responsibility
- Segregation of duties
- Documentation procedures
- Physical controls
- Independent internal verification
- Human resource controls

Bank Reconciliation

Bank	Books
Balance per bank statement Add: Deposit in transit Deduct: Outstanding checks Adjusted cash balance	Balance per books Add: Unrecorded credit memoranda from bank statement Deduct: Unrecorded debit memoranda from bank statement Adjusted cash balance

Note: 1. Errors should be offset (added or deducted) on the side that made the error.
2. Adjusting journal entries should only be made on the books.

STOP AND CHECK: Does the adjusted cash balance in the Cash account equal the reconciled balance?

RAPID REVIEW
Chapter Content

RECEIVABLES (Chapter 9)

Methods to Account for Uncollectible Accounts

Direct write-off method	Record bad debt expense when the company determines a particular account to be uncollectible.
Allowance methods: **Percentage-of-sales**	At the end of each period, estimate the amount of credit sales uncollectible. Debit Bad Debt Expense and credit Allowance for Doubtful Accounts for this amount. As specific accounts become uncollectible, debit Allowance for Doubtful Accounts and credit Accounts Receivable.
Percentage-of-receivables	At the end of each period, estimate the amount of uncollectible receivables. Debit Bad Debt Expense and credit Allowance for Doubtful Accounts in an amount that results in a balance in the allowance account equal to the estimate of uncollectibles. As specific accounts become uncollectible, debit Allowance for Doubtful Accounts and credit Accounts Receivable.

PLANT ASSETS (Chapter 10)

Presentation

Tangible Assets	Intangible Assets
Property, plant, and equipment	Intangible assets (patents, copyrights, trademarks, franchises, goodwill)
Natural resources	

Computation of Annual Depreciation Expense

Straight-line	$\dfrac{\text{Cost} - \text{Salvage value}}{\text{Useful life (in years)}}$
Units-of-activity	$\dfrac{\text{Depreciable cost}}{\text{Useful life (in units)}} \times \text{Units of activity during year}$
Declining-balance	Book value at beginning of year × Declining balance rate* *Declining-balance rate = 1 ÷ Useful life (in years)

Note: If depreciation is calculated for partial periods, the straight-line and declining-balance methods must be adjusted for the relevant proportion of the year. Multiply the annual depreciation expense by the number of months expired in the year divided by 12 months.

SHAREHOLDERS' EQUITY (Chapter 13)

Comparison of Equity Accounts

Proprietorship	Partnership	Corporation
Owner's equity Owner's capital	Partner's equity Name, Capital Name, Capital	Stockholders' equity Common stock Retained earnings

No-Par Value vs. Par Value Stock Journal Entries

No-Par Value	Par Value
Cash Common Stock	Cash Common Stock (par value) Paid-in Capital in Excess of Par—Common Stock

DIVIDENDS (Chapter 14)

Comparison of Dividend Effects

	Cash	Common Stock	Retained Earnings
Cash dividend	↓	No effect	↓
Stock dividend	No effect	↑	↓
Stock split	No effect	No effect	No effect

BONDS (Chapter 15)

Premium	Market interest rate < Contractual interest rate
Face Value	Market interest rate = Contractual interest rate
Discount	Market interest rate > Contractual interest rate

INVESTMENTS (Chapter 16)

Comparison of Long-Term Bond Investment and Liability Journal Entries

Event	Investor	Investee
Purchase / issue of bonds	Debt Investments Cash	Cash Bonds Payable
Interest receipt / payment	Cash Interest Revenue	Interest Expense Cash

Comparison of Cost and Equity Methods of Accounting for Long-Term Stock Investments

Event	Cost	Equity
Acquisition	Stock Investments Cash	Stock Investments Cash
Investee reports earnings	No entry	Stock Investments Revenue from Stock Investments
Investee pays dividends	Cash Dividend Revenue	Cash Stock Investments

Trading and Available-for-Sale Securities

Trading	Report at fair value with changes reported in net income.
Available-for-sale	Report at fair value with changes reported in the stockholders' equity section.

STATEMENT OF CASH FLOWS (Chapter 17)

Cash flows from operating activities (**indirect method**)

Net income			
Add:	Losses on disposals of assets	$ X	
	Amortization and depreciation	X	
	Decreases in current assets	X	
	Increases in current liabilities	X	
Deduct:	Gains on disposals of assets	(X)	
	Increases in current assets	(X)	
	Decreases in current liabilities	(X)	
Net cash provided (used) by operating activities			$ X

Cash flows from operating activities (**direct method**)

Cash receipts (Examples: from sales of goods and services to customers, from receipts of interest and dividends on loans and investments)	$ X	
Cash payments (Examples: to suppliers, for operating expenses, for interest, for taxes)	(X)	
Net cash provided (used) by operating activities		$ X

PRESENTATION OF NON-TYPICAL ITEMS (Chapter 18)

Prior period adjustments (Chapter 14)	Statement of retained earnings (adjustment of beginning retained earnings)
Discontinued operations	Income statement (presented separately after "Income from continuing operations")
Changes in accounting principle	In most instances, use the new method in current period and restate previous year's results using new method. For changes in depreciation and amortization methods, use the new method in the current period but do not restate previous periods.

RAPID REVIEW
Chapter Content

MANAGERIAL ACCOUNTING (Chapter 19)

Characteristics of Managerial Accounting

Primary users	Internal users
Reports	Internal reports issued as needed
Purpose	Special purpose for a particular user
Content	Pertains to subunits, may be detailed, use of relevant data
Verification	No independent audits

Types of Manufacturing Costs

Direct materials	Raw materials directly associated with finished product
Direct labor	Work of employees directly associated with turning raw materials into finished product
Manufacturing overhead	Costs indirectly associated with manufacture of finished product

JOB ORDER AND PROCESS COSTING (Chapters 20 and 21)

Types of Accounting Systems

Job order	Costs are assigned to each unit or each batch of goods
Process cost	Costs are applied to similar products that are mass-produced in a continuous fashion

Job Order and Process Cost Flow

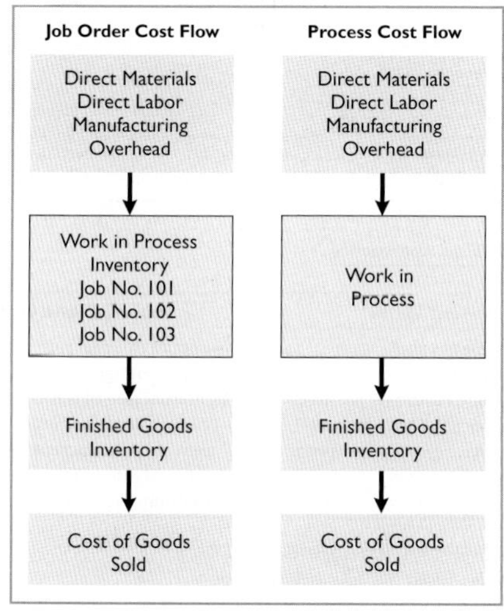

COST-VOLUME-PROFIT (Chapter 22)

Types of Costs

Variable costs	Vary in total directly and proportionately with changes in activity level
Fixed costs	Remain the same in total regardless of change in activity level
Mixed costs	Contain both a fixed and a variable element

CVP Income Statement Format

	Total	Per Unit
Sales	$xx	$xx
Variable costs	xx	xx
Contribution margin	xx	$xx
Fixed costs	xx	
Net income	$xx	

Unit contribution margin = Unit selling price − Unit variable costs

Break-even point in units = Fixed costs ÷ Unit contribution margin

Required sales in units for target net income = (Fixed costs + Target net income) ÷ Unit contribution margin

RAPID REVIEW
Chapter Content

BUDGETS (Chapter 23)

Components of the Master Budget

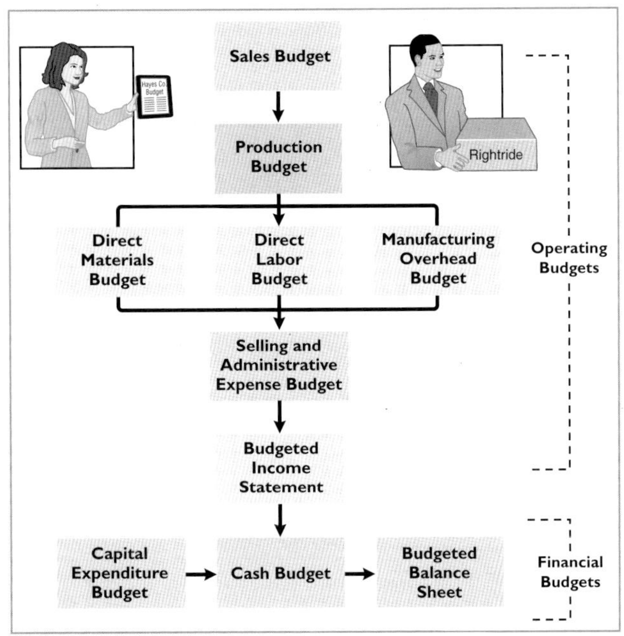

RESPONSIBILITY ACCOUNTING (Chapter 24)

Types of Responsibility Centers

Cost	Profit	Investment
Expenses only	Expenses and Revenues	Expenses and Revenues and ROI

Return on Investment

Return on investment (ROI) = Investment center controllable margin ÷ Average investment center operating assets

STANDARD COSTS (Chapter 25)

Standard Cost Variances

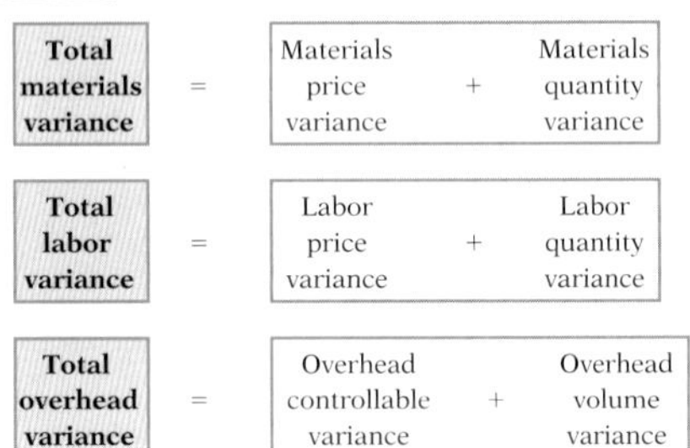

Total materials variance = Materials price variance + Materials quantity variance

Total labor variance = Labor price variance + Labor quantity variance

Total overhead variance = Overhead controllable variance + Overhead volume variance

Materials price variance = AQ × AP − AQ × SP

Materials quantity variance = AQ × SP − SQ × SP

Labor price variance = AH × AR − AH × SR

Labor quantity variance = AH × SR − SH × SR

* **Overhead controllable variance** = Actual overhead − Overhead budgeted

* **Overhead volume variance** = Fixed overhead rate × Normal capacity hours − Standard hours allowed

*Appendix coverage

Balanced Scorecard

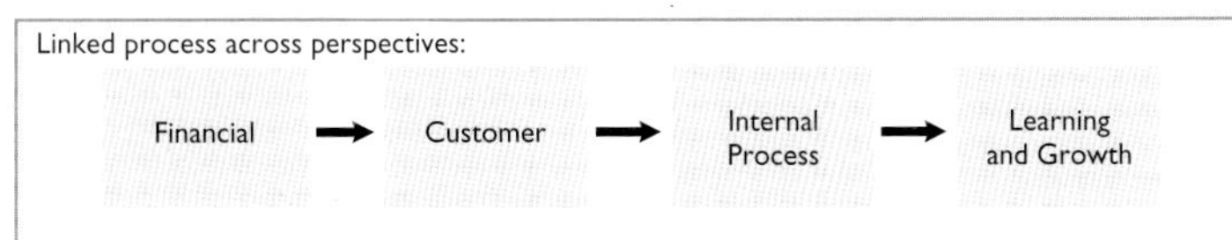

INCREMENTAL ANALYSIS AND CAPITAL BUDGETING (Chapter 26)

Incremental Analysis

1. Identify the relevant costs associated with each alternative. Relevant costs are those costs and revenues that differ across alternatives. Choose the alternative that maximizes net income.
2. Opportunity costs are those benefits that are given up when one alternative is chosen instead of another one. Opportunity costs are relevant costs.
3. Sunk costs have already been incurred and will not be changed or avoided by any future decision. Sunk costs are not relevant costs.

Annual Rate of Return

Annual rate of return = Expected annual net income ÷ Average investment

Cash Payback

Cash payback period = Cost of capital investment ÷ Net annual cash flow

Discounted Cash Flow Approaches

Net Present Value	Internal Rate of Return
Compute net present value (a dollar amount). If net present value is zero or positive, accept the proposal. If net present value is negative, reject the proposal.	Compute internal rate of return (a percentage). If internal rate of return is equal to or greater than the minimum required rate of return, accept the proposal. If internal rate of return is less than the minimum rate, reject the proposal.

RAPID REVIEW
Financial Statements

Order of Preparation

Statement Type	Date
1. Income statement	For the period ended
2. Retained earnings statement	For the period ended
3. Balance sheet	As of the end of the period
4. Statement of cash flows	For the period ended

Income Statement (perpetual inventory system)

COMPANY NAME
Income Statement
For the Period Ended

Sales		
Sales revenue	$X	
Less: Sales returns and allowances	X	
Sales discounts	X	
Net sales		$X
Cost of goods sold		X
Gross profit		X
Operating expenses		
(Examples: store salaries, advertising, delivery, rent, depreciation, utilities, insurance)		X
Income from operations		X
Other revenues and gains		
(Examples: interest, gains)	X	
Other expenses and losses		
(Examples: interest, losses)	X	X
Income before income taxes		X
Income tax expense		X
Net income		$X

Income Statement (periodic inventory system)

COMPANY NAME
Income Statement
For the Period Ended

Sales			
Sales revenue		$X	
Less: Sales returns and allowances		X	
Sales discounts		X	
Net sales			$X
Cost of goods sold			
Beginning inventory		X	
Purchases	$X		
Less: Purchase returns and allowances	X		
Net purchases	X		
Add: Freight-in	X		
Cost of goods purchased		X	
Cost of goods available for sale		X	
Less: Ending inventory		X	
Cost of goods sold			X
Gross profit			X
Operating expenses			
(Examples: store salaries, advertising, delivery, rent, depreciation, utilities, insurance)			X
Income from operations			X
Other revenues and gains			
(Examples: interest, gains)		X	
Other expenses and losses			
(Examples: interest, losses)		X	X
Income before income taxes			X
Income tax expense			X
Net income			$X

Retained Earnings Statement

COMPANY NAME
Retained Earnings Statement
For the Period Ended

Retained earnings, beginning of period	$X
Add: Net income (or deduct net loss)	X
	X
Deduct: Dividends	X
Retained earnings, end of period	$X

STOP AND CHECK: Net income (loss) presented on the retained earnings statement must equal the net income (loss) presented on the income statement.

Balance Sheet

COMPANY NAME
Balance Sheet
As of the End of the Period

Assets

Current assets			
(Examples: cash, short-term debt investments, accounts receivable, inventory, prepaids)			$X
Long-term investments			
(Examples: investments in bonds, investments in stocks)			X
Property, plant, and equipment			
Land		$X	
Buildings and equipment	$X		
Less: Accumulated depreciation	X	X	X
Intangible assets			X
Total assets			$X

Liabilities and Stockholders' Equity

Liabilities	
Current liabilities	
(Examples: notes payable, accounts payable, accruals, unearned revenues, current portion of notes payable)	$X
Long-term liabilities	
(Examples: notes payable, bonds payable)	X
Total liabilities	X
Stockholders' equity	
Common stock	X
Retained earnings	X
Total liabilities and stockholders' equity	$X

STOP AND CHECK: Total assets on the balance sheet must equal total liabilities and stockholders' equity; and, ending retained earnings on the balance sheet must equal ending retained earnings on the retained earnings statement.

Statement of Cash Flows

COMPANY NAME
Statement of Cash Flows
For the Period Ended

Cash flows from operating activities	
(*Note:* May be prepared using the direct or indirect method)	
Net cash provided (used) by operating activities	$X
Cash flows from investing activities	
(Examples: purchase / sale of long-term assets)	
Net cash provided (used) by investing activities	X
Cash flows from financing activities	
(Examples: issue / repayment of long-term liabilities, issue of stock, payment of dividends)	
Net cash provided (used) by financing activities	X
Net increase (decrease) in cash	X
Cash, beginning of the period	X
Cash, end of the period	$X

STOP AND CHECK: Cash, end of the period, on the statement of cash flows must equal cash presented on the balance sheet.

RAPID REVIEW
Using the Information in the Financial Statements

Ratio	Formula	Purpose or Use
Liquidity Ratios		
1. Current ratio	$\frac{\text{Current assets}}{\text{Current liabilities}}$	Measures short-term debt-paying ability.
2. Acid-test (quick) ratio	$\frac{\text{Cash + Short-term investments + Accounts receivable (net)}}{\text{Current liabilities}}$	Measures immediate short-term liquidity.
3. Accounts receivable turnover	$\frac{\text{Net credit sales}}{\text{Average net accounts receivable}}$	Measures liquidity of receivables.
4. Inventory turnover	$\frac{\text{Cost of goods sold}}{\text{Average inventory}}$	Measures liquidity of inventory.
Profitability Ratios		
5. Profit margin	$\frac{\text{Net income}}{\text{Net sales}}$	Measures net income generated by each dollar of sales.
6. Asset turnover	$\frac{\text{Net sales}}{\text{Average total assets}}$	Measures how efficiently assets are used to generate sales.
7. Return on assets	$\frac{\text{Net income}}{\text{Average total assets}}$	Measures overall profitability of assets.
8. Return on common stockholders' equity	$\frac{\text{Net income} - \text{Preferred dividends}}{\text{Average common stockholders' equity}}$	Measures profitability of owners' investment.
9. Earnings per share (EPS)	$\frac{\text{Net income} - \text{Preferred dividends}}{\text{Weighted-average common shares outstanding}}$	Measures net income earned on each share of common stock.
10. Price-earnings (P-E) ratio	$\frac{\text{Market price per share of stock}}{\text{Earnings per share}}$	Measures ratio of the market price per share to earnings per share.
11. Payout ratio	$\frac{\text{Cash dividends}}{\text{Net income}}$	Measures percentage of earnings distributed in the form of cash dividends.
Solvency Ratios		
12. Debt to assets ratio	$\frac{\text{Total liabilities}}{\text{Total assets}}$	Measures percentage of total assets provided by creditors.
13. Times interest earned	$\frac{\text{Net income + Interest expense + Income tax expense}}{\text{Interest expense}}$	Measures ability to meet interest payments as they come due.
14. Free cash flow	Net cash provided by operating activities − Capital expenditures − Cash dividends	Measures the amount of cash generated during the current year that is available for the payment of additional dividends or for expansion.